the EXPLORERS LTD. source book

COMPILED AND WRITTEN BY
Explorers Ltd.

EDITED BY
Alwyn T. Perrin

HARPER & ROW, PUBLISHERS

NEW YORK, HAGERSTOWN, SAN FRANCISCO, LONDON

1817

Explorers Ltd. (ETM) was established in 1966 as a data clearinghouse to provide research and consulting services for fields of activity that concern or contribute to exploring by land, sea and air. Areas of interest include wilderness recreation, marine and aviation fields, history and travel, archeology and the natural sciences.

Explorers Ltd., Gwinhurst, Wilmington, Delaware 19809

NOTE: All products discussed in this book have been evaluated by Explorers Ltd. and its associates to the best of their ability, and all those products recommended meet, to their best knowledge, the highest standards of quality. However, neither Explorers Ltd. nor Harper & Row in any way warrants as to the safety of materials or products recommended, since conditions of use may vary, and possible variability in manufacturers' statements cannot be vouched for.

Library of Congress Cataloging in Publication Data

Explorers Ltd.
    Explorers Ltd. Source Book

    Includes index
    1. Outdoor recreation—Handbooks, manuals, etc.
I. Perrin, Alwyn T.   II. Title.   III.   Title: Source Book.
GV 191.3.E95   1977   790'.028   75-26224
ISBN 0-06-011252-2

table of contents

contributors to 2nd ed.

John Broadwater (Virginia) - *Diving*
Doug Finley (California) - *Bicycle Touring, Photography*
Charles Garrett (Texas) - *Treasure Hunting*
Richard Gitz (New Jersey) - *River Touring*
Yvonne Johnson (British Columbia) - *Dog Packing, Dog Sledding, Foraging*
Bob Livingston (West Virginia) - *Ski Touring, Snowshoeing, Backpacking*
John Markwell (West Virginia) - *Backpacking, Climbing*
Waldo Nielsen (New York) - *Wilderness Areas & Trails*
Tom Oerman (Iowa) - *Ballooning*
Dan Poynter (California) - *Hang Gliding*

John Rhoads (Massachusetts) - *Land Navigation, Maps, Aerial Photographs*
Jim Shaw (Iran) - *Vagabonding*
John Shortall III (Florida) - *Offshore Sailing*

2nd ed. staff

Mary Darby
  Typing, copy editing, proofing, composition, layout and paste up
Al Perrin
  Editing (after a fashion) and art

WILDERNESS

Here's where you can find yourself in Mother Nature's arms ... no one to serve you a meal ... no traffic cop to whistle you off the hidden rock in the next rapids ... no friendly roof to keep you dry when you have misguessed the weather ... no tour guide (most of the time) to show you which bivouac spot threatens a night-long wind ... and no easy escape from the misery of mosquitos and black flies—what you sees is what you gets. This is the place—mountain, forest, desert, jungle, swamp—the country beyond, the wilderness.

Wild, wilderness, and primitive are terms hung on particular types of topography, and you'll hear them quite often if you get involved in camping, backpacking, climbing, and canoeing. The terms can lead to a bit of confusion unless you happen to know whence they came—the government. Then it all becomes clear, in a manner of speaking. Ask the typical forester (U.S. Forest type, since they run the wild, wilderness, primitive show) what the difference is between a wild and a primitive area, or a primitive and wilderness area, and he'll probably say..."Gee, I dunno??? They all look the same to me!"

Actually, the only difference is in the way they are administered. With respect to wild and wilderness areas there *is* a difference in size. A wild area is from 5,000 to 100,000 acres in size, and a wilderness area 100,000 acres and over. There are also National Parks and the Public Lands to consider. There's a lot of land we own and maybe the following definitions will help you to understand how they're categorized and used.

Wilderness and Wild Areas are administered by the Forest Service (Department of Agriculture) and in some cases the National Park Service. The land is maintained essentially free of permanent improvements so as to remain in a natural wild state. No motorized equipment or permanent structures are allowed; logging is not permitted. Mineral prospecting, hunting, and fishing are permitted in Forest Wilderness; fishing only is permitted in Park Wilderness. Roughly, there are about 37 million acres of wilderness in the United States.

Primitive Areas are administered by the Forest Service and their status and usage is the same as the above type areas with one exception: Primitive Areas are sort of in an administrative limbo awaiting reclassification as either Wilderness Areas or back to National Forest status. National Forest status would allow mining, camping, hunting, fishing, logging, leasing of land for cabins, and other permanent structures like roads.

The Wilderness Act of 1964 was a Congressional Act officially establishing some nine million acres of these Wilderness and Wild Areas as part of the National Wilderness Preservation System. This took care of just about all the Wilderness and Wild Areas the Forest Service had established as far back as 1926. You gotta hand it to the Forest Service boys, they were looking out for us backpackers way before there were any backpackers; in those days they were known as mountain men. Incidentally, the Act also directs the Secretary of Agriculture to review, within 10 years, the lands classified by the Forest Service as Primitive and recommend to Congress either reclassification as Wilderness or return to National Forest Land.

National Parks are under the administration of the National Park Service (Department of Interior) and are preserved strictly for recreational purposes, no multi-use concepts are applied here.

Public Lands are Federal Property under the administration of the Interior's Bureau of Land Management (BLM). Much of them could be classified as wilderness, and are for multi-purpose uses.

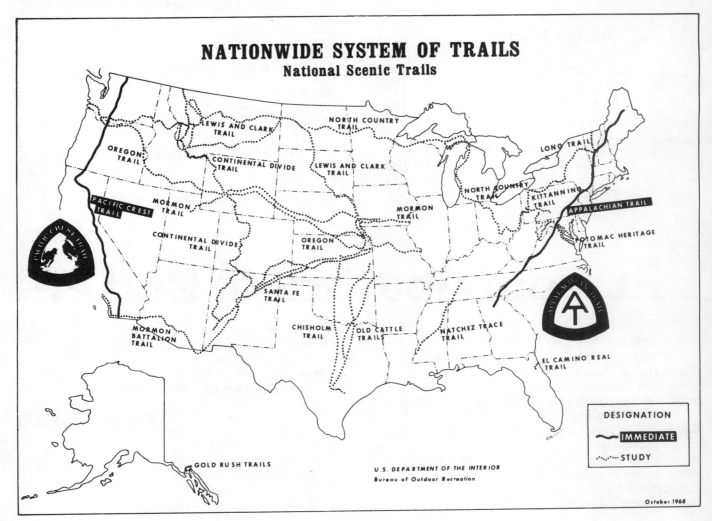

NATIONWIDE SYSTEM OF TRAILS
National Scenic Trails

LEWIS AND CLARK TRAIL

NORTH COUNTRY TRAIL

OREGON TRAIL

LONG TRAIL

CONTINENTAL DIVIDE TRAIL

LEWIS AND CLARK TRAIL

NORTH COUNTRY TRAIL

KITTANNING TRAIL

PACIFIC CREST TRAIL

MORMON TRAIL

MORMON TRAIL

APPALACHIAN TRAIL

CONTINENTAL DIVIDE TRAIL

OREGON TRAIL

POTOMAC HERITAGE TRAIL

SANTA FE TRAIL

MORMON BATTALION TRAIL

CHISHOLM TRAIL

OLD CATTLE TRAILS

NATCHEZ TRACE TRAIL

EL CAMINO REAL TRAIL

GOLD RUSH TRAILS

U.S. DEPARTMENT OF THE INTERIOR
Bureau of Outdoor Recreation

DESIGNATION
⌒ IMMEDIATE
⋯ STUDY

October 1968

AREAS and TRAILS

TRAILS

Throughout the U.S. there exist hundreds of marked trails for use on foot or horseback. Some are so well marked as to require neither map nor compass. Others are rough enough to require both, plus a lot of stamina and experience. Many are reasonably "civilized" and heavily traveled, while others are so remote and difficult that a traveler can go for days without human contact.

There are also many unmarked, but easy to follow trails. These are the narrow strips of land once used for transportation, communication or distribution—the abandoned railroad rights-of-way, canal towpaths, utility rights-of-way, etc. These are generally level and many of them are close to urban areas; some of them are being incorporated into marked trail systems.

National Symposium on Trails

On June 2-6, 1971, the U.S. Department of Interior, the U.S. Department of Agriculture, and the Open Lands Project of Chicago tri-sponsored the National Symposium on Trails in Washington, D.C. The meetings and speeches had over 350 individual participants from 37 states and the District of Columbia. All types of trails were considered: foot, canoe and kayak, bicycle, horse, and motor. A resolution was passed to establish a permanent trails organization. On 25 February 1972 the National Trails Council was formed. Future national and regional trails symposiums will be organized by the National Trails Council.

For a detailed report on the Symposium, you can get the 132-page *Proceedings of the National Symposium on Trails,* stock number 2416-0042, $1.60 from the Superintendent of Documents, U.S. Gov. Printing Office, Washington, D.C. 20402.

NATIONAL SCENIC TRAILS

The National Trails System Act of 1968 designated a *National Scenic Trail* as "... an extended trail which has natural, scenic, or historic qualities that give the trail recreation use potential of national significance." At the present time there are two trails that enjoy this distinction: the Appalachian Trail and the Pacific Crest Trail. Fourteen others, having a total of about 18,000 miles of trails, are under consideration. Here is a short rundown on the two National Scenic Trails:

Appalachian Trail (AT)

The Appalachian Trail is a 2,053-mile footpath along the backbone of the Appalachian Mountains, originating at Mount Katahdin in Maine and terminating at Springer Mountain, Georgia. It was proposed by architect Benton MacKaye in 1921. The first mile of it was cut and marked in Palisades Interstate Park, N.Y. in 1922, and the trail was completed on 15 August 1937.

The work of building the trail was done primarily by private clubs and groups along with the U.S. Forest Service and other public agencies. Efforts were coordinated by the Appalacian Trail Conference (ATC), a private organization which was set up in 1925 expressly for that purpose. Much of the trail follows previously marked routes and 866 miles of it passes over private land. Portions which cross Federal and state lands are for the most part financed and maintained by their appropriate agencies. Private areas are cared for by private clubs and organizations to which the ATC assigns a given stretch for which they are responsible.

The Trail is dotted with shelters spaced every five to ten miles, which are maintained by local clubs and are generally open to the public.

The Appalachian Trail enjoys the statistical distinction of being the longest continually marked recreational pathway in the world.

Zowie! However, its greatest distinction is that it exists as the results of the efforts of public and private individuals working together.

For information on using the Trail, write:

THE APPALACHIAN TRAIL CONFERENCE
P.O.Box 236, Harpers Ferry, W. Va. 25425

Pacific Crest Trail (PCT)

The 2,404-mile Pacific Crest Trail is the West Coast counterpart of the Appalachian Trail. It follows the backbone of mountain ranges that stretch from the Canadian to the Mexican border, traversing glaciers at its northernmost reaches and deserts in the south.

Unlike the Appalachian, the PCT crosses land that is for the most part Federally owned, although 444 miles of it is on private land belonging mostly to lumber companies. In addition to travel by foot, the Trail is suited to horseback and pack train. There are some shelters along the way and designated grazing areas for stock.

The PCT incorporates in its network, seven previously established trails:

Washington: Cascade Crest Trail—514 miles.
Oregon: Oregon Skyline Trail—436 miles.
California: Lava Crest Trail, Tahoe-Yosemite Trail, John Muir Trail, Sierra Trail, and Desert Crest Trail—total of 1,454 miles.

It passes through twenty-five National Forests and six National Parks. Administration and maintenance of the Trail is in the hands of the National Park Service, the Bureau of Land Management, the Forest Service, and individual states.

For information on using the Trail, write:

PACIFIC NORTHWEST REGION (Washington and Oregon)
Regional Forester, P.O. Box 3623, Portland, Ore. 97208

CALIFORNIA REGION (California)
Regional Forester, 630 Sansome St., San Francisco, Calif. 94111

NATIONAL RECREATION TRAILS

Included under the same Trails Act is a recommendation to the Secretaries of Interior and Agriculture that existing recreation trails be expanded and new ones developed for a National Recreational Trails System. In order to be so designated, a trail must be continuous, of any length, guaranteed available to the public for at least ten years, and be in or reasonably accessible to urban areas.

There are, at present, 40 such trails. Most of these run through civilized, even metropolitan areas, and few through any true wilderness areas. They are included here for their own specific value as an attempt to improve metropolitan outdoor recreation.

If you know of such a trail that you feel should be included in the National Recreational Trails System or if you would like further information on the National Scenic Trails System, write:

Secretary, DEPARTMENT OF THE INTERIOR
Attention: Bureau of Outdoor Recreation, Washington, D.C. 20240

or: **Secretary, DEPARTMENT OF AGRICULTURE**
Attention: Forest Service, Washington, D.C. 20250

STATE SCENIC TRAIL SYSTEMS

Many states are now establishing state scenic trail systems that are similiar to the national system. To the best of our knowledge, the states that currently have a scenic trails system, or are actively considering one, are California, Connecticut, Colorado, Florida, Georgia, Illinois, Maine, Maryland, Massachusettes, New Jersey, New Hampshire, New Mexico, New York, North Carolina, Ohio, Tennessee, Vermont, Virginia, and Washington. Write to your state park commission, conservation agency, or whatever for more information (state recreation and tourist bureaus are listed a little further on).

CANADA

Information Services, PARKS CANADA
Dept. of Indian and Northern Affairs
400 Laurier Ave. West, Ottawa, Ontario, Canada K1A 0H4
These are the people who administer the national parks of Canada.
Information requests regarding facilities and use of the parks should
be directed to them at the above address.

There are 29 national parks in Canada covering a total of 49,800
square miles. Most of this land, zoned as wilderness, is restricted to
the likes of hiking, backpacking, primitive camping, and such. A
motor vehicle fee of $10 is good for unlimited use during one season,
and if you want to fish, it'll cost you another whopping $4 per person
for all the parks. Going into the back country (and there's a lot of
lonely land up there) requires registering with park officials, but after
that, it's heaven.

Map Distribution Office, SURVEYS AND MAPPING BRANCH
Dept. of Energy, Mines, and Resources
615 Booth St., Ottawa, Ontario, Canada
Contact the Map Distribution Office for indexes of topo maps to
Canada's national parks. Indexes are free and maps run 25¢ to $2.50
each depending on the scale desired.

CANADIAN GOVERNMENT TRAVEL BUREAU
150 Kent St., Ottawa, Ontario, Canada K1A 0H6
Just about any and all information on backpacking, hiking, wilderness
areas, national and provincial parks can be secured through the Canadian Government Travel Bureau. A letter detailing your requirements
will get a prompt and friendly answer accompanied by much helpful
literature, and if necessary, referrals to other sources of information.
They publish a couple of free booklets you might wish for your files:
Canada National Parks Accommodation Guide, 36 p.
Canada Campgrounds, 52 p.

THE RIDEAU TRAIL ASSOCIATION
P.O.Box 15, Kingston, Ontario, Canada K7L 4V6
The Rideau Trail follows the historic Rideau Canal through lake-strewn
forests and quiet countryside for 200 miles to Ottawa, the capital of
Canada. If hiking isn't your thing, you can always canoe the Rideau
Canal.

GANARASKA TRAIL ASSOCIATION
Box 1136, Barrie, Ontario, Canada L4M 5E2
A new trail, not yet completed, will provide a route from Port Hope on
Lake Ontario, through the old home of the Huron Indians, skirting the
north end of Lake Simcoe and linking up with the Bruce Trail near Col-
lingwood.

CANADIAN YOUTH HOSTELS ASSOCIATION (CYHA)
1406 West Broadway, Vancouver 9, B.C., Canada
CYHA has hostels spread throughout Canada where members may
stay the night when traveling through. Many hostels are also used as

meeting places for local members who engage in backpacking, mountaineering, cycling, canoeing, and skiing, via scheduled outings. Five
membership classes are offered ranging from $5 to $50. Regional
groups publish their own newsletters and bulletins. For complete
information write the above address.

The Bruce Trail

BRUCE TRAIL ASSOCIATION
33 Hardale Crescent, Hamilton, Ontario, Canada L8T 1X7
Made up of eleven member clubs, the association takes care of the
430-mile Bruce Trail which extends along the Niagara escarpment
from Niagara to Tobermory in Ontario. Each member club has its own
activities aside from trail maintenance. You can join directly or
through one of the member clubs. The fee is the same—$5 for adults.
There are publications by each member club, plus *Bruce Trail News*
(about 4 issues per year) which covers activities of general interest
and a calendar of upcoming events.

The *Bruce Trail Guidebook* is available to members for $4 and non-
members for $6.

GREB HIKING BUREAU, c/o Greb Shoes Ltd.
51 Adelt Ave., Kitchener, Ontario, Canada
Greb, who manufacturers hiking boots, has set up an information
facility for hikers and backpackers. They can answer your questions
on Canadian backcountry subjects, and they publish a number of
helpful pamphlets which include *Equipment for the Trail* (free), *Foot
Care for the Trail* (free), and a 52-page booklet *Hiking Trails in
Canada* (25¢)—Excellent! Write the above address.

PROVINCIAL RECREATION AND TOURIST BUREAUS

These agencies will be able to assist with backcountry travel and camping information for their provinces:

Alberta - Travel Alberta, 10065 Jasper Ave., Edmonton, T5J 0H4

British Columbia - Dept. of Travel Industry, 1019 Wharf St., Victoria, V8W 2Z2

Manitoba - Dept. of Tourism, Recreation & Cultural Affairs, Tourist Branch, Winnipeg, R3C 0V8

New Brunswick - Dept. of Tourism, P.O.Box 12345, Fredericton, E3B 5C3

Northwest Territories - Travelarctic, Government, Northwest Territories, Yellowknife, X1A 2L9

Nova Scotia - Dept. of Tourism, P.O.Box 456, Halifax, B3J 2R5

Ontario - Ministry of Industry and Tourism, Travel Services, 3rd Floor, Hearst Block, Queen's Park, 900 Bay St., Toronto, M7A 2E5

Prince Edward Island - Tourist Information Centre, P.O.Box 940, Charlottetown, C1A 7M5

Quebec - Dept. of Tourism, Fish & Game, Place de la Capitale, 150 Est Boulevard Saint-Cyrille, Quebec, G1R 2B2

Saskatchewan - Dept. of Tourism, 1825 Lorne St., Regina, S4P 3N1

MEXICO

MEXICAN NATIONAL TOURIST COUNCIL
405 Park Ave., New York, N.Y. 10022

Mexico's National Park System differs from our own in several major respects. Only a few have facilities of any kind. The Mexican National Park System is roughly the equivalent of our National Forest System—large tracts of scenic areas set aside to avoid commercial exploitation.

At the present time there are approximately 30 national areas, with most of them clustered in the Valley of Mexico. Some of them, particularly the remote and seldom visited Parque de San Pedro de Martir in Baja California, are spectacular. From one high peak it is possible to view both the Pacific Ocean and the vivid blue waters of the Sea of Cortez. Wild and primitive, it is doubtful that more than fifty people a year visit this park. In many of Mexico's parklands, road conditions vary drastically, and it is advisable to check conditions with either the local police or park wardens before making a trip.

Mexico is oriented to tourism, not to wilderness recreation because it doesn't bring in the dollars, and few Mexicans consider living out of a pack in the wilds to be recreation. So hikers, backpackers, and campers will find little, if any, government literature on the subject—no national park directories, campground or trail guides (Mexico has no organized trail systems), or such. There is, however, a *Mapa Turisco de Carreteras*, a detailed road map showing the locations of Mexico's national parks. This is free from the Mexican Tourist Council. As far as hiking maps go, check the Navigation Section for Operational Navigation Charts. This is the best we can do for you, at the moment. What we're really trying to say is that Mexico, in many ways, is very much like it was in the eighteen hundreds—wild, rugged, and waiting to be explored. Here, the American backpacker will find few "apron strings" like guides, directories, and detailed descriptions of what to expect around every corner to hang onto for security. Kinda wish the United States had followed their example a little more. Nevertheless, if you need that kind of stuff (and most of us part-time mountainmen do), don't let this stop you from trying to get specific information from the Tourist Council. Quite often they'll surprise you.

UNITED STATES

FOREST SERVICE, U.S. DEPT. OF AGRICULTURE
14th St. and Independence Ave., S.W., Washington, D.C. 20250

The U.S. Forest Service under the Department of Agriculture rides herd on some 187 million acres designated as the National Forest System. These lands are spread throughout 47 states, Puerto Rico, and the Virgin Islands and are classed under the headings of National Forests, National Forest Purchase Units, National Grasslands, and other specified lands. Within the National Forest System the National Forests make up about 183 million acres located in 40 states and Puerto Rico. It's all open to backpacking, either on trails, of which there are over 105,000 miles, or if you're the adventurous type, by bushwhacking (walking cross country using no trails). You'll have to share much of this land though, because the Forest Service is "dedicated to the principle of multiple use management ... for sustained yields of wood, water, forage, wildlife, and recreation." There's plenty of back country, however, where you can hoof it out into momentary oblivion for a week or two, especially if you venture into

some of the more remote areas of the 14½ million acres of National Forest Wildernesses and Primitive Areas which were set aside by Congress in 1964 as the National Wilderness Preservation System. This also includes the Boundary Waters Canoe Area in Minnesota. No roads, no mass recreation developments, and no timber cutting—just natural wilderness. Well, at least it's left alone now, but there have been non-wilderness activities on much of it in the past, such as logging.

The National Forest System offers some of the best backpacking in the country, and information on taking advantage of this is in the following booklets:

Backpacking in the National Forest Wilderness, PA-585, 25¢.
Camping, PA-502, 65¢.
National Forest Vacations, PA-1037, 90¢.
The National Forests, FS-25, 15¢.
Search for Solitude, PA-942, 65¢.

From: Sup. of Doc., U.S. Gov. Printing Off., Washington, D.C. 20402

For detailed information on national forests and wilderness areas, see the map below for the name of the Forest Service region you're interested in, and address your query to **Regional Forester, Forest Service:**

1. P.O. Box 1628, Juneau, Alaska 99801
2. P.O. Box 3623, Portland, Oreg. 97208
3. 630 Sansome St., San Francisco, Calif. 94111
4. Federal Bldg., Missoula, Mont. 59801
5. 324 25th St., Ogden, Utah 84401
6. Federal Center, Bldg. 85, Denver, Colo. 80225
7. 517 Gold Ave., SW, Albuquerque, N. Mex. 87101
8. 633 West Wisconsin Ave., Milwaukee, Wisc. 53203
9. 1720 Peachtree Road, NW, Atlanta, Ga. 30309

NATIONAL PARK SERVICE
C St., between 18th & 19th Sts., N.W., Washington, D.C. 20240

Unlike the U.S. Forest Service, the National Park Service does not cater to the multi-use concern of the nation. It was established "exclusively to preserve outstanding recreational, scenic, inspirational, geological and historical values on the American scene and make them available permanently for public use and enjoyment," and oversees 285 natural, historical and recreational areas of national significance. The Park Service restricts uses that are not compatible with the basic purposes of the parks; although after viewing concessions at some of the parks, you begin to wonder.

There is much wilderness within the park system's natural and recreational areas for backpacking and even with the increase of hikers, the back country is still relatively free of people. Entrance fees are usually charged, and if you go often, it may be worthwhile to get a Golden Eagle Passport. The cost is $10 and admits you and your car to a National Park, U.S. Forest lands, or Bureau of Land Reclamation areas which charge a fee. The Golden Age Passport is essentially the same thing but is issued free to anyone over the age of 62. You can get either pass at major post offices or directly from the National Park Service, the U.S. Forest Service, or the regional offices of either. The pass is good from January 1 to December 31 of any given year.

The booklets which introduce you to backpacking in the National Parks are:

National Parks of the U.S. (map & guide), (S/N 024-005-00546-3), 75¢.
Back-Country Travel in the National Park System, (S/N 2405-0267), 35¢.
Outdoor Safety Tips, (S/N 001-000-03427), 35¢.
Camping in the National Park System, (S/N 024-005-00627-3), 85¢.
From: Superintendent of Documents, U.S. Gov. Printing Office, Washington, D.C. 20402

BUREAU OF LAND MANAGEMENT, DEPT. OF THE INTERIOR
1800 C St., N.W., Washington, D.C. 20240

In 12 western states there are 457 million acres of Public Lands, which is that part of the original public lands of the United States still in Federal ownership and which hasn't been set aside for national forests, parks, or other special uses. That's about 60% of the nation's federal lands, and consists mostly of desert, mountain, and scrubland-type wilderness so typical of the West, where most of it's found. The government still has it because during the early expansion of the U.S., no one else wanted it. These lands are managed by the Bureau of Land Management for multiple uses, including mining, logging, research, and recreation (hunting, fishing, off-road vehicle travel, canoeing, camping, mountaineering, and backpacking). The Bureau of Land Management doesn't have quite the profusion of recreational literature that other government agencies have, but it does put out two very worthwhile publications: *Our Public Lands,* $2/yr., a quarterly magazine; and *Room to Roam,* 50¢. Both of these can be obtained from: Sup. of Documents, U.S. Gov. Printing Office, Washington, D.C. 20402. Backpacking can be done on trails or off bushwhacking into the back country. More than 2,500 Federal recreation areas are open for public use. You can pay a daily fee or you can get a single $10 Federal Recreation Permit called the Golden Eagle Passport which is good for one year (see under National Park Service). Information about the wilderness lands of the Bureau can be had by writing to the appropriate regional office for the states listed below.

State Director, Bureau of Land Management:

Alaska - 555 Cordova St., Anchorage 99501
Arizona - Federal Bldg., Room 3022, Phoenix 85025
California - Federal Bldg., Room E–2841, 2800 Cottage Way, Sacramento 95825
Colorado - Room 700, l600 Broadway, Denver 80202
Idaho - Federal Bldg., Room 334, 550 W. Fort St., Boise 83702
Montana, North Dakota, South Dakota, and Minnesota - Federal Bldg., 316 N. 26th St., Billings, Mont. 59101
Nevada - Federal Bldg., Room 3008, 300 Booth St., Reno 89502
New Mexico and Oklahoma - Federal Building, South Federal Place, P.O. Box 1449, Santa Fe, N. Mex. 87501
Oregon and Washington - 729 Northeast Oregon St., P.O. Box 2965, Portland, Ore. 97208
Utah - 8217 Federal Building, P.O. Box 11505, 125 South State, Salt Lake City 84111
Wyoming, Nebraska, and Kansas - P.O. Box 1828, Cheyenne, Wyo. 82001
EASTERN STATES (All states not listed above).
7981 Eastern Ave., Silver Spring, Md. 20910

NATIONAL PARKS AND CONSERVATION ASSOCIATION
1701 18th St., N.W. Washington, D.C. 20009

The NPCA is a private group which works closely with government agencies for the protection and enlargement of our National Parks system and for world-wide conservation practices in every area of environmental concern. It was founded in 1919 and at present has over 50,000 members. Membership is open to anyone interested in the organization and its goals. Dues are: student—$8 and associate—$10 per year. The monthly *National Parks and Conservation Magazine*, put out by the NPCA, comes with membership. It focuses on conservation, including endangered species, forestry, and other topics, mostly within the National Parks.

NATIONAL TRAILS COUNCIL
P.O.Box 1042, St. Charles, Ill. 60174

The National Trails Council was formed 2 June 1972 as a result of a resolution at the First National Symposium on Trails. The stated purpose of the Council is "...to support the planning, promotion and execution of trails systems at the local, county, state, regional and national levels." They will also function as a clearinghouse for all types of trail information and related activities. Any person or qualified organization interested in supporting the objectives of the National Trails Council shall be eligible for membership upon payment of dues. Annual dues are: student, $5; member, $10; club or organization, $25;

commercial, $100; industrial or foundation, by gift only.

Members receive the *National Trails Council Newsletter,* quarterly, 10 p., an informative newsletter about new and old trails throughout the country.

The National Trails Council will also be organizing future national and regional trails symposiums. Proceedings of the Second National Trails Symposium, held in Colorado Springs in 1973 can be obtained for $8.

STATE RECREATION AND TOURIST BUREAUS

These agencies can provide a variety of information on wilderness areas, forests, parks, trails, plus camping, canoeing, and other recreational activities for their state. A good one-stop-spot for securing information and literature.

Alabama - Bur. of Publicity and Info., Rm. 403, State Hwy. Bldg., Montgomery 36104
Alaska - Travel Div., Pouch E, Juneau 99891
American Samoa - Office of Tourism, P.O. Box 1147, Pago Pago 96920
Arizona - Office of Economic Planning & Development, Visitor Development Section, 1645 W. Jefferson St., Rm. 428, Phoenix 85007
Arkansas - Dept. of Parks & Tourism, 149 State Capitol, Little Rock 72201
California - State Office of Tourism, 1400 Tenth St., Sacramento 95814
Colorado - Div. of Commerce & Development, 602 State Capitol Annex, Denver 80203
Connecticut - Development Comm., State Office Bldg., P.O. Box 865, Hartford 06115
Delaware - Div. of Economic Development, 45 The Green, Dover 19901
District of Columbia - Washington Convention & Visitors Bur., 1129 20th St., N.W., Washington, D.C. 20036
Florida - Dept. of Commerce, Collins Bldg., 107 W. Gaines St., Tallahassee 32304
Georgia - Dept. of Community Development, P.O. Box 38097, Atlanta 30334
Guam - Visitors Bur., P.O. Box 3520, Agana 96910
Hawaii - Visitors Bur., 2270 Kalakaua Ave., Suite 801, Honolulu 96815
Idaho - Div. of Tourism, Rm. 108, State Capitol, Boise 83720
Illinois - Dept. of Business & Economic Development, 205 W. Wacker Dr., Suite 1122, Chicago 60606
Indiana - Div. of Tourism, Rm. 336-State House, Indianapolis 46204
Iowa - Development Comm., Tourism & Travel Div., 250 Jewett Bldg., Des Moines 50309
Kansas - Dept. of Economic Development, Rm. 122-S, State Office Bldg., Topeka 66612
Kentucky - Dept. of Public Info. Advertising & Travel Production, Capitol Annex, Frankfort 40601
Louisiana - Tourist Comm., P.O.Box 44291, Baton Rouge 70804
Maine - Dept. of Commerce & Industry, State House, Augusta 04330
Maryland - Dept. of Economic & Community Development, 2525 Riva Rd., Annapolis 21401
Massachusetts - Dept. of Commerce & Development, 100 Cambridge St.—Leverett Saltonstall, Boston 02202
Michigan - Tourist Council, 300 S. Capitol Ave., Rm. 102, Lansing 48926
Minnesota - Dept. of Economic Development, 480 Cedar St., Hanover Bldg., St. Paul 55101
Mississippi - Agricultural & Industrial Board, 1504 State Office Bldg., P.O.Box 849, Jackson 39205
Missouri - Div. of Tourism, 308 E. High St., P.O. Box 1055, Jefferson City 65101
Montana - Dept. of Highways, Helena 59601
Nebraska - Dept. of Economic Development, P.O.Box 94666, State Capitol, Lincoln 68509
Nevada - Dept. of Economic Development, Travel-Tourism Div., Carson City 89701
New Hampshire - Div. of Economic Development, Vacation Travel Promotion, P.O.Box 856, Concord 03301
New Jersey - Div. of Economic Development, Dept. of Labor & Industry, P.O.Box 2766, Trenton 08625
New Mexico - Dept. of Development, Travel Bur., 113 Washington Ave., Santa Fe 87501
New York - State Dept. of Commerce, Travel Bur., 99 Washington Ave., Albany 12210
North Carolina - Dept. of Natural & Economic Resources, Travel & Promotion, P. O. Box 27685, Raleigh 27611
North Dakota - Highway Dept., Capitol Grounds, Bismarck 58501
Ohio - Dept. of Economic & Community Development, 30 E. Broad St., Columbus 43215

Oklahoma - Tourism & Recreation Div., 500 Will Rogers Bldg., Oklahoma City 73105

Oregon - Travel Info. Section, 104 State Hwy. Bldg., Salem 97310

Pennsylvania - Dept. of Commerce, Bur. of Travel Development, 431 S. Office Bldg., Harrisburg 17120

Puerto Rico - Tourism Development Company, GPO Box "EN", San Juan 00936

Rhode Island - Dept. of Economic Development—Tourism, One Weybosset Hill, Providence 02903

South Carolina - Dept. of Parks, Recreation & Tourism, P.O.Box 113, 1205 Pendleton St., Columbia 29201

South Dakota - Dept. of Economic & Tourism Development, Div. of Tourism, Pierre 57501

Tennessee - Tourism Development, 1007 Andrew Jackson State Office Bldg., Nashville 37211

Texas - Travel & Info. Div., Highway Dept., Austin 78701

Utah - Travel Council, Council Hall—Capitol Hill, Salt Lake City 84114

Vermont - Agency of Development & Community Affairs, Info.—Travel Development, 61 Elm St., Montpelier 05602

Virgin Islands - Dept. of Commerce, P.O.Box 1692—Charlotte Amalie, St. Thomas 00801

Virginia - State Travel Serv., 6 N. Sixth St., Richmond 23219

Washington - Dept. of Commerce & Economic Development, Gen. Administration Bldg., Olympia 98504

West Virginia - Dept. of Commerce, Travel Development Div., Rm. B-553, 1900 Washington St. East, Charleston 25305

Wisconsin - Dept. of Natural Resources, Vacation & Travel Development, P.O.Box 450, Madison 53701

Wyoming - Travel Comm., 2320 Capitol Ave., Cheyenne 82002

ADIRONDACK MOUNTAIN CLUB, INC. (ADK)
172 Ridge St., Glen Falls, N.Y. 12801

New York's outdoor club for nature lovers, rock climbers, and backpackers. Concentrating most of its efforts in the beautiful Adirondack Mountains of New York, the club believes that the wilderness lands' "beauty, charms, and its stillness may be savored most fully with least damage to natural cause ON FOOT." Although supporting conserva-

tion and ecological practices nationwide, their immediate concern is the Adirondack Forest Preserve and New York's acquisition of additional forest lands for more wilderness. There are over 6,000 members with 18 chapters. Activities are formed on a club and/or chapter basis with the major emphasis on backpacking and camping trips throughout the entire year. Most chapters publish outing schedules. They maintain a library of rare Adirondack books at one of their lodges. To become a member you have to have concerns similar to the club's and sign a pledge supporting the club's objectives and vowing to be conservation conscious when out in the wilderness. Each chapter also has its own membership qualifications. Dues are $10 per year for active membership, which includes *Adirondac*, bimonthly, 16 p. il., $3 per year to nonmembers. This periodical covers club activities and conservation news of the Adirondacks.

The ADK also sells its *"Guide to the Adirondack Trails"* and *"Climbers Guide to the Adirondacks"* as well as other books and trail maps. Write for publication list.

THE ADIRONDACK FORTY-SIXERS
Adirondack, N.Y. 12808

A rather unique hiking and backpacking club because membership is based solely upon the successful climbing (hiking) of the 46 Adirondack peaks which are over 4,000 feet high. The $2 annual dues are optional, but must be paid in order to become an active member. The club publishes a pamphlet *Mountain Manners* and a book, *The Adirondack High Peaks and the Forty-Sixers*, $12.95.

APPALACHIAN MOUNTAIN CLUB (AMC)
5 Joy St., Boston, Mass. 02108

Founded in 1876, the AMC is the oldest mountain club in America, and it is also one of the largest with well over 23,000 members, worldwide. The club's primary interest has been the preservation and recreational enhancement of the mountain country of New England, and "it represents the spirit of giving opportunities to the outdoor public to share our natural heritage through common efforts and experiences." The club maintains hundreds of miles of trails, 20 back country campsites and shelters, and 9 huts. It also conducts workshops in hiking

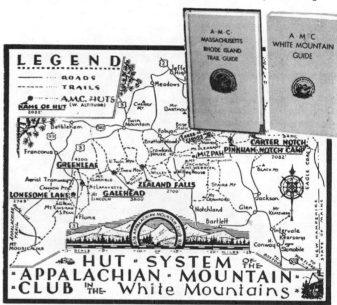

and safety. Aside from hiking and backpacking, the club sponsors outings and instruction in snowshoeing, cross-country skiing, smooth and white water paddling, and rock climbing and mountaineering activities. Each of the 10 chapters also has its own programs. Membership requirements include a desire to support club activities, sponsorship by two members, and approval by the Membership Committee. The AMC publishes (free to members) the *Appalachia Bulletin*, quarterly, which reports on issues concerning the New England and New York areas; the *AMC Times*, 10 times a year, which covers club activities; and the *Appalachia Journal*, semi-annually, "for those who enjoy the outdoors, exploration and adventure." Dues for those 23 years and older are $20 per year plus a $5 admission fee, and for those under 23 it's $10 (or $5 without club publications). Nonmembers can receive both the *Times* and *Bulletin* for $7 (cannot be ordered separately), and the *Journal* for $5. All three can be had for $10 a year. Newsletters are also put out by the individual chapters. It almost pays to become a member.

THE COLORADO MOUNTAIN CLUB (CMC)
2530 W. Alameda Ave., Denver, Colo. 80219

The Colorado Mountain Club, which is composed of 12 autonomous groups, is highly active in conservation issues in Colorado, especially in the Colorado Rockies. Their activities run the gamut of outdoor mountain fun: hiking and backpacking, from day-long hikes to three-week backpacking trips. Membership has to be approved and the dues structure is variable among the groups. The following publications are available to nonmembers:

Trail and Timberline, monthly, 12 p. il., $4/yr.

Summer Schedule, annually, 236 p., $2.50. Six months of CMC summer outdoor events.

Winter Schedule, annually, 150 p., $2. Six months of CMC winter outdoor events.

FINGER LAKES TRAIL CONFERENCE (FLTC)
P.O.Box 18048, Rochester, N.Y. 14618

The FLTC oversees the planning and construction of the Finger Lakes Trail, which is a 350-mile wilderness foottrail through the Southern Tier of New York State, from the Catskills to Allegheny State Park. There are also another 300 miles of branch trails, one of them connecting to the Bruce Trail in Canada. Well over half complete, it is an outstanding example of what a few dedicated citizens can do; most of the trail is on private property, for which trail easements have been obtained. A large, stamped, self-addressed envelope will get you a *Buyers Guide to Maps.*

GREEN MOUNTAIN CLUB INC.
P.O.Box 94, Rutland, Vt. 05701
Protects and helps to maintain the Long Trail system in Vermont. Made up of sections which plan outdoor recreational activities year round. Publishes several guidebooks and *Long Trail News* with information on club activities and pertinent trail and shelter matters. Membership is for "all those who love the out-of-doors and have a pride in the mountains of Vermont."

THE IOWA MOUNTAINEERS (IM)
P.O. Box 163, Iowa City, Iowa 52240
The Iowa Mountaineers is primarily a mountaineering club but is active enough in hiking and backpacking to fulfill the needs of most backpackers. Major foreign and U.S. trips are scheduled each year. Anyone is eligible for membership; dues are $7 for active, $6 for expedition and $5 for associate. Members receive *The Iowa Climber* semi-annually, 40 p. il., containing articles on club events and trips, schedules of future outings and expeditions.

NEW ENGLAND TRAIL CONFERENCE
c/o Anne Mausolff, Sec.-Treas., Box 145, Weston, Vt. 05161
Made up of four dozen New England hiking clubs and is a clearinghouse for information in its area. Publishes *New England Trails* annually, $1 per copy, relating trail conditions, annual meeting summary, and other pertinent club information and *Hiking Trails of New England* every now and then, 50¢ per copy, which has sketch maps of trails and trail-related information. Membership is through one of the constituent clubs.

NEW YORK-NEW JERSEY TRAIL CONFERENCE, INC.
G.P.O.Box 2250, New York, N.Y. 10001
Federation of hiking clubs in New York and New Jersey, which maintains more than 450 miles of trails with shelters, and supports needed conservation measures. Membership is through member clubs or membership at large for $5, which gets you the bimonthly *Trail Walker.* List of trail guides and maps for large, stamped, self-addressed envelope.

THE POTOMAC APPALACHIAN TRAIL CLUB (PATC)
1718 N St., N.W., Washington, D.C. 20036
The Club maintains 500 miles of trails in the Washington area, 226 of which are on the Appalachian Trail (AT); and maintains 17 shelters and 15 cabins along the trail, both types may be used by non-members (a fee is charged for cabins). Despite this arduous task, PATC members have a full schedule of hiking, backpacking, climbing, and other mountaineering activities the year round. They are particularly active in hiking and backpacking on the AT and often combine outings with work excursions. Along with these doings, conservation issues are also a major activity. Anyone interested in working with the

club is welcome to join, but sponsorship by a member and approval by the council are required. Dues are $10 for adults plus $5 application fee, and $4 for juniors. Members receive the *Potomac Appalachian* (formally *Forecast*), monthly, 6 p., which now includes the quarterly *PATC Bulletin.* The PATC now publishes a special yearly issue of the *Potomac Appalachian,* approximately 150 pages and full of interesting, well-written articles. Available for $2 and well worth it.

THE SIERRA CLUB
530 Bush St., San Francisco, Calif. 94108
Though the Sierra Club is most noted for its environmental and conservation work to preserve wilderness areas where civilization appears to be encroaching irresponsibly, it is also quite active in using the wilderness throughout the United States via its regional chapters. A note to the above address will get you a list of the chapters to find the one closest to you.

Benefits of membership include wilderness outings throughout the year; educational trips with optional university credit; whitewater trips, ski touring, mountaineering and bike hikes; local hiking and climbing trips, clean-up and trail maintenance activities, and the use of huts and lodges—14 in the U.S. and 1 in Canada.

There are several classes of membership open, though the most common type, Regular Membership, runs $15 annually plus a one-time $5 admission fee. Each of the chapters has its own newsletter which is free to members. In addition, the home office puts out:

Sierra Club Bulletin, ten times per year, $8 (free to members). Official club magazine containing conservation and ecology articles, book reviews, club news and a schedule of major trips.

Ascent, annually, $6 (member's price, $5). The Club's mountaineering journal containing outstanding photographs of mountains and accounts by the people who climb them.

THE NATIONAL HIKING AND SKI TOURING ASSOCIATION (NAHSTA)
P.O.Box 7421, Colorado Springs, Colo. 80907
The National Hiking and Ski Touring Association is devoted to the research, planning and rebuilding of America's trails. It has established a Volunteer Conservation Corps. Volunteers participate in trail building and trail maintenance in the National Forests. NAHSTA also runs an outdoor school at Vail. Dues are $5 a year and include a newsletter.

APPALACHIAN TRAIL CONFERENCE (ATC)
P.O.Box 236, Harpers Ferry, W. Va. 25425

The Appalachian Trail Conference is a private, non-profit, national organization which represents citizen's interests in the Appalachian Trail. Through its member clubs, the Conference keeps much of the Trail cleared and marked. The ATC works in cooperation with the National Park Service and the Forest Service in the planning, operation and maintenance of the Trail. Membership dues are $10 (plus a first year fee of $2.50); members receive the quarterly *Appalachian Trailway News* and an ATC patch.

The ATC also publishes guidebooks, maps and other descriptive literature on the Trail. Available from the ATC are:

The Appalachian Trail (folder, incl. list of publications), Pub. No. 17, 25¢.

Suggestions for Appalachian Trail Users, Pub. No. 15, 70¢.

The Appalachian Trail (65-page booklet), Pub. No. 5, $1.25.

There are dozens and dozens of trail guides. Some are very good and many are poor. It would be impossible to list them all, so we'll just list a few, including some regional guidebooks and the only trails bibliography that we know of.

Clubs and organizations often publish and sell guidebooks and maps of trails or trail systems they are involved with. These have been listed. Government agencies publish small guides and maps which should be useful. Outstanding are the approximately 5 miles-to-the-inch scale maps of the different National Forests which are available from the appropriate Regional Forest Service Agency (see page 9 for addresses).

INTRODUCTION TO FOOT TRAILS IN AMERICA
Robert Colwell
1972 - 224 p. il. - $3.95

This is about the only book available which attempts to cover hiking trails throughout the entire country under one cover. It is still very limited since it describes only 81 selected trails, most of which are suited for family hiking. Only a few are accompanied by rough sketch maps. However it is a beginning. Now available in paperbound for $3.95.
From: Stackpole Books, Cameron & Kelker Sts., Harrisburg, Pa. 17105

HIKING AND HIKING TRAILS—A TRAILS AND TRAIL-BASED ACTIVITIES BIBLIOGRAPHY, Bibliography Series Number 20
Mary Ellen Barkauskas
December, 1970 - 58 p. - $3

This bibliography, the only one of its kind, includes general hiking books, congressional hearings and reports, sources of info on trail construction and maintenance, as well as guides and general trail literature. The number and scope of the listings is impressive, 470, but the information needed to go out and buy the things is deficient—no price, no address, only the publisher. Nonetheless, it's still a good source.
From: National Technical Information Service, 5285 Port Royal Rd., Springfield, Va. 22151

HANDBOOK OF WILDERNESS TRAVEL
George and Iris Wells
1968 - 306 p. il. - $3.75

First published in 1956, a second "revised" edition, now available in paperback, was issued in 1968. Actually, the book is exactly the same, page for page, and word for word, except for the lists and weights of food and equipment, which reflect the advent of lightweight equipment and freeze-dried foods. Nevertheless it is still a very valuable addition to the backpacker's library. It includes a list of 371 wilderness areas in the U.S.
From: Gerry, 5450 North Valley Hwy., Denver, Colo. 80216

RIGHT-OF-WAY, A GUIDE TO ABANDONED RAILROADS IN THE UNITED STATES
Waldo J. Nielsen
1973 - 119 p. il. - $5.95

There are over 35,000 miles of railroad right-of-way, abandoned between 1937 and 1973, well distributed over the entire country. If you are looking for a hiking trail in your backyard, or while you are travel-

FLORIDA TRAIL ASSOCIATION
P.O.Box 13708, Gainesville, Fla. 32604

The Florida Trail Association was formed to establish the first footpath in the state of Florida. The Trail is scheduled to run some 1,300 miles when completed, from the Alabama state line west of Pensacola to the Tamiami Trail (U.S. 41). Four hundred miles of the Trail have already been completed and pass through pine woods, cypress stands and swamps of scenic beauty unmatched anywhere. Membership in the Association, which runs $5 a year, brings a quarterly newsletter with news and activity schedules; however, more important, it allows the member to use those sections of the Trail that pass over private property. The Association, by accepting responsibility for members' actions, has been able to secure this "privilege of trespass" for card-holding hikers. Because of this, the Association's trail guides and maps can only be purchased by members.

For more info, drop a card to the above address.

GUIDE BOOKS

ing, this is the book to show you where. Walking these roadbeds (ties and tracks have been removed) is like walking through history. As one rambles along, one sees the abandoned stations, the abandoned farms and ghost towns. On some rights-of-way the tunnels are still there to walk through and the switchbacks to climb.

This "atlas" has a map for each state on which the abandoned railroads are mapped. Plus a lot of useful introductory material.
From: Maverick Publications, Box 243, Bend, Oreg. 97791

sources of books & maps

Most of the mountaineering shops listed elsewhere in this book carry some of the books and trail guides. Books are probably stocked on a regional basis. Unfortunately, there are very few book dealers who deal exclusively in trail guides, hiking books and maps. Among the few:

BACKPACKER BOOKS
Bellows Falls, Vt. 15101

An affiliate of *Backpacker* magazine and the only outlet we know of that will attempt to supply just about anything and everything on trails. They handle over 600 titles (and more to come) including 193 trail guides, books on backpacking, mountaineering, mapping, survival, biking, caving, skiing, canoeing and even city walks.

By all means send for their *Book List No. 1, No. 2* and *No. 3.* And if you know of a trail guide they haven't included (doubtful), let them know and they will stock it.

WALKING NEWS, INC.
P.O.Box 352, New York, N.Y. 10013

For a self-addressed, stamped envelope, you can get a Hikers Region Key Map that shows the areas covered by 80 different 17" x 11" trail maps for New Jersey and Catskill region of New York State. List also includes other trail guides and regional books. Nice thing about the Hikers Regional Maps is that they're very well drawn, clear and easy to follow—and, they are printed on waterproof and tearproof paper (if you don't believe it, try and tear one of the damn things—won't work!). Maps run 50¢ to 75¢ each depending on the region covered.

NOAMTRAC
Box 805, Bloomington, Ind. 47401

Translation: North America Trail Complex. The intent of this group is to develop an interest in an "International Network of Expeditionary Foot Trails." The guide maps developed to date are copies of U.S.G.S. topo maps with suggested trail study corridors sketched in. Whether or not this ever takes off, it is an interesting concept. An inquiry will bring a list of guide maps for 9 proposed cross-country and coast-to-coast trails.

WILDERNESS PRESS
2440 Bancroft Way, Berkeley, Calif. 94704

Books about the outdoors is their business, but they publish and sell only their own. Actually, they specialize in trail guides, most of which are of California, but they're expanding their geographical coverage. Free pamphlet includes about 24 books and some maps.

land navigation

Pathfinding and land navigation are often used interchangeably to describe the process of determining one's own position with respect to camp or known landmarks, or finding where an objective lies so as to set a compass course to it. Actually, pathfinding is not so much concerned with determining position and direction as it is with choosing the best route to take across country to reach the objective. Both pathfinding and land navigation require a background in the use of map and compass, but the pathfinder must be especially good at translating map data to the physical lay of the land, and he must know the workings of nature so as to be able to determine where water can be found; on which side of a mountain travel will be the easiest with respect to terrain, weather, providing shelter, etc.; the possibilities of going directly across a swamp to save time, as opposed to going around it; where to ford a river, traverse a snowfield, or cross a desert most advantageously, and so forth. Very often the pathfinder of an expedition will also be the one who provides the camp with food, thus he must not only know how to hunt and trap, but also where to route the party to provide the best access to game.

It would seem that the only way to develope proficiency in pathfinding would be to spend a heck of a lot time in the field. Actually, much good information can be gotten from several books presently available on the market. Two of them are by Vinson Brown, a professional biologist and naturalist who lives in California. *Reading the Woods,* $7.95, is concerned with interpretive reading of the landscape, trees, rocks, rivers, swamps, etc., and *Knowing the Outdoors in the Dark,* $7.95, discusses the sounds, movement and shapes of the wilderness night and how they can be used to identify wildlife and their activity, weather trends, position, and so forth. A third book, *Things Maps Don't Tell Us,* by Armin K. Lobeck, $6.95, which covers the mechanics of how the shape and form of the landscape came to be, would complete the set and give you a well-rounded source of pathfinding study material.

The land navigator, like a surveyor, wants to know the numbers. Direction, time, rate of travel, and relative position — where one thing is located with respect to another — are all of prime importance to him. His tools are compass, map, dividers, pencil with a little penknife, watch, and a notebook. In his head he keeps facts and figures on wilderness travel determined from his own experimentation or from notes taken on previous expeditions. For example, he can tell you that it will take approximately 30 minutes for the average person with a 10-pound day pack to cover a mile and a half of path on a particular section of the Appalachian Trail, and that the actual distance made good would only be three-quarters of a mile. If the person's pack weight is increased, he knows at what rate to proportionately increase the time for travel. He can tell you that an expedition of 5 people, each carrying 35 to 40- pound packs, will be able to travel at a rate of 3 miles per hour over a particular terrain, and that in 2 hours time they will walk 6 miles, equal to only 2 miles made good on the map. Knowing that sunset occurs at, say, 6:32 p.m., and taking into consideration that the chosen campsite is on the east side of a particular mountain, which means for all practical purposes it'll be too dark for travel by 6:00 p.m., the competent land navigator can tell you what time you should leave the jump-off point to arrive at the site with sufficient light to set up camp and prepare chow.

The good wilderness navigator realizes the most important tool is his notebook and the facts he's written down. When the party takes off he's careful to record the number in the group, each person's pack weight, time of departure, weather, temperature, type of terrain, and other pertinent data. Enroute he will continue to make notes, and record bearings and locations of discoveries not on the map — an underground spring, a neat bivouacking area, a black raspberry patch, an overhanging rock ledge as a possible emergency shelter, and so on. By taking notes the navigator forces himself not only to learn the area he's traveling in,

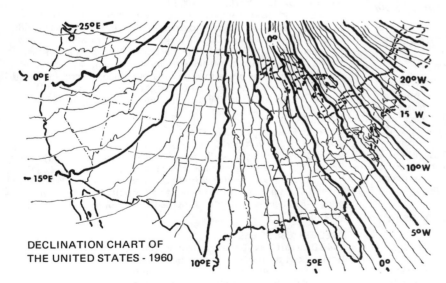

DECLINATION CHART OF
THE UNITED STATES - 1960

This chart shows the number of degrees that a compass is off true north for different parts of the United States. True and magnetic north coincide along the line running east of Florida and on north through Illinois and Michigan. Along this line of 0° declination you won't have to adjust your map (true) course to obtain a compass (magnetic) heading. But in other localities you will have to add west declination (or subtract east declination) to your map course to get a correct compass heading. An easy way to remember whether to add or subtract the declination error is via the mnemonic (memory jogging) device, *CHAW* — (from map to) *C*ompass *H*eading, *A*dd *W*est (declination).

All topographic maps show the declination at the lower left hand corner for a particular year. The annual change in declination will also be shown, and this annual change should be applied to the declination to bring it up to date.

Here's some data regarding declination error for your navigator's notebook: an error of 10° in your compass heading will put you off course 950 feet for each mile you walk.

but also to sharpen his powers of observation. Soon he'll find that he's seeing and remembering 50 to 60 percent more about a region than the other people in the group.

Note-taking may seem a bit tedious at first, but once you get the swing of it, it's as easy as scratching your head. And if you're conscientious in making your entries, you'll have something to bring back from the trip that's a lot more useful and permanent than just pleasant memories. Any notebook that's small and handy can be used for a journal, but the best is a civil engineer's field book. One in particular, that's available through Forestry Suppliers, Inc., can be recommended: the Dietzgen, Hi-visibility orange cover model with 80 waterproof pages and 4 x 4 grid. The field book is 5 in. x 7½ in., weighs 8½ oz., and all left-hand pages are lined for note taking and right-hand pages have a ¼" grid suitable for route-sketching or drawing

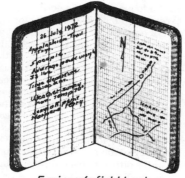

Engineer's field book

up local maps. A 16-page supplement in the back includes much useful geometry data and a table of trigonometric functions. If you happen to be in a university area, you can sometimes find these field books (also called transit books) in the university bookstore.

The best book we've come across for the practical land navigator, which very well covers the whole subject, is Calvin Rutstrum's *The Wilderness Route Finder*, $5.95. It's the only wilderness nav book that not only discusses seat-of-the-pants navigation in detail, but also the use of sextant and transit for determining latitude and longitude of position by the stars.

Learning land navigation is mostly OJT, which some of you lucky stiffs may remember means "on the job training." Since use of map and compass is not considered useful or practical enough to be taught in school you'll have to do this on your own or perhaps through the Scouts. Interestingly enough, Sweden thinks otherwise about the practicality of land navigation and teaches the subject in their elementary schools. Bjorn Kjellstrom, one of their citizens, has been pushing this attitude in the U.S., and to make it more in-

teresting, he's thrown in a competitive aspect and called the process Orienteering, which basically runs along the same lines as sports car rallying, except you do it on foot with map and compass. The whole deal is explained in Kjellstrom's Orienteering handbook, *Be Expert With Map And Compass*, $6.95, which makes a good companion book to Rutstrum's *Wilderness Route Finder.*

Silva, Inc., a Swedish manufacturing concern, which among other things builds an excellent and very popular line of compasses, has gotten involved in the Orienteering push with training aids, films, Orienteering kits, and advice for groups desiring to set up a local program. As a matter of fact, if your backpacking group is tired of the same old trails, an Orienteering rally would certainly make an interesting adjunct to a weekend outing.

We haven't said much about land navigation and getting lost. Frankly, if that's the only time it would be used, you'd best forget it. Land navigation is not a remedy, rather it is a process used before the fact, and if done properly, will prevent you from ever crossing into that foggy zone of not knowing where you are or where to go.

---

sources of information

U.S. ORIENTEERING FEDERATION
Box 1081, Athens, Ohio 45701
and
THE CANADIAN ORIENTEERING FEDERATION
P.O. Box 6206, Terminal, Toronto 1, Ontario, Canada
These people can supply information on competitive Orienteering Racing, setting up an Orienteering club, where to get maps, instruments, and so forth.

AMERICAN ORIENTEERING SERVICE
P.O. Box 547, La Porte, Ind. 46350
and
CANADIAN ORIENTEERING SERVICE
446 McNicolls Ave., Willowdale, Ontario, Canada

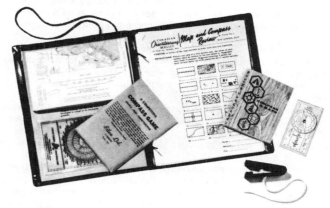

This is the service division of Silva, Inc., in the U.S. and Canada. They will provide you with information on Orienteering plus teaching and training aids, such as practice compasses, protractors, training topo maps, visual aid material, and textbooks.

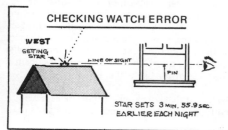

CHECKING WATCH ERROR

WEST

SETTING STAR

LINE OF SIGHT

PIN

STAR SETS 3 MIN. 55.9 SEC. EARLIER EACH NIGHT

A simple method of determining how accurately your watch keeps time can be done by checking it against the movement of a selected star past a given point over a period of two or three nights. The procedure is to find a bright star that sets behind a roof or something, in the west, and note the position where it sets (meridian) by sticking a pin in the windowsill from which you're observing and sighting directly across the head. The moment the star goes behind the roof (occults), note the hour, minute, and second on your watch. The next night do the same thing. Note the exact time the star occults — one instant you'll see it, then it'll be gone. "Then" is when you mark the time. Next, sharpen your pencil and subtract today's time from yesterday's. If you find that the star set 3 minutes, 55.90644 seconds earlier today than yesterday, you've got a pretty damn accurate watch. (Pick a star that's higher than 40° above the horizon.)

Pathfinding

One can often learn the direction by noticing the hill ranges and the rocks. On the first going into a hilly locality, pay particular attention to the bearing of the hill ranges. This can often be determined by the map. On your map find the main water channel. For example, if the main waterway runs westward, and you intend to travel and camp on the north side of this, notice the direction in which the northern tributaries flow into the main waterway. These tributaries flow between the hill ranges.

In determining this, look at the small tributaries and not the main channel. If the tributaries flow southwest, then the hill ranges lie northeast and southwest. Verify this on the ground. Many good woodsmen, if in a country well known to them, depend almost solely on this.

If, in the case cited above, you find on a cloudy day that you have difficulty in distinguishing the southwest from the northeast, you can frequently decide the matter by studying the geologic dip. The strata of the rock seldom lie level, but dip in some one direction. Now if in the case with which we are dealing, you have found that the strata dip downward to the north or northwest, then the southeast side of the hill range will show a cross section of the stratum. This disposes of your difficulty at once.

In some places in Canada and the Northern States a knowledge of the glacial drift will answer the same purpose. A great ice cap moved across the northern part of our continent and left scratches and grooves in many places on the rocks. In some places these are coarse scratches; in others they are grooves several inches wide. It is a good idea to get a map of the glacial drift, and notice the direction in which the ice moved in the country you intend to visit. Of course there are only some places where you can see these marks, but where they can be found they are all exactly parallel for a given locality.

The glacial drift left us two other evidences which we can use. The ice, in sliding over a hill, seems to have smoothed off the side which it first reached and to have left the other side abruptly. Thus if the drift came from the northwest, the northwest side of the hill will slope gradually while the southeastern side will be more abrupt. This ice sheet carried boulders, and after carrying them up a hill often dropped them on the other side at the foot of the slope.

Moss on rocky hills and on boulders, when these are not under the shade of trees, is more luxuriant and covers more area on the north side than on the south. The center of the mossy area is slightly east of north.

The trees are great aids to the traveler in finding his way. In studying them, always remember that their peculiarities of form are due to the sun and the wind. The most intense light comes from the south, and in most parts of our country the prevailing winds come from the west.

If, from its position, a tree is shaded from the west wind and from the southern light, it will not develop the characteristics which can be of use to us. Keeping this in mind, you will study large numbers of trees, tall trees, and those in open places. Then the following rules can be very useful:

The heaviest branches are on the south and east sides of the trees. The thickest bark is on the north and west sides. When a tree is cut down the growth rings are found to be widest on the northeast. Saplings can be used to establish this. The lines on the bark of a tree are closer together and deeper on the north and west than on the south and east. The roots on the west side are horizontal while on the east side they are more nearly vertical. Trees growing on rocks may have horizontal roots on both east and west sides. In this case the roots on the west sides are larger than on the east.

More trees lean to the southeast than to any other direction. Some trees, such as poplar, are darker on one side than on the other. The center of the dark part is slightly east of north. The north and west sides of a tree are harder than the other sides. This can be tested by using a knife blade.

Much has been said of moss on the trees. This is of use in some cases but one must bear in mind that only the trees which are exposed to the south can be considered. The moss forms only on trees that are damp. The northern side of the tree is not exposed to the direct rays of the sun and so that side of the tree is kept more moist than the other. As a result it should have more moss than the other. But if the tree is shaded from the south and there is a pool on that side, then the moss will be found not on the north but on the south. Of course this is the exception to the rule. As a rule, the center of the mossy area is slightly east of north. Dead trees usually give a better indication than trees with moss. The bark on a dead tree holds the moisture on the northern side. For this reason, under the bark on this side the tree is wet while the other side is dry. This damp side is the first to rot. The center of the damp or rotted area is usually slightly east of north.

Cocoons are sometimes to be found under the bark of dead trees. After the bark becomes quite loose they may be found on all sides, but in the early stages they are on the side of the looser bark. That is on the damp side. Tall, pointed trees such as spruce, usually have their tips leaning slightly to the north of east. One is not likely to get lost in a small maple wood such as is usually used for sugar-bush, but if this does occur the difficulty may sometimes be overcome by noticing the tap-holes. These are oftenest to be found on the southern side, from the southeast to the southwest, as the sap runs best on this side.

Sometimes an opening in the forest will be strewn with flowers. These have their faces turned to the brightest light. Notice the ones near the center of the opening. They are not so likely to have been shaded by trees, so their faces will turn to the south.

Grasses, especially in the spring and fall, are real pointers. The prevailing wind is from the west, and this acting on the grass in the later stages of its growth causes it, when mature and dry, to lean to the east. In the late fall it is often broken, and the broken ends point east. In the spring, the dry, leaning grass remains, while the young growth shoots up between. In a wet or average season, the growth on a southern slope will be more dense, and the grass longer than on the northern slope. On the other hand, in an extremely dry season, the grass on a southern slope may be baked.

Bird's nests and animal burrows may be studied to advantage. Doubtlessly every one has noticed that barn swallows build their nests under the eaves on the south side of a building. Sometimes they will use the east side, but they never use the north. Kingfishers tunnel into sand banks, and make homes at the ends of the tunnels. These tunnels never face the west wind, but where possible they are in a hillside facing south.

Some animals, such as groundhogs, show the same taste in their homemaking. Nests and burrows are so scarce, and circumstances so alter their construction, that they can be taken only as a general aid, and too much confidence must not be placed in them.

To find one's direction in winter, the position and hardness of the snow banks should be observed. The banks on the east side of hills are generally deepest, while the crust on the west side is hardest. This fact can be used in traveling on the ice on a winding stream. Points of land jut out into the water. If the stream runs east or west, the snow on the sides of these points indicates the direction. If the stream runs north or south, the snow on the faces of the banks themselves gives the information.

In case of need one will find that some one of these devices will straighten out the difficulty, but it is well to employ several so as to make no mistake.

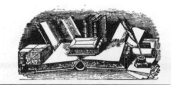
READING THE WOODS
Vinson Brown
1969 - 160 p. il. - $7.95

There are many other signs to watch for that tell us about the effects of climate. For example, many ferns, much moss, and many large-leaved vines in the undergrowth of a forest are a sign of heavy rainfall in the area. Widely spaced trees with few shrubs below them tell us that here the rainfall is probably rather low or between 15 and 30 inches per year. Still more widely spaced desert trees with numerous spines, such as the saguaro cacti and the Joshua tree ... tell us of extreme desert conditions with rainfall usually well below 10 inches a year.

Another sign of a recent severe earthquake is a line of trees standing at a strange angle and yet giving no evidence of having been attacked by a strong wind, which would have bent their branches or trunks out of shape. The roll of an earthquake across the ground may have stopped at a point where the trees were tipped at an angle. The trunk of such a tree, if it continues to live, will then turn at an angle in order to grow straight up once more, an elbowlike effect that lasts for all of its life.

If you've ever wondered how the old Indian scout could casually glance over a section of terrain, then pop off with a 25-minute read-out of interpretive data, here's the book that'll tell you what goes into his program. It covers the effects of climate, weather, animals and man on the wilderness, and discusses the many clues they leave behind which tells the story of what occurred. Really an unusual and interesting book.
From: Stackpole Books, Harrisburg, Pa. 17105

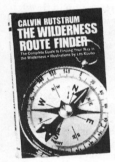

THE WILDERNESS ROUTE FINDER
Calvin Rutstrum
1967 - 214 p. il. - $5.95

This is probably the most comprehensive book on wilderness navigation yet available. Cal gets right with it in the opening chapters of the book by debunking some of the popular myths: no one has an innate sense of direction, moss does not grow more heavily on the shady side of trees, and the like. He tells why one gets lost and how to prevent it; how to use a map, a compass, and even a sextant; how to define and figure base lines and lines of position; how to use celestial bodies as route finders during the day and at night. He explains the use of a common transistor radio for homing back to the departure point or fixing a position. A full-scale appendix discusses some of the more involved ways of finding direction, but in 99 percent of the cases, the main body of the book is all one needs to ensure absolute safety on any trip by land or water. The book is well illustrated and contains much of Cal's wilderness wisdom, which you find in his other books on canoeing, cabin building, and so forth. Definitely recommended for anyone seriously interested in wilderness navigation.
From: Macmillan Co., Front & Brown Sts., Riverside, N.J. 08075

MAP READING FM 21-26
U.S. Army Field Manual
1969 - 155 p. il. - $6.75
Cat. No. D 101.20:21-26/4

An excellent book on all phases of land navigation, but for a government book, it's way overpriced. We're including it, because despite its price it is a very good reference work on the subject. The book contains information on the purpose and use of various types of maps, aerial photographs, photomosaics, photomaps, and pictomaps. Included are such subjects as marginal data, grids, map scales, terrain forms and contours, the compass and its application, land navigation and pathfinding field techniques, and field map sketching. The appendix contains a list of reference texts and tables of measure with conversion factors. Four maps in color are supplied with the book for practicing and screwing around with.
From: Superintendent of Documents, U.S. Government Printing Office, Washington, D.C. 20402

KNOWING THE OUTDOORS IN THE DARK
Vinson Brown
1972 - 191 p. il. - $7.95

It is easier to see in the dark than most people think ... a human being generally has eyes that can see better in the gloom of night than those of a bear, and almost as well as those of a cat ... in the first fifteen minutes a person stands in the dark his iris spreads to its widest extent ..., but it takes another half-hour, or three-quarters of an hour altogether, for the retina behind the iris to become fully adjusted to the night and able to make full use of that wide-open iris.

This is the companion volume to Brown's other work *Reading the Woods*. Whereas Brown's first book is concerned with the inanimate environment and reading clues left behind from some previous activity, this book is concerned with the animate environment — animals and reading the clues to their present activity, particularly at night. Since sight is rather marginal in the nighttime wilderness, other senses must be used to determine what is going on. Interpretive reading of sounds, smells, flashes and glowing lights, silhouettes against the night sky, even the feel of particular textures are all discussed, in addition to ways of developing your night vision, and sense of hearing and smell. A fantastic book.
From: Stackpole Books, Harrisburg, Pa. 17105

BE EXPERT WITH MAP AND COMPASS
Bjorn Kjellstrom
1976 - 214 p. il. - $6.95 (pb)

NUMBER OF MINUTES TO COVER 1 MILE	HIGHWAY	OPEN FIELD	OPEN WOODS	MOUNTAIN & FOREST
WALK	15	25	30	40
RUN	10	13	16	22

You can estimate the distance you have traveled by the number of minutes elapsed. Various speeds and terrains influence time to cover 1 mile.

Originally published in 1955, this one's been through a couple of publishers. Stackpole put it out first for American Orienteering Service, a division of Silva, Inc. (which Kjellstrom heads up). Then it went back to Silva, Inc., and now Scribner's Sons have it out in paperback. A couple of revisions have been made, but essentially it's still the same book Stackpole was publishing, though not quite as nice a binding. Kjellstrom places emphasis on use of map and compass for fast and efficient cross-country travel, and the discussions of topographical maps and the use of Silva compasses are all oriented to this end. After you've gotten the basics of all of this, Kjellstrom introduces you to Orienteering racing, which is competitive cross-country travel via specified check points. Route Orienteering is won by the person finding the most check points within a given time period, and Point Orienteering is won by the person going through all check points in the shortest period of time. Well illustrated and lotsa good techniques to help speed up your land navigating.
From: Chas. Scribner's Sons, Vreeland Ave., Totowa, N.J. 07512

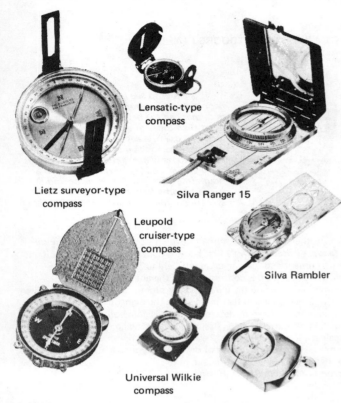

Lietz surveyor-type compass

Lensatic-type compass

Silva Ranger 15

Leupold cruiser-type compass

Silva Rambler

Universal Wilkie compass

Suunto KB-14

LAND NAVIGATION

COMPASSES
$5 - $25

The compass is used essentially to determine the direction of magnetic north, which is located slightly north of the Hudson Bay area in Canada. A compass is subject to two errors: (1) declination, also called variation, which is the difference between magnetic north and true north, and can be as great as 180° off true north in some parts of the world (in the United States the error ranges from 20° east of north to 20° west of north); and (2) deviation, which is caused by a ferrous object placed too close to the compass, causing the needle to deflect. Deviation is usually not a problem for the wilderness trekker, but declination should always be taken into account when using compass with map. All maps are oriented true north, and if you follow a compass course taken from a map without accounting for declination, you could be a half mile off course after a mile of walking at an error of 20° declination.

A good compass should have jeweled bearings upon which the needle rotates (in some cases the needle is actually a circular card). To prevent the needle from swinging wildly every time the instrument is moved to take a bearing, the needle should be immersed in a liquid which will not freeze at low temperatures. This is called liquid damping. Another method, not as popular as using liquid, is also employed called induction damping. Here the swing of the needle sets up an electric field which tends to oppose the movement of the needle. When the needle stops the field disappears. The field, as might be supposed, does not interfere with the magnetic attraction of the needle. If a compass is to be used at night, the needle as well as calibrations should be luminous. For working with maps and plotting courses it's best that the compass be calibrated in degrees, 0° to 360°. There should always be some means of sighting with the instrument, such as two vanes, in order to take bearings.

Silva makes a good range of low- to medium-priced compasses with a variety of arrangements and features. These are widely available in camping and sporting goods stores. The Suunto is a good medium-priced compact sighting compass. Some surplus Army and Marine Corps compasses are excellent (especially the artillery type) and are often sold at bargain prices.

Serious outdoor professionals and near-professionals will want to consider the Brunton compass. Trade-named the "pocket transit," this is actually just a tried-and-true, rugged compass with a strange but effective sighting arrangement, and an accurate built-in clinometer (for measuring vertical angles and slopes, and for leveling). See any textbook of field geology for details of how they can be used. Brunton is just the name of the original model (made ages ago); over the years they have been put out by several manufacturers (notably by Ainsworth, and by Keuffel and Esser). Most field geologists feel naked without one. Current production models, made by a firm in Riverton, Wyoming, which has taken on the original Brunton name, cost upwards of $80, depending on features. There is nothing wrong with the old ones, though, if you can find them. Also, ex-military Bruntons sometimes turn up surplus for quite cheap prices. There's no difference except for the olive-drab paint job.

PLOTTING INSTRUMENTS
$3 - $6

For plotting bearings in your field book or on a map, you will want a scale (or ruler), a straightedge, and a protractor, as well as (obviously) a pencil. If you enjoy juggling, or like spending your field time hunting for all these things, you can use all the gadgets in the illustration. Altogether they will run you about $8 to $12. Or, if you are not quite so masochistic, you will get a six-inch clear plastic engineer's scale by the C-Thru Company at a drafting supply or stationery store. They make a model that serves as a protractor and straightedge, and is graduated 20 to the inch so that you can read distances in feet from USGS 7.5 minute topo maps. It also slips neatly into a field book and costs about thirty cents, so you don't have quite so much to mourn when you lose it in the underbrush. Some compasses also have built-in protractors and scales.

If you require something larger, aviation supply places sell a transparent plastic flight plotter which makes an excellent combination protractor and straightedge, though the graduations aren't quite as useful unless you are using aeronautical charts.

READING THE SURVEYOR'S COMPASS

Occasionally you might run across a compass like the surveyor's type shown above with the "E" and "W" in the wrong place. Actually they're in the right place for this type of compass. Here's why. The calibrated ring with the four cardinal points is attached to the compass housing instead of floating freely. Only the needle swings. The "N" and "S" are directly under the sighting vanes. Hence "N" is always in the direction of the object being sighted. As you can see from the diagram, if the object being sighted lies in a westerly direction the needle would swing into the eastern quadrant. Since the needle indicates the bearing of the object it should point toward the "W." That's why

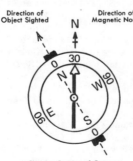

Direction of Object Sighted

Direction of Magnetic North

Showing Position of Compass Needle Indicating a Sight N 30° W.

the "W" is on the wrong side of the compass. The compass ring is numbered from "N" and from "S" to 90° at "E" and at "W." In the illustration, the needle is pointing to the magnetic north and the instrument is set to sight an object 30° west of this point. Since the needle points to 30° in the quadrant between "N" and "W," the bearing of this sight is N 30° W. Similarly, if the needle pointed to 62° in the quadrant between "S" and "E," the bearing of the sight would be S 62° E. Whenever a survey plat is drawn up the direction of the boundary lines is noted on the drawing in this manner.

NAVIGATION GEAR

TOPOGRAPHICAL MAPS
$1.25 - $2.50

Maps come in countless categories and variations, all more or less useful in land navigation, but the most valuable general-purpose type is the modern "topo." These show the form of the land with contour lines, plot the course of streams and rivers, and show the locations of roads and trails. As you gain skill in interpreting them, they reveal more and more information about the landscape, the best ways to travel over it, and even its origins and history. At $1.25 a sheet, these are about the best bargain the government turns out. See the Maps Section for further information. The topo map takes precedence as the most precise "instrument" the backpacker can carry.

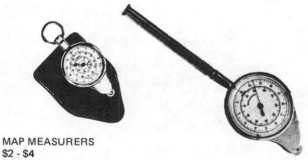

MAP MEASURERS
$2 - $4

These are for measuring the lengths of unstraight paths on a map by counting the turns of a little wheel. Entertaining little gadgets to play with at home, but not a great deal more accurate than eyeballing it (remember, too, that they give you distances as though the trail were flat which can be deceiving in mountainous country).

MAP CASES
$1 - $15

These come in several forms. Some protect the folded-up map while allowing you to look at part of it through clear plastic, which can also be marked up with a wax pencil without dirtying the map. A standard surveyor's or geologist's leather field book case hangs from the belt and will accommodate USGS 1:24,000 topo maps with the borders trimmed off and the maps folded or chopped into

ninths (the tiny 2.5' tick-marks at the edges of the map can be used as cutting or folding guides). This is a lot of work, though, and I use the simple no-cost alternative: fold them however you like, stick them wherever they'll fit, and write whatever you please on them with a soft pencil. They'll get filthy and possibly wrinkled (if you let them get wet), but they're printed on good strong paper and won't fall apart, at least not before you've gotten well over $1.25 worth of use out of them. You can clean off dirt and earlier scribblings with an art-gum eraser. You may not *want* to erase earlier scribblings; it's often interesting to know what you did or found out the last time you were there.

 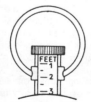 

Calibrating scale for setting pedometer to match length of stride

PEDOMETERS
$6 - $8

The empiricist's trail-measurer. Works by counting your paces. It is therefore only as accurate as the length of your stride, which can be

quite variable over rough ground or on the slope. It is OK for looking at so you can say, "Gee, I walked sixteen miles today," but it is definitely not a precision instrument.

The alternative is tracking yourself on a good topographic map and measuring the distance with the scale. In the absence of a map or a long tape, distances up to a few thousand feet can be measured reasonably well by pacing. Calibrate the length of your stride *over the kind of ground you will be covering.* To do this measure a hundred feet, walk it several times counting strides, and then compute the average length of your stride. When out on the trail, count your steps in your head or with a tally counter and multiply them by the length of your average stride. Counting only every second or fourth step makes it easier to keep track.

Lufft altimeter

Thommen "Everest" altimeter

ALTIMETERS
$50 - $400

This is merely a barometer calibrated for altitude instead of weather, utilizing the well-known fact that air pressure decreases with altitude. It will give you a rough idea of what it's supposed to measure (among the problems: as the weather changes, so does your "altitude"), but you will have a much more accurate idea if you have been following your path on a map. Unless you do a lot of mountain climbing in unmapped regions, it rates as an expensive toy at $50 to $100 (to $400 and more for a good surveyor's aneroid).

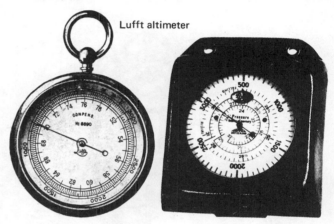

Rangematic Mark V range finder
range: 50 yds to 2 miles

Davis Ranger stadimeter
range: unlimited

RANGE FINDERS
About $30

More gewgaws of limited practical use. Of course it would be nice to be able to measure distances without having to go anywhere, but the laws of trigonometry are not on your side. To use a stadimeter, you need to know the height of the thing you're sighting. This unfortunately is usually just as unknown as the distance. Two-lens coincidence range finders (which work like oversized camera range finders) have an accuracy dependent on the length of the instrument. The six-foot-long ones used on warships are quite accurate, but are not a convenient backpacking item. In any case, accuracy falls off rapidly with increasing distance.

The very inexpensive alternative is to train yourself to estimate distances. Your eye and brain continually use a lot of subtle clues to estimate distances for your own subconscious purposes, so this is easier than you might think. You can learn to estimate distances as accurately as a pocket range finder, or better, by iteration: take a guess, then check it (with a tape, on a map, or by pacing).

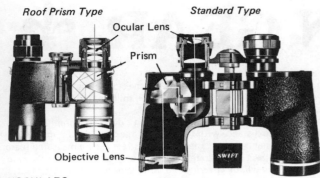

Roof Prism Type   *Standard Type*

Ocular Lens

Prism

Objective Lens

SWIFT

BINOCULARS
$20 - $350
Binoculars provide two services. The most obvious is the magnification of distant objects. The not so obvious, is their light-gathering qualities, which can increase night vision. The best size glass for

zine such as **Audubon.** Some used dealers, like I. Miller in Philadelphia, are competent and reliable optical shops and check out what they sell, but in general be careful of used glasses and have them checked, and a-ligned if needed, by a repairman. Poorly aligned binoculars are a headache, both figuratively and literally.

SURVEYING INSTRUMENTS
$125 - $1,000 plus
These include levels, transits, theodolites, alidades and astrolabes. The most important in exploration work is probably the plane table alidade. Plane-tabling is a method of drawing a map right in the field, using simple geometric methods. The plane table is a drawing board mounted on a tripod, and the alidade is basically just a ruler with sights. You can make good maps with an alidade you can construct yourself or with your Silva compass (see Greenhood's book, **Mapping,** reviewed in the Maps Section). More refined commercial versions of the alidade feature a telescope instead of peep sights, for accurate pointing of the ruler, a graduated vertical circle, for measuring vertical angles and for leveling, and stadia lines in the telescope (an optical method for approximate distance measurement). Unfortunately these

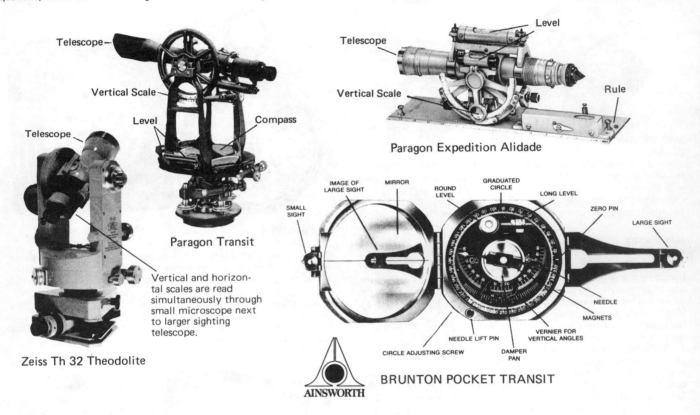

Telescope

Vertical Scale

Telescope

Level

Compass

Paragon Transit

Vertical and horizontal scales are read simultaneously through small microscope next to larger sighting telescope.

Zeiss Th 32 Theodolite

Telescope

Level

Vertical Scale

Rule

Paragon Expedition Alidade

IMAGE OF LARGE SIGHT   MIRROR   ROUND LEVEL   GRADUATED CIRCLE   LONG LEVEL

SMALL SIGHT

ZERO PIN

LARGE SIGHT

NEEDLE

MAGNETS

NEEDLE LIFT PIN

CIRCLE ADJUSTING SCREW

DAMPER PAN

VERNIER FOR VERTICAL ANGLES

AINSWORTH

BRUNTON POCKET TRANSIT

general field use is the 6 x 30 (6 power by 30 millimeters objective lens). You could stretch it to 7 x 35, but the extra weight and size makes the advantage of an additional 1x power questionable. If you haven't been following the binocular market too closely, you might be interested in knowing of the new "barrel" or "roof prism" glass. It looks very much like the old style Galilean binocular, but uses a new design roof prism to increase optically the binocular's focal length. Its advantage over the standard style prism types is reduced weight and size for the same and power and objective diameter. Very much recommended, but they ain't cheap. Least expensive (Swift, Neptune model, 7 x 35) starts at $87, and the prices go up well over $200. Checking over the general run of recreational outfitters' catalogs, we didn't find anyone that really carried a decent inventory of field glasses, unless you're interested in the Lietz brand and have the cash to fork out for a pair of 'em. Recreational Equipment, Inc. carries their line. Otherwise, the best bet is go direct to the manufacturers like Swift, Bushnell, or if you can afford the higher-priced spread, Bausch & Lomb, Carl Zeiss, or Ross. Sears has some fair glasses in the low price range. A good source of information on dealers in new and used binoculars is the classified section of a birder's maga-

precision types run to around a thousand dollars.

Transits and theodolites do basically the same jobs, measuring horizontal and vertical angles with varying degrees of precision. The price tag varies with the accuracy attainable (cheaper models can be read to one minute of arc, which is a sixtieth of a degree, and the most expensive can be read to one second, which is a sixtieth of *that,* or even smaller increments) and with the convenience features, such as instant optical read out, that high-priced engineers are willing to pay for. Transits and theodolites are used for control surveying (locating a few points with high precision, for later use as "control" points in topographic mapping or compiling maps from aerial photographs), or for determining your location astronomically (seldom necessary in this day and age). They can also be used for topographic mapping, though they are in some ways inferior to the plane-table rig for this.

You can read about techniques for using these and more exotic instruments in a text such as Philip Kissam's **Surveying: Instruments and Methods** (New York, McGraw-Hill). The best information on plane-tabling is in books for field geologists (Robert Compton's **Manual of Field Geology,** New York, Wiley, $9.95, is good on both plane-tabling and control surveying).

sources of land navigation gear

Your local outfitter may have an adequate stock of basic land navigation equipment, and will usually be the most convenient source of local topo maps (though he may mark the price up since the USGS gives him less of a margin of profit on them than he prefers to get).

Another source not to overlook is your local engineer's and surveyor's supply store (often combined with a blueprint service so look that up in the yellow pages if it isn't under the other name). There is one of these stores in every large town, and in a lot of fairly small towns if there is some oil field or mining activity in the area. They usually carry high-quality field books, all kinds of drafting supplies, and instruments from hand compasses through the fanciest surveying gear. Most of these stores are affiliated with one of the big engineering supply companies (Keuffel & Esser, Dietzgen, or Lietz), and handle premium-quality equipment at fairly high prices. When you deal with them there is some consolation in the fact that the equipment is built to last, and they will stand behind it (at least in my experience, instant repair or replacement is the norm).

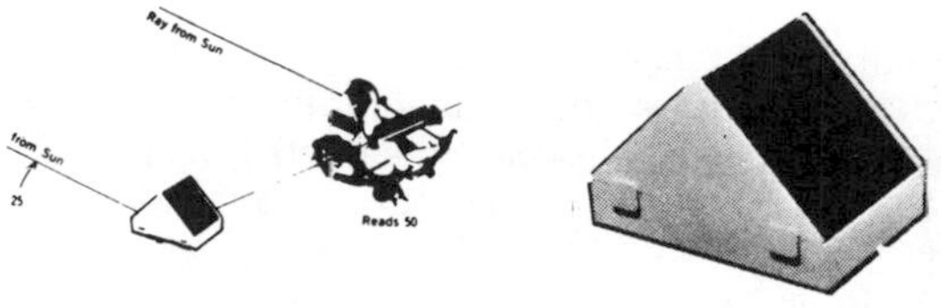

Artificial Horizon

DAVIS INSTRUMENTS CORP.
857 Thornton, San Leandro, Calif. 94577
Though Davis' gear is primarily designed for marine use, there's no reason why it cannot be applied to land navigation. Through the use of high-impact strength plastic, Davis has reduced the cost of many navigational instruments by more than 90%. Some of their gear includes the Mark 3 practice sextant, $19; a 6 in. x 4 in. x 1½ in. artificial horizon device (used with a sextant for taking star or sun altitudes in areas where there is no visible horizon, i.e., the woods); hand bearing compass with sighting vanes; stadimeter; and a variety of plotting instruments. Eight-page brochure with prices and order blank available on request.

Sextants are useful for taking horizontal angles in rough reconnaissance surveys, but if you are thinking of using them for getting your location from celestial observations, keep in mind that even with a good one you will be lucky to determine your location within one or two miles. If you don't know your location within one or two miles, you are usually in need of more than a sextant.—John Rhoads (1976).

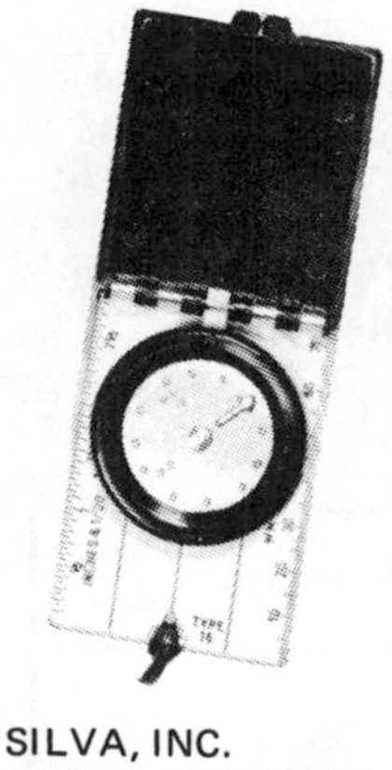

HOW TO USE THE BRAILLE COMPASS

The way the Type 16B is used is for the blind person to hold it level in front of him with the cover wide open and pointing straight ahead. Holding the compass in that position, he closes the cover for 6 to 8 seconds which permits the dial to float freely and be attracted by the earth's North Pole. He then opens the cover wide which locks the dial in position and he can then feel the direction on the Braille graduation. In this way he is able to determine which direction he is standing.

SILVA, INC.
La Porte, Ind. 46350
Complete line of compasses; Orienteering training aids including films for class discussion; books on compass use, Orienteering, and pathfinding. Compasses are all of high quality, liquid-filled, and with declination-adjusting set screw. Prices range from $4 to $20. This line is the most popular with backpackers and campers because of its economical price and professional construction. Silva also manufactures a unique braille compass for the blind, $12. Eight-page brochure available.

GOLDBERGS' MARINE DISTRIBUTORS, INC.
202 Market St., Philadelphia, Pa. 19106
Pocket range finder (50 yds. to 2 miles), $28; stadimeter, $20; complete line of plotting instruments; plastic map cases. Goldbergs' is a marine equipment discount house which sells name-brand gear. Their 195-page catalog is well worth the $1 they ask, particularly if you include boating among your activities.

FORESTRY SUPPLIERS, INC.
P.O. Box 8397, Jackson, Miss. 39204
Complete line of pocket compasses and transits including Suunto, Silva, Leupold, Brunton, Warren-Knight, and K & E; pocket altimeters, including Thommens and Lufft; pedometers, rolling map measures and plotting instruments; leather map cases, $13 to $26. Foresters' equipment catalog of 448 pages available.

I've heard reports that Forestry Suppliers has gone sour on sending catalogs to whoever asks for them (reasonable, considering it must run them upwards of a couple of bucks to service a request with that nice catalog of theirs). They only seem to want professional foresters as accounts and are sending rude letters to that effect to other people requesting the catalog.—John Rhoads (1976).

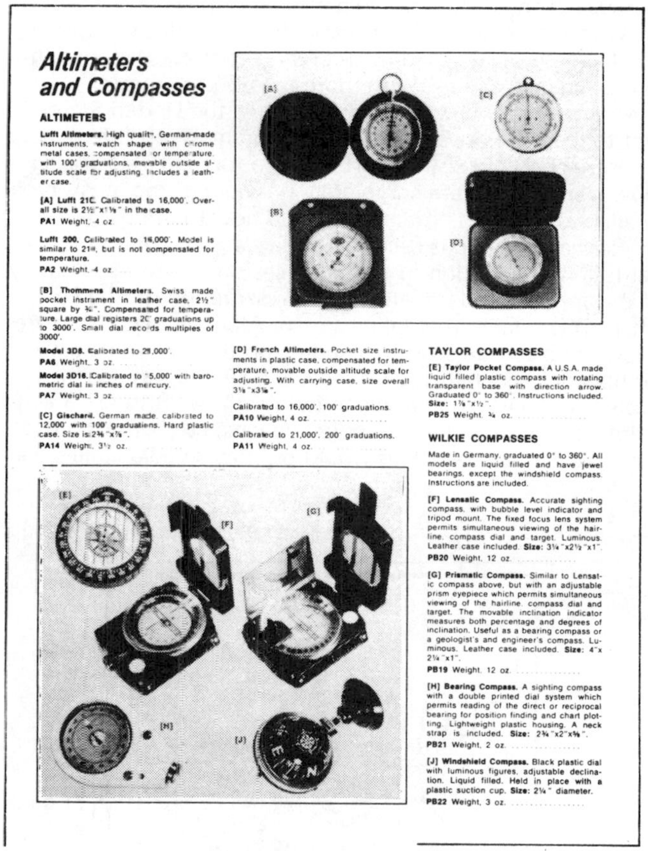

Altimeters and Compasses

ALTIMETERS

Lufft Altimeters. High quality, German-made instruments, watch shape with chrome metal cases, compensated for temperature, with 100' graduations, movable outside altitude scale for adjusting. Includes a leather case.

[A] Lufft 21C. Calibrated to 16,000'. Overall size is 2½"x1⅛" in the case.
PA1 Weight, 4 oz. ....

Lufft 200. Calibrated to 16,000'. Model is similar to 21C, but is not compensated for temperature.
PA2 Weight, 4 oz. ....

[B] Thommens Altimeters. Swiss made pocket instrument in leather case, 2½" square by ¾". Compensated for temperature. Large dial registers 20' graduations up to 3000'. Small dial records multiples of 3000'.

Model 3D8. Calibrated to 25,000'.
PA6 Weight, 3 oz. ....

Model 3D16. Calibrated to 15,000' with barometric dial in inches of mercury.
PA7 Weight, 3 oz. ....

[C] Gischard. German made, calibrated to 12,000' with 100' graduations. Hard plastic case. Size is 2⅜"x⅞".
PA14 Weight, 3½ oz. ....

[D] French Altimeters. Pocket size instruments in plastic case, compensated for temperature, movable outside altitude scale for adjusting. With carrying case, size overall 3⅛"x3⅛".

Calibrated to 16,000', 100' graduations.
PA10 Weight, 4 oz. ....

Calibrated to 21,000', 200' graduations.
PA11 Weight, 4 oz. ....

TAYLOR COMPASSES

[E] Taylor Pocket Compass. A U.S.A. made liquid filled plastic compass with rotating transparent base with direction arrow. Graduated 0° to 360°. Instructions included. **Size:** 1⅞"x½".
PB25 Weight, ¾ oz. ....

WILKIE COMPASSES

Made in Germany, graduated 0° to 360°. All models are liquid filled and have jewel bearings, except the windshield compass. Instructions are included.

[F] Lensatic Compass. Accurate sighting compass, with bubble level indicator and tripod mount. The fixed focus lens system permits simultaneous viewing of the hairline, compass dial and target. Luminous. Leather case included. **Size:** 3¼"x2½"x1".
PB20 Weight, 12 oz. ....

[G] Prismatic Compass. Similar to Lensatic compass above, but with an adjustable prism eyepiece which permits simultaneous viewing of the hairline, compass dial and target. The movable inclination indicator measures both percentage and degrees of inclination. Useful as a bearing compass or a geologist's and engineer's compass. Luminous. Leather case included. **Size:** 4"x 2¼"x1".
PB19 Weight, 12 oz. ....

[H] Bearing Compass. A sighting compass with a double printed dial system which permits reading of the direct or reciprocal bearing for position finding and chart plotting. Lightweight plastic housing. A neck strap is included. **Size:** 2¾"x2"x⅝".
PB21 Weight, 2 oz. ....

[J] Windshield Compass. Black plastic dial with luminous figures, adjustable declination. Liquid filled. Held in place with a plastic suction cup. **Size:** 2¼" diameter.
PB22 Weight, 3 oz. ....

RECREATIONAL EQUIPMENT, INC.
1525 11th Ave., Seattle, Wash. 98122
Handles Silva (Swedish), Wilkie (German), and Suunto (Finnish) compasses in several models of each. Prices range from $3 to $30. They also handle plastic map cases; Lufft, Gischard (German), Thommens (Swiss), and several French altimeters ranging from $17 to $65; pedometers and rolling-type map measurers. Recreational Co-op (or The Co-op, as it is sometimes called in backpacking circles) is by far the only recreational outfitter with this diversified a line of wilderness nav gear. Seventy-four-page catalog of wilderness recreation equipment available.

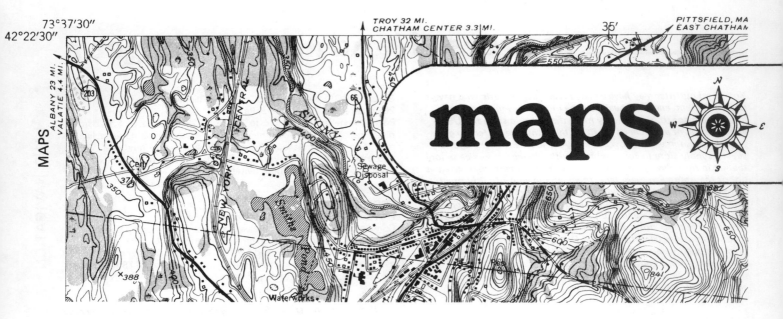

73°37'30"
42°22'30"

TROY 32 MI.
CHATHAM CENTER 3.3 MI.

35'

PITTSFIELD, MA
EAST CHATHAM

maps

Under the ground, approximately 15 miles southeast of the intersection of 38º 00' N. latitude and 86º 00' W. longitude lies more than a million dollars in gold. No lie! It's been there for some time, and there are even some people who know its location within probably 500 feet. As far as is known, it is still there and probably will remain for a long time to come because of the difficulties in getting it out.

Without a map you'll probably have little luck in finding the location of this gold, and it serves to show just how important a map can be. With more than 500 different government agencies producing maps in the United States, not to mention private individuals who make up fishing maps, treasure charts, cruising charts, and so forth, it's surprising how many people are completely unaware of the many types available, where to obtain them, and how to use them.

Basically, a map is designed to give a geographical representation of a section of terrain as seen from the air. Usually, if the area covered is water the representation is called a chart; if it is land, it is called a map. All maps and charts are drawn to a certain scale, depending on the area to be covered or how much detail is to be shown. A simple way to think of scale is to consider an airplane flying at low altitude. The pilot can see trees, people, dogs and cats, but his vision does not cover much area. This would be considered a large-scale

(large-detail) map. When the pilot goes up to a higher altitude, the visible area is increased, but there is less detail. This would represent the small-scale (small-detail) map.

The analogy of the pilot may make it easier to remember the difference between the small- and large-scale maps, since this seems to be a confusing definition, and it is much used in map work. Actually, scale is a fraction or ratio of the distance measured on the map compared with the actual distance on the ground.

On a map the distance from Chicago to somewhere may be measured off at 7 in., whereas in actual miles it is 700. Taking a mile to the inch as our scale this would be written 1:63,360, because 1 mile is equal to 63,360 inches.

Topography and elevation are two other things you should be familiar with in addition to map scales. Topography is another name for the lay of the land, in other words, trees, rivers, orchards, houses, beaches, and so forth. Color and symbols are used to represent these items on the map. Elevations are also part of the topography and are shown by brown lines that follow the ground surface at a constant elevation above sea level. These are called contour lines, and the vertical distance (elevation) between them is called the contour interval, the value of which is always found next to the scale on a map.

Of all the maps available for exploring activities, the easiest to acquire and the least expensive are the ones put out by government agencies. In the United States they are the U.S. Geological Survey and the Army Map Service, and in Canada the Surveys and Mapping Branch of the Department of Mines and Technical Surveys.

The U.S. Geological Survey, formed in 1878, has charge of all the topographical mapping in the United States. It works closely with the Army Map Service, which is part of

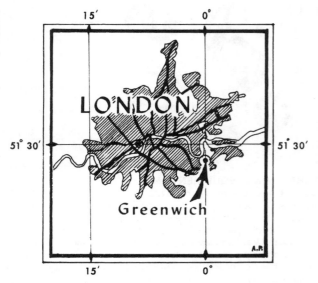

The prime meridian passes through Greenwich, a small suburb of London, England, where the Royal Observatory is located.

Scale	1 inch represents
1:24,000	2,000 feet
1:20,000	about 1,667 feet
1:62,500	nearly 1 mile
1:63,360	1 mile
1:250,000	nearly 4 miles
1:1,000,000	nearly 16 miles

A comparison of map scales.

the Corps of Engineers, in producing topo maps of the country. These maps are the ones you'll find readily available at any map store in your city, at prices ranging from 75¢ to $1. Incidentally, you might remember that these are the prices the government sells the maps for. Many map dealers will increase the sale price, because they can't make a profit at 75¢ and $1.

For maps to be of any use they must be referable to the portion of the globe they represent. This is done through latitude and longitude, which can be seen as an imaginary grid covering the earth. All vertical lines that run north and south are lines of longitude, and all horizontal lines running east and west are lines of latitude. Lines of latitude are parallel to each other and are numbered from 0° at the equator to 90° at the North Pole and likewise from the equator to the South Pole. The equator is the 0° point of reference for these lines. Lines of longitude are measured from 0° at the prime meridian to 180° going west to the international date line and likewise going east to the international date line. The prime meridian serves as a reference point for lines of longitude, just as the equator does for latitude. The prime meridian was assigned to the line of longitude running through Greenwich, England, a small suburb of London, by international agreement, in 1884. Before that the United

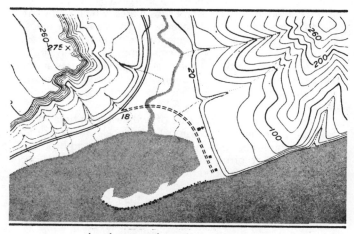

Landscape as shown by contour lines.

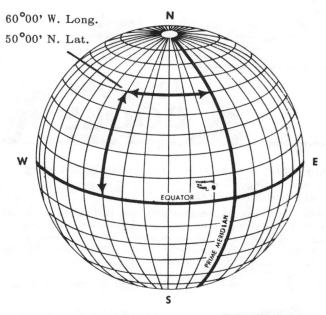

60°00' W. Long.
50°00' N. Lat.

The globe with lines of reference.

ence to a location is not a sure thing because of the elements and the bulldozer.

Topographical maps are an invaluable source of information for the explorer, but it requires a thorough knowledge of all the symbols, notation, and colorings used. And a little deductive reasoning. For instance, an open pit, mine, or quarry is shown by a ⚒. This would be a natural for the rockhound and paleontologist. Contour lines shown so close together that they're almost solid or a road running through a cut in a mountain could be places where strata would be showing, and perhaps some geological specimens. Depression contours could mean a sinkhole and maybe a cave below. If you're a fisherman and familiar with the environment that some fish live in, you might be able to locate a good spot by noting the way a marsh lies in relation to a steep bank or a

States used the meridian running through Washington, D.C., for the 0° reference point, France, the one running through Paris, and so forth. You can imagine what a screwed-up mess it must have been when whaling captains from these different countries got together to plan a joint voyage. Incidentally, as a point of interest, the 0° – 0° reference point at which the prime meridian crosses the equator today, is located about 500 miles southeast of Nigeria, Africa, in the middle of the Gulf of Guinea.

When the cartographer or map maker draws a map, he uses lines of latitude and longitude to co-ordinate the area he is mapping to the larger area of the world. You'll find the notations for latitude and longitude along the borders of all maps, even road maps. The notations are given in degrees, minutes and seconds of arc, which is written 42° 31' 12''. Minutes and seconds have nothing to do with time here; they are measurements of a curved surface. Experienced map users always refer to a location by latitude and longitude, because they realize that such a location can always be found at a later date. Using natural or man-made landmarks as a refer-

Unimproved dirt road		==========
Trail		– – – – – –
U.S. mineral or location monument — Prospect	▲	x
Quarry — Gravel pit	⚒	⚔
Shaft—Tunnel entrance	▫	Y
Campsite — Picnic area	🏕	⚮
Located or landmark object—Windmill	○	⚚
Exposed wreck		
Rock or coral reef		
Depression contours	Rapids	
Mine dump	Glacier	
Dune area	Dry lake	

Map symbols.

beach at the bend in a river. You might be able to find an exciting fly-fishing spot with rapids and quiet pools in the same area and not a road or house for miles. Hiking trails and old abandoned dirt roads or railroad right-of-ways are almost always shown. These are usually what backpackers or the guy who wants to put his jeep though its paces is looking for.

When purchasing a topographical map ask for the topographical map symbols sheet also. It's free and explains all the symbols, colors, and notations on the maps. To determine the map you want, ask the dealer for a topographical map index to your state. This is free, too. It will show your state broken down into squares and subsquares, which represent the different scales of maps available. The squares or maps are called quadrangles, or quads for short, and the large ones measure 15' on their edge, the small ones 7½'. When you order a map, give the size of the quadrangle in minutes and its name. Incidentally, if you buy a series of topographical maps, you can cut the borders off and tape them together to make one large map.

Maps, if properly taken care of, will last a lifetime. If you only use your map for occasional reference at home or in the office, it should be rolled, rather than folded, and if possible kept in a tube to protect it from dust, sunlight, and moisture. A map's days are numbered as soon as it is taken into the field, but its life can be extended by proper folding, taping, and storing. Folding a map weakens the paper at the folds, but it can be strengthened by putting masking tape on the

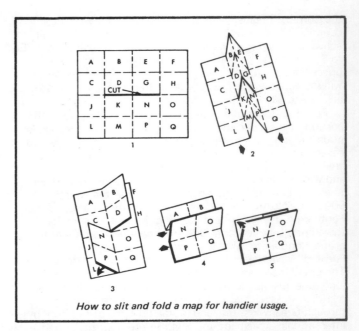

How to slit and fold a map for handier usage.

back of the map over the creases. When marking a map, use a light line so that it can be erased easily and will not tear the paper and leave confusing marks. It takes a little more time to do things right, but in the long run the results are worth it.

BOOKS

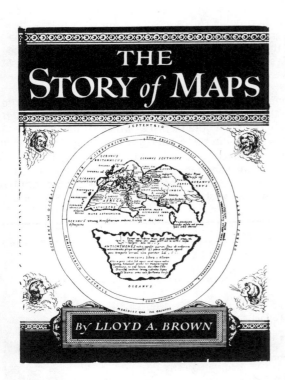

THE STORY OF MAPS
Lloyd A. Brown
1949 - 393 p. il. - $3.95

A comprehensive and readable history of the art and science of map making with beautiful black-and-white reproductions of early maps. An extensive 64-page section of notes and bibliography in fine print probably makes this one the last word as a reference source for the serious map collector. To write this book, Brown spent four years delving into every source of material available on maps. It was originally published by Little, Brown & Co. at $12.95 and has since been reprinted by Bonanza Books at the above price.
From: Bonanza Books, 419 Park Ave. South, New York, N.Y. 10016

NOTES ON THE CARE AND CATALOGUING OF OLD MAPS
Lloyd A. Brown
1971 - Repr. of 1941 ed. - $6.25

Here's Brown with another gem for the map buff. A former curator of the magnificent collection of maps at the William L. Clements Library, University of Michigan, he worked out his own system of classifying and cataloging some 25,000 old and rare maps. After putting his methods to the test in the Clements map room, he published them for other map collectors.
From: Kennikat Press, Inc., Box 270, Port Washington, N.Y. 11050

THINGS MAPS DON'T TELL US
Armin K. Lobeck
1956 - 160 p. il. - $5.95

This is the geological story of how the topography shown on today's map developed from something completely different over a period of many years. Informative reading for anyone interested in map interpretation or anyone who needs a geological background to regress a topo map for historical purposes.
From: Macmillan Co., Front and Brown Streets, Riverside, N.J. 08075

ELEMENTS OF CARTOGRAPHY
A.H. Robinson and R.D. Sale
1969 - 3rd ed. - 415 p. il. - $11.95

A rather technical tome on the subject of map making, using today's technology and tools. Covers everything from scale, air photographs, and grid systems to generalization, symbolization, cartographic topography and drawing, and map reproduction techniques. Good but deep.
From: John Wiley & Sons, Inc., One Wiley Dr., Somerset, N.J. 08873

MAPPING
David Greenhood
1964 - 288 p. il. - $2.95 (pb)

A terrifically useful nontechnical introduction to getting the most out of maps and making your own. Chapters on the basics of co-ordinates, great circles, distance, direction, projections, and more. Covers map compilation, maps from field surveys, map making tools, materials, and equipment. (Recommended by Nach Waxman).
From: University of Chicago Press, Univ. of Chicago, Chicago, Ill. 60637

THE NATIONAL ATLAS OF THE UNITED STATES
U.S. Geological Survey
1971 - 431 p. il. - $100

This 14-pound, hard-bound volume is the last word in atlases for the United States. It contains 336 pages of multicolored maps, as well as an index with more than 41,000 entries, including geographic co-ordinates, finding code and where appropriate, population of places named. Each page is 19″ x 14″ and many open double fold. The publication of this atlas in 1971 was the culmination of eight years of planning and involved the co-operation of more than eighty federal agencies and numerous commercial firms, specialists, and consultants. The book describes the nation's salient characteristics, such as *Physical* (relief, geology, climate, water resource, soils, and vegetation); *History* (discovery, exploration, territorial growth, settlement, battlefields, and scientific expeditions); *Economic* (agriculture, industry, resources, and transportation); *Social* (population distribution and structure, educational achievement); *Administrative* (counties, judicial and election districts, time zones, and districts and regions for more than fifty federal agencies); and *Map Coverage* (showing status of aerial photography, geodetic control, and published maps with representative samples). If you've got the jack to spare, it's certainly worth the price.

Sections of the *Atlas* are available at prices ranging from $1 to $1.75 per sheet. These are actually 19″ x 28″ copies of selected maps contained in the big book. A descriptive list of these with prices is available upon request. Ask for "National Atlas Separate Sales Editions."
From: Distribution Section, U.S. Geological Survey, 1200 South Eads St., Arlington, Va. 22202

NATIONAL ATLAS OF CANADA
Surveys and Mapping Branch
Dept. of Energy, Mines and Resources
$36, loose sheets; $56, bound

We don't have a lot of information on this one, but from the schedule of maps and data that are included it looks to be pretty good. These are the sheets contained, which by the way, can be purchased separately at 50¢ each from the Canada Map Office, 615 Booth St., Ottawa, Ontario, Canada K1A 0E9. The *Atlas* itself should be ordered from the address given below.

1. Routes of Explorers, 1534 - 1870
2. Mapping the Coasts, 1492 - 1874
3. Mapping the Interior, 1630 - 1870
4. Extent of Mapping Surveys —1955
5. Extent of Topographical Mapping—1955
6. Comparison of Scales
7. Aeronautical Charts
8. Hydrographic Charts
9. Bathy-Orography—Canada
10. Bathy-Orography—Eastern Canada
11. Bathy-Orography—Western Canada
12. Bathy-Orography—Northern Canada
13. Physiographic Regions
14. Physiography of Southern Ontario
15. Glacial Geology
16. Bedrock Geology
17. Principal Minerals
18. Earthquakes, Magnetism and Tides
19. Atmospheric Pressure
20. Wind and Sunshine
21. Seasonal Temperatures
22. Temperature Ranges
23. Frost
24. Growing Seasons
25. Annual Precipitation

26. Precipitation Days and Precipitation Variability
27. Seasonal Precipitation
28. Snow Cover
29. Humidity and Fog
30. Climatic Regions
31. Typical Weather Situations
32. Weather Stations and Forecast Regions
33. Drainage Basins and River Flow
34. Profiles of Major Rivers
35. Soil Regions
36. Soil Survey Maps
37. Ranges of Representative Insects, Ticks and Spiders
38. Natural Vegetation and Flora
39. Forest Regions
40. Forest Inventory Maps
41. Ranges of Principal Commercial Trees
42. Ranges of Principal Mammals
43. Ranges of Principal Birds
44. Ranges of Principal Commercial Inland Fish
45. Parks and Faunal Reserves
46. Distribution of Population 1851 - 1941
47. Distribution of Population —1951
48. Density of Population —1951

49. Rates of Population Change 1851 - 1951
50. Births, Marriages and Deaths, Etc.
51. Age and Sex Ratios
52. Aboriginal Population
53. French and British Origins
54. Other Origins and Citizenship
55. Principal Religions
56. Urban Population
57. Rural Population
58. Furs, Whaling and Fish Processing
59. East Coast Fisheries
60. West Coast Fisheries
61. Forestry and Woodworking
62. Sawmills
63. Pulp and Paper Mills
64. Farm Livestock
65. Wheat and Barley
66. Other Grains and Oil Seeds
67. Fodder Crops and Intensive Crops
68. Farms
69. Agricultural Regions
70. Agricultural Labour Force and Services
71. Food Industries
72. Primary Iron and Steel
73. Non-Ferrous Metals—Eastern Canada
74. Non-Ferrous Metals—Western Canada
75. Industrial Minerals
76. Mineral Fuels, Pipelines and Refineries
77. Hydro and Fuel Electric Power —Eastern Canada
78. Hydro and Fuel Electric Power—Western Canada

79. Fabricated Metal Industries
80. Textiles, Clothing and Rubber Products
81. Manufacturing Centres
82. Navigable Waterways
83. Railways
84. Railway Freight Traffic
85. Major Roads
86. Civil Airports, Aerodromes and Time Zones
87. Air Lines
88. Air Passenger Traffic
89. Domestic Trade, Finance and Construction
90. Shipping
91. Television and Radio
92. Hospitals
93. Education
94. Public Libraries, Museums and Art Galleries
95. Populated Places—Gulf of St. Lawrence Area
96. Populated Places—Great Lakes Area
97. Populated Places—Prairies
98. Populated Places—The Far West
99. Populated Places—Northern Canada
100. Quebec City and Montreal
101. Ottawa and Toronto
102. Winnipeg and Edmonton
103. Vancouver and Victoria
104. Rural Municipalities—Eastern Canada
105. Rural Municipalities—Great Lakes—St. Lawrence Area
106. Rural Municipalities—Western Canada
107. Census Divisions
108. Federal Electoral Districts
109. Political Evolution
110. Canada and the World

Note: The following Atlas Maps are out of print: 16, 23, 25, 30, 41, 43, 44, 47, 53, 58, 59, 60, and 87.

From: Information Canada, 171 Slater St., Ottawa, Ontario, Canada K1A 0S9

MAPS

CANADA MAP OFFICE
Dept. of Energy, Mines and Resources
Ottawa, Ontario
Canada K1A 0E9
This is the source of all Canadian topographical maps and general map information for Canada. As you'll note in the accompanying blocks on this page, there are quite a number of indexes for the different maps available. They can be had free of charge from the above address. For the standard topo series, the best bet is to pick the regional index that covers the area you're interested in, from one of the 17 shown on the master index map on this page, and request it from the Map Office. Regional indexes are for maps at scales of 1¼-inch to one mile (1:50,000) and one inch to one mile (1:63,360). All available maps at these scales are named and numbered on the regional indexes, and the procedures for ordering them are given. These maps measure 22 in. x 29 in. and cost 75¢ for each half sheet and $1.50 for each full sheet.

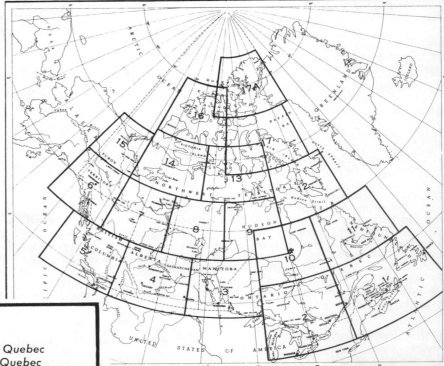

INDEXES TO MAPS
1:50,000 (See Map)

No. 1   *Eastern Provinces and part of Quebec*
No. 2   *Part of Ontario and Western Quebec*
No. 3   *Part of Ontario, Manitoba, Saskatchewan*
No. 4   *Part of Alberta and Saskatchewan*
No. 5   *Part of British Columbia*
No. 6   *Part of British Columbia and Yukon*
No. 7   *Part of British Columbia, Alberta, Yukon and Northwest Territories*
No. 8   *Part of Alberta, Saskatchewan, Manitoba and Northwest Territories*
No. 9   *Part of Manitoba and Northwest Territories*
No. 10 *Part of Northwestern Quebec and Northeastern Ontario*
No. 11 *Part of Labrador and Northeastern Quebec*
No. 12 *Part of Northern Quebec and Northwest Territories*
No. 13 *Part of Northwest Territories*
No. 14 *Part of Northwest Territories*
No. 15 *Part of Yukon and Northwest Territories*
No. 16 *Part of Northwest Territories*
No. 17 *Part of Northwest Territories*
No. 17A *Northern Part of Northwest Territories*

OTHER INDEXES

1:250,000
No. 18 *Eastern Canada*
No. 19 *Western Canada*
No. 20 *Northern Canada*

1:500,000 & 1:506,880
No. 21 *All Canada*

1:1,000,000
No. 22 *All Canada*

1:125,000 & 1:126,720
No. 23 *Eastern Canada*
No. 24 *Western Canada*

GENERAL

M.C.R. No. 53: Index to General National Topographic System

MISCELLANEOUS

List of General Maps
List of Maps Covering National Parks
List of Maps Covering Algonquin Park
List of Maps Covering La Verendrye Park
List of Electoral Maps

CANADIAN PROVINCIAL MAP SOURCES
If you're interested in general provincial maps, county maps, legal survey plans, etc., the addresses given below are the places to check. In most cases maps of this kind will be available at prices from 25¢ to $2.50 per sheet. When writing for information be specific about the location and type of data you're after.

Alberta - Dept. of Lands & Forests - Natural Resources Bldg. - Edmonton T5K 2E1
British Columbia - Dept. of Lands, Forests & Water Resources - Parliament Bldgs. - Victoria
Manitoba - Dept. of Mines & Natural Resources - Rm. 816 - Norquay Bldg. - 401 York Ave. - Winnipeg R3C 0P8
New Brunswick - Dept. of Natural Resources - Map & Photo Library - Rm. 575 - Centennial Bldg. - Fredericton
Newfoundland and **Labrador** - Dept. of Mines, Agriculture & Resources - Confederation Bldg. - St. John's - Newfoundland
Nova Scotia - Communications & Information Centre - P.O. Box 2206 - Halifax
Ontario - Ministry of Natural Resources - Surveys & Engineering Branch - Parliament Bldgs. - Toronto 182
Prince Edward Island - Dept. of the Environment & Tourism - Map Library - P.O. Box 2000 - Charlottetown
Quebec - Photogrammetry & Cartography Div. - Dept. of Lands & Forests - 200 Chemin Ste-Foy, 7th Floor - Quebec City
Saskatchewan - Lands & Surveys Branch - Dept. of Natural Resources - 2340 Albert St. - Regina S4P 2V7

government sources of maps

For more and more of the world, getting good topographic maps is a simple matter of writing the government's geological survey or other principal mapping agency. A selection of addresses for the most important of these follows. Sometimes, though, these agencies cannot provide adequate maps for the area you are interested in. Do not give up hope right away, though. Use the infallible general rule for map-finding: ask yourself what agency of what government or colonial power has, or has had, a vested interest in this place. *They will have maps.* Do not confine yourself to the obvious, if you are having trouble locating maps, and do not give up too easily. Often when a government agency says they have no such maps, it really means they didn't find them in the most obvious place and don't feel like checking further. You may have to do some of your own detective work.

Examples of less obvious map sources in the U.S.: if the land belongs to the government or formerly did, the Bureau of Land Management, Department of the Interior, will have at least a crude map of it. Is the land in or near a mining district? Ask the U. S. Geological Survey or the state geological survey about maps. Is it near the ocean or a navigable waterway? Ask the National Ocean Survey and the Corps of Engineers. In or near a national forest? Check with the U.S. Forest Service. The Bureau of Reclamation maps land near dams and irrigation works. State highway departments and county surveyors produce useful maps, and so on.

For maps of foreign lands, check with former as well as present governing powers. For example, the island of New Guinea is now divided between the nations of Papua, New Guinea and Indonesia, but government maps of sections of the island were also produced by Australia, Great Britain, the Netherlands and Germany during the various times these powers were in control.

Check also in any large library you have access to. They will often have out-of-print maps that are nonetheless useful, or special-purpose maps bound in with books or articles. Such holdings cannot usually be borrowed, but they can be photocopied.—*John Rhoads (1976).*

FRANCE

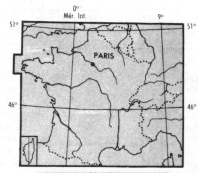

CARTE AU 1/1 000 000
1 mm sur la carte représente 1 000 m sur le terrain.
CARTE EN 12 COULEURS - 1 feuille : 101 x 125 cm.
(Edition aviation en 10 couleurs avec surcharge aéronautique et quadrillage GEOREF).

L'INSTITUT GEOGRAPHIQUE NATIONAL
Direction General
136 bis, Rue de Grenelle
Paris VII
France

L'Institut has perhaps the most informative and useful map catalog available of any country we've seen so far. No eight ways about it. Only problem is it's all in French. Over 170 pages of indexes to topographic maps of France and countries that are or at one time were French colonies or possessions in Africa, the Caribbean, and the South Pacific. Maps for the Antarctic are there, too. Topo maps are just one type featured; others are aeronautical charts, plastic relief maps, and tourist maps. Beautiful catalog. A separate price sheet is included with the book (in French and with prices in francs, of course). The catalog is available free upon request and is definitely recommended for your foreign map source files; add a good French dictionary while you're at it.

GREAT BRITAIN

The Director General
ORDNANCE SURVEY
Chessington
Surrey
England

This is the source of British topo, historical, and tourist maps. Their 40-page catalog is most informative and includes descriptions of various scale and types of maps, books, atlases, plus prices. Very interesting section on archaeological and historical maps, and national park maps of Great Britain. The catalog is available upon request and is a good reference source for maps of the British Isles.

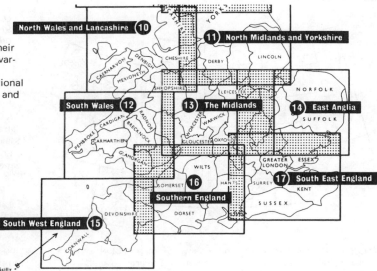

QUARTER-INCH FIFTH SERIES

SNOWDONIA NATIONAL PARK

MAP OF ROMAN BRITAIN
SCALE: 16 MILES TO ONE INCH
PUBLISHED BY THE ORDNANCE SURVEY
THIRD EDITION

MAPS

U.S. ARMY TOPOGRAPHIC COMMAND
Corps of Engineers, Washington, D.C. 20315
USATOPOCOM handles a rather varied selection of political and topographical road maps to areas and countries around the world, in addition to lunar topo maps and pictorial maps of Mars. Well worth a 13¢ stamp to request their 4-page catalog. Incidentally, they no longer handle the 1:250,000 plastic relief maps of the United States. The only ones they sell are one of the world at 1:1,000,000 and one of Puerto Rico at 1:250,000. Each costs $8.75 plus postage.

GEOGRAPHIC AREA	SCALE	PRICE PER SHEET
Continental Southeast Asia	1:2,500,000	$1.00
World Road Map	1:1,000,000	1.00
East Asia Road Maps	1:1,250,000	1.00
Middle East Briefing Map	1:1,500,000	1.00
Africa	1:2,000,000	1.00
Philippine Road Map	1:1,000,000	1.00
Iran Road Map	1:2,500,000	1.00

U.S. GEOLOGICAL SURVEY
Map Information Office, National Center, Reston, Va. 22092
This is your one-stop shop for, among other things, the best and most economical supply of topographical maps in the United States. The diversity of material and literature available from USGS on maps alone is so extensive that probably the best approach is to provide the keys to the locks and let you do the door opening where it best suits your needs.

Indexes and Topographic Maps of the United States

The following indexes are available free from the Survey and are well worth getting for your map reference files. As noted, several of the indexes have interesting and valuable information on them regarding the maps they list.

State Maps Series. State maps published by the Survey are available in base, topographic, and in a number of cases in shaded-relief editions generally at a scale of 1:500,000. A 20-page list describes the maps available for each state with ordering information. Prices range from $1.50 to $2.75. As a point of interest, if you order from a state's geological survey, this will more than likely be the same map you get.

Shaded Relief Series. The Survey has available shaded relief editions of certain topographic quadrangle maps showing physiographic features of special interest. There are about 150 of them and included are (note: climbers, backpackers) a number of mountains and national parks. On these editions shading accentuates the physical features by simulating in color the appearance of sunlight and shadow on the terrain, creating the illusion of a solid three-dimensional land surface. This is another group of maps the USGS is letting slide, as few have been updated. The index consists of an 8-page brochure that lists the maps, scale, survey date, paper size, and price, plus description of the series and ordering information.

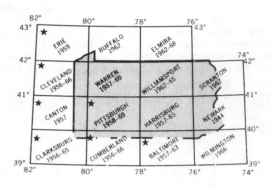

1:250,000 Scale Series. This is the next largest scale of topo map available for the United States, and it takes 473 of these to make a complete map of the country. This is the best scale to get if you're planning a trip to some area but have not decided exactly where you want to go. There is enough detail here to help you make a decision; at the same time the map gives you a lot of terrain coverage on one piece of paper. Once you've found your spot, then pick up the necessary 7½-minute quads that cover it. Map size for this scale is 34" x 22" and the price is $2 each. The index is in the form of a United States map with black grid overlay showing areas covered by each map in this series. It includes a description of the series and ordering data, plus list of other United States maps available.

Four 7½'s make up one 15-minute quadrangle, and 32 15-minute quads make up a 1:250,000 series map. Total 7½'s needed to make up a complete map of the U.S. would be 60,544, requiring a wall 910 ft. wide by 468 ft. high. Cost of these maps would be $45,399.

7½- and 15-Minute Series. There are 48 of these indexes available, each taking the name of the state(s) it applies to (except for the Antarctica index). This is by far your most important index, because it shows both the 7½- and 15-minute quads available and the 1:250,000 scale series for the state. More types of maps on one sheet than anywhere else. As you may note from inspecting one of these indexes, the Survey isn't particularly excited about the 15-minute series. For one thing, they're not publishing many of them, and those that are available are not being updated at the same priority as the 7½'s. Frankly, you'd do just as well to skip the 15's, unless there are no 7½'s available for the area. Besides, you get detail with the 7½'s, at 1 in. equaling less than half a mile (2,000 ft.). The index for this series is in the form of a state map with a black grid overlay showing the areas covered by each map. Information included on the index pertains to the state and consists of libraries where you may inspect topo maps, retail dealers that handle USGS maps, special maps with complete descriptions and prices (good info here, be sure to look it over), plus, of course, description of the series and ordering data. Maps for the 7½-minute quads are 22" x 27"; for the 15-minute quads, 17" x 21". Both types run $1.25 per map.

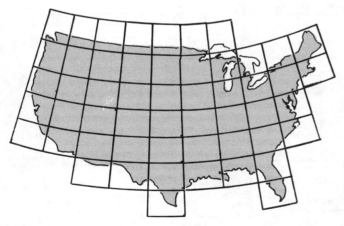

1:1,000,000 Scale Series. This index shows 55 maps that when put together make a complete map of the country. The area covered by each map is shown as a black overlay on a green base map of the United States. Sheet size for this series of maps is 27" x 27", and cost runs $1.50 per map. Index includes a description of the series and ordering data plus a list of other United States maps available.

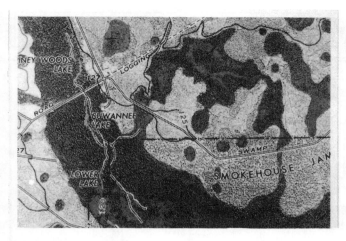

Topographical Photomaps

A new photomap technique called orthophoto mapping is being experimented with by the Geological Survey. It consists of topographic mapping symbols and colors being overprinted on aerial photographs. The beauty of the arrangement is that a detailed natural protrayal of trees, grass, rock outcroppings, cultivated fields, and so forth, can be shown. It's now possible, for example, to spot individual trees on a map and to make a distinction between pine trees growing on land and cypress trees growing in a swamp. Nature's patterns, rather than the conventional map symbols, are what make this series so unique. Several areas have been mapped using this technique, and sheets are available, most on a scale of 1:24,000. One of the areas for which maps are available is the Okefenokee Swamp of Georgia and Florida; a set of 16 maps for this one, each selling for $1.25. As far as we know, there have been no indexes issued for this series yet, but you can check with the Survey for more info.

Index to a Set of 100 Topographic Maps Illustrating Specific Physiographic Features

Sort of a long title, huh. This is an index to a special set of maps that illustrate land features found throughout the United States, such as different types of mountains, plains, plateaus, valleys, volcanic configurations, lakes, streams, rivers, wind-created forms (like sand dunes), coasts and shorelines, escarpments (cliffs, cuestas, hogbacks, etc.), and glaciation. It's more of a topographical study item than anything else. The maps in this set consist of both 7½- and 15-minute types and may be purchased as a set or individually. The price is $1.25 per map, and, as far as we know, you don't get a break if you buy the complete set. The index is in the form of a United States base map with overlay showing locations of each of the 100 maps. On the reverse side is a description and ordering information, plus a wealth of physiographic data pertaining to each of the maps. Worth picking up if you're a map buff.

Status Index of Topographic Mapping (issued semiannually)

This large overlaid base map of the United States shows what parts of the country have been mapped and what parts have not; the map scales that are available with respect to the 7½-minute series

(1:24,000) and the 15-minute series (1:62,500) for each part of the country; the surveying method used and the agency doing the work. Surprising as it may seem, there are a number of spots in the United States for which there are no 7½- or 15-minute quads available. From a practical standpoint this index can tell you what the availability status is on a particular area for which you may require a map.

Free Publications from U.S. Geological Survey

Here are some free publications on maps and mapping that are available from the U.S. Geological Survey's Map Information Office.

Topographic Maps. This little 24-pager has the complete scoop on topo maps, including data on map scale, the National Topographic Map Series, control surveys, mapping procedures, national standards for topo maps, symbols, how and when maps are revised, and how to order maps. Excellent.

Topographic Maps — Silent Guides for Outdoorsmen. Has a number of good tips on what a topo map can tell you about the hunting and fishing environment of an area. Also has procedures for mounting your maps on a cloth backing to make them last a bit longer. Eight pages.

Elevations and Distances in the United States. A 24-page booklet that lists geographic statistics on the fifty states. Includes the elevations of prominent mountains and cities, defines geographic centers, and indicates distances between various geographic localities. Lots of interesting statistical data.

Maps of the United States. Selected United States maps published by various federal agencies are described in this 8-pager, which includes descriptions of map, paper size, scale, price, and the address of where to order. Types of maps described include base and outline maps, aeronautical charts, coal fields, congressional districts, electric facilities, forest, geologic, gravity anomaly, great circle, ground conductivity, highway, isogonic, national parks, natural gas pipelines, oil and gas fields, physical divisions, population distribution, railroads, reclamation activities, shaded relief, status indexes (topographic, aerial photography and aerial mosaic), tectonic, time zones, waterways, and weather. Hey, that ought to keep you going for a little bit. Excellent reference source.

Types of Maps Published by Government Agencies. This is *the* directory of *all* government map sources. Includes the type of map(s) published, publishing agency and the address of where to get more information or to buy.

Publications of the Geological Survey (monthly catalog). If you want to keep up to date on the new maps being issued by USGS, as well as geological publications, your best source of information is this 12- to 20-page annotated monthly catalog. It's free and requires only that you put in a request for a subscription to Washington. Information contained in the catalog is pretty dry and is mainly oriented to technical reports and professional papers of interest to geologists. The map data consists only of four to six pages of lists giving quad name, latitude and longitude, scale, and contour interval of the new or revised sheets. Pretty ho-hum. The other map info included is new national park and monument maps issued and new state indexes for the 7½- and 15-minute series.

U.S. GOVERNMENT PRINTING OFFICE
Superintendent of Documents, Washington, D.C. 20402

Sup Docs, as the Government Printing Office (GPO) is known among insiders, handles a fantastic assortment of maps, charts, atlases, and cartographic publications. All are reasonably priced and listed in a free catalog known as *PL-53 Maps, Engineering, Surveying.* Just send a note to Sup Docs at the above address requesting it, and they'll mail a copy right out to you before you can say Jack Robinson (which shouldn't take any longer than eight weeks).

BOUNDARIES.

Boundaries of the United States and the several States. 1966. 291 p. il. map. $1.75.

Catalog No. I 19.3 : 1212

This bulletin serves as a reference work on boundaries of the United States and the several States and Territories and gives information on their source and their marking. Miscellaneous geographic information concerning areas, altitudes, geographic centers, and a map of the United States showing routes of the principal explorers from 1501 to 1844 are also included.

United States wall map. 1964. Scale 1 : 3,168,000, 1 in.=50 mi. 65 x 42 in. $2.00. Catalog No. I 53.11 : Un 3/964

This colorful map showing current distribution of Federally-owned lands, affords quick location of National Parks and Monuments, National Forests, Indian Reservations, Wildlife Refuges and Public Domain Lands. Printed on one sheet in 12 colors, this edition, measures 65 x 42 inches and can be mounted for classroom, office or home.

Maps showing explorers' routes, trails and early roads in the United States, an annotated list. 1962. 137 p. map. $1.50. Catalog No. LC 5.2 : Ex 7

LAND OWNERSHIP MAPS, a checklist of 19th century U.S. county maps in the Library of Congress. 1967. 86 p. il. $1.25. Cat. No. LC 5.2 : L 22

OPERATIONAL NAVIGATION CHARTS

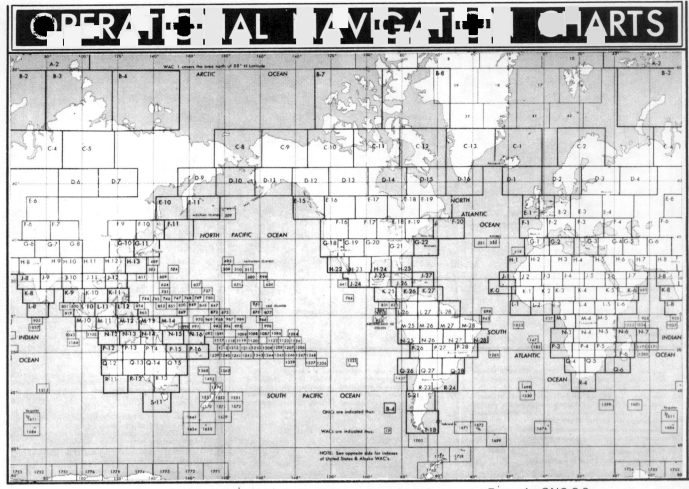

Price: $1.85   **How to order:** Indicate code and number   **Example:** ONC C-8

NATIONAL OCEAN SURVEY
Distribution Div., C-44
Washington, D.C. 20235
One source of topographical info for any part of the world is the (air) Operational Navigation Charts (ONC) published by the National Ocean Survey. Their purpose in aviation is to help the low, slow-flying pilot find his way by landmarks, and they're just as useful to the man on foot, especially for areas of the world where no other maps exist. Here's the scoop on the ONC's: *Projection,* Lambert Conformal Conic;

U.S. STATE GEOLOGICAL SURVEYS
Every state except Rhode Island has a geological survey. State surveys handle maps, books, and often mineral specimens native to the state, and it's certainly worth the investment of 13¢ to familiarize yourself with the material your state's survey has available. They'll be glad to supply you with literature, catalogs, and price lists on request. Here's where to write:

Alabama - Geological Survey of Alabama
P.O. Drawer O, University, 35486
Alaska - Dept. of Natural Resources
3001 Porcupine Dr., Anchorage, 99504
Arizona - Arizona Bureau of Mines
Univ. of Arizona, Tucson, 85721
Arkansas - Arkansas Geological Commission
3815 W. Roosevelt Rd., Little Rock, 72204
California - Div. of Mines & Geology, Dept. of Conservation
Resources Bldg., Rm. 1341, 1416 9th St., Sacramento, 95814
Colorado - Colorado Geological Survey
254 Columbine Bldg., 1845 Sherman St., Denver, 80203
Connecticut - Conn. Geological & Natural History Survey, Dept. of Environmental Protection, State Office Bldg., Hartford, 06115
Delaware - Delaware Geological Survey
Univ. of Delaware, 16 Robinson Hall, Newark, 19711
Florida - Dept. of Natural Resources, Bur. of Geology
P.O. Box 631, Tallahassee, 32302

Scale, 1:1,000,000 (13.7 nautical miles to the inch); *Description,* topographic information includes cities and towns, principal roads, railroads, distinctive landmarks, drainage, and relief. Relief and elevations are shown by spot elevations, contour lines and shading, which makes mountains look like mountains on a flat piece of paper. These charts are revised on a regular schedule. *Price,* $1.85 each. For complete information on ordering, request *Catalog of Aeronautical Charts and Related Publications* from NOS.

Georgia - Dept. of Mines, Mining & Geology
19 Hunter St., S.W., Atlanta, 30334
Hawaii - Div. of Water & Land Dev., Dept. of Land & Nat. Res.
P.O. Box 373, Honolulu, 96809
Idaho - Idaho Bureau of Mines & Geology
Moscow, 83843
Illinois - Illinois State Geological Survey
121 Natural Resources Bldg., Urbana, 61801
Indiana - Dept. of Natural Resources, Geological Survey
611 N. Walnut Grove, Bloomington, 47401
Iowa - Iowa Geological Survey
16 W. Jefferson St., Iowa City, 52240
Kansas - Geological Survey
1930 Avenue "A", Campus West, Univ. of Kansas, Lawrence, 66044
Kentucky - Kentucky Geological Survey
Univ. of Kentucky, 307 Mineral Ind. Bldg., Lexington, 40506
Louisiana - Louisiana Geological Survey
Box G, University Station, Baton Rouge, 70803
Maine - Maine Geological Survey
State Office Bldg., Rm. 211, Augusta, 04330
Maryland - Maryland Geological Survey
214 Latrobe Hall, Johns Hopkins Univ., Baltimore, 21218
Massachusetts - Mass. Dept. of Pub. Wks., Research & Material Div.
99 Worcester St., Wellesley, 02181
Michigan - Dept. of Nat. Res., Geological Survey Div.
Stevens T. Mason Bldg., Lansing, 48926

Minnesota - Minnesota Geological Survey
Univ. of Minnesota, 1633 Eustis St., St. Paul, 55108
Mississippi - Mississippi Geological, Economic & Topographical Survey
P.O. Box 4915, Jackson, 39216
Missouri - Div. of Geological Survey & Water Resources
P.O. Box 250, Rolla, 65401
Montana - Montana Bur. of Mines & Geology
Montana College of Mineral Science & Tech., Butte, 59701
Nebraska - Conservation & Survey Div.
Univ. of Nebraska, 113 Nebraska Hall, Lincoln, 68588
Nevada - Nevada Bureau of Mines & Geology
Univ. of Nevada, Reno, 89507
New Hampshire - Geologic Branch, Dept. of Geology
James Hall, Univ. of N.H., Durham, 03824
New Jersey - New Jersey Bur. of Geology & Topography, Dept. of
Environmental Protection, P.O. Box 2809, Trenton, 08625
New Mexico - N. Mex. Bur. of Mines & Mineral Resources
Campus Station, Socorro, 87801
New York - Geological Survey
New York State Education Bldg. Annex, Hawk St., Albany, 12234
North Carolina - Mineral Resources Section, Dept. of Nat. & Econ. Res.
P.O. Box 27687, Raleigh, 27611
North Dakota - North Dakota Geological Survey
University Station, Grand Forks, 58202
Ohio - Ohio Div. of Geological Survey
Fountain Square, Columbus, 43224
Oklahoma - Oklahoma Geological Survey
Univ. of Oklahoma, 830 Van Vleet Oval, Rm. 163, Norman, 73069

Oregon - State Dept. of Geology & Mineral Industries
1069 State Office Bldg., 1400 S.W. Fifth Ave., Portland, 97201
Pennsylvania - Bur. of Topographic & Geological Survey
Harrisburg, 17120
South Carolina - Div. of Geology
P.O. Box 927, Columbia, 29202
South Dakota - South Dakota State Geological Survey
Science Center, Univ. of S. Dak., Vermillion, 57069
Tennessee - Dept. of Conservation, Div. of Geology
Rm. G-5 State Office Bldg., Nashville, 37219
Texas - Bur. of Economic Geology
Univ. of Texas at Austin, Austin, 78712
Utah - Utah Geological & Mineral Survey
606 Black Hawk Way, Salt Lake City, 84108
Vermont - Vermont Geological Survey, Agency of Environmental
Conservation, Geology Bldg., Univ. of Vermont, Burlington, 05401
Virginia - Virginia Div. of Mineral Resources
P.O. Box 3667, Charlottesville, 22903
Washington - Washington Div. of Mines & Geology
P.O. Box 168, Olympia, 98501
West Virginia - W. Va. Geological Survey
P.O. Box 879, Morgantown, 26505
Wisconsin - Wis. Geological & Natural History Survey
Univ. of Wis. Extn., 1815 Univ. Ave., Madison, 53706
Wyoming - Geological Survey of Wyoming
P.O. Box 3008, Univ. Station, Univ. of Wyo., Laramie, 82071

OTHER COUNTRIES

GEOLOGICAL SURVEYS (foreign)

When it appears that no domestic source of maps is available for a particular country, the next step is to contact the country's national geological survey or whatever agency is involved in the country's geological research. Sometimes it may be a department of the national university. The usual difficulty that crops up here is language and ascertaining whether exactly what you want is available. And, believe me, it's worthwhile to make sure the survey, or whoever, knows exactly what you're after so they can advise you. It will save a lot of time and frustration. Okay, so what do you do if English is the only thing you can handle? In the **Yellow Pages** is a section called "Trans-

lators and Interpreters." Start here, then move on to the language department of the local college, travel agents, and finally a dictionary. When composing your letter, be sure to describe precisely what you would like the map(s) to show, approximate scale, areas covered (bounded by what lines of latitude and longitude), whether map indexes are available, and what the prices are in American money. Incidentally, when making payment for the maps, the best thing to use is an international (postal) money order. Info on this can be secured through your local post office.

A list of geological surveys for different countries of the world follows:

North America

Canada	Mexico
Geological Survey	Instituto de Geologia
Department of Energy, Mines and Resources	Universidad Nacional Autonoma de Mexico
601 Booth Street	Ciudad Universitaria
Ottawa K1A 0E9	Mexico 20, D.F.
Greenland	**United States**
Grønlands Geologiske Undersøgelse	Map Information Office U.S. Geological Survey
Østervoldgade 7	National Center
Kobenhavn K, Denmark	Reston, Va. 22092

Caribbean Islands

Cuba	Jamaica
Instituto Nacional de Investigaciones Cientificas	Geological Survey Department Hope Gardens
Cerro 827	Kingston 6,
Havana	
	Puerto Rico
Dominican Republic	Economic Development
Servicio de Mineria	Administration
Ministerio de Industria y Comercio	Industrial Research Mineralogy and Geology Section
Santo Domingo	Box 38, Roosevelt Station Hato Rey
Guadeloupe	
Arrondissement Mineralogique de la Guyane	**Martinique** Arrondissement Mineralogique
Boite Postal 448	de la Guyane
Pointe-a-Pitre	Boite Postale 458 Fort-de-France
Haiti	
Geological Survey	**Trinidad and Tobago**
Department of Agriculture	Ministry of Petroleum and Mines
Damiens pres Port-au-Prince	P.O. Box 96 Port-of-Spain, Trinidad

Central America

Costa Rica	Honduras
Geological Survey of Costa Rica	Departamento Minas e
Geologic Department	Hidrocarburos
University of Costa Rica	Direccion General de Recursos
San Pedro de Montes de Oca	Naturales
San Jose	Tegucigalpa, D.C.
El Salvador	**Nicaragua**
Centro de Estudios e	Servicio Geologico Nacional
Investigaciones Geotecnicas	Ministerio de Economia
Apartado Postal 109	Apartado Postal No. 1347
San Salvador	Managua, D.N.
Guatemala	**Panama**
Seccion de Geologia	Departamento de Recursos
Direccion General de Cartografia	Minerales
Avenida Los Americos 5-76,	Apartado Postal 1631
Zona 13	Panama, Panama
Guatemala, Guatemala	

South America

Argentina	Chile
Instituto Nacional de Geologia y Mineria	Instituto de Investigaciones Geologicas
Avada Julio A., Roca 651	Augustinas 785, 5º Pisa
Buenos Aires	Casilla 10465
	Santiago
Bolivia	
Ministerio de Minas y Petroleo	**Colombia**
Servicio Geologico de Bolivia	Instituto Nacional de
Avenida 16 de Julio No. 1769	Investigaciones Mineras
Casilla Cerreo 2729	Carrera 30, No. 51-59
La Paz	Bogota
Brazil	**Ecuador**
Departamento Nacional da	Servicio Nacional de Geologia y
Producao Mineral	Mineria
Avenida Pasteur 404	Casilla 23-A
Rio de Janeiro	Quito

French Guiana
Bureau des Recherches
   Geologiques et Minieres
B.P. 42
Cayenne

Guyana
Geological Survey Department
P.O. Box 789
Brickdam, Georgetown

Paraguay
Direccion de la Produccion
   Mineral
Tucari 271
Asuncion

Peru
Servicio de Geologia y Mineria
Apartado 889
Lima

Surinam
Geologisch Mijnbouwkundige
   Dienst
Dept. van Opbouw
Klein Wasserstraat 1
Paramaribo

Uruguay
Instituto Geologico del Uruguay
Calle J. Herrer y Obes 1239
Montevideo

Venezuela
Ministerio de Minas e
   Hidrocarburos
Direccion de Geologia
Torre Norte, Piso 19
Caracas

Europe

Austria
Geologische Bundesanstalt
Rasumofskygasse 23
1031 Vienna 3.

Belgium
Service Geologique de Belgique
13 rue Jenner, Parc Leopold
Brussels 4

Bulgaria
Direction des Mines
Ministere des Mines et des
   Richesses du Sous-sol
Sofia

Czechoslovakia
Ustredni Ustav Geologicky
Malostranske Nam. 19
Prague 1

Denmark
Danmarks Geologiske
   Undersogelse
Roadhusvej 36
Charlottenlund

Finland
Geologinen Tutkimuslaitos
Otaniemi, Near Helsinki

France
Bureau des Recherches
   Geologiques et Minieres
74 rue de la Federation
Paris XVe

Germany
Bundesanstalt fur
   Bodenforschung
Alfred-Bentz-Haus
Postfach 54, Buchholz
Hannover 3

Great Britain
Institute of Geological Sciences
Exhibition Road
South Kensington
London, S.W. 7

Greece
Institute of Geology and
   Subsurface Research
Ministry of Industry
6, Amerikis Str.
Athens (134)

Hungary
Magyar Allami
Foldtani Intezet
Nepstadion-ut 14
Budapest XIV

Iceland
Department of Geology and
   Geography
Museum of Natural History
P.O. Box 532
Reykjavik

Ireland
Geological Survey of Ireland
14 Hume Street
Dublin 2, Eire

Italy
Servizio Geologico D'Italia
Largo S. Susanna N. 13 - 00187
Roma

Liechtenstein
Geological Survey of
   Liechtenstein
Vaduz

Luxembourg
Service Geologique
Direction des Ponts et Chaussees
13, rue J.P. Koenig
Luxembourg

Netherlands
Geologische Stichting
Spaarne 17
Haarlem

Norway
Norges Geologiske Undersokelse
P.B. 3006 Ostmarkneset
Trondheim

Poland
Instytut Geologiczny
ul. Rakowiecka 4
Warsaw

Portugal
Servicos Geologicos de Portugal
Rua da Academia das Ciencias
   19-2o
Lisboa 2

Romania
Comitetul de Stat al Geologiei
Calea Grivitei 64
Bucuresti 12

Spain
Instituto Geologico y Minero
   de Espana
Rios Rosas 23
Madrid 3

Sweden
Sverges Geologiska
   Undersokning Frescati
Stockholm 50

Switzerland
Schweizerische Geologische
   Kommission
Bernoullianum
CH 4000 Basle

USSR
Ministry of Geology and
   Conservation of Mineral
   Resources
B. Gruzinskaya, 4/6
Moscow

Yugoslavia
Institute for Geological and
   Geophysical Research
Belgrade

Africa

Algeria
Direction des Mines et de
   la Geologie
Service Geologique
Immeuble Mauretania - Agha
Algiers

Angola
Servicio de Geologia y Minas
Caixa Postal No. 1260-C
Luanda

Botswana
Geological Survey
P.O. Box 94
Lobatsi

Burundi
Ministere des Affaires
   Economiques et Financieres
Department de Geologie et
   Mines
Boite Postal 745
Bujumbura

Cameroon
Ministere des Transports,
   des Mines, des Postes, et
   des Telecommunications
Direction des Mines et de
   la Geologie
Boite Postale 70
Yaounde

Chad
La Service des Mines et de
   la Republique des Tchad
Service des Travaux Publiques
Fort Lamy

Congo, Republic of
Service des Mines et de
   la Geologie
Boite Postale 12
Brazzaville

Congo (now Zaire)
Service Geologique National de
   la Republique du Congo
Boite Postale 898
Kinshasa

Dahomey
Service of Mines and Geology
Ministry of Public Works,
   Transport and
   Telecommunications
Box 249
Contonou

Egypt
Geological Survey and
   Mineral Department
Dawawin Post Office
Cairo

Ethiopia
Imperial Ethiopian Government
Ministry of Mines
P.O. Box 486
Addis Ababa

**French Territory of Afars and
   Issas**
Service des Travaux Publiques
   du Territoire Francais des
   Afars et des Issas
Djibouti

Gabon Republic
Direction des Mines
B.P. 576
Libreville

Ghana
Ghana Geological Survey
P.O. Box M 80
Accra

Guinea
Service des Mines et de
   la Geologie
Conakry

Ivory Coast
Service Geologique
Boite Postal 1368
Abidjan

Kenya
Ministry of Natural Resources
Mines and Geological
   Department
P.O. Box 30009
Nairobi

Lebanon
Direction Generale des
   Travaux Publiques
Beirut

Liberia
Liberia Geological Survey
Ministry of Lands and Mines
P.O. Box 9024
Monrovia

Libya
Geologic Division
Ministry of Industry
Tripoli

Malagasy
Ministere de L'Industrie et
   des Mines
Direction des Mines et
   de l'Energie
Service Geologique
B.P. 280
Tananarive

Malawi
Geological Survey Department
P.O. Box 27
Zomba

Mali
Ministere des Travaux Publiques
   des Telecommunications, de
   l'Habitat, et des Resources
   Energetiques
Bamako

Mauritania
Direction des Mines et de
   la Geologie
Nouakchott

Morocco
Division de la Geologie
Direction des Mines et de
   la Geologie
Rabat (Chellah)

Mozambique
Servicos de Geologia e Minas
Caixa Postal 217
Lourenco Marques

Niger
Service des Mines et de
   la Geologie
Ministere des Travaux Publiques
Niamey

Nigeria
Ministry of Mines and Power
Geological Survey Division
P.M.B. 2007
Kaduna South

Reunion
Service des Travaux Publiques
St. Denis

Rhodesia
Ministry of Mines and Lands
Geological Survey Office
Causeway P.O. Box 8039
Salisbury

Rwanda
Service Geologique
B.P. 15
Ruhengeri

Saudi Arabia
Ministry of Petroleum and
Mineral Resources
Directorate General of Mineral
Resources
P.O. Box 345
Jiddah

Senegal
Direction des Mines et de
la Geologie
B.P. 1238
Dakar

Sierra Leone
Geological Survey Division
Freetown

Somali
Geological Survey Department
Box 4l
Hargeisa

South Africa, Republic of
Geological Survey
P.B. 112
Pretoria

Southwest Africa
Geological Survey
P.O. Box 2168
Windhoek

Spanish Sahara
Direccion General de Plazas y
Provincias Africanas
Servicio Minerio y Geologico
Castellana No. 5
Madrid 1

Sudan
Geological Survey Department
Ministry of Mining and Industry
P.O. Box 410
Khartoum

Swaziland
Geological Survey and Mines
P.O. Box 9
Mbabane

Tanzania
Ministry of Commerce
Mineral Resources Division
P.O. Box 903
Dodoma

Togo
Ministere des Travaux Publiques,
Mines, Transports, et
Telecommunications
Direction des Mines et de
la Geologie
B.P. 356
Lome

Tunisia
Geological Survey of Tunisia
95, Avenue Mohamed V
Tunis

Uganda
Geological Survey and Mines
Department
P.O. Box 9
Entebbe

Upper Volta
Direction de la Geologie
et des Mines
Ouagadougou

Zambia
Ministry of Labour and Mines
Geological Survey Department
P.O. Box R.W. 135
Ridgeway, Lusaka

Asia

Afghanistan
Ministry of Mines and Industry
Mines and Geological Survey
Department
Kabul

Borneo
Geological Survey Department
Borneo Region, Malaysia
Kuching, Sarawak

Brunei
The Government Geologist
Brunei Town

Burma
Geological Department
226 Mahabandoola Street
Box 843
Rangoon

Cambodia
Service des Mines
Phnom-Penh

Ceylon (now Sri Lanka)
Geological Survey Department
48, Sri Jinaratana Road
Colombo 2

China
Chinese Ministry of Geology
Peking

India
Geological Survey of India
29 Jawaharlal Nehru Road
Calcutta 16

Indonesia
Geological Survey of Indonesia
Djalan Diponegoro 57
Bandung

Japan
Geological Survey of Japan
135 Hisamoto-cho
Kawasaki, Kanagawa

Korea
Geological Survey of Korea
125 Namyoung-dong
Seoul

Laos
Department of Mines
Ministere du Plan
B.P. 46
Vientiane

Malaysia (West)
Geological Survey
Scrivenor Road
P.O. Box 1015
Ipoh

Nepal
Ministry of Industry and
Commerce
Nepal Geological Survey
Lainchaur, Kathmandu

Pakistan
Geological Survey of Pakistan
P.O. Box 15
Quetta

Philippines
Dept. of Agriculture and
Natural Resources
Bureau of Mines
P.O. Box No. 1595
Manila

Taiwan (Republic of China)
Geological Survey of Taiwan
P.O. Box 31
Taipei

Thailand
Royal Department of
Mineral Resources
Rama VI Road
Bangkok

Vietnam
Direction Generale des Mines de
l'Industrie et de l'Artisanat
Service Geologique
59, rue Gia-Long
Saigon

Middle East

Cyprus
Geological Survey Department
3, Electra Street
P.O. Box 809
Nicosia

Iran
Iranian Geological Survey
P.O. Box 1964
Teheran

Iraq
Geological Survey Department
Directorate of Minerals
Ministry of Oil
Baghdad

Israel
Geological Survey of Israel
30, Malkhei Israel Street
Jerusalem

Jordan
Natural Resources Authority
Mines and Geological Survey
Department
Box 2220
Amman

Kuwait
Kuwait Oil Affairs Department
Ahmadi 94

Syria
Directorate of Geological
Research and
Mineral Resources
Ministry of Petroleum
Fardos Street
Damascus

Turkey
Maden Tetkik ve Arama
Enstitusu
Posta Kutusu 116
Eskisehir Road
Ankara

Yemen
Office of Mineral Resources
Ministry of Public Works
Sana

Australia and Pacific Islands

Australia
Bureau of Mineral Resources,
Geology, and Geophysics
Box 378, P.O.
Canberra City, 2601

Borneo
Geological Survey, Borneo
Region (East Malaysia)
Kuching, Sarawak

British Solomon Islands
Geological Survey Department
P.O. Box G-24
Honiara, Guadalcanal

Fiji
Director of Geological Survey
P.M.B., G.P.O.
Suva

New Caledonia
Service des Mines
Noumea

New Hebrides
New Hebrides Condominium
Geological Survey
British Residency
Vila

New South Wales
Department of Mines
11 Loftus Street
Sydney, N.S.W.

New Zealand
Department of Scientific and
Industrial Research
New Zealand Geological Survey
P.O. Box 30368 - Andrews Ave.
Lower Hutt, Wellington

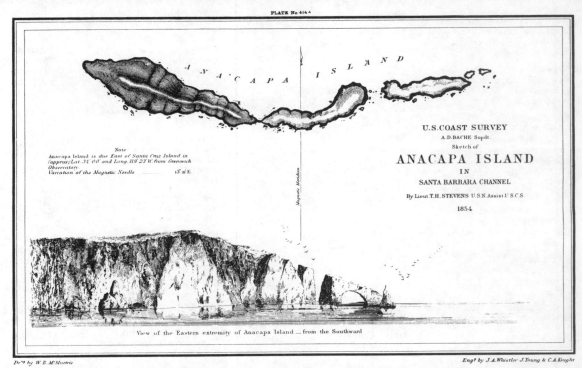

PLATE No.414 A

Note
Anacapa Island is due East of Santa Cruz Island in
(approx) Lat. 34.00 and Long. 119 23 W. from Greenwich
Observatory.
Variation of the Magnetic Needle   13°21'E.

U.S.COAST SURVEY
A.D.BACHE Supdt.
Sketch of
ANACAPA ISLAND
IN
SANTA BARBARA CHANNEL
By Lieut.T.H.STEVENS U.S.N.Assist U.S.C.S.
1854

View of the Eastern extremity of Anacapa Island — from the Southward

Dr'n by W.B.M'Murtrie   Eng'd by J.A.Whistler J.Young & C.A.Knight

Engraving of Anacapa Island, California, by James M. Whistler, J. Young, and C.A. Knight. Whistler, perhaps best known for the portrait of his mother, was employed as an engraver with the U.S. Coast Survey for three months during the winter of 1854—55. In the above engraving, he was responsible for adding the two flocks of gulls in flight, which the Survey wasn't too happy about.

NATIONAL OCEAN SURVEY (NOS)
Rockville, Md. 20852

Over 23,000 individual surveys going back to 1835 are on file in the National Ocean Survey Archives, and copies of these as well as original maps and aerial photographs (from 1927 on) are available to the public.

The surveys represent a unique and comprehensive record of the United States coastline and adjacent waters, showing conditions existing at any particular date over more than a century and providing a quite detailed record of the changes that have occurred from both natural and man-made causes during this time. If you are interested in studies of the shoreline and adjacent land areas, topographic surveys should be requested; such surveys are identified by a number with the prefix T. Indexes of these surveys are available and will be furnished free upon request. The area covered by any individual survey is indicated approximately on the index and will vary, depending on the needs of the survey at the time it was made.

Topographic surveys vary not only in coverage but in content. Many show only the shoreline and planimetric features immediately adjacent thereto. Others are complete planimetric maps covering an area from the shoreline inland to as much as five or more miles, or up to the 7½-minute quadrangle limit. The indexes show the type of information as well as the coverage.

From 1835 to 1927 practically all of the topographic surveys were made by planetable, and the original planetable sheets are filed in the Archives. Photographic copies (photostats or bromides) are furnished of these. Since 1927, aerial photographs and photogrammetric methods have been utilized. Photographic copies of these are furnished as ozalid prints. The indexes also indicate whether a topographic survey was made by planetable or by photogrammetric methods.

When a copy of the entire survey is desired, a bromide copy is made. A few surveys will require more than one bromide, depending on size and available negative. Upon request, a survey will be enlarged photographically to any scale up to twice, but not more than twice its original scale and down to one-half its original scale. Charges will be based on the number of prints required in reproducing the surveys. A plain language "Descriptive Report" exists for most surveys and is available at additional cost.

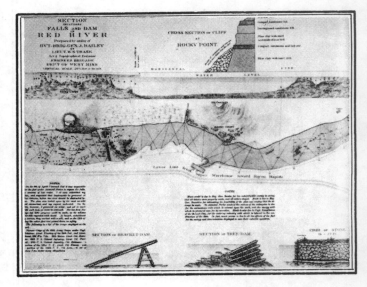

Bromide prints (up to 40 in. x 80 in.).............$15.00 ea.
Ozalid of topographic map, compiled
    from aerial photographs............................$ 8.50 ea.
"Descriptive Reports" (page size copies).........$ 1.00 ea.
Ocean Survey Sheets (OSS) (To be used
    as plotting sheets only)............................$ 1.00 ea.

For indexes and other information on:
Surveys — Attn: Hydrographic Data Section, C3233
Aerial Photographs — Attn: Coastal Mapping Division, C34
Topographic Maps — Attn: Physical Science Services Branch, C513

All should be addressed to: Director, National Ocean Survey, Rockville, Md. 20852

sources of old maps & surveys

THE WINDSOR COLLECTION
111 Canterbury Drive, Wilmington, Del. 19803

Old maps and atlases from around the world, some up to 400 years old—that's the Windsor Collection. These people specialize in original engravings of maps produced by well-known and not so well-known cartographers of Europe, America and Asia. A beautifully illustrated, descriptive catalog is available to serious map collectors. The Windsor Collection is also interested in acquiring maps and atlases, and would be glad to quote on any that you may have to sell. For more information, write them at the above address.

Southwest. L'Ancien et le Nouveau Mexique, M. Bonne, Paris, 1788. Southern California, present Arizona, New Mexico, western Texas, and northern Mexico, much of which is terra incognita. Santa Fe is shown and the River Colorado with obviously unknown origins. Locations of Indian nations (Yumas, Apaches, Cenis, etc.) are given. Hand colored in outline. 14 x 9¼ ins. + margins. $65.

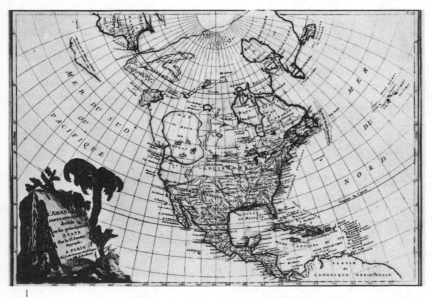

North America. L'Amerique Septentrionale divisee en ses principaux Etats, Janvier, Paris, 1762. A fine map of North America which offers the English, French, and Spanish territorial holdings, divisions into colonies, and a curious choice of cities. In Virginia the only towns are Jamestown (!) and Elisabeth, in New England Harford (sic) and Boston, and in Nova Scotia (Acadie), Annapolis. The courses of major rivers still seem to be unknown. An extraordinary error occurs in the northwest, with the rendering of a vast "Mer ou Baie de L'Ouest", a fictitious sea larger than the Gulf of Mexico, presumably derived from a mistaken understanding of Puget Sound. Alaska is drawn fancifully and with great inaccuracy. Hand colored. 12¼ x 17¾ ins. + margins. Phillips. $150.

MIDCONTINENT MAPS AND REPRODUCTIONS, INC.
P.O. Box 3157, Tulsa, Okla. 74101

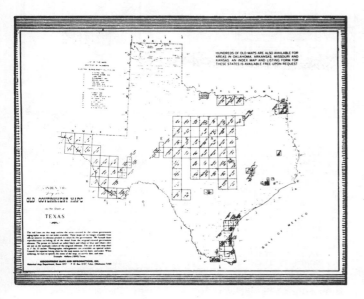

"We offer rare old maps of areas surveyed by United States Government agencies. These are authentic topographic maps originally published 50 to 100 years ago. They were made initially to show the exact locations of towns, schools, cemeteries; roads, trails, mines, isolated buildings, rivers, streams, mountains and other features. These surveys were actually made on the ground by pioneering surveyors who endured all kinds of hardships in the accomplishment of what then was a monumental task. These maps are of areas in Arkansas, Kansas, Missouri, Oklahoma and Texas. We are adding other states as rapidly as possible. Most of the maps are approximately 17 in. x 22 in. size and scaled about ½ in. to one mile. They are used extensively by historians and researchers in establishing the exact locations of events recorded in the history of the past century. We have spent a lot of time and money to locate copies of these valuable old maps and to make reproductions available to everyone at a very low cost. Some of the copies we found were torn or faded, but most of them were in good condition and the reproductions are good to excellent.

"We have prepared index maps of Arkansas, Kansas, Missouri, Oklahoma and Texas (free upon request) which show the areas covered by these rare old government maps in the various states. The index maps show the names and survey dates of each of the oldest topographic maps we could find—those still available in editions printed by the government and those no longer available from official sources but now reproduced and sold by our Historical Map Department.

"We fill all orders for old government maps with editions printed by the government if available. However, there are not many of these left, and, when they are not available, we send copies we have reproduced in black and white or in blue and white. Please request our combination listing sheets and order forms to determine the status of particular maps. Prices are: $1.25 per map ($5 minimum order) or 10 or more maps at $1 each.

"We also carry in stock all USGS topo maps currently published by the government for all of Oklahoma, western Arkansas, southwest Missouri and the mountainous areas of Colorado."

JOHN BARTHOLOMEW & SON, LTD.
12 Duncan Street
Edinburgh
Scotland EH9 1TA

Bartholomew & Son, Ltd. is one of the old line cartographic houses. It produces internationally recognized maps of all types for just about every country. Definitely good people. Their catalog of general maps, topo maps, historical reproductions, tourist (road) maps, and atlases is available free upon request. We also suggest that if you need any help obtaining information on a map of anywhere, new or old, J.B.&S., will help you as best they can.

CHATHAM LAMINATING CO.
P.O. Box 5171 - Sta. A, Savannah, Ga. 31403
Chatham Laminating is presently providing waterproof, plastic laminated charts to boatmen. Seems to be pretty good. Though we have not checked with them, perhaps they might also buy and laminate USGS quadrangles on special order.

U.S./CANADIAN MAP SERVICE BUREAU
Midwest Distribution Center, Box 249, Neenah, Wis. 54956
This is *the* one-stop-spot to service all of your map and chart needs. These people handle a selection of virtually a quarter million up-to-date topographic maps and hydrographic charts plus related publications for the United States and Canada, all conveniently listed and indexed in their two catalogs: *Official Eastern North America Map and Chart Index Catalog* and *Official Western North America Map and Chart Index Catalog.* Also listed are many specialized maps including lunar maps, plastic raised relief maps, and national park maps of the U.S. and Canada. It's all there in the two catalogs which run $5.85 each, postpaid. Incidentally, these 160-page catalogs are the best reference sources yet available (we know of no other) on maps and charts of North America. Beautifully arranged, clean, clear and easy to use, they're a definite *must* for any serious explorer or outdoorsman's reference library.

Prices for most of U.S./Canadian's maps and charts are a little higher than what the government sells them for. Publications are about the same as government prices. For more information, request U.S./Canadian's brochure describing their services and catalogs.

HAMMOND MAP STORE, INC.
10 E. 4lst St., New York, N.Y. 10017
World, road and travel, sales-planning maps. American and world atlases. Political wall maps of foreign countries. Bible, history, moon, and weather charts. Reproductions of antique maps of the world. North America and Europe, moon and world globes. Specific literature available on request.

KISTLER GRAPHICS, INC.
P.O. Box 5467, Denver, Colo. 80217
Plastic relief maps of the world, United States, and Mexico. Maps of certain states and national parks are available including: Alaska, Arizona, California, Colorado, Hawaii, Idaho, Montana, New England, New Mexico, Oregon, Texas, Utah, Washington, Wisconsin, Wyoming, Grand Teton National Park, Mount Rainier National Park, Rocky Mountain National Park, Vail Ski Area, Monument Valley, Utah. These maps average 17 in. x 22 in. and cost about $6 each. Complete literature available on request.

MICHELIN GUIDES AND MAPS
P.O. Box 188, Roslyn Heights, N.Y. 11577
Michelin, well-known for their motorcar tyres, are just as well-known for their road maps, usually the first choice of anyone planning a motoring trip on the Continent. In addition to their very well-draughted maps, Michelin publishes the *Red Guide* series featuring road maps, city plans and a wealth of information and advice, as well as selected listings and ratings of hotels and restaurants. Titles available are: France, Germany, Italy, Spain and Portugal, Great Britain and others. Their other series, the *Green Guides,* offers touristic and cultural information on main places of interest and suggestions for sightseeing.

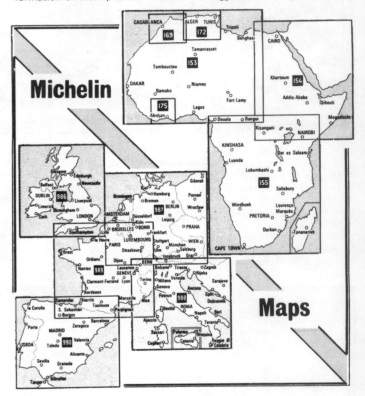

MAPS — EUROPE

MICHELIN'S MOTORING MAPS:	
M801 FRANCE	1.30
M802 GERMANY, HOLLAND, BELGIUM, LUXEMBOURG, AUSTRIA...	1.30
M803 GREAT BRITAIN	1.30
M804 ITALY & SWITZERLAND	1.30
M805 SPAIN & PORTUGAL	1.30
MAPS BY HALLWAG, LTD.:	
M806 ADRIATIC	1.50
M807 BERNE TOWN MAP	1.50
M808 DALMATIA I	1.50
M809 DALMATIA II	1.50
M810 DALMATIA III	1.50
M811 NORTHERN ITALY I	1.50
M812 NORTHERN ITALY II	1.50
M813 OLYMPIC MAP: 1972 SUMMER OLYMPIC GAMES IN MUNICH.	2.50

English edition titles include: Austria, Brittany, Chateaux Loire, French Riviera, Germany, Italy, New York City, Normandy, Paris, Portugal, Spain and Switzerland. Michelin publications are available at most bookstores. For prices and other information, write to the above address.

sources of maps & supplies

NATIONAL GEOGRAPHIC SOCIETY
17th and M Streets, N.W., Washington, D.C. 20036

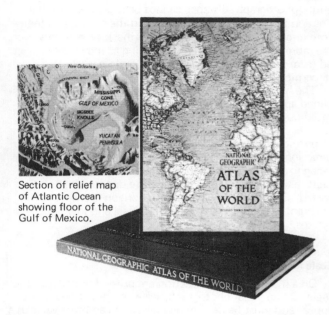

Section of relief map
of Atlantic Ocean
showing floor of the
Gulf of Mexico.

Wall and atlas maps of foreign countries, United States and the world
in color. Special relief maps of Atlantic, Pacific, and Indian Ocean
floors. Historical, moon, United States vacationlands, Holy Land,
archaeological sites of Mexico, mural maps, and globes of the world.
Literature available on request.

A.J. NYSTROM AND CO.
3333 North Elston Ave., Chicago, Ill. 60618

U. S. Geological Survey quadrangle formed in plastic relief. 17 x 22" — weight. 4 oz.

TRUE RAISED RELIEF MAPS

U.S.G.S. QUADRANGLES

A set of 12 quadrangles, formed in dura
ble vinyl plastic, showing topography of
the following areas.

Soda Canyon, Colorado

Princeton, Indiana-Illinois

Harrisburg, Pennsylvania

Loveland, Colorado

Kaaterskill, New York

Mammoth Cave, Kentucky

Whitewater, Wisconsin

Chief Mountain, Montana

Mount Rainier, Washington

Oceanside, California

Point Reyes, California

Toms River, New Jersey

Plastic relief maps of the world, United States, Europe, Asia, Africa,
North America, South America, Canada, the Eastern United States
continental shelf, California, New Jersey, New York, Pennsylvania,
and Wisconsin. Plastic relief and physical-political globes of the world.
Relief globes of the moon. Nystrom has twelve USGS quadrangle
maps in relief representative of topography studied in geology and
geography classes. They're 17 in. x 22 in. and cost $9 each. Literature
and catalog available on request.

SKI HUT
1615 University Ave., Berkeley, Calif. 94703
Specialized topo and relief maps of selected United States and
Canadian national parks, trails, and mountains. Clear contact plastic
for laminating your own maps. It's 18" wide, pressure applied, and
costs less than a buck per running yard. Recreational equipment
catalog available.

RAND McNALLY AND CO.
P.O. Box 7600, Chicago, Ill. 60680

United States reference maps, atlases, and guides for geographic and
marketing data. World, continent, and foreign country maps. Vacation, camping, national park, and archaeological atlases and guides.
Atlases of the world, United States, history, and universe. Educational and decorative globes. Catalogs available on request. Rand McNally
operates a nice map store in New York City at 10 East 53rd Street,
which carries all the above and is well worth visiting.

RECREATIONAL EQUIPMENT, INC.
1525 11th Ave., Seattle, Wash. 98122
Specialized topo and relief maps of selected United States and
Canadian national parks, trails, and mountains. Recreational equipment catalog available.

T.N. HUBBARD SCIENTIFIC CO.
P.O. Box 105, Northbrook, Ill. 60062

RAISED RELIEF
TOPO MAPS

You may recall we mentioned several pages back that USATOPOCOM
did not handle plastic relief maps anymore, except for one of Puerto
Rico and one of the world. Hubbard picked them up from the Army,
and as far as we know, is now the only source of these maps. They
have over 300 different quadrangles available at a scale of 1:250,000
and selling for $12 each. Descriptive literature can be had by writing
Hubbard at the above address.

aerial photographs

Most people rarely think of an aerial photograph when considering ways to get information on a piece of terrain. The reason for this is probably that they're not as handy to the public as maps are. But once you get the inside dope on sources and ordering procedure, you'll find there's no more of a problem to getting an aerial photo than there is to getting a topo map. The only thing is, they're a bit more expensive. To make you feel more at ease about them, here's some background information on the types available, how they're made, and what aerial photos can do for you.

The aerial photographs most commonly available today are of two major types: vertical and oblique. They are distinguished by the altitude and angle of the camera in relation to the earth's surface at the time the photograph is taken.

Of the two types, vertical photos are the most frequently used. A vertical photograph is taken with the camera pointed straight down. Its primary uses are as a map supplement or substitute, and in making new maps or revising old ones. A vertical shot has certain distinctive characteristics: it covers a relatively small area, maybe 3 by 3 miles; it gives an unfamiliar view of the ground, because it is shot from straight overhead; distance and directions may approach the accuracy of maps if the photo is taken over flat terrain; and relief is not readily apparent.

The low oblique is a photograph taken with the camera inclined approximately 20º to 30º from the vertical. Its characteristics are: it covers a relatively small area; the terrain pictured is a trapezoid, although the photo is square or rectangular (this means that no scale is applicable to the entire photograph, distance cannot be measured, parallel lines on the ground are not parallel in the photo, and therefore direction cannot be measured either); objects, however, are more easily recognizable, appearing as they might if viewed from the top of a high hill or tall building; relief is discernible but distorted.

The high oblique photograph is taken with the camera inclined approximately 60º from vertical. This type is most often used in making aeronautical charts. Characteristics: it covers a very large area, though not all of it is usable; trapezoidal attitude negates measurement of distance and direction; the view varies from the recognizable to the unrecognizable, depending on the height from which the picture was taken; relief may be quite discernible, but distorted, as in any oblique view; the horizon is always apparent, whereas it is not in the vertical and low oblique photos.

Scale and Direction

On a map, scale and direction are printed directly on the sheet. On an aerial photograph, scale and direction do not appear and must be determined before it can be of value as a map substitute. Usually this data will be available from the agency where you purchased the photo.

Identification of Features

The identification of features on aerial photographs de-

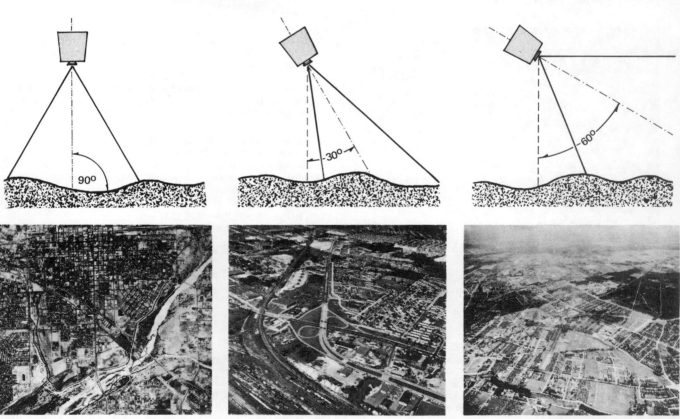

Vertical.   Low Oblique.   High Oblique.

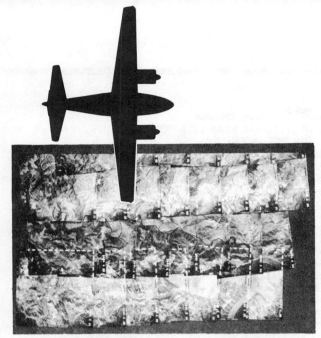

Adjacent parallel flight run showing overlap and sidelap of aerial photographs.

pends upon a careful application of five factors of recognition.

1. Size. The size of unknown objects and a clue to their identity can be determined from the scale of the photo or a comparison with known objects of known size. For example, in a built-up area the smaller buildings are usually dwellings, and the larger buildings commercial or community buildings.

2. Shape and Pattern. Objects in aerial photographs are greatly reduced in size, hence will appear distorted. Nevertheless, many features have characteristic shapes that readily identify them. Man-made features usually appear as straight or smooth curved lines, while natural features appear irregular. Some of the most prominent man-made features are highways, railroads, bridges, canals, and buildings. Compare the regular shapes of these with the irregular shapes of such natural features as streams and timber lines.

3. Shadows. Shadows are helpful in identifying features, since they show the familiar side view of the object. Some excellent examples are the shadows of water towers or smokestacks; viewed from overhead, only a round circle or dot is seen, whereas the shadow shows the profile. Relative lengths of shadows can also give a good indication of the heights of objects.

4. Shade, Tone, and Texture. Of the many different types of photographic film in use today, the film used for most aerial photography, except for special purposes, is panchromatic film. Panchromatic film is sensitive to all the colors of the spectrum; it registers them as shades of gray, ranging from white to black. This lighter or darker shade of features is known as tone. The tone is also dependent on the roughness or texture of the features; a paved highway has a smooth texture and produces an even tone on the photograph, while a recently plowed field or a marsh has a rough, choppy texture and results in a rough or grainy tone. It is also important to remember that similar features may have different tones on different photographs, depending on the reflection of sunlight. For example, a river or body of water appears light if it is reflecting sunlight directly toward the camera, but appears dark otherwise. Its texture may be smooth or rough, depending on the surface of the water itself. As long as the variables are kept in mind, tone and texture may be used to great advantage.

5. Surrounding Objects. Quite often, an object not easily recognized by itself may be identified by its relative position to surrounding objects. Large buildings located beside railroads or railroad sidings are usually factories or warehouses. Schools may be identified by baseball or football fields. It would be hard to tell the difference between a water tower next to a railroad station and a silo next to a barn unless the surrounding objects, such as the railroad tracks or cultivated fields, were considered.

Orientation

Before a vertical photograph can be studied or used for proper identification of features, it must be oriented for perspective. This orientation is different from the north/south, east/west type. The orientation for perspective consists of rotating the photograph so that the shadows on the photograph point toward you. You then face a source of light. This orientation places the source of light, and an object and its shadow in a natural relationship. Failure to orient a photograph properly may cause the height or depth of an object to appear reversed. For example, a mine or quarry may appear to be a hill instead of a depression.

Mirror stereoscope.

Stereovision

One of the limitations of the vertical aerial photograph is the lack of apparent relief. Stereoscopic vision or, as it is more commonly known, stereovision or depth perception, is the ability to see three-dimensionally—to see length, width, and depth (distance) at the same time. This requires two views of a single object from two slightly different positions. Most people have the ability to see three-dimensionally. Whenever an object is viewed, it is seen twice—once with the left eye and once with the right eye. The fusion or blending together of these two images in the brain results in the judgement of depth or distance.

In taking aerial photographs, it is rare for only a single picture to be taken (at least when the government does it). Generally, the aircraft flies over the area to be photographed, taking a series of pictures, each of which overlaps the photograph preceding it and the one following, so that an unbroken coverage of the area is obtained. The amount of overlap is usually 56%, which means that 56% of the ground detail appearing on one photo also appears on the next photograph. When a single flight does not give the necessary coverage of an area, additional flights must be made. These additional flights are parallel to the first and must have an overlap between them, This overlap between flights is known as sidelap and usually the amount is between 15% and 20%.

The requirements for stereovision, i.e., seeing two views of an object from two slightly different places, can be satisfied by overlapping photographs if one eye sees the object on one photograph and the other eye sees the object on another photograph. While this can be done after practice with the eyes alone, it can be done more easily if an optical aid is used. These optical aids are known as stereoscopes.

Lens stereoscope positioned over aerial photographs for viewing.

Alignment of Photos for Stereovision

For the best three-dimensional viewing, pairs of aerial photographs should be arranged as follows:

1. Place the selected pair of photos in such a way that the shadows on them generally appear to fall toward the viewer. It is also desirable that the light source used during the study of the photographs originates from the side opposite the viewer.

2. The photos should be on a flat surface so that the detail on one is directly over the same detail on the other photo.

3. Place the stereoscope over the photographs so that the left lens is over the left photograph and right lens over the right photo.

4. Separate the photographs along the line of flight until a piece of detail appearing in the overlap area of the left photograph is directly under the left lens and the same piece of detail on the right photo is directly under the right lens.

5. With the photograph and stereoscope in this position, a three-dimensional image should be seen. A few minor adjustments of scope or photos may be necessary to obtain the correct position for your eyes. The hills then will appear to rise and the valleys to sink, so that there is the impression of being in an aircraft looking down at the ground.

The identification of features on photographs is much easier and more accurate with this three-dimensional view. However, the same five factors of recognition must still be applied, but now with the added advantage of depth and relief.

STEREOSCOPES
$7 - $200

Several types of stereoscopes are available, but essentially all serve the same purpose, and that is as an aid to stereoscopic vision in the examination of aerial photographs. The least expensive type is the lens stereoscope, which consists of two magnifying lenses mounted in a metal or plastic frame. This is the most portable and is usually available in folding pocket models. The other types are the mirror and prism scopes. They offer greater versatility in viewing and are much better suited to contour interpretation than the lens type, which has a tendency to distort the image at the edges of the photo.

Lightweight Pocket Stereoscope

Can be used with any matched pair of stereo photographs to provide clear, sharply-defined 3-D images. Legs fold for easy storage.

Each $4.00.

A good source of these intruments is Forestry Suppliers. They handle more than ten different types and models in addition to other photogrammetry aids. It's all in their 448-page catalog.
From: Forestry Suppliers, Inc., Box 8397, Jackson, Miss. 39204.

Aerial Photography Division
AGRICULTURAL STABILIZATION AND CONSERVATION SERVICE (ASCS)
U.S. Department of Agriculture
Washington, D.C. 20250

ASCS has more aerial photo coverage of the Nation (about 80%) than any other federal agency. Reason is they are involved in the farm production-adjustment program and need some means of keeping track of what farm acreage is being used for. Because of their coverage, ASCS would be the best people to check with first when you're in the need of an aerial photo. Their negative files date back to 1933, so this would also be the place to come when you're looking for visual data on how the landscape has changed over a period of years. ASCS photography is of the vertical type at scales of 1:20,000 and 1:40,000. Negatives are 9"x 9". Camera focal length is generally 6, 8¼, or 12 inches with the longer focal lengths used for areas with greater differences in high and low ground elevations. Flight lines are either north/south or east/west with 65% overlap in sequential photos and 30% sidelap in flight lines. Contact prints and enlargements of the complete negative are available ranging in size from 9½"x 9½" to 38"x 38" on water-resistant stable base paper. Here's the price schedule:

Size (inches)	9½ x 9½	13 x 13	17 x 17	24 x 24	38 x 38
Cost (per print)	$1.75	3.00	3.50	4.50	9.00

Other available products include copy negatives, glass plates and types of film positives for light table use or for making diazo blueprint copies. Extra services include photography certified as to the date of exposure, prints with geodetic control located on them, and controlled or uncontrolled mosaics constructed from photography. To determine the aerial photos you need, it's best to purchase a photo index of the county or parish (that's for you Louisiana boys) in which the area you're interested lies. Cost is $3 per index, which consists of a composite picture of the county showing each of the aerial photographs and the area of the county each covers. Indexes are usually at a scale of one inch to one mile on 20"x 24" paper. Therefore, one or more index sheets may be required to give complete coverage for a county. The following free literature is available and worth requesting to familiarize yourself with the ASCS setup: *Aerial Photo-Maps of Your Farm—A Bonus for You, ASCS Aerial Photography—Supplemental Data, ASCS Aerial Photography Status Map of _____* (insert name of your state).

ASCS is pretty good about service, and will normally have your order processed and on its way within two to four weeks if you use their order form and post it to the appropriate address shown below. Use the same address for requesting information, pamphlets, and indexes:

Eastern Aerial Photography Laboratory   for aerial photographs
Program Performance Division   of these states...
ASCS-USDA
45 South French Broad Avenue
Asheville, N.C. 28801

			Pennsylvania
Alabama	Iowa	Mississippi	Rhode Island
Connecticut	Kentucky	Missouri	South Carolina
Delaware	Maine	New Hampshire	South Dakota
Florida	Maryland	New Jersey	Tennessee
Georgia	Massachusetts	New York	Virginia
Illinois	Michigan	North Carolina	West Virginia
Indiana	Minnesota	Ohio	Wisconsin

Western Aerial Photography Laboratory   for aerial photographs
Program Performance Division   of these states...
ASCS-USDA
2505 Parley's Way
Salt Lake City, Utah 84109

Arizona	Idaho	Nevada	
Arkansas	Kansas	New Mexico	Texas
California	Louisiana	North Dakota	Utah
Colorado	Montana	Oklahoma	Washington
Hawaii	Nebraska	Oregon	Wyoming

Coastal Mapping Div. (C3415)
NATIONAL OCEAN SURVEY (NOAA)
Rockville, Md. 20852

The National Ocean Survey has developed its aerial photo files around nautical and aeronautical charting programs. Their inventory is mostly of coastal areas and flight areas, such as airfields. The Survey's photographs are of the single-lens type, some panchromatic, some color, and a smaller portion infrared. Their panchromatic stuff is usually taken at scales of 1:10,000, 1:20,000, 1:24,000, 1:30,000, and 1:40,000. Point to remember here is that the scales are larger than those available through USGS. Contact prints are black and white, 9" x 9" and on double-weight glossy paper. Their infrared photos are water-line surveys (strictly coastal); the water photographs as black, thereby showing a sharp cutoff line between land and water areas, a most useful feature for making nautical charts. Contacts for infrared are the same specs as for panchromatic, and regardless of type, contact prints (9" x 9") run the same—$3 each. Enlargements are available at slightly higher prices, and the Survey will enlarge selected portions of a negative upon special request. Color aerial photographs (contact prints) are available at $9 each. Color enlargements (prints or transparencies) are also available at higher prices and enlargements of selected portions are available upon special request. The Survey has photo indexes on 1:250,000 scale base maps that cover an area of 1° of longitude by 1° of latitude with individual exposure indicated by a dot. Separate series of indexes are maintained for panchromatic, infrared and color, so specify which you want when requesting an index. Ozalid prints of indexes are available at 50¢ each. As with USGS, your best move is to request information on what is available, study it, and then make your decision. Get a copy of *Reproductions of Aerial Photographs* from the above address for all the info—free.

U.S. GEOLOGICAL SURVEY
507 National Center, Reston, Va. 22092

The Survey handles two types of aerial photographs: vertical and low oblique. The low oblique type, taken approximately 20° from vertical, is the result of special mapping projects, hence may not be available for the particular area you're interested in. USGS recommends, that before ordering prints, you obtain a free copy of *Twin Low-Oblique Photography* from the above office if you're not familiar with this type. Aerial photographs come in the form of contact prints 9" x 9", the same size as the negative, and are available with or without stereoscopic overlap. Stereoscopic coverage requires about twice as many prints as those without (pictorial photos). Enlargements to an exact ratio or specific scale can be had, but prints are usually made at scales of 1:24,000 (about 12 square miles of coverage per photo) and 1:63,360 (about 81 square miles coverage). Prints are of the whole negative. You won't get anywhere asking for blow-ups of special sections or cropping. To determine just what you're after, photo indexes can be requested for practically all USGS aerial photos. These show assembled prints in standard quadrangle units, generally 7½-minute units, but in some cases 15-minute units. Your best bet, to avoid confusion, is to put in a request for information. Tell them what you're going to use the photos for and define the specific area(s) you're interested in; best way is to submit an outline drawn on a topo map; second-best is to give them the latitude and longitude of each of the four corners (or whatever number) of the area. Be sure and specify the scale or enlargement and whether you want pictorial or stereographic coverage. Prices run $3 per 9" x 9" print and $5 per photo index. Incidentally, prints aren't stocked, but are custom-processed for each order. This can mean a waiting period of from three to six weeks. But hang in there.

Free USGS Aerial Photo Publications

The following publications are recommended for your aerial photo reference files. They're available free from the USGS Washington Office:

Aerial Photographic Reproductions. This accordion-folded brochure has the complete scoop on the USGS aerial-photo services, including descriptions and prices. Nine pages, illustrated.

Twin Low-Oblique Photography. Background data on this type of aerial photography.

Status of Aerial Photography. This 27" x 41" overlaid base map of the United States shows what parts of the country have had aerial-photo surveys made and who has the negatives. In some cases, it's the government, in others commercial firms. Their addresses are given, in addition to quite a bit of technical data regarding the photos. This index could save time by directing you to the source of the photos.

Status of Aerial Mosaics. This is essentially the same type of index as the above (same size, too), except that it shows the parts of the country for which there are complete photomaps available, as opposed to just single photos. A mosaic is simply a batch of aerial photographs that have been carefully matched along their edges, clipped and taped together to make an aerial photo covering a larger area. This index describes the scale of the negatives, dates of photography, and agencies from which copies of photomaps may be obtained. Color coding on the index indicates who holds what originals among federal agencies and commercial firms. All addresses are given.

AERIAL PHOTOGRAPHS IN GEOLOGIC INTERPRETATION AND MAPPING
U.S. Geological Survey
1960 - 230 p. il. - $3.00

Someone recommended this book as being really great for the price, but we can't find his letter with the data. (Marvin please send another letter).
From: Superintendent of Documents, U.S. Government Printing Office, Washington, D.C. 20402

INTERPRETATION OF AERIAL PHOTOGRAPHS
T. Eugene Avery
1968 - 324 p. il. - $10.95

This highly recommended book is designed for courses in photo interpretation, remote-sensing, photogrammetry, and so forth, as taught in schools of geology, forestry, engineering, agriculture, and at military posts. There are about 250 references to current literature; more than 250 black-and-white illustrations; a special eight-page insert of color aerial photographs; exercises for student use or self-instruction, and a glossary of photogrammetric terms.
From: Burgess Publishing Co., 426 South 6th St., Minneapolis, Minn. 55415

BOOKS

FORESTER'S GUIDE TO AERIAL PHOTO INTERPRETATION
T. Eugene Avery
1969 - 40 p. il. - 75¢

Another one by Avery written as a practical reference on techniques of aerial-photo interpretation for someone with rudimentary knowledge of the subject. It emphasizes stereoscopic interpretation of vertical aerial photos and discusses types and preparation of aerial photos for stereo viewing; photo scale, bearings and distance; identification of forest types and tree species; mapping; measuring areas; aerial cruising and photo stratification for ground cruising. Even though this is written primarily for the forester, it's good, inexpensive information on the subject.
From: Superintendent of Documents, U.S. Government Printing Office, Washington, D.C. 20402

weather

It's remarkable the number of people who take off for several days in the woods or mountains without a thought as to what the weather will bring while they're out there. The way things look when they leave is what counts, and the only important future considerations are the status of chow and insect repellent. So they spend three days in a tent counting raindrops and are never the wiser for their experience.

Weather is a critical factor that should be taken into account for any outing by land or water, and advance warning of what is to come is available to anyone who will just watch the clues Mother Nature provides. Clouds, for example, are a primary source of clues. Rapidly moving clouds that lower and increase in number by evening foretell not-so-nice weather by morning. A cloud-filled sky in the summer evening will blanket the day's heat to earth, which means maybe you'd better plan on using two fans that night. And by the same token, a cloudless winter evening will allow the day's heat to escape, so double up on the blankets. Clouds moving in separate directions at different heights indicate unsettled weather, and large fluffy clouds heaped and scattered throughout the summer sky indicate fair and pleasant weather for several days.

There are a multitude of natural weather signs, from the way dew lies on grass in the morning to how high a swallow flies, that if memorized can help you in determining what the future weather will be. Of course the daily paper, the radio, or a call to the airport or Weather Bureau (their new name, by the way, is the National Weather Service) will get you a 6- to 12-hour forecast. In some cities the telephone company has a number that can be dialed to hear the latest prediction. Just dial 411 and ask the operator if this service is available, and the number. It's more fun though, to do your own observing and predicting, even if just to keep the weatherman honest. The tools you need are thermometer, barometer, and maybe a humidity indicator. With these you can keep track of the most important things happening with the air: temperature, pressure and water content. If you can afford it, a wind direction and wind speed indicator would be nice, but it's just as easy to estimate these. If you get serious about recording your weather observations, we've made up pads of observation forms which are available through ETM.

Even with the most sophisticated batch of instruments available, you'll not get far unless you can tie your observations into some practical conclusion. For this we can recommend no better book as a starter than Lehr, Burnett, and Zim's 160-page *Weather*. It's one of the soft-bound Golden Nature Guides available at just about all book stores for less than $2.

Wind—Barometer Table

Wind Direction	Barometer Reduced to Sea Level	Character of Weather
SW to NW	30.10 to 30.20 and steady	Fair, with slight temperature changes for 1 or 2 days.
SW to NW	30.10 to 30.20 and rising rapidly	Fair followed within 2 days by rain.
SW to NW	30.20 and above and stationary	Continued fair with no decided temperature change.
SW to NW	30.20 and above and falling slowly	Slowly rising temperature and fair for 2 days.
S to SE	30.10 to 30.20 and falling slowly	Rain within 24 hours.
S to SE	30.10 to 30.20 and falling rapidly	Wind increasing in force, with rain within 12 to 24 hours.
SE to NE	30.10 to 30.20 and falling slowly	Rain in 12 to 18 hours.
SE to NE	30.10 to 30.20 and falling rapidly	Increasing wind and rain within 12 hours.
E to NE	30.10 and above and falling slowly	In summer, with light winds, rain may not fall for several days. In winter, rain in 24 hours.
E to NE	30.10 and above and falling fast	In summer, rain probably in 12 hours. In winter, rain or snow with increasing winds will often set in when the barometer begins to fall and the wind set in NE.
SE to NE	30.00 or below and falling slowly	Rain will continue 1 or 2 days.
SE to NE	30.00 or below and falling rapidly	Rain with high wind, followed within 36 hours by clearing and, in winter, colder.
S to SW	30.00 or below and rising slowly	Clearing in a few hours and fair for several days.
S to E	29.80 or below and falling rapidly	Severe storm imminent, followed in 24 hours by clearing and, in winter, colder.
E to N	29.80 or below and falling rapidly	Severe NE gale and heavy rain; winter, heavy snow and cold wave.
Going to W	29.80 or below and rising rapidly	Clearing and colder.

This table, prepared by the National Weather Service, is a general summary of observations taken all over the country. It is, therefore, an average, and will not apply to your back yard without some alteration. However, it will help you to correlate wind and barometeric tendencies with changes in the coming weather.

THE ANEROID BAROMETER
1957 - 10 p. il. - 15¢
C 30.2:B26/2

A fine little pamphlet describing the two types of barometers—aneroid and mercurial—and their use and adjustment. Includes methods of checking accuracy and adjusting for different heights above sea level. If a barometer is hanging on your bulkhead for something other than decoration, you ought to get this.

CLIMATIC ATLAS OF THE UNITED STATES
1968 - 76 p. il. - $4.25
C 52.2:C6 1/2

One of the largest and most interesting weather books we've seen. It's a huge 16 by 22 inches and contains 231 maps, 13 tables, and 21 graphs, which show collective weather conditions over a period of many years. Included in the statistics are average and extreme temperatures, precipitation, wind, barometric pressure, relative humidity, dew point, sunshine, sky cover, degree days, solar radiation and evaporation. You can find the mean dates for the last frost in spring and the first autumn frost in the atlas. High and low temperature and temperature range for each month of the year for many cities are recorded. Other maps show the mean annual and monthly number of days with maximum temperatures of 90 degrees or below. If you're planning to move to a new area, this would be a good book to check for getting an idea of the climate to expect.

CLOUDS
1969 - 25¢
C 52.2:C62

This is a four-color fold-out which describes the different types of clouds, how they formed and their approximate height above sea level. Weather station symbols, abbreviations, and a photograph are shown for each cloud type. An excellent study aid for this subject.

PSYCHROMETRIC TABLES
1941 - 87 p. il. - 45¢
C 30.2:P95/941

These tables would be useful to anyone running an amateur weather station for obtaining vapor pressure, relative humidity, and temperature of the dew point from readings of a wet bulb and dry bulb thermometer. And talk about some good reading, this one's terrific for a long winter's evening.

SURFACE OBSERVATIONS
1969 - 328 p. il. - $2.50
C 1.8/4:1

Federal Meteorological Handbook No. 1, formerly issued as WBAN Circular N. This handbook prescribes uniform instructions for standard weather observing and reporting techniques. It is intended to provide a framework within which the observer can find a system for identifying meteorological phenomena and reporting their occurrence in an understandable format. In other words, this is the Weather Service's principal manual for weather observations, and it's certainly worth having as a reference source.

EXPLANATION OF THE WEATHER MAP
1969 - Free

This 19-by 24-inch chart, available free from the National Weather Service, explains how a weather map is constructed, the symbols and abbreviations used, and what they mean. Framed and hanging on the wall of the den next to your ship's wheel barometer, it's very impressive, believe me.
From: National Weather Service, NOAA, Silver Spring, Md. 20910

DAILY WEATHER MAPS (weekly series)
Annual subscription $16.50
C 55.213

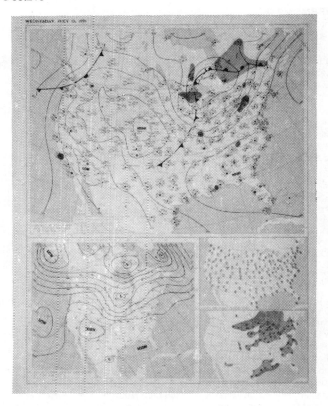

Features for each day of the weekly period, Monday through Sunday, a surface weather map of the United States showing weather conditions observed daily at 7 A.M. EST, the highest and lowest temperatures for the previous day, at selected stations in the United States, and the areas over which precipitation was reported in the preceding 24 hours. A complete explanation of the maps and weather symbols used is included.

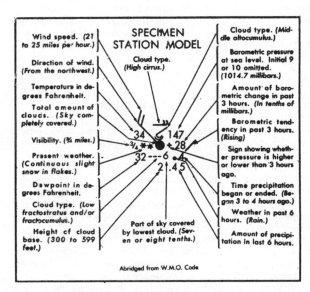

This is the way you would write up a report of your weather observations if you were running a station. *Explanation of the Weather Map*, available from the National Weather Service, covers all of the symbols and how they are used in detail.

WEATHER INSTRUMENTS

WEATHER

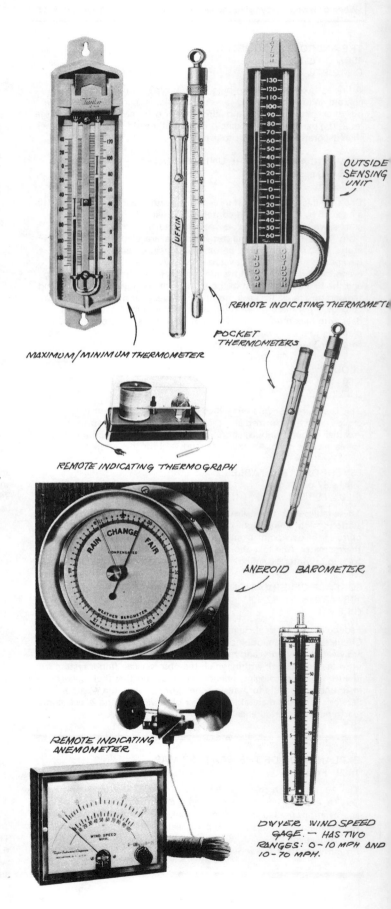

THERMOMETERS
$1 to $200

Thermometers measure the ambient (surrounding, encompassing, moving freely about) air temperature. Several different kinds are available. The best known is the standard type which you can pick up at any hardware store for a buck. The maximum/minimum (max/min) type records the lowest and highest temperatures reached over a certain period of time. Taylor Instruments has a very good one for $13. The thermograph gives a continuous reading of the temperature over a seven-day period on a moving graph. The cost of one of these gems is around $150. The remote indicating thermometer is like the standard except that a sensing unit is placed outside the house and the thermometer is inside. This way you don't have to go outside to tell what the temperature is. The remote indicating type can be found in most hardware stores for $5 to $10. For the backpacker or camper who is weather conscious and who also might want to know how his 2½ lb. down bag is doing on the top of Mt. Monadnock in midwinter, there are several brands of good pocket thermometers costing between $3 and $5. Most outfitters carry them. You can also order through Recreational Equipment, Inc., or Forestry Suppliers, Inc. These people have the most to choose from and the best prices.

BAROMETERS
$20 to $400

A barometer is probably your most important instrument, because it will tell you more about the weather and what's going to happen than any other. Its function is to show changes in air pressure, which is directly related to highs and lows, which in turn is directly related to good weather and bad weather. There are two basic kinds of barometers. The most accurate (to 1/1000th of an inch) is the mercurial, which consists of a 32-inch high column of mercury that rises and falls with changes in air pressure. Robert E. White, Instruments, Inc., can fix you up with one for as little as 250 bills, which is about the average cost. The other type is the aneroid (from Greek: not wet), which relies on air pressure to squish a vacuum-filled metal box that activates a dial. The aneroid isn't as accurate as the mercurial, but it's accurate enough. And any worth having will run you at least $20 to $24. Incidentally, a very good publication on barometers is **The Aneroid Barometer**, from the U.S. Government Printing Office (ordering information is in this section). Recording barometers, or barographs, which record data the same way as thermographs, are available and run about $150. We haven't run across any economical pocket-type barometer for the outdoorsman, but we do know where you can get some expensive ones that are combination barometer/altimeter: Recreational Equipment, Inc., $45 to $65; Forestry Suppliers, Inc., $55 to $200.

WIND SPEED AND WIND DIRECTION INDICATORS
$6 to $150

Wind speed is measured by the anemometer and wind direction by a wind or weather vane. They haven't come up with a Greek name for that one yet. Maybe we could call it an anemovane. Maybe. The most common type of anemometer is the remote indicating. It consists of three spinning cups on the roof of a building and the dial indicator inside. Price-wise this type of rig costs about $75. R.A. Simerl has an electrically operated, hand-held anemometer, that's really quality gear, for $45. But the best and the neatest anemometer for us poor-type people comes from Dwyer Instruments, Inc., for 7 bucks, and you can't beat it for the price. It's made of plastic, a handy size, and certainly suitable for packing into the woods, using on a sailboat, or wherever one needs to know the speed of the wind. Wind vanes you can find in most hardware stores. Remote indicating types with vane on the roof and directional indicator in the house are a little harder to find and more expensive. They run about $75. Combination units consisting of both wind speed and wind direction indicators are manufactured, and their cost is slightly lower than the cost of the two individual units by themselves, about $130.

MAXIMUM/MINIMUM THERMOMETER

REMOTE INDICATING THERMOMETER

POCKET THERMOMETERS

REMOTE INDICATING THERMOGRAPH

OUTSIDE SENSING UNIT

ANEROID BAROMETER

REMOTE INDICATING ANEMOMETER

DWYER WIND SPEED GAGE. — HAS TWO RANGES: 0-10 MPH AND 10-70 MPH.

42

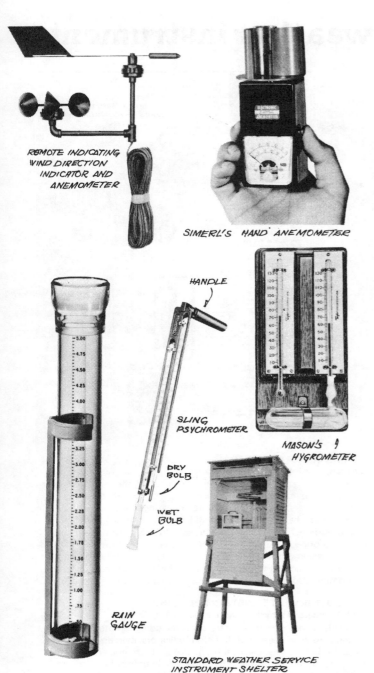

REMOTE INDICATING WIND DIRECTION INDICATOR AND ANEMOMETER

SIMERL'S HAND ANEMOMETER

HANDLE

SLING PSYCHROMETER

DRY BULB

WET BULB

MASON'S HYGROMETER

RAIN GAUGE

STANDARD WEATHER SERVICE INSTRUMENT SHELTER

HUMIDITY INSTRUMENTS
$3 to $350

Humidity is the amount of water vapor the air is holding. And relative humidity is the amount of water vapor the air is holding, expressed as a percentage of the amount the air could hold at that particular temperature. As it happens, warm air can hold more water vapor than cold air. That's why it feels a lot stickier in summer at 70 percent humidity than it does in winter at the same percentage. The most accurate instrument for measuring humidity is the psychrometer. This is actually two thermometers, one of which has a wet sock over its bulb. As water evaporates from the sock it cools the bulb. The difference in temperature between the wet bulb and dry bulb is taken, and reference is made to a set of psychrometric tables to determine relative humidity. A psychrometer that's twirled through the air is called a sling psychrometer. Twirling prevents any build-up of water vapor about the sock, which would give an inaccurate reading. Sling psychrometers cost about $20. Another kind of humidity instrument is the hygrometer. One type uses a bundle of blonde human hair, which expands and contracts with changes in the air's water vapor content. Hair is most often used in hygrographs (recording hygrometers). Robert E. White, Instruments, Inc., handles both recording and dial-type hygrometers using hair. The only problem with human hair types is that they lack accuracy, lag behind changes in relative humidity, and require frequent calibration. The type of hygrometer most often found in homes uses a synthetic hygroscopic element instead of hair, and likewise is less expensive. Price-wise, hygrographs run about $160, human hair hygrometers $15 to $35, and synthetic element hygrometers, or humidity indicators as they are more popularly called, $6 to $12.

RAIN GAUGES
$5 to $30

This is the least complicated of all the weather instruments. Basically it's a transparent cylinder with a scale on its side. When it rains it collects water just like any ol' farm bucket. And when the rain stops you simply check where the water level lays with respect to the scale and directly read the inches of rain that fell. Ho hum. Perhaps you also knew that one inch of rain falling over an acre of ground is equal to twenty seven thousand two hundred and five gallons of water. Yawn!

INSTRUMENT SHELTERS
$26 to $130

If you're going to handle your weather observations in a professional manner, a shelter is a good thing to have. It protects the instruments from pilferage and direct exposure to the elements, yet puts them out where the action is. Actually you could build your own out of some old louvered shutters. Just make sure you have 360° ventilation. Forestry Suppliers, Inc., handles the standard Weather Service type (large), they also have a smaller one, 16½" x 8" x 5½" ID.

OLD FARMER'S ALMANAC
Robert B. Thomas
Pub. Annually - 148 p. il. - 75¢

Farmer's calendar, recipes, planting dates, zodiac secrets, weather forecast for the whole year. Illustrated with old engravings. Published since 1792. Fun to read.
From: The Old Farmer's Almanac, Dublin, N.H. 03444

JULY hath 31 days.

D.M.	D.W.	Dates, Feasts, Fasts, Aspects, Tide Heights	Weather ↓	Farmer's Calendar.
1	Tu.	Dominion Day · R 34 Ireland to N.Y. 1919 (2nd)	Hot	When I was a boy, our market, "Mister Healey's," had something of the flavor of cracker-barrel days. In winter it was toasty from the generous heat of floor registers. In summer, ponderous wooden fans revolved leisurely.
2	W.	Visit. of Mary · Yrs. highest A.M. {11.6 high tide {10.0	with	
3	Th.	Tammuz *Little strokes fell great oaks* {11.8 {10.0	rain	
4	Fr.	Ind. Day Hawaii bec. rep. 1894 Tides {10.8 {10.0	that is	
5	Sa.	☾ on Eq. Sun farthest from earth Tides {10.2 {9.9	plain.	

TO THE WEATHER-WISE

M. Toalda of Padua (circa 1720) asserted that the weather changes most often (85.8% of the time) when the new moon comes in; 83.4% with the full, and 66.7% with the other two phase changes. Recent studies by scientists with the U.S.W.B. and N.Y.U. show heaviest rainfall comes 3 to 5 days after the new and the full moons.

Many blossoms on plum trees in the Spring, heavy fruit crops in the Fall, oak (and other) leaves remaining on trees in December indicate a severe Winter is coming up. The thickness of Fall fur on most animals, goose bones, pigs' melts, distance between caterpillar stripes also are Winter predictors. Birds, particularly owls, pileated woodpeckers, and swallows are predictors — as is, of course, the woodchuck. When hornets build nests high off the ground, expect deep snows. Bees, spiders, and ants — as well as certain flowers — are useful as short-term predictors. Nature, on the whole, however, is not easily understood and birds and animals, who should know, are often as misled by her as is mankind.

6. Close weather with a southerly wind presages rain.

7. A red sky at sun set indicates wind.

8. When the wind suddenly shifts and blows in a different course to the sun's apparent motion in the heavens, which is from east to west, it foretells wet and blowing weather.

9. A circle round the moon, at some distance, is generally followed with rain the next day.

sources of weather instruments

R.A. SIMERL
238 West St., Annapolis, Md. 21401
Electronic hand-held and remote indicating anemometers for land and marine use. Very high quality. $59 to $280. Brochure available from the above address.

RECREATIONAL EQUIPMENT, INC.
1525 11th Ave., Seattle, Wash. 98122
Pocket thermometers, hand-held wind speed gauge, pocket barometers (classified as altimeters in their catalog). Fat catalog of outdoor recreational equipment available.

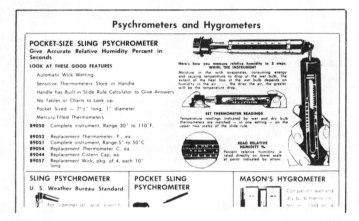

FORESTRY SUPPLIERS, INC.
Box 8397, Jackson, Miss. 39204
Complete line of weather instruments including pyranometers and pyranographs, hygrographs, standard and pocket sling psychrometers, 3″ OD engineer's barometer $200, barographs, remote reading and regular rain and snow gauges, remote reading and hand-held wind speed and direction indicators, max/min thermometers, pocket thermometers, thermographs, standard Weather Service instrument shelters, small 16½ in. x 8 in. x 5½ in. ID instrument shelters.

We've had some negative reports from *Source Book* readers on the way Forestry Suppliers has been handling requests for information and literature on their products. They didn't answer our inquiry for information for the second edition.

DON KENT INSTRUMENTS
283 Washington St., Weymouth, Mass. 02188
Several models of wind speed and wind direction indicators, $70, combination units, $150, matching panel barometers, hygrometers, and thermometers; remote indicating and recording instruments. Don has some good prices on his wind instruments and he's the only one we've seen that has a nice range of matching meters for custom building a weather instrument panel. Literature available.

STURBRIDGE YANKEE WORKSHOP
Brimfield Turnpike
Sturbridge, Massachusetts 01566
Cape Cod weather glass, $5. This is a colonial whaling barometer made of glass and designed to hang from a bulkhead. A liquid-filled tube indicates pressure changes. Nice colonial crafts catalog available.

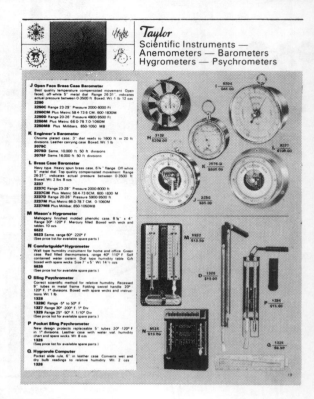

TAYLOR INSTRUMENTS
Arden, North Carolina 28704
Complete line of weather instruments including thermometers, thermographs, barometers, barographs, Mason's hygrometer, sling psychrometers, rain gauges, remote indicating anemometers, and wind vanes, and a handy little pocket slide rule for converting wet and dry bulb readings to relative humidity, called the Hygrorule Computer, $7 (overpriced). It might be worth your while to know that most of the people in this list, who handle a variety of instruments, have diversified by adding the Taylor line. Taylor's 20-page catalog is recommended for the weather observer's equipment reference shelf.

ROBERT E. WHITE, INSTRUMENTS, INC.
33 Commercial Wharf, Boston, Mass. 02110
Complete line of weather instruments including remote sensing and hand-held wind speed and direction indicators, mercurial and aneroid barometers, barographs, max/min thermometers, thermographs, hair and durotherm hygrometers, hygrographs, sling and hand-aspirated psychrometers, hygrothermographs, and other combo recording instruments, rain and snow gauges, standard Weather Service instrument shelters, and a 16″ x 24″ magnetic hurricane tracking chart, $17. White has a $3 psychrometric slide rule. Instrument literature available. Recommended for the professional weather observer's equipment reference shelf. Damn good service!

DWYER INSTRUMENTS, INC.
P.O. Box 373, Michigan City, Ind. 46360
Hand-held plastic windmeter, $7, remote indicating windmeter using liquid-filled tube, $25. Good quality, low-priced instruments. Literature available.

WEATHER MEASURE CORP.
P.O. Box 41257, Sacramento, Calif. 95841
Complete inventory of instruments for the amateur and professional meteorologist. Selection includes thermometers, barometers, hygrometers, psychrometers, anemometers, and so forth. Complete collection of chart recording instruments for all phenomena, instrument shelters, towers, remote tracking, transmitting and receiving gear, data loggers and anything else your little weather-wise heart could desire. Weather Measure also handles hydrological, water quality and air pollution instruments. Literature is available, but when you write be specific as to your needs.

CLIMATE THROUGH THE AGES
C.E.P. Brooks
1970; 395 p. il. - $3.00 (soft bound)

The classical study of paleoclimatology. Part One begins with a thorough discussion of the various factors which operate on climate and the changes they may effect, virtually a self-contained text book of meteorology. Part Two evaluates the Wegener theory of continental drift in terms of paleometeorology and paleoclimatology, among the few sciences that can validate it. Part Three, drawing on many different sources, examines actual climatic changes that have occurred since about 5200 B.C. in the five major continents and Greenland. 36 diagrams.
From: Dover Publications, Inc., 180 Varick St., New York, N.Y. 10014

SNOW CRYSTALS
W. A. Bentley and W. D. Humphreys
1931 - 226 p. il. - $4.00 (soft bound)

Over 2,000 beautiful crystals shown in photomicrographs and printed on coated stock for clarity. Introduction to photographing techniques, crystallography, classification, and meteorology. 202 plates.
From: Dover Publications, Inc., 180 Varick St., New York, N.Y. 10014

INSTANT WEATHER FORECASTING
Alan Watts
1968 - 64 p. il. - $3.75

Here's a revolutionary book, with twenty-four cloud pictures in color. It is a basic guide to forecasting the weather hours ahead and provides information on what likely weather trends will be. It will enable the user to foretell with reasonable accuracy whether it will rain or blow, not change much or clear up soon. The photographs are arranged to show skies associated with bad weather, with no immediate change, with sudden change, with temporary deterioration, and with improvement. A simple scientific introduction in the front of the book explains how to use the pictures, while the actual forecasts are set out in tables facing each photograph. The book is good because it synthesizes sky clues into the different resulting weather patterns, something it would take the average person a long time to do through observation. Don't get this as your first book on weather though, because it won't do anything for you. Read and understand *Weather* first, then you'll have the background necessary to work with Watts' book.
From: Dodd, Mead & Co., 79 Madison Ave., New York, N.Y. 10016

BOOKS

WEATHER
Lehr, Burnett and Zim
1957 - 160 p. il. - $1.95

This is the first book anyone cracking weather should buy. Excellent coverage of all the important things you need to know about weather in theory and practice, but light and interesting reading. Contents include different forms of precipitation, their nature, types and origin; the atmosphere and its structure in weather functions; the earth's motions and its effect on the atmosphere; high and low fronts and associated weather; storms, their origin and development; instruments and how they are used; setting up the amateur weather station; weather maps and their interpretation; and weather forecasting principles. The book has beautiful color illustrations, which make the subject so easy to understand. There's a complete index and a flatly out-of-date reading list in the back.
From: Golden Press, P.O. Box 700, Racine, Wis. 53404

WEATHER AND WEATHER FORECASTING
A. G. Forsdyke
1970 - 159 p. il. - $3.95

This book is written by a meteorologist who approaches the subject from a practical layman's point of view. No heavy math, physics, or atmospheric data. But there is the jargon, which you've got to know to work with weather, and Forsdyke gets right into that at the beginning. He then covers the basic equipment, the causes of weather and its changes, including cloud formations and their meanings, probably the most important aspect of getting the "feel" of weather casting. There's 240 full-color drawings which do much to aid in understanding principles. Only problem is a lot of the cloud drawings don't quite look like the real thing. Even so, this is another good reference book for one who wants to be in the know about weather.
From: Grosset & Dunlap, Inc., 51 Madison Ave., New York, N.Y. 10010

SAGER WEATHERCASTER
Raymond M. Sager
1975 - 25 p. il. - $7.95

A spiral-bound booklet with a dial computer on the front cover, the *Weathercaster* is designed to allow you to predict local weather conditions 12 to 24 hours in advance. Used with barometric readings, wind directions, and visual observations, it predicts wind speed and direction, temperature, cloud conditions and precipitation within a 30-mile radius. Pretty accurate little device, and fun to use.
From: International Marine Pub. Co., 21 Elm St., Camden, Maine 04843

backpacking

To borrow the words of Colin Fletcher, backpacking can best be described as camping with "your house on your back." Anyone in good physical condition with a desire to get away from the crowds can backpack, if they're just willing to exert the effort.

The best way to get started, as with many other activities, is slowly. Pick up some good books on the subject (see Books section) and start taking short walks near home in one of those parks you've always been meaning to visit. These walks are more for conditioning than anything else. From here, you'll want to progress to an overnight or weekend hike in an area that's not too remote and has established trails. This will allow you to learn to live with your equipment in a relaxed setting. Summer is the best time of year for this. If you're an experienced packer taking a friend on a first trip, a tip worth noting is: take it easy on anyone you want to get into backpacking! Nobody is going to come back for more if the initial experience is bad.

As far as the equipment you'll want to buy goes, the best advice we can give, again, is to take it slow. You can blow between $100 and $500 on an initial outfit easily, and unless you're loaded (with money), the chances of getting gear that doesn't suit you or your needs are pretty high. Having

to buy certain items a second time doubles the price, and although you can usually unload gear you've made a bad choice on, you rarely get your money out of it. You should rent or borrow gear initially. This way you can try different brands and styles of everything from packs to tents to pots, and so forth. Then, when you decide that a certain item is what you really want and need, you only have to buy it once, and are assured it will do the job for you.

Backpacking offers many rewards to those who would rather walk than ride. Trails are to be found almost everywhere in the world. State parks, national parks and national forests all offer the hiker unlimited opportunities to get out and explore new country. It doesn't seem to matter how remote the area is as long as the backpacker goes out with an attitude of discovery. Whether you're hiking in the park near home or traversing one of the large wilderness areas of the West, there's always something new to see either in nature or yourself.

But, alas, the backpacking scene has changed considerably in the last ten years and, unfortunately, many trails are overcrowded and many back-country areas are overused and abused. Some areas (the Great Smokie Mountain National Park, for example) require reservations to get on the trail

Camping at Crater Creek, Three Sisters Wilderness Area, Deschutes National Forest, Oregon. Photo: U.S. Forest Service.

during peak seasons, and others require permits which control the number of people going into certain areas. So, be forewarned, and check with Rangers or whoever before you go.

If bumping into people on the trail isn't your bag, there's still lots of untracked wilderness to see out there. We won't tell you where it is, but it's there, and if you really want to get out and away, you'll find it. Or on the other hand, if you're into group outings, there are many organizations offering trips for people of all experience levels (see Sources of Information).

We of Explorers Ltd. would now like to enter a plea to all who travel the back country. These areas are fragile and suffer greatly from even minor abuse. Leave each campsite as clean or cleaner than you found it. Carry a stove and build fewer fires. And, *pack out all of your trash and some extra, besides!!!*

In this section we are concerned with backpacking in the purest sense: getting out and getting into the world of nature. There are many other endeavors—mountaineering, rock climbing and ski touring, to name a few—where backpacking is secondary, a means to those ends. These activities are dealt with in separate sections of the Source Book.

sources of information

As it happens, all the groups that would have been listed here—government agencies, clubs and associations—are oriented toward trail and wilderness activities more than the academic or technical aspects of backpacking. This means you've got to back up several sections to the Wilderness Areas and Trails section, where we've listed them all.

BACKPACKER
Craig Evans, Ed.
Bimonthly - $12/yr. - $2.50/issue - 85 p. il.

This is the definitive magazine devoted to backpacking and related topics of interest. Articles are diverse and regularly include equipment tests and comparisons. For example, issue No. 13 contained a rundown of available compasses and their relative merits. Quality of articles and photography are quite good. A good magazine for entertainment as well as information.
From: Backpacker, 65 Adams St., Bedford Hills, N.Y. 10507

WILDERNESS CAMPING
Harry N. Roberts, Ed.
Bimonthly - $6.50/yr. - $1.25/issue - 55 p. il.

Still going strong after some six years of publication, though not getting any bigger, *Wilderness Camping* continues its crusade against the use of motorized vehicles and the misuse of the wilderness. Editorial slant is toward the self-propelled, who enjoys hiking, backpacking, ski touring, snowshoeing, canoeing, kayaking and bicycling. Articles tend to be a fair blend of "my favorite adventure," equipment reports and usage, techniques and where to go. Regular features include columns on cross-country skiing, wilderness politics and legislation, book reviews, new equipment reports, and the latest news from the U.S. Canoe Association and the American Youth Hostels; also a small classifieds section. All in all, the magazine isn't bad.
From: Wilderness Camping, 1255 Portland Pl., Boulder, Colo. 80302

PERIODICALS

Comments

"*Better Camping is defunct,* Wilderness Camping *continues to be nearly worthless, and* Backpacker *has nice pictures, but no substance—it's definitely for the armchair hiker.*"—Ed Lawson (1975).

"*Been reading* Wilderness Camping *for 4 years, and it just keeps getting better.*"—Reader from Lincoln, Neb. (1974).

"Wilderness Camping—*good magazine;* Backpacker—*better magazine.*"—Reader from Bay City, Mich. (1974).

"Backpacker—*delightful—their first issues were better than more recent ones.*"—Deborah Finch (1974).

"Mountain Gazette—*Good service, and they seem to be very concerned about their subscribers.*"—Reader from Saratoga, Calif. (1974).

BACKPACKING JOURNAL
Quarterly (?) - $1.35/issue

The people who publish *Camping Journal* (Davis Pub., Inc.) must have figured they were missing a good part of their market, since not a helluva lot of wilderness types read it. So spring of '76 they came out with *Backpacking Journal.* It's O.K., better than *Camping Journal,* but still typical of the run-of-the-mill. Here's what the editors say they're gonna do, "...satisfy your interests—whether you're a beginner, intermediate or expert...explore all aspects of hiking and backpacking, giving you helpful rundowns on equipment, the places where backpackers/climbers/hikers can go, plus timely and informative interviews with well-known outdoorsmen...provide absorbing and instructive articles on physical fitness and survival...news on conservation, trail organizations, and land acquisition." Should be fun...ho-hum.
From: Backpacking Journal, 229 Park Ave. So., New York, N.Y. 10003

MOUNTAIN GAZETTE
Gaylord T. Guenin and Allan Rabinowitz, Eds.
Monthly - $10/yr. - 36 p. il.

Mountain Gazette is not strictly a backpacking magazine, although it does have its share of backpacking-oriented articles. Slightly off-the-wall, *Mountain Gazette* features stories on an individual experience level, some of which are provocative, others pretentious; but all topics are fair game. The magazine seems oriented toward the western mountain-desert areas. *Mountain Gazette* probably has the highest-quality writing of any outdoor publication. You never know what you'll find.
From: Mountain Gazette, 2025 York St., Denver, Colo. 80205

BOOKS

THE NEW COMPLETE WALKER
Colin Fletcher
1974, 2nd ed. - 512 p. il. - $10

Fletcher came out with the first edition of this book in 1968, and it's been a success ever since. The author has been able to present a thorough and logical approach to equipment and the organization involved in backpacking, while maintaining an amusing and very reasonable style. Useful drawings and charts serve to illustrate his points, where needed. Fletcher has his definite preferences in gear, and includes brand names and prices. He seems to have good taste. This is an entertaining, as well as informative, book. After reading it you'll want to read his other two: *The Thousand Mile Summer,* a log of his walk along the Pacific Crest Trail, and *The Man Who Walked Through Time,* a description of a walk through the Grand Canyon.
From: Alfred A. Knopf, 201 E. 50th St., New York, N.Y. 10022

BACKPACKING: ONE STEP AT A TIME
Harvey Manning
1972 - 356 p. il. - $2.95 (pb)

Here is a book which explores backpacking from start to finish, with a sound grasp of the subject. Fine photography and drawings add to the effect. This should be one of the more complete and thorough books on the market.
From: Recreational Equipment Inc. Press, 1525 11th Ave., Seattle, Wash. 98122

THE BEST ABOUT BACKPACKING
Denise Van Lear, Ed.
1974 - 384 p. il. - $6.95

Here's another of the popular Sierra Club Totebook Series. It's a collection of articles covering all aspects of backpacking gear and conditions, even traveling with a child. The authors include Colin Fletcher, Harvey Manning, and several others who are well qualified to write on their subjects. Among the appendices are biographical information about the authors, a list of backpacking organizations and wilderness areas.
From: Sierra Club Books, 530 Bush St., San Francisco, Calif. 94108

AMERICA'S BACKPACKING BOOK
Raymond Bridge
1973 - 417 p. il. - $5.95

This is another fairly comprehensive book—almost a manual. It is divided into four parts. Part I is the art and folklore of backpacking; Part II, equipment; Part III, special skills; and Part IV, where to go. The author suggests a lot of lower-cost alternatives to some of the more expensive gear—a definite help. Patterns for make-it-yourself parkas and packs are included. Altogether, a thorough introduction to the activity.
From: Charles Scribner's Sons, 597 Fifth Ave., New York, N.Y. 10017

BACKPACKING
R. C. Rethmel
1974 - 185 p. il. - $5.95

Rethmel's book is now in its 5th edition. Coverage includes chapters on equipment; clothing; food, menu planning and cooking; safety; tips for on the trail and in camp; and preparing for a backpacking trip. Many useful tables and an extensive appendix have been added. The appendix gives, among other things, sources of gear and foods, maps and trail info, and the locations of Wilderness and Primitive Areas in National Forests. Book is oriented toward the weekend packer who wants a good basic background on the subject.
From: Burgess Publishing Co., 7108 Ohms Lane, Minneapolis, Minn. 55435

THE MASTER BACKPACKER
Russ Mohney
1976 - 288 p. il. - $3.50

The first of a series of small "packit-along" books by Stackpole, *Master Backpacker* is like a grad course for those ready to tackle primitive terrain. It covers what first must be known about trip planning, maps, compass, equipment, clothing, nutrition, meal planning, innovative cooking, ridge and waterway crossing, wildlife encounters, camp sitting, health, first aid, safety, climbing techniques, winter backpacking, snowshoeing and cross-country skiing. Ecology is the watchword throughout.
From: Stackpole Books, Cameron & Kelker Sts., Harrisburg, Pa. 17105

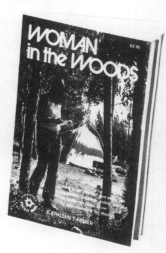

WOMAN IN THE WOODS
Kathleen Farmer
1976 - 256 p. il. - $2.95

Not a libber book that tries to convince women to get out there, but a practical one with needed information for those who want to go. There are basics on minitrips (to ease into it), guided trips and outdoor hobbies. There's also lots of help for staying comfortable, acquiring camping skills, and keeping clean and well groomed on the trail—you know, like those ladies in the Westerns of the 50's—after riding hellbent for leather for three days through two dust storms and a thunder shower to outrun the sheriff's posse, Veronica DiMilo (the boss's broad, played in the movie by Sylvia Sterling) dismounts, jauntily kicks a grimy vaquero in the gut for being too slow in helping her, and saunters over toward the boss (camera zooms in on freshly pressed cullotes, gleaming white, starched blouse w/ruffles, new make-up and a half-hour old permanent). Ever wonder how she did that? Read *Woman in the Woods.*
From: Stackpole Books, Cameron & Kelker Sts., Harrisburg, Pa. 17105

THE WILDERNESS HANDBOOK
Paul Petzoldt
1974 - 288 p. il. - $7.95

Petzoldt, founder-director of the National Outdoor Leadership School, has finally put it all together in this 288-pager. Most emphasis is placed on group and expedition techniques, rather than for the individual. He also tends to concentrate more on winter mountaineering than other areas, and there's quite a bit of philosophizing. Unfortunately, as other reviews have shown, not everyone tends to agree with some of Paul's convictions. Be that as it may, the man's background and experience are top-of-the-line, and both novice and well-seasoned packer will find much of value here.
From: Backpacker Books, Bellows Falls, Vt. 05101

BACKPACKING GEAR

PACKS and BAGS

The best way to approach the subject of pack types is to look at the types of walking one may be doing. Hikes can run the gamut from half-day rambles behind the house or in the park, to multiday or even multiweek epics on longer trails, or the ultimate—an extended trip into true wilderness involving both on- and off-trail hiking as well as some basic mountaineering.

The belt pouches and fanny packs offered by many outfitters are ideal for carrying most of the dayhiker's needs: a light lunch, water bottle, and maybe an extra camera lens. For rock climbing or carrying more camera gear, you can't beat one of the frameless teardrop packs or a larger frameless rucksack. These should be contoured to hug the back in a way that reduces shifting to a minimum (you haven't lived until your sack has shifted, throwing you off balance, in a difficult move on a rock climb). For ski touring, the new and larger contoured packs are just the ticket. Most have a waistbelt and are designed to not hinder the movement of the skier. They come in both divided and undivided styles, with or without side pockets, and usually have a provision for attaching your skis to the pack should you have to walk or climb. Check to see if the side pockets interfere with your arm movement. For carrying maximum loads on extended trips, the tubular packframe with suitable sack attached is the obvious way to go. Frames distribute the majority of the load to the hips and offer the most comfort—if the waistbelt is used properly and the pack fits. Bags made to fit packframes come in an assortment of sizes and styles. The most basic is the single, full-length bag with outside pockets. With no built-in dividers, this bag offers greater carrying capacity than any other. This is a real boon to the winter backpacker or snowshoer, who often carries lots of bulky down gear. You can also use three-quarter-length bags, with or without pockets and with or without built-in dividers. With these, though, the sleeping bag, and often the tent, are carried on the outside of the pack attached to the bottom of the frame.

Most of today's packs are made of nylon. Material weight runs from around 6 ounces per yard to about 22 in some climbing sacks (see Forrest Mountaineering in the Climbing section). Nylon duck is the most common material, although many manufacturers are offering rucksacks in a highly durable nylon material called Cordura. Generally, the harder the intended use of the pack, the tougher (heavier) the material should be. There are some packs, mainly European, that are still made from cotton duck. These are mostly climbing rucksacks and are extremely durable but considerably heavier than most nylon models.

Some manufacturers still offer leather as a bottom material on some of their daypacks, climbing packs and rucksacks. When you think of how many times you can set a pack down in just a day, this could be a feature to consider. If the bottom is made of the same material as the pack, make sure it's a double thickness.

The pack fabric, as well as being durable, should be waterproof. You can test this by trying to blow through it; if you can, it's not good enough. The weakest point in the structure of most packs is the sewing. Quality stitching in packs should be small (7 to 10 stitches per inch). The stitches should run straight and stress points (corners, etc.) should be double- or triple-stitched and if necessary, reinforcing material should be used in areas requiring extra strength, i.e., where shoulder straps are attached. Most companies are now using Dacron thread with a cotton sheath for most of their sewing. The Dacron gives the thread strength and the cotton swells when wet to seal the needle holes in the material as well as prevent cutting. You'll still probably want to seal the seams of your pack with one of the commercial preparations designed for this to insure watertightness.

There are other features one should look for in selecting a quality pack. Outside pockets should have a protective rain flap over the zipper. Also, check the zipper to see if it's nylon, either teeth or coil. Metal zippers tend to freeze up in cold, wet weather. Nylon zippers are prone to easier sliding under normal circumstances, anyway.

Below you'll find discussions of the different classes of packs divided into the following categories based on capacity and/or use: belt pouches and fanny packs, knapsacks and daypacks (frameless), framed rucksacks, frameless contour packs, packframes and bags,

BOOKS

BACKPACKING EQUIPMENT - A Consumer's Guide
William Kemsley, Jr., and editors of *Backpacker* magazine
1975 - 160 p. il. - $4.95

Here's a book which covers the spectrum of backpacking equipment—almost! Only the basics are included—packs, sleeping bags, tents, boots and freeze-dried foods—but, frankly, these are the items that are the most important and dearest. This consumer's guide takes a look at what is available while exploring the relative merits of each brand. Reports are very similar to what one would find within the pages of *Backpacker,* and just as helpful. Certainly the best reference source available if you're in the market for a complete outfit or even a particular item. Much good info on insulating materials and fabrics. Only thing we didn't find—and most noticeably so—was the lack of addresses. Where do you write for more input...or to buy?
From: Collier Books, 866 Third Ave., New York, N.Y. 10022

LIGHT WEIGHT CAMPING EQUIPMENT AND HOW TO MAKE IT
Gerry Cunningham and Margaret Hansson
1976, 5th ed. - 150 p. il. - $5.95

Cunningham and Hansson's book has gone into its 5th edition, or maybe it's the 6th (title page doesn't say—?). Anywhoo...it's still one of the best books around for doing it yourself, i.e., making packs, sleeping bags, tents, and so forth, at home. Materials and fabrics, sewing methods, insulation data, closures, hardware and waterproofing are covered in the first part of the book to provide you with all the fundamentals. Following that are chapters with detailed patterns and instructions for building packs, bags, tents and jackets. Good info. Now then...the current ('76) edition has a chapter on modern camping methods (so-so) and one on building a down sweater (fair), which are new. But for all intents and purposes, nothing else has been added to the earlier ('68) edition. So, if you've got a copy of the '68 one, you're in good shape. If you don't, it'd be worth your while to pick up the '76 one, if you're serious about getting into this area of packing.
From: Charles Scribner's Sons, 597 Fifth Ave., New York, N.Y. 10017

MAKING YOUR OWN CAMPING EQUIPMENT
Robert Sumner
1976 - 168 p. il. - $6.95

This is the other best book around for doing it yourself. Sumner covers just about the same fundamentals as Cunningham and Hansson, but in a somewhat broader scope. He also tells who amongst the top outfitters (REI, EMS, Ski Hut, Kelty, etc.) have what in fabrics and insulation. In his patterns and design part of the book, Bob provides plans and instructions for building packs, sleeping bags, tents and jackets—and—a packframe, down booties, rain pants, shell clothing, a down vest and gaiters. Even in this department, Bob seems to have covered a bit more ground than Cunningham and Hansson. Also he has a fair number of b&w photos whereas C & H only have line drawings. Make no mistake, though, both are good books. It's just that you can be sure Sumner (his being the newest book on the market) has picked over Cunningham and Hansson's book and incorporated what he felt was the best of what they had to offer.
From: Drake Publishers, Inc., 801 Second Ave., New York, N.Y. 10017

and children's packs and child carriers.

BELT POUCHES and FANNY PACKS
$6 - $25
A belt pouch is simply a zippered pouch that either clips or threads

onto the wearer's belt and is used on short walks to carry just the few items you think you'll need. It is also ideal attached to the waistbelt of a larger pack to carry often-wanted items, such as ski wax, extra lenses, light meter or trail snacks. This way you don't need to remove your pack to get at 'em.

If what you usually take on short walks won't fit into a belt

Belt pouch

Fanny pack

pouch, then a fanny pack is the ticket, as it offers a greater carrying capacity than a pouch. A fanny pack is nothing more than a large belt pouch with the belt already attached. It is usually carried behind you (on your fanny). When you need to get something, just slide the pack around to your front. Zippers that pull in two directions or that have a double slider are a feature of great value in this type of pack, as it makes access easier and lets you get at a certain section of the pack without exposing the entire contents to rain or snow.

Belt and fanny packs are to be had all over the place now that ski touring has become so popular in the U.S. Check out the variety available and you'll surely find one to suit your needs and wants. Bean's Belt Pack (24 ozs.) has inner and outer zippered compartments, $25 from L. L. Bean. Moor and Mountain offers their Norwegian Touring Ski Belt with three separate compartments (7 ozs.), $24. Eddie Bauer, Recreational Equipment, Holubar, Ski Hut and most other outfitters offer a fanny pack of some sort. Weight runs from 4 to 24 ozs. and prices from $6 to $25.

RUCKSACKS

Probably the most versatile type of pack made is the rucksack. For trips of one or two days, ski touring, rock climbing or vagabonding, there's a pack designed for each, but it's also possible to find one that can do for all these activities. If you're into more than just hiking, a multipurpose rucksack is a good thing to own. If diversification of use is what you're looking for, get a sack a bit bigger than what you think you need and you'll find that sooner or later you'll appreciate the extra space. Features such as ski slots, leather bottoms, hauling loops, ice axe attachments, and so on, just add to the versatility of the rucksack. Sizes vary from those that junior can carry to some with the capacity of a packframe and bag, but we've found those in between to be the best choice.

We've divided rucksacks into three categories to make discussing them easier: knapsacks (frameless rucksacks), framed rucksacks and contour packs (large, soft packs with the capacity of a packframe and bag).

Backpacker's rucksack

Climber's style daypack

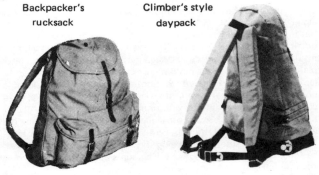

Knapsacks (frameless rucksacks or daypacks), $10 to $30. These are little more than cotton canvas or nylon bags with shoulder straps attached for carrying. There are all sorts of sizes and shapes but capacity is usually small. Teardrop packs are popular with rock climbers for day climbs and also make for good daypacks. Those with one zipper for the main closure can cause trouble, though, if the zipper goes. Sacks with a drawstring closure at the top of a slightly tapered bag are more foolproof. A flap that covers the top opening of the pack not only keeps out the rain and snow, but also gives one a great-

er flexibility in packing. Outside pockets are a good feature for carrying items you need frequently, such as extra lenses, but can get in the way if you're going to do any climbing. If you need a pack for a kid (that's a good excuse to buy a pack), these small sacks work very well.

Here are three of the most versatile knapsacks to check out: the Ski Hut water-repellent knapsack in either canvas or nylon with two outside zipper-closure pockets (18 ozs.), $10 for the canvas model, $12 for the nylon, from Ski Hut; the Millet 525 day rucksack of coated nylon with head-flap pocket, waist strap, crampon and ice axe straps (1 lb. 4 ozs.), $21, from REI; and, in the slightly larger category, the Chuck Roast Nameless Frameless Rucksack of 9-oz. coated Cordura nylon with three outside pockets, two on the sides and one in the flap, ski slots and ice axe carrier (2 lbs. 9 ozs.), $30, from EMS.

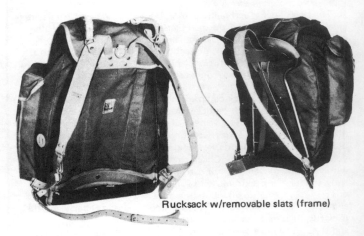

Rucksack w/removable slats (frame)

Framed Rucksacks, $35 to $69. For trips up to a week (yes, a week), mountaineering, or heavier load carrying (up to about forty pounds), the framed rucksack is the way to go. These are usually larger than knapsacks and have internal frames or stays of plywood, aluminum or fiberglass sewn into slots within the pack. These give it stiffness up the back to aid in the carrying of heavier loads. For easier stowage, some frames are removable. As with knapsacks, these packs come with or without features which will extend their versatility: outside pockets; crampon, ice axe and ski slots; waistbelts to keep the pack from shifting around; and load compressor straps. There are lots of these on the market, so things can get pretty confusing when you try to decide which is for you. Let simplicity, function and your needs be your guide.

Here are some really good framed rucksacks you might want to look at: the Eiger Standard by Alpine Designs in urethane-coated nylon duck with two side pockets and one in the flap closure (2 lbs. 5 ozs.), $43, from The Gendarme; the North Face Kaksack of 10-oz. coated Cordura nylon with fiberglass frame, slots for skis, leather patch for crampons and leather bottom (3 lbs. 8 ozs.), $65, from EMS; the Caribou Tourpack with padded waistbelt, load adjustment straps and fiberglass frame which they claim allows you to carry up to fifty pounds (3 lbs. 5 ozs.), $69, from Sierra Designs; and the Joe Brown, in either water-repellent canvas or coated nylon duck, with detachable pockets, bivouac/load extension and single-stay frame (3 lbs.), $50, from Swallows' Nest or The Gendarme.

Contour Packs, $55 to $75. Contour packs are relatively new on the market but have gained great popularity with many backpackers and ski tourers. They are nothing more than extremely large soft packs that distribute the load over the wearer's back, shoulders and hips uniformly without the use of a frame. Capacity is about the same as a frame-and-bag combination, and the comfort is very good. The only drawback to the contours is that they're unwieldly when partially loaded. Developed by Don Jenson originally, there are now quite a few folks manufacturing contour packs of one sort or another. If you're looking for an alternative to a packframe, this may be the best choice. These packs have one big plus for those who hitchhike, and that is there's no frame protruding to tear the upholstery in the car that just picked you up; they're also easier to hold on your lap.

The following are the contours available: the Rivendell Jenson Pack (the original design), $55, from Swallows' Nest; the Chouinard Ultima Thule with vertical compartment divider, drawstring closure at top, zippered sleeping bag compartment at the bottom and a generous flap pocket (3 lbs. 2 ozs.), $70, from Ski Hut or The Great Pacific Iron Works (Chouinard); and the Greatsack by Jan Sport featuring aluminum stays that conform to the wearer's back and foam hip pads (3 lbs. 13 ozs.), $75, from Co-op Wilderness Supply.

PACKBAGS WITH TUBULAR FRAMES
$33 - $100

Since frames and bags are most often used as a unit, we're discussing them together. For most extended backpacking trips involving several days or more carrying relatively heavy loads over pretty *even* terrain, the frame-and-bag combo is hard to beat. If you plan on doing a lot of cross-country travel involving lots of bushwhacking, you may want to consider one of the contour packs as in thick brush, such as laurel thickets or young aspen groves, the packframe tends to be an abominable pain in the ass.

Packframe. The rigid packframe has the greatest load-carrying potential of all pack systems. Instead of concentrating the weight on the neck and shoulder muscles, the frame, when fitted with a good padded waistbelt, transfers it to the hips, thus putting the strain of carrying on the strongest part of the anatomy—the legs.

The frame also keeps all those sharp, cornered items in the pack from coming in contact with the wearer's back, and eliminates the forward lean so common to toting rucksacks. What all this amounts to, over the long haul, is more comfort for the packer.

The old Trapper Nelson wooden packboard was the forerunner of the modern packframe. It was heavy, clumsy and its capacity limited. Haven't seen one on the trail anywhere for years!

Today's packframes are mostly aluminum alloy tubing either ¾ or 1 inch in diameter. Most have heliarc-welded joints (Kelty, Trailwise and Camp Trails), but some incorporate mechanical coupling systems to hold the frame together (Alpine Designs uses Lexan). The welded frames are rigid and don't flex. Flexible frame manufacturers (Jan Sport and Alpine Designs) claim that flexing makes the frame more comfortable to carry. Regardless of which you choose, the frame should resemble an elongated S (viewed from the side) that conforms to the spinal curve of the wearer.

The packframe system also allows for ventilation of the back through the use of either horizontal bands 5 to 6 inches wide or a full-length nylon mesh backband as the point of contact between the wearer's back and the frame. The lower band, if bands are used, is best padded. Backbands or mesh back panels, if they are to do the job, should be kept tight. This is accomplished by using either turn-buckles or a sound lacing system to take up any slack.

Some frames are equipped with simple padded shoulder straps; others have a yolk assembly for increased comfort. Either should be 2½ to 3 inches wide, well-padded with Ensolite or similar material, and cloth-covered.

A well-fitted waistbelt is the key to the packframe system when you're talking about comfort. The waistbelt serves as the weight transfer point between the frame and your hips. Two types are available. The first is the two-piece waistbelt that doesn't completely encircle the hips. It attaches to the frame at the bottom of each side

of the lower frame extensions. This type of belt tends to clamp the frame to your back with considerable pressure and discomfort. The second and preferred type is the waistbelt that completely encircles your waist. The two lower extensions of the frame are attached to the belt only to provide a point of contact to transfer the load of the pack to the hips. In this way, the frame is not clamped to your back—it merely rests on the waistbelt.

There are also some frames on the market with wraparound frames, frames with handlebars protruding forward from the bottom of the frame so your arms can help lift the load, and there's even one where you carry half your load in front and half in back on a frame that looks like one of those "walkers" that some old people use. Does anyone make one with training wheels? Probably...

Packbag. Packbags made to mount on frames are so plentiful, and varied in their features, that it's impossible even to begin to discuss them all. Most bags are made of coated nylon (waterproof) except for the Kelty bags, which are water-repellent (they'll leak in a hard rain) so they can "breathe." Kelty will sell you a waterproof rain cover, though. Don't buy a cotton canvas bag for your frame unless you like to get your gear wet.

The style of bag chosen is up to the individual, but generally speaking, the simpler, the better. Beware of packs which depend on zippers for closing their main compartments. We've said this elsewhere, but you haven't lived until you've tried to pack up a bag with a huge flap closure on the back that won't close (that's the principal hangup). There are three-quarter-length bags and full-length ones; bags with vertical dividers and those with horizontal ones. If you camp only in summer, you won't need as much capacity for bulk (a BIG bag) as does the guy who goes out alot in winter. Do you like lots of outside pockets or just a few? No matter what you're looking for, you can probably find it if you just look around, but don't just rush out and buy "a pack." Look at and use as many different ones as you can before you buy to be sure of what you want.

This has been a relatively rambling discussion of packframes and their bags, and some of you are undoubtedly confused (I am and I wrote it—yours truly, John Markwell). For clarification on the finer points, consult a few good books and browse through any catalogs you can get ahold of (some are extremely educational), and it won't be long 'til you can argue the pros and cons of packs with the best. Following is a list of some of the better outfits available: Trailwise

BACKPACKERS CHECK LIST

FLAP POCKET
Maps — Fire Permit — Fishing License
Notebook - Pencil — Hunting License
Identification — Medical Allergies & restrictions

BACK POCKET
Plastic Bowl
Plastic or Sierra Cup
Pot Tongs
Tablespoon
Waterproof Matches
Sunglasses
Lunch & trail snacks
The following items are so important they should be carried on your person: Knife, Compass, Waterproof matches.

UPPER LEFT POCKET
1 Quart Conteen

UPPER RIGHT POCKET
1 Quart Conteen

UPPER COMPARTMENT
Cook Kit — Condiment Kit
Backpackers Grill — Sugar - Milk
Stove if needed — Coffee — Tea
Bags of Food — Powdered Juice
Extra bags — Cooking Oil
G.I. Can Opener — Salt - Pepper
Rubber Bands
(Tent - if too big for lower compartment)

LOWER LEFT POCKET
Toilet Kit
Toothbrush
Toothpaste
Soap (Hotel Size)
Paper towels
Toilet paper
Scouring pad
Flashlight
Spare bulb and batteries

LOWER COMPARTMENT
Air Mattress & Repair Kit or
Foam Pad
Tarp & Ground Cloth or
Tent or Tube Tent
30' Nylon Cord
Underwear - Socks
Bandanas (2)
Windbreaker Jacket
Stocking Cap
Rainwear

LOWER RIGHT POCKET
First Aid Kit (over)
Sunburn Ointment
Repellent
Chap stick
Whistle
Matches in w p case
Candle
2 Dimes
Needles - Thread
Signal Mirror
Safety Pins
Water Purification

Camp Trail's recommended pack arrangement.

packframe with the Model 72 packbag—frame is welded aluminum with nylon mesh back panel, padded shoulder yoke and padded full-circle waistbelt (medium-size frame, 37 ozs.), $50; the Model 72 is an extremely cavernous sack and the one preferred by Colin Fletcher, five outside pockets and a generous storm flap (30 ozs.), $40; both $84, from Ski Hut and other Trailwise dealers. Kelty Mountaineer frame with A4 packbag—aluminum frame, $34; nylon bag with three compartments at top and one at bottom with zipper, $32; both from Kelty or other dealers. EMS Heliomaster frame and Expedition bag—aluminum frame, $29; large, three-quarter-length bag, nine outside pockets, $40; both from EMS. REI Super-pak—contoured aluminum frame with three-quarter-length coated nylon bag with five outside pockets. This is good for those on a tight budget—it's worth the money—(4lbs. 4 ozs.), $53 for the combo, from REI.

CHILDREN'S PACKS
$8 - $40

When your kid wants to carry her own stuff, the best thing you can do is to buy that small daypack you've been wanting, if it'll fit her. There aren't many packs made especially for kids, that's why it's simpler to go the daypack route. Framewise, you're better off if you can get to a large shop and try several on, as both Kelty and Trailwise have small frames and bag combinations; the small Kelty Basic weighs just 3 lbs. 2 ozs. and runs only $37 from EMS. Other packs you might want to consider are the EMS Child's Knapsack (7 ozs.), $8, from EMS, or the Kelty Sleeping Bag Carrier, a short teardrop model made to carry a sleeping bag strapped to the bottom (5 ozs.), $9, from Kelty.

soon run you short on space. Enter the stuff bag to save the day. A stuff bag is just that—a bag to stuff down stuff in (not rolled or folded, but stuffed—get it? That's the stuff!). Stuffing down gear in a stuff bag is the best way to reduce its bulkiness. That's one of the beauties of down. Like nothing else known, it has the ability to bounce right back (regain its loft) after being compressed. Stuff bags not only reduce the volume of down articles but offer protection as well. To do the job properly, stuff bags should be made of at least 5-oz. coated nylon, and the seams should be sealed to keep water from leaking in. This is especially important if you're carrying your sleeping bag in one outside the pack. Wet sleeping bags don't make for a very snuggly nighty-nite. Another advantage of stuff bags is they make organizing the contents of a pack a much simpler and more tolerable chore. Stuff bags come in all sizes from 3″ x 4″ x 6″ giving you 72 cubic inches of capacity, to those offering as much as 400 cubic inches of space. Most backpackers never seem to have enough stuff bags. It's a good idea to get an assortment of sizes and colors when you buy, and be sure to put a good drawstring clamp on the drawstring of each bag; knots can play hell with one's composure when trying nonchalantly, but urgently, for the toilet paper. Stuff bags have a few not-so-common uses, also; here are some from our experience: serving as booties to keep the dew off the tootsies when you finally get that TP and make the run outside the tent; if you have a stuff bag that leaks just enough, you can rig a shower; filled with rocks, a stuff bag makes a dynamite anchor for a collapsible boat, if you packed one in for lake fishing; and stuff bags are also good for packing out the catch. Of all backpacking accessories there's nothing, except nylon cord, that has as many uses as a bunch of different-size stuff bags. Cost for stuff bags ranges from about a buck to four or so, and they're available at most all outfitters. Both Frostline and Carikit offer stuff bags in kit form for the do-it-yourselfers.

CHILD CARRIERS
$4 - $25

If you walk with little ones very much, you'll end up carrying them at least part of the way, no question about it. Infants, too, can go along on day hikes if you've got the right kind of setup. Here are a couple of items to make your and junior's day more pleasurable: Gerry Kiddie Pack with stand (the nicest we've seen) lets you set your child down just about anywhere (at the edge of a cliff—ho, ho, hoooo...), and pack which includes a storage compartment below seat (1 lb. 8 ozs.), $25, from Moor and Mountain; Gerry Pleatshell, adjustable side carrier for infants, leaves the arms of the person doing the toting free to move (3 ozs.), $5 from EMS.

STUFF SACKS
$1 - $5

Though packs have a pretty fair amount of room for the most part, you'll find that putting a down sleeping bag and jacket in, too, will

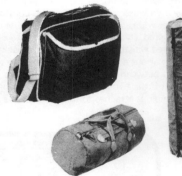

DUFFLE BAGS and KIT BAGS
$5 - $60

Duffle bags are hardly the apple of the backpacker's eye, but they are useful in transporting gear to the roadhead. The big ones are great for storing down gear at home (though it's not a good idea to store down in a compressed attitude for long periods of time) and the little ones are convenient for carrying those items needed often on the trip to wherever.

Most duffle bags now available are made of tough nylon duck with a zippered opening, reinforced carrying handles, and sometimes a shoulder strap. Quality and construction should be the equal of a good pack and the same criteria apply. For added convenience, many have zippered outside pockets for carrying small, frequently used items. Kelty makes three that are about as nice as any we've seen: small, 9″ x 13″, 12 ozs., $14; medium, 10½″ x 20″, $17; and large, 12″ x 26″ at $21; all are Cordura nylon and have at least one outside pocket. Available from Kelty or Kelty dealers. For air travel with fully-loaded packframes, Gerry makes the foam-padded Air Bags of heavy nylon duck with waterproof zippers, reinforced handles and leather grips. The Gerry Air Bags come in two sizes: small, 9″ x 16″

x 25" (1 lb. 12 ozs.), $35; large, 11½" x 16" x 32½" (2 lbs. 2 ozs.), $40, from EMS. For those wanting just a plain old duffle bag, EMS has one with a drawstring made from coated 6-oz. nylon duck with hand and shoulder carrying straps (14 ozs.), $10, from EMS.

Kit bags are a lot like big purses with a shoulder strap. Some are elaborate and expensive, most are more stylish than functional. One brand you might want to look at is Eddie Bauer's Sportsmans shoulder bags: four styles with varying numbers of pockets and compartments, 15-oz. cotton duck with cowhide trim; prices run from $23 to $30 and are worth the money.

GUIDE AND MAP POCKET
$7

Colin Fletcher swears by this little number. Many have become enamored by it and it went into the catalogs to meet demand. The pocket is just that—a pocket sewn onto the shoulder strap of the pack that provides for convenient storage of, and easy access to, items like pens, maps, sunglasses, and so forth. Moor & Mountain makes one that weighs 4 ozs. and has a flap that closes with Velcro; dimensions are 7" x 5" x 1" and it sells for $7. That seems steep, but they're the only ones who make one. Available from Moor & Mountain.

SLEEPING

SLEEPING BAGS
$50 - $200

A sleeping bag is a very important piece of your backpacking equipment, and also one of the most expensive. The state of the art in sleeping bag construction has reached a very high level, as has the variety of models, styles and features. This is good for the consumer, but also confusing when it comes time to select one. The biggest single consideration should be quality. A sleeping bag becomes a liability when baffles tear out, the fill shifts, or zippers break. Better to shell out a few extra bucks for a topnotch bag than to regret buying an el cheapo. This does not mean buying extra features or gizmos which aren't necessary to warmth and comfort, or a specialized use.

The most important function of a sleeping bag is to insulate against the cold. Lots of materials insulate. Crumpled newspaper, sawdust and lava are pretty good. But a bag must be lightweight, compressible and resilient. These factors rule out a lot of materials, narrowing down the selection to only two: goose or duck down and some synthetics. The thickness of insulation is proportional to the amount of heat conserved. This is shown by U.S. Army Quartermaster research data for the amount of insulation needed to retain the body heat of an "average" sleeping person at various temperatures:

$40°$ 1½" insulation
$20°$ 2 "   "
$0°$ 2½"   "
$-20°$ 3 "   "
$-40°$ 3½"   "

Down has the edge in the amount of loft provided per ounce—one reason it has been so popular with backpackers. In addition to thickness, or loft, the ability to pass water vapor plays a large part in an insulator's effectiveness. Mr. Average puts out about 1 pint of water vapor each night. Some of this is in the breath, some in the form of insensible perspiration. Water conducts heat from the body about 20 times faster than a dry medium. Two inches of a closed-cell foam would insulate well, but the trapped moisture would greatly reduce its effectiveness. Under usual conditions, down will allow moisture to pass through very well. Breathing inside a down bag, however, will add more moisture than the bag can get rid of. The same applies to using a bag which is too warm for conditions. A person will tend to sweat, thereby dampening the fill. In this respect, synthetic insulators, such as Fiberfill II, PolarGuard and Dacron 88, hold the advantage. A synthetic-filled bag will not absorb water directly into its structure; therefore, the moisture will be much easier to remove by drying or sublimation. A wet down bag is worthless and may be a liability—care should be taken at all times to protect it from wetness of any sort.

As for compressibility and resiliency, down, again, holds an edge over synthetics. A down bag will occupy about 25% less space than a

 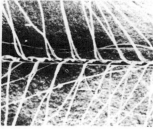

Magnified 10x   Magnified 1000x

Down fibers.

synthetic bag of equal weight, an important consideration when space is at a premium. Over an extended period of time, down will tend to lose some of its loft, or resiliency; but this is usually a matter of oil and dirt accumulation. The better grades of down will be affected less by this. A synthetic bag will be more uniform in its performance, but only if the insulating material is properly sewn to the bag shell, so that it is stabilized.

The term "down" needs a little clarification. Technically, down is the small, fluffy feathers close to the body of a goose or duck. It provides these animals with their primary source of insulation. Down has no quills, as do feathers which provide the fowl with their flight and water repellency capabilities. Down as a commercial product, however, is not pure down. Quality control on this would be prohibitively expensive. The Federal Trade Commission has determined that, by law, down should be: down, 80% minimum; feathers, 18% maximum; and residue, 2% maximum. Down, as defined, is subdivided into two grades: garment and bag. Feather and residue percentage varies from 8 to 12% in garment, from 12 to 20% in bag. Originally, down was a by-product of geese raised in Scandinavian countries for food, hence the term "prime northern." However, demand for down has surpassed the demand for cooked goose, so duck down is becoming increasingly popular. Aside from duck down's grey color, there is little difference between the two. As geographic terms for a particular down's quality have disappeared, most manufacturers are using fill properties to describe their product. For instance, 600 cu. in. per ounce would be superior to 500 cu. in. per ounce. Before, fill was described in terms of weight only. In many cases today a manufacturer's bag will contain less fill by weight than several years ago, but the volume numbers appear better. It's a way of saving bucks.

Synthetics have been around for awhile, especially Dacron 88, the standard Boy Scout and el cheapo bag fill; however, it wasn't up to par for serious cold weather use. Currently, Fiberfill II and PolarGuard are the most widely used synthetic insulators for sleeping bags. While not as effective as down, in terms of weight per loft and compressibility, their resistance to moisture absorption can be particularly important if wet conditions with minimal shelter are to be encountered. In addition, synthetic bags are about 40% cheaper than down, per inch of loft, which can be an important consideration on a limited budget. For additional discussions on down vs. synthetic, and goose down vs. duck down, check out the EMS, Sierra Designs, North Face and Holubar catalogs. Below are some additional considerations to keep in mind in choosing a sleeping bag:

Shell Fabric. The shell of just about all bags is constructed entirely of nylon fabric. It's light, tear-resistant, and permeable to water vapor. To a naked body, nylon feels cold—real cold, initially—but warms up within a surprisingly short period of time. Two basic fabric types are used: ripstop and taffeta. Ripstop is a fabric weighing about 1.5 to 1.9 ozs. per sq. yd. Its tear strength is greatly increased by a crisscross pattern of heavier threads incorporated at about ¼" intervals. Taffeta is a tight, flat, smooth tabby weave, usually weighing about 2.3 ozs. While taffeta does not have the tear resistance of ripstop, it's a lot more abrasion-resistant. Neither type of fabric is coated for waterproofness, although a silicone preparation is added to increase water repellency. This wears off in time, and should be replaced with a new treatment.

An interesting development in fabric is Goretex. It's basically a nylon cloth with a semipermeable coating. The coating is porous enough to let water vapor escape, yet the pores are small enough to prevent water droplets from entering. Its application to down sleeping bags has much potential.

Zippers. Nylon zippers are the way to go. They're lighter than metal, self-lubricating and less prone to freezing, and tend not to damage fabric should they become caught. There are two types of nylon zippers: tooth and coil. Tooth zippers are similar to the standard metal design. Their only drawback seems to be that they're not as durable as the coil type. The coil, instead of utilizing individual teeth, consists of two long spiral loops of nylon which mesh together. They're self-repairing and do not get out of alignment. However, care must be taken to start them at the proper position, otherwise the coils will mismatch and the sliders will become difficult to operate. Nylon zippers are numbered according to size: the smaller the number, the smaller the zipper. Number 10 zippers are usually used in sleeping bags for ease of operation. Zippers which open from either end are a convenience. The top or bottom or both may be unzipped for ventilation, while maintaining the bag's basic shape. In addition, two bags with similar zippers may be connected for, uh, coziness.

Baffles. Baffles keep the down from shifting all to one side, underneath or to the top or bottom. Otherwise, the value of the insulation decreases and the bag loses its efficiency. The simplest method is the *sewn-through* construction, whereby the top and bottom shell layers are sewn directly together to form down-filled tubes. Unfortunately, each seam has no loft thickness and the insulation suffers by forming cold spots. A better way is to insert verticle baffles between the outer and inner shell. This way the down is compartmentalized while still retaining uniform loft. More work and material (and weight) are involved, but the results are well worth it. The three basic types of baffled compartments are *square box, slant box,* and *overlapping V tube.* The individual tubes of down formed by the baffle should not be more than 6" apart. Some winter expedition bags have 3" separation for precise down control. Trailwise uses a chevron V-shaped baffle design, which tends to cancel out the body forces that cause down to shift. Baffle material is either a very light ripstop nylon or mosquito netting. Sierra Designs stitches the baffles internally—there are no exterior threads to wear.

The *double-quilted* or *laminated* construction is seldom used, due to its weight. It's basically two sewn-through bags offset and sewn together. A similar principle is used in ski parkas, substituting a single unbroken layer of nylon for one sewn-through layer.

Cut. Cut refers to the width of the inner shell vs. the outer shell. *Space-filler* cut has both shells the same size. The idea is that any excess fabric inside will drape over the body, reducing the amount of space necessary to heat. *Differential* cut has the inner shell smaller than the outside. The idea is that elbows and knees can't poke and touch the outside shell and create a cold spot. This is most assuredly a moot point, since either arrangement depends upon the ideal quiet, nonrestless sleeper. Check the catalogs for the manufacturers' opinions. They may be useful in making a decision.

Size. Most bag models are offered in two sizes. Regular and large. Regular fits people up to about 6'. Large fits people up to 6'3" or 6'4". Don't buy a bag larger than you need—it's only extra room to heat and weight to carry. The girth of a bag is generally a function of

the style.

Style. Style refers to the cut or shape of the bag. There are several variations, each serving a specialized function of its own. Below are some of the more common styles.

Mummy bags: By far the most common and popular style, mummy bags are cut to fit close to the body—broader at the shoulders and narrower around the hips and legs. With a fairly snug fit, there is less unoccupied air space inside, which improves the efficiency of the insulation. There is also a savings in material weight. However, this style is fairly constricting and does not allow for much body movement. Mummy bags are available from heavy expedition weights to very lightweight, snug models. North Face, Sierra Designs, Camp 7, Holubar and Snow Lion are companies noted for their quality and wide selection of models.

Barrel bags: These have a semimummy shape, not being so snug around the shoulders and hips. While not as efficient as a mummy, barrel bags offer more freedom of movement for restless sleepers. REI is a good source for this type.

Rectangular bags: As their name implies, these are straightforward bags with virtually no cut at all—most don't incorporate a hood. The ultimate for stretching out, they are somewhat heavy and bulky. Some rectangular bags will have a zipper running along one side and across the bottom. When fully unzipped, the bag becomes an excellent down comforter—a nice double-duty feature.

Double mummy bags: If you're pretty sure you want to be close with someone, this type might be the one to consider in lieu of zipping two bags together. The double is a mummy shape expanded to

CYMKOLD SPOTS diagram — SEWN-THROUGH; BAFFLES — SQUARE BOX; SLANT BOX; OVERLAPPING V-TUBE; **SLEEPING BAG CONSTRUCTION**; LAMINATED; DOWN-FILLED TUBE, BAFFLE, ZIPPERS — DIFFERENTIAL CUT; SPACE-FILLER CUT

fit two people. Zippers are located on the sides. Their weight, expense and lack of versatility limit them severely. They might be great for car camping.

Sleeping bag covers

Half bags and children's bags: The half bag or footsack is a shortened sleeping bag designed to be worn in combination with a down parka for overnight bivouacs or ultralight camping. Its construction is the same as a regular-sized bag. The back is cut a little longer so your back won't be exposed when in a sitting position. The top has a drawstring, which forms it into a hood. This way it can serve double duty as a child's bag. Most children's bags come in kit form, which means you've got to sew 'em yourself. Holubar and Frostline, both of whom are kit manufacturers, feature bags which can be extended by adding extra length as the child grows. Keep in mind that most types of sleeping bags, which includes adult sizes, can be obtained in kits at a substantial savings (usually about 30% cheaper). Of course, it helps to enjoy sewing; otherwise, it may not be worth your while. Some companies offering kits for sleeping bags (and other outdoor gear) are:

Holubar, Box 7, Boulder, Colo. 80306

Frostline, 452 Burbank, Broomfield, Colo. 80020

Care and Cleaning. Aside from wear and tear, most damage to a bag will occur from handling. A down sleeping bag that has been stuffed into a nylon sack will regain its loft quickly when removed and fluffed up. Leaving it stuffed in a bag for long periods of time can damage the down's ability to recover. It's a good idea to store a bag by hanging it up unconstricted. Frequent airing will make sure all moisture is out of the down and render the bag a lot more inviting to sleep in.

Dirt and body oils will eventually contaminate the down and affect its ability to loft. Approximately once a year, then, a down bag should be cleaned. If done improperly, however, it can be ruined. Down gear may be washed and dried at home easily enough. The cardinal rule is to use soap, not detergent. Detergent removes natural oils from the down, harming its resiliency. The easiest place to wash it is in a bathtub. Prepare a warm, soapy solution several inches deep. Roll the bag snugly to force out as much air as possible. Place the bag in the tub and unroll underwater. This insures that the soapy water penetrates into all the down compartments. Gently wash the bag and *rinse several times.* This is important because any leftover soap will tend to mat the down. Let the bag drain where it lies. When it's drained, lift it out, carefully supporting it; otherwise, the weight of the wet down may tear out some of the baffles. Let the bag air-dry outside for awhile, then transfer carefully to a dryer. Dry at very low heat for as long as necessary. Some folks throw in a tennis shoe to help break up wet down clumps.

Down gear may be dry-cleaned; but only petroleum-based solvents, such as Stoddard fluid, should be used. The chlorinated hydrocarbon solvents, such as perchloroethylene (perk), will ruin down. Check around at various cleaners; if the people there don't have any experience cleaning down products or do not know what type of solvent they use, better to do it yourself or send it to a cleaner that specializes in down gear (see Down East in "Sources of Backpacking Gear"). Incidentally, if you decide to do it yourself, be absolutely certain that all cleaning fluid fumes are out of the bag—air it thoroughly. These fumes are poisonous and could cause death.

BAG COVERS AND LINERS
$10 - $30
Covers and liners offer a degree of extra protection against dirt and abrasion. Liners serve mainly to keep the interior of the bag clean. Few people seem to use them, as they are an extra item and weight to carry around. Holubar is one of few companies offering liners as an option with their bags. A cover helps to improve the efficiency of a bag by reducing heat loss from the wind. This can be helpful when

camping without a tent. In addition, a cover doubles as a ground cloth. Generally, the bottom is waterproof nylon; the top, breathable.

SLEEPING PADS
$8 - $20
Because the down underneath a sleeper is compressed and loses its insulating properties, some substitute must be used. A foam pad will

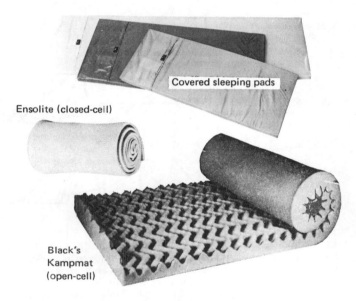

Covered sleeping pads

Ensolite (closed-cell)

Black's Kampmat (open-cell)

supply a bit of cushioning as well as insulation. Foams used in sleeping pads come in two categories: open- and closed-cell. Open-cell foam is the same type of material as an ordinary kitchen sponge. Due to its porosity, some means is needed to keep it from absorbing moisture. An envelope of waterproof nylon is used for this purpose. While comfortable and effective, these pads are hard to compress and tend to take up a lot of space. If water should leak into the foam past the nylon cover, the moisture is very hard to remove. With closed-cell pads, the air pockets are individually sealed to the outside. This eliminates the problem of water absorption. These pads are equally effective in insulating properties as the open-cell, but are thinner, though denser. They will not compress, but may be rolled up and tied outside the pack without harm. For 3-season use, 1 inch of open-cell or 3/8" of closed-cell foam is adequate. For winter, 2" or ½" is better. Foam pads come in several lengths. While a 3½' length will insulate the back area, a longer 5' piece will, in the long run, be more comfortable and versatile. Some pads will have a nylon-cotton blend for the top surface. This helps prevent the sleeping bag from sliding around with the slightest movement.

GROUND CLOTH
$4 - $10
A waterproof sheet of some sort is necessary under the bag to prevent ground condensation from wetting it. Any sheet of lightweight plastic will work if camping is done without a tent. A large enough sheet of plastic can double as a shelter. (Try to use plastic 4 to 6 mils [thou-

sandths of an inch] in thickness, as it will resist punctures better.) Coated-nylon tarps are excellent and most durable, but more expensive.

Tube tent

SHELTER

The best sleeping bag in the world is useless if it's not dry and sheltered from the wind. Nature provides little in the way of natural shelters and unless the weather is warm, still, and dry, you'll want to carry some form of shelter with you. Due to weight considerations, polyethylene and light nylon are the prime materials used in shelters for backpackers.

When you browse through the catalogs you'll see everything from plastic tarps and tube tents to palatial mountain tents with princely price tags. Choice usually comes down to the question of how much weight you're willing to carry for a given amount of comfort.

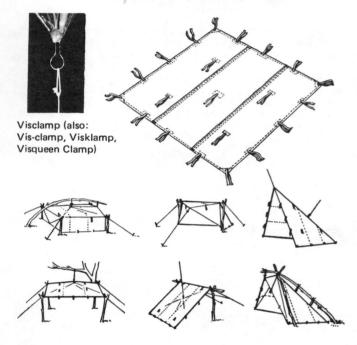

Visclamp (also:
Vis-clamp, Visklamp,
Visqueen Clamp)

TARPS
$3 - $30
Polyethylene has been the backpacker's stand-by for years. It can be used for tarps or ground sheets, and comes in an assortment of sizes and colors (it should be opaque if you plan to use it for shelter from the sun). Thickness ranges from 2 to 6 mils (1 mil = one-thousandth of one inch) and generally you're going to pick the heavier for most uses, as experience has shown the thin stuff can turn to holes really quick. REI sells three sizes of white, 4-mil Visqueen tarps which reflect sunlight: 8' x 9' size (1 lb. 8 ozs.), $3; 9' x 12', (2 lbs.), $4; and 12' x 12' (3 lbs.), $6. The addition of grommets or the use of Vis-clamps makes these tarps a lot more versatile. REI sells Tarp-Tys (2 ozs.), 6 for $1. These are sections of vinyl tape with a grommet at one end. The vinyl is coated with an adhesive and attaches easily to the plastic tarp. Just stick one anywhere you want a grommet. Vis-clamps are a better bet, though. Vis-Clamps (½ oz.), 18¢ each, from REI, and Versa Ties, pkg. of 20 (3 ozs.), $3, from EMS, are little devices for attaching nylon cord to any point on a plastic tarp. They operate on the same principle as a garter belt hook (those things that hold up gentlemen's socks) and do wonders to increase the versatility of plastic tarps.

For those wanting a tougher poly tarp, EMS offers their Griffolyn Reinforced Polytarp. This is not something out of **The Lord Of The Rings,** but it is a big improvement on the standard plastic sheet. Essentially, it's a laminated deal with crossed nylon threads sandwiched between two layers of plastic. They are available in three sizes: 8' x 12' (2 lbs. 10 ozs.), $10; 8' x 16' (3 lbs. 10 ozs.), $14; and 12' x 12' (3 lbs. 12 ozs.), $15.

For long trips or those where you need extra strength and dependability, a coated nylon tarp is the answer. The best and lightest are made of ripstop and are urethane-coated. They usually have grommets set into the seam around the edge and some have attach-

ment points strategically located at other areas. Typical are those offered by REI in the following sizes: 7' x 9' (1 lb. 8 ozs.), $15; 9' x 11' (2 lbs.), $20; 11' x 13½' (3 lbs. 8 ozs.), $30. One caution: check out the seams and stitching—should be French with tight stitches. If a tarp leaks, this is where it's most likely to happen.

TUBE TENTS
$4 - $50
These are just what the name implies, tents made in the shape of a tube. Most are of polyethylene and come in two sizes. These make good shelters, but are prone to condensation if you close up the ends. All you need to set them up is a piece of nylon cord rigged between two trees to form a ridge line, and you're set. Available from most outfitters, REI has the following: 1-Person Instant Tent, 3'3" x 9' (1 lb. 4 ozs.), $5; 2-Person Instant Tent, 4'10" x 9', (2 lbs. 6 ozs.), $7.

As with tarps, the answer to the problem of how to build a tougher tube tent is to use nylon. Ski Hut offers the Trailwise Ultimate Tube Tent featuring all-nylon construction. It has urethane-coated nylon for the roof with a heavier material of contrasting color for the floor. The ends are of mosquito netting with the rear sewn in place and the front featuring a zippered opening. The Ultimate Tube Tent is 86" long and the floor tapers from 58" in the front to 42" wide in the rear; height is 45" in the front tapering to 38" in the rear. Complete with poles and rigging, it weighs 50 ozs. and costs a dollar an ounce ($50). Available from Ski Hut.

REI also offers a nylon tube tent that rigs between two trees. Dimensions are very similar to the Trailwise model and it also has mosquito netting at each end. Weight is 2 lbs. 10 ozs. and the price tag is $32. Available from Recreational Equipment.

TENTS
Tarps, tube tents and the like all have one thing in common—they don't offer the backpacker total protection from the elements. With a tarp, you not only get blasted by the wind but drenched by any accompanying rain. The tube tent offers a little more protection from wind and windblown rain; but if you close them up, you drown from the condensation inside. The answer to these problems is the nylon mountain tent. Depending on the size and shape of the tent, its weight can run anywhere from 4 to 10 pounds complete, which isn't that much extra for a backpacker to include in his load.

The best tents are those with a waterproof floor and side walls that extend at least 8 inches up the sides of the tent. Urethane-coated nylon at least 2.5 ozs. in weight should be used for floors and side walls, and the fewer seams in the floor, the better.

The main body of the tent should be 1.9-oz. ripstop nylon that will breathe. This eliminates the condensation problem, in all but the coldest weather, by allowing moisture-laden air inside the tent to "breathe" (pass) through the nylon to the outside.

Now you're asking yourself how the rain stays out if the fabric in the tent body can pass water by breathing. Well, the answer is the rain fly. This is a form-fitted tarp, ideally of an extremely light, coated ripstop nylon that is placed over the tent. There should be at least six inches of clearance between the fly and the tent body to allow for the circulation of air. Not only will the fly keep the rain off, but if it's made of a light colored material, it will also reflect some of the heat of the sun.

Nylon is the only material to consider for a backpacking tent for many reasons. Unlike cotton, nylon is not susceptible to rot or mildew. Nylon is also stronger, lighter, considerably more waterproof, and it doesn't shrink like cotton does.

The opening of the tent will be either a triangular zippered door or a tunnel entrance which resembles a bottomless duffle bag. Some tents come with one or the other type, and some have both. Tents with two entrances have the potential for better air circulation in hot weather than do those with only one. Needless to say, the doors should also have mosquito netting to keep out the bugs. Some tents also have window-like or sleeve-type air vents. These should be closable in some way for really foul weather and also be mosquito-netted.

Construction criteria for tents are much the same as for other backpacking equipment. Stitching should be with nylon or Dacron thread with all stress points reinforced. Seams should be double-stitched and of the overlapped and turned type. Zippers should be of nylon to prevent freezing.

In choosing a tent, as with most other gear, consideration must be given to the type of use it will be given. Overkill is a common fault with most gear freaks and they usually pay the price in added weight.

There are many features available in tents which the backpacker may or may not really need; again this depends on where one is going, the time of year, altitude, and so forth. Snow flaps that prevent wind from getting under the tent are a nice feature if you do a lot of high-altitude or winter backpacking, but are just added weight if you use the tent mostly in the summer on the AT. Likewise for the frostliner, offered with many tents, to cut down on inside frost accumulation during the winter. Features that many packers do like for their convenience are inside pockets for stowing small stuff within the tent. Clothesline attachment points inside the tent are also nice if you hit a spell of bad weather. The zippered cookhole is often nice to have also, but make sure it's under the highest point in the tent, so that if the stove flares up while cooking inside you don't do in your own shelter. Speaking of fire, some manufacturers are now offering their tents in a flame-retardant nylon as an added safety feature. If you do a lot of winter traveling, a vestibule (an extra space at either the front or rear of the tent) can be exceptionally useful for stowing gear and keeping snow out of the living area of the tent. It's also a good place for the dog, kids, wandering peddlers or minstrels to sleep. You may also want to equip the tent guys with shock cord tighteners to absorb gusts of wind and lessen the strain on the tent. Shock cord tighteners also let you put even tension on all the tent pullouts to avoid any sagging, and the accompanying need to readjust guylines.

You may decide that a mountain tent is a bit heavy, considering the other gear you plan to haul—O.K., there are other lighter backpacking tents available. These usually lack many of the features of the mountain tents, but provide perfectly adequate shelter for the weight-conscious packer.

Below are some of the tents offered that are suitable for backpacking. Some are light (read Basic Shelter) and others may appear ridiculously heavy (read The Ritz). As we said before, the weight/comfort ratio is what you've got to balance out to make a choice.

Basic Shelter. In the Volkswagen category, you might want to look at the following tents: Two-Person Tent, a light, compact tent for the weight-watching packer, with all accessories (6 lbs.), $84, from REI; Biker/Packer two-man tent, one of the lightest tents available with all the features, a good sound shelter (4 lbs. 4 ozs.), including fly, poles and stakes, an outstanding buy at $110, from Moor and Mountain.

Basic Shelter Plus. Moving on to the midsize models: Trailwise's Fitzroy II, a self-supporting tent requiring no guylines under normal conditions, has many features of the Cadillacs but in reduced size (7 lbs. 2 ozs.), complete with fly, poles and stakes, $165, from Ski Hut; the Sierra Designs Wilderness Two-Man Tent, available with either a tunnel or zippered entrance, cookhole, sleeve vents and double A-frame poles (6 lbs. 10 ozs.), $157, from Sierra Designs. Gerry offers the Year-Round II with zippered opening covered by a floorless vestibule for stowage of gear, and cooking (7 lbs. 6 ozs.), $140, from EMS.

The Ritz. If you're into real luxury, you'll want to check out these: Sierra Designs Glacier Tent, all the comforts of home (7 lbs. 11 ozs.), $185, or the Three-Man Tent, all the comforts of the Glacier with a little more room (8 lbs.), $199, either from Sierra Designs. The Crestline Expedition Tent is the least expensive of the Cadillac models (7 lbs. 4 ozs.), $100, from REI. Last but not least,

Backpacker's tent w/fly

Mountaineer's style tent

we've got one for the man with a harem, the Mariposa. A bit heavy (14 lbs.) for most backpacking, but if you're into room or traveling with a group of friends, this would be like traveling with the Hilton on your back, $350, from Sierra Designs.

TENT ACCESSORIES

Pegs, 16¢ to $1. Most tents come with pegs. Tarp tenters and those with tube tents will have to buy them or make do with rocks, twigs or whatever. Pegs come in all sizes, materials and shapes: 1/8''-dia. aluminum wire skewers, 7'' (½ oz.), 10'' (5/8 oz.), 17¢ and 22¢, from EMS; chrome-moly steel wire, 10'' (1½ ozs.), 25¢, REI; 8-oz. plastic tent stake, 9'', 25¢, Moor and Mountain; SMC aluminum tent stake, 8'' (1 oz.), 20¢, from REI. In snow, many folks utilize the deadman concept for anchoring guylines. This amounts to tying something to the guy and burying it in the snow to keep it from being pulled out. It also works well for pitching a tent on sand. If you can't get a stake in the ground, you can always use a rock for an anchor point—make sure they're big enough.

Poles, $2 to $18. Most poles are made of aluminum and some from fiberglass. Those mentioned below are mainly of interest to tube and tarp tenters who may be traveling in an area without convenient trees from which to rig. Some of these poles nest together, others telescope. The more reliable seem to be the nesting type, and for convenience, those with a shock cord joining assembly can't be beat. REI sells a collapsible pole set with a long nylon spike on one end joined by shock cord that gives an overall height of 56'' from four 16'' sections (6 ozs.) that sells for $5. EMS sells single-pole sections which may be cut to length to achieve desired height. Each pole is 14½'' long, 12'' net when joined (1¼ ozs.), 60¢ in single-end form and 70¢ in double-end form. If you need an extendible pole, REI has one that goes from 4' to 8' (22 ozs.) and sells for only $3. If you need replacement poles for your tent, you can make your own from single-pole sections or buy ready-made replacements from the

CANOE TENT   WALL TENT   BAKER TENT

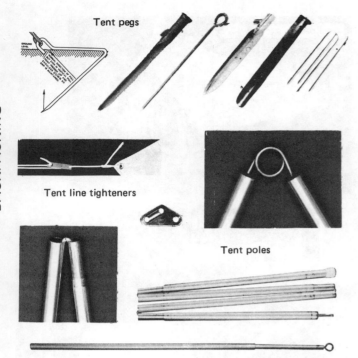

Tent pegs

Tent line tighteners

Tent poles

tent manufacturer. Ready-mades for a Trailwise Fitzroy II will set you back $22, and those for the REI Crestline run $20. It may pay to go the single-pole section route, should you break one.

Line, $1 to $2 per 100 ft. It's just about an absolute must for tarp and tube tenters to carry nylon line. It won't take long to find at least a thousand other uses for it besides stringing up a shelter. The most suitable for ridgelines and guylines on tarps and tube tents is a ¼", but you'll also find the smaller sizes useful. The ¼" tests out to 1000 lbs., 1/8" to 500 lbs., and 3/32" to 300 lbs. You can get this stuff at any outfitters. Be sure to buy twice as much as you think you'll need!

Line Tighteners, 10¢ to $1. Gizmos of nylon or aluminum that work as mechanical grippers. They slide on the guylines to control tension of main guys and pullouts. Weight is about 1/8 oz. each. EMS sells six nylon ones for 95¢.

Shock Cord, 33¢ to $5. If you camp a lot above timberline, this stuff can save you much grief. It's used on guylines to help absorb the shock of gusts of wind as they buffet tent, tent fly or tarp. When properly applied, they are surprisingly effective and save considerable wear and tear on the fabric of the shelter. The most useful seems to be the Figure 8 shock cord sold by REI (¾ oz.); a package of four costs only 33¢. If you'd like to make your own, you can buy bulk shock cord at most hardware and sporting goods shops for around 5¢ per foot for 3/16" diameter, and 14¢ per foot for 7/16".

Ripstop Nylon Adhesive Tape, 75¢ per yard. Handiest thing going for fixing tears in any light nylon fabric. To make it permanent, it must be sewn on; but for emergency repairs, the adhesive seems to work pretty well. Ski Hut sells it for 75¢ per yard for the 2"-wide stuff, and REI has it in 25' rolls for $6.

___ FIELD KITCHEN

These days, the rule for outdoor cooking is a lightweight backpacking stove. Of course, fires can be used, and have been for several thousand years. Trouble is, fires have a number of drawbacks. They're time-consuming, and awkward to prepare and maintain. Uniform cooking is difficult, and most backpacking cookpots will buckle with the heat. The greatest problem has to do with the people themselves. With more and more of us in the woods, building more and more fires, some campsites look like the Third Army just left.

Lightweight stoves are easy to carry and use. Fuels include white gas, kerosene and bottled gas (either propane or butane). As a rule, one stove is sufficient for two people—three people would be stretching it a bit. For larger groups, an extra stove will facilitate cooking and offset any disadvantage from extra weight.

Selection of a stove should be based on the intended use and

availability of fuels.

The characteristics of the different stoves are determined primarily by the type of fuel they use. Gasoline stoves must be primed to start them. A small amount of gasoline must be squirted into the depression on top of the fuel tank and ignited. As this gas burns off, it heats the fuel supply and air inside, generating enough vapor pressure to force gas out at the burner. As the stove burns, it generates enough additional heat to maintain pressure. Kerosene stoves work in much the same manner. However, as kerosene is less volatile than gasoline, a small pump is fitted to the fuel tank. This provides the needed additional pressure. Incidentally, never fill the fuel tank of either stove completely full—about 2/3 to 3/4 will do. Otherwise, there will be no room for vapor to develop, only frustration.

Propane-butane stoves are in a class by themselves in that they use self-contained, disposable cartridges, and need no priming. Propane, being more volatile, must utilize a sturdier, heavier container, similar to those used for propane torches. Because of its weight, it's not too popular. Butane, because it is less volatile, gets away with a lighter cartridge. Trouble is, butane won't vaporize below 30° F., which makes it a hassle for winter use unless the stove is kept warm via another heat source.

White gas at the pump is becoming increasingly hard to find. Coleman fuel or its equivalent is as good or better, but more expensive. Do not use automotive gasoline—it contains additives which will eventually gum up the stove's orifice, or lead which can be fatal in large enough quantities. Kerosene is less common than white gas, but in foreign countries, is likely to be a lot easier to find. Bottled gas usually can only be obtained through an outdoors supplier, so it's best to have an adequate supply for any intended trip.

In order to compare these fuels, below is a chart showing approximate burning time and cost for a pint of the more popular ones:

Fuel	Burning Time/Pint	Cost/Pint
Coleman fuel	2½-3 hrs.	.20
Kerosene	2½-3 hrs.	.06
Butane	4 hrs.	3.00

GASOLINE STOVES
$20 - $50

These are by far the most common type in use. Gasoline is widely available and relatively cheap. It is, however, volatile and care should be exercised in filling and priming the stove. As a rule, gas stoves don't usually have a pressure pump. In cold weather, the fuel tank should be insulated from any cold surface with a piece of Masonite backed with foam. For extended winter camping or expeditionary cooking for large numbers of people, larger gas stoves with pumps are a better choice than those without.

Perhaps the most widely used stove is the Svea 123, or Optimus 80. The only difference is tank capacity and the type of windscreen-pot support provided. The Svea weighs 17.5 ozs. and has a 1/3-pt. capacity. The Optimus weighs a little more and holds ½ pt. Prices are about $26 and $25, respectively, from Kelty. Similar in construction to the above, but different in arrangement, are the Optimus 8R and 99. These have the burner mounted in a square metal box with the fuel tank on the side, a more stable design. Both weigh 23 ozs. and hold 3.2 ozs. fuel. The 8R costs $26; the 99 has a removable lid and windscreen and goes for $29. The Optimus 111B is similar to the 8R and 99 only larger (56 ozs., 16 ozs. fuel). In addition, it has a pump on the fuel tank. $50 will buy one. All three available from EMS and most other outfitters.

Phoebus sells two stoves, the 625 (32 ozs., 16 ozs. fuel) and the 725 (23 ozs., 10 ozs. fuel). The 625 is a fairly large, stable winter stove with a pressure pump. The 725 is the smaller backpacking version. The 625 is $26; the 725, $21; both from EMS.

Mountain Safety Research has come up with an interesting idea: instead of building the stove and fuel tank as one unit, utilize the fuel bottle as the tank and have a separate burner unit. The MSR 9A consists of stove (burner unit) and a pump-feed tube which threads into the standard Sigg fuel bottle. The burner and pump weigh only 12 ozs. The fuel bottle is more, of course, but it would be carried anyway. Price from MSR is $45. MSR also sells a burner which will use kerosene, Stoddard solvent, No. 1 stove oil, No. 1 diesel, white gas

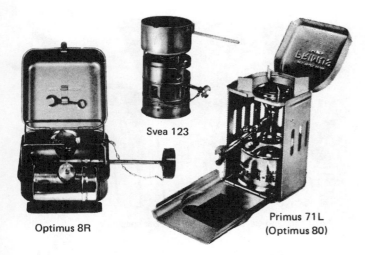

Svea 123

Optimus 8R

Primus 71L
(Optimus 80)

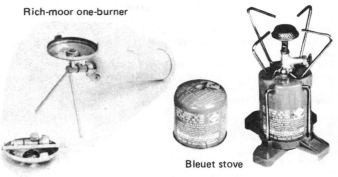

Rich-moor one-burner

Bleuet stove

and alcohol. Weight is the same, but the cost for burner and pump is $48.

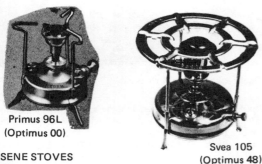

Primus 96L
(Optimus 00)

Svea 105
(Optimus 48)

KEROSENE STOVES
$34 - $50

Kerosene stoves are good for large amounts of cooking, melting snow for water, and so forth, as they have a larger fuel capacity and are cheaper to run. In addition, kerosene is less dangerous than gasoline. However, they do have their disadvantages—the stoves must be primed with a fluid other than kerosene, usually alcohol. Kerosene is smelly; the odor will tend to linger in places exposed to it. Also, it is not as common in some areas of the U.S. as others. It is more common in foreign countries and should be considered for use on any trips out of the U.S.

Optimus makes a model 111, similar in size, price, capacity and weight to the 111B gasoline stove. Its stability and low profile make pots less prone to tip over. EMS carries it. Two other popular stoves are the Optimus 48 (Svea 105) and Optimus 00 (Primus 96L). Both have a 1-pt. capacity, but the Optimus 48 has a couple of burner plates incorporated into the pot support. For this reason, its weight (40 ozs.) is more than that of the Optimus 00 (26 ozs.). Both stoves have pumps and feature partial disassembly for transport. Both from REI for about $35.

As noted above, MSR offers their model 9A ($48), which burns kerosene as well as other fuels.

Alcohol stoves

ALCOHOL STOVES
$2 - $18

Alcohol stoves haven't received much mention mostly because they aren't used very often. The stoves are lightweight because they are simpler—no moving parts. Alcohol isn't as efficient as gasoline for its weight, however. REI sells a simple burner for $3 (4 ozs.), which

might be good for emergencies. EMS has the Optimus 77A, which consists of a burner, two pots, a lid-fry pan and windscreen for $18 (24 ozs. total).

BOTTLED GAS STOVES (butane and propane)
$10 - $40

Bottled gas stoves have one big attraction—they are convenient. Just turn the knob and light them. The fuel is expensive, so there is a trade off. Also, the empty containers must be carried out. Fuel cylinders are not commonly available, so an adequate supply must be carried. On some stoves such as the Bleuet, the cartridge may not be removed once it is attached to the burner. Other cartridges, such as the LP gas and propane type, may be removed after each use. Keep in mind that butane won't vaporize below 30° F. at sea level. The higher one goes, the lower the atmospheric pressure and temperature of vaporization.

The French-made Bleuet S-200 was one of the first popular butane stoves. It weighs 15 ozs. and costs $10 from EMS. Cartridges (11 ozs.) cost $1.35 and last for 3 hrs. at full blast. The Universal Sierra (Kelty) and ERI Mini (EMS) are probably the most compact stoves going—4½" diameter and 7 ozs. LP fuel containers weigh 10 ozs., burn 3 hrs., cost about $1.40, and are removable. Both stoves sell for sixteen bucks. Rich-moor, the food people, market an interesting stove using the same type cartridge in a two-burner stove. One burner can be removed and a gas lantern mounted in its place. Light to eat by! This outfit, from EMS, weighs 29 ozs. without the cartridge, and costs close to $40. On the propane end, Rich-moor has one- and two-burner models, from $10 to $25. Cylinders are $2.50 and weigh 2 lbs., which is one drawback. The stoves, themselves, are fairly light, going at 8 ozs. and 16 ozs. for the one- and two-burner models, respectively. Moor & Mountain handles these.

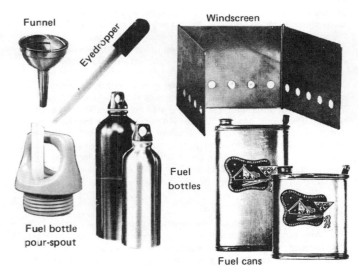

Funnel

Eyedropper

Windscreen

Fuel bottles

Fuel bottle pour-spout

Fuel cans

STOVE ACCESSORIES

These may be obtained from just about any supplier.

Cleaning Needles, 10¢ to 50¢. These are useful for unclogging the orifice of your stove. Most new stoves will come with one. A carbide lamp tip cleaner can also be used. The small gauge wire should be handled with care.

Fuel Bottles, $3 to $5. A quart or pint aluminum bottle is a necessary accessory. Sigg makes the nicest (and most expensive). The quart size is better for trips longer than a weekend. Some bottles are available anodized—this is unnecessary for gasoline. A nice addition that goes with the Sigg bottle is a pour-spout cap which interchanges with the original cap. It facilitates pouring fuel into the stove tank.

Funnels, 10¢ to 25¢. A small, plastic funnel is useful for filling the stove's fuel tank. Some have a fine mesh wire screen in them to trap any moisture which might have collected in the fuel bottle.

Eyedropper, 10¢. This is another handy gadget, used for placing fuel in the priming cup on top of the stove tank prior to preheating. The alternative is to pour fuel directly from the fuel bottle—kinda sloppy—and problems you might not be interested in can develop, such as burning up the tent or yourself. Of course, these things are part of the fun of backpacking.

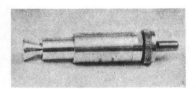

Optimus Mini Pump   Stove cleaning needles

Optimus Mini Pump, $5. Designed to fit any Optimus, Svea or Primus stove. This screws onto the tank filler opening and allows fuel to be pumped out into the priming cup for preheating. It is removed before lighting. A little complicated, but cuts down on waste. From Moor & Mountain or Kelty.

Metal Match

Plastic match case   Metal match case   WINDPROOF

FIRE ACCESSORIES

Should you decide to cook on an open fire, you might do well to carry a few things to help out. No, firewood is not one of them, though some have done it.

Plastic and metal waterproof match holders are available. They're worth the 50¢ to $1 they cost for the assurance of a warm fire and cooked food.

If an ordinary match won't do, there are lots of fire starters. A metal match works by shaving off pieces of it into a pile of tinder. Then by striking the match sharply, sparks are generated that light the pile. These cost around $2. Fire Ribbon is a paste for smearing on damp wood to get it going. Cost is under $1. Tinderdry, a crumbled fire starter, does the same thing for about the same price. There are wind and waterproof matches that burn even in gale winds and rain. They're approximately 25¢ a box. Just about every mountain shop will carry all these things.

COOKING AND MESS GEAR

The backpacker has a lot of leeway when it comes to selecting cook gear. Anything from common kitchen utensils to elaborate cook sets may be used, although weight and bulk are always a consideration. As a minimum, each person should have a cup, spoon and knife. A durable plastic cup is best, as it won't break or burn your mouth. Any spoon will do, preferably a tablespoon. A knife will normally be carried anyway. (Stay away from the machetes.) One cookpot per two people is the bare minimum; two pots will make preparing the main course and a hot beverage a lot easier.

Obviously, there are a lot of accessory items which are either convenient or may be necessary depending on the type of food selected. Avoid the temptation to include a lot of easily misplaced or seldom used paraphernalia.

Feed bag, 2nd Cavalry, 1 ea.   Backpacker's grill   Plastic water bottle

Backpacker's cook & mess kit   Plastic canteen

Just about all outdoor suppliers include a stove-cooking gear section in their catalogs. Most of the items listed below can easily be found from one or several sources.

Eating Utensils (knife, fork, spoon), about 75¢ to $1. Aside from ordinary kitchenware, stainless steel knife-fork-spoon sets are popular. These are designed so that all three will clip together for storage and usually include a plastic case. Weight is about 3 ozs. The attaching studs on the spoon can be hooked on a pot rim to prevent it from slipping into several inches of glop.

Plates and Bowls, 50¢ to $1. Most cookpots come with a lid which may be used as a plate; a cup will do just as well, although it may not have the capacity. For those who aren't choosy, one person can eat out of the pot, another from the lid. For those who are, inexpensive and lightweight plastic or aluminum bowls and plates are available. Plastic seems better, as it will not lose heat as rapidly. These weigh about 3 ozs.

Mess Kits and Nesting Pot Sets, $5 to $30. There is a lot of variety with these items, from one-man sets to gear for six or more people. The old classic, the Boy Scout outfit, consists of a frying pan, dish, plastic cup and small pot with lid. The frying pan handle folds to hold the set together. EMS wants $5 for one; weight, 1 lb. 8 ozs.

Perhaps the most nicely made (and expensive) are the spun-aluminum nesting pots by Sigg of Switzerland. These are available in five sizes, 1 to 5 qts., and come with lids. The bail locks in an upright position for pouring. A Svea 123 stove will fit inside the smallest pot, with room left over for a pot gripper, pot scratcher, salt and pepper, etc. They average about $9 and weigh 14 ozs. apiece. Sigg also makes the Tourister Cookset, consisting of two pots, lid and base-windscreen which will accept the basic Svea burner unit. Price is $23 and weight, 1½ lbs., minus stove. Sigg cookware is carried by Ski Hut, EMS and Moor & Mountain.

A good alternative to the higher-priced Sigg ware is the Hope Cookset from Japan and imported by Mountain Paraphernalia. It costs $15 and contains two pots and lids, and a smaller sauce pot with lid. A zippered nylon case is provided to keep stove soot from contaminating the rest of your pack interior. Kelty has a couple of good two- and four-person sets, around $10 and $13. REI has a good selection of individual pots for putting together a custom outfit.

There is one important thing to keep in mind about cookware: aluminum pots, by virtue of their light weight, have poor heat-dissipating qualities. An unattended pot of whatever cooking can stick and burn to the bottom very quickly. A coffee can lid (with edges filed smooth) will help greatly to spread the heat. Better yet, find one of those asbestos-impregnated wire screens used in chem labs.

Cups, 50¢ to $3. The steel Sierra cup has long been a favorite for

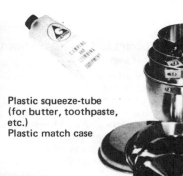

Reflector oven (folding)

Plastic squeeze-tube
(for butter, toothpaste,
etc.)
Plastic match case

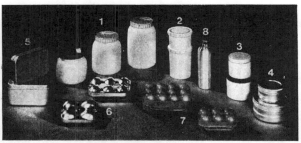

Assorted aluminum and plastic provision containers

Aluminum skillet

Sigg nesting pots

G.I. can opener, 1 ea.

Folding water bag

Pot clamp

Sierra cup

its durability and ease of use. The wire rim helps to prevent burning. Current issue U.S. Army cups are good, although somewhat heavy. It's handy to have an extra 1-cup level marked on any cup for ease in preparing dehydrated or freeze-dried foods.

Pot Gripper, 50¢ to $2. This is a handy gadget, especially if your cookpot doesn't have a bail. Most will clamp on the rim of the pot, either by manual pressure or spring action. The handles can usually be shortened to fit better inside the cookset. Some cook kits come with an el cheapo lightweight pot gripper—impress the salesperson when you buy the kit (the rest of the kit is usually O.K., just the gripper is bad news) by asking if there's a trash can around, and throw the damn thing away.

Other Cooking Utensils, 50¢ to $2. A small spatula can come in handy when using a frying pan. Kelty has a 2-oz. stainless steel model with a hardwood handle for $1.75. Teflon-coated frying pans are becoming more popular since they are less hassle, but a nylon spatula must be used, to prevent scratching the surface. REI and Moor & Mountain have them for about 75¢. A cook spoon and soup ladle could be useful, but usually not enough to justify their presence.

Frying Pans, about $8. Cast iron is out, due to its weight, even though it gives the best results. Steel is better, but still pretty hefty. Aluminum is the best bet, particularly with a Teflon coating, as it's lightweight, less likely to burn and maintenance-free. Kelty and Moor & Mountain offer 8-oz. models with a folding aluminum handle; they are 8 in. in diameter—large enough for a few trout.

Pressure Cooker, $30. This is not one of your frequently used items, but can be very important at high altitudes, where cooking time is longer. EMS sells a British Skyline Cooker, made of cast aluminum, which weighs 3 lbs. 4 ozs. It comes with three removable partitions so that several foods may be cooked separately. Capacity is 5½ quarts.

Can Opener, 50¢. Ranks 10 on the Richter (temper-blowout) scale of most commonly forgotten items. The best is the G.I. P-38 opener. It weighs a fraction of an ounce and does a surprisingly good job. Folks who pack a Swiss Army knife will usually have an opener, but their effectiveness is doubtful.

Water Bottles, 50¢ to $2. The most important thing to look for is a bottle that won't leak around the cap. The ribbed plastic bottles from Moor & Mountain are good, and have an attached cap which can't be lost. Among the best are the Nalgene lab bottles from Ski Hut. They are very strong and the cap has an excellent seal. Wide-mouthed bottles have several advantages over narrow-mouthed ones. It's easier to inspect the inside for bugs, crud, etc., and easier to add powdered drinks. Small streams may make it necessary to fill the bottle with a cup—easier again.

Large folding, polyethylene water carriers are handy to have along, particularly if you don't know whether you'll be able to, or want to, camp next to a water supply. A 1- or 2-gallon collapsible jug (10 ozs. or so) can save many long trips to the spring that's a half-mile or so down the trail from your tent. Huh? Oh sure, dummy, fill the jug at home and pack it loaded on the trail—be sure to fill it with the lightweight-type water mentioned on the next page, though.

Provision Containers, 50¢ to $5. A number of small, wide- and narrow-mouthed plastic jars can come in handy for storing beverages, spices and other foodstuffs. Again, a good seal is important. Plastic

bags can be used. They are light, but very prone to breaking. Most suppliers carry a good selection of these items. Gerry makes a handy gadget called a squeeze tube. Similar to a large toothpaste tube, it can be filled from the bottom by removing a plastic clip. Perfect for peanut butter, Crisco, honey, toothpaste... From EMS, 50¢.

Cleaning Stuff. A pot scratcher is a good idea, especially for those morning-after cleanups. Nylon is best, as steel tends to score the inside of the pot. A quantity of biodegradable soap will make things easier.

LIGHTWEIGHT FOOD

Short hikes seldom require any food other than maybe a trail snack or, in the case of a full day's jaunt, you might want to take along the fixings for one full meal. For the most part, provisions for short hikes, even those for weekend trips, can be put together right out of the kitchen cupboard. These short trips can be real gourmet's delights since weight and bulk are not a problem; you can usually even find room for a bottle of wine.

It's when you start planning major trips, say four days or more, that weight and bulk problems begin to surface. There are several approaches to the problem and no one in particular is applicable to all trips. Depending on the location, time of year and type of climate you're backpacking in, you may want to try the following approaches or a combination of them. Let's start at the Spartan end of the scale. There has been a big turn to natural foods recently and many who have read Euell Gibbons think they can just pack up their camping gear, head out and live off the land (see Foraging). Well, you could, but foraging for survival would be pretty much a full-time job and little time would be left for all of the other activities so important to the enjoyment of a backpacking trip, i.e., watching bumblebees, swimming in mountain streams, scratching PI (poison ivy), daydreaming and just plain walking. Eating wild berries or picking a few to add to the pancakes doesn't take much time, but foraging for survival does. At the opposite end of the scale is the approach of being completely self-contained and having to depend only on what you're carrying for sustenance. This is where lightweight dehydrated and freeze-dried foods really come into their own. Not only do they offer light weight, but the bulk of a day's food's needs can also be held to the absolute minimum. Variety is about as great as anyone could ask for, including such things as freeze-dried ice cream and strawberries. Generally, the longer the trip, the lighter and more compact your food load must be. Two pounds per person per day is the rule of thumb most folks use in planning menus for long trips, and it seems to be a sound one. You have to plan your meals well to keep within this rule, but with a little thought it can be done. Another approach to the food problem is a combination of the foregoing two. There's nothing like fresh mountain trout to add some

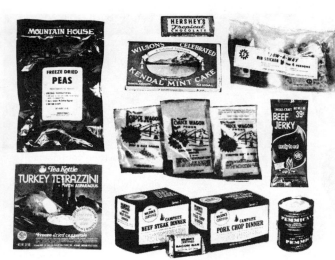

BOOK

THE COMPLETE GUIDE TO TRAIL FOOD USE
Wm. W. Forgey - $3.95

Here's another source for those seeking nutritional information for help in planning menus for back-country trips. This is a definitive study of both human nutritional and caloric needs, and the ability of various prepared and natural foods to meet those needs. The book covers all aspects of trail foods, including calorie content, weight, water and cooking time requirements. Information on sources and prices of various prepared and natural foods is included.
From: Indiana Camp Supply, P.O. Box 344B, Pittsboro, Ind. 46167

zest, not to mention variety, to your dehydrated or freeze-dried meals, so you may want to weigh the advantages of carrying fishing gear with you (weigh that, too) if you happen to be traveling in trout country.

Achieving a balanced diet while backpacking and insuring that you ingest all the recommended daily requirements of vitamins, minerals, and such, can be done. With two full meals per day and trail snacks, it shouldn't present any problem. Calories are the important thing to watch. A 165-lb. backpacker will need around 4500 calories per day to keep going under normal conditions and somewhat more in the winter. You get calories from eating fats, protein and carbohydrates, with the latter providing most of the caloric needs. Fats should provide about 20% of your caloric intake (100 mg. or 3.6 ozs. per day for a 165-lb. person), and protein should account for 5% or so (54 mg. or 1.9 ozs. per day) with the carbohydrates picking up the slack.

The above figures are only approximations, and you can vary them considerably without suffering any ill effects. If you really want to get into figuring nutritional and caloric needs, and intake, we suggest you look at *The Complete Walker,* pp. 82, 83, or obtain a copy of Agricultural Handbook No. 8: *Composition of Foods,* $1.50, from the Superintendent of Documents, U.S. Government Printing Office, Washington, D.C. 20402. The latter will probably have more information than you'll ever need to plan a normal menu for a normal trip of a week to ten days. Many of the manufacturers of lightweight foods also have pamphlets on the nutritional and caloric values of the foods they sell, and these also can be of considerable help in planning menus. Remember, though, that these guys are out to sell their product and are not likely to knock it themselves if it's not what it should be.

Backpacking and mountaineering outfitters, although they are the most obvious source of lightweight foods, are not the cheapest source nor do they often have a great variety to choose from. They are, however, one of the best sources of information on quality and ease of preparation of many items, and they are often the only source of lightweight freeze-dried meats and high-energy specialty foods. Since most of the folks who staff these shops (not all shops) are into a variety of outdoor activities and because they probably get a lot of feedback from many people, they are usually quite willing and capable to counsel you on your food needs for a specific trip. If you have special problems such as diet, large groups of people, availability of water (or lack of it) or an extremely long trip, most manufacturers and suppliers can help you in planning around their products which can best fill your needs.

It won't take long for you to find out that lightweight foods are pretty expensive. You can get around much of the cost by substituting supermarket items for many things, for instance, rice, dried soup mixes, biscuit mixes, beans, gravy and sauce bases, noodles, macaroni, instant potatoes, hard breads and crackers, dried fruits and nuts, and powdered drink mixes. Most of this stuff comes bulk-packed and needs to be broken down into portions of two or more, depending on the number of people involved in the trip. Even with the cost of plastic bags for repackaging, buying food this way works out to a lot less dollarwise than buying all processed food for a trip. Smoked sausage, cheeses and other items for trail snacks are available from delicatessens and specialty shops. Farmers markets are also a good source for this type of food.

Regardless of where you get your food, pretrip menu planning can really simplify things once you're out on the trail. Plan out every meal, bag them up and then bag three meals to a larger bag for each day of the trip. Then you're all set and don't have the hassle of digging around in the pack for whatever meal you've decided on. Another thing to keep in mind when planning meals is KISS (Keep It Simple, Stupid). One-dish meals are ideal for the bush, with maybe soup before and a sweet snack after. Not only are elaborate meals hard to prepare on the trail, but they leave you with a lot of pots to wash in cold water. Lastly, we'd like to recommend that you take a slight excess of whatever hot drink you prefer—tea, coffee ($$$) or whatever—as that extra cup can often be appreciated in the middle of a very cold, wet, miserable day.

Most people order their low-moisture foods from mail-order houses or buy from local outfitters. Usually if you order direct, you can achieve a savings or at least get a better selection to choose from. Below is a list of lightweight food dealers and manufacturers. (* indicates those who are particularly helpful or cooperative.)

*NATIONAL PACKAGED TRAIL FOODS—SEIDEL
632 East 185th St., Cleveland, Ohio 44119
Minimum order, $10. Mail-order price list available on request. They offer a trial order, which is a sampling of many of their items, but offer no discounts. Some of this stuff is hard to prepare at high altitudes.

DRI-LITE FOODS
11333 Atlantic, Lynwood, Calif. 90262
We've heard most of this food is extremely palatable. Minimum order, $10. Brochure available on request.

*TRIP-LITE

S. Gumpert Co. of Canada, Ltd.	S. Gumpert & Co.
31 Brock Ave.	812 Jersey Ave.
Toronto 3, Ontario, Canada	Jersey City, N.J. 07302

This outfit was originally organized to provide food for the Boy Scouts of Canada. Most things are simple to prepare and are designed to feed 4- to 12-year-olds. They sell direct, but only in case lots.

RICH-MOOR
P.O. Box 2728, Van Nuys, Calif. 91404
Some of the best low-moisture food we've eaten—and enjoyed. Available through many outfitters or by mail direct. Literature and price sheet on request.

*FREEZE-DRY FOODS LTD.

| 579 Speers Rd. | 201 Savings Bank Bldg. |
| Oarville, Ontario, Canada | Ithaca, N.Y. 14850 |

Catalog available and they pay shipping on all orders over $25.

*STOW-A-WAY
166 Cushing Hwy., Cohasset, Mass. 02025
These folks have no minimum order, a free catalog, discounts of 10% on orders over $100 and 20% on those over $300, and they pay shipping on all orders over $10.

*CHUCK WAGON FOODS
Nucro Dr., Woburn, Mass. 01801
These guys have a good catalog, will mail order, and will even drop-ship to any point in the U.S. They can't ship to Canada because of a Canadian Dept. of Agriculture rule, but will ship to points on the border. Discounts offered: 20% on orders between $50 and $100, 30% over $100; minimum order is $10.

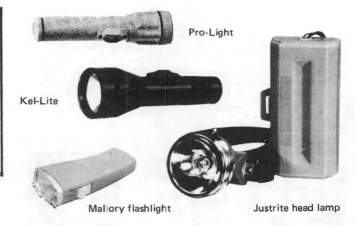

Pro-Light

Kel-Lite

Mallory flashlight

Justrite head lamp

DEHYDRATOR

TITCOMB BASIN PRODUCTS, INC.
P.O. Box 291, Wilmette, Ill. 60091
For those of you who are really hard to please foodwise, here's a gadget that'll allow you to plan your menus around the foods you like. It's the Drykit Food Dehydrator Kit for drying your own fruits and vegetables. It will shrink their size and weight from 70% to 40% of the original with no loss of nutritional value. It won't work on meats (at least they don't say it will), but at $50 it looks like just the ticket for those who do a lot of packing and prefer fruits and vegetables.

PERMAPAK
40 East 2430 South, Salt Lake City, Utah 84155
Catalog available, retail store in Salt Lake or you can order by mail. No minimum order.

*OREGON FREEZE DRY FOODS INC.
P.O. Box 666, Albany, Oreg. 97321
These fellows manufacture the Mountain House and Teakettle brands. Their strawberries and freeze-dried peas are almost like fresh. Anyway, you can buy this stuff locally at most outfitters or order direct. They have bulk-packed foods for large groups or those planning long trips. Literature and list of dealers on request.

KAMP PACK FOODS, SELECT FOOD PRODUCTS, LTD.
120 Sunrise Ave., Toronto 16, Ontario, Canada
Literature available, no minimum order, will pay shipping on orders over $50.

LIGHTWEIGHT WATER
You can live for quite a long time with little or no food. Without water, though, you would probably die within a few days or even quicker in the desert. Intake of water is important and obvious in the desert, but it is equally important in most other climates as well, especially in the mountains where the air is really dry. You should drink at least two quarts of water per day, even in cold weather. Needless to say, under desert conditions you could double that easily. Even in well-watered country, it's advisable to keep at least a quart bottle of water in your pack for those times between water sources, when it seems you get the greatest thirst. Not only is water critical to survival, but it often is an essential ingredient in preparing most lightweight foods.

These days you have to be really out in the bush to trust water sources. Unless you're in an area where springs or streams are monitored for drinkability, we would suggest that you purify it before using. You can use chlorine-releasing Halazone tablets for this, if you want to do it chemically. The other method is to boil the water: one minute at a rolling boil plus one additional minute for each thousand feet of elevation above sea level. To clear it, use a filter. See the Survival section.

If you're really lucky, you won't have to do anything to your water but dip it out of a cold, clear stream. You'll have to be pretty far back in the bush to do it safely, but it's one of the greatest joys known to man.

LIGHTING

FLASHLIGHTS
$2 - $18
Most backpackers will carry at least one source of light, and the flashlight is by far the most common type. They are usually compact, self-contained, and generally reliable. Either two AA size or two C or D size batteries are used.

The lightest and most compact flashlight is the Mallory, a flat, plastic job which uses two AA alkaline batteries (included). It throws a fairly good beam of light for its size—but don't drop it too far or let it get wet. The sides press-fit together, and once opened, all manner of parts can fall out. Might be hard finding them in the dark. It has no particular moisture-proofing. The Mallory (with its batteries) sells for $2.59 and can be obtained from Moor & Mountain, Ski Hut, REI and EMS.

There are a heck of a lot of conventional flashlights, using either two C or D cell batteries. While they weigh more, they are usually more durable, though resistance to moisture is still a problem on most. Moor & Mountain offers two waterproof flashlights. One is made of a rubber-jacketed metal and uses two D cells. It has a spare bulb and holder built in. Weight is 9 ozs. and it costs $4. The other is a plastic model using rubber gaskets to eliminate moisture. It weighs 4 ozs. and uses 2 C cells; price is $3.

Lately, a few really excellent flashlights have been adopted by backpackers. These are machined from aluminum or molded of unbreakable plastic with Lexan lenses, waterproof switches, and O-ring seals on all threaded parts. They can be run over with a car and not break. Cops have been using the longer 6- and 7-cell versions for a combination light and billy club. Moor & Mountain offers the Pro-Light, molded of cycolac plastic. It contains a spare bulb and a replaceable switch. The Pro-Light uses 2 D cells and weighs 8 ozs., empty; price is $18.

The Kel-Lite is machined aluminum and completely waterproof, with a spare bulb in the base. It comes with a lifetime warranty for the original owner. Weight, empty, is 4 ozs. for the 2 C cell model. Price is about $12 and it's available from Ski Hut, EMS and REI.

Herretts Stocks, Inc., Box 741, Twin Falls, Idaho 83301, sells the Hi-Lite, very similar to the Kel-Lite above, including warranty. Price for a 2 C cell model is $19.

While the above flashlights represent a considerable investment, you should only have to buy one unless, of course, you lose it. Unfortunately, none of the above have a lanyard ring to help prevent loss.

HEAD LAMPS
$6 - $11
Head lamps are frequently used by mountaineers, rock climbers, and those whose nighttime activities require having both hands free. They weigh no more empty than a regular-sized flashlight and can make night chores more convenient. A head lamp consists of a light fixture mounted on an elastic headband; a battery pack is carried on the belt or in a pocket, and current is supplied by a cord running between the two. An advantage of a head lamp over a hand-held lamp is that the battery case may be kept warm in an inside pocket. This will greatly improve battery power and the quality of light in cold weather. EMS and Ski Hut sell the Justrite ($9; 10 ozs., empty) and the Wonder ($7; 6 ozs., empty). Both lamps feature a focus for the beam, from a narrow spot to wide illumination. The Justrite case takes four D cells, which adds considerably to its weight. The Wonder lamp takes a special Wonder battery, which is not readily available at most places. The Wonder lamp is more versatile in that the battery case has its own attached lamp. The head lamp and cord can be detached and the battery case becomes a self-contained flashlight. Mountain Safety Research, 631 S. 96th St., Seattle, Wash. 98108, offers an interesting conversion of the Wonder lamp. The standard battery has been eliminated and either two alkaline C cells or one lithium D cell may be used. A lithium D cell costs $8, but it will supply 3 to 4 times as many light-hours as the alkaline battery. The conversion without battery costs $11. The total package may be expensive, but it looks worth it in the long run.

CARBIDE LAMP
$12
This old caver's stand-by may have its uses for backpacking trips.

Carbide lamps provide a bright, diffuse light and will burn for 2½ hours on a charge of calcium carbide (about $2 for 2 lbs.). The lamps are mechanically simple and reliable. Spare parts should include a tip, felt filter, lighter flint, and tip cleaner. The lamps are fairly heavy (9 ozs.) and carbide must be carried. About 1 oz. per hour of light is a general rule. In addition, spent carbide must be carried out. It is poisonous to plant and animal life. (Premier lamps are the best currently available [EMS, $10], although an old brass Justrite or Autolight are better, if you can find one.) See a more detailed explanation in the Caving section.

Liquid light

Candle lantern, 1 ea.

French candle lantern

CANDLE LANTERNS
$4 - $10
Lightweight and cheap to use, these little numbers are great for illumination and, during cold weather, some added warmth inside a tent. They use styrene candles (dripless and smokeless) which burn for several hours and cost about 10¢ each. The folding variety of lantern may be placed on its base or suspended (Moor & Mountain, 8 ozs., $7). The round telescoping type must be suspended (REI, 5 ozs., $4). EMS offers a round variety which may be placed either way (5 ozs., $10). All are aluminum. The telescoping and round types have glass chimneys. The folding type has windows of mica, somewhat fragile.

LIQUID LIGHT
About $2
Recently available, these plastic tubes (6" x 1") work on the "firefly" principle of chemical fluorescence. By bending the outer tube, an inner tube containing a catalyst is broken. The resulting reaction provides a strong greenish glow for about 3 hrs., diminishing over the next 10 hrs. These could be useful for emergency situations. From Moor & Mountain (2 ozs.), $1.25.

BATTERIES
25¢ - $8
When most folks get hold of a flashlight, they generally continue to use the same battery-bulb combination. It works, surely, but it may not be the most functional. The greatest advance has been in battery types. The carbon-zinc battery is the most familiar and the most primitive. The alternatives are the alkaline cell and the lithium cell. One initial difference among these choices is that one lithium cell contains twice the working voltage (2.7 V) of the other two (1.3 V). Below are comparisons of weight, efficiency at 20° F., and price:

	Weight (ozs.)	Efficiency at 20° F.	Price
1 Lithium D Cell	2.8	96%	1 for $7.75
2 Alkaline D Cells	9.5	15%	2 for $2.00
2 Carbon-Zinc D Cells	6.0	5%	2 for $ .50

It becomes apparent that the lithium cell is lighter, more efficient and—more expensive. However, the working life of a lithium cell is about 3 to 4 times that of an alkaline cell, and the alkaline about 10 times that of the carbon-zinc; so, the advantages tend to outweigh the disadvantages. Also, lithium cells don't fade. They retain peak brightness for 90% of their life. Alkaline cells fade to half-brightness after a short time. Since flashlights and head lamps are equipped to handle 2 or 4 batteries, MSR sells dummy C and D cells to take up the extra

room lithium cells provide. They cost 75¢ each. Two lithium cells can be used, but require the type of bulb used in standard 4-cell flashlights.

MSR and EMS both sell lithium and alkaline batteries and a variety of bulbs suitable for both. Their catalogs contain charts for determining candle power, bulb and battery life.

CAMP TOOLS

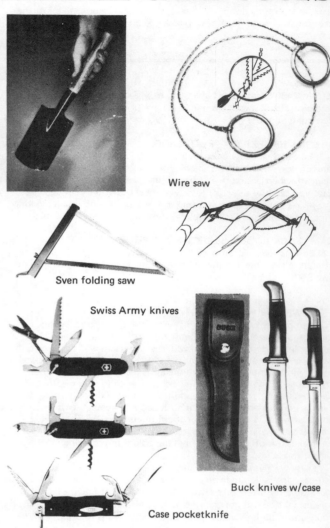

Wire saw

Sven folding saw

Swiss Army knives

Buck knives w/case

Case pocketknife

TOOLS
Contrary to what the catalogs tell you, the only tool the backpacker really needs is a good, heavy-duty pocketknife. Not a machete or a Bowie, but a pocketknife. Ideally, it should have two blades, and maybe a can opener, although many prefer the P-38 opener (see Field Kitchen) to those found on most pocketknives.

Swiss Army-style knives are extremely popular with outdoorsmen everywhere. Not only can you get your two blades and a can opener, but they also make models incorporating screwdrivers, tweezers, saws, files, magnifying glasses, toothpicks, fishhook disgorgers, ad infinitum. Many of these are a bit absurd; but if you're into gadgets, it's the only way to go. Victorinox is the best make of Swiss Army knives available. As it happens, these are also the people who supply the Swiss army. They are available from most good outfitters, but beware of imitations—look for the name "Victorinox" engraved at the base of the large blade. The Ski Hut catalog lists the following popular Victorinox models: Bijou, one blade and three tools (¾ oz.), $9; Pioneer, two blades and five tools plus lanyard ring (2.5 ozs.), $8, Spartan, two blades and nine tools (2.25 ozs.), $11; Champion, two blades plus everything conceivable (5.25 ozs.), $29.

For those more interested in just a cutting tool (that's a knife), there are lots to choose from. Names such as Case, Buck, Gerber, Henkels, and Kabar all offer a selection of both folding and sheath knives. Sheath knives may look flashy but they are also heavy. If you really want to carry one, get a light one like the Gerber Shorty from Ski Hut (7.5 ozs.), $18, or the Buck Personal from REI (7 ozs.), $16.

For those wanting a folding knife, the classic is the old Boy Scout style as made by Case. It has one blade, an awl, screwdriver-bottle cap lifter, and can opener and is available from REI at $7 and weighs only 4.5 ozs. Other good choices include: Henkels' Folding Knife, from Ski Hut (3.5 ozs.), $15; Gerber's Sportsman III, also from Ski Hut (12 ozs.), $30; and, of course, the Buck Folding Hunter, available everywhere (8 ozs.), $22. Regardless of which you choose, if you keep it sharp, don't use it for a screwdriver unless so designed, and don't lend it out, your knife should give you years of service.

Gone are the days of cutting bough beds and poles for erecting tents, digging trenches around tents, and all those other environmentally unsound practices that our fathers could get away with because they knew no one would see the scars for five years. With the heavy traffic now seen in most back-country areas, nothing, and we mean NOTHING, should be done to harm the wilderness, because there are, as we now know, others as well as mother earth to consider. So, you don't really need things like axes, shovels, and such. With them, you only have a greater potential for ruining the landscape.

There are other tools that may be of value to the backpacker. A small trowel (like those used by gardeners) is useful for covering up fire scars and digging latrines. Moor and Mountain sells one (2 ozs.) for 50¢. People used to use a stick for this, but times change. If you camp in the winter alot, you may want to consider carrying a snow shovel. They're useful for digging drifting snow from around tents, digging snow caves, if you prefer them or need one in an emergency, leveling a platform for a tent, and as a bonus, they make great anchors for tent guylines in snow. A good snow shovel with detachable 14'' ash handle (1 lb. 5 ozs.) is sold by EMS for $11. Last, but not least, you might want to consider carrying one of the ultralight wire saws for cutting small pieces of wood for the occasional small campfire. Ski Hut has one that weighs just ½ oz. and sells for $2. Be sure you get, or make, a case of some sort in which to carry these guys, as they are hell on nylon pack material if carried loose in a pack pocket. Before you jump into the accessory end of backpacking, consider very carefully what you need in the way of tools other than a good sharp pocketknife.

DUDS

Other than a poncho for keeping off the rain, backpacking requires little in the way of specialized clothing. Any rugged clothing lying around the house will do for most outings except winter ones.

Goodwill stores, the Salvation Army, thrift and surplus stores are all good sources of quality shirts, pants, sweaters and hats at reasonable prices. Many folks throw away some awfully good stuff, and if you're willing to scrounge a little to save some bucks, you can find some amazing buys in these places. I recently got a 100% Australian wool sweater for 25¢ at a Salvation Army store in Virginia.

Another good way to save money on clothing, especially down gear, is to get one of the many kits on the market and sew your own. This presumes you're handy with a sewing machine. If not, look around, you can usually find someone to help with sewing a kit. Frostline, Carikit and EMS kits are the best known of the sew-your-own companies. Kits come with all the materials necessary to do the job—complete instructions, precut fabric, thread—the works.

If you buy ready-made backpacking clothing, be sure to check for quality, as most of the stuff is quite expensive, and some of it can be a real rip. The more specialized items like ponchos, down jackets, wind shirts, chaps, and such, should be as well constructed as your tent, sleeping bag or pack—the same construction criteria apply. Most of the weights mentioned in the following discussions are for average sizes, and the prices given may fluctuate with the whims of the manufacturer or the seasons. Speaking of seasons, check out the end-of-season sales for some good buys at your larger retailers.

The Layer System. Many layers of light garments will trap more dead air than one heavy one, and that's what comfort on the trail is all about. With layers of clothing, you can regulate your comfort by adding or removing a layer or layers as the temperature and activity dictate. Looking at it from a warmth-for-the-weight point of view, you're ahead weightwise by using this method and, excepting down gear, you get greater versatility from your clothing.

The following discussion deals mainly with ready-made items as found in outfitters' catalogs. Needless to say, in many cases, you can find good alternatives to the items mentioned by doing a little scrounging.

Duofold long johns

Net underwear

UNDERWEAR
$5 - $22

The basis for the layering system of keeping warm is underwear. Traditionally, Norwegian net underwear has been the standard, but many other types are also popular. Wool is best for winter conditions; however, it's expensive and often hard to come by—and the damn stuff can drive you up a wall with itching, if you start getting a bit warm.

Net-type underwear insulates on the dead-air principle, though the cotton material it's made of readily soaks up perspiration and gives the wearer that cold, clammy feeling when activity ceases. REI offers a wool, net undershirt (no pants) (8 ozs.), for $8. Regular cotton, net underwear is available from most outfitters. Pants and shirts run about $5 and weigh 9 ozs. and 8 ozs., respectively.

If you can stand it, 100% wool underwear is about the best you can come up with. Often available at surplus stores are GI surplus union suits in gray wool for about $6. They're scarce, but worth the effort to find. Janus makes a set of underwear in 58% wool and 42% nylon that reportedly doesn't itch. Color is navy and it's available in both men's and women's sizes; tops weigh 11 ozs. and bottoms, 9 ozs.; cost for either is $14 from Ski Hut. Stil-longs are an 85% wool, 15% orlon outfit offered by EMS. Men's are navy, women's, blue; price is $14 from EMS. If you're really into luxury, then Angora Sports Underwear is for you. Made from 20% Angora, 45% lamb's wool and 35% acrylic, it is reputed to be some of the best long underwear in the world. Advertising claims it will absorb 40% of its own weight in moisture, and is sure to keep you warm no matter how hard you're working. Men's and women's sizes are available in white or blue; weight is only 6 ozs. for top or bottom, and they're priced at $20 and $22, respectively, from EMS.

Duofold underwear is a layered material with cotton next to the skin and a wool, cotton and nylon material on the outside. Duofold is supposed to be quite absorbent, and traps warm air between the layers to insulate. Two types are available: the straight Thermal Duofold sells for $9 for tops and bottoms, and the Mount Everest, which has a higher wool content in the outer layer, sells for $11 for the tops and $10 for the bottoms. Weight on either is about 11 ozs. for the tops and 9 ozs. for the bottoms; from Ski Hut.

You'll also see down insulated underwear in many of the catalogs; however, they're not much for backpacking, unless it would be for wearing around camp at night, and I doubt that many would find the weight equal to the luxury.

SHIRTS
50¢ - $35

Shirts can encompass everything from 50¢ T-shirts to the $35 wool-lies. For the most part, any shirt will do for the usual summer trip. Many folks like the Chambray work shirts as sold by Moor and Mountain (8 ozs.), $7, or at Sears for $5.

Most backpackers carry a wool shirt of some sort for that occasional drop in temperature, wearing around camp in the evenings, and always in the winter. Light wool shirts are generally to be preferred to the Alaskan type, and for the given weight, a light shirt

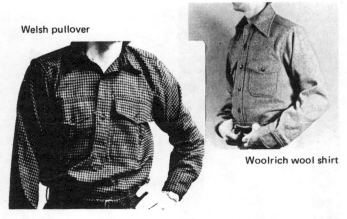

Welsh pullover

Woolrich wool shirt

and sweater give you more versatility than one heavy shirt. Woolrich and Pendleton are the usual shirt offered by most outfitters. EMS has Pendletons (1 lb.), for $28, and Ski Hut offers the Woolrich Ranger (22 ozs.), for $20. If you have trouble keeping it tucked in, the Joe Brown shirt from Wales is worth looking at. It's a pullover with super-long tails. Austral Enterprises sells them for $25 and The Gendarme has them for $22. (See Index.)

Chamois cloth shirts are available most everywhere, and are extremely popular with many folks. They sell for around $16 everywhere.

Oiled wool sweaters (10W30)

SWEATERS
50¢ - $50
There are all sorts of sweaters available in most every catalog, and at sports shops, clothing stores, and the Goodwill or equivalents. Wool is to be preferred, as with shirts, since it is warm even when wet. Light to medium weights seem to be the best, but some people prefer the heavy, oiled wool sweaters for wear in really wet or damp areas like the Pacific Northwest. Style is a matter of preference, but open or V-necks should be avoided because they don't protect your neck very well. With a little experimentation, it shouldn't take too long to find what suits you.

SHORT PANTS
$0 - $22
Being basically cheap ourselves, we prefer the zero price tag on our shorts. This means cut-offs. Seems like a lot of others think the same way, as you see a lot of 'em on the trail. All you need is a worn-out pair of jeans and some scissors or a pocketknife—et voilá!

For the sportier look, there are cotton stretch shorts, denim shorts, twill shorts, canvas shorts, and so on. The main thing to consider is weight and durability. The number of pockets is up to you, but we can't find a pair with more than seven (including a watch pocket). Flaps over the rear pockets are a nice feature to look for, as is a double seat (for sitting on rocks) which adds considerably to the wearability factor. Some shorts you might want to look at include: British Corduroy Shorts (12 ozs.), $22, from Ski Hut; Rough Rider

Bavarian Shorts (12 ozs.), $11, from REI; and EMS's twill Trail Shorts (10 ozs.), $13. For you gals on the trail who are tired of being caught with your pants down, there's a pair of shorts on the market with a Velcro crotch; price tag of $18 seems a bit much, though, when you consider how easily and cheaply a pair of cut-offs can be modified to achieve the same results. And unless girl's underwear manufacturers adapt their construction to the same idea, the Velcro crotch won't really solve a thing—will it. Another problem apparently missed by Q-P Pants—the manufacturer—is, what happens during a rough-and-tumble hike when the young lady stoutly swings her leg up high for a foothold? Hmmm, betcha a lotta guys'll be going on that hike.

Q-P pants

Knickers

Hiker's shorts and trousers

LONG PANTS
$5 - $30
Everything from jeans to army pants is seen on the trail nowadays and the catalogs abound with trail pants of all sorts. Cotton or a cotton blend is perfectly adequate for most outings except during winter, and for that we suggest wool. Add about 25% to the cost of most shorts and you'll be in the ball park on pants prices. Here's where a run to the Goodwill store can really pay for itself.

KNICKERS
$19 - $45
Allowing more freedom of movement than long pants, these ¾-length britches are available in many different fabrics. Not much weight is saved over long pants, as you need to carry long, knicker socks for colder weather. One advantage of knickers is that they're cooler than long pants, and if left open at the gathering below the knee, they can provide a lot of ventilation when the going gets warm on those long uphill slogs. Knee closures are usually either Velcro or a buckle and strap, although if you get lucky, you may find a pair that laces at the knee. Some knickers designed for climbers are really rugged and have double seats and knees. Cost of knickers is slightly more than the ordinary pair of trail pants, but if you're economy-minded and handy with needle and thread, you can make a great pair of knickers from old, wool army pants found at most surplus stores.

Poncho

Rain suit

Pack poncho

Anorak

Wind parka

Wind pants

RAIN GEAR

There are all kinds of plastic, rubberized canvas, coated nylon and coated cotton materials used in the construction of rain gear these days. The one thing that everybody has been trying to lick for years, though, is the condensation problem. So far, coated nylon is the predominant material used in ponchos, cagoules and anoraks. It definitely keeps water out, but it's also terribly prone to condensation. The newest thing to get around this is a material called Goretex. According to what we've read and seen in the way of tests, Goretex could be the answer to the problem of drowning in your rain gear while keeping out the rain. Synergy Works has pioneered the use of Goretex in waterproof gear for climbers, and has published a twenty-page report on this amazing "microporous polymeric film of polytetrafluoroethylene (PTFE)" (feel like you just had your jaw jacked, huh). For more information, write to Synergy Works, 6440 Valley View, Oakland, Calif. 94611. If any of you have had experiences with Goretex fabric garments, we'd like to hear about them.

Rain Pants (Chaps) and Shirts (Parkas), $4 to $125. If you're really concerned about keeping out the rain, then pants, chaps and rain jackets are about as effective as foul-weather gear comes. These garments, most of which are made of urethane-coated nylon, have one drawback, in that condensation is severe if you are doing any strenuous activity; so look for good ventilation features to help dissipate that water vapor (supposedly Goretex garments don't have this problem). Between the chaps and the shirts, chaps seem to have the most practical application for the backpacker traveling through wet brush. Prices run from $4 to $28 for rain pants or chaps, and from $10 to $125 for rain jackets or parkas. Rain shirts usually lack a hood, whereas parkas have one; both are available with pockets of some sort. If you wear a rain shirt, you'll probably want to buy a rain hat of some kind, $3 to $15. REI has several rain hats and they, as well as Ski Hut, EMS, Moor and Mountain, Holubar, and Sierra Designs, offer rain pants, chaps, parkas and rain shirts in various styles and price ranges. And if you're for trying the new Goretex, contact the Synergy Works.

Ponchos, $5 to $25. This is the most versatile garment a backpacker can own. It can be used as a raincoat, shelter or a ground cloth; and because it is open at the sides, it offers very good ventilation preventing condensation. Most ponchos for backpacking are made of coated nylon, about 2.5 ozs. in weight per yard, and most have snaps along the side for closing against windblown rain or combining with another to make a large shelter. Grommets at the corners and a hood are also standard on most good ponchos. The most popular type covers not only the wearer, but also his pack by being longer in the back. There is a provision for taking up the extra material, by way of snaps, if worn without the pack. Weights run from 10 ozs. to about 1 lb. 9 ozs. or so. Available from any and all dealers. Don't use a poncho for a ground sheet, if you expect it to last very long; they can turn to holes easily.

SHELL CLOTHING
(Wind Pants and Shirts, Parkas and Anoraks)
$5 - $62

The purpose of shell clothing is to keep wind from penetrating the dead-air space created by the layers of clothing underneath. For the most part, these items are water-repellent rather than waterproof as they are also designed to breathe. They're not supposed to keep out the rain (use rain gear), but the wind. The simplest form of wind protection is thin, tightly-woven nylon pants and jackets. REI has both lightweight wind jackets and pants (8 ozs.) for $9 each. EMS sells wind shirts and pants in kit form for $14 and $11, respectively.

For heavier duty, wear a wind parka or anorak of either ventile, nylon or 60-40 cloth (a blend of 60% cotton and 40% nylon). Both of these garments have hoods and they are heavier on the average than the ultralight nylon versions. The parkas have a full-length front zipper, and usually abound with pockets. Both pockets and zippers should have either snap or Velcro-closing storm flaps. Anoraks are a pullover version of the parka, and if they have a zipper, it's usually a short one at the throat for ventilation. Kangaroo pockets (a pouch on the upper front) seem to be standard on anoraks and should be covered by a storm flap. Both of these garments are hip-length in the best designs, and have drawstrings at both the waist and hood. Sierra Designs sells the Original 60/40 Mountain Parka. It has seven pockets, is double-layered throughout, has an extremely well-designed hood, and is tough as hell. At 1 lb. 12 ozs., it sells for $62 and is worth every penny. REI sells an English Ventile Anorak, which is fully lined with Egyptian cotton. This is an extremely windproof garment, though a little on the heavy side. It has three pockets and a drawstring at the hood and waist (2 lbs.), $45. EMS sells several models of parkas in kit form; the nicest appears to be the EMS All-Weather 60/40 Shell Kit. At 1 lb. 5 ozs. and $18, this looks like a good bargain for those who would rather sew their own.

For those of you looking for heavy-duty wind pants, best bet is to check the surplus stores. There are military combat fatigues available in a 60/40 ripstop material that is incredibly tough. They come with two cargo pockets and drawstrings at the cuffs. Sorry, camouflage only, about $8.

Balaclava

Crusher hat

Watch cap

Akubra sheepherder

HATS
$1 - $35

For protection against sun, rain, cold or wind, you need a good hat. Felt hats are hard to beat for versatility. Any high-crowned hat with a brim of from 2½" to 4" will serve for most of the above purposes. Moor and Mountain has the ever-popular Crusher hat for $4. For those of you who are really into hats, you might want to take a look at the Akubra hats imported by Austral Enterprises. These are the Australian version of the Stetson and are truly a dandy of a buy.

There are seven different styles ranging in price from $27 to $35. For cold weather or winter use, a wool Balaclava can't be beat. They're of Scottish origin and can be worn rolled up like a watch cap or pulled down to protect the neck and face. Balaclavas come in both wool and synthetic models, with the wool to be preferred; available from most backpacking and climbing shops for around $5.

If you have a hard time keeping your head warm, you might want to look at Eddie Bauer's down insulated caps. Their Arctic Cap (5 ozs.) sells for $21.

GLOVES
$1 - $10
Many folks often carry work gloves of some type to protect the hands while working around camp gathering firewood and such. Any lightweight work glove is adequate. For working in cold temperatures, especially when handling metal objects or manipulating a camera, thin nylon or silk gloves are good worn under mittens. They'll protect your hands if you have to do something that can't be done with your mittens on—and keep your fingers from freezing to metal objects. Ski Hut sells a silk glove liner (1 oz.) for $9. If you find that silk gloves don't provide enough tactile sense, then fingerless gloves may be the way to go. We've found them to be invaluable for fly-fishing in cold weather. It's really hard to tie knots in fine leaders with silk gloves. Fingerless gloves are available in all wool (4 ozs.) at $5 from The Gendarme. Also available are Millar Mitts, which have a wool back for warmth and a treated cotton knit on the palm for a better grip. Millar Mitts (4 ozs.) are available at most outfitters for around $11.

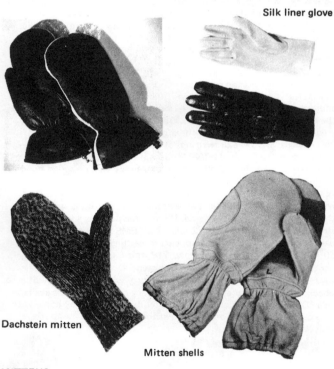

Silk liner glove

Dachstein mitten

Mitten shells

MITTENS
$4 - $13
Because they keep the fingers together, mittens are warmer than gloves. Wool, again, is the most common and desirable material. Dachstein Mitts are some of the finest (6 ozs.), $11, from most outfitters. Forrest Mountaineering recently came out with a mitten with a wool pile lining and a knitted wool outer shell. Weight is about 7 ozs. and they sell for $8. Available from Forrest Mountaineering (see Climbing—Sources of Gear for address). For those who get really cold hands, down mittens may be the answer (see Winter Bivouacking).

MITTEN SHELLS
$5 - $12
Wind can cut right through a wool mitten, and to keep it out, you need a mitten shell. The most economical is the old GI gauntlet mitts with leather palm, long gauntlet, and index-finger slot for shooting a camera or AR-15. These can usually be picked up at surplus stores for around $4. Most manufacturers of outdoor clothing make a mitten shell. Some you might want to look at are: EMS Mitten Shell

(5 ozs.), $7; Sierra Designs (2½ ozs.), $9; and REI's Leather Palm Overmitt (3 ozs.), $8.

———————— FOOTWEAR

BOOTS
$20 - $100
If you walk very much with a pack on your back, it won't be long before you decide to invest in a pair of good boots. Tennis shoes are O.K. for short outings, but once you progress beyond the weekend hike stage, you'll want something a bit more on the sturdy side.

Although boots won't be your most expensive piece of gear, they'll surely be your most important. Deciding what style, weight and, most important, the size you need is going to be one of the toughest decisions on equipment you must make.

There are a lot of boots on the market suitable for backpacking and some not so suitable. There are lightweight boots, heavy boots, flexible boots and stiff ones. There are also high-altitude mountaineering boots and, believe it or not, some folks wear them in the summer to backpack in. What we're concerned with here is a boot suitable for hiking, priced in the $20-to-$100 range. If you're looking for a climbing boot, check out the Climbing section.

Construction. Leather is the primary material used for making hiking boots. It will be either chrome-tanned or oil-tanned. Chrome-tanned is preferred, because it holds its shape better and is stiffer than the more supple oil-tanned, which is often used for harness making. Medium- and heavyweight boots will be made from full-grain leather, which is just that—a full thickness of the cowhide. For the uppers of lighter boots, split-grained leather is used. The thinner, lighter leather for these boots is obtained by taking a full-grained piece and splitting it into layers called (not surprisingly) splits. Split-grained leather, being thinner than full-grained, is not as waterproof, nor does it offer the protection and support the thicker, full-grained leather will.

Full-grained leather and certain splits have a smooth and a rough side to them. The smooth surface provides a waterproof barrier. It is usually placed on the upper part of the boot with the rough side out (hence the term "rough out") to protect it from damage. Your better and more expensive boots will have the upper made of a single piece of full-grained leather with the rough side out. By using one piece of leather the number of seams (read: weak points and leaks) is reduced to a minimum. Generally, the fewer seams a boot has, the better it is—the best only have a seam running up the back of the boot. Where there are seams at the instep and toe area, they should be double- or triple-stitched. The tongue of the boot should also be an integral part of the boot's upper, and not stitched in.

For protection, the heel and toe areas of the boot should be relatively stiff or rigid. Trails in many areas can be rocky and, after a day on a rough section, a stiff toe and heel will be much appreciated. The toe section is usually protected by thick leather and the heel by either a fiber or leather heel counter.

To protect the foot from the stitching inside the boot, a soft leather lining is sewn in many models. In addition to the liner, many boots have foam padding at the heel, ankle and tongue areas for added comfort and protection. For protection of the boot itself, extra thicknesses of leather are sometimes sewn over the toe and heel and are called caps.

The height of the boot is an important thing for the hiker to consider. If a boot is lower than six inches, the ankle is exposed to roots, rocks and snags. If it's much higher than 8", it will restrict comfort by constricting the lower leg and adding unneeded weight. So what we end up with is an ideal boot height of about 7" or 8". Some boots come with a scree collar or cuff which is supposed to help keep pebbles and dirt out of the boot. They do this pretty well 'til they bag out (loose their elasticity).

On heavy mountain boots, D-rings and speed laces are about all that's available in the way of hardware for lacing. On some light- and mediumweight hiking boots, eyelets are available, and are to be preferred. Hooks tend to snag on things and break off in rugged terrain, and sometimes they snag on the laces of the boots themselves, usually promoting a fall. Falls aren't funny with a fifty-pound pack. Neither is having a pair of boots that you can't tighten properly because of a couple of busted hooks that can't be fixed except by a cobbler. If you have to buy boots with lacing hooks, try to get a pair with only a few for tightening the ankle section of the boot. They'll give you less trouble than if they're located higher up.

Soles are fastened in various ways to the upper portion of the boot. Generally, any system which uses as many fastenings as possible on the inside of the boot is better than one using outside fastenings. (For more information on this, see "Climbing Footwear," by Steve Komito, *Climbing* magazine, July, 1970, pp. 15-17.) Sole material is almost exclusively of the neoprene lug type, today. Vibram is the most popular brand and has almost eliminated the nailed soles of old. Lugs hold pretty well on all surfaces, except for wet wood and ice, so be careful on logs over streams and strap on crampons for ice.

Selection. There are lots of neat boots and shoes for walking and, as such, the first thing to do, as with any other item you select for backpacking, is to determine what type of use it will get, and what you want the boot to do for you and with you. The general rule is: "the rougher the walking, the heavier the boot." Logic is the best guide. You don't need a heavy mountain boot to walk on the AT through Shenandoah National Park. Nor do you want a lightweight split-leather boot for the rugged trails of Colorado or Wyoming, where the walking can be over boulder fields and snow. Many times your choice will be a compromise or, if you can afford it, you may want to buy more than one pair for different conditions.

Once you've decided on the type, the proper fitting of the boot becomes your next concern, and an important one it is. Regardless of the quality you buy, the boot won't be worth a damn if it doesn't fit properly. Best advice we can give is to try on as many pairs as you can before deciding. After you've settled on a particular model, try on several pairs of the *same* size you believe to be a proper fit. Many boots vary a little from pair to pair in a given size, and one pair may feel better than another. Here are a few other guidelines that may be helpful in selecting and fitting.

When trying on boots, be sure to wear the socks you'll be wearing on the trail. With your toe against the front of the boot, you should be able to insert no more than two fingers and no less than one finger behind the heel of the foot. Next, lace up the boots. Check to see if they pinch or bind anywhere, especially at the ball of the foot. Kick something with the toe. If your foot slides forward, it's gonna do the same when walking downhill. If your toe hits the end of the boot, check to see if they're laced properly. If they are, it's probably a bum fit. Check the width of the boot carefully and decide if there's room for your feet to swell (they will after a long slog) or the addition of an extra pair of socks. Does the foot tend to roll around inside when you stand on the edge of the sole? If it does, try a narrower boot. When you think you've about got it, just stand around in the boots for awhile. Be sensitive to subtle pressures, the feel of the arch, the tightness of the ankle collar—and can you wiggle your toes. If you're convinced the boots fit, run through the whole process with a pair a size smaller and a pair a size larger to be sure. Don't get exasperated with this long, drawn-out process—it's important. The boot you decide on isn't going to be a nickle-and-dime investment. And once used, even if only for a short trip—the one that kills your feet—they can't be returned! So make sure they fit comfortably. Boots will stretch slightly during the breaking-in period and will conform to your feet. Initially, they should fit rather snugly, but comfortably, and give you support in the arch and ankle areas.

As we said, there are lots of boots on the market now. Below is a sampling from some of the better-known outfitters.

Children's Boots: Bambino—by Munari, fully lined and padded, nonscuffing sole, $29, from REI. Youth's Backpacking/Climbing Boot—made like pop's boots, good and rugged (2 lbs.), $27, from Moor and Mountain.

Lightweight Boots: Clarks Rhino—a canvas boot for those who prefer sneakers for the trail; upper is heavy canvas, cleated sole is bonded to upper; looks like an ideal boot/shoe for swamping; 7" high, $25, from EMS. Pivetta "Muir Trail"—a light trail boot made of one-piece suede leather; it has good padding and a steel shank; $50, from Ski Hut. Raichle offers the Zermatt in a lightweight boot for women. This is a really nice boot, and we know lots of packers who have used them and been well pleased; smooth, brown leather uppers with a Vibram sole, an outstanding buy at $45 from REI.

Mediumweight Boots: EMS Wasatch—made by Raichle, heavy full-grain, rough-out, leather upper, fully lined and padded; a good buy at $43, from EMS. Pivetta "5"—a smooth-finished boot very similar to the "Muir Trail," but of sturdier construction; fully lined, with a steel shank and a medium-stiff sole; $68, from Ski Hut. Cariolo—by Munari of Italy; lined and padded, hard toe; $44, from REI.

Heavyweight Boots: Pivetta "Eiger"—a heavyweight boot for tough treks and occasional mountaineering; full-grained, one-piece leather uppers, inside-fastened sole with no exposed stitching; $75, from Ski Hut. EMS Grimsel—full-grained leather upper, scree collar,

Pivetta 5

Muir Trail

Moor & Mountain Youth's Boot

Vibram lug sole

lug sole with steel shank; $55, from EMS. Galibier Super Guide—a mountaineering boot that's popular with many backpackers. Top quality in all respects, this is a fine piece of footwear, but it's pretty heavy and should be considered only for the most rugged of trips; $89, from most outfitters.

Ordering Boots Through the Mail
Don't!

O.K., so you're working out of Waterproof, Louisiana, and there's no trail shop nearby to visit (that's for sure!). What then? Well, you'd best be forewarned that buying boots sight-unseen can be one of the most exasperating experiences ever imagined.

With the proliferation of outfitters around the country now, it should be possible for most people to find a shop carrying boots, even a specific model. If this isn't true in your case (Waterproof), and you must order through the mail, the following tips may help to ensure a correct fit. First, you'll have to make a tracing of your foot. Put on the socks you plan to wear with the boots, and stand on a piece of paper on a hard surface (like, for example, the floor!) (John...you're a real wit.) and have someone trace the outline of each foot while you distribute your weight evenly between both feet. Be sure the pencil is held vertical, or if that's uncomfortable, perpendicular. On the tracing, be sure to mark any corns, bunions, or other anomalies, and on the same piece of paper list your regular shoe size, any measurements asked for by the mail-order dealer, and any other information you feel may be of help to the salespeople to fill your order. In most catalogs, there is ordering information, and it may vary from one outfit to another, so be sure you give all the information asked for. When the boots arrive, wear them around your house for a few days to make sure they fit. If you wear them outside and then decide they don't fit, you're out of luck, as no place allows the return of "used boots" no matter how little they've been used.

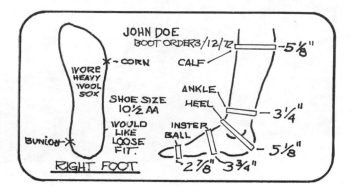

JOHN DOE
BOOT ORDER 3/12/72
— 5 1/8"
CALF
X—CORN
WORE HEAVY WOOL SOX
SHOE SIZE 10 1/2 AA
WOULD LIKE LOOSE FIT.
ANKLE
HEEL
— 3 1/4"
INSTEP BALL
— 5 1/8"
BUNION—X
RIGHT FOOT
2 7/8" 3 3/4"

Care of Boots

Boots are expensive items. In order to get long life and proper service from them, they must be well cared for. Drying wet boots probably destroys more of them than all other abuses combined. If your boots get soaked, hang them upside down and let them dry slowly in a well-ventilated place at room temperature. Heat of any kind, fires, ovens, heating ducts and such should be avoided, as exposure to direct heat cracks leather and breaks down the bonding materials used to secure soles and midsoles to uppers. For really wet boots, crumpled newspaper may be stuffed inside to help absorb the excess moisture, but be sure you don't leave it in the boot for a long period of time. Air needs to circulate within the boot to assure complete drying.

You'll want to put some type of boot dressing on your boots, both to preserve the leather and to help keep out the water. What you use will depend on the type of boot, the leather used and the tanning process used on the leather. Manufacturers recommend what they feel is best for their product, so it's hard to go wrong by following their advice. Most climbing and hiking boots are chrome-tanned and a silicone (wax) dressing is used on these, because it protects the leather without softening it. Sno Seal is the standard here. It's a paste wax that's best applied when slightly warmed to a semiliquid state. This allows the leather to absorb it easier. Leath-R-Seal is a liquid and is applied with a brush furnished in the container. Being a liquid, Leath-R-Seal is exceptionally well suited to application around welts

Wigwam
boot sox

and stitching. It flows into needle holes as well as being absorbed into stitching and leather alike. Although it costs more, Leath-R-Seal is preferred by many backpackers because it is not nearly as messy to apply as Sno Seal. Leath-R-Seal is $1.25 for an 11-oz. bottle, and Sno Seal is 95¢ for an 8-oz. can, both from REI. Oil-tanned boots are best treated with a quality boot oil or grease. Huberd's shoe grease is really good, 60¢ for a 7-oz. can, from REI. Pecards oil, $1.10 for 8 ozs., and Original Mink Oil, $2 for a 7-oz. jar, are also good for oil-tanned boots. Both are available from Moor and Mountain. Before applying any dressing to boots, be sure they are clean and dry. If they're dirty, an application of saddle soap will help remove a lot of the dirt that's been ground into the leather. After using the saddle soap, be sure to let the boots dry before applying any dressing. When your boots are cleaned and dressed for your next outing, store them in a cool, dry place. Keep the soles flattened with boot trees, if you can.

BOOT LACES (see Climbing section)

SOCKS

If you've ever walked far in boots without socks (100 yards is enough), you'll know they're important. Socks protect the feet from abrasion, the constant pounding of walking, and help absorb moisture. Wool seems to be the best, as it resists compression better than most materials, and is relatively warm even when wet. It also dries fast. Good wool socks should be several inches higher than the boots you're wearing, and for longer life, should have a nylon reinforced heel and toe, 'cause these areas tend to wear out fast. Some find wool to be too scratchy to wear next to the skin. The answer here is to wear either an inner sock of cotton, nylon or silk, or a wool sock with a high orlon or nylon content to cut down on the scratchy feeling. REI sells the Ripon Thermal Stretch (3 ozs.), for $2, and it's supposed to be excellent for those who can't stand wool. Solaris Silk Socks (1 oz.) are available from EMS at $4 for those looking for the ultimate in an inner sock.

Although "Wick Dry" is a trade name, there are lots of socks made of cotton, orlon, nylon and polypropylene blends that are supposed to wick moisture away from the feet into an absorbent outer layer. What happens when the outer layer gets soaked, they don't say (?). "Wicking" socks are available from the following: Wigwam Dry Foot Sock (12 ozs.), $1.65, from REI; Medium Wicking Socks (3 ozs.), $2.75, and Super Heavy Wicking Socks (5 ozs.), $3, both from EMS; Wick Dry (1½ ozs.) $1.95, from Ski Hut.

MISCELLANY

Believe it or not, a pack loaded with the essential components for a trip into the woods and mountains will always have a few empty nooks and crannies. These spots can be filled with various odds and ends and gizmos which may or may not be necessary to the backpacker's well-being.

Most people pack with an eye toward eliminating weight. The advantage of this is obvious. However, by the same token, there are items which, though not strictly necessities, are useful enough to con-

Bivouacking at Cathedral Lake Park, British Columbia. British Columbia Government Photo.

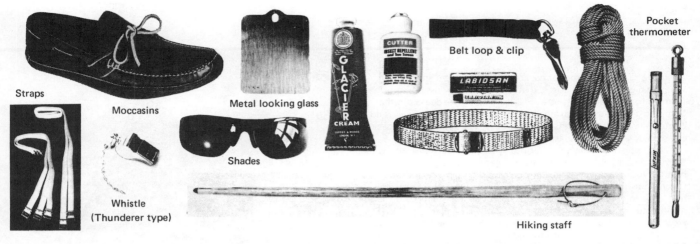

Straps

Moccasins

Metal looking glass

Shades

Whistle
(Thunderer type)

Belt loop & clip

Pocket
thermometer

Hiking staff

sider including with your kit despite the weight penalty. After all, the idea is to also have a comfortable trip, right? Right!

Belt Loop and Clip. A small cotton or nylon loop with an attached dog leash-type clip is useful for keeping frequently needed items handy. A compass, cup, pedometer, small camera, or monocular are all considerations. One can easily be made at home, or purchased from Ski Hut for 75¢.

Belt. Although not needing much introduction, beware—wide, thick leather belts with large metal buckles weigh a lot and will interfere with a backpack waiststrap. When the lower edge of a belt starts digging into the hips, the problem is apparent. A web belt with a small buckle (recommended is the Marine Corps-style buckle) will give a lot more comfort, and provide a convenient emergency strap for many jobs.

Camera. Personal preference here. Large, bulky cameras may take excellent photographs, but they weigh a lot. Instamatic types are cheap and light, but are limited in what they can do. A small 35mm, such as the Olympus, may be a good compromise. See Photography section for more info.

Cord. 1/8" nylon cord is a must for a variety of purposes. Use it to string up a tarp, suspend a food bag from a limb, tie stuff to the outside of a pack, and so forth. Fifty feet ought to do. Cost is about 3¢ per foot. EMS has a variety of diameters in 100-ft. lengths, running from $1.50 to $3.

First-Aid Kit. A must, if for no other reason than it's *the* place to carry moleskin for blisters. See the First Aid and Medical section for ideas and recommendations.

Hiking Staff. When the going gets rough, a lot of people end up wishing they had a third leg. A strong staff is just the ticket for maintaining balance on talus, among deadfalls, and when fording a stream. It can also be used as a support pole for a tarp, a prop for your backpack, and for goosing deer. An old hickory or ash rake handle about 50" long will do nicely. Holubar offers an ash staff in three lengths for $10.

Insect Repellent. If flies and mosquitos are around, there's going to be a hassle, period! Repellent can make quite a difference, especially when the backpacker has stopped. Cutters is one of the best at $1.75 for one ounce. Moor & Mountain carries the "Ole Time Woodsman's Fly Dope," a classic concoction, for $1.10 per 2 ozs.

Lip Protection. This may be necessary at higher elevations or in very dry conditions. Ordinary Chap Stick works well and will allow you to smile without thinking twice.

Moccasins or Tennis Shoes. After a 15-mile day, it's a real treat to slip into something soft. A pair of these may be in order. Moccasins are light and soft, and will give some protection from rocks, branches, etc. Tennis shoes, 'though heavier, give more protection. (Some folks hike in their tennies when the going is easy.) Tennis shoes may also come in handy for fording streams—to keep your boots dry (no, dummy, you don't put 'em on over your boots...!).

'Most everyone has tennis shoes—so let's check moccasins. They run anywhere from $10 to $40. Casco Bay Trading Post and L. L. Bean Inc., both of Freeport, Maine 04033, have good selections.

Monocular or Binoculars. Another luxury, but they're good for viewing wildlife or mountain route-finding. There are a number of good quality, lightweight binoculars on the market, but a monocular is cheaper, and one eye will see the same view as two—when it's a case of adding more weight to your pack. Kelty has a Bushnell 8-power monocular for $25. EMS offers the Zeiss 8-power for $100. Each weighs about 4 ozs. More about optics in the Land Navigation section.

Repair Kit. This ought to be a catchall for small repair parts and notions needed for a variety of purposes. Possible inclusions might be spare parts for a stove or carbide lamp, ripstop tape for patching down gear or tent, nylon thread and a couple or medium-sized needles for clothes, and spare bulbs for a flashlight. (Note: the stickum on ripstop tape doesn't work too well. It's better to take a little time and sew patches on.) The more complicated Swiss Army knives include a variety of potentially useful tools, such as scissors, awl, corkscrew, and so forth. Small, folding scissors are available from Ski Hut and REI for about $4. Ski Hut also offers a combination tool featuring pliers, adjustable wrench, and screwdriver for $6; it weighs 5 ozs. EMS has a sewing kit for $1, which contains thread, scissors, needle, pins, buttons and a thimble.

Straps. Straps serve several definite functions. A short strap can be used to hold the top and bottom parts of a cookset together. Longer ones are popular for attaching a sleeping bag to the bottom of a packframe. Any leather accessory patch sewn onto a pack is a potential site for strapping extra gear. Watch out for shock or Bungi cords—they work, but items can be pulled loose when walking through heavy brush. Nylon or cotton straps with metal buckles are available through most backpacking suppliers and generally cost 50¢ to 75¢ each.

Sunglasses. If your trip takes you through a lot of open areas or into snow-covered high country, sunglasses are a must. Snow blindness is painful and can impair vision for several days. While just about any type will do, a pair of glasses with hooked earpieces will prevent them from falling off your face. Prices run from el cheapo $2 types through the Mountain Spectacles (Ski Hut, $18) to Vuarnet glasses (Kelty, $30). Most good sunglasses will come with a hard, protective case—a must for protecting your investment.

Sunburn Cream. An effective sunburn preventive is essential at high altitudes due to the greater amount of ultraviolet light getting through the atmosphere. Ordinary zinc oxide ointment is cheap and is available at drugstores. Glacier creams are sold by REI and EMS from 80¢ to $2 per ounce.

Thermometer. Ever wonder how cold you were? Remove any doubt, but be sure the thermometer comes with a protective case. Most suppliers carry them, at prices ranging from $3 to $5.

35mm Film Cans. Good for stashing small parts, salt and pepper, and such. The older ones were aluminum; newer cans are plastic. Check around at camera shops or with photographer friends.

Toilet Kit. Some backpackers like to travel scroungy, others can't live with themselves if they do. Perhaps a bottle of Dr. Bronners Soap, toothbrush, metal mirror, small towel, and talcum powder could be considered a basic kit. Again, most suppliers sell all kinds of backpacker toilet articles for those who want light, compact equipment.

Water Purifiers. There are not many things worse than a case of the trots in the woods. When in doubt, purify your drinking water by boiling or adding a couple of Halazone tablets per quart. Halazone is found in drugstores, and costs about $2/bottle. Check the Survival section for packable water filters.

Whistle. Good for keeping track of someone who might have strayed, or drawing attention to yourself if in trouble. Make sure it's a loud one.

Writing Materials. If you feel the need to record observations, insights and experiences, a small notebook and pencil won't take up much room. Pens are O.K., but they've been known not to work when needed.

There are so many sources of backpacking gear, from small local shops to big mail-order houses, that it would be impossible to list them all in the space we have available. Most of the dealers in the Climbing, Ski Touring, Caving, First Aid and Medical, Survival, and Winter Bivouacking sections sell equipment of interest to backpackers, so check these places, too.

The discussions below are not nearly as complete as we would like them to be, so you'll have to write and get the catalogs you think will best fill your needs for detailed information on individual products. Often you will be able to find items on display in local shops, enabling you to make a firsthand evaluation of similar items by different manufacturers. We heartily suggest you do this, if you can. If you write to all the dealers listed in the *Source Book* who handle some sort of backpacking gear, you should have enough reading material to keep you wishing for many a cold winter evening. Most of the catalogs are free and where there is a cost involved we've tried to indicate such. As always, we would appreciate hearing from you about your experiences in dealing with the folks listed (and those not listed), and your comments on their gear, good and bad.

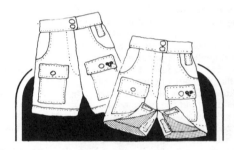

Q-P PANTS
3300 Atlantic Blvd., Jacksonville, Fla. 32207
This is the place to get those Velcro-crotch pants, girls! Available in denim or khaki at $18 a copy. Incidentally, Q-P has a contest running to see who can guess what Q-P means...and what their stylized Q-P logo symbolizes... What fun!

SWALLOWS' NEST
3320 Meridian Ave. North, Seattle, Wash. 98103
Backpacking and climbing gear. Nice little catalog.

EARLY WINTERS LTD.
110 Prefontaine Place South, Seattle, Wash. 98104
Manufacturers and retailers of down gear and accessories for the backpacker using Goretex for their external coverings. They claim you can have waterproof down gear that breathes(?). If you have any experience with this gear, we'd like to hear about it. They also have a Goretex tent, The Light Dimension, that weighs only 3½ lbs. and sells for $195. And for those of you who would like to make your own gear from Goretex, they sell both a 1.5-oz. and a 1.9-oz. Goretex laminate material at $1.75 and $1.95 per yard.

ALPENLITE
108 S. Spring St., Claremont, Calif. 91711
This outfit manufactures what they call a hip-carry wraparound frame. The Paczip is their deluxe bag and features a full zipper for access to the main compartment. Frame and bag are priced at just under $90. Catalog on request.

ALPINE DESIGNS
P.O. Box 3561, Boulder, Colo. 80303
Famous for their nice rucksacks and packs (the rucksacks still come with good leather bottoms), Alpine Designs gear is hard to beat. For a long while their gear was hard to come by, but now it's available at most outfitters (they no longer sell direct), and much of it is still very reasonable. Their catalog is worth writing for, even though it lacks certain pertinent information, like construction details.

ALPINE PRODUCTS
1309 Windward Circle, West Sacramento, Calif. 95691
Manufacturers of PolarGuard bags and jackets. Construction is said to be some of the finest around. Illustrated catalog on request.

ASCENTE
P.O. Box 2028, Fresno, Calif. 93718
Manufacturers of fine down gear, tents, shell clothing, and so on. They offer fourteen types of bags, and one of the few one-man tents around for $67 (2 lbs. 8 ozs.). Their gear is widely available in mountain shops, or you can order direct. Catalog is free.

CLEAR CREEK BACKPACKING & WILDERNESS SUPPLY
14361 Catalina St., San Leandro, Calif. 94577
These folks manufacture and sell one of the nicest and lightest three-man tents we've seen. The Mt. Shasta tent at 8 lbs., complete, sells for $188 and is backed by an unconditional guarantee on materials and workmanship.

EDDIE BAUER
P.O. Box 3700, Seattle, Wash. 98124
Most of what is offered in the Bauer catalog is of more interest to the gentleman sportsman than the backpacker. They do, however, manufacture some of the best down gear anywhere, and they also sell good tents and packs. Prices are not cheap, but their gear is all high-quality.

L. L. BEAN, INC.
997 Main St., Freeport, Maine 04033
Bean's shop is the only place we know of where you can go and buy a pair of boots anytime of the day or night—they're open 24 hours a day, 365 days a year. Most of what they sell for the backpacker is available from other dealers and a good part of their goods are geared towards the gentleman sportsman. Bean's 128-page catalog is really nice. It comes out twice a year. Everything they sell is backed by a 100% guarantee and the catalog is free.

BISHOP'S ULTIMATE OUTDOOR EQUIPMENT
2938 Chain Bridge Rd., Oakton, Va. 22124
Barry Bishop manufactures The Ultimate tents and the Bishop Packlite tents. Having traveled the world over and climbed Mt. Everest in 1963, he knows what tents are all about and what they should do out in the bush. The Packlite is the most applicable to backpacking, and The Ultimate is more for mountaineering. Prices are a bit steep, but the workmanship and materials are superb. Brochure runs 25¢.

THOMAS BLACK AND SON
225 Strathcona Ave., Ottawa, Ontario K1S 1X7, Canada
Black's no longer maintains a shop in the U.S. Although some of

sources of backpacking gear

their gear is rather traditional in design and materials, their down gear is excellent and not overly expensive. The catalog is free and, although it has been getting better year by year, they could still beef up their technical information.

CAMP 7
802 S. Sherman, Longmont, Colo. 80501
The Camp 7 folks specialize in high-quality and high-dollar down gear. They offer a complete line of down clothing as well as some of the best sleeping bags on the market. They also will do custom work. Send for free brochure.

CO-OP WILDERNESS SUPPLY
1607 Shattuck Ave., Berkeley, Calif. 94709
These folks offer the complete line of Jansport packs as well as Jansport and Eureka tents. They sell their own line of bags and jackets, and offer a choice of down or PolarGuard in both. Other items include a good selection of freeze-dried foods, and lots of backpacking accessories. Prices are average and the catalog is free.

EASTERN MOUNTAIN SPORTS (EMS)
1041 Commonwealth Ave., Boston, Mass. 02215
Probably the largest outdoor recreation supplier in the country, EMS has managed to maintain a fine reputation despite its bigness. They sell only top-quality gear. The illustrations and technical information in their huge catalog are the best of any we've seen, bar none. There are comparison charts to aid in the selection of packs, sleeping bags, tents, and so on. Not only does EMS carry most of the established brands of backpacking gear, but they also manufacture their own. Kits (EMS Kits) are also offered for the do-it-yourselfers. I doubt seriously that there's anything a backpacker could want that he couldn't find in this catalog. They have a fine offering at good prices and the catalog only costs a buck (but they seem to keep coming after you buy the first one); anyway, the information is worth that much.

EUREKA TENT AND AWNING CO., INC.
Box 966, Binghamton, N.Y. 13902
The Eureka people make everything in the way of tents. Of most interest to backpackers are the Exo-frame Blanchard-design tents and the new Aleutian. If you're into making your own tent, Eureka offers no less than 14 kinds of tent and awning material by the yard. Prices (remarkably) have remained reasonable over the years. Literature on request.

KELTY PACK, INC.
P.O. Box 639, Sun Valley, Calif. 91352
Kelty is another old and famous name in the backpacking equipment world. Kelty packs and frames have been used around the world (like on top of Everest) and have set a standard of performance that's hard to beat. The Kelty catalog, which is free, offers much more than just the Kelty line of packs. North Face, Alpine Designs, Camp 7, Gerry, Sierra Designs and other products are offered to round out the gear you can compare and select from. Quality of an item and not price seems to be the criterion for inclusion in the catalog, and if you buy from the Kelty folks you can be assured you're getting mighty good equipment. Kelty recently added two new bags to their packbag line: The Serac and The Tioga. If you've been looking for a larger-capacity bag for your Kelty frame, these are the way to go.

ADVENTURE 16
10064 Bert Acosta St., Santee, Calif. 92071
Best known for their packs and frames, which are of the hip-hugger suspension design. The frames are also custom fitted and can be altered to fit growing packers. They carry one style sleeping bag and two pack kits (for building your own) and manufacture two half-dome tents. Prices are about 15% below retail. Pamphlet available.

THE SMILIE CO.
575 Howard St., San Francisco, Calif. 94105
Not only do they maintain a full line of backpacking equipment and accessories, but they also have some mule packing gear complete with a 2-lb. gold pan; far out. Their own sleeping bags are featured, but they also carry some Sierra Designs bags. On a few things prices seem a little high. The catalog is 63 pages, illustrated, and costs 10¢.

PETER LIMMER AND SONS, INC.
Intervale, N.H. 03845
Peter Limmer and his sons make custom hiking and light mountain boots for backpackers. They're a bit of a status symbol in places, but are extremely good and exceptionally comfortable, as they are made exclusively to the individual's measurements. Limmer's brochure also lists other items, like packs and ropes and stoves, but boots are their mainstay. If you don't mind the wait, Limmer boots are worth the money; and this is about the only place to go if you've got odd feet.

PAK FOAM PRODUCTS
390 Pine St., Pawtucket, R.I. 02862
This outfit sells what is probably the best foam pad on the market for backpackers. It's made by sandwiching open and closed foam together to give you the advantages of both—a waterproof bottom layer and a breathable top one to lie on. Write for their free catalog.

CHARBON OUTFITTERS
257 W. Broad St., Athens, Ga. 30601
An outfitter in the Southeast that carries a good line: North Face, Trailwise, Mountain House, and so on. These guys ship all orders over $10 free and guarantee two-week processing with a refund on out-of-stock items. Write for their free catalog.

UPTOWN SEWING INC.
Box 700, Jackson, Wyo. 83001
Manufacturers of gear for winter travel. They also offer custom work, if your ideas are not too far out. The outfit is run by Pete Carman, the fellow who invented the Super Gaitor. Brochure is free.

THE NORTH FACE
Box 2399 Sta. A, Berkeley, Calif. 94702
The North Face is one of those outfits that started small and made it to the big time by producing high-quality sleeping bags, jackets, tents and packs. Most of their stuff is pretty good, and so's the other stuff listed in their catalog—Kelty packs, Buck knives, and so on. Prices on North Face gear seem to be a bit high when compared to

other makers, but the quality is generally high. Catalog, which is free, is very nice and product descriptions are excellent. You can also see their goods in many local shops.

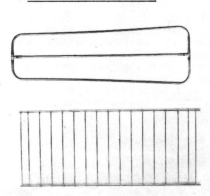

BACKPACKER GRILL
Lightweight tubular stainless steel. 5" x 15" (width tapers to 4") comes with nylon case.
Wt. 4½ oz. $6.75

SKI HUT
1615 University Ave., Berkeley, Calif. 94703
If you read much of Colin Fletcher's work, you'll soon find he is enamored with Trailwise equipment from the Ski Hut. He probably walks as much as any man alive, and expresses nothing but satisfaction with their products. All Trailwise stuff is good. You can't say much more, because it really is. They manufacture tents, packs, sleeping bags and clothing, and all of it is well presented in their catalog, along with a host of other good gear for mountaineering and backpacking by other makers. Costs sometimes seem a bit high; but if you talk with people who've bought Trailwise gear, they usually say it's worth the money. Their gear is well constructed, tough, and pleasing to the eye.

SNOW LION
P.O. Box 9056, Berkeley, Calif. 94701
Formerly Snowline, this outfit is now offering PolarGuard as well as down gear. They have a nice catalog that'll tell you some things you probably didn't know about down and PolarGuard. Their sleeping bags, both down and PolarGuard, are reasonable in price and backed by a good guarantee. They also have a pretty nice PolarGuard half-bag or *pied d'elephant*. Forty expeditions have chosen Snow Lion gear in the last year and that alone says something about the quality and reliability of the insulation system used in their bags and garments. Snow Lion gear is widely available at most outfitters, and their free catalog gives you all the dope on their equipment.

STEPHENSON'S
Box 398, Gilford, N.H. 03246
Much to the chagrin of many feminists, these folks sell their goods with sex, at least in their advertising. Products are the Warmlite tents, sleeping bags, some clothing, a pack and frame, and an inflatable raft for backpackers. They also sell fabrics, and some hardware and accessories. Stephenson claims his tent material breathes and, therefore, needs no fly; but we'll be interested in seeing what happens now that Goretex is on the market. So far it's been just about impossible to get a waterproof fabric that breathes, but maybe these folks have the answer. Anyway, their catalog of wonder equipment is free, so write for one.

COUNTRY WAYS
3500A Hwy. 101 South, Minnetonka, Minn. 55343
These people are strictly a kit company for outdoor folks with sewing ability. They specialize in PolarGuard insulated jackets, sleeping bags, mittens, booties and vests, and also sell shell clothing kits, like anoraks. They also sell a kit for a PolarGuard quilt. Prices seem reasonable, and they've got dealers in 50 cities across the U.S. Catalog is free.

FROSTLINE OUTDOOR EQUIPMENT
452 Burbank, Broomfield, Colo. 80020
One of the first and certainly one of the best quality dealers in kits for backpacking gear and clothing. See Winter Bivouacking Section.

NORTHWEST RECREATIONAL SUPPLY
P.O. Box 70105, Seattle, Wash. 98107
This outfit used to sell the Mountain Master packs (defunct). Their catalog now features Kelty, Mountain Products Corp. (sleeping bags, tents and clothing), and the Ascente line of bags and clothes. They have a good general selection of backpacking gear and accessories, including stoves and snowshoes, at pretty good prices. Catalog is free.

POWDERHORN MOUNTAINEERING
Box 1660, Jackson, Wyo. 83001
For those of you heading out to the Tetons, this place is a must to visit. They have current information on trail conditions in the park and surrounding area, as well as a good selection of backpacking and mountaineering gear. Run by outdoor folks, they sell top-quality gear only. Product literature on request.

TRAILTECH, Div. of Gibraltar Industries
10 W. 33rd St., New York, N.Y. 10001
Manufacturers of PolarGuard gear of very good quality. They have jackets, bags and shell clothing in their fall and winter clothing, as well as other backpacking items. Catalog is free.

HOLUBAR
Box 7, Boulder, Colo. 80302
Holubar is one of the oldest producers of down gear in the country. Roy and Alice set a standard of quality that has survived despite the growth of the company. Today, if you buy a Holubar bag or jacket you can be assured of getting top quality for your money. They use only the finest down and their designs are all time-proven. Construction is impeccable. They also sell tents, boots and climbing gear as well as a complete selection of accessories for the back-country camper. They offer kits through their Carikit division (see Winter Bivouacking), and we have heard excellent reports on the simplicity of these. You can order direct from the catalog or buy in any of their retail shops in the Denver-Boulder area. Catalog is free.

CHILD'S SLEEPING BAG — This bag is mummy shaped 22" x 68" filled with 1½ lbs. of 100% continuous filament fortrel polyester Polarguard. Single layer bat construction, full-length around the foot nylon zipper, snap closure and draw-string hood. Completely washable. For the 5—10 yr. old backpacker. Good to about 32° F.
Cat. No. 344: (Fits Med. stuff bag.)   Wt.: 2.38 .bs.   **$36.00**

MOOR & MOUNTAIN
63 Park St., Andover, Mass. 01850
Dealing in backpacking, ski touring, and paddling (canoe and kayak), Moor & Mountain handles their own line of sleeping bags, tents, packs and frames, down garments, and other clothing. They're a complete supplier of backpacking gear. The catalog comes out two times a year, is about 48 pages, illustrated, and free.

SYNERGY WORKS
255 Fourth St., Suite 2B, Oakland, Calif. 94607
Dan Sherman and his crew were one of the early users of Goretex. Their clothing is exceptionally well made, and the waterproof gear is just that—waterproof! They also manufacture a unique line of packs. Needless to say, high quality equals high dollar; but the gear these guys make is worth every penny. Unlike some manufacturers, they are interested in how their gear performs, and if you buy any of it, they'll be in touch for a product evaluation. It's nice to know someone cares about the opinions of the people who buy and use their gear. These folks seem not only genuinely concerned, but willing to listen to suggestions. Their catalog will cost you a buck, but it'll give you all the dope on the new Goretex material; it's interesting reading.

RECREATIONAL EQUIPMENT, INC. (REI)
1525 11th Ave., Seattle, Wash. 98122
REI is a well-known and long-established firm in the Northwest. Their store in Seattle is like a supermarket, and anyone into outdoor activities at all can while away many hours fondling gear there. This outfit is a true co-op. It costs you $2 to join and you get a 10% return on the total dollars spent during the year, around March of the following year—not bad. They manufacture and job out many of the items sold under their own label and offer a wide variety of other people's gear as well. Much of their gear, despite the low price, is of excellent quality; but, alas, some of it is exactly worth what you're paying. They have good prices on many items and, if you need only light-duty gear, some of the stuff is a real bargain. In recent years, though, the overall quality of their goods has gone up, mainly because of consumer demands and criticism. REI does offer the lowest prices around on many name-brand items; and they handle a great variety of gear for all outdoor activities, from paddling to climbing to ski touring to bicycling. As far as accessory-type items go, they've got one of the largest selections anywhere and offer great variety in both price and quality. They also offer some organized hikes and tours, if you're interested. Their 100-plus-page catalog is free.

SIERRA DESIGNS
Fourth and Addison Sts., Berkeley, Calif. 94710
It's hard to talk about backpacking gear without the name Sierra Designs coming up. They were the originators of the 60/40 Parka and still sell it in an updated version that's just as good, if not better than the original. They also manufacture down sleeping bags, down clothing, rain gear and tents. Their Glacier model tent is one of the best, most popular and reasonably-priced quality mountain tents on the market today. The catalog is a pleasure to read and offers equipment by Kelty, Buck, Sigg and a host of other manufacturers of accoutrements for the quality-conscious backpacker. They import a real nice bunch of sweaters (all-wool, of course), and also offer cross-country ski equipment. Catalog runs 50¢.

TODD'S
5 S. Wabash Ave., Chicago, Ill. 60603
Sells name brand shoes and boots, some of which (mostly of the Chippewa brand) are suitable for backpacking. A small illustrated 24-page booklet is free on request.

DON GLEASON CAMPERS SUPPLY, INC.
9 Pearl St., Northampton, Mass. 01060
Handles lightweight gear from Kelty, Ascente, Camp Trails and Gerry, at competitive prices. Gleason also has an awful lot of car and camper stuff—if you happen to need any for backpacking (?). Fat catalog of 100 pages for 50¢.

WILDERNESS EXPERIENCE
20120 Plummer St., Chatsworth, Calif. 91311
This outfit is run by Jim Thompsen, who used to work with Kelty some years back. Jim's specialty is packs and nothing else, and you can tell it by the craftsmanship that goes into the frames and packbags. Frames are made of 6061-T6 aircraft-quality aluminum with wall thickness of .049 in. All joints are heliarc-welded and then radiused to assure a perfect match at the weld point. Two types are available—the S-Frame and Wrap-around and include full-circumference padded hipbelts. Packbags to fit either frame are available in a front-opening or back-opening style made of 8-oz. Parapack. Thompsen also manufactures rucksacks and mountaineering packs, daypacks, flight bags and one style of bike-hiking bag. Prices range from $75 for pack/frame combo to $10 for the bike bag. A very detailed catalog s available on request to the above address.

ANTARCTIC PRODUCTS CO., LTD.
P.O. Box 223, Nelson, New Zealand
The guarantee is impressive: if you're not satisfied, you are refunded full purchase price plus postage, immediately. Sorry, no quality info to date. Antarctic carries two sleeping bags and some down clothing, down blankets, and wool sweaters. Send for free 17-page booklet.

GERRY, Div. of Outdoor Sports Industries, Inc.
5450 Valley Hwy., Denver, Colo. 80216
Gerry no longer sells mail order, but his unique gear is available almost everywhere. He has designed packs, tents, stoves, and many other pieces of gear, all of which have stood the test of time. The Gerry Himalayan tent is one of the best available, and their child carrier is the original design, which has yet to be equaled. Catalog of products upon request.

THE GENDARME
P.O. Box 15, Mouth of Seneca, W. Va. 26884
Heavy on climbing, light on backpacking (pun—smile!). Run by the Hole in the Wall Gang—Butch "Suds" Markwell and Sundance Livingston. No catalog.

Repair & Cleaning Services

DOWN EAST ENTERPRISES LTD.
93 Spring St., New York, N.Y. 10012
Down East is Leon Greenman's latest innovation to supply what appears to be the only service of its kind under one roof for the wilderness recreation fraternity. Leon calls it the "Outdoor Service Center." Objective is to provide cleaning, repair, maintenance and modification services for outdoor gear. Specialty is dry cleaning down bags and garments, which includes minor repairs of small rips, before cleaning, at no extra charge. The other services include repairing backpacking and camping gear—applying patches, grommets, hooks, straps and buckles—and resoling hiking, climbing and mountaineering boots, plus repairing hooks and eyelets.

Looks like just the ticket for those "Gee, who do I go to, to get *this* taken care of?"-problems. Have no data on prices, but write to Leon—he'll gladly provide you with info on the full scoop.

INSTRUCTION and EXPEDITIONS

Outward Bound

The following groups offer instruction and/or excursions for back-packers. We've only been able to provide a brief description of their operations and suggest that you write the ones you're interested in for complete details. Incidentally, for other groups that have backpacking-oriented activities check the Climbing and the Survival Sections.

ADIRONDACK MOUNTAIN SCHOOL, INC.
Long Lake, N.Y. 12847
Located near the six-million-acre Adirondack Park, the institution has a summer wilderness camping program (6 weeks, $800; 7 weeks, $850) for ages 11 to 16, and a special camping trip in Colorado and Wyoming for boys aged 14 to 16 years ($1000).

THE ASHEVILLE SCHOOL MOUNTAINEERING PROGRAM
Asheville, N.C. 28806
The Asheville School offers out-door activities in the form of backpacking, mountaineering and canoeing trips for girls and boys from 14 to 18 years of age. There are five trips during the summer that range from two weeks, $325, to three weeks, $325 to $750. Two of the trips are in Wyoming, one in northern Minnesota and two in the southern Appalachians. The school also has a mountaineer program during the regular school year to supplement their academic program.

BACKPACKING WITH BARROW
P.O. Box 183, Whitefish, Mont. 59937
Basically, Barrow has a five-day backpacking trip into the Bob Marshall Wilderness of Montana for $120 with equipment furnished and $90 without. Books and personal gear are not provided. There are also twelve-day trips in the same area for $270 with equipment and $195 without. Trips are during the months of July, August and September.

COOPERATIVE WILDERNESS ADVENTURES
Contact: Gary Grimm, Room 23, Erb Memorial Union
University of Oregon, Eugene, Oregon 97403
Here's a group which acts as a coordinating agent for wilderness trips conceived and planned by different individuals throughout western and midwestern U.S. and Canada. The idea is to offer low cost, cooperative wilderness excursions in which all participants can be involved in planning and expenses. The trip leader (someone who wants to get a group together) sends his schedule in to CWA and the proposed trip is presented in a calendar brochure called *Cooperative Wilderness Adventures.* This is mailed out to people who've gotten on CWA's mailing list. Next step is for those who want to go on a trip to contact the trip leader of the excursion they're interested in and get details, schedules, and so forth. Don't know whether CWA has gone east, but if you want to find out, write 'em. If you have a trip in mind that you'd like to get some other people involved in, work up the following particulars and send them to CWA:
   Initiating Person - Name and address.
   Destination
   Activities available
   Dates - Departing time and place, deadline for applying, returning
      time and place.

   Equipment List
   Cost
   Maximum number of participants
   Experience necessary
If you'd like to get the CWA trip schedules, which are published on a seasonal basis, write to the above address. As far as we know, there's no fee.
   Here's a couple of trips which were presented in the CWA brochure:

JULY 1-4   Seven Devils & Hell's Canyon, Idaho—Backpacking
Ernie Naftzger, 454 Fairmount, Pocatello, Idaho 83201. Family camping, hiking, photography, fishing. Departing from Pocatello 8 a.m. July 1. Maximum participants: open. Apply before June 23. No previous experience necessary.

JULY 12-19   Current River, South Central Missouri—Canoeing
Jackie Kerr, Route 3, Box 537, Springfield, Missouri 65804. Canoeing, caving, hiking, swimming. Departing from Akers Ferry, Hwy. K, 10 a.m. July 12. Maximum participants: 14. Apply before July 1. No previous experience necessary.

ODYSSEY LTD.
26 Hilltop Ave., Berkeley Heights, N.J. 07922
Art Fitch and Denise Van Lear run this outfit which offers backpacking, ski touring, canoeing, rock climbing, mountaineering and ski mountaineering excursions. In the backpacking department, trips of various lengths are conducted overseas and in the western U.S., with prices ranging from $100 to $950. Write for their current trip schedule.

HIGH HORIZONS
Box 1166, Banff, Alberta, Canada T0L 0C0
They have scheduled trips for teenagers in mountaineering, cycling, kayaking and backpacking. The two wilderness backpacking trips are two-week excursions into the Canadian Rockies and cost from $250 to $525. If you're an adult, don't be discouraged; you can get together with them and plan a customized trip for your group at anytime.

KILLINGTON TRAIL CAMP
Killington, Vt. 05715
Two-week hiking and backpacking sessions are offered through the summer. Tuition is $200 for adult sessions and $250 for teenage sessions. Basic rock climbing is included in the instruction, which lasts four days and is followed by eight days of wilderness travel.

MOUNTAIN TRAVEL (USA)
1398 Soluno Ave., Albany, Calif. 94706
Of all the outfitters, Mountain Travel probably has one of the most varied offerings. Trips to Africa, Asia, Europe, Nepal, Polynesia; and South America, as well as North America, are a continuing thing throughout the entire year. Backpacking is a large part of many of the outings. Prices are as low as $1069 for an 11-day trip to Hawaiian beaches, rain forests and volcanoes, and as high as $4911 for 49 days of exploring Siberia and the Far East. They also operate the Palisade School of Mountaineering (see Climbing section).

NATIONAL OUTDOOR LEADERSHIP SCHOOL
Box AA, Lander, Wyo. 82520
One of the best outdoor wilderness schools in the country, with an outstanding staff. There are about 14 courses given by this outfit, that run from two to five weeks and cost from $200 to $2800. Rock climbing, logistics, rescue, first aid, map reading, advanced camping, conservation and ecology are only a few of the areas covered in the courses, which are given in the summer months. All trips are for people over 16 years except one, the Adventure Expedition, which is for 13-, 14- and 15-year-olds. Enrollment is limited and is on a first-come basis—so plan far ahead. It's a school worth attending.

OUTWARD BOUND, INC.
165 West Putnam Ave., Greenwich, Conn. 06830
Besides having an excellent staff and being one of the best wilderness experience schools, it is also one of the oldest, founded in 1941 in Wales. The first American Outward Bound school was established in 1962. Today, there are 28 schools on five continents and six of these are located in the United States. Their courses last from 21 to 28 days and include a week of training and conditioning at the beginning of a session, groups activities, and up to 3-day solo expedition near the end of the course. The lower age limit is 16½ years. Instruction includes first aid, route finding, rock climbing, canoeing, and many other activities and varies from school to school. For more information contact the office above or one of the six schools listed below.

Colorado Outward Bound School
945 Pennsylvania St., Denver, Colo. 80203

Minnesota Outward Bound School
1055 E. Wayzata Blvd., Wayzata, Minn. 55391

Hurricane Island Outward Bound School
P.O. Box 429, Rockland, Me. 04841

Northwest Outward Bound School
3200 Judkins Rd., Eugend, Ore. 97403

North Carolina Outward Bound School
P.O. Box 817, Morganton, N.C. 28655

Southwest Outward Bound School
P.O. Box 2840, Santa Fe, N. Mex. 87501

RECREATION UNLIMITED
Jackson, Wyo. 83001
Two, five-day backpacking trips are held during the summer in the Tetons. Cost is $8 per day for one-day trips and $15 per day for multi-day trips. You can furnish much of your own equipment but for an extra fee, meals will be provided.

REI (RECREATIONAL EQUIPMENT) TRAVEL, INC.
P.O. Box 22404, Seattle, Wash. 98125
REI has several tours and at least three of them involve hiking and backpacking. These include several Asian treks (prices vary), a photography trek ($1000) and two European treks (about $350 plus air fare).

RICK HORN WILDERNESS EXPEDITIONS
Box 471, Jackson Hole, Wyo. 83001
All major equipment and food are furnished for ski touring and wilderness expedition tours. Backpacking is a large part of the scheduled wilderness expeditions which vary from 10 to 35 days and include all phases of mountain experiences and activities. There are also private expeditions, which can be of any length and include any of the mountaineering activities. Prices vary with the length and type of trip but will average under $200 per week. The lower age limit is 15 years for the scheduled trips; private trips can accommodate any ages.

ROCKY MOUNTAIN EXPEDITIONS, INC.
P.O. Box CC, Buena Vista, Colo. 81211
Outings are held throughout the year, both winter and summer, and you can operate in cr out of a base camp if you like. A 7-day backpacking trip will be about $170. Custom trips can be arranged for any group who wants them. They've also started to give educational courses through the Colorado Mountain College.

THE WILDERNESS INSTITUTE, INC.
P.O. Box 338, Bonners Ferry, Idaho 83805
For the jaunts provided by the Wilderness Institute, all you need is a pair of boots, clothes and personal gear; they supply everything else and even cook for you so you can be out enjoying the wilderness. The excursions are in various parts of the country; most of them run 10 days and cost around $235. Age limits are 15 to 55 years. The Institute also conducts a Survival and Mountaineering School for those seeking training as wilderness guides. Five trips are offered averaging 14 days each. Cost is just under $300 per trip.

WILDERNESS SHACK
515 S. La Grange Rd., La Grange, Ill. 60525
The Shack has a newsletter that lists clinics, discussions and slide shows scheduled throughout the year. These are free to anyone who wants to come and are on wilderness living, climbing, winter camping, ski touring and backpack techniques. You can also attend their 3-day weekend Climbing or Wilderness Living School. Write 'em for more info.

WILDERNESS SOUTHEAST, INC.
Route 3, Box 619, Savannah, Ga. 31406
They have backpacking trips in the Great Smoky Mountains, and a one-week base camp experience on the coastal islands of Georgia. The other two trips are an aquatic (scuba diving) trip off the coast of Florida and a canoe trip in Okefenokee Swamp.

WILDERNESS VENTURES
8560 Concord Hills Circle,
Cincinnati, Ohio 45243
This group, run by Mike and Helen Cottingham, conduct backpacking, mountaineering, rafting and wilderness living expeditions for young people ages 14 thru 18. Actually, all these expeditions are part of one summer-long trip which the group spends living out-of-doors and exploring a particular section of the country. Travel is via passenger van and en route, between jump-off points, the group camps at state parks and private campgrounds; otherwise, it's trekking and living in the wilderness. Sounds like a great way to spend two months of the summer. Cost, all inclusive, is under $1400.

climbing

There are two ways climbing may be approached. The practical way for the outdoors enthusiast, whether hunter, backpacker, fisherman, or naturalist, involves traveling across natural obstacles like vertical rock, ledges and cliffs or steep snow and ice and can be of value to anyone navigating through a back country area. The other way, seemingly impractical (although that's hardly the case), is climbing for the sake of climbing.

The reasons people climb have been bantered about for years, but suffice it to say that most people climb for the pure joy and excitement of it, and the self-satisfaction of accomplishment.

People from all walks of life are attracted to climbing, and although one should be in reasonably good physical condition, he certainly needn't possess super human strength. Some of the best climbers are women, who make up for their lesser strength through grace and dexterity of movement and through the mastery of good climbing technique. Technique is really the key, and though it takes time, patience, and practice to develop, it'll get you through many problems which cannot be overcome by strength alone.

You don't have to take a course or even have a license to climb, but if you're just starting out it would be mighty smart to get an experienced person or group to train you. To become a competent and, above all, safe climber, takes time, exposure to successively more difficult problems, and an experienced and patient person to climb with and learn from. Climbing is most dangerous for the person who reads one book, buys a rope and hits the rocks. Don't make the mistake of trying to learn by this self-taught, trial and error method; you probably won't live long enough to find out what you did wrong.

One of the best ways to meet climbers is to go where they climb, and there's a place to climb almost everywhere. The high mountains and most of the best rocks are in the West; the East has a few fair mountains and some good rock, and just about anywhere there's a decent contour to the land, you can find small vertical rock outcroppings that offer much in the way of practice climbing. These "practice areas" are not only a good place to tune up for the big time climbs, but they're also the gathering and meeting places for all local climbers and climbing clubs. Of course if you're new in an area, you might have a little trouble finding out where they are, but a call to one of the local outing or hiking clubs should get you directions.

Getting in with a climbing club shouldn't present a problem, and you'll have plenty of new climbers just learning the ropes to keep you company. As a matter of fact, the popularity of climbing has resulted in such a staggering number of participants, that not only are the practice areas overcrowed, but the big rocks and high mountains everywhere are fast becoming the same way.

Overuse has caused the National Park Service, which administers many of the challenging peaks in the country, to limit the number of people using certain back country climbing sections, and to require registration and an entrance fee from anyone entering a National Park.

Along with the problem of too many people there has been a corresponding increase in the number of accidents resulting from falls, exposure, and falling rock. In an effort to remedy this, many climbers and climbing clubs have set up climbing guidelines for themselves (and hopefully others), which stress helping fellow climbers in trouble and preserving the rocks and environment in general.

Mountains and rockfaces are fragile and we urge all who climb to use good conservation at all times. Rock scarred by the repeated placement of pitons is just as unsightly as trash left at a campsite—and impossible to repair. Bolts should be avoided at all costs—except life and limb. The use of chalk is a relatively recent development and feelings are mixed on the use of it. We personally don't like to climb routes with all the holds marked.

Divisions of Mountaineering

Mountaineering has become sort of a catch-all word that includes everything from mild hill walking to an Everest ascent. In this section, though, we're only concerned with mountaineering in its purest sense (climbing), and that is negotiating the steep or vertical surfaces of a mountain (regardless of size) by means of special techniques and equipment, the summit being the ultimate objective.

I. **CLIMBING.** Usually denotes short excursions or practice ascents, and for recreation rather than for expeditionary purposes as in mountaineering.

   A. **ROCK CLIMBING.** Ascents on broken or solid rock surfaces.

      1. **Scrambling.** Ascents over steep, but not vertical surfaces, which present no technical difficulties, and which do not require ropes or other artificial aids.

      2. **Technical Climbing.** Ascents over surfaces that present technical difficulties, and which require special techniques and/or equipment to overcome. An example of such a surface would be a vertical wall of rock with a 12-ft. ledge cantilevered from its face 120 ft. above the base of the wall.

         a. *Free Climbing.* Negotiating vertical surfaces without the aid of rope or other gear, but employing special techniques such as jamming (wedging hand or foot in a crack to get a hold on the rock).

         b. *Aid or Artificial Climbing.* Using rope and other gear such as pitons (devices to which rope is attached after they are pounded into cracks in the rock's surface) to assist the climber up over vertical walls, under and over ledges, and across other technical difficulties.

   B. **SNOW and ICE CLIMBING.** Ascents over snow and/or ice-covered surfaces which generally present technical difficulties and require the use of aids. Where the surface is soft, such as with snow, an ice axe will usually suffice, but as the surface becomes harder and steeper additional aids such as rope, special ice axes, crampons, ice pitons, and ice screws are needed to secure holds on the surface while ascending. As a catagory, snow and ice climbing is a technical aid-type of climbing.

II. **MOUNTAINEERING.** An expeditionary type ascent on a large and prominent mountain usually conducted by professionals, which not only involves the use of technical climbing skills and equipment, but also requires the use of a base camp and succeedingly higher bivouac camps, fixed ropes and ladders, and sometimes special high-altitude aids such as oxygen. These "assaults" are usually of long duration often lasting four to five weeks, and require such an outlay of supportive gear—food, fuel, tents, medical supplies—in addition to ropes and other climbing aids, that more often than not, financial backers are a must.

On Brenta-Bugaboo. **British Columbia Government Photo**

___sources of information

Since the last edition, the list of clubs has been enlarged a bit, and we've included as many foreign Alpine clubs as we could come up with for those of you planning foreign climbs. Most of these clubs are open to all for membership, especially the European ones. Hut facilities are usually available and some groups have a reciprocal arrangement with their neighbors. The Austrian Alpine Club offers rescue insurance to members (rescues are expensive in the Alps—if they'll come get you!).

When writing U.S. clubs include a stamped self-addressed envelope to help speed up the reply.

Incidentally, the Chicago Mountaineering Club has the International Directory of Mountaineering Clubs & Organizations. Contact: Geo. Pokerny, 739 Forest Ave., Glen Ellyn, Illinois 60137 for info on getting a copy, if you're interested. —John Markwell (1976)

CANADA

ALPINE CLUB OF CANADA
P.O. Box 1026, Banff, Alberta, Canada T0L 0C0
Since the last edition came out we (and the publisher) received correspondence from E. S. Moorehouse of the ACC correcting some of the information we ran on them, so here goes.

First of all, this is the Canadian equivalent of the American Alpine Club, but it has a two-step membership. Associate or Junior membership is open to anyone with an interest in the Club. Senior membership is only open to those who have established their qualifications as mountaineers. (How 'bout that, ACC?). Dues are $20 per year plus a $10 entrance fee for Seniors and Associates and for Juniors (under 25 years) $10 per year, no entrance fee. There is no longer a visiting members category.

The Club sponsors climbing and ski mountaineering programs from the family type to major expeditioning. They also sell climbing guides to Canadian ranges.
Periodicals: *The Gazette* - A semiannual bulletin of Club information.
Canadian Alpine Journal - The yearly chronicle of Canadian Mountaineering with a wide variety of articles on climbing throughout the world. Free to associate and senior members.

BRITISH COLUMBIA MOUNTAINEERING CLUB
P.O. Box 2674, Vancouver, B.C., Canada VGB 3W8
Founded in 1907 this club has a reputation for being the most active in British Columbia. They have a schedule of climbing activities every weekend.

UNITED STATES

AMERICAN ALPINE CLUB
113 E. 90th St., New York, N.Y. 10028
Activities: If not the most influential mountaineering club in the country, it is the most prestigious, being the United States member of the UIAA. The club was founded in 1902 and has five sections throughout the country with a total of about 900 members. Its objectives include "the encouragement of mountain climbing and exploration and the dissemination of information to the public at large on mountains and mountaineering through publications."
Projects involve publishing guidebooks, extensive work in mountaineering safety and rescue, and assistance to expeditions through monies, information and research facilities. It maintains a museum and the most complete mountaineering library in the country, both of which are open to the public. Evening lectures are held approximately once a month at the AAC New York clubhouse from September through May. These are also open to the public.
Membership: At least 20 yrs. old and sponsored by two AAC members. Requirements also include at least 3 years of technical mountaineering experience. Dues are $10 for initiation and $20 a year thereafter.
Periodicals: A club newsletter, $2.50/yr., quarterly, and...
American Alpine Journal - Over 400 p. - $5/copy - annually. Compendium of world mountaineering activities. Probably the

best source of information on ascents of the more remote and difficult routes in the world. Excellent book reviews.

Accidents in North American Moutaineering - About 50 p. - $2.50/copy - annually. Analysis of major mountaineering accidents in North America. Each accident discussed has a valuable lesson to be learned in it. Reading this will keep you on your toes and maybe keep you alive and injury free. A comprehensive list of qualified mountain rescue groups is included in the back of the book.

THE ADIRONDACK MOUNTAIN CLUB
RD 1, Ridge Rd., Glen Falls, N.Y. 12801
Activities: Mostly a hiking and ski touring club, but it does organize winter mounteering and rock climbing trips and even conducts a rock climbing school in the summer. Has a large membership of over 6,000 with 18 chapters

Membership: Each chapter has its own requirements. Active membership dues are $10 per year.
Periodicals: *Adirondack* - Bi-monthly, 16 p. il., $3 per year. Consists of club news and activities.

APPALACHIAN MOUNTAIN CLUB
5 Joy St., Boston, Mass. 02108
Activities: Founded in 1876, making it the oldest U.S. mountain club, AMC boasts over 23,000 members for 1976 (a mighty jump from 8,500 in 1969). This makes it one of the largest as well. Involved in mountaineering in all of its forms—ski mountaineering, snowshoeing, and rock, snow, and ice climbing. Publications are many and include several mountain guidebooks. The club sponsors informal and semiformal climbing sessions, and climbing and mountaineering outings and trips.
Membership: A desire to participate in the club's activities. Dues for those 23 and older are $20 per year with a $5 admission fee.
Periodicals: *Appalachia Bulletin* - Four issues per year.
Appalachia Journal - Two issues per year. The AMC's mountaineering journal.
AMC Times - Ten times per year. Club activities.
Cost to nonmembers for both the *Bulletin* and *Times* is $7; *Journal*, $5; all three, $10.

ARIZONA MOUNTAINEERING CLUB
P.O. Box 1695, Phoenix, Ariz. 85001
Got a letter from Fritz Huls the other day and these guys down in the desert seem to do alot. Anyone can join this club. The emphasis is on rock climbing and meetings are held on the 3rd Monday of each month. They support and participate in local rescue operations and have equipment rentals available to members as well as a reference library.
Periodicals: *Arizona Mountaineer* - Monthly publication on club activities.

COLORADO MOUNTAIN CLUB
1723 East 16th Ave., Denver, Colo. 80218
Activities: Organized in autonomous groups located throughout Colorado. The club's purpose is to collect and disseminate info regarding the Rocky Mountains. Has outings, mountaineering schools and seminars. Each section has its own newsletter and pamphlets.
Membership: "Anyone of good standing in his community who supports the club's purposes..." Endorsement by two members. Dues vary from section to section.
Periodicals: *Trail and Timberline* - Monthly, 24 p. il., $3 per year. The official club magazine.
Summer Schedule Annual, over 200 p., $2 per copy (6" x 3½"). Six months' line up of outdoor summer events.
Winter Schedule - Annual, over 100 p., $1 per copy (6" x 3½"). Six months of outdoor winter events.

IOWA MOUNTAINEERS
P.O. Box 163, Iowa City, Iowa 52240
Activities: An extremely active group. Many local and weekend outings: hiking, climbing, canoeing, ice skating, and skiing. A major summer mountaineering outing at least once a year to Western U.S. or Canada. An annual foreign expedition for pioneer climbing and exploration takes place for interested members. Wilderness and mountaineering classes are sponsored, and college credit is given for them by the University of Iowa. The number of people interested dictates what type and how many courses are offered. Fees are nominal for all activities and courses, but most of the activities are limited to members.
Membership: At least 18 years old for active, $7 per year, or expedition membership, $6 per year.
Periodicals: *The Iowa Climber* - Semiannually, 30 p. il., free to members. Media for club news and activities.

CHICAGO MOUNTAINEERING CLUB
2901 South Parkway, Chicago, Ill. 60616
Activities: Publish an annual roster of North American mountaineering clubs and their publications. Worth getting: $1.

THE MAZAMAS
909 N.W. 19th Ave., Portland, Ore. 97209

M.I.T. OUTING CLUB
M.I.T., Cambridge, Mass. 02139

MOUNTAIN RESCUE AND SAFETY COUNCIL OF OREGON
c/o C. H. "Chuck" Adams, 405 Cedar St., Portland, Ore. 97207
Activities: MRSCO is made up of 19 search, rescue, and climbing organizations throughout the state of Oregon.

MOUNTAIN RESCUE ASSOCIATION
P.O. Box 67, Seattle, Wash. 98111
Promotes mountain safety education and acts as a central coordinating agency for member units. The Association attempts to standardize units, equipment, and techniques wherever possible. Their federation is composed of 37 rescue teams throughout the U.S. and Canada, with a total membership of 1700. Each unit has a minimum of 25 members, at least five of whom have climbing experience at altitudes of 10,000 feet and above. The American Alpine Club has given them grants to help standardize mountain rescue reports and develop a portable rescue winch.
Periodicals: A newsletter four times a year.

MOUNTAINEERING CLUB OF ALASKA, INC.
P.O. Box 2037, Anchorage, Alaska 99501

THE MOUNTAINEERS
P.O. Box 122, Seattle, Wash. 98111
Activities: The counterpart of the Appalachian Mountain Club in the northwestern U.S. is the Mountaineers, with over 6,000 members. They were organized in 1906 with 152 charter members as a mountain exploring club to explore, record, and preserve the natural heritage of the Northwest and "to encourage a spirit of good fellowship among all lovers of outdoor life." They've pretty much done this by annually sponsoring many outings and expeditions; publishing books, pamphlets, and maps; and backing many conservation causes. They also offer various instruction and courses in mountaineering and climbing which are considered excellent. And they have an outstanding mountaineering library.
Membership: Fourteen or older and sympathetic with the club's objectives. Dues for regular members are $9 per year, with a $6 initiation fee.
Periodicals: *The Mountaineer* - Monthly (except June and July), 30 p. il., $5/yr. Official mouthpiece of the club. Contains information on conservation and club activities, and has numerous book reviews.

POTOMAC APPALACHIAN TRAIL CLUB
1718 N St. N.W., Washington, D.C. 20036
Activities: The Potomac Appalachian Trail Club, or PATC (pronounced "patsy") sponsors climbing and mountaineering activities in the form of outings, courses, and practice sessions. They maintain a library at their office which is open to the public, and publish many books, guides, maps and pamphlets. One of their recent publications is a climbing guide to Seneca Rocks in West Virginia.

Membership: Interest in helping with the club's activities. Two sponsors are required. Dues are $10 a year and a $5 application fee.
Periodicals: *Potomac Appalachian* - free to members. Monthly newsletter with information on club events.

Up Rope - Monthly, 4 p. il. Subscriptions for members of PATC's Mountaineering Section are included in dues; $3.50 per year to outsiders. News and activities of the PATC Mountaineering Section: a brief rundown on club climbing.

other countries

UNION INTERNATIONALE DES ASSOCIATIONS d'ALPINISME
29-31, rue des Delices, 1211 Geneve, 11, Suisse
Coordinating body for the Alpine Clubs of the world. Sets minimum standards for strength of equipment, i.e., rope and carabiners, and tests same. Has a neat little booklet available on the UIAA climbing classification system as well as a bulletin dedicated to the cause of Alpinism.

BRITISH MOUNTAINEERING COUNCIL
Crawford House, Precinct Centre, Manchester Univ., Booth St. E., Manchester 13, England
Activities: Made up mainly of British mountaineering clubs, the BMC strives to enhance the sport of mountaineering. Member of UIAA (Union Internationale des Associations d'Alpinisme). Will supply on request a list of available films on mountaineering and rescue.
Membership: Full membership is for mountaineering and climbing clubs only. Associate membership is open to individuals and other bodies.
Periodicals: *Mountaineering* - Contains information on "safety, a code of conduct and other matters."

Argentina - Fed. Argentina De Montanismo Y Afines, Jose P. Varela 3948, Buenos-Aires
Austria - Oesterreichischer Alpenverein, Wilhelm-Greil-Str. 15, 6010, Innsbruck 1
Belgium - Club Alpin Belge, 19, rue de l'Aurore, 1050 Bruxelles
Bolivia - Club Andino Bolivano, Ave. 16 de Julio 1473, Casilla 1346, La Paz
Brazil - Fed. De Montanhismo Do Estado Do Rio De Janeiro, Av. Almirante Barroso 2/8, 2000 Rio De Janeiro ZC-P RJ
Bulgaria - Fed. D'Alpinisme Bulgare, Bd Tolboukhine 18, Sofia 1
Chile - Fed. De Andinismo De Chile, Vicuna Mackena 44, Casilla 2239, Santiago
Czechoslovakia - Ceskoslovenski Horolezecky Svaz, Na Porici 12, Praha
Ecuador - Assoc. De Excurs. Y Andinismo De Pichincha, Concentracion Deportiva, Apartado A 108, Quito
France - Fed. Franc. De La Montagne, Rue de la Boetie 7, 75008 Paris
Germany - Deutscher Alpenverein, Praterinsel 5, 8 Munchen 22
Greece - Club Alpin Hellenique, Karageorgi Servias 7, Athens 126
Guatemala - Fed. De Andinismo De Guatemala, Palacio de los Deportes, Guatemala C.A.
Hungary - Magyar Hegymaszo Klub, Bajcsy Zsilinsky, Budapest 6, Postfach 614 1374, Budapest 5
India - Himalayan Mountaineering Institute, Darjeeling
Indonesia - Wisata Ria Remaja, Jalan Alhambra 63, Jakarta - Barat
Iran - Iranian Mountaineering Federation, Post Box 11 - 1642, Teheran
Ireland - Fed. of Moun. Clubs of Ire., Sorbonne 7, Ardilea Est., Dublin 14
Israel - Club Alpin Israelien, Bd Rothschild 60, Tel-Aviv
Italy - Federazione Italiana Sport Invernali, Via Cerva 30, Milano
Japan - Japanese Alpine Club, Sukura Bldg., 7th floor 6-1 Yushima, 1-Chome Bunkyo-Ku, Tokyo 113
Korea - Korean Alpine Fed., 22-2 2-Ka Ulchiro Chung-Ku, Seoul 100
Liechtenstein - Liechtensteiner Alpenverein, FL - 9490 Vaduz
Luxembourg - Groupe Alpin Luxembourgeois, Place d'Armes 18, boite postale 363, Luxembourg
Mexico - Fed. Mex. De Excurs., San Juan de Letran 80, Despacho 408, Mexico 1, DF
Nepal - Nepal Moun. Assn., Sport Coun. Bldg., Kathmandu
New Zealand - New Zealand Alpine Club, POB 41-038, Eastbourne
Norway - Norsk Tindeklub, Post Boks 1727, Vika, Oslo 1
Peru - Club Andino Peruano, Las Begonias 630 - 11 San Isidro, Lima
Poland - Polski Zwiazek Alpinizmu, Ul. Sienkiewicza 12/439, Warszawa
Portugal - Club National De Montanhismo, Rua Formosa 303, Porto
Russia - Fed. D'Alpinisme D'URSS, Skatertnyi pereoulok 4, Moscou 69
Spain - Fed. Espanola De Mont., Alberto Aguilera 3 pizo 4 izq., Madrid 15
Sweden - Svenska Klatterforbundet, Box 14036, 70014 Orebro
Switzerland - Schweizer Alpenklub, Obergrundstrasse 42, 6003 Luzern
Turkey - Turk. Dagcilik Fed. Ulus, Is Hani, Blok a Kat 3, Ankara-Ulus
Yugoslavia - Planinarski Savez Jugoslavije, Dobrinjska 10/1, Belgrad

___ PERIODICALS

Climbing periodicals are about 40% advertising, 30% entertainment, and 30% information. The information is generally good and most of the time it's of some value. The advertising is necessary and the entertainment...well? Here are the commercial publications and a couple of nonprofit ones directed to climbers. If we missed any, let us know. Club publications are listed with their respective organizations.

OFF BELAY
Ray Smutek, Ed.
Bimonthly - $7.50/yr. - 56 p. il.

Variety is the spice of climbing rags and Ray Smutek is surely putting it into *Off Belay*. There is a good balance between technical, historical, practical and entertaining articles. Coverage seems to be somewhat oriented towards the Northwest. The articles on mountain medicine and equipment are of particular interest to most serious mountaineers as are the historical articles on selected mountains and climbing areas. News coverage is oriented more to issues, like what the Park Service is doing, than to what was climbed by whom—and that's a real nice change.
From: Off Belay, 15630 S.E. 124th St., Renton, Wash. 98055

MOUNTAIN
Ken Wilson, Ed.
Bimonthly - $8/yr. - 60 p. il.

This is the International Herald Tribune of the climbing periodicals. Typically British, which means meticulously thorough and accurate, *Mountain* offers the best in international climbing of any mag. Coverage of significant ascents is its specialty as are interviews with famous or infamous contemporary greats of the climbing world. Historical articles, such as the one on Geoffrey Winthrop Young, which appeared in the January 1976 issue, are of particular interest. Most issues close with an excellent treatise on equipment or book reviews, providing important and much needed information on new climbing gear and on the voluminous quantity of climbing literature available today.
From: Mountain Magazine Ltd., 56 Sylvester Rd., London N.2 England

SUMMIT
Jene M. Crenshaw & H. V. J. Kilness, Eds.
Monthly, except Nov., Feb. and Aug.
$7/yr. - 44 p. il.

It is entertaining and the pictures are beautiful. The poems are nice, too. But almost at once you miss the well-written, matter-of-fact exposition of *Mountain* (qv), which contains so much concise and accurate information that it borders on being a technical journal. *Summit* seems almost as loose and disjointed as most of the independent climbers in the United States. There is a similarity between the two—wild, informal, eager. It's value is not so much in technical information as it is in portraying the style and spirit of the American climber. *Summit* has grown with American climbing over the years, and their earlier issues contained much excellent technical and "how-to" information which has now, for the most part disappeared. Those of you who may have a collection of back issues might be interested in getting Chuck Pease's excellent *Index to Summit Magazine*, Vols. 1–15, Nov. '55 to Dec. '69; seventy-one pages covering book reviews, "Know Your Mountains" series, obituaries, people, places, poems, and subjects, each category arranged alphabetically giving issue number and page. Price is $5 and should be ordered from Chuck Pease, 766 33rd Ave. B, N.E., Great Falls, Mont. 59404. Requests for back issues of *Summit* and subscription orders should be sent directly to *Summit* Magazine.
From: Summit, P.O. Box 1889, Big Bear Lake, Calif. 92315

MOUNTAIN GAZETTE
Mike Moore and Nan Babb, Eds.
Monthly - $6/yr. - 60¢/issue - 36 p. il.

The *Gazette* has come a ways since the first edition appeared in '72. Though still the large tabloid size, it now has a stiff glossy cover and looks slightly more like a magazine than a newspaper. Coverage is still oriented toward the whole mountain and wilderness scene—conservation, ecology, recreation, travel and natural history—yesterday, today and tomorrow. The "Mountain Notebook" department covers current trends and directions—newsy briefs on what's happening with conservation groups vs. government and industry, plus tidbits on equipment, techniques, people, achievements, and so forth. Book section is good, and the reviews are thorough and comprehensive. Feature articles now tend to be philosophically-oriented human interest accounts (1st or 2nd person) of experiences—traveling, on the slopes, river tripping, packing or just plain living; whereas in earlier editions there was a little more practical material—equipment rundowns, technique debates and "how-to" articles, area reports, and so forth.
From: Mountain Gazette, 2025 York St., Denver, Colo. 80205

SENECA ROCKS LETTER
John F. Christian, Ed.
Now and again* - Free, but donations are accepted

Dedicated to preserving Seneca Rocks and environs, and keeping concerned climbers informed of USFS antics in the Seneca Rocks, Spruce Knob National Recreation Area. Safety, rescue, appropriate development, and overuse are the prime focus of this much needed and appreciated newsletter.

*It hasn't been published for a long time but it will come out again. Anyone interested in working on it with John should get in touch with him.
From: Seneca Rocks Letter, 6502 Ridge Rd., Bethesda, Md. 20016

NORTH AMERICAN CLIMBER
Paul Baird, Ed.
Bimonthly - $7.50/yr. - 26 p. il.

If you're not esoterically inclined and want to find out what your friends at the local cliff have been doing, then this is the one for you. Obviously styled after a certain British magazine we all read, it's analogous to reading the **National Observer** after having read the *Times*. Paul Baird has some good folks lined up as correspondents, so things are likely to improve, and we certainly hope so.
From: North American Climber, P.O. Box 9131, Providence, R.I. 02940

EASTERN TRADE
John Stannard, Ed.
As it comes - No charge, but donations are welcome

Dedicated to the preservation of the Shawangunks in New York. If you climb at the Gunks you should read this and help with some of the work they're doing up there to keep the place open for climbers.
From: The Eastern Trade, 13003 Daley St., Silver Springs, Md. 20906

CLIMBING
Michael Kennedy, Ed.
Bimonthly - $5.50/yr. - 36 p. il.

A typical article might start out: " 'Think it'll rain? No huh? Well let's get started.' We then started up this fabulous ice pitted wall for what proved to be another day of terrific climbing." And so it goes—very informally, recounting climbing experiences and adventures throughout. It has some occasional fiction as well. For an entertaining magazine about mountaineering, *Climbing* does a fine job, and one that is necessary to help present an accurate and overall picture of climbing to the expert and novice alike. However, it slips a bit in the current information department. Not much on equipment testing and evaluation reports, and marginal coverage of significant expeditions and climbs. Entertainment is its main contribution to the sport.
From: Climbing, Box E, Aspen, Colo. 81611

There's so much climbing literature around we decided to categorize the books so that novices (or those who dislike reading) could sort out those to read for good basic information. You old-timers will have to bear with us. And by the way if we've missed what you feel is a good and important book, let us know what it is and where to get it.

 BOOKS

MOUNTAINEERING: FREEDOM OF THE HILLS
Ferber, Chairman of Eds.
1974 - 485 p. il. - $9.95

This book should be an essential part of every mountaineer's library. The new third edition is completely revised from earlier editions to reflect changes in techniques, equipment, attitudes and ethics. A complete and up-to-date source of information for the climber.
From: The Mountaineers, P.O. Box 122, Seattle, Wash. 98111

BASIC ROCKCRAFT
Royal Robbins
1971 - 71 p. il. - $1.95

This book has now stood the test of time. It is considered *the* source of information for the beginning climber and provides enjoyable reading for the veteran. Written by one of the masters of American climbing, it provides, with typical Robbins' wit, all the essential information an aspiring rock climber could ask for.
From: LaSiesta Press, Box 406, Glendale, Calif. 91209

BIG WALL CLIMBING
Doug Scott
1975 - 348 p. il. - $12.50

This one addresses itself to the Biggies, walls that is, from Yosemite to

the Himalayas. Scott is a recognized expert in the field of big-wall climbing and covers all aspects of dealing with them from planning, routes, bivouacking, and aid and siege climbing to the historical aspects of climbing big walls, its appeal and the pioneers in the field. An important reference for those inclined towards epics.
From: Eastern Mountain Sports, 1041 Commonwealth Ave., Boston, Mass. 02215

THE CLIMBER'S SOURCEBOOK
Anne Schneider and Steve Schneider
1976 - 320 p. il. - $4.95

The Climber's Sourcebook has been the subject of a bit of bad press from the climbing community before and after its publication. Well we're gonna hafta stand somewhat apart from the crowd and give compliments where compliments are due—and, likewise, criticism where it is due! The good news: Anne and Steve have put together one of the best annotated directories of climbing organizations, schools (including universities offering climbing), instruction and expedition services; manufacturers, importers and dealers in mountaineering gear; climbing areas and guides; books and periodicals; and films, slide shows and lectures yet available—better than our Climbing Section in many respects. Their book is particularly strong in the organizations, schools, and equipment sources areas, and also the periodicals and book dealers areas. As far as their book list goes, it's as they say, "...*some* mountaineering books."

So what's all the bad press about? It concerns Part IV - "Climbing

Areas and Local Guidebooks," which lists places to climb, and where available, accompanying guidebooks. In climbing, as in caving, as in just about any other activity there is a greater percentage of unconcerned (inconsiderate) than concerned participants. In the climbing community it has been learned the hard way that if a virgin climbing spot is discovered, particularly on private property, you just don't go out and blab the word around—not even a hint that it exists—or you can most assuredly kiss it off. If the information is not controlled and limited to concerned individuals, the word will spread to the marginal element (especially when written up in a national publication) and invariably these people will troop through, create a bad image and leave the local climbers holding the bag! Steve is concerned about this also—for his home ground of New Hampshire! For this state, he lists *only* those climbing areas which *already* have been publicized in two regional guides. Hmmm, funny thing! Fortunately, the damage done to areas in the other states isn't that bad...specific directions for reaching those controversial sites listed are not given.
From: Anchor Press/Doubleday, 245 Park Ave., New York, N.Y. 10017

BELAYING THE LEADER
Richard Leonard and Arnold Wexler
1956 - 96 p. il. - $1.95

With the advent of all sorts of mechanical belay devices (see equipment section), this work is a bit out-of-date but we feel most climbers can value from reading it. After all, what happens if you drop your Sticht Plate halfway up the N. A. wall.
From: Sierra Club, 530 Bush St., San Francisco, Calif. 94108

MOUNTAINEERING—From Hill Walking to Alpine Climbing
Alan Blackshaw
1970 - 552 p. il. - $4.95 (pb)

Covers a lot of ground, and generally very soundly, but it is sometimes vague; you're not always sure of exactly what Blackshaw is trying to say. A very complete bibliography is included at the end containing books, periodicals and films on mountaineering, and 13 other related subjects such as orienteering and backpacking. Being an English publication, however, this compilation is of more use to those climbing in Great Britain.
From: Penguin Books, Inc., 7110 Ambassador Rd., Baltimore, Md. 20207

ON ICE AND SNOW AND ROCK
Gaston Rebuffat
1971 - 187 p. il. - $15

An up-dated version of his earlier work, *On Snow and Rock.* This is excellent for the person interested in snow and ice technique. The strength of this book lies in its fine and thorough text and excellent photographs of the various techniques in application. It is probably the best book now available on alpine methods.
From: Oxford Univ. Press, 16–00 Pollitt Dr., Fair Lawn, N.J. 07410

ENCYCLOPEDIA OF MOUNTAINEERING
Walt Unsworth
1975 - 272 p. il. - $12.95

This exhaustive work deals with explaining, defining and discussing places, people, techniques and equipment, and miscellanea associated with the sport of mountaineering on an international basis. If you can't find it in this book, it's got nothing to do with climbing. This would be a valuable book for people heading to Europe for their first Alpine season—all those weird European terms are in here.
From: St. Martin's Press, Inc., 175 5th Ave., New York, N.Y. 10010

BASIC MOUNTAINEERING
Henry I. Mandolf, Ed.
1970 - 136 p. il. - $2.50 (pb)

A good buy at $2.50. It has good sound information on most aspects of mountaineering, but for 136 pages you can only get so much. To start you off, a better book on the basics would be hard to find.
From: San Diego Chap., Sierra Club, Box 525, San Diego, Calif. 92112

CHOUINARD
The Great Pacific Iron Works
1976 - 70 p. il. - $1

This is probably the most esoteric catalog ever produced. Thus we have included it once again with the Literature. As well as advertising the line of Chouinard wares, the material in this catalog has set the standard for the clean-climbing ethic in America. It also contains much specific information on the proper use of equipment and a very good treatise by Doug Robinson on running talus. You have to read this to appreciate it.
From: The Great Pacific Iron Works, P.O. Box 150, Ventura, Calif. 93001

Knots and Slings

ROPES, KNOTS, AND SLINGS FOR CLIMBERS
Walt Wheelock, revised by Royal Robbins
1967 - 36 p. il. - $1

An excellent booklet describing the basic knots needed for climbing. The illustrations are so good the knots can be learned almost without reading the instructions. Includes short sections on ropes and the selection and care of them. Here's something to impress upon the fickle subconcious—the importance of a correctly tied knot;
> "A young mountaineer named McPott
> Tied an insecure butterfly knot;
>   He screamed as he fell
>   (A maniacal yell ...)
> My God! I'll just be a spot."
From: La Siesta Press, Box 406, Glendale, Calif. 91209

KNOTS FOR MOUNTAINEERING
Phil D. Smith
1967

Describes and diagrams 55 useful knots for the mountaineer.
From: Phil D. Smith, Twentynine Palms, Calif. 92277

First Aid and Survival

MEDICINE FOR MOUNTAINEERING
James A. Wilkerson, M.D., Ed.
1967 - 309 p. il. - $7.50

The only book of its kind. See First Aid and Medical Section for review.
From: The Mountaineers, P.O. Box 122, Seattle, Wash. 98111

ACCIDENTS IN NORTH AMERICAN MOUNTAINEERING
The American Alpine Club Safety Committee
Annually - 30 p. il. - $1

A compilation of accident reports and analysis of the situations. This stuff provides real food for thought.
From: The American Alpine Club, 113 E. 90th St., New York, N.Y. 10028

HYPOTHERMIA: KILLER OF THE UNPREPARED
Theodore G. Lathrope, M.D.
1970 - 23 p. - $1

A short treatise on death as a result of lowered body temperature: something every climber should know about, be able to recognize, and know how to cope with.
From: Mazamas, 19th Ave., Portland, Oreg. 97209

MOUNTAINEERING MEDICINE
Fred Darvill, M.D.
1969 - 48 p. il. - $1

Designed to be carried in the first aid kit. See First Aid and Medical Section for critique.
From: Skaget Mountain Rescue Unit, Inc., P.O. Box 2, Mount Vernon, Wash. 98273

MOUNTAINEERING FIRST AID
Harvey Manning, Ed.
1967 - 50¢

A miniaturized reprint of chapter 18 of *Mountaineering: Freedom of the Hills.* Designed to be carried in the first aid kit.
From: The Mountaineers, P.O. Box 122, Seattle, Wash. 98111

MOUNTAIN SEARCH AND RESCUE OPERATIONS
Ernest K. Field, Ed.
1958 (6th printing, 1969) - 87 p. il. - $1.25

Gives a fairly broad and thorough rundown on the search and rescue area of mountaineering, though it tends to leave you hanging with not quite enough information on some topics and items. For example, it tells you the Stokes rescue litter is the best, but not much else—no leads as to where, what models, if any, etc. You're even more at a loss after reading "pully blocks." All in all, however, it is a valuble contribution to mountaineering literature.
From: Grand Teton Natural History Assoc., Grand Teton Nat. Park, Moose, Wyo. 83012

ABC OF AVALANCHE SAFETY
Edward R. LaChapelle
1961 - $1

How to steer clear of and survive avalanches. Safety rules. Equipment to use. Search and rescue operations.
From: Colo. Outdoor Sports Corp., P.O. Box 5544, Denver Colo. 80217

THE SNOWY TORRENTS: AVALANCHE ACCIDENTS IN THE UNITED STATES, 1910–1966
Dale Gallagher, Ed.
1967

Much like the American Alpine Club's *Accidents in North American Mountaineering*, the U.S. Forest Service's *Snowy Torrents* scrutinizes some 60 life-involving avalanches and rescues, describing the events in detail and providing a rational, unbiased analysis of each for the reader. The Forest Service is continually soliciting information on avalanches and rescues, and as data is compiled, reports are published.
From: Alta Avalanche Study Center, Alta, Utah 84070

SNOW AVALANCHES
1968 - 84 p. il. - $1
FSH 2309.14

Forest Service handbook on forecasting and control measures that can be applied to snow avalanches.
From: Superintendent of Documents, U.S. Government Printing Off., Washington, D.C. 20402

FROSTBITE—WHAT IT IS—HOW TO PREVENT IT—EMERGENCY TREATMENT
Bradford Washburn
1963 - 25 p. - 75¢

A more thorough treatise on frostbite is not to be found anywhere. This pamphlet is a reprint of Washburn's June 1962 article in the *American Alpine Journal.* A more technical version appeared in *The New England Journal of Medicine,* May 10, 1962. Both of these articles were well illustrated. Unfortunately, only one illustration was used from the articles for this pamphlet, so you will have to refer to them for the pictorial presentation.
From: The American Alpine Club, 113 E. 90th St., N.Y., N.Y. 10028

MOUNTAIN RESCUE TECHNIQUES
Wastl Mariner
1963 - 195 p. il. - $3.50

First English translation of Mariner's world-famous volume, which is recognized as the official manual of the International Commission for Alpine Rescue. Covers all phases of alpine rescue with both specialized and improved equipment. Its first appendix, in the form of a trouble-shooting chart, is valuble to all mountaineers. Translated by Dr. Otto Trott and Kurt Beam.
From: The Mountaineers, P.O. Box 122, Seattle, Wash. 98111

MOUNTAIN SEARCH & RESCUE TECHNIQUES
W. G. May
1973 - 301 p. il. - $4

We believe this to be the most complete work on search and rescue available. The book covers virtually every aspect of technical rescue work on all types of terrain, and it goes into not only organized rescues but deals with emergencies through improvisations as well. It's well worth the effort to read this, especially if you get into hot water somewhere.
From: Rock Mt. Rescue Group, Inc., P.O. Box Y, Boulder, Colo. 80302

TREATMENT OF HIGH ALTITUDE PULMONARY EDEMA
Herbert N. Hultgren, M.D.
1965 - American Alpine Journal reprint - $1

From: The American Alpine Club, 113 E. 90th St., New York, N.Y. 10028

—————— sources of books

Most outfitters sell some climbing literature. Here are some good sources from whom you should be able to get anything you want in the way of books.
If you don't want to buy, you can check the libraries of climbing clubs. We know PATC in Washington, D.C., has a pretty good mountaineering library as does the American Alpine Club in New York.

OUTDOOR BOOKWORKS
2118 N. Main Ave., Scranton, Pa. 18503
All sorts of climbing books, guides, technique, mountain rescue, etc. Price list on request. Prices run 10 to 15% below retail.

AUDREY SALDELD
21 Dartmouth Row, London S.E. 10, England
New and second-hand books, journals and articles on mountaineering and allied subjects. They also buy books, journals and articles. Monthly lists, free.

GASTON'S ALPINE BOOKS
Brooklands, Unicorn St., Bloxham, OX15 4PX, England
Deals in old and new books, club journals, and special maps of the mountaineering world. They buy used books and will purchase whole libraries.

DAWSON'S BOOK SHOP
535 North Larchmont Blvd., Los Angeles, Calif. 90004
Dawson's handles "rare and unusual books at bargain prices" in quite a range of subjects including mountaineering.

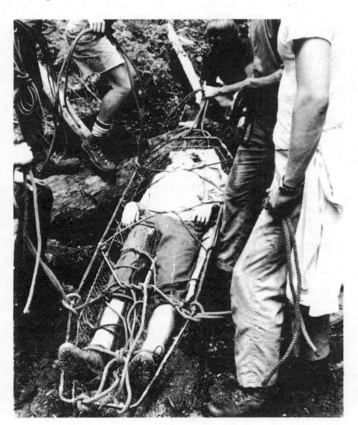

SCHOOLS and INSTRUCTION

As you can see from the listing below there are lots of folks out there willing to teach you to climb. For many only an address is available and with few exceptions, the information presented on each outfit is from their own literature. What we'd like to have is some feedback from those of you who have attended a specific school or schools on the quality of their training, instructors, and so forth. How about it you guys? Some of you must go to these schools! (Or are all the people running them starving?)

A commercial outfit will charge about $190 for a one-week course and may offer instruction on a daily basis at about $25 a day. An alternative to these outfits is to check with the local club. Most clubs offer both formal and informal training sessions and the cost is generally a lot less than a school.

One word of caution. Check out the reputation of the group from which you decide to get your training!

CANADA

ADVENTURE UNLIMITED
Entrance Toe Oro, Alberta, Canada
Pete Austen runs this outfit and apparently offers mountaineering and rock climbing instruction. The ditto sheet he sent was sort of hard to decipher.

ALPINE CRAFTS
Box 86597, North Vancouver, British Columbia, Canada
Mountaineering and rock climbing courses. Tours up to three weeks for climbers with some experience. Expensive.

CANADIAN MOUNTAIN HOLIDAYS
132 Banff Ave., Box 1660, Banff, Alberta, Canada
Instruction and tours for rich folks. If you like to go climbing (or skiing) in style, this is the outfit for you.

UNITED STATES

COLORADO MOUNTAIN SCHOOL
2402 Dotsero, Loveland, Colo. 80537
These guys offer a course oriented toward those interested in mountaineering and small-scale expeditioning. Program covers climbing on ice, snow and rock as well as route finding in the mountains, first aid equipment selection and backpacking skills. Cost for their one-week seminar is $195.

HERBERT CRETTON ROCKY MOUNTAIN CLIMBING SCHOOL AND GUIDE SERVICE
Box 769, Estes Park, Colo. 80517
Instruction and guided climbs in Rocky Mountain National Park. Inquire at Outdoor World in Estes Park.

THE BOB CULP CLIMBING SCHOOL
1329 Broadway, Boulder, Colo. 80302
Instruction in technical rock and ice climbing by some of America's top climbers. Maximum of two students per instructor at $16 per day Or you can get private instruction at $26. An exceptionally good place to learn the technical aspects of climbing. Advanced lessons also available. Bob's a good fellow and a good climber.

Photos: Yosemite Mountaineering

BASIC ROCK SCHOOL

Lesson I, for those with little or no previous experience or those who desire a review of the elements of climbing, covers such topics as knots, rope handling, belays, equipment, climbing safety, and basic free climbing techniques. An introductory climb will be made.

Lesson II involves the rappel, placing emphasis upon anchors and realistic situations. The student will practice numerous methods of rappeling on rocks ranging from slabs to overhangs, learning to place his own piton and sling anchors. In addition there will be practice climbing on faces of intermediate difficulty. The student should bring a pair of leather gloves and a durable jacket.

Lesson III is devoted to belaying the leader, self-rescue techniques such as the "baboon hang", prussiking, jumaring, and aiding the fallen leader. The leader belay will be practiced. There will be a session on intermediate crack and chimney climbing.

Lesson IV is concerned with leader protection and problems associated with leading such as route-finding and the development and exercise of good judgement. The student will climb second over a pitch on which various devices for leader protection will be demonstrated. Those who wish will lead a pitch under the observation of the instructor. There will be practice in advanced climbing techniques.

Lesson V is an introduction to artificial climbing. Modern techniques of direct aid will be taught and practiced on slabs and near-verticle pitches. The ethics of sportsmanship will be discussed in relation to artificial methods in general, particularly the use of bolts.

Lesson VI covers in depth all aspects of artificial climbing. Practice climbs will be conducted on vertical and overhanging rock and roofs. The techniques of belaying in slings, jamaring second, penduluming, and hauling equipment will be demonstrated. Advanced nut, piton, sling, and hook placement will be practiced.

The **SOLO LESSON** is a private presentation of the methods of solo climbing. These techniques are not only of interest to the solo enthusiast but could be of crucial importance to any climber in an emergency. Self-protection techniques and equipment management will be demonstrated and practiced in both free and artificial climbing situations. The student will be encouraged to climb a pitch under the close observation of the instructor. This lesson is not meant to be an endorsement of soloing and will clearly outline the potential hazards of climbing alone.

Bob Culp Climbing School

EASTERN MOUNTAIN SPORTS CLIMBING SCHOOL
Main St., N. Conway, N.H. 03860
Offers basic and intermediate training in rock and ice climbing as well as courses in winter mountaineering. We understand their instructors are quite capable.

EE-DA-HOW MOUNTAINEERING AND GUIDE SERVICE
Box 207, Ucon, Idaho 85454
One-day courses averaging $15 per day. Six and thirteen-day instructional expeditions are also offered at $165 and $325, respectively. If you are interested in expeditioning these guys offer a 21-day mountain leadership course which sounds pretty good at $450.

EXUM MOUNTAIN GUIDE SERVICE AND SCHOOL OF MOUNTAINEERING
Moose, Wyo. 83012
Authorized by the National Park Service, Department of the Interior, to provide guide services within Grand Teton National Park. People in good shape can usually climb the Grand (with a guide for $50 each) after taking the basic and intermediate courses. Joanne Bruno went through both courses in 1975 and found them tiring, but extremely fun and educational. Cost of the two one-day courses, $20 per day.

FANTASY RIDGE SCHOOL OF ALPINISM
Box 2106, Estes Park, Colo. 80517
Mike Covington offers good instruction on a daily basis in ice, snow and rock climbing as well as five-day mountaineering seminars. The prices are a bit steep, but knowing Mike, you get what you pay for.

Photo: Yosemite Mountaineering

HIGH WAYS
Box 1744, Boulder, Colo. 80302
Twenty-one-day courses covering all the skills and techniques of mountain craft. An excellent introduction to the pursuit of wilderness mountaineering. $400 covers all expenses except clothing and boots.

INTERNATIONAL ALPINE SCHOOL
1752 N. 55th, Boulder, Colo. 80301
Winter ice climbing courses taught by Jeff Lowe. The five-day course including room and board (home-cooked meals) ''and night-life forays into the town of Ouray'' will cost you $200.

JACKSON HOLE MOUNTAIN GUIDES
Teton Village, Wyo. 83025
Basic, intermediate and advanced climbing instruction in the Tetons. The most interesting offering these guys have is a three-day seminar on climbing and photography for $70.

LUTE JERSTAD/ELITE ADVENTURES
4525 S. W. Lee St., Portland, Oreg. 97221
Basic rock climbing, ice seminars and Himalayan trekking. Jerstad has something to interest almost everybody. Details on the treks are in the Backpacking Section and the expeditions in the outfitters part of this, the Climbing Section.

MOUNT ADAMS WILDERNESS INSTITUTE
Flying L Ranch, Glenwood, Wash. 98619
Eight- and twelve-day sessions on mountaineering geared to the Northwest.

THE MOUNTAIN SCHOOL
P.O. Box 728, Renton, Wash. 98055
Comprehensive training in mountain travel and mountaineering with an emphasis on the type of climbing found in the Northwest. This is a good place to learn snow climbing and glacier travel. The emphasis on rock is minimal.

MOUNTAINEERING SCHOOL OF VAIL, INC.
P.O. Box 931, Vail, Colo. 81657
Dick Pownall's group. Six-day course in basic and advanced mountaineering in the Gore Range of Colorado. $195 includes meals and all technical equipment.

PALISADE SCHOOL OF MOUNTAINEERING
1398 Solano Ave., Albany, Calif. 94706
Week-long climbing schools conducted from a wilderness base camp. You must be 18 or older and in sound physical condition. Cost per session is $250 including meals and technical equipment.

Commercial schools are rarely ever worth the money. To properly train someone in the techniques of climbing during one or two courses would take more time and money than most novices could spare. This obviously means something's running short somewhere, since commercial outfits are still doing business the way they've always been. For the climber who knows the basics, and wishes only to more fully develope his technique, a school might be worthwhile, but I feel the time and money could be better spent in travelling to a good climbing area and climbing. —John Markwell.

POTOMAC VALLEY CLIMBING SCHOOL
P.O. Box 5652, Washington, D.C. 20016
Bob Norris offers some of the most reasonably priced instruction in the East. Courses cover all phases of rock climbing, and he offers a basic ice climbing course in winter.

RAINIER MOUNTAINEERING, INC.
201 St. Helens, Tacoma, Wash. 98402
Rock, snow and ice climbing instruction as well as mountain medicine and photography seminars. Courses of instruction run 5 days. Ascents of Mount Rainier are the specialty of these guys.

RECREATION UNLIMITED
Jackson, Wyo. 83001
This is the last of the schools in the Tetons that we know of. These folks offer all the basic rock stuff and a 1½-day snow climbing course. Prices are reasonable.

ROCKCRAFT
906 Durant St., Modesto, Calif. 95350
Four-day courses of instruction from one of the great American climbers, Royal Robbins. Courses offered to fit all your needs and interests from $175 up.

SAWTOOTH MOUNTAINEERING
5200 Fairview Ave., Boise, Idaho 83704
Four-day sessions in the Lost River Range in Idaho teach rock climbing and snow travel in the field. This is the only group to mention teaching about mountain weather as well as the other phases of small-scale expeditioning. $50 per four-day course.

SOUTHEASTERN SCHOOL OF MOUNTAINEERING
RR2, Dahlonega, Ga. 30533
Basic to advanced rock and ice climbing throughout the East. Prices are a bit steep, but they do supply all equipment.

TELLURIDE MOUNTAINEERING SCHOOL
Box 4, Aspen, Colo. 81611
Basic mountaineering courses; river rafting; a guide school; and a special mountaineering school for girls. Courses run six weeks for $650. Sounds a lot like Outward Bound.

WILDLIFE
P.O. Box 669, Silverton, Colo. 81433
Three-week, Outward Bound-type course; some mountaineering is taught.

YOSEMITE MOUNTAINEERING
Yosemite National Park, Calif. 95389
Rock and ice climbing instruction amidst the beauties of Yosemite. Special seminars, guided climbs and reasonable prices.

Other Countries

ALPINE SPORTSCHULE GOTTHARD
Ch-6490, Andermatt, Switzerland
Courses covering rock, snow, ice, and so on; emphasis, as with ISM, is on Alpine climbing.

INTERNATIONAL SCHOOL OF MOUNTAINEERING (ISM)
P.O. Box 25, Leysin, Switzerland
Emphasis is on Alpine climbing with speed, safety and style. Some specialized rock and ice climbing courses, as well as training in glacier travel. Prices are reasonable once you are there.

LOC EIL CENTER
Fort William, Inverness-shire, Scotland
Rock climbing mountaineering, snow and ice climbing. Brochure on request.

MOUNTAIN HOLIDAYS
29 John Adam Street, London, England
This is a program of the Youth Hostels Association. They offer training in all phases of climbing, mountain travel, etc. They also sponsor climbing tours to the Alps, Dolomites and other good areas, at reasonable charter-type rates. Other activities include canoe and kayak trips to Scandinavia, archeological expeditions and treks to all parts of the world.

CLIMBING GEAR

One of the hardest things for the beginning climber to cope with is equipment. There are well over a hundred different types and sizes of pitons, chocks, screws, etc.; over fifty different types of carabiners with several styles of shapes, gates, and locking arrangements in a raft of different breaking strengths; six to seven styles of hammers; eight to ten of crampons; and on, and on, not to mention the many different brands that are available.

Each piece of equipment has a particular use in a given situation, very often based upon an individual's preference, and cost-wise none of it is nickel and dime stuff. All of which leads to the natural question: how does the novice save his pocketbook, while wisely trying to purchase only the gear he will need and can use when he doesn't know a nut from a bolt, or a Jumar from a Bong? Answer: Experience. Familiarize yourself with all the various types of hardware by using it in a variety of problem ascents employing different techniques, and you'll know how and what to buy.

But,... but,...

Sorry about that. It's the only way to go. Understand, however, that you don't do this all at once.

Start out by investing in climbing shoes, a harness or swami seat, and a helmet. That's really the bare minimum for a beginning climber. Once you have these and have mastered a few basic ascents at the local climbing area (under experienced guidance), try to get in with a bunch of climbers who have a full complement of gear that you can use and discuss the merits of. If these guys also happen to have the means of getting to places like Boulder, the Gunks, or Seneca, try and wangle your way in on the next trip; it all adds up in experience. If you handle yourself well, you'll probably be welcomed on other trips.

Where do you meet these guys? Most of the action is probably going on with the local climbing club. Ask around at the practice area or check the organizations listed in this section to find out how to get in touch with one. A club is a good place to meet experienced climbing partners, too.

If you can't get in with a club, you can try a good climbing school. Here equipment is lent or rented, and the instructors really know their stuff and can make recommendations. The only problem is the tuition can be a pretty expensive proposition.

Finally, when you are ready to buy your own rope, carabiners, and other hardware, remember not to cut corners on quality in order to save money. Your life will be hanging from that stuff, so only get the best. Talk to experienced climbers and glean all the information you can from available literature to help guide you in your choice.

Once the initial expenditure has been made, there is little in the way of maintenance and repair costs to speak of, except for occasionally having your boots resoled. Probably the biggest expense will be

Basic Climbing Kits

ROCK

Basic gear required by one man for rock climbing:

1. Rope (Perlon or Goldline)
2. Rock hammer
3. Hammer holster
4. Carabiners
5. Pitons
6. Chocks and nuts
7. Kletterschuhe
8. Swami belt
9. Helmet (see no. 12 in other photo)

ICE and SNOW

Basic gear required by one man for an alpine-style ascent:

1. Boots (RD Super Guide)
2. Crampons (Chouinard)
3. Gaiters
4. Mittens (Dachstiens)
5. Fingerless mittens (Millar)
6. Slings, runners, rappel anchors, seats, etc.
7. Rock pitons—bong, blades, ¾" angle
8. Tubular ice screws (Salewa)
9. Rucksack w/bivouack extension (Joe Brown)
10. Down jacket
11. Balaclava
12. Helmet
13. Rope
14. Carabiners
15. Alpine Hammer
16. Hammer holster
17. Ice axe
18. Cagoule

adding new gear to your kit and replacing broken or bent items. And what to do with worn out hardware? Well, John Markwell made a wind-chime with some of his.

When you get a little further on into the equipment discussions, you might find that some items of gear are missing, like in the clothing, tent, and pack listings. Reason is that some of these things are used more in backpacking than in climbing, and we had to draw the line somewhere. So look for the missing items in the Backpacking Section, and refer to the Climbing Section when you're trying to get more out of backpacking, but don't refer to both sections at once, or you might lose track of which section you're being referred from... or to... or vice versa, you know.

Before getting into gear, here's a brief essay on how climbers climb and how they protect themselves from falls while doing it.

HOW CLIMBERS CLIMB

This is a general overview of what climbing actually entails for people who aren't into climbing, but who are curious as to how it is done.

Two climbers are preparing for a climb at the base of a high, almost vertical granite cliff. Halfway up is a ledge wide enough for two to sit on. The next resting spot would be at the top of the cliff. The face of the rock is fairly rough with numerous small cracks, some wide enough to get a handhold in, and projections and ledges sufficient for a minimal foothold. The leader has checked all this out, determined the best route to the first ledge and commences to climb.

Tied to the leader's waist is a rope that leads to the second man below on the ground who acts as the belayer. He pays out the rope slowly as the leader climbs using the cracks and ledges for hand- and footholds.

At a height of about 10 feet, the leader takes a piton and hammers it tightly into a crack. He snaps a carabiner (see p. 91) through the hole in the piton (see p. 92) and then snaps the trailing part of the rope tied to him through the carabiner.

If the leader had slipped while hammering the piton, he would have fallen 10 feet to the ground, and nothing could have been done to prevent it. Now, with the piton in place and the rope attached and held tightly by the belayer, if the leader slipped, he'd probably not fall more than a foot or two.

The leader has secured his first pitch (distance from ground level to the first piton) of the climb and is now ready to climb again. He calls down to the belayer, "Climbing."

"On belay," calls back the belayer, which is the go-ahead signal to the leader. It also means the belayer is ready to hold the rope in the event of a slip.

The leader starts climbing and the belayer slowly pays out the rope maintaining slight tension to prevent any slackness. On this pitch of the climb, the leader feels he can safely make it to 15 feet above the first piton before setting his second piton. He realizes that if he has made an error in judgement and falls from that height, he'll fall 15 feet to the first piton (accumulating 15 feet of slack in the rope) and then continue to fall another 15 feet before the slack is used up and the first piton yanks the rope to a stop. Only problem is, the distance from the first piton to the ground is 10 feet and he'd hit the ground before the rope tightened up. As far as the belayer being able to reel in that 15 feet of slack, there's no way he could do it fast enough during the short space of the fall. Splat! The moral here is: don't overclimb

your first pitch if you're not absolutely confident of your position.

Luckily, though, the leader makes the second pitch safely and sets his piton. The third, fourth, fifth, and on up to ten pitches are handled as the first and second—no hitches (poetic: problems).

The route, unfortunately, was not able to be run directly to the ledge because there were no cracks in the rockface in that area where pitons could be set. What the leader did was to angle his route as close as possible and climb higher than the level of the ledge. He then set the tenth piton about 20 feet above the ledge and 20 feet to the left of it.

With the tenth piton secure, the leader signals to the belayer, way below him, to ease him down. Hanging 25 feet below the tenth piton, the leader starts to swing himself back and forth like a pendulum, till finally he is able to swing over to the ledge and get a handhold. He then climbs onto the ledge and prepares to set himself up as the belayer so his partner below can climb to the ledge. The leader sets a piton in a crack behind him and ties himself to it. Next he takes a coil of rope he had been carrying on his back while climbing, ties one end to the piton and drops the other end to the man below.

Meanwhile, the man below has been preparing to climb. He takes the rope he'd been holding onto while the leader was climbing and ties one end around his waist (this rope still runs through all the pitons to the leader up on the ledge). Then he takes the end of the other rope the leader just dropped and ties this around his waist, also. Now he has two ropes tied to him, one going directly to the leader and the other through the pitons to the leader.

At this point, the belayer calls up to the leader, "Ready."

The leader answers, "On belay." The leader now becomes the belayer, and the guy at the bottom, the climber. As he begins his ascent to the first piton the belayer takes up the slack on both ropes. At the end of the first pitch the climber removes the piton with a piton hammer and snaps it to a shoulder sling he carries. At the end of the second pitch, the same thing, on up to the ninth piton. After removing the ninth piton the climber must decide whether he can safely remove the tenth and make his way over to the ledge, or leave the tenth in place and run a pendulum traverse to the ledge as his partner did. In this case, since there were insufficient hand- and footholds, the tenth was left and the climber pendulum-traversed to the ledge.

The rest of the climb to the top would be handled essentially in the same manner as the climb to the ledge.

Name	Description	Price	Weight
Galibier "RR"	Stiff lug sole; rubber over heel and toe counter; excellent for edging and long aid climbs.	28.50	3 1/4 lb
Galibier "RD"	Somewhat flexible smooth rubber sole; rubber toe; rubber encircling the entire lower edge of shoe; excellent for friction and thin jam cracks.	20.00	2 lb, 6

Climbing Shoes

LIGHTWEIGHT EQUIPMENT FOR HIKING, CAMPING, AND MOUNTAINEERING
Equipment Committee, Potomac Appalachian Trail Club (PATC)
April, 1972 - 13th Ed. - 78 p. - $1.

Trying to get all the information together on prices, descriptions, and

sources of information

sources of climbing equipment available today could be a tedious and long-range project. But you don't have to, because the 1,800 members of PATC and their Equipment Committee have done it already in the Technical Mountaineering section of their lightweight equipment "buying guide." Even though it is a bit dated, the info is still pretty good. The TM section begins with a discussion of what's happening in climbing equipment development, testing and use. Following this are subsections dealing with each major type of gear—ropes, boots, pitons, and so forth. Each subsection starts by covering general considerations, characteristics, and applications of the equipment, and follows through with a list, in chart form, of a goodly number of what PATC considers satisfactory makes and models. Each item includes a description, appropriate specifications, price and source. In other sections climbing packs, backpacking gear and clothing are dealt with in the same manner. *Lightweight Equipment* is particularly useful for the newcomer to climbing, and serves as a useful reference for old hands.

THE EQUIPMENT (itself)

Equipment-wise I prefer mostly Chouinard for hardware. (For down gear and tents I like the workmanship of Sierra Designs.) It's the best of all the lines I've seen and used. Their attention to detail is superb, and there are few, if any, horror stories to be heard about their stuff. —John Markwell.

BOOTS

Boots are boots, but not all boots are mountaineering boots, and not all mountaineering boots are good rock boots, nor will each rock boot work with equal efficiency on all types of rock. It can be a specialist's problem. But most climbers get around it through ignorance of the finer points or by simply avoiding them. They carefully choose a pair of klettershuhe* that will give good service on the majority of rock, and a pair of mountain boots that will do the same for snow, ice, and general mountaineering work.

There are certain criteria, however, that apply to all climbing boots regardless of how they're used. And one of the first you should be aware of is that they are not made for street walking and everyday wear—they're made for climbing. The other factors that distinguish a climbing boot from a hiking boot or street shoe are:

Narrow Welt. The edge of the sole that sticks out slightly around the perimeter of a shoe should be almost nonexistent on a climbing boot. A welt can apply leverage against your foot, particularly when you're "edging," that is, have the edge of your sole on just a ½" or ¼" nubbin of rock for a foothold—quite common in climbing, and the wider the welt, the more strain it will take to keep your foot level so as to maintain a grip on that tiny nub. A wide welt also has a tendency to bend, which could very well mean a slip and a fall.

Narrow Toe. This makes it easier to get your boot into narrow cracks, steps, and stirrups than with a wide toe. One of the problems with European-made boots, which are the most readily available climbing boots on the U.S. market, is that they're made for European feet—too damn narrow—and many Americans, with their wider feet, have trouble finding a boot to fit. The problem is not as bad as it used to be, and many European boots now come in two or more widths. If you find a pair that still seems a tad too tight, you might be able to have a shoemaker stretch the sides out a little.

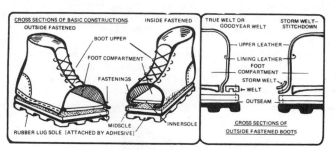

CROSS SECTIONS OF BASIC CONSTRUCTIONS
OUTSIDE FASTENED — INSIDE FASTENED

BOOT UPPER
FOOT COMPARTMENT
FASTENINGS
MIDSOLE
INNERSOLE
RUBBER LUG SOLE (ATTACHED BY ADHESIVE)

TRUE WELT OR GOODYEAR WELT — STORM WELT—STITCHDOWN
UPPER LEATHER
LINING LEATHER
FOOT COMPARTMENT
STORM WELT
WELT
OUTSEAM
CROSS SECTIONS OF OUTSIDE FASTENED BOOTS

Construction. Most shoes and hiking boots have the sole stitched or fastened to the uppers on the outside around the perimeter of the sole, but in better quality climbing boots the sole is fastened from the inside. Inside fastened soles are superior to any other design and for several reasons: one, there is virtually no welt; two, there is no thread on the outside to be worn; and three, repair and resoling are much easier. Thread is still the common means of fastening, but far better are wooden pegs or clinch nails.

Seams are more susceptible to damage than any other part of the boot and are a good place for water to leak in, so, the fewer the better. A good boot will be of one-piece construction with only one seam at the back; even the tongue will be an integral part of the leather and not stitched in.

For more detailed information on climbing boot construction refer to the article, "Climbing Footwear," by Steve Komito in *Climbing* magazine, July, 1970, pp. 15-17.

Lacing. Boots should lace all the way down to the toes. This will make it easier to get your foot in and out under adverse conditions like in cold weather. Full-length lacing also makes possible a wider range of adjustment. On the boot, hooks make lacing easier, but they tend to break or catch on things like rocks and etriers if too near the toe; hooks are best used only at the top. Most kletterschuhe have regular eyelets while mountain boots use D rings and hooks. A neat little device found on some of the heavier kletterschuhe and mountain boots is the lace locker (gripper). It's simply a compressed hook in the 3rd or 4th position from the top, which grips the lace when it's forced into it. Thus you can loosen the top of your boot for walking and still keep the bottom snugged up. As far as the laces go, they can be either cotton or a flat or round-braided nylon. Many of the nylon brands have a waxy texture which helps them to hold knots better. Both types are satisfactory, but the nylon type are preferred by most climbers. Incidentally, leather is never used because of its stretch and the way it's affected by water. It's not very strong either.

If you're looking for more ankle support, the ladder as opposed to the diagonal method of lacing will give it to you. Here's how to do it:

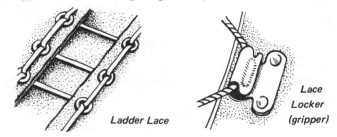

Ladder Lace

Lace Locker (gripper)

Here are the two basic styles of climbing boots—the kletterschuh and the mountain boot.

Kletterschuhe, $27 to $55. These are often referred to as rock or rock-climbing shoes or boots and are designed especially for rock climbing. How 'bout that! They're light and tight, and give the foot the closest thing to barefoot control available without sacrificing the support and protection needed for this type of climbing.

Kletterschuhe weigh at the most 3 to 4 lbs. On the heavier types, the upper part is made from the flesh side of split cowhide (called splits) or of canvas, or a combination of the two. The lighter types usually have split uppers without a lining. The best manner of construction is a combination of leather and canvas or straight canvas uppers that lace to the toes and have rubber over the heel counters and toes. On the rock they'll outperform just about any of the other models. The uppers should also be flexible enough at the ankles so the climber can bend his foot easily when edging, jamming, and tension climbing.

Rock boots will have one of three types of soles: crepe, flat-smooth, or shallow lug. On rough sandstone or granite, a crepe or flat-smooth rubber sole will give better traction, whereas on smoothly polished granite, lugs are best.

There is a great deal of variation in the stiffness of soles in different models of kletterschuhe, and the presence or lack of stiffness is largely a matter of personal choice. The more flexible soles are better for certain types of friction work such as slab climbing. However, on long artificial climbs where one spends much of his time standing in stirrups or etriers, stiff soles have a definite advantage. To increase rigidity, materials from stiff leather to steel rods may be incorporated into the sole.

* *Kletterschuhe.* German, *kletter* climb, *schuhe* shoes; the singular is *kletterschuh.*

Fitting a kletterschuh will be a little different from fitting most other types of shoes. An extremely snug, though not painful, fit is desired with a light or medium wool sock. Actually, a properly fitted rock shoe should be too tight and uncomfortable for long walks—over a mile, and one that's 1 to 1½ sizes smaller than your street shoe would provide the best service on the rock. Another thing to keep in mind is that unless you get ones with really stiff soles and a rubber coating over the toes and heel counters, they'll normally stretch to a half-size larger after a bit of use.

Of the better kletterschuhe, here are some we're familiar with and can recommend:

ROYAL ROBBINS "RR"

"RR" Yosemite, by Galibier, $49, 3 lbs., 4 oz. This was designed by Royal Robins to meet American rock climbing conditions and techniques, and has been successfully used on many big wall climbs. It's a heavy duty kletterschuh with stiff soles for edging and standing in etriers, yet flexible enough for good friction work. Heel and toe are rubber coated and upper part is of suede splits. From Holubar.

PA Varappe, by Galibier, $36. Designed by Pierre Allain and thought by many to be one of the best rock shoes on the market. Rubber covered toe, canvas uppers, and a flat-smooth rubber sole that is medium stiff and very good for friction climbing. From Ski Hut.

RD Varappe, by Galibier, $44, 2 lbs., 14 oz. Similar to the PA but with leather uppers and rubber covered heel as well as toe. From Recreational Equipment, Inc.

EB's, $45, 2 lbs. This is a British smooth-soled shoe similar to the PA, but much softer. It has, in recent years, become the "fad shoe" and, like chalk bags, it's sort of the sign of really being there in the climbing scene. Considering the difficulty of many climbs recently done in EB's though, they must be an O.K. shoe, or could it be that there are a lot of O.K. climbers wearing them.

Mountain Boots, $45 to $115. There are three weights of mountain boots on the market, but for the most part the light- and medium-weight models are better suited to mountain walking than climbing. Thus our discussion here will only concern the heavy-weight models which run about 6 to 7 lbs. These have more demands put on them than any kletterschuh has even thought of: they must protect the foot from cold and wet as well as the scrapes and bangs of walking and climbing over rough rock and sharp ice, they must be comfortable for extended periods of walking, and have the characteristics necessary for technical rock and ice climbing.

To satisfy these requirements a mountain boot should be fairly stiff particularly at the toe and heel for maximum foot protection. The sides should also be rigid though not so much as to restrict ankle flexibility, and they shouldn't come much over the ankle bone for the same reason; about 6 to 8 in. above the sole.

The upper part of the boot should be made from one piece of chrome-tanned, full-grain hide with only one seam at the back covered for protection with another piece of leather. This type of construction is the most waterproof and durable available. The inside of the boot should be padded and lined with a soft glove leather for cushioning and insulation.

As previously mentioned, light and medium-weight mountain boots are not satisfactory for all-round mountaineering work. The reason for this is their soles are too flexible for technical climbing. A flexible sole has a tendency to bend, which greatly reduces positive control of the foot and likewise increases the chance of slipping; it makes standing in etriers for any length of time fatiguing and uncomfortable; and when using crampons, control is reduced, leg fatigue is increased and so is the chance of crampon breakage.

Traction is another important consideration in the mountain boot.

In the early days of climbing various styles of nails were used. Even in Europe today, tricounis nails are very popular, and for grassy or moss-covered rock and ice they're still tops. Nails are rarely found in the U.S., though, having been completely replaced by hard rubber (neoprene) lugs that are a composite part of the sole itself. One of the reasons for this is that the use of crampons, which can be strapped on whenever spiked traction is needed, has rendered nails almost superfluous. All in all, the composite lug sole, of which Vibram is the leading name, is the most versatile traction arrangement. That's why you'll find it on the majority of hiking and climbing boots sold in the States.

A mountain boot should not fit as tightly as a kletterschuh because you'll often be walking long distances in it, but nevertheless, it must fit snugly since you'll also be climbing in it. In general this boot should fit comfortably snug when worn with two pairs of wool socks without being constrictive. Do a ballet toe stand with the laces loosened. You should be able to fit one finger between your heel and the back of the boot. Next, lace them up and do a toe stand again. Your toes shouldn't touch the front of the boot and you should be able to wiggle them freely. If you can do both of these, you've probable got a pretty good fit. In any event, if inexperienced, lean heavily on the advice of someone who knows how a boot should fit—like (hopefully) the boot salesman.

Needless to say, the above doesn't much fit in with ordering boots through the mail, which if at all possible you shouldn't do. If this is your only alternative, however, check under "Boots" in the Backpacking Section for suggestions on how best to order to get a proper fit. You'll also find information there on boot care and the use of various preservatives.

Okay, if you're in the market for a good pair of mountain boots, here are some you might check out first:

"RD" Super Guide, by Galibier, $85, 5 lbs., 14 oz. A heavy-duty technical mountaineering boot with stiff sole, narrow welt, double chrome tanned roughout (flesh side out) leather, and one-piece uppers. It has a double tongue, a steel shank running the full length of the sole, Vibram soles, and lace locks. Eight inches high. From Ski Hut.

Haderer, by Haderer of Innsbruck, Austria. Little can be said about this boot except that it's terrific and expensive—$140. The arch support is an integral part of the midsole which is held together with hand-whittled wooden pegs. Available from Teton Mountaineering.

HIVERNALE DOUBLE BOOT

Double and Triple Mountain Boots, $85 to $155. These, in most respects, are identical to single mountain boots, and construction and use criteria are the same. Weight is a tad heavier, between 7 and 8 lbs.

What sets them apart, however is the separate inner boot, which provides for extra insulation under severe conditions. Made of felt, leather, or both, the inner boots also work nicely as tent and apres-climbing wear. The outer boot cannot be worn without the inner, so it's a good idea to buy two pair of inners at the same time. Then, for example, if one pair gets wet, you'll have the other to wear while it's drying. Fitting is the same as with the single boot. You should be able to wear two pair of wool socks in the inner boot comfortably. There are not really very many of these boots made, but here's one we can recommend:

Hivernale Double Boot, by Galibier, $130, 6½ lbs. Has two sets of inner boots for different conditions: the "artic" inner has felt soles, leather uppers, and is lined with synthetic fur; "alpine" inner has a smooth black leather exterior and is lined with felt. Outer boot is smooth black leather, has narrow welts and hinged heel.

For really extreme conditions, there are even triple boots. These are like the double boots except they include a third, innermost boot, of felt.

There are many good climbing and mountaineering boots on the market in addition to the ones we've listed. The following chart gives some of the other acceptable ones to be found in U.S. climbing shops:

Manufacturer	MOUNTAIN BOOTS	KLETTERSCHUHE
Fabiano, Italy	Mountain boot, med. wt., $50 Cragman, heavy wt., $60	TRC Black Beauty, $38 Fabiano Blue, $34 Madre no. 90, $34
Galibier, France	Hivernale, double boot, $130 Walker Payot, stiff, $95 Peuterey, stiff, $70 Super Guide RD, stiff, $85	PA Verappe, friction shoe, $34 RD Verappe, friction shoe, $44 RR Yosemite, $29
Hanwag, Germany	Rondoy, $60	Friction, $34
Henke, Swiss	Monte Blanc, $48	Berina, $20 Tundra, $19
Kronhoffer, Germany		Kletterschuh, $38
Lowa, Germany	Civetta, stiff, $80 Hiebler Triplex, triple boot, $160 Everest, double boot, $105 Alspitz, med. wt., $54 Scout, flexible, $41	
Richle, Swiss	Palu, med. wt., $52 Lucendro, plastic & leather, $90 Poly Deluxe, $56	
Vasque, United States	Whitney, med. wt. $48 Glacier, very heavy, $67	Shoenard, $45

BOOT REPAIR AND RESOLING

All boots will now and again require repairs or resoling. Here's a list of cobblers we know of who will work on mountain boots and climbing shoes. Steve's the only guy we've personally met, and we can vouch for his craftsmanship. The others have been recommended, but we'd certainly appreciate any candid qualitative data you have on them.

Steve Komito
Box 2106
Estes Park, Colo. 80517

Mike Harding
Mountain Traders
1711 Grove St.
Berkeley, Calif. 94709

Table Mesa Shoe Repair
665 S. Broadway
Boulder, Colo. 80303

ROPE
$49 - $120 for 165 ft. (50 m.)

Rope used for climbing must be light, strong, and have a high energy (impact) absorption factor. If it meets these criteria it can perform its job well as both a tool and a safety device. As a tool, rope is used for ascending and descending, for swinging from one point to another, and to hold the climber in position while he attends to another task. As a safety device, it is used to prevent the climber from slipping or falling, and if he does fall, to absorb the shock, somewhat like a spring, and prevent him from getting splattered below. Of the many kinds of rope material available (manila, nylon, dacron, and polyethylene), nylon is by far the best for mountaineering work. Here's how it compares to the familiar manila:

	Manila	Nylon
Strength/Weight Ratio	*1.0*	*2.8*

Comment: Nylon is nearly three times as strong as manila of the same diameter. This means a lighter weight for the same strength.

Energy Absorption	*1.0*	*8.6*

Comment: This is the shock absorbing factor— the ability of a rope to act like a rubber band in absorbing the shock of a fall instead of passing it on to the climber which could injure or kill him, or passing it on to the pin the rope is attached to, which will break it or pop it out of the rock, again injuring or killing the climber.

Stretch	10%	40%

Comment: This is directly proportional to energy absorption. Nylon by itself stretches about 40% but because of the construction (weave), some nylon rope made for climbing will stretch up to 80% of its length. From a practical standpoint, rope does not begin to stretch as soon as a weight or force is put on it. Some ropes require more than a 200 lb. pull (static load) before they'll start to give. A rope with this property and a high energy absorption factor is ideal for climbing.

Water Absorption	25%	4.5%

Comment: In rain, snow, ice—wet climbing, manila would greatly increase its weight from the absorption of water.

Resistance to Chemical and Biological Deterioration	Fair	Exc.

Resistance to Abrasion	Good	Exc.

Comment: Only problem with nylon is that it melts at 480°, a temperature that can be reached relatively easily from the friction of a rope running across a 'biner or another rope too fast. Pay it out slowly.

In nylon mountaineering rope two kinds are available: three-strand (hawser) laid, where three strands of smaller nylon filaments are tightly wound around each other, and kernmantle laid, which consists of a core of long continuous strands of nylon filament enclosed in a woven sheath. Kernmantle (often erroneously called Perlon—German tradename for the type of nylon used in the ropes) appears to be gaining in popularity over three-strand, because it resists abrasion better, is more pliable with less of a tendency to twist and kink, has a higher resistance to static load stretch (about 200 lbs.), and has a higher energy absorption factor than three-strand of the same diameter, though a mite heavier in weight. Kernmantle ropes are rated by the UIAA as to a fall factor. This is the number of leader falls, based on the UIAA standard drop which simulates the most severe fall possible. Generally, the higher the fall factor the more durable the rope. Also available now are Everdry ropes which do not absorb water. These are ideal for winter climbing.

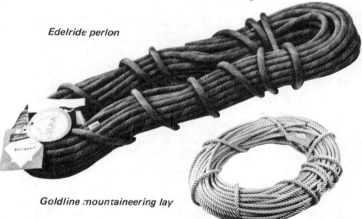

Edelride perlon

Goldline mountaineering lay

The best (and only*) three-strand rope acceptable for mountaineering is Plymouth's Goldline which is made in the United States. In kernmantle, there are Chouinard, Edelrid, Mammut, Edelweiss, Joanny, and Rocca, all European make. Chouinard's kernmantle is the one preferred by many in the U.S. Climbing rope comes in standard lengths of 120 ft., 150 ft., and 165 ft., and the more popular diameters are 3/8" and 7/16" for three-strand and 9 mm and 11 mm for kernmantle. Rope sold by reputable climbing dealers will carry a Union Internationale des Associations d'Alpinisme (UIAA) label indicating it has met certain standards for climbing. Look for it.

CARABINERS
$1 - $4

Carabiners are oval or D shaped links made either of steel or aluminum alloy with a spring-loaded gate. They weigh from 2 to 7 oz., and

* Yeah, we know about Columbian—Plymouth Cordage Co. owns 'em.

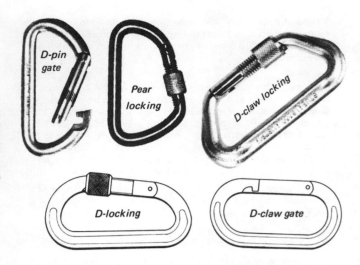

D-pin gate

Pear locking

D-claw locking

D-locking

D-claw gate

made of iron) are made of various steel alloys (mostly chrome nickel and chrome molybdenum), aluminum alloy, or soft iron, and are available in a variety of shapes and sizes. It's impossible to find a crack for which some type of piton has not been designed, unless it's over 6 in. wide.

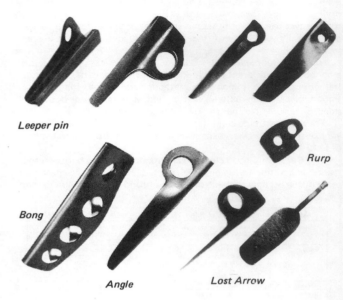

Leeper pin

Rurp

Bong

Angle

Lost Arrow

are approximately 4 in. long by 2 in. wide. Their purpose is to link two or more things together without having to cut, tie or thread them through each other. For example, a climber can attach his rope to a piton in the rock by using a carabiner rather than by threading it through the piton's eye. 'Biners have many uses such as carrying a batch of other 'biners (like on a key ring), attaching ropes to hauling sacks, making rappel-braking devices, rigging hammocks, and opening beer bottles at the end of a hard day's climb. Some models have a threaded sleeve that can be screwed across the gate which locks it and assures that it won't open accidentally. Although steel 'biners are still made, aluminum ones now predominate because of their lighter weight. The body of a carabiner is either bent from aluminum rod or die forged, depending on the cross-sectional shape desired. Gates should have stainless steel pins and springs and close in a notched tang. All carabiners should have their rated strength stamped on the body. If you have one that doesn't, use it to open beer bottles at home—*Do Not Use It For Climbing!*

Following is a chart rating the better carabiners available on the U.S. market. All are aluminum unless otherwise stated. Prices are average.

Manufacturer/Model	Wt./oz.	Min. Breaking Strength	Opens Under Load	Price
CASSIN				
Bonati-D	2-3/4	4000	no	$3.25
Red gate	3	4450	yes	4.10
Blue gate	3-1/5	4450	yes	4.10
Gold Gate	2-1/2	4500	x	5.00
Locking-D	7-1/8	4200	x	4.35
Steel-D	4-1/2	3600		No longer sold
CHOUINARD				
Caribiner	2-1/2	5000	yes	3.65
HIATT				
Steel-D	4-1/2	5000	no	2.90
Locking	4-1/2	5000	x	3.00
Regular-D	2-1/2	4000	yes	3.98
Locking-D	2-1/2	4000	x	4.25
RECREATIONAL EQUIP.				
Oval	2	2700	no	2.05
Locking Oval		(removed from market)		
Standard-D	2.1	4770	no	2.30
Locking-D	2.3	2835	x	2.95
SMC				
Standard Oval	2	2810	no	2.00
Standard-D	2.1	4000	no	2.25
STUBAI				
Standard-D	2-3/4	6000	x	3.00
Locking-D	3	3190	x	3.25
Lg. Steel-D	8-1/4	5200	x	3.50
Chrome vanadium	6-1/2	11,000	x	4.50
EIGER				
Standard Oval	2	2700	no	2.50

All carabiners are aluminum unless otherwise stated. Prices are an average.
X indicates no data available.

PITONS
$1 - $4

Pieces of metal designed to be hammered into cracks in the rock to serve as points of attachment and protection for the climber. Once the piton is pounded into a crack, a carabiner is attached through a hole in it, and a rope, sling, or whatever can be snapped into the 'biner. When finished, the piton is pulled out of the rock with a piton hammer that has a short blunt pick in place of a claw. Pitons or iron-ware (a term carried over from the old days when all pitons were

Cassin is probably the classic name in the history of the piton. Still an active climber at over sixty, Cassin was the first to manufacture pitons, and for many years his were the only available. These were of soft iron, and most could be used only once or twice before they were banged up so badly they had to be discarded; often just left behind in the rock. Soft iron became outmoded with the advent of stronger and lighter materials, chrome moly in particular. Along with the new alloy steels came new designs and methods of application. Pioneers in this area were John Salthe, Yvon Chouinard, Dick Long, and Ed Leeper. Salthe was the first to use the Lost Arrow pattern, now being used by Chouinard; Long's pitons dropped out of sight in the mid-sixties, never to be seen again; Ed Leeper designed the Z-section piton, which he now manufactures at Wallstreet, Colorado; and there are others not so well known. But of all ironmongery available today, Chouinard's and Leeper's pins stand out as truly the best.

Forrest Copperhead chock set in place.

Their design and workmanship are superb, and all are the lightest and strongest possible for any given design. Here's a chart of the better piton manufacturers and a sample of what they offer:

Manufacturer	Material	Model & Price	Comments
CHOUINARD United States	chrome moly	Lost Arrow, $2.25 3/4" Angle, $1.10 4" Bong, $3.25 1/2" Rurp, $1.00 Bugaboos, $1.75	Well designed and manufactured. Care given to quality and dependability.
SMC United States	chrome moly, chrome nickle, and aluminum.	1/2" Angle, $1.25 2" Bong, $2.05 4" Bong, $3.45	Similar to Chouinard; some small angles have been found with forging flaws.
HIATT Great Britain	chrome moly	Blade, $1.98 3/4" Angle, $1.30	Thin blades to 3/4" angle.
CLOG Great Briatin	chrome moly	Similar to Chouinard	Short thin blades to 4-1/2" long blades. Poorly finished.
PECK Great Britain	chrome moly	Angles, $1.60 ea.	Similar to most angles, but designed to be used with Peck nuts.
LEEPER United States	chrome moly	Z-sections, $1.05 to $1.25	Tremendous holding power in vertical cracks. Well made and strong.

Hold it a minute before going out to load up with ironware. Read the next part and consider the use of chocks as an alternative. Why? Because pitons play hell with mountains. When hammered in or jerked and pounded from a crack they break and damage the rock. Often they're driven in so tightly they can't be pulled free and are left on the rockface as unsightly climbing litter.

Kirk's Kamm

Chouinard wired stopper

Chouinard Hexcentric

CHOCKS
55¢ - $5

For many years the piton was the standard bearer for a lead climber. The British, however, frowned upon their exclusive use, because they were not always the most efficient means of attaching for protection and they damaged the rock. So they substituted knotted slings (loops of nylon webbing or rope), and slings with carabiners, or natural chockstones (wedge-shaped pieces of stone) attached; devices which could easily be placed and jammed in a crack, and likewise removed with less damage than a piton. The box-shaped machine nut with a sling threaded through was the next natural step in the movement to pitonless protection. Today there are wedges, knurled cylinders, truncated pyramids, small I-beams, and serrated bits of copper, employed with nylon rope and webbing and stainless steel cable as chocks. Even the old machinist's nut has become sophisticated, and there are all kinds of sizes and shapes available to fit the needs of almost any situation. There's such a variety of them, that in America, climbers are calling everything nuts, when in fact, a nut is still a particular type of chock (with all due respect for the British, who led the way).

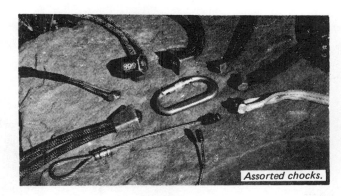

Assorted chocks.

A new trend is underway to "climb clean" using few if any pitons, and instead, relying on chocks, runners, tied-off chockstones, and the like for protection. Climbing areas must be protected and preserved from the thoughtless and selfish acts that are ruining them for today's and tomorrow's climbers. Although the damage already done by bolts and pitons cannot be mended, the rate of damage can be slowed to a snail's pace or even halted completely by an increased reliance on chocks and "fixed" pitons for protection.

Most chocks are made of high-strength aluminum and fitted with either a web, rope, or cable in the form of a loop to provide for the attachment of a carabiner. The theory of placing chocks is relatively simple. Locate the wide part of a crack and insert the chock, loop downward. It should be positioned so that when a downward force is applied as in a fall, the chock will be jammed into the narrower portion of the crack, thus holding it fast. Although particularly applicable to vertical cracks, they can be used in horizontal ones if placed with care.

One of the hottest new ideas in clean climbing goes to Ron Kirk, the brains behind a new nut design brought out by CMI this summer. We've been testing a prototype for three years and find they are the best solution yet to placements in parallel-sided cracks, weird slots and some flaring cracks.

The following is a comparison chart of the better chocks available in the U.S.:

Manufacturer Model	Comments	Sizes	Wt. oz.	Price
CHOUINARD Stoppers	Aluminum wedges with double taper. Sizes 1 to 4 are cabled.	1/8 to 1-1/2"	1/4 to 2 lbs.	$1.50 to $2.65
Hexcentrics	Irregular hexagons that will fit three ways. Very versatile shape and a good alternative to the Bong.	7/16 to 3-3/4"	1/4 to 6-3/4	80¢ to $4.40
Crack-N-Ups	Anchor-like devices for thin cracks. Usable mostly for aid. They're neat but scary.	1/16 to 5/16"	1-1/2	$2.50 ea.
FORREST Copperhead	Nuts of copper swages on steel aircraft cable. Very functional for constricting cracks.	3/16 to 1/2"	.5 to 2.5	$1.50 to $2.25
Foxhead	Die-forged aluminum wedge on single-strand steel cable.	3/4 to 1-1/4"	2.5	$2.65
Arrowhead	Single cable wedges that simplify many placements.	3/16 to 7/16"	1/4 to 1-1/4	$2.35
COLORADO Nut	Aluminum I-beam, tapered for large cracks. Alternative to the Bong and Hexcentric.	1-1/2 to 4"	n/d	$1.50 to $4.50
PECK Nuts	Aluminum; round and knurled shapes, extremely useful in both sandstone and granite.	1/4 to 1-1/4"	n/d	40¢ to $1.50
GENDARME Steve's Stones	Unique dual-taper wedges, similar to Stoppers and Moac, overlapping size range, hard to get, but good. Available Gendarme, Mouth of Seneca, W. Va.	5/8 to 1-1/4"	.4 to 2.1	75¢ to $2
TROLL Nuts	Similar to Clog line. Placement often difficult in shallow cracks.			30¢ to 90¢
MOAC Nuts	Aluminum dual-taper wedge of great utility. Very versatile chock.	5/8 to 1-1/4"	1	$1
CMI Kirk's Kamms	Eccentric, cammable nuts on wire sling. The best thing yet for solution holes and both vertical and horizontal cracks with parallel sides.	3/4 to 2-1/2"	3/4 to 3-1/2	$20 set

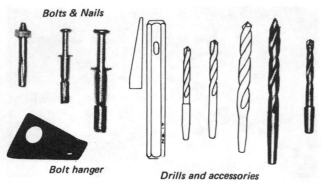

Bolts & Nails

Bolt hanger

Drills and accessories

BOLTS
75¢ - $1; about $7.50 for drill, etc.

There's not much one can say about these destructive and ugly little beggars. They're used when there is no place to drive a piton, for example, where there is no crack in the rockface, or where the crack is too big to safely use a piton or chock. They resemble machinist's bolts, and you have to drill a hole and pound them in, defacing the rock in the process. Once set, the protruding stud is a permanent fixture and reminder of someone's passing. There is a method of partially correcting this by clipping the stud, or pulling the whole bolt with a special bolt puller, and then filling the hole with a mixture of epoxy and local sand. It's hard work and will cut in on your climbing time. But it does a fair job of hiding the hole, and that makes it worth the trouble of doing. The placing of bolts, to say the least, makes a route less natural. Although necessary in some extreme situations, the average climber would be better off not wasting his money on them. It may also be worthwhile to note that many of the major climbing retailers do not carry bolts.

HARDWARE SLINGS
$1 - $24

A load of pitons can get pretty heavy and the sling on which racked pins are carried can cut mercilessly into the shoulder. Several people have come up with gear slings that have wide shoulder straps to distribute the load over a greater area. Forrest Mountaineering has one with a wide shoulder band attached to a loop of 7 mm kernmantle to make removal of 'biners easier. Chouinard has made one out of 2 in. seat belt webbing which has been rolled and sewn to make access to hardware easier. Both are very functional and run $4 and $2 respectively.

Forrest sling and Pin Bin

An interesting innovation in hardware slings is Forrest's Pin Bins. They're individual racks with a spring-loaded plunger gate, and are supposed to work pretty well, but you've got to buy his Pin Bin bandolier to put the racks on; holds ten of 'em. Pin Bins are a little less than $3 each, and bandolier, $4.

Incidentally, for fun and excitement on the rocks try using webbing for a sling, say a 2 in. width. Just kidding. Using webbing of any width for a hardware sling, rather than driving you up a wall, will be a good incentive to jump from a wall. Try it, you won't like it.

POINTS OF PROTECTION—Snow and Ice

The recent renaissance in snow and ice climbing has led to the development of anchors especially suited to this surface for protecting the leader and belayer. Of course, the most secure anchor even for climbing on snow or ice is a piton or nut placed in a rock outcrop if one is available. Lacking this, which often is the case, the climber must resort to innovations such as deadmen, ice pitons, and ice screws.

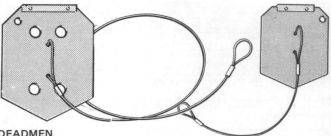

DEADMEN
$4 - $7

These are 4- to 9-in. square plates made of heavy aluminum sheeting. They sort of resemble a perforated shovel blade with a reinforced top edge; makes it easier to drive them into snow or soft ice. A two-wire bridle is attached at the center line of the plate, one end near the top, the other near the bottom, in such a fashion that any force applied to the bridle tends to pull the deadman downward and deeper into the snow. With its wide surface area, it makes for a very secure anchor if properly placed. Deadmen are made by Clog, SMC, MSR, and Troll, and are available at most mountain shops. Also check REI's catalog.

MSR tubular screw

Wart Hog

Salewa ice screw

Chouinard tubular screws

ICE PITONS AND SCREWS
$6 - $10

When it comes to hard ice, forget the deadmen, you'll never drive 'em. Here the ice piton (or screw) is the ticket. They look pretty much the same as a rock piton, but of a bit harder material and usually the edges are serrated or notched to grip the ice better.

There are only two really good hammer-driven ice pitons available to the climber today. These are the Salewa and the Chouinard Wart Hog. Both work well in hard-water ice, but the Chouinard seems to be the better of the two being investment cast in stainless steel for a greater resistance to bending, and it has an elliptically shaped eye to reduce carabiner shifting under a load.

Salewa tubular ice screws were the standard for years, but once again Chouinard comes up with better... In this case it's a better ice screw, offering 40% more holding power. He uses a larger diameter tube of chrome-moly with thinner walls. This screw bends under a higher load than the Salewa and due to the larger diameter, it doesn't shear as easily through rotten ice. These new tubes come in lengths from 13 to 28 cm. and sell for $6.50.

MSR also came up with a new ice screw this year and they ran some pretty impressive tests on it. It's a bit steep at $9.50 but if it's as good as they say, it should be worth it.

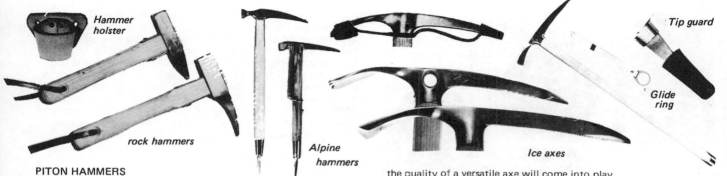

Hammer holster

rock hammers

Alpine hammers

Tip guard

Glide ring

ice axes

PITON HAMMERS
$5 - $16

These hammers are specially designed for the driving (placing) and removal of pitons. Most hammers fall into two distinct catagories: rock hammers and alpine hammers. *Rock hammers* are those designed to be used on technical rock climbs where no ice or snow is to be encountered. On this type of hammer a blunt pick opposite the face, or striking surface, is desirable for driving and removing pins in tight cracks. *Alpine hammers* are those designed for use on mixed or alpine style climbs where rock, snow, and ice are encountered. They should have a longer and more pointed pick. Picks on the best alpine hammers are drooped (curved down) and serrated to give a good bite in the ice. The longer pick is also used for clearing ice and moss from prospective piton cracks, extracting nuts from deep cracks, and cutting an occasional step in ice. More appropriately, the alpine hammer is used as an aid in technical ice climbing, serving not only as a piton hammer, but also as an ice dagger on technical ice. For placing ice pitons, which are hammered in, the alpine hammer is a virtual necessity. For placing ice screws, it's a great convenience. With the pick, a pilot hole for the screw can be started, and after the screw has been started by hand, the pick can be inserted into the eye and used as a lever to turn it into the ice.

The ideal weight for either hammer is from 15 to 20 ounces. The handle, if wood, should be of straight-grained hickory and from 10 to 13 in. in length. If the handle is metal or fiber glass with a rubber grip, the shaft must be *permanently* bonded to the head; a reliable manufacturer's guarantee is a good indicator of the quality of this bond. All hammers should have a safety sling for wrist or shoulder attached to the handle or a provision for attaching one. Here's a chart of the hammers available in the U.S.

Manufacturer Model	Wt. oz.	Handle	Length	Carrying	Pick	Useful on	Price
CHOUINARD							
Yosemite	22	Hickory	11"	Sling	Blunt	Rock	$16
Crag	19	Hickory	11"	Sling	Long	Rock	18
Alpine	27	Hickory	11"	Sling	Drooped & serrated	Ice	18
FORREST	26	Fiberglass	11"	Provision	Blunt	Rock	18
INTERLAP							
North Wall	28	Hickory	23"	Provision	Ice axe-pick	Ice	24
Fitzroy	28	Hickory	22"	Provision	pick	Ice	27
PECK							
Terrordactyl	27	Steel	15"	Provision	55° pick	Ice	55
SALEWA							
Rock Hammer	22	Steel	12"	Provision	Blunt	Rock	9
Alpine Hammer	22	Steel	12"	Provision	Drooped & serrated	Ice	16

Hammer Holsters, $2 to $4. Carrying a hammer in the back pocket has proven to be expensive for most climbers; if you don't lose it, you'll sure as hell wear your pants out quickly. Besides, it's hard to get a hammer in and out of a back pocket. Therefore, a hammer holster should be considered an essential climbing item. The best were made by Bill Dolt in California, but since his death, these are no longer available. Chouinard sells a nylon and leather one which is very good for $4. The Clog holster, a British import, is very similar to the old Dolt and runs about $6.

ICE AXES
$24 - $60

The ice axe, long the symbol of the mountaineer, has undergone tremendous development over the last four years as a result of increased interest in alpine style routes and severe ice climbing. For those who just plan to tromp around in the snow, almost any ice axe of walking cane length will do, but the serious climber has more to consider if he wants to tackle steep snow and ice in good form; here

the quality of a versatile axe will come into play.

Ice axes are used for cutting steps (also called stance or pigeon holes), as a walking aid, for belaying by sinking the shaft up to the hilt in snow or the pick into ice, and on glaciers to probe for crevasses. The parts of an ice axe are the head, composed of an adze and a pick; the shaft; and a spike at the end of the shaft. Certain characteristics are necessary for an ice axe to perform well on steep snow and ice. It should have a curved pick with serrations or notches on the cutting edge and with sufficient holding power to safely support a climber. Although of secondary importance, the adze must above all be sharp so that it will cut and not shatter the ice when used to chop an occasional stance hole. A strong handle is also necessary. The axes obtainable in the U.S. that meet these criteria are listed here:

Chouinard Axe. This is highly regarded among leading climbers. It has a good droop to the deeply notched pick and a strong laminated split bamboo handle. Most good retailers handle it. Lengths are 55, 70, and 80 cm. and the price is $60.

Ralling Everest Axe. Similar to the Chouinard, but the head is of a lower quality carbon steel. The adze is scalloped and slightly curved longitudinally. Lengths are from 70 to 95 cm. Handled by most climbing shops at around $25.

Stubai Ashenbrenner. If Stubai would add a droop to the deeply-notched pick it would be a fine axe. Word is that they will. Available in lengths of 60, and 75 to 95 cm., from Recreational Equipment for $24. Incidentally, ice axe shafts increase in length by increments of 5 cm.

Mountain Safety Research Thunderbird. An axe designed by Larry Penberthy in Seattle. It is the only one of his axes that has the potential of being a good technical climbing tool, that is, if you get the head case-hardened for $2.50 extra. The tubular aluminum shaft tests out to be very strong. Five lengths from 18 to 37.5 in. From Mountain Safety Research for $43.

In addition to the above axes, there are two specialist's types of note. They are designed for use on the severest ice climbs in conjunction with the German front pointing technique. Designed to bite and hold in steep ice, they provide direct support in the way of a hand-hold.

Chouinard Climaxe. Basically, a scaled-down version of the Chouinard-Frost Axe on a hickory hammer handle. This is an extremely useful tool on severe ice climbs when used in conjunction with an alpine hammer. A group could even replace one of their conventional ice axes with it on a long alpine-style climb. Length, 11 in.; cost, $27.

MacInnes Terrordactyl. A short shaft ice axe with an adze opposite a 55° angled pick. These axes have proven themselves on some very hard climbs. Length, 38 cm., $55. Not readily available in the U.S.

Ice Axe Accessories, 50¢ to $2. A *glide ring* consists of a metal ring with a nylon or canvas strap attached. The ring slides on the ice axe shaft, and you slip the strap over your wrist; helps to keep you from losing your axe. Some axes are sold with glide rings, others without. If you want to pick one up, they're available through Recreational Equipment, as are the rest of these accesories. *Ice Axe Guards* are leather or rubber sheaths to be slipped over pick and adze for protection during transportation and storage. A *spike guard*, made of rubber or plastic, serves the same purpose.

To describe the ice axe it was necessary to show how it functioned as a cutting and chopping tool; however, remember the new ethic of ice climbing, which is very much the same as that of rock climbing— leave little or no sign of your passage. To accomplish this the modern ice climber has to eliminate the need to cut steps. One way is to use the French technique of ice climbing, which is very similar to pure friction climbing on rock, but instead of boot soles against rock for friction, it's crampons against ice with the axe used as a hold for balance and security.

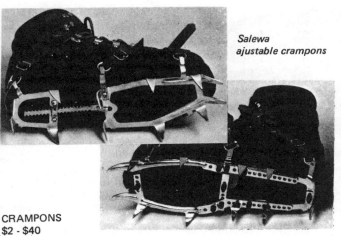

Salewa ajustable crampons

CRAMPONS
$2 - $40

Crampons are spiked frames that are strapped to the bottom of mountain boots to provide a better grip on hard snow and ice, and to reduce or eliminate the need for step-cutting when climbing steep slopes. There are three types of crampons: instep, lobster claw, and regular crampons. *Instep* crampons are small frames with two or four points that are strapped directly to the instep of a shoe or boot to provide better traction on level ice. They're designed for glacier walking and are of little use to the modern climber. *Lobster claws*, also called front pointers or twelve-pointers, seem to be the best investment for the modern climber because they are applicable to all types of terrain from snow slogs to technical ice. The best type have a rigid frame with twelve points, two of them protruding horizontally beyond the toe of the boot. They're adjustable so the climber with two pairs of boots need not own two pairs of crampons. When adjusted to fit correctly, a crampon should remain attached to a raised boot without the aid of straps. Lobster claws with rigid frames have to be worn with stiff-soled boots or they'll flex and break. *Regular* crampons have only ten points, all vertical, and although useful for the French style of ice climbing, cannot be used to front point (German style), because they lack the lobster claws. Except for this, regular crampons are similar to the twelve-point style.

The following chart lists the twelve-point crampons available in the U.S. Note that after the price of each is a number. This is a rating of the crampon's performance on all types of terrain from snow slogs to technical ice, with more emphasis given to the latter. The scale is from 1 to 5, with 5 being tops:

Chouinard Crampons, $60, (5). Rigid frame which must be used with stiff-soled boot; fully adjustable; sizes 7 thru 13; neoprene-nylon straps provided.

SMC Rigid Crampons, $52, (4). Similar to the Chouinard but not enjoying equal popularity. Comes in two sizes: one fits boots size 8 and up; the other, 8 and down.

Salewa Crampons, $30, (4). Hinged frame; adjustable for length; extremely popular on Scottish ice; no straps.

SMC Chrome Moly Crampons, $20, (3). Hinged frame; no straps.

REI Chrome Moly Crampons, $21, (3). Hinged frame; not adjustable; no straps.

Simond Everest Crampons, $27, (2). Hinged frame; no straps; very strong.

Grivel Crampons, $20, (1). Hinged frame; no straps.

Ralling Crampons, $27, (1). Hinged frame; no straps; very strong.

Crampon Bindings, $2 to $6. When wet, leather crampon bindings are too stretchy to be of great value, and nylon bindings tend to slip. Both make readjustment a constant hassle. Bruce Beck came up with a neoprene-coated nylon strap that has proven superior to all others on the market. Chouinard crampons come fitted with these, and they can be obtained for any other crampon by writing Beck Outdoor Projects (check "Sources of Equipment"). Beck's Regular model straps are $5.25, and the Professional model runs $6.

CLIMBING ACCESSORIES

WEBBING

5¢ - 75¢ per running foot

One of the most useful materials to the climber is nylon webbing. Two types are available, tubular (hollow) and flat (solid), in widths of ½" to 3", and tensile strengths up to 7000 lbs. Tubular webbing is the more versatile of the two, is easier to work with, and will hold knots better. It's used for stringing chocks, making harnesses and swami belts, and for the ever useful general purpose sling (runner) of various sizes. Incidentally, Chouinard has some good information on constructing and using runners in his catalog. Flat webbing is also good for making swami belts, and best for making etriers and short "rope" ladders for direct aid climbing. Eastern Mountain Sports probably has the best selection of webbing, and at good prices. Another group that handles a good deal of webbing is Parachutes, Inc. (check Parachuting Section), though the majority of theirs is of the flat type; however, they also have beaucoup webbing, sewing and fastening gear, plus all types of hardware, buckles, links, and so forth which might prove useful. Check 'em out. Whatever, though, always buy plenty of webbing. You never have enough.

HARNESSES
$6 - $20

Harnesses are used by most climbers today, because they're safer to fall in than the traditional rope loop around the body. There are several styles of harnesses, some of which are manufactured commercially, and others which you make up yourself from webbing, like the seat sling, the diaper sling, and the swami. The swami is interesting in that it has become a catch-all term for any type of seat harness, when in fact it is simply a wide piece of webbing wrapped around the waist five or six times, and the climbing rope tied to it. Yvon Chouinard and T. M. Herbert devised the swami belt, and knowing the way Chouinard comes up with names, he probably associated the length and method of donning it with the swami's turban.

Harnesses distribute the force of a fall over a large area of the body reducing the shock of impact and the chance of injury from the rope cutting into you. They're manufactured by several firms, and the two best, in our humble opinion, are the Forrest Swamibelt and the Whillans Sit Harness. They're available at most good climbing shops or respectively from Forrest Mountaineering, $25, and Chouinard, $25. If you choose another brand, make sure the harness has a minimum of metal parts, especially at the point where the climbing rope is attached. Bending a rope through a ring or carabiner and then subjecting it to a severe load greatly reduces its strength. Chest harnesses, although popular in Europe, have never caught on in the United States. Anyone who's ever taken a fall while wearing one can tell you why. It's an unnecessarily painful experience. We hear that a combination seat and chest harness is in the making. Should prove interesting.

Williams harness

BELAY SEATS
$4 - $6

This is a must for those planning longer climbs on difficult artificial pitches (such as Yosemite-type climbs) where both ledgeless belays and bivouacs may be encountered. Belay seats are somewhat akin to harnesses, though their purpose is different. They allow the climber to sit in relative comfort while suspended from an anchor in the rockface. The most popular, and the original, is the Robbins belay seat available from most outfitters for about $5. Others have been patterned after the Robbins, and are produced under the names of "Bat," "Dolt," and "Clog." All of these are reliable and perform well.

BELAYING ACCESSORIES
60¢ - $6

Mechanical belaying devices are now in widespread use. There are two models of the Sticht plate out now, one with a spring to hold the plate away from the attaching carabiner which seems to be more hassle than it's worth and one without the spring. They also come in single- and double-hole models. The double, fitting both 9 and 11mm ropes, is not only more versatile, but is also lighter than the single-hole 11mm model. Many folks are also using 8 rings to belay with; see the section on descenders.

ASCENDERS
$13 - $55

Ascenders are valuable aids for quickly ascending high, vertical stretches of rock with a rope once the leader has established a safe anchor point at the top. If you get into caving you'll find them used quite frequently.

Today's ascenders are mechanical substitutes for the prusik knot, which while slower and more tedious, provided a reliable method of ascending. Indeed, the prusik is still used, if not for the actual ascent, in conjunction with an ascender as a safety "self-belay" in the event of mechanical failure.

Three acceptable makes of ascenders are sold on the U.S. market: the Jumar, the Gibbs, and the Clog. All employ the use of an eccentric (cam) which compresses against the rope when pressure is applied (downward) and releases when pressure is removed. Two ascenders are always required so the climber's weight can be switched from one to the other, thus leaving an ascender free of tension to be slid up the rope by hand. The usual set-up is to rig each ascender with a foot stirrup and one ascender with a safety chest loop. An alternative method for long climbs is to attach your harness to one or both of the ascenders, and when you get tired you can sit and rest a spell. An excellent treatise on ascenders appeared in the January-February, 1972 issue of *Off Belay*, pp. 14-21, 52. The most popular ascenders in the U.S. are the Jumars, sold at most stores for about $55 a pair. Clog, of England, has redesigned their ascender. It is now very similar to the Jumar but has a better handle configuration. They are widely available at $41.50 a pair. Gibbs ascenders can be ordered direct from the factory; $9 each for the regular model, and $11 each for the quick-release pin model. More data is given in the Sources of Equipment subsection.

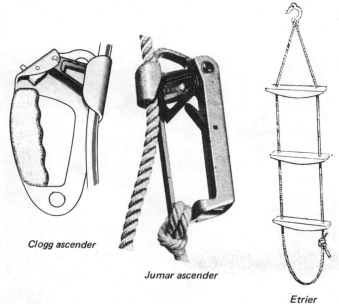

Clogg ascender

Jumar ascender

Etrier

ETRIERS*
About $7

Etriers are short flexible ladders about 6 ft. long with 3 to 6 rungs. They're used in pairs for direct aid climbing. Here's what a climber does if he's the leader: first he places an anchor and snaps in an etrier. Then he climbs up the etrier and places a second anchor. To this he attaches his second etrier, climbs it and places a third anchor. He retrieves his first etrier and snaps it in the third anchor just placed. The second climber, who follows, will have his own etriers, and his job will be to remove the anchors as he climbs past them. This continues until the leader ascends to an area where he can again use cracks and ledges with his hands and feet to continue working upward. There are other applications of the etrier, but they all add up to providing the climber with freedom of movement to place or remove anchors.

Like harnesses, etriers can be purchased ready made or the climber can build his own. Some have metal rungs, which are considered a bit easier to get your feet into when resting against a flat surface, and others are made of webbing stitched or knotted to form stirrups. Of the two, the webbing type is by far the more popular. Forrest Mountaineering has a 64-in. etrier of 1-in. webbing, four stirrups, stitched, with nylon sheath over carabiner pocket to protect it, tensile strength

* Etriers: French, stirrups. Pronounced "A-tree-A."

is 4000 lbs. They have another model just about the same as the preceding one but of ¾-in. webbing and 3000 lbs. test. Either model runs $7.

DESCENDERS
$1 - $9

Contrary to popular belief, the rappel (abseil) is *not* the best nor the safest manner of descent, even though to some it may be the most thrilling (particularly to the observer safe on the ground). For the Jack Armstrong, all-American mountaineer types we quote the following, from *Mountaineering, The Freedom of the Hills*, Harvey Manning, Ed.: "Photographs often show 'jump rappels,' the climber bounding far out into space, sliding many feet down the rope, coming back into the cliff with sprung knees and bounding out once more. Such rappels are not only spectacular to watch but frequently spectacular in their consequences. The jerky descent places tremendous strains on the anchor, whose failure may make the last bound a very long one. Rope burns are more frequent, and finally the rappeller who in one of his bounds passes an overhang often gets rather badly battered around the head and chest when he comes back to the cliff. In recent years there have been so many rappelling accidents that the supposed, theoretical safety of the technique has been called into serious question. First, there are numerous points of possible failure, any one of which can cause a fall. Second, since rappelling is ordinarily done over great exposure a fall is frequently fatal." And from Alan Blackshaw's *Mountaineering*, "It is an unhappy fact that abseiling is a major cause of alpine accidents." The moral of the story is downclimb whenever possible, and if you have to rappel do it carefully. Use a belay rope as an additional precaution in the event something pulls loose.

There are numerous devices on the market made to slow one's descent when rappelling. The simplest is the *break bar*, which fits across a carabiner and increases friction on the rope passing through the 'biner. An alternative to the break bar is a braking system made up of several carabiners arranged at right angles to each other through which the rope is threaded. It creates more friction than the break bar and is probably the most popular method now in use. Giving some competition to the carabiner brake is CMI's Figure-8 descender. It's highly efficient and similar to, but better than, the old Clog. At $7.50 it's a real bargain. It also makes a good belay device and is excellent for lowering loads, i.e., a litter.

CMI 8-Ring

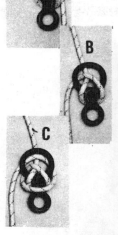

BELAY, LOAD LOWERING, RESCUE

Figure A: Normal configuration for applying friction.

Figure B: Rope lock for 7/16 laid or 11 mm single or double Kernmantle, doubled 7-9 mm.

Figure C: Double lock for more security on smaller single ropes, heavy loads etc.

Biner descender

Markwell using a biner descender

MSR climbing helmet

Ultimate climbing helmet

HELMETS
$8 - $22

Statistically, if you're within two standard deviations of the mean on the normal curve (that's 95.46% of the population), you'll have one of two reactions to helmets: "It's about time," or "Gag!" The other 4.54% don't even give it a second thought. Aesthetically they're ugly and unappealing. Practically they're cumbersome and hot. Safety-wise they do offer a certain amount of head protection against small falling stones and cracking your dome in a fall. But regardless of how you feel about 'em, helmets are coming into vogue. Most of the helmets on the market now are pretty good. Here's a rundown on what's available.

German plastic rock helmet: from REI, $7.95. It's better than nothing.

Ultimate helmet: REI and others, $21.95. This is a light helmet similar to the Joe Brown, but has recently fallen suspect due to a large recall of helmets sold since January of 1975.

Joe Brown helmet: EMS and others, $21.50. Long a popular helmet with a good reputation and it is approved by the British Mountaineering Council.

MSR helmet: MSR and others, $20. According to Larry Penberthy, this is the safest helmet around. His tests have yet to be duplicated and he found something wrong with all of the above. Read his newsletter for the full skinny.

GOGGLES
$2 - $11

A pair of tinted goggles is an absolute necessity when venturing out onto a snowfield to prevent snow blindness regardless of whether it's sunny or overcast. People who wear glasses may have a problem, since goggles are not available with prescription lenses. Best bet here is a pair of ski goggles and wear your glasses under them. Goggles are preferred over sunglasses, and they should have a good quality, solid glass lens. No plastic and no glass-plastic laminated lenses. Plastic scratches and the other type is subject to moisture condensing between the laminations. Goggle frames should be ventilated to prevent moisture build-up. Recreational Equipment, Inc. (REI) sells Anti-Dim Stick, an anti-fogging glycerin stick for 35¢. REI also sells a really good pair of goggles for the economy minded. These are the Swiss Everest glasses and are one of the best around for the money. Price is $8. The Chouinard Annapurna goggles are also excellent, and are the top of the line at $11. There are other brands available which are pretty good, but be sure that whatever you get has lenses of good optical quality.

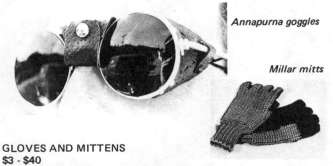

Annapurna goggles

Millar mitts

GLOVES AND MITTENS
$3 - $40

In cold weather the hands are often the first part of the body to cause discomfort, and this is particularly true for the rock climber who must have his fingers exposed and free to maneuver. Any glove with the fingers cut out could be used for protection, but the only one that has proven itself in use on technical climbs is the Millar mitt, an English made fingerless glove. The back is silicone treated wool and the palm is slip-resistant cotton. They look as if your fingers would freeze right off, but they're highly efficient in keeping the hands warm when negotiating technical rock or doing work that would be impossible to handle with your fingers covered. Sizes: small, medium, and large. Price: $6. Best deal: REI. Where the fingers are not required to be exposed, mittens provide the best warmth, better than gloves because they keep the fingers all together. In wool, the Dachstien mitten is the best around. It comes in two weights, medium and heavy, for about $5 at most dealers, or check with EMS. Down mittens are made by damn near everybody, and you should be able to get a good pair for $25 to $40. If you plan on being in a lot of wet snow, use wool mittens; down is useless as an insulator when wet. You might want to check the Winter Bivouacking Section for more information.

GAITERS
$3 - $10

Another requirement for snow climbing is a good pair of gaiters. These serve to seal the space between pant leg and boot top to keep out snow as well as small rocks on scree slopes. Eastern Mountain Sports (EMS) offers a good line ranging from $6 to $9. Sierra Designs also has a fine pair for $11. High gaiters have proven to be more useful than low types. If the highs happen to get too hot, just shove 'em down to your ankles.

Pete Carman's Supergators have been out for several years now and have stood the test of time. Design changes have been minor, and they are available in only one model now—$25, and a liner is available for really severe conditions, at $8.50.

New from Chouinard this year is the Watergator, a really rugged knee-length gaiter with a waterproof bottom section and a breathable, pack-cloth upper to cut down on condensation, $16, anywhere.

Sierra West cagoule

Gaiters

CAGOULES
$18 - $40

Protection from the elements can often be a minor annoyance, or it can be a matter of survival. For protection against the rain and light summer snows in the mountains or for emergency bivouac use, a cagoule is recommended. Somewhat resembling a poncho, a cagoule is a hooded, calf-length sack, but with sleeves. The bottom can be closed off with a drawstring to protect the legs and feet, which are drawn up into it. These garments provide good protection for sitting out a shower and can be of value as a shelter if one is caught on a peak after nightfall. Most cagoules now on the market are made of thin nylon, coated for water repellency. When purchasing, buy big, so you'll have plenty of room to wear down gear underneath. Sierra Designs sells an excellent one for $34. Chouinard has his made in

Scotland where they know what rain's all about. It sells for $35. Other good cagoules are available from Ski Hut, $27; North Face, $33; and Holubar, $34. There is a shorter version of the cagoule available, about waist length, but these rain "shirts" just don't cut the mustard in the mountains.

BIVOUACKING GEAR

FOOT SACKS
$28 - $55

Planned bivouacs usually dictate some sort of protection against the night air. As everyone knows, even as far back as the sixteenth century, night air has been considered unhealthy—especially at high altitudes where it's not unusual to see the bottom drop out of a thermometer. In these circumstances Jack Nicklaus and Johnny Miller both recommend the down-filled foot sack or *elephant's foot* (Scottish golf courses are pretty rough), or even if you're just out for an overnighter on Annapurna, an elephant's foot combined with a down parka will provide almost "sleeping bag" comfort. Actually, an elephant's foot, which reaches from feet to slightly above the waist, could be considered somewhat of a half-sleeping bag. A number of outfitters are handling an innovation called bivouac pants, which are down-filled expedition pants that can be converted to an elephant's foot by zipping the legs together.

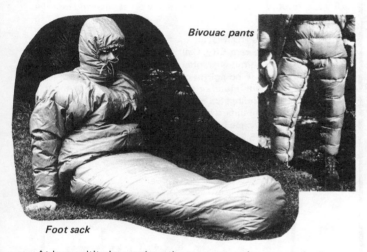

Bivouac pants

Foot sack

At lower altitudes or where the temperature is more moderate, a waterproof, nylon foot sack should be satisfactory, and if used with a cagoule, will provide adequate protection from the elements for a safe night out. Forrest sells a good one for $27.

People experienced enough to do multiple-day climbs generally know what they're looking for in foot sacks. However, if you would prefer to rush into it, you ought to be able to get a good nylon one for under $30 (Chouinard has a nice one for $21), and a good down-filled foot sack for under $50. A good pair of down expedition pants that convert into a foot sack will run you a bit more—up to $95 or so. Most of the dealers mentioned so far in this subsection sell foot sacks and bivouac pants.

BIVOUAC SACKS
$18 - $26

These could be considered sort of like small, box-shaped tents. They are made of waterproof nylon and are large enough for one or two men to crawl in for an overnight bivouac on a ledge or large crack in the rockface. Until recently they were difficult to obtain in this country, but now two really good ones are on the market. Chouinard imports a nice two-man bivouac sack from Germany which sells for $35, and Forrest Mountaineering has a one-man sack of coated nylon for $29.

CLIMBING HAMMOCKS
$13 - $50

On a big wall climb a hammock can mean the difference between a sleepless, seemingly unending night, and sweet dreams. The difference between a climbing hammock and a regular one is that they're designed to be suspended from one or several anchors on the rockface, they close over the top of the climber like... well, a pea pod, and

Forrest Mountaineering bivouack hammock

they're made of very light, but sturdy rip-stop nylon. Chouinard, in fact, has the Pea Pod, a two-point suspension hammock designed by Chuck Kroger to eliminate the squashed shoulders effect associated with hanging bivouacs. Price is $22. The nicest and most sleepable, as well as the most expensive, is the Forrest all-weather hammock. It has a fly of waterproof nylon and is guaranteed weathertight, yet breathable. Designed to be suspended from a single anchor point, it eliminates the need to hunt for a horizontal crack in order to hang it. From Forrest Mountaineering, $30 for the hammock and $20 for the fly. Ummm... ahh... oh yes, use something more than a cliff hanger when rigging this one, lads.

CLIMBING PACKS

Before closing down this equipment discussion, let's consider how you're gonna get all the good stuff you been reading about up the mountain. Mountain goats are now being imported by Forrest in the Oreamnos Americanus model for the American climbing market. Here's what Bill Forrest has to say about them: (quoted from the *Furnace Creek Daily Telegraph*, Furnace Creek, Calif.). "Better than Sherpas or caddies, these Oreamnos models we are now importing (and have an exclusive on, by the way) will revolutionize the climbing scene. Absolutely and unconditionally guaranteed for 1000 pitches or six months (whichever comes first), the Oreamnos is a top-gun mountaineer. It is very well adapted to rock and narrow ledge work. Sheer cliffs and great heights seem to have no effect on the Oreamnos, and it has a cool head and very little imagination—the ideal climbing partner! Yessiree Bob, with its net load capacity of 300 lbs., you'll be able to carry more nets than ever before on even the most difficult of ascents. This is no goat in a poke." For more data contact William Forrest, Underwater Specialties, Furnace Creek, Calif. (Sorry, but Furnace Creek has not qualified for a zip code.)

For those of you who still prefer the old fashioned method of toting your own, there are a number of packs on the market particularly suited to climbing, and others specifically designed for the mountaineer. We've listed these here. The rest of the packs are listed in the Backpacking Section.

RUCKSACKS (frameless)
$15 - $40

These small, teardrop-shaped sacks are ideal for day climbs when only food, water, and rain gear are to be taken along, in addition to ordinary climbing gear. Some on the market are divided into upper and lower compartments, a real convenience since you don't have to dig through sandwiches, yesterday's socks, old skivvies and such to get to the beer (German climbing staple), ale (British climbing staple), wine

(French climbing staple), or Gatorade (American climbing staple). The rucksack's teardrop shape is ideal for technical climbing because its low profile is not likely to jam when negotiating chimneys or while being hauled up a wall. The best are made of waterproof nylon duck, have good durable leather bottoms, and padded leather shoulder straps. Alpine Designs makes two models of this type, the Rock Climber Standard, $18, and the Special, $20. The latter is the larger, and is capable of carrying just about everything you'll need for a one-day climb (see 5th, 6th, and 7th lines above), including hardware. Other good models are made by North Face, $21, and Holubar, whose small size costs $13, and large (with leather bottom), $22.

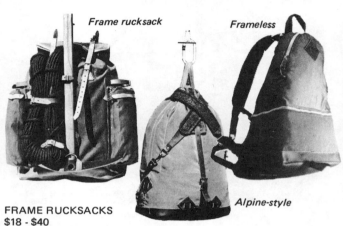

Frame rucksack

Frameless

Alpine-style

FRAME RUCKSACKS
$18 - $40

These are considerably larger than the standard rucksacks, and can be somewhat cumbersome affairs to wear if you're on an extremely technical climb. Most of the time they're just used to bring gear to the base of the climb, and if taken on the ascent itself, are hauled up after the climbers. For long one-day climbs on rock that doesn't present any great technical difficulties such as the type found in the Colorado Rockies where a down jacket, cagoule, rope, and some hardware are often taken as insurance along with lunch, Pepto-Bismol, and a first aid kit.. ah, I forgot what I was going to say.. Oh yeah—frame rucksacks are pretty handy. Most of them have two or three extra pockets attached on the outside so you can carry all that stuff. The larger capacity of these sacks also lets them double nicely as a child's pack for backpacking. There are a good number of these rucksacks on the market, so, not to bore you, we've only listed the better makes here. The Alpine Designs Eiger Pack is probably the best of the whole lot in terms of materials used, workmanship, and durability. They use the heaviest leather of any company around for the bottoms and shoulder straps. For $30 it's a real steal. The Millet sack has been around for a long time, and in frame models they offer some real nice ones but without the leather bottoms. Even so, craftsmanship is very good and prices vary from $18 to $39 depending on the carrying capacity you're after. Another good one is the Holubar Royal Pack; very similar to the Eiger and sells for $39.

ALPINE-STYLE SACKS
$30 - $60

For big time climbing, the alpine-style sack is better than either of the two previous types because of its greater carrying capacity. The best has a sleeve or collar sewn around the top opening, which is normally kept tucked in the sack, but when it's pulled out it can increase the carrying capacity by as much as 75%. This sleeve is also called a "bivouac" extension because it enables the sack to alternate as a foot sack during bivouacs. Another nice feature some of these sacks have is detachable outside pockets; helps save weight. It's unfortunate that only a few models of this type are available in the U.S. The Millet 294 is an excellent one which extends to 36" and has attachments for an ice axe and crampons; $44, from Thomas Black & Sons. Salewa used to make a fine sack of this type, but for some reason it has disappeared from the American market. Among those without the extendable sleeve is one by Forrest Mountaineering. The Grade VI Hauling Bag is a super, heavy duty pack primarily designed for hauling gear up walls. It's made of 22 oz. neoprene-coated nylon (heavy stuff), is 32" high, has removable padded shoulder straps, and a 3-ft. long daisy chain sewn to the outside for attaching climbing gear, $38. The other sack is by North Face. It's roomy, but lacks the detachable pockets and a bivouac extension. It does have arrangements though for attaching skis, ice axe, crampons, and other items. Cost is $50.

Since there's almost a google of retailers who sell climbing gear, we've had to be a bit selective in whom to list. Most of these people also handle backpacking equipment, so we decided that only those carrying a substantial stock of good climbing merchandise would be listed here and the rest would be relegated to the Backpacking Section.

ALPINE RECREATION WAREHOUSE
4B Henshaw St., Woburn, Mass. 01801

Consisting of a mail order house and seven stores in Massachusetts and New York, ARW carries an impressive array of commodities. They put out a mimeographed pamphlet (free on request) for each type of equipment they sell by mail: tents, packs, food, books, sleeping bags, and climbing hardware. All other wares are sold only at the store sites. In the tent, sleeping bag, and pack pamphlets, there are brief but informative write-ups covering basic considerations to keep in mind when selecting the particular type of gear. It would be nice if they'd do this for their hardware pamphlet as well. Their selection of hardware is large enough for the most discriminating climber. Major brands include Chouinard, Forrest, SMC, and Troll. Climbing packs are offered in a variety of makes—Lafume, Alpine Designs, Forrest, Gerry, and Kelty. Retail prices are usually set at what the manufacturer suggests.

BECK OUTDOOR PROJECTS
P.O. Box 1038, Crescent City, Calif. 95531

Beck has a no-time-limit guarantee on their product—a neoprene coated nylon strap (binding) for crampons and snowshoes. If you are dissatisfied, they will refund or replace at your request. Without reservation their bindings are among the best, and far superior to any made of leather. Chouinard believes this and has them riveted onto his crampons. Snowshoe bindings are $7 to $11, crampon bindings are $3 for instep, $5.25 for the regular model, and $7 for the professional model. If you have any special designs you'd like made up, Beck also does custom work. Literature and a sample of the strap material are available on request.

THOMAS BLACK AND SONS, INC.
225 Strathcoma Ave., Ottawa K1S 1X7, Canada

The parent firm and control of Blacks is in Scotland. They carry a good line of exclusive import products including tents, sleeping bags, packs, boots, stoves and clothing. Most of their climbing hardware is Stubai and Hiatt; some is Salewa, Karrimor, and Moac. They only carry three models of boots (a mountaineering, a climbing, and a hiking) by Blax, good but not of outstanding quality. Their ropes are Goldline and Viking Kernmantle, and meet standards set by the Union Internationale des Associations d'Alpinisme (UIAA). A 22-page color catalogue is available, but many of the items could be described a little better. Sometimes an item's weight or the amount of fill for down clothing is omitted and occasionally an item is listed, but not pictured.

GREAT PACIFIC IRON WORKS
P.O. Box 150, Ventura, Calif. 93001

Chouinard's outfit. Manufactures pitons, carabiners, hammers, chocks, and other climbing hardware and software for the discriminating climber. Some of Chouinard's staple is made in Europe to their exact specifications. This includes their crampons and rope. Chouinard is

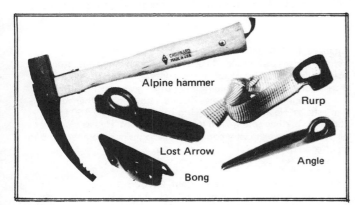

Alpine hammer

Rurp

Lost Arrow

Angle

Bong

probably the finest line of alpine climbing equipment in the world, and their crampons are unquestionably the best. They'll handle other manufacturers' products providing they consider them of superior quality. In footwear, Chouinard handles the Royal Robbins rock-climbing boot by Galibier, $45. In other words, if you buy something from Chouinard, there ain't no problem of whether it'll do the job or not—it will! As a result of the unusual pains taken to assure that they sell only the best, their equipment is sometimes hard to get, which is particularly true of the hardware. Their 96-page catalog costs $1, but you'll get more than $2 worth of information and inspiration from it—lotsa good tips on the proper use of Chouinard equipment and experts' views on the new climbing ethics.

EASTERN MOUNTAIN SPORTS, INC. (EMS)
1041 Commonwealth Ave., Boston, Mass. 02215
EMS handles a range of merchandise from good to best for almost every wilderness recreation activity, and their illustrated 240-page catalog is virtually a textbook of this type equipment. Each section of gear begins with an introduction that covers much of the basic info one needs to make a proper selection of what they have to offer, even down to handy charts comparing different brands and types. And from where we read it, they don't seem to be playing any favorites—just the facts. As a much welcomed feature EMS has started testing technical climbing rope and hardware. Test procedures and results are also written up in the catalog. If you have questions or would like to make comments concerning the testing program, write Dr. J. C. Kohr in care of EMS. The gear that EMS carries is mostly Chouinard, Forrest, SMC, Stubai, and Bonaiti as well as a few commodities of other manufacturers, such as the Joe Brown helmet and the Millar mitt, a fingerless glove made in England. Boots are Fabiano, Vasque, and Galibier makes with some being specially made for EMS by West German and Swiss bootmakers. Prices are sometimes competitive, but generally conform to suggested retail. Occasionally, EMS will have a clearance sale and offer some far out (in this instance, good) deals. So get on their mailing list, 'cause they send out a big flier on these clearances. And while you're at it don't forget to request a copy of their catalog—$1.

FORREST MOUNTAINEERING
1517 Platte St., Denver, Colo. 80202
Forrest Mountaineering, like Chouinard, is a specialist manufacturer of climbing equipment. A comment by Bill Forrest typifies the integrity and sincere dealings inherent in his outfit, "No item gets listed in this catalogue unless I have personally used it on a grade V or VI climb [that's a class 5.6 to 5.9 in the YDS system], and that's part of the Forrest guarantee." Except for chocks and a hammer, Forrest hasn't gotten into much hardware, but the equipment they do make is distinguished by many innovative and interesting characteristics. Their packs, for instance, have deviated from the traditional and incorporated, among other things, the following features; 22 oz. per square yard vinyl coated nylon (that's heavy stuff, man), one strap to hold down the top flap, daisy chains sewn to the outside for attaching equipment, and inner pockets for load separation. Five types of packs are now made. Forrest also has bivouacking hammocks. Generally considered among the best on the market, their two hammocks, the regular, $30, and the all weather, $40, have now been

combined into one hammock, $42, with an optional rain fly for $42. A 68-page catalog is available.

GIBBS PRODUCTS
854 Padley St., Salt Lake City, Utah 84108
Their main claim to fame is the Gibbs Ascender. Two versions are made—the standard, $10, and the quick-release pin model, $13. Both are simply constructed and use body weight instead of a spring to set the gripper. They cannot come off the rope as some ascenders do, and frank reports reaching us have it they perform exceptionally well on icy or muddy rope. Spare parts are available. Other wares sold are Plymouth Goldline rope, 37¢ per foot, and Mammut Dynamic rope,

$88 for 165 feet of 11mm; SMC 'biners; and webbing. A four-page pamphlet is gotten with an inquiry.

HOLUBAR
P.O. Box 7, Boulder, Colo. 80302
Manufacturers and retailers of what is probably one of the best and most complete lines of mountaineering and backpacking equipment in the United States. Their down gear and tents are of the highest quality; they sell "seconds" at substantial savings, and if you want to make your own, they're the sole distributor for Carikit. But more of that in the Backpacking and Winter Bivouacing Sections. Their selection of climbing ware comes from the best: Chouinard, SMC, Forrest, and others. Galibier's Hivernale double mountaineering boot, $110, and the Royal Robbins rock-climbing boot, $45, are featured. For mountaineering boots lighter than the double, they carry the Vasque line. You can see all this for yourself in the 64-page catalog which they will supply on notice of your desideratum.

MOUNTAIN SAFETY RESEARCH (MSR)
631 S. 96th St., Seattle, Wash. 98108
Larry Penberthy founded MSR back in 1969 as "a volunteer organization of persons interested in promoting mountaineering safety," and elected himself the Ralph Nader of the climbing community. Some manufacturers and retailers of climbing gear think him the devil's advocate; however, he has had legitimate gripes concerning unsafe and questionable equipment on the market. And he has been instrumental in having some removed, or advertising claims corrected, through legal action. Where this has failed, he has tried to apply "economic pressure on merchants and manufacturers to improve their products by (having

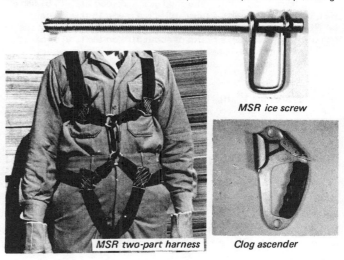

MSR ice screw

MSR two-part harness

Clog ascender

MSR offer) better products to the mountaineering fraternity." In some cases MSR has come up with a better product, in others...

The point, though, is that Penberthy, despite what many feel is self-esteemed horn-tooting, is doing something to try and make climbing safer. So he's not polished; so he's made some mistakes—it's a lot better than sitting by the wayside with a shrug of the shoulders and, "...can't fight city hall, baby."

MSR has grown quite a bit since '69 and handles a fair line of climbing gear both of their own and others' manufacture, including Chouinard, Leeper, CMI, Salewa and Bonaiti. Periodically they issue a "Newsletter & Catalog" of about 50 pages. Half is devoted to listing and describing the equipment and books MSR handles, and the other half to editorial comment by Penberthy on such subjects as mountain sickness, climbers' food needs, unfair attitudes of the government concerning climbing on public property, environmental issues, book reviews, equipment tests and evaluations, and so forth. Makes for some interesting and informative reading. If you'd like to get on MSR's mailing list to get the newsletter/catalog combo, send $1.50 (donation) to the above address.

RECREATIONAL EQUIPMENT, INC. (REI)
1525 11th Ave., Seattle, Wash. 98122

In the first edition of the *Source Book* we listed REI as selling everything for the self-propelled—some good stuff and some bad—you have to watch what you buy or you'll end up with less than adequate equipment. Well, Huh Boy! Did we get some static back on that one, in addition to the statement that REI would not sell one copy of the *SB* till we got our facts up-to-date. We were also sent a copy of "View Point" (72-73 cat.) which stressed REI's never-ending emphasis on quality control. Among other things we read, "In April 1971, REI established its own Quality Control Department to investigate charges by a few members that some climbing equipment and other merchandise were inadequate. We hired Cal Magnusson, a mechanical engineer and mountaineer, to look into complaints and eliminate or improve defective equipment.

"The policy of REI has always been to supply our members with the best merchandise available for the price."...so forth and so on.

Well, we're happy to report that, among other things, REI is still listing and selling the best Austrian corkscrew* available (for the price), by Stubai, on pgs. 62-63 of their '76 catalog...in three sizes. The 3¼" is for small bottles with short corks such as Mateus or Grenache Rose; the 5", for medium-size bottles, any fine porto (Ficklin California; York House), burgundy (Beaulieu, 1970; Sebastiani, 1967) or sauterne (Korbe Dry; Wente Dry Semillion, '68 & '69), and the 7", of course, for only the finest of champagnes (Schransberg Blanc de Blanc, 1966; Korbell Natural). Some climbers, on reaching the summit, have been known to pop a bottle of rhine with a 7-incher, but this certainly shows a lack of good taste!

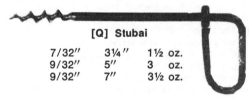

[Q] Stubai		
7/32"	3¼"	1½ oz.
9/32"	5"	3 oz.
9/32"	7"	3½ oz.

Yes, there is definitely some good gear and good deals to be had at REI, but unfortunately we must still add a caveat to this listing.

REI is a co-op organization with a membership fee of $2. At the end of the year you get a return of about 10% on the total price of what you bought. Membership is open to anyone with two bucks. A fully-illustrated 96-page catalog of their gear is available on request.

SWALLOWS NEST
909 N.E. Boat St., Seattle, Wash. 98105

These guys put out a very informative equipment guide/catalog for free. They deal with equipment for all types of environments and situations from day-tripping to expeditions. They handle a good, time-proven selection of articles from Forrest, Chouinard, Trailwise and Snow Lion, as well as being one of the few outfits to deal in Haderer boots. If you're looking for guidance in buying gear, their guide is truly worth getting and reading.

*Austrian (Stubai) ice screw. Considered unreliable. L. Penberthy (MSR) asked Stubai about them breaking. Stubai replied that they got *only* 4 to 5 reports of this nature per year. (Ref: *MSR Newsletter*, Vol. 4, pg. 17).

MOUNTAIN SPORTS
821 Pearl St., Boulder, Colo. 80302

A small store in Boulder that handles high quality climbing and mountaineering merchandise. There are no cheap, junk articles offered for sale. Prices are sometimes very good. Literature is available.

PETER LIMMER, INC.
Intervale, N.H. 03845

Pete carries his own brand of custom made climbing boots (some made in Europe to his specs). Price ranges from $45 to $65. In his 8-page catalog, he lists a minimum of other gear: down clothing, sleeping bags (most are Thomas Black's), stoves, and other concomitant articles. He also handles Edelrid ropes, 11 mm. by 150 ft. for $55, and Goldline ropes, 7/16-in. at 24¢ per foot. He has more gear in his store. Prices seem very competitive, and his boots are reported to be of good quality.

THE SKI HUT
1615 University Ave., Berkeley, Calif. 94703

Along with a fine selection of quality climbing gear, Ski Hut has a very good line of packs, down gear, clothing, and accessories. Their climbing stock is from Chouinard, Peck, Bonaiti, Salewa, and others. They also carry the Stitch Belay Plate for $6. Boots from lightweight rock climbing and hiking boots to heavyweight double boots—by Galibier, Pivetta, and Vasque. Sometimes they assess the value of their goods a bit high. A postcard request will bring their 60-page, well-illustrated catalog.

Stitch belay plate

Joe Brown helmet

SKIMEISTER SKI SHOP, INC.
Main St., North Woodstock, N.H. 03262

A good all around selection of mountaineering, backpacking, and ski touring equipment. Climbing merchandise from Chouinard, Leeper, SMC, Salewa, Bonaiti, Forrest, and Stubai. Ropes: Goldline, Edelrid, Mammut, and Chouinard. Shoes by Fabiano, Vasque, and Lowa. Joe Brown Helmet, $19.50 as opposed to EMS's $21.50. Jumars, $30 a pair to Ski Hut's $32. Other values are retail or lower. Thirty-six pages for the '72-'73 catalog. It's free.

ENGLAND

A few of the articles mentioned on the previous pages may not be readily available in the United States just yet, such as the Clog descender, the Terrordactyl ice axe, and a variety of bivouac sacs. Too bad, you say? Not really; we're listing a few dealers in Britain who sell these items. Just write them for their catalog (costs 31¢ for an air mail letter); make the money conversion according to the current exchange rate (inquire about this information in your letter to the dealer); order your stuff; and pay the duty, if any. Simple.

BRYAN G. STOKES
2 High Court, High St., Sheffield, England

ELLIS BRIGHAM
6-14 Cathedral St. M4 3FU, Manchester, England

L. D. MOUNTAIN CENTRE LTD.
34 Dean St., Newcastle, England

Y. H. A. SALES
29 John Adam St., W.C.2., London, England

TOURS & EXPEDITIONS

Going to a new climbing area can be both an exciting and exasperating experience. Exciting, because new problems and new challenges always are to the climber. Exasperating, because who's to say that halfway up a new route, the climber won't be forced to turn back because, through ignorance of the situation, he didn't have the right gear or ran out of experience.

A guidebook is the logical answer to this; however, if none is available, the local climbing shop should be able to give you some info, or refer you to local climbers who can tell you what you need to know. If it's impossible to get any information on a certain area, then you'll have your own personal little adventure going. Exploring a new area "blind" is more fun than it sounds, but be prepared to back off (or peel off) some climbs.

There is, in some circles, an anti-guidebook movement. While we agree that some climbs are best left out-of-print, guidebooks to popular areas serve their purpose if for no other reason than safety. With their descriptions and ratings of climbs for different areas, the climber can choose those within his technical experience instead of getting into something over his head.

Climb Grading Systems

Since guidebooks use grading systems to tell a climber what kind of route he's chosen and the difficulties he should expect to encounter, it seems in order to discuss grading systems. In the United States the National Climbing Classification System (NCCS) and the Yosemite Decimal System (YDS) are used. Of the two, the Yosemite is more precise in the information it gives, and likewise is the more popular. This is what a typical classification number looks like (note the three parts):

IV - 5.7 - A4 (YDS)   or   *IV - F7 - A4* (NCCS)

When a climbing route is graded three things must be rated: first, the overall difficulty of the route (IV); second, the hardest free climbing section of the route (5.7 or F7); third, the hardest aid climbing section of the route (A4). In general conversation, however, a climber usually will give only the hardest free climbing section (pitch), to wit, "He told me on the phone Class 4, and when I shows up at the rocks with just my boots, he says, 'I meant a Class F4.'—dumbass!"

Overall Rating of Route. This takes into account the length and time of the complete climb, weather problems to be encountered, ease of escape, the average difficulty of all of the pitches (the sections between the belay points on a given climb), and the difficulty of the hardest pitch. Both the NCCS and the YDS systems rate the climb from Roman numeral *I* (easy; half-day climb) to *VI* (hard; multi-day climb). The overall rating for the climb graded above is *IV*.

Hardest Free Pitch Rating. A rating of the most difficult free climbing pitch. The YDS starts with the number *1* and continues in whole numbers to *5*, from there it goes up in gradations of tenths (.1) until reaching *5.11*. Thus, *1* is walking on level ground, *5.0* starts the roped free climbing, and *5.11* is the hardest free climbing imaginable. The NCCS assigns this part the letter *F* followed by a whole number from *1* to *10* in order of difficulty. The above rated climb gives this a *5.7* (YDS) or an *F7* (NCCS) classification.

Hardest Aid Pitch Rating. If there is any aid work on a climb, the hardest aid, or artificial, pitch encountered is rated. Both the YDS and the NCCS systems have delegated this part the letter *A* followed by a whole number from *1* to *5*, five being the hardest. The climb rated above is given an *A4* in this area. If no aid is found on a climb, this designation is usually not included in the classification number.

When using either one of these systems, you must bear in mind that the second and third catagories rate only the hardest free pitch and the hardest aid pitch for a given route up the mountain. While these are important to keep you from getting over your head in free or aid climbing, you must give the first part, the general overall rating, careful attention to find out how difficult and sustaining the *entire* climb is. Take a *I 5.5 A2* climb. By the overall rating of *I* you can tell this is a short climb which is not very demanding, but the *5.5* indicates that there is a fairly difficult free climbing pitch. It also has some aid climbing, but it is not very hard as you can see by the *A2*

designation. Now, if the overall rating on this climb was *III*, making it a *III 5.5 A2* climb, you would have to be prepared for a much longer climb that would probably include a bivouac. And if the overall rating was *VI*, making it a *VI 5.5 A2* climb, you would definitely have to make extensive food and bivouac preparations for three or more days. For the NCSS system the equivalent ratings would read: *I F4 A2*; *III F4 A2*; and *VI F4 A2*.

If your climbing takes you to Europe, there is another classification system you will have to contend with, or I guess I should say two, if you also climb in England. The English use a system of descriptive adjectives to grade their rock climbs. It is hard to explain, so I refer you to the chart following this discussion for a comparison with the YDS and NCCS systems. The Union Internationale des Associations d'Alpinisme (UIAA) has a different system from the British and is the standard one used on the Continent. The UIAA system rates only the hardest free climbing problem but requires that a complete pitch by pitch description of the climb be included and graded in the text so that one may ascertain the overall commitment to the route.

With a little practice you'll be able to pick up a basic working knowledge of these systems. A fairly good discussion that may help you to better understand the difficulties of using classification systems is to be found in Blackshaw's *Mountaineering—From Hill Walking to Alpine Climbing*, pp. 136-139 and 364-367.

The following chart will help to orient you toward the systems discussed, both at home and abroad. —John Markwell.

CLIMBING DIFFICULTY CLASSIFICATIONS

Overall Difficulty		Free Climbing Difficulty					Aid Climbing Difficulty	
YDS	NCCS		YDS	NCCS	UIAA	British	YDS	NCCS
I	I	Level walking	1		I		A1	A1
II	II	Uphill walking	2				A2	A2
III	III	Scrambling	3	F1	II		A3	A3
IV	IV	Scrambling, rope should be available	4		III—	Easy	A4	A4
V	V	Beginning of roped climbing	5.0		III		A5	A5
VI	VI		5.1	F2	III+	Moderate		
			5.2		IV—			
			5.3	F3	IV	Difficult		
			5.4		IV+	Very difficult		
			5.5	F4	V—	Severe		
			5.6	F5&6	V	Very severe		
			5.7	F7	V+			
			5.8	F8	VI—	Hard very severe		
			5.9	F9	VI			
			5.10	F10	VI+	Extremely severe		
			5.11					

CLIMBING GUIDES

ARTIFICIAL CLIMBING WALLS,
Kim Meldrum and Brian Royle, 1970 - $5.74.
From: Transatlantic Arts, Inc., North Village Green, Levittown, Long Island, N.Y. 11756

MOUNTAINS OF THE WORLD: A HANDBOOK FOR HIKERS AND CLIMBERS, William M. Bueler, 1970 - 279 p. il. - $4.75

Not really a climbing guide, *Mountains'* value is in its broad coverage of the world's "high spots" and its brief, but useful, general information.
From: Charles E. Tuttle Co., Inc., Rutland, Vt. 05701

WORLD ATLAS OF MOUNTAINEERING,
Wilfrid Noyce and Ian McMorrin, eds., $14.95.
From: St. Martin's Press, 175 Fifth Ave., New York, N.Y. 10010

CANADA

A CLIMBER'S GUIDE TO THE COASTAL RANGES OF BRITISH COLUMBIA, Dick Culbert, 425 p. - $7.00.
From: Alpine Club of Canada, P.O. Box 1026, Banff, Alberta, Can.

A CLIMBER'S GUIDE TO THE INTERIOR RANGES OF BRITISH COLUMBIA, William L. Putnam, $7.00.
From: American Alpine Club, 113 E. 90th St., N.Y., N.Y. 10028
10028

A CLIMBER'S GUIDE TO THE ROCKY MOUNTAINS OF CANADA, J. Monroe Thorington, $6.00.
From: American Alpine Club, 113 E. 90th St., N.Y., N.Y. 10028

A CLIMBER'S GUIDE TO YAMNUSKA,
Brian Greenwood and Urs Kallen, $2.50.
From: Alpine Club of Canada, P.O. Box 1026, Banff, Alberta, Can.

PURCELL RANGE OF BRITISH COLUMBIA, (?), $5.00.
From: American Alpine Club, 113 E. 90th St., N.Y., N.Y. 10028

UNITED STATES

Northwest

BOULDERS AND CLIFFS, A CLIMBER'S GUIDE TO LOWLAND ROCK IN SKAGIT AND WHATCOM COUNTIES
Dallas Kloke, 80 p. il. - $2.50.
From: Signpost Publications, 16812 36th Ave. West, Lynwood, Wash. 98036

GUIDE TO THE LEAVENWORTH ROCK CLIMBING AREAS
Beckey and Byornstad, $2.50.
From: Eastern Mountain Sports, Inc., 1041 Commonwealth Ave., Boston, Mass. 02215

A CLIMBER'S GUIDE TO GLACIER NATIONAL PARK
J. Gordon Edwards, 144 p. il. - $5.25.
From: Sierra Club, 1050 Mills Tower, San Francisco, Calif. 94104

A CLIMBER'S GUIDE TO THE CASCADE AND OLYMPIC MOUNTAINS OF WASHINGTON, 1961 - 386 p. - $5.00.
From: American Alpine Club, 113 E. 90th St., N.Y., N.Y. 10028

A CLIMBER'S GUIDE TO OLYMPIC MOUNTAINS
Olympic Mountain Rescue, $4.95.
From: Eastern Mountain Sports, Inc., 1041 Commonwealth Ave., Boston, Mass. 02215

A CLIMBER'S GUIDE TO OREGON
Dodge, $3.95.
From: Eastern Mountain Sports, Inc., 1041 Commonwealth Ave., Boston, Mass. 02215

A CLIMBER'S GUIDE TO THE TETON RANGE
Leigh Ortenburger, 336 p. il. - $6.00.
From: Sierra Club, 1050 Mills Tower, San Francisco, Calif. 94104

West

A CLIMBER'S GUIDE TO PINNACLES NATIONAL MONUMENT
Steve Roper, ed., $2.75.
From: Ski Hut, 1615 University Ave., Berkeley, Calif. 94703

A CLIMBER'S GUIDE TO THE HIGH SIERRA
Harvey Voge, ed., 298 p. il. - $6.50
From: Sierra Club, 1050 Mills Tower, San Francisco, Calif. 94104

A CLIMBER'S GUIDE TO ROCKY MOUNTAIN NATIONAL PARK AREA, Walter W. Frickle, $6.00.
From: Ski Hut, 1615 University Ave., Berkeley, Calif. 94703

A CLIMBER'S GUIDE TO TAHQUITZ AND SUICIDE ROCKS
Chick Wilts, Callis, and Raymond, eds., $3.75.
From: American Alpine Club, 113 E. 90th St., N.Y., N.Y. 10028

A CLIMBER'S GUIDE TO YOSEMITE VALLEY
Steve Roper, ed., 1970 - 190 p. il. - $6.95.
From: Sierra Club, 1050 Mills Tower, San Francisco, Calif. 94104

GUIDE TO THE COLORADO MOUNTAINS
Robert Ornes, ed., 1970 - 250 p. - $6.00.
From: Swallow Press, Inc., 1139 S. Wabash Ave., Chicago, Ill. 60605

GUIDE TO NEW MEXICO MOUNTAINS
Ungnade, $3.95
From: Eastern Mountain Sports, Inc., 1041 Commonwealth Ave., Boston, Mass. 02215

GUIDE TO THE SANDIA MOUNTAINS
Lawrence G. Kline, $1.75.
From: Ski Hut, 1615 University Ave., Berkeley, Calif. 94703

HIGH OVER BOULDER
Pat Ament and Cleveland McCarty, $5.50.
From: Pruett Publishing Co., Box 1560, Boulder, Colo. 80302

LONGS PEAK—ITS STORY AND A CLIMBING GUIDE
Paul W. Nesbit, $1.50.
From: Paul W. Nesbit, 711 Columbia Rd., Colorado Springs, Colo. 80904

Midwest

A CLIMBER'S AND HIKER'S GUIDE TO DEVIL'S LAKE
Smith, $1.50.
From: Leon R. Greenman, Inc., 132 Spring St., N.Y., N.Y. 10012

A CLIMBER'S GUIDE TO MISSISSIPPI PALISADES
J. Kolocotronis, $1.00.
From: Leon R. Greenman, Inc., 132 Spring St., N.Y., N.Y. 10012

A CLIMBER'S GUIDE TO THE NEEDLES IN THE BLACK HILLS OF SOUTH DAKOTA, Bob Kamps, 96 p. il. - $5.50
From: American Alpine Club, 113 E. 90th St., N.Y., N.Y. 10028

Northeast

A CLIMBER'S GUIDE TO CATHEDRAL AND WHITE HORSE LEDGES, Joseph and Karen Cote, 1969 - 76 p. il. - $1.50.
From: The Outdoorsman, Back Bay, Box 447, Boston, Mass. 02117

A CLIMBER'S GUIDE TO RAGGED MOUNTAIN
Reppy and Streibert, $1.00.
From: Yale Outing Club, New Haven, Conn. 06520

A CLIMBER'S GUIDE TO THE ADIRONDACKS
T. Healy, ed., $3.00.
From: Eastern Mountain Sports, Inc., 1041 Commonwealth Ave., Boston, Mass. 02215

A CLIMBER'S GUIDE TO THE QUINCY QUARRIES
Crowther and Thompson, $1.00
From: Leon R. Greenman, Inc., 132 Spring St., N.Y., N.Y. 10012

A CLIMBER'S GUIDE TO THE SHAWANGUNKS
Arthur Gran, 1964 - $5.00.
From: American Alpine Club, 113 E. 90th St., N.Y., N.Y. 10028

PITTSBURG AREA CLIMBER'S GUIDE
Jirak, $1.50.
From: Leon R. Greenman, Inc., 132 Spring St., N.Y., N.Y. 10012

Mideast

A CLIMBER'S GUIDE TO SENECA ROCKS, WEST VIRGINIA
Guides to this area come and go so fast it's hard to tell which ones are currently available. As of press time, there are none. We suggest you write to the Gendarme, Box 53, Mouth of Seneca, W. Va. 26884, for the latest info.

The Classification Problem.

As often happens when you start classifying things, you get confusion. Well, that's what we got when we tried to separate (clearly) commercial groups, clubs, associations, and so on, as to what services and programs they offered. Often they put equal emphasis on two or more programs and that makes it hard to decide where to list some groups.

In this subsection we've listed those groups who are primarily into leading, organizing and directing tours and expeditions. It wouldn't hurt to check back through the section on schools though to get the full rundown on what's offered in the way of commercial expeditioning.

ADVENTURE GUIDES, INC.
36 E. 57th St., New York, N.Y. 10022
These people are a good source of information for just about any type of wilderness excursion. They publish a 224-page illustrated guide which lists and describes "adventures" by land, water, and air conducted by over 700 groups across the nation. Climbing and mountaineering are included. Names and addresses of organizations are listed by activity and then geographically, which, if you're looking for a group by their name alone, can make them a little difficult to locate. Other than that, *Adventure Travel USA* is a great little directory. It's available from the above address for $3.95.

ALPINE RECREATION
135 Saranac Dr., Missoula, Mont. 59801
Tom Kumpf and Rich Larcom offer backpacking-mountaineering trips for experienced as well as novice climbers in the Selway-Bitterroot Wilderness area of Montana. They provide an opportunity for families, individuals and groups to enjoy the wilderness in a safe, clean manner. Trips average around 5 days at $70 per day.

ALASKA MOUNTAIN GUIDES
Talkeetna, Alaska 99672
15- to 20-day trips in which you climb South Peak; survival treks that emphasize rock and glacier work. Guided climbs in McKinley area. Expensive.

CAMP DENALI
Box D, College, Alaska 99701
Offer 1-week mountaineering trips within Mt. McKinley National Park with an emphasis on the appreciation of the Far North's echo systems. They don't "spoon-feed guests" and they have no bar (but you can bring your own). Sounds like a good place to go if you'd like to get into the world of the Tundra.

DOLOMITES 76
2421 Spruce St., Boulder, Colo. 80302
Twenty-one-day technical climbing expeditions to the Italian Alps.

EARTH EXPLORERS
1560 Sandburg Terrace, Chicago, Ill. 60610
Definitely an alternative to an "Acapulco-style" vacation. Not only do they offer climbing excursions throughout Europe but they also have treks, Land Rover excursions and sailing cruises in every area of the world imaginable. Prices seem reasonable, too.

HONDO RAST & CO.
857 N. 8th, Laramie, Wyo. 82070
Mountaineering expeditions throughout North and South America. Lots of trips offered to Alaska.

THE INFINITE ODYSSEY
14 Union Park St., Boston, Mass. 02118
These guys offer 3- to 6-week trips for teenagers. Mountaineering in the Tetons, Colorado, and Wind River range. Some secondary schools will grant academic credit for these trips. Place sounds neat but expensive, although they say they have financial aid available for a few kids.

INTERNATIONAL MOUNTAIN EQUIPMENT
Box 494, North Conway, N.H. 03860
Offer guided climbs in The Presidential Range and winter mountaineering trips (Presidential Traverse) at reasonable costs. They also offer some instruction.

JOHANN MT. GUIDES
P.O. Box 19171, Portland, Oreg. 97219
Ed Johann offers guided climbs on Mt. Hood, Mt. St. Helens and other peaks in the Northwest as well as mountaineering seminars and a trip around Mt. Hood taking 5 days. Prices seem reasonable.

MT. HOOD CLIMBING & GUIDE SERVICE
9120 W. Stark St., Portland, Oreg. 97229
Phil Dean and his crew offer a really extensive expeditioning and guide service throughout the Northwest. Luxury accommodations at Timberline Lodge are available if you're into that and can afford it.

MOUNTAIN TRAVEL (USA)
1398 Solano Ave., Albany, Calif. 94706
Probably has one of the most versatile offerings of any of the expeditionary groups in the United States. Trips to North and South America, Europe, and nine countries in other parts of the world. Prices, which include air fare, can go as low as $475 per excursion, but usually they run over $1000. Mountain Travel will send you a beautifully illustrated booklet with all the details on each expedition package they offer. Also, they operate the Palisade School of Mountaineering— see under "Schools."

NORTHERN LIGHTS ALPINE RECREATION
Box 399, Invermere, British Columbia, Canada V0A 1K0
Mountaineering camps similar to those offered by The Alpine Club of Canada. These trips afford a good chance to see some really beautiful mountain country. Guided winter trips also available.

NORTHWEST ALPINE GUIDE SERVICE, INC.
P.O. Box 80345, Seattle, Wash. 98109
Mountaineering in the Northwest and also Mexico. Have some trips geared to youngsters between 11 and 17.

NORTHWEST MOUNTAINEERING GUIDE SERVICE
P.O. Box 19171, Portland, Ore. 97219
Summer, one to ten days, and up to twenty people at a time. Each day will cost you from $15 to $25. Group rates. Includes all mountaineering gear.

RECREATION UNLIMITED
Jackson, Wyo.
These fellows offer guided climbs on most of the peaks in Grand Teton National Park. Also have a neat Ice Cave trip.

RICK HORN WILDERNESS EXPEDITIONS
Box 471, Jackson Hole, Wyo. 83001
Expeditions include camping, backpacking, fishing, mountaineering and rock climbing, ski touring, and natural history. All special clothing and equipment is supplied. Moderate rates. Information pamphlets covering their program are easy to get—just send them a postcard.

THE WILDERNESS INSTITUTE
P.O. Box 1843, Jackson, Wyo. 83001
Guided trips throughout the Tetons again. Also offer family treks anywhere in the Western Rockies, and some instruction.

dog packing

Dog packing solves one of the backpacker's biggest problems: what to do with the household pet when the urge to take to the hills strikes. Instead of putting your pet in a costly kennel, you can enjoy the companionship of man's best friend without adding his food and gear to the forty or fifty pounds you're already toting around on your back. The exercise and fresh air are just as good for the dog as they are for you. And besides such rational considerations, it's nice to have his warm, furry body and his friendly breath at night, when the great dark forest with its anonymous noises closes in around you.

A dog can comfortably carry one-half to two-thirds of his own body weight if he's active and in good health. In addition to his own food, a pack of half his weight should allow him to carry his bowls, leash, and emergency veterinary supplies. In some cases, you may even be able to squeeze in some of your gear. A dog is physically capable of carrying much more than this amount. Some hunters and trappers load their dogs with up to twice their body weight, but that is strictly a matter of work and not of pleasure.

Training the Dog. A dog can easily be taught to wear a pack. Start a few weeks before your trip to allow time for him to adjust to it. The first step is to let him familiarize himself with the pack. Let him sniff it for a minute or two. If you can be sure he won't nibble, you can even let him sleep with it at night. Then put it on him, petting and reassuring him as you do. If he seems nervous, stop until the next day and then try again. In other words play it by ear, letting the dog set the pace. If you force the issue, chances are you'll end up losing.

Once the dog is familiar with the pack, you can start adding things to the pockets to accustom him to carrying some weight. Take him for walks with the pack and praise him when he performs well. Once he becomes comfortable with the idea, it's just a matter of practice before he's ready to go. Add objects to the pack, gradually increasing the weight on each walk. On his first trip go a little easy with weight and bulk; as his experience grows, he'll be able to carry more.

Choosing the Pack. The dog pack resembles saddlebags used behind Western saddles and consists of one bag on each side of the dog, connected with a band or strap across the dog's back. Some packs are made of canvas or duck, but the nylon used in backpacks is now becoming more popular. The advantages of nylon are light weight, durability, and strength. And there's another factor—while most dogs find canvas a nice snack, few seem to have much taste for nylon.

Some packers use a blanket or pad under the pack to protect the dog from sharp edges or chafing. A cardboard liner for the bags can offer similar protection from edges, but a pad is still a good idea.

A 16-in. pack is considered standard for a dog of sixty to seventy pounds and corresponding height—20 to 21 inches. The 16-in. pack measures 16 in. wide by 12 in. deep by 4 in. thick. The Gerry Doggie Pack, the most popular and the only widely distributed one, is slightly smaller, measuring 11 in. by 9 in. by 3 in. Properly loaded, the 16-in. pack will enable a dog to carry one-half to two-thirds of his weight.

Securing the Pack. One of the most important things to remember in placing a pack is to position it so that it lies properly, the front edge resting over the dog's shoulders to allow the weight to be carried well forward and not so far back as to interfere with the dog's rear action.

The Smilie Company's dog pack

The Gerry and most ready-made packs come complete with fastenings, but if you're making your own or find the fastenings provided unworkable, here are some suggestions. A permanently attached breast band is the simplest and most effective method of assuring proper placement of the pack at all times. Position the pack properly on the dog's back, then stretch a 2- to 3-in. band of webbing across his chest, attaching the ends of the band to the front of each bag. Remove the pack and stitch the webbing to the bags and the pack is permanently fitted. When you're ready to move out, simply slip the pack on, and the breast band will prevent it from slipping too far back.

Many packers use a long strap or rope with a squaw hitch to lash the pack to the dog. Although this works adequately, there are easier methods that are just as effective. One good one, used with the breast band, consists of a strap with a snap at each end and two D-rings. A D-ring is attached to the bottom of each bag and the strap is hooked onto one of them, passed under the dog's belly, through the second ring, and back to the first where it is snapped. This rig will serve if the pack does not shift or roll with the dog's motion. However, if shifting is a problem, a longer strap can be used. After it is brought back to the first ring, instead of fastening it, pass the strap through the ring and over the dog's back to the second ring, and then pass it through the second ring once and secure it.

If the pack is tied down, a breakaway knot with a small stick through it may be better than the commonly used saddle hitch. The stick will prevent accidental untying of the knot. In an emergency, a hard yank on the end of the rope will snap the stick and undo the knot. Such emergencies are certainly rare—but still...

What to Pack. A dog's needs in the wilderness (or anywhere else for that matter) are so much less complicated than a human's that filling his pack is a simple affair. All he'll really need is dry or canned food and a bowl or bowls for food and water, unless you want to be Spartan about it and let him eat out of the cooking pots after you've served supper. As a matter of fact, that isn't such a bad idea, since it will save a lot of scraping and scrubbing. Other items that might prove useful are a 15- to 20-ft. lead, in case you have to tie him for any reason. For easy access, you can let him carry his own first aid gear, or you can add it to your own kit. In either case, it should consist of a sturdy pair of tweezers for removing thorns and splinters, adhesive tape and gauze, and, for lengthy trips, possibly some cortisone and antibiotics. Check with a vet for suggestions on what to take if your trek will be an extended one. He can supply you with

Happiness is a full pack.

medicines, or you may order them from one of the veterinary suppliers listed in this section—if you know what you're doing. Make sure your dog's rabies and distemper shots are up to date, too.

Controlling Your Dog. Before taking to the woods with your dog, there are certain basic things he should be able to do. He should have some fundamental obedience training so that he will come when called, sit and stay put on command, and walk at heel. Most of the time he'll be running free, so his manners won't matter. But if you encounter other outdoorsmen, or if he decides to take off after a rabbit, you'll have to be able to control him without a leash. In short, if you can control your dog verbally, you won't waste time chasing after him as he vanishes in pursuit of some critter. Also, the few people you may run into won't have to cope with a barking, snarling dog on what should be a peaceful wilderness outing.

Regulations Regarding Dogs. There are restrictions regarding dogs in some national parks. Many completely prohibit the entry of pets, while others require that the dog be on a leash at all times. There are few restrictions in national forests and wilderness areas, but it's always best to check in advance, so you won't have to turn back at the last minute. State parks have varying policies with respect to pets.

PERIODICALS

OFF-LEAD
Lorenz D. Arner, Ed.
Monthly - $7.50/yr. - 46 p. il.

This is the only magazine we've come across that's devoted solely to obedience training, and it looks like a good one. Editorial slant is "how to" with emphasis on training techniques, use of equipment, hints and tips, and so forth. Coverage runs the whole spectrum of the various types of training for different jobs from farm work to sentry duty. Almost the whole of each issue has "save for future reference"-type articles.
From: Off-Lead, 8140 Coronado Lane, Rome, N.Y. 13440

NATIONAL STOCK DOG MAGAZINE
E. G. Emanuel, Ed.
Quarterly - S3/yr. - 35 p.

Publication slanted toward farmers, ranchers, stockmen and dog owners, with emphasis on the livestock working dog.
From: National Stock Dog Magazine, Rural Route 1, Butler, Ind. 46721

Gerry's nylon, waterproof panniers.

OBEDIENCE CLASS INSTRUCTION FOR DOGS
Winifred Gibson Strickland
1972 - $8.95

Though this book is for instructors of dog obedience classes, the amateur who is trying to train his dog can pick up many tips here. The objective is, through the use of psychology and proper handling methods, to get the dog interested in learning. Covers a lot of the mistakes that can be made through harsh, incorrect or dull training methods with photos illustrating the right and wrong techniques. Very thorough—even tells what to do when a dog flunks his examination at an obedience trial. The author, Winifred Strickland, conceived this method and through it earned 81 AKC obedience titles with high scores including 40 Perfect's.
From: Macmillan Publishing Co., Inc., Front & Brown Sts., Riverside, N.J. 08075

THE NEW DOG ENCYCLOPEDIA
Henry P. Davis, Ed.
736 p. il. - $24.95

This is the revised version of Henry P. Davis' classic *The Modern Dog Encyclopedia*. If there is one good book with nearly everything in it, this is it. Included is material on nutrition, breeding, training, showing, grooming, and dog psychology plus a full listing of publications, clubs and organizations around the world, stud books and registers, etc. A comprehensive reference tool for the laymen or professional trainer.

From: Stackpole Books, Cameron & Kelker Sts., Harrisburg, Pa. 17105

TRAINING YOU TO TRAIN YOUR DOG
Blanche Saunders
1952 - 301 p. il. - $5.95

A comprehensive, well-illustrated guide to every phase of obedience training from sitting and staying to trailing and tracking. The author discusses all aspects of dog care and discipline with emphasis on making the owner a good trainer. Includes AKC standards for various Companion Dog ratings. A good reference book.
From: Doubleday & Co., Inc., 501 Franklin Ave., Garden City, N.Y. 11530

THE NEW KNOWLEDGE OF DOG BEHAVIOR
Clarence Pfaffenberger
1972 - $7.95

An illustrated book analyzing how dogs act in terms of the modern knowledge of dog psychology. Based upon Pfaffenberger's work at Guide Dogs for the Blind and collaboration with the Behavior Research Laboratory at Hamilton Station. Well-written and practical information for amateur dog shrinks.
From: Howell Book House, Inc., 730 Fifth Ave., New York, N.Y. 10019

SLED DOG BULLETIN: PACKING DOGS
12 p. il. - $1.65

Short booklet giving the basics for training your dog to the pack and for properly packing him. Detailed instructions for making your own pack are also included. You'll find mention of Ray Thompson's packs here, too, though he no longer makes them. All inquiries are now referred to Wenaha Dog Packs.
From: Raymond Thompson Co., 15815 2nd Place West, Lynnwood, Wash. 98036

YOUR DOG'S HEALTH BOOK
Jack Denton Scott, Ed.
1962 - 317 p. - 95¢ (pb)

Forty-two chapters, each written by a different veterinarian, describe common health problems and their treatment, what symptoms to look for, and how to prevent illness. This is a compact, thorough source of reference for the dog owner, sort of the *Baby and Child Care* of the canine world.
From: Collier Books, The Macmillan Co., 866 Third Ave., New York, N.Y. 10022

USAF MILITARY WORKING DOG PROGRAM—Training
U.S. Air Force
1973 - 138 p. il. - $2 (looseleaf)
S/N 008-070-00337-6

In addition to serving as a guide to the techniques and methods for obedience, scout and sentry dog training, this book discusses the history of military dogs, health care and feeding, building obstacle courses and kennels, and a little military red-tape gobbledygook such as what form to fill out if your dog is killed in action. A lot of good info for the dog trainer at a low price.
From: Superintendent of Documents, U.S. Government Printing Office, Washington, D.C. 20402

other books

THE KOEHLER METHOD OF DOG TRAINING
W.R. Koehler
208 p. il. - $5.95

From: Howell Book House, Inc., 730 Fifth Ave., New York, N.Y. 10019

THE COMPLETE BOOK OF DOG TRAINING AND CARE
Joseph J. McCoy
Rev. Ed. - $6.95
From: Coward, McCann and Geoghegan, Inc., 200 Madison Ave., New York, N.Y. 10016

DOG PACKING

EASTERN MOUNTAIN SPORTS
1041 Commonwealth Ave., Boston, Mass. 02215
Sells the Gerry Doggie pack for the same price, $25, as Gerry. Beautiful outdoor equipment catalog available, $1.

NORDKYN OUTFITTERS
P.O.Box 1118, Moses Lake, Wash. 98837
Nordkyn has three pack styles (made by Wenaha)—the Chinook for occasional use, the Explorer for heavy-duty use, and the Cascade which incorporates their recreational harness with a canvas saddle allowing the dog to pack and pull at the same time. Prices range from $25 to $32. Free catalog.

Explorer Pack

Dave Chenette designed this pack for the serious packer, who carries bulky, heavy loads through all kinds of terrain. The Explorer Pack carries more food and equipment than the Chinook and Cascade with its new cross-top saddlebag that laces up the middle. Rainflap attaches with Velcro fastener.

WENAHA DOG PACKS
4518 Maltby Rd., Bothell, Wash. 98011
Wenaha specializes in dog packs. Their standard ones are waterproof nylon pouches on a canvas saddle. Three styles are available: Style A, the original Wenaha design with buckle flaps over pockets and neoprene about the bottom of each pack to act as a brush guard; Style B, similar to A but with zippered flaps; and the Explorer Pack, designed for the hiker who is packing a big bulky fixed load. The two outside pocket covers are joined together over the top of the load with strong lacing which holds the load securely in place. The laces are covered by an attached top cover with a built-in rain fly. Comes with detachable saddle. Cost is $30. Style A runs $22.50 and B, $25. Models A and B come in small, medium and large sizes, and the Explorer in medium and large; prices are the same. Drop Dave or Lynn Chenette a card, and they'll be glad to send you an illustrated brochure describing their dog packs.

GERRY DIV., Outdoor Sports Industries, Inc.
5450 North Valley Hwy., Denver, Colo. 80216
Manufactures and sells a sturdy, nylon pack called the Doggie Pack. It's the standard pannier (saddlebag) style with zippers and leather reinforcements at the corners. Available in one size only; dimensions are 10 in. x 9 in. x 4 in. for each bag. Price: $20. Lightweight equipment catalog available, free.

OUTFITTERS, INC.
78 Grove St., Peterborough, N.H. 03458
Another dealer for Gerry Doggie Pack ($19.95). Offers a wide selection of top line gear for backpack and mountain travel. Issues a 32-page catalog, free.

THE SMILIE CO.
575 Howard St., San Francisco, Calif. 94105
Dog packs in four different sizes for small, medium, large and extra large dogs, ranging in price from $22 to $25. Packs consist of two zippered pouches of waterproof nylon with a padded pack saddle joining them. The catalog states that these packs will enable the dog to carry up to one-fifth of his body weight, but no dimensions are given. Outdoor equipment catalog available, 15¢.

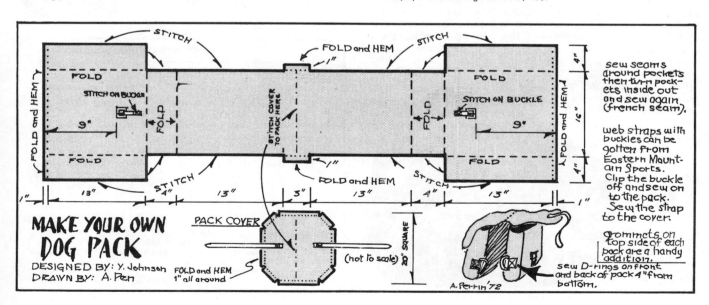

MAKE YOUR OWN DOG PACK
DESIGNED BY: Y. Johnson
DRAWN BY: A. Perrin

sew seams around pockets then turn pockets inside out and sew again (french seam).

web straps with buckles can be gotten from Eastern Mountain Sports. Clip the buckle off and sew on to the pack. Sew the strap to the cover.

grommets on top side of each pack are a handy addition.

sew D-rings on front and back of pack 4" from bottom.

109

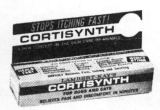

DOG PACKING

TUBE FEEDER for feeding weak or "fading" puppies. Better than a bottle because food can be delivered directly to the stomach.

ANIMAL VETERINARY PRODUCTS, INC.
P.O. Box 1267, Galesburg, Ill. 61401

A complete selection of health products for dogs and cats, including veterinary medicines, instruments and supplies, grooming aids, vitamins, leashes, chain choke, leather collars, and feeding bowls. Each product shown has a description of its use and purpose. Good reference source for dog medicinal and health supplies. A 96-page catalog available.

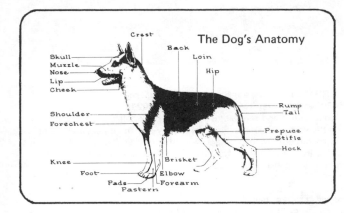

The Dog's Anatomy

NASCO
Fort Atkinson, Wisc. 53538

These people deal in a broad range of farm and ranch supplies with emphasis on horses, livestock, and poultry. Good selection of dog items such as grooming aids, leashes, collars, and so forth, and small dog cages. They carry some handy-looking automatic watering valves for dogs, and an extensive line of veterinary medicines, surgical instruments and supplies. A 334-page *Farm and Ranch Catalog* is available upon request.

ELWOOD HURFORD
21 Cricket Terrace, Ardmore, Penna. 19003

Hurford supplies obedience training and attack training protective equipment. In the training area he has high jumps, broad jumps, and bar jumps ranging from $25 to $90; dumbells; nylon choke collars, about $2; chrome over brass choke chains, $3 to $6 depending on size, and various types of leads—all very high quality. In protective equipment he has sleeves, jackets, trousers and complete suits in leather from Germany, $150 to $475, also in 3-ply jute and in burlap at lower prices. For complete information and prices, write Elwood at the above address.

Heavy Plastic Dish, 5 qt., $4

Nylon Training Leads, 1-ft. to 40-ft., $4 to $9.

Self-Waterer, $8

Super Duper Pooper Scooper, $6.

Nylon Training Collar, $2.

SPORTING DOG SPECIALTIES, INC.
Box 68, Spencerport, N.Y. 14559

Though definitely oriented toward the hunting-dog owner, this company carries general use accessories such as leads, leashes, collars, chains, general grooming aids, and a good selection of vitamins and medicines. They also handle leather dog boots. Their 64-page catalog is free.

BILL BOATMAN & CO.
South Maple St., Bainbridge, Ohio 45612

Hunting dog equipment. Good selection of general use accessories. A 46-page catalog–free.

CABELA'S
P.O.Box 199, 812 13th Ave., Sidney, Nebr. 69162

Cabela handles a wide line of hunting and fishing gear. The fall/winter catalog covers hunting gear and includes several pages of general use accessories for the dog (leather dog boots included). Limited selection but good prices. A 156-page catalog—free.

PET INDUSTRIES
1405 Midmeadow Rd., Baltimore, Md. 21204
Stainless steel dog identification tags for $2.

JAYEM ENGRAVING CO.
P.O. Box 5554, Madison, Wis. 53705
ID tags—$2.

WEIGHT OF DOG	MEAL OR OTHER DRY TYPE FOOD[1]				CANNED DOG FOOD[2]			
	Daily Food Requirements for Maintenance		Daily Food Requirements for Growth		Daily Food Requirements for Maintenance		Daily Food Requirements for Growth	
Lbs.	Per lb. body wt.	Per dog	Per lb. body wt.	Per puppy	Per lb. body wt.	Per dog	Per lb. body wt.	Per puppy
	(lbs.)	(lbs.)	(lbs.)	(lbs.)	(lbs.)	(lbs.)	(lbs.)	(lbs.)
5	0.040	0.20	0.080	0.40	0.111	0.55	0.222	1.10
10	0.034	0.34	0.068	0.68	0.093	0.93	0.186	1.86
15	0.028	0.42	0.056	0.84	0.078	1.18	0.156	2.34
20	0.027	0.54	0.054	1.08	0.076	1.52	0.152	3.04
30	0.026	0.78	0.052	1.56	0.071	2.14	0.142	4.26
50	0.025	1.25	0.050	2.50	0.069	3.44	0.138	6.90
70	0.025	1.75	0.050	3.50	0.069	4.83	0.128	9.68
110	0.025	2.75	—	—	0.069	7.60	—	—

ESTIMATED FOOD INTAKES REQUIRED BY DOGS OF VARIOUS SIZES

[1] Calculations of weights of food required have been based on a food containing 10 per cent moisture and yielding 1240 available calories per pound.
[2] Calculated on a basis of 70 per cent moisture with total and available calories estimated as 525 and 450 per pound.

From: *Your Dog's Health Book*

OBEDIENCE TRAINING

Obedience training, as the American Kennel Club puts it, "...is to demonstrate the usefulness of the ... dog as a companion and guardian of man, and not the ability of the dog to acquire facility in the performance of mere tricks."

Both the Canadian and the American Kennel Club have adopted standards of performance for obedience-trained dogs that have been divided into three grades: Companion Dog (novice class), Companion Dog Excellent (open class), and Utility Dog (utility class). Each of these represents a progressive development of the dog's ability. There is another classification: Tracking. However, this is really more of an endorsement than a grade, because it can be obtained at any time after the dog has received his Companion Dog rating.

Obedience trials are held periodically by kennel clubs in most of the big cities, and if you're interested in seeing how well you've trained your buddy, you might consider entering him in one. The only requirement is that he be purebred, which means papers (AKC registered). If this is your first time, your dog will be entered in the novice-class trials, asked to perform certain tasks before several judges, and if both you and he do well, your dog will receive his Companion Dog (C.D.) rating. Rover, C.D., will be his new title then. This rating, incidentally, is recognized throughout the United States and Canada among kennel clubs and serious dog buffs. Once your dog has his C.D. rating, he's eligible to participate in the open-class trials for his Companion Dog Excellent (C.D.X.) rating.

Here's the basic performance requirements for each rating:

COMPANION DOG (C.D.)

Heel on Leash. Dog is required to move at heel on loose leash close to handler's left side, walking at slow, normal, and fast paces, and making right turns, left turns, about turns, and figure eight turns. Any time the command "Halt" is given by a judge, the dog must come smartly to sit at heel without command or signal from his handler.

Stand for Examination. The handler "stands" his dog, moves away to the end of a loose leash, and stands facing his dog, while a judge touches the dog on his head, body, and hindquarters. The dog must not move out of position nor show shyness or resentment.

Heel Free. Same as "Heel on Leash," except that no leash is used, and the figure eight is not required.

Long Sit. Handler leaves his dog in sitting position for one minute and stands off to the side 30 feet away. The dog must remain in position until released by his handler. This test is usually done with from six to fifteen dogs at a time.

Long Down. Same as "Long Sit," except that the dog is left lying on his haunches for three minutes.

Recall. The dog is left in a sitting position while handler moves about 30 feet away. The handler then signals his dog to come. The dog moves at a smart pace to the handler and sits directly in front of him. At a second command the dog then moves smartly to sit at heel on the handler's left side.

COMPANION DOG EXCELLENT (C.D.X.)

Heel Free. Same as in Companion Dog requirements, except that the figure eight is included.

Drop on Recall. Same as "Recall" in Companion Dog requirements, but with this modification: while the dog is returning to the handler from his sitting position (at about the halfway point), the handler signals his dog to "Drop," that is, come *immediately* to a lying position on his haunches. Another signal is given, and the dog continues on his way to the handler, sitting in front of him and on command coming to heel at his left side.

Retrieve on Flat. The handler commands his dog to sit, throws a dumbbell, and then commands his dog to "retrieve." Whereupon the dog moves out at a smart clip, retrieves the dumbbell, and returns to sit in front of the handler. A command to release is given, and the dog releases the dumbbell to the handler. Another command is given, and the dog moves to heel position. The dog must make no move, except upon command, and there should be no unnecessary mouthing of the dumbbell.

Retrieve Over High Jump. Same as "Retrieve on Flat," except that the dog must clear a hurdle one and a half times the height of his back or 3 feet (whichever is less), going to the dumbbell and returning.

Broad Jump. The handler stands his dog 10 feet from the jump, which consists of four hurdles each measuring 7 inches high by 5 feet wide, spaced evenly apart; the maximum width of the jump (distance between first and last hurdles) being equal to three times the height of the dog at his back. The handler then moves to the side of the hurdles and gives the command to jump. The dog must clear the complete jump without touching a hurdle, return to the handler, and sit before him.

Long Sit. Same as in the Companion Dog requirements except that the dog must remain for three minutes, and the handler must be out of sight of the dog.

Long Down. Same as in the Companion Dog requirements, except that the dog must remain for five minutes, and the handler must be out of sight of the dog.

UTILITY DOG (U.D.)

Scent Discrimination. This trial is conducted in three parts, all essentially the same, except for the item to be retrieved. The basic drill is that the handler has three items: one of wood, one of leather, and one of metal. One of the items is selected and handled by the trainer and then placed about 30 feet away among ten to twelve similar articles that have not been handled. The dog sits at heel by his trainer and is given the command "Fetch." He then goes to the articles at a brisk pace, retrieves the handled object, returns to sit before his trainer, on command releases the object, and on another command goes to sit at heel. This is done for all three items.

Seek Back. The handler and dog execute the same movements as in "Heel Free." However, while walking the dog at heel, the handler surreptitiously drops an article and continues on his way for about 30 feet. The handler then halts and commands the dog to seek back and fetch the article (on his own). By either sight or scent the dog retrieves the article and promptly returns to the handler, following through in the same manner as with "Scent Discrimination."

Signal Exercises. The handler performs the same maneuvers with the dog as in "Heel Free," except that no voice commands are given, only hand signals.

Directed Jumping. Two jumps are placed on a line east and west about 40 feet apart. One jump is a bar type and the other is solid (like a wall), both set at one and a half times the dog's height at his back. The handler and dog (sitting at heel) are in between the jumps about 20 feet south of the east/west line. The dog is commanded to go north about 40 feet and sit. The judge indicates which jump is to be taken, and the handler signals his dog to take the particular jump indicated. When the jump is completed, the dog comes smartly to sit in front of his handler and thence, on command, to heel. The same procedure is followed for the second jump. Both jumps must be taken to complete this test.

Group Examination. Same procedure as "Stand for Examination," except that from six to fifteen dogs are examined in a group. The judge goes from one dog to the next. Each dog must remain standing in his position in line and exhibit no concern upon being examined.

TRACKING DOG (T.D.)*

A course about 450 yards long is laid out in the absence of handler and dog. A stranger wearing leather shoes walks the course somewhat randomly and leaves a wallet or glove at the finish (in the test stakes are used to indicate the course, and as the stranger walks he picks up all stakes except the one at the start and one about 30 feet from the start; these are left to indicate the general direction of the course). When the trail is at least a half-hour old, but no more than two-hours old, the dog is brought to the scene on a 30- to 60- foot leash. The handler then commands the dog to track. The scent must be picked up before the dog has passed the second marker.

* A Companion Dog who earns a T.D. appends C.D., T.D. to his name. However, a Utility Dog appends only U.D.T.—Utility Dog Tracker— which is the highest classification a dog can earn in obedience training.

Complete information on obedience trial procedures and requirements plus registration requirements for purebred dogs, can be secured from: American Kennel Club, 51 Madison Ave., New York, N.Y. 10010.

horse packing

British Columbia Government Photo.

After a decline in the early 1900's, the use of the horse is on the increase again and the outdoorsman who has a good mount under him will never envy the trail biker or four-wheeler. These are the inventions of civilization, but the horse is a product of the wilderness. After all, what mechanical device could carry you through thick forest and over rugged mountain trails, live off the land, provide companionship and even protection?

Trail riding is a popular activity with many horseowners, though most often "trail riding" means an afternoon's excursion in the country rather than a three to four day camping-type expedition. The equipment and style of riding most often associated with trail riding is Western, although along the Atlantic Coast one will see English gear used because of the popularity of the style in this region. Actually the difference in riding styles is more in the equipment used than the actual relationship between horse and rider. Certainly there are different methods of training to produce different end results from cutting out calves to performing the precision *dressage*; however, the fundamental principles of training and riding are the same. As a matter of fact, it's worth noting that the movements of a western cow pony in action at high speed are precisely those that are carried out in *dressage* tests.

Western or English will get you on the trail, but if you go out to Colorado, Montana, or Wyoming to do boonie riding with an English rig, be ready for the old fisheye and some raspberries from the local cowpokes.

To trail ride you need a horse, and keeping a horse isn't the problem you might think. Most cities have boarding stables with rates that vary from $25 to $85 per month depending on whether it's strictly a stall and pasture arrangement, or includes feeding, exercise, and the works. Farmers and rural neighbors are other alternatives that can be checked for boarding, and often leads can be gotten from local riding clubs. Of course you can take care of the horse yourself if you've got the room (even a 50- x 100-ft. lot) and there are no city ordnances.

Getting the horse to the boonies for trail riding and weekend excursions requires a trailer, and a used one could run as little as $150. Many are designed with compartments for tack and feed, so you can keep everything together

As far as places to trail ride go, pick up a topographic map and head for the country. Many states have horse trails in their parks and forests, and New York is one we've run across that publishes a guide to them—*Horse Trails in New York State.*

There's no question that the West is the best place for horsing around and ideal for extended adventures into the wilderness backcountry. If you live here, you might even think of adding another horse to your stable and getting into packing. Before doing it however, it would be worth the investment of $100 to $150 to take your first pack trip with a knowledgeable outfitter for the experience. You'll learn a lot of stuff you won't find in a book and have a great time, plus you can ask questions—something else you can't do with a book.

If you live in the East and dig horses, packing can offer some unique experiences, and is a great way to see the Western backcountry (all the packers are in the West or Northwest). It also might be the only way you'll ever get to do some packing.

At any rate, no matter why you decide to make a trip, there are a few things you should know about the packing and outfitting business before shopping around for an outfitter.

First of all, most of the guys are in it to make an honest buck providing equestrian transportation and, in some cases, collaterally to provide experience and guidance for certain types of activities on a trip, such as hunting, fishing, rockhounding, sightseeing, photography, and so forth. The ones who provide *only* transportation for you and your equipment are known as packers. These are the guys whose motto is "Have horses, will travel." Those who, in addition to supplying transportation also supply tents, camp gear, and often even food for an expedition, are the outfitters, because they outfit the pack trip. You, of course, provide your own personal gear, which usually includes a sleeping bag. Some outfitters have programmed excursions to certain local areas just to give the dudes a chance to get some saddle sores, see the country, and sleep out under the stars in a tent. Other outfitters have programmed trips, if you'd like them, but they're loose enough in schedule and attitude to handle anything you want.

There are five basic services offered by outfitters; some guys handle the whole bag, others only a couple of them.

First and simplest is the *trail ride*, which can last from one day to maybe three. The outfitter provides you with a saddle horse, and you carry your kit with you. No pack horses are involved. Trail rides are often conducted by local riding stables, and you can either use your own horse or they'll provide everything, including chow.

The second type is the *tour*, which like the trail ride is for sightseeing and the pleasure of riding and camping. The tour can be a simple trail ride to a base camp of previously erected tents, from which you make excursions (trail rides) to different areas, returning in the evening, or it can be a base camp pack trip, which is a legitimate pack trip.

Here, saddle and pack horse travel to a pre-selected site, everything is unloaded and set up, and for the duration of the trip trail rides are taken daily out of the base camp. At the end of the tour everything's loaded back up, and the pack train returns to the ranch.

A tour can also be a *moving pack trip*, which is the most fun and the most work. Camp is set up for one day, maybe for three, then torn down and packed to another location. The tour is conducted while the pack train moves along, and during the camping intervals by saddle trips from camp.

The third type is the *hunting and/or fishing pack trip*, which to be worthwhile requires an experienced guide. Most states require such guides to be licensed. These trips are conducted in about the same manner as the tour, except, of course, the objectives are different. Also, you supply your own tackle or weapons and ammo.

The fourth type is the *contract pack trip*, in which the outfitter provides what the client needs for transportation and camp, and the client sets the itinerary. This type of arrangement is used for surveying, geologic investigations, scientific expeditions, and so forth.

The fifth type is a modification of the contract trip called the *spot* or *drop pack trip*. Here, the client (backpacker, camper, hunter) arranges with the outfitter to pack him in to a particular site, leave him there, and at some pre-arranged date meet and pack him back out again, or he can make it a one-way drop and walk out himself.

Rates for trail rides, tours, and drop trips range from $25 to $50 per person per day, depending on the number in your group (the more people the less per person), the number of days, the terrain, and so forth. A good round figure for estimating is $40 per day per person. For hunting/fishing and contract trips add, say, $35 per day for each guide or wrangler. Naturally, if you bring the gear and the food, the price per person will be a lot less than if the outfitter supplies it.

A few words on packing gear. A pack saddle rides on the back of a pack horse or mule as a framework to attach containers or other items. There are several designs of pack saddles available, but probably the sawbuck and the Decker are the most popular. Attached to the pack saddle are panniers, kyacks, or alforjas (in order of popularity), words quite often used interchangeably for a horse-toted container. Strictly speaking a pannier is a rigid container (basket, box, oil drum), a kyack is a pliable container (cloth, canvas, leather), and an alforjas is a leather container. But don't try mincin' words with a cowpoke, he could care less as long as *he* knows what he means.

The only other commonly used packing item you might not be familiar with are hobbles. These are employed like shackles and are used to prevent a horse from running, though they will allow him to walk slowly. Hobbles are put on the horse while at camp to keep him from wandering too far. They can be made of two leather bands attached to each other by a couple of links of chain or even from a piece of rope.

___ sources of information

AMERICAN QUARTER HORSE ASSOCIATION
P.O. Box 200, Amarillo, Tex. 79105

This group is oriented toward maintaining the pedigree of the quarter horse breed, and if you're looking to buy one of these, they would be the people to contact for background information. They've also got some good literature that you might like to look over:

Judging Quarter Horses, 8 p. il. This booklet is designed to acquaint you with the physical standards of the breed, and would be worth checking over before you buy a quarter horse.

Ride a Quarter Horse, 28 p. il. The complete skinny on the quarter horse, its history and use, and on the American Quarter Horse Association and its activities.

Training Riding Horses, 28 p. il. A nice picture story on what's involved in training. Step-by-step procedures from start to finish, accompanied by some really salty photos taken at King Ranch. This isn't a manual, but it'll sure give you some practical information on what it's all about. Prepared by Wayne Dinsmore.

Publications Div., Office of Information
U.S. DEPT. OF AGRICULTURE
Washington, D.C. 20250

Several good publications on horses are available free upon request from USDA. When you ask for them be sure to include the order number we've shown.

Light Horses, 1965, F 2127. This 56-pager should be your first investment in reading material if your library is shy on horsy stuff. A 13¢ stamp will get it for you. Really a fantastic collection of right-to-the-point data on saddle horses by M. E. Ensminger. Coverage includes breeds and their characteristics, with photos of each type; selecting a horse with everything from teeth to hoofs discussed, including personality traits; data on breeding horses with the whole bit on feeding and managing; plus buildings, fences, and equipment. Real nice architectural rendering and floor plans for a two-stall stable. If you pass this up for the price of a stamp, you ought to be shot.

The rest of their material looks pretty good, and since they're all free, here's the list:

Horse Equipment for Field Events, 1968, M 1085. Plans, designs, and construction data.

Infectious Anemia (swamp fever) of Horses, Mules and Donkeys, 1968, F 2088.

Saddle Horse Barn, Plan No. 5994, 1966, M 1029.

Two-Horse Trailer, Plan No. 5943, 1964, M 977. Four-wheel tandem axle rig.

PERIODICALS

THE HORSETRADER
Jerry Goldberg, Ed.
Monthly - $4/yr. - 50¢/issue - 64 p. il.

This tabloid size (17" x 11") newspaper is solid advertising covering everything of interest to the horseman: horses, trailers, tack, ranch equipment, auctions and sales. Tremendous place to look for used stuff and bargains.
From: The Horsetrader, 4131 Erie St., Willoughby, Ohio 44094

THE WESTERN HORSEMAN
Chan Bergan. Ed.
Monthly - 175 p. il. - $6/yr. - 75¢/issue

One thing about Chan Bergan, he realizes there's more to horses than just riding, and *Western Horseman* shows it through its diversified and interesting coverage of ranching, rodeos, trail riding and packing, both today and yesterday. Many how-to articles on breaking, training, shoeing, and horse care, as well as the building and repair of tack and gear, and construction around the stables and ranch. Good place to keep up with equipment and who's selling what.
From: The Western Horseman, 3850 N. Nevada Ave., Colorado Springs, Colo. 80933

HORSE PACKING

HORSES, HITCHES AND ROCKY TRAILS
Joe Back
1959 - 118 p. il. - $6.95

Well, pardner, this is one of the few books—if not the only one—available on horse and mule packing. Joe Back tells it like it is, starting on page 1. Here's the drill: what makes a camp good; packing horses; getting along with a pack horse; gear; pack saddles; equipment; balancing a load; packing up right; finishing hitches and final ties; rope shortage; repairs and makeshifts; on the trail; making camp; and getting along in the wilderness. This book reads like Joe talks, good old-fashioned back-trail humor and good horse sense and not one page is wasted on filler, either. Includes many pen-and-ink sketches (based on the old Chinese adage about a thousand words and so on). There are about 500 pages of prime information crammed into 118. Damn good book for the amateur and professional packer.
From: Swallow Press, Inc., 1139 S. Wabash Ave., Chicago, Ill. 60605

PRACTICAL WESTERN TRAINING
Dave Jones
1968 - 160 p. il. - $5.95

Have you ever had anyone talk to *you* in a book? Well, Dave does: "... sure, sometimes you have to get a little rough with a rough horse, and I'll tell you how to do this. But I won't tell you how to beat up a horse." There are 25 years of experience in this book, describing just how, why, and what to do to train a horse correctly. Starting with what to look for in a horse, Dave proceeds to explain every step of the training procedures he's found best, everything from the first handling and breaking of the colt on through the development of a finished reining, roping, or cutting horse. Nothing is neglected—not even the ornery critters and the awkward problems they present.
From: Van Nostrand Reinhold Co., Order Dept., 300 Pike St., Cincinnati, Ohio 45202

HORSES: THEIR SELECTION, CARE, AND HANDLING
Margaret Cabell Self
1943 - 170 p. il. - $5.95

This book, written almost thirty years ago, has flat stood the test of time. As a matter of fact, the American Booksellers Association recommends that bookstores include it in their basic stock of titles, because it's so popular. *Horses* is the next best thing to experience. The first part of the book, more than two-thirds of it, covers selecting the horse; selection and care of equipment; the stable; general care—feeding, bedding, grooming, shoeing, etc.; first aid, handling the horse; causes and control of vices. Last part of the book is devoted to a brief discussion of Eastern riding and showing.
From: A. S. Barnes & Co., Box 421, Cranbury, N.J. 08512

BREAKING AND TRAINING THE STOCK HORSE
Charles O. Williamson
1950 - 123 p. il. - $8.50

Many manuals on horse training sort of approach the subject with Newton's third law as their underlying attitude. Charlie's attitude is to relate to the horse in a more subtle way, so that it is tuned to deft signals, movements, and pressures from you. If you train yourself and your mount to "blend" in this manner, you'll have no need of a bridle. Really, no tricks or gimmicks, just patience, sensitivity, and an awareness of the horse's psyche. Charlie, incidentally, operates a school in horse training and horsemanship at Hamilton, Montana.
From: C. O. Williamson, Hamilton, Mont. 59840

A HORSE OF YOUR OWN
M. A. Stoneridge
$9.95

Whether you already own a horse or are thinking of buying one, you'll find the information you need in this book. Covers choosing, caring for, training, and showing your horse, both English and Western style. With drawings by Sam Savitt and over 200 photographs.
From: Doubleday & Co., 501 Franklin Ave., Garden City, N.Y. 11530

OUTDOORSMAN'S HANDBOOK
Clyde Ormond
1971 - 336 p. il. - $5.95

This Outdoor Life book is the companion to Ormond's earlier *Complete Book of Outdoor Lore* (1964 - $5.95 - Harper & Row). Like its predecessor, it is a fine outdoor how-to-do-it or make-it book containing hundreds of individual items. The book covers seven major areas—hunting, fishing, camping, cooking, backpacking, photography, and horsepacking. The horse section presents some good material on

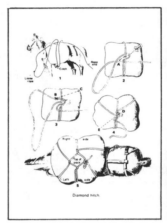

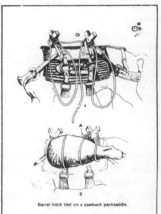

Barrel hitch tied on a sawbuck packsaddle.

the basics of riding, handling, and packing—choosing the horse, saddling, staking, tethering, hobbling, feeding, currying, riding, shoeing, tying a string of horses, making a hackamore, throwing various pack hitches, and choosing boots, and making chaps. The coverage of the other areas is similar with plenty of tips on the camp, cooking, hunting, and fishing sides of the pack trip.
From: E. P. Dutton & Co., 201 Park Ave. South, New York, N.Y. 10003

HORSE PACKING IN PICTURES
Francis W. Davis
1975 - 91 p. il. - $8.95

Looks like Joe Back and his *Horses, Hitches and Rocky Trails* almost has some real solid competition in *Horse Packing In Pictures*. Davis, who is a writer/illustrator and a very knowledgeable packer, has it all together in his book. Ninety percent of the material is annotated illustrations covering everything from choosing the correct horse for packing to a multitude of ideas for camp-making. In between are shorts on training the horse; replacing a shoe; ropes, rope work and knot tying; various types of pack saddles and panniers; slings, hitches and methods of loading an assortment of cargo; packing the packer's saddle; logistics and planning the trip; inventories of food and gear; trail-packing techniques; and so forth. A lot of info in 91 pages. Davis' writing style is not homespun like Joe's nor half as much fun to read, but his drawings are almost as good and they present a lot more visual info than Joe's. Which of the two to get? Pretty hard question to answer. If you can afford both, you ought to get 'em. If only one, then

considering the price and all-round content, I think I'd go Joe Back's book first. Though you may not get as much sideline info as with Davis, you're darn well not going to miss anything important.
From: Charles Scribner's Sons, 597 Fifth Ave., New York, N.Y. 10017

THE LAW AND YOUR HORSE
Edward H. Greene
1970 - 340 p. il. - $8.50

In this one you'll find, with the aid of case histories and court precedents, the things you should know about the laws regarding horse ownership. There's a brief guide to the history and development of the statutes governing horses; a chapter dealing with laws regarding selling and buying horses; a discussion of open stock laws; and explanations about liability in cases where horses croak under a vet's care or while in transit.
From: A. S. Barnes & Co., Box 421, Cranbury, N.J. 08512

THE PROBLEM HORSE
Reginald S. Summerhays
$3.95

Twenty-five chapters by a leading trainer deal with the particular idiosyncrasies and vices of the problem horse, with recommendations for the best cures or treatment of each.
From: A.S. Barnes & Co., Box 421, Cranbury, N.J. 08512

VETERINARY NOTES FOR HORSE OWNERS
Capt. M. Horace Hayes and J. F. D. Tutt
1964, 15th ed. - 676 p. il. - $15

If a poll were to be taken, you'd probably find *Veterinary Notes* to be the best known manual of horse medicine and surgery. First published in 1877, this step-by-step guide for the detection and treatment of all diseases found in horses is now in its fifteenth enlarged, revised, and up-to-date edition. Chapters on lameness, blood bruises, skin diseases, fractures, eyes, breathing, digestion, nerves, the mouth, heart, common horse parasites, diseases of the nervous system, shoeing, operations, nursing, and basic nutrition for horses are the most authoritative ever published anywhere. Innumerable drawings and photographs help clarify the authors' points.
From: Arco Publishing Co., Inc., 219 Park Ave. S., New York, N.Y. 10003

FIRST AID HINTS FOR THE HORSE OWNER
W. E. Lyon
$9.95

A simply written and comprehensive guide to the first aid treatment of horses. Covers diseases, lameness, cuts and wounds, teeth, etc. Good illustrations.
From: Wm. Collins Sons & Co., 215 Park Ave. S., New York, N.Y. 10003

STABLE MANAGEMENT AND EXERCISE
Capt. M. Horace Hayes
1968, Rev. Ed. - 382 p. il. - $10.00

Here is a completely up-to-date, revised edition of the classic volume on stable management, first published in 1900. A companion book to Capt. Hayes's *Veterinary Notes for Horse Owners*. The author, who is recognized as the most competent authority on matters relating to the horse, has covered every aspect of horse care. Separate chapters deal with watering, varieties of food, feeding techniques, bedding, clothing, handling and leading horses, grooming, stable routine, exercise for the various kinds of horses, caring for gear, and many other subjects of importance to anyone maintaining his own horse.
From: Arco Publishing Co., Inc., 219 Park Ave. S., New York, N.Y. 10003

DESIGN AND CONSTRUCTION OF STABLES
Peter C. Smith
$9.00

A practicing architect and enthusiastic horseman has written this book for the benefit of everyone who is interested in the construction of new stables or the extension, alteration, or adaptation of existing buildings. The general principles of stable planning and construction are adhered to, but the differences of opinion likely to be found among individual horse owners and breeders are considered and discussed as well.
From: Albert Saifer, Box 56, West Orange, N.J. 07052

TIPS ON HORSE BARNS
Bill Ryan
16 p. il. - $1.50

Sixteen pages of help for the new or experienced horseman who plans to build a horse barn. Tips on site, layout, orientation, building materials, roof, etc. Sample layouts, special barn features, horse barn plan list, and miscellaneous plans list for hurdles, gates, racks, doors, and fencing.
From: Bill Ryan Enterprises, 65 Mechanics St., Putnam, Conn. 06260

HOW TO MAKE COWBOY HORSE GEAR
Bruce Grant and Lee M. Rice
1956 - 192 p. il. - $3.50

Clear and detailed illustrations and instructions on making all kinds of tack and other items from leather, including bridles, hackamores, hobbles, reins, reatas, quirts, cinchas, etc. Another section of the book contains step-by-step instructions on making your own saddle, from the construction of the drawdown stand to the finished thing. Very well illustrated.
From: Cornell Maritime Press, Inc., Box 109, Cambridge, Md. 21613

ELEMENTS OF FARRIER SCIENCE
Donald M. Canfield
$11.95

An outstandingly valuable textbook used by Middle Tennessee State University in their Farrier Science course. Well written and illustrated. With this book you'll be able to get into the business of shoeing your own horse without reservation. Covers the functions of the farrier as well as how they are performed, plus everything from the anatomy of the horse to corrective shoeing. Twenty-one different subjects.
From: Nasco, Fort Atkinson, Wisc. 53538

THE ART OF BLACKSMITHING
Alex W. Bealer
1969 - 425 p. il. - $10.00

Fairly thorough discussion of the history and methods of blacksmithing. Has an extremely good coverage of the smith's tools and instructions for making most of them.
From: Funk & Wagnalls, Vreeland Ave., Totowa, N.J. 07512

HOW TO SHOE A HORSE
Marion C. Manwill
$4.50

A good little reference and how-to book on the art and science of the farrier that makes a seemingly difficult subject easy, so you can do your own shoeing. Complete coverage of the equipment and its use, types of shoes, nails, etc., plus safety tips. Well illustrated.
From: A. S. Barnes & Co., Box 421, Cranbury, N.J. 08512

HORSES, TACK, and PACKING GEAR

Morgan

Quarter Horse

Appalosa

HORSES
$100 to $2,000

Anyone thinking about getting his own horse would do well to spend some time at a nearby riding stable, preferably working there for a while, to see what he's letting himself in for. If you've decided to go ahead and get a horse anyway, it would be best to start out with a 5- to 7-year-old mare or gelding (castrated horse). Horses live to be about 25 to 28 years old, so this wouldn't be a very old one. Often, a good saddle horse this age, well broken and trained, can be had for between $200 and $400. The quarter horse is probably the most popular type for trail riding, and much information can be had on this breed from the American Quarter Horse Association. Another good breed is the Appalosa, although they aren't as easily found in all parts of the East as they are in the West. The Morgan is another possibility. This is an American breed that was developed in New England from the prepotent stallion Justin Morgan. Before getting too hot to trot, though, pick up a copy of *Light Horses* (free) from the U.S. Department of Agriculture and find out more about the breeds, their characteristics, and the care of them.

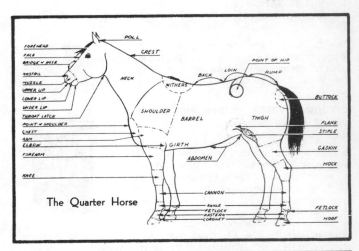

The Quarter Horse

TACK
$50 to $300

Tack is a collective term for the riding gear that outfits a horse. This includes what goes on the horse's back with its accessories and what goes on the horse's head, with its accessories. Normally, all one needs to start is a bridle and a saddle; used, they can be picked up for $5 and $25 respectively, which, incidentally, would be the best way to start out. As you go along, you'll pick up a halter (this is sort of a bridle without bit or reins that gives you something to attach a lead to for moving the horse from stall to pasture or wherever), lead, curry brush or comb, feed and water buckets, and so forth. You can familiarize yourself with most of this gear by picking up, say, Tex Tan's *Saddlelog* and by reading *Horses: Their Selection, Care and Handling.*

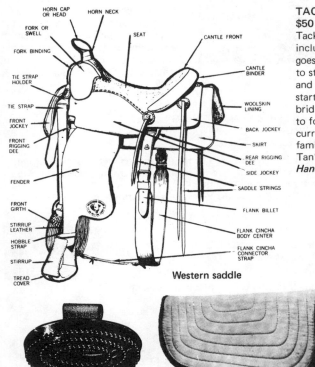

Western saddle

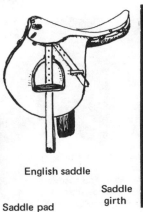

English saddle

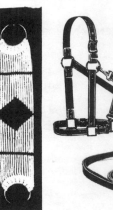

Saddle girth

Halter

Bridle

Hard rubber curry comb

Saddle pad

PACKING GEAR
$7 to $100

Packing gear includes everything from saddlebags to packsaddles. For the average guy who'll be riding the same horse he packs, there are some nice canvas and leather saddlebags and over-the-saddle kyacks available. Tex Tan has a selection of both canvas and leather types, plus a thing they call a saddle pocket that fits directly behind the cantle ($11). Good for a day's run. If you're to be out longer, say, two or three days, you might look into Gerry's pannier. By definition, it's a kyack consisting of two compartments per side and one top-loading compartment, all nylon with zipper closures ($28). Going into something a bit bigger, Beckle Canvas has an over-the-saddle kyack (no top loading, because you sit there), which, as they put it, "will hold more than your horse should carry" ($40). Speaking of loads, the recommended maximum net weight for a pack horse in steep mountain country is about 150 lbs. distributed approximately 50/50/50, side/top/side.

TRAILERS
$700 to $1,600

You've got to have some way of getting your horse to the trail, and unless you use a trailer, you'll ride him. There are about as many types of horse trailers as there are outboard runabouts, so making a choice will depend more on the coins you have than anything else. Nevertheless, there are certain criteria for a good trailer. To wit: springs under each wheel; tandem wheels for best distribution of weight; spare tire mounted outside; ample cross-ventilation; a good roof and weather-proof side curtains (if upper sides are open); an independent braking system; and room for storage of tack and feed. And if you're really planning to get out there and do some riding and camping with your horse, don't get a single stall trailer—you'll be making your outings by yourself. Much better to have a two-stall rig and always be able to take along a friend with her horse or a saddle horse and a pack horse. As far as finding a trailer, your best bet would be to look for a used one first ($150 to $300). Try the newspaper classifieds, call around to nearby stables and tack shops, and check *The Horsetrader*. If it's a new one you're after, there are a lot of them advertised in *Western Horseman*. When writing to manufacturers, don't just request literature and prices; get right to the point and ask why they feel their trailers are better than the others on the market (if they don't feel confident in their own products, you'd better steer clear of them). You'll be surprised at the results, learn a helluva lot about trailers double quick, and, if you're any judge of a businessman, you'll be able to separate the pikers from the pros with no trouble at all.

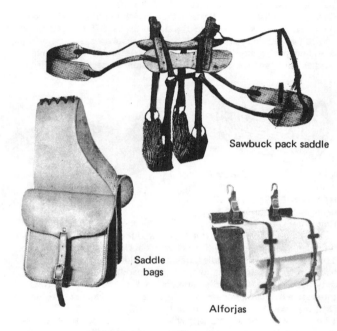

Sawbuck pack saddle

Saddle bags

Alforjas

Stirrup Length

The proper stirrup leather length can best be decided while mounted on your horse. As the first adjustment, raise yourself in a standing position so there is enough space between crotch and saddle for the clearance of the palm of your hand when laid flat. As a second check adjustment, lower yourself to a sitting position with your knees slightly bent so you can just see the tip of your toe, as illustrated.

After your stirrups have been adjusted for length, lay the saddle flat on the floor with the stirrup leather and fender also stretched flat on the floor. Wet the stirrup leather and fender about half way up with water. This is to make the leather flexible. It is suggested the leather be dampened only on the underside to avoid staining the finish on the outside.

Now, with the leather wet, turn each stirrup back in the direction of the rear skirt at an angle that is flat, so the lower front part of the fender will lie flat against the calf of your leg. Place a weight on each stirrup that is heavy enough to hold it in place firm while drying. A sandbag, feed bag, or something of that sort does fine. The drying should be slow, so leave the saddle in a shady place of moderate temperature.
—Tex Tan.

Hobbles

Over-the-saddle pannier

Stake-out hobble

Decker pack saddle

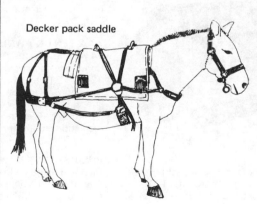

Gerry saddle pannier

HORSE PACKING

H. KAUFMAN & SONS SADDLERY CO.
139-141 East 24th St., New York, N.Y. 10010
Generally English. Some Western. Good selection of veterinary equipment and supplies. Nice range of jodhpur boots, $25 to $70; leather and canvas saddlebags, $13 to $25; saddle scabbards, $39; interesting branding iron, custom-made with your three initials—brand your saddles, tack, and roommate, $6. Two-color, 71-page catalog.

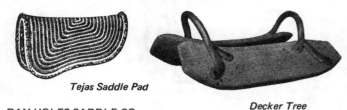

Tejas Saddle Pad

Decker Tree

RAY HOLES SADDLE CO.
Grangeville, Idaho 83530
Ray Holes is the packer's friend. If you're the type, his catalog, with its pen-and-ink sketches of trail scenes and his straight talk about his riding and packing gear, will make you feel right at home. He makes a nice line of Western saddles, flank and saddle cinchas, stirrups, hackamores, headstalls, halters, etc., and handles light- and heavy-duty hobbles, Navajo saddle blankets, pack saddle pads; he offers three styles of leather chaps, too. In the packing department, Ray has Decker packsaddles and Decker trees, plus 6' x 6' and 6' x 7', 18 oz. canvas mantas. Four bits will get you his 32-page catalog. *Recommended by everyone west of the Mississippi.*

NASCO
Fort Atkinson, Wisc. 53538
If you own a horse and take care of him yourself, you should have Nasco's Farm and Ranch catalog on your bookshelf. They don't have any packing gear, but they do handle a basic line of English and Western tack that will more than take care of the average rider's needs. This includes tack repair parts, saddle blankets and pads, horse blankets, chain and rawhide hobbles, chaps, stable and feeding necessities, farriers' equipment and supplies, and 26 pages of veterinary instruments, equipment, and supplies. Their 336-page catalog is fully indexed and amply describes all their products. Available upon request.

BECKEL CANVAS PRODUCTS
P.O. Box 20491, Portland, Ore. 97220
One model of pannier that fits over the saddle (riding or pack) made of heavy white canvas with blaze orange trim, pretty roomy, $40. Nice little 8-page brochure of canvas products (tents, stuff bags, tarps, etc.) available on request.

MILLERS HARNESS CO., INC.
131 Varick St., New York, N.Y. 10013
Pretty well-rounded outfit, though mostly English. Nice selection of tack, tack room and stable necessities. Good line of veterinary, health, and grooming supplies. Some farrier's equipment and fair batch of books. Their 96-page color catalog would be worth picking up for the books and vet supplies.

Sheepherder Stove

COLORADO TENT AND AWNING CO.
3333 E. 52nd Ave., Denver, Colo. 80216
Colorado handles a number of canvas items for packers, including feed bags (for the horse); 14.9 oz., 11'' x 12'' saddlebags, $15; kyacks in No. 8, 6, and 4 duck, handmade, and strapped with heavy harness leather, $30 to $56 per pair; various weights of canvas from which you can make up your own kyacks. They also handle other stuff for trail expeditions, including tents, bedrolls, cots, sheepherder's stoves, tent stove pipe rings, etc. Their catalog, which is available on request, sort of reminds you of the old days, when camping had nothing to do with two or four wheels. Good equipment, and they offer a 50% discount on their merchandise if there's no dealer in your area. *Recommended by R. C. Gutshall.*

Food Bags

Press-top Tins

Kyack

THE SMILIE CO.
575 Howard St., San Francisco, Calif. 94105
Sawbuck-type packsaddle complete with breast collar, lash cincha, saddle pad, halter, pair of kyacks, and 59 feet of ½-inch manila, "everything you need except the mule," $90; No. 4 duck canvas kyacks, leather-bound, $100. Smilie has a nice line of packing gear for camp and field kitchens, including tents, sheepherder's and Campers Companion (wood-burning) stoves, food sacks and tins, etc. Sixty-three-page recreational equipment catalog available, 10¢.

AAA TENT & AWNING CO.
24 West 5th South, Salt Lake City, Utah 84101
Conestoga and sheep wagon covers in sizes ranging from 12' x 12' to 12' x 14', 12 to 15 oz. canvas duck. Stockman's special heavy duty lined horse blankets for winter use, heavy leather breast and belly straps, 3'' web reinforced, full coverage of tail, various sizes from $23 to $29. These really look rugged. Forty-six page outdoor recreation equipment catalog available.

PUEBLO TENT & AWNING CO., INC.
First and Santa Fe Sts., Pueblo, Colo. 81002
Over-the-saddle-type panniers of 18-oz. canvas—no flaps to keep out rain, two sizes, $52 and $57. Eight-page tent and canvas products catalog available.

GERRY DIVISION, Outdoor Sports Industries, Inc.
5450 North Valley Hwy., Denver, Colo. 80216
Gerry has one model of a nylon pannier that fits behind the saddle
and hangs over the horse's back, good for about 20 lbs. of gear. In
keeping with Gerry's style, it has zippers all over the place. Full-color,
26-page recreational equipment catalog available on request.

OUTDOOR WORLD
P.O. Box 1880, Estes Park, Colo. 80517
Really a nice selection of Western-type apparel; actually, a more
appropriate term would be bush clothing, since it's not strictly cow-
boy. Outdoor World carries the **complete** Levi line; all types of
leather clothing, including hats, jackets, vests, trousers, moccasins, and
boots; genuine raccoon caps ($43), sheepskin jackets, bush jackets,
short and long trousers, CPO wool shirts, parkas, and some down
gear. A good, well-rounded inventory of outdoor and riding clothing.
Prices are average, what you would expect to pay at a local department store. Well-illustrated 26-page catalog available upon request.

TEX TAN WESTERN LEATHER CO.
Box 711, Yoakum, Tex. 77995
Complete selection of Western saddles and accessories, blankets, pads,
bridles, halters and other tack, training equipment, duck and leather
saddlebags, $17 to $22, saddle scabbards, $17, regular and stake-out
hobbles, $3 to $8, horse blankets and hoods, stable and feeding necessities, grooming aids, and a nice selection of farriers' equipment.
Other items include lariat rope, several styles of rain slickers and
leather chaps. Tex Tan's 120-page color *Saddlelog* is certainly worth
the asking price of 50¢. *Recommended by Charlie Stoel.*

TOURS and EXPEDITIONS

sources of information

Here is a list of groups and professional organizations (and some publications) that will be of value in securing more information on trails,
trail riding, and pack trips. The first batch is involved in tours for
pleasure and exploring; the last batch is more oriented to hunting and
fishing. Incidentally, a good source of hunting and fishing pack outfitters can be found in the back sections ("Where To Go") of *Field
and Stream, Outdoor Life,* and *Sports Afield.* Only problem is, from
their ads it's not always obvious that they use pack animals.

AMERICAN GUIDES ASSOCIATION (DBA: ADVENTOURS, INC.)
Box B, Woodland, Calif. 95695
These people are really river runners, but they offer (based on their
'72 schedule) four to five five-day trail rides, mainly in Idaho. If they
supply everything, the price will be about $250 per person. If you
bring everything, including your horse, you can join up for nothing—
this includes bringing your own food, too. Really a flexible good-guy
group. Ask them for their wilderness expeditions schedule.

WILDERNESS SOCIETY
1901 Pennsylvania Ave. N.W., Washington, D.C. 20006
About the same drill as American Forestry Association, except they
go to different areas in the West. The problem with trying to give you
a rundown on where any of these people go is that their schedules
change every year. Best bet is to get current literature. The Wilderness
Society's pack trips are called *A Way to the Wilderness*, and a 24-page
brochure on same is available for the asking.

THE SIERRA CLUB
530 Bush St., San Francisco, Calif. 94108
The Sierra Club handles, among many other things, a couple of pack
rides to areas in the West. They can also supply information on outfitters and packers who run private tours in California and Oregon.

TRAIL RIDERS OF THE WILDERNESS

Bridger Wilderness, Wyoming
$355 from Pinedale
Limited to twenty riders.

AMERICAN FORESTRY ASSOCIATION
1319 Eighteenth St., N.W., Washington, D.C. 20036
Moving pack tours of about ten days per trip with twenty people or
so are scheduled from March through September to selected wilderness areas and national parks in the East and West. Average cost per
person is $335. Trip itineraries, schedules, prices, etc., are in the 21-
page *Trail Riders of the Wilderness* brochure, available on request.

NATIONAL WILDLIFE FEDERATION
1412 Sixteenth St. N.W., Washington, D.C. 20036
Same setup as American Forestry Association and Wilderness Society.
NWF's tours are called Conservation Safaris and run about two weeks
for $400 per person. Brochure available on request.

119

On the Kaibab Trail. Mule team ascending north rim of the Grand Canyon. **Photo by Gene Ahrens.**

AMERICAN YOUTH HOSTELS
National Campus, Delaplane, Va. 22205
No pack trips, but an annual trail ride through Pennsylvania Dutch country. Five days for $120. The American Youth Hostels and the American Forestry Association are the only two groups that run riding trips in the East.

HIGHWAY 50 ASSOCIATION OF CALIFORNIA
P.O. Box 454, Placerville, Calif. 95667
Here's an interesting group that runs an annual wagon train from Round Hill, Nevada to Placerville, California along U.S. Highway 50. It's about a five-day trail ride type affair, more for fun than anything else. Everyone is required to wear 1849 style attire and supply his own transportation whether it be saddle horse, mule, horse and buggy, Conestoga wagon, or what have you. Hay for the horses is provided, but your food either has to be brought or bought along the way. Costs to join up are $5 registration and $2 per day. Usually the affair is held around mid-July. Drop 'em a card for details if you're interested.

TRAIL RIDERS OF THE CANADIAN ROCKIES
P.O. Box 6742—Station D, Calgary, Alberta, Canada T2P 2E6
Moving pack tours in the Canadian Rockies. Average run is about six days at $180 per person. Complete schedule on request.

IDAHO OUTFITTERS AND GUIDES ASSOCIATION
P.O. Box 95, Boise, Idaho 83701

MONTANA OUTFITTERS AND DUDE RANCHES ASSOCIATION
Box 382, Bozeman, Mont. 59715

WYOMING OUTFITTERS ASSOCIATION
Box A1, Jackson, Wyo. 83001

The above three are professional organizations of outfitters, guides, and packers involved in hunting, fishing, trail riding, canoeing, river rafting, etc. A letter to any will bring you information on pack horse outfits and their services in the respective states.

EASTERN HIGH SIERRA PACKERS ASSOCIATION
Box 147, Bishop, Calif. 93514
This is a confederation of nineteen outfits operating in the eastern Sierra Nevadas in the vicinity of Kings Canyon and Sequoia National Parks. You work with an individual outfitter, but the group as a whole offers a complete range of trips, prices averaging $20 to $30 per day per person. A list of the outfitters showing general operating areas plus description of their services is available from the above address.

Kit For Pack Trips

To be packed on canvas duffle or safari bag (which will ride on pack horse):

- ● *Pack in stuff bag*
  Down sleeping bag (good to 0° F.)
  Air mattress or ensolite pad
- ● *Loose*
  Two-piece wool or thermal long johns, 1 pair
  Skivvies and T-shirts, 2 pair
  Wool socks, 3 pair
  Neckerchiefs, 2
  Swim suit
  Long-sleeve khaki or chambray shirts, 2
  Jeans, 2 pair
  Wool sweater, 1
  Down jacket, 1
  Moccasins or tennis shoes, 1 pair
  Small laundry sack
- ● *Toilet kit*
  Comb
  Soap
  Toothbrush and paste
  Metal mirror
  Shaving gear
  Towels, 2
  Washcloth, 1
  Leather or rubber chaps (optional in heavy brush country; pack near top of duffle to be handy when you mount up)
- ● *If outfitter does not supply camp gear, add the following:*
  Two-man backpacker tent
  Cook kit and eating utensils
  Svea or Optimus stove with 2 quart fuel bottles
  Chow for one week

To be packed in *your* saddlebags:

  Rain jacket (preferably long Western rain-slicker type)—lash behind cantle
  Rain pants
  CPO or heavy wool shirt-jacket
  Flashlight with spare batteries
  Pliers
  Insect repellent
  Shades (sunglasses)
  First aid kit
  Sheath or jackknife (experience recommends you don't wear your sheath knife while riding)
  Funny paper (toilet paper)
- ● *Optional items*
  Camera wrapped in thick towel
  Film (1 roll per day) in black change bag
  Camera accessories (flash bulbs, filters, etc.)
  Binoculars wrapped in thick towel
  7½-minute topo map(s) of area
  Jawbreakers, mixed, 1 lb.
  Portable typewriter with spare ribbons
  Spare horseshoes with nails
  Forge, hammer, and anvil
  Small hydraulic jack for changing horse shoes
  Bugle with sheet music for "Retreat" and "Taps"

To be worn:

  Felt Western-style hat (felt is the preferred material)
  Jeans
  Shirt
  Wool socks
  Hiking boots, 6 to 8 inch (these are preferred to riding boots because they're a helluva lot easier to walk in, unless you're really used to riding boots.)

Your kit should consist of a duffle bag and a pair of saddlebags weighing, all told, 50 lbs. or less (if you left most of that optional crap out).

HORSEBACK VACATION GUIDE
Steven D. Price
1975 - 180 p. il. - $5.95

Nice little directory covering the whole horsing-around scene. It includes names, addresses and info for dude ranches and pack trips; pleasure riding, fox hunting, riding vacations abroad; horse racing, rodeos and horse shows; summer riding camps and unusual horseback vacations like covered-wagon trips, working on a ranch, sleigh rides, and so forth. Really some good resource information here if you're into horses.
From: Stephen Greene Press, P.O. Box 1000, Brattleboro, Vt. 05301

NEW YORK DEPT. OF ENVIRONMENTAL CONSERVATION
50 Wolf Road, Albany, N.Y. 12201
Horse Trails in New York State, 17 p. il. - Free. If the other states put out something like this, Man, would it be great. Covers all the trails, shelters, things to see, route guides, plus a fold-out map of the Adirondack region and smaller maps of the Catskills, Bear Spring Mountain, and Pharsalia Trail Systems.

British Columbia Government Photo.

PACK OUTFITTERS

Here's a list of outfitters, which is by no means complete. We've tried to include those who have a broad range of services. Get in touch with those who are closest to the area you want to pack into. If their brochures don't give you the complete story, then ask questions—exactly what you are getting for what price. Most outfitters are good guys, but there are a few who aren't—and you ain't no expert, so *caveat emptor.*

In our list, the only guys we know enough about to recommend are Bill Crader of Wilderness Safaris (Arizona), Don Hinton (Oregon), Ed Nixon (Montana), and Glidden McNeel (Wyoming). The rest of them, no comments at this time, but please give us yours if you have any.

ALASKA
Wes Nelson & Sons, Box 182, Skagway 99840

ARIZONA
Fred Harvey, Inc., Grand Canyon 86023
Price Canyon Ranch, P.O. Box 1065, Douglas 85607
Mardean Waymire, Grand Canyon 86023
Wilderness Safaris, P.O. Box 742, Apache Junction 85220

CALIFORNIA
William E. DeCarteret, 30547 Mehsten Dr., Exeter 93221
Little Antelope Pack Sta., 10435 Jimenez, Lake View Terrace 91342
George Mallet, Star Rt. Box 56, Lewiston 96052
Allen R. Simmons, Squaw Valley 93646
Dick R. Wilson, 1716 Meadow Lane, Visalia 93277

COLORADO
American Wilderness Experience, Inc., Box 1108, Boulder 80302
Arapaho Valley Ranch, Granby 80446
Big Creek Outpost, Box 21, Cowdrey 80434
Colorado Back Country Pack Trips, P.O. Box 110, La Jara 81140
William R. Hellyer, Box 412-G, Heyden 81639
Emmet C. Koppenhafer, 320 South Market, Cortez 81321
Rawah Ranch, Glendevey 80485
Seven W Ranch, Gypsum 81637
South Fork Resort, Box 71, Glenwood Springs 81601
Paul Van Horn, P.O. Box 1111, Estes Park 80517
West Fork Guide Service, Rt. 1—Box 170-A, Parker 80134
Wilderness Safaris, (see Arizona for address)

HAWAII
Kauai Guides, P.O. Box 122, Koloa, Kauai 96756

IDAHO
Clearwater Outfitters, P.O. Box H, Elk River 83827
Devil's Bedstead Ranch, Box 328, Mackay 83251
Bill Guth, Box 212, Salmon 83467
Bruce Henderson, Rt. 1, New Meadows 83654
Holcomb's Packing Service, North Fork 83466
Nitz Brothers, Outfitters, Elk City 83525
Palisades Creek Ranch, P.O. Box 594, Palisades 83437
Park's Pack Trips, Irwin 83428
Peck's Ponderosa, P.O. Box 493-I, Challis 83226
Primitive Area Camps, 1105 S. Owyhee, Boise 83705
Red River Corrals, Elk City 83525
Gerald Ritchie, (see Montana for address)
Bob Smith, Box 1485, Salmon 83466
Al Tice, Box 481, Notus 83656

MONTANA
Black Otter Guide Service, Box 1135, Cooke City 59020
Canyon Creek Ranch, Box 126, Melrose 59743
Cheff Ranch, Rt. F-1, Charlo 59824
Circle Eight Ranch, P.O. Box 457, Choteau 59422
Double Arrow Outfitters, Box 104, Seeley Lake 59868
Elk Creek Ranch, P.O. Box 323, Augusta 59410
Glacier Outfitters, Box 219, Ronan 59864
High Country Outfitters, Rt. 1, Box 1266, Hamilton 59840
KNL Spotted Bear Resort, Hungry Horse 59919
L Lazy F Outfitters, 11 Cloudrest, Dillon 59725
Ed Nixon, Box 279, Condon 59868
Rawhide Outfitters, Hoffman Rt., Livingston 59047
Gerald Ritchie, Star Rt., Darby 59864
Robert Toelke, P.O. Box 714, Ronan 59864
Rocky Mountain Outfitters, Rt. 2—Box 39, Columbia Falls 59912
Triple Tree Ranch, Rt. 3—Box 74, Bozeman 59715
White Tail Ranch, Ovando 59854

NEW MEXICO
Los Pintos Ranch, Cowles 87525

OREGON
Boulder Park Resort, Box 417, La Grand 97860
Don Hinton, P.O. Box 71, Rogue River 97537
Sharkey Ranch, Joseph 97846

UTAH
Jack H. Church, P.O. Box 370, Kanab 84741
Triple R Farms, RFD 258, Payson 84651
Mitchell M. Williams, 156 North First West, Moab 84532

WASHINGTON
Frey's Pack Service, Trout Lake 98650
River Trails Ranch, Quilcene 98376

WYOMING
A & L Outfitters, Pavillion 82523
Boulder Lake Ranch, P.O. Box 725, Pinedale 82941
Cliff Brewer, P.O. Box 369, Pinedale 82941
Roy Coleman, Box 1272, Cody 82414
Cross Mill Iron Ranch, Burris 82511
Elk Horn Ranch, Cody 82414
Fall Creek Ranch, Box 181, Pinedale 82941
L. D. Frome, Afton 83110
Vaughn Haderlie, Box 126, Freedom 83120
Lava Creek Ranch, Box 514, Dubois 82513
Glidden McNeel, Alpine 83127
Rimrock Ranch, Box 485, Jackson 83001
Raymond Risser, Pinedale 82941
SeTeton Pack Ranch, Box 648, Pinedale 82941
Sheep Mountain Outfitters, Box 1365, Cody 82414
Stanley Siggins, Cody 82414
Skinner Brothers, Inc., Box B, Pinedale 82941
Glen B. Taylor, P.O. Box 37, Kelly 83011
Triple X Ranch, Moose 83012
Two Bar Spear Ranch, Box 251, Pinedale 82941
Vagabond Camps, 1127 8th St., Rawlins 82301
Wilderness Trails, Box 1113, Jackson 83001

BRITISH COLUMBIA, CANADA
Tom Mould, Fort Nelson, B.C.

121

off-road touring

Jeep Renegade. (American Motors.)

There are several different types of off-road vehicles, or ORV's, as they're sometimes called, available to the back-country traveler. The most popular are the two-wheelers—trail bikes—and four-wheelers—four-wheel drive automobiles. Others are the all-terrain vehicles, ATV's, which include six-wheelers, articulated vehicles, tracked vehicles, and by some people's definition even hovercraft.

Trail bikes (off-road motorcycles) are the most maneuverable and responsive of the off-road vehicle family. Their small size and excellent traction make them the ideal machine for rough and mountainous country. On flat and rolling terrain, they're almost an extension of the individual, highly responsive to all his movements and almost on a par with a well-trained horse, which also makes them the fun machine of the ORV's.

A trail bike has the special advantage of being able to operate on the road, as well as off, legally and practically (some ORV types cannot be legally operated on the highway, nor are they practical for it). Thus it can take you directly from home clear back into the boonies without having to mess with a trailer or leave your car parked in some out of

the way spot. However, don't feel that because it can be used on the highway that it's just a modified street bike—it isn't. A trail bike is a totally distinct machine which reflects the special character of off-road riding.

In a street bike, horsepower and speed are the main criteria; not so in off-road work. Pulling power is far more important, which means that torque rather than horsepower is the primary consideration. An ideal off-road engine setup gives a broad, flat, torque curve or nearly a constant torque output over a wide range of engine rpm to provide good pulling power at all times. The Honda 125 engine is an excellent example of such an output. Street bikes, on the other hand, are set up more for high-end speed than wide-band torque. Maneuverability, that is, the ability to weave through tight spots and to avoid obstacles quickly and easily while moving along at a fair clip, is a principal characteristic of the trail bike; the street bike normally sacrifices quick response in favor of greater stability. The trail bike also offers a specialized suspension system, and you can stand on the pegs for extended distances without coming away bowlegged. Finally, it has brakes that won't lock up in loose gravel (which can

122

definitely smart), greater ground clearance and less weight for improved handling (a big help when you've sunk to the handlebars in quicksand). All of which goes to show that while a trail bike will operate satisfactorily on the street, it is still a true off-road vehicle.

The 4WD, although the least specialized of the ORV's, has a lot of good things going for it. Unlike the other ORV's, the 4WD can carry a lot of gear and several people in safety and relative comfort. The 4WD is, more than any of the others, a transport vehicle. It can go where others can't, in particular on public thoroughfares, city streets, or freeways, without getting you a ticket and still take you through some mighty rugged terrain.

The 4WD's essential difference from a 2WD is its ability, as its name states, to deliver power to all four wheels. Because all four wheels pull, each only has to supply one-half the traction force required by a 2WD. In addition, it is more solidly built, a bit higher off the ground, and has an extra set of low gears available to give more power in really tough situations.

The 4WD driver, in common with most ORV types, often finds himself in some pretty rugged country, and it is extremely important that he really understand the workings of his vehicle—what it can and cannot do. The *4WD Handbook* (discussed under Books) is a good investment for anyone who contemplates purchasing one of these happy hybrids.

The other ORV's, the all-terrain vehicles, lack the dual nature—off-road and highway capabilities—of the two- and four-wheelers, thus unless you have a specialized job you'd need one for, the return on the investment can be questionable. In the early '70's, small six-wheeler amphibious vehicles were the "in" fun thing to have, but for the most part they were expensive adult toys—not that they were junky ma-

chines. It's just that more people bought them to mess around with than for practical reasons. Seems, though, that today the fad has died out and there aren't many to be found around.

sources of information

NATIONAL 4 WHEEL DRIVE ASSOCIATION (N4WDA)
P.O. Box 386, Rosemead, Calif. 91770
N4WDA serves as a clearinghouse for information on four wheel drive vehicles and acts at the national level to maintain the rights of all four wheelers. N4WDA also serves as the sanctioning body for official races and sets all competition standards. A monthly newsletter, *N4WDA News*, is sent to all members. N4WDA also publishes a special conservation bulletin, *Four Wheel Drive Trail Tips*.

PERIODICALS

and a special 4x4 troubleshooting clinic covering such questions as the feasibility of dropping a V-8 in your Land Rover or an overdrive in your Toyota.
From: Off-Road Vehicles, 12301 Wilshire Blvd., Los Angeles, Calif. 90025

TRAIL BIKE
Mike Griffin, Ed.
Quarterly - Newsstand sales only - $1/issue - 98 p.

This is the only mag devoted strictly to trail biking. It is put out by the *Popular Cycling* people and offers a good range of material, including trail tests of new bikes, technical material, bike packing data and tips, riding tips, and accessories and gear. Solid. Unfortunately, it is not available by subscription, but back issues are available.
From: Delta Distributing Co., 131 S. Barrington Place, Los Angeles, Calif. 90049

PICKUP, VAN & 4WD (PV4)
Monthly - $9/yr. - $1/issue - 82 p.

PV4 is the newest of the 4WD mags and one of the best. All the information is solid nuts and bolts material—off-road driving technique, fundamentals of vehicle systems and components, road tests, and rundowns of new vehicles and equipment. Concentration is on technique and equipment—how to drive the back country and with what. Vehicle coverage is split between pickups, vans and 4WD's. No dune buggies or racing here.
From: PV4, 555 Crowe Rd., Marion, Ohio 43302

FOUR WHEELER
Monthly - $9/yr. - $1.25/issue - 74 p.

Mostly 4WD with an occassional glance at the pickups and vans. Racing and the club scene are about evenly matched with general off-road material and vehicle rundowns. Vehicle tests and data are very well done, interesting articles, and lotsa ads for off-road goodies.
From: Four Wheeler, P.O. Box 978, North Hollywood, Calif. 91603

OFF-ROAD VEHICLES
Monthly - $9/yr. - $1/issue - 74 p.

Monthly mag for the ORV set. Emphasis is on 4WD and dune buggies with subsidiary coverage of such areas as snowmobiling. Four-wheel coverage includes 1000-mile test results presented for various vehicles

OFF-ROAD ADVERTISER
Monthly - $5/yr.

The monthly magazine for off-road enthusiasts with info on equipment, new and used parts, information on local events, features, legislation and laws. A buyer's and seller's guide for services, dealer closeouts and pages of individual classified ads. Good place to find or sell four-wheeling gear.
From: Off-Road Advertiser, P.O. Box 340, Lakewood, Calif. 90741

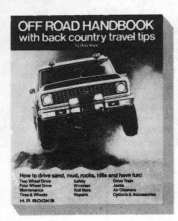

OFF ROAD HANDBOOK
Bob Waar
1975 - 192 p. il. - $4.95 (pb)

The complete title of this book is *Off Road Handbook with Back Country Travel Tips,* and it does give you a good overview of operating four-wheelers in God's country with many excellent tips. Coverage also includes info on the vehicles themselves, options and accessories. Lotsa pictures. As a matter of fact, you kinda get the idea that many of the photos were used as filler to get the book up to 192 pages. Info is good, as far as it goes, but it hardly deserves the title "Handbook." There just isn't that much hard-core material. However, if you're just getting into off-roading, you won't go wrong with this one at $4.95.
From: H. P. Books, Box 50640, Tucson, Ariz. 85703

FOUR WHEEL DRIVE HANDBOOK
James T. Crow & Cameron A. Warren
1972 - 96 p. il. - $3.95

This happens to be the only four wheeling book; so that obviously makes it the best. Even if it weren't the only one, it would still rate well. It's a basic book that assumes you know nothing of four wheeling and covers from the ground up all the material on vehicles, equipment, tools, special driving techniques, troubles and cures, and even suppliers. It's revised annually to keep all material current. Must reading for the novice and worthwhile for the experienced hand.
From: Parkhurst Publishing Co., P.O. Box 1757, Newport Beach, Calif. 92663

HOW TO SELECT, RIDE, AND MAINTAIN YOUR TRAIL BIKE
Doug Richmond
1972 - 160 p. il. - $5.95 (pb)

Hot off the press and looking good. How to select a new or used bike, learning to ride, riding techniques, safety, clothing, maintenance and repair, and camping. Excellent basic book for the novice with plenty of good material for the experienced hand.
From: H. P. Books, Box 50640, Tucson, Ariz. 85703

RIDING THE DIRT
Bob Sanford
1972 - 221 p. il. - $6.95

A year or so ago, you would have been hard pressed to find much in the way of good books on trail biking and off-road riding. However, the gestation period has now passed and such books are rolling off the presses. *Riding the Dirt* is one of the best of these new books. It is a text of intermediate and advanced techniques for the full range of dirt riding—trail, fireroading, motocross, enduro, and trials, Admittedly, a lot of this is racing material, but that's the place where off-road riding techniques and equipment are developed to their fullest, and every trail rider can benefit from the knowledge available in these areas. Sanford starts off with elementary dirt riding, which includes such basic movements as the wheelie, spinning the donut, and the power and brake slide. Regardless of the image associated with such maneuvers, they are truly basic trail techniques which you should know. From there it's into advanced trail riding, a good look at the characteristics of dirt bike geometry and design, and then the fine points of racing. Other sections cover maintenance, clothing, and physical fitness. Interesting, informative, and eminently readable. Recommended.
From: Bond-Parkhurst Publications, 1499 Monrovia Ave., Newport Beach, Calif. 92663

TWO-WHEEL

RANGER
The Ranger is a unique two-wheel drive bike. It has an automatic torque converter transmission which gives a 3-speed range selection of the following gear ratios: low, 115 to 45; medium, 67 to 27; and high, 34 to 13. Large low-pressure tractor-type tires give excellent traction, and by using the wheel drums for storage, 11 gallons of fuel can be carried. The Ranger is a true expedition bike. Doesn't go fast, but it does go. Top speed is 40 mph; load, 400 lbs. plus rider; weight, 185 lbs.; suspension, low-pressure tires; grade-climbing ability, 45°. Rokon also has the Scout model, which is essentially the same as the Ranger except for the gear ratios and the wheel drum fuel tanks. Price on the Ranger is $1,495 and the Scout, $1,395.
From: Rokon, Inc., 160 Emerald St., Keene, N.H. 03431

The following is a list of trail bikes with the manufacturer's name and address. Contact them for literature and more information.

BENELLI
   Cosmopolitan Motors, Jacksonville & Meadowbrook Rds., Hatboro, Pa. 19040
BRONCO
   Engine Specialties Inc., P.O. Box 260, Cornwells Heights, Pa. 19020
DKW
   Hercules Distributing, 9825 Mason Ave., Chatsworth, Calif. 91311
HARLEY DAVIDSON
   Harley-Davidson Motor Co., 3700 W. Juneau Ave., Milwaukee, Wis. 53201
HODAKA
   Pabatco, P.O. Box 327, Athena, Oreg. 97813
HONDA
   American Honda Motor Co., 100 W. Alondra, P.O. Box 50, Gardena, Calif. 90247
HUSQVARNA
   West—Husqvarna Motor Corp., 4790 Palm Ave., La Mesa, Calif. 92401; East—1906 Broadway Ave., Lorain, Ohio 44052
INDIAN
   Indian Motorcycles Inc., 1535 W. Rosecrans, Gardena, Calif. 90249
JAWA/CZ
   West—American Jawa Ltd., 3745 Overland Ave., Los Angeles, Calif. 90034; East—185 Express St., Plainview, N.Y. 11803
KAWASAKI
   Kawasaki Motor Corp., 1062 McGraw Ave., Santa Ana, Calif. 92705
MZ
   International Accessories, 102 Park St., Hampshire, Ill. 60140
PUCH
   Hercules Dist. above under DKW
SUZUKI
   U.S. Suzuki Motor Corp., 13767 Freeway Dr., Santa Fe Springs, Calif. 90670
YAMAHA
   Yamaha International Corp., 6600 Orangethorpe Blvd., Buena Park, Calif. 90620
ZUNDAPP
   Rockford Motors, 1911 Harrison, Rockford, Ill. 61101

In the 2-wheel ORV's, there is only one vehicle truly designed for back-country exploration, and that's the Rokon Ranger; however, its great off-road characteristics are also its weak spot for highway use—in a word, 40 mph top speed. If you want a more versatile trail bike, that is, versatile from the standpoint of off-road and highway use, then you'll have many to choose from. Listed are the manufacturers you can contact for literature with which to make comparisons.

In the 4-wheel line-up, there are only eight major manufacturers of 4x4's offering some 10 basic vehicles, but when you consider that some manufacturers offer four different engines, four transmissions, two transfer cases and three axles, then you really have something like 500 vehicles to sort through and choose from. Throw in on top of that all the decisions that have to be made about limited slip differentials, heavy-duty suspensions, assorted tires, winches, locking hubs, plus all the other options offered, and you've got a heavy load of homework to do in making an intelligent choice.

Probably the best route to follow would be to choose 2 or 3 vehicles that really interest you, write to the editors of the dirt bike magazines or 4WD magazines (as the case may be) and ask them to send you reprints or back issues carrying the latest vehicle reports and road tests for those vehicles. While waiting for mail time on that, drop by your local dealer and get sales literature, prices and answers to your questions.

FOUR-WHEEL

BLAZER/JIMMY and SUBURBAN

The Blazer (Chevrolet) and Jimmy (GMC), which are essentially the same vehicles, are offered in '77 with a 250 cu. in., in-line 6, with a 3.73 rear end and a 3-speed manual transmission as a standard package. The standard top (over the rear) is a removable fiberglass-reinforced plastic closure. Base price is $5,680. Options available for the Blazer/Jimmy power package are a V-8 engine in choices of 305, 350, and 400 cu. in.; rear axles in 3.07:1 and 4.11:1; and a 4-speed manual or 3-speed automatic transmission. Rag top is also available as an option.

The Suburban (Chevy and GMC both call it the same thing) is a longer, heavier wagon available in two models, the K-10 and the K-20 (these are GMC designations; the respective model numbers for the Chevy Suburban are K-1500 and K-2500; we're gonna use K-10 and K-20 for both GMC *and* Chevy [Jeez, but ain't it a bunch of corporate Mickey Mouse!]). Anywhoo..., the standard power package for both is the 305 cu. in. V-8 with a 3.73 (K-10) or 4.10 (K-20) rear end. Transmission is a 3-speed manual. Main difference between the K-10 and K-20 is load capacity, i.e., beefier suspension system. Base price for the K-10 is $6,290 and for the K-20, $6,655.

Options available for the Suburban power package include V-8's in 350 and 400 cu. in. for both models and rear ends in ratios of 2.76:1,

3.07:1, and 4.11:1 (K-10) and 4.56:1 (K-20).

Four Wheeler checked out a Chevy Suburban K-20 with a 400 cu. in. V-8 and 4.10 rear end, and had nothing bad to say about it (Hmmm?). Gas consumption on the road was 10 mpg and off the road, 9.

From: Chevrolet Motor Div., General Motors Corp., Detroit, Mich. 48202 (Blazer & Suburban)

Truck and Coach Div., General Motors Corp., Pontiac, Mich. 48053 (Jimmy & Suburban)

BRONCO

The 302 cu. in. V-8, 3.50 rear end and 3-speed manual transmission continue as the standard package with the Bronco for '77. Improvements for '77 include a solid-state ignition system called DuraSpark, 14-gallon plastic gas tank, and a new variable venturi carburetor. Engine changes include an intake manifold with higher-velocity air passages and revised combustion chambers and pistons. Base price is $5,323.

From: Ford Trucks & Recreational Vehicles, P.O. Box 1509, Dearborn, Mich. 48121

RAMCHARGER/TRAIL DUSTER

The Ramcharger and Trail Duster, like the Blazer and Jimmy, are essentially the same vehicle except Chrysler sells the Ramcharger, and Plymouth, the Trail Duster. In the standard package, this little wagon is offered with a 225 cu. in., 6 cyl. or 318 cu. in. V-8 and a 3.55:1 rear axle. Transmission is a 3-speed manual. Base price for the 6 is $4,860 and for the V-8, $5,053. Power package options include 360, 400, 440 cu. in. V-8 engines; 4-speed manual and 3-speed automatic transmissions; and 3.20 and 3.90 rear axles.

In general, no major body or chassis changes have been made for 1977. Roof is either the dealer-installed soft top or the factory-option removable steel roof of double-wall construction.

Pick Up, Van & 4WD test-drove a 360 cu. in. V-8 Trail Duster with a 3.2 rear end (see Jan. '77 issue, pg. 42) and had problems with the emissionized V-8 overheating which caused prevaporization of the fuel before reaching the carb. Lotsa engine kills in off-road stop-and-go

crawling. Other items of interest noted were 0-60 mph in 14.8 sec., which ain't exactly hot for merging with freeway traffic at the entrance ramp. Also, an oversensitive vacuum-boosted hydraulic braking system which was excellent for rear wheel lockup. Other than that, the Trail Duster was A-O.K., though the test crew recommended going for the 440 cu. in. with the 3.2 rear axle as a better buy.

From: Automotive Sales Div., Chrysler Corp., P.O. Box 1919, Detroit, Mich. 48231 (both vehicles)

The Wagoneer, available in the 4-door model only, is essentially the same size and configuration as the Cherokee, but has more of a "city" look to it. Standard package is a 360 cu. in. V-8 with two-barrel carb, 3.54 rear end and 3-speed automatic transmission. Base price is $6,966. Options include a 360 cu. in. four-barrel carb V-8, a 401 cu. in. four-barrel carb V-8 and a 3.07:1 rear end.

From: Jeep Corp., 27777 Franklin Rd., Southfield, Mich. 48076

JEEP CJ-5 and CJ-7

The Jeep CJ-5 is offered in the standard package with a 6 cyl., 232 cu. in. OHV engine, a 3.54 rear end and 3-speed manual transmission for $4,400 (lowest price of all the 4WD's).

Problems with the CJ-5, according to Steve Bigwood who ran a road test on the '76 model (see *Off Road*, Sept. '76, pg. 36), are the use of unleaded gas, which ain't easy to come by in Mexico or Canada, in case you're thinking of a run in these countries; undesirable heat from the catalytic converters—though this did not seem to have any great effect on performance, just passenger comfort; lousy braking, "...provided about as much peace of mind as a wooden drag on a pioneer wagon"; and a suspension system that doesn't handle cornering well. Hopefully some of this will be remedied in '77; however, we've found out that AMC has already pulled a nifty which ain't so neat: they've done away with the slotted hinges that would let you remove almost everything without a wrench. Now tailgates and such are bolted. Certainly a step in the wrong direction for '77.

On the plus side, power, handling, steering and gas economy are good—16 mpg on the highway and 15 off the road.

Options available for the CJ-5 are a 258 cu. in., 6 cyl. and a 304 cu. in., V-8 engine; 4.09:1 rear axle; and a 4-speed transmission. Disc brakes, power or manual, are also available—may help with the pioneer wagon act.

The CJ-7 is just a longer version (about 10") of the CJ-5, and it has the same standard package and options plus an additional option of a 3-speed automatic transmission. Base price for the CJ-7 is $4,500.

From: Jeep Corp., 27777 Franklin Rd., Southfield, Mich. 48076

SCOUT II and SCOUT TRAVELER

International offers the Scout in two models this year, the Scout II, 166.2" overall and the Traveler, 184.2". Standard power package for both is a 4-cylinder, 196 cu. in. engine and 4.09:1 rear axle with a 3-speed manual transmission. Base price for the II is $5,751 and for the Traveler, $6,122.

Options for the power package include a V-8, 304 or 345 cu. in. engine, 3.07 or 3.54 rear end, and a 4-speed manual or 3-speed automatic transmission. Both the Scout II and Traveler are also available with a Nissan 6 cylinder, 198 cu. in. diesel engine, a 3.54 rear end and 4-speed manual transmission. Base price for the II with diesel is $8,394 and the Traveler, $8,770.

International had the diesel available in '76, its first year, and except for the price, the results have been very intriguing: low maintenance, mainly oil and filter changes; excellent mileage (w/the 3.54 rear end)—on the highway, 22 to 28 mpg with a fuel that's cheaper than gasoline (diesel runs from 45¢ to 50¢ per gallon), and no problems with low engine efficiency because of pollution devices. Doesn't need 'em—very efficient combustion. Main problem with the diesel engine is that it's designed to run most efficiently in a narrow RPM range (high), so unless the revs are kept up, performance tends to be sluggish. In a word: low response. But as a workhorse, and for low maintenance, few problems and fuel economy you can't beat, the diesel is at the top of the line, even with the high price tag. Incidentally, International has reprints available of the April '76 issue of *Four Wheeler* which carried a report on the diesel and included a road test of the Traveler.

From: International Harvester Co., 401 N. Michigan Ave., Chicago, Ill. 60611

CHEROKEE and WAGONEER

Cherokee is American Motors' station wagon, available in 2- and 4-door, which comes in the standard package with a 258 cu. in., 6 cyl. engine and a 3.54 rear axle. Transmission is 3-speed manual. Power disc brakes are standard on both models. Base price is $5,673. Options for the power package include a 360 and 401 cu. in. V-8; 4-speed manual transmission and 3-speed automatic transmission; and 3.07 and 4.09 rear axles.

TOYOTA

The Land Cruisers for '77 are virtually the same as for '76, the year in which power disc brakes for the front wheels were introduced and the rear brake drums widened. Also, '76 saw a change in the rear cab: side-hinge, swing-out rear doors for the hardtop.

Standard power package is a 258 cu. in. 6 cylinder, with a 4.11 rear end and a 4-speed manual transmission both for the hardtop and the wagon. No options. Base price for the hardtop is $5,698 and for the wagon, $6,638.

From: Toyota Motor Sales U.S.A., Inc., 2055 W. 190th St., Torrance, Calif. 90509

Components Discussion

AUTOMATIC TRANSMISSION

An automatic is going to cost you in power available at the wheels. Going to an automatic transmission from a three-speed manual can cut the maximum torque by 950 ft.-lbs. or nearly 17%. On the other hand, the automatic is convenient and will allow you to easily perform some maneuvers that you can't with a manual—unless you happen to have two left feet. The inherent slippage in the automatic may keep you from digging in where you well might with a stick shift. All this is good if you can afford the power loss.

FOUR-SPEED TRANSMISSION

Going to a four-speed will substantially increase the maximum torque and acceleration for low-low. However, quite often you don't need the extra torque, and in these cases, it's likely to dig you into more holes than it will ever get you out of. In general, the small six-cylinder engines can use a bit more heft and a four-speed may be good. Most of the V-8's don't need a four-speed transmission, but with a couple of them, a four-speed will give a better vehicle.

LIMITED SLIP & LOCKING DIFFERENTIALS

In general, limited slip and locking differentials are definitely the way to go. With a decent power train package, the limiting factor in where you can go will usually be either clearance or traction. With limited slip all four wheels must loose traction before the vehicle is stuck.

AXLES

Changing to a different axle ratio lets you trade off speed against acceleration (or torque). A higher ratio will give more torque but less speed; a lower ratio gives more speed but less torque. Normally the standard ratios are a fine compromise for general use. If you need more speed or torque, the best bet may be a lower ratio axle combined with a four speed transmission (improves both speed and acceleration).

FREEWHEELING OR LOCKING HUBS

Freewheeling or locking hubs allow you to disconnect the front wheels from the drive train for highway driving. Without locking hubs, the entire front drive train is dragged along by the wheels even though the vehicle is in two-wheel drive. With locking hubs, the front wheels spin freely on their bearings, and the front drive train need not rotate. This cuts wear on the drive train, reduces gear whine and improves power slightly. Unfortunately, to shift the hubs, one must stop the vehicle and get out—a bit of a nuisance. Still if most of your driving is on the highway, they are well worth the trouble.

Automatic hubs lock automatically whenever power is applied to the front axle and disengage whenever you shift back to 2WD. You will have to stop to shift into 4WD, but you don't have to get out. However, the hubs will automatically unlock whenever you let off the gas and thus there will be no compression braking from the front wheels going down a steep hill or stopping on a slippery surface. If you want compression braking or wish to shift in and out of 4WD without stopping every time, you must manually lock the automatics just as with regular hubs.

The best arrangement is the constant four wheel drive systems. These use an extra differential between the front and rear drive shafts which allows the use of 4WD on all road surfaces at all times. Any time you hit an unexpected slippery spot on the road, you've got the 4WD working for you. For maximum off-road traction, the differential can be locked and will act just like a regular 4WD setup.

TRACTION CHART

2-WHEEL-DRIVE	4.5%
4-WHEEL-DRIVE	10%
4-WHEEL-DRIVE WITH LOCKED REAR DIFFERENTIAL	32%

Grade-climbing ability on low traction surfaces.

SURPLUS VEHICLES

Maybe you're leaning toward a military surplus vehicle. In general, surplus vehicles are not what they've been cracked up to be. The usual vehicle is in only fair condition, is not particularly cheap, and parts and equipment are military spec and very hard to come by. You will normally do far better on the second-hand civilian market.

However, if your heart is set on a command car, a weapons carrier, or a Dodge Power Wagon, you can either bid directly on government sales or buy from one of the surplus dealers who specialize in these rigs. You'll probably do best with the dealers, because you can usually pick your vehicle out of a group of them, and many dealers will rebuild the vehicle if needed—for a price, of course. Remember that these guys do most of their business in heavy equipment, so don't expect too much from them. They're not geared to the little man.

Most surplus dealers do not offer specific literature since their line varies considerably. If you request information on a particular type, they will be able to handle that. Better yet, drop in on one; it can be a blast sorting through several hundred acres of assorted wheels.

A good way to run down a surplus dealer is to subscribe to either *Rock & Dirt* or *Construction Bargaineer.* These are both straight advertising newspapers devoted to equipment for the construction industry—mostly surplus and used vehicles and equipment. Worth the price just to look at what's available.

sources of information

If you'd rather buy straight from the government, contact Defense Surplus Bidders Control Office, The Federal Center, Battle Creek, Mich. 48117. Tell them that you would like to be placed on the Department of Defense Surplus Property Bidders List. They'll send information. You pick out the areas you want to bid on and then settle back and have at it. If you'd like a bit more initial information as to what to expect, send 25¢ to: Superintendent of Documents, U.S. Government Printing Office, Washington, D.C. 20402, with a request for *How to Buy Surplus Personal Property.*

ROCK & DIRT
36 issues/yr. - $2.50/6 mo. - 80 p. il.
From: Rock & Dirt, Crossville, Tenn. 38555

CONSTRUCTION BARGAINEER
24 issues/yr. - $8/yr. - 80 p. il.
From: Construction Bargaineer, P.O. Box 16365, St. Paul, Minn. 55116

Two dealers who do offer literature on surplus vehicles are:

WILENSKY AUTO PARTS CO.
1226 Washington Ave., North, Minneapolis, Minn. 55401
6x6 trucks, half tracks, power wagons—one page listing only.

Dodge ¾-ton personnel carrier

Continental 13-ton tractor, M5

sources of surplus vehicles

SOUTHEASTERN EQUIPMENT CO., INC.
P.O. Box 5438, Augusta, Ga. 30906
Tracked vehicles, heavy trucks, Canadian 4x4 trucks, weapons carriers, command cars, personnel carriers, and winches and tires.

Mack 6x6 5-ton truck

Dodge ½-ton command car

MAINTENANCE
BOOKS

A basic understanding of what makes your wheels tick and how to apply this to practical repair problems is essential in the back country. Either you fix it or you walk out, so a little preparation now could save serious trouble later. The following are a couple of good books on two-wheel and four-wheel operation and repair:

MOTORCYCLE REPAIR MANUAL
Bob Greene and the editors of *Motorcyclist* magazine
Annual - 288 p. il. - $3.95

Another goodie from the Petersen stable. All the data on how each system works and how to fix it, tune it, and maintain it, including specific tune-up techniques for 13 makes of bikes. Straightforward and plenty of helpful photos to explain all the words. Combine this one with one of the foregoing specialty manuals on your bike, and you'll have it all there.
From: Petersen Pub. Co., 8490 Sunset Blvd., Los Angeles, Calif. 90069

CLYMER SERIES

Clymer offers a fine series of service and repair handbooks for specific models, though they are mostly oriented toward the big racing machines. There are, however, several in the series that do include trail bike models, so it might be worth your while to look into them. Prices range from $4 to $6. J. C. Whitney handles some of these books at a discount.
From: Clymer Publications, 222 N. Virgil, Los Angeles, Calif. 90004

CHILTON MOTORCYCLE SERIES

Chilton has a series of excellent repair and tune-up guides for most of the popular bike lines—BSA, BMW, Harley, Honda, Kawasaki, Suzuki, Triumph, and Yamaha. Chilton also has specialized books on motorcycle carburetors, electrical systems, and engine trouble shooting. Prices range from $5 to $7.
From: Chilton Book Co., 401 Walnut St., Philadelphia, Pa. 19106

MOTORCYCLE MAINTENANCE MADNESS
Bill Schissler
1972 - 150 p. il. - $4

A humorous approach to motorcycle maintenance. Specifically written for 2-strokers but with plenty of good material for everyone. Dedicated to keeping fun in all phases of biking.
From: Cyclo Cycle Publications, P.O. Box 1176, Indio, Calif. 92201

MOTOR'S TRUCK AND DIESEL REPAIR MANUAL
Annual - 1100 p. il. - $17 - 8½" x 11"
From: Motor Book Dept., 250 W. 55th St., New York, N.Y. 10019

CHILTON'S AUTO REPAIR MANUAL
Annual - 1500 p. il. - $10.95 - 8½" x 11"

CHILTON'S TRUCK REPAIR MANUAL
Annual - 1300 p. il. - $18.00 - 8½" x 11"
Both from: Chilton Book Co., Automotive Book Dept., 401 Walnut St., Philadelphia, Pa. 19106

These three are the reference books on detailed maintenance for your particular 4x4. They are really professional shop manuals, and if you are into serious repair items, you'll find them invaluable. They won't tell you how it works or what's wrong, but they cover the details of taking it apart and putting it back together after you've decided what needs taking apart. They only cover the U.S. 4x4's, however. Motor has put all the 4WD's into their *Auto Manual*, while Chilton has split them—Jeep in the *Auto Manual* and the others, including Jeep trucks, in the *Truck Manual*. The Chilton books are discounted by several dealers. The best price on their *Auto Manual* is offered by U.S. General Supply Corp. at $8.45 while J. C. Whitney offers the *Truck Manual* at $17.49. The Motor books are also available through discount dealers, but the price is not discounted. Sorry!

BASIC AUTO REPAIR MANUAL
1971 - 384 p. il. - $3.95
From: Petersen Publishing Co., 8490 Sunset Blvd., Los Angeles, Calif. 90069

AUTO ENGINES AND ELECTRICAL SYSTEMS
600 p. il. - $10
From: Motor Book Dept., 250 W. 55th St., New York, N.Y. 10019

These are both excellent basic books put out by people who know the business. The Petersen book was put together by the *Motor Trend* magazine people and Motor specializes in automotive shop manuals. Both provide excellent coverage of operation and design, diagnosis of problems, and repair procedure and technique. Take your pick.

REPAIR & TUNE-UP GUIDE FOR TOYOTA
Annual - 175 p. il. - $5.95

General maintenance information for the full Toyota line including the Land cruiser.
From: Chilton Book Co., Automotive Book Dept., 401 Walnut St., Philadelphia, Pa. 19106
[Also available from J. C. Whitney ($5.79) and Sears, Roebuck and Co. ($5.88)]

INSTRUCTION

If you want to invest the money, several correspondence schools offer courses in automotive maintenance and repair. The courses cover the operation and maintenance of all major systems and include both gasoline and diesel engines. In general, the value received from these, for the cost, is questionable. You'd probably do well to check your local school district first for possible adult courses. But if you want to look into the correspondence schools, here are two with automotive courses.

AMERICAN TECHNICAL SOCIETY
Drexel and 58th St., Chicago, Ill. 60637
Full course including diesel engines is 86 lessons. Full course costs $289. Individual sections are available.

NATIONAL TECHNICAL SCHOOLS
4000 South Figueroa St., Los Angeles, Calif. 90037
Full courses including heavy equipment and diesel is 82 lessons. Full course cost is $235. Individual sections not offered.

J. C. WHITNEY & CO.
1917-19 Archer Ave.
Chicago, Ill. 60616

WARSHAWSKY & CO.
1900-24 So. State St.
Chicago, Ill. 60616

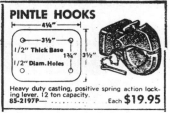

These two are really the same operation. They use essentially the same catalog with a different cover and a little different arrangement. The Warshawsky catalog is free while the first J. C. Whitney catalog is nominally $1. You can probably get both free though. They offer a very wide range of general automotive parts and accessories, books, and tools at very good prices. Except for a fair selection of Jeep items, they do not offer a lot of specialized 4WD gear, but they are still the best source for many items in this area. Also offer motorcycle gear. 178-page catalogs.

SOLIDOX
Here's an item for your basic kit. A seven pound gas welding outfit

sources of books

For something that's a little more practical to carry along and every bit as good as the big shop manuals above, the manufacturer's service and shop manuals are the answer. These will cover everything you need to know about your particular vehicle—which is all you care about anyway. If you buy a new vehicle, be sure to order a shop manual. Dealers are sometimes reluctant to provide this as they would rather handle all repairs themselves—for a price. Insist. If you have a used vehicle, the manufacturer will either supply a manual or direct you to a dealer. The usual cost is from $6 to $10.

JEEP SERVICE MANUALS

ORIGINAL REPRODUCTIONS
P.O. Box 74, Upland, Calif. 91786
Offers copies of Jeep service manuals covering the Jeep Universal and J Series, the old Utility Wagon and the M38-A1. Prices range from $12 to $13. A little steep, maybe.

E. S. SCHECHTER & CO.
181 Glen Ave., Sea Cliff, N.Y. 11579
Complete line of service manuals for all the popular makes of 4WD vehicles and vans. Also books and manuals on tune-up, engine maintenance, electrical systems, clutches and transmissions, and so forth. Prices average about $8 a book.

TOTAL SERVICE MANUALS	
0503 BLAZER 69-73 all 2 & 4 whl dr inc GMC Jimmy	$7.95
0504 BRONCO, Ford 66-73 all 2 & 4 wheel drive models	$7.95
8200 CHEVY GMC pick-ups 70-75 all models to ¾ ton	$7.95
8201 CHEVY GMC vans & sport vans 67-74 for all models	$7.95
0378 CHEVROLET LUV 72-75 covers all models	$7.95
8202 DATSUN pick-up 75 covers all models	$7.95
8430 DATSUN pick-up 68-74 PL521, PL620 models	$7.95
1719 LANDROVER 48-61 covers series 1 & 2 models	$9.95
1254 LANDROVER 59-76 covers series 2, 2A & 3 models	$9.95
0880 MAZDA pick-up 72-75 all 1600 & Wankel engine mdls	$7.95
8208 RAMCHARGER & TRAILDUSTER 74-75 all models	$7.95
E342 RANGE ROVER 70-76 covers 3500 model	$9.95
C881 TOYOTA HI-LUX 70-74 for all pick-up models	$7.95
C882 TOYOTA LAND-CRUISER 66-74 covers all models	$7.95

PETERSEN PUBLISHING CO.
6725 Sunset Blvd., Los Angeles, Calif. 90028
Nice selection of automotive and motorcycle maintenance books averaging from $3 to $4 apiece.

sources of parts and tools

that uses propane (the standard small tank) and oxygen from special solid pellets to produce a 5,000°F flame. No fancy and expensive piping or big heavy tanks. Obviously the unit will not do everything that the big oxy-acetylene outfits will, but then it costs only about

one quarter as much. It will do light welding, medium brazing, and silver soldering. It really works.
From: Cleanweld Products, P.O. Box 1108, Alhambra, Calif. 91802

SEARS, ROEBUCK AND CO.
4640 Roosevelt Blvd., Philadelphia, Pa. 19124

Sears is probably the best source of automotive tools and general maintenance supplies. Their Craftsman tools are exceptional and unconditionally guaranteed—if you break one for any reason, take it back at any time for a new one. They also have a good selection of automotive accessories and some parts, all at good prices, and a specialized catalog of Jeep parts and accessories. Although the Jeep selection is good, the prices are generally high. The big catalog (1100 pages plus) covers the tools and general items. Special parts are in the specialty catalogs listed below. All the catalogs are free from the nearest catalog sales office or write to the address above.

Replacement Parts for Jeep Catalog, 40 pages.
Automobile, Truck and Dune Buggy Catalog, 135 pages.

U.S. GENERAL SUPPLY CORP.
100 General Place, Jericho, N.Y. 11753

Offers a very wide selection of tools of all types at good prices. Brand names at discount prices. Be sure to note that the catalog uses a special coded pricing (they want to be sure that you appreciate the savings). 204-page catalog, $1.

SILVO HARDWARE
107 Walnut St., Philadelphia, Pa. 19106

Silvo offers the same general line of tools as U.S. General. Some things are better in one, some in the other. Both catalogs are worth the investment. 166-page catalog, 50¢. Minimum order is $10.

T. J. VAN DER BOSCH & ASSOC.
P.O. Box 91, Lake Zurich, Ill. 60047

If your old Jeep body has had it, you might want to consider replacing it with a fiberglass one. T. J. Van Der Bosch manufactures glass bodies for the CJ-2A, 3A, MB, M-38, M38-A1, CJ-5 and 6. Parts and complete bodies are available. Prices run from 6 to 7 bills depending on the model.

Here's what Jerry Driscoll, T. J.'s sales manager, has to say about doing it yourself: "Replacing a body and body parts is relatively simple and people without mechanical experience are usually able to handle it on a weekend at home. Two problems that must be faced directly are the removal of the old and rusted parts and the wiring system. Once the body is removed, sandblasting the frame should be given affirmative consideration on the older vehicles. Once these hurdles are passed, your rig is ready for its new body and the only tools needed are a hand drill, coping saw and basic straight wrenches. To rebuild at this point is relatively simple. Our one-piece body is constructed from the firewall back, to include glassed-in supports in the floor pan, wheel well areas and tail section. Shim to level and bolt in place. Our reinforced body weighs approximately 175 pounds. Metal parts, still in good shape on the Jeep, are interchangeable with our fiberglass replacement parts. The front end is the same. All holes are marked for drilling and bolting to the body and fenders. The hood comes with supports to give added strength."

Write Jerry at the above address for sales lit and prices and any questions you may have.

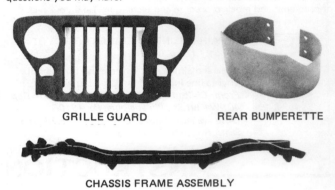

GRILLE GUARD   REAR BUMPERETTE

CHASSIS FRAME ASSEMBLY

ACME TRUCK PARTS & SALES
P.O. Box 49, Gardena, Calif. 90247

If you'd prefer sticking with metal for replacing your rusted-out Jeep body, then Acme's got it all: complete body kits and parts for the CJ-2A, 3A, 3B, M38 and MB. Price for a complete body which includes body, hood, fenders, tailgate, grille and windshield (w/o glass) runs $800; just the body shell alone, $600. Acme can also supply a chassis frame and a fair number of mechanical parts, too, if you need 'em—clutches, distributors, coils, W/S wipers, motor mounts, rear axle shafts, etc. Jeep bodies are made in Manila, mechanical parts in Japan. For illustrated price list, write the above address.

FOUR WHEEL PARTS WHOLESALERS
P.O. Box 54572, Terminal Annex, Los Angeles, Calif. 90054

Has essentially the same selection of Jeep parts as American Auto Parts Co. but offers a much more complete line of accessories. Has best prices available on many items. American does have better prices on some parts, however, so you really need both catalogs. Ninety-two-page catalog, $1.00.

G. H. MEISER & CO.
P.O. Box B, Posen, Ill. 60469

Meiser manufactures the Enginair tire pump which screws into the spark plug hole and uses cylinder pressure to pump air up to 130 psi. The manifold vacuum prevents the gas mixture from being sucked into the cylinder, so it pumps only fresh air. It can save a lot of sweat on a hot day. Literature available. Pump costs $13.50 plus $1 handling. Also carried by J. C. Whitney.

OVERDRIVE
$210 - $325

The overdrive is an extra transmission that adds on to the existing setup. It gives one extra gear on the high side which can be used in conjunction with any of the regular gears. Thus it provides a gear range between each of your regular gears and on top for a high-high gear which will increase top speed. The overdrive is most useful in this respect where a small engine limits highway capability. In such a case, an overdrive will both improve top speed and reduce engine wear since the engine

can turn slower for the same speed. However, if you have a good power train to start with, it won't do much for you.

STEERING STABILIZER
$13 - $18

The steering stabilizer is a shock absorber attached to the steering arm to damp out any sudden lurches of the wheel while traversing rough terrain. When a wheel slides off a rock it can put a terrific strain on the steering system. The stabilizer softens the shock and protects the system so that you are less likely to have to walk back home.

Winches

A winch is insurance. It will allow you to go into country that you might otherwise pass up, secure in the knowledge that if you do get stuck, you will have an extra edge on getting out.

There are two basic kinds of winches—the power take-off (PTO) and the electric. The PTO winch uses the engine for power by means of a special drive shaft from the transmission or transfer case. The electric winch is driven by an electric motor operating off the battery. Both come in sizes up to 8000 pounds pull. However, because the PTO winch can draw on a much larger power source, it can reel in much faster under full load and run for a much longer time than an electric. On the other hand, the electric winch will operate even if the engine won't.

By using a block and a double line hook-up you can easily reduce the load on your winch or pull a heavier load with a smaller one. In this arrangement, a pulley block is attached to the fixed pulling point and the cable goes from the winch, through the pulley block, and back to the vehicle where it is attached. Now the force on the vehicle will be 8000 pounds when the winch is only pulling with 4000 pounds. This load reduction is important with an electric winch, as it can be run only for a short time under full load but much longer at reduced loads.

RAMSEY WINCH CO.
P.O. Box 15829, Tulsa, Okla. 74115
Very complete line of all types and complete mounting kits. Great 120-page catalog, free.

WARN INDUSTRIES
9050 Empire Way So., Seattle, Wash. 98118
Two 8000 pound electric winches. Mounting kits for most vehicles, also hubs. Literature free. Warn offers the most winch for the money. Their abbreviated mounting kits will cut another $50 off the price. Four Wheel Parts discounts the Warn even further. Specific price available on request.

WAREHOUSE SALES
P.O. Box 36, Rossford, Ohio 43460
8000 pound Viking & Rhino winches—both electric and PTO. Kits for Rhino winches. Also good line of jacks, pintle hooks, etc. Free catalog.

sources of winches

SUPERWINCH, INC.
Pomfret, Conn. 06258
Small electric winches, 750 pounds to 1500 pounds. Literature 50¢. These will give close to 3000 pounds on double line operation. They are truly portable (18 lbs.), easily shifted from front to rear, and they may be mounted in any position—bolted directly to your present bumper or dropped over a standard ball hitch. They will only handle 45 feet of 5/32" cable, but you can always carry extra. Four Wheel Parts offers the complete 1500 pound unit for $110.

KOENIG IRON WORKS, INC.
P.O. Box 7726, Houston, Tex. 77007
PTO & Electric, 8000 lb. standard. Complete mounting kits for most vehicles. Literature free.

BERENS ASSOCIATES, INC.
5885 Hollis St., Emeryville, Calif. 94608
Catalog: $1 (for 2)

MASTER MECHANIC MFG. CO.
P.O. Box A, Burlington, Wisc. 53105
Catalog: free - 80 p.

SURPLUS CENTER
P.O. Box 82209, Lincoln, Neb. 68501
Catalog: free - 68 p.

AIRBORNE SALES CO.
P.O. Box 2727, Culver City, Calif. 90230
Catalog: 50¢ - 88 p.

sources of accessories

SUZUKI FUN CENTER
515 N. Victory Blvd., Burbank, Calif. 91502
The Fun Center has an excellent selection of cycle gear and accessories. Their 120-page catalog is packed with something for everyone—helmets, leather jackets and boots, tools, skid plates, fairings, conversion kits, tires, and a full range of parts from gas tanks to exhaust pipes, and handle bars to sprockets. They also handle the Clymer repair manuals. Catalog investment is $1 and worth it.

CUSTOM GAS TANKS
11719 McBean Dr., El Monte, Calif. 91732
Replacement and auxiliary gas tanks for Toyotas, Jimmy/Blazer, Suburban, Bronco, Scout and most Jeep models. Tanks are stainless steel or aluminum, heliarc welded with baffles. Catalog available for $1.

EDGEWOOD NATIONAL, INC.
6603 N. Meridian, Puyallup, Wash. 98371
Loose-leaf catalog available of off-road parts and accessories. One buck gets you Edgewood's current catalog and your name on their mailing list for catalog supplements mailed out twice a year.

HUSKY DUALMATIC MFG. CORP.
P.O. Box 1119, Longmont, Colo. 80501
This company offers products under the names Husky and Dualmatic—freewheeling hubs, overdrives, soft tops, steering stabilizers, tire carriers, carpeting, rear seats and tire covers. Info available.

DICK CEPEK, INC.
9201 California Ave., South Gate, Calif. 90280
Specializes in off-road and high floation tires. Also offers a fair range of general 4WD accessories and some basic camping gear.

BERENS ASSOCIATES, INC.
5885 Hollis St.
Emeryville, Calif. 94608

HICKEY ENTERPRISES, INC.
1645 Callens Rd.
Ventura, Calif. 93003

Neither of the above two dealers sells directly to the public. Hickey, however, will sell to individuals if there is no dealer in the area. Berens will send catalogs (2) for $1. Hickey's 24-page catalog is free.

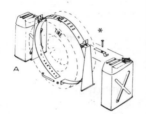

A. Saddle Bag Can & Accessory Carrier
• Encircles your spare tire with steel, creating a basic support system for many accessories • No holes to drill in your vehicle • Easily adjusts to mount around all diameter 15" tires • Doesn't require tail light relocation on new C.J.'s • Carries one or two Jerry cans (curb theft with vinyl-coated cable 5.95)

MOUNTAIN MAN INDUSTRIES, INC.
P.O. Box 2400, Boulder, Colo. 80302
Cargo carrying accessories to fit most four-wheelers. 18-page catalog (loose sheets) runs $2 which is applied toward purchase. Info in catalog isn't worth the cost—mostly isometric line drawings with info on how the various carriers can be put to use. Scarce on construction, materials and dimensions data. Gear is supposed to be pretty good, but you couldn't prove it by their sales literature.

KELLY MANUFACTURING CO.
5611 Raritan Rd., Denver, Colo. 80221
Jeep accessories—steel and soft tops, rear seats, tire carriers, doors, and tire covers. Literature free.

WESTERN TIRE CENTERS
3645 S. Palo Verde Blvd., Tucson, Ariz. 85713
Good source of back-country tires and off-road vehicle accessories. Catalog available free.

NOREMCO LEISURE PROD.
151 Birge St., Hamilton, Ontario, Canada L8L 7V4
Makers of the Unstucker. With this unit you bolt an adapter to your rear wheels when you get the unit and leave it there. Now if you get stuck, attach a special drum to each adapter, fasten lines to a solid object, and spin the wheels. The line will wind up tight on the drum and pull you out—8,000 pounds of pull—$210.

BACK-COUNTRY TRAVEL

How about some information on places to go? If you're interested in Baja California, you have a good choice of specialized off-roading books for the area—obviously, Baja is an "in" place. For other areas, however, things are tight. One of the best sources of material are the various books offered by treasure hunting, prospecting and rock-hounding dealers. Many of these people offer detailed information on getting into some fine back country and what to expect there.

Maps are, of course, one of the best sources of information on any area. The U.S. Geological Survey topographical maps are normally the most comprehensive. Aerial photos may also prove helpful. For areas not covered by topo maps (such as Mexico and Central America), aeronautical maps and guides are probably the best bet.

Local off-roading clubs are a good potential source for the most current information. Local clubs are also a good place to pick up back-country experience and tips. Most members are real founts of information for the novice.

BOOKS

The Trip

FOR YEARS the usual place to start the Baja shot was at the Shell station in San Ysidro, and for those who ride their bikes down to the border, it is still the logical place for commencement. And even if you truck the bike down to the border, this is a good place to top up the tanks on both the bike and the truck. As you approach the border at San Ysidro, locate wherever, keep an eye out for Sanborn's insurance agency for Sanborn is the only reliable source of Mexican insurance for motorcycles that I've been able to locate so far.

It is only about half a mile or so to the International Border, and here you will encounter the nearest thing to the East Berlin Volkspolizei to be found under the U.S. flag in the form of a contingent of San Diego City cops who have a pronounced tendency to harass younger citizens and motorcyclists. They have been known to hand out traffic tickets for not having mirrors to motorcyclists who unloaded their Baja sleds from trucks at the border, in spite of remonstrances on the rider's part that the mirrors were removed as a safety measure. I can think of nothing less enjoyable than getting the stalk of a rear-view mirror jabbed into the brisket when comes a spill — and a spill will come!

By contrast, the Mexican authorities are very polite and helpful, and the formalities at the border itself are almost non-existent. Follow the signs out of Tijuana past the insurance-and-divorce traps (auto insurance, that is) — you're going to Ensenada!

There is now a new "Freeway" from Tijuana to Ensenada but it is far from free — it is a toll road. But the old road to Ensenada is still open and it's a better road for motorcyclists. The views are prettier and it has lots of curves and carries most of the traffic, because most Mexicans fail to see the loss of paying a couple of dollars or so for the privilege of saving ten or fifteen minutes on the trip. The rich Americans with their poor handling, overpowered, bulky of cars will

BAJA
Doug Richmond
1970 - 112 p. il. - $4

Doug Richmond puts out some damn fine hard-nosed material. Straight. Almost two-thirds of *Baja* covers specifics for the trail bike although he doesn't skimp on details of the gear needed for a trip—all the little items that make the difference (like why detergent instead of soap). The rest covers the full trip down the peninsula. All the dope. Most of the book is applicable to any extended back country trip from Baja to northern Maine. Don't pass it by.
From: Bagnall Publishing Co., Box 507, Lake Arrowhead, Calif. 92352

A GUIDE TO LAND-ROVER EXPEDITIONS
1972 - 15 p. - free

An excellent little booklet. Specifically written for the Land Rover but applicable to any off-road expedition. Gives a rundown on recommended vehicle equipment, spare parts to be carried, hints for cross-country driving, and general info on visas, maps, health, finance, documents, and insurance. Whether you're planning a weekend junket or a true expedition into the real wild regions of the world, there is some fine material here.
From: British Leyland Motors, 600 Willow Tree Rd., Leonia, N.J. 07605

BAJA HANDBOOK
James T. Crow
96 p. il. - $2.50

One of the better books on the Baja area. Written for four wheelers. What to take, where to go, and what to expect. Good solid material.
From: Haessner Literary Service, Box 89, Newfoundland, N.J. 07435

ADVENTURE TRAVEL USA
1976 - 224 p. - $3.95

The **Adventure Travel USA** includes a good listing of some forty outfitters around the country who offer special guided 4WD trips. Many of these are the only way to get into the area in question. Average cost is about $20 per day for a one day trip and $30 to $50 per person per day for overnight trips. These prices are based on the use of the outfitter's 4WD and driver. Whether you can bring your own rig or not, it doesn't say.
From: Adventure Guides, Inc., 36 East 57th St., New York, N.Y. 10022

tion, it's filled with articles on choosing a bike (new or used), riding techniques, tips for packing your gear, magazine and book reviews, and materials on maps, credit cards, and the like. The style is free and easy throughout. **The** source for information on motorcycle camping.
From: Tobey Publishing Co., Box 428, New Canaan, Conn. 06840

OVERLANDING
John Steele Gordon
1975 - 328 p. - $4.95

If you're planning any long-distance runs, say, across Europe or Africa or down to Central and South America, with a four-wheeler, **Overlanding** is your handbook. Gordon covers the whole shmear from A to Z and then some. Nine chapters discuss trip planning and logistics, costs and making arrangements—insurance, passports and visas, misc papers, also health and medical requirements. Two chapters are devoted to vehicles, accessories and maintenance, which ain't a helluva lot, but the information that's there is good. Other chapters include maps and guidebooks, daily overland expedition chores, customs and immigration, expedition business matters, i.e., mail forwarding, consulates, legal aid, banking, etc., and photography. Nice little book, and well indexed.
From: Harper & Row, 10 E. 53rd St., New York, N.Y. 10022

TWO WHEEL TRAVEL—MOTORCYCLE CAMPING AND TOURING
Peter W. Tobey, Ed.
1972 - 128 p. il. - $3

This one is right down our line. **Two Wheel Travel** is the **Whole Earth Catalog** of motorcycle camping and touring. It delves primarily into gear and equipment—what you need and why, how to judge and choose, who has it and for how much, and what to do with it. In addi-

TWO-WHEEL TOURING & CAMPING
Cliff Boswell and George Hays
1970 - 110 p. il. - $3.50

Don't confuse this with **Two Wheel Travel.** Both of these deal with motorcycle touring and camping, but **Two Wheel Travel** concentrates on the equipment end, while **Two-Wheel Touring** is heavier on the how-to and travel information. Where they do overlap, **Two Wheel Travel** provides superior coverage, but in general, each complements the other nicely. **Two-Wheel Touring** has some good specifics on travel in Mexico, Canada, and Europe and includes a full listing of sources for additional travel material. There isn't a lot of specific trail bike information here, but if you're interested in touring, it offers some good background.
From: Bagnall Publishing Co., Box 507, Lake Arrowhead, Calif. 92352

EXPEDITIONS

SIERRA ADVENTURES, INC.
331 E. Indian School Rd., Phoenix, Ariz. 85018

Sierra Adventures is one outfitter who does offer guided 4WD and trail bike tours into the Sierra Madre Mountains of Northern Mexico where you use your vehicle. These are ten-day tours into some of the finest wilderness on the continent. The trip features fantastic waterfalls, canyons deeper than the Grand Canyon and primitive Indians. The cost is $100 plus per vehicle with up to four people. This one looks well worth it, and this country is something else. Free literature available.

river

River running in a C-1 slalom canoe at Farmington, Conn.

Rivers, streams, bayous, lakes, all form a vast complex of wilderness waterways that, barring a few dams here and a little pollution there, can take you throughout North America—deep into the Canadian wilderness, through the thousands of lakes in northern Minnesota, down the wild canyons of the West, and across the sleepy prairies of the Midwest. Few people would consider traveling this way today, but in earlier days, these were the highways for exploration, commerce, and communication. The rivers are still there, but now they are the realm of the outdoor recreationist—the canoeist, the kayaker, and the river rafter—who looks to the river more as an end in itself than as a wilderness highway.

River running. People who ply the rivers can be grouped into two classes: the river runners and the river tourers. The river runners do just that—run rivers, particularly fast-moving ones with jagged rocks, boulders and much white water. It takes skill, judgment, and foresight and certainly could be considered dangerous since a number of people have been killed doing it. In spite of the risks involved, or perhaps because of them, white-water enthusiasts find excitement in thundering rapids, meeting the wet challenge of heavy water paddling.

The first choice of boats for river running is the modern kayak, a slim fiberglass shell weighing under 30 pounds with just enough room for two legs and two cheeks. A kayak is extremely sensitive and highly maneuverable. The sensation when paddling a kayak is akin to skiing; you feel as if you are wearing the boat.

The river runner's next choice for a boat would be the white-water or decked canoe. These recently developed craft are something of a cross between the more traditional open canoe and a kayak. White-water canoes are completely decked, with cockpit holes in which the paddler(s) kneel.

A large group of river runners still prefer the standard open canoe for tackling the white water. Although kayakers mockingly liken this to a "barge" by comparison, the same thrills are still to be had, and a deft hand and cool brain are still required.

Yet another variety of river runner is the rafter. Raft travel is mostly limited to the canyon rivers of the West where giant standing waves, fast currents, and waterfalls would overwhelm other craft. Raft travel requires a lesser degree of skill than the other forms of river running since most everybody on a raft is just a passenger.

Few people rent white-water kayaks or decked canoes, and fewer will outfit trips (provide the boats, gear, etc.). The reason is that proper control of a craft in white water requires a certain degree of skill, and even with this, it's still easy to rip up a boat (not to mention yourself) in the rapids.

Many beginners first learn the technique of river running from friends who have boats. Serious kayakers often have more than one boat and are usually willing to introduce buddies to the sport, so take it from there. At the very worst you may have to buy a boat and learn on your own. Used kayaks can be had for less than $100, but they may be a little hard to scrounge up. Usually canoe club poop sheets will carry a few classifieds listing them.

Take it easy while learning and practice on flat water until you can handle the craft reasonably well, then try your hand at easy white water. One thing you should perfect as quickly as possible is the Eskimo roll. Capsizes are not infrequent, and recovery is best done by rolling out; the paddle is used to push yourself upright. Many canoe clubs have made arrangements to use indoor swimming pools during the winter for rolling practice. Look into it. Rolling is not that difficult to learn and could be vital.

River touring is best done with two groups so you can spot one car at the put-in and one at the take-out. (Cartopping—Montana, 1912)

touring

Photos courtesy
Old Town Canoe Co.

*Canoeing the waters of Marsh Lake,
Yukon Territory. (This photo looks
pretty good upside down, too.)*

One of the problems with white-water canoeing and kayaking is that the best water levels occur in early spring, when weather and water are as cold as a witch's tit. Capsizing in warm weather is hardly a problem, but going over in cold weather can be dangerous because of exposure. Even if you don't dump, expect to get wet from spray and splash. So pick up a wet suit similar to the type divers wear. Other gear you should have are a kayaker's helmet for head protection, a life vest and a pair of tennies; rapids and sharp rocks can be tough on the tootsies. One thing that everyone seems to tell you "after it happens"—after you dump and smack your gourd on a boulder—is to turn your body so your feet are pointed downstream and use your legs to protect yourself from rocks and boulders. We're telling you now.

Gaining skill in river running takes practice, lots of it, while slowly progressing from the easy to the difficult. When you get to the top, like with the fast draw, you'll always find a run that'll beat you.

When you get tired of it all, bailing out's relatively easy. Investment-wise, you've got a boat and some accessories that can be readily sold through canoe club news bulletins or even the local newspaper. Expect to realize 60–70 per cent of their cost, as the market's pretty good for used equipment.

River touring. Our other group, the river tourers, are less interested in being labeled as "harebrained thrill seekers who will tackle any rapid." These are the canoe travelers who explore Canadian lakes, fish, camp, and enjoy the total experience of wilderness travel by canoe. Sure they shoot the rapids but only as part of the trip rather than as an end in itself.

The boat for this is the open canoe, the most versatile of all river craft. It can be handled by one man yet carry three people plus a fair quantity of gear. It can maneuver across quiet pools as well as roaring rapids and even serve as a makeshift shelter on shore.

Another touring craft, which is more popular in Europe than here in the U.S., is the two man touring kayak. Although the touring kayak holds less gear than a canoe, proponents argue that the craft is more stable because of its low center of gravity.

Getting into touring is fairly easy since almost every city has at least one canoe livery. You can begin by renting a canoe (usually from $5 to $10 a day) to familiarize yourself with its handling characteristics, and with a couple of afternoon pack-your-lunch trips, you'll get a feel for what touring can be like. If you can make arrangements for an overnight or weekend rental, the next thing to do is plan a trip. There are many places to get information on rivers and streams to paddle—for example, fish and game departments, state tourist bureaus, canoe dealers and clubs, as well as river guidebooks and charts. The easiest river and stream charts to get hold of are the U.S. Geological Survey topographical maps (check the Maps Section), which generally show such details as rapids, falls, and beaches. With a little background in map reading you'll soon be able to determine the best runs for touring, where to put in and take out (the boat), and choice spots for camping overnight. Frankly it's always best to start planning a trip with a topo map.

Downriver touring (few people make upriver trips) is best done with two groups for safety and so that you can spot a car at the put-in and one at the take-out.

Paddling a canoe is a team effort, with the more experienced person taking the stern position. In white-water paddling, the bow and stern positions are equally important. The bow man can see the rocks better and must make the first move to avoid them and initiate a course; the stern paddler must sense what the bow man is doing and follow through. White-water travel involves skill that comes only with experience. As you learn to read the river and realize how different paddle strokes control the boat, you'll soon discover a rapid improvement in your canoeing ability. Incidentally, capsizing is part of the learning process, so enjoy it.

Eventually you might want to purchase a canoe, and with the popularity of the craft, you shouldn't have any trouble in locating a new or used one. Good spots to check for used ones are canoe rental places, newspapers, and club newsletters. If you're seriously interested in canoeing, buy a good canoe to begin with. In kayaking you should work up from one grade of boat to another as you gain experience; this doesn't apply in canoeing.

If you get bored with the whole business, you'll find the used market is very good for top-quality canoes, and you can expect to realize up to 75 per cent of the original price. Keep this in mind when purchasing; you and your canoe will do better in the long run.

RIVER TOURING

The national clubs are made up of affiliated local clubs and individual memberships. They provide the best single source of information on the various aspects of canoeing, kayaking and rafting. These organizations can put you in touch with a local club. All publish periodicals which keep members abreast of activities on a national level.

AMERICAN CANOE ASSOCIATION (ACA)
4260 E. Evans Ave., Denver, Colo. 80222
The ACA is divided into 13 geographic divisions around the country. The activities of each division are determined by members' interests and the nature of the local water. A national office is maintained in Denver to coordinate activities and centralize information services. Annual membership dues are $10 to $14. This includes subscription to the bimonthly, *Canoe,* official magazine of the ACA. *Canoe* is an attractive, well-done-up slick, weak in feature article content, though the news items are worth the price. Infidels may subscribe to *Canoe* for $6 a year. Write: Canoe Magazine, 1999 Shepard Rd., St. Paul, Minn. 55116.

UNITED STATES CANOE ASSOCIATION (USCA)
Sandy Zellers, Membership Chairman
R.R. 1, Winamac, Ind. 46996
Organized in 1968, membership is much like that of the ACA and AWA, made up of affiliated clubs and individuals. Dues for the year run $7.50 to $15. The USCA's *Canoe News,* a bimonthly publication, appears as an inclusion in *Wilderness Camping.* The USCA portion of *Wilderness Camping* magazine, which retains the name *Canoe News,* is received by USCA members only.

AMERICAN WHITEWATER AFFILIATION (AFA)
Box 51, Wallingford, Conn. 06492
This is a volunteer organization made up of individuals and local clubs interested in white water. Yearly dues of $5 include subscription to AWA's bimonthly magazine, *American Whitewater Journal.* This is probably the best periodical available to river runners. Loaded with up-to-date detailed info on techniques, equipment, safety, conservation and river access developments. Send name, address and 24¢ in stamps for copy of *Journal.*

RIVER DEFENSE GROUPS

These organizations are actively involved in river conservation, lobbying for rivers and against river damaging dams, diversions and development. Many put out quarterly newsletters reporting conservation issues and who to contact to make your biggest impact. The old thing about writing your congressman really works, especially when enough of us give a damn. Write them for details.

AMERICAN RIVER TOURING ASSOCIATION
1016 Jackson St., Oakland, Calif. 94607

AMERICAN RIVERS CONSERVATION COUNCIL
324 C St. SE, Washington, D.C. 20005

APPALACHIAN MOUNTAIN CLUB
5 Joy St., Boston, Mass. 02108

FRIENDS OF THE EARTH
529 Commercial St., San Francisco, Calif. 94111

THE SIERRA CLUB, RIVER TOURING SECTION
3962 Fordham Way, Livermore, Calif. 94550

PERIODICALS

CANOEING
Mrs. Karl L. Ketter
Quarterly - $1/yr. - 30 p. il.

Articles run from trip reports to some very good equipment comparison tests. Put out by two people who sell and love canoes. No avenging angels.
From: Ketter Canoeing, 101-79th Ave. N., Minneapolis, Minn. 55430

CHE-MUN
Nick Nickels
Quarterly - $3.50/yr. - 6 p.

International canoeing newsletter. Picks up canoeing news from around the world. From a prison break attempt in a canoe to good information on remote rivers in the far north. Informal and interesting. More enjoyable than most of the mags.
From: Nick Nickels, Box 479, Lakefield, Ontario, Canada K0L 2H0

NATIONAL SLALOM COMMITTEE NEWSLETTER
Eric Evans, Ed.
Monthly - $2.25/yr. - 2-4 p.

Strictly for the racing enthusiast, race schedules and results.
From: Bonnie Bliss, 11 Larchdell Way, Mountain Lakes, N.J. 07046

THE WILDERNESS CANOEIST
Roger Smith, Ed.
Quarterly - $6/yr. - 12 p. il.

Newsletter of the Wilderness Canoe Association, a club in southern Ontario, it covers techniques used in the bush, trip reports, conservation issues in Ontario and club news. Winter coverage deals with cross-country skiing and snowshoeing. Provides an interesting view of Canadian canoeing and brief peeks into the furry wilderness up north.
From: Wilderness Canoe Assn., R.R. 3, Cavan, Ontario, Canada L0A 1C0

DOWN RIVER
Eric Evans, Ed.
Monthly - $8/yr. - 48 p. il.

A relatively new magazine which for its first two years received its share of criticism for exploiting the river experience. It gives a balanced coverage to canoes, kayaks and rafts, and contains some very informative articles on techniques and river conservation, though pieces on somebody's boat trip to the Calgary Stampede seem to appear with the same frequency. As an independent magazine this publication could transcend the party politics that have mucked up some of the club rags.
From: World Publications, P.O. Box 366, Mountain View, Calif. 94040

RIO GRANDE GURGLE
Ms. Helen F. Redman, Ed.
8 issues/yr. - $3.50/yr. - 4-10 p.

A New Mexico newsletter covering part of Colorado. The stress is on river news, local and otherwise. Reports on safety, techniques, conservation and water levels for southwestern river runners. Extremely well written.
From: Rio Grande Gurgle, Route 1, Box 177, Santa Fe, N. Mex. 87501

WHITE WATER MAGAZINE
Stuart Fisher, Ed.
Quarterly - $5/yr. (U.S. air mail) - 28 p. il.

Official rag of the British Canoe Union Slalom and Wild Water Racing Committee. British and European racing news, tips on training and club news. Not recommended for the casual reader, though of possible interest to the dedicated competitor. Cheques should be made out to the Manchester Canoe Club.
From: C. M. Rothwell, 21 Windsor Rd., Clayton Bridge, Manchester M10 6QQ England

BASIC RIVER CANOEING
Robert E. McNair
1972, 3rd ed. - 103 p. il. - $2.95 (pb)

Many groups and schools use this book as a text to complement river instruction. Primarily written for open canoes, the chapters on reading water and river strategy would benefit all river runners.
From: American Camping Assn., Inc., Bradford Woods, Martinsville, Ind. 46151

A WHITE WATER HANDBOOK FOR CANOE AND KAYAK
John T. Urban
1974 - 77 p. il. - $2 (pb)

John Urban has been running rivers for eons. This book came out ten years ago and hasn't changed a note. It offers sound advice on managing open and decked boats in fast water. It also contains the best presentation of how to do the Eskimo roll ever to appear in print, though understand, no one yet has learned to do the Eskimo roll by reading about it. Excellent chapters on the variety of water conditions and deviations found on a river.
From: Appalachian Mountain Club, 5 Joy St., Boston, Mass. 02108

THE COMPLETE WILDERNESS PADDLER
James West Davidson and John Rugge
1975 - 259 p. il. - $10 (hb)

Primarily for the open canoeist. Told in the context of the authors' own expedition down the Moisie River in Labrador. Davidson and Rugge take you through the many steps of preparing for and running expeditions into wilderness areas, from how to find a river, the right partners, equipment, portaging where no portage exists and heavy-water techniques. The chapter on navigation explains this science in such clarity and humor that you will actually enjoy yourself while learning to navigate. A delightfully human narrative written in a most entertaining style; a good book for all.
From: Alfred A. Knopf, 201 E. 50th St., New York, N.Y. 10022

CANOE POLING
Al, Syl and Frank Beletz
1974 - 136 p. il. - $4.95 (pb)

The only book devoted to the art of poling a canoe. If you've ever tried poling and have had some difficulty you might check this tome out. It will not teach you how, but contains a number of tips that will help you on your way.
From: A. C. Mackenzie Press, Box 9301, Richmond Heights Sta., Richmond Heights, Mo. 63117

CANOEING WILDERNESS WATERS
G. Heberton Evans III
1975 - 211 p. il. - $15 (hb)

Written with the serious wilderness tripper in mind, this book covers subjects from choice of canoes to weather without any of the usual B.S. You can actually learn something here. Forty-four pages are devoted to portages, with an excellent chapter on lake travel and jury-rigged canoe sails, plus solid advice on upstream and downstream travel; profusely illustrated. Evans has 16 years experience in the Canadian bush as a trip leader for the go-for-the-distance Keewaydin Camp.
From: A. S. Barnes & Co., Inc., P.O.Box 421, Cranbury, N.J. 08512

BUILDERS OF BIRCH BARK CANOES
William Rossman
24 p. il. - $1.50 (pb)

This booklet is about Bill Hafeman and his techniques and methods of building bark canoes. Hafeman has been building these canoes on the Chippewa and Voyageur design for over forty years, and in this 24-pager he tells you how to do it.
From: The Chicagoland Canoe Base, Inc., 4019 N. Narragansett Ave., Chicago, Ill. 60634

LIVING CANOEING
Alan Byde
1974, 2nd ed. - 266 p. il. - $9.50 (hb)

The most comprehensive treatise on kayaking available. A British book requiring a little translating, but the information is clear and to the point. Recommended for beginners and experienced paddlers. Very good chapters on basic and advanced strokes, and four chapters devoted to deep-water and open-sea cruising—a subject you'll find discussed nowhere else. Byde has devoted his life to the sport.
From: Transatlantic Arts, Inc., N. Village Green, Levittown, N.Y. 11756

KAYAKING
Jay Evans and Robert R. Anderson
1975 - 192 p. il. - $4.95 (pb)

A very basic introduction to decked craft for beginners. The best chapter is "Basic Paddling Technique." Unfortunately there is a good deal of filler in this book which will probably frustrate the more advanced paddler. "Tips on Training, Cruising" and "Racing" chapters are totally inadequate for those beyond the intermediate stage.
From: The Stephen Greene Press, P.O.Box 1000, Brattleboro, Vt. 05301

RIVER RUNNING
Verne Huser
1975 - 294 p. il. - $4.95 (pb), $10 (hb)

An authoritative work on rafting in general, and on Western rivers in particular. Covering equipment, safety and emergency techniques. Really oriented towards folks going on commercial raft trips. Mr. Huser devotes the major portion of his book to a study of regulatory agencies and the progress being made to preserve our rivers. Informative and well written. The appendices themselves, as a reference source, are worth the price of the book!
From: Henry Regnery Co., 180 N. Michigan Ave., Chicago, Ill. 60601

WHITEWATER RAFTING
William McGinnis
1975 - 361 p. il. - $12.50 (hb)

A definitive work on rafting. Divided into three parts, the first 176 pages of the book deal with inflatable craft, accessories, how to make your own, wild-water techniques and river camping, including how to build your own riverside sauna. Top marks go to a very good first aid chapter. The second part is a general river guidebook to 26 rivers around the U.S. suitable for rafting. The third section is a massive appendix, 46 pages of inflatable boat manufacturers and commercial rafting outfitters.
From: Quadrangle Books, 10 E. 53rd St., New York, N.Y. 10022

RUSHTON & HIS TIMES IN AMERICAN CANOEING
Atwood Manley
1968 - 203 p. il. - $14 (hb)

This is a biography of John Rushton, a famous canoe builder of the latter part of the 19th century. For those dreaming of constructing a canoe with classic lines, Manley's book has a fine appendix containing line drawings of Rushton's canoes with offsets, center-line elevations and some details on construction. The beginning builder might get a headache tackling this but those proficient at lofting and good with tools could build a craft unlike any other available today.

For the less ambitious, there is much enjoyable reading—actually, the real purpose of the book. It contains a history of modern canoeing, from the long-distance cruises of MacGregor, Neide and Bishop, to the formation of the American Canoe Association. The only thing lacking is a bibliography.
From: Syracuse Univ. Press, P.O.Box 8, University Sta., Syracuse, N.Y. 13210

POLE, PADDLE & PORTAGE
Bill Riviere
1974 - 258 p. il. - $3.95 (pb)

Full coverage of the many aspects of canoe handling and camping. Written by a Maine guide
who knows his business. Includes an interesting
chapter outlining canoe trails throughout
North America.
*From: Little, Brown & Co., 200 West St.,
Waltham, Mass. 02154*

BARK CANOES AND SKIN BOATS OF NORTH AMERICA
Edwin Tappan Adney and Howard I. Chappelle
1964 - 242 p. il. - $6.75 (hb)
SN 4701-0021

A handsomely-done documentary with many black-and-white photographs and construction drawings by the master naval draftsman,
Howard I. Chappelle, on watercraft of the North American Indian.
Early history, materials and tools, form and construction, plus examples of finished work are included for craft of the Eastern Maritime
Region, Central Canada, Northwestern Canada and the Arctic. Excellent book for those wishing to build their own canoe or kayak the
old way, maybe the best way. In the appendix John Heath gives instructions for executing the Greenland kayak roll accompanied by
step-by-step photos. A steal for the price of $6.75.
*From: Sup. of Doc., U.S. Gov. Printing Office, Washington, D.C.
20402*

THE SURVIVAL OF THE BARK CANOE
John McPhee
1975 - 114 p. - $7.95 (hb)

Survival is intended as a profile of Henri Vailliancourt, who builds
birch bark canoes based on the Malecite design. The book goes into
such detail on his methods and techniques that it would make a good
primer for builders.

Aside from its more practical aspects, *Survival* is highly recommended to anyone interested in the outdoors. It conveys a feeling of
freedom and balsam-scented air, and contains some of the finest passages in canoeing literature. John McPhee is considered one of America's best outdoors writers.
*From: Farrar, Straus & Giroux, Inc., 19 Union Sq. W., New York,
N.Y. 10003*

sources of books

WESTWATER BOOKS
Box 365, Boulder City, Nev. 89005
Besides publishing an excellent series of river guides, Westwater Books
carries a complete selection of river guides to the Western U.S. and a
number of how-to books. Write for free mail-order catalog.

MOOR & MOUNTAIN
63 Park St., Andover, Mass. 01810
Mainly a wilderness equipment retailer, Moor & Mountain carries a
large number of technique books and an extensive selection of river
and trail guides. Catalog is free.

FILMS

WHITEWATER SELF DEFENSE: THE ESKIMO ROLL
A Russ Nichols film
14 min. - Super 8mm, color, sound - rental, $15; purchase, $120

The foundation of efficient and safe kayaking is the Eskimo roll (not
to be confused with the Arctic bagel). This is *the* basic "stroke" to
learn when you first get into the sport despite the fact that you never
plan to go near heavy, class IV or V water. An accidental upset in the
middle of a large lake is not unheard of, and unless you can properly
execute the Eskimo roll, you've got a long, dreary swim ahead of you!
While books tell how to do it, this film shows you. An ideal training
aid.
From: Russ Nichols Productions, Box 192, Lemont, Pa. 16851

*One can gain basic instruction in river running at local clubs. The na-
tional organizations also provide very good instructional programs.
The following listed courses are a selection of more specialized training: from ground zero, i.e., don't-know-elbow-from-gunwale, to opportunities to run real hair. Minimum age is usually 14. For those with
less exotic taste it is suggested you check the Learn-to-Canoe Directory, free from Grumman Allied Industries, Inc., Marathon, N.Y. 13803.
It lists 250 locations where you can learn which end of a canoe is the
front and which the back.*

CANOE & KAYAK COURSES

MONDAMIN WILDERNESS ADVENTURES
P.O.Box 8, Tuxedo, N.C. 28784
Five-day, white-water open-canoe clinics at novice and intermediate
levels, $190. Price includes use of boats, gear, room and board. Cours-
es in April, May, August and September. This instruction gives you a
solid understanding of operating open canoes in fast water. Brochure
available.

MADAWASKA KANU CAMP
2 Tuna Court, Don Mills, Ontario, Canada M3A 3L1
Intensive six-day white-water training for K-1, C-1 and C-2 paddlers,
novice to expert levels. Beginners can rent boats for $80 per six-day
course, everybody else must bring their own. $165 for course and
room and board. If you camp and cook off school grounds, course is
$90. Christa and Hermann Kerckhoff who run this school both hold
Canadian National Championship titles in K-1.

RAFT KAYAK SCHOOL
440 N. First St., San Jose, Calif. 95112
For the aspiring kayakist, a two-day pool session is offered year-
round, $40. Other year-round kayak courses are a weekend of white-
water training for $80 which includes the works, and for those who
have mastered the Eskimo roll, a two-day surfing class for $80. From
April till October five-day, white-water kayak classes are available for
$200 including meals, gear and open-air lodging. Instruction for be-
ginner to intermediate. Kayak groups can also charter support craft
from these people for trips longer than a day. Write for details.

Other Canoe & Kayak Schools

ASPEN KAYAK SCHOOL
Box 1520, Aspen, Colo. 81611

NANTAHALA OUTDOOR CENTER, INC.
Star Route, Box 68, Bryson City, N.C. 28713

NORTHERN WATERS, INC.
Fryeburg, Maine 04037

ROGER PARIS KAYAK SCHOOL
Colorado Rocky Mountain School, Carbondale, Colo. 81623

SUNDANCE OLYMPIC KAYAK SCHOOL
665 Hunt Lane, Grants Pass, Oreg. 97525

ROWING COURSES

AMERICAN WHITE-WATER SCHOOL
1016 Jackson St., Oakland, Calif. 94607
These courses are offered by the American River Touring Association, a nonprofit organization, to teach the basic skills necessary to
enjoy and protect our wilderness rivers. They represent a high point
in river-running instruction. Minimum age is 17 and no experience is
required to attend, though they recommend you have completed a
Red Cross first-aid course (see First Aid and Medical section). A
seven-day rowing workshop in April on the American and Stanislaus
Rivers provides an introduction for the beginner, $250. Two-week
rowing workshops are available throughout the summer, costing
$250 to $450. In June and July there is a twenty-seven-day complete workshop for $750. Instruction is given in oar boats, paddle

SCHOOLS and INSTRUCTION

boats and kayaks, and the course moves to various rivers throughout Oregon and northern California. Also offered are a series of paddle experiences throughout the summer from a relaxed, six-day Eel River run, $160, to a nineteen-day paddle through the Grand Canyon, $675. There are a number of courses offered for academic credit. Brochures on request.

CANYONEERS, INC.
Gaylord Staveley
P.O.Box 2997, Flagstaff, Ariz. 86001

Instruction in running small rowboats down the Colorado and Rio Grande taught by Gaylord Staveley who has twenty years' experience in sliding down rivers. Three courses are offered: an introduction to white-water boating, white-water oarsmanship and intermediate white-water oarsmanship. They may be taken separately or in an unbroken sequence. Prices are based on the number of people attending each class. In a class of five the cost per student is $339 for the complete nine-day, oar-flogging experience. This is definitely a good buy; Staveley knows his stuff and you'll learn.

An interesting book on Gaylord Staveley is his account of a rowing expedition down the Green and Colorado Rivers, *Broken Waters Sing,* published by Little, Brown & Co.

FASTWATER EXPEDITIONS
Box 365, Boulder City, Nev. 89005

Nine-day instruction and recreational trips down Utah's Green River in 7-ft. Sportyaks. Cost includes food, boats, gear and a neat ride, $385. Runs from July to October. Write for brochure.

WILDERNESS ENCOUNTERS, INC.
Box 232, Cambridge, Idaho 83610

Six-day Sportyak runs on the Lower Salmon and Snake Rivers, July through September, $395.

AMERICAN GUIDES ASSOCIATION
Box B, Woodland, Calif. 95695

This organization supplies trained crewmen to professional rafting companies. Their annual training schedule is broken into three separate sessions: five weekends beginning in March, $300; eight days in April, $250; and eight days in June, $300. Requirements to attend and costs are a bit stiff. If you don't have the hots to become a commercial boatman, you'd do better going elsewhere. Write for details.

WILDERNESS WORLD
1342 Jewell Ave., Pacific Grove, Calif. 93950

Primarily a commercial raft-trip outfit, they offer two, five-day basic introduction courses to rafting. In April the course is held on the Stanislaus; in June, on the Rogue. Minimum age is 18. Good experience if you're thinking about buying your own inflatable boat. $195.

Photo: Courtesy of Old Town Canoe Co.

139

WATERCRAFT

KAYAKS

KAYAKS
$200 - $555

The kayak's heritage goes back to the Eskimo skin boat, which was built of stitched seal or walrus hides stretched over a wood frame, and designed for hunting and fishing the rough seas of the Arctic. With the aid of modern plastics and fiberglass, the Eskimo's design has been adapted to today's light and highly maneuverable sport kayak.

There is a variety of basic designs for sport kayaks, each tailored to meet special requirements. The categories include downriver and flat-water racing, slalom racing, touring, and surfing.

Phantom Sprint downriver kayak

Speed is the characteristic desired of downriver and flat-water racing boats. This is achieved through a long narrow hull with a V-shaped bottom. Carrying these characteristics to the extreme results in a highly unstable boat that is difficult to maneuver; however, since racing is a contest of speed, maneuverability is of secondary importance, just as long as there's enough for the paddler to avoid obstacles.

Prijon Special slalom kayak

In slalom racing (comes from the Scandinavian and means zig-zag course or race) the paddler must maneuver his craft through a stretch of rapids while passing through a series of gates (marker poles suspended above the river). To achieve the greatest efficiency, a slalom kayak uses a fully rounded bottom, making the boat highly maneuverable, easily controlled, and responsive to the slightest touch of the paddle. However, this also makes it slow and often difficult to paddle in a straight line.

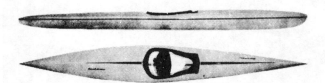

Combi 2000 touring kayak

Touring kayaks are used for recreational paddling and represent a balance between maneuverability and speed. As might be expected, many different touring kayak designs are available to fit different points on the speed-maneuverability spectrum. When maneuverability is emphasized, the kayak's design is similar to that of a slalom boat, except there is more V in the hull for straighter running and longer glides between paddle strokes. As the length is increased and more V added, the boat becomes faster and takes on the characteristics of the downriver kayak. Fourteen feet is about the optimum length for a touring kayak. At this length, glide characteristics are maintained and the craft has sufficient load-carrying capacity for extended trips.

Though there are some two-man (K-2) kayaks made, the majority of them, particularly wild-water types, are one-man (K-1) craft. Hulls are designed with only enough room for the paddler to sit with his legs stretched out before him. The hull has one opening in the deck, an oval hole just large enough for the paddler to fit through. A waterproof skirt fits over the hole and around the paddler's waist to keep water out of the craft.

Fiberglass-reinforced plastics are the predominant materials used in kayak construction because they lend themselves well to the complex hull configurations. Considerable research is still being done on plastics to improve the craft's lightness, flexibility, and durability.

A number of special design features incorporated into better kayaks include:

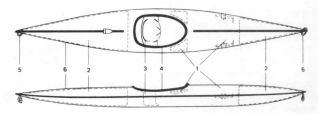

(1) Foot and knee braces—used to brace the paddler so that body motions can be used to help control the kayak.

(2) Flotation bags—used to provide buoyancy and additional hull support. Bags are contoured to hull shape.

(3) Hanging seat—provides lateral hip bracing and prevents hull damage by keeping paddler's weight suspended above the hull.

(4) Cockpit rim—provides lip for fastening elastic spray skirt closure.

(5) Grab loop—built in rope loop for more handling convenience and safety.

(6) Construction—special molded fiberglass formulation that produces a strong boat with resilience to withstand the hazards of whitewater, making it exceptionally sturdy for recreational paddling.

FOLDING KAYAKS (foldboats)
$200 - $700

Before fiberglass came into widespread use, most kayaks were similar in construction to the original skin-covered Eskimo craft. They consisted of a wood frame over which a canvas or rubberized skin was stretched. Known as cruising kayaks, these craft still find considerable use, especially in Europe, where many are made.

The most popular varieties are called foldboats. Their chief advantage is that the wood frame is hinged and can be assembled easily. A rubberized canvas covering slips onto the assembled frame and is fastened with snaps and inflatable tubes. The foldboat disassembles just as easily and can be packed up to fit in a car trunk for travel and stored in a closet when you get home. The foldboat's chief advantage is also its chief disadvantage if you get tired of the 25- to 45- minute assembly time.

Foldboats have been successfully used in white water, but the risk

Alaskan Eskimo skin boat **Photo: Bureau of Indian Affairs**

of ripping the canvas skin is great, so beware. Foldboats also make excellent sailing craft and have proved themselves in lengthy flat-water and coastal touring trips. Both Klepper and Folbot, two of the largest manufacturers of these craft, offer sailing rigs as standard accessories.

For a more complete look at this type of boat, write for a copy of *Folbot Holidays*, by Folbot Corp., P.O. Box 7097, Charleston, S.C. 29405. The book contains 308 pages of trip reports, tips and general B.S. attesting to the advantages of cruising kayaks. Cost is $2.

Assembling a Folbot

INFLATABLE KAYAKS (rubber duckies)
$80 - $375

By the time you get down to these boats, you've come a long way from the fine lines of the swift, lightweight fiberglass jobs. Nevertheless, inflatable kayaks have much to recommend them, particularly to beginners. Available in one- and two-man models, these boats are slightly more clumsy than fiberglass kayaks and a little harder to paddle, but you sure can bang them around in white water without worrying about destroying a $100–$200 investment. Great boat for learning in, but frankly, for extended cruising or any big-lake paddling, these craft are hopeless.

A high state of the art has been reached by the West German firm, Metzler. They have developed a 13-ft. inflatable kayak, the Spezi, complete with decking, knee braces, foot pegs and bucket seat. Fitted with a spray skirt you can roll this boat, though its 29-in. beam makes it a roll you'll remember. The hull material and seaming process are superior to any other inflatable kayak on the market.

Manufacturers of the less costly craft state hull materials will last ten years. The more popular brands even have one-year guarantees. The hull fabric will, if protected from sharp objects, last indefinitely. The real problem with these boats is the seams, which usually start going in their second year. But they're working on it.

Pyrawa two-man kayak

SPORTYAKS
$175 - $250

Sportyaks, while relatively unknown in the East, enjoy a certain amount of use throughout the western U.S. They come in two models, the 7 ft. x 36 in. Sportyak II-C, $175, and the 8 ft. x 45 in. Sportyak III-C, $250. They're molded of high-impact polyethylene, and feature a permanently-bonded double hull which provides integral flotation.

The shape is best described as rectangular—they're rowing dinghies.

The 44-lb. Sportyak II-C is the more popular for river running and has surprising white-water capabilities. The hull is strong and stable, and quite forgiving of mistakes. Many of the schools in the West use this craft for their courses.

While not suited for extended wilderness cruising, these boats fulfill the same function as rubber duckies and the cheaper inflatable rafts. And they might be considered a degree safer. The advantages are low cost and high durability.

Price, despite the above, depends on where you buy one. Most of the large marine supply houses carry them, and they usually allow a discount. Sportyaks are made by Dayton Marine.

CANOES

Heading out in Lake Michigan in a 25-ft. fiberglass birchbark replica

(Ralph Frese)

CANOES
$200 - $1,150

The canoe is the most versatile of all river touring craft, though it cannot handle the heavy water, where rafts perform best, or the most difficult white water, where kayaks shine. Essentially an open two-man craft, the canoe can carry large amounts of duffel on extended river trips. It is fast in the water, is easy to maneuver, and can navigate moderate white water with little difficulty.

For one-man paddling in white water or flat water a 15-foot canoe is best. For two men, 16 to 17 feet is a good length, and for extended flat water travel, 18- to 20-foot canoes are used. For all-around general purposes, the 17 footer is most popular.

Many canoes are available with a choice of two different keels. The lake keel is thin and extends a full inch below the hull. It prevents side slippage while paddling and is best for lake canoeing, where maneuverability is not important. The shoe keel, which is thick and extends only a quarter of an inch below the hull, is best in white water, where you need to turn the craft rapidly to avoid hitting rocks.

Some canoes do not have sufficient freeboard (distance from the waterline to the top of the hull). Six inches is the absolute minimum; 8 to 10 is preferred. These days, few canoes have much of an upturned bow or stern. Though they look nice and cut into the waves effectively, they also catch the wind and are expensive to manufacture.

All aluminum and many fiberglass canoes could be called flat bottom. Their chief advantage is stability and greater carrying capacity. The disadvantage is that they are slower and harder to paddle. If you are into racing, look for more V in the hull.

Which canoe is best? Actually there is no one answer. It depends on how and where you plan on using it. However, some are better than others and recommendations can be made.

Wood-canvas, $500 to $700. Traditionally, canoes were built with vertical wood ribs and cross planking and covered with canvas. These have withstood the test of time and are still readily available from Old Town, Chestnut, and a number of smaller manufacturers. Wood-canvas canoes have a rustic air about them, look nice, and if properly maintained will last a lifetime. However, their popularity has declined for several reasons: (1) they are expensive because they're handcrafted; (2) they require periodic maintenance and must be protected from severe weather; (3) they are easily damaged in white water; and (4) they soak up water. By the end of an active season, a wood-canvas canoe may weigh 20 pounds more than at the season's beginning.

Aluminum, $150 to $280. These are currently the most popular canoes for a number of good reasons: (1) aluminum is a tough material

Chestnut's 15' Bob's Special wood-canvas canoe

which will resist even the roughest white water; (2) aluminum requires no maintenance, and the canoe can be stored outside without fear of damage from weather; and (3) aluminum will not deteriorate over time.

Despite aluminum's leadership as a canoe material, there are several valid complaints: (1) aluminum is cold to the touch, especially on a cold day; (2) paddling an aluminum canoe is noisy because of wave slap and scraping over rocks; (3) aluminum tends to "stick" when it rides over a rock—that is, it flexes and holds tight to the rock, whereas the more rigid fiberglass will slip off or crack.

One traditional argument against aluminum canoes is that they are difficult to repair. This is no longer considered a problem since many airplane welders around large cities have taken up canoe repair as a spare time business. Grumman, the largest canoe manufacturer, carries a complete line of aluminum replacement parts so that even the worst wrecks can be revived.

Grumman's 15' aluminum canoe

When examining aluminum canoes, look at the gunwale rivet spacing, ribs, keel, and bow and stern plates; you'll notice quite a difference between el cheapo canoes and the more expensive Grumman ones (for some reason Grumman Allied Industries is the only manufacturer of high-quality aluminum canoes). There's no question that price is a reflection of quality here. If you chose a Grumman for white-water use, order it with a shoe keel and additional ribs; the extra $15 is well spent.

Sawyer's 17' Canadian fiberglass canoe.

Fiberglass, $200 - $780. With today's technology in materials and advanced methods of application, fiberglass, or fiber-reinforced plastics, is taking the lead in fine canoe construction. Fiberglass can be easily molded to hull designs unattainable in other materials.

Mad River and Sawyer Canoe are leading builders and designers in this material. Their hull shapes have more vee and are designed to move through the water with more ease and speed than any aluminum canoe built. With well-designed hulls the question of to keel or not to keel becomes a moot point. The better canoes now track, and when needed, sideslip with a dancer's agility. Cost is about the same as aluminum.

Two offshoots of fiberglass are UniRoyal's Royalex and DuPont's Kevlar 49.

Royalex, which weighs about the same as glass or aluminum but more expensive, is a composite of materials: cross-linked vinyl, acrylonitrile-butadiene-styrene (ABS), and a closed-cellular foam. This forms a multi-laminated hull of high strength able to withstand as much, if not more, abuse as aluminum. And it doesn't have aluminum's rock fetish. Royalex is a bit more difficult to mold to fine lines, though over the last three years much progress has been made along these lines

(pun!). Old Town's 17-ft. Chipewyan is an especially successful application. It possesses a very fine bow configuration, giving it a smooth water entry. Mad River Canoe Inc. is probably the leader in Royalex construction. Their 16 ft.-6 in. Explorer model is a total success in regard to achieving fine hull lines using Royalex. The Explorer has a beautiful shape utilizing a vee hull design.

Kevlar 49, or Kevlar, is a high-modulus organic aramid developed by DuPont. It's as easily worked as fiberglass. Kevlar has two outstanding advantages over all other materials. On a pound-for-pound basis it's five times stronger than steel, which means that maintaining the same strength factor, a craft can be made dramatically lighter. A canoe in Kevlar will be 15 to 20 lbs. lighter than a canoe of the same size in any other material. Its chief drawback, however, is cost—$150 to $200 more than a fiberglass model.

PACK CANOES
$90 - $375
The one-man pack canoe, a small, light, and easily backpacked craft, which was popular at the turn of the century, has been rediscovered. Now molded in fiberglass, these have become a favorite with Canadian fishermen and hunters who want to reach remote ponds and streams where a canoe must be packed in. Many are also used by auto campers who want to carry along a boat for occasional use but don't have room for a full-size canoe.

Rushton replica with Rushton original. Note size of paddle in background—pack canoes are small boats.

Old Town builds the Rushton canoe, after a design by Bart Hauthaway. Hauthaway also builds this boat and undersells Old Town every time—$250 as opposed to $295. John Rushton originally built the canoe, on which the Rushton is based, for George W. Sears, alias Nessmuk. Pack canoeists might be interested in Nessmuk's book, *Woodcraft,* from Dover Publications, Inc., 180 Varick St., New York, N.Y. 10014, $1.25 (paperback). It contains a delightful chapter on the perfect canoe.

WHITE-WATER CANOES
$200 to $500
These are canoes that have been somewhat modified to make them more suitable for rough and tumble wild-water paddling. They have slightly less freeboard and a lower profile than a standard canoe, almost a straight sheer (top edge of hull) with just a slight upturn at the bow and stern. The lines are finer, and the hull is not quite as full as in a regular canoe. These boats are fully decked, in fact the decking is molded to the fiberglass hull just like on a kayak. White-water canoes are available in both one and two man models. Paddlers sit in cockpit holes and wear spray skirts as in a kayak. On some boats there is a cargo hole amidships for gear. C-1 and C-2 design is the result of efforts to meet specific requirements for slalom and downriver competition. As with kayaks, which the uninitiated would mistake them for, there are three main categories: the slalom, the downriver and the touring.

The slalom C-1, or C-2, is a few inches beamier than a kayak, but has a similar hull shape. It's designed with extreme rocker for high maneuverability. These craft demand more stamina and greater skill than do kayaks. C-2's, in addition, require a high level of teamwork. A slalom C-boat is not bullish on straight lines or speed.

The downriver C-1 or C-2 machine, with slightly longer water line and sharper hull lines, compromises stability for speed. Suited only as a racing craft, it cannot be recommended for any other use.

Touring C-1 and C-2 canoes do not exhibit the extremes found in the competition class design, though some of the less intense slalom types can be used with great success in white-water touring. The C-2 models tend to be flushed out, allowing for more stability and better tracking. In general, touring craft have the same disadvantages found in kayaks. Flotation bags are required, portages are to be avoided, and some folks might find them uncomfortable due to lack of spacious seating arrangements. However, their white-water capabilities far exceed those of open canoes.

SAILING CANOES
$300 - $1,145

Most canoes make fast, sporty sailing craft with the addition of a sail, a rudder, and leeboards. A majority of the canoe manufacturers offer one or two styles of sailing rigs for their stock boats. A sailing rig will cost about $200, but savings can be realized if some of the parts can be scrounged or home-built. Often spars, sails, hardware, and such can be gotten from a Sunfish or similar small sailboat. Both plans and kits are available if you want to build a sailing rig from scratch.

Most sailing rigs are of the "bolt-on" variety. The idea is to car-top the entire rig and install it in about 30 minutes or less. Lateen rigs are most popular because they lend themselves best to easy setting up. They're also easy and cheap to build. The Marconi and other rigs are more often encountered when the canoe is set up as a permanent sailboat.

If you decide to build your own rig, here's what you'll need:

Sails. Either Dacron or nylon is preferred since they're lighter and dry faster than canvas after a wetting. The average 17-foot canoe carries a lateen sail of between 45 and 75 square feet, which is a simple triangle and easily sewed by the average homemaker.

Spars. These consist of a mast, gaff, and boom, which support the sail. Tubing of maintenance-free aluminum has almost replaced the traditional wooden spars.

Mast step and partners. The mast step is where the base of the mast seats against the keel. Normally this is a mortised block attached to the keel. Better-quality canoes will often have the step built in. A thwart with a hole in it serves as partners to support the mast above the step. Some canoe sailors have found that combining the mast step and the partners in one assemblage works best.

Rudder. The tilting type is considered best since it'll pop up when scraping bottom. Sailing a canoe in shallow water and up to a beach is not uncommon. Controlling the rudder is done via tiller, ropes, or even a foot treadle arrangement, depending on what you like.

Leeboards. These can be made of either wood, fiberglass, or aluminum. Their purpose, like that of a centerboard on a sailboat, is to keep the boat from slipping sideways (downwind) when tacking into the wind. Although only one board is needed on the lee side of the canoe, you'll have to figure out a way to move it quickly each time you change tack, or have one board on each side of the canoe. Most canoe sailors use two boards. The location of the leeboards and the

Old Town Otca

Grumman

mast are critical to the sailing balance of the canoe. If the boards are too far aft, you'll have to fight the rudder to keep the bow from falling off the wind; too far forward and you'll have the same problem, but in keeping the bow from coming up into the wind. The ideal spot for the leeboards is where you can release the tiller while sailing close hauled, and the canoe will tend to head up into the wind by itself.

A number of canoes are specifically manufactured to take sailing rigs. For example Old Town's 16-foot fiberglass Wahoo canoe has built-in slots on both sides to mount dagger-type leeboards. It is also equipped with a mast step and mast-thwart for stepping the mast, and mountings for the rudder. Cost for everything, including the sails, is $1,145.

While occasional sailors can have a great time with bolt-on sail rigs, there are some who take the sport much more seriously. An entire sailing fraternity has developed around the International 12-Meter as a basis for competitive racing. These canoes are completely decked, have sliding seats and hiking boards, and carry lots of sail. Strictly wet competition sailing.

Basic canoe lines (symmetrical bow and stern, long, narrow hull) have also proved a successful combination for larger, multiple-sail craft. It's not entirely by accident that some intrepid sea voyagers chose the "canoe" for transoceanic travel. Viking longboats and Polynesian outriggers are actually canoes. These vessels, developed in entirely different cultures, were among the first to venture beyond sight of land on the wide ocean. If you're ready to head to sea this way, contact AMF, Alcort Div., South Leanard St., Waterbury, Conn. 06720, for details on its Hilu Outrigger, a 14-foot Polynesian-type sailing craft.

RAFTS

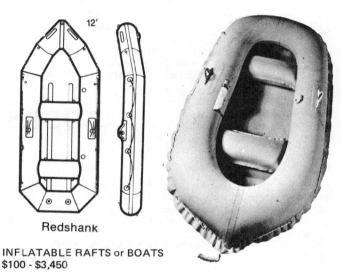

12'

Redshank

INFLATABLE RAFTS or BOATS
$100 - $3,450

River touring often calls for special craft tailored to certain water conditions. The inflatable raft is one that's best suited to rivers with big waves and numerous rocks. Because of its large flat area, a raft is fairly stable, and because of its inherent flexibility, it can bend and twist over small falls, will give on impact with rocks, and can ride over large standing waves. Inflatable rafts can definitely take abuse, lots of it. That's why they're best suited to the fast-flowing, rough and tumble, canyon rivers of the West.

Inflatable rafts specifically designed for white-water touring have little in common with the two- and four-man rafts found in surplus and sporting goods stores. These $30-$120 fisherman's pals are suited for small ponds and casual use. River-running types are much larger and stoutly constructed with heavy materials.

Although sometimes used on slower streams, here the inflatable raft's shortcomings soon become apparent. Without a swift current its ability to flex around boulders is a disadvantage because it just bends around a rock and hangs there. In quiet water, rafts are difficult to maneuver and slow—paddling really becomes a chore because of the large surface area they present to the water. In white water, paddling isn't so bad with a small raft, but the only way to handle a big boat effectively is with oars. Unfortunately the oarlocks on most standard rafts are inadequate to handle this type of duty and the boatman will have to custom-build himself a rowing frame.

Qualitywise, for raft construction and materials, the dividing line seems to be at 10 feet. Boats under this length often are cheaply built of thin materials, whereas those over 10 feet are of heavier material and closer attention is paid to seams, fastening tabs, valves, and so forth. Manufacturers of boats over 10 feet for river running include Avon (very good quality), Camp Ways (popular with commercial rafting companies) and Maravia (see "sources of river gear").

CANOE and KAYAK BUILDING

PLANS and KITS

Building a kayak or canoe at home can save you quite a bit of money over a factory-built boat, and it can be done with a minimum number of hand tools and a few weekends. Plans are available if you want to start from scratch, or you can go the kit route with precut materials that require only a little shaping before assembly.

Wood-canvas boats are the easiest to build, and the simplest of these are the horizontal rib variety. Kits are available. For more advanced canoes, such as the laminated wood-strip or birch-bark types, you'll have to build from scratch, because the only thing available for these are plans.

In the fiberglass department, things are a little easier. Boats can be built by either assembling premolded fiberglass kits or molding your own. Many canoe clubs and individuals have fiberglass kayak molds which can be rented for about $35. A kayak done this way will cost only about $75 to $100. If it's a fiberglass canoe you're after, you can lay it up right on the hull of another canoe. Cost will be a little higher than for a kayak, since a reinforcing frame must be added.

Rather than duplicate the boatbuilding information that's written up in the Offshore Sailing Section, we suggest that you sort of thumb your way over in that direction (toward the back of the book) and look it over. There you'll find several amateur boatbuilding organizations that can assist you, books on wood and fiberglass construction techniques, and sources of boating supplies.

As far as specific info on kayak and canoe building, we've listed it here. Many are not listed because they're no longer in print. Please contact us if you know of additional books which should be listed.

BOOKS

BOATBUILDER'S MANUAL
Charles Walbridge
1975, 2nd ed. - 70 p. il. - $4.50 (pb)

An in-depth guide to building fiberglass kayaks and C-boats. If you know nothing about working with fiberglass, or need to know more, this is a superb straightforward presentation. Good rundown on resin systems and the various cloths. For those facing repair jobs this book would also be of help.
From: Wildwater Designs, Penllyn Pike & Morris Rd., Penllyn, Pa. 19422

CANOE BUILDING, Part I, Soft Skin and Moulded Veneer Canoes, No. 7A
1968 - 51 p. il. - $1.50 (pb)

CANOE BUILDING, Part II, Glass Fibre Canoes, No. 7B
1972 - 42 p. il. - $1.50 (pb)

Two of a series of pamphlets published on canoeing and kayaking by the British Canoe (Kayak) Union, 26/29 Park Cresent, London, W.I.
From: Moor & Mountain, 63 Park St., Andover, Mass. 01810

THE STRIPPER'S GUIDE TO CANOE-BUILDING
David Hazen
1976 - 88 p. il. - $7.95 (pb)

Step-by-step detailed instructions for beautiful laminated wood-strip and fiberglass canoes and kayaks. The book comes with six sheets of full-size templates for seven canoes and two kayaks. This method of boat construction requires a great deal of time and patience. While it's not especially difficult, you must approach your work with care and vigilance. Considering the price of wood canoes today, you could save a bundle.
From: The Book Bin, 547 Howard St., San Francisco, Calif. 94105

BUILDERS OF BIRCH BARK CANOES
William Rossman
24 p. il. - $1

A booklet on Bill Hafeman and his building of birchbark canoes. Describes the entire process from stripping the tree to applying the pitch.
From: Chicagoland Canoe Base, 4019 North Narragansett Ave., Chicago, Ill. 60634

OUTDOOR SPORTS
P.O.Box 1213, Tuscaloosa, Ala. 35401
Books, plans and full-size patterns for 25 wood-and-canvas and ply-wood boats. Among the plans are three kayaks well suited for open-sea cruising. This is a type rarely seen in the U.S. as nobody makes them outside of Europe. Many other interesting canoe and kayak plans to be had. Ask for the catalog, it's free.

BALDWIN BOAT CO.
Hoxie Hill Rd., Orrington, Maine 04474
Besides a line of factory-completed boats, they offer three fiberglass kayak kits at $70 savings from factory jobs. Baldwin also has a 20 ft.-6 in. canoe you can get as a fiberglass shell to finish, it's $320, a $120 savings over completed model. They say all you need to complete the kits is a quart of resin.

COUNTRY WAYS, INC.
3500 Highway 101 S., Minnetonka, Minn. 55343
These people handle the highly-reputed English Ottersports, Ltd. brand. Five canoe and kayak models. Wood-and-canvas construction, easy to put together and inexpensive. Send for catalog.

CHEM TECH
4481 Greenwold Rd., Cleveland, Ohio 44121
Real alchemists, they've developed epoxy systems that can be used with damp wood and at damn near any temperature you feel like building a boat in.

DEFENDER INDUSTRIES
255 Main St., New Rochelle, N.Y. 10810
For fiberglass construction, lots of cloths, microballoons, release waxes, resins and tools. Defender is a big discount marine supply house. Catalog $1.

FOLBOT CORP.
Stark Industrial Park, P.O.Box 7097, Charleston, S.C. 29405
Prefab kits of wood-and-canvas and fiberglass kayaks. Savings is about $150 from factory jobs. The wood-and-canvas kits require a lot of work, and a full complement of hand tools. Eight models.

HYPERFORM
25 Industrial Park Rd., Hingham, Mass. 02043
Two fiberglass kayaks. The Lettmann Mark I, a good beginner's slalom boat, and the Prijon 420, a touring model. $250 each. Kits come with everything and they estimate you can stick 'em together in 10 hours. Write for catalog.

PHOENIX PRODUCTS, INC.
U.S. Route 421, Tyner, Ky. 40486
Five glass prefab kayaks, $75 difference in price from completed boat. Kits come with the works, 12- to 14-hour job.

PLASTICRAFTS, INC.
2800 Speer Blvd., Denver, Colo. 80211
Fiberglass supplies, some kayak and paddle kits. Free catalog.

RIVER TOURING ACCESSORIES

PERSONAL FLOTATION DEVICE (PFD)
$10 - $35

As of 1 October 1973 all recreational watercraft are required to carry one PFD for each person on the boat. These PFD's must carry the U.S. Coast Guard's stamp of approval for use.

Type I - Life Jacket. Type I's are capable of turning an unconscious person face up, and are the most buoyant and the largest. Unfortunately they get in the way of paddling movements. They are used to great extent among rafters, and for good reason, they are the most able PFD to float you in hair.

Type II - Buoyant Vest. These have somewhat less flotation than Type I, but are not capable of turning an unconscious person face up as quickly.

Type III - Buoyant Device. Will not turn an unconscious person face up. These are the most popular among the paddling fraternity. They're comfortable and fit closer to the body than Types I and II.

Type IV - Throwable Device. Seat cushions and ring buoys.

Type V - Open Classification. The USCG reserves this type to provide special circumstances. Stearns and Maravia both have Type V jackets approved for white-water use.

HELMETS
$12 - $25

The ideal white-water hard hat has yet to be designed. Any helmet is better than none. Cooper's converted hockey hat now retails at $20. Joe Brown's Ultimate Helmet, a rock-climbing helmet is a pretty good white-water hat. It has a superior suspension system and is lined with closed-cell foam, but side protection could be better and it doesn't have drain holes, $22. Seda also puts out a decent pot, but it has the same deficiencies as the Ultimate, $25. Like in the old motorcycle saw, when you look at prices and groan, ask yourself how much your head is worth.

WET SUITS
$30 - $100

Ice-cold water and survival don't go hand in hand. Immersion in water below 40°F for only five minutes can render you helpless; over seven minutes can be deadly. Since the opportunities for this kind of dunking on cold weather canoe and kayak trips are common, cold weather exposure and immersion suits are recommended. A wet suit is not waterproof, but it is snug-fitting enough so that water seeps in slowly and can be warmed by the body without the wearer even noticing it. Besides the insulating qualities there are other advantages to a wet suit. It provides additional buoyancy and protection against abrasion from boulders. Wet suits 3/16-inch thick and over restrict movement while paddling, so go for 1/8-inch. Some paddlers will layer certain parts of an 1/8-inch suit with additional 1/8-inch material glued on to provide extra insulation where it's needed (and won't interfere with the suit's flexibility). Wet suits can be bought complete or in individual pieces—gloves, boots, hood, pants, and jacket.

For a more detailed commentary on wet suits, check the Diving Section.

POGIES
$7 - $22

For all paddlers in early and late seasons this innovative aid allows direct contact with the paddle or oar shaft, yet gives complete protection to hand, wrist and forearm. Pogies can be used on both oars and paddles. They fasten on the shaft, then you insert your hands. They provide greater warmth and sensitivity than wet-suit gloves. Think about how many gloves went downriver while you were fitting your spray skirt. They are made in nylon and in neoprene.

SPRAY SKIRTS
$16 - $43

Spray skirts are like mini skirts. Step into one, pull it up to your waist, hop into the cockpit, and stretch the bottom of the skirt around the cockpit rim. Keeps out the water when the going gets rough or if you flip and have to pull an Eskimo roll. Water adds weight, changes momentum, can cause loss of stability, and it ain't very comfortable in cold temperatures. Neoprene is the way to go; nylon skirts, while cheaper, don't fit as snugly on the coaming or you. And after a time, nylon leaks. Northwest River Supply has developed a short-sleeved wet suit jacket-spray skirt combination. They've taken a neoprene

Type III vest

Stearns

Helmet

Spray Skirt

Wet Suit

Flotation Bags

skirt and sewn it to the bottom of a jacket, the Centaur. For those who have a good roll this combo assures a warm and dry cockpit. The Eskimos had a similar rig called the tuvilik.

FLOTATION BAGS
$6 - $30

Air bags are highly recommended to prevent a kayak from sinking after a spill. A buoyant boat is less vulnerable to impact against a rock than a submerged one and is a lot easier to fish out of the drink. Vinyl plastic bags are available for bow, stern, and midship sections. HIPP manufactures a heavy-duty type with a plastic tube attached so the bag can be blown up tighter once placed in position. Hyperform also manufactures heavy gauge bags. An alternative to factory-made flotation bags is blow-up-type beach balls.

DECKING
$81 - $365

Mad River Canoe is the only company offering spray covers for each of their models, $81-$124, depending on size. Old Town offers a cover for all their models at a flat rate, $365. Old Town's cover is Hypalon and snaps onto the hull just below the outwale. Mad River's is urethane-coated nylon and attaches by a shock cord running around the canoe under the outwale. Both are good at keeping you and your gear dry in a variety of situations. For those who don't own a Mad River, or can't go Old Town's price, Wayfarer Recreational Products makes spray covers to fit all canoes for $99.50. They're nylon and attach with snaps. For weekend white-water runs, when there's no gear to get wet, a good alternative to decking is blocking—and it's cheaper. Go to your local plastics manufacturer, or packaging material supplier, (they're in the phone book) and get some nice big 1 ft. x 3 ft. x 5 ft.

Old Town deck

blocks of styrofoam. Put these in your canoe with a little carving and tie down. Blocking limits the possibility of getting swamped and it provides for an extremely buoyant boat.

KAYAK PADDLES
$18 - $65

Your "blade" is what provides propulsion and maneuverability, and in kayaking the double-blade type (one at each end) is used. Most experienced kayakers prefer paddles with blades set 90 degrees from each other. This sounds strange, but once you get the hang of it, the wrist motion involved is easier. Paddles without this feature are also available, as are those that break in the center for easier storage. Many varieties of paddles are available in combinations of wood, fiberglass, aluminum, plastic and Kevlar 49. Wood paddles seem to have a better feel than fiberglass and are warmer to the hands. Fiberglass is stronger, however. There are also different size blades and blade curves. Blade curve is a matter of experience and personal preference. As to brands, most experts agree that Prijon makes the finest paddles in the world, but they are in short supply and hard to come by. Next are Triton, Kober and Old Town.

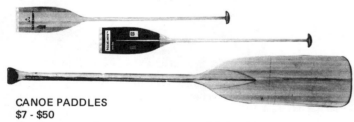

CANOE PADDLES
$7 - $50

Open-boat canoeists are not as concerned as kayakers about blade quality, because they don't operate in extremely heavy waters where every paddle stroke counts. Undecked boaters also resort to using the paddle as a rock pry if all else fails. Although fiberglass blades are available and many are to be seen on the river, particularly Iliad and Nona, many canoeists still stick with wood. Ash or spruce is the best. When selecting a paddle, a rule of thumb is to pick one that comes to your chin. Blade widths will range from 5 to 12 inches, and if you have no particular preference, 8 inches is a good width. Sawyer, Smoker, and Clement paddles are good brands, but be careful when selecting because paddle quality seems to vary from one batch to the next.

CANOE ROWING ATTACHMENT
$45 - $200

Canoes can be rowed, and special rigs consisting of a combination seat and oarlocks are made that clamp amidships in the canoe. Old Town makes a good unit.

Poling on Churchill Lake, Maine Photo: National Park Service

POLES
$5 - $30

Canoeing upriver is best done by poling. It's easier than it sounds and works well up through class III rapids. Good poles are from 10 to 12 feet long, 1 to 2½ inches in diameter, strong, light, and flexible. Clear spruce, ash, and aluminum are considered excellent, but maple and pine work very well, too. Metal "shoes" are usually attached to the pole to protect it from bottom rocks, and sometimes thin steel rods are inserted into the foot of the pole to aid in sweeping it up against the current. Old Town offers a setting pole with pick for $20. The A. C. Mackenzie River Co. produces a take-apart aluminum for a little over $29 including postage.

RAFT OARS
$15 - $80

Oar length varies according to raft size and water conditions. Rafts of 12 feet are comfortable with 8- to 10-ft. oars; a 16-ft. inflatable could also be handled well with 10-ft. sticks. Oars should be stout and flawless, with straight grain. Dense hardwoods like ash are recommended. While heavy, they don't usually break... as often. All oars should be secured to the raft in event of an upset. Sticks over 8 feet are difficult to locate. For sources, check out marine supply houses and various rafting supply houses.

RAFT OARLOCKS
$8 - $24

There are three main oarlock types being used in white-water rafting, each with good and bad points.

The pin-type oarlock holds the oar in position with a bolt through the oar shaft. This fits into a socket on the rowing frame. It's the sort of oarlock found on the rowboats in the park. You can't feather the oar, but under pressure the oar will come out of the socket. This may prevent damage to the oar or frame.

The ring-type oarlock is a simple ring slipped on the oar and placed in the socket. It allows feathering, and if need be, the oar can be drawn inboard. On this type you must fit a stopper on the shaft to keep it from sliding through the ring.

The clip-type oarlock requires a pin set in the socket on the frame. Then a clip is clamped onto the oar shaft and clipped to the pin. A variation of this is clamping a piece of rubber on the shaft. Under pressure the clip or rubber will pop off the pin, hopefully saving the oar.

RAFT ROWING FRAMES
$0 - $200

A small party of two or three on an extended rafting junket would benefit by installing a frame on their raft. Rowing is a lot easier. Frames also help stiffen and stabilize the boat. Commercial rigs are available in wood, aluminum and fiberglass. You can also build one without a great deal of trouble. Bill McGinnis' ***Whitewater Rafting*** contains a series of excellent sketches and elevations for just this purpose. Aluminum frames last longer and take more punishment than do wood or fiberglass. The disadvantage of aluminum is it's just about impossible to repair on the river.

OUTBOARD MOTORS
$100 - $600

A 1½- to 6-horsepower outboard motor mounted to the side of a canoe may not be in keeping with the romantic traditions of the craft, but it sure can come in handy if you've got a large lake to cross or a good distance to go upstream on a river.

Conventional propeller-driven outboards are the fastest but are also the most vulnerable to rocks and obstructions. Fork-like propeller guards help beat the problem. Air-cooled outboards are best in shallow water since the engine must frequently be operated at a tilt in order to clear obstructions. Water-cooled engines require that the water inlet always be submerged. Johnson, Evinrude, and Mercury all have small engines suitable for canoes, but they're water-cooled. Chrysler manufactures one 3.6-hp air-cooled engine and Sears has five air-cooled ones in the 3- to 7-hp range.

Small water jet motors are not quite as efficient as prop-driven types, but they solve the problem of rocks, logs, and weeds. Otterbine Industries has three air-cooled models from 3.5 to 8 hp.

Carrying Yoke

OUTBOARD MOTOR BRACKETS
$15 - $20

A lot of people falsely assume that an outboard motor must be mounted directly on the stern of a boat. This is not true, especially for a canoe, and it will work just as well clamped to the side on a mounting bracket. Shifting your body weight easily compensates for the imbalance. Brackets are usually simple affairs designed to be temporarily or permanently attached to the canoe. Most dealers carry them. You could make one yourself quite easily from angle iron.

DUCKBOARDS
About $18

Wood-slat floorboards for canoes to keep feet and gear out of the bilges. They're easy enough to make yourself out of 1 in. x 2 in. pine, but you can get manufactured ones from some of the canoe firms. Or just throw brush in the bottom of the canoe, put your gear on top and call it a day.

AIR PUMP
$10 - $200

Inflatables are designed to operate at specific air pressures. A good pump is mandatory and with a pump, a pressure gauge. The size of your raft will dictate what volume pump you need. The ideal, of course, is a large air volume at low pressure.

YOKE
$18 - $34

A yoke is a straight piece of wood or aluminum with shoulder pads that clamps amidships across the canoe. With it one man can balance

and carry a canoe for some distance. A yoke is a simple thing, and you ought to be able to build one yourself. If buying, be sure to check the spacing of the shoulder pads for fit. If your boat has two thwarts, in lieu of a yoke, lay two paddles fore and aft with the blades projecting slightly beyond the forward thwart. Be sure the blades are spaced wide enough to fit your shoulders, then lash the paddles in place. When carrying the canoe, rest the paddle blades on your shoulders.

CAR-TOP CARRIER RACKS
$16 - $40

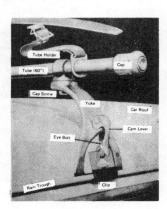

Car-top carriers for hauling canoes and kayaks should be designed to firmly grip the auto gutter. Avoid cars without gutters, especially station wagons where some design genius thought the car would look swifter without them. As for carriers, Quik-N-Easy brackets are far and away the best. The units are made of cast aluminum and have a positive acting clamp that never needs adjustment en route, yet the entire rack can be removed in seconds. We've found that buying the brackets and adding oak bars is the best route—cheaper, too. Brackets run $19. Curved brackets that fit the hull of a kayak can be had from Eastern Mountain Sports. Grumman and Eastern Mountain Sports have also introduced a new carrier design using aluminum extrusion bars and stamped brackets. These seem to be a good deal and are cheaper than the Quik-N-Easy system. Suction-cup car-top rigs aren't even worth discussing.

WATERPROOF PACKS
$2 - $28

Check out army surplus stores for ammo boxes and delousing bags. A couple of river supply houses carry surplus boxes and bags, they're cheap and watertight.

Voyageur Enterprises' waterproof canoe bags run $8.95. If you throw away the other protective bag, or lose it, the inner bag is clear and makes a beautiful (and expensive) map case. It's large enough to carry 20 unfolded USGS topos, and they'll be waterproofed in a way no other map case provides.

Hefty trash can liners can be used inside a tightly packed rucksack. For pack canoeists this is the lightest way to go. Line your rucksack with two Heftys, then stuff your gear in and strap down. This will keep your gear dry in heavy rain and anything else short of holding it underwater for 15 minutes.

GRAY TAPE
$1 - $3

Sticky cloth tape that comes in various widths and is used for emergency river repairs and whatever. Voyageur sells a 30-ft. roll for $1.

RIVER TOURING KITS

Canoeing	Kayaking
Canoe	Kayak
Paddles (3, one as a spare)	Paddle
Life vests	Life vest
Rope (two 10-foot lengths)	Spray skirt
Knee pads	Helmet
Gray tape	Flotation bags
Waterproof pack	Gray tape
Change of clothes	Wet suit
Lunch and snack	Lunch and snack
Flashlight	Spare car keys
Spare car keys	
Polarized sunglasses	

BOATS

OLD TOWN CANOE CO.
Old Town, Me. 04468

One of the last remaining builders of the traditional wood-plank-canvas canoes, Old Town is now gaining leadership in quality fiberglass canoes and white-water kayaks. The company offers a wide range of models including fiberglass pack canoes, specialized sailing canoes, wood-canvas models including a war canoe, C–1 and C–2 decked white-water (WW) canoes, and a boat shed of slalom, downriver, touring, and surfing kayaks. Old Town also has quite an assortment of accessories for canoeing and kayaking, even replica jewelry.

Known for quality construction throughout, Old Town kayaks and WW canoes were designed by Bert Hauthway. The fiberglass canoes are made of a special reinforced fiberglass–balsa sandwich, a technique pioneered by Old Town. Even more exotic is the company's use of vacuum-molded ABS plastic with foam center on one canoe and one kayak model. Known as Royalex, the material is said to be far tougher than other fiberglass compositions. As an option to the fiberglass craft you can get Kevlar, though Old Town's application of this material is limited to one reinforcing layer replacing the final layer of roving in their normal fiberglass lay-ups.

Fourteen different models are available in fiberglass. They range from the 10 ft.-6 in. Rushton to a new 18 ft.-4 in. Racer, for downriver competition. For middle of the road tastes there is a more traditional 16-ft. open model, it costs $385, and weighs a hefty 79 lbs.

The six Chipewyan models are constructed of Oltonar (Royalex). Many trippers use the 17-ft. Chipewyan. It has a good shape and can carry an exceptional load. Hull depth is 15 inches. It weighs 74 lbs. and is priced $480. All the Chipewyan models are good river-touring craft.

The wood-and-canvas canoes are now in the same price range as baby grand pianos. The least expensive, the Lightweight, goes for $835. The 18-ft. Guide, which for years was considered the ultimate tripping canoe, now costs $920. You get what you pay for.

GRUMMAN ALLIED INDUSTRIES, INC.
Marathon, N.Y. 13803

If you must have an aluminum canoe, this is the one to get. They make a dependable product at a fair price. For river touring it is suggested you forsake the standard keel versions and order the shallow keel. Grumman designates their shoe-keel models as white-water canoes and on an average they cost $25 more than the standard model. The 15-footer is $339; 17-footer, $359; and the 18-footer, $377. A spray cover for the 17-ft. boat is available, as are a number of other aluminum canoe goodies including 2 sailing rigs. They have a few free booklets you can write for: *The Grumman Book Rack,* a bibliography of canoeing literature; *Learn-to-Canoe Directory,* listing 250 locations where you can learn; and that old favorite, *Rent-a-Canoe Directory.*

FOLBOT CORP.
Stark Industrial Park, P.O. Box 7097, Charleston, S.C. 29405

This is the only builder of folding kayaks in the U.S. These craft have been used in white water, surf and long-distance river cruises. They consist of a wood frame covered with a heavy-duty canvas skin that is heavily impregnated and coated with vinyl. On some models the skin can be slipped off the frame, the frame disassembled, and both packed up for easy transporting or storage.

They offer three folding models. The Sporty, a 15-footer for $299, is capable of carrying one person and enough gear to miss Thanksgiving. Accepting its limitations in white water, this is an excellent boat. The complaint most often heard though is that it's a real pain to assemble. The other two models are double-place craft: the 16-ft. Big Glider for $332 and the 17 ft.-6 in. Super for $354. Sail rigs are available for these boats. Their catalog is free.

Sometimes you see Folbot ads in magazines saying send two bucks and get catalog and the book, *Fabulous Folbot Holidays.* This book, now a paperback, was first published in 1940 by the William Byrd Press. It's a little seedy. If you want to get the book free, write Folbot saying you saw their ad in *National Geographic.* It seems they send the book out free to *Geographic* readers who request their catalog.

Folbot makes a good product at a reasonable price. This is the craft NOLS uses on their Alaskan expeditions.

Kamerad W

HANS KLEPPER CORP.
35 Union Square W., New York, N.Y. 10003

Almost 60 years ago a German, Johann Klepper, designed the first practical folding boat. Today his company builds a line of top-quality folding kayaks, a runabout and a sailboat as well as tents and fiberglass white-water kayaks.

Assembly time for Klepper folding boats is down to 15 minutes on some models, thanks to special snap locks and built-in sponson-like air tubes that provide added flotation. The company offers five folding models, from a very nice 15-ft., one-man job suitable for extended cruising to a big 18-footer. Prices are on the steep side, $399 to $699, and that's before you start tacking on accessories. These boats are built in Germany, and compared to the offerings of Folbot, the workmanship is telling. Klepper gives you a beautifully-made boat, the put-together-take-apart sequence involves only 17 pieces. Accessories include sailing rigs, a collapsible boat cart, a foot-controlled rudder assembly and spray cover.

Fiberglass kayak models cover the entire spectrum and include an 11-ft. junior version for 8- to 14-year-olds. Another unusual fiberglass kayak is the Kamerad W, a 16-ft. two-seater with one large open cockpit. It's something of a cross between a white-water and cruising kayak. Klepper's colorful, well-illustrated catalog is free.

SAWYER CANOE CO.
234 S. State St., Oscoda, Mich. 48750

Quality fiberglass construction at economic prices. A nice tripping canoe, the 17 ft.-9 in. Cruiser weighs 68 lbs. in fiberglass and costs $330. You can get it in Kevlar at only 39 lbs. for $480. It should be noted that Sawyer leans toward racing designs. Many of the models offered have considerably less load capacity than other brands. This shouldn't stop you from purchasing a Sawyer canoe, as the overall workmanship and handling characteristics of these boats are very good. But definitely keep this shortcoming in mind when planning longer cruises.

Another nice bit of work is the Canadian, 16 feet long with a 33-in. beam, it weighs 67 lbs. and costs $310. In Kevlar it goes for $460 and weighs only 38 lbs. Six other models are available, plus two kayaks. The kayaks, $269, have an interesting feature. They're equipped with built-in foam flotation.

BART HAUTHAWAY
640 Boston Post Rd., Weston, Mass. 02193

Complete selection of quality kayaks built to order; 10 models to choose from. Slalom and surf kayaks, $300; downriver touring model, $325. In the canoe department, Hauthaway has the distinction of being the only builder to specialize in pack canoes. His smallest is the 18-lb. Pack Canoe, only 10 ft. 6 in. long. Despite its length, this boat tracks in a manner unwarranted for its size. This is due to the meticulous attention paid to hull shape and overall design. There are other 10-ft. canoes on the market, but it's doubtful that they handle like this craft. Hauthaway's largest is the 2-man, 14-ft. Allagash weighing 45 lbs. Cost is $375. Six other models are available from $290 to $350. Fiberglass only.

MILLBROOK BOATS
Riparius, N.Y. 12862

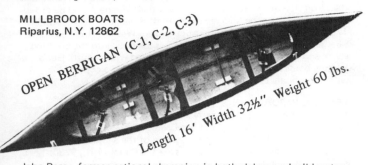

OPEN BERRIGAN (C-1, C-2, C-3)
Length 16' Width 32½" Weight 60 lbs.

John Berry, former national champion in both slalom and wild-water C-1 and C-2 canoeing, operates Millbrook specializing in C-1 and C-2 boats exclusively. Each canoe is built to order. C-1's in fiberglass cost $260, C-2's average $430. All models can be had in Kevlar. Millbrook Boats is a small operation which does not have a dealer network, it is mentioned here because of the quality of workmanship and thought that goes into each boat. If you want a boat bad enough, they'll get it out to you, somehow.

Millbrook conducts a C-1 canoeing clinic during the summer for beginners and intermediates. Three-day course of instruction costs $45.

CHESTNUT CANOE CO.
Oromocto, N.B., Canada E2V 2G5

Chestnut is one of the largest manufacturers of canoes in Canada. The company is best known for its wood-canvas models, which are very popular in the Canadian back country. A wide selection is available ranging from the 16-ft. Kruger, $567, to a 26-ft. freighter-type, the Salmo, $1,542.

Chestnut also manufacturers fiberglass and aluminum canoes, though none of the models appears to be as outstanding as the wood-canvas boats.

Many accessories, including sailing rigs, are offered. A nicely-illustrated brochure is available.

HYPERFORM
25 Industrial Park Rd., Hingham, Mass. 02042

One of the leading manufacturers of competition and recreational-type kayaks in the country. Majority of K-1 models cost $350; they offer an extensive selection. Also available are two K-2 models at $550, three C-2 boats from $475 to $550 and two C-1's, $350. Kits are offered representing a $100 savings over ready-built.

MAD RIVER CANOE, INC.
P.O.Box 363, Spring Hill, Waitsfield, Vt. 05673

The most distinctive feature of Mad River canoes is the design of their hull. With one exception they all have a unique vee bottom that combines the best properties of both keel and keelless boats—tracking ability in flat water and maneuvering ability in white water. The company has three models that are particularly well-suited to extended wilderness river touring. The largest is the 18-ft. fiberglass T-W Special, $569, which is fast, paddles effortlessly and maneuvers well. Next, the 16-ft. fiberglass Malecite, $409, which has one of the finest hull shapes available. It handles superbly and is well-suited for the weekender and tripper. Last is the Explorer, $469, which is based on the Malecite design but made of Royalex and is 2 inches wider and deeper to allow for a greater cargo capacity. These three models are also available in Kevlar. Of interest to the pack canoeist would be Mad River's 13-ft. Compatriot, $335, in glass. She's designed along the same lines as the Malecite and is probably the sweetest handling 13-ft. canoe in existence; has a 30-in. beam and load capacity of 385 lbs. at 6 inches of freeboard. Mad River also has a number of other craft suited to rock garden specialists, racers, families and fishermen. Spray covers are available for all boats at good prices. Drop 'em a line for details.

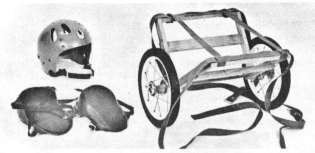

Helmet, knee pads, and canoe dolly

MOOR & MOUNTAIN
63 Park St., Andover, Mass. 01810

Moor & Mountain stocks a number of glass and ABS canoes from Old Town and Mad River, two models of the Klepper folding kayak, the British line of Tyne boats—folding and glass kayaks—plus the Sea Eagle Explorer and Metzeler inflatable kayaks. You get the option at M & M! In the tripping accessories department, Moor & Mountain has several styles of life vests, helmets, knee pads, wet suits, canoe and kayak paddles, repair tape and kits, the Quik-N-Easy car-top carrier, a two-wheel boat dolly and the Voyageur waterproof bag line. In the reference department it handles canoeing and kayaking books, river tour guides and sets of river maps. A 64-page outdoor recreation catalog is available for the asking.

WHITEWATER BOATS BY DICK HELD
P.O. Box 483, Cedar City, Utah 84720

Free and independent enterprise is alive, well and living in Utah. Dick Held makes top-quality boats at yesterday's prices. Competition class, low-volume slalom kayak for $285. Good cruising kayak capable of carrying 250 to 270 lbs., paddler and gear, $325. Two surf kayak models at $285. An enormous 18-ft. K-2 touring boat for $425. Fine boats at great prices.

THE BLUE HOLE CANOE CO.
Sunbright, Tenn. 37872

The super dreadnaught of the white-water fanatics. Blue Hole is a small company offering three canoes. A 16-ft. heavy cruiser at $445, and two 17-ft. pocket battleships, one armed for wild water, the other a cruising model. These boats, all Royalex hulls, are absolute gluttons for punishment and can be used in rough water with confidence. Blue Hole also makes a paddle of frightening proportions and strength, $38. Good dealer network.

WATER MEISTER SPORTS
P.O. Box 5026, Fort Wayne, Ind. 46805

Water Meister specializes in river running and touring gear and handles everything from boats to club jackets. It handles the Old Town line, and Pavel Bone, one of the leading white-water canoe and kayak designers and manufacturers in Europe, has selected Water Meister as a distributor. In the accessories department there are paddles, life jackets, helmets, spray covers, wet suits (custom-fitted), dunnage gear—waterproof bags, pack baskets, and rucksacks—camping gear, car top carriers, books, and club items. The catalog consists of a folder of manufacturers' literature and price lists; it's all there, but a bit confusing. Available upon request.

CHICAGOLAND CANOE BASE
4019 North Narragansett Ave., Chicago, Ill. 60634

Chicagoland is probably the Midwest's largest river boat and accessories dealer. Though Ralph Frese, the owner, is a Canadian voyageur buff, he does handle quite a number of white-water canoes and kayaks, including the Old Town line, Sawyer, and the Klepper folding boats and rigid kayaks. Chicagoland's emphasis, though, is on cruising canoes like the Grumman aluminum, Old Town wood-canvas, Canadian fiberglass, and Pere Marquette fiberglass canoes. If you want an authentic fiberglass birchbark replica of the 26-ft. North Canoe ($2,995), or the 34-ft. Montreal Canoe ($4,995), these are available on special order. Chicagoland handles a complete line of accessories, including sailing rigs, paddles, helmets, life jackets, packing and bivouacking gear for canoe cruising and repair supplies. In the reference department Frese is more than happy to supply information on canoeing clubs, river data, books, and so on, much of it on mimeographed sheets. Literature, brochure, specs and price sheets available on request.

149

AVON RUBBER CO., LTD.
Seagull Marine Sales (Western U.S. distributor)
1851 McGaw Ave., Irving, Calif. 92705
Inland Marine Co. (Midwest and Central Eastern U.S. distributor)
79 E. Jackson St., Wilkes-Barre, Pa. 18701
Avon builds the highest quality boat in the rafting industry. They offer 11 models from 9 to 17 feet. Prices range from $585 to $1,750. All Avon rafts are constructed using heavy-duty nylon coated with DuPont Hypalon which is resistant to oil, sunlight and abrasion. All rafts have a five-year guarantee against fabric deterioration, plus a one-year guarantee for defects in material and workmanship. Two good choices for river touring are the 12-ft. Redshank, $745, and the 15-ft.

Avon's REDSHANK

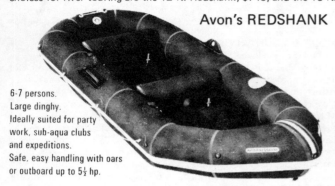

6-7 persons.
Large dinghy.
Ideally suited for party work, sub-aqua clubs and expeditions.
Safe, easy handling with oars or outboard up to 5½ hp.

Professional Mark II, $1,395. The Redshank is a very good all-around craft rowed or paddled, and the price includes inflatable cross thwarts, repair kit, pump and carrying sack. The Professional Mark II has a very good reputation among professional rafters. A full line of accessories is available through dealers. Write Seagull or Inland for more info.

AMERICAN SAFETY EQUIPMENT CORP.
7652 Burnet Ave., Van Nuys, Calif. 91405
This firm makes the Pack Raft III, a 3¼-lb. number being marketed as the backpacker's dream. It costs $110. The hull is extremely thin neoprene-coated nylon and should be kept away from rocks and other sharp objects. Write for info.

CAMP-WAYS
12915 S. Spring St., Los Angeles, Calif. 90061
This brand is very popular with commercial rafting companies. Hypalon-coated nylon hulls and heavy construction throughout. Camp-Ways has their boats built in Japan, and compared to the British Avon rafts, model for model, Camp-Ways is about $100 less. They've had some trouble with seams, but over the last year design improvements have cleared this up. Boats range from 9 to 17 feet, and prices from $175 to $1,700. The Hopi, 12 ft. x 6 ft., with 17-in. tubes is a little drier than Avon's Redshank due to its slightly larger buoyancy tubes; $625. The Shoshoni III, 16 ft. x 7 ft. 8 in. with 21-in. tubes, weighs 160 lbs. and runs $1,149. Camp-Ways has a big selection of rafting accessories including an aluminum rowing frame. Write for free catalog.

MARAVIA CORP.
857 Thornton St., P.O.Box 395, San Leandro, Calif. 94577
A relatively new company producing rafts of advanced design and extremely tough material; all craft are built using ballistic nylon coated with urethane. They specialize in larger boats and straight outrigger tubes. The Mistral, a 17 ft. 6 in. x 8 ft. raft with 23-in. tubes, has a nice rise to her bow and stern and goes for $1,750. Three other rafts are available ranging up to 27 feet. Outrigger tubes are available in three sizes from 22 to 30 feet; all are 36-in. diameter and made of the same materials as the rafts. Prices run from $550 to $725. Maravia has also developed a new life jacket, approved by the Coast Guard under their Type V rating. They call it the Type V Professional Whitewater Life Jacket. This jacket tests out as good as a Type I in buoyancy and has some features not found in any other personal flotation device, the best of which is its quick-release buckling system. There are times when you can't get out of a jacket fast enough.

THE INFLATABLE BOAT CENTER
510 Santa Monica Blvd., Santa Monica, Calif. 90406
Helmut Peters imports the Metzeler Spezi, which up till quite recently, was difficult to find. Now there are several dealers around the country and, depending from whom you buy, the Spezi can range from $330 to $375. It should be noted that this craft requires a specified air pressure to be operated safely, so you'll need a pump and pressure gauge.

WILDERNESS BOATS
Rt. 1, Box 101-A, Carlton, Oreg. 97111
David Hazen, who is Wilderness Boats, presents himself as a real craftsman from the old school with a product that anyone would be proud to own. He makes the Micmac canoe in three lengths: 16-ft., $665; 17-ft., $680; 18-ft., $690. Construction is of Western Red Cedar strips fiberglassed inside and out. Air chambers are built into the bow and stern, and all exposed woodwork triple-coated with varnish. Good-looking boats and tough. Write him for details and a copy of his wilderness boats broadside.

LEISURE IMPORTS, INC.
104 Arlington Ave., St. James, N.Y. 10780
Imports the French Pyrawa and Sea Eagle series, 9- to 12-ft. inflatable kayaks, $80 to $160. A beefed-up version of the Sea Eagle is the Explorer; hull material is heavier, seams are the same; 11-ft., $230; 12-ft., $250. Costs include a repair kit.

SEVYLOR U.S.A. INC.
6279 E. Slauson Ave., Los Angeles, Calif. 90040
Imports the Tahiti from France; available in four sizes. Very similar to the Pyrawa and Sea Eagle, but costs about $20 more. Sevylor offers a sail rig for the 12-ft. Tahiti.

DAYTON MARINE PRODUCTS
7565 E. McNichols Rd., Detroit, Mich. 48234
Manufactures the Sportyak rowing boat. Write for address of local dealer, but don't hold your breath. Some marine supply houses carry the boat. Check around.

ACCESSORIES

OTTERBINE INDUSTRIES, INC.
Fourth and Madison, Malta, Ill. 60150
Outboard water jet 3.5-hp motor good for canoes and small rafts, $249.

VOYAGEUR ENTERPRISES
P.O.Box 512, Shawnee Mission, Kans. 66201
Waterproof dunnage bags of woven polypropylene in two sizes, $8.95 and $12.50. They also have a kayak tour-pak, a combination waterproof gear sack and flotation bag. Once gear is stowed and the sack placed in the boat, you inflate it. Bow and stern set costs $29.50. For the shutterbug, Voyageur has an airtight, waterproof polyvinyl camera bag fully lined with closed-cell cloth-covered foam. Tested AOK by USN at 200 feet; $8.95. Voyageur also handles other tripping accessories. Write for complete literature.

NORTHERN STAR MARINE
1972 Grand Ave., St. Paul, Minn. 55105
Clamp-on sailing rigs for most standard canoes. Write for info.

WILDWATER DESIGNS KITS
Penllyn Pike & Morris Rd., Penllyn, Pa. 19422
Life vest (not USCG-approved), paddle jacket, wet suits, pogies and spray skirts all in kit form. Sells neoprene by the foot or sheet. Send for free catalog—Now!!!

THE BONNIE HOT POGIE
B. A. Losick, Ely, Vt. 05044
The only manufacturers of pogies. Handcrafted for paddles or oars. Pogies for kayaking cost $21.50 in neoprene and $12 in nylon, which is almost as warm as the neoprene. Write for flyer and sizing info.

NORTHWEST RIVER SUPPLIES
540 N. Grant St., Moscow, Idaho 83843
Total range of kayak and rafting supplies. Only source for the Centaur wet suit jacket-spray skirt combination. Carries Avon, Camp-Ways and other less expensive rafts. Some inflatable kayaks. Also rowing frames, oars, pumps, and repair items. The catalog is a source book on rafting and to some extent, kayaking. Really well done. Free.

WAYFARER RECREATIONAL PRODUCTS
1208 E. Elm St., Springfield, Mo. 65802
Manufactures canoe spray covers custom-fitted to any canoe. You furnish name, model and description of canoe. Covers are made of 10-oz.

Executing the ESKIMO ROLL

This maneuver is as old as the kayak itself and has been handed down to us by the seal hunters of the far north. A primitive version of this craft is still used in remote areas of Greenland for hunting and the Eskimo roll is common work-a-day procedure.

THIS ROLL CANNOT BE MASTERED BY READING ABOUT IT. Only through diligent practice, trial and error can anyone become proficient. For this reason, it is recommended that after reviewing what is said here, go out and get wet. Then, refer back several times as you practice.

Before proceeding, the following suggestions should be noted:

(a) Learning the Eskimo roll should be practiced in shallow water with sufficient clearance between the surface and bottom to execute the maneuver without striking. Waist deep is about right.

(b) Learning to roll should be done with an assistant, when possible, one who understands the maneuver himself. This is considered normal safety practice and will save much time otherwise wasted in beaching and emptying the kayak of water.

(c) The use of a face mask or nose plugs is helpful while learning unless you happen to have a taste for large quantities of water.

(d) To acquaint yourself with the feel of being upside down in your kayak, deliberately roll over while sitting in the cockpit and hang there for a few moments before leaving for the surface. Practice leaving the cockpit several times by pushing yourself downward, thrusting on the deck with both hands. The spray skirt will disengage itself automatically. This practice will lend confidence to your ability to free yourself.

There are many acceptable methods of accomplishing the roll. We have found the following method to be one which is easily mastered, and with practice will add to your skill and versatility. The roll can and should be mastered with equal facility on either side, however, for clarity, only the right hand roll is described here.

(1) The paddle should be held over the right side, its shaft nearly parallel with the surface and the active blade flat above the water well forward. The left hand should grasp the paddle shaft forward, with knuckles out. The right hand (also with knuckles out) should grasp the shaft and hold it at a point slightly behind the body. The inactive blade (toward the stern) should be raised slightly and kept out of water as long as possible to avoid drag and fouling with the kayak.

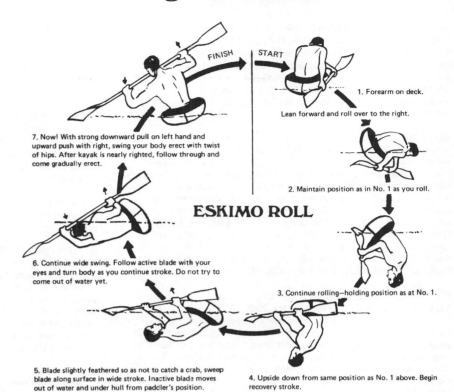

ESKIMO ROLL

START

1. Forearm on deck.

Lean forward and roll over to the right.

2. Maintain position as in No. 1 as you roll.

3. Continue rolling—holding position as at No. 1.

4. Upside down from same position as No. 1 above. Begin recovery stroke.

5. Blade slightly feathered so as not to catch a crab, sweep blade along surface in wide stroke. Inactive blade moves out of water and under hull from paddler's position.

6. Continue wide swing. Follow active blade with your eyes and turn body as you continue stroke. Do not try to come out of water yet.

7. Now! With strong downward pull on left hand and upward push with right, swing your body erect with twist of hips. After kayak is nearly righted, follow through and come gradually erect.

FINISH

(2) With the paddle in position, lean forward and to the right rolling the craft upside down. When in a full upside down position begin the recovery stroke by twisting at the waist in the same direction. The recovery stroke should be a smooth continuous movement in which the active blade describes a sweeping motion from its point of beginning at the bow along the surface of the water as you roll.

(3) When the body is almost parallel with the surface and nearly awash after completing three-quarters of the roll, the active blade should be well out at about 90 degrees from the keel line and skimming along the surface. The paddler then levers himself upright with a strong upward thrust on the paddle shaft with the right hand, the left still sweeping, but now with a downward thrust. With reference to the paddler's position the inactive blade is in the air beneath the hull. As the stroke continues beyond a 90 degree deflection from the keel line, coordinate a push upward with the right hand while the left sweeps out and downward levering the body gradually erect following the kayak onto an even keel.

Assuming that everything has been done correctly, the paddler is again in an upright position ready to proceed. This will not be the case on the first attempt, or the second. Be prepared for several failures while learning. The Eskimo roll is mastered only through practice. It is a "MUST" for those who aspire to white water competition. It will be found that once learned, it will add greatly to your skill as a kayaker because any fear of overturning will have been overcome.

Courtesy: Old Town Canoe Co.

---

waterproof nylon, $99.50, complete with attachments. They also do up a line of open-cell foam clothing. Write for brochures.

A. C. MACKENZIE RIVER CO.
P.O. Box 9301, Richmond Hts. Sta., Richmond Heights, Mo. 63117
Offers a 12-ft., 3-lb. floating aluminum canoe pole that can be dismantled; $29.11 includes air mail delivery. They put on a two-day free poling clinic once a year, in August, for intermediates and above; info costs two bits!

RIVER GEAR/RIVER EXPLORATION LTD.
1225 Liberty St., El Cerrito, Calif. 94530
Manufactures wooden rowing frames. Provides either finished or unfinished versions. Poop decks, oar clips, watertight wooden boxes. Lotsa hardware for those building frames. Catalog free.

CANOE CALIFORNIA
P.O. Box 61A, Kentfield, Calif. 94904
Large number of really fine waterproof bags and packs, waterproof nylon with plastic liners. Plus custom-made nylon and neoprene spray skirts. Free brochure.

QUIK-N-EASY PRODUCTS, INC.
934 West Foothill Blvd., Monrovia, Calif. 91016
Quik-N-Easy has one of the best-designed car top carrier racks around. It attaches to the car roof gutters via four adjustable clamp units, each operated by an eccentric lever. No fuss, no muss. Boat hold downs, ski clamps, and utility straps are available for tying down odd-shaped items. An illustrated price sheet is available on request.

Rafters, Canoeists—No more takin' a dump in the Grand Canyon or Okefenokee. Bring your own head.—Uncle Sam (1976).

GARELICK MFG., INC.
644 2nd St., St. Paul, Minn. 55071
Port-O-Biff, portable folding aluminum toilet, uses plastic bags, $9.95.

ZURN INDUSTRIES, INC., Recreational Prod. Div.
5533 Perry Hwy., Erie, Pa. 16509
Sani-Mate, portable chemical toilet, $85.50. Also has economy model for quick squats; folding metal frame, plastic seat, uses plastic bags, $8.

TOURS and EXPEDITIONS

NATIONAL PARK SERVICE (NPS)
Dept. of the Interior, Washington, D.C. 20240
Check with regional NPS offices before running any of the rivers under their jurisdiction. Good source for up-to-date info on conditions and what, if any, regulations exist. Here are some of "their" rivers: Buffalo (AR), Colorado (UT & AZ), Current (MO), Green (UT & CO), Jacks Fork (MO), Rio Grande (TX), San Juan (UT), Snake (WY) and the Yampa (UT & CO).

U.S. FOREST SERVICE
Dept. of Agriculture, Washington, D.C. 20250
When running any river that flows through a national forest contact the superintendent of that forest (see Wilderness Areas and Trails for regional addresses). River maps are distributed at local levels usually for the asking, though in certain areas you may get soaked (another pun!) for 50¢. The Forest Service has more rivers under its administration than you can count. This will give you an idea: the AuSable (MI), Black Creek (MS), Chattooga (GA), Clearwater (ID), Eagle (CO), Eleven Point (MO), Grande Ronde (OR), Grays (WY), Green (UT), Illinois (OR), Kings (CA), Lochsa (ID), Rice (MN), Rogue (OR), Salmon (ID), Selway (ID), Tuolumne (CA), Turtle (MN).

U.S. GEOLOGICAL SURVEY
12201 Sunrise Valley Dr., Reston, Va. 22092
Besides publishing the best touring maps (topographical maps) for rivers and lakes, USGS also issues the monthly **Water Resources Review** of about 18 pages, which covers stream flow and ground-water conditions for rivers and river basins throughout the United States. Though the information is somewhat dry (charts, graphs, and the like), it can provide enough data for you to add two and two to determine where the action is—particularly for white water. The **Review** is available free of charge at the above address. Incidentally, USGS is a good place to get specific info on rivers, streams and general water conditions. These people will refer you to other sources if they can't handle your problem.

STATE AND PROVINCIAL TOURIST AND TRAVEL BUREAUS
Much good information can be had from these people on canoe trails, river conditions, launch areas and camping spots. Just about every state and province has a canoeable stream, though not every one has literature specifically devoted to canoeing and kayaking. The addresses to write for state and provincial information will be found in the Wilderness Areas and Trails section.

Rail Travel Bureau
CANADIAN NATIONAL RAILWAYS
P.O. Box 8100, Montreal, Quebec, Canada H3C 3N4
It's pretty hard setting up car shuttles in the Canadian wilds. Sometimes the only way into a place, or out of it, is by rail. Check with these people about bringing your boat back from James Bay, or anywhere else that track runs. Write early.

SPECIAL CANOE ROUTES DATA SERVICE
Nick Nickels
Box 479, Lakefield, Ontario, Canada K0L 2H0
For the canoeist planning a far-flung expedition into the wilder Canadas, Nickels has compiled extensive research files on this part of the world. If you're having difficulty getting info on which way the Coppermine flows and who flies in there, this service could help you. It includes a complete set of topos for the area to which you are headed, regional temperature and rainfall figures, break-up and freeze-up dates, preliminary field contacts and other source info. The service isn't intended for people going to Algonquin Provincial for a week, but for those headed back into the real "God's country." Cost is dependent on the amount of digging Nick has to do; you'll get a quote beforehand. It's suggested you contact him well in advance of your trip. Write for details.

BRITISH CANOE UNION (BCU)
70 Brompton Rd., London, England SW3 1DT
If you're going abroad on a canoeing trip the BCU sells canoeing books and river maps of a large number of rivers in Britain and on the Continent. If you write them from the states enclose a couple of International Reply Coupons, which can be gotten at any post office.

GRUMMAN ALLIED INDUSTRIES
Marathon, N.Y. 13803
Grumman has compiled a **Rent-A-Canoe Directory** to the United States, which gives a state by state listing of several hundred liveries where canoes may be rented. Available free on request.

U-PADDLE CANOE RENTAL SERVICE
Hudson's Bay Co.
800 Baker Centre, 10025 106th St., Edmonton, Alberta, Canada T5J 1G7
U-Paddle will supply a 17-ft. Grumman canoe with carrying yoke and three paddles to experienced canoeists for canoe cruises in the Canadian Northwest. Rental is $70 per canoe per week for a minimum of two weeks. The Hudson's Bay Co. does not supply food or camping gear with its canoes. Further particulars can be had at the above address.

ADVENTURE GUIDES, INC.
36 E. 57th St., New York, N.Y. 10022
Adventure Guides has put together a 224-page directory of all types of wilderness land and water excursions. In the water division 52 pages of canoeing, kayaking and river-float trips are listed with the name and address of the outfitter, trip schedules or rental services, prices and descriptive commentary. Some really good information. The directory is called **Adventure Travel USA** and sells for $3.95. Available at the above address.

River Classifications

Canoe trail and river guidebooks use a number system to grade the difficulty of various stretches of a waterway. Through this a paddler will know what to expect, from flat water paddling to dangerous rough and tumble wild water, and whether he has the experience to handle it. The American Whitewater Affiliation has developed a rating chart which has become a standard for grading rivers. It gives from one to six points to various factors affecting negotiability and safety. The chart is reproduced here so that you can see exactly what determines the difficulty of a river. The more points a river gets, the rougher its conditions:

Class	River Description	Skill Required
I	*Very easy.* Relatively smooth small waves, few if any obstructions, perhaps a sandbar or a bridge or two.	Beginner
II	*Easy.* Some rapids though with wide and clear passages, low waves, a few easy ledges.	Experienced beginner
III	*Medium.* Numerous high and irregular waves, short rapids with clear though narrow passages, rocks and boulders, eddies.	Intermediate
IV	*Difficult.* Many powerful and irregular waves, strong currents and boiling eddies. Long rapids with difficult passages and dangerous rocks. Requires inspection from shore before tackling.	Experienced
V	*Very difficult.* Solid waves, powerful crosscurrents and eddies, long violent rapids one right after the other, dangerous boulders and rocks, many obstructions, passages difficult and often impossible to determine, *must* be inspected from shore before tackling.	Expert
VI	*Extraordinarily difficult.* A class V situation carried to the limits of navigability, very dangerous and just about impossible. Complete course requires very careful scrutiny from shore and due consideration to water level must be given.	Team of experts taking every possible precaution.

NORTH AMERICA

WILD RIVERS OF NORTH AMERICA
Michael Jenkinson
1973 - 413 p. il. - $12.95 (hb)

Eight rivers are featured in depth, with 106 others presented in sketches, from Nicaragua to the Arctic Ocean. Good appendices provide source material for further research.
From: E. P. Dutton & Co., 201 Park Ave. S., New York, N.Y. 10003

CANADA

CANOE CANADA
Nick Nickels
1976 - 256 p. il. - $9.95 (pb)

Over 600 canoe routes throughout Canada, featuring 50 in detail. A storehouse of information.
From: Van Nostrand Reinhold Co., 450 W. 33rd St., New York, N.Y. 10001

FUR TRADE CANOE ROUTES OF CANADA—THEN AND NOW
Eric Morse
1968 - 128 p. il. - $3.75 (hb)

Covers old routes from Montreal to the Columbia River, linking these trails with today's highway system. Good for planning a trip.
From: Minnesota Historical Society, Cedar & Central, St. Paul, Minn. 55101

Yukon

YUKON RIVER TRAIL GUIDE
Archie Satterfield
1975 - 159 p. il. - $4.95 (pb)

Lake Bennett to Dawson City.
From: Stackpole Books, Cameron & Kelker Sts., Harrisburg, Pa. 17105

UNITED STATES

MAKENS' GUIDE TO U.S. CANOE TRAILS
James C. Makens
1971 - 86 p. - $4.95 (pb)

This is primarily a research guide describing some 1,040 canoeable rivers and streams in the United States. The book is organized alphabetically by waterway and state and includes data on flat-water and white-water runs. Makens took two years of extensive research to put this all together, and the wealth of information in the book's bibliography certainly shows it.
From: Le Voyageur Pub. Co., 1319 Wentwood Dr., Irving, Tex. 75061

INTRODUCTION TO WATER TRAILS IN AMERICA
Robert Colwell
1973 - 217 p. il. - $2.95 (pb)

Information on 112 rivers around the country within three hours' drive from 150 cities? Mostly nice, quiet streams for beginners.
From: Stackpole Books, Cameron & Kelker Sts., Harrisburg, Pa. 17105

Alaska

DISCOVER SOUTHEAST ALASKA WITH PACK & PADDLE
Margaret Piggot
1974 - 269 p. il. - $7.95 (pb)

From: The Mountaineers, P.O. Box 122, Seattle, Wash. 98111

Northwest

KAYAK & CANOE TRIPS IN WASHINGTON
Werner Furrer
1971 - 31 p. il. - $2 (pb)

From: Signpost Pubs., 16812 36th Ave. W., Lynnwood, Wash. 98036

SIERRA WHITEWATER
Charles Martin
1974 - 192 p. il. - $5.95

California rivers.
From: Fiddleneck Press, P.O. Box 114, Sunnydale, Calif. 94086

SNAKE RIVER GUIDE
Verne Huser and Buzz Belknap
1972 - 72 p. il. - $4.95 (pb)

Wyoming.
From: Westwater Books, Box 365, Boulder City, Nev. 89005

WATER TRAILS OF WASHINGTON
Werner Furrer
1973 - 31 p. il. - $2.50 (pb)

From: Signpost Pubs., 16812 36th Ave., W. Lynwood, Wash. 98036

WEST COAST RIVER TOURING
Richard Schwind
1975 - 222 p. il. - $5.95 (pb)

Rogue River Canyon and South.
From: Touchstone Press, P.O. Box 81, Beaverton, Oreg. 97005

WILDWATER TOURING
Scott and Margaret Arighi
1974 - 334 p. il. - $8.95 (hb)

"How-to" book with an excellent river guide section to the West.
From: Macmillan Co., Inc., 366 Third Ave., New York, N.Y. 10022

DIFFICULTY RATING CHART FOR RIVER SECTIONS OR INDIVIDUAL RAPIDS
Prepared By Guidebook Committee, American White-Water Affiliation — H. J. Wilhoyte   February 12, 1956

	Factors Related Primarily To Success in Negotiating			Factors Affecting Both Success & Safety				Factors Related Primarily To Safe Rescue			
	SECONDARY FACTORS			PRIMARY FACTORS				SECONDARY FACTORS			
POINTS	Bends	Length, Ft.	Gradient, Ft./Mi.	Obstacles Rocks, Trees	Waves	Turbulence	Resting or Rescue Spots	Water Vel. Mi./Hr.	Width/Depth	Water Temp. °F	Accessibility
ONE	Few Very Gradual	Less Than 100	Less Than 5 Regular Slope	None	Few Inches High Avoidable	None	Almost Anywhere	Less Than 3	Narrow ⟋75' and Shallow ⟍3'	Above 65	Road Along River
1	Many Gradual	100 - 700	5 - 15 Regular Slope	Few: Passage Almost Straight Through	Low (Up to 1') Regular Avoidable	Minor Eddies		3 - 6	Wide ⟍ 75' and Shallow ⟍3'	55 - 65	Less Than 1 Hrs. Travel By Foot or Water
2	Few Sharp-Blind Scouting Req'd.	700 - 5000	15 - 40 Ledges or Steep Drops	Courses Easily Recognizable	Low to Med. (Up to 3') Regular Avoidable	Medium Eddies		6 - 10	Narrow ⟋75' and Deep ⟍ 3'	45 - 55	1 Hr. to 1 Days Travel By Foot or Water
3		5000+	40+ Steep Drops Small Falls	Maneuvering Required. Course Not Easily Recognizable	Med. to Lge. (Up to 5') Mostly Reg. Avoidable	Strong Eddies Cross Currents	A good One Below Every Danger Spot	10+ or Flood	Wide ⟍ 75' and Deep ⟍ 3'	Less Than 45°	Greater Than 1 Days Travel By Foot or Water
4				Intricate Maneuvering Course Hard to Recognize	Lge.-Irreg. Avoid. or Med. to Lge. Unavoidable	V. Strong Eddies Strong Cross Currents					
5				Course Torturous Frequent Scouting Required	Large Irregular Unavoidable	Large Scale Eddies & Cross C's. Some Up & Down C's.					
6				Very Torturous Always Scout from Shore	V. Lg. (5'+) Irregular Unavoidable Required	V. Lge. Scale Strong Up & Down Currents	Almost None				

Rating	Approximate Difficulty	Total Points (From Above Chart)	Approximate Skill Required
I	Easy	0 - 7	Practiced Beginner
II	Requires Care	8 - 14	Intermediate
III	Difficult	15 - 21	Experienced
IV	Very Difficult	22 - 28	Highly Skilled (Several Years with Organized Group)
V	Exceedingly Difficult	29 - 35	Team of Experts
VI	Utmost Difficulty — Near Limit of Navigability	36 - 42	Team of Experts Taking Every Precaution

(chart from *AMC New England Canoeing Guide*)

Southwest

CANYONLANDS RIVER GUIDE
Bill and Buzz Belknap
1974 - 63 p. il. - $4.95 (pb), $6.95 (waterproof ed.)

Green and Colorado Rivers in Utah.
From: Westwater Books, Box 365, Boulder City, Nev. 89005

DESOLATION RIVER GUIDE
Laura Evans and Buzz Belknap
1974 - 56 p. il. - $4.95 (pb), $6.95 (waterproof ed.)

Green River in Utah.
From: Westwater Books, Box 365, Boulder City, Nev. 89005

DINOSAUR RIVER GUIDE
Laura Evans and Buzz Belknap
1975 - 64 p. il. - $4.95 (pb), $6.95 (waterproof ed.)

Green and Colorado Rivers in Wyoming, Utah and Colorado.
From: Westwater Books, Box 365, Boulder City, Nev. 89005

GRAND CANYON RIVER GUIDE
Buzz Belknap
1975 - 52 p. il. - $4.95 (pb), $6.95 (waterproof ed.)

Colorado River.
From: Westwater Books, Box 365, Boulder City, Nev. 89005

NEW MEXICO RIVER NOTES
Doug Murphy
10 p. - $2

From: Get Down Rivers, 9212 Bellehaven NE, Albuquerque, N. Mex. 87112

TEXAS RIVERS & RAPIDS VOL. I & II
Ben M. Nolen
1974 - $5.95 (pb)

From: Ben M. Nolen, P.O. Box 673, Humble, Tex. 77338

Midwest

CANOE TRAILS OF SOUTHERN WISCONSIN
Michael Duncanson
1974 - 64 p. il. - $4.95 (pb)

From: Wisconsin Tales & Trails, Inc., P.O. Box 5650, Madison, Wis. 53705

MISSOURI OZARK WATERWAYS
Oz Hawksley
1972 - 114 p. il. - $1 (pb)

From: Missouri Conservation Commission, Jefferson City, Mo. 65101

WHITEWATER; QUIETWATER
Bob and Jody Palzer
1974, 2nd ed. - 152 p. il. - $7.95 (pb)

Rivers of Wisconsin, Upper Michigan and N.E. Minnesota.
From: Evergreen Paddleways, 1416 21st St., Two Rivers, Wis. 54241

Northeast

ADIRONDACK CANOE WATERS; NORTH FLOW
Paul F. Jamieson
1975 - 299 p. il. - $6.95 (pb)

From: Adirondack Mountain Club, 172 Ridge St., Glen Falls, N.Y. 12801

AMC NEW ENGLAND CANOEING GUIDE
Appalachian Mountain Club
1971, 3rd ed. - 600 p. il. - $6.50 (hb)

A pocket-size, hard-cover canoeing guide covering all the New England rivers. Includes three removable maps—*A Canoeist's Map of Southern New England, A Canoeist's Map of Vermont and New Hampshire,* and *A Canoeist's Map of Maine.* River descriptions include put-ins, take-outs, river conditions including rapid classes, type of scenery, and historical data for towns, mills, dams, bridges, and so forth along the way. The *New England Canoeing Guide* has been a-round since '36 and is probably one of the best-known river guides in the country.
From: Appalachian Mountain Club, 5 Joy St., Boston, Mass. 02108

AMC RIVER GUIDE VOL. I
Appalachian Mountain Club
1976 - il. - $6 (pb)

Northeastern New England.
From: Appalachian Mountain Club, 5 Joy St., Boston, Mass. 02108

APPALACHIAN WATERS VOL. I
W. F. Burmeister
1974 - 274 p. - $6.95 (pb)

Delaware River and tributaries. Pennsylvania, New York and New Jersey.
From: Appalachian Books, P.O. Box 248, Oakton, Va. 22124

APPALACHIAN WATERS VOL. II
W. F. Burmeister
1975 - $7.50 (pb)

Hudson River and tributaries, and New York.
From: Appalachian Books, P.O. Box 248, Oakton, Va. 22124

Catching forty winks at the first rapids on the Eastman River, Quebec. Photo: Old Town Canoe Co.

APPALACHIAN WATERS VOL. III
W. F. Burmeister
1975 - $8.50 (pb)

Susquehanna and tributaries, and Pennsylvania.
From: Appalachian Books, P.O. Box 248, Oakton, Va. 22124

EXPLORING THE LITTLE RIVERS OF NEW JERSEY
James and Margaret Cawley
1971, 3rd ed. - 252 p. il. - $2.75 (pb)

From: Rutgers Univ. Press, 30 College Ave., New Brunswick, N.J. 08903

NEW ENGLAND WHITE WATER RIVER GUIDE
Ray Gabler
1975 - 236 p. il. - $5.95 (pb)

From: Tobey Publishing Co., Inc., Box 428, New Canaan, Conn. 06840

NO HORNS BLOWING
Eben Thomas
1973 - 134 p. il. - $3.95 (pb)

Maine.
From: Hallowell Printing Co., 145 Water St., Hallowell, Maine 04347

THE WEEKENDER
Eben Thomas
1975 - 134 p. il. - $3.95

Maine.
From: Hallowell Printing Co., 145 Water St., Hallowell, Maine 04347

Southeast

APPALACHIAN WATERS VOL. IV
W. F. Burmeister
1976 - 812 p. - $10 (pb)

Chattooga River, plus rivers throughout Virginia, North and South Carolina, Tennessee, Georgia and Florida.
From: Appalachian Books, P.O. Box 248, Oakton, Va. 22124

BLUE RIDGE VOYAGES VOL. I
H. Roger Corbett and Louis Matacia
1973, 4th ed. - 75 p. il. - $3.95 (pb)

Ten selected canoe trips within a 150-mile radius of Washington, D.C. in Maryland, Virginia and West Virginia. Includes maps and photographs. Plastic spiral binding.
From: Louis Matacia, 2700 Gallows Rd., Vienna, Va. 22180

BLUE RIDGE VOYAGES VOL. II
H. Roger Corbett and Louis Matacia
1972, 2nd ed. - 84 p. il. - $3.50 (pb)

Selected canoe trips in the Smoke Hole Recreation Area with hikes (including three pocket folding maps) and one- and two-day trips within a 160-mi. radius of Washington, D.C. in Maryland, Virginia and West Virginia, on the Potomac River, the Cacapon River, Cedar Creek, Catocin Creek, Antietam Creek, and the South Branch of the Potomac River.
From: Louis Matacia, 2700 Gallows Rd., Vienna, Va. 22180

BLUE RIDGE VOYAGES
VOLUME TWO
BY
CORBETT AND MATACIA
FIRST EDITION
1968

BLUE RIDGE VOYAGES VOL. III
H. Roger Corbett and Louis Matacia
1972 - 116 p. il. - $3.50 (pb)

Virginia, West Virginia.
From: Louis Matacia, 2700 Gallows Rd., Vienna, Va. 22180

CANOEING WHITEWATER
Randy Carter
1974, 8th ed. - 267 p. il. - $5 (pb)

Canoeing info on 2,000 miles of rivers in Virginia, eastern West Virginia, and the Great Smoky Mountain area of North Carolina.
From: Appalachian Books, P.O. Box 248, Oakton, Va. 22124

A GUIDE TO THE WILDERNESS WATERWAY OF THE EVERGLADES NATIONAL PARK
William G. Truesdell
1973 - 64 p. il. - $2.50 (pb)

From: Univ. of Miami Press, Drawer 9088, Coral Gables, Fla. 33124

WILDWATER WEST VIRGINIA
Bob Burrell and Paul Davidson
1975, 2nd ed. - 162 p. il. - $5.25 (pb)

This is a paddler's guide to more than 1,500 miles of white-water rivers in the mountain state. The rivers are arranged in nine chapters according to key watersheds or basins. Each chapter is prefaced by a regional introduction which points out the history, scenic attractions, economics, natural history and environmental threats. For white-water paddlers, detailed information on each river is provided which carefully explains put-in and take-out access points, general hydrologic characteristics, key rapids, danger points and difficulties, and other characteristics helpful in planning trips. Unlike most books, this guide attempts to tell the whole truth, and if some of the areas are an environmental disgrace, it says so.
From: Paul Davidson, Dept. of Medicine, West Virginia University, Morgantown, W. Va. 26506

MAPS

LESLIE ALLEN JONES
Star Route, Box 13, Heber City, Utah 84032
Carefully made strip-scroll maps for Western river runners. Each map comes with a special plastic bag to use as a case, allowing a waterproof look at the next ten miles of river. Jones has put together 11 different maps covering various areas of the Colorado River Basin: two Oregon River maps, five of the Snake River Basin and three rivers in British Columbia. Each map shows the river's course in detail, giving difficulty ratings at serious rapids with running and scouting advice. Also points out campsites. Prices range from $2 to $5 per map. Write for list.

U.S./CANADIAN MAP SERVICE BUREAU
Midwest Distribution Center, Box 249, Neenah, Wis. 54956
This is a private company authorized by the United States and Canadian governments to act as their agent for the sale of maps, charts and related material. They stock 22,500 U.S. and Canadian topographic and hydrographic charts which have been cataloged into two books: *Official Eastern North America Map and Chart Index Catalog* and *Official Western North America Map and Chart Index Catalog,* $5.85 each, postpaid. The division between east and west is a line running up the Mississippi River due north to Hudson Bay. The catalogs are a collection of all the map indexes for each state and province, and chart indexes for the Atlantic, Pacific and Gulf coasts and Great Lakes; several order blanks are included with each catalog. U.S./Canadian's prices are more than those of the government map offices, but waiting time is considerably shorter. Even if you don't order through these people, it's worth buying their catalogs to have on hand for reference. The sheer bulk of maps that is offered is really impressive. You feel like you've got it all there at your fingertips. You do! Write for a descriptive brochure of their services.

"See ya on a river...!"

winter bivouacking

When cold weather arrives in the wilderness and the crowds leave, this is the time for those who love winter, the hearty souls with a touch of iron in their blood, to pack up and move into action. But be prepared for a whole new thing—landmarks and trails will have vanished under a blanket of snow; making camp and building a fire will present new problems, even walking won't be the same. And along with the difficulties of providing food and shelter, the winter traveler will have to cope with hazards of hypothermia, frostbite, and avalanches.

There are two books that deal realistically with the very special conditions encountered in winter camping and travel. Both are heartily recommended: *Paradise Below Zero*, by Calvin Rutstrum, The Macmillan Co., $5.95, and *Arctic Manual*, by Vilhjalmur Stefansson, The Macmillan Co., apparently out of print but available through many libraries. Between these two, enough information is given so you can use the winter environment to your advantage.

Clothing is given prime coverage in both books because it's really the most important category of equipment. Eskimo and Indian garments and footwear are lauded—mukluks, skin parkas, mitts—and while there's no question about their efficiency (who'd question an Eskimo's idea of how to keep warm?), genuine Eskimo clothing is scarce and expensive. So the choice for most poeple will fall among the latest in down or wool or G.I. surplus. All are equally warm in the proper application.

Warmth isn't the only consideration, however. If you plan to propel yourself through the winter wonderland with any exertion, you'll need clothing that is reasonably light in weight and breathable. The light weight makes for comfort and maneuverability. The breathability prevents body moisture from condensing in the material. Ideally, moisture passes or "wicks" through the clothing and you stay dry. Even clothing that breathes will get soaked, however, if you work yourself into a lather pushing along on snowshoes or skis. So don't get overheated. Wear layers of clothing instead of one bulky jacket and take off or add pieces as the temperature or your level of exertion changes. Stay on the cool side while moving.

The need for a breathable garment that supplies maximum warmth with a minimum of weight is best filled by goose down. Warmth is provided by the layer of dead air that's between you and the cold, and a very small weight of down will fluff out or "loft" to provide this layer better than any other material. Its biggest drawback is the expense, but if you can afford the initial investment, which, incidentally, doesn't have to be so great if you buy a kit and make your own clothing, you'll be repaid with years of wear and service.

Wool, though heavier, is also an excellent material for its insulative qualities and breathability. It even does the job when it's wet or dirty, and in addition to its use in jackets and trousers, it's still the best material possible for mittens, socks, and headgear.

Armed forces surplus clothing made from wool, cotton, and synthetics, is heavier than down garments, but equally efficient from the standpoint of warmth and wicking properties. A lot of research and experimenting has gone into G.I. clothing. Arctic parkas, anoraks, deck jackets, field jackets, gloves, mittens, socks, and boots are available at surplus stores for a fraction of the cost of new clothing.

The kind of footwear you choose will depend on how you're traveling. For some uses, such as travel through wet snow, boots will need to be completely waterproof. In any case, they should be warm and non-binding. Good ones are the L.L. Bean Maine boot, the Canadian Sorel boot, and the surplus G.I. Korea boot. If your activities center around winter climbing and you've got the money, the mountaineer's double boot is a good investment. Boot cuffs or gaiters are a good idea also, to keep the snow out.

Travel through deep snow for any distance is just about impossible without snowshoes or skis. You should become acquainted with the use of both, and the white stuff you'll be traveling on.

Snow is shaped and molded by wind, sun, and temperature in different ways depending on the lay of the land, so that its character changes daily. Understanding the effects of weather and terrain on snow, and learning to read its surface texture is of vital importance to safe and speedy travel.

How about the length of a trip? From a practical standpoint, it shouldn't be longer than four days or so. Here's why. Clothing will get salted up from perspiration and after four days it just won't dry very well. Wearing damp clothes is asking for big trouble. The practical limit on packs, even if you are in good shape, is 50 to 60 pounds. With this weight, and all the extra gear involved in winter bivouacking, you'll have just about enough room for four days worth of chow.

To keep weight down, freeze dried foods are the ticket. Or if you can spare the weight here's an idea. Freeze a rich stew in several smallish breadpans. When frozen remove and wrap in plastic bags. Out in the field just drop one of these "stew bars" in a pot and heat it up for a tasty meal. It can be eaten for breakfast and supper, with a high-energy food bar for lunch. Wash it all down with a lot of liquids, at least 1½ quarts per day, to prevent dehydration which'll sneak up on you in the dry cold of a sub-zero environment. And a note on the merits of alcoholic beverages: liquor in strict moderation can work wonders toward boosting chilled spirits. But take just a snort when the stuff is minus 20 or 30 degrees (it stays liquid that far down the thermometer) and it'll freeze your throat instantly. A frozen throat can mean almost instant death.

When picking a campsite, head for protection from the wind. Watch out for lees where snow will drift and for overhanging branches loaded with the stuff. A quick shelter is the hollow under a fir tree, or you can dig a snow cave. For more permanent camps that merit the effort, build an igloo. For less innovative people, a well-designed tent is the answer. Be sure to pick one with a good durable waterproof floor, and a coated waterproof fly which will give a double wall effect. This way the space between the tent and the fly traps a layer of dead air that acts as added insulation against the cold. The tent itself, except for the floor, should be of a breathable fabric so moisture from your breath and body won't condense on the inside. Mountaineering tents usually have a drawstring, tube-type opening which eliminates the zipper, an item that can jam or be hard to work with cold fingers. These small openings retain warmth better than flap types and keep out snow and scree too.

Next—sleeping bags. All good cold weather bags are rated for effectiveness. Know what you'll be needing when you buy. Don't be a "hindsighter." One bag inserted in another will increase its warmth. Wear dry clothes or nothing to bed. Moisture is really your biggest problem in keeping warm in the super cold. Another thing, if a catalytic or other type of heater is taken along to warm the tent, make sure you can get along without it in the event it doesn't work. Be leery of depending too heavily on mechanical gadgets in the cold. If you use a wood fire, bank it and keep those coals going all night. Have a sufficient supply of fuel close at hand which can be reached without having to get out of your bag. There's nothing better for morale than being able to crawl out of the sack to a nice crackling warm fire in the morning.

One last reminder: the winter scene is well worth all the effort it takes to get there compared to the relatively tame summer scene. But in the same proportions it can be very brutal and swift in its punishment for carelessness. Good advance planning, common sense, and a few well-chosen alternatives and escape routes can mean the difference between an exhilarating adventure with nature, a few missing toes, or disaster.

BOOKS

THE ABC OF AVALANCHE SAFETY
Edward R. LaChapelle
1961 - $1.00

Basic handbook of avalanche safety—how to steer clear of avalanches and how to survive them. Included are general safety rules, rescue procedures, and suggested equipment for mountain touring. LaChapelle is a snow ranger with the U.S. Forest Service, is on the faculty of the University of Washington, and is actively involved in avalanche research.
From: Colorado Outdoor Sports Corp., P.O. Box 5544, Denver, Colo. 80217

BASIC COLD WEATHER MANUAL FM 31-7
U.S. Army
198 p. il. - $5.50

A lot of good information on how to survive and function in the severe cold. If you can get over the military stuff like how to stand at attention on skis, it does a good job on clothing, shelter, cold weather travel, and how to make war in the snow.
From: The Adobe Hacienda, Box 517, Glendale, Ariz. 85301

HOW TO KEEP WARM
Gerry Cunningham
15 p. il. - free

Explains the basic physical principles involved in keeping warm, with recommendations on the best way to achieve warmth. Insulation, ventilation, and evaporation are discussed along with the science of properly clothing each part of the body. This booklet is given away at many stores, or you can write and request one. It contains a lot of good technical information.
From: Colorado Outdoor Sports Corp., P.O. Box 5544, Denver, Colo. 80217

FROSTBITE
Bradford Washburn
1962 - $1.00

Most complete information available on frostbite: what it is, how to avoid it, and how to treat it. This booklet is a reprint from the 1962 *American Alpine Journal.*
From: The American Alpine Club, 113 E. 90th St., New York, N.Y. 10028

COLD-WEATHER CAMPING
Ray Stebbins
1975 - 228 p. il. - $4.95 (pb)

Ray Stebbins, a former editor of *Colorado Magazine,* has put together a good batch of cold-weather travel and bivouacking information which includes clothing and basic winter camping gear; travel tools: snowshoes, skis, sleds and snowmobiles; route planning and logistics; setting up camp, building shelters and how to work out of a base camp; staying out of trouble and survival situations; and things to do out in the snowy wilderness like tracking and photographing animals, ice fishing and so forth. If you're wondering where to go, Ray's covered that, too, with a listing of popular areas around the country.
From: Henry Regnery Co., 180 N. Michigan Ave., Chicago, Ill. 60601

HYPOTHERMIA: KILLER OF THE UNPREPARED
Theodore G. Lathrope, M.D.
13 p. - $1.00

Hypothermia is a condition of sub-normal body temperature with associated deceleration of metabolic processes that results in death by freezing (how's that for a nifty definition?). This little book describes the condition, how to deal with it, and how to avoid it. A good book for winter travelers.

From: Eastern Mountain Sports, 1041 Commonwealth Ave., Boston, Mass. 02215

PARADISE BELOW ZERO
Calvin Rutstrum
1968 - il. - $5.95

Calvin Rutstrum has fifty years of winter wilderness travel experience to his credit and his enthusiasm for cold weather ventures is infectious. He discusses equipment, shelters, snowshoeing, dog sledding, food, and emergencies. Accounts of notable incidents of sub-zero survival among Eskimos, Indians, and prospectors are included. Anecdotal in tone, fun to read, and full of useful information.

From: The Macmillan Co., Front and Brown Sts., Riverside, N.J. 08077

COMPLETE SNOW CAMPER'S GUIDE
Raymond Bridge
1973 - 390 p. il. - $8.95 (hb), $3.95 (pb)

The information that this book contains appears sound enough, and it does seem to cover every possible aspect of winter camping, from how to travel, to how to make winter clothing. It's just the presentation that's a little hard to take. The "how to" approach is carried to a ridiculous extreme making it over-simplified, to say the least, and a little painful to read. Am still pondering such sweeping statements as: "Watery regions are often passable on foot only when temperatures remain below freezing." and "However you start, winter travel is not very expensive, once you buy the equipment."

From: Charles Scribner's Sons, Vreeland Ave., Totowa, N.J. 07512

ARCTIC MANUAL
Vilhjalmur Stefansson
1944

The *Arctic Manual* was specifically written as a survival handbook for the U.S. Army Air Corps, whose operations took pilots over the polar regions as early as 1929. Stefansson, a noted Arctic explorer, spent many years in northern regions on exploratory and anthropological expeditions, and his manual covers every conceivable aspect of sub-zero living: shelter, hygiene, travel, care of pack animals, emergency rations, hunting, diet, camping, Arctic fuels and how to use them, clothing and its care. Though Arctic conditions are the extreme, the information that this book contains has a broad range of application for the cold weather traveler anywhere.

From: (The Macmillan Co., Front and Brown Sts., Riverside, N.J. 08077); out of print but available from many libraries.

WINTER HIKING AND CAMPING
John Danielson
1972 - 192 p. il. - $4.50

This is a basic manual on wilderness excursions in winter. Discussions of the body's reaction to cold, first aid, clothing, equipment, food, travel by foot, skis, and snowshoes, orienteering, survival, and rescue are included along with over 100 diagrams and photographs.

From: The Adirondack Mountain Club, Inc., R.D. 1, Ridge Rd., Glen Falls, N.Y. 12801

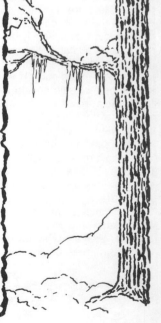

WIND-CHILL CHART

Estimated Wind Speed MPH	ACTUAL THERMOMETER READING °F.											
	50	40	30	20	10	0	—10	—20	—30	—40	—50	—60
	EQUIVALENT TEMPERATURE °F.											
Calm	50	40	30	20	10	0	—10	—20	—30	—40	—50	—60
5	48	37	27	16	6	—5	—15	—26	—36	—47	—57	—68
10	40	28	16	4	—9	—21	—33	—46	—58	—70	—83	—95
15	36	22	9	—5	—18	—36	—45	—58	—72	—85	—99	—112
20	32	18	4	—10	—25	—39	—53	—67	—82	—96	—110	—124
25	50	16	0	—15	—29	—44	—59	—74	—88	—104	—118	—133
30	28	13	—2	—18	—33	—48	—63	—79	—94	—109	—125	—140
35	27	11	—4	—20	—35	—49	—67	—82	—98	—113	—129	—145
40	26	10	—6	—21	—37	—53	—69	—85	—100	—116	—132	—148

Wind speeds greater than 40 MPH have little additional effect	LITTLE DANGER FOR PROPERLY CLOTHED PERSON	INCREASING DANGER	GREAT DANGER
		DANGER FROM FREEZING OF EXPOSED FLESH	

To use the chart, find the estimated or actual wind speed in the left-hand column and the actual temperature in degrees F. in the top row. The equivalent temperature is found where these two intersect. For example, with a wind speed of 10 mph and a temperature of —10°F., the equivalent temperature is —33°F. This lies within the zone of increasing danger of frostbite, and protective measures should be taken.

CLOTHING & EQUIPMENT

DOWN CLOTHING

Down is the most efficient insulative material available at this time for use in cold weather garments. It provides a large volume of insulation for a proportionately small weight, is highly compressable and resilient which facilitates storage, and possesses good wicking properties. And for the benefit of conservationists, down is harvested from birds being raised for the meat market, so a down jacket isn't on the same ecologically frivolous level as a mink coat.

There are two types of down in use: *goose* down and *duck* down. Pound for pound, duck down is about 85% as efficient as goose—efficient here refering to the amount of space a given weight will fill.

Prime down of either type is that which comes from mature birds grown in northern climates and specially processed to assure a minimal quill and feather content.

The *color* is irrelevant to its quality, so you needn't be concerned about whether your're getting gray down or white.

Most wilderness winter jackets on the market are down-filled ones made of light, strong nylon and fitted with zippers, snaps, and hoods. They offer the ultimate in warmth and at the same time maximum comfort and freedom of movement. (A jacket weighing under 2 lbs. can keep a person comfortable at temperatures as low as minus 15°). To aid the prospective buyer, the following are construction features to look for:

Fabric. The most widely used and the most practical is ripstop nylon. In addition to resisting tears, it is also down-proof, that is, the down filling can't leak out between its fibers.

Method of Construction. There are three types of construction used in down jackets: quilt, double-quilt, and baffle.

A *quilted* jacket is one in which the outer jacket fabric is stitched through to the lining at regular intervals to create compartments for the down in much the same way a bed quilt is made.

A *double-quilted* jacket is essentially two jackets, one sewn inside the other, with seam lines alternating so that a uniform thickness of down prevails throughout. This makes for a warmer jacket than the simple quilt construction, because it eliminates the cold spots created by stitched-through seams where the down is compressed by the stitching to a thickness of a fraction of an inch (remember that it's the loft, not the quantity, of the down that creates its insulating properties). The double quilt method is used on expedition parkas, or any jacket designed for use in sub-zero environments.

Baffle construction consists of two pieces of material—an outer shell and an inner liner—with cloth dividers (baffles) sewn between them to form compartments for the down stuffing. This arrangement provides for a continuous thickness of insulation throughout the garment. Since the inner and outer materials are not sewn together, but are sewn instead to the baffles, cold spots are eliminated. Also weight is reduced since an additional layer of material isn't needed as in double quilting.

Cut. Jackets, again, like sleeping bags, should be differentially cut, that is, the lining should be smaller than the outer fabric. This creates the space in between lining and shell for the down.

Fastenings. Zippers on cold weather garments should be non-metal (nylon, Delrin, etc.) since at low temperatures, metal tends to freeze up and jam. Most jackets use snaps in addition, mainly to close a down flap over the zipper to eliminate a cold spot down the front of the jacket. This is also an extra fastening device in case the zipper breaks or jams.

Pockets may be fastened with Velcro or snaps. Velcro is better since it seals the entire pocket shut so nothing can slip out, and because it's easier to open and close with mittens or gloves on.

To conserve body warmth and keep cold breezes out, most jackets have a drawstring at the bottom. One can be added pretty easily if the jacket isn't so equipped.

Sleeve cuffs should be snugly closed with either a nylon stretch cuff or elastic, though most people find elastic uncomfortable. An alternative is a Velcro-fastened strap that wraps around the cuff.

Hoods. Hoods are usually optional on sweaters, light jackets, and expedition parkas. Though they tend to restrict lateral vision, they add considerably to the warmth of the garment. Often they are designed so they can be rolled and fastened under the collar when not in use.

Pockets. The more expensive jackets have pockets that are down filled so that they can be used as hand warmers. Light jackets and

sweaters usually skip the down filling.

An excellent source of information on jacket construction and on the properties of down and other insulative materials is Cunningham and Hansson's *Lightweight Camping Equipment and How To Make It* ($2.50; Colorado Outdoor Sports Corp., P.O. Box 5544, Denver, Colo. 80217). Down jackets can be purchased at considerable savings from the two New Zealand outfitters, Arthur Ellis and Antarctic Products, or in kit form from Frostline or Carikit.

DOWN VEST
$18 - $38
Can be worn alone or under a jacket. Small enough to stuff in a belt pack for ski or bicycle touring where you need a little extra warmth when you stop. Quilt construction.

DOWN SWEATER
$30 - $65
A light down jacket suitable for summer nights in the mountains or autumn wear. Cover it with a windproof parka, and it can double as a winter jacket. Quilt construction.

EXPEDITION PARKAS
$80 - $138
These are made for use in sub-zero conditions such as those encountered in winter mountaineering. The Alpine Designs Expedition Parka and the MPC Frosty Parka (available from The North Face) are examples of this type. Both cost in the neighborhood of $95 and are suitable for temperatures as low as minus 40°, depending on your level of activity. Double-quilt or baffle construction.

DOWN JACKET
$45 - $90
Suitable for moderate to cold conditions, depending on the quantity of down and whether quilt or double-quilt construction is employed. The North Face Puma ($47) and the Sierra Designs Whitney Parka ($57), both quilt-type jackets, are rated for temperatures as low as 10° to 15°. The Gerry Makalu ($73) and the Alpine Designs Glacier Jacket ($75), both double-quilt types, are rated to around minus 20°. Again, a windproof shell increases the range of use by as much as 20°

DOWN PANTS
$35 - $74
These are of two types: regular pants and pants that convert to a half-bag (a sleeping bag that reaches to the waist) by means of special zippers or snap arrangements. Both types are available from Holubar and other suppliers. Quilt construction.

ONE-PIECE DOWN SUITS
$85 - $125
One-piece suits are good for icy high wind conditions, though they don't allow as much freedom of movement as separate jacket and pants. They're well suited to snowmobiling where a lot of movement isn't involved and wind is a factor. Maybe they'd be good for winter motorcycling, too. Eddie Bauer sells snowmobile suits, $87 to $120. Holubar makes a one-piece Supersuit, which provides an all-over 2 inches of down insulation, $125.

DOWN BOOTS
$9 - $15
Down boots can be worn around camp, in a sleeping bag for extra warmth, or for what Colin Fletcher calls "brief excursions out of your tent into snow."

OTHER CLOTHES

UNDERWEAR
$5 - $15
There are lots of different kinds of underwear. Fishnet is considered by many to be the most efficient, because the mesh traps air against the skin which acts as insulation. Other kinds of underwear are available in various mixtures of synthetics, wool, and cotton, and there's always the classic woolen long johns. Of course, half their success results from the body heat generated by all the scratching and squirming that commences about ten seconds after you put them on.

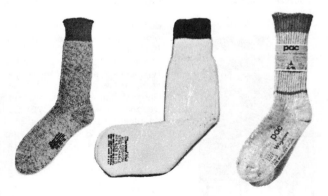

SOCKS
$1 - $6
Here, too, wool is the best material available. Wear two pairs: a thin finely woven wool inner sock and a heavy, coarsely woven outer sock. If boot space permits, a third pair can be added for extra warmth. Just remember to keep them loose-fitting so the toes are always free to wiggle (this boosts circulation). Silk or Olefin liner socks offer an alternative to the wool liner, but wool is the warmest.

BOOTS
$6 - $100
Winter boots, very simply, have to keep the feet warm and dry. The all-time favorite is the G.I. Korea boot, a double vapor rubber boot that sells for around $20 in surplus stores. A standard hiking or work boot with a couple pair of wool socks and some sort of waterproof cover for wet snow is fine, or there's the L.L. Bean Maine Hunting Shoe or the Canadian Sorel style boot, both of which have leather uppers and waterproof lowers. Incidentally, when snowshoeing with boots, watch the sharp edges of your soles. They can chafe through webbing in a hurry.

Canadian
Sorel Boot

L.L. Bean
Maine Hunting Boot

MUKLUKS
$35 - $60
A mukluk is a soft cold-weather boot invented by the Eskimos. Often it is lined with fur and usually made of sealskin or reindeer hide. Authentic Eskimo and Indian mukluks are beautiful, expensive, and hard to find. Iroqrafts, Ltd. and the Alaska Native Arts and Crafts Cooperative Assn. occasionally have them for sale. Modern versions in synthetics and leather are for sale by Eddie Bauer and other suppliers.

LEATHER COMPOUNDS
All leather boots need occasional treatment with some leather compound to restore natural oils and especially in winter use for waterproofing. The kind of compound used depends on the boot design and how the leather was tanned. Rock climbing, mountain boots, and many hiking boots are chrome or silicone tanned to achieve a fairly rigid leather for maximum foot support. Hunting and moccasin type boots are more apt to be oil tanned for suppleness. So when purchasing a boot, be sure to find out what tanning process was used. Chrome and silicone tanned boots require wax or silicone compounds like Sno-Seal or Leath-R-Seal. Use Snow-Proof, shoe oil or neatsfoot oil for oil-tanned leathers. A word of caution: be extremely careful in using any preparation requiring that the boot itself be heated. Overdoing it just a little could ruin the leather completely, so be sure you know what you're doing before you start.

Watch Cap

Face Mask

Balaclava

Avalanche

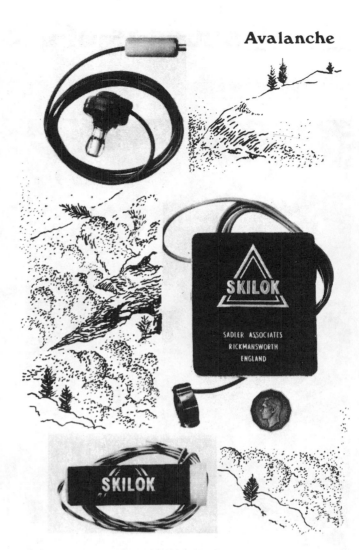

HEADGEAR
$1 and up

There are a couple of great Army surplus hats that have visors to shield the eyes and lined flaps that can be pulled down over the ears. These aren't real easy to find, but if you can get your hands on one, grab it. Eddie Bauer's Arctic Cap, $13, is a near match. Climbers generally prefer a visorless hat that allows for full upward vision. A wool watchcap ($1 on up) can be worn alone, under a hood, or as a nightcap. Wool balaclavas cover the entire head and most of the face, roll up into a cap, are super warm, and cost about $4. Eddie Bauer's sells down-filled watch caps, $10, and even a down-filled face mask, $15. Deerskin face masks run about $5 and are sold by most winter sports dealers. Ski shops sell wool face masks for a couple of bucks, and Army surplus ones are even cheaper.

MITTENS, GLOVES
$3 - $5

Mittens are warmer than gloves because they keep the four fingers together, combining their warmth. The only problem with them is that they limit manual dexterity (try tying knots or loading a camera with a pair on). An efficient solution to this is to wear a pair of light gloves under the mittens so that you can pull the mittens off and still work with a reasonable amount of protection to your hands. With respect to materials, wool is by far the best for the outer mitten. It keeps its insulative qualities even when wet and dirty. Down-filled mittens are extremely warm, but lose their insulative properties completely when wet. Waterproof shell mittens of coated nylon can be carried along to wear over regular ones for use in rain or wet snow. A good material for the inner glove is silk or nylon. Though these gloves aren't very warm, they don't restrict the use of the fingers and can protect the skin for up to four or five minutes at a time in sub-zero weather.

HANDWARMERS
$3 - $10

Nice to warm up with. Some run on a fluid and others on solid stick fuel. Great World, P.O. Box 250, West Simsbury, Conn. 06092, sells one for $3 that runs on charcoal sticks. The sticks are $1.50 a dozen.

AVALANCHE VICTIM LOCATOR
About $68

Saddler Associates, a British outfit, manufactures an electronic locating device called the Skilok detection system. It consists of a 5 oz. beacon, 3-1/2" long by 2" diameter, and a 4 oz. receiver with earpiece and 65' of search wire. The beacon transmits very low frequency signals, which when covered by an avalanche are capacitively coupled into the snow. The electrostatic field thus produced is detected by the receiver and converted into an audible tone. The intensity of the tone is used to locate the victim. During tests in the Alps, beacons were buried in snow at depths of 5 feet and were detected from an average range of 60 feet. Cost of the beacon is $18, and the receiver, $50. For more information check with Eugene Huber of Deep Powder House Ski Shop, 671 East 9620 South, Sandy, Utah 84070. He's the U.S. distributor for Skilok.

AVALANCHE CORD
About $2

This is a bright colored cord carried by climbers and skiers in areas where an avalanche might be expected. The cord is tied around the waist and drags behind as you move along. The idea is that if an avalanche does hit, enough of the cord will remain unburied to guide rescuers to your aid. Holubar sells it in 50 foot lengths marked at 6 foot intervals.

sources of clothing & equipment

SIERRA DESIGNS

ORIGINAL 60/40 MOUNTAIN PARKA

Glacier

Our most popular 2-man tent, the Glacier sets up neatly, tightly and quickly in all terrain and weather. Inside, catenary-cut lower side walls, consistently high ridge seam and triangular alcove create space for two and gear, room for three in a pinch. The Glacier's A-frame pole construction with balanced guy-line fastenings and taut pitch give a low tent profile, little flap in the wind. Inside, it's a comfortable tent. One end has a large zippered door. At the other end is a fully enclosed alcove with tunnel door and cookhole. Both doors are backed by insect netting for summertime ventilation. Inside, net pockets hold miscellaneous gear. The custom-fitted waterproof fly-sheet overlaps the waterproof lower side walls to protect against all angles of foul weather.

Colors: Blue, Green or Orange Total weight: 7 lbs. 11 oz. Packed size: 8" × 20" Price: $170.00

Parka has four, large velcro-closed pockets on front and a full back pocket with zipper closing. Cuffs are gusseted and close with velcro. They can be operated with gloves and snugly adjusted over gloves or left wide open for ventilation. Hood draw sliders are on inner facing and will not beat you to death in the wind. Front closure is snap/flap set over a no. 10 Y.K.K. nylon zipper. Parka is fully lined through sleeves and body with nylon. Hood is double layer of 60/40.

Sizes: XS(30-32), S(34-36), M(38-40), L(42-44), XL(46-48)
Colors: Navy, Green, Orange Aver. total wgt.: -1 lb. 12 oz.
Price: $57.00

SIERRA DESIGNS
4th & Addison Sts., Berkeley, Calif. 94710
Sierra Designs is a beautiful outfit. Everything we hear about their products and service is very positive—innovative designs, finest materials and workmanship, and orders promptly filled. Their sleeping bags are all 1.5 oz. ripstop nylon, differentially cut, with baffled construction. The Omni, a mummy with 36 oz. prime duck down fill, costs about $120 (all specs are for large size). Their warmest is the Model 200 mummy, 42 oz. prime goose down fill, V-tube baffle construction; cost, about $145. In the clothing line, their 60/40 parka, a windbreaker, runs about $57, and is probably the best to be found anywhere. Other garments include a down vest for about $31; the Whitney Parka, $45; and the Inyo Parka, $82. Except for the Inyo, which features an outer windbreaker shell of 60/40 cloth, Sierra Designs jackets have Supernyl shells and linings. All are duck down filled and of quilted construction. Their tents are of the finest workmanship available. All three are suited to cold-weather use, feature tube-type openings and waterproof fly and floor. They run from $40 to $300. Write for a copy of their 51-page color catalog, 50¢.

Powderhorn Mountaineering

Wind River Parka

POWDERHORN MOUNTAINEERING
Box 1660, Jackson, Wyo. 83001
Powderhorn has been in operation for about 10 years now, but still they keep their product range small and quality high. Their line consists mainly of jackets and parkas including the Wind River Parka, a 60/40 windbreaker with waterproof nylon yoke, $66; the Down River Parka, same as the Wind River, but with 6.7 oz. of down, $94; the Bighorn, a short down jacket appropriate for general wear or skiing, $73; and the Hornito, a pullover windbreaker, $44. Powderhorn also manufactures children's jackets and snowsuits, rain ponchos, wind pants, mittens and down booties. Write the above address for their descriptive literature.

Royalight II

The "Go-Anywhere" Two Man Tent!

107003A: ROYALIGHT II TENT (Complete w/poles, rainfly, stakes)
Av. Wt. 6 lbs. 14 oz. (complete) **$135.00**

HOLUBAR
Box 7, Boulder, Colo. 80302
Good line of down clothing including the Paragon Incalescent Parka, $180, and the Expedition II Pants, which can be changed into a half-bag in a snap, $54; wool duds, mountain tents, glacier cream, snow goggles, the Hivernale double boot, $90; leather snow-proofing compounds, high altitude sleeping bags, and half-bags. Nice 64-page color catalog, free.

Alpine Designs™
A GENERAL RECREATION, INC. COMPANY

ARCTIC SLEEPER
This is the most popular sleeper we make. It has all of the "High Loft" features, a 5-inch slant wall construction and is filled with 2 lbs. of Prime Northern Goose Down (medium size bag), which lofts to a full 8 inches. The Arctic is a bag which can be used year-round, though you might get pretty hot in it on a warm summer night. Available in Royal Blue..$140

ALPINE DESIGNS
6185 East Arapahoe, Boulder, Colo. 80303
Manufacturer of high-quality general recreation equipment: clothing, packs, sleeping bags, and tents. Their Cirque Jacket is very popular. It's a goose down-filled nylon jacket with double-quilt construction, lined hood and snap-closed, down-filled pockets. Price, about $55. Other items include a down sweater, jacket, vest, wind parka and gaiters. Their cold-weather bags are goose down mummies of 1.9 oz. nylon that run from $115 to $170. Their fine mountain tents cost from $125 to $165. Send for their free color catalog and price list.

ORLON BALACLAVA. Looks good and gives maximum all-weather face protection. 100% Orlon double fabric knit. Colors: black, navy, red.
.........wt. 3 oz. $2.75

SKI HUT
1615 University Ave., Berkeley, Calif. 94703
Ski Hut is the manufacturer of Trailwise recreational equipment, and they handle other people's stuff too. In the cold weather department they include high altitude tents with flap door on one end, and tunnel door on the other, sleeping bags, a complete line of down and wool clothing, gaiters, snowshoes and bindings, and skis. Good quality gear though prices seem a little high. 60-page color catalog, free.

SKI HUT FITZROY.... 3 lbs. 3 oz. ......$160 ....

THE NORTH FACE

Down Vest

Mountain Parka

The North Face mountain parka is designed to combine insulation, wind resistance, and protection from rain into one article of clothing. It is a two-ply garment, with 60/40 cloth on the outside and 1.9 oz. Ripstop nylon lining. The blend of 60% nylon, 40% cotton breathes in dry weather, yet swells slightly in rain to provide water-resistance. The zipper is a double slider nylon coil type, with a 2″ wide snap flap.

The mountain parka's four pockets include two bellows pockets with storm flaps, a vertical zippered outside pocket and a zippered inside pocket. The hood has a drawstring closure, and an inner drawstring at the waist provides temperature control.

Sizes	S, M, L, XL
Colors	Navy blue, Flaming orange, tan
Weight	20 oz. average
Price	$49.50

Sizes	S, M, L
Colors	Heavy Cobalt Blue, Flaming Orange
Weight	12 oz. average
Price	$29.50

THE NORTH FACE
P.O. Box 2399, Station A, Berkeley, Calif. 94702
North Face makes good stuff, and their on-the-move catalog will make you feel like you're not with it if you're not out climbing a mountain or skiing across a glacier. Their sleeping bags, available in a wide comfort range, are made of 1.9 oz. ripstop nylon with continuous coil nylon zippers, differential cut, and interior slant-wall baffle construction. Their cold-weather bags have goose down filling, and run from about $98 for the Superlight, a mummy bag with 24 oz. of down (comfortable to about 10°), to about $175 for the North Face bag which has 42 oz. of filling (comfortable to about -30°). North Face's winter clothing includes the Mountain Parka, a 60/40 cloth windbreaker parka, $50; a down vest for around $30; the Serow, a down-filled 60/40 parka suitable for sub-zero temperatures, $80; the Puma parka, $47; and the North Face parka, $95. They also sell fishnet underwear, $9 per set; socks and wool shirts. Write for their free 45-page color catalog.

The Alaska Native Arts & Crafts Cooperative Assn., Inc.

ALASKA NATIVE ARTS COOPERATIVE ASSN.
Box 889, Juneau, Alaska 99801
Authentic Aleut, Eskimo, and Indian handicrafts. Beautiful baskets and ivory figures. Eskimo mukluks of seal or reindeer skin are occasionally offered for sale, depending on their availability from individual craftsmen. This is the only source of the real thing that we have on hand. Can anyone help out? 24-page catalog, $1.

Waban PolarGuard Parka - $48

Mansfield PolorGuard Parka - $58

EASTERN MOUNTAIN SPORTS
1041 Commonwealth Ave., Boston, Mass. 02215
If you want to know how good and informative a catalog can be, send for Eastern Mountain Sports'. It's fully indexed, completely illustrated, and the descriptions of each item are thorough, with exact specifications, weights and dimensions given for everything sold. The manufacturer's name is also given for every item listed, which is something a lot of catalogs, for some mysterious reason, don't do. In addition, for ease of comparison, EMS includes tables of comparative specifications for things like tents, stoves, sleeping bags and down parkas. Along with equipment by major manufacturers (Sierra Designs, The North Face, Alpine Designs, etc.), EMS sells its own brands at very reasonable prices. Their Dhaulagiri sleeping bag, a ripstop mummy, contains 3 lbs. of duck down for a total loft of 11 inches and is rated to around minus 50°. The large size costs about $140, and weighs 5 lbs. 11 ozs. The EMS Mt. Robson is rated to minus 20°, costs about $170 for the large size, and weighs 4 lbs. 9 ozs. EMS brand jackets include the Flume sweater, $32; the Nylon Down Parka, $40; and the Yeti, a 60/40 parka, $60. Other winter gear includes snowshoes, cross-country skis, winter boots, gaiters, overboots, socks, hats and gloves. Their catalog is a great reference source, $1.

Down Hood

G315—(Taffeta)
G316—(Ripstop)
Designed to fit our Down Sweater, Super Sweater and Makalu Jacket. the down hood is very warm and functional. Made of Prime down with all nylon fabrics. Fits all sizes.

Approx. Weight: 3 ozs.
Colors: G315 Taffeta: Blue Grass, Chocolate Brown, Print, Gold, Midnight Blue
        G316 Ripstop: Blue, Green, Vail, Red, Beige, Orange

Net Underwear

100% cotton in wide mesh pattern that creates hundreds of small airways for efficient ventilation. Makes air barrier between body and outer clothing. Allows perspiration to vaporize instead of dampening clothing.
C701—Undershirt
Sizes: Small, Medium, Large, Extra Large
Approx. Weight: 8 ozs.
Color: White
C702—Underpants
Sizes: Small, Medium, Large
Approx. Weight: 8 ozs.
Color: White

GERRY DIV., Outdoor Sports Industries, Inc.
P.O. Box 5544, Denver, Colo. 80217
Gerry Cunningham is the Thomas Edison of the wilderness recreation field. He's designed and invented some of the cleverest lightweight equipment around and co-authored with Margaret Hansson the very useful *Lightweight Camping Equipment and How to Make It.* His winter clothing includes a down vest, light down sweater, Super Sweater, Makalu jacket and Arctic Jacket. His cold-weather bags range from the Backpacker, a mummy bag comfortable to around 0°F, to the Expedition sleeper, comfortable to around minus 40°. The Himalayan tent is especially designed for high altitude and polar use where strong winds are a constant factor. It comes complete with rain fly, frost liner, snow flaps, poles and wands, totaling 12 lbs. 12 ozs. Gerry knows all about keeping warm and gives you all the technical details in his excellent booklet, *How to Keep Warm* (free from the above address). Write for the free 16-page color catalog. (Incidentally, Cunningham himself has sold out to Outdoor Sports Industries, Inc., and is now making gear for the small sailboat racing crowd.)

Arctic Jacket

G300—The ultimate in down parkas. the Arctic has been designed to handle the toughest expedition conditions. Double quilt construction that is actually two jackets in one. Prime northern down throughout. Extra heavy-duty front zipper covered by a large flap. Two rows of snaps designed for bivouacking. Sleeves have zippers for controlled ventilation. Handwarmer down-filled pockets with zippers under large cargo pockets on outside with velcro closures. Drawstring with delrin cord lock at bottom of jacket. Attached down-filled hood with velcro and drawstring closure. Fabric of 1.9 ripstop nylon.

Sizes: Small: Chest 32"-36": Arm 32"
       Medium: Chest 36"-40": Arm 33"
       Large: Chest 40"-44": Arm 34"
       X Large: Chest 44"-48": Arm 35"
Approx. Weight: 2 lbs. 11 ozs.
Loft: 3"
Colors: Orange, Blue, Green

Makalu Jacket

G250—Just one step down from the expedition parka. the Makalu is constructed with a double quilt of prime down so there are no cold spots. Very generously cut for additional warmth and comfort. Overlapping snap flap covers a tough nylon zipper. Down-filled pockets with velcro closure flaps. Sleeves are amply filled with down. Cuffs have snaps and elastic to control ventilation. Drawstring in hem at bottom of jacket with lace locks. Shell of 1.9 luxurious ripstop nylon. Snaps on collar for optional down-filled hood.

Sizes: Small: Chest 32"-36": Arm 32"
       Medium: Chest 36"-40": Arm 33"
       Large: Chest 40"-44": Arm 34"
       X-Large: Chest 44"-48": Arm 35"
Approx. Weight: 2 lbs. 6 ozs.
Loft: 2½"
Colors: Blue, Green, Orange

165

Fairy down

ARTHUR ELLIS AND CO., LTD.
Private Bag, Dunedin, New Zealand

Here's another New Zealand dealer with good prices on quality down products. Sir Edmund Hillary used their bags in Antarctica, New Zealand, the Swiss Alps and on his Everest expedition. Their cold-weather sleeping bags range from the Arctic, a cambric mummy with 2 lbs. duck down fill, chevron compartments, box wall construction, and hood (total approximate weight, 5 lbs.; price, about $45), to the Everest Sierra, a ripstop nylon mummy, with chevron compartments, box wall construction, 3½ lbs. goose down (total weight 4 lbs. 15 ozs.; price, about $97). Winter jackets include the Stratton Ski Jacket, a lightweight down quilt construction jacket with hood, $40; the Camp V Duvet, a goose down double-quilt nylon jacket with zippered down pockets and hood, $93; the Alpine Jacket, a nylon expedition jacket of goose down with baffled construction, down hood and pockets, $97. The warmest of their jackets is the Polar which features a wind-breaker shell, ripstop nylon liner, and two hoods: a nylon fur-lined inner hood and an outer windbreaker hood. Fill is goose down. Price is $138 with fur-trimmed hood, $130 without trim. Other items: down trousers, $57; down mitts, $24; down boots, $33. All items are subject to a 7% duty. Their 21-page catalog is free.

POLAR DOWN JACKET

Qual. No.	Size ft.	in.		ft.	in.	Price
WITH FUR TRIMMED HOOD						
468011	5	10	to	6	0	**$137.80**
468012	5	8	to	5	10	**$137.80**
468013	5	6	to	5	8	**$137.80**
WITHOUT FUR TRIMMED HOOD						
468061	5	10	to	6	0	**$129.60**
468062	5	8	to	5	10	**$129.60**
468063	5	6	to	5	8	**$129.60**

ANTARCTIC PRODUCTS

Highest expedition quality

THE ANTARCTICA MUMMY   PRICE $51

100% Down Filled

Rip stop nylon throughout. Top grade pure selected goose down filled. Built in hood and full taper. Exceptionally small fully baffled down compartments. Differentially cut. 30 inch heavy duty nylon zipper (bags do not zip together). Down flap prevents heat loss at zipper. Expedition designed and tested. Color blue. Please see pages 5 and 6 for further details.

for heights to:	order size:	bag length	total Wgt.	down Wgt.
5ft 8in	standard	80in	3lb 12oz	2lb 4oz
6ft 4in	large	85in	4lb 4oz	2lb 8oz

over 6ft 4in   not made (order Antarctica in X large)

ANTARCTIC PRODUCTS
P.O. Box 223, Nelson, New Zealand

If you can wait the four to eight weeks it takes for delivery, you won't find better prices on top-notch down sleeping bags and clothing anywhere. Antarctic's South Polar 1 Parka is a nylon chevroned expedition jacket with box baffling construction, wool cuffs, nylon zipper, and drawstrings at hood, waist, and bottom. Large size weighs 2 lbs., 6 oz. It compares to American-made jackets in the $70 to $100 price range but only costs about $55. They have a goose down ski jacket for $36, down mittens for $15, pile-lined down boots with leather soles for about $20, and a down vest for about $18. Their expedition sleeping bags are of ripstop nylon, differentially cut, goose down filled, feature baffled construction, and have nylon zippers and drawstring tops. The bag's overall loft exceeds 4 inches. The Antarctica Mummy, large size, contains 2 lbs., 12 oz. down and costs $55. Catalog prices include postage and insurance. You pay a duty that amounts to about 7% of the purchase price, but even at that, their parkas and bags are close to one-third less than the price of comparable American gear. Send an airmail letter, 31¢, requesting their free 17-page catalog, and if you place an order be sure to also send it airmail. Surface mail to New Zealand can take as long as eight weeks.

PALLEY SUPPLY CO.

11630 Burke St., Los Nietos, Calif. 90606

Palley claims to be the world's largest surplus dealer, and you'll believe it when you see their catalog. Unfortunately it's mostly machinery, but they do have some good, genuine, surplus cold weather gear, including sheepskin flying pants, $9, white ski troop parkas, $4, goggles, arctic face masks, cross country skis, and a variety of jackets. Their 256-page catalog is available on request.

WHITE ARMY CAMOUFLAGE SKI PARKA

Made of pure white, water-resistant twill slipover style. Large and roomy to be worn over other clothing if desired. Has drawstring in hood for snug fit around the face.

Two breast pockets with flaps and drawstring bottom. Adjustable wrist straps on cuffs. Ideal for protection from rain, snow, etc.

$3.95

USAF WHITE WINTER BOOT

Heavy grade felt uppers with sturdy canvas cuff trimmed in white leather with straps and buckles. Midsole is extra thick felt with non-skid rubber tap sole. Special heavy duty cord stitching. Sizes: extra large only

CL-12SU   **$3.95 pr.**

Northwest

"EIS" PARKA by ASCENTE

MPC WIND PANTS
(recommended for breaking wind)

NORTHWEST RECREATIONAL SUPPLY
P.O. Box 70105, Seattle, Wash. 98107

Northwest is a general outfitter with an emphasis on cold weather gear. They carry tents and sleeping bags by Mountain Products Corp (MPC). MPC tents with waterproof fly and floor run from $80 for the two-man Pocket Tent (4 lbs., 14 oz.) to $150 for the two-man Mountain Tent (8 lbs.). MPC cold weather sleeping bags range from the Sierra, a ripstop mummy with 1-1/2 lbs. of goose down, $90, to the Northarc Twin, a ripstop tapered rectangular bag with 4 lbs. of goose down in the large size, $140. Northwest also carries Tubbs snowshoes and bindings, and avalanche cord of red braided nylon (also suitable for lashing gear or for tent guy lines) for under a nickle a foot. Winter jackets by Ascente are made of ripstop nylon with goose down filling and non-metal zippers, run from $20 for a vest to around $55 for the EIS Parka with hood. Northwest's catalog is free.

MOOR & MOUNTAIN

MOOR & MOUNTAIN
63 Park St., Andover, Mass. 01810

A full selection of winter wilderness equipment—parkas, tents, sleeping bags, skis, snowshoes, boots—we could go on forever. Their cold weather bags are ripstop nylon, goose down filled and are reasonably priced from $50 to $180. The Moor & Mountain Down Jacket costs about $64, the Expedition Parka, about $120. Insulated winter boots (similar to the G.I. Korea boot) run around $72. Their 64-page Fall-Winter catalog is free.

CANNONDALE 2-MAN BACKPACKING TENT (Flame-retardant) — We've taken this tent backpacking in the Adirondacks, and winter camping in the White Mountains with good results. With its unique pole structure and roomy vestibule, this is a 3½-season tent. It has much to offer for backpacking, canoe camping, and moderate winter camping.

$175

M & M M M

MOOR & MOUNTAIN HAS "REAL" MICKEY MOUSE BOOTS — New production to exact specifications of the Korean sub-zero boot. Multi-layers of felt between two layers of neoprene rubber. Third layer of rubber with inflatable air channel (not of use to mountaineers). Sizes: 7-14

Cat. No. 636: M & M M.M. Boot   Wt.:9.00 lbs./pr. Sz. 9 $88.50

1 **INSULATED BOOTS** — For winter walking, work or sport where the foot is apt to be in ice, snow or water; double layer felt insulation with a separating air space around foot and 6" up the ankle. The soles are of Vibram composition with deep lugs similar to that used on our climbing and hiking boots; will give a superior grip and outlast two standard rubber boot soles. Boots are 12" high; have steel arch support; olive. They will keep feet comfortable with one pair of heavy socks and some foot movement in zero temperatures. Speed laces. Sizes: 6 to 14 whole sizes.

Cat. No. 617   Wt.: 5.00 lbs. $72.00

167

WINTER BIVOUACKING

FROSTLINE
452 Burbank, Broomfield, Colo. 80020

Buy a kit and make your own down gear, and save some money. Frostline has kits for parkas, pants, booties, vests, hoods, and gloves. Particularly worthy of mention are their children's down clothing kits. They also have kits for cold weather sleeping bags. Prices average about half the cost of ready-made gear. Materials are top quality. Good, descriptive 31-page catalog is free.

DOWN BOOTIE   KIT $5.95

Designed to keep your feet warm! Not down socks to be worn inside boots, but rugged Down Booties. Wear them around camp or in the cabin, summer or winter. **Vinyl-impregnated waterproof Nylon soles** are textured so you can stand up in slick snow. Ripstop Nylon uppers and prime goose down make these soft and warm. ¼" foam Ensolite insole insulation. Elastic at ankle prevents the Bootie from working down under your heel. No cold seams. All parts are pre-cut everything included. Colors: Uppers—Navy Blue, Medium Blue, Forest Green and Red. Sole and Welt strip is bright Gold with all colors of uppers. Five sizes available: For correct fit SEND YOUR FOOT OUTLINE MADE WITH SOCKS ON—the socks you will be wearing inside the Booties.

Weight: (size 9-10) 8 oz.

Aspen Jackets

A hip-length, light down jacket with down baffled Nylon zipper extending up into the collar. Sizes Sm-X-Lg open from bottom as well as top. Pre-set snaps on collar allow you to attach the C-11 Down Hood, not included. All Ripstop Nylon materials. Two-layer quilt construction, plump, high collar, elastic cuffs, feather light, toasty warm. Average thickness is 1" with 8 oz. of down (medium). **Velcro-flap-closed down-filled patch pockets included.** A belt may be added to this jacket (illustrated) with the purchase of Belt Kit No. C-22, page 10. Colors: Navy Blue, Medium Blue, Forest Green and Red. Fits into a B-27 Stuff Sack, not included. See "How to Determine Your Size" to get best fit. Sleeve lengths are maximum and may be shortened to fit during construction.

$25.95

Children's Highland Parka
HC 110

colors: navy or red Supernyl
sizes: ages 6, 9, 12

CARIKIT
P.O. Box 7, Boulder, Colo. 80302

Another supplier of kits for down clothing including parkas, vests, sweaters, booties, mittens, and hoods. Also cold weather bags. Prices are about 15 to 20 percent higher than Frostline's. Carikit also has children's parkas. Sixteen-page color catalog is available on request.

L. L. Bean, Inc.

L.L. BEAN
Freeport, Maine 04032

Bean is an old (60 years) reputable woodsman's outfitter. Their gear runs on more or less traditional lines with a lot of fine wool garments, moccasins and moccasin boots, and the like. Of special interest to the winter traveler are their Icelandic wool toques—one of the warmest wools available—$8; wool shirts, $20 to $21; complete line of cold-weather underwear; snowshoes, $44 to $80; Splitkein Touring Skis, $52 to $63, and accessories; and the Bean Down Mackinaw, a hooded windbreaker jacket with prime goose down fill, $74. If we had to pick just one Bean item to recommend, it would have to be the Insulated Hunting Shoe, one of the best winter boots around. It has rubber bottoms and leather uppers. The bottoms are lined with close-celled foam with an additional thick foam innersole. Uppers are of water resistant silicone tanned top-grain leather. Prices are $37 for 10-inch and $40 for 12-inch boots. Bean also carries Silva compasses, Gerry and Blacks sleeping bags, and Kelty packs and frames, several tents, and many backpacking items. Free 120-page catalog.

Eddie Bauer

DOWN FACE MASK

Size: One size fits all.
Color: Beige.
0154 Face Mask.....

ppd. **$16.95**

RECREATIONAL EQUIPMENT, INC.

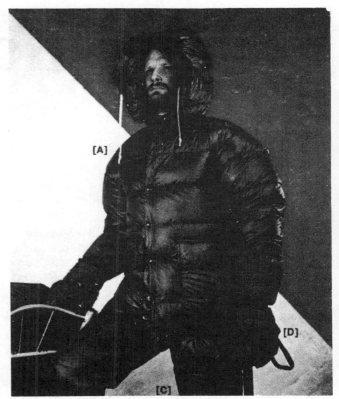

RECREATIONAL EQUIPMENT, INC. (REI)
1525 11th Ave., Seattle, Wash. 98122
Recreational Equipment is a membership co-op through which members receive dividends based on their purchases over a given period. The dividends can be applied to the purchase of more equipment. Jim Whittaker, one of the guys who runs the place, was a member of the first successful American assault on Everest, and as might be expected, the co-op sells a lot of mountaineering and cold weather equipment and clothing—some they make themselves and some they buy from other people. They sell a complete selection of downhill and touring ski wear, expedition down parkas and pants, down jackets, vests, sweaters, and bivouac pants (convert to a half bag), parkas, wool shirts, downhill and touring skis, boots and accessories, snowshoes and bindings, Raichle hiking boots, cold-weather sleeping bags that run from $70 to $140 and the Crestline Expedition, a cold weather tent, $127. There is a Fall-Winter catalog and a Spring-Summer catalog, both free, both complete reference sources for wilderness recreation equipment.

[A] **Denali Expedition Parka.** No expense has been spared in producing our finest quality, cold weather parka. This parka is made using double quilt construction which has proven to be the simplest yet most efficient design to insure maximum warmth. Both the outer and inner layers are made of 1.9 oz. ripstop nylon and filled with Prime Northern *Silvergrey* Goose Down; the Medium size contains 27¾ oz. of Down. A large No. 10 *Delrin* zipper with a 3″ snap-down overflap completely seals the front from the cold while a second row of snaps inside the zipper allows for ventilation during periods of warmer weather.
FE1 Medium Size Weight, 4 lbs. $109.00

Bean's Insulated Hunting Shoe

MOUNTAIN SAFETY RESEARCH (MSR)
631 S. 96th St., Seattle, Wash. 98108
MSR features a nice 3- to 4-man tunnel tent with 3 supporting hoops complete with snow flaps. It has a double-layer roof to prevent condensation. The inner roof is of uncoated 1.5 oz. ripstop nylon, outer is .75 oz. coated ripstop. Floor is coated 2 oz. taffeta which extends 2 in. up the sides. Price is $236 with two zip doors. Other MSR winter expeditioning gear includes foot sacks and sleeping bags, parkas, down vests, overpants, booties and mittens, plus hand and body warmers. For more info, drop a card to the above address.

EDDIE BAUER
P.O. Box 3700, Seattle, Wash. 98124
Bauer's catalog is slick, glossy, and gentlemanly with a hunter-fisherman-country squire image. Their products aren't cheap, but they have a long-standing reputation for quality. Bauer has a wider variety of down garments than we've seen anywhere else—down watch caps, $12; down face masks, $17; down socks, $8, and four different down vests, $20 to $30; in addition to basic down stuff like sleeping bags, parkas, underwear, pillows, and comforters. Snowmobile suits, Sorel boots, and mukluks of silicone-treated cowhide, $36, are some items of special interest. Write for their free 144-page un-indexed color catalog.

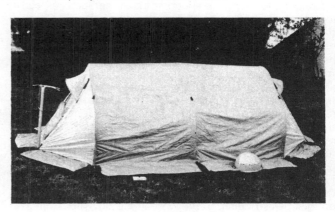

snowshoeing

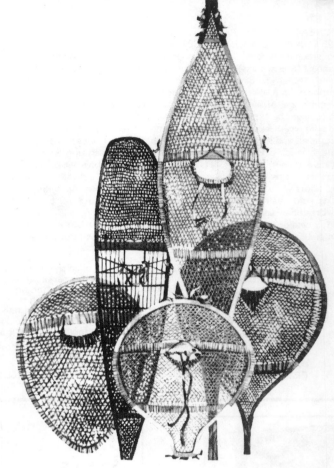

For the modern outdoorsman snowshoes still represent a prime means of locomotion in deep snow. While skis partially offset the advantages of snowshoes, their use in back country is limited. Considerable skill is required to handle skis in unbroken snow and on wooded slopes—especially uphill. Also, many say that a heavy pack reduces any of the advantages of skis over snowshoes in rough country. In addition snowshoes are lighter than skis and one is less apt to sprain an ankle from a fall—a definite safety factor when far back in the mountains.

The bearpaw snowshoe is the easiest to use and is excellent for extremely rough country where great maneuverability is required. It is standard with surveyors and hunters. The beavertail or Maine shoe is the most popular type. It gives a little better weight distribution than the bearpaw and is good for varying conditions. The Alaskan finds limited use and is for fast travel on flat country—where skis can do just as well.

Generally the snowshoe should be balanced but not at the physical center of the shoe. As the foot is lifted in the harness the tail of the snowshoe should drop back and trail in the snow. If this were not the case, the shoe would spill the runner forward with each step. The toe of the shoe should be slightly curved up. This allows better horizontal control and avoids any slicing through snow banks. In hill climbing, however, a large upward curve means greater difficulty. So a happy medium must be reached, as has been done with most commercially available snowshoes.

To improve the maneuverability of some types of snowshoes, the extreme tail may be sawed off. This should be done only with the greatest care, and reinforcement should be added to the frame. Snowshoe traction is of course considerably less than that of boots. This lack of traction can become a problem when climbing, though it can be noticeably boosted by wrapping rawhide around the frame.

The Frame. The best woods for frame construction are, in order of desirability: hickory, white ash and yellow birch. Hickory is heavier but most reliable. Make sure that the grain is straight and that there are no knots in the frame; especially look for knots covered with a thick coat of varnish. Check the mortising for strong joints. The crosspiece in front of your toe and the other parallel and behind your heel must bear your weight and hence be firmly joined to the outer frame.

The Webbing. The webbing gives the snowshoe its flotation and bears much of the weight of the runner. Caribou rawhide makes the best webbing owing to its long life. Since this is difficult to find nowadays, most manufacturers have resorted to moose, horse, or cow hide. All of these hides are tough enough not to sag or absorb water. The mesh size depends largely on where the snowshoe is to be used. In the East snow is comparatively wet and heavy, so a large mesh is desirable, because this wet snow will not easily accumulate on the open stringing. In the West and North, snow falls at very low temperatures and is either granular or very fluffy; hence, a small mesh is desirable in these areas.

The Harness. The harness serves to fasten the foot to the snowshoe and is the most important part of it. If it is loose and poorly fitted, the snowshoe will be difficult to control. Good ready-made harnesses are available through most outfitters with the Beck neoprene harness being a popular choice. Trappers, Indians and other seasoned snowshoers, however, usually prefer the "snowshoer" knot and their own strings. These strings, made of either moosehide, calfskin, or one-inch lamp wick material, include one strip about four feet long and another optional two-foot strip for the toe strap. One of the advantages of this rig is the ease with which the snowshoer can free himself in the event of a fall. Also, the strap is readily replaceable when worn out.

Footwear. The best footwear for snowshoeing is a pair of high pack or doe skin moccasins. These, with additional insulated socks, are just as warm as regular boots and somewhat more comfortable. It's a good idea to buy your high packs about one half to a full size larger than normal to allow for additional socks. One advantage of moccasins is that they serve to protect the snowshoe webbing and thus add extra years of life to the shoe.

The snow mountaineer has somewhat of a problem, since moccasins do not make for such good climbing once the snowshoes are discarded. Changing to boots in midroute is out, so the only solution is to wear boots with your snowshoes. With proper care this is not as bad as some would have you believe, but be sure there isn't any metal on the boot bottoms that might cut the rawhide lacing.

Snowshoeing Technique. Of the three major winter

sports—skiing, skating and snowshoeing—the last is by far the easiest to learn. Snowshoeing requires only that you step a little higher, wider and farther. The basic technique can be picked up in a hundred yards of your first trip and it is not necessary that you walk with your feet spread too wide apart, as it is okay if the inner edges of the frames glide over each other with each step. The trick is to limber up and achieve an easy swinging motion. Avoid tensing your muscles and you will be able to go miles on the deepest snow without undue fatigue.

Snowshoes don't always float on the very top surface of the snow. In soft snow they will sink as much as eight or ten inches, so when traveling through the bush, especially in deep soft snow, strive to keep an eye out for submerged snags which could cause a broken shoe. Watch also for snow pockets around trees and over little evergreens which might cause you to plummet head first into the snow. The ability to recognize these hidden hollows is mostly a matter of experience and of knowing the woods.

If you're planning to travel any distance remember to carry some spare rawhide strings and buckskin thongs as an emergency repair kit.

As one becomes more adept with snowshoes, he will probably want to find out how fast he can really move on the "webs." Up Canada ways, snowshoe races have become a regular part of the winter scene. The record stands at 100 yards in 10 seconds; one mile in 4½ minutes, and five miles in 31 minutes—facts to contemplate as you plod along.—Mike Blevins.

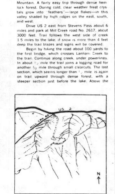

SNOWSHOEING HIKES IN THE CASCADES AND OLYMPICS
Gene Prater
1970 - 95 p. il. - $3.50 (pb)

The Mountaineers publish good books. This is a fine guide to eighty-one hikes in the beautiful Olympics and Cascades. Each trail is detailed, giving access routes and maps. There's extensive information on selection, use, and maintenance of snowshoes, plus hints on cold weather clothing.
From: The Mountaineers, 719 Pike St., Seattle, Wash. 98111

CROSS-COUNTRY SKIING AND SNOWSHOEING
Erwin A. Bauer
1975 - 205 p. il. - $8.95 (hb)

Although this book starts to leave the subject at hand, it offers an interesting comparison of cross-country skiing and snowshoeing. While it's a little hard to find specific snowshoeing information due to the dual nature of the book, all aspects of the sport are covered. About one quarter of the book is devoted to a "where-to-go" guide, plus addresses for specific area information.
From: Winchester Press, 205 E. 42nd St., New York, N.Y. 10017

BOOKS

SNOWSHOEING
Gene Prater
1974 - 110 p. il. - $3.95 (pb)

Gene Prater has drawn on extensive experience to present this very sound snowshoeing book. Equipment and technique are fully covered, aided by useful drawings and photographs. This is another must book on snowshoeing.
From: The Mountaineers, 719 Pike St., Seattle, Wash. 98111

THE SNOWSHOE BOOK
William Osgood and Leslie Hurley
1975, 2nd ed. - 168 p. il. - $4.50 (pb)

An interesting and informative book that says just about everything that can be said about snowshoes. It describes very thoroughly their history and function, the selection of the right type for a particular terrain and purpose, and proper maintenance procedures. Includes an evaluation of modern innovations, such as the use of neoprene, plastic, and aluminum in snowshoe construction, and gives simple directions for fashioning homemade bindings out of leather strips or old inner tubes. Even has a section devoted to snowshoe races. Nicely illustrated; fun to read.
From: The Stephen Greene Press, Box 1000, Brattleboro, Vt. 05301

SNOWSHOEING

SNOWSHOES
$32 - $89

Snowshoes distribute the wearer's weight over a wide area to allow him to walk on the surface of the snow instead of sinking into it. The traditional types consist of wood frames with rawhide stretched and woven across to form an intricate webbing. Snowshoes come in various shapes, each suited to a particular terrain. At one extreme is the Alaska snowshoe, a long narrow shoe designed for use in open country relatively free of snags and obstructions. Its shape facilitates swift movement and long, graceful strides across the snow. This type, by the way, is the granddaddy of the ski. At the other extreme is the bearpaw, a short, tailless oblong shoe suited to country with heavy overgrowth and bush that would defeat a long-tailed shoe. In between are the beavertail or Michigan styles which are short enough to be maneuverable in overgrown areas, but long enough to provide good stability. Some manufacturers have departed from traditional materials, using aluminum for frames, neoprene for webbing, or making the entire shoe of plastic. The one material that represents any substantial improvement is neoprene-coated nylon for webbing. Neoprene resists snow build-up, doesn't stretch much, and isn't subject to rot. Still, the majority of manufacturers are sticking to the time-tested wood and rawhide, offering neoprene webbing as an option.

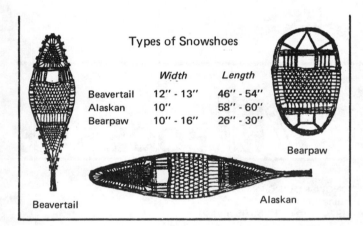

Types of Snowshoes

	Width	Length
Beavertail	12" - 13"	46" - 54"
Alaskan	10"	58" - 60"
Bearpaw	10" - 16"	26" - 30"

Bearpaw

Beavertail

Alaskan

BINDINGS (Harnesses, sandals)
$7 - $30

Snowshoe bindings are made of leather or neoprene. They are supple harness-like affairs that bind the toe of the boot to the shoe, leaving the heel free to hinge. In lieu of a ready-made binding, a length of leather can be used to tie boot toe to snowshoe.

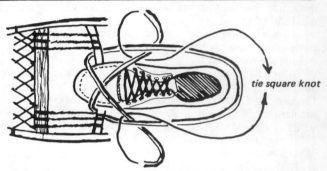

tie square knot

How to tie the Snowshoer Harness used by Indians and Trappers.

TRACTION DEVICES
$5 - $13

For extra grip in icy conditions or on slopes, rope or rawhide string can be wrapped around the frame on both sides of the shoe. Veteran snowshoers have come up with a variety of useful gripping devices for additional traction. Gene Prater offers several good suggestions for making your own in his introduction to *Snowshoe Hikes In The Olympic and Cascades.* Eastern Mountain Sports sells ready made snowshoe crampons that lace onto the bottom of the shoe.

sources of snowshoes

SHERPA DESIGN, INC.
3109 Brookdale Rd. East, Tacoma, Wash. 98446

These folks have come up with some very innovative ideas about snowshoes and bindings. Frames are aluminum tube, and neoprene decking is laced to them. To offset lack of traction due to the decking, a traction device is attached under the shoe. The secure bindings are attached with a metal hinge rod for ease of movement. Snowshoes are from $45-$84, harnesses $14-$30. Kits, including bindings, range from $40-$89. Although more expensive than traditional snowshoes, the Sherpas fit the bill for light weight and durability. Write Sherpa for descriptive literature.

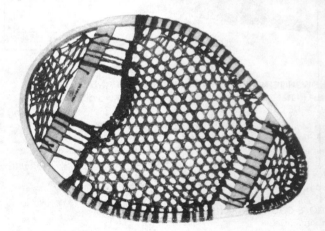

RAQUETTES AIGLE NOIR, INC.
251 Boul. La Rivere, C.P. 250, Loretteville, P.Q., Canada

This Canadian firm offers a wide variety of types and sizes of snowshoes, including racing, children's and surveyor's models. Their first quality snowshoes are laced with treated leather, and are guaranteed. Their others are made with a lower grade leather and are not guaranteed, although care in construction is equal. The frames are ash. Prices are around $50 per pair. Literature available.

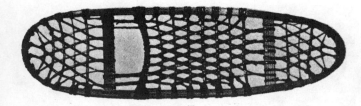

Green Mountain Bear Paw—10 x 36

This shoe, designed by Tubbs, is the most versatile shoe on the market. Its unique design makes it easy for the beginner and is a favorite of the Vermont Fish & Game Department. It is designed for New England snow conditions and is best in the woods and the brush. Very popular with hunters, it will support weights up to 200 lbs.

VERMONT TUBBS
18 Elm St., Wallingford, Vt. 05773
Tubbs is one of the older names in snowshoes, offering a variety of types and sizes, and rawhide or neoprene lacing and bindings. Their snowshoes are in the $50 range. For those of you really into snowshoes, Tubbs makes snowshoe chairs and rockers which are partially disassembled, needing only a screwdriver for completion. Free brochure available.

SPORTSMEN PRODUCTS, INC.
P.O. Box 1082, Boulder, Colo. 80302
Manufacturers of Snowtreads, molded plastic snowshoes. They're not as inexpensive as might be expected for plastic—about $26 for the short ones (29 in. x 11¾ in.) and $35 for the long (38 in. x 12 ¼ in.). This is about the same price as a pair of Indian handmade wood and rawhide shoes from Iroqrafts, Inc. Though they are extremely light (22 oz. each for the short size and 40 oz. for the long) and require none of the maintenance procedures that attend conventional snowshoes, the advantages seem to end there. One user complained that the hinged piece under the binding broke while he was wearing them. Another became livid at the mention of the name Snowtreads, and described a trip on which he wore these shoes and landed every fourth or fifth step face down in the snow with his 70 lb. pack on top of him. Seems the bindings stretch badly when wet and his boot kept slipping out. One important note: Snowtreads and other plastic snowshoes are promoted as being especially handy to carry along on a snowmobile for emergency use. If a pair of snowshoes aren't dependable, all they can do to an emergency is compound it.

BILL WABO
RFD 1, Berlin, N.H. 03570
Manufacturer of traditional snowshoes with ash frames and rawhide or neoprene webbing. Also two aluminum frame shoes. Don't know what retail prices are, but the dealer prices he sent us were incredibly low. Write for a free brochure and price list.

LEONARD JOSEPH CO.
Box 204, Denver, Colo. 80201
Leonard Joseph, although primarily a surplus-type distributor, handles the Canadian Faber & Company brand of traditional snowshoe under the name "North Woods." They also handle the U.S. "Safesport" brand. The Faber snowshoes are ash with rawhide lacing and run $32-$38. The Safesport is also ash with rawhide or neoprene lacing, from $39-$45. Check with them for more information.

BLACK FOREST ENTERPRISES
Box 1007, Nevada City, Calif. 95959
Black Forest manufactures aluminum frame snowshoes laced with 800-pound test nylon cord which is coated with resin for abrasion resistance. Available either finished or in kit form. The finished version sells for $53. Brochure with a post card.

BECK OUTDOOR PRODUCTS
Box 1038, Crescent City, Calif. 95531
Beck turns out some excellent neoprene-nylon bindings to complement any snowshoe. A regular model and one with a toepiece for steep descents are available. Prices run from $7 for the standard to $13 for the special. Catalog and fabric samples are free.

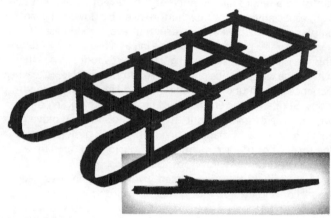

SNOCRAFT
Oak Hill Plaza, Box 487, Scarboro, Maine 04074
This is the oldest of the snowshoe companies, offering much the same line as Tubbs. Construction is white ash frame with rawhide or neoprene web. Leather bindings are offered. Snowshoes run $47-$63, harnesses $13-$20. Snocraft also manufactures snowshoe chairs and tables, and a folding sled—$38, which can be pulled behind for load carrying. For more info, write to the above address.

Snowshoes, bindings and accessories are also available from the following mail order suppliers:

SKI HUT
Box 309, Berkeley, Calif. 94701
Catalog free.

RECREATIONAL EQUIPMENT, INC.
1525 11th Ave., Seattle, Wash. 98122
Catalog free.

EASTERN MOUNTAIN SPORTS, INC.
1041 Commonwealth Ave., Boston, Mass. 02215
Catalog $1.

MOOR AND MOUNTAIN
63 Park St., Andover, Mass. 01810
Catalog free.

KELTY
1801 Victory Blvd., Glendale, Calif. 91201
Catalog free.

IROQRAFTS, LTD.
R.R. 2, Ohsweken, Ontario, Canada
Catalog 25¢.

ski touring

Ski touring opens a wide realm of winter recreational possibilities, from gentle tours through the woods to demanding high mountain skiing; from competition racing to downhill ski area-type instruction and accommodations. All forms have a common ground in that travel through the winter environment is achieved by one's effort; the rewards are of one's making.

Although overshadowed by Alpine skiing until recently, ski touring has been around a long time as a way of winter travel and communication, primarily in the Scandinavian countries. The term 'Nordic skiing' reflects this origin, although ski touring and cross-country skiing are commonly used interchangeably. Racing, using ultra-light skis and gear, has developed from this traditional method, as has ski mountaineering, incorporating techniques and equipment very similar to Alpine skiing. Although traditional touring gear has established a secure niche, much of the current equipment design, especially skis, has been influenced by downhill gear. Examples are the fiberglass construction and the ski bases which need either no preparation or waxing at all—a trend to take the "hassle" out of ski touring. However, waxing is a skill which one can practice and acquire; if nothing else, it teaches patience and an understanding of the different snow conditions. Similarly, the entire act of cross-country skiing offers a wide degree of involvement, from a basic shuffling movement to a high degree of maneuvering skill. This is a most rewarding form of outdoor recreation; ski touring can open up a whole spectrum of winter possibilities.

Although ski touring by itself involves certain basic gear (see "Touring Equipment"), there is more to it than what to get and how it works. Any person venturing into the woods should have some emergency gear and knowledge to fall back upon if circumstances require. Equally important is knowing what is available for a given outing. Different sections of this book give information of specialized aspects of touring, such as climbing, winter bivouacking, backpacking, first aid, survival, and so forth. These topics will supplement the basic information in this section. With adequate knowledge, ski touring can be a challenging, rewarding and addicting winter experience.

Looking south from Big Sky Mt., Lolo National Forest, Montana.

U.S. Dept. of Agriculture

sources of information

SKI TOURING COUNCIL
c/o Rudolf F. Mattesich, West Hill Rd., Troy, Vt. 05868
The Ski Touring Council is a nonprofit organization committed to fostering ski touring as recreation. As such, they offer a variety of information and clinics. Workshops and tours are sponsored in all New England states plus Pennsylvania, New York and New Jersey. Their *Schedule,* about 100 pages, costs $2.50 and lists these sponsored activities which are free of charge except for a registration fee of about $2. Also included is information on areas offering instruction, citizen's races, lodging and travel directions. Also available is the $2 *Ski Touring Guide* booklet, which covers basic touring areas in the eastern United States. The Council is a good source of information for the eastern part of the country.

U.S. SKI ASSOCIATION (USSA)
1726 Champa St., Suite 300, Denver, Colo. 80202
USSA is the major skiing organization of the country, coordinating races and events in both Alpine and Nordic skiing. Although a national organization, it is divided into regional affiliates. For instance, the

Eastern Ski Association is one of the geographic subdivisions which handles Nordic activities. A tour racing schedule is available for the northeastern United States, along with information on sanctioned competition. A magazine, *Skier,* is devoted to Eastern skiing, giving information on ESA and related activities. ESA handles applications for the Nordic Ski Patrol system. Membership in ESA ($10 individual) enables one to classify for competition in USSA events, purchase ski theft and accident insurance, participate in charter ski flights, and receive *Skier.* Write for information on your area.

NATIONAL HIKING AND SKI TOURING ASSOCIATION
Box 7421, Colorado Springs, Colo. 80918
This organization is dedicated to the construction of hiking and ski-touring trails in various parts of the country. A pilot program was successfully run near the Colorado headquarters using volunteer effort. It is hoped that a number of similar projects can be initiated by the involvement of these members, with the cooperation of federal, state and local interests. Write for literature on their trail projects and activities.

AMERICAN YOUTH HOSTELS, INC.
National Campus, Delaplane, Va. 22025

Nonprofit organization maintaining chapters throughout the country that engage in various outdoor activities including ski touring. Don't let the name mislead you. There are no age limits whatsoever in this group. Members make use of a network of hostels maintained by chapters. Write for address of chapter nearest you.

SIERRA CLUB
530 Bush St., San Francisco, Calif. 94108

By now everyone knows about the Sierra Club. In addition to their monumental work in conservation, they have thirty-odd chapters from coast to coast that engage in wilderness outings, among them ski touring and ski mountaineering. Write the Winter Sports Committee at the above address for information on activities and the address of the chapter nearest you.

CANADIAN YOUTH HOSTELS ASSOCIATION, 333 River Road
Vanier City, Ottawa, Ontario K1L 8B9
Canada

A nonprofit organization with regional offices and hostels across Canada that engage in a wide variety of outdoor activities. Really into ski touring and other winter sports.

The following wilderness groups conduct ski touring outings. Get in touch with one in your area for information on tours.

The Adirondack Mountain Club - Box 52 - Keene Valley, N.Y. 12943
The Appalachian Mountain Club - 5 Joy St. - Boston, Mass. 02108
The Dartmouth Outing Club - Hanover, N.H. 03755
The Green Mountain Club - 108 Merchants Row - Rutland, Vt. 05701
The Mountaineers - P.O. Box 122 - Seattle, Wash. 98101
The Nordic Ski Club - Fairbanks, Alaska 99701
The North Star Ski Touring Club - 4231 Oakdale Ave. So. - Minneapolis, Minn. 55416
Putney Ski Club - Putney, Vt. 05346
Skicrosse Touring Club - 135 Albertson St. - Rochester, Mich. 48063
The Viking Ski Club - Box 57 - Morin Heights, Quebec - Canada

CROSS-COUNTRY SKIING AND SKI TOURING
William J. Lederer and Joe Pete Wilson
1972, 2nd ed. - 189 p. il. - $4.95 (pb)

This is written from an instructor's point of view. Rather than begin with the "means," the author touches on equipment and concentrates on instruction—the "how to." Particularly useful are information and charts on waxing, snow conditions and ski preparations. It's definitely a good choice for skiers who would like to teach themselves.
From: W. W. Norton & Co., 500 Fifth Ave., New York, N.Y. 10036

SKI TOURING: AN INTRODUCTORY GUIDE
William E. Osgood and Leslie J. Hurley
1972 - 148 p. il. - $5

A good basic touring book, putting most of its emphasis on technique, safety and winter camping. Attention is paid to planning and detail of preparations.
From: Charles E. Tuttle Co., 28 S. Main St., Rutland, Vt. 05701

NORDIC SKIING GEAR
1974 - 64 p. il. - $1.75 (pb)

DISCOVER CROSS-COUNTRY SKIING
1974 - 48 p. il. - $1.50 (pb)
both by Nordic World Magazine

World Publications offers an excellent line of touring literature. In addition to their magazine, **Nordic World,** they include a series of six booklets covering virtually every aspect of the sport. The first two mentioned here are especially useful as they cover the areas of equipment and technique. **Nordic Skiing Gear** offers very good advice on gear selection and comparative tables of available equipment and suppliers. Write for information on their full line of touring publications.
From: World Publications, Box 360, Mountain View, Calif. 94040

SKI TOURING IN NEW ENGLAND
Lance Tapley
1973 - 192 p. il. - $3.95 (pb)

Although this one contains the important equipment, technique, waxing and related information, it is more than just a how-to book. Fully one third is a guide to popular touring areas in New England, complete with addresses of area clubs, information on state parks, cross-country ski equipment shops and other accommodations. Although regional in nature, this book gives an idea of "how it's done and where to do it."
From: Stone Wall Press, 19 Muzzey St., Lexington, Mass. 02173

NORTHWEST SKI TRAILS
Ted Mueller
224 p. il. - $4.95

This is a guide to the best places to ski in the Northwest, from resort skiing to touring and ski mountaineering. On touring alone, the book includes forty-one scenic trails in Washington, Oregon, and British Columbia. Special 20-page section on ski touring equipment, techniques, and hazards.
From: The Mountaineers, P.O. Box 122, Seattle, Wash. 98111

THE NEW CROSS-COUNTRY SKI BOOK
1973, 4th ed. - 144 p. il. - $3.95 (pb)

CALDWELL ON CROSS-COUNTRY
1975 - 160 p. il. - $8.95 (hb)
both by John Caldwell

Here are two books which distill the ski-touring experience of John Caldwell, formerly an Olympic skier and U.S. team coach. Caldwell has presented his knowledge in a very readable style.
The New Cross-Country Ski Book deals primarily with the basics of the sport. Equipment and clothing selection and care are treated with the necessary attention, without becoming mired in detail. The technique involved in using the equipment is developed well in the book, ending with basic turns and maneuvers. Waxing, being all-important, has some of the mystery removed. All in all, this is a very good introductory book for the cross-country skier.
Caldwell on Cross-Country leads into the realm of racing. While not necessary for the purely recreational skier, this book is loaded with information on distance, speed and related training. Diet, exercise, theory and off-season activities are all covered to provide a well-balanced whole.
From: Stephen Greene Press, Box 1000, Brattleboro, Vt. 05301

THE CROSS-COUNTRY SKI, COOK, LOOK, AND PLEASURE BOOK
Hal Painter
1973 - 156 p. il. - $4.95 (pb)

If you're looking for an unconventional approach to cross-country skiing, this is it. While the book has an irreverent and humorous tone, the author skillfully incorporates sound advice on the stuff that's technical while never skimping on the most important part—fun! If you're not in a good mood when you begin the book, you will be when you finish, and the better for it.
From: Wilderness Press, 2440 Bancroft Way, Berkeley, Calif. 94704

WILDERNESS SKIING
Lito Tesada-Flores and Allen Steck
1972 - 310 p. il. - $6.95 (pb)

Somewhere along the way the cross-country skier may wonder about the attraction of Alpine skiing, that ultra-controlled descent of steep snow. This book points the way to the essence of the cross-country equivalent, Alpine touring. Part one focuses on equipment and techniques, both for one-day and multi-day tours. Part two contains information on snow conditions and terrain, as well as first aid and the potential avalanche dangers of the high mountains. Basic climbing skills, location of touring areas in the country, and equipment lists round off this well-written book. For the person who intends to ski away from it all, this book is a must.
From: Sierra Club, 530 Bush St., San Francisco, Calif. 94108

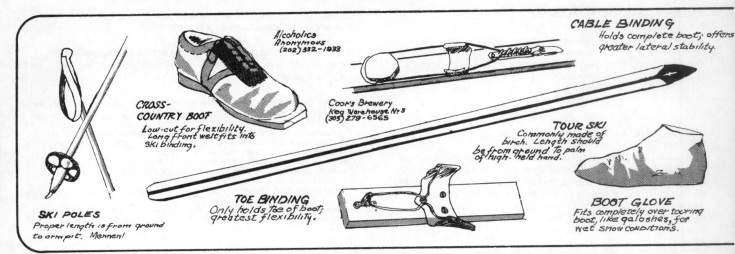

CABLE BINDING
Holds complete boot; offers greater lateral stability.

Alcoholics Anonymous (202) 332-1933

CROSS-COUNTRY BOOT
Low-cut for flexibility. Long front welt fits into ski binding.

Coor's Brewery Keg Warehouse Nº 3 (305) 279-6565

TOUR SKI
Commonly made of birch. Length should be from ground to palm of high-held hand.

SKI POLES
Proper length is from ground to armpit. Mennen!

TOE BINDING
Only holds toe of boot; greatest flexibility.

BOOT GLOVE
Fits completely over touring boot, like galoshes, for wet snow conditions.

SKIS
$45 - $160
Touring skis can be divided into four basic categories: racing, light touring, general touring, and ski mountaineering. Racing skis are light (3 lbs.) and narrow (45 mm) at the waist. They are used primarily on prepared tracks and are too fragile for rougher travel. Light touring skis are more substantial and suitable for general cruising over moderate terrain. General touring models are the heavy-duty ones, being wider (55 mm) and heavier (5½ lbs.) for added strength. Although the added weight is sometimes a burden, these skis are sturdy enough for cross-country travel and hold up pretty well under the forces of higher speed crashes. Mountaineering skis are the way to go for those who intend to travel through high country and require better control for the steeper runs found there. Although general touring skis with metal edges are commonly used for this type of skiing, specialized mountaineering skis are to be preferred. These resemble downhill equipment in appearance, construction and price. Shorter and wider than most, they are stable and quick to maneuver.

Common to most skis is the use of laminations and layers of different woods for strength and flexibility. Softer woods such as beech, birch and spruce form the core for lightness, while the top and bottom surfaces are hickory for durability. The number of laminations is generally a factor of strength; a light touring ski will have about 18, while a general touring ski will have about 28. A desirable feature is edges of lignostone (resin-impregnated compressed beechwood), which are very durable. Increasingly popular are skis with a fiberglass or fiberglass-wood construction. Good flex and lightness are their chief merits. Most will have either a plastic base capable of holding wax, or a "mechanical" base which imitates the grip-guide of a waxed ski.

BINDINGS
$6 - $85
As with skis, bindings take their characteristics from intended usage. The 3-pin toe binding is commonly used for racing, and light and general touring. Racing bindings are very lightweight, while light and general touring toe bindings are more substantial. Cable bindings, by utilizing a toepiece and cable around the heel, allow a wider selection of footwear. Some cable bindings can be used with either a hiking boot or a regular touring boot, while others are intended for a hiking or mountaineering boot only. The cable binding seems to find most of its use in the general touring and ski mountaineering areas, although sophisticated release bindings of a downhill type are now used for ski mountaineering, adapted so that the heel of the boot can rise for the walking motion necessary in ski touring.

HEEL PLATES
60¢ - $1
These are little plates in the shape of a heel that can be attached to the ski under the boot heel to provide extra lateral stability.

BOOTS
$30 - $85
Boots fall pretty much into the same categories as skis and bindings. Racing boots are little more than track shoes, while light and general touring boots are heavier and more rugged. Touring boots which use a pin binding have an elongated welt in front to accept the binding clamp, and may have a groove around the heel for use with a cable binding. Many have a sole molded to the uppers which is suitable for moderate skiing; however, a shoe with a sewn Norwegian welt will be more lasting in the long run. Lug-soled climbing boots or special ski mountaineering boots are necessary for certain cable bindings and most alpine-type release bindings. Footwear of this sort has the advantages of warmth, ankle support and versatility in case rock is encountered during off-ski trekking.

BOOT CUFF
$2 - $4
This is a kind of gaiter which is worn to keep snow out of the boot. They can be made of waterproof coated nylon (best in wet snow conditions) or of breathable cotton or nylon duck (when snow is dry enough not to soak through). Regular gaiters may be used instead and are actually preferred for mountain touring.

RUBBER BOOT GLOVE
$2 - $3
This is a snug rubber sock that slips over the ski boot. It keeps the feet dry when skiing in wet snow conditions.

POLES
$4 - $25
Bamboo and aluminum are the two basic materials for poles. Those made of Tonkin cane are the best of the bamboo, and are strong and flexible. However, they do break, and that's where aluminum comes in. A metal pole will tend to bend, but can be straightened, while a bamboo pole must be taped to work at all. Wrist straps are useful for push, but should not be used on downhill runs.

CLIMBING SKINS
$15 - $22
These are attached to the bottoms of the skis with the nap going backward to provide extra grip for climbing steep grades, preventing the ski from sliding backward yet allowing it to slide forward. Original types were of sealskin but are now mostly made of synthetics. The Smilie Company is the only source of real sealskin climbers that we know of.

SPARE PARTS KIT
About $5
Luckily, most damage to a touring system can be jury-rigged, although replacement parts are a good investment. A spare cable or spare bale should be carried in case either of these are lost or broken. Stout nylon cord can be used to hold the boot in the binding if nothing else is available. Occasionally a binding will tear free from the ski in a fall, and steel wool stuffed into the hole and a replacement screw will help you get back on your way. A roll of tape will repair a split bamboo pole until it can be replaced.

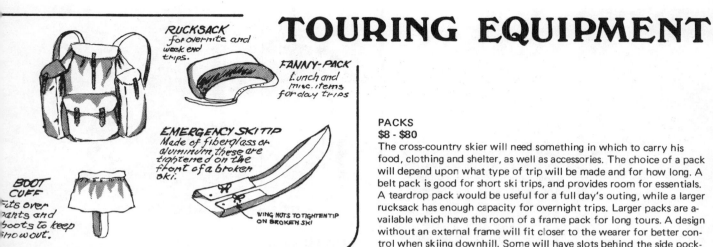

TOURING EQUIPMENT

RUCKSACK for overnite and week end trips.

FANNY-PACK Lunch and misc. items for day trips

EMERGENCY SKI TIP Made of fiberglass or aluminum, these are tightened on the front of a broken ski.

WING NUTS TO TIGHTEN TIP ON BROKEN SKI

BOOT CUFF Fits over pants and boots to keep snow out.

PACKS
$8 - $80

The cross-country skier will need something in which to carry his food, clothing and shelter, as well as accessories. The choice of a pack will depend upon what type of trip will be made and for how long. A belt pack is good for short ski trips, and provides room for essentials. A teardrop pack would be useful for a full day's outing, while a larger rucksack has enough capacity for overnight trips. Larger packs are available which have the room of a frame pack for long tours. A design without an external frame will fit closer to the wearer for better control when skiing downhill. Some will have slots behind the side pockets so that the skis may be carried if rock or hard-packed snow is encountered and you have to remove your skis and walk.

SPARE TIP
$2 - $7

If you ever break a tip (the most common ski breakage), replacement is a must. Tips are usually plastic and come in widths to fit light and general touring skis. When they are slipped on, a row of metal teeth grab and keep them from backing off. Some are aluminum and are screw-adjustable.

WAX
80¢ - $3

Waxing is one of the so-called "mysteries" of ski touring; however, it is a skill which one can easily acquire through practice. Waxes run from very hard to a toothpaste consistency. These match snow conditions from very dry powder to virtual slush. If a wax is property matched to the snow, it will grab on the snow crystals when standing weight is applied, providing kick. Whenever the ski moves along the surface, the wax will "float" over the crystals, giving a guide. The harder waxes are used below freezing, while the softer klister waxes are used above freezing. The ski bottom should be wiped off with a thinner to remove any factory sealer. Pine tar is then brushed on thinly and heated in short sections with a torch, being careful not to scorch the wood. After the tar has bubbled a bit, any excess is wiped off. The wax is applied over this base. Some ski-bottom preparations are brush-on only; however, heated-on pine tar lasts longer. A softer wax will go onto a harder one, but not the reverse. Always wax for the coldest snow conditions expected. Most wax brands are color-coded for snow temperature—light green being coldest, then green, blue, violet, red and yellow. Klisters run from red (coldest) to violet to blue. Since klisters are soft and extremely sticky, they are also packaged in spray cans for convenience.

SCRAPER
$1

A scraper is a must for removing old wax or one which is too sticky for conditions. It is a necessary item for all tours.

CORK
40¢ - $1

Corks are useful for smoothing a newly-waxed ski bottom; the smoother the wax, the more consistent its performance. Some folks use the palm of their hand, while others will use the cork handle of a ski pole.

WAXING TORCH
$7 - $17

These torches come with a flame-spreading head and use disposable butane cartridges. They help to even a wax coat prior to corking. They are a must for pine tarring a ski bottom. Although fairly light (1 lb.), butane doesn't produce much pressure below freezing, so the torch would have to be kept warm if carried along.

WAXING ACCESSORIES

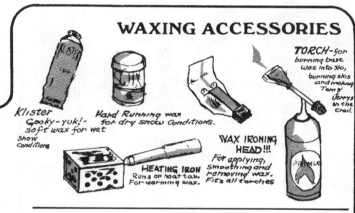

TORCH-for burning base wax into ski, burning skis and making Tom & Jerrys on the trail.

Klister-Gooky-yuk!-Soft wax for wet snow conditions

Hard Running wax for dry snow conditions.

WAX IRONING HEAD!!! For applying, smoothing and removing wax. Fits all torches

HEATING IRON Runs on heat tab. For warming wax.

SCIA WAXING GUIDE

The proper wax for touring and cross-country skiing depends on the type of snow, how long it has settled on the ground and the moisture content. By selecting a number from each of the questions below, in sequence, you can identify a snow type. Waxes for that snow type are then listed in the table by manufacturer; only numbers corresponding to real snow types appear.

Is the surface...
1. Snow?
2. Ice, crust, corn or pellets?

Is it snowing or has it snowed in the last few days?
1. Yes!
2. No!

A handful of snow...
1. is very powdery.
2. blows easily.
3. blows with difficulty.
4. forms a loose clump.
5. balls up easily.
6. drips water when squeezed.
7. is a mixture of snow and water.
8. cannot be had.

EXAMPLE: 1 1 1

SNOW TYPE	BRAND			
	RODE	EX-ELIT	SWIX	REX
111	Dk Gn	Lt Gn	Lt Gn	Turqoise
112	Lt Gn	Green	Green	Lt Gn/Gn
113	Blue	Blue	Blue	Blue
114	Violet	Violet	Violet	Violet
115	Yellow	Tö Klis	Red Klis	Yellow
116	Red Klis Yel Klis	Tö Med Tjara K	Yel Klis	Red Klis
123	Lt Gn	Green	Green	Green
124	Blue	Blue	Blue	Blue
125	Violet	Violet	Violet	Violet
126	Red	Red	Red	Red
127	Red Klis	Tö Med Tjara K	Red Klis	Red Klis
226	Vio Klis	Tö Klis	Vio Klis	Vio Klis
227	Vio Klis Silv Kl	Tö Med Tjara K	Red Klis	Silver K
228	Blue Klis	Skare K	Blue Klis	Blue Klis

N.B. Type 124 is the most common!

Copyright, 1971 - Scia, Inc.

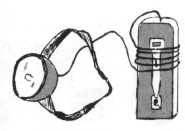

SLEDS
$30 - $40

Sometimes skiers and snowshoers use small sleds to carry extra gear pulling them along behind them. The only supplier we've come across is Garland Mfg. Co., Box 487, Scarboro, Maine 04074. Under their trade name, Snocraft, they sell a folding sled for about $38.

HEADLAMPS
$5 - $7

For night skiing, a lightweight headlamp can be used. These lamps have bands that fit around the head and run on batteries that are worn in a case on the belt or in a pocket. Justrite makes a nice one for about $7 which can be focused in either a short, wide-angle beam or a long, narrow beam. Available from most suppliers.

Bow Summit area looking toward Mount Patterson, Alberta, Canada. Photo: Canadian Youth Hostel Assn.

CLOTHING
0 - $35

Except for boots, no special clothing is really required for ski touring any more than for backpacking. A lot of dealers sell touring suits that consist of knickers and a sweatshirt-like top ($25 - $35), and they're nice to have, but not necessary. Knickers are generally preferred because the fabric in regular trousers chafes as the legs move back and forth. But whatever clothes you choose, remember that ski touring involves a great deal of exertion which increases body heat and perspiration. Garments should be lightweight, allow freedom of movement, and be of a breathable fabric. A good rule is to wear layers of lightweight clothing that can be added or removed as required. A warm jacket or down vest should be carried along to keep warm when stopped.

A Basic Ski Touring Kit

Skis	Two Pair Socks
Bindings	Sweater or Quilted Vest
Boots	Shirt
Poles	Ski Wax
Gloves or Mittens	Scraper
Knickers	Sunburn Ointment
Fish-net Underwear	Flashlight or Headlamp
Knee Socks	Rucksack
Hooded Parka	Paraffin
Earband or Wool Cap	Waxing Cork
Sunglasses or Goggles	Blowtorch

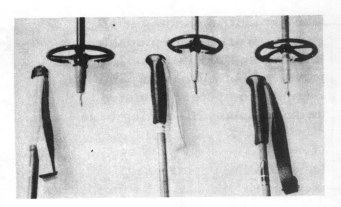

TONKIN TOURING POLES

AKERS SKI
Andover, Maine 04216

The only thing these folks sell is touring gear, and they manage to display a very comprehensive selection of makes and models. Most items are shipped postpaid, a nice gesture these days. Their catalog, which is free, contains boot, pole and ski selection charts.

B-44 ALPHA LOW LIGHT TOURING BOOT
Same great Alpha quality but lower cut and without nylon fur lining. An ideal boot for the weekend racer. Sizes 35 - 47 (4½ - 12).

C-44 FABIANO TOURING BOOT
This boot offers freedom of movement, yet high enough to give excellent support. Roomy toe, trim fitting instep, snug fitting heel. Features Goodyear welt, sewn with nylon thread for strength. Fully insulated throughout for warmth. Foam padded water-tight bellows tongue. Sizes 6 - 13½.

ALPINEER
Box 208, Crested Butte, Colo. 81224

Although not one of the giant chain stores, Alpineer does sell quality touring equipment, as reflected in their Bonna, Fischer and Landsem skis and Alfa and Fabiano boots. They offer clothing and all necessary touring paraphernalia. Catalog free.

EASTERN MOUNTAIN SPORTS
1041 Commonwealth Ave., Boston, Mass. 02215

One of the nice things about EMS is the clear layout of their catalogs. This one covers the gamut of outdoor gear, with suitable emphasis on ski touring. EMS features Lovett skis, of foam-fiberglass construction, as well as Madshus, Bonna, Asnes, and Fischer makes. Boots, bindings and accessories are adequately covered, although not in much depth. The catalog, $1, has a good supply of comparative information on touring as well as other gear.

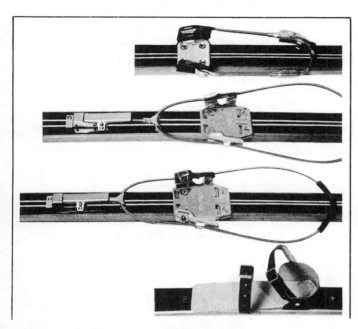

RAMER BINDING

Mountaineering binding with vertical toe release and heel release. Binding can be used with most heavy mountaineering and ski-mountaineering boots. Binding has two climbing positions for steep and moderate climbing and should be used on Rossignol Haute Route or similar alpine touring ski. Wt. 48 oz./pr. $75.00

RECREATIONAL EQUIPMENT, INC.
1525 11th Ave., Seattle, Wash. 98112
The Co-op is one of the oldest and largest outdoor suppliers, and as such carries an extensive line covering all phases of cross-country skiing. A good source for touring-related clothing and equipment. Their illustrated 100-page catalog is free.

MOOR AND MOUNTAIN
63 Park St., Andover, Mass. 01810
Carrying basic touring gear as well as a variety of other outdoor gear, this company features Alfa boots and Trak and Trysil Knut skis. Basic ski outfits are sold in sets, with a selection for children. Catalog free.

FABIANO SHOE CO., INC.
850 Summer St., S. Boston, Mass. 02127
Fabiano offers well-made touring shoes with both sewn and injection molded soles, running from $30 to $50. Catalog free.

GREAT WORLD
Box 250, 250 Farms Village Rd., West Simsbury, Conn. 06092
These folks offer a complete line of touring gear and accessories from waxes to clothing. A good selection of brands is offered; however, most of the skis are Sandstrom. Information and maps to the area's facilities and trails are also available. Catalog is free.

SILVRETTA BINDING

A heavy-duty touring binding. Excellent for ski mountaineering. Easily converts for downhill skiing with double cable hooks. Pivots forward to a 90-degree maximum angle. The binding is designed to allow use of mountaineering boots on skis. Ideal for mountaineering and heavy touring skis. Wt. 25 oz. $33.50

SKI HUT
Box 309, 1615 University Ave., Berkeley, Calif. 94701
Although Ski Hut's catalog features primarily ski mountaineering skis and bindings, a separate Nordic supplement is available. Fischer, Salewa, and Rossignol skis and Ramer, Silvretta, and Iser bindings are featured, as well as a good selection of backpacking and outdoors gear including the Ski Hut's own Trailwise line. Catalog free.

COMPANY 3
530 E. Bleeker, Box 1859, Aspen, Colo. 81611
This is the place for ski mountaineering equipment. Company 3 offers the Ramer binding, designed specifically for mountaineering or alpine boots. Also featured are Trucker skis, of ABS plastic-fiberglass construction, in touring or mountaineering design. Poles, skins, clothing, winter camping gear and avalanche rescue equipment round out their line. Catalog 50¢.

Cross-section: Hexcel Ski.

THE BIKE AND SPORT SHOPPE
772 N. Main St., Bishop, Calif. 93514
The Hexcel mountaineer ski, very light with an aluminum honeycomb-fiberglass construction, is available here for $98 plus shipping.

Instruction in Nordic skiing is offered through specialized schools and at ski lodges that have ski touring divisions. Following are the names of some schools and lodges that offer cross-country clinics. Write for their brochures, but be sure to specify an interest in Nordic skiing since most offer Alpine skiing as well. Independent schools that do not offer lodging will supply information on inns in their area if you request it.

UNITED STATES SKI ASSOCIATION, 1726 Champa St., Suite 300 Denver, Colo. 80202

Through its Nordic Committee, USSA sponsors ski touring clinics, including instruction in ski mountaineering. A recent back country clinic sponsored by the Rocky Mountain Division of USSA included orienteering, waxing for special conditions, avalanche recognition, and route selection. It lasted four days in the Colorado wilderness with overnight shelters varying each night to include snow caves, igloos, and lean-to's. Tuition for four days was $20 with skiers supplying their own equipment. USSA is an organization of skiers devoted to the encouragement, advancement, and improvement of all phases of the sport. Write for their brochure describing current activities in your general area.

LODGES and CLINICS

BURKE MOUNTAIN RECREATION, INC.
East Burke, Vt. 05832
Burke Mountain is a highly developed touring area, with lodging, instruction, rentals, special topics and races all available in almost any combination. Group lessons run from $6, and lodging in apartments from $36 nightly. The area has a good selection of trails.

BLUEBERRY HILL FARM
Goshen, Vt. 05733
Tony and Martha Clark run an inn with a touring shop in Vermont's Green Mountains, and deal exclusively with ski tourers. Accommodations are family style, and a network of 40 miles of trails offers plenty of opportunity for the accomplished skier and novice alike. Reservations are a must.

VIKING SKI TOURING CENTER
Little Pond Rd., Londonderry, Vt. 05148
Rentals, sales, instruction and trails are offered here. $4 per person covers instruction for two hours and gear is $5 per day. Accommodations can be obtained locally, and other good touring areas are nearby.

ROYAL GORGE SKI TOURING SCHOOL, INC.
Box 178, Soda Springs, Calif. 95728
Royal Gorge offers just about every aspect of touring instruction, from rentals and day lessons to trans-Sierra trips over five days. Weekend trips are run out of a dormitory lodge and include everything but personal clothing and accessories. Prices start at $48 per person for a weekend trip. Special weekend courses in mountain medicine, avalanches and ski orienteering are offered occasionally with the same structure. The country tours involve wilderness travel in various parts of the area and of various lengths. Weekend trips start at $45 and longer ones at $200.

MOOSE MOUNTAIN CROSS COUNTRY LODGE
Etna, N.H. 03750
Moose Mountain is a family-type lodge offering a comfortable stay in intimate surroundings. Rentals and sales are available at the ski shop, with instruction on weekends. Many trails are in the immediate area. Reservations are advisable. Write for current prices on lodging and meals, which are available separately.

JACKSON SKI TOURING FOUNDATION
Jackson, N.H. 03846
This is not so much any one organization as it is a Nordic "ski area." A wide variety of rooms and lodges, instructions, rentals and sales, transportation and trails, and related services abound. Three Alpine ski areas and miles of touring country put a lot of different activities within reach in a fairly compact area.

SCANDINAVIAN LODGE
Steamboat Springs, Colo. 80477
Located at the Mt. Werner Ski Area, this lodge provides a large array of services and comforts, including touring instruction in specialized fields, such as coaching, ski patrol, and ski sales techniques. Rooms at the lodge start at about $30 per person per day, including meals. Instruction starts at $4.50 per person for a group lesson.

X-C SKI EXPEDITIONS

The following people conduct guided ski tours for a price. Tours range from gentle cross-country wilderness runs to breathtaking jaunts in the Canadian Rockies. Most have standard tours planned around various levels of ability but can arrange a custom tour to suit your wishes. Many rent equipment. For full details on each, write for their brochures.

For a state-by-state listing of ski-touring outfitters, get a copy of Adventure Travel U.S.A., $3.50, from Adventure Guides, Inc., 36 E. 57th St., New York, N.Y. 10022. This book is a fantastic source of information if you're interested in just about any type of adventure from kayaking to sky diving.

CANADIAN MOUNTAIN HOLIDAYS
130 Banff Ave., Box 583, Banff, Alberta, Canada T0L 0C0
For wild and dramatic ski tours, try this one. These guys will fly you by helicopter with guide to a remote British Columbia mountain area for a week of skiing. Write for free schedule and description of trips.

NORTHERN LIGHTS ALPINE RECREATION
Box 399, Invermere, British Columbia, Canada V0A 1K0
Arnor Larson runs outdoor programs year-round in the Canadian Rockies. His winter activities include snowshoeing, ski touring and ski mountaineering. Basic courses can be daily, while more involved outings of a week or more are available. Lodging must be found in the Invermere area. This is not your "luxury lodging"-type outfit. Weekly rates range from $75 for Alpine hiking to $200 for ski mountaineering, which includes snow, ice and rock climbing.

YOSEMITE MOUNTAINEERING
Yosemite Park and Curry Co., Yosemite N. P., Calif. 95389
This is ski touring in one of the country's most scenic areas. Day instructions in basic, children's classes and touring survival are available as well as overnight or longer tours. Overnight trips stay at huts, and breakfast and dinner are provided. Prices run from $6 for children's classes to $85 for extended stays.

WILDERNESS INSTITUTE
Box 1843, Jackson, Wyo. 83001
The Wilderness Institute offers multi-day touring instruction in Yellowstone National Park. Equipment and lunches are provided on the trail; dormitory-style cabins are used at night, with available facilities at Old Faithful. They also offer a full spectrum of summer activities. Prices start at $150 per person for a day tour.

NORTHWEST ALPINE GUIDE SERVICE, INC.
Box 80345, Seattle, Wash. 98108
This outfit takes care of you from start to finish, with transportation to and from the Seattle airport, accommodations, a rental car, and either independent or guided tours. Needless to say, this treatment is fairly expensive. Prices run from $60 per two people for a weekend unguided to $150 per two people for six days of escorted touring.

RICK HORN WILDERNESS EXPEDITIONS, Box 471
Jackson Hole, Wy. 83001
Rick and Judy Horn operate in an area famous for its rugged, dramatic beauty. They offer just about every type of wilderness experience, ranging from pack trips to mountain climbing. Ski tours are available on a scheduled and private basis, the only prerequisite being "a desire to know the mountains and wilderness." Good campfire and mountain stove cooking, conservation, and identification of edible wild plants are stressed. All clothing, food, equipment, guide service, and instruction necessary for expeditions are supplied. Write for a free brochure, specifying winter or summer trip information.

The National Ski Patrol System is always in need of skiers to serve in their first aid and winter rescue efforts. The Ski Patrol assists in the handling of accidents at ski areas and works with municipal and federal agencies in cold weather disasters such as air crashes, mountain accidents and blizzards. Members are trained in advanced American Red Cross first aid and in cold weather rescue and survival, including avalanche recognition and rescue. Every Ski Patrol has a 12-hour refresher course in the fall. Even if you don't join, ask permission to sit in. For the name and address of your local patrol write: National Ski Patrol System, 29 Westwood Terrace, Dedham, Mass. 02026, and in Canada: Canadian Ski Patrol, 136 Ballantyne Ave., Stratford, Ontario.

dog sledding

There has been a recent resurgence of interest in exploring and enjoying the wilderness in winter—snow camping, cross-country skiing, nature hikes, and snowshoeing. In any winter travel by foot, a dog can be a real asset—far more than just a companion. Hitched to a small sled, a dog can haul not only his own gear, but yours as well, leaving you to travel free and unencumbered. With a team of three to five dogs you can even ride for much of the trip. For a little extra excitement you might try *skijoring*, which is essentially winter water skiing with one dog power—attach a tow rope to your dog, put on your cross-country skis, and grab hold. For real fun hook up to a team of two or three dogs.

In the purest sense, though, dog sledding is a dog team and sled headed crosscountry. Such a team offers a fine and thoroughly ecological alternative to the snowmobile. Dog power may be a bit slower (a racing team can maintain a pace of 15 mph over a stretch of five miles), but they're more dependable. For the price of a decent snowmobile today, one can well afford to maintain a small team for a good number of years. Outfitting the team requires only a small investment, for example, ganglines will run only $10 per dog. A good sled though will be a bit more, usually over $100, but you can easily make a simple

but fully functional one of your own for under $20. Top line dogs, of course, are expensive, but there are really few restrictions on the types of dogs suitable for a team. Almost any dog over forty pounds can make a fine sled animal (although he should be suited to cold weather if you intend to camp out much).

Admittedly the commitment to a team is greater than that to a snowmobile. You can't simply stuff the dogs in a garage and ignore them from one weekend to the next or from April to November, but then the rewards are commensurately greater also. A good working relationship between you and your dogs on a wilderness trip brings a special pride and satisfaction.

Even without snow you can use a team. A dog is just as happy pulling a wheeled cart, a small wagon, or even a light dune buggy. You can mush down the beach just as easily as through the North woods. You can even hook up to your bicycle—let the dog pull you five miles down the road and pedal back. Good for both of you. If you're truly adventurous, try *skijoring* on roller skates. There are really no limitations. Give yourself and your dog a break and open up new vistas for the both of you. Good Mushing!

—Yvonne Johnson.

Training Sled Dogs

Any dog of medium size (17" to 20" high) or larger and in good general health can be trained to pull a sled or cart, although how easy he will be to train is another matter. This depends on the dog's temperament, the trainer's patience and the relationship between dog and trainer. An easy-going, eager-to-please dog will adjust much more quickly than one that is shy and easily intimidated, but the shy dog

will usually turn out well if care is taken not to rush him.

The first step is to introduce the dog to his harness—let him sniff it a bit, then put it on him and let him walk around the house and yard for awhile. Keep an eye out to see that he doesn't get tangled and thus becomes badly frightened. Once the first shock is over, he probably won't pay much attention to the harness. Occasionally he may try to rub it off (prevent this immediately), but that's about all. If he does seem very upset or intimidated, take it off and try again later—don't push him.

Assuming that all is going well, the next step is to attach the harness via long traces to an old tire, log, or similar object that's light enough for him to pull easily, but heavy enough to enable him to feel the drag (be certain that the traces are long enough and the object heavy enough that it doesn't leap forward and bang into him). Now step back a few paces (no more than 5 or 10 feet) and call him. The odds are that as soon as he feels the drag he'll strain and bark but not move (especially if he's been tied for any length of time). Call him again. Tell him it's all right, that he can come if he pulls. If necessary, hold the harness and help him get started—he should keep it up once he feels it move. As soon as he succeeds in pulling the object to you,

While I was in the Arctic, an Eskimo friend told me that there was one cardinal rule of dog sledding—at least with Eskimo dogs. Simply stated it is, "Never take a crap upwind of your dogs while on the trail." The problem seems to be that the dogs will get one whiff and that quick you're going to have the whole team fighting right there where you're squatting. Could get kinda dangerous.

I never had a chance to test this in practice, but it sounds worth keeping in mind even if your dogs are well fed and even if my friend was drunk at the time.

—John Wagner.

praise and reward him in whatever manner he's used to. Keep this up for awhile, but only as long as he seems willing. This exercise can be repeated until he'll pull for quite a distance without balking. If your dog has been through obedience training, you will probably have more trouble getting him to pull than if he hasn't. Just be patient and work towards teaching him that it's all right to pull when he's in harness—but not on the leash.

As soon as he's cooperative about pulling, you can start teaching him to respond to verbal (and manual) commands. Basically this is just a matter of giving the command and initiating the correct response and can be achieved very easily by putting a lead onto the harness and walking with him, using physical control where necessary. Always use the same word phrase for each action to avoid confusing him, and it's a good idea to preface all commands with his name (Fred, let's go). This eliminates the probability that he'll take off every time he hears certain words. A word to the wise; every idiot in town is liable to yell mush when he sees a sled dog, so unless you enjoy chasing runaways, you had best choose another command to start him. The basic commands are go, stop, turn right and turn left— you can use any terms you want but try to keep them short and distinct.

Your dog is now ready to hook to the sled or cart if you're going to continue working him alone. If you plan to use two or more dogs, you must now decide whether you're going to get them used to each other while pulling the log or whatever, or if you're going to go whole hog and introduce them to the sled and each other at once. Whichever you choose, remember that the sled is much easier to pull than a log or tire, and that two dogs can pull more than twice as much as one. So whatever you choose make sure it's heavy enough that it takes a fair amount of effort to move it. There's very little chance of frightening the dogs with too heavy a load at this point, and the heavier it is (within reason), the less chance the dogs will have to get tangled or run off faster than you can keep up.

When using two or more dogs, you also have to decide which will be the lead dog. One determining factor will be which dog is willing to lead (many dogs won't), and the other is which is best at obeying commands. Most team lead dogs don't pull except in emergencies— I mean really pull any weight—when they lead. This isn't true in two or three dog teams though, or in most recreational situations.

A bitch is just as good a sled dog (and leader) as a male and often better. Many professional racing drivers use nothing but bitches. Just don't work her too hard if she's pregnant.

As a hint in governing weight, one medium-size dog in good condition, but a bit out of shape (like most pets), can easily pull a fair-size child on a sled; two dogs can pull a child and an adult.

Be sure to check the harnesses occasionally to see that they are not chafing the dogs and check paws for stones and cuts. As long as you're working your dogs, you have to make certain they're getting enough of the right things to eat. I buy frozen blocks of meat from the fur breeders co-op and mix it with dry kibble. Meat packers and butchers often make up dog food out of meat scraps at reasonable prices. Even table scraps are all right just so long as the dogs get some meat, bones, fat and even vegetables. Dry or canned food alone isn't sufficient for physically active dogs—at least not for mine.

—Yvonne Johnson.

sources of information

INTERNATIONAL SLED DOG RACING ASSOCIATION (ISDRA)
Dick Molberg, Secretary
Center Harbor, N.H. 03226

ISDRA handles the racing scene, sets competition rules for sled and cart racing and weight pulling, sanctions events, etc. For data on local clubs and racing info, this is the place. Annual dues are $7.50.

PERIODICALS

NORTHERN DOG NEWS
Leatha Braden, Ed.
Monthly (except August)
$7.50/yr. - 75¢/issue - 28 p. il.

A far out magazine dealing with northern dogs, mainly Samoyeds, Malamutes, and Siberians, and related activities such as sledding and packing. General interest articles cover health, breeding, training, snow safety, skijoring, etc. They also have a good selection of books. Nice, helpful people; recommended.
From: Northern Dog News, 6436 Mullen Rd., Olympia, Wash. 98503

TEAM & TRAIL
Cynthia Molburg, Ed.
Monthly - $7.50/yr. - 32 p.

T&T is devoted solely to the sport of sled dog racing on an international basis. It's strictly racing and training with maybe an occasional column on how to build a portable dog box or the like. If you're into racing, this is it. Even if you're not, *T&T* is a good place to run down data on clubs or sources of gear or dogs (lots of top line dogs advertised).
From: Team & Trail, Center Harbor, N.H. 03226

NORTH STAR SLED DOG CLUB
Rt. 1, Box 289, Bemidji, Minn. 56601

Since there are some 50 sled dog clubs in North America (ISDRA can supply you with a list of just about all the clubs), perhaps it's unfair to single out one. However, the North Star Club has been particularly helpful in answering our questions and has shown a special desire to help those with an interest in dog sledding. The club has members throughout the United States and their activities are largely aimed toward racing, but the only requirement for membership is an interest in dogs. Associate membership runs $5 a year. The club's monthly newsletter, *The Tug Line*, goes to all members. For further information or specific questions, write the above address.

ALASKA
Monthly - $12/yr. - $1/issue - 78 p.

Mostly general interest articles about Alaska, but occasionally they have an article of special interest on dog sledding or packing. Their book catalog (50¢) contains a good collection of north country books including several on dog sledding.
From: Alaska Northwest Publishing Co., 130 Second Ave., South, Edmonds, Wash. 98020

TUNDRA TIMES
Weekly - $15/yr. - $8.50/6 mos.

Northern newspaper put out by Alaska native group.
From: Eskimo, Indian, Aleut Publishing Co., Box 1287, Fairbanks, Alaska 99701

BOOKS

The following books have all been written by Raymond Thompson and are available through his company (which specializes in books on dog sledding, trapping, and related subjects). Most of these are also available from several other sources in this section, but Mr. Thompson, as the author, deserves listing as the primary source.

CART AND SLED DOG TRAINING MANUAL
1969 - 42 p. il. - $3.15 (pb)

More on cart training than sled training, but since the principle is the same, this is no disadvantage. Good but not superior to Fishback's *Novice Sled Dog Training.* If both books are ordered together, the cost is only $4.

SLED DOG BULLETIN SERIES:
Sled and Harness Styles - $2.15
Sled Building Plans - $2.15
Skijoring With Dogs - $1.65

The first two of these are good companion aids to the books on sled dog training, giving additional information on sleds and harness styles. They are necessary aids to building your own.

HOW TO BUILD A TRAINING CART
$2.50

Plans and materials list for constructing a heavy duty cart suitable for three to nine dogs.

Several other books on working with specific breeds are also available. All from: Raymond Thompson Co., 15815 2nd Place West, Lynnwood, Wash. 98036

NOVICE SLED DOG TRAINING
Mel Fishback
1961 - 32 p. il. - $3.15

This is an excellent book for the novice driver and for anyone who has to train a novice dog. It covers equipment, obedience, lead dog training, problem dogs, and so forth. A good thorough introduction to sledding for the amateur.
From: Raymond Thompson Co., 15815 2nd Place West, Lynnwood, Wash. 98036

TRAINING SLED DOGS
Frank and Nettie Hall
22 p. il. - $1.95

Booklet giving hints and help on training one dog or a team.
From: Hall's Alaskan Cache Kennel, 5875 McCrum Rd., Jackson, Mich. 49201

PARADISE BELOW ZERO
Calvin Rutstrum
1968 - 244 p. - $5.95

While generally covering winter living and camping, this book does have a very complete section on dogs and sledding.
From: Macmillan Company, 866 Third Ave., New York, N.Y. 10022

Two Young Alaskan Huskies

DOGS
$50 to $200

Almost any medium-size or large dog can be trained to pull a sled. Shepherds, setters, pointers, and collies have all been used. The larger hounds make excellent racing teams, since they are among the few varieties to combine size (to 70 or 80 pounds) with good speed and endurance. Traditionally, of course, the northern breeds have been the the backbone of dog sledding and for winter touring, a northern breed is the best choice simply because the dogs can sleep outside in cold weather without any special shelter. The four popular breeds used in sledding are the Siberian Husky, the Samoyed, the Alaskan Malamute, and the Alaskan Husky. The first three of these are pure bred and recognized by the American Kennel Club while the Alaskan Husky is a mixed breed. Here are details on each:

   Siberian Husky, average height 22 in., average weight 45 lbs. Good racing dog, lightweight, fast and with good endurance. They tend to be shy and a bit high strung, requiring easy handling, but are gentle and make good pets. Recommended as a good dog for the beginner.

   Samoyed, average height 21 in., average weight 55 lbs. Fair racing dog. Very heavily furred for cold weather. Seems to prefer trotting to the hard running of a race circuit, and thus might make a good tour dog. Least popular of the northern breeds.

   Alaskan Malamute, average height 24 in., average weight 75 lbs. Freight dog (too slow for racing) with excellent strength and determination. Usually hardheaded—they love to fight, so a definite requirement is a big person with firm control to run the team. Much of the ruggedness has gone out of some southern strains bred for show, but most northern strains are still solid. Raymond Thompson has individual books on the raising and training of each of these three breeds, $1.50 each.

   Alaskan Husky. As a mixed breed, Alaskan Huskies come in a variety of sizes and temperaments. They tend to be less high strung and less prone to ailments such as dysplacia (somewhat similar to arthritis) found in the pure breds. The best racing dogs are Alaskan Huskies but so are some of the worst sled dogs.

   There are two other types of dogs you may find being used in sledding circles. The first is the Eskimo dog. This is a rather loose term usually applied to any large northern dog of somewhat uncertain breeding (which may be in their favor). The other is the Akita

ARCTIC MANUAL
Vilhjalmur Steffansson
1944 - 556 p. (out of print)

This manual, originally prepared in 1935 for the use of downed fliers, has an extensive section on dog sledding and makes mention of packing methods as well. Out of print now so check your library or used book stores. Originally published by Macmillan.

MUSH: A BEGINNER'S MANUAL OF SLED DOG TRAINING
Bella Levorsen, Ed.
1970 - 39 p. il. - $3.00 (pb)

Solid instructions on how to train from one to three dogs. Describes training methods using leash, bicycle, and automobile; delves into advanced training for competition. Considers feeding, health, housing, and skijoring plus an appendix on equipment. Published by the Sierra Nevada Dog Drivers.
From: Nordkyn Outfitters, P.O. Box 1118, Moses Lake, Wash. 98837

DOGS, SLEDS, and GEAR

which is a relatively new pure bred becoming popular on the race circuit. Check periodicals for kennels handling northern breeds.

If you're putting together a team, the dogs should be reasonably well-matched for size and speed if you expect them to work together. Perhaps most important, the dogs should match the driver. The type of handling required ought to match your personality if you wish to avoid a lot of frustration and build up a good working relationship.

SLEDS
$60 to $300

There are two basic types of sleds, the flat toboggan and the runner sled. Toboggans are good on wet, unpacked snow of varying depths where the runner sled could bog down. Trails with hard packed snow or ice call for a sled with runners for increased speed and maneuverability. Runner sleds are the most popular and the most fun to drive. There are two styles, the racing sled and the freight sled. The racing sled is small (less than 8 ft. long with a basket less than 5 ft. long) and lightweight (under 40 lbs.). The freight sled is bigger (8 ft. to 12 ft. long with a full basket up to 10 ft. long), heavier (60 lbs. and up), and capable of carrying several hundred pounds of gear. For most recreational use a racing style is the best choice, being cheaper, easier to handle and pull, and fully capable of carrying your basic

FREIGHT SLED (Central Arctic)
Illustrated is a typical central Arctic Eskimo sled. It's simplicity is a reflection of the region it comes from—flat open tundra country where wood is scarce and maneuverability relatively unimportant. Cross pieces are lashed to the runners for flexibility. Simply stack your gear on, lash it down, get her rolling, and hop on. The brake is a snow anchor. Easily home-built for open country use.

bivouac equipment. The freight sled is the answer for an extended expedition.

The best sleds are constructed of hardwood (ash or oak is most common) with all joints lashed (usually with either leather or nylon) for maximum flexibility. Runners are steel shod for durability with spring steel being tops. A number of less expensive sleds are available using bolted construction for the joints (or sometimes a combination of bolted and lashed joints).

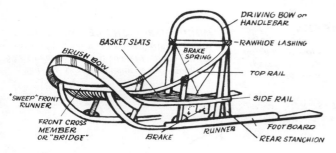

STANDARD RACING SLED
The racing sled has a much shorter bed than the freight type as it traditionally carries little if anything—except perhaps bivouac gear. Note drag brake, which is stepped on and driven into the snow to keep the sled from running into the dogs.

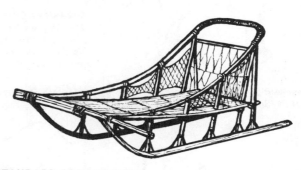

STANDARD FREIGHT SLED
The freight sled is designed for heavy long distance hauling over rough country.

Make Your Own Sled

The toboggan shown in the sketch can be built for an investment of less than $10 and is suitable for general recreational use (I wouldn't recommend that you show up at an ISDRA race with it, though). It is certainly not the best or most efficient design, but it is cheap and simple, and it works.

First cut two pieces of ¾-in. plywood to a curvature suitable for front upsweep (we use a curvature the same as that of a circle with a 6-ft. diameter). Now nail these pieces to the ¼-in. plywood at the base of the curve (see the sketch) and then attach 5-ft. two-by-three's to both the ¼-in. and the ¾-in. pieces as shown. Now the hard part—

the ¼-in. plywood at the front must be bent to the curvature of the ¾-in. pieces and nailed. This is most easily done by turning the whole thing upside down, pouring boiling water over the areas to be bent, bend some and nail some, and repeat. When this is done, nail a 2'6'' two-by-three across the inside top of the curve (nail it to both the ¼-in. and the ¾-in. pieces).

The remaining work is simple although it may be time consuming if you decide to mortise all the joints for a good fit and ease of lacing. All remaining joints should be laced to provide sufficient flexibility in the finished product. Either leather or nylon boot laces should be satisfactory. When that's finished, add two eyebolts to the front, and you're ready to go.

As a variation, you may want to add wheels for year-round use (stop laughing—what do you expect for $10 these days). Anyway, the conversion to a cart will cost another $10 or so, and look totally absurd but go like the wind.

What you'll need are four wheels (8-in. wheelbarrow type), two axles (3-ft. threaded rods or a couple of good hardwood rods), and hardware to put the wheels on the axles. The procedure is to drill four holes through the side two-by-three's, insert the axle rods, and slap on the wheels. The cart is now ready to roll, and roll it does, You might want to add more braking than is available by simply standing on the rear wheels, and some strengthening of the bed will be necessary to carry any weight since the ¼-in. plywood is not supported.

With this rig two medium-size dogs (40 to 70 lbs.) can pull one adult and one child easily in snow, and two adults and one child with the wheels on—not the first time though! Give the dogs a break by working them up to it.   —Yvonne Johnson.

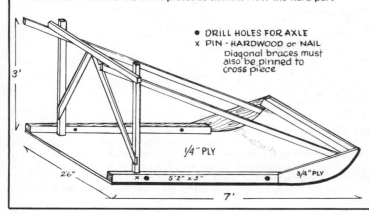

HIGH DRAFT HARNESS

HARNESSES
$3 to $13

There are two basic types of harness—the high draft and the low draft. The true racing harness is a high draft type, with the traces attached high on the dog's back to allow the most freedom of movement. The freighting harness is of the low draft variety, with the traces attached quite low on the dog to allow the most efficient use of force. All others are a cross between these two.

For a novice dog or handler, the best choice is probably a harness with a minimum of material for the dog to become tangled in. We prefer a harness with a low draft pull because it is a bit more difficult for the dog to back out of. The double traces (quite rare on a true racing harness) also help somewhat to keep the dog headed in a straight line.

Any harness should be made to fit the dog that's to wear it. The custom harness is nearly always more comfortable, and the dog is less apt to object quite so strenuously. The best harness materials are leather and nylon webbing. Nylon is actually the better choice for the simple reason that even hungry dogs won't eat it.

MODIFIED SIWASH RACING HARNESS
There are a number of different modifications of the standard Siwash harness in use today. This is one of the more popular. Often called high draft because the pull is high on the dog.

LOW DRAFT HARNESS

 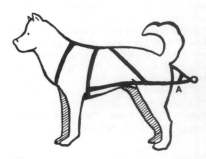

X-BACK
Popular racing harness. Another modification of the Siwash.

SIWASH FREIGHT HARNESS
The full Siwash harness. Called low draft because the force of pull is low on the dog. Used for pulling heavy loads over rugged terrain. Note the wooden spreader bar.

MODIFIED SIWASH FREIGHT HARNESS
Another variation on the Siwash. Spreader bar at A helps prevent the dog from crossing his lines. Uses a single line from the ring.

COMBINATION HARNESS

CANADIAN RACING HARNESS
Recommended for beginners due to its simplicity—not as much material for the dog to become tangled in. Uses a single tug line off the back.

MODIFIED RACING HARNESS
Tug lines or traces attach on each side of the dog at the rings. Well suited to tandem hitch. This was our first harness and is relatively simple to make. The harness is stitched to itself at A where the lines cross. This theoretically allows the forces to be exerted against the shoulders and chest of the dog. The cinch strap is optional, but we noticed a tendency of the harness to slip without it.

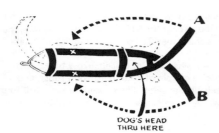

DOG'S HEAD
THRU HERE

EASTERN ARCTIC ESKIMO HARNESS
Pulls off the back with double tug lines. Used on both the fan and double (feather) hitch. A and B attach to the main harness at X with snaps. Said to be easy to make and fit.

COLLAR TYPE HARNESS
The collar is usually of soft leather and is well padded to lessen chances of abrasion from rubbing. Tug lines or traces attach to each side at ring X. This harness is used extensively in the Northern prairies for freighting. It's also considered one of the easiest for the novice dog and handler to use. Buckles may be added at A and B so the harness can be adjusted to fit various dogs. However, if the collar is not properly fitted to the individual dog, heavy work will result in collar sores.

TRAINING CARTS
$150 to $350

A three-wheeled cart is used to train and exercise dogs when there's no snow. It's operated and used much like the sled. Training carts are not suitable for rough country, but can be used on open ground, beaches, or back wood roads, and they are good for extended trips. The standard training cart is of tubular frame construction and has a drag brake. Some have shoe brakes as well and a steerable front wheel.

GANGLINES
$6 to $13 (for a three dog hookup)

The gangline is the arrangement of lines which connects the dog team together and to the sled. Most lines are simply 3/8- to 1/2-in. polyethylene rope (size depends on load, number of dogs, and particular segment of the line). There are three basic gangline arrangements in common use today—the feather (or double) hitch, the tandem hitch, and the fan hitch. The lines are normally attached to the dog harnesses by means of snaps (brass snaps being the best). A snub line, sometimes considered as part of the gangline, is attached to the main tow line near the sled, and is used to tie the team to a stationary object so they won't run off while left unattended. Some manufacturers include a shock link in their ganglines, which is a short section of elastic material to help cushion the dogs from sudden jerks.

If you purchase a gangline, the dog spacing is pre-set for you. However, if you're making your own, be sure to leave sufficient room between dogs so that they don't bump into each other. Room is especially needed between the wheel dog and the sled (you don't want the sled constantly running into him).

COMMON GANGLINE HITCHES

FEATHER HITCH (DOUBLE HITCH)
The common method of hitching a team of five or more dogs (works well with three dogs, too). Occasionally a double lead for two lead dogs is used. This is mainly a racing hitch and isn't particularly efficient if any great weight is to be pulled but does allow the dogs ample freedom of movement.

TANDEM HITCH
This is a method of running small teams—usually from one to four dogs. The double tow line theoretically helps keep the dogs all headed forward. This is the method used by many freighters because it allows each dog to pull directly ahead for maximum efficiency. Up to eight or ten dogs can be used—more than that and two teams would be more efficient. This is the hitch that we use.

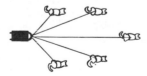

FAN HITCH
This hitch works best for fast travel in open country. It's not a particularly efficient one, and control is more difficult than with the others. As a result, it isn't seen too much today.

Making a Collar Harness

The most commonly seen harness is a racing or modified racing type, and its adherents swear by it. Personally I prefer a collar type. The harness is made to fit the individual dog, but it can be bought or made with buckles instead of rings so that it's adjustable. This is the only harness we were able to get our Elkhound to pull in although the Siberians would pull in anything. Even they seem to prefer this rig (possibly the elimination of the straps across the chest and under the legs allows for greater comfort).

The collar harness can be easily made at home. The collar presents the most problems since it must be rigid enough to keep its shape while withstanding a great deal of force (hopefully at any rate), and it must be soft enough so as to be reasonably comfortable and not chafe the dog.

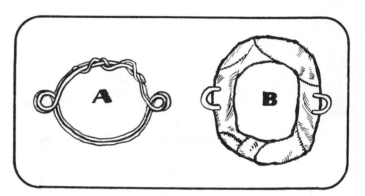

What we did was take bailing wire of a bit heavier gauge than coat hanger wire and bend it to form a circle with two small loops, one on each side (sketch A). Run the wire around twice and double up on everything. Now wrap around the loops and where the wire stops and starts with fine wire and solder. The next step is to cover the collar with some suitable padding. I used wool yarn for a base with strips torn from an old sheet for a top covering. When finished, the wire should have between one-half inch and one inch of padding all the way around. This is now covered with some abrasive-resistant (and preferably waterproof) material (we used scraps of pack and sail nylon). The finished collar should look like sketch B. Don't forget to leave the two small loops uncovered as the traces are attached to these.

There are two schools of thought as to the placement of the small loops. One method is to place the loops in the exact center of the circle. This allows the collar to be turned completely over and the wear to be evenly distributed (also prevents compaction of the padding). The second method is to place the loops approximately two-thirds of the way down from the top (one-third of the way from the bottom if you prefer), thus placing the greatest loading lower on the chest for more efficient pulling. For merely recreational use, I doubt that there is much difference. It is important, however, to make the large circle more oval than round to achieve a good fit.

Now for the rest of the harness. The first step is to put the collar on the dog and take some measurements. Measure from collar ring to approximately the end of the rib cage (being sure that you are not too close to the dog's tassel if he's a male; remember that the harness will be pulled back as soon as a strain is placed on it.), from the center of the side across the back to the center of the other side, and the same under the belly.

Now take some 1- to 1½-in. soft nylon webbing and cut to the measurements you just made (except for the belly strap which must be several inches longer if it is to be tied). After checking again for fit, stitch one of the side pieces to the ring (loop) on the collar and the other end to a D ring. Repeat for the other side. Then stitch the back band from one side ring to the other and the belly band to one of the rings only. The harness should now fit on the dog, allowing the belly band to be drawn up under him and tied or snapped to the other side ring. Check for final fit, and you're ready to go.

This is one of the easiest harnesses to both put on the dog and to hook up to traces. Simply slip the collar over the dog's head, pull back on the side rings, cinch the belly strap, and snap the tug line to each side. That's all there is to it.   —Yvonne Johnson.

____ sources of sledding gear

HALL'S ALASKAN CACHE KENNEL
5875 McCrum Rd., Jackson, Mich. 49201
Ten sled models from a 6½-ft. Kiddie to a 9-ft. freight sled for recreation, racing or freight hauling. Standard sleds are bolted construction with double runners, standing platform, cold rolled steel on runners, brake and bridle. One freight model and race model are full-tied construction, and all models are offered with swivel construction as an option. Price range is $50 to $275. Hall also handles a pair of wheeled trainers, harnesses (including an adjustable one), ganglines and collars. Catalog, free.

FRANK C. THOMPSON
Rt. 3, Mira, Minn. 55051
Top line, training cart with 16-in. motorcycle wheels (steerable front wheel), lockable drag brake, as well as shoe brakes on the rear wheels, torsion bar suspension, and folding handle bar. Price, $330. Literature available, free.

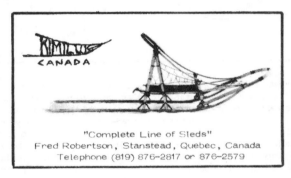

"Complete Line of Sleds"
Fred Robertson, Stanstead, Quebec, Canada
Telephone (819) 876-2817 or 876-2579

KIMILUK
Fred Robertson, Stanstead, Quebec, Canada
Five models from 7½-ft. Quebec Junior to 10½-ft. freighter. All except the Quebec Junior have 100% mortise-and-tenon joints and are lashed with babiche and nylon. Runners are laminated, and wood is plastic coated. Price range is $90 to $290. They look good. Literature free.

SNOWCRAFT CORP.
P.O. Box 487, Scarboro, Me. 04074
Used to be Garland Mfg. Co. Their principal line is Snocraft snowshoes, but they also make toboggans and a 4-ft. folding sled (which looks about right for ski touring with your dog). The folding sled goes for $38. Literature available free. (L.L. Bean handles the same sled for $28—listed in their fall catalog only).

JOE VENNEWITZ
20370 Ostrum Ave. North, Marine-on-St. Croix, Minn. 55047
Swiftfoot sleds. Apparently only one model 8-ft. long, 22-in. wide, 36-in. high with high driving bow, $200. The last word was that Joe has no current literature and answers by personal letter. If you want specific details, be sure to specify what you want.

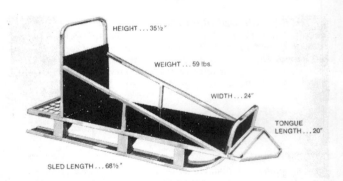

HEIGHT ... 35½"

WEIGHT ... 59 lbs.

WIDTH ... 24"

TONGUE LENGTH ... 20"

SLED LENGTH ... 68½"

TUN-DRA
KENNELS

SYLVAN INDUSTRIES, INC.
201 W. Elm St., Millersburg, Ind. 46543
Sylvan makes a couple of aluminium sleds which look pretty interesting. Runners are 3/8-in. steel for durability. The Husky (photo shown) is designed for use with dogs. The Kodiak is more for riding behind a snowmobile (torsion suspension and a windshield of questionable value). Literature available, free. (We have no price on these).

TUN-DRA KENNELS & OUTFITTERS
16438 96th Ave., Nunica, Mich. 49448
Dealers for Snow Paw sleds. Two working sizes. Adult Racer (94 in. x 37 in. x 27 in., 37 lbs.) for $139 and Junior Racer for $120. Construction is a combination of wood and polyethelene plastic (looks to be about half-and-half) and bolted. Harnesses from $7 to $14. Carts for $395. Tun-dra also handles everything from bumper stickers to wool dog socks to brass belt buckles, plus a fair selection of books. Write for their free catalog—it's a doozie.

The North Star Sled Dog Club has informed us that sleds are also available from the following members of the club:

Sleds	Wheeled Carts
John Cooper	Vince Hartigan
10821 Normandale Rd.	Rt. 1
Minneapolis, Minn. 55424	Big Lake, Minn. 55309

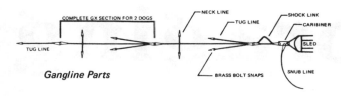

Gangline Parts

Labels in diagram: COMPLETE GX SECTION FOR 2 DOGS, NECK LINE, TUG LINE, SHOCK LINK, CARIBINER, TUG LINE, SLED, BRASS BOLT SNAPS, SNUB LINE

NORDKYN OUTFITTERS
P.O.Box 1118, Moses Lake, Wash. 98837
Modified Siwash recreational harness and full Siwash freight harness offered. Available in heavy 1-in. nylon webbing or 1-3/8-in. cotton webbing. Also complete ganglines of polyethylene rope with brass bolt snaps, snub rope, carabiner hookup, and special shock link. Tuglines and neck lines are 1/4-in. line; center line and snub lines are 5/16-in. line. All harness and gangline materials are available separately if you wish to make your own, and Nordkyn will even sew up your harness for you after you've cut it out (in case you don't want to tackle the sewing). In addition, Nordkyn handles Montgomery sleds (both recreational and freight), leashes and collars, sled utility bags, dog packs, and a number of good books. They also are the only people to offer a skijoring tow rope with handle and a bicycle tow line with handle and shock link. Nice gear. Literature available, free.

IROQRAFTS
RR 2, Ohsweken, Ontario, Canada
Primarily genuine Iroquois crafts and arts from the Six Nations Reserve and some items from the northern Indians and Eskimos. The regular catalog (25¢) has few items specifically for dog sledding, but they do have some good cold weather clothing—mukluks, moose hide jackets, Cowichan raw wool sweaters, and Cree dog sledding mitts (fur trimmed, fringed and beaded for $16 and up depending on the amount of beading). Catalog includes such other items as birchbark canoes, snow shoes, and even snow snakes, which are polished lead-weighted javelins thrown along a trough in the snow. This is a favorite winter game among the Iroquois with the greatest distance winning (catalog claims over 1 mile is possible). Good catalog.

A special mimeo listing of Collector's Specials is also available at $1 for 10 mailings. Covers mostly scarce, one of a kind art pieces and genuine old craft items. The following are drawn from one listing: model Ojibwa trapper sled with gun, snow shoes and lashed-in fur pack (8-in. $5); pair of matching dog covers, blue wool with fringe, floral embroidery ($28); dog sled whip, 9½-in. wood handle, topped with braided wool section, 48-in. braided leather whip, 10-in. cracker ($12); dog harness, sinew sewn seal skin with ivory toggle bar ($14); two old, used bone toggles from dog harness, 2¾-in. ($14). Worth the money just to read.

Snow Hook

ZIMA
P.O.Box 57, Kila, Mont. 59920   5959
Three styles of harness are offered—modified Siwash racing harness (slightly different modification from Nordkyn's), X-back racing harness, and a full Siwash freight harness. Available in 1-in. cotton web or 1-in. nylon web (light web for racing harness, heavy web for freight harness) and hand sewn. Ganglines are poly rope with a choice of 5/16-in. or 3/8-in. center line and 3/16-in. or 1/4-in. neck lines and tug lines. Snap lines are standard, but toggles and neck loops are available on request. Zima also offers a racing and recreational sled, a wheeled training cart, leashes and collars, and both snow hooks and brush hooks to increase the odds of finding your rig when you return. Literature available, free.

AUSTRAL ENTERPRISES
P.O. Box 70190, Seattle, Wash. 98107
Leather leads, signal whips, quirts, and dog boots (four sizes). Also handle a fine selection of other leather goods and several wool items plus some great Aussie felt hats. 64-page fun catalog, 25¢.

Suppliers of veterinary items and general accessories for dogs are covered in the Dog Packing Section.

Kelson Reg'd.

KELSON REG'D.
P.O.Box 208, Hudson, Quebec, Canada J0P 1H0 Canada
Kelson offers three styles of racing harness, standard, semi-pro, and pro. Details on the exact style and materials are not included in their literature. Ganglines of braided poly using 1/4-in. tug and neck lines and a 3/8-in. center line are available along with their racing sled (manufactured by Kimiluk to Kelson design), snow hooks (standard and heavy duty), collars, and a full line of materials and miscellaneous hardware. Occasionally they also have young Siberian and Alaskan huskies. Literature available free.

KATMAI
Rt. 1, Box 562, Cambridge, Minn. 55008
Nylon webbing racing harness and X-back freight harness. Also collar, canvas sled bag, and nylon webbing. Literature available, free.

Commander J.L. Blades tries his hand with a dog sled and team of huskies on the Antarctic icecap. "Come on you guys, shape up."

189

foraging

Foraging is a pastime requiring little equipment, few skills and no cost. Anyone can forage almost anywhere. Successful foraging needs a certain investment in time and energy—and the right attitude! Most of us in North America—especially city dwellers—are not accustomed to the idea of gathering food, beverages, home medicines and other useful commodities from plants growing wild. The very word "foraging" conjures up images of starving bush pilots grubbing up unpalatable roots with a pointed stick or munching desperately on a handful of lichen. Surely no one would do that unless forced to!

But wait...is that really the way it is? All of us can remember at one time or another taking a drive in the country to pick blueberries—that's foraging, and it's fun!

Foraging can add an exciting and useful dimension to a great many outdoors pastimes. For example on backpacking and camping expeditions knowledge of wild edibles can be used to cut down on the amount of food to be carried and to vary your diet. On lengthy expeditions, some foraging skill is almost a necessity because the food/weight carrying capabilities of a person may not be sufficient to handle the distance being covered. Short trip or long, the importance of looking on foraging as a supplement to basic supplies cannot really be stressed enough. While it is certainly possible to gather all your needs from the wild in most parts of the continent, especially in summer, such an undertaking is time-consuming and can be a heavy delay factor to a travel schedule—best to use it as a supplement.

Foraging is, of course, an important survival skill if you ever need (or want) to live totally without supplies. An industrious forager, even in the city, can cut down considerably on food bills—and in these days that could be considered a survival skill in itself.

Some common questions. Don't wild plants taste funny? Our tastes are usually set by what we are "used to," and it may take a certain amount of courage and imagination to try new foods. It may help to remember that most of our cultivated vegetables have been domesticated from wild plants. Read Euell Gibbons for mouth-watering descriptions of "wild feasts" and try it. Start out with plants you know you will like—a bowl of sun-warmed blackberries with cream—or simply add a small amount of the new food to your already familiar one—a handful of dandelion greens to your spinach or a spoonful of dried chicory roots to your pot of store-bought coffee. Keep on experimenting until you find the level of

What about poisonous plants? Some plants are poisonous. Mushrooms in particular must be gathered with care. Parts of many garden plants are also poisonous—tomato and rhubarb leaves for example—and careless people have gotten sick. The answer is knowledge—gather and use only plants that you know and have positively identified. If you are just beginning, stick to well-known varieties until your knowledge and experience increase. **Never eat or drink anything without knowing exactly what it is.** If you scrupulously adhere to this rule, the chances of poisoning yourself are very slight. Of course, some people are allergic to various kinds of plants. If you suspect you might be, eat or drink only a very small amount of the unfamiliar food the first few times.

Numerous plants, instead of being poisonous, actually can provide remedies for many common ailments. Mint (fresh or tea) is soothing to an upset stomach; plantain, dock or sorrel leaves rubbed on the skin will relieve the sting of an insect bite or stinging nettle.

How to forage. The successful forager looks at every tree, shrub and flower with one question: What can I use it for? To find out, it is necessary first of all to identify the plant. If you can find a person who is wise in the ways of plants and their uses attach yourself and learn. Otherwise, invest in a supply of plant identification guides specifically written for your part of the country and a couple of foraging books which will tell you of known uses for many plants. Incidentally, most state and provincial departments of agriculture or forestry put out booklets on local plants. They're sometimes free, but if not, they usually don't cost much. Look up the number in the *white pages* and give 'em a call.

Where to forage. In the city—vacant lots, old-fashioned back lanes, along railroad tracks, anywhere that has stayed or gone "wild" are good places to forage. Many valuable foraging plants are escapes from cultivation so be on the lookout especially for old abandoned gardens, fruit trees, and such. Be aware of where you are finding your plants. If close to roads or industrial developments, they may have unhealthy pollution residues.

In the country—anywhere, especially along fence lines, abandoned homesteads and orchards are good foraging sites. Once you become knowledgeable of the habits and habitats of different plants you'll have a good idea of where and when (what season or month) to look for what.

BOOKS

STALKING THE WILD ASPARAGUS
1962 - 303 p. il. - $2.95

STALKING THE BLUE-EYED SCALLOP
1964 - 332 p. il. - $3.95

STALKING THE HEALTHFUL HERBS
1968 - 295 p. il. - $2.95
all by Euell P. Gibbons

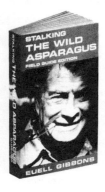

Within these three top-selling books are descriptions and illustrations of how to recognize, obtain and prepare a hell of a lot of wild plants, useful herbs and sea creatures for delicious consumption. Gibbons has put this foraging business within practical reach of any who will take the time to read and practice his teachings. If done, his words will come alive with the beautiful smell and taste of what you have created from the wilds. Even with all this goodness floating around, however, plant identification in some cases is poor, so you may also require a good field manual for recognition. Gibbons' books are good for foraging in eastern North America, the Midwest and along the West Coast. *Stalking the Blue-Eyed Scallop* is a must for tidewater seafoods.
From: David McKay Co., 750 Third Ave., New York, N.Y. 10017

CHICKWEED (Stellaria media)

Description: A small annual with weak stems up to 1 ft. long, which are much-branched and usually reclining. However, the plants frequently grow so densely that the stems support each other. Pointed, oval leaves about ½ in. long grow in opposite pairs along the stem. Small, white, star-shaped flowers have 5 petals which are deeply cleft.

Habitat: Waste places and cultivated ground, especially in shaded areas. Grows throughout the world and is widespread in the United States. Young chickweed usually can be found throughout the year except in freezing weather.

Uses: Cook young, tender stems like spinach or use them raw in salads. Chickweed makes an excellent potherb if used before the stems become tough.

44

EDIBLE AND POISONOUS PLANTS OF THE EASTERN STATES
1973 - 52 cards il. - $4.95

EDIBLE AND POISONOUS PLANTS OF THE WESTERN STATES
1974 - 52 cards il. - $4.95
both by Calvin Burt and Frank Heyl

This is a great system for learning plants. It consists of 52 flashcards (playing card size) with a full-color shot of the plant on one side, and a description of the plant, its habitat, and uses on the other. Next best thing to having a teacher, and they're waterproof, too.
From: Plant Deck, Inc., 2134 S.W. Wembley Park Rd., Lake Oswego, Ore. 97034

WILD EDIBLE PLANTS OF THE WESTERN UNITED STATES
Donald and Janice Kirk
1970 - 307 p. il. - $3.95

This is one of the few foraging books floating around that has both a good plant identification key and the best ways to use plants. A lot of line drawings, and they're done accurately enough to make field identification fairly easy. Once you've got the greens, the Kirks provide recipes and cooking instructions for fixing them up. Like the title says, this one's for the western U.S., and for western Canada, too. The vegetation doesn't change at the border, incidentally.
From: Naturegraph Publishers, Healdsburg, Calif. 95448

FIELD GUIDE TO EDIBLE WILD PLANTS
Bradford Angier
1974 - 256 p. il. - $4.95 (pb)

Angier's latest on plants, and his best—and the best we've seen for identification purposes. Reason is the fabulous full-page watercolor illustrations done by Arthur J. Anderson. No chance now of not being able to recognize delicacies from Mother Nature's produce basket. More than 100 of the common wild edibles are listed including those of trees and marine plants for the United States and Canada. Each listing covers the scientific name of the plant, just about all the common names, description, distribution and what can be done with it for eating, drinking, medicinal and other purposes. Really the best book on the market for the amateur forager.
From: Stackpole Books, Cameron & Kelker Sts., Harrisburg, Pa. 17105

EDIBLE NATIVE PLANTS OF THE ROCKY MOUNTAINS
Harold D. Harrington
1967 - 388 p. il. - $10.00

Now here's a book that comes closer than most to having what we've been looking for —good, usable, plant pictures. You can take this book in the field and do some identifying without a lot of doubt and double checking. Drawings are representative of the flowering and fruiting stages. Besides a bunch of run-of-the-mill recipes, there are ones for beer, wine, jams, preserves, and dyes. Add to that the history of the uses of these plants, and you've got a very comprehensive book.
From: University of New Mexico Press, Albuquerque, N.M. 87106

EDIBLE WILD PLANTS OF EASTERN NORTH AMERICA
Meritt L. Fernald and Alfred C. Kinsey, Rev. by Reed C. Collins
1958 - 452 p. il. - $10.95

If you are in the eastern part of the U.S. and north of Florida, you couldn't be in better hands than those of Fernald, Kinsey, and Rollins (this Kinsey, by the way, is the same man who later did the Kinsey Report on human sexuality — how's that for a Renaissance man!). The book covers all of the edible plants including seaweed and lichens in this region, telling how to find and then prepare them into delicious dishes. The line illustrations are O.K. but leave out familiar well-known plants such as milkweed and cattail. Taking the opportunity to help the reader organize his thoughts, the authors have categorized the plants into handy sections according to use. Something unique here also — an excellent chapter on poisonous plants that are sometimes mistaken for edible or harmless ones: even includes that famous Socrates killer, poison hemlock.
From: Harper & Row, Inc., Keystone Industrial Park, Scranton, Pa. 18512

A FIELD GUIDE TO ROCKY MOUNTAIN WILDFLOWERS
J. J. Craighead, F. C. Craighead, and R. J. Davis
1963 - 277 p. il. - $5.95

In addition to a foraging book you need a good, separate field identification key. Such a key would readily allow you to identify a plant by the simple process of elimination. And after verifying the name you can turn to your foraging book for the full scoop on the plant. *Rocky Mountain Wild Flowers* is one such key that meets all the standards required of an A-number- one field book. Aside from just giving you the name it also has other interesting and often useful facts about the plant.
From: Houghton Mifflin Co., 2 Park St., Boston, Mass. 02107

OTHER BOOKS

Not being able to review all the pertinent books, we've included an additional list of other texts which have been recommended to us or otherwise seem to have merit.

FRUITS OF HAWAII
C.D. Miller, K. Bazore, M. Bartow
1965 - 299 p. il. - $4.50
From: University of Hawaii Press, 535 Ward Ave., Honolulu, Hawaii 96814

THE MUSHROOM HUNTER'S FIELD GUIDE
Alexander H. Smith
1967 - 264 p. il. - $8.95
From: University of Michigan Press, 615 East University, Ann Arbor, Mich. 48106

EDIBLE WILD PLANTS
Oliver P. Medsger
il. - $7.50
From: The Macmillan Co., 866 Third Ave., New York, N.Y. 10022

COMMON EDIBLE MUSHROOMS
Clyde M. Christensen
Reprint of 1943 ed., il. - $5.95 (hb), $1.50 (pb)
From: University of Minnesota Press, 2037 University Ave. S.E., Minneapolis, Minn. 55455

COMMON EDIBLE AND USEFUL PLANTS OF THE WEST
Muriel Sweet
il. - $3.50 (hb), $1.50 (pb)
From: Naturegraph Publishers, Heraldsburg, Cal. 95448

EDIBLE WILD WESTERN PLANTS
Harold D. Harrington
il. - $3.45 (pb)
From: University of New Mexico Press, Albuquerque, N.M. 87106

fishing

Fooling a fish, which is what angling is all about, can be a real challenge with the diversity of tackle available today. It's not so much a question of catching the fish, but of what to use to do it. Back in the old days it was simply a cane pole, line, bobber, hook and a can of worms. If you had a little spare cash, you might even go so far as to pick up a rod and reel, and there was only one kind that everyone used — bait casting. Then along about 1940, maybe a little earlier, came the spinning reel and from that the spin cast reel. It didn't stop there. Every angler had his own ideas on innovations, modifications and adjustments that were necessary to a better rig to catch better fish, so that today one fools the fish with a precisely balanced "system." Most people, however, avoid the complications that have developed around chosing appropriate systems by just simply buying individual pieces of tackle, a good looking rod, a smooth operating reel, line of sufficient test to handle the largest fish expected to be caught, and several pretty lures. Sounds ridiculous? You're right.

The best way to get into fishing is to do some reading on the subject before buying tackle or stepping into the water. Get a background on fish, what baits or lures can be used to catch the different types in your area, and the best tackle to use in presenting this bait to the fish. A good book for this, which can usually be found in most tackle shops, is Tom McNally's *Fisherman's Bible,* $7.95. Very good coverage of fishing systems and individual articles of tackle. This one is recommended as your first book to buy if you're just getting into angling.

The diversity of tackle is not the only thing that'll keep you hopping. Since manufacturers do not seem to set retail prices anymore, you'll find the cost of an item to vary from state to state, even from store to store. Impulse buying without first checking four or five mail order catalogs can lead to paying more than you might have had to. Pick up a copy of *Outdoor Life* and check the ads, especially the ones in the classifieds section. You'll find many tackle dealers that issue catalogs. We have a number listed in "Sources of Tackle," whom you can also contact.

What is the best fishing system to use — spin casting, spinning, bait casting or fly fishing? There's no "best," but spinning is the most versatile, because of the weight range of the lures that can be used ranging from plugs to flies; fly fishing is the most difficult but the most rewarding; and bait casting is somewhat of a specialist's system and not very popular with the novice because of the backlash problem.

The important thing is not so much the system, but having a balanced outfit. This is important with all systems, but more so with fly fishing than any other. Balance starts with the fish and the lure, and from there continues with the strength, weight, diameter and length of the leader and line; the type, weight, and line capacity of the reel; and the types, length and action of the rod, all of which must be matched or "balanced" to the lure. Complicated? Yes, if you're going to worry about all the different tackle manufacturers. But luckily most people only have two or three outfits and it's easy to memorize the weights and sizes of line, leaders and lures that go together with them for efficient fishing under different conditions. Tackle manufacturers will supply you with this information for their rods and reels. They're also pretty good about recommending the best outfit for the type of fishing you'll be doing.

FISHERMAN'S KNOTS

Blood Knot
One of the oldest and still one of the best knots for tying two pieces of equal diameter monofilament together. Notice that the two strands are wrapped in opposite directions for maximum strength.

Improved Clinch Knot
Similar to tying one-half of a blood knot, with the exception of running the end of the line through the loop. This is an excellent knot for attaching lures or swivels to monofilament line.

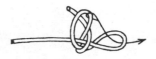

Perfection Loop
A popular knot for tying a loop in the end of a line or leader. To tie, make two separate loops, run the line through both of them and pull tight.

Surgeon's Knot
This easy-to-tie knot is ideal for joining two pieces of monofilament leader or tying a "shock" leader to a spinning line. Lay the two ends of line together with ample line to spare. Treating the two as a single line, tie a simple overhand knot. Now, tie the same overhand knot again and pull the two strands through the loop; pull tight and clip ends.

Fishing in the United States is regulated by state fish and wildlife departments. A written request to a state agency will bring much useful information besides the standard license and fishing regulations data, like fishing maps, outfitters and lodges' literature and sometimes even booklets or pamphlets with practical tips.

Canada and Mexico have no special requirements for bringing tackle into their countries. However, do make a list in duplicate of your gear, with serial numbers, and leave a copy with the U.S. Customs official at your point of entry. This will save arguments on whether you did or did not buy the tackle outside the U.S.

Non-resident license fees in Canada are set by provincial governments and vary from province to province. Incidentally, provincial wildlife departments will also supply you with lotsa goodies, literature-wise, if you'll drop 'em a card.

Compared to the U.S. and Canada, Mexico just doesn't have that much sport fishing activity, hence the federal government is the regulatory body for the whole country. Non-resident fees are charged on the following basis: three days, 48¢; one month, 80¢; three months, $2; one year, $4. Licenses can be secured from border authorities at principal seaports and resorts, and from local game and fish wardens. For additional information write the Mexican Government Department of Tourism, 630 Fifth Ave., New York, N.Y. 10020.

TROUT UNLIMITED (TU)
P.O. Box 361, Denver, Colo. 80201

Trout Unlimited's principal goal is the protection, and where needed, the enhancement of the cold-water environment. Otto Teiler, one of TU's past presidents, put it succinctly, "Trout are comparable to the canary in the mine, a healthy trout fishery is one sign of a well-managed stream environment. However, if the water becomes polluted and clogged with elements that destroy that clean-water environment, these trout will die." Thus, TU members in more than 280 chapters spend much of their leisure time in "watchdog" activities. This requires constant surveillance of streams, rivers and ponds which must be protected from the ravages of those who, by either ignorance or design, would destroy one of our greatest natural resources, the cold-water fishery.

Trout Unlimited publishes a quarterly magazine, *Trout,* with articles on fishing, stream management and conservation. They also publish a biannual newspaper called *Action Line* which covers national and chapter activities, projects, and so forth. Members receive both of these as part of their membership. Dues run $10 annually for U.S. residents and $12 for Canadians. For more info, contact TU at the above address. They've got a good cause going.

BASS ANGLERS SPORTSMAN SOCIETY (BASS)
1 Bell Rd., Montgomery, Ala. 36109

Objectives of BASS, which has a membership of upwards to 160,000 in more than 750 regional chapters, are to bring together avid bass fishermen to improve their skills through the exchange of techniques and ideas, and to provide government and private conservation groups with their organized expertise, support and encouragement to help actualize good conservation practices. BASS members are active in detecting and reporting water and stream polluters, and are quick to call public and political attention to the situation.

The organization's bimonthly magazine, *Bass Master,* is full of practical articles, tips and info on all aspects of bass fishing. Membership, which includes a subscription to *Bass Master* and some other goodies, runs $10 per year. For complete info, write the above address.

INTERNATIONAL SPIN FISHING ASSOCIATION
P.O. Box 81, Downey, Calif. 90241

More of a record-keeping organization than anything else, but it does issue some interesting bulletins and newsletters. Drop 'em a card for information on membership and services.

DIVISION OF FISHERY SERVICES
U.S. Bureau of Sport Fisheries and Wildlife, Washington, D.C. 20240

These are the people to contact if you're interested in getting fingerlings for your trout pond. Normally they work through state fish and wildlife agencies with their distribution program. Check with them for information on the program or any problems you may have in stocking or raising fish.

U.S. TROUT FARMERS ASSOCIATION
Box 681, Buhl, Idaho 83316

Though this group is mainly oriented to serving the needs of commercial trout raisers, there's no reason why you couldn't make use of their information services if you've got a trout pond. They've got a lot of "how to" publications available. If you're not in the business of raising trout an associate membership runs $6. If you are, the fee is higher. This will bring you their bimonthly *U.S. Trout News,* lists of helpful publications, and books on fish and trout farming plus their advice and assistance in getting started with your own trout pond project. Definitely worth checking into.

SPORT FISHING INSTITUTE
719 Thirteenth St., N.W., Suite 503, Washington, D.C. 20005

A conservation agency supported by manufacturers of fishing tackle and related products. Their areas of interest are all aspects of fish conservation, fishery biology and resource management, water pollution and conservation, fishing laws and regulations, and conservation education. They publish the monthly *SFI Bulletin* and biennial *Fish Conservation Highlights,* plus other educational material. For more information on their activities and a price list of their publications, drop a card to the above address.

BROTHERHOOD OF THE JUNGLE COCK
10 E. Fayette St., Baltimore, Md. 21202

Small group of anglers dedicated to conserving game fish and teaching angling technique and good sportsmanship. Founded in 1939, but that's all we've got on 'em.

AMERICAN CASTING ASSOCIATION
P.O. Box 51, Nashville, Tenn. 37202

This group, founded in 1906, is composed of some 45 regional clubs, several state associations, some local groups of amateur tournament fly and bait casters, and colleges and universities that teach angling and casting. Their primary objective is to promote angling and casting as a recreational activity. Their official publication is the bimonthly *Creel.* Membership info is available from the above address.

STATE DEPARTMENTS of FISH and GAME

For current regulations and license data, plus much helpful literature, contact these departments.

Alabama - Dept. of Conservation & Natural Resources - 64 N. Union St. - Montgomery 36130
Alaska - Dept. of Fish & Game - Subport Bldg. - Juneau 99801
Arizona - Game & Fish Dept. - 2222 W. Greenway Rd. - P.O. Box 9099 - Phoenix 85068
Arkansas - Game & Fish Com. - Game & Fish Bldg. - 2 State Capitol Mall - Little Rock 72201
California - Dept. of Fish & Game - The Resources Agency - 1416 Ninth St. - Sacramento 95814
Colorado - Dept. of Natural Resources - Div. of Wildlife - 6060 Broadway - Denver 80216
Connecticut - Dept. of Environmental Protection - State Office Bldg. - Hartford 06115
Delaware - Div. of Fish & Wildlife - Dept. of Natural Resources & Environmental Control - Tatnall Bldg. - Dover 19901
District of Columbia - Metropolitan Police - 300 Indiana Ave., N.W. - Washington 20001
Florida - Game & Fresh-Water Fish Com. - Dept. of Natural Resources - 620 S. Meridian - Tallahassee 32304
Georgia - State Game & Fish Div. - Trinity-Washington Bldg. - 270 Washington St., S.W. - Atlanta 30334
Hawaii - Div. of Fish & Game - Dept. of Land and Natural Resources - 1151 Punchbowl St. - Honolulu 96813
Idaho - Fish & Game Dept. - 600 S. Walnut - Box 25 - Boise 83707
Illinois - Dept. of Conservation - 605 State Office Bldg. - Springfield 62706
Indiana - Div. of Fish & Wildlife - Dept. of Natural Resources - 608 State Office Bldg. - Indianapolis 46204
Iowa - Fish & Game Div. - State Conservation Com. - State Office Bldg. - 300 Fourth St. - Des Moines 50319
Kansas - Forestry, Fish & Game Com. - Box 1028 - Pratt 67124
Kentucky - Dept. of Fish & Wildlife Resources - Capital Plaza - Frankfort 40601
Louisiana - Wildlife & Fisheries Com. - 126 Wildlife & Fisheries Bldg. - 400 Royal St. - New Orleans 70130
Maine - Dept. of Inland Fisheries & Wildlife - 284 State St. - Augusta 04333
Maryland - Dept. of Natural Resources - Tawes State Office Bldg. - Annapolis 21401
Massachusetts - Dept. of Environmental Resources - Div. of Fisheries & Wildlife - 100 Cambridge St. - Boston 02202
Michigan - Dept. of Natural Resources - Mason Bldg. - Lansing 48926
Minnesota - Div. of Game & Fish - Dept. of Natural Resources - 301 Centennial Bldg. - 658 Cedar St. - St. Paul 55101
Mississippi - Game & Fish Com. - Robert E. Lee Office Bldg. - 239 N. Lamar St. - Box 451 - Jackson 39205
Missouri - Fisheries Div. (or) Game Div. - Dept. of Conservation - 2901 N. Ten Mile Dr. - Jefferson City 65101
Montana - Fish & Game Dept. - Helena 59601
Nebraska - Game & Parks Com. - P.O. Box 30370 - 2200 N. 33rd - Lincoln 68503
Nevada - Dept. of Fish & Game - Box 10678 - Reno 89510
New Hampshire - Fish & Game Dept. - Box 2003 - 34 Bridge St. - Concord 03301
New Jersey - Dept. of Environmental Protection - Div. of Fish, Game & Shellfisheries - Box 1390 - Trenton 08625
New Mexico - Dept. of Game & Fish - State Capitol - Santa Fe 87501
New York - Fish & Wildlife Div. - Dept. of Environmental Conservation - 50 Wolf Rd. - Albany 12201
North Carolina - Wildlife Resources Com. - Albemarle Bldg. - 325 N. Salisbury St. - Raleigh 27611
North Dakota - State Game & Fish Dept. - 2121 Lovett Ave. - Bismarck 58501
Ohio - Dept. of Natural Resources - Div. of Wildlife - Fountain Square - Columbus 43224
Oklahoma - Fisheries Div. (or) Game Div. - Dept. of Wildlife Conservation - 1801 N. Lincoln - P.O. Box 53465 - Oklahoma City 73105
Oregon - Dept. of Fish & Wildlife - Box 3503 - Portland 97208
Pennsylvania - Fish Com. - P.O. Box 1673 - Harrisburg 17120
     Game Com. - P.O. Box 1567 - Harrisburg 17120
Rhode Island - Div. of Fish & Wildlife - Dept. of Natural Resources - 83 Park St. - Providence 02903
South Carolina - Wildlife & Marine Resources Dept. - 1015 Main St. - Box 167 - Dutch Plaza - Bldg. D - Columbia 29202
South Dakota - Dept. of Game, Fish & Parks - State Office Bldg. No. 1 - Pierre 57501
Tennessee - Game & Fish Com. - Wildlife Resources Agency - Box 40747 - Ellington Agricultural Center - Nashville 37204
Texas - Parks & Wildlife Dept. - John H. Reagan Bldg. - Austin 78701
Utah - State Dept. of Natural Resources - Div. of Wildlife Resources - 1596 W.N. Temple - Salt Lake City 84116
Vermont - Agency of Environmental Conservation - Fish & Game Dept. - 151 Main St. - Montpelier 05602
Virginia - Com. of Game & Inland Fisheries - 4010 W. Broad St. - Box 11104 - Richmond 23230
Washington - Dept. of Game - 600 N. Capitol Way - Olympia 98504
     Dept. of Fisheries - 115 General Admin. Bldg. - Olympia 98504
West Virginia - Dept. of Natural Resources - 1800 Washington St., East - Charleston 25305
Wisconsin - Dept. of Natural Resources - Box 450 - Madison 53701
Wyoming - Game & Fish Dept. - Box 1589 - Cheyenne 82002
Guam - Div. of Fish & Wildlife - Dept. of Agriculture - Agana 96910
Puerto Rico - Div. of Fisheries & Wildlife - Dept. of Natural Resources - Box 11488 - Santurce - San Juan 00910

CANADIAN FISH and WILDLIFE DEPARTMENTS

Alberta - Fish & Wildlife Div. - Dept. of Recreation, Parks & Wildlife - Edmonton 6
British Columbia - Fish & Wildlife Branch - Dept. of Recreation & Conservation - Parliament Bldgs. - Victoria V8V 1X4
Manitoba - Tourist Branch - Dept. of Tourism, Recreation & Cultural Affairs - 200 Vaughan St. - Winnipeg R3C 0P8
New Brunswick - Fish & Wildlife Branch - Dept. of Natural Resources - Centennial Bldg. - Fredericton
Newfoundland - Dept. of Mines, Agriculture & Resources - Confederation Bldg. - St. John's
Northwest Territories - TravelArctic - Yellowknife
Nova Scotia - Wildlife Div. - Dept. of Lands & Forests - P.O. Box 516 - Kentville B4N 3X3
Ontario - Fish & Wildlife Branch - Dept. of Lands & Forests - Parliament Bldgs. - Toronto 5
Prince Edward Island - Fish & Wildlife Div. - Dept. of the Environment - P.O. Box 2000 - Charlottetown C1A 7N8
Quebec - Fish & Game Branch - Dept. of Tourism, Fish & Game - 150 Est - Boul. Saint-Cyrille - Quebec G1R 4Y3
Saskatchewan - Dir. Fisheries & Wildlife - Dept. of Natural Resources - Gov. Admin. Bldg. - Regina
Yukon Territory - Fisheries Service - 122 Industrial Rd. - Whitehorse
     Dir. of Game - Box 2703 - Whitehorse

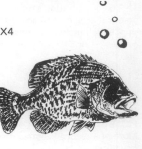

FISHING

ORVIS FLY FISHING SCHOOL
10 River Rd., Manchester, Vt. 05254

Three-day sessions (actually two days, from lunch the first to lunch the third) which include meals and a room at a mountain lodge with swimming pool. Course consists of casting lessons and practice at the Orvis trout ponds; illustrated lectures on fly selection, stream entomology, knot tying; tour of the Orvis rod factory, and free use and try-out of Orvis' fly rods. Cost is $165. Write Ms. Pam Newhouse at the above address for the Orvis school booklet.

FENWICK FLY FISHING SCHOOLS
P.O. Box 729, Westminster, Calif. 92683

If you've been concerned about improving your fly technique to insure a good trout breakfast on the trail, here's a good place to do it! The courses which usually run two days, 9 to 5, cover fly line, rod and reel construction; choosing the right tackle; insects, their life cycles, what to look for, where and when; artificial fly construction, choices of flies and "how to match the hatch"; fishing knots, use of leaders; and reading a stream to determine where the fish lie, why, how to approach them and with what. Textbook is *Fly Fishing From The Beginning* by Jim Green. Tackle is supplied by Fenwick or bring your own. Lunch and dinner are included in the fee of $125, but lodging is your gig—a motel or camp out (courses are usually held where you can do this). For more complete information and a schedule of dates and states where the classes are being held throughout the year, write Cheri Hayes at the above address.

PENNSYLVANIA ANGLER
James F. Yoder, Ed.
Monthly - $2/yr. - 25¢ issue - 32 p. il.

Most states of the Union have conservation or fish and wildlife magazines published by their natural resources agencies, but Pennsylvania is the only state that has a magazine devoted to just fishing (and boating). They also have one covering just hunting and wildlife. The *Pennsylvania Angler* is a good, down-to-earth periodical with much practical information on tackle, rigs, bait, do-it-yourself projects, and useful regional information on fishing spots. There's also fisherman-oriented boating and camping information, plus the latest skinny on who's screwing up what conservation-wise. Any Pennsylvania angler — frankly, any angler — who hasn't got a subscription to this one, is missing a sure bet for two bucks.
From: Pennsylvania Angler, 3532 Walnut St., Harrisburg, Pa. 17120

FLY FISHERMAN
Don Zahner, Ed.
7 issues/yr. - $10/yr. - $1.50/issue - 100 p. il.

Fly Fisherman is published seven times a year to fit in with the fly fisherman's cycle of activity. The "Spring Special" (March) issue is a big doubleheader of information. This very nicely laid out and well-illustrated magazine is for those anglers who fish primarily with a fly rod, and for those who would like to learn about fly fishing. Articles cover both fresh- and salt-water techniques, fly tying, angling tradition and history, rod making and tackle fussing, where-to-go features, and regular, extensive coverage of new products for the fly fisherman.
From: Fly Fisherman, Manchester Village, Vt. 05254

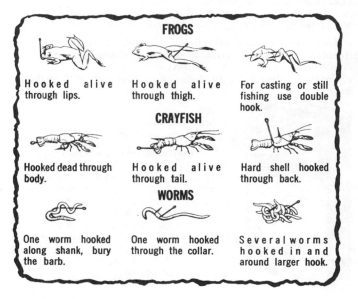

FROGS		
Hooked alive through lips.	Hooked alive through thigh.	For casting or still fishing use double hook.
CRAYFISH		
Hooked dead through body.	Hooked alive through tail.	Hard shell hooked through back.
WORMS		
One worm hooked along shank, bury the barb.	One worm hooked through the collar.	Several worms hooked in and around larger hook.

FISHING WORLD
Keith Gardner, Ed.
Bi-monthly - $4/yr. - 75¢/issue - 64 p. il.

Nice four-color fishing rag with good "how to" columns on freshwater, offshore, trout and salmon, and inshore fishing. Tom McNally is their "offshore" columnist. Articles cover fresh and saltwater fishing, are generally regional in nature, and flavored with typical fishing "jaw" and some practical information. Each issue usually carries at least one fly fishing article. Information on new tackle and fishing gear is a regular two-page feature. All in all, it looks pretty good.
From: Fishing World, 51 Atlantic Ave., Floral Park, N.Y. 11001.

SALMON TROUT STEELHEADER
Frank W. Amato, Ed.
Bi-monthly - $3/yr. - 60¢/issue - 46 p. il.

For wilderness fishing, *Salmon Trout Steelheader* is the one. It carries articles on technique, equipment, history, and regional fishing data; well illustrated with photos and technical drawings, and their ads are informative. Unfortunately, as far as regional information goes, they only cover the northwestern part of the United States and British Columbia. The STS people also have three good books on the market: *Steelhead Drift Fishing and Fly Fishing,* $2.50; *The Steelhead Trout,* $5.95; *Fishing the Sea-Run Cutthroat Trout,* $2.00. Check with 'em for more information on these books.
From: Salmon Trout Steelheader, P.O. Box 2112, Portland, Oreg. 97202

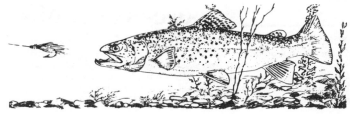

McCLANE'S NEW STANDARD FISHING ENCYCLOPEDIA
160 contributing authors
1974, rev. - 1,200 p. il. - $40

Originally published in 1965, this revised edition brings you nearly 9 lbs. of instant information on everything about fish and fishing. It covers every fish you'll find in the Americas, Europe and Africa, plus it explains in detail every kind of tackle, bait, lure and fishing technique there is from yesterday to today, and on and on. Really a fantastic book even at the stiff price of $40.
From: Holt, Rinehart and Winston, 383 Madison Ave., New York, N.Y. 10017

BOOKS

COMPLETE BOOK OF FLY FISHING
Joe Brooks
1965 - Rev. Ed. - $9.95

What Lucas can do to bass, Joe can also do to trout. And this is his collection of notes, techniques, and ideas on fly fishing gleaned from years of experience.
From: A.S. Barnes & Co., Box 421, Cranbury, N.J. 08512

LUCAS ON BASS FISHING
Jason Lucas
1962 - Rev. Ed. - $6.00

If there's a master bass angler, Lucas is most surely the man. And this book contains all the notes, techniques, and ideas Lucas has developed over the years to catch this baby.
From: Dodd, Mead & Co., 79 Madison Ave., New York, N.Y. 10016

FLIES
J. Edson Leonard
1950 - 340 p. il. - $7.95

One of the classics on flies and fly tying. Very complete, detailed, including chapters on hook design, tools, and materials, as well as construction. Leonard's dictionary of fly patterns runs some 80 pages, and it'll keep you tying for years. An excellent chapter on entomology, fifty plus pages. If you can only get one book on the subject, this is the book.
From: A.S. Barnes & Co., Box 421, Cranbury, N.J. 08512

THE ART OF PLUG FISHING
Homer Circle
1965 - 224 p. il. - $3.95 (pb)

Now here's a book that puts its arm around you and sez, "Let's us talk about fishing and no monkey business." Just like some old timer passing on 60 years of fishing wisdom. How to do it, where to do it, and best of all—why! Just great reading.
From: Stackpole Books, Harrisburg, Pa. 17105

TROUT
Ray Bergman
1964 - 500 p. il. - $12.50

This is, and undoubtedly will continue to be the authoritative work on trout and trout fishing. Includes color plates of 500 fly patterns, tying techniques, and angling methods, plus many stories of Bergman's experiences in the field.
From: Alfred A. Knopf, Inc., 457 Hahn Rd., Westminster, Md. 21157

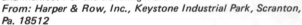

sources of books

ANGLER'S AND SHOOTER'S BOOKSHELF
Goshen, Conn. 06756
Angler's latest catalog lists over 4,000 books on hunting and fishing. Good source of hard-to-find, out-of-print books, and of course, current, popular titles. Send $2 for their catalog, which is refundable on any $10 order.

FLY TYING, SPINNING AND TACKLE MAKING
George Leonard Herter
200,000 words - $4.39

Highly recommended, especially by Herters. Complete information on building your own tackle, lures, and flies. Much good info on the fish themselves and their habits too. *Fly Tying* is a 192-page condensed version, and sells for $1.20. It concentrates on the subject of its title, and for the price, will supply you with all the background you need to really get into fly tying. Excellent.
From: Herter's, Inc., RFD 2, I-90, Mitchell, S.D. 57301

COMPLETE GUIDE TO FISHING ACROSS NORTH AMERICA
Joe Brooks
1966 - 613 p. il. - $7.95

Everyone knows Joe, and that's a pretty good recommendation in itself. Here's the inside skinny, and all of it, on where to go, how to get there, where to stay, plus tips and techniques. State by state coverage plus Canada and Mexico. For the traveling man.
From: Harper & Row, Inc., Keystone Industrial Park, Scranton, Pa. 18512

GILL OR SET NET

POPULAR NETCRAFT

POPULAR NETCRAFT
H.T. Ludgate
1948 - 72 p. il. - $1

Really a neat manual for making all kinds of nets and net-type gear. Covers the tools, types of twine, setting up, and mesh making techniques. Very thorough on this. Includes plans for landing nets, turtle and minnow trapping nets, a South Seas casting net, gill nets, and seines. Also details on repairing and preserving nets. Beautiful, easy to understand illustrations and instructions.
From: Netcraft Co., 3101 Sylvania Ave., Toledo, Ohio 43613

COMPLETE BOOK OF FRESH WATER FISHING
P. Allen Parsons
1963 - 332 p. il. - $7.95

If you want to get a general education on all the fresh-water tackle types and how best to fish with them, then here's your book. Loads of practical tips, angling techniques for the popular species, plus a list of the 100 best trout streams in the U.S.
From: Harper & Row, Inc., Keystone Industrial Park, Scranton, Pa. 18512

RODS
$9 to $130

Though there are three basic types of rods — *spinning* ($10 to $50), *casting* ($9 to $30), and *fly* ($10 to $130) — all are designed to be an extension of the angler's arm in casting, manipulating the lure and playing the fish. The longer the rod, the greater the leverage for casting; the more flexible the rod the better the "feel" for working the lure and playing the fish once he's caught. Also, when the flex is right, the rod helps to drive out the lure with comparative ease and accuracy. The lure, more than anything else, sets the criteria for rod length and flexibility, and the type of reel to be used. Though there is a heck of a lot of overlap, the scheme generally runs: the heavier the lure, the shorter and stiffer the rod; the lighter the lure, the longer and more flexible the rod, and the lighter the weight of the whole outfit. In order from heaviest to lightest, the outfits would run: bait casting, spin casting, spinning, and fly fishing. Since most fish can be caught on a variety of lures (weight-wise), the type of outfit to use is really a matter of personal choice.

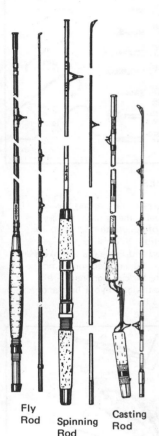

Fly Rod   **Spinning Rod**   **Casting Rod**

The majority of rods made today are of fiberglass, though steel casting rods are to be found, and bamboo is sometimes used, particularly in high quality fly rods. Tonkin bamboo is considered to be the most desirable. Guides are made of an extremely hard steel alloy to prevent wear from the moving line. This is particularly important at the tip guide. Handles are covered with cork for lightness and grip, and are of two types: straight, used on spinning and fly rods, and off-set, used on casting rods. Some rods come in sections and are joined by ferrules, which incidentally, should never be put together or taken apart by twisting; use a direct pull or push and you won't weaken the ferrule's binding to the rod.

Pack rods break down into 4 or 5 sections for convenience of packing into back-country fishing areas. Wright & McGill's Eagle Claw Trailmaster rods are the most popular of this type, and come in spinning, casting, fly, and a spinning/fly combo; just flip the handle around. Price is about $23.

Amongst the top names in rods are Garcia, Wright & McGill (Eagle Claw), Fenwick, and Orvis (particularly for fly rods). If you're into making your own rods or just want to keep them in good repair, Fenwick can supply you with fiberglass rod blanks of all descriptions. Reed Tackle is a good source of parts, supplies and tools, including rod kits. They're mostly oriented toward the fly man though. Orvis has some nice fly rod kits as well as parts and supplies.

REELS
$3 - $50

Reels fall into five different classes. Fly fishing reels include the *single action* ($6 to $50) and the *automatic* ($6 to $20). Casting

SINGLE ACTION REEL
Pflueger Medalist

systems use the *multiplier*, also known as the Kentucky or bait casting reel ($6 to $50) and the *spin cast* reel ($3 to $25). And the *spinning* reel ($6 to $50) is used in spinning.

The single action is the progenitor of all reels and is simply a spool with a handle. Its purpose is to store line, not to reel in or play the fish. The automatic is a single action type with springs in the reel housing that wind up as line is run out. Tension thus built up will reel the line back on the spool when a release is activated. The single action is preferred over the automatic, because it is more versatile, lighter, and is easier to change spools and dismantel for cleaning. Amongst the brands of single action reels the Pflueger Medalist series ($13 to $18) is well regarded, as are the Hardy reels manufactured in England ($40 to $49). Scientific Anglers and Orvis both have good lines of fly reels.

Bait casting reels are geared for faster line retrieval in playing the fish. They also have more spool friction than other reels, hence it takes a heavier lure to gain distance in casting, actually, just to get the line off the spool. Probably the biggest problem with this reel is back-lash, where the spool continues to feed line when the cast is finished and a tangled mess results about the reel. Quite a few of the newer reels have anti-backlash drags, but not all of them

AUTOMATIC FLY REEL
Garcia Mitchell 710

work that well. Trouble is when they're tightened up they reduce casting distance as well. Two of the top names in bait casting reels are Garcia and Pflueger.

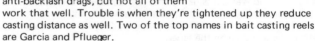

MULTIPLIER REEL
Pflueger 2000 Bond

The spin cast reel, also called the closed-face, is an offshoot of the spinning type developed to give both the advantage of the bait caster (without backlash) and the spinning reel. Casting is a cinch because of a push-button release that gives positive line run-off control, and there is less friction. Because of the reduced friction lighter lures and line are used and the reel is normally matched to a slightly longer and more flexible rod than the bait casting reel. Johnson is one of the top names in spin cast reels, as well as Garcia with its well-known Abu-Matic 170. In the lower price range Zebco is a popular brand.

THE COMPLETE GUIDE TO SALT AND FRESH WATER FISHING EQUIPMENT
Bill Wisner
1976 - 256 p. il. - $9.95

Really a thorough and complete guide to fishing tackle and accessories. Wisner starts off with fishing lore and anecdotes and then goes on to explain the rudiments of salt- and fresh-water fishing, basic angling methods, and types and care of tackle and lures. Next is the "Tackle Showroom" wherein salt-water rods, reels and line are covered on a company-by-company basis with a critique on each of their more popular models; prices are also given as well as the company's address.

Covered in the same manner are fresh-water rods, reels, line and ice-fishing gear; fly-fishing rods, reels, line and lures; hooks, terminal tackle and lures for all types of fishing; fishing accessories and boat gear; electronic aids to fishing, and clothing for fishing. This is not a guide to all the companies catering to the fisherman, but rather a guide to those manufacturers who have made a reputation for themselves in the business. Even so, coverage of their gear, at least for the models listed, is fairly detailed. A fabulous buy for the real fishing buff who wants to know the best place to spend his money wisely.
From: E.P. Dutton & Co., Inc., 201 Park Ave., S., New York, N.Y. 10003

The spinning or open face reel has many advantages which no doubt have been responsible for its tremendous popularity, and they all focus on the spool. In the spinning reel the spool does not turn. Instead the line uncoils off the end of the spool in large loops and the rod guides, large at the reel growing smaller toward the tip, act as a funnel to straighten the line out. This design permits almost frictionless run-off, which is why such light lures can be used. When reeling in, a pick-up bar or bail snaps in position and coils the line back around the spool. Advantages of the spinning outfit, in addition to the light lures that can be used, are no backlash, excellent balance because the reel is directly under the hand, the rod doesn't have to be shifted from one

SPIN CAST REEL
Garcia ABU 505

hand to the other at the end of a cast, and the technique is relatively easy to learn compared to other systems. It's definitely a good first choice for someone just getting started. Garcia's Mitchell line of spinning reels is a favorite, with the Mitchell 300 ($18) considered to be a very good buy.

SPINNING REEL
Mitchell 300

LINE
$1 to $13

There are two basic types of line: fly line, which is quite specialized, and the other kind used for spinning and casting, usually called monofilament. In fly casting it's the weight of the line that gets out the lure, since the fly hardly weighs anything. Fly line comes in 12 weights from 60 to 380 grains, and must be carefully matched to the rod. The weight is based on the first 30 feet of line for all types ("tapers"), and there are a number of them. The most popular three are the double taper, in which the line weight is concentrated in the 30-foot mid-section; the end taper, with weight concentrated in the forward 20-foot section; and level, with weight and diameter uniform throughout. Each type, which is also designed to float, sink, or do both, is used to cast or "present" the lure in a special way. Before Scientific Anglers, Inc., came along you only had a choice of silk or nylon for fly line, which required periodic attention to get it to perform properly. Scientific Angler's Air Cel (floating line) and Wet Cel (sinking line) has done away with the old fly line problems, and has become the top selling line in the country. It's availalbe just about everywhere, a 30-yard coil selling for $4 to $9 depending on the taper.

Casting and spinning line is available in braided materials such as dacron, about $2/100 yds./12 lb. test, and in monofilament made of various plastic-type synthetics, nylon being the most common. Stren, a DuPont product, seems to be overriding nylon in popularity, however, because of its greater durability, strength and flexibility. It sells for about the same as monofilament. Cabella's is a source of these lines if you can't find them elsewhere.

LEADERS
25¢ - 45¢

Leaders come ready made or are custom made by the angler. Here again DuPont's Stren is a good material, unless you're angling for the bigger toothy types, then wire's the ticket. The leader is important because it saves wear and tear on the business end of the line, and the less visible it is the better your chances of getting a fish to accept the lure. So keep in mind length, diameter, color, and the fishing conditions when deciding what to get. With respect to fly fishing, leaders are just as critical as the choice of fly.

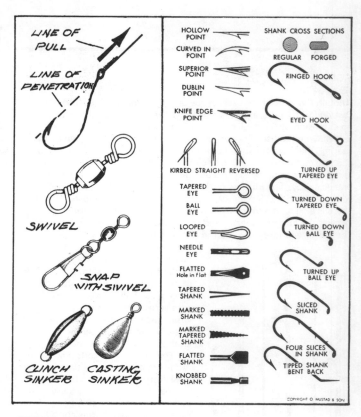

HOOKS, SINKERS, SNAPS & SWIVELS
1¢ - 20¢

The hook is the business end of any piece of tackle, and though you may feel any will do, the fact is that some designs are very inefficient. The reason is that the line of penetration of the hook does not coincide with the line of traction. You follow me? The two top names in hooks are Mustad and Eagle Claw. Sinkers get the line down where it's supposed to be, and can sometimes be used to heavy up an otherwise light lure for casting. Snaps are convenience items to save having to tie things on your line, and swivels prevent lures from twisting up a line.

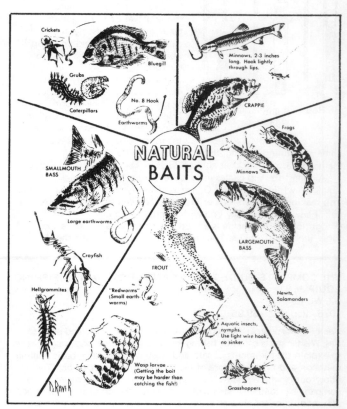

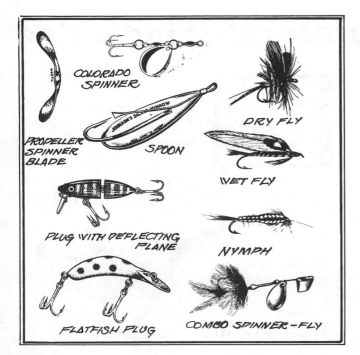

COLORADO SPINNER

PROPELLER SPINNER BLADE

SPOON

DRY FLY

WET FLY

PLUG WITH DEFLECTING PLANE

NYMPH

FLATFISH PLUG

COMBO SPINNER - FLY

LURES
15¢ - $3

Artificial bait comes in four families: spoons, spinners, plugs, and flies. The simplest of the four is the spoon, shaped very much like the bowl of a spoon. This shape makes it wobble and flash when drawn through the water. Spoons are sub-surface type lures used in casting for pike, muskies, northerns, pickerels, bass, and trout. Some anglers say that if they had only one choice of lure, they'd pick a simple wobbler spoon over all others.

Spinners come in two types. The single blade, which sometimes looks and acts like a spoon, is one. The propeller blade is the other. Sometimes these little props are used with plugs or flies to give additional flash and movement to the lure for trolling. Spinners are good lures for pike, walleye, lake trout and pan fish.

Plugs, next to flies, are the most complicated of lures. These are broken down into three types: surface, sub-surface, and deep or sinking, which is determined by the plug's weight and deflecting-plane angle. Just about all plugs today are made of plastic to resemble a small fish or some other form of live bait. Colors, if chosen carefully, can be of value in attracting fish. For example, bass, which are associated with plug fishing more so than with other types, are responsive to the red end of the spectrum rather than the blue. Plugs are used in casting and trolling for bass, pike, and pan fish.

Flies are a combination of feather, hook, and sometimes fur tied to resemble an insect. Two general groups are recognized, the dry, which is treated to float on the water, and the wet, which absorbs water and sinks. Flies are also divided according to the form they take (fan-wing), the material used to make them (hackles), or the type of insect they represent (spiders). Some flies do not represent insects at all, rather they are dressed to depict minnows or other small bait fish. These are the bucktails and streamers. There are more than three hundred nationally or locally well-known patterns with a diversity of odd-ball names that'd run Rube Goldberg up a tree, hence it's always wise to recon prospective fishing spots and check with local anglers to see what's eatin'.

Flies tied by professional dressers, such as those sold by Orvis and Rangeley Region Sport Shop, can be pretty dear, running up to a buck and a half each, hence a lot of people get into the business of tying flies themselves. A good book to get you started in this is George L. Herter's *Professional Fly Tying, Spinning and Tackle Making Manual*, $4.39, and if you really get serious about it, your next purchase ought to be J. Edson Leonard's *Flies*, $7.95. As to fly tying tools and supplies, you'd be missing a good bet if you didn't try Reed Tackle—top-gun inventory and good prices. Normally, you can pick a pattern that will do the trick out of a well-rounded assortment such as those sold by Orvis Co., Inc., $5 to $65. When you get right down to it, though, nine times out of ten, presentation of the fly is the key to success rather than its color and pattern.

ACCESSORIES

Fishing accessories are limitless, and since we're trying to hold this section to the practical aspects of angling (wilderness food source) as much as possible, we'll just cover the more practical items. If you have any recommendations, we'd be happy to have them for the next issue of the *Source Book.*

Some sort of kit for your tackle is of first import. If you're going by canoe a tackle box is not too much to carry along. Most brands are pretty good, with the average price for a small to medium box running $5 to $8. If you're packing in, it has to be a handier and lighter size. Cabela's has several sizes of Tenite compartmented boxes, $1 to $3. Tenite looks like plastic, but is a helluva lot stronger and won't crack. Rangeley has Fletcher's Tote Bag, a compartmented canvas/leather shoulder bag that might appeal to the serious packer/angler, $13. Flies can be kept in aluminum fly boxes on clips or via magnetic hook keepers. Perrine is the brand here. Prices range from $3 to $5, Cabela's, Rangeley, Reed and Orvis all handle 'em, but Cabela's is your best price. You can also go the fly book route. This is a soft zipper pack with wool "pages" into which the flies are hooked, $5. Reed and Rangeley have several styles. Some people (fly types) cram their gear in fishing vests and wear 'em with their packs, which doesn't seem like a bad idea. A good vest will run you $12 to $20. For your rod there are polyethelene and aluminum telescoping cases ranging from $7 to $18. Orvis sells a beautiful leather job for $37. Wright & McGill supplies an aluminum case with their Trailmaster models. Be sure to get it when buying through a dealer. Reels are carried in leather pouches, about $4. A landing net may seem superfluous, but many a beauty has been lost through lack of one. The only landing net we can recommend is the folding type; the others are too cumbersome to pack in. Rangeley has two styles, $6 to $12, and Orvis a fourth, $28. When stream fishing, you've got to have someplace to stash them trout and the Japanese split willow creel, $15 to $30, is the traditional item for this, though a tad out of place for the packer. A better choice would be the Arctic Creel, $8 to $10, made of flax water bag canvas. Does a good job of keeping fish fresh, too. Netcraft has two types of creels, split willow and Chinese reed, and Cabela's has a good price on the Arctic Creel. Line dressing is a must for the fly fisherman, and highly recommended is Mucilin, an English preparation, in liquid or paste form for adding buoyancy and durability to lines and flies. Available through Rangeley for less than a buck.

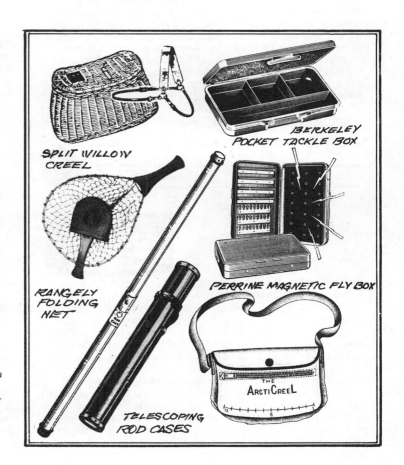

SPLIT WILLOW CREEL

BERKELEY POCKET TACKLE BOX

RANGELY FOLDING NET

PERRINE MAGNETIC FLY BOX

THE ARCTICREEL

TELESCOPING ROD CASES

FISHING

SCIENTIFIC ANGLERS
Box 2007, Midland, Mich. 48640
These guys invented a process for manufacturing fly line with millions of tiny air bubbles in it to make it float, and just about revolutionized the fly line industry. Before they came along compounds were required to make the line float or sink, and ... well, to make a long story short, the whole business was a pain in the butt. Anyway, Scientific Anglers has taken the pain out of it, and have the top flylines in the business. They've also developed 8 matched fly fishing rigs. Rods are bamboo, and reels are by Hardy. Their 14-page color catalog of fly lines, rods and reels is free. Also ask for their fly fishing bulletin. Good information.

FIRESIDE ANGLER
P.O. Box 823, Melville, N.Y. 11746
Complete selection of fly tackle including the Scott PowR-ply glass rod which supposedly has the same "feel" as bamboo—they've got the tapers all worked out (Hmmm?). Free catalog from the above address.

RAYMOND C. RUMPF & SON
Ferndale, Pa. 18921
Very large selection of fly-tying materials including hooks, feathers, furs, tinsel, chenille, wool, plus tools, jig heads, and so forth, at discount prices. Write for free catalog.

GARCIA CORP.
329 Alfred Ave., Teaneck, N.J. 07666
Garcia is probably best known for their Mitchell spinning reels, Ambassadeur bait casting reels, and Abu-Matic spin casting reels. Though Garcia does not sell directly to the public, they will provide you with the name of a local who handles their gear. Cabela's and Netcraft both handle the Garcia line through mail order. In the repair department, Garcia has over 550 service centers that can handle any rod or reel problem. Their addresses are available from Garcia upon request. Each year Garcia puts out their *Fishing Annual*, which is a combination fishing magazine and product catalog of their equipment. It runs $1, and has a lot of "how I did it" type stories plus 70 to 80 pages describing the complete Garcia line of tackle. In addition to their *Annual*, Garcia also publishes 16 soft-bound instruction books of 100 pages or so on different types of fishing and fishing rigs. Several that can be recommended are: *Freshwater Fishing, Pan Fishing, Fly Fishing,* and *Artificial Lures*; cost is $1 each.

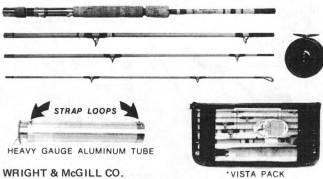

STRAP LOOPS

HEAVY GAUGE ALUMINUM TUBE

*VISTA PACK

WRIGHT & McGILL CO.
P.O. Box 16011, Denver, Colo. 80216
Wright & McGill is better known under their trade name: Eagle Claw. They don't sell directly to the public, rather they distribute through local retailers and mail order outfits. You can get a 60-page color catalog of all the Wright & McGill tackle, though, by writing to the above address; pictures and descriptions, but no prices. Wright & McGill's fame came with their Eagle Claw design hooks back in the 1920's. Since then they've added rods, reels, and line to their hooks. Particularly noteworthy and very popular are their pack rods in the Trailmaster series, for spinning, fly fishing, or a combo rod for both. Wright & McGill publish a paperback book called *Elementary Fishing* by Joseph D. Bates, Jr., for 75¢. Everything the beginner should know about fresh-water fishing. It's supposed to be pretty good.

ANGLER'S LOG
Keep a factual record of how, when, where, weather conditions, size, and species of fish caught. Such fun to look back and reminisce.
Price $6.00
Refills $4.00

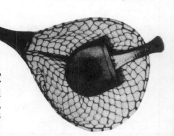

HANDY PAK NET
Completely collapsible net, which folds into leather belt pouch. Spring steel hoop, cherry wood handle, cotton net. 15" x 11" net — 18" deep. Price...... $11.95

RANGELEY REGION SPORTS SHOP
28 Main St., Rangeley, Maine 04970
Complete line of fly tying materials and tools, plus a fair inventory of ready made flies. Really oriented toward the professional fly man. Equipment-wise, Rangeley handles Fenwick and Phillipson rods, Hardy reels, and Orvis tackle among others. Lotsa neat angling gadgets and accessories, plus a nice selection of books. Prices are a little high on some items, but all their stuff is first class. Black-and-white, 28-page catalog available, free.

H. L. LEONARD ROD CO.
25 Cottage St., Midland Park, N.J. 07432
One of the oldest rod companies in the United States and probably the best. Their rods are about twice the price of Orvis', but truly remarkable.—Richard Davis 1974.

THE ANGLERS ART
1055 Thomas Jefferson St., N.W., Washington, D.C. 20007
Complete selection and a wide range of fly-fishing tackle and fly-tying supplies, plus over 2,000 books on angling and a very nice collection of wildlife originals and prints.

Triangular Rod Cases
Non-rolling triangular rod cases give first-rate protection; available in rich brown hard plastic with white trim and flip-top lid.

SEVENSTRAND TACKLE MFG. CO.
P.O. Box 729, Westminster, Calif. 92683
Ever hear of Fenwick fiberglass rods? Well, these are the people who build 'em, and they're reputed to be one of the top rods available. Sevenstrand makes Fenwick rods for all fishing systems, and if you want to build your own, they'll supply you with blanks and accessories. Literature and prices available on request. Sevenstrand also publishes a couple of books, *Fly Casting* by Jim Green, $2, and *Saltwater Fishing: Beginner to Expert* by Chuck Garrison and Bill Rice, $1; plus an interesting and informative 8-page *Newsletter* which comes out now and again. It's available free. If you want to get taught fly fishing, request the Fenwick Fly Fishing School brochure.

REED TACKLE
Box 390, Caldwell, N.J. 07006

This is strictly a part's shop for anglers, the home craftsman-type who digs making his own plugs, flies, and rods. Only about 10% of the merchandise in Reed's 96-page catalog is "ready-to-wear" tackle, being mainly tools, jigs, supplies, hardware, and compounds. Excellent selection of fur and feathers, hooks (Mustad), rod blanks, guides, handles, cork, reel bands, lure parts, blades, beads, spoons, jig heads, etc. If you prefer a kit to building from scratch, they've got 'em for fly tying and rod making. Good prices on all their stuff.

Tenacious

For

Quality

HERTER'S FREEZE DRIED BAITS

It is effective, fish love it, it is odorless when stored. Once the bait is put into water it regains its original shape, flavors and aromas. Complete with instructions. Shpg. wt. each box 4 ozs.

No.	Type of Bait	Price Per Box
BC12A	Blood Worms	$1.04
BC12C	Crickets	.74
BC12D	Frogs	1.04
BC12E	Golden Shiners	.96
BC12F	Minnows	.85
BC12G	Nite Crawlers	.94

HERTER'S, INC.
RFD 2, I-90, Mitchell, S.D. 57301

Herter's, in addition to a million other things for the sportsman, also handles fishing tackle and accessories for spinning, casting, and fly fishing. Also much gear and supplies for making your own — fly tying, lure making, and rod building. George Leonard Herter's book on fly tying is considered tops (one of the top, anyway) in fly dressing circles, so they've got something going for them. Good prices, and for the most part, good quality. Pick up a copy of their 352-page catalog for a buck—loaded with tackle and "no-two-ways-about-it!" reading.

Fly Tying Desk.................$11.95

THE ORVIS CO., INC.
Manchester, Vt. 05254

An old line company dedicated to the fly fishing specialist, Orvis not only sells gear, but they teach you how to use it. For $165 you can take a 3-day fly fishing course up at their place in Vermont. In the equipment department, they have their own line of fly and spinning tackle, fly tying tools and materials, and one of the best selections of ready made flies we've seen, all beautifully illustrated in their free 100-page color catalog. Accessory-wise Orvis has a nice selection of clothes, fishing vests, waders, and gadgets, all top quality. They also have some camping gear (Camp Trails stuff). Oh yeah, they publish a little 8-page newspaper every two months or so with good angling and product info. One thing you've got to remember when dealing with Orvis — in the words of old J.P. Morgan, "If you have to ask what it costs, you can't afford it."

CABELA'S, INC.
P.O. Box 199, Sidney, Neb. 69162

Cabela's has the best inventory and prices for general fishing tackle and accessories around. They have an excellent range of rod and reel models from just about all the top manufacturers for spinning, casting, and fly fishing rigs. Lure-wise, they're heavy on plugs and light on flies. Fine assortment of lines of all types including Scientific Anglers' and DuPont Stren. Numerous accessories including knives, vests, waders, creels, and tackle and lure boxes. For the do-it-yourselfer, Cabela's sells quite a batch of lure and rod making supplies, tools, and accessories. In addition to fishing stuff, Cabela's catalog includes camping and boating gear and clothing for the fisherman. Excellent prices, good quality, and indexed, which will make it easy to find stuff in those 175 pages.

FLY FISHERMAN'S BOOKCASE AND TACKLE SERVICE
Rt. 9, Croton-on-Hudson, N.Y. 10520

Very nice selection of tackle including Scientific Anglers, Hardy, Pflueger, Vince Cummings, Fenwick, Maxima, Berkeley, Wheatley, Perrine and DeWitt. Prices are low, averaging 15 to 25% off list.

NETCRAFT CO.
3101 Sylvania Ave., Toledo, Ohio 43613

Netcraft originally started in the net making business back in '41, since then has expanded into a real general line of angling merchandise. They've got just about something of everything, though more oriented toward gadgets than straight tackle, and the quality ranges all over the map. Inventory includes: netmaking supplies and instruction booklets; plug and soft bait making supplies and kits; fly tying supplies, kits, tools, jigs; rod making and repairing stuff, including rod blanks, handles, cork, guides, wrapping and winding equipment; rod and reel cases, in all materials and types; rods by shakespeare, Wright & McGill, True Temper; reels by Garcia, South Bend, Zebco, Pflueger, Heddon, Johnson, Shakespeare, and Penn (limited range of models for any one manufacturer, though); ice fishing accessories, stoves; fish smoking equipment, et cetera and so forth. Their 69-page catalog will fit in your vest pocket sos you can check their stuff out on lunch break. Good prices, worth checking before buying elsewhere, and you'll be able to find them — the catalog has a good index.

falconry

Falconry is alive and thriving. The ancient sport, which emerged 2,000 years before Christ and reached its prime in the Middle Ages, is practiced today by a growing number of devotees, men and women who spend a large share of their time and patience capturing, training, and hunting with hawks.

Falconers are a funny bunch of people. Dedicated, clannish almost to the point of functioning as a secret society, they get their thrills from experiencing the beauty, grace, and efficiency of the bird of prey in action. And they are conservationists by nature and by necessity. By nature, because they are totally committed to the image and the reality of the creatures they work with. By necessity, because in order for their avocation to remain viable, the bird of prey—and the prey itself—must survive and flourish.

Unfortunately, in recent years, birds of prey along with other animals have not been faring very well. The peregrine falcon, that noble bird of medieval falconry, and even the bald eagle are threatened with extinction. Along with every other wild creature, hawks have had to cope with the effects of pesticides and the encroachment of civilization on breeding grounds and habitats. In addition, they've had to survive "varmit" shooters and deliberately poisoned carrion.

The decline of these species has been a factor in the political/environmental controversy that has arisen between falconers and environmental protectionists. The gist of it is that falconers have been labeled villians by association. What the protectionists (those ten percent who have educated themselves in the attitudes and concepts of falconry) don't tell you though, is that the falconer captures, never kills the bird, that he trains, but never tames it, and that ultimately he returns the bird to the wild. They also fail to mention the rigorous apprenticeship a tyro must go through to learn the bird's habits, veterinary techniques, diets and feeding procedures, and all that is necessary to keep the animal in the peak of health.

Still, falconers have suffered from the adverse publicity. While some have come forward as a group to defend the sport and educate the public, others have withdrawn even more to exclude outsiders. The situation creates a problem for someone who is seriously interested in falconry, since the only acceptable way to learn the art is through apprenticeship to an experienced falconer. Just try and find one! You can write to the North American Falconers Association for the name of a group in your vicinity. They might be willing and able to help you, but don't count on it. Another thing you should do is check your state's laws. Many subject falconry to strict seasons, much like hunting; others simply prohibit it.

The main expenditure in falconry is time—lots of it—and in that respect, it is an expensive proposition. Most falconers make their own gear—perches, bags, leashes, jesses, and so forth—so the cost there is minimal. But even buying new, ready made stuff shouldn't set you back any more than $50, excluding books. The cost of building a mews (the falcon's living quarters), will vary depending on what you want to put into it. Like any other home-built project, it can be simple or ornate. The falconer also purchases and administers medications when necessary, since most vets know very little about raptors, and even fewer will touch them. From beginning to end falconry is a time-consuming, demanding avocation, but one with unique rewards.

THE ART OF FALCONRY
Frederick II of Hohenstaufen, ed. by Casey A. Wood & Marjorie Fyfe
$20 or $200 (see text)

The classic work on the practice of falconry, written in the 13th century by a poet, scientist, and authority on hawking. The first section deals with ornithology, the second, with procuring, breeding, and taming of falcons, and the third, with training. Three remaining sections are devoted to crane hawking, wild-duck hawking, and heron hawking. A special collector's edition which is a facsimile of the 13th century original, handcut, with 111 folios and full leather binding, along with a companion volume (in German) that explains the original treatise, is available from William R. Hecht for $200. An edited English edition is available from Stanford University Press, Stanford, Calif. 94305 for $20.

NORTH AMERICAN FALCONRY & HUNTING HAWKS
Frank L. Beebe & Harold M. Webster II. - $30

This is probably the best book available for the novice falconer. Training and trapping techniques for different types of birds are discussed along with care, feeding, and diseases. Well worth the price.
From: North American Falconry and Hunting Hawks, P.O. Box 1484, Denver, Colo. 80201

FALCONRY
Humphrey ap Evans
1973 - 160 p. il. - $10

The newest treatise on the ancient art by the author of *Falconry for You.* This work, though presented as an "illustrated introduction," goes far beyond that to cover in detail the proper way of getting into falconry, the rigors of apprenticeship and the overall practice of the sport from caring for and feeding the hawk to training and flying it. Though many of the references are to British organizations and sources, the actual practical information is universal. Many, many beautiful photographs.
From: John Bartholomew & Son Ltd., 12 Duncan St., Edinburgh, Scotland EH9 1TA

NORTH AMERICAN FALCONERS ASSOCIATION
Rt. 2, Hawley, Minn. 56549

NAFA has fought for years for the recognition of falconry as a legal field sport, and through their hard work have succeeded at the federal level and in a vast majority of the states. Their purpose is "...to provide communication among and to disseminate relevant information to interested members; to promote scientific study of the raptorial species, their care, welfare and training; to promote conservation of the birds of prey, and an appreciation of their value in nature and in wildlife conservation programs; to urge recognition of falconry as a legal field sport; and, to establish traditions which will aid, perpetuate, and further the welfare of falconry and the raptors it employs." Their publications, *Hawk Chalk* and the *Journal* are available to members only. Publication totals four times a year. Membership is by sponsorship and is open to all falconers and those sincerely interested in the conservation of birds of prey. We were given no information on dues.

THE FALCONRY CENTRE
Newent, Gloucestershire, England

Founded and under the directorship of Phillip Glasier, "The Falconry Centre has been established not only as a rendezvous for hawking enthusiasts, whether old hands, or students of this ancient sport, but also for anyone interested in a country pursuit which has for centuries formed part of the traditional pattern of the British heritage. The aim of the Centre is to be a clearing house for the exchange of information, experience, advice and news between falconers everywhere, as well as being an interesting place to visit. There is a museum showing the different birds used in falconry, their equipment and how it is made, methods of training and ways of trapping."

CANADIAN RAPTOR SOCIETY
Box 37, Saanichton, British Columbia, Canada

The Canadian counterpart to the North American Falconers Assn.

FEDERAL FALCONRY REGULATIONS

New regulations requiring federal permits for falconers and setting standards for falconry became effective 17 February 1976. The regulations require that persons entering the sport have a basic knowledge of raptor identification, biology, regulations, care and training. They establish three classes of falconry permits depending upon the individual's level of competence: apprentice, general and master. They also set housing and marking requirements for raptors and identify species and the number of birds which can be used for sport. Finally, they establish minimum standards to be used by the states for issuing the permits. For more information write: U.S. Fish and Wildlife Service, Dept. of the Interior, Washington, D.C. 20240 and your state Fish and Wildlife Dept.

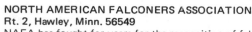

(Photo-art courtesy of California Hawking Club)

BOOKS

HINTS ON THE MANAGEMENT OF HAWKS
James E. Harting
$9

In addition to basic information on the care and management of the hawking establishment, this book includes a section on the training of eagles for large quarry. The author is considered one of the finest falconers in the sport.
From: North American Falconry and Hunting Hawks, Box 1484, Denver, Colo. 80201

ART & PRACTICE OF HAWKING
E.B. Mitchell
$7

An excellent beginner's book which discusses techniques used in training most of the birds used in falconry. Only possible point of confusion for the novice are the Old World names by which the birds are called. This is a poor source of info on diseases since it was written in the early 1900's when little was known of cures and the use of drugs.
From: Chas. T. Blanford Co., 28 Union St., Newton Centre, Mass. 02159

FALCONRY IN THE BRITISH ISLES
Francis H. Salvin and William Brodrick
Reprint of 1855 edition - il. - $22.50

Though not recommended for beginners, this is one of the leading books in the field and required reading for the serious falconer. It includes 23 color illustrations of the raptors utilized in falconry.
From: North American Falconry and Hunting Hawks, Box 1484, Denver, Colo. 80201

sources of books

Falconry books are not easy to come by. Because of the limited practice of the sport, there isn't a sufficient demand for them to be standard bookstore stock, though most shops will order them for you. Metropolitan area libraries usually have at least three or four on hand and the USAF Academy Library, U.S. Air Force Academy, Colorado 80840 is said to have an extensive collection devoted to falconry. Their services are normally limited to Academy students and personnel, but they participate in inter-library loans. Two book dealers specialize in books on falconry: North American Falconry and Hunting Hawks (P.O. Box 1484, Denver, Colo. 80201), which is in the publishing and reprint business, and William R. Hecht (Box 67, Scottsdale, Ariz. 85252), who probably has the most extensive listing available. Not only does Hecht have all of today's popular titles, but also rare first editions and foreign works on falconry. Write for his latest list.

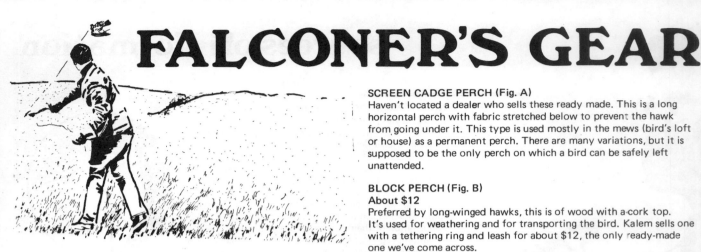

FALCONER'S GEAR

SCREEN CADGE PERCH (Fig. A)

Haven't located a dealer who sells these ready made. This is a long horizontal perch with fabric stretched below to prevent the hawk from going under it. This type is used mostly in the mews (bird's loft or house) as a permanent perch. There are many variations, but it is supposed to be the only perch on which a bird can be safely left unattended.

BLOCK PERCH (Fig. B)
About $12
Preferred by long-winged hawks, this is of wood with a cork top. It's used for weathering and for transporting the bird. Kalem sells one with a tethering ring and leash for about $12, the only ready-made one we've come across.

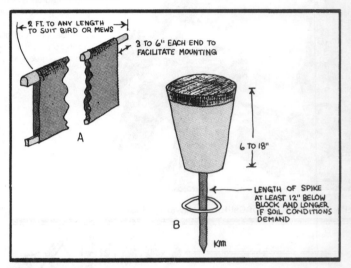

JESSES (Fig. A & B)
About $2
Strips of soft, strong leather about 9" long that are attached to the bird's legs to restrict its flight. A bird must never be allowed to escape with his jesses, for they can become entangled in tree branches or the like and trap him to die of starvation. Repeat the previous sentence 20 times a day.

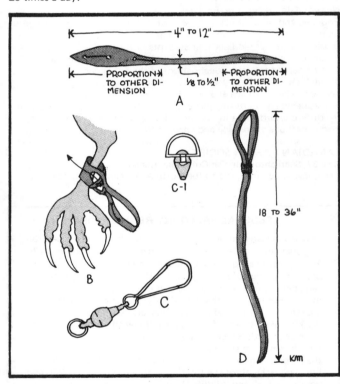

BOW PERCH (Fig. C)
About $15
You can buy one from Kalem Glove Manufacturing Company or make your own from a concrete reinforcing rod. A ring is attached for tethering, and the perch is padded with canvas or a similar material.

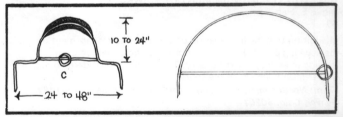

SWIVELS (Fig. C)
90¢ to $1
Used with leash, lure, or jesses to enable the line or leather strap to move freely without tangling. The type with a snap hook and ring is available in most sport fishing stores.

LEASH (Fig. D)
75¢ to $1
A strip of leather about three feet long used for "weathering" the falcon, i.e., tying it outside.

LURE
$6 to $10
Used in training and for recalling the bird after an unsuccessful flight. Usually a small leather bag filled with sand and covered with feathers, and attached to a line three or four yards long. The falconer swings the lure over his head until the bird sees and comes for it.

Falconry and Conservation

Falconers are concerned, more than anybody else, about the welfare of the raptorial bird populations. With our own self interests in mind, without any hawks our sport would cease to exist except in some obscure books in a library.

Most of the birds a falconer uses are returned back to the wild after a season of hunting. In effect, we are only borrowing our birds temporarily from nature.

Falconry can actually increase our hawk population. It is common knowledge that the mortality rate for hawk species is unusually high in nature. In the case of the Peregrine and the Prairie falcon the yearly natural mortality rate of the young is eighty to ninety percent. An eyess taken out of the nest by a falconer, on the other hand, stands a greater probability (eighty to ninety percent) to *survive* to maturity in captivity. This inverse relationship would mean that if every captive eyess was released to the wild (released when the bird is sexually mature and when it can fend for itself) a population increase

Drawings of equipment were made up by Wally Green to show how you might build your own. Artist—Ken Mentel.

BELLS
$2 to $3

Some falconers attach these to the bird's legs to aid in locating it if it gets lost in the brush. Everyone seems to agree that the best ones come from Pakistan. They're attached by pieces of leather called bewits.

CREANCE
About $1.25 for 30 yards

A long piece of nylon cord that is tied to the swivel and the jesses and used in training the bird to fly to the fist or to the lure.

FALCONER'S BAG
$25 to $50

Worn on the belt or a shoulder strap, this is used to hold game and to carry meat to reward the hawk. Types vary from plain to decorative.

GAUNTLET
$13 to $17

A heavy glove with an extended cuff used to protect the falconer's hand and arm from the bird's talons. A heavy welder's glove may be substituted.

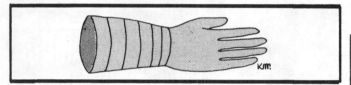

HOOD
$7 to $10

This covers the hawk's head to keep it calm while being transported. H. Eugene Johnson sells deluxe leather hoods with feather plumes that are tooled and dyed, around $10.

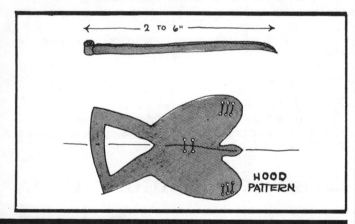

HOOD PATTERN

would result. The increased number of adult breeders could further accelerate a population growth in a non-regenerating population.

In England, the Goshawk has come back as a breeding species after years of extinction. British falconers, after a number of years of flying and losing their imported Goshawks found the bird reestablishing itself as a nesting species. This was an unconscious effort on the behalf of the falconers in the British Isles and look at the impact it had on reintroducing this bird.

If falconers were allowed to continue taking immature or passage falcons with a provision that the birds have to be released at the end of their second winter, the wild populations would be benefited. Diseases that are fatal in the wild are easily curable in captivity. The food that is fed to these captive hawks is relatively free of pesticides. When these charges are released to the wild there is a better chance that their egg shells will not be affected by chlorinated hydrocarbons. Again, the immediate effect of such a program would be an increased number of birds surviving to breeding age.

—Ray Linder, California Hawking Club (1971).

(Photo-art courtesy of California Hawking Club)

sources of gear

ALLCOCK MANUFACTURING CO.
Box 551, Ossining, N.Y. 10562
Manufactures Havahart traps, including sparrow and pigeon traps, in which animals are taken alive. Write for free brochure or check a local hardware store.

PRAIRIE HAWKING
2344 Nomad Ave., Dayton, Ohio 45414
Gene Johnson makes bags, hoods and lures—all handsewn of fine leather. He uses his own designs or will custom-make to your order. They really look like they're right out of Sherwood Forest. Write for literature and prices. NAFA members get 10% off.

PETER J. ASBORNO
4530 W. 31st Ave., Denver, Colo. 80212
Bells in silver, bronze, brass, and monel. Write for current prices.

CH. MOHAMMAD DIN & CO.
Prem Gali No. 4, Railway Rd., Lahore, W. Pakistan
Bells, swivels, hoods, gloves, etc. Prices we have are by the dozen, but this is one case where it really is cheaper by the dozen (sometimes cheaper than single items bought here in the U.S.). They also sell birds. Prices run from $40 for a Luggar to $260 for a female Peregrin (only $80 for a male). Equipment list with prices, free.

H. EUGENE JOHNSON
2344 Nomad Ave., Dayton, Ohio 45414
Deluxe hoods tooled and dyed, with a feather plume; plain hoods; Indian bells; bags; leashes; jesses; name tags; kangaroo leather for bewits. Equipment list with prices, free.

KALEM GLOVE MANUFACTURING CO.
2557 North Dubonnet Ave., Rosemead, Calif. 91770
Gloves, jesses, bells, perches, lures. Free brochure.

MICHERO'S
P.O. Box 1315, Fort Worth, Tex. 76101
Imported and domestic falconry supplies including bells, swivels, leashes, leather for jesses and bewits, falconer's bags and creance line. Free brochure.

ROGER UPTON
The Leather Shop, 78 High St., Marlborough, Wiltshire, England
Hoods, gloves, falconer's bags, lures, swivels, leashes, bells. Equipment list with prices, free.

wilderness living

Vanzer homestead, Washington state, late 1800's. Photo: Darius Kinsey.

Wilderness living can take many different forms. It may indeed be a true wilderness cabin located miles from the nearest road and hand-built of natural materials, or it can be a hunting cabin, a vacation home, or a small country farm—any place that offers an alternative to the 9 to 5 punch clock technology for even a short period. We're not going to go into all the various alternatives, but just want to present the basic information sources for each so that you can develop the background to make your own choice.

There are three basic considerations involved in wilderness living. The first is finding and buying the land, the second is building the cabin itself, and the third is living in the cabin and sustaining your new lifestyle. Each of these areas is treated as somewhat of a separate section, with its own sources of information. A few sources are of interest for all three and are covered below.

U.S. DEPARTMENT OF AGRICULTURE (USDA)
Office of Communication, Washington, D.C. 20250
If your questions have anything to do with farming or general rural living, USDA is the source for whatever material the government may have. Every year the USDA puts out hundreds of publications on all aspects of rural living at very reasonable prices. For a rundown of current available publications, request a free copy of List 5.

For specific questions, write the appropriate USDA agency listed below. The proper address is Information Division, name of agency (as shown), U.S. Dept. of Agriculture, Washington, D.C. 20250.

Federal Extension Service. This is the rural information agency, and here you can reach the county agricultural agent (maybe you remember him from 4-H). The local agent can be a store-house of info on local agricultural problems and land availability.

Soil Conservation Service. This is the place for guides, maps, land surveys, etc. They also will provide help in planning conservation programs for your land.

Agricultural Stabilization and Conservation Service. These people run the cost-sharing program (usually 50-50) for certain land and conservation projects (at least they did before the recent federal budget cuts).

Forest Service. Everything to do with national forests and trees in general.

Farmers Home Administration. Loans to farmers and rural folk. .

— sources of information

AMERICAN FORESTRY ASSOC. (AFA)
1319 18th St., N.W., Wash., D.C. 20036
AFA is a conservation organization whose aim is the intelligent management and use of our natural resources, especially forests, and the promotion of public appreciation of these resources. The principal organ for the latter is the monthly magazine *American Forests,* which is sent to all members. The articles are mostly of general interest, usually on the use and conservation of the outdoors, and as such, do not provide much specific information on wilderness  living. (The magazine does do a good job of presenting balanced views of emotional environmental issues). The AFA, however, publishes a number of excellent books on trees, wood, and forests, including *Knowing Your Trees* (covered in Log Cabin Section), and maintains a special department to answer forestry and conservation questions. AFA also conducts a series of wilderness trail rides and canoe trips to promote knowledge of the wilderness. Membership fee is $7.50 per year.

I get *American Forests* and I don't think it's so balanced. It is the organ of the lumber and paper companies and reflects their views about timbering; a lot of conservationists reject their view substantially.

—Nach Waxman (1973)

AMERICAN FOREST INSTITUTE (AFI)
1619 Massachusetts Ave., N.W. Washington, D.C. 20036

AFI is the forest industry organization, which is made up of lumber companies and small wood-lot owners. As such, it is not particularly oriented to hard public information, but for data on member organizations who may have specific info this should be a good place to start.

PERIODICALS

THE MOTHER EARTH NEWS (Mother or TMEN, as you prefer)
John Shuttleworth, Ed.
Bimonthly - $10/yr. - $2/issue - 180 p. il.

Basically *Mother* deals with the homestead, which to quote her, is the "small, relatively self-sufficient farm or mini-farm on which food crops and farm animals are raised as naturally and as chemical-free as possible." That's *Mother*'s area—the how-to of finding, developing and living on such a homestead. Straight and solid. Special sections include excerpts from *Grow It* and Ken Kern's *The Owner-Built Home* and *The Owner-Built Homestead*, which when completed will give you the full content of these books. Other sections are Access (where to get it), Positions & Situations, and Swaps. Feature articles cover such areas as low-cost houses (like a home of straw), windmills and water wheels, home businesses, gardening, raising stock, butchering, etc. Most of this info is timeless, so the many back issues are a storehouse of good material. *Mother* got her start in 1970 and has hit high gear now. She's also started the Mother Earth News Research Center, which will develop new methods of ecologically compatible lifestyles. *Mother* is a great source of wilderness living books, so when writing them, don't forget to request a copy of the current book catalog.
From: Mother Earth News, P.O. Box 70, Henderson, N.C. 28739

FOXFIRE
Quarterly - $4/yr.

Foxfire presents the folklore, customs, and old-time crafts of the Southern Appalachian region. The material was collected, compiled, and published by the high school students of Rabun Gap, Ga. as part of their English course, and they have done a magnificent job of preserving a vanishing lifestyle. We could dwell on the content of the magazine for some time, but if you really want to understand it, get a copy of *The Foxfire Book* published by Doubleday and covered in Log Cabin Section. This book is a compilation of the magazine material. If you're into any type of wilderness life, you will want a copy anyway. A second and third book, *Foxfire 2* and *3*, are now available, by the way (see below).
From: Southern Highlands Literary Fund, Rabun Gap, Ga. 30568

BOOKS

THE LAST UPDATED WHOLE EARTH CATALOG
1975 - 447 p. il. - $5.00

WHOLE EARTH EPILOGUE
1974 - 320 p. il. - $4.00
Both edited by Stuart Brand

Two huge catalogs of sources—information, tools, gear. If you want to do it with your own hands or head, the *Catalog* and the *Epilogue* have the starting points, and you need both books for the complete picture (no repeats in the *Epilogue*). Whole systems, land use, shelter, industry, craft community, nomadics, communications and learning. Sources for everything from understanding the universe to building a banjo and back again.
From: Whole Earth, Box 428, Sausalito, Calif. 94965

FOXFIRE 2
Eliot Wigginton, Ed.
1973 - 410 p. il. - $4.50 (pb)

Ghost stories, spring wild plant foods, spinning and weaving, midwifing, burial customs, corn shucking, wagon making, and more affairs of plain living are brought together in volume two of the *Foxfire* set.

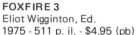
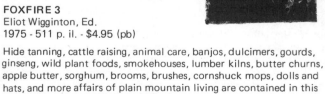

FOXFIRE 3
Eliot Wigginton, Ed.
1975 - 511 p. il. - $4.95 (pb)

Hide tanning, cattle raising, animal care, banjos, dulcimers, gourds, ginseng, wild plant foods, smokehouses, lumber kilns, butter churns, apple butter, sorghum, brooms, brushes, cornshuck mops, dolls and hats, and more affairs of plain mountain living are contained in this third volume in the *Foxfire* series.
All from: Anchor/Doubleday, 245 Park Ave., New York, N.Y. 10017

THE NEW PIONEER'S HANDBOOK
James Bohlen
1975 - 276 p. il. - $8.95 (hb)

Bohlen's book is not the typical "soft" back-to-the-land homesteader's guide. In fact, it should be called, "The New Pioneer's Engineering Guide," because it covers the technological economics of operating an efficient homestead, and Bohlen doesn't spare the numbers. Land operation from purchasing to developing; resource economics—machines, electricity, heat, and other work/energy aspects; renewable energy sources from solar through wind, water, wood, methane to human muscles; and design and construction factors from grass shack to stone barn. It's all there with an excellent annotated bibliography and an energy-oriented appendix. Funny thing, though—all the good info in this book comes from what everyone is trying to get away from...?
From: Schocken Books, Inc., 200 Madison Ave., New York, N.Y. 10016

THE HOMESTEADER'S HANDBOOK
James E. Churchill
1974 - 224 p. il. - $7.95 (hb)

Land, tools, home construction and repair, water, gardening, animal husbandry including working a farm with horses; food growing, gathering, processing and preserving; spinning and weaving; and miscellaneous matters from soap-making to first aid and health problems is Churchill's coverage of what you should know about to secure and run a handy country home. And he comes across very well with useful info that's applicable to almost any homestead operation. Lotsa names and addresses of people to write to, too, and the book is indexed.
From: Stackpole Books, Cameron & Kelker Sts., Harrisburg, Pa. 17105

REAL ESTATE

Thoughts on evaluating and purchasing ...

The first thing to remember when thinking about wilderness land is that the basic requirements are the same as for any other type of land. There are certain variables that must be examined before the property can be finally evaluated: water availability and accessibility, soil quality, access, tree and ground cover, exposure, temperature extremes, types and probable future of surrounding land parcels, and so forth. To ignore these considerations is to invite trouble later on.

Deciding what kind of land you want as far as terrain, distance from populated areas, topography and vegetation, etc. is one of the early concerns of any prospective homesteader. It can make it a lot easier to find what you want and help cut down considerably on your research if you know what you want to begin with. For instance, a few years ago we were looking for homestead type land in northern British Columbia. Just a subsistence-type homestead, but it had to be remote, unlikely to be a prospect for development, esthetically satisfying, and so on. Here's how we went about it.

First we talked to the provincial government department of lands and forests and got copies of all the literature we could on the area, including data on land use, facilities, weather, plus recently published land status maps showing all timber leases, public and private land ownership, roads and trails, parks, towns, and so forth. At the same time we picked up copies of corresponding topographic and forest cover maps, plus material from the department of mines and resources with information on known and suspected mineral deposits in the B.C. area.

After studying this stuff we were able to narrow down our choice to a couple of sites on the north coast and a couple in the interior, just south of the Yukon border. Then we made a trip to the provincial capital and talked with several people in the lands and forests, mines and natural resources, and agricultural departments, and anyone else we could find who knew the areas under consideration. Most of the departments were extremely helpful giving us updated information and allowing us the use of their libraries, files, and other facilities.

As a result of this legwork, we eliminated our coastal spots in favor of those further inland and started preparing for the next step— an on-site inspection. Like everything else, the on-site inspection is a compromise between the ideal and the possible; it *should* be made during the most difficult or unpleasant season of the year—late summer if there is likely to be a drought, winter if cold or snow cover is going to be a problem. Remember that late spring and early summer will make even the most inhospitable areas look and feel just great.

It isn't always possible to make a trip during ideal times, however, so you may have to do some digging in other places. Talk with as many local residents as possible, read back issues of the local papers, read books or histories that could be helpful, and so on. You want— and need—to find out about the bad times, because if they are acceptable, the good will surely be.

What exactly are you looking for in this inspection? During all seasons, no matter what the extremes in temperature, there must be adequate water for yourself, stock, and a garden; enough suitable trees for building and fuel; good drainage and soil of adequate quality to support your plans; natural shelter from the elements; accessibility via land or water, as well as assurance that you will have access rights if you need to cross private land. Check the exposure and slope to determine quality of sunlight, and of course, be sure of the esthetic appeal. Does it feel good to you?

If the land passes your inspection, it's time to look into getting a hold of it. There are basically four methods available: (1) buying outright from the owner; (2) leasing on either a long-term or short-term basis with or without option to purchase; (3) homesteading, if legal; (4) squatting with or without the owner's permission. A squatter has no legal rights and can be forced to move at any time regardless of whether the owner gave him permission—at least in most areas.

Let's assume you've gotten the property and are planning your setup. While making your original inspection of the land, presumably, you took photos from several angles to identify special features, along with pages of notes identifying the pictures and describing various aspects of the property. If at all possible, you should now take all of this material and sketch it up into a property plot. On it locate streams, rapids, meadows, tree cover and type, predominant wind direction, slope and exposure, identifying characteristics, spots with best soil, drainage, worst soil and so forth, anything that might be helpful. Don't skimp on photos, maps, and drawings, because they'll all add up to efficency and economy in planning landscaping, locations of buildings, gardens, and pathways. If done with care and foresight, it will pay off in the long haul.

—Yvonne Johnson (1972).

United States PUBLIC LANDS

Technically all lands held by federal, state, or local governments are public property. However, only those held by the federal government truly belong to all the people of the country. Public land as used here will refer to that part of the original public lands of the United States which are still under federal ownership and have not been set aside for special uses—and thus are still available for conversion to private ownership. Originally the Federal Government obtained most of the western United States and Alaska through a series of purchases and agreements (Louisiana Purchase, Oregon Compromise, Gadsden Purchase, Mexican Cession, and Alaska Purchase) from foreign governments who controlled or claimed the land at the time. This was then held in trust as sort of a land bank for the citizens and was known as public domain or public lands. As the nation subsequently expanded westward, much of this land was transferred to private ownership and to the states when they entered the Union. Other areas were reserved for special uses, such as national parks and national forests, and the balance remaining became public lands.

There are still some 450 million acres of public lands available with 280 million acres in Alaska and 170 million acres in the lower 48. Nearly all of the latter is located in the 11 western states with only small amounts left in the mid-western and southern states. There never was any public land in the original 13 states or in Texas or Hawaii.

All the public lands are administered by the Bureau of Land Management, and any questions on public lands should be directed to it. Questions on a specific area should go to the appropriate state office of the BLM.

The Alaskan land situation deserves special mention both because two thirds of all public land is in Alaska, and because the situation is not normal at this time. As a matter of fact, it is a bit of a hairy ball of wax. Prior to statehood, Alaska was 99% public domain. The Statehood Act allowed Alaska 25 years to choose some 104 million acres of public lands for state use and disposition. Thus far the state has chosen less than a quarter of its allotment. A couple of years ago, the native Alaskans, Indians, Aleuts, and Eskimo, filed claim for the return of their native lands. The result has been that with both state and native claims pending and outstanding, the BLM has frozen all federal lands in Alaska until the claims are properly settled and agreed upon. So for the past couple of years, no new federal lands have been released to the state or to individuals. However, the situation should open up again before too long. You'll just have to check with the Alaskan BLM office for the latest details.

sources of information

BUREAU OF LAND MANAGEMENT (BLM)
U.S. Dept. of the Interior, Wash., D.C. 20240
The following are the addresses of BLM regional offices which should be contacted for local information. Address your letter to:

State Director, Bureau of Land Management:

Alaska - 555 Cordova St., Anchorage 99501
Arizona - Federal Building, Room 3022, Phoenix 85025
California - Federal Building, Room E-2841, 2800 Cottage Way, Sacramento 95825
Colorado - Room 700, 1600 Broadway, Denver 80202
Idaho - Federal Building, Room 334, 550 W. Fort St., Boise 83702
Montana, North Dakota, South Dakota, and Minnesota - Federal Building, 316 N. 26th St., Billings, Mont. 59101
Nevada - Federal Building, Room 3008, 300 Booth St., Reno 89502
New Mexico and Oklahoma - Federal Building, South Federal Place, P.O. Box 1449, Santa Fe, N. Mex. 87501
Oregon and Washington - 729 Northeast Oregon St., P.O. Box 2965, Portland, Ore. 97208
Utah - 8217 Federal Building, P.O. Box 11505, 125 South State, Salt Lake City 84111
Wyoming, Nebraska, and Kansas - P.O. Box 1828, Cheyenne, Wyo. 82001
EASTERN STATES (All states with public lands not listed above) - 7981 Eastern Ave., Silver Spring, Md. 20910

PUBLIC LAND STATISTICS
Annual - 188 p. il. - $2
S/N 2411-0036

Annual statistical summary of public land information, including a listing of federal acreage in each state and definitions of public land terms.
From: Superintendent of Documents, U.S. Government Printing Office, Washington, D.C. 20402

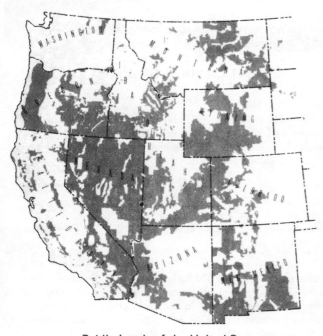

Public Lands of the United States

WHAT ARE "THE PUBLIC LANDS" (Info. Bulletin No. 1)
Bureau of Land Management
1971 - 4 p. - 25¢
I 53.9: 1/6

Brief rundown on public lands, where they are located and how they are managed.
From: Superintendent of Documents, U.S. Government Printing Office, Washington, D.C. 20402

—— HOMESTEAD LAND

The word on homesteading isn't particularly encouraging. For many years, homesteading was the principal method of transferring public lic lands to private ownership.

The Homestead Act of 1862 opened up undeveloped public lands to settlement and agricultural development. It specified that any United States citizen who was at least 21 years old or the head of a household could settle up to 160 acres of public domain, and by building a house, living on the land for five years, and farming a specified part of it, he would receive clear title to the land (the only cost being the minimal filing fee). (The information we have on homesteading public land in Alaska calls for economic cultivation of at least one eighth of the land and residence for at least seven months a year for three years. We don't know whether this time period represents a special regulation for Alaska or not.)

The Act, which is still on the books, was designed specifically to turn undeveloped public land into operating private farmland. This is why homesteading is so rough today. All the reasonable agricultural lands have long since been homesteaded or have otherwise passed out of the public domain—at least in the lower 48. Those remaining 170 million acres in the lower 48 are 99 and 44/100 per cent desert and mountain country, and while there is farmland in Alaska, you can't get at it now (and you can be sure that the state and natives will grab the best of what there is when they are turned loose). So it's an uphill fight all the way.

Still you might find something everyone else has missed or you just might like to buck the problems. If so here's how it works. First you must find suitable public domain land—this is your problem, the government has no designated areas or any aids. Next file an application with the BLM land office in the state where the land is located. It's all pretty straightforward, but it does take some leg work. Now comes the hooker. The BLM must classify the land as "suitable for agricultural purposes and suitable for development as a home and farm for a man and his family" before the application can be approved. This means the government people must decide whether your land has suitable soil and sufficient rainfall or irrigation water to support you. And the government isn't talking subsistence level—it doesn't give away land so that you can live off welfare. If irrigation is required (and it is on much of the land now available), you must show that you have the resources to properly develop it. This can be expected to run in the upper five figure bracket. For that kind of bread, you can buy an existing farm in a hell of a lot better location than homestead land. Enter the vicious circle.

One way you might break that circle is to come up with a gimmick. Maybe you can show a profitable way to raise maguay in the desert without irrigation (set up your own tequila factory) or how about growing Christmas trees in the mountains (if raising cotton is farming, Christmas trees should qualify also). Still, official policy is "forget it," and the dudes have made up their minds—it won't be easy to change them. The challenge flag is flying.

sources of information

WHAT ABOUT LAND IN ALASKA (Info. Bulletin No. 2)
Bureau of Land Management
4 p. - 20¢
0-792-665

A short pamplet covering the basics of homesteading in Alaska and general information on conditions in Alaska.
From: Superintendent of Documents, U.S. Government Printing Office, Washington, D.C. 20402

THE HARD FACTS OF HOMESTEADING
3 p. - free

Dope on homesteading today—the situation and how to go about it.
From: Bureau of Land Management, Washington, D.C. 20240

─────── LEASE LAND

The Forest Service sometimes offers recreational leases in certain national forest areas which are either not required or not suitable for general public use. The average parcel is about half an acre, and a number of lots are grouped together in a tract-type arrangement to facilitate administration and access. The leases are carefully controlled for kind and location of buildings allowed, waste disposal, etc. and are restricted to summer use. The usual rent is $50 to $200 per year, depending on the desirability of the plot.

Only a few sites are presently available, so you may have trouble locating an undeveloped site. However, while the leases themselves are non-transferable, one may purchase the improvements on the property from the present lessee and thus obtain the right to use the property. But be sure to check with the district ranger or forest supervisor before closing any such deal to be certain that the lease is not about to run out without an option for renewal. The district ranger or forest supervisor should be able to tell you of anyone interested in selling his improvements. Local real estate agents may also have listings on these. For more information, contact Forest Service, U.S. Dept. of Agriculture, Washington, D.C. 20250

sources of information

FEDERAL HOUSING ADMINISTRATION (FHA) and FARMERS HOME ADMINISTRATION (FmHA) REPOSSESSED LAND
This crew finances a raft of country property, and when someone can't pay up, they have to foreclose the mortgage and try to unload the property. The nice thing—at least by the info that we have—is that they are not looking to make any profit on the deal, and properties are sold for the outstanding balance on the mortgage (plus costs, we presume). You just might be able to find a deal here.

FHA deals with a wide variety of housing whereas FmHA specializes in farm and country property. Specific requests on properties available should go to the state and local offices (in the case of FHA request a listing of "Secretary-held properties"). General information should be available through the Washington office.

Farmers Home Administration
U.S. Dept. of Agriculture
Washington, D.C. 20250

Federal Housing Administration
Dept. of Housing and Urban Dev.
Washington, D.C. 20410

─────── AUCTION LAND

Periodically the Bureau of Land Management puts up parcels of public land at public auction. These parcels usually run from 40 to 120 acres, but they can range from a fraction of an acre to 5,000 acres. The sales are either by sealed bid or oral bid (most commonly) and are held at the appropriate state BLM office. Don't look for any real steals here, though. The land is first appraised at fair market value by BLM, and the bidding starts at this figure—no land is sold for less. Appraised values range from $20 to over $600 an acre, depending on the type of land, location, water availability, access, and size. The average is around $100 an acre, but remember that this is just the starting point for bidding.

Notices of these auctions are placed in local newspapers and recorded in the *Federal Register*. However, the simplest way to keep abreast of the auction lands being offered is through *Our Public Lands*, BLM's quarterly magazine. Each issue contains the current listing of parcels coming up for auction along with a general description. If a parcel interests you, you may request a prospectus on it from the appropriate state BLM office for complete details. There is no charge for this. Then you can start thinking about an on-site inspection and finally about submitting your bid.

Remember that this is a government operation—so even if you are the successful bidder, you still have one more hurdle to cross. The law under which most of these parcels are sold specifies that landowners adjacent to the parcel have the right of preference. This means that all such landowners may purchase the property within thirty days of the sale by either matching your winning bid or paying three times the appraised value, whichever is less. In other words, adjacent landowners are guaranteed the final bid.

O.K., if you made it through that one, the land is now yours free and clear, to do with as you please (assuming, of course, that your check didn't bounce—neglected to mention that you must pay in full at the time of sale. Makes financing mighty difficult).

There are two special classes of auction land that may be of interest. One is the special request type. Occasionally land, particularly extensive mountain parcels, is put on the auction block at the request of the adjacent property owner, and normally only this person will have his request honored. But if you have a particular piece of real estate in mind, you can't lose anything by at least talking to the boys at the state land office about the possibility.

The other special class covers "small tract homesites," which are normally 5-acre parcels located adjacent to national parks or forests. These are designed specifically for residential or recreational use (primarily suited to the vacation cabin) and are limited to one per customer. Prior to 1963, one could file a request to have particular parcels offered, but the speculators jumped on this (which is why BLM is a bit uptight on specific requests). Now you just have to wait until an area is classified and opened to auction.

sources of information

OUR PUBLIC LANDS
Quarterly - $3/yr. - 75¢/copy - 24 p. il.

Official publication of the Bureau of Land Management. In addition to listing all auction lands to be offered, it includes a variety of articles and news items on the wildlife, conservation, history, and use of public lands.
From: Superintendent of Documents, U.S. Gov. Printing Off., Washington, D.C. 20402

AUCTION BULLETIN BOARD

ARIZONA

3.75 A, 16 miles east of Tombstone in ghost town of Gleeson, Cochise Cty. El 4,900 ft. Good dirt roads from Tombstone, Bisbee, and Pearce. Moderately rolling. Rights-of-way reserved to US. App $562 plus pub $34.31.

CALIFORNIA

2 isolated tracts, 40 A each, 7 air miles west of Angels Camp, Calavaras Cty. No legal access. Rough terrain; veg is brush, scattered digger pine and native grasses; no water. App $4,900 for both.

COLORADO

29 tracts, 14.25, A to 320 A, Larimer Cty. Moderately rolling to rough; grazing pot. Two tracts join national forests; one corners on graded and maintained road; others have no access. Two have permanent streams; one crossed by intermittent stream with seeps and springs. App $155 to $6,250.

HOW TO BUY PUBLIC LANDS (Info. Bulletin No. 4)
Bureau of Land Management
4 p. - 15¢
O-265-484

Presents basic data on buying auction land.
*From: Bureau of Land Management, Dept. of the Interior,
Washington, D.C. 20240*

BLM STATE OFFICES
For specific information, contact the appropriate state land office of
the Bureau of Land Management. On request they will provide notification of auction lands available through their office.

_____ MINERAL LAND

This is not a way to get land for a wilderness cabin, but rather a warning. Mineral claims are intended strictly for mining a valuable mineral.
To file such a claim, one must first prove color, and to retain the
claim, $100 worth of assessment work must be done on the claim
each year. To file a claim or buy a quit-claim for use as a homesite or
vacation site is illegal. You may live on the site only while working
the claim, so don't be talked into a "good" deal.

State & County PUBLIC LANDS

A number of states have small programs offering state land for sale or
lease. However, most of these are occasional offerings, and details
vary considerably from state to state. With its extensive landholdings,
Alaska is the only state with a truly comprehensive land program.
Therefore, the emphasis in this section will be on Alaskan offerings.

__TAX ARREARS LAND

Tax delinquent land is normally sold by the county at public auction.
If the supply is sufficient, such auctions may be held on a regular
basis, but more often the sales are intermittent. Notice is normally
given in the local papers and posted at the courthouse. If you are
interested in a particular area, you can usually arrange with the
county auditor or tax collector to be notified of upcoming sales.

   Tread very carefully in dealing with tax arrears land, however. A
careful check prior to the auction is an absolute necessity. You may
buy the place for a song only to find that you have assumed several
thousand dollars worth of mortgage or other liability assessed against
the land. Or the survey may be old and inaccurate—some land sold
has actually turned out to be in the middle of a lake. The previous
owner may also have the right of redemption for a period of a year or
more, which means that at any time during this period he may
reclaim the property for the taxes owed. Any improvements you may
have added are your loss. T.S., baby. Check the pertinent regulations
for the state in question first.

_____ LEASE LAND

A number of states have lease programs similar to those of the
Forest Service. Most of the leases are recreational areas and are
usually restricted to summer occupancy. Details vary considerably,
and your best bet is to inquire at the appropriate state's Department
of Forestry or the state Chamber of Commerce.

   Alaska has an extensive leasing program. The usual term is 55
years and is subject to renewal with preference given to the current
lessee. These lease lands are normally auctioned to the person
offering the highest annual rate, with the bidding starting at 6% of
the assessed value of the land. Lands not leased at auction may be
leased across the counter for the minimum rental (6% of assessed
value) on a first-come, first-served basis. You may lease as much
land as desired, but in this case it must be used for its classified
purpose. Leases may be assigned and improvements sold to the
assignee.

   As a separate class, small leases for five years or less with an
annual rental under $250 may be negotiated directly with the Div-
ision of Lands at any time. With such a lease, you have preference
rights whenever the parcel comes up for sale or long-term lease, i.e.,
you have the final bid this time and need only match the top bid to
buy the parcel.

sources of information

SOUTH CAROLINA PUBLIC SERVICE AUTHORITY
P.O. Box 398, Monck Corner, S.C. 29461
These cats are in charge of all the lease property in the five-county
area on and around the Santee-Cooper Lakes in South Carolina.

ALASKA DEPT. OF NATURAL RESOURCES, Div. of Lands
323 E. Fourth Ave., Anchorage, Alaska 99501
Division of Lands handles all the Alaskan land programs including
lease lands. Details are under Auction Lands section. *Alaska Land
Lines* also lists ease lands.

ALASKA LAND LINES

LAND AVAILABLE FOR OVER-THE-COUNTER SALE OR LEASE

All lands available for immediate purchase or lease are shown on this list. Land not sold or
leased at an auction is available over the counter at the Division offices in Anchorage, Fairbanks and Juneau. Mail orders should be sent to the Anchorage office.

Brochures are available upon request. Please specify locality and type of land in which you
are interested. The general localities as given in this list indicate the general areas in
which the land is located using where possible a designation found on the latest map of the
state. Each brochure has a map or maps showing the lots or tracts offered.

TYPE OF LAND	LOCALITY	SIZE IN ACRES	PRICE RANGE
For Sale:			
Residential	Kenai, Kodiak	1.06 to 3.55	$900 to $6,100
Recreational	Kenai	14.37 to 29.45	$9,550 to $14,100
Utility	Kenai, Talkeetna, Fairbanks	17 to 149.82	$21,950 to $32,200
			Annual Rental:
For 55-Year Lease:			
Recreational	Harding Lake, Talkeetna	.34 to 74.73	$40 to $1,095
Industrial	Kenai	32.74	$3,275
Commercial-Industrial	Kenai	20	$2,300
Utility	Talkeetna, West Matanuska Valley	37.04 to 160	$560 to $2,765

NOTE: All improvement credit (homestead) lands have been sold. It may be several years before more is available because of lack of survey in agriculturally potential areas.

_____ AUCTION LAND

States occasionally offer land for sale at public auction, much as
BLM auctions of public lands. The bidding starts at the assessed
value, but as far as we know, there are no preference rights for
adjacent landowners. Such state lands are often included with
county sales. For information on these sales check the local papers
or contact the Department of Lands and Natural Resources for the
state that interests you.

ALASKA

   Alaska puts up state lands for auction on a regular basis. However,
don't be misled into thinking that Alaskan land is supercheap. The
average appraised value at this time is probably close to $200 per
acre. Right now land is scare in Alaska because of the freeze on Federal lands and because the Federal Government will not turn the land
over to the state until it is surveyed into at least township size.

Thus not only is the state not receiving any new land, but it's only slowly receiving that which it has already chosen. This scarcity has driven prices up sharply. Things may improve somewhat when the freeze is removed, but don't expect any sudden change.

To be eligible to purchase land in Alaska from the state (or for that matter to obtain state land under any of Alaska's programs) one must be at least 19 years old and a United States citizen or have filed a declaration of intent to become a citizen. As a further restriction, an individual is limited to a total of 640 acres of auction land, although your roommate may also purchase up to 640 acres.

Alaska does wish to attract new people and recognizes that its land prices are not particularly cheap. In an effort to compensate, the state offers a special deal for all land purchased at auction. If you cannot or do not wish to make the entire payment for the land at the time of purchase, you may pay 10% down and 10% annually for the next nine years, plus 6% interest on the unpaid balance. In effect, the state will finance the purchase with a 90% 10-year mortgage at 6% interest. The contract may be paid off at any time without penalty, or it may be transferred. As land mortgages go, this is a pretty good deal.

Land for sale or lease in Alaska is listed by classification, such as residential, recreational, utility, or industrial. These classifications reflect the general nature and location of the land, as well as the basis for the appraisal, but they do not restrict the owner's use of his land after purchase—except insofar as what local zoning laws may require. Full details on the various classes are given in *Facts About Alaska Lands*.

One final item. Any land not sold at auction is available over the land office counter at the appraised price on a first come, first-served basis. The Division of Lands will send details on such parcels upon request.

Homestead or Improvement Credit Land

Since the State of Alaska has chosen or expects to choose most of the best farmland out of the federal lands, it is offering its own homesteading plan for prospective farmers. The program applies only to areas designated as improvement credit lands. The initial procedure and regulations are the same as for buying land at public auction on the 90%, 10-year contract plan. You must bid on the land (up to 640 acres) and pay 10% down if you are high bidder. Now the difference. The subsequent annual payments may be offset by credits allowed for improvements to the land according to a set schedule. Thus for your first few critical years, it should be possible to completely offset the annual payments (in effect, the state will subsidize the improvements). With land prices what they are at the moment, it is unlikely that you can offset any more than 30-40% of the total land cost, but that is still a help. Unfortunately, the latest word from Alaska is that there are presently no improvement credit lands available, nor are any new ones expected to open up for the next couple of years. Still you might keep it in mind for the future. Check with the Division of Lands if you want more info.

IMPROVEMENT CREDITS ALLOWED

1. Land brought to cultivation (including clearing and drainage when necessary)...$ 40 per acre
2. Fencing...$ 3 per 100 ft.
3. Permanent family dwelling (not to exceed $1,000)..$ 4 per sq. ft.
4. Farm buildings (not to exceed $1,000)...............$ 2 per sq. ft.
5. Well, producing water approved for domestic purposes...$ 5 per foot
6. Access road (not to exceed $1,000)....................$500 per mile

Open-to-Entry Recreational Site Program

This is another program which is unique to Alaska and looks particularly interesting. Lease and auction lands must be surveyed before being auctioned off, so the open-to-entry program was instituted to bypass the surveying problem and speed up land disposition. Under this program, anyone qualified to purchase state land may enter upon and occupy any land classified as open to entry (which presently includes some 2.5 million acres of state land). The individual must personally enter upon his parcel and stake it (much like staking a claim), then file application for a lease and pay the first year's rent ($40) and the filing fee ($10). If the application is approved, he receives a five-year lease ($40 per year rental), renewable for an additional five years. The entry may not exceed 5 acres in size or have more than 400 feet of water frontage. It must be reasonably compact and mate to adjoining parcels already filed. Only one parcel of open-to-entry land is available per individual, but a husband and wife may both acquire a parcel. At any time during the ten years of the lease, the entryman (that's you) may become eligible to purchase the land at the appraised market value at the time of entry by having the parcel surveyed by a qualified surveyor (thus saving the state the trouble and expense). The cost of the survey should run close to $1,000 (possibly less if adjacent entries have already been surveyed).

Locating open-to-entry areas and determining which land is vacant and unappropriated is your responsibility. Township status plats are available at Division of Lands offices and may be purchased for $2. At the moment most of the lands available are in the Susitna Valley between Anchorage and Fairbanks and along the Tanana River southeast of Fairbanks. If you have your eye on a special parcel outside the open-to-entry lands, you may petition for a public hearing to have it declared open.

sources of information

ALASKA DEPT. OF NATURAL RESOURCES
Division of Lands, 323 E. Fourth Ave., Anchorage, Alaska 99501
This is the place for full details on all the Alaskan land programs. For general information, request a copy of their free booklet *Facts*

Average Alaska Temperature and Rainfall

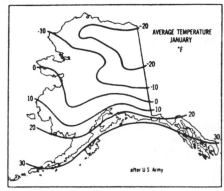
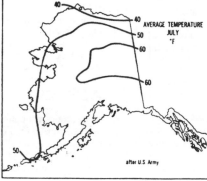
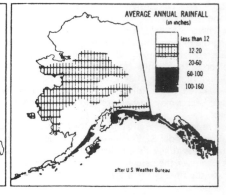

About Alaska Lands. This contains an exceptionally complete rundown on the Alaskan programs, plus a listing of other specialized sources of information.

ALASKA LAND LINES
Alaska Dept. of Natural Resources
Monthly - 6 p. - free (ZIP code required for subscription)

Alaska Land Lines gives the monthly rundown of the Alaskan Land situation and provides a listing of state lands for sale or lease. Someone has told us that *Land Lines* is sent only to Alaskan addresses, but there's no mention of this restriction in any of the literature. So give it a try.
From: Alaska Dept. of Natural Resources, 323 E. Fourth Ave., Anchorage, Alaska 99501.

ADDITIONAL SOURCES OF INFORMATION ON ALASKAN LAND AND AGRICULTURE

Alaska Dept. of Natural Resources
 Dept. of Agriculture, P.O. Box 800, Palmer, Alaska 99645
Cooperative Extension Service
 University of Alaska College, Alaska 99701
 Their *Land and Living in Alaska* booklet contains some good material. Other good booklets include *Building a Log House* (43 p. - $1.00; 25¢ for Alaskan address).
U.S. Soil Conservation Service
 P.O. Box F, Palmer, Alaska 99645
Farmers Home Administration
 945 Cowles, Fairbanks, Alaska 99701
Office of the Governor
 Rural Development Agency, 338 Denali, Anchorage, Alaska 99501

PRIVATE LANDS

Whether you intend to deal through an agent or strike out on your own, it would still be wise to check with several local agents first. They can be a regular treasure house of info on real estate conditions in the area, showing you what is available, how prices are running, and what to look for. I once spent four full days going through used car lots and in doing so received a fantastic cram course in judging used cars, all for free. It's the same for real estate. Shop around, listen, ask questions, and learn.

If you haven't narrowed your search to any specific areas, there are several national and international agencies that put out country-wide catalogs. Their nationwide network of local agents should be able to help you with additional information on particular areas.

realtors

STROUT REALTY
P.O. Box 2757, Springfield, Mo. 65803
Strout is one of two nationwide firms that regularly publish a catalog of properties for sale throughout the U.S. They have some 500 local offices in 41 states who furnish listings for the catalog and can supply full details on properties of interest. The listings include farm, ranch, town, city, recreation, retirement, income, and business properties. The vast majority of these are developed land with existing houses, and only occasionally is an undeveloped wilderness plot found. Strout does offer some good farm and ranch listings. The catalog is published quarterly and runs around 225 pages with lots of pictures. Sent free on request.

No. 354 - 160a. Close-in, on state hwy.
50a tillable, 100 wooded: Well. 7-rm
hse w/pt bsmt; garage. Part down pmt...$5000

No. 348 - 156a riverfront farm. Minutes
to town. 75a tillable pasture. 8-rm, bath
hse; pt bsmt, furnace. Barn, shop, garage.$15,600

UNITED FARM AGENCY
612 W. 47th St., Kansas City, Mo. 64112
United Farm has just about the same setup as Strout and offers the same type of properties. They have some 500 local offices that are concentrated in 33 states. Catalog is about 225 pages and is free on request. Both United's and Strout's catalogs are recommended even if you don't want developed land—they'll give you some good background on how prices are running in various areas.

PREVIEWS, INC.
49 East 53rd St., New York, N.Y. 10022
Previews is a high-priced Strout or United Farm. They are real estate agents handling property throughout the United States and Canada, plus the Caribbean, Mexico, South America, and Europe. They handle only upper-class developed land, with prices starting at close to $50,000 and going up—way up. A 250-page catalog is available for $3 (sold on newsstands also). This isn't exactly wilderness cabin territory, but the catalog does carry advertisements and a listing of local real estate agents in all these areas who should be helpful no matter what you are looking for. The pictures in the catalog are beautiful, and you can always dream a little with an 11,000-acre ranch in New Mexico, a plantation in Jamaica, an out-island in the Bahamas, or a castle in England.

WILDERNESS TRACTS

There are a number of operators who buy up large parcels of wilderness land and then sell off smaller pieces ranging from a fraction of an acre to a couple of hundred acres. Generally what you get is more suitable for a vacation cabin than a wilderness home, but you do get such conveniences as access roads. Prices are not what you could do on your own but usually aren't too bad. So if you have more bread than free time, this might be the way to go. Just be sure to inspect the land before putting down your cash.

tract dealers

NATIONAL ASSOCIATED PROPERTIES, INC.
Box 1322, Coeur d'Alene, Idaho 83814
These fellows offer land parcels of 5 to 20 acres in northern Idaho and eastern Washington at prices from $200 to $300 per acre. What they do is buy a big parcel and split it into blocks for resale. Thus you can expect neighbors. A time-payment plan is standard with 10% reduction for cash payment. Roads are constructed to all blocks in each tract, so you are at least guaranteed access. Should be in some nice mountain country here. Listing available free.

TIMBER RESOURCES INC.
P.O. Box 4246, Spokane, Wash. 99202
This is another tract dealer with land in Montana, Idaho, and Washington. Lot sizes range up to 80 acres, and prices are $25 to something over $100 per acre (larger lots are usually cheaper per acre). This is a good bit below National Associated Properties prices. Initial literature and tract listing available free.

REFORESTATION INC.
P.O. Box 14006 Opportunity Station, Spokane, Wash. 99214
Reforestation is another tract dealer operating in northern Idaho, northeastern Washington, and Montana (must be a reason they all operate in this area). Lots range from 5 acres to 160 acres, and prices from $100 to $500 per acre. Again, time payments are offered as standard policy, and a 15% discount is available for cash payment. Road access is provided to all lots (upkeep is usually the owner's

responsibility). Literature and a listing of current tracts are available free.

REPOSSESSED LAND

Property repossessed by banks and savings and loans institutions for mortgage default is usually sold at public auction locally. Check the newspapers for sheriff's sales and the like.

LEASE LAND

A number of lumber companies around the country have recreational land available for lease. Leases range up to 99 years, and costs are usually reasonable. The best bet for running these down is the local chamber of commerce. You might cross your fingers and drop a line to the American Forest Institute (beginning of section).

Caretaker Positions

These won't get you any land, but they will let you sample country life before you commit yourself completely. For maintaining a farm, you get a small wage, plus the right to live in the farmhouse and raise your own garden. Can be a good deal. Older couples are usually preferred, but if you're responsible people, you should be able to come through regardless.

_____ Canada GOVERNMENT LANDS

Our information on Canadian government land programs is still somewhat sketchy. The situation is a bit confused because each province apparently administers the disposition of all lands within its boundaries, resulting in a variety of programs and regulations. Even in the Yukon and Northwest Territories, where all the land is federal, dispositions and inquiries are handled by the individual territorial offices of the Dept. of Indian Affairs and Northern Development.

In general, government lands are available for sale only to Canadian citizens or landed immigrants, which is the designation applied to those who have been granted permanent residence status on entry to Canada. The Canadian immigration people have instituted a point system to ascertain whether you are likely to be a help or hindrance to the country. You receive points based on your educational and occupational background, available finances, fluency in both English and French, certainty of a Canadian job, etc. The maximum score is 100 points, and to qualify for landed immigrant status, you must score at least 50. Further details may be obtained from the Canadian Immigration Office, Ottawa, Ontario, or from the Canadian Immigration Offices in Los Angeles, San Francisco, Chicago, Denver, or New York (all c/o the Canadian Consulate General).

ALBERTA

Alberta has a homesteading package, but you must be a Canadian citizen. Also you have to be between the ages of 18 and 71 and have resided in Alberta for one year of the last three. After you've met these qualifications, you may homestead up to 640 acres. You must break and bring to cultivation 10 acres per quarter section per year for the first four years and end up with 60 acres per quarter section under cultivation by the end of the eighth year. Having done so, you have fulfilled the contract and supposedly receive title to the land.

Alberta also offers other lands for sale and lease and offers land at public auction. Anyone, regardless of nationality or immigrant status, may bid on auction lands. You may also submit a request to have specific lands offered at auction (fee is $5 per quarter section). As usual, the bidding starts with the appraised value. Auctions are held once a year.

All Alberta land programs are handled through the Dept. of Land and Forests, Natural Resources Building, 109th St. and 99th Ave., Edmonton, Alberta T5K 2E1.

BRITISH COLUMBIA

Anyone 19 or older may lease up to two sections (1280 acres) of government land in British Columbia. The usual lease is for 20 years with an annual rent of 5% of the assessed value (minimum $40 per year). All these leases are with option to buy, but only a Canadian citizen may exercise this option. We have no specific information on the sale process or price (presume the land is available at assessed value), when the option may be exercised, whether a survey is required, or how assessed values are running (an estimate for remote northern lands would be $10-$15 per acre). For these and other questions, you should contact the Minister of Lands, Forests and Water Resources, Parliament Buildings, Victoria, B.C. British Columbia is broken up into some 25 land recording districts, and any application for lease must be made through the appropriate local land commissioner.

YUKON and NORTHWEST TERRITORIES

Most government land in the Yukon and Northwest Territories is federal Crown land and is administered through the Dept. of Indian Affairs and Northern Development. Any Canadian citizen or landed immigrant may select a parcel of land and apply for a lease. You must personally select your own parcel. Upon approval, you are granted a two-year lease with the annual rate based on the assessed value of the land. During the period of the lease, you must occupy the property and make certain improvements (like building a permanent dwelling). If you have complied with the requirements, you may purchase the land at the appraised value at the end of the lease. However, final title requires that the parcel be surveyed—either hire your own surveyor or pay the government to have it surveyed. We have no specific data on the amount of land you can choose under this program. Information is available from the Department of Indian Affairs and Northern Development, Yellowknife, NWT X0E 1H0, or Whitehorse, Yukon.

ONTARIO

A person who has the financial resources, experience and knowledge to set up and operate a full-time farming operation may qualify, before the Public Agricultural Lands Committee, to obtain Crown lands for farming. If so, the land is made available on condition that it will be used solely for agricultural purposes. Land for homesteading is not available in Ontario, the homestead and free grant legislation having been repealed in 1961. For more information contact Div. of Lands, Lands Administration Branch, Whitney Block, Parliament Bldgs., Toronto, Canada.

SASKATCHEWAN

The Department of Agriculture, Land Branch, Regina, offers agricultural lands for sale to leaseholders who have brought a minimum of 40 acres per quarter section into cultivation. Prices begin at $22 per acre for cultivated land and $11 per acre for uncultivated land. The government will accept a mortgage on the land, taking 20% down and the remainder over a period of up to 30 years (or until your 70th birthday) at 6.5% interest. The Land Branch also will sell up to 3300 acres of grazing land at a minimum price of $11 per acre to leaseholders who have worked the land for five years.

LANDS BRANCH, DEPT. OF LANDS AND NATURAL RESOURCES
810 Norquay Bldg., Winnipeg 1, Manitoba

LANDS SERVICE SECTION, DEPT. OF LANDS AND FORESTS
Parliament Buildings, Quebec, Quebec

DEPT. OF AGRICULTURE AND COLONIZATION
201 Cremazie Blvd. E., Montreal, Quebec

TAX ARREARS LAND

As elsewhere, Canadian tax arrears land is sold at public auction by the government whose taxes were not forthcoming (usually the township). We don't have details on the other provinces, but at least in Ontario, notice of all such sales are published in the *Ontario Gazette,* issued by the Queen's Printer (details below).

For a bit more money, you can get the same information by subscribing to Sovereign Publishing's *Ontario Journal and Tax Sale Register* (details follow). Besides listing properties offered by municipalities at their annual auctions, it presents selected properties available "for immediate sale" by the Municipal Tax Land Disposal Agency, which handles lands from municipalities that do not hold their own auctions. We have no details on these properties, but the implication is that they are not sold by auction.

Apparently Canadian tax laws specify that a tax deed represents free and unencumbered title, guaranteeing that no mortages or other liens against the property may be passed on to you, and

insuring that the previous owner has no redemption rights (except in rural New Brunswick where he does have a one year redemption right). Therefore the only thing you need watch is that the survey is reasonably accurate—normally not too big a risk. If all this is really true, Canadian tax lands could offer some good deals. As a matter of fact, a number of the people listed as tract dealers obtain at least part of their lands through tax sales. If they can do it, you can too.

sources of information

THE ONTARIO GAZETTE
Published on the first Saturday of each month - 15¢/copy

Provides details on all tax sale auctions in Ontario
From: Queen's Printer, Dept. of Public Works, Ferguson Block, Parliament Buildings, Toronto, Ontario, Canada

SOVEREIGN PUBLISHING CO.
110 Church St., Toronto 1, Canada
Sovereign publishes the monthly *Tax Sale Register* for Ontario which lists all the tax arrears property being offered by the local governments of the province. They also put out issues for New Brunswick and Prince Edward Island which are the only sources we know of for these areas. What Sovereign does is take the local government lists as they come out, compile them, and shoot them off to subscribers "in advance of closing date." Sovereign doesn't sell any land—all deals are direct with the appropriate local officials. Cost of the Ontario listing is $4.98 per year. The New Brunswick and Prince Edward Island listings run $9.50 each per year. Literature available free.

PRIVATE LANDS

realtors

There are no national real estate agencies covering Canada now. Two good sources for listings of local agents are the Real Estate Institute of British Columbia, 608-626 West Pender St., Vancouver 2, British Columbia, and the Ontario Association of Real Estate Boards, 20 Eglinton Ave. East, Toronto, Ontario.

tract dealers

There are a number of tract dealers handling Canadian land. Unlike their U.S. counterparts many of these specialize in smaller, more isolated parcels and may offer complete parcels rather than tract setups. No access roads or the like are included, but prices tend to be a good bit lower. Many of the parcels are timberland that has been cut over. Some of the major dealers are listed below.

CANADIAN ESTATE LAND CORP.
286 Lawrence Ave. West, Toronto 20, Ontario, Canada
These folks sell undeveloped wilderness land throughout southern Canada (emphasis is on the eastern provinces, though). They own the land and offer parcels from a fraction of an acre to over 300 acres, with those 40 acres and up being the most common. Prices run from around $20 per acre for the larger, remote parcels to well over $100 per acre for ones close to towns. Most of the land is in timber areas (logged over) but some river and lake front lots are offered. A time payment package is offered as standard with a 10% reduc-

---

PARCEL TK71322 ●

South part, Broken lot 7, Concession 6, Henwood Township, Temiskaming District. Ontario — **157 acres.**

Six hundred feet of this parcel's eastern border are formed by the shores of a small, unnamed lake. Some marshland fringes the lake, promising good duck and geese hunting right on the lot. Most of the parcel is dry land, however, and it is in the stamping grounds of moose,

---

bear, deer and other wild animals. In a versatile district, the parcel has access to trout fishing in Evanturel Creek which passes 600 yards north of the lot. Just over half a mile south is another nameless lake and between one and two miles southeast are two other lakes, headwaters of Wabi Creek.

PRICE: $4,995.00 payable $270.00 cash with order and 62 monthly payments of $95.00 each with a final payment of $15.72 OR $4,495.00 being 10% off if paid $270.00 cash with order and $4,225.00 in ten days.

---

tion for straight cash. Their 120-page catalog listing properties has some good prices, but no specific pictures are presented and only rough details are given on access, water availability, and so forth, so a personal inspection would certainly be recommended. Catalog costs $5 per year, but they don't say how often it comes out. They may push a bit hard, but they can show you what is available.

REED AND ZELSMAN LTD.
3768 Bathurst St., Downsview, Ontario, Canada
Here we find the same deal and type of land as Canadian Estate Land Corp.—they must use the same writer or else they copy pages, because the presentation, description, and financial arrangements are damn near identical. Reed and Zelsman have only about eight pages in their listing, but then they'll send it free. Maybe you'll want to check them out first before scrounging a five for Canadian Estate's catalog. (Listing is mostly Ontario land.)

H.M. DIGNAM CORP. LTD.
85 Bloor St. East, Toronto, Ontario
Here's the third one in the set. Dignam puts out a 15-page catalog, called their *Tax Sale List* on an irregular basis (they claim to pick up most of their land through tax sales). The presentation and arrangements are the same as the others with emphasis on Ontario but with some listings in Nova Scotia, Prince Edward Island, and the western provinces. The current *Tax Sale List* is free, and $1 will buy you a subscription to the next four issues.

From: *The Foxfire Book*

THE CABIN

The wilderness cabin can take a variety of forms. It may be built of logs, adobe, stone, or cement; it may be a standard frame construction, a dome, a tipi, or a yurt; it may be made of such exotic materials as bamboo, straw, sandbags, or bottles. It can be an authentic crafted cabin built only with hand tools and natural materials, or it may be a vacation home constructed entirely of lumberyard materials by professionals. Cost, time, working knowledge, available material, personal preference, and permanence desired will all affect your choice. This section touches on the necessary material and information for all these areas so that you may quickly develop the background needed to make an intelligent choice and to follow through on the building of your own cabin.

BOOKS

THE FOXFIRE BOOK (1)
Eliot Wigginton, Ed.
1972 - 384 p. il. - $4.95 (pb)

The Foxfire Book is one of the best sources of material on log cabin living. It is in many ways a unique book. The contents were collected and compiled by high school students in Rabun Gap, Ga., as part of an English course and were originally presented in *Foxfire* magazine. The aim was to collect and preserve the traditional arts and crafts of the southern Appalachian region, and the students have succeeded admirably. The result is an engaging insight into a vanishing lifestyle.

The section on log cabin building is exceptional. The techniques are presented in a clear step-by-step fashion with plenty of photographs showing details of actual cabins. Each stage of construction is described for three types of cabin—the crafted cabin, which is a creation of genuine beauty and distinction built using only hand tools and natural materials; the less complicated but fully functional cabin, which allows the use of power tools and sawmill materials; and the cabin with special variations which you may wish to incorporate. The result is exceptionally clear and concise. The idea is not really to show how to build a cabin, but how cabins were actually built.

The same approach is applied throughout the book—showing various aspects of country living and presenting detailed how-to information. The areas considered range from such luxuries as soap-making to such necessities as turning out moonshine. Examples are quilting, hog butchering, canning, butter-making, hunting, home remedies, faith healing, snake folklore, and anecdotes. Whether you actually want to try the wilderness life or just want to learn what it was like, this book is a must.
From: Doubleday & Co., Inc., 501 Franklin Ave., Garden City, L.I., N.Y. 11530

THE INDIAN TIPI—ITS HISTORY, CONSTRUCTION AND USE
Reginald and Gladys Laubin
1957 - 208 p. il. - $1.65 (pb)

A properly constructed Indian tipi is one of the simplest and finest wilderness dwellings for year-round use and has the particular advantage of being highly portable. *The Indian Tipi* is *the* authoritative book on the subject, presenting full details on construction, setup, furnishing, and just plain living in a tipi. The main emphasis is on the Sioux tipi with subsidiary coverage of other types. The plans presented are the ones used by nearly all manufacturers of authentic tipis.

The book also presents a good look at Indian philosophy and customs, as well as information on Indian tanning methods, jerky making,

and constructing a sweat lodge. All of this should be of interest no matter what type of wilderness home you want. The overall presentation makes a fascinating account, and the book is a fine investment.
From: Ballantine Books, Inc., 101 Fifth Ave., New York, N.Y. 10003

THE WILDERNESS CABIN
Calvin Rutstrum
1961 - 169 p. il. - $5.95

Covers the whole range. Location and selection of site, construction of both log and frame cabins, use of heavy timber tools for making log cabins, building of fireplaces, directions on water supply and sewage disposal, and advice on living in the cabin. All based on Rutstrum's personal experience with cabins.
From: The Macmillan Co., 866 Third Ave., New York, N.Y. 10022

DOMEBOOK TWO
Lloyd Kahn
1971 - 128 p. il. - $5

The book on geodesics. From people who build domes and live domes. Coverage from mathematics to domes that have been built—how they were done and how they turned out. A dome offers wide possibilities to the home builder—cover yours with glass and plastic, ferro-cement, or hand-hewn cedar shakes.
From: Book People, 2940 Seventh St., Berkeley, Calif. 94710

KNOWING YOUR TREES
G. H. Collingwood and Warren D. Brush
Rev. & ed. by Devereux Butcher
1964 - 349 p. il. - $7.50

Certain types of wood are particularly suitable for certain uses. If you are going to build a wilderness cabin, you need to know not only which type wood you should be using for a particular job, but also how to identify that tree in the wild. *Knowing Your Trees* is your identification manual. Photographs are used throughout the book and are easier to work with than the usual sketches. More than 170 trees are covered, and in each case, the full standing tree (both in summer and winter for the deciduous varieties), the flowers, leaves, fruits, buds, and bark are clearly depicted and explained. The natural range in the United States and southern Canada is also shown on a map. This full spread of clear photos makes identification easy.

The book is put out by the American Forestry Association, and so it covers only commercially valuable trees—which fortunately are exactly those we wish. In addition to identifying data, full details are provided on the properties of the wood—color, weight per cubic foot when dry, hardness, ease with which it is worked, and common uses. An indispensable addition to your cabin library.
From: American Forestry Association, 919 17th St., N.W., Washington, D.C. 20006

CONSTRUCTION

YOUR ENGINEERED HOUSE
Rex Roberts
1964 - 239 p. il. - $4.95 (pb)

Mostly post and beam work as far as actual construction methods discussed, but Roberts does go very thoroughly into positioning the house, room layout, heating, ventilation, etc. Invaluable.
From: J. B. Lippincott Co., East Washington Sq., Philadelphia, Pa. 19106

THE OWNER-BUILT HOME
Ken Kern
1961 - 281 p. il. - $7.50

Collection of low-cost building techniques from around the world. Includes details on construction using such materials as woven bamboo and bottles, rock and earth, and concrete sheet and contemporary wood framing. Fantastic collection of ideas. For an additional $5, Kern will supply a preliminary design to your specifications (send a sketch of site, space requirements, and personal preferences) either with order for book or after you've had a chance to look it over. A second book, *The Owner-Built Homestead* is due out shortly. Both are being serialized in *The Mother Earth News.*
From: Ken Kern, Sierra Rt., Oakhurst, Calif. 93644

BUILD YOUR OWN STONE HOUSE
Karl and Sue Schwenke
1975 - 156 p. il. - $4.95 (pb)

"The traditional methods of dry laying (laying stones atop one another without bonding agent so they remain in place by their own weight), and hand laying (same as dry laying except that it uses mortar) required too long a time in construction. Therefore we finally settled upon the slipform method of building with fieldstone." And with this, Karl and Sue take you through the step-by-step process of building a stone house as they did theirs, from choosing the site to shingling the roof, via the slipform method. This method uses wooden forms to retain the stones and concrete in place till set. As each course is built, the forms are "slipped" (moved) up to the next course level and the wall built higher. Karl, who has an engineering background, lets it show throughout the book with his many tables and construction drawings. If you're planning to build in New England or any other place with an overabundance of fieldstone, this would really be the way to go, and the Schwenkes's book can give you just about all the info you need to do it.
From: RPM Distributors, 5862 Wicomico Ave., Rockville, Md. 20852

STONE SHELTERS
Edward Allen
1969 - 199 p. il. - $4.95 (pb)

Building with stone—or at least how it is done in southern Italy. Basically concerned with how the architectural styles and techniques derive from the local geography and lifestyle of the people. Excellent photos.
From: MIT Press, 28 Carleton St., Cambridge, Mass. 02142

HOW TO BUILD YOUR HOME IN THE WOODS
Bradford Angier
1952 - 310 p. il. - $3.95 (pb)

Angier has a regular series of books on wilderness living, and this is his handbook on building a log cabin. The actual construction techniques are carefully presented step-by-step. Angier's is not the purist's cabin covered in *The Foxfire Book* but rather the somewhat simpler (but fully functional) type made with some sawmill lumber, nails, glass windows, and roll roofing. The explanations and illustrations are not always as clear as those in *The Foxfire Book,* but the information is all there. On the other hand, Angier does delve into the construction of such items as doors, window shutters, furnishings, fences, lights, stoves, beds, swings, hot-water heaters, and the like, which are not covered in *Foxfire.* All of these, of course, are useful additions to a fully functional year-round home.

There are also several sections giving basics of constructing frame shelters and camping shelters as well as a raft of good tips for living off the wilds. All good material.
From: Hart Publishing Co., Inc., 719 Broadway, N.Y., N.Y. 10003

BUILDING WITH LOGS
B. Allen Machie
1971 - 40 p. il. - $5

Most of the material in this spiral-bound soft-cover book concerns constructing a cabin on one basic design. Each building problem is discussed, with several solutions. Good how-to info for anyone interested in more than a temporary cabin.
From: B. Allen Mackie, P.O. Box 1205, Prince George, B.C. Canada

SHELTERS, SHACKS AND SHANTIES
D. C. Beard
1914 - 243 p. il. - $2.75

This reprint of D. C. Beard's wilderness home construction handbook for boys has got to be one of the best books available on the subject. Particularly for the wilderness purist who wouldn't dream of using anything but what nature supplies. While there are other books that are useful for housing in the wilds, only Beard's gives details for those that can be constructed totally from materials found on the site, with only the axe, crosscut saw, mason's hammer and rope having to be carried in. The book's chapters cover projects ranging from a simple balsam bed to a tree house to a permanent totem cabin. Included is information on how to build hearths and chimneys, and how to lay a fire; instructions for using the tools required, and details for setting up gates, latches, locks, catches, log ladders, and so forth. One chapter entitled, "How to Make a Concealed Log Cabin Inside of a Modern House," discusses the idea of having a log cabin room as a den, complete with fireplace and the works. Pretty spiffy thought, particularly if there's no hint that such a room exists before you open the door to it. Throughout the book Dan Beard's own rustic drawings illustrate design and construction methods. Really a great book for $2.75.
From: Charles Scribner's Sons, 597 Fifth Ave., New York, N.Y. 10017

BUILD WITH ADOBE
Marcia Southwick
184 p. il. - $2.50

Construction with adobe. Also includes hints on such areas as financing, landscaping, interior decorating.
From: Swallow Press Inc., 1139 S. Wabash Ave., Chicago, Ill. 60605

VILLAGE TECHNOLOGY HANDBOOK
1970 - 400 p. il. - $7.00

Put out by Volunteers for International Technical Assistance, who specialize in technical assistance to poverty areas around the world. Building your own tools, buildings, and appliances—from washing machines to plows, refrigerators to waterwheels—from available materials.
From: VITA, College Campus, Schenectady, N.Y. 12308

TOOLS

SURVEYING
Charles B. Breed
1957 - 495 p. il. - $7.95

All the details of actually operating the gear and finding the answers.
From: John Wiley and Sons, 605 Third Ave., New York, N.Y. 10016

HOW TO USE TRANSITS AND LEVELS FOR FASTER, MORE ACCURATE BUILDING
1966 - 24 p. il. - free

This is a small booklet put out by C. L. Berger & Sons, who manufacture transits. It presents the basics of transit use—what you can measure with a transit and how to do it. This is no detailed step-by-step approach. Rather the basic setup for each type of measurement is illustrated and briefly explained.
From: C. L. Berger & Sons, Inc., 43A William St., Boston, Mass. 02119 02119

THE COMPLETE WOODWORKING HDBK
J. T. Adams and E. Stieri
595 p. il. - $5.95

The full spread. Selection of proper wood and tools and their use and care; also covers adhesives and finishing techniques. Recommended.
From: Arco Publishing Co., Inc., 219 Park Ave., South, New York, N.Y. 10003

MODERN CARPENTRY
W. H. Wagner
480 p. il. - $5.97 (pb)

Encyclopedia of modern building methods and materials. Mostly framing procedures. Good reference.
From: Goodheart-Wilcox Co., 123 W. Taft Dr., Holland, Ill. 60473

HOW TO WORK WITH TOOLS AND WOOD
Robert Campbell and N. H. Mager, Eds.
1965 - 488 p. il. - $1.25 (pb)

This one is an updated version of the very popular book originally put out by Stanley Tool Co. It provides a complete rundown of basic hand and power tools and the proper techniques for using and caring for them. In addition, it includes sections on choosing the right wood for the job, joining and fastening techniques, and finishing, as well as a number of plans for small household items. The woodworking techniques are primarily aimed at the home handyman, but construction principles and tool choice and use are the same whether you're building an end table or a whole house.
From: Pocket Books, Inc., 630 Fifth Ave., New York, N.Y. 10020

FUNDAMENTALS OF CARPENTRY, VOL. 2
Walter E. Durbahn and E. W. Sundberg
1970 - 504 p. il. - $7.40

Professional textbook of modern techniques. Know your basics before you tackle this one.
From: Am. Technical Society, 848 E. 58th St., Chicago, Ill. 60637

COUNTRY TOOLS
Fred Davis
1974 - 152 p. il. - $3.95 (pb)

Here it is, 152 pages of where to get essential hardware and livery for the wilderness homestead: adzes, apple peelers, burlap bags, oak barrels, cast-iron bean pot tripods, bottling and canning implements, horse-drawn buckboards, butter churns, hand (push) cultivators, fireplace tools, cranes, implements, etc., cast-iron irons (iron clothes—betcha didn't think you could get these anymore!), froes, goat harnesses, cider presses, praying mantises and ladybugs (live), razors and strops, meat smokers, soil test kits, hand seed broadcasters, sugar buckets, traps, water wheels (over- or undershot), wooden baby cradles, wooden toys, and more. Though the items, themselves, are illustrated with hand drawings and described, only the address is given for the supplier—no prices or dealer description. Nevertheless, the book is definitely worth the price.
From: Oliver Press, 1400 Ryan Creek Rd., Willits, Calif. 95490

> The following books and publications are available from:
>
> Superintendent of Documents
> U.S. Government Printing Office
> Washington, D.C. 20402
>
> When ordering, always give the catalog number listed after the price.

HOMES—CONSTRUCTION, MAINTENANCE, COMMUNITY DEVELOPMENT - PL 72
Price List - 72 - free

If you want the complete list of books the Government puts out on home construction, et al, request this free price list.

CARPENTRY AND BUILDING CONSTRUCTION
1960 - 198 p. il. - 75¢
D 101.11:5–460

Don't have any details on this one. Soon's we can scrounge up six bits we'll buy it and let you know.

LOW-COST WOOD HOMES FOR RURAL AMERICA— CONSTRUCTION MANUAL
L. O. Anderson
1969 - 112 p. il. - $1
A 1.76:364

Details for constructing wood frame buildings and pole houses.

GOV. PUBLICATIONS

WOOD-FRAME HOUSE CONSTRUCTION
L. O. Anderson and O. C. Heyer
U.S. Dept. of Agriculture, Forest Service
1970 - 223 p. il. - $2.25
A 1.76:73/97.0

Complete construction techniques for a wood-frame house, from checking the site to final painting. Carefully details how each section is properly put together and mated to the others.

PROTECTING LOG CABINS, RUSTIC WORK AND UNSEASONED WOOD FROM INJURIOUS INSECTS IN EASTERN UNITED STATES
U.S. Dept. of Agriculture
1970 - 18 p. il. - 15¢
A 1.9:2104/4

Considers the three main boring beetles which attack and destroy newly felled timber—bark beetles, ambrosia beetles, and wood borers. Tells how to recognize each type and how to avoid and prevent infestation.

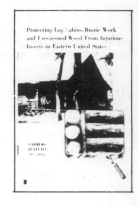

SUBTERRANEAN TERMITES, Their Prevention & Control in Bldgs.
Rev. 1972 - 30 p. il. - 20¢
A 1.77:64/4 S/N 0100-1507

Provides information on the appearance, biology, and habits of termites. This pamphlet discusses the prevention of termite attack during the construction of buildings; methods of controlling termites in existing structures; and other insects that damage wood in buildings.

EARTH FOR HOMES: IDEAS AND METHODS EXCHANGE
$3 PB 188918

HANDBOOK FOR BUILDING HOMES OF EARTH
$3 PB 179 327

BUILDING WITH ADOBE AND STABILIZED-EARTH BLOCKS
U. S. Department of Agriculture
1972 - 8 p. il. - 10¢
A 1.35:535/3 S/N 0100-1563

Concise presentation of the principles and techniques of making and building with adobe or stabilized-earth blocks. Covers proper foundation, making and laying block, putting on roof, and coating block for protection. In a dry climate with few trees at hand, an adobe or earth-block house is the simplest way to go.

ELEMENTS OF SURVEYING
1971 - 304 p. il. - $2.25
D 101.11:5-232/3 S/N 0820-0388

This Department of the Army Technical Manual provides instructional guidance and reference in the principles and procedures of basic surveying, and in the care, use, and adjustment of surveying instruments. Discussions are also included on some of the computations and adjustments, calibrations, and graphic portrayals of survey data.

CONCRETE AND MASONRY
Dept. of Army Technical Manual—TM 5-742
1964 - 198 p. il. - $1.00
D 101.11:5-742

The Army way of working with concrete and masonry. Contains a lot of technical material and graphs covering all the variables that affect the properties of concrete. Assorted field tests are described for evaluation of various components and finished products as well. A fair amount of the material is aimed at heavy construction, but they haven't left out anything that applies to the little man. Complete, if not always applicable.

FIREPLACES AND CHIMNEYS
U.S. Dept. of Agriculture
1971 - 24 p. il. - 20¢
A 1.9:1889/6 S/N 0100-1520

Good rundown on proper construction details for building a fireplace and chimney in your cabin.

MANUAL OF INDIVIDUAL WATER SUPPLY SYSTEMS
1962 - 121 p. il. - 60¢
FS 2.6/2:W29/2

All kinds of wells from hand dug to jetted.

FARMSTEAD SEWAGE AND REFUSE DISPOSAL
U.S. Dept. of Agriculture
1963 - 25 p. il. - 20¢
A 1.75:274

Construction, design, and operation requirements for various sewage systems including septic tank, cesspool, privies, and chemical closets. Also covers proper disposal techniques for general refuse.

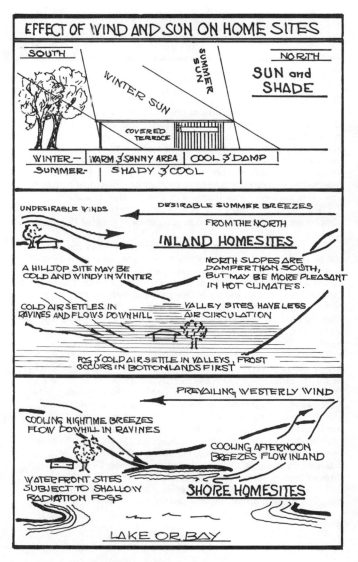

MANUAL OF SEPTIC TANK PRACTICE
U.S. Dept. of Health, Education, and Welfare
1967 - 92 p. il. - 50¢
FS 2.6/2: Se 6/967

Presents the Government standards and requirements for the construction of a septic tank system or seepage pit. Tells how to conduct a percolation test, construct the drainage field, etc. This book is used as the standard by most localities in establishing regulations and by contractors in installing the systems.

BASIC HANDTOOLS
1963 - 227 p. il. - $1.50
D 208.11:H19/963

Proper use, care, and sharpening. Covers woodworking, metalworking, and machinists tools.

TOOLS AND THEIR USES
1971 - 179 p. il. - $1.50
S/N 0847-00145

Provides descriptions, general uses, correct operation, and maintenance procedures for the hand and power tools commonly used in the Navy.

USE AND CARE OF HANDTOOLS AND MEASURING TOOLS
1961 - 223 p. il. - $1
D 101.11:9-243

WOODWORKING TOOLS, 1600-1900
1966 - 48 p. il. - 70¢
SI 3.3:241/paper 51

LOG CABINS

So you're into log cabins, but your site is a barren island in the Arctic Ocean, or maybe you just don't dig the Paul Bunyan bit. O.K., so there's a bunch of manufacturers who specialize in log cabin kits and who can supply you with everything you need for your cabin or log home. Here's how it works. The logs and other materials are all precut and ready to assemble on delivery. A minimum of construction experience is necessary to put the cabin together so you can do most of it yourself or hire a local contractor. The plans available range from a 7' x 7' minicabin to a 20-room inn, and if you don't like any of these, you can design your own. The options are there and you can do as much or as little of the total work as you wish.

The simplest kit consists of all the logs called for in the plan, but no roofing, no floors, no doors or windows, no electricity or plumbing or anything like that—just the four walls and the roof rafters and sometimes the floor joists and interior walls. The idea behind this is that all the other items are standard lumberyard or home supply materials and can usually be bought cheaper locally than they can be shipped over a long haul. Smart. Gives you a good chance to do some scrounging on these things, too. As a general guideline, the price on a basic kit for a single level cabin, 24' x 32', will run you between $3,300 and $5,500. Specific prices for a similar size cabin are given for each dealer later, but don't lean on these too heavily because no one includes exactly the same things in the kits.

Many dealers offer a shell or standard kit. These include all the stuff like flooring, roofing, windows, exterior and interior doors, interior walls, and often paneling, ceilings, and insulation. They do *not* include plumbing, wiring, fixtures or appliances, kitchen cabinets, foundations, disposal systems, and heating. You still have to take care of these locally. The prices on shell kits for the same 24' x 32' cabin start around $6,000 and work up to around $9,000 depending on how fancy you get. These prices do not include shipping, which will run between 50¢ and $1.00 per mile by truck and a bit less by rail. This can add up. As another general rule of thumb, if you hire someone to finish the house and buy all the other items needed to complete it, the total cost will run about double the shell cost, plus maybe 10% for good measure. Of course, if you do a lot of the work yourself, you can save a bundle—that's one of the objectives of the kits.

In looking over the available kits, you will note that a variety of logs are employed. Far and away the most common are cedar, either northern white cedar (in the East) or western red cedar. Others use eastern white pine, lodgepole pine, red spruce, and redwood. The big thing with cedar is its exceptional resistance to rot and decay, making it extremely durable. In this regard cedar ranks with redwood and cypress as the best commercial wood. In addition, cedar is attractive, easily worked, and shows small shrinkage and checking when dried. This is not to put down the other types, however. They are all good structural woods and are normally treated chemically to resist both rot and insects. Thus with a proper foundation to keep the logs well off the ground, they should all serve perfectly well. The accompanying table details the characteristics for each type of wood.

One final thought—if you intend to use your cabin year-round in cold country, the size of the logs is important for insulation. Dry wood is a good insulator, but it is still only about one-third as good as fiberglass for the same thickness. Thus one should have at least 6-in. logs for comfortable cold weather living—unless, of course, you have plenty of free firewood and like cutting it. Also, make certain the logs fit together tightly and are properly sealed.

sources of log cabins

AIR-LOCK LOG CO., INC.
P.O. Box 2506, Las Vegas, N. Mex. 87701
Air-Lock offers a unique system—the logs are hollowed and lathe-turned to a standard 6-inch diameter (7" and 8" are available). Construction is horizontal tongue and groove with full overlap and interlocking corners. The hollowed logs are lighter than solid ones for ease of handling and shipping, and because they can dry at both the center and outside, Air-Lock claims there is less cracking and checking. The type of log is not specified though we expect it's pine.

Air-Lock has about 57 standard plans ranging from a 7' x 7' minicabin to an 8,700 sq. ft. inn. They offer both log material kits and shell kits for all of these. The log material kit for 24' x 32' single-floor cabin (768 sq. ft.) costs $5,780 plus shipping. Many of the smaller units have been designed for airlifting into remote sites. A number of unusual and intriguing designs are offered. Catalog costs $2.

NATIONAL LOG CONSTRUCTION CO. OF MONTANA
P.O. Box 68, Thompson Falls, Mont. 59873
National manufactures the same system as Air-Lock and has the same catalog (would guess they have a franchise with Air-Lock). Prices seem to be a bit higher.

L. C. ANDREW, INC.
South Windham, Maine 04082
Andrew uses white cedar logs in a horizontal tongue-and-groove arrangement. The insides of the logs are flattened for a smooth interior wall. Logs vary in size (not milled to a uniform size) for a more rustic appearance, but there is no traditional overlapping at the corners. Material packages and packages of prefabricated 8-ft. sections (including roof and floor) are offered. L. C. Andrew also manufactures rustic cedar furniture and a complete line of rustic cedar fencing—stockade-style and traditional post and rail. For more information write the above address.

BELLAIRE LOG CABIN MANUFACTURING CO.
P.O. Box 322, Bellaire, Mich. 49615
Bellaire uses white cedar logs in a vertical spline construction. An assortment of 4-, 5-, and 6-inch logs is provided for each house so that you can juggle them around to get the windows and doors to fall where you want and the corners to match (at least until you get to the last corner). The logs are flattened on the inside to give a smooth interior wall. The material kit for their 24' x 36' Riverside model (they don't have a 24' x 32' model) includes roof materials. Bellaire also offers materials for flooring, windows, insulated roofs, paneled walls, storm windows, gable porches and exterior paneling as options. Full literature is available for $1.

GREEN MOUNTAIN CABINS, INC.
Box 190, Chester, Vt. 05143
For its cabins Green Mountain uses hand-peeled spruce logs splined together. The logs are left rounded on the inside and are square-notched and overlapped at the corners in traditional fashion. The standard kit for their 20' x 34' Sebago costs $8,000, but this includes floor and roof materials. Literature is available free.

NORTHERN PRODUCTS INC.
Bomarc Rd., Bangor, Me. 04401
Here we find white pine log walls and spruce support timbers in a horizontal tongue-and-groove setup. The corners are also tongue-and-groove with no overlap, but there is alternate log extension beyond

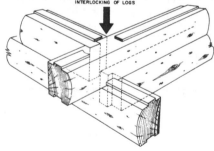

INTERLOCKING OF LOGS

the corners. Once again the logs are flattened on the inside and are 6" x 8" which we presume means 6 inches thick (with flattened side) and 8 inches high. Catalog is available for 2 bills.

Comparative Table of Woods Used in Log Cabin Construction						
Log	Color	Color after weathering	Weight lbs./ft.^{3}	Decay resistance	Shrinking	Checking
western red cedar	red	dark gray	24–30	very high	low	little
northern white cedar	yellow-brown	gray	19	very high	low	little
eastern white pine	cream to brown	light gray	24–27	medium	low	conspicuous
lodgepole pine	light brown	gray	25–36	high	—	—
red spruce	off-white	light gray	28	low	medium	conspicuous
redwood	reddish brown	dark gray	24–26	very high	medium low	little

TIMBERLODGE INC.
105 W. 8th Ave., North Kansas City, Mo. 64116
These people, located in the heart of the timber country, put out red-wood log or plank kits for homes and cabins. The arrangement is horizontal tongue-and-groove, but the basic construction is post-and-beam. To elaborate on that, the logs or planks come in 4-foot sections and are stacked tongue-and-groove with the ends tongue-and-groove into redwood box posts. The roof rafters are box beams supported by the posts, so the log walls carry no loading. The logs are apparently milled full round and left so on the inside, but they don't tell you that. Since everything is built on multiples of 4 feet in this setup, the plans all go by changes of 4 feet in length and width, and it is easy to add or subtract, as you wish. Since the walls carry no load, large glass areas are possible on any wall. Their basic log kit for the 24' x 32' cabin includes the roof and windows (no floor). Stronger roof systems are offered for heavy snow areas. Literature available, free.

WARD CABIN CO.
Box 72, Houlton, Me. 04730
Ward cabins represent a return to the by now familiar white cedar logs, tongue and grooved, horizontal construction, with tongue and groove corners and alternate log extension beyond the corner. The logs are 4¼ in., rough peeled on the outside, flattened on the inside. In case you are interested, the purlins are spruce for greater strength. Ward has both cabin kits and year-round home kits. The 24' x 32' Vacationer cabin kit includes roof, flooring, interior partitions and windows (really a shell kit). The catalog runs $2, but only covers year-round models. Cabin literature is available free (ask for Allagash Rustic Camp lit.).

MILLER VACATION HOMES
Rt. 67, RFD 3, Ballston Spa, N.Y. 12020
Miller handles the Ward line at Ward prices. Might save on shipping if he is closer to your site.

VERMONT LOG BUILDINGS, INC.
Hartland, Vt. 05048
Vermont Log employs white pine logs for the walls and red pine for the rafters and joists. The logs are splined together as are the corners. The logs are nominally six-inch diameter, but are hand-peeled and may range up to 8 in. or more. Inside walls are left rounded. A unique sealing system is used with two polyurethane gaskets providing the seal between logs rather than the usual messy caulking. The log material kit for the standard Cavendish cabin (16' x 32') is $7,450. Catalog of plans for cabins, homes and business is $2. Some real rustic cabins here.

Starting erection.

Two and a half hour's progress with four men.

AMERICAN TIMBER HOMES, INC.
Escanaba, Mich. 49829
American offers primarily year-round vacation cabins and homes using white cedar planks 2-3/8 in. thick and splined together. Their 24' x 32' Villager, which is a full shell kit, includes floor, insulated roof and all the rest, which is the only package offered. Catalog is $1.

CEDAR FOREST PRODUCTS CO.
Polo, Ill. 61064
Western Red cedar planks, 4'' x 8'', tongue-and-groove. The basic literature has some good looking plans but not much specific info. We have no prices on these. Literature free.

LINDAL CEDAR HOMES
P.O. Box 8839, Seattle, Wash. 98178
Lindal uses 2-in. Western red cedar planking and post and beam construction 5' 4'' on center. Full catalog is $1.

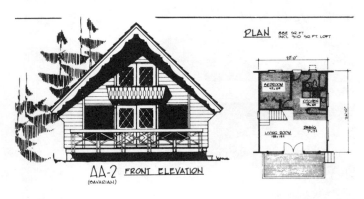

PLAN 885 SQ FT
INCL 510 SQ FT LOFT

AA-2 FRONT ELEVATION
(BAVARIAN)

JUSTUS CO., INC.
P.O. Box 91515, Tacoma, Wash. 98491
Justus uses 4'' x 8'' Western red cedar planks, double tongue-and-groove, for the walls and Douglas fir for the joists and beams. Again only full shell kits are offered, that include flooring and an insulated roof. Emphasis is on homes, but there are some good cabins offered. Catalog is $1.

INTERNATIONAL HOMES OF CEDAR
P.O. Box 268, Woodinville, Wash. 98072
International Homes uses laminated cedar planks in a choice of three thicknesses depending on whether you want 3-, 4- or 5-piece lamination. Actual thicknesses are 2¼'', 2¾'' and 3¾'' (nominal 3 x 8 and 4 x 8). Single or double tongue-and-groove is used depending on plank thickness. Again only full shell kits are offered. Literature is available free.

PAN-ABODE INC.
4350 Lake Washington Blvd., Renton, Wash. 98055
Here we have 3'' x 6'' cedar planking, tongue-and-groove, extending beyond the corners which are square-joint and overlapping. The shell kit for the 24' x 33' cabin, $9,000 (includes roof and floor). Literature available, free.

RONDESICS, INC.
527 McDowell St., Asheville, N.C. 28803
Rondesics offers their Rondette in a variety of sizes from 8 sides enclosing 335 sq. ft. to 15 sides enclosing 1165 sq. ft. The unit is shipped as prefabricated 8' panels to be assembled on site. The exterior is redwood siding. The house is available as a shell or as a complete package house, fully insulated, and includes kitchen cabinets and appliances, bathroom fixtures, and electric heating units. It does not include hook-up plumbing, electrical wiring, foundation, sewage system, water heater or setup. The price on the 12-side Rondette (735 sq. ft.) shell package (complete floor and roof) is $9,300.

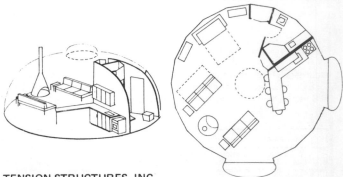

TENSION STRUCTURES, INC.
9800 Ann Arbor Rd., Plymouth, Mich. 48170
These cats offer a 25' fiberglass O'Dome which comes in 18 wall panel sections including one sliding glass door and skylight. You put it together on your own foundation (it has no floor) and add what you want. Area is 505 sq. ft. It can easily be taken down and stored or moved anytime you wish. You can connect two or three together for more room. If you want to use this in a populated area, better be sure of building regs. A lot of city fathers are down on this sort of home. Literature available, free.

NOMADICS
Star Route, Box 41, Cloverdale, Oreg. 97112
Nomadics has four different-sized tipis from 16 ft. to 22 ft. in diameter in either 10-oz. marine-treated Terrasol canvas, 14-oz. cold duck canvas, or 14-oz. flame-resistant canvas. They also have each of these sizes in pre-cut kits ready for sewing if you'd rather do it yourself. The basic design is Sioux with a number of modifications. Their 16-ft. tipi in 10-oz. Terrasol runs $178, the liner costs another $64. The kit for this tipi is $132 and $53 for the liner. Nomadics should have something for everybody. Prices are low and the quality of workmanship very good. For more info, write Jeb Barton at the above address.

Design of Nomadics Tipi

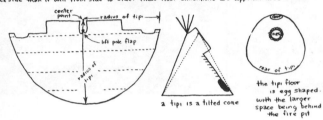

The design we use is the basic Sioux design as explained in the Laubin's book, The Indian Tipi. The center point for the arc is located at the very top middle of the smoke flaps. The dotted lines represent 36" wide strips of material. Notice that the bottom of the lift pole flap is 36" below the center point of the tipi when measuring along the radius down the middle or backbone of the outspread tipi cover. Therefore, when set-up the back of the tipi will be 3 ft. shorter than the front side where the door hole is. This difference causes the tipi to tilt to the rear rather than being a perfectly symetrical cone. As a result of this tilt, the floor of the tipi is egg shaped. The tipi will therefore be longer from the front door to the middle of the backside than it will from side to side. These floor dimentions are approximated below.

a tipi is a tilted cone

the tipi floor is egg shaped, with the larger space being behind the fire pit

GOODWIN-COLE, TENTMAKERS
1315 Alhambra Blvd., Sacramento, Calif. 95816
These people offer a stock Sioux tipi employing several of their own modifications, but they will also build tipis to the Cheyenne, Arapaho, Kah-Nee-Ta, Blackfeet, Laubin, Crow and Dakota designs on special order. The Sioux tipi is available in 14', 16', 18', 20', 22' and 24' diameters of 10- and 12-oz. duck, 10-oz. flame-resistant army duck and 13-oz. "winterized" army duck. Their 16', 12-oz. duck tipi runs $130, an 18-oz. water-resistant floor runs another $60, and a door flap, $9, for a total of $199. A 6', 12-oz. duck liner for this tipi costs $64. Kits are available for all their tipis. For the 16-footer, deduct $33 from the cost of the tipi. Almost pays to have them handle the sewing. Amongst all the tipi makers, Goodwin-Cole is the only one we've seen that also offers an ozan (an extension of the liner, almost like a smaller tent within the tipi, sometimes with extra curtains for compartmen-

talizing the tipi or for hanging as a canopy over the sleeping area to help retain heat). An ozan of 10-oz. flame-resistant army duck for the 16' tipi would run $38. For more information, write the above address for Goodwin-Cole's two-page brochure describing their tipis. It's free and includes much interesting info on setting up and using tipis.

WESTERN TRADING POST, INC.
P.O. Box 9070, Denver, Colo. 80209
Western has some seven different-sized tipis from 10 ft. to 22 ft. of 10-, 12- and 14.9-oz. canvas. All must be made to order—their design or yours. The price for their 16-ft. design is $193, which is getting up there, but the liners go for more than half the price of the tipi—$109 for this one! Better buy your liner somewhere else. From the info we have available, these look to be made by Goodwin-Cole. Western's catalog also contains a good selection of Indian crafts, books and craft materials, including willow backrests made by Frank Billy, a Chippewa Cree, $90. Catalog is free. Write for it at the above address.

WEBB MANUFACTURING CO.
Fourth and Cambria Sts., Philadelphia, Pa. 19133
Webb makes Sioux Indian tipis based on the Laubin drawings. Five sizes (12', 16', 18', 20' and 22') are offered in 10.10- and 12.65-oz. NoBlaze army duck. Price on the 10.10-oz., 16-footer is $230 and $86 for the liner. Webb also makes a Hogan or Longhouse in sizes up to 12' x 23' x 8' and an assortment of more conventional tents. Catalog is free.

WINONA AMERICAN INDIAN TRADING POST
P.O. Box 324, Santa Fe, N. Mex. 87501
Pierre Bovis, who specializes in Indian history, culture and artifacts, offers the 1876 Powder River Sioux Tipi, an 18', 12-oz. canvas duck tipi patterned after the Sioux tipis made during the period when canvas was substituted for buffalo hides on the great western plains. Price is $355 including 6-ft. liner made of 7-oz. tight-weave cotton satin, water-repellent, DuPont-treated Zepel. In '75 Bovis was supplying, on special order, 12', 15', 18' and 21' tipis in several styles—Crow, Blackfeet, Cheyenne and Sioux—all traditional, constructed of 10-oz. duck, but his current literature ('76) makes no mention of this.

In addition to the Powder River Tipi, Winona offers a wide range of materials for Indian crafts and a good collection of authentic Indian relics. Their catalog of Indian books is also exceptional. The annual *Supply Catalog*, which contains info on the tipi and is published each January, runs $2. The book catalog costs $1. A separate brochure is available on the tipi for free. Write Pierre at the above address for more info.

THE COLORADO TENT & AWNING CO.
3333 E. 52nd Ave., Denver, Colo. 80216
Colorado makes tipis in 12', 14', 16' and 20' diameters of white single filled duck, either 12- or 14.9-oz. They are after a design by E. T. Seaton, who lived among the plains Indians and provided Colorado the pattern in 1934. List price on the 12-oz., 16-footer is $318 and the 12-oz. liner is $191—a tad steep for both of them. Colorado's catalog provides a fine assortment of other canvas products including tents, tarps, water bags, duffle bags, folding cots and chairs, panniers and saddlebags, aprons and chaps, grommets, canvas, water-repellent compounds, chuck wagon covers and more. 34-page catalog free.

DOMES

DYNA DOME
22226 North 23rd Ave., Phoenix, Ariz. 85027
Dyna Dome makes domes, and within 500 miles of Phoenix they will build you one. Beyond that you may buy a complete kit and set up your own or just buy the hub connectors and a set of plans, and really work from the basics. Watch your local building codes again. There is no appreciation of personal initiative. Literature available, free.

WILDERNESS LIVING

House Plan No. FS-SE-6

DESIGNS FOR LOW-COST WOOD HOMES - SUMMARY SHEET
U.S. Dept. of Agriculture, Forest Service
32p. - 25¢

The Forest Service people have whipped up 11 separate designs for low-cost wood homes, and the complete working plans for each of these are now available from the Government Printing Office. The summary sheet gives you the basic details of each design so that you can tell which of the plans you would like to invest further in. Designs are all oriented toward rural areas and reflect a special effort to optimize the use of low-cost materials and simple techniques. Styles run the gamut from conventional through a duplex to a round house and a tubular home. The working plans themselves cost between $1 to $1.75.
From: Sup. of Doc., U.S. Government Printing Office, Washington, D.C. 20402

MASTER PLAN SERVICE
89 E. Jericho Tnpk., Mineola, N.Y. 11501
Plans and blueprints - "Leisure Homes Portfolio" - $1 (catalog)

THE GARLINGHOUSE CO.
2320 Kansas Ave., Box 299, Topeka, Kans. 66601
Plans and blueprints - "Holiday Homes" catalog - 120 designs, mostly chalet and A-frame - $1.35.

L. M. BRUINER & ASSOCIATES, INC.
1304 S.W. Bertha Blvd., Portland, Oreg. 97219
Plans and blueprints - "250 New Non-basement 1 & 2 Story Homes and Vacation Homes" catalog - $1.50

MASONITE CORP.
111 W. Washington St., Chicago, Ill. 60602

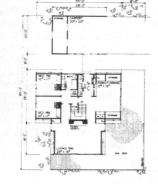

156 VACATION HOMES
Richard B. Pollman
Annual - 130 p. il. - $3.95 (pb)

This is really a catalog covering some 156 vacation home designs for which Home Planners, Inc. sells construction blueprints. An exceptional range and variety of designs are included, from log cabins on up, making the book a good reference source for designs even if you don't want to buy their blueprints. By the way, the blueprints ran $25 for a single set and $5 per additional set in 1968, which is the last price we have. If you know someone looking for a new home, these guys have several other catalogs of plans that cover the full range, from traditional ante-bellum plantation mansions to contemporary redwood and glass, cliffhanging bungalows.
From: Home Planners, Inc., 16310 Grand River Ave., Detroit, Mich. 48227

BUILD YOUR OWN LOW-COST HOME
L. O. Anderson & H. F. Zornig
1972 - 206 p. il. - $4.95 (pb)

What we have here is the complete construction plans for the same eleven designs that are available from the U.S. Gov. Printing Office (*Designs for Low-Cost Wood Homes*). For the price of four of the plans from the government, you can get all eleven in this book—if you really want that many. As a little extra frosting, Dover has included Anderson's construction manual for wood frame houses (presume that this is the same as his *Wood-Frame House Construction* book, also available through the Government Printing Office). It's a nice convenient way to collect it all, anyway.
From: Dover Publications, Inc., 180 Varick St., New York, N.Y. 10014

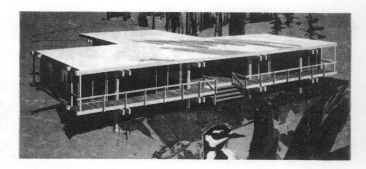

GREAT IDEAS FOR SECOND HOMES
36 p. il. - 50¢ - (No. T610)

Another catalog, this one put out by the American Plywood Association. Details some 20 vacation homes for which plans are available. To confuse the issue a little, the catalog is put out by the American Plywood people, but the blueprints are sold by the Home Building Plan Service. As you might expect, the plans all favor the use of plywood, so don't expect any log cabins. Still they look good. Blueprint costs are $25 for one set or $35 for four sets. The American Plywood people also offer plans for an assortment of small projects including a portable kennel, a gun and tackle cabinet, a simple pickup cab, and several boats, if you wish to inquire for these at the same time.
Book available from: American Plywood Association, 1119 A St., Tacoma, Wash. 98401
Blueprints available from: Home Building Plan Service, 2235 N.E. Sandy Blvd., Portland, Ore. 97232 (they also have several other catalogs of their own plans.)

OTHER SOURCES

The following are all reported to offer vacation home plans. We haven't checked any of them personally yet, but our sources are current and hopefully reliable.

NATIONAL PLAN SERVICE, INC.
1700 West Hubbard St., Chicago, Ill. 60622
Plans and blueprints - "Selected Leisure Time Living - Second Homes" catalog - $1.50 (65 designs)

THE WICKES CORP.
P.O. Box 3244, Saginaw, Mich. 48605
"Quick & Easy" Planning Guide - gives six basic floor plans and complete materials listing for shell and finishing kits using low-cost materials (24' x 30' shell, materials run $3,000) - $1.

U.S. PLYWOOD CORP.
Nancy Stuart Service Bureau, 777 Third Ave., New York, N.Y. 10017

WESTERN WOOD PRODUCTS ASSOCIATION
1500 Yeon Bldg., Portland, Oreg. 97204

WEYERHAUSER CO., Lumber and Plywood Div.
First National Bank Building, St. Paul, Minn. 55402

THE YURT FOUNDATION
Bill Coperthwaithe, Bucks Harbor, Maine 04618
Yurt Plans, $3.50.

TIMBER and CARPENTRY TOOLS

SEARS, ROEBUCK AND CO.
4640 Roosevelt Blvd., Philadelphia, Pa. 19132
Sears Craftsman line of hand and power tools is probably the best
tools available and also usually the cheapest (for comparable quality
at least). All the hand tools are unconditionally guaranteed—no time
limit, no limitations. If you bust it, you get a new one, no hassle, no
questions. Hard to beat a combination like that. Tools are covered in
both the big catalog and the subsidiary Power and Hand Tool Catalog.
Get both but order from the big catalog whenever possible because
a lot of prices are higher in the little catalog (to help pay for the extra
printing, we guess). The big catalog includes all sorts of other goodies
like surveying equipment and hardware items. Catalogs are available,
free from your local Sears outlet or from the above address.

SILVO HARDWARE CO.
107-109 Walnut St., Philadelphia, Pa. 19106
Silvo has a whole raft of brand-name tools (hand and power) at discount prices. Lines handled include Stanley, Rockwell, Skil, Millers
Falls, Dremel, Estwing, Disston, Wellsaw, Marshalltown, Rigid,
General, and Cresent. Mostly first-rate equipment at good prices.
166-page catalog, $1.

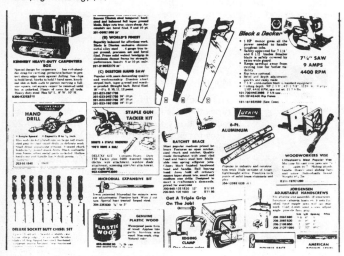

U.S. GENERAL SUPPLY CORP.
100 General Place, Jerico, N.Y. 11753
U.S. General offers the same deal as Silvo. They handle some of the
same lines as Silvo (Stanley, Skil, and Millers Falls) and some which
Silvo does not carry like Black & Decker, Wen, and Ram. U.S. General
has branched out into areas like office equipment, watches, and binoculars. Mostly good stuff, with an occasional piece of junk. With both
of these catalogs, you should be able to buy most of the brand-name
gear at the best price available, and even if you don't buy from them,
it's worth the cost to be able to check and make sure that you've gotten the best deal available. Don't let the U.S. General catalog throw
you. All items are listed at retail. The real price is coded to make you
feel good when you finally manage to figure it out. 204-page catalog
costs $1.

WOODCRAFT SUPPLY CORP.
313 Montvale Ave., Woburn, Mass.
01801
Woodcraft specializes in fine hand
tools for woodworking—carving tools,
turning tools, bow saws, and the like.
They also sell many of the Stanley
hand tools, but not at reduced prices.
What they do have for the cabin builder is an excellent assortment of books
on woodworking, and specialty tools
like draw knives, broad axes, and adz
heads that you'll be hard pressed to
find elsewhere. Nice equipment; 68-
page catalog, 50¢.

PRUNING SAW
Use in your hand

Use on lightweight
extension poles.

SAW WEDGES

FORESTRY SUPPLIERS INC.
Box 8397, 205 W. Rankin St., Jackson, Miss. 39204
Though these people don't want to deal with anyone who's not legiti-
mately in the industry, this is still a good catalog to have if you can
get it. If it's a tool remotely connected with trees and forests or the
environment, it's here. Equipment for seeding, spraying, pruning, cutting, fire fighting, surveying, weather, mapping, trapping, backpacking,
and even geology and oceanography. Say your neighbor has just set
your lower forty afire (just because your dead horse happened to fall
into his well) and you need a fire swatter fast (that's a giant 15" fly
swatter for beating out grass fires—or oversize mosquitoes). This is the
place. Your neighbor can order his water pollution detector and water
carriers from them, too. Or maybe you're just looking for brush cutters, post hole diggers, elephant traps, tree climbers, range finders,
timber tools, a Handyman jack, a Warn capstan winch, a Woodsman's
Pal, or surveying gear from hand levels through the Brunton pocket
transit to topline pro gear. Prices are not spectacular but are below
retail.

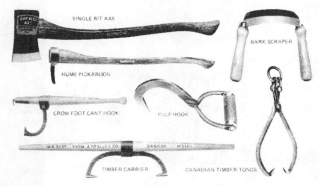

SNOW & NEALLEY CO.
155 Perry Rd., Bangor, Maine 04401
This outfit is strictly steel timber tools—all sorts of things like cant
dogs, crow foot mill dogs, pickaroons, bark spuds, pickpoles, wiffletree
woods, and bunk hooks as well as such common items as axes, wedges,
and buck saw blades. All classic equipment. They are still using their
1963 catalog with a new price list (which includes their one concession
to progress, plastic chain saw wedges). Good tools, good prices, good
people, and a fun catalog—12 pages, free.

BARTLETT MANUFACTURING CO.
3003 East Grand Blvd., Detroit, Mich. 48202
Bartlett is tree trimming and pruning gear—with every kind of tree saw
imaginable. Most of their products can be found cheaper elsewhere,
but they do have some specialty items like two-man crosscut saws
that we've only found here. 32-page catalog, free.

TSI CO.
P.O. Box 151, Flanders, N.J. 07836
Just ran across this one, and naturally they are out of catalogs at the
moment, so all we can say is that they're supposed to sell forestry
supplies. Add their address to your file anyway. Catalog is free.

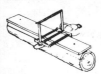
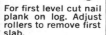
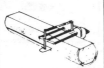

For first level cut nail plank on log. Adjust rollers to remove first slab.	Then use sawn surface as guide to remove bottom slab.	Turn log. Use plank squared up with side. Remove third slab.

GRANBERG INDUSTRIES
200 S. Garrard Blvd., Richmond, Calif. 94804

The *Alaska Jr.* "chain saw lumber making attachment" is the name of the product here. Attach the *Alaska Jr.* to your chain saw, and you have your own sawmill. Converts raw logs into planks, posts, beams or any piece of lumber you need. Use it to smooth your cabin logs for a tight fit. The *Alaska Jr.* will fit any chain saw with a blade between 18" and 32" long. Price for blades up to 24" is $95 and $105 for blades 24" to 32". Granberg also sells an assortment of chain saw service tools. Literature available, free.

WARN INDUSTRIES
9050 Empire Way South, Seattle, Wash. 98118

Since we're making concessions to chain saws, a few other gas-powered tools may be of special interest. The Warn winch model 800G is a beautiful little gas powered capstan winch weighing only 19 lbs., but capable of lifting 800 pounds in single line operation (all from a one horsepower, two cycle engine operating through a gear ratio of 186:1). Just the ticket for any heavy hauling and lifting around the cabin and easily packed into remote areas. Forestry Suppliers sells this winch with attachment chain for $145. Literature available, free.

TRIWAY MANUFACTURING CO., INC.
P.O. Box 37, Marysville, Wash. 98270

Triway makes a portable capstan winch; this one designed to operate off your chain saw engine. Remove the chain and bar from your saw, bolt on the MiniWinch, and you're ready to start hauling. The maximum line pull depends on the size of your chain saw engine, but it is designed for over 200 pounds (gear reduction is 100:1 so you should expect roughly 400 pounds per horsepower). MiniWinch weighs 12 pounds and sells for $120. Literature available, free.

Living in the wilderness or even just in the country as a regular thing can present a number of problems, particularly for modern Americans, who have hardly been brought up in the simple ways. Most of us, whether we like it or not, are too acclimated to the fast pace of things to change easily. In the boonies the lack of people and "things to do" is probably the biggest problem, though it may take a couple of months before you begin to realize it. Second to this is the lack of handy conveniences, both practical and entertaining—groceries, shopping centers, movies, nightclubs, and the all-consuming TV. And last is the requirement of being self-sufficient.

These are serious enough to think about before firming up plans, because like the wind and rain, they can slowly erode attitudes and concepts and bring to ruin the most "ideal" of wilderness living situations.

YANKEE
Monthly - $4/yr. - 50¢/issue - 225 p. il.

The articles found here are simple general interest types that are not especially applicable to this section, but you don't get a fat little mag of 225 pages for 50¢ unless it's packed with ads. And *Yankee* is, and that's how it fits—as a source of dealers for such things as spinning wheels, wood stoves, cast-iron cookware, weather vanes, leather products, etc.
From: Yankee, Dublin, N.H. 03444

ORGANIC GARDENING AND FARMING
Monthly - $5.85/yr. (1971 price at least)

These cats are *the* source for organic gardening material, both to turn you on to it and to tell you how. Besides the magazine, they put out a couple of the best books we've seen on the subject—*How to Grow Vegetables and Fruits by Organic Methods,* which gives you all the basics; *The Basic Book of Organic Gardening,* which is the smaller paperback edition of the same book; and *The Encyclopedia of Organic Gardening,* which is the bible for the experienced hand.
All from: Rodale Books, Inc., 33 E. Minor St., Emmaus, Pa. 18049

THE WILDCRAFTERS WORLD
Annual - $1.70/yr. - 32 p. il.

This small booklet is full of old-time tips and techniques for wilderness living, woodcraft, or just plain surviving. Much of it is drawn straight from readers' letters and gives you the feeling of sitting around the potbellied stove listening to the old timers telling how it was and how they did it when times were hard. Wildcrafters also puts out a passel of woodsmen's manuals and other publications worth checking out. Two 8¢ stamps will get you a listing of the contents of back issues. A real storehouse of goodies.
From: Wildcrafters Publications, RR 3 - Box 118, Rockville, Ind. 47872

NATURAL LIFE STYLES
Sally Freeman, Ed.
Bimonthly - $9/yr. - $1.50/issue - 80 p.

Natural Life Styles is just beginning to come back after some hard times last year. Thus far they are doing a fine job with good hard material covering the realm. Try a copy. We think you'll like it.
From: Gorden & Beach Science Publishers, Inc., 440 Park Ave. South, New York, N.Y. 10016

THE HOMESTEAD

BOOKS

If you know your psyche and can handle it, then adapting to the inconveniences will be manageable except for earning a living. Because regardless of how well everything else works out, you still need a medium of exchange to purchase certain necessities, pay property taxes, keep your transportation in repair, and secure medical services, supplies, and other things you may not be able to trade for. Consider your income producing projects carefully and be especially concerned about their bad points. It would be a good idea to have at least five *solid* programs in mind.

Since money is important, we've oriented the data in this section of Wilderness Living to saving it and earning it with respect to the publications, dealers, and sources of information listed. We'd like to hear your ideas and suggestions, too.

PERIODICALS

OUTDOOR CAREERS
Quarterly - $4/year - $1.25/issue - 35 p. il.

Outdoor Careers is basically a catalog of books on such money-making outdoor pursuits as fur farming and trapping, forestry, raising sheep, goats, hogs, horses, cattle, dogs, cats, rabbits, mushrooms, fish, pigeons and chinchillas, fur and leather craft, taxidermy, etc. The book collection offered is perhaps the most complete available for these areas, making the magazine a good source of material. All books are available through the magazine. There is a good bit of overlap between issues.
From: Clay Publishing Co., Ltd., Bewdley, Ontario, Canada

ALASKA
Bob Henning, Ed.
Monthly - $12/yr. - 79 p. il.   79 p. il.

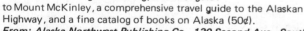

The articles in *Alaska* are about life in Alaska and what's happening there. Unlike most of the other magazines in this section, they don't have much how-to material, but if you are interested in settling in Alaska, you can get some good background material here. The same people also publish a number of books on Alaskan hunting and fishing, a tourist guide to Mount McKinley, a comprehensive travel guide to the Alaskan Highway, and a fine catalog of books on Alaska (50¢).
From: Alaska Northwest Publishing Co., 130 Second Ave., South, Edmonds, Wash. 98020

The following magazines are listed as other possible sources. They have been recommended in other publications, but we have no current information of our own on them. We'll just have to beat harder on the door next time.

WOOD HEAT QUARTERLY - $3/yr. - Vermont living.
From: Lowther Press, RD 1, Wolcott, Vt. 05680

MAKE IT - Quarterly - $3/yr. - Building things.
From: Make It, Box 526, Old Chelsea St., New York, N.Y. 10011

NATURAL LIVING - Monthly - $9/yr.
From: Magnum Royal Publications, Inc., 1560 Broadway, New York, N.Y. 10036

Suggest maybe you write ahead before you send them your check just to make sure they're still there.

ONE ACRE AND SECURITY
Bradford Angier
1972 - 319 p. il. - $7.95

In *One Acre and Security,* Angier is more interested in country living than in wilderness living, but the material is of interest to both. The book is directed to the problems of growing your own food and small-scale cash crops. It presents the basics for raising sheep, pigs, bees, cows, goats, rabbits, poultry, and even fish, frogs, turtles, and earthworms along with material on growing grapes and herb cultures and producing wine, juices, jellies, and raisins. All of these can provide both sustenance and spending money. Even in a wilderness home, you may well wish to have a small garden and some chickens, a cow or two, and maybe some pigs, so the material should be of interest to anyone contemplating a return to the earth.

Angier has also included sections on choosing your locale, checking the title, etc., and as always, has managed subsidiary sections—this time—on hiking, hunting, fishing, and wild foods. The result is a book full of ideas for insuring the continued success of your home in the country.
From: Stackpole Books, Cameron & Kelker Sts., Harrisburg, Pa. 17105

THE BOOK OF COUNTRY CRAFTS
Randolph Wardell Johnson
1964 - 211 p. il. - $3.95

Mr. Johnson very much enjoys doing these things and makes you feel you'd do the same.
From: A. S. Barnes & Co., Box 421, Cranbury, N.J. 08512

A BOOK OF COUNTRY THINGS
Told by Walter Needham; recorded by Barrows Mussey
1965 - 166 p. il. - $5.95

Sit around the fireplace on a winter night or on the front porch on a warm summer evening and listen to Walter Needham reminisce about his Grandpa's life in Vermont during the 1800's. That's the way the material for this book was collected and that's the way it's presented. As Needham says, "My knowledge of doing things was from Grandpa, from the way he done things. This story is just going to be the country things that Gramp taught me; I think they'd ought to be put down before they're forgotten altogether." Not quite a step-by-step how-to book but plenty of material on making fences, soap, tools, tanning, sugaring, grafting trees, country medicine, and hundreds of other topics. It is good just to sit back and listen to Needham talk.
From: Stephen Greene Press, Box 1000, Brattleboro, Vt. 05301

TRADITIONAL COUNTRY CRAFTS MAN
J. Geraint Jenkins
1965 - 236 p. il. - $8.75

Mostly interesting English country crafts, some of possible value to the wilderness resident. Blacksmithing, cooperage, furniture making, and so forth.
From: Praeger Publishers, Inc., 111 Fourth Ave., N.Y., N.Y. 10003

OUTDOORSMAN'S FIX-IT BOOK
Monte Burch
1971 - 274 p. il. - $6.95

Here's the book to keep you busy during those long winter evenings in front of the fire. It has all the data on repairing and maintaining such outdoor equipment as axes, knives and saws; canvas, leather, and rubber goods; appliances; fishing tackle from plugs to reel; boats and canoes; guns and scopes; cameras; archery gear; snowmobiles, outboard motors, and trailers; and chain saws. Burch doesn't get into any of these very heavily, but he does cover the standard maintenance precedures and basic repair techniques which should be sufficient 95% of the time.
From: Harper & Row, Keystone Industrial Park, Scranton, Pa. 18512

HENLEY'S 20TH CENTURY BOOK OF 10,000 FORMULAS, PROCESSES & TRADE SECRETS
Gardner D. Hiscox, Ed.
867 p. il. - $6.95

No die-hard, do-it-yourselfer home or camp owner should be caught without a copy of this truly fascinating book. It tells you how to make, treat, or process just about anything you can think of. For instance, it tells you how to make cheese (although after reading about how it's done, you'll probably give up the stuff). How to make insect repellent, powders, and traps; how to make about twenty different kinds of soap—powders, flakes, blocks, and liquids; how to make safe fireworks for the kids (sparklers); how to sterilize water, soften water, settle mud in water, remove iron from water, drink water ... drink water (?). Well, it does tell you how to do a lot of things, and it has trade secrets too (whisper)—do you know what German silver is made of? Okay then smarty, did you know that you can solder *glass* together with a metal solder??? Hah!!! Look on page 662. I didn't know you could either, but I do know one thing; this book is guaranteed to have you smelling up the house with a batch of gooey-gook, merrily bubbling over on the stove top in short order. P.S. It's full of factual, functional, and informative reading, too. —R. Lancy Burn (1971).
From: Books, Inc., 5530 Wisconsin Ave., N.W., Washington, D.C. 20015

HOME TANNING AND LEATHERMAKING GUIDE
1950 - 176 p. il. - $1.50 (pb)

HOME MANUFACTURE OF FURS AND SKINS
283 p. il. - $1.50 (pb)

Two good guides by Albert B. Farnham, a trapper and taxidermist, on the treatment of skins, tanning, and leathermaking for the rural resident.
From: A. R. Harding Publishing Co., 2878 E. Main St., Columbus, Ohio 43209

This valuable tree has a Bark that will dye twelve distinct colours—one for each month in which it may be collected. It is reported that a farmer's wife discovered this method of dyeing by noticing that a piece of cloth well coloured in the month of January assumed a new colour as it passed through each succeeding month of the year—besides several agreeable shades as it terminates one month and begins another!

BUTTERNUT TREE DYE

FORMULAS, METHODS, TIPS AND DATA FOR HOME AND WORKSHOP
Kenneth M. Swezey
1969 - 691 p. il. - $7.95

This book is a fascinating collection of formulas for making your own compounds for household use—a regular workshop cookbook. It very clearly tells you how to concoct such items as paints, stains, and whitewashes; glues, adhesives, and sealers; cleaning and polishing solutions; detergents, soaps, and medicinal preparations; and pesticides. On the construction end, it tells how to mix concrete, plaster,

and mortar. A variety of other items included are photographic chemicals, metal etching, working with metals, preserving wooden fence posts, cleaning and waterproofing leather, and even reading the Latin on your prescription and mixing your own. All this is topped off with a listing of sources for the materials and a rundown of weights and measures, nail, pipe, and wire sizes; data on various kinds of lumber; and so on. A thoroughly useful book for just about everything—especially when the local store may be a fair hike.
From: Harper & Row, Keystone Industrial Park, Scranton, Pa. 18512

BUTCHERING, PROCESSING AND PRESERVATION OF MEAT
Frank G. Ashbrook
1955 - 318 p. il. - $8.50

Excellent for anyone wanting to make full use of the meat animal. Butchering of hogs, cattle, sheep, and lambs, dressing game animals, cutting the carcass, dressing poultry and wild fowl, fish, various methods of preserving—in other words, everything you need to know about butchering, processing, and preserving meat!
From: Van Nostrand Reinhold Co., 300 Pike St., Cincinnati, Ohio 45202

GROW IT
Richard W. Langer
1972 - 365 p. il. - $8.95

The subtitle for this book is "The Beginner's Small Farm Guide," and that pretty well wraps it up. Very simply *Grow It* tells how to get started in small-scale farming. The book was serialized a chapter a month in *The Mother Earth News,* so if you really want a better feel for it, check a copy of *Mother.* You know if she's running it, it's good hard-core material.
From: Saturday Review Press, 230 Park Ave., New York, N.Y. 10017

DRIED FRUITS
Dr. Bernard Jensen
23 p. il. - 50¢

A very complete pamphlet on the sun drying of fruit.
From: Hidden Valley Health Ranch, Rt. 4 - Box 822, Escondido, Calif. 92025

STOCKING UP
Carol Stoner, Ed.
1973 - 351 p. il. - $8.95 (hb)

This one represents over 30 years of information accumulated by the editors of *Organic Gardening and Farming* and it teaches how to preserve home-grown foods the natural way. Covered are the traditional methods of home preservation that were used before insecticides and food additives were household words, combined with the safety and efficiency of modern developments in home food storage. Complete step-by-step instructions are given for preserving everything from fruits and vegetables to dairy products, to nuts and grains, to meats, without chemicals (like sulphur) and without overrefined ingredients (like sugar). *Stocking Up* starts at the beginning by helping you to choose the fruits and vegetables best suited for the method of storage you have in mind and tells you where you can obtain the seeds for your garden. It tells you how to harvest and prepare your plant foods and how to dress (but not butcher) your animals for maximum taste, food value and keeping qualities. It teaches you how to build your own smokehouse and food dryer, how to convert your basement into a root cellar, and how to turn your garage into a temporary butchering room. A very practical book with scads of good illustrative black-and-white photographs.
From: Rodale Books, Inc., 33 E. Minor St., Emmaus, Pa. 18049

LIST OF AVAILABLE PUBLICATIONS OF THE U.S. DEPARTMENT OF AGRICULTURE
1973 - 190 p. - Free

Latest list of all the books, booklets, pamphlets and other material published by USDA, current to July 1973. Of the several thousand titles listed on farming, forestry, animal husbandry, home building, home economics, conservation, and so forth, roughly sixty percent are free or available for less than two bits. Fantastic catalog, and full information is included for ordering the publications listed.
From: USDA Office of Communication, Washington, D.C. 20250

FARM and RANCH EQUIPMENT

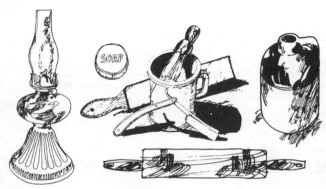

MOTHER'S TRUCK STORE
Box 506, Flat Rock, N.C. 28731

This is the *Mother Earth News* people's entry into the retail sales world. Their aim is to make available a full line of old-time tools and household items for the homestead. Thus far they have succeeded admirably. The store opened in 1971 with a 28-page catalog which has grown in two years to over 100 pages of great items ranging from windmills to tipis and straight razors to Franklin stoves. All prices are retail, but this is no rip-off. All profits are slated for the establishment of a research center to seek solutions to the problems of ecological living and alternative lifestyles. Support a good cause and good people. A must catalog, 25¢.

R. F. KROLL CORP.
Wautoma, Wisc. 54982

Kroll offers a series of power attachments for your chain saw. Presently available are an air compressor (to run paint sprayers and the like), a water pump and a drill chuck. Prices run $135 for the compressor, $170 for the pump, and between $21 and $27 for the drill chuck and adapter. Not cheap. Literature available, free.

STROMBERG'S
Box 717, Fort Dodge, Iowa 50501

Stromberg sells animals—ducks, chickens, pigeons, rabbits, geese, turkeys, guinea pigs and assorted pets, both wild and domestic. Many of the breeds are exotic. Also sells some basic equipment like pens and a good assortment of books. 48-page catalog, 50¢.

MELLINGER'S INC.
2310 West South Range Rd., North Lima, Ohio 44452

Horticulture, man. Every kind of tree, shrub, and bush including fruit trees, berry bushes, grape vines, nut trees, garden seeds, and grass seeds in addition to the normal run of ornamentals. Horticulture tools, sprays, fertilizers, and books are also included in their 71-page catalog. Don't look for a lot of pretty pictures, but if you know what you want, it is probably here. Good selection and good prices. Catalog, free.

NATIONAL FARM EQUIPMENT CO.
645 Broadway, New York, N.Y. 10012

The equipment here is better suited to the country home and garden than the farm. The catalog features lawnmowers, garden tractors, rototillers, snowblowers, chain saws, and small sprayers, but it does get into poultry supplies, brush cutters, cement mixers, and feed mixers. 74-page catalog, free.

KANSAS CITY VACCINE COMPANY
Stock Yards, Kansas City, Mo. 64102

Good line of veterinary supplies and instruments for livestock, poultry, and pets—serums, vaccines, bacterins, insecticides, and drugs included. Catalog details the uses for each medicine and also gives a rundown of the common diseases—what it is, symptoms, cause, prevention, and treatment. Good reference source in itself. 106-page catalog, free.

Package bees pictured here
not included in A12.

Cat. No.		Price
A12	Beginner's Outfit, Wt. 42 lbs. (See above, less package of bees)	$35.30

A. I. ROOT CO.
623 West Liberty St., Medina, Ohio 44256

Root has been operating since 1896, and is probably one of the best known suppliers of beekeeping gear. Their indexed, 32-page catalog lists hives and accessories; beekeepers' tools and clothing; honey processing, packaging, and selling aids (for roadside stands); and a number of books on bee culture and the beekeeping and honey business. For the beginner, A.I. Root offers a $36 outfit consisting of a standard hive with accessories, feeder, bee smoker hive tool, bee veil and gloves, and *Starting Right With Bees*. Root also buys beeswax. Catalog is available at no charge from the above address.

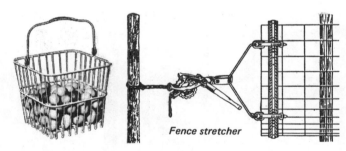

Fence stretcher

NASCO
Fort Atkinson, Wisc. 53538

Nasco is *the* source of farm and ranch equipment. Everything but the truly heavy gear. Two-thirds of the big 335-page catalog is devoted to livestock related equipment—tagging, branding, grooming, feeding, breeding, and health care items for dairy cattle, hogs, sheep, horses, and poultry. Everything from ear tags to the Kelver Training Cow (which is a mock-up of the business end of a cow allowing you to practice artifical insemination in case you aren't sure.) The remainder of the catalog has gear for spraying, water and soil testing, fencing, safety, shop, garden, and forest, including a full line of timber handling tools. Prices are not particularly low but they do have the stuff. Catalog is free.

OTHER DEALERS IN MEDICINES AND DRUGS
We have not personally checked the following dealers, but they are reported to offer a good selection of serums, vaccines, drugs, and instruments. Catalog is free from both.

UNITED PHARMACAL CO.
306 Cherokee St., St. Joseph, Mo. 64504

EASTERN STATES SERUM CO.
1727 Harden St., Columbia, S.C. 29204

PRECISION and CRAFT TOOLS

BROOKSTONE CO.
123 Vose Farm Rd., Peterborough, N.H. 03458
Brookstone is the place for precision and specialty tools and other hard-to-find tools. Jewelers' tools, typewriter and camera tools, glass cutters and glass drills, rangefinders, hand levels, sharpening tools, leather strops for tools, three-way clamps, tweezers, nut splitters, side action funnels, and even collapsible canteens are included in their 68-page catalog. Good quality, good prices. Catalog, 25¢.

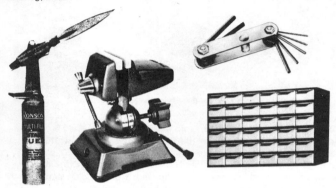

NATIONAL CAMERA SUPPLY
2000 West Union Ave., Englewood, Colo. 80110
Another good assortment of precision tools plus some good photography books. 58-page catalog, *Flasher,* comes out quarterly. Subscription is $1 per year. Sample copies are free on request.

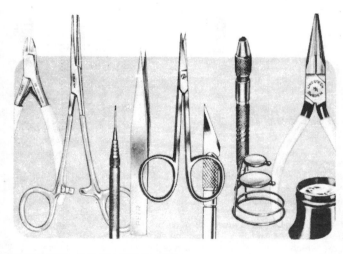

OTTO FREI - JULES BOREL, INC.
P.O. Box 796, Oakland, Calif. 94604
More good precision tools but pretty much restricted to specific types—pliers, nippers, tweezers, scissors, pin vises, knives, screwdrivers, magnifiers. They also put out a separate catalog on jewelry making tools and supplies (including items for wax casting, sand casting, and electroplating). 32-page catalog, free.

ALLCRAFT TOOL & SUPPLY CO., INC.
100 Frank Rd., Hicksville, N.Y. 11801
An excellent collection of metalworking and jewelry tools and supplies. Best selection of specialty hammers, anvils, and stakes around. They even handle lathes and engraving machinery. Separate catalogs available on casting and enameling equipment. Main catalog is 97 pages, $1.

CRAFTSMAN WOOD SERVICE CO.
2727 South Mary St., Chicago, Ill. 60608
Woodworking tools and supplies for the home craftsman. Both hand and power tools, including a number from the Stanley line; a good selection of hardware items, specialty woods, veneers, finishing products and stains, cements, and woodworking books is offered. Kits for making your own guitar, dulcimer, mandolin, or grandfather clock are also found in the 144-page catalog (35¢). Prices fair.

ALBERT CONSTANTINE AND SONS, INC.
2050 East Chester Rd., Bronx, N.Y. 10461
Constantine is oriented to the same market as Craftsman with the same general line of tools, woods and wood products, and kits (guitar, dulcimer, clocks, and ship models). If you use either of these, you need the other. Some things are handled by one, some by the other, some prices are better with one, some with the other. 94-page catalog, 25¢.

LEATHER TOOLS and SUPPLIES

AUSTRAL ENTERPRISES
P.O. Box 70190, Seattle, Wash. 98107
Austral has hides and horsehair for braiding and lacing, and they offer a variety of fine Australian products made of felt, leather and wool. Their Akubra felt hats are outstanding and include the famous Aussie slouch hat and a genuine sombrero. Leather products include belts, watchbands, fine whips, lanyards, and even dog boots. An assortment of books, pewter buttons and jewelry, yarn and patterns, Puma knives and a boomerang round out the general line. Fun catalog, 64 pages, 25¢.

TANDY LEATHER CO.
1001 Foch St., Fort Worth, Tex. 76107
Tandy is leather craft kits, supplies, and basic tools, but mostly kits. Kits for handbags, wallets, boots, mocs, belts, watchbands, chairs, chaps, saddles, holsters, etc. Some OK and some so-so. They can supply a variety of leather. 95-page catalog.

UPHOLSTERITE KIT

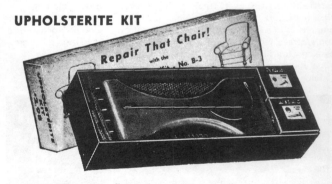

With Step-by-Step Instructions

C.S. OSBORNE & CO.
125 Jersey St., Harrison, N.J. 07029
If you're into leather, Osborne has the tools. Even if you're not into leather, you may find some of these tools of value. The catalog also contains some mortar and cement tools, cold chisels, and punches. 44-page catalog, free.

230

WATER PURIFICATION

ALVO CORP.
P.O. Box 19087, Cincinnati, Ohio 45219

Alvo produces special home and travel water filters which use the oligodynamic process of purification—couldn't resist putting that in. This means that the purifying agent is a special form of silver deposited on activated charcoal. The silver loves to kill bacteria and the charcoal soaks up bad tastes and odors. This combination teamed up with mechanical filters to remove solid particles is the full package. Mostly it kills bacteria although Alvo claims the carbon will also remove such baddies as DDT and detergent as well. Three units are available: the travel purifier ($40), the Mark I or countertop unit ($140), and the Mark II ($220) for home installation. Lifetime will depend on how fast the filters plug up, but they should run 4,000 gallons or better for Mark II and 500 gallons for Travel unit. Replacement units for the Mark II cost $80. Literature available, free.

SUNWATER CO.
10404 San Diego Mission Rd., San Diego, Calif. 92108

Here we have solar stills for home use. Sizes range from ½ to 2 gallons per day per unit output. Just add any dirty old water and clean sunlight, and out comes pure distilled water. They will even give you marble chips to put some mineral taste back into the water. A one-gallon-per-day unit costs $100 plus crating and freight. Collection reservoir, automatic or semiautomatic feed systems, and special faucets are available at extra cost. Literature available, free.

ELECTRIC GENERATORS

AMERICAN HONDA MOTOR CO.
100 West Alondra Blvd., Gardena, Calif. 90247

Besides everything else they're into, Honda makes a series of small gasoline-powered portable electric generators for cabin or camper. Standard sizes range from 300 watts to 800 watts rated output at 115 V.A.C., with an additional 100 watts available for short duration such as motor startup. These units also supply 12-volt D.C. for battery charging (the E900, which is the 800 watt unit, will supply 8 amps at 12 volts). Do not try to operate 12-volt appliances off the generator as the output is a very dirty 12 volts designed for battery charging only. The E900 weighs in at 82 pounds. Literature is available, free.

WINPOWER MANUFACTURING CO.
Newton, Iowa 50208

Winpower also makes portable gasoline electric generators. Their smallest generator, the model GM2B2-B, puts out a maximum of 2000 watts at 120 volts A.C. or 180 watts at 12 volts D.C. (15 amps) for battery charging. This unit is powered by a 5-horse Briggs & Stratton engine that automatically idles when no power is being drawn. It weighs in at 75 pounds and sells for $360. Winpower puts out a variety of other units with outputs to 20,000 watts and higher if you happen to dig on electricity. Literature available, free.

KEROSENE LAMPS and HEATERS

ALADDIN INDUSTRIES, INC.
P.O. Box 7235, Nashville, Tenn. 37210

Aladdin makes some really beautiful kerosene mantle lamps. These lamps give the bright light of a gasoline mantle lamp, but without most of the disadvantages—no pumping or pressurizing, no hissing, no smoking flame, no uncontrollable brightness, and no dangerous gasoline. Kerosene is drawn up by a wick and apparently vaporized and mixed with air in a generator before burning within the mantle. The adjustment of the wick controls brightness with the maximum output being equivalent to a 100-watt light bulb. In normal use, the lamp will run for 50 hours on a gallon of kerosene. Aladdin also makes an electric conversion for several of these lamps which allow you to replace the mantle assembly with a light bulb screw-in socket for 110-volt operation. A variety of styles is offered, including table, wall, and hanging units. The average price on the aluminum models is $29 for the kerosene lamp and another $10 for the electric convertor. Brass models will run you around $55 for the lamp. Aladdin also makes some good kerosene heaters if you're interested. Literature is available, free.

A reader of the Last Whole Earth Catalog *has a couple of tips on the operation of the Aladdin lamps that are worth passing along in case you haven't seen them. If the lamp is turned up too high, the mantle will soot up. To rectify this, sprinkle a little salt down the chimney and the soot will burn right off. This may seem a bit too simple to be true, but there are commercial salts available to burn the soot out of oil stoves, and I can tell you that they certainly work. So whether it is the salt itself or other trace salts that do the job doesn't really matter. For the next trick, to increase the brightness of the lamp, increase the chimney height—like put another chimney on top of the present one. It draws better and burns brighter.*

GREENFORD PRODUCTS, INC.
64 Old Orchard, Skokie, Ill. 60076

Greenford is the national distributor for Aladdin kerosene heaters and parts. As such they deal mostly with jobbers, but if you can't find a local outlet, they will sell you a heater. They have five different models with heat outputs from 3,350 BTU per hour to 9,300 BTU per hour (equivalent to electric heating units of 1,750 watts to 2,750 watts). Units are manufactured in England and are top notch. Literature available, free.

WOOD and COAL STOVES

SHIPMATE STOVE DIVISION
Richmond Ring Co., Souderton, Pa. 18964

Shipmate is synonymous with fine marine stoves. Whether you want to burn wood, coal, kerosene, alcohol, or bottled gas, Shipmate makes a stove that will handle the job in either modern or classic style. They even make a couple of small wood or coal burning cabin heaters. Literature available, free.

PORTLAND FRANKLIN STOVE FOUNDRY INC.
Box 1156, Portland, Me. 04104

If you'd rather get your literature straight from the manufacturer, this is the place. Portland makes a fine line of cast-iron stoves, including the ultimate in wood burning kitchen ranges—The Queen Atlantic. Not cheap (the Queen can run to $750 with accessories), but good. Literature available, free.

PRESTON DISTRIBUTING CO.
No. 1 Whidden St., Lowell, Mass. 01852

Preston is the distributor for a variety of wood and coal stoves, ranges, and heaters, including the complete Portland line. They also handle colonial hardware and cast cookware to go with the stoves. Literature available, free.

WASHINGTON STOVE WORKS
P.O. Box 687, Everett, Wash. 98201

Nice assortment of wood or coal stoves, including pot bellies, arctic stoves (used by Alaskan gold miners), heavy-duty folding camp stove (cast iron), and even a kit to convert a 55-gallon oil drum into a cheap cabin heater. Nothing fancy—just good basic stoves. Literature available.

MISCELLANEOUS

Fruit Press for Making Wine, Cider and Fruit Juices

Old-fashioned Apple Parer

THE ORIGINAL VERMONT COUNTRY STORE, INC.
Weston, Vt. 05161

The Country Store catalog is just a little too "tourist" not to be suspect, but it does contain far too many useful old-time items to be passed by—like mustache brushes, goose quill tooth picks, straight razors, fireplace bellows, Aladdin kerosene lamps (brass models only, but under retail), oil lamps, candle kits, sickles, assorted whole-grain cereals and flour, old-fashioned candy, cheeses, and an excellent selection of kitchen utensils. 95-page catalog - 25¢.

Kitchen in the Chateau at Fortress Louisbourg, Nova Scotia, Canada.

232

by the HEARTH

Fireplace Logs

Beech wood fires are bright and clear
   If the logs are kept a year.
Chestnut's only good, they say,
   If for long it's laid away.
Birch and fir logs burn too fast,
   Blaze up bright and do not last.
Elm wood burns like a churchyard mould;
   E'en the very flames are cold.
Poplar gives a bitter smoke,
   Fills your eyes and makes you choke.
Apple wood will scent your room
   With an incense like perfume.
Oak and maple, if dry and old,
   Keep away the winter cold.
But ash wood wet and ash wood dry,
   A King shall warm his slippers by.

—ANON

RUSSIAN TEA

This is a great hot spicy drink for sippin' round the fire in late autumn. We haven't been able to dig up any data on the origin of the name or recipe. Actually, there are a number of versions floating around, but of the lot, we figure this one's best.

Here's what you need—

½ cup of sugar	3 tea bags or equivalent
1 orange	4½ cups water
1 lemon	6 whole cloves
3 cinnamon sticks	and one 6-cup tea pot

Here's what to do—

Boil up the water and pour half a cup of it into the sugar; stir until dissolved. Pour the rest of the water into the tea pot, and dump in the tea bags, cloves, and broken up cinnamon sticks. Next, pare off a complete ring of rind from the orange and the lemon; break the rinds into small pieces and pinch 'em so the oils go into the water. Then drop the rinds in the water. Stir a couple of times and let the whole mess steep for about 6 minutes.

Phase Two: While the tea steeps, cut and juice the orange and lemon, pulp and all (not the seeds, Ace), into the sugar water you've got sittin' on the side. Leave that for a sec, and get your mugs ready by pouring boiling water into each. Right before serving the tea, dump the water, and you'll have some nice hot mugs.

Six minutes ought to be up by now, so pull the tea bags out, and pour in the orange-lemon juice mix; stir a tad, and serve her up.

Place smells just like Marco Polo walked in—don't it.

To make *Russian Bivouac Tea* add 5 jiggers (1½-ounce size) of Remy Martin or Courvoisier; to make *Russian Naval Tea* (for home-sick salts temporarily lost in the woods), add 2 teaspoons salt and 5 jiggers Myer's Planters Punch. Booze should be added to the pot at the last possible moment before serving, or to the mugs on a pro-rata basis of 1 jigger each. Hey!

Firewood

Firewood is measured in cords which is a standardized stack of 4-foot logs 4 feet high and 8 feet long—128 cubic feet altogether. This doesn't mean that you actually get 128 cu. ft. of wood, since there is a lot of space between the logs (an average cord may only contain 80 cu. ft. of wood). For cooking and heating a wilderness cabin in winter, one will need four cubic feet of wood per day or a cord a month. Actually you should be able to keep warm most of the winter by cutting, sawing, splitting, and piling that much wood.

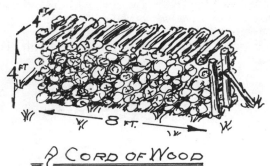

A CORD OF WOOD

The actual amount of wood needed will depend mainly on the type of wood you use. Two pounds of dry nonresinous wood contain about as much heat value as one pound of coal. The denser and heavier your wood, the greater the heat value per cord. This can vary by as much as a factor of two. Resin, by the way, gives twice as much heat as wood, weight for weight. Resinous woods, which may be 15% resin, thus give more heat than would be expected from the weight, but they also burn faster. Such quick burning woods are best for rapid heating and kindling but not good for long-lasting low heat. Your best kindling woods are the pines, cedars, aspen, basswood, and cottonwood. The best general heating woods are ash, oak, hard maple, hickory, and locust. The following table shows the relative heat content of various woods.

RELATIVE HEAT VALUE OF VARIOUS WOOD	
Ash, red oak, white oak, beech, birch, hickory, hard maple, pecan, dogwood, locust, southern yellow pine, Douglas fir	High (approximately 1 cord equals 1 ton of coal)
Soft maple, cherry, walnut, elm, sycamore, gum, cypress, redwood, cedar	Medium (approximately 1½ cord equals 1 ton of coal)
Aspen, basswood, cottonwood, chestnut, poplar, white pine, sugar pine, ponderosa pine, true firs, spruce	Low (approximately 2 cords equals 1 ton of coal)

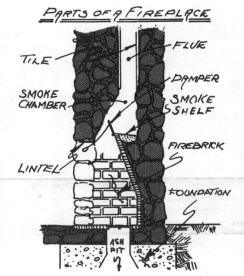

PARTS OF A FIREPLACE

FLUE

TILE

DAMPER

SMOKE CHAMBER

SMOKE SHELF

FIREBRICK

LINTEL

FOUNDATION

ASH PIT

diving

There are still caverns, canyons, and mountains which have never been explored. They, as well as ancient cities, lost ships, and undiscovered plants and animals, lie hidden beneath the world's oceans. Scuba diving is the key to these uncharted mysteries.

Because of the innumerable experiences available through diving, it has become a very popular sport, and no matter where you live there's probably someplace close by to dive. Even inland there are lakes, rivers, springs, quarries, and occasionally caves.

Diving is divided into three categories. *Skin or free diving* is usually done in shallow water with only mask, snorkel, and flippers (if any equipment is used) where the diver swims along the surface observing the bottom until he notes something of interest, gulps a deep breath of air, and plunges down to investigate. In *scuba diving* (for *s*elf-*c*ontained *u*nderwater *b*reathing *a*pparatus), the diver carries his air with him compressed in a tank or in a closed system which purifies the air so that it may be rebreathed. *Surface-supplied diving* is done by commercial outfits—the deep-sea diver with his brass hard hat—and air is supplied to the diver via hose from the surface.

Recreational diving is mostly limited to skin and scuba diving. It can be fun and safe as long as you have due respect for the sea or whatever waters you're diving in. Though it may be getting a little wearisome to hear the same old cautions on using good judgment—always dive with a buddy,

don't dive in bad weather, be supercareful in strange waters, especially when visibility is poor or zero, blah, blah—a study by the University of Rhode Island, shows that the major cause of diving deaths is poor judgment. Something's not getting through somewhere.

Unfortunately, formal training is not required of the recreational diver, particularly those using scuba. It's a simple matter to order gear from a mail-order outfit and take the plunge. We hope, however, that no one would begin diving this way, since there are a number of reputable and helpful organizations around the country dedicated to assisting anyone with half the interest in becoming a safe, certified diver. For some time, concerned individuals have recognized the need of proper training and certification of divers. As a result, in many areas it's becoming increasingly difficult to buy air and sometimes even diving gear without a valid certification card from some approved course.

Certification is achieved by taking a training course which teaches diving physics, the use of scuba gear, safety practices, underwater swimming, and knowledge of the underwater environment. Many of the training courses are conducted at local YMCA's and cost from $30 to $50. And although everyone is welcome to take a course, 14 is the minimum age for certification (in some areas, 15).

If you want a better background on diving before committing yourself to the course, your local library can supply some good books on the subject. For a fine presentation of the adventure and spirit of diving, a book like *Diving to Adventure* by Hans Haas is the answer. It deals strictly with free diving—no special equipment or techniques—and truly captures the feeling and mood of diving. For a look at the more technical aspects of scuba diving, *The New Science of Skin and Scuba Diving* is the best intermediate source available. This will most likely be the textbook for your course, so you might want to get a copy ahead of time. And if you really want to delve into diving theory and practice, you should get a copy of the *U.S. Navy Diving Manual*. This is a composite

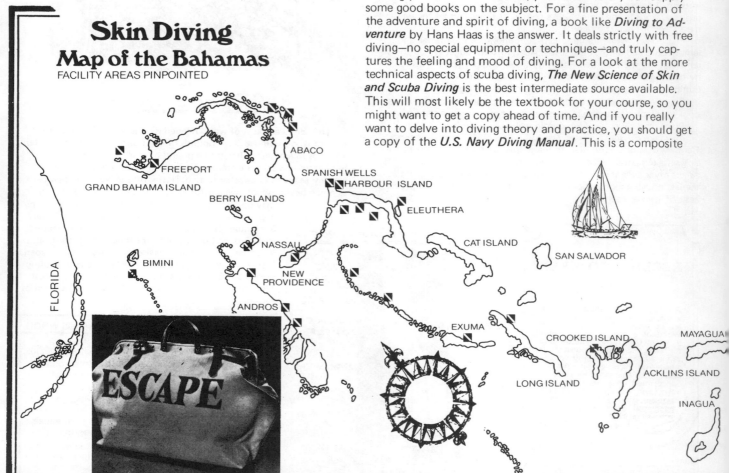

Skin Diving
Map of the Bahamas
FACILITY AREAS PINPOINTED

ABACO
FREEPORT
GRAND BAHAMA ISLAND
SPANISH WELLS
HARBOUR ISLAND
BERRY ISLANDS
ELEUTHERA
NASSAU
CAT ISLAND
SAN SALVADOR
BIMINI
NEW PROVIDENCE
FLORIDA
ANDROS
EXUMA
CROOKED ISLAND
MAYAGUA
LONG ISLAND
ACKLINS ISLAND
INAGUA
ESCAPE

Bahamas Tourist News Bureau

of all the Navy's research on the subject and is the bible for serious diving.

Once you've completed a basic training course, get some practical experience in the company of knowledgeable divers. All waters present their own special hazards. Coastal waters usually have very limited visibility, often only a few inches, and surf and currents can smash you about or pull you out to sea. Further offshore, ocean waters offer better visibility, but dives are often deep and of long duration, which brings on the problems of time limits while down and decompression

while coming up.

When diving in a new area, consult a local club or dive shop for information on good spots, danger areas, and legal restrictions, especially on spearfishing. You can always find a dive shop in the yellow pages. And don't have any hang-ups about approaching a club. They're usually good guys and will be glad to include you in their dive plans (especially if you walk in with a couple of six-packs in hand); they know the best spots and can show you a fine time.

sources of information

UNDERWATER SOCIETY OF AMERICA
427 Chestnut St., Philadelphia, Pa. 19106
This is primarily an association of the diving councils of Canada, Mexico, and the United States, though it does have a membership program for individuals. The society looks out for the diver's interests at the national level and provides a forum for the exchange of information. It also functions as the sanctioning and regulating body for underwater competition. The society's official publication is the *Underwater Reporter*, which comes out quarterly and goes to all members. Members of individual diving councils may become regular members of the society by paying annual dues of $5 through their councils. Individuals not affiliated with a club or council may become associate members by paying the dues directly to the society.

COUNCIL FOR NATIONAL COOPERATION IN AQUATICS (CNCA)
220 Ashton Rd., Ashton, Md. 20702
CNCA is a council of national organizations active in aquatic sports and water safety, with the objective of coordinating programs and studies in this area. With respect to diving, CNCA has put out several excellent publications, one of which has been adopted as a standard training manual for many scuba instruction courses, *The New Science of Skin and Scuba Diving* (see Book section). For specific information on diving principles and safety, this group should be a good bet.

NATIONAL ASSOCIATION FOR CAVE DIVING (NACD)
3001 West Tennessee St., Tallahassee, Fla. 32304
NACD acts as a clearinghouse for information on cave diving. In addition to this, it's trying to establish proper controls and training courses and develop special equipment and techniques for this type of diving. Cave diving is a specialized and dangerous activity for which few divers are properly trained. NACD is out to change this.

MARINE TECHNOLOGICAL SOCIETY (MTS)
1730 M St., N.W., Washington, D.C. 20036
MTS is a society for oceanographers and others interested in ocean science and technology. Previously, MTS served only professionals, and the American Society of Oceanography (ASO) served the general public and interested layman. In 1971 the two joined forces, and now they span the entire range of interest in ocean science. MTS publishes the bimonthly *MTS Journal*, which is restricted to certain member classes, and the monthly newsletter *Ocean Soundings*, which goes to all members. Numerous other books and pamphlets are available, several on commercial diving and underwater work.

Reflecting the '71 merger, the society offers a variety of memberships. The general public has a choice of an ASO membership for $12 a year, which does not include the technical *MTS Journal*, or an associate membership, which does, for $20 a year. Other classes of membership are available for students, professionals, and institutions. A request to the above address will get you complete information.

Diving Laws and Regulations

The laws and regulations governing skin and scuba diving and spearfishing vary so greatly from one location to another that it's always best to check with local authorities for information. If they're not familiar with some of these relatively obscure laws, then check with the local dive shops or clubs. We've listed the addresses of state and provincial authorities (fish and game departments) that can be reached by mail in the Fishing Section, and below are listed general sources of information for the Bahamas, Canada, and Mexico.

Spearfishing—the equipment used and the types of fish shot—seems to be the biggest concern of authorities. Presently there is a great deal of sentiment against sport spearfishing, especially among divers themselves—and with good reason. There's little sport in killing fish while on scuba. Spearfishing competition, which involves killing as many fish as possible in a certain time period, is an ecologically senseless and wasteful sport. Thus, don't be surprised to find stringent laws limiting spearfishing activities. For example, the Bahamian government flatly states, "Spear guns are not allowed in the Bahamas. For spearfishing, only Hawaiian slings and pole spears are permitted. Scuba gear may not be used while spearfishing."

Collecting of abalone, clams, oysters, all types of shellfish, free-swimming fish, plants and corals is often regulated. Check with local authorities or dive clubs before removing any living creatures from the water.

Another subject which is becoming increasingly regulated is the disturbance of sites which have historical or archeological importance. Shipwrecks, sunken piers, wharves and buildings all fall into these categories. Due to the carelessness of a few divers, many important historic shipwrecks have been destroyed, and authorities in many parts of this and other countries are taking steps to protect these sites. Familiarize yourself with local restrictions.

BAHAMAS MINISTRY OF TOURISM
30 Rockefeller Plaza, New York, N.Y. 10020

CANADIAN GOVERNMENT OFFICE OF TOURISM
150 Kent St., Ottawa, Ontario, Canada K1A 0H6

MEXICAN GOVERNMENT DEPARTMENT OF TOURISM
630 Fifth Ave., New York, N.Y. 10020

Maps and Charts

The most useful charts to divers are nautical types which indicate shorelines, boating channels, water depths, bottom conditions, and certain wreck sites that are hazards to navigation. There's a chart for each coastal area of the United States; for example, Chart No. 426 covers the Cape Fear River from Cape Fear to Wilmington, N.C. Most charts are available from local boating sources or may be ordered directly from the National Ocean Survey (U.S. waters), Hydrographic Chart Distribution Office (Canadian waters), and U.S. Naval Oceanographic Office (high seas and foreign coastal waters). These agencies and others are described in detail under Navigation in the Offshore Sailing Section.

When visiting stores, museums, and parks, watch for local area maps which show good fishing and diving spots as well as other information that may not be available elsewhere. The best chart of an area is generally the one you make yourself by compiling data from local divers and from other charts.

PERIODICALS

SKIN DIVER
Paul J. Tzimoulis, Ed.
Monthly - $9/yr. - $1/issue - 72 p. il.

This is the best source of general information on diving and current diving activities and equipment. Articles are usually non-fiction diving adventure stories, equipment reports, technical information, and editorial comments.
From: Petersen Publishing Co., 8490 Sunset Blvd., Los Angeles, Calif. 90069

SEA FRONTIERS and SEA SECRETS
F. G. Walton Smith, Ed.
Bimonthly - $15/yr.

For the person interested in oceanography and ecology, these two excellent publications are a must. A subscription to both comes with a $7.50 annual membership in the International Oceanographic Foundation.

Sea Frontiers is a beautiful 60-page slick, color magazine that discusses the sea, its animals and plants, ships and seafaring, diving, conservation, and so forth in a non-technical manner.

Sea Secrets is a 16-page tag-along booklet that comes with *Sea Frontiers*. One part of it is written up in a question and answer arrangement, readers providing the questions and editors the answers. The other part features short news items on oceanography.

Both magazines are well written, interesting, and very informative. Definitely worth the $7.50 investment, which, incidentally, will get you book discounts and other benefits through the foundation.
From: The International Oceanographic Foundation, 10 Rickenbacker Causeway, Virginia Key, Miami, Fla. 33149

UNDERCURRENTS
Monthly - $5/yr.

This magazine specializes in information on commercial diving. Featured are articles on equipment tests and safety reports.
From: Undercurrents, Inc., P.O. Box 2383, New Orleans, La. 70116

OCEANS
Keith K. Howell, Ed.
Bimonthly - $12/yr. - $2/issue - 80 p. il.

This is the *National Geographic* of the oceans. It combines general coverage of the entire ocean scene with spectacular photography to provide a fine magazine for the layman. Topics featured include natural history, marine archaeology, sailing, diving, technology, oceanographic research, island areas, and business and investment aspects of the ocean science industry. If you're looking for a good general overview of what's happening with the sea and if you like beautiful photography, subscribe to *Oceans*.
From: Oceans Magazine Co., Bldg. 240, Ft. Mason, San Francisco, Calif. 94123

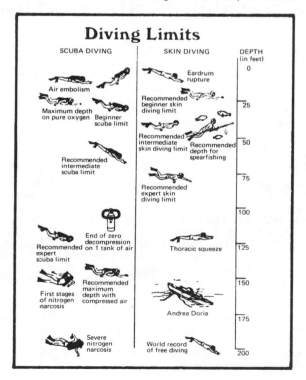

Diving Limits

SCUBA DIVING	SKIN DIVING	DEPTH (in feet)
	Eardrum rupture	0
Air embolism		
	Recommended beginner skin diving limit	25
Maximum depth on pure oxygen / Beginner scuba limit		
	Recommended intermediate skin diving limit / Recommended depth for spearfishing	50
Recommended intermediate scuba limit		75
	Recommended expert skin diving limit	100
End of zero decompression on 1 tank of air		
Recommended expert scuba limit	Thoracic squeeze	125
First stages of nitrogen narcosis	Recommended maximum depth with compressed air	150
	Andrea Doria	175
Severe nitrogen narcosis	World record of free diving	200

THE NEW SCIENCE OF SKIN AND SCUBA DIVING

Council for Nat. Cooperation in Aquatics
1974 - 288 p. il. - $4.95 (pb)

This book is probably used in more scuba courses than any other book, and with good reason. It is not full of witty prose or colorful pictures, but without going into as much detail as the *U.S. Navy Diving Manual*, it covers all the basic theory and practical information needed to explain the physics and physiology of diving, first aid for diving accidents, dangerous marine life, and equipment used in the sport. Examples and illustrations are included in all chapters. Absolutely a must for every diver's library.
From: Association Press, 291 Broadway, New York, N.Y. 10007

U.S. NAVY DIVING MANUAL

U.S. Navy
1970 - 687 p. il. - $16.70
S/N 0846-00072

This excellent manual, recently revised, is the bible for serious diving—sport, military, or commercial. In addition to the facts needed for basic sport diving, there is information on saturation diving, mixed-gas diving, closed-circuit breathing apparatus, hard-hat practices, and much more. An extensive first aid section is also included. As a reference book for detailed information on diving, you can't find a better source than the *Navy Diving Manual*.
From: Sup. of Doc., U.S. Gov. Printing Office, Washington, D.C. 20402

MEDICAL ASPECTS OF SPORT DIVING

Christopher W. Dueker
1974 - 232 p. il. - $7.95

Dueker discusses in detail the causes, symptoms and treatment of all diving-related medical problems for the layman. Of value to both the sport and commercial diver.
From: A. S. Barnes and Co., Box 421, Cranbury, N.J. 08512

MARINE SALVAGE OPERATIONS

Edward M. Brady
1960 - 237 p. il. - $10

An excellent practical handbook covering the basic equipment, techniques, and problems of ship salvage operations. It gets right into the specific how-to's for salvaging stranded and sunken ships or towing disabled ones—rigging patches, building a cofferdam, shoring and sealing for compressed air lifting, and rigging a liverpool bridle. Obviously a professional's handbook, but there is plenty of information for any wreck diver in the sections on naval architecture, welding and cutting, air lifts, and propeller salvage.
From: Cornell Maritime Press, Box 109, Cambridge, Md. 21613

NOAA DIVING MANUAL

1975 - 448 p. il. - $8.55
S/N 003-017-00283

This new manual from NOAA is an excellent reference source, similar to the *U.S. Navy Diving Manual.*
From: Superintendent of Documents, U.S. Gov. Printing Office, Washington, D.C. 20402

DANGEROUS MARINE ANIMALS

Bruce W. Halstead, M.D.
1959 - 146 p. il. - $5

An excellent source of sound information on the dangerous animals that inhabit the oceans of the world. *Dangerous Marine Animals* includes photographs and illustrations of marine creatures, discusses the mechanisms with which they harm human beings and gives first aid information for treating injuries.
From: Cornell Maritime Press, Box 109, Cambridge, Md. 21613

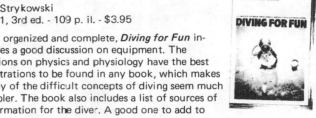

DIVING FOR FUN

Joe Strykowski
1971, 3rd ed. - 109 p. il. - $3.95

Well organized and complete, *Diving for Fun* includes a good discussion on equipment. The sections on physics and physiology have the best illustrations to be found in any book, which makes many of the difficult concepts of diving seem much simpler. The book also includes a list of sources of information for the diver. A good one to add to your library.
From: Dacor Corp., 161 Northfield Rd., Northfield, Ill. 60093

BUSINESS OF DIVING

John E. Kenny
1972 - 302 p. il. - $14.95

The emphasis here is on the various uses of diving as a tool for the exploitation and understanding of the ocean's resources. This is a what's doing book— what's doing in sport, commercial, military, and scientific diving and what we can expect in the future. The main sections are semitechnical, with appendices covering such items as the Navy decompression tables, equipment operation details, the Navy diver training course, and listings of commercial diving companies and schools offering scientific diving programs. It's fairly heavy on the technical end, but if you want to see what the state of the art in diving is, this is a good start.
From: Gulf Publishing Co., 3301 Allen Parkway, Houston, Tex. 77001

FISHWATCHERS GUIDE TO WEST ATLANTIC CORAL REEFS

Charles C. G. Chaplin and Sir Peter Scott
1972 - 65 p. il. - $6.95

This book has color illustrations of 184 species of fish and is *waterproof* so it can be taken underwater by divers
From: Harrowood Books, Box 397, Valley Forge, Pa. 19481

SPORT DIVER MANUAL

Jeppesen
1975 - il. - $8.95

This scuba training manual comes complete with a separate workbook for diving study.
From: Jeppesen, 8025 E. 40th Ave., Denver, Colo. 80207

SWIMMING AND WATER SAFETY

American National Red Cross
1968 - 142 p. il. - $1

From: American Nat. Red Cross, 17th and D Sts., N.W., Washington, D.C. 20006

RESEARCH DIVER'S MANUAL (Tech. Rep. 16)

Lee H. Somers
1972 - il. - $12.95

This is an excellent manual of diving skills for the serious diver.
From: The University of Michigan, Ann Arbor, Mich. 48104

UNDERWATER NAVIGATION FOR SCUBA DIVERS

Jack E. Glatt
1962 - 63 p. il. - $1.50

Determination of speed and direction underwater; use of compass.
From: Chicago Aligraphy and Lithographing Co., 633 S. Plymouth Ave., Chicago, Ill. 60620

DIVER TRAINING

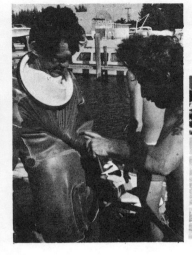

the United States. NAUI instructors are located in all parts of the world and certify hundreds of divers every year. Before becoming instructors, they must undergo a rigorous training and certification program themselves. NAUI certification cards (C-cards) are probably more widely accepted than any other type. A letter to the above address will get you information on the programs and location of the nearest diver training course.

YOUNG MEN'S CHRISTIAN ASSOCIATION (YMCA)
(Check your phone directory for nearest YMCA or YWCA)
Since this organization has swimming pool facilities in most parts of the United States, you're likely to take your scuba course in a "Y" pool regardless of who's offering it. Many "Y's" offer their own courses, and if you're a member, you'll find their prices lower than others. YMCA certification is also universally accepted by dive shops as proof of scuba competence.

PROFESSIONAL ASSOCIATION OF DIVING INSTRUCTORS (PADI)
2064 N. Bush St., Santa Ana, Calif. 92706
PADI offers an excellent program based on sound and up-to-date training methods, and has become the largest of the certifying organizations. PADI is unique in offering its Mossback program for the "forgotten diver," which allows certifying an experienced diver through an abbreviated testing program. This allows an experienced diver to become certified without having to spend the full amount of time and money required for a complete basic course. More information on the Mossback program and other PADI Basic and Specialty courses is available from PADI headquarters at the above address.

NATIONAL ASSOCIATION OF SKIN DIVING SCHOOLS (NASDS)
1757 Long Beach Blvd., Long Beach, Calif. 90813
NASDS certification is widely known and accepted, and they offer just about the same type of instruction and certification programs as NAUI and PADI. However, unlike these other certifying organizations, NASDS is associated exclusively with dive shops, and sometimes you'll get an instructor who tends to place more emphasis on acquiring diving gear rather than diving skill. If you take a course associated with a dive shop, be certain you don't end up buying more equipment or more expensive equipment than you really need. Get some advice from senior members of a dive club not associated with a shop.

FLORIDA STATE SKINDIVING SCHOOLS, INC. (FSDA)
1300 North Mills Ave., Orlando, Fla. 32803

SCUBA CERTIFICATION

If you're interested in learning to dive, your local YMCA or dive shop can tell you about the various organizations for training and certifying divers in your area.

A scuba course generally lasts several weeks and is divided into four broad areas: classroom theory, skin diving, scuba diving, and open-water diving. The cost of a course runs from $40 to $60.

Divers who have completed a basic course may want to go for an advanced or senior diver training program. In addition, many of these programs, including the pioneering program started by Los Angeles County, offer specialized training in areas like underwater photography, spearfishing, wreck diving, surf diving, and so forth. Often local diving clubs and organizations offer these specialty courses, taught by senior members.

If you want professional training, there are several commercial schools offering scuba and hard-hat courses.

Remember, though, the most important part of any course is the instructor, so check around the local shops and talk it up with divers to get some input on who can be recommended.

The groups listed below are the main ones in the United States offering diver certification programs.

NATIONAL ASSOC. OF UNDERWATER INSTRUCTORS (NAUI)
22809 Barton Rd., Grand Terrace, Colton, Calif. 92324
This group is the most popular and respected diving organization in

---

Commercial diving courses are expensive, starting at $1,000, and last several weeks or months, depending on the extent of the training. However, a good commercial diver can make as much as $190 a day on the West Coast and probably just as much on the East Coast, so a course is worth the investment if you're seriously interested.

COASTAL SCHOOL OF DEEP SEA DIVING
320 29th Ave., Oakland, Calif. 94601
The "oldest and largest in the world," this school offers training in all phases of deep-sea diving. Its basic 427-hour (11½-week) course runs $1,095. Other instruction includes a 150-hour (4-week) advanced course in helium diving for $1,395 and a one-week submersible operator's course for $375, plus the standard NASDS 25-hour scuba course for $50. Send $1 for information and the book, *Your Future in Deep Sea Diving.*

COMMERCIAL DIVING CENTER (CDC)
272 South Fries Ave., Wilmington, Calif. 90744
CDC offers a complete 436-hour, 15-week deep-sea diving course for $1,700. CDC is the exclusive diver training center for their parent company, Oceaneering International, Inc., the largest independent diving contractor in the world. School facilities are excellent. Courses cover the entire range of diving activities, including NAUI scuba certification. A course is also offered on Bell/Saturation Diving. A free brochure is available, but if you're serious, best get the $2 catalog.

COMMERCIAL DIVING

DIVERS TRAINING ACADEMY (DTA)
Link Port, RFD 1, Box 193 C, Fort Pierce, Fla. 33450
Two basic courses are offered: 218-hour commercial salvage/repair diver course, including scuba, $1,050, and a 218-hour commercial deep-sea diver course which requires taking the salvage/repair course first. The total package is 436 hours and costs $1,560. Send $2 for their catalog.

DIVERS INSTITUTE OF TECHNOLOGY (DIT)
P.O. Box 70312, Seattle, Wash. 98107
DIT offers a basic 14-week, 420-hour course for $1,925, plus an advanced Professional Deep-Sea Diving Course, a 6-month, 750-hour course for $2,900. The advanced training is an "add-on" to the basic 14-week course and a student can return at any time to complete the 11-week advanced segment. Catalog, $1.50.

THE OCEAN CORPORATION
5709 Glenmont, Houston, Tex. 77036
Ocean offers a full 480-hour, 16-week course covering all commonly-used commercial systems for $1,650. Free literature is available from the above address.

DIVING GEAR

AIR CYLINDERS
$100 - $150

The scuba air cylinder is a steel or aluminum high-pressure vessel which contains compressed air for diving. Steel cylinders, which have been in use for many years, generally contain 71.2 cu. ft. of compressed air at 2,475 pounds per square inch (psi). The relatively new aluminum tanks hold as much as 80 cu. ft. of air at 3,000 psi. Because of this extremely high pressure, the Department of Transportation requires that tanks be pressure tested ("hydroed") every five years. The usual cost is about $8. In addition, many dive shops are requiring a yearly visual inspection of the inside of the tank before they'll fill it. If the tank doesn't pass, you may have to have it "tumbled"—that is, rotated with an abrasive compound inside to remove rust and corrosion. Visual inspection runs $2 to $3 and tumbling a few bucks more.

There are many brands of tanks, but only a few tank manufacturers, so don't expect much variation except in valves. The one exception is the aluminum cylinder just introduced by U.S. Divers.

Valves are attached to the top of tanks to regulate the flow of compressed air and are generally grouped into two classifications:

K valve. This is just a straight valve with a knob to control airflow.

J valve. This valve has the additional feature of a reserve air supply lever which can be set to hold 300 psi of air in reserve for emergency use. (Note: Some regulators also have reserve valves.)

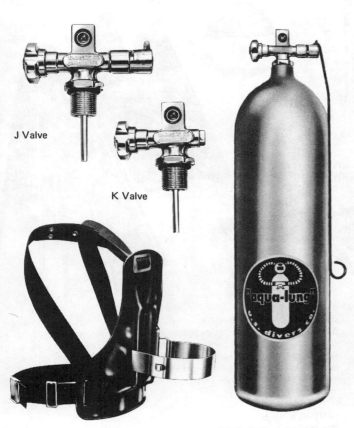

J Valve

K Valve

Single Tank Backpack

Air Cylinder with J Valve

BACKPACK
$18 - $32

A backpack is a device used to hold the air cylinder comfortably on the diver's back. Quick-release clamps make changing tanks simple, and a quick-release harness (standard on most packs) is a must for safety. Backpacks come in a single or double model which holds two tanks side by side. These tanks are then connected by a special valve assembly to which a regulator can be attached. Double tanks give you twice as much air but are heavy and somewhat clumsy in and out of the water.

Single Hose Regulator

Double Hose Regulator

REGULATOR
$50 - $130

The regulator is the heart of the scuba outfit. By regulating pressure and airflow from the tank to the diver, it makes breathing safe and effortless. Most modern regulators bring the pressure down to that required by the diver in two "stages" of regulation. The first stage lowers the high tank pressure to an intermediate pressure (about 100 psi), while the second stage is a "demand" stage which supplies air to the diver as he needs it. The diver merely has to inhale normally to activate the valve. In addition to looking for a two-stage regulator, look for a balanced first stage (for easier breathing over a range of tank pressures) and a downstream second stage (for safety). A trained diver or a dive shop salesman can usually explain these terms to you in more detail.

Regulators are divided into two general categories:

Double hose. This type of regulator has both stages contained in one unit, which mounts on the tank valve. Two large, flexible hoses extend from the unit to the mouthpiece, one for inhalation and the other for exhaust. Although somewhat difficult to use, the double hose does keep bubbles away from the face making for better vision and hearing.

Single hose. In this regulator the first stage is connected to the tank, but the second stage is attached to the mouthpiece. One thin high-pressure hose runs between the two stages. The single-hose regulator is the overwhelming favorite among sport divers because of its easier breathing and convenience.

Only single-hose regulators can be bought with built-in reserve valves, so if you choose a double-hose regulator, be sure to buy a tank with J valves. If you borrow a tank, try to borrow one with a reserve, so you won't have to dive without one.

A new concept now being offered by most manufacturers is the *octopus regulator.* This is simply a single-hose regulator with two hoses and second-stage units that allows two divers to breathe off one tank and regulator system in an emergency.

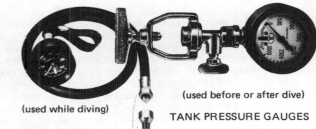

(used while diving)

(used before or after dive)

TANK PRESSURE GAUGES

TANK PRESSURE GAUGES
$14 - $40

This gauge, when attached to the regulator, allows the diver to monitor his tank air pressure throughout his dive. The gauge is easily mounted on a single-hose regulator and requires only a small adapter for attaching to a double-hose rig. On deep dives a pressure gauge is essential to assure that enough air remains for a normal ascent and, if necessary, decompression. Reserve valves (already discussed) are not completely reliable for this, since the reserve lever could be accidentally tripped to the "on" position, thus allowing the reserve air to be used up. Should this happen on a deep dive or in a confined space, the results could be disastrous. Even in shallow-water diving, the pressure gauge, though not a necessity, is a convenience which allows the diver to plan his remaining dive time wisely.

FACE MASKS
$6 - $26

A mask covers the diver's eyes and nose and allows him to see clearly underwater. A good seal is essential for comfort; otherwise, you'll have water trickling into the mask—a real problem for mustache-wearers. A double skirt inside will help prevent leaks. Some masks have purge valves, which allow water to be cleared out of the mask easily. Some divers prefer them, others don't.

Masks come in a variety of sizes and shapes. The important thing is to choose one that fits. Here's how to do it: Place the mask on your face without putting the strap in place, then inhale. Release the mask. If it clings to your face, you have a good fit. Incidentally, one way to keep a mask from fogging up while diving is to spit into it, rub the saliva around the lens, rinse out, and put it on.

Good news for those who wear glasses. Large-size prescription lenses are available for masks at under $30, installed.

SNORKELS
$2 - $10

A snorkel is a hollow, curved plastic tube with a mouthpiece at one end. It allows a diver to breathe while swimming along the surface with his head underwater and for handiness attaches directly to one

chafing.

Open-heel. This type slips on over the foot and is secured by an adjustable rubber strap that fits around the heel. Either socks or wet-suit boots should be worn for protection since the heel of the fin is open. Generally speaking, open-heel fins are stiffer than closed-heel ones and consequently harder on the beginner.

FLOTATION DEVICES
$30 - $185

A flotation device goes by many names—Mae West, life vest, buoyancy compensator (BC)—all of which refer to a vest that can be inflated by a CO_2 cartridge, by compressed air, or by mouth (all vests should have a provision for oral inflation) to provide emergency flotation for the diver.

One vest, the buoyancy compensator, has the additional advantage of allowing you to regulate the amount of air, and therefore the buoyancy of the vest. This allows the diver to maintain proper buoyancy without changing the amount of weight he carries—essential for cave diving and many types of wreck diving. Some BC's offer only oral inflation plus CO_2 cartridge, while some have connections to fit a low-pressure port on the regulator, and others have their own small com-

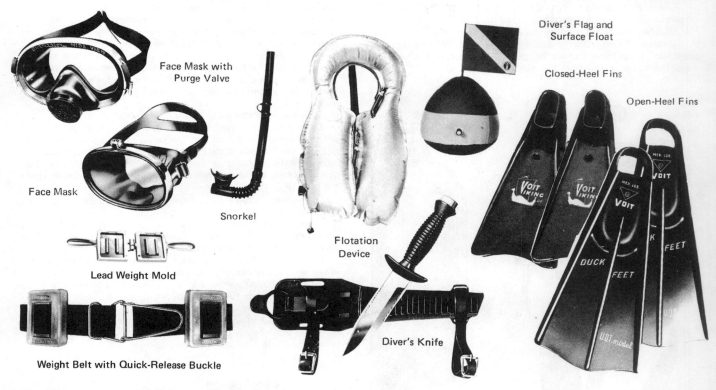

Face Mask with Purge Valve

Face Mask

Snorkel

Lead Weight Mold

Weight Belt with Quick-Release Buckle

Flotation Device

Diver's Knife

Diver's Flag and Surface Float

Closed-Heel Fins

Open-Heel Fins

of the mask straps. Most snorkels are rigid, but some have a flexible tube leading to the mouthpiece. The advantage with this is that when using scuba gear, the snorkel mouthpiece will spring out of the way and not interfere with the regulator mouthpiece. The only problem is that the flexible tube has a tendency to collect water, which can be irritating.

The diameters of snorkel tubes or "barrels" vary considerably. Big barrels allow more air to pass through but are more difficult to clear than small barrels. It's a matter of preference, but in general, the best barrels are rigid, with a moderate-sized diameter. One caution: A snorkel with a barrel too long or too large in diameter can cause a buildup of stale air, leaving the diver short of breath. This condition, if allowed to persist, could cause a blackout.

SWIM FINS
$15 - $60

Rubber fins increase the diver's efficiency underwater. Stiff ones give power and speed; flexible ones are best if you're not a strong swimmer or do not dive often. Design-wise fins can be classed into two groups:

Full-foot (or closed-heel). These come in shoe sizes usually covering a size and a half. So be sure to check for fit. Keep in mind that you might want to wear socks or wet-suit boots with them to prevent

pressed air bottle. Since BC's cost several times as much as a simple life vest, consider your needs before investing. For most diving, an oral inflator with a CO_2 backup is sufficient, but make sure you have a large, flexible hose and a purge valve which will allow you to inflate and empty the vest rapidly. Most BC's are also equipped with a "pop-off" valve to prevent over-inflation.

DIVING KNIFE
$9 - $27

The diving knife is more than a toy; it is a tool which can be used to free a diver trapped by seaweed, rope, fishing line, or other obstructions. Most cheap diving knives will rust easily if not washed and dried carefully after each dive. Care should be taken to keep a sharp edge on the blade. A knife is no good if it won't cut when you need it.

DIVING WATCH
$40 - $275

Any waterproof watch could be used for diving, but to classify as a diving watch, it should have a rotating bezel numerically marked from 1 to 60 either in a clockwise or counterclockwise direction. The former is a regular diving or elapsed-time bezel which allows the diver to set a pointer to the time he starts his dive. The counterclockwise, or "countdown," bezel is generally considered superior for deeper dives, since it allows the diver to set the bezel to the time he wishes to finish the dive and thus monitor his time remaining at any point in the dive. This bezel eliminates the need for computing remaining dive time, which on a deep dive, can be difficult because of the intoxicating effects of nitrogen narcosis. A watch should be easy to read, have a bezel, and be waterproof to a depth in excess of the number of feet to which you expect to dive.

DEPTH GAUGE
$7 - $225

A depth gauge allows the diver to monitor water depth at any time, which can be particularly important for deep diving because of decompression problems. When you buy a depth gauge, make sure it is accurate and easy to read. A gauge which is difficult to read on the surface may be impossible at 100 feet, when nitrogen narcosis has set in. Look for a large dial with scale divisions marked in even increments, such as every 10 feet. Any gauge that you select can be checked periodically for accuracy. Inexpensive capillary gauges are very accurate for shallow diving, and may be all the gauge you need. More ex-

Compass

Wet Suit   Damp Suit
(not shown)

Depth Gauge

Watch   Dry Suit

pensive gauges are available for deep diving, ranging all the way up to the $225 digital depth gauge/ascent rate meter made by Farallon Industries.

WET SUITS
$80 - $300

In most areas of the world, a wet suit is necessary for comfortable diving. It is essential for survival in cold waters. Wet suits are made of a rubber foam material, lined with a strong, elastic cloth. The thickness of the suit is generally 3/16 or 1/4 inch. A wet suit does not prevent the diver's body from getting wet; instead, it allows the water to seep into the suit. The water is then warmed by the diver's body and provides an extra layer of insulation. A wet suit can be a sleeveless pullover jacket or a full suit with boots and gloves. Various makes and styles are available and prices can run as much as $300 for a full suit. Heavy-duty suits, made with the working diver in mind, have linings and a cloth covering on top of the rubber to add strength and are even more expensive.

DRY SUITS
$80 - $350

Another type of protective clothing is the dry suit. Before wet suits,

dry suits were used to dive in cold waters. Dry suits are made of thin rubber and have seals at the face, waist, wrists, and ankles to keep the diver's body completely dry. Long underwear is often worn under the suit for extra protection. These suits are not used much today because they are difficult to put on and easy to tear.

INFLATABLE DRY SUITS
$250 - $640

A recent innovation in diving suits is the inflatable dry suit. It has the outward appearance of a wet suit and has the same neoprene material; however, all openings are fitted with watertight seals and waterproof zippers (or no zippers at all) are used. For inflation, manual and/or hose-supplied fittings are employed. The objective of the inflatable suit is to be able to add air as a means of adjusting buoyancy and to provide a thermal layer for insulation against cold. They've been used in Arctic waters with great success. Only problem with them for the weekend diver is they're pretty dear.

WEIGHT BELT and WEIGHTS
$15 - $30

Since wet suits are made of foam rubber they increase a diver's buoyancy because of the thousands of tiny air bubbles. To compensate for this buoyancy, you can strap lead weights to the waist on a belt. The amount of weight depends upon the person, the type of diving, and the type of diving suit and equipment worn. Generally, a diver with a wet suit and buoyancy compensator will require a minimum of 10 to 20 lbs. of weight. An inflatable dry suit can add quite a bit of extra weight to this requirement. A weight belt should always have a quick-release buckle so it can be dropped at once in an emergency.

DIVING FLAG (and/or Surface Float)
$4 - $15

A surface marker lets boatmen and other people in the area know where a diver is. The proper method of marking your location when diving is to tow a surface marker bearing the standard white-stripe-on-red diver's flag. When diving from a boat, the flag should be clearly displayed from a mast or pole. Diving flags and surface floats are cheap (the float can be an old inner tube) and can save your life.

ACCESSORIES

Gloves, $2.50 to $12. For most diving, gloves are advisable to prevent cuts, bruises, and stings. A full wet suit comes with a pair of rubber gloves, but these are thick and clumsy. In warm water, leather or cloth gloves can be easier to use. Buy gloves that will hold up against sharp rocks and broken glass.

Diving light, $15 to $140. Essential for cave diving and most wreck diving, a light guides the way in dark and enclosed places. If you plan to make deep dives, a strong case and O-ring seals are a must. Cheaper lights will crush or fail to operate under the pressures of these depths.

Safety line, about $3 for 100 feet of 1/4-in. polypropylene. An essential item for cave and wreck diving to help guide you out.

Tools, $5 to $50. You'll find that shelling, abalone hunting, wreck diving, and other underwater activities are much more productive when you have the right tools. Most standard tools, such as knives, hammers, wrenches, etc., can be used underwater *IF* they are properly cleaned after diving. Tools made especially for diving are more resistant to rust but are expensive. With a good rust preventive and a little ingenuity, you can fill your tool bag from common or homemade tools and save money.

Slate and Pencil, about $3. Underwater, there is no need to wave your arms around trying to tell your diving buddy something when you can write him a note instead. A slate and pencil are inexpensive, easy to carry, and invaluable for underwater communication.

Compass, $4 to $27. An inexpensive accessory which can increase your ability to navigate underwater. (Be careful when using it near ferrous metals, such as around a shipwreck, because it will give erroneous readings.)

Camera equipment, $70 to $1,000 plus. Housings are available for cameras ranging from inexpensive Instamatics all the way up to professional still and movie cameras. Underwater photography and equipment are covered in the Field Photography Section.

sources of diving gear

In most areas of the United States, you're probably near a shop that sells scuba gear. This is where you should start looking for equipment, but keep in mind that there's a wide variation in the prices of different brands and even of the same brand at different stores. Therefore, compare prices at one or more stores and check through the catalogs of the dealers listed below before deciding. If you shop around, you can find discounts of 25 to 33 per cent on scuba equipment of major brands without any reduction in quality. As a matter of fact, many retail outlets will sell at prices below the manufacturer's suggested list price.

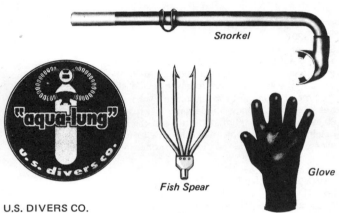

Snorkel

Fish Spear

Glove

U.S. DIVERS CO.

3323 West Warner Ave., Santa Ana, Calif. 92702
U.S. Divers is the "world's largest and oldest manufacturer of sport, commercial, and military diving equipment." It handles a complete inventory of scuba gear and accessories of excellent quality. The regulators bear the trademark Aqua-Lung, the name commonly applied to all scuba gear by nondivers. U.S. Divers offers excellent service on orders, warranties, and repairs. For $1.50, you can get a copy of the company's catalog with a colorful and complete listing of all its gear and prices. You can order directly from the above address, but substantial discounts are usually available from local sources and mail-order houses. U.S. Divers also deals in commercial diving equipment. This gear is highly rated and includes items from the Kirby-Morgan shallow-water mask to hard hats and communication systems. In addition, U.S. Divers also maintains an excellent information and public relations staff who will send speedy replies to questions about diving, equipment, and instruction.

Compressor

NEW ENGLAND DIVERS, INC. (NED)

Tozer Rd., Beverly, Mass. 01915
New England Divers, now operating 8 retail outlets plus a catalog department, carries most major brands of scuba gear. A complete inventory of equipment and accessories is shown in the catalog, which you can order for $1. Catalog prices are wholesale and generally reflect a savings of 25 to 40 percent off retail. New England Divers has one unique offering: with any purchase of a New England Divers air cylinder, you get a card entitling you to receive free air refills for life at any NED store. NED has an excellent service record and is one of the best known and most respected of all mail-order houses. New England Divers has the largest inventory of diving equipment to be found, and orders are shipped the same day they are received. On orders of $75 or more, you can call collect and have your order shipped the same day, COD. Items under 60 lbs. are shipped freight-paid.

TANK GAUGE

TANK BOOT

Extra heavy boot for "permanent" bottom protection of your tank. Tank stands by itself for easy storage and very handy when attaching regulator.

NEO-FUSE GLUE
World's finest neoprene glue.

CENTRAL SKINDIVERS

2608 Merrick Rd., Bellmore, N.Y. 11710
Central's catalog has a broad selection of brand-name gear at good prices. In addition to the basics, it offers assorted accessories, photographic equipment, and some professional items. Prices look to be the best of the lot. Catalog is free.

Basic Kit

SKIN DIVING

Face Mask
Snorkel
Fins

Knife
Inflatable vest

SCUBA DIVING
(add to the above)

Air cylinder with reserve
Backpack

Regulator
Trained buddy!

SCUBA ACCESSORIES

Weight belt
Depth gauge
Diving watch
Compass

Wet suit
Tank pressure gauge
Diver's flag-surface marker

Here's some of my thoughts on a basic kit:

I prefer the straight-tube snorkel because it allows for easier breathing. If night diving is planned, a strip of Scotchlite reflector tape wrapped around the top of the snorkel is a good safety precaution.

I'd suggest a life vest that does not have the CO_2 cylinder next to the body. If the cylinder is in contact with the bare skin, a freeze-burn can develop when the cartridge is activated.

A mask with double skirting inside is best to prevent leaks, and is a must for the diver who sports a moustache. Also, a purge valve is helpful, though some divers I know don't care for them.

Make sure fins will fit snugly over boots, but are not tight enough to cut off circulation.

Most commercially made "diving" knives will not keep a keen edge. A U.S. Navy survival knife or a serrated steak knife in a home-made sheath would probably give better service.

Here's my recommendations on the brands of gear to buy:

Wet Suit: Sharkskin II, U.S. Divers, Healthways

Mask: Cressi, Nemrod, Voit

Fins: Voit, U.S. Divers, Healthways

Tank &

Regulator: U.S. Divers

Watch: Zodiac, Rolex (if you can afford it!!!)

—Rick "the Rock" Reinecker (1972)

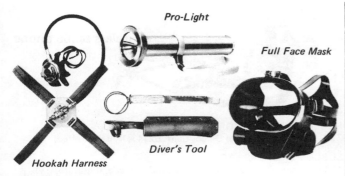

Pro-Light

Full Face Mask

Diver's Tool

Hookah Harness

BERRY DISTRIBUTORS
12003 S. Cicero, Alsip, Ill. 60658

Berry offers U.S. Divers, Voit, Healthways, and Nemrod/Seamless lines of diving gear at 25 to 33 per cent off the retail price. The company will send you the manufacturers' catalogs ($4.25 worth right off the top) and a list of discounts. Berry also handles the Voit Swimaster and Nemrod Professional gear but not at discount. Sorry! To make it up, Berry has a separate Professional Divers Equipment Catalog which contains a wide variety of accessories, underwater photographic gear, and a fine pro line—hard hats, communications, metal detectors, compressors, decompression chambers, propulsion units, and the Unisuit system. Prices on many of the sport items are cheaper than New England Divers', and Berry pays all postage for an additional plus. Don't know how the service stacks up though. Catalog, $1. Berry operates five stores in the Midwest in addition to its mail-order operation.

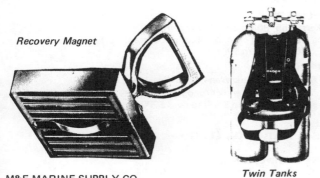

Recovery Magnet

Twin Tanks

M&E MARINE SUPPLY CO.
P.O. Box 601, Camden, N.J. 08101

M&E's 165-page commercial catalog is the largest catalog of brand-name sport and professional diving gear and accessories to be found anywhere and, at $1.50, is the best single source on diving gear and prices available. M&E has been serving divers since 1947, selling wholesale and retail from their store on Route 130, Collingswood, N.J. Their catalog lists almost every conceivable item of diving equipment from underwater chain saws to high-pressure compressors to decompression chambers, hard-hat equipment, and underwater communications and photography equipment. When ordering the catalog, specify the "MAR-VEL Diving Catalog," since M&E also has a boating catalog.

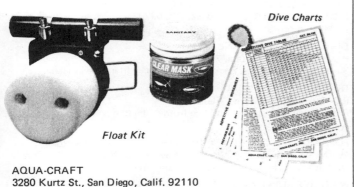

Dive Charts

Float Kit

AQUA-CRAFT
3280 Kurtz St., San Diego, Calif. 92110

Aqua-Craft is accessories—books, general accessories, spearguns and parts, accessories for tanks, weight belts, wet suits, and photographic gear. Twenty-three-page catalog, 50¢.

MANUFACTURERS

In addition to the major suppliers of scuba gear listed above, the following companies all sell equipment through dealers and by mail. Catalogs may be obtained by writing:

DACOR CORP.
161 Northfield Rd., Northfield, Ill. 60093
Complete line of scuba gear; catalog, $2.

HEALTHWAYS, INC.
P.O. Box 45055, Los Angeles, Calif. 90045
Complete line of scuba gear; catalog, $1.

IMPERIAL MFG. CO.
Box 4119, Bremerton, Wash. 98310
Wet suits; fins masks, snorkels; catalog, $1.

PARKWAY FABRICATORS
291 New Brunswick Ave., Perth Amboy, N.J. 08861
Wet suits; catalog, $1.

SCUBAPRO
3105 East Harcourt, Compton, Calif. 90221
Excellent and complete line of scuba equipment; catalog, $2; equipment fair-traded (no discounts).

U.S. NEMROD, INC.
P.O. Box 5188, Hamden, Conn. 06518
Complete line of scuba gear; catalog, $1.25.

SPORTSWAYS
P.O. Box 2407, Huntington Park, Calif. 90255
Complete line of scuba gear; catalog, $1.

WHITE STAG
5203 South East Johnson Creek Blvd., Portland, Ore. 97206
Complete line of scuba gear; Catalog, 25¢.

AMF SWIMASTER
3801 S. Harbor Blvd., Santa Ana, Calif. 92704
Complete line of scuba gear; catalog, $1.50.

GLOBAL MANUFACTURING CORP.
P.O. Box 4714, Milwaukee, Wisc. 53215
Full line of accessories; catalog, 25¢.

SEA QUEST
722 Genevieve St., Solana Beach, Calif. 92075
Wet suits and general accessories; catalog, free.

SPECIALIZED GEAR

The following dealers offer the specialized gear indicated by the heading.

Custom Wet Suits

SEA SUITS OF CALIFORNIA
P.O. Box 245, Costa Mesa, Calif. 92627; literature, free.

DIVE N' SURF
504 North Broadway, Redondo Beach, Calif. 90277; literature, free.

HARVEY'S SUITS
2505 S. 252nd St., Kent, Wash. 98031; catalog, $1.50.

Prescription Face Plates

Large wide-angle lenses are ground to your prescription and bonded to the inside of your own mask. Cost is about $35.

PRESCRIPTION FACE PLATES

LEONARD MAGGIORE
1702 Gates Ave., Brooklyn, N.Y. 11227; literature, free.

AQUA OPTICS
A. S. Newton, 575 West 6th St., San Pedro, Calif. 90731; lit., free.

UNDERWATER VISION INC.
950 Cooper St., Venice, Fla. 33595; literature, free.

Wet Submersibles

FARALLON INDUSTRIES
1333 Old Country Rd., Belmont, Calif. 94002
DPV MK-II, III, IV, V & VI propulsion vehicles; literature, $1.

UNDERWATER WAYS, INC.
211 Broadway, Lynbrook, N.Y. 11563
Sea Scuta propulsion device; literature, free.

W. KENT MARKHAM
1147 Greenridge Rd., Jacksonville, Fla. 32207
Plans for building your own wet sub, $10; literature, free.

PERRY OCEANOGRAPHICS, INC.
Perry Bldg., Riviera Beach, Fla. 33404
Wet submersibles; literature, free.

Spearguns & Power Heads

YIKES

TAPMATIC CORP.
P.O. Box 66, Costa Mesa, Calif. 92627
Multibarrel .22 blank-powered spear gun; literature, free.

BAYFRONT INDUSTRIES, INC.
4225 Ponce de Leon Blvd., Coral Gables, Fla. 33146
Power heads; literature, free.

Underwater Communications

ALPINE PIONEER, INC.
Winter St., Hanover, Mass. 02339

HYDRO PRODUCTS
Box 2528, San Diego, Calif. 92112; literature, free.

Wireless scuba phone

HELLE ENGINEERING INC.
7198 Convoy Court, San Diego, Calif. 92111; literature, free.

SUBCOM SYSTEMS LTD.
153 Riverside Dr., North Vancouver, B.C. Canada; literature, free.

IMAGINEERED PRODUCTS CORP.
3737 North 35th St., Milwaukee, Wisc. 53216; literature, free.

Diving Watches

The following foreign dealers offer good diving watches at savings of 50 per cent over U.S. retail prices. All will ship directly to your home, and the mailman will collect the customs duty on delivery (normal duty is about $4 for a watch with 17 jewels or less; duty increases rapidly for watches with more than 17 jewels). Air mail shipping costs are about $3, and delivery should be within two weeks.

ITRACO WATCH CO., LTD.
8027 Zurich, Switzerland
Good selection of diving watches and chronographs in the $25 to $50 range; free catalog.

OLLECH & WAJS
Stockerstr. 55, 8039, Zurich, Switzerland
Diving watches and chronographs; prices seem a bit higher than Itraco's. Catalogs run $2.

T. M. CHAN
P.O. Box 3881 Sheung Wan Post Office, Hong Kong
Seiko diving watches and chronographs for less than $60; also handles Omega and Rolex from $100 to over $200. Free catalog.

Miscellaneous Items

KEENE ENGINEERING, INC.
9330 Corbin Ave., Northridge, Calif. 91324
Gold-diving gear—hookas, dredges, jet pumps; catalog, free.

IDEAL REEL CO.
823 Harrison St., Paducah, Ky. 42001
SAFLINE diving reel for safety line; literature, free.

APPLETON PAPERS, INC.
P.O. Box 348, Appleton, Wisc. 54911
Resin-coated waterproof paper that can be written on with a regular lead pencil while underwater. Cost varies from 3½¢ to 10¢ a sheet depending on quantity. Available in 25-sheet tablets. Looks just like regular paper, but it works. Literature, free.

PROFESSIONAL GEAR

DIVING EQUIPMENT & SUPPLY CO., INC. (DESCO)
240 N. Milwaukee St., Milwaukee, Wis. 53202
Full line of pro gear—top-line stuff; catalog available.

DIVER'S EXCHANGE INC.
P.O. Box 504, Harvey, La. 70058
Mixed-gas hard hat and Beckman Electrolung; literature available.

DIVEQUIP
P.O. Box 339, Melbourne, Fla. 32901
Professional dive service. Full line from scuba to mixed gas. Catalog, available.

POSEIDON SYSTEMS U.S.A. (Division of Parkway Fabricators)
291 New Brunswick Ave., Perth Amboy, N.J. 08861
Unisuit system and accessories; literature, free.

WILDLIFE SUPPLY CO.
301 Cass St., Saginaw, Mich. 18602
Excellent assortment of oceanographic equipment and sampling kits. Catalog, $1.

TOURS & EXPEDITIONS

There are many parts of the world that offer diving opportunities to lure the underwater explorer. Beginning with the lower Florida Keys and extending to tropical waters around the globe, these areas beckon to the adventurous diver with tales of virgin shipwrecks, 200-foot visibility, and water temperatures in the high 80's. These areas offer splendid opportunities for diving vacations, but transportation and diving costs are just about prohibitive for the average person. To get around this, go with a group and take advantage of the lower rates. Often local clubs will sponsor package trips, and travel agencies can keep you posted on now-and-again group diving tours sponsored by airlines, hotels, and so forth. We've listed tour agencies that specialize in diving tours below.

Another way to drum up information on new diving areas, facilities, and, possibly, package tour deals is to write to tourist information bureaus. Check the Backpacking Section for the names and addresses of those in the United States and the front part of this section for the national tourist bureaus of Canada, the Bahamas, and Mexico.

ATLANTIS SAFARIS
Lee Turcotte, P.O. Box 303, Miami Shores, Fla. 33153
Atlantis Safaris offers a variety of one- and two-week diving tours throughout the Caribbean and Mediterranean. In the past, regular trips have run to Bonaire and Curacao, Haiti, Greece, Roatan, Honduras, British Honduras, Jamaica, Cayman Islands, and Italy. The one-week Bonaire-Curacao trip runs around $260 per person plus air fare for the summer season. Literature available, free.

Exploring a sunken wreck in Bonaire.

LEE TURCOTTE'S
ATLANTIS SAFARIS

Day 2 thru 5—*Enjoy four full days of diving in the warm, clear waters of the Caribbean exploring different sites which have been especially selected for you. Included is a diving excursion to the nearby island of Klein Bonaire. For the advanced diver there's an intriguing sunken ship still intact from 1911 to be explored and photographed.*

BAY TRAVEL, INC.
2435 East Coast Hwy., Corona del Mar, Calif. 92625
Bay Travel has a series of two-week cruises to major diving spots like the Bahamas, the Great Barrier Reef, Jamaica, Samoa, Cozumel, Fiji, and the Greek islands. Cruise costs run from $20 to $40 a day plus air fare.

KIRK ANDERS TRAVEL
P.O. Box 1418, Fort Lauderdale, Fla. 33302
Kirk Anders offers a variety of one-week tours throughout the Caribbean to such areas as British Honduras, Andros Island, Cozumel, Antigua, the Virgin Islands, and Bonaire. These are not strictly diving trips, but rather trips for shell collectors (Anders also operates Shells of the Seas, which sells seashells by mail). However, some of the best shells are obtained by diving, so full diving facilities are always provided on tours. For the best shells the tours go into the more remote areas of the places visited; because of this you could say that Anders' trips offer more virgin diving country to the underwater explorer than any other tours. The prices are exceptional, too—$325, and this includes round-trip air fare from Fort Lauderdale. All you have to do is get to Fort Lauderdale.

INTERNATIONAL DIVERS GUIDE
M. T. O'Keefe, Ed.
1975 - 208 p. il. - $6.95

Good guide, includes "Yellow Pages" of dive shops and services.
From: Toss, Inc., P.O. Box 1889, Winter Park, Fla. 32789

GREAT DIVING - I (Eastern U.S.)
Judy and Dean May
1974 - 256 p. il. - $3.95 (pb)

The first of a planned two-volume set covering the best inland, river, coastal and open-sea diving sites in the East. Included are dive shops, decompression chambers and charter boat operators for each state along the Atlantic and Gulf coasts, plus applicable salvage and spearfishing regulations. Very good guide for the price.
From: Stackpole Books, Cameron & Kelker Sts., Harrisburg, Pa. 17105

—————————— **TOURS**

SEE & SEA TRAVEL SERVICE, INC.
680 Beach St., Suite 340, San Francisco, Calif. 94109

COZUMEL

For several years our Cozumel diving trips have featured a 2-day visit to the Yucatan mainland, diving on the Spanish Galleon (The Mantanceros), visits to the Mayan citadel of Tulum, virgin reef diving and just beachcombing. Since the first of the year we have stayed at Club Akumal, a new development pioneered by Pablo Bush of CEDAM. This new arrangement has proved so attractive that our 1972/73 trips are redesigned to feature a longer stay of four days at Akumal. There is a lot of diving and adventure around Akumal and the Quintana Roo coastline.

See & Sea is another agency specializing in all-inclusive diving trips around the world, concentrating on the Caribbean and the Pacific. The 1973 schedule calls for trips to Cozumel, Cayman Islands, Curacao-Bonaire, and Australia's Great Barrier Reef. Previous trips have included British Honduras, the Galapagos, Tahiti, and Bora Bora. Most of the trips are for 11 days, with costs ranging from around $525 to $1,000 plus air fare. Literature available, free.

KIRK ANDERS

British Honduras, Central America
Here's your chance to see the Caribbean the way it "really was." A beautiful week at Glover's Reef Village, a unique tropical island resort on a remote coral atoll. Of the 26 atolls in the Caribbean, Glover's Reef is the only one comparable to the Pacific atolls. Eighty-one square miles of shallow lagoon, only ten miles away from the Great Barrier Reef of the Caribbean, 150 miles long and second only to the Barrier Reef of Australia. Includes round trip air fare, transportation to the resort, cabin (double occupancy), daily boat trips around the reef with guides, all meals, one tank w/back pack, lead weights, unlimited air, use of dugout canoes, motor skiff, tips, etc.; $325.

offshore sailing

Stephen Bleinberger

Ringy

Offshore sailing is offshore cruising—ocean voyaging, and though this may certainly be done in a powerboat, we've slanted the section toward sail because a sailboat is better suited to long ocean passages. One of the reasons is that it's more economical—a sailboat's fuel, the wind, is free. Other reasons for sail as a better choice are that it's quiet and tranquil, but yet at the same time exciting because it calls for a unique involvement between man, boat, and the sea. With power you just can't get this. It's simply crank up the engine and steer a course. Ho hum. Four to five days at sea like this with the racket of an engine and the smell of diesel (stink, if you will) can really get you down. All of which pretty well explains why there is a preponderance of sailboats appearing on the roll of notable ocean cruising vessels. In all fairness, however, it should be stated that power has a lot to recommend it for cruising along the coast, but offshore, for long passages, a windjammer's the only way to go.

Of all the activities in the *Source Book*, offshore sailing is probably the most involved; there's more of a variety of things to know and a greater number of capabilities required of a person. For example, here's the type of background knowledge and experience a good offshore cruising man will have regardless of whether he's sailing a 25' sloop or a 60' schooner: sailboats—their construction, maintenance, and operation; boat and sail handling under all sea conditions and circumstances; auxiliary engines—their operation and maintenance; coastwise and offshore navigation—use of instruments, methods, and aids; communications—operation and maintenance of electronic gear and other signaling devices; weather forecasting and use of instruments; first aid and survival at sea; legal—rules of the road, Coast Guard requirements, state requirements, plus registration, documentation, entering, clearing, and dealing with foreign governments; business—purchasing and selling a boat, brokers, insurance, boatyard practices, equipment and supplies scrounging practices, chartering practices; and last but not least, handiness at cooking, sewing, carpentry, metalworking, mechanics, plumbing, and painting—just to name a few abilities.

To the uninitiated, this may seem a bit excessive; however, the more you get into this cruising business, the more you find that you have only yourself to depend upon—so make it a point not to have a ding-a-ling for counsel.

Setting a proper course to achieve this is simple as pie. As a matter of fact, there are boating groups out there just begging to help you do it the right way. One of them, the U.S. Power Squadrons, even has a toll-free number to call to learn where you can take their free boating course, which is excellent. The Coast Guard Auxiliary, a civilian boating group

246

associated with the U.S. Coast Guard, also offers free boating classes and, if you request it, will inspect your boat to make sure it has the proper equipment (this is free and there are no strings attached).

Successful cruising depends on equal amounts of book study and experience at the helm. Here are several good books that we can recommend for starting your ship's library. *Hand, Reef and Steer* by Richard Henderson is fine for beginners and for teaching young people how to sail. Royce's *Sailing Illustrated* will be useful for a lifetime of sailing. *Basic Sailing* by M. B. George is a comprehensive and profusely illustrated book covering sailboats and their handling. *Piloting, Seamanship and Small Boat Handling* by Chapman covers in encyclopedic detail much of what you should know, although it is primarily useful for reference rather than systematic study. Hiscock's *Cruising Under Sail* is his best book and will give you a good feeling for the problems of cruising and recommended solutions. Donald Street's *The Ocean Sail-*

ing Yacht is very practical and well worth considerable study early in the game. All of these books are more fully described further on.

For the experience end of things, nothing does it like having your own boat. A small sloop of from 12 feet to 20 feet would be about right to cut your teeth on, and a used one should be easy to locate for $800 or so. Try to buy a type which is raced locally. Probably the best way to learn how to sail a big cruising boat is to start by racing small ones. You might also consider chartering a larger boat to see how you and your family react to the whole experience. It may not be for you.

With a good boating course under your belt, a well-rounded marine library for reference, and a fine little ship from which to gain practical sailing and maintenance experience, you could say an intelligent first step has been taken toward tomorrow's long voyage to the South Seas aboard your next boat.

sources of information

U.S. COAST GUARD
400 Seventh St., S.W., Washington, D.C. 20590
These are the federal water cops who fly their helicopters directly over you when you're close hauled, issue citations for running aground when their buoys drift off mark, but are the best all-around guys to drop in on and visit for a couple of days when cruising in the vicinity of their island lighthouses. The Coast Guard is involved in enforcing navigation and boating safety regulations, search and rescue operations, maintaining aids to navigation, inspecting merchant and other vessels engaged in commercial trade, and licensing seamen and officers. If you plan to take people out on your boat for charter trips, these are the government boys you'll be dealing with when you go for your Motorboat Operator's License and for the inspection of your vessel if you intend to carry more than five passengers for hire. To get complete info on what the Coast Guard does with respect to enforcing navigation laws and pleasure boating safety, licensing and inspection, search and rescue, and so forth, pick up a copy of *Recreational Boating Guide, CG-340* (listed with the books), or drop them a letter at the above address with a specific request for information. The Coast Guard publishes quite a number of free pamphlets and booklets, which might be worth considering for your ship's library; some of them, anyway. You'll find them listed in other parts of the Offshore Sailing Section.

For information, publications and to be placed on mailing list to receive free weekly *Local Notice to Mariners,* write the Commandant of your Coast Guard district. Addresses are given below:

- COMMANDER
  1st Coast Guard District (b)
  J.F. Kennedy Federal Bldg.
  Government Center
  Boston, MA 02203

- COMMANDER
  2nd Coast Guard District (o)
  Federal Building
  1520 Market Street
  St. Louis, MO 63103

- COMMANDER
  3rd Coast Guard District (o)
  Governors Island
  New York, N.Y. 10004

- COMMANDER
  5th Coast Guard District (o)
  431 Crawford Street
  Portsmouth, VA 23705

- COMMANDER
  7th Coast Guard District (b)
  51 S.W. First Avenue
  Miami, FL 33130

- COMMANDER
  8th Coast Guard District (o)
  Custom House
  New Orleans, LA 70130

- COMMANDER
  9th Coast Guard District (b)
  Room 2021, New Federal Bldg.
  1240 E. 9th Street
  Cleveland, OH 44199

- COMMANDER
  11th Coast Guard District (o)
  19 Pine Avenue
  Long Beach, CA 90802

- COMMANDER
  12th Coast Guard District (b)
  630 Sansome Street
  San Francisco, CA 94126

- COMMANDER
  13th Coast Guard District (b)
  915 2nd Avenue
  Seattle, WA 98104

- COMMANDER
  14th Coast Guard District (b)
  677 Ala Moana Boulevard
  Honolulu, HI 96813

- COMMANDER
  17th Coast Guard District (o)
  P.O. Box 35000
  Juneau, AL 90801

Commandant G-BAU
U.S. COAST GUARD AUXILIARY (USCGAUX)
U.S. Coast Guard Headquarters, Washington, D.C. 20590
The Coast Guard Auxiliary was created by an act of Congress some 36 years ago to assist the Coast Guard in promoting safety on the water. It's closely affiliated with the Coast Guard, though not actually a part of it. Auxiliarists are all civilian volunteers.

The Auxiliary has three basic functions: teaching boating courses for the pleasure-boating public; conducting Courtesy Motorboat Examinations; and conducting miscellaneous operations such as search and rescue, chart updating, regatta and safety patrolling, and other Coast Guard operational support missions.

Probably the most noted of the Auxiliary's activities is the Courtesy Motorboat Examination, which if passed wins the boat a USCGAUX "Seal of Safety" decal—very good for discouraging Coast Guard BOSDETS (Boating Safety Detachments) from routinely stopping and boarding your boat for equipment checks. Quite often you'll find a couple Auxiliarists, set up with a card table at some popular dock or marina, on call for anyone who would like his boat examined. If invited aboard, they'll check for the required safety equipment, lights, ventilation system, fire extinguishers, and so forth for the size of the boat. If all goes well, they'll stick a decal on the windshield. If it doesn't, they'll present a list of things to be corrected. But if that happens to you don't worry, they won't report you to the Coast Guard or any other law enforcement agency; the program's a positive one designed for your benefit only.

Membership in the Auxiliary is open to any United States citizen who is 17 years or older and who owns at least 25% interest in a boat, aircraft, or amateur radio station, or who has other skills important to the Auxiliary program. Applicants are usually enrolled as Conditional Members until they pass the examination for Basic Qualification which means displaying practical knowledge of boating and boat handling. If you meet the age and ownership or skill requirements, it's certainly worth joining up for the opportunity for advanced boating training, for being of service to your fellow boatmen, and contacts in boating circles. Get full details, contact the Auxiliary Flotilla or Coast Guard unit nearest you. Or write the above address for pamphlets on the Auxiliary and its programs. Ask for *This Is The Seal of Safety, Free Boating Courses,* or *A Helping Hand—The Coast Guard Auxiliary,* or *Federal Requirements For Recreational Boats.* Also available in limited quantities is the *Auxiliary Bibliography of Publications, CG-336-1,* containing listing of boating safety literature and material.

U.S. POWER SQUADRONS (USPS)
P.O. Box 30423, Raleigh, N.C. 27612
Founded in 1914, the USPS is a little older than the Coast Guard Auxiliary, but both have the common objectives of promoting safe boating and instructing the public in boat handling, navi-

gation, seamanship, first aid, and so forth. USPS, however, is more in-volved in education than anything else. USPS is a national fraternity of boatmen with over 86,000 members in some 442 squadrons throughout the U.S. Membership is by invitation only after successful completion of their Basic Boating course. *The Ensign* is a 56-page monthly magazine published for members. See page 253 for more in-formation on courses offered.

STATE BOATING AUTHORITIES

Each state has its own boating authority set up to administer registra-tion and numbering regulations and to provide the public with boating info for the state, which includes charts, pamphlets, marina and ramp lists, and so forth. If you haven't contacted your state's department, it would be worth doing so just to familiarize yourself with what's going on.

Alabama - Dept. of Cons., State Admin. Bldg., Montgomery 36104
Alaska - Com. of Public Safety, Pouch "N", Capitol Bldg., Juneau 99801
Arizona - Game & Fish Dept., P.O. Box 9099, Phoenix 85023
Arkansas - Game & Fish Com., State Capitol Grounds, Little Rock 72201
California - Dept. of Navigation & Ocean Development, 1416 9th St., Sacramento 95814
Colorado - Div. of Parks & Outdoor Recreation, 1845 Sherman, Denver 80203
Connecticut - Dept. of Environmental Protection, State Office Bldg., Hartford 06115
Delaware - Dept. of Natural Resources & Environmental Control, D St., Dover 19901
Dist. of Columbia - Metropolitan Police Dept., Harbor Section, SOD, 550 Waterfront St., S.W., Washington 20024
Florida - Dept. of Natural Resources, Larson Bldg., Tallahassee 32304
Georgia - Game & Fish Div., Dept. of Natural Resources, Rm. 707-C, Trinity-Washington Bldg., Atlanta 30334
Hawaii - Dept. of Trans., Harbors Div., 79 S. Nimitz Hwy., Honolulu 96813
Idaho - Dept. of Law Enforcement, P.O. Box 34, Boise 83731
Illinois - Cons. Dept., 400 S. Spring St., Springfield 62706
Indiana - Dept. of Natural Resources, 606 State Office Bldg., Indianapolis 46204
Iowa - State Cons. Com., 300 4th St., Des Moines 50319
Kansas - Forestry, Fish & Game Com., Box 1028, Pratt 67124
Kentucky - Div. of Water Enforcement, State Office Bldg., Frankfort 40601
Louisiana - Wildlife & Fisheries Com., 400 Royal St., New Orleans 70130
Maine - Bur. of Watercraft Registration & Safety, State Office Bldg., Augusta 04330
Maryland - Dept. of Natural Resources, Tawes State Office Bldg., Taylor Ave., Annapolis 21404
Massachusetts - Marine & Recreation Div., 64 Causeway St., Boston 02114
Michigan - Dept. of Natural Resources, Stevens T. Mason Bldg., Lansing 48926
Minnesota - Dept. of Natural Resources, 350 Centennial Blvd., St. Paul 55155
Mississippi - Boat & Water Safety Com., Rm. 403, Robert E. Lee Bldg., Jackson 39201
Missouri - Div. of Water Safety, P.O. Box 603, Jefferson City 65101
Montana - State Fish & Game Dept., Law Enforcement Div., Helena 59601
Nebraska - State Game & Parks Com., 2200 N. 3rd St., Lincoln 68503
Nevada - Fish & Game Dept., P.O. Box 10678, Reno 89510
New Hampshire - Div. of Safety Services, 85 Loudon Rd., Concord 03301
New Jersey - Dept. of Environmental Protection, P.O. Box 1889, Trenton 08625
New Mexico - Park & Recreation Com., P.O. Box 1147, Santa Fe 87501
New York - Marine & Recreational Vehicles, South Mall, Albany 12223
North Carolina - Wildlife Resources Com., Albemarle Bldg., Raleigh 27611
North Dakota - State Game & Fish Dept., Bismarck 58501
Ohio - Dept. of Natural Resources, Fountain Square, Columbus 43224
Oklahoma - Dept. of Public Safety, Box 11415, Oklahoma City 73111
Oregon - State Marine Bd., 3000 Market St., N.E. No. 505, Salem 97310
Pennsylvania - Bur. of Waterways, Fish Com., 3532 Walnut St., P.O. Box 1673, Harrisburg 17120
Rhode Island - Dept. of Natural Resources, Veterans' Memorial Bldg., 83 Park St., Providence 02903
South Carolina - Wildlife & Marine Resources Dept., P.O. Box 12559, Charleston 29412
South Dakota - Dept. of Game, Fish & Parks, State Office Bldg. No. 1, Pierre 57501
Tennessee - Boating Div., P.O. Box 40747, Nashville 37204
Texas - Parks & Wildlife Dept., John H. Reagan Bldg., Austin 78701
Utah - Div. of Parks & Recreation, 1596 W. North Temple St., Salt Lake City 84116
Vermont - Marine Div., Dept. of Public Safety, Montpelier 05602
Virginia - Com. of Game & Inland Fisheries, P.O. Box 11104, Richmond 23230
Washington - State Parks & Recreation, P.O. Box 1128, Olympia 98504
West Virginia - Dept. of Natural Resources, State Office Bldg., 1800 E. Washington St., Charleston 25305
Wisconsin - Dept. of Natural Resources, P.O. Box 450, Madison 53701
Wyoming - Game & Fish Dept., P.O. Box 1589, Cheyenne 82001
Puerto Rico - Maritime Dept., Ports Authority, GPO Box 2829, San Juan 00936
Virgin Islands - Dept. of Cons. & Cultural Affairs, Charlotte Amalie, St. Thomas 00801

BOAT OWNERS ASSOCIATION OF THE U.S. (BOAT/US)
5261 Port Royal Rd., Springfield, Va. 22151

Ten years old and with 41,000 members, this is the American Auto-mobile Association of the boating world. They offer members a well-rounded batch of services including discounts on equipment and books, consumer protection ala Ralph Nader and representation of the interests of boat owners when our galloping government bureauc-racy threatens to sink their yachts. Recent problems attacked includ-ed the marine toilet farce and the attempt by the U.S. Coast Guard to stop documentation of pleasure yachts. BOAT/US also has marine fi-nancing and insurance programs for members only. I saved a good bit of cash in the purchase of two Optimus pressurized kerosene lanterns. However, I found their insurance rates to be excessive in my case. If

PERIODICALS

BOAT OWNERS BUYERS GUIDE
Frank T. Moss, Ed.
Annually - $2.50 - 365 p. il.

The most complete and comprehensive listing of source information for sailing and power boating available in the United States. It might even be better than the *Explorers Ltd. Source Book*—a helluva admission! *BOBG* or *Bob's Guide*, as it's known, includes listings, descriptions, and prices on all types of boats and water craft, engines and acces-sories, communication and electronic apparatus, navigation devices and instru-ments, hardware, fastenings, fittings, rope, cable, sails, rigging, paint, chemicals and maintenance supplies, anchors and mooring gear, deck and hull accessories, construction materials, kits, plans, tools, cabin and galley gear, clothing, baggy wrinkle, gilhikies, shoreline, doldrums, irons, cat's paws, mare's tails, kites and royals, lee shores and oh, oh's, architects, brokers and used gams, charters and boat rentals, schools and instruction, financing, hedges against acts of God, publications, organizations, surveying, transportation, and special services (of course). Addresses of where to get all this stuff is included, set in three point type.
From: Bob's Guide—Yachting, 50 West 44th St., New York, N.Y. 10036

YACHTING
Marcia Wiley, Ed.
Monthly - $12/yr. - $1.50/issue - 270 p. il.

Yachting has held out against changing its body type face to a "modern" style, which is why you might think it looks old fashioned compared to *Motor Boat-ing* or *Sail*. Its editorial slant is pretty conservative too, although they are con-tinuing to expand their already broad coverage of the racing scene. If you're primarily interested in what's happening in sailing competition circles, *Yachting's* got it. Of secondary importance, but still good, is the coverage of practical boating, ship's business, main-tenance, navigation, cruising info, and technical data. Book reviews are done by individuals and are fair; new products and techniques, o.k.; hardly any current nav data (chart, sailing directions, coast pilot, and notice to mariners-type stuff), though there is good cover-age of the Washington scene and boating legislation; very good brokerage section; and an excellent classifieds department just reeking with crew positions—needed and available—used boats, charters, equipment, and much more. Each January issue of *Yachting* covers the major boat show (new) products, with descriptions, specifications, and much visual material. *Yachting* is nice, but it would not appear to be a good first choice magazine for the cruising man.
From: Yachting, 50 West 44th St., New York, N.Y. 10036

you have a boat and are pretty active with it, it would be worth the investment to join. If you don't have one, BOAT/US would be a good place to take your first step into the boating world and begin to col-lect, at good prices, some of the basic books. Annual dues are $17. Definitely worth checking into.

CANADA

CANADIAN COAST GUARD (CCG)
Transport Canada
Ottawa, Ontario, Canada K1A 0N7

CCG is the federal boating regulatory body for Canada, and will sup-ply you with information directly or refer you to other federal or provincial departments. CCG publishes a free *Boating Safety Guide,* which might be worth requesting for the information it has on Canadi-an boating practices.

MOTOR BOATING AND SAILING

Jeff Hammond, Ed.
Monthly - $10/yr. - $1.25/issue - 160 p. il.

With a circulation of 156,000, *MB&S* has to have something to offer subscribers. Color presentation is pleasant and effective and makes for quick and easy reading. Articles are oriented toward applied boating with equal treatment for power and sailing yachts. Each issue carries something on cruising, boat handling, maintenance, marine electronics, new charts and navigational publications, and ship's business. "Boatkeeper's Notebook" by Jack Dillon contained in the "yellow pages" in the center of each issue is worth the price of the whole magazine. This section is printed on heavy paper and is suitable for punching and binding into a notebook. *MB&S* is in the consumer's game with its monthly "Product Log." The brokerage section has improved but still isn't quite as good as *Yachting's*, nor is their classified section as good either. The January number covers the majority of new gear and boats that'll be on the market for the coming year—runs about 400 pages.
From: Motor Boating & Sailing, P.O. Box 544, New York, N.Y. 10019

SAIL

Keith Taylor, Ed.
Monthly - $12/yr. - $1.25/issue - 200 p. il.

Sail is one hundred per cent devoted to sailing with nary the smell of a stink pot on one of its pages. Regular departments include "Ocean Racing and Ocean Cruising," "Weather," "Navigation," "Sail Trimming," "Learning to Sail," "Hull," "Construction," and "Electronics." Really a broad spread of technical and practical information. Good features, too, on history, cruising, boats, and personal experiences. Artwork, though all black and white, is very well done, particularly graphs and technical drawings. Not a whole lot of news-type material; book reviews are limited (one or two per issue), though very comprehensive; new products coverage is fair; brokerage and classifieds departments are excellent. *Sail* is published by the Institute for the Advancement of Sailing.
From: Sail, 126 Blaine Ave., Marion, Ohio 43302

NATIONAL FISHERMAN

David R. Getchell, Ed.
Monthly - $8/yr. - 75¢/issue - 40 p. il.

NF has to be about the best thing that ever happened on the American boating scene. Although much is dedicated to commercial fishing, there is considerable information on legislation, Coast Guard activities, marine history, seafood cooking and a delightful column on "God's Tugboat." Along with the *AYRS Journal* and *The Woodenboat Magazine*, *NF* contains much information for amateur boatbuilders. Technical Editor John Gardner writes one or two longish articles each month on such, and building plans for small boats are often included. International Marine publisher Roger Taylor supplies an article in each issue on older yachts complete with lines drawings— another rarity in the modern boating press. You'll find many ads for custom-designed sailing and power vessels and a goodly number of classifieds for used boats and marine equipment. There is a 16-page centerfold on books and marine prints available from International Marine with excellent descriptions of most of the best marine books in print.
From: National Fisherman, 21 Elm St., Camden, Maine 04843

CRUISING WORLD

Murray Davis, Ed.
Monthly - $9/yr. - $1/issue - 105 p. il.

At last a magazine solely for the cruising sailor! The former editor of *Sail* has done a beautiful job with this publication. A typical issue contains 15 or so articles on all aspects of cruising including navigation, seamanship, rigging, trailering, coast-hopping and ocean-crossing. Special problems facing cruising people are covered, such as corrosion, dinghies, anchoring, engines, radios and the costs of cruising, plus Murray's wife, Barbara, writes a feature on the galley. *CW* publishes

some of the best reviews of marine books, and each November the 170-page *Sailboat Show Annual* appears in place of a regular number. Classifieds are good, but not yet as comprehensive as the older magazines. Highly recommended for both the cruising man and those with just a gleam in their eye.
From: Cruising World Pubs., P.O. Box 734, Manchester, N.H. 03105

THE WOODENBOAT

W. Lyman Phillips, Ed.
Bimonthly - $9/yr. - $1.75/issue - 76 p. il.

For devotees of the only renewable natural resource we have—wood— this magazine is a real delight. The black-and-white artwork is great. Although some articles on modern yachts are run, emphasis is given to those glorious sailing yachts of yesteryear and in many cases modern reproductions or restorations of same. There are occasional articles on boatbuilding techniques in wood, scantling rules and specialized tools. Lines drawings are often included. All aspects of wooden boat construction and ownership are covered including the restoration of salvaged hulls, often of considerable historical interest and value.
From: The Woodenboat Magazine, P.O. Box 268, Brooksville, Maine 04617

MULTIHULLS

Charles Chiodi, Ed.
Quarterly - $6/yr. - $1.50/issue - 80 p. il.

A fascinating magazine for those attracted to the many advantages of trimaran, catamaran and proa sailing. *Multihulls* is well illustrated with many black-and-white photographs and drawings. Articles include cruising accounts, new designs, analyses of rating rules, building of multihulls and race news. "News Across the Country" features reports from over 20 multihull associations in the U.S. and abroad. The magazine organizes the World Multihull Symposium, the first of which was held in June, 1976 in Toronto. Well worth subscribing to for those who sail one-man racing catamarans as well as cruising catamarans and trimarans. The only U.S. magazine now in print on the subject.
From: Multihulls, 91 Newbury Ave., No. Quincy, Mass. 02171

SOUNDINGS

John P. Turner, Pub.
Monthly - $5/yr. - 50¢/issue - 80 p. il.

This is in newspaper format with a vast number of used sailboats advertised—more than any other periodical we've come across. Some ads for hardware, equipment, nav instruments, plans and books and a few articles are included. The latter are on the light side concerning boating news, legislation, galley department and people. Emphasis is on the New England scene.
From: Soundings, Box 210, Wethersfield, Conn. 06109

PRACTICAL BOAT OWNER

Denny Desoutter, Ed.
Monthly - $18/yr. - 200 p.

This is a unique how-to-do-it yachting magazine. Our British cousins seem to be ahead again, as there is nothing remotely like this periodical in the U.S. Emphasis is on maintaining your own boat with much information on amateur boatbuilding, diesel engine conversions, renovating old hulls, making boat cushions, DIY electronic speedometer and rope fenders among the many topics covered. Plans are occasionally published as well as frequent evaluations of European yachts. Classified ads are very extensive.
From: Practical Boat Owner, Hatfield House, 54 Stamford St., London, England SE1 9LX

other periodicals

BOATING
   P.O. Box 2773, Boulder, Colo. 80302
RUDDER
   Fawcett Bldg., Greenwich, Conn. 06830
SAILING
   125 E. Main St., Port Washington, Wis. 53074
SEA
   1499 Monrovia Ave., Newport Beach, Calif. 92663
YACHTSMAN
   P.O. Box 819, Rio Vista, Calif. 94571

BASIC SAILING
M. B. George
1965 - 112 p. il. - $2.50

If you want a comprehensive elementary text on handling a boat under sail, this is the one. The presentation is systematic, and through the extensive use of photographs and diagrams it's almost like being aboard with a tutor. Discussions include types of sailboats, parts of the boat and sails, theory of how a boat sails, preparing to sail, different positions of sailing and why they're used, things to look for while sailing to get the "feel" of how well she's performing, setting and working different types of sails from spinnaker to storm canvas—breaking new ones in, caring for them, furling, and stowing; handling a capsize, coiling and taking care of rope, and adjusting standing rigging for best performance. Also a section on handling multihull boats. The nice thing about George is that he keeps it simple and to the point. There's a lot more that he could have included in the book, but frankly, the book is quite adequate as is for learning the rudiments of sailing.
From: Motor Boating & Sailing Books, Box 2319, FDR Station, New York, N.Y. 10022

HAND, REEF AND STEER—A PRACTICAL HANDBOOK ON SAILING
Richard Henderson
1965 - 95 p. il. - $7.95

Intended for beginners, this is probably the best book available for young people new to sailing. With the author's very clear sketches, it is easy for young and old to understand the basics of sailing and seamanship. I have no patience with those who say that sailing is just a matter of "getting out there." In my opinion, learning to become a good sailor is a matter of 50% experience and 50% study. This book is a good place to begin.
From: Henry Regnery Co., 114 W. Illinois St., Chicago, Ill. 60610

THE GLENANS SAILING MANUAL
Philippe Harle
1967 - 446 p. il. - $10

Textbook for the Glenans School in Brittany, this one is considered the most complete single volume on the care and handling of small sail boats and the scientific principles of their operation. This would be the book to move up to after *Basic Sailing.*
From: John De Graff, 34 Oak Ave., Tuckahoe, N.Y. 10707

TEXT-BOOK OF SEAMANSHIP
Stephen B. Luce
1898, rep. 1950 - 720 p. il. - $10

A reprinted 1898 manual of seamanship, long a necessary reference for the naval and merchant services. Contains much general knowledge, valuable technical information and interesting sea lore.
From: Cornell Maritime Press, Box 109, Cambridge, Md. 21613

SAILING ILLUSTRATED
Pat Royce
1971, 5th ed. - 352 p. il. - $4

Royce *touches* on just about every aspect of sailing in sort of a ramble of hints, tips, and methods, accompanied by many, many drawings, graphs, and charts. If anything, it's Pat's excellent annotated artwork that makes the book. The text is randomly organized with a lot of good information, but likewise a lot of jaw. *Sailing Illustrated* might be called a light reference book.
From: Nourse Publishing Co., Box 398, Old Country Rd., San Carlos, Calif. 94070

YACHTMAN'S OMNIBUS
H. A. Calahan
1968 - 1000 p. il. - $9.95

This is Calahan's classic work, which up until the late 1950's graced the bookshelf of anybody who claimed to be a serious small boat sailor. The *Omnibus* is a collection of three of Calahan's earlier books: *Learning to Sail*, *Learning to Race*, and *Learning to Cruise*, and though many new books have come on the scene with the rise in popularity of boating, and sailing in particular, Calahan's *Omnibus* is still very much to be recommended. First of all, it's the only book I know of that has a good thorough coverage of the total sailing picture. You have to learn the rudiments, and after that you either go the racing route or the cruising route or both; there is nowhere else to go. Second, it has something that seems to be missing today in many a non-fiction book that those of the 40's and 50's had. The easiest way to explain it is to think of a log cabin in the wilderness without a fireplace. Well, Calahan's book is like a log cabin with a fireplace. Do you follow me? There's not a helluva lot of photos or drawings (200 in 1000 pages), but the text is readable, interesting, and instructive. Personally, this is the first book I would read if I were just getting into sailing and cruising (in fact, it was the first).
—Al Perrin (1972).
From: The Macmillan Co., Order Dept., Front and Brown Sts., Riverside, N.J. 08075

SEA SENSE
Richard Henderson
1972 - 302 p. il. - $15

This is probably the best of several books by the same author. He tells us what to look for in hull design and construction as well as how to prepare for sea, handle emergencies, and heavy-weather seamanship in both sail and power yachts.
From: International Marine Pub. Co., 21 Elm St. Camden, Maine 04843

THE BOATMAN'S HANDBOOK
Tom Bottomley
1972 - $3.95

This almanac of useful boating information covers emergency procedures, safety afloat, seamanship, rules of the road, piloting and navigation, weather, federal and state boating laws, marine electronics, useful tables, organizations, schools (sailing, boating, navigation), marine museums, etc. complete with addresses. Really a nice source book of boating data. Maintenance section includes full-size illustrations showing bolt, screw, and nail types. Provisions have even been made for the boat owner to record all critical boat data and names and addresses of service and repair personnel.
From: Motor Boating & Sailing Books, Box 2319, FDR Station, New York, N.Y. 10022

THE KEDGE ANCHOR
William N. Brady
1879, rep. 1950 - 720 p. il. - $11.95

This is a facsimile reprint edition of the classic handbook on seamanship originally published in 1879. It covers 544 numbered topics from the launching of a ship to the recipe for making black varnish, to turning in deadeyes, to taking in a lower studding sail—"a blwin' fresh." Definitely recommended for bosuns of barques and brigantines.
From: Library Editions Ltd., 200 W. 72nd St., New York, N.Y. 10023

SENSIBLE CRUISING DESIGNS
L. Francis Herreshoff
1973 - 393 p. il. - $20

This is a really great book with complete descriptions of some of the most famous of the Herreshoff-designed yachts interwoven with Herreshoff's practical and earthy comments on boatbuilding, cruising equipment, floating gin palaces, and rigging. His preference for the cedar bucket over the modern marine toilet is best described by his quotation: "They bored a hole below her line to let the water out,

But more and more, with awful roar, the water in did spout." Complete building instructions and construction drawings are given for nine boats including *Rozinante, H-28, Meadowlark, Golden Ball, Nereia, Mobjack* and *Marco Polo.* An additional 150 pages are devoted to a portfolio of Herreshoff designs including his famous *Tioga.*
From: International Marine Pub. Co., 21 Elm St., Camden, Maine 04843

BOOKS

PILOTING, SEAMANSHIP AND SMALL BOAT HANDLING
Charles F. Chapman
1971, 49th ed. - 638 p. il. - $8.95

Chapman's, as this book is popularly called, has been around since the early 1900's as one of the foremost texts on boating for the powerboatman. It's usually updated about every two years and covers just about everything you need to know to operate a power boat safely and efficiently. As a matter of fact, it's such a good book that the only two really big boatmen's organizations, the U.S. Power Squadron and the U.S. Coast Guard Auxiliary, use *Chapman's* as one of the texts for boating courses they offer. One reason is that it is current and it's kept that way by the backup facilities of the *Motor Boating & Sailing* editorial staff. For in-depth coverage of boating laws and regulations, equipment, rules of the road, lights, weather, the compass and its errors and use, charts, aids to navigation, coast navigation: piloting, dead reckoning, currents and tides, and the operation, maneuvering and seamanship of power cruisers, both single and twin screw—you couldn't find a better one-source book of information. All your government requirements for boats (up to 65') and licensing of personnel are included. There are 2,000 lbs. of info in this 4½-lb. book.
From: Motor Boating & Sailing Books, Box 2319, FDR Station, New York, N.Y. 10022

HEAVY WEATHER SAILING
K. Adlard Coles
1968 - 304 p. il. - $12.50

A collection of experiences of yachtsmen and yachts caught up in extreme storms, gales, and hurricanes with thoughts on the best maneuvering techniques for survival. Analysis of weather conditions and sea conditions produced by a storm, with sound life-saving advice. Written in first rate narrative form.
From: John De Graff, Inc., 34 Oak Ave., Tuckahoe, N.Y. 10707

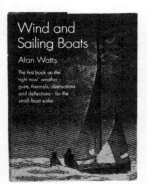

WIND AND SAILING BOATS
Alan Watts
1967 - 224 p. il. - $10

Based on extensive scientific research by meteorologist Alan Watts, this book offers a treasure of information about the micro-structure of the wind, the very small or very localized changes in wind speed and direction that are so important to the performance of a sailing vessel. After reading this one, you should have the ability to anticipate wind-shifts, gusts and lulls, and relate them to course and sail trim decisions to get the most out of your boat. Very well-illustrated with diagrams and meteorological photographs.
From: World Publishing Co., Order Dept., 2231 W. 110th St., Cleveland, Ohio 44102

EAGLE SEAMANSHIP: SQUARE RIGGER SAILING
Lt. William Norton
1969 - 172 p. il. - $5.95

This is the modern book on old fashioned seamanship covering the management and operation of square riggers—the *Eagle* in particular. It describes the rig and functions of the Coast Guard Academy's barque with details on sailing orders, maneuvering methods, and techniques under normal and adverse conditions. It's a great owner/operator's manual for everyone who has a ship of this type. Complete with diagrams, photos, and instructions.
From: Lippincott, East Washington Sq., Philadelphia, Pa. 19105

RECREATIONAL BOATING GUIDE CG-340
U.S. Coast Guard
1971 - 93 p. il. - 60¢
S/N 5012-0056

This is a must for every sailor's reference library. It covers numbering requirements; minimum equipment requirements for the different classes of motorboats (which includes all auxiliary sailboats); operating responsibilities and what the Guard will do to you if you screw up, accident reports, and data on Coast Guard patrols; aids to navigation; safety hints and tips; requirements for boats under straight sail, oars, or paddles; various emergency procedures including distress signaling and use of the marine radiotelephone; plus a little background on the U.S. Coast Guard Auxiliary and their courtesy motorboat examinations. This is the legal dope from the guys who back it up.
From: Sup. of Doc., U.S. Gov. Printing Off., Washington, D.C. 20402

THIS BUSINESS OF BOATING
Elwell B. Thomas
1949 - 320 p. il. - $2.50

Though a little dated, much of the information in this book is just as good today as it was yesterday. Chapters include all aspects of buying and selling a boat; legal and business considerations on boat and ship operation; dealing with architects, boatyards, charter parties, the government, and so forth; yacht club organization, marina management, and the ins and outs of salvage. Really a thorough coverage of the whole business of boating.
From: Cornell Maritime Press, Box 109, Cambridge, Md. 21613

SEA SURVIVAL: A MANUAL
Dougal Robertson
1975 - 148 p. il. - $15

A practical book on staying alive after a yacht sinking. For those concerned with the worst the sea can offer, this is a good book to have although it is the stuff of which nightmares are made.
From: International Marine Pub. Co., 21 Elm St., Camden, Maine 04843

THE MARINER'S CATALOG
Volume I - 1973 - 192 p. il. - $4.95 - David R. Getchell, Ed.
Volume II - 1974 - 191 p. il. - $4.95 - David R. Getchell, Ed.
Volume III - 1975 - 192 p. il. - $5.95 - George Putz and Peter Spectre, Eds.

A wonderful series of where-to-get-it "catalogs" without advertising and well recommended for all interested in boatbuilding, models, gear and fittings, tools, engines, sources of plans, fishing equipment, and a host of related topics. From the people who publish *National Fisherman.*
From: International Marine Pub. Co., 21 Elm St., Camden, Maine 04843

BOAT OWNER'S LEGAL MANUAL
William P. Crawford
1975 - 102 p. il. - $5.95 (pb)

Chapters include buying a boat, marine insurance, financing, safety and water pollution control. Good bit of info if you're in the market for a new boat.
From: International Marine Pub. Co., 21 Elm St., Camden, Maine 04843

OFFSHORE SAILING

IMP's
Book
Catalog

INTERNATIONAL MARINE PUBLISHING CO. (IMP)
21 Elm St., Camden, Me. 04843

IMP gets a ★★★★ rating, Jack! Their catalog (really a newspaper) is the most interesting, the saltiest, and the best laid out of all we've seen—in true Bristol fashion, sir. They leave nothing to be desired in the descriptions of their titles, and last but not least, Roger Taylor, who is chief honcho at IMP, lists only the best books on commercial fishing, merchant shipping, boat building and design (mainly small craft), practical boating and seamanship, sailing, and maritime history—no garbage. IMP is associated with *National Fisherman*, and you can get the book supplement (catalog) as part of the *National Fisherman* or by dropping a card to Roger and requesting the book supplement by itself.

CORNELL MARITIME PRESS, INC.
Box 109, Cambridge, Md. 21613

Cornell covers the complete marine scene, though it is more oriented to the merchant service and shipping than to pleasure boating. Included amongst its more than 150 titles are books on cargo and ocean shipping, marine insurance, seamanship, deck officer's guides, ship's business, specimen examinations for merchant officer license tests, navigation, meteorology, marine engineering (all aspects), naval architecture and ship construction, marine history and nautical lore, marine encyclopedias and dictionaries, small craft design and boatbuilding, knotting, macrame, cordage and wire rope work, and hard hat and scuba diving. If you're serious about boating, it would be worth your while to have their 30-page catalog on hand for reference. Books are very well described.

UNITED STATES NAVAL INSTITUTE
Annapolis, Md. 21402

Contrary to popular belief, the Institute doesn't just publish books of interest to Navy personnel. As a matter of fact, they cover navigation, naval architecture, engineering, maritime history, and a number of subjects that are not at all nautical. Here are some of the titles that are circulating around the yachting mob: *Dutton's Navigation and Piloting, Heavy Weather Guide, Sail and Power, Piloting and Dead Reckoning, Polar Operations* (the skipper's handbook on all aspects of seamanship, navigation, and survival in the latitudes where dem big ice cubes is), and *Marine Fouling and Its Prevention*. Ask for their latest catalog, you'll find a lot of good reading.

CARAVAN-MARITIME BOOKS
87–06 168th Place, Jamaica, N.Y. 11432

If you've been looking for a hard-to-find or very old nautical book of any type—history, technical, biography, or what have you, Caravan-Maritime would be a good place to check. Periodically, they issue a 30-page list of the titles on hand giving the author, title, a brief commentary, and the price of the book. The lists are available on request. Caravan is also in the book-buying business and will purchase entire collections or single items on maritime subjects.

BOAT/US
5261 Port Royal Rd., Springfield, Va. 22151

See page 248 for details on this association for boat owners. A large book catalog is published for members only, offering some of the best discounts available.

ROBERT & SUSAN PYKE (BOOKS)
2 Beaufort Villas, Claremont Rd., Bath, Avon, England BA1 6LY

Prices for used books are less in England than here, and there are considerable savings in asking for quotations on titles of interest. Write Bob and Susan for a copy of their catalog.

MOTOR BOATING & SAILING BOOKS
Box 2319, FDR Station, New York, N.Y. 10022

This is a split-off from *Motor Boating and Sailing* magazine. Their stable consists mainly of small craft design and construction titles and quite a number of plans for the amateur builder. The big seller, of course, is *Piloting, Seamanship and Small Boat Handling*. A post card will get you their 18-page catalog.

NAUTICAL BOOK SERVICE
2825 Newport Blvd., Newport Beach, Calif. 92660

A very good selection of all types of nautical books including government navigation tables. The major section of their catalog gives only title, author, date of publication, and price. No description. There're two arrangements: alphabetical and by subject matter. A small section in the back lists some of the more popular books with description and cover photo. You can get their 37-page catalog for $1.

KARL F. WEDE, INC.
RFD 3, Box 344, Saugerties, N.Y. 12477

Karl, who is an old friend of Explorers, Ltd., is in the same business as Caravan-Maritime, except that he doesn't stop with old and rare marine books. Karl has an extensive collection of ship models, scrimshaw, old binnacles, cannon, navigation instruments, and so forth. Really a fantastic collection, which makes his shop in Saugerties virtually a museum—except it's all for sale, and dear! He buys books, charts, and marine antiques, so if you have got something in the attic you're not interested in, he might be. If you'd like to get a good idea of what his collection is like, request a free copy of Karl's latest illustrated catalog. It's updated periodically as new things come in and others are sold.

THE DOLPHIN BOOK CLUB
Book-of-the-Month Club, Camp Hill, Pa. 17012

Well worth joining for its book discounts. Watch the yachting magazines for their advertisements. New members are offered the choice of any three of a large number of boating books for only $3 plus handling. Recent choices have included *Dutton's Navigation & Piloting, The Ocean Sailing Yacht, Sensible Cruising Designs,* and *A Cruising Guide to the Lesser Antilles,* among others.

STANFORD MARITIME LTD.
12 Long Acre, London, England WC2E 9LP

Books on navigation, racing, engines, electronics, sailing and cruising, charts of United Kingdom and English Channel waters. Free catalog.

SCHOOLS and INSTRUCTION

There are many groups around the country offering resident or correspondence instruction on various aspects of boating. We've listed in this section those we're familiar with who teach general boating and sailing courses. Others teaching navigation, meteorology, and boat design are listed under Navigation and Naval Architecture.

There are no licensing requirements for the operation of private pleasure craft—yet, and one way to keep it this way is for every boatman to sign up voluntarily for the Coast Guard Auxiliary or U.S. Power Squadron courses. Even if you do have a good boating background, the certificate issued at the end of the course will be proof of this and make things a lot easier for you if boarded by the Guard or involved in an accident.

If you intend to carry passengers for hire on fishing or sailing excursions, you'll have to have a Motor Boat Operator's License. There are schools that will prepare you for this, but most people find after checking with the Coast Guard, which administers the examination for this license, that the study requirements are not that involved and can be handled on one's own.

A word about correspondence courses. There is no government agency or other regulatory body presently operating that can guarantee the quality of commercial mail-order courses (we're not speaking of university or college extension courses). And the well-known National Home Study Council is no exception. Even though it has set certain standards for its member schools, which include just about all correspondence institutions, it has no way of enforcing them. Indeed, the Council has compromised its position in several cases. If you're interested in the details ask the *New York Times* to send you a copy of the story they did on correspondence schools in the 31 May 1970 issue of the paper. With respect to the ones listed here, we've given all data we have and would certainly appreciate any input from those of you who are familiar with these schools, or others not listed, for use in the next edition of the *Source Book*.

Incidentally, for a fairly complete state by state listing of all types of boating schools and instruction, check the back part of *Boat Owners Buyers Guide*.

UNITED STATES POWER SQUADRONS (USPS)
P.O. Box 30423, Raleigh, N.C. 27612
USPS offers a free boating course to the general public covering the following subjects: boat handling under normal and adverse conditions, seamanship and common emergencies, rules of the road, aids to navigation, compass and chart familiarization, running lights and equipment, boat trailering, river boating, and the mariner's compass and piloting. To make it real easy for you, the Power Squadrons have provided for a toll-free number—800-243-6000—which can be called for information on these courses, class schedules, and the locations of the one being given nearest you.

Members of the Power Squadron are eligible to take other boating courses offered by the USPS which include *Seamanship, Advanced Piloting, Junior Navigator, Navigator, Engine Maintenance, Marine Electronics, Sailing, Weather, Instruction Techniques* and *Instructional Aids*. All look to be excellent, and you can find out more about them by writing the above address.

U.S. COAST GUARD AUXILIARY
Commandant G-BAU
U.S. Coast Guard Headquarters, Washington, D.C. 20590
The Auxiliary conducts a wide range of boating safety courses—from in-depth courses for the serious skipper to shorter courses to get the novice off to a good start. There are courses for adults and for youths, courses for power boaters and for sailors. The price is right—free—except for a minimal charge for materials.

Boating Skills and Seamanship. Six to thirteen lessons. The first six lessons are the nucleus of the course and cover boat handling, boating laws, rules of the road, aids to navigation, safe boating techniques and sailor's terminology. Upon successful completion of the course, the student is awarded the respected "Basic Seamanship Certificate." Lessons seven through thirteen are optional, and one or more of these one-session classes may be offered at the conclusion of the first six lessons:

Charts and Compass. Marine charts, compass and basic piloting

Marine Engines. Basic theory on operation of internal combustion engines, inboard and outboard, including troubleshooting and maintenance suggestions

Marlinspike Seamanship. Instructions on uses and limitations of rope and lines aboard ship, including classroom practice on basic knots and splices

Introduction to Sailing. Handling of small sailboats

Weather. Introduction to factors affecting weather and what the sailor may expect under certain weather conditions

Marine Radiotelephone. Rules, regulations and proper marine communications procedures

Locks and Dams. River and canal navigation, with explanation of operation and use of locks and dams

Principles of Sailing. Seven-lesson course on basic sailboat handling, sailing terminology, lines and knots, rough weather procedures and handling emergency situations.

Basic Boating. Compact three-lesson course covering seamanship, aids to navigation, rules of the road, knots and safety techniques.

Skipper's Outboard Special. An excellent one-lesson starter course to give the novice or occasional boater an understanding of safety devices, boating equipment and potentially hazardous situations.

Introduction to Sailing. One-lesson course covering basics of handling sailboats (also offered as a BS & S lesson).

Young People's Boating Course. One-lesson course for 10-15-year-olds, featuring pupil participation in demonstrations.

First Aid for the Boatman. One-lesson course developed in cooperation with the American National Red Cross.

MASSACHUSETTS DEPT. OF ADULT EDUCATION
182 Tremont St., Boston, Mass. 02111
Here's a great correspondence course covering all aspects of boat handling. When you've finished it, you'll be fully prepared to sit for the U.S. Coast Guard's Motorboat Operator License examination. It's called "Small Boat Handling, Part 1 and 2," and consists of 20 lessons and examination (no college credits). Cost of the course is $68 for out-of-state students; a little less for those living in Massachusetts. Cost of textbooks runs about $10. Check with the above address for more information.

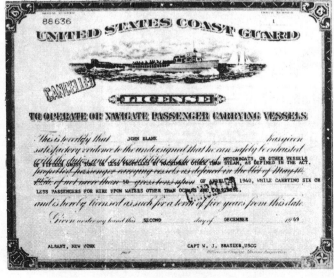

USCG Motorboat Operator's License

253

COAST NAVIGATION SCHOOL
418 East Canon Perdido, Santa Barbara, Calif. 93102

These people are best known for their celestial and coastwise navigation courses (discussed in the Nav subsection); however, they also offer two boating correspondence courses: Introduction to the Art of Sailing, $50, and Boating and Seamanship, 20 lessons, $140. Both are good, but overpriced compared to what you can get through the Auxiliary or the Power Squadron in a classroom. CNS also offers a course to prepare you for the Motorboat Operator License examination, $245, and one for the Third Officer, CW (coastwise) examination, $370.

CAPTAIN VAN'S NAUTICAL SCHOOLS
P.O. Box 66, Port Arthur, Tex. 77640

This is probably one of the oldest marine correspondence schools in the nation. It was started back in 1920 to assist merchant seamen and officers desiring to advance in grade with the more academic side of their profession—mathematics, spherical trigonometry, physics, mechanics, engineering, admiralty law, and so forth. All of these, in one degree or another, are required knowledge of masters, mates, engineers, and AB's. Here's a list of the courses offered:

	Tuition Fees
License Titles - Deck Officers:	
Master, Ocean, Unlimited Waters, Unlimited Tonnage, Inspected Vessels	$ 450.00
Master, Ocean Passenger Vessels of not over 300 gross tons, Inspected Vessels	450.00
Master, Ocean Oil Industry Vessels of not over 500 gross tons, Inspected	400.00
Ocean Towboat Operator, Waters of Oceans, Uninspected, tonnage limit 200 g/t	400.00
** Master, Oceans, Uninspected Ocean Vessels of less than 300 gross tons	400.00
Master, Limited Oceans, Freight & Towing Vessels of 1000 gross tons	400.00
Ocean Endorsement Navigation Course for Coastal Oil Industry & Towing Vessels	200.00
Master, Coastwise, Oil Industry and/or 1000 g/t Freight & Towing Vessels	300.00
Towboat Operator, Uninspected Vessels, Inland/C'wise/W'rivers/G'Lakes-(each)	250.00
Towboat Operator, two combined limited waters courses taken at same time	300.00
Upgrade, Ocean, Chief Mate, Second Mate, or Third Mate (Unlimited Tonnage)	400.00
Original Second Mate, Oceans Unlimited,	450.00
Mate, Coastwise, Oil and Mineral Vessels of not over 500 gross tons, Inspected	250.00
Mate, Coastal Waters, Freight & Towing Vessels of less than 1000 g/t Inspected	250.00
** Mate, Oceans, Uninspected Vessels of less than 300 gross tons	350.00
License Titles - Engineer Officers:	
Engineers, All Grades, Over 2000 Horsepower Steam and/or Motor	$ 400.00
Engineers, All Grades, 2000 Horsepower and Less, Steam and /or Motor	350.00
** Engineers, All Grades, Uninspected Motor Vessels	300.00
Motorboat Operators of Small Motor Passenger Carrying vessels of 100 g/t or less:	
Basic Motorboat Operator License (6 passenger/15 gross tons) Inland or Coastal	$ 50.00
Inland Operator (Limited to 100 gross tons/No specified passenger limits) Inland	75.00
Ocean Operator(100 miles out/100 gross tons/No specified passenger limits) Ocean	100.00
Miscellaneous Short Courses for Certificates, License Renewal & Computer Navigation - Radar:	
Captain Van's Short Course on Coastal Navigation with the SR-50 Pocket Calculator	$ 25.00
Captain Van's Radar, or Loran, License Endorsement Exam Prep-Courses	75.00
Special License Renewal, Rapid Radar, Pollution, and Rules Road Exam Prep-Kit	50.00
Tankerman, Able Bodied Seaman, and QMED Certificates - pre-exam courses (each)	75.00

**NOTE: "Inspected Vessel Licenses" are good on all "Uninspected Vessels" (within the restrictions, if any, on your "Inspected Vessel" license). Don't fall into the "Dead End" trap of going for an 'Uninspected Vessel' license...they can get you into a "Dead End" corner... The new "Towboat License" is "Uninspected" but, right now, there is no other way for the Towboatman to go...So...if you have a choice... ALWAYS...shoot for the Inspected Vessel License...! Remember...The very top-of-the-heap is the Inspected Vessel, Unlimited Waters, Unlimited Tonnage Licenses...and in the Engineroom it is Inspected Steam or Motor, Any Horsepower.

If you'll drop Capt. John Vandegrift, Sr. a card, He'll be glad to send you his catalog, which gives a complete description of the Coast Guard's requirements for a Motorboat Operator License with its various endorsements, and other officer's licenses. His literature is the best source of orientation information on this we've come across (other than going straight to the Coast Guard and requesting their free books: *Rules and Regulations for Licensing and Certificating of Merchant Marine Personnel, CG-191* and *Rules and Regulations for Manning of Vessels, CG-268).*

CARIBBEAN SAILING YACHTS LTD. (CSY)
Box 491, Tenafly, N.J. 07670

Primarily a charter yacht firm with locations in the Virgin Islands and the Grenadines, CSY also offers sailing and cruising lessons at their marinas. They have a yacht leasing program where they handle all the details of chartering (leasing) your yacht, in your absence, if you purchase the yacht they specify and equip her to their rigorous charter specifications. For those contemplating building or buying a large yacht to sail the world, it might be a good idea to charter first to see how the realities of sailing jibe with pre-conceived notions of loafing in the sun.

ANNAPOLIS SAILING SCHOOL
P.O. Box 14414, St. Petersburg, Fla. 33733

Annapolis Sailing School does operate out of Annapolis, but only during the summer; St. Petersburg is their year-round headquarters.

They also have a set-up at Key Largo and one in the Virgin Islands. Sailing instruction offered ranges from a two-day weekend introductory course aboard your own private 34' auxiliary sloop—a Carib 34. Here several boats go on an excursion at one time with an "instructor" vessel. During the day the instructors sail with the students, and in the evening at anchoring, they move aboard their own boat. Other courses include a two-day class on handling auxiliaries and a five-day cruising course. Schedules and locations of classes—Chesapeake Bay, Tampa Bay, Biscayne Bay, or the Virgin Islands—are pretty flexible and can be tailored to individual parties. Arrangements for lodgings during the course are made by the school unless you'll be living aboard. Course fees, which do not include lodging expenses, range from $85 to $558 per person depending on the course selected and the number of people in the party. Literature and full details are available from the above address.

AMERICAN SAILING COUNCIL
537 Steamboat Rd., Greenwich, Conn. 06830

This is a division of the National Association of Engine and Boat Manufacturers, which can supply free sailing movies, data on organizing a sailing instruction course, general sailing information, and literature on class boats; and for those desiring to locate a sailing school in their vicinity (rather than starting one), a complete listing of all the sailing schools in the country.

Schooner *Westward*

SEA EDUCATION ASSOCIATION (SEA)
P.O. Box 6, Woods Hole, Mass. 02543

This non-profit, educational group operates a 100' steel stays'l schooner, the *Westward* (sailing out of the East), which goes to sea on contract oceanographic assignments. This isn't anything unusual; however, the neat thing is that *you* can join her as a student member of the crew. SEA runs about six expeditions a year averaging a month each in summer and two in winter. The vessel is staffed by professional seamen and scientists, and manned by 20 oceanographic apprentices 16 years or older (average age runs more like 20). Students are instructed in oceanography, seamanship, navigation, and ship handling during the voyage, while assisting in the research work. We weren't able to get details on student requirements or the tuition fees, but financial aid is available in some cases. Write 'em. They've got a grand program, and we hope to hell they can keep it financed.

HARRY LUNDEBERG SCHOOL OF SEAMANSHIP
Piney Point, Md. 20674

The Lundeberg School is a cooperative venture between the Seafarers International Union and the operators of privately owned American Flag vessels under contract with the union. Its purpose is to train young lads in the ways of the sea and possibly a career in the merchant service. The school owns several large sailing vessels including the 130' gaff schooner *Richard Henry Dana*, the 128' Grand Banks schooner *Freedom*, plus a number of motor vessels—one in particular of note is the 257' yacht *Dauntless*, formerly the *Delphine* of Great Lakes registry. Students attending the school are instructed in seamanship, navigation, ship handling, and engineering, and pay no fees of any kind. In fact, they receive a cash spending allowance in addition to room, board, and clothing. If you're interested in the merchant service, this might be a good place to start.

BOATS

The prospective boat owner has two ways of getting a boat. He can buy it or build it. In buying he has the choice of new or used, and in building, the choice of starting from scratch or working from a kit. Regardless of which route is taken, however, he should familiarize himself with boats, their design, the materials used in construction, and the general costs and time involved in working on a boat—whether to build it or just to get it back in condition. A very good book which covers much of this is Brewer and Betts' *Understanding Boat Design*, $3.95 (discussed under Naval Architecture which is a

little further on).

Learning about boats is only part of it. The business and legal aspects of buying or building are important, too, and can affect your decision of how to go. Since there's no handy source of info on this like Brewer and Betts' book, we've gone into it here in the *Source Book*. Following is data on surveying, purchasing, insurance, and so forth, and under Naval Architecture & Design we've covered some of the things you should know about when dealing with architects and buying plans.

SURVEYING

This is the process of checking over thoroughly a used boat prior to purchasing. Usually the more money involved, particularly when financing will be required, the more professional the checkerover, i.e., the surveyor. A good list of marine surveyors can be found in the back of *Boat Owners Buyers Guide*. Another place to look is the yellow pages in large coastal towns. How do you get the name of a good man?—through referrals. Call all the marinas and ask 'em each if they can recommend a good surveyor; do the same with naval architects and marine insurance agents. All of these people deal with surveyors in their daily business. By the time you finish calling around, you ought to have the low-down on just about every surveyor in town. Since surveyors charge up to $25 per hour, or $50 and up flat rate, for their services (which is well worth it), it's best that you handle the initial process of elimination of the boats you're considering. Use the surveyor for the last one—the boat you feel sure of. Incidentally, a haul out to inspect the hull is common practice—do it—and be prepared to pay the charges. To locate a qualified surveyor in your area, you can write the National Association of Marine Surveyors, P.O. Box 55, Peck Slip Station, New York, N.Y. 10038, for a copy of their membership list.

sources of information

SURVEYING SMALL CRAFT
Ian Nicholson
1974 - 224 p. il. + supp. - $10.95

While this book will not teach you all the ins and outs of yacht surveying, it goes a long way toward that goal and improves the chances that you will not get stuck when buying a used boat. This is an English book, and a welcome addition is the 27-page supplement by Bob Wallstrom on surveying small craft in North America.
From: International Marine Pub. Co., 21 Elm St., Camden, Maine 04843

MARINE SURVEY MANUAL FOR FIBERGLASS REINFORCED PLASTICS
Gibbs & Cox, Inc
1962 - 92 p. il. - $10

This flexible-bound handbook provides guidelines for the inspection and evaluation of fiberglass boats by surveyors and the layman boat buyer. Gives a good checklist of what to look for and where to look.
From: John De Graff, Inc., 34 Oak Ave., Tuckahoe, N.Y. 10707

PURCHASING

Purchasing a boat can be almost as involved as purchasing real estate, depending on whether it's new, used, of U.S. or foreign registry. But it seems to us that, when all is said and done, the best way to go about purchasing a boat is to go through a yacht broker. He can help you find the boat and handle the paperwork and details to insure all is done that is supposed to be done—that the title is clear and there are no hidden encumbrances on her. (In admiralty law, for example, if a boatyard bill isn't paid, the bill follows the boat, not the owner, and if you become the new owner, you may just find the sheriff seizing your boat for the bill *it* owes—a good broker covers things like this.) Also, the broker can help you find financing and insurance, and it won't cost you a cent extra. It's all part of the job for which the broker gets a commission from the guy who sells you the boat. The *Boat Owners Buyers Guide* has a pretty good list of brokers, which includes data on the types and sizes of boats they deal in.

Financing a new boat isn't much different from financing a car and the interest rates are comparable; term is usually 7 years with 25% to 30% down. A used boat 10 years or older, especially if of wood, however is out of the question.

If you buy a boat outside the States and plan to sail her back, it would be best to write a letter to the U.S. Customs Service prior to making the purchase so you'll know what kind of duty is to be paid and some of the things you can and cannot do. Tell them what you're buying including size, type, hull material, cost, and other particulars, where you're buying, how you will bring the boat into the United States, where, and what you intend to do with it once it's here. Then ask what your responsibilities are. They'll give you a pretty detailed account of what the law is and how it affects you. The address to write is Commissioner of Customs, U.S. Customs Service, Dept. of the Treasury, Washington, D.C. 20229.

INSURANCE

Marine insurance isn't quite the same as auto insurance nor is it as easy to get, particularly if you intend to go far offshore, say, to the South Pacific. As you'll see, the experience of the owner and his intended cruising grounds have much to do with the price of the premiums or whether you'll even be considered for insurance.

A marine underwriter (insurance agent) bases his decision of whether a boat is a good risk or not on the following factors: (a) type of craft (power or sail) and type of engine; (b) age and condition; (c) value; (d) months used out of the year; (e) geographical cruising

limits (further offshore, the harder to get coverage and the more...)
(f) experience of owner and age (a certificate from a U.S. Coast Guard
Auxiliary or U.S. Power Squadrons boating course really greases the
way and can help cut premiums).

The Yacht Policy

This is a very simplified explanation of what the different parts of a
yacht policy are and what they cover without all the ramifications.
Incidentally, the phraseology used in marine insurance policies goes
way back to the early 1600's and remains virtually unchanged today.
Ask your agent for a blank policy—makes for great reading.

Hull Insurance. This covers the hull, machinery, rigging, sails,
spars, equipment, instruments, etc. against loss, damage, or breakage
due to latent defects. It also will pay the other fellow for any damage
you cause his boat through collision, up to the amount your boat is
insured. But it will not pay for other property damaged (like to the
owner of a dock or seawall) or for personal injury.

Protection and Indemnity (P&I) Insurance. This is the liability
part of the policy and it requires a separate premium. It covers what
you might have to pay the other guy for bodily injury or property
damage to his boat (over what Hull Insurance covers) or anything else,
like his dock or seawall, which results from being hit by your boat.

Medical Payments Insurance. This supplements P&I Insurance and
covers the medical expenses you may have to pay for people injured
on your boat, but it doesn't cover you unless you so request it at an
additional premium.

Federal Compensation Act Insurance. This covers medical expenses
for people injured while working on your boat such as dock workers,
boatyard employees, and so forth.

sources of information

CHUBB & SON, INC.
90 John St., New York, N.Y. 10038
Chubb's been in the marine insurance business for a long time. As an
aid to potential customers, they've issued a 20-page booklet, *The ABC
of Yacht Insurance*, which is available on request from the above
address. Got some good info in it.

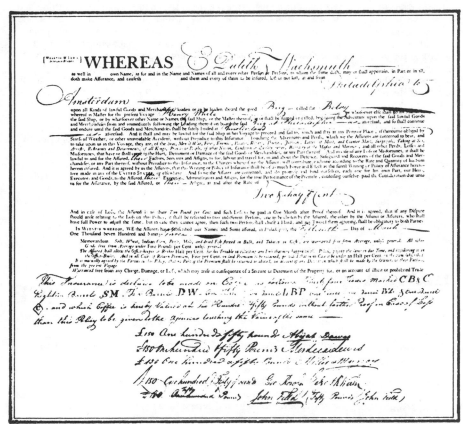

BOAT/US
5261 Port Royal Rd., Springfield, Va. 22151
These people, mentioned earlier in this section, will send you a
detailed "Marine Insurance Primer" if you request it when asking for
membership information. BOAT/US offers both boat financing and
insurance programs for members, but I found in my case that their
insurance quotation was higher than some others.

REGISTRATION

Once you've got your boat you ought to give her a good seafaring
name like *Wind Song* or *Pequod*, not some garbage like *Cocktail Boss*
or *Playin' Hooky*—though, happily, you very rarely find a handle like
this on a sailboat. Next, if your boat has an engine or uses an outboard, you must get her numbered (registered) with the state where
she'll be docked, or if she's 5 net tons or over, you may have her
documented as a yacht or documented as a commercial vessel with
the U.S. Coast Guard. Ton is not a measurement of weight in this
case, but of volume, and historically is derived from the tun, or wine
keg, which took up approximately 100 cubic feet of space in a ship's
hold. You can roughly determine a sailboat's net tons via the following formula:

$$.45 \left(\frac{LBD}{100} \right) = \text{net tons}$$

where L is the overall length, B is the overall breadth amidships, and
D is the overall depth amidship (but not including the solid keel).

Numbering a boat through the state doesn't give you any particular benefits worth mentioning and that's why most skippers who
cruise offshore and can meet the 5 net ton minimum requirement go
the documented route. Some of the benefits of documentation are:
it obligates the United States to protect the vessel in foreign waters;
facilitates travel (with respect to government authorities, in particular, customs) between U.S. and foreign ports; provides for recording
mortgages, bills of sale, and other instruments of title and keeping
permanent records of same in the Coast Guard Documentation Office
(this can make it easier to sell a boat); and in the case of yachts, if the
owner is sailing foreign and belongs to a bona fide yacht club, he can
ask the local Coast Guard Office for a Yacht Commission to identify
his vessel. Such a commission is a token of credit to any United States
official and to the authorities of any foreign power for the privileges
enjoyed under it.

The following are the forms of documentation available to United
States vessels:

Registry. Only vessels sailing the *high seas*
are registered. They must enter and clear with
customs and may pay certain fees when doing
this. Yachts can be registered as "vessels of
pleasure," but they may not engage in any
commercial activity and are treated as any
other registered vessel. Because of this, not
too many yachts are registered. The U.S. Coast
Guard handles the paper work on this type of
documentation.

License. All vessels of between 5 and 20
net tons sailing the *coastal waters*, rivers and
lakes of the United States must be licensed.
This is a "license" to engage in coastwise
trade or the fisheries or to operate as a yacht.
Vessels licensed in coastwise trade or the fisheries may not leave U.S. waters without first
clearing customs and surrendering their license
for a certificate of registry. A vessel licensed
to operate as a yacht, however, may sail foreign anytime without clearing customs or
surrendering her license, and she may enter
(return) without going through the formalities
of customs unless she carries dutiable merchandise. In this case an informal entry is required
(see Cruising for particulars). Needless to say,
the yacht license is the most popular form of
documentation among pleasure boatmen as
long as their boats are not over 20 net tons.
If they are, then they must go ...

Enrollment and License. Vessels of 20 net
tons and over sailing *coastal* and inland waters
are enrolled and licensed. They're enrolled in
a particular district (home port) and licensed

OFFSHORE SAILING

256

to engage in a trade or the fisheries or to operate as a yacht. When any of these vessels leave U.S. waters they must go through the same process as a licensed vessel; however, the exception again is the yacht (same freedom as a licensed yacht).

The thing to remember about documenting as a yacht is that you can't use the boat to earn money directly or indirectly, which cuts out chartering. If you want to do this you'll have to get registered, licensed, or enrolled and licensed as a commercial vessel, depending on (a) whether you plan to go offshore or hang around the coast, and (b) your tonnage.

The U.S. Coast Guard handles the yacht license as well as the yacht enrollment *and* license, and commercial license.

sources of information

U.S. COAST GUARD
400 Seventh St., S.W.
Washington, D.C. 20590
The Coast Guard issues numbers to undocumented boats propelled by machinery of over 10 hp if used in New Hampshire, Washington, Alaska, District of Columbia, or Guam. All other states issue their own numbers, and the appropriate state agency should be contacted. The Guard also issues yacht licenses and handles the admeasuring (measuring the volume of the hull to determine the yacht's true tonnage). Info on numbering and documentation can be found in the following pubs available free from the above address:

Pleasure Craft—Federal Requirements for Boats, CG-290.

Yacht Admeasurement and Documentation, CG-177.

ventilation, fire extinguishers, life jackets, and numbering (discussed previously). What you require will depend on the class of motorboat you own; Class 3's require more gear than Class A's.

The requirements affecting construction only concern boats carrying cargo or more than 6 passengers for hire—inspected vessels.

The following booklets, available free from the Coast Guard, cover in depth the requirements for various types of vessels;

Rules of the Road, International - Inland, CG-169. This 102-page, free book gives all the information necessary to obtain your commercial USCG motorboat operator's license for carrying passengers for hire.

Pleasure Craft, CG-290. Covers legal requirements for uninspected motorboats, Classes A through 3, including numbering, lights, flotation devices, fire extinguishers, and so forth. Also discusses reporting boating accidents and law enforcement procedures used by the Coast Guard. This pamphlet should be thoroughly read by every boatman.

Rules and Regulations for Uninspected Vessels, CG-258. A 44-page booklet discussing in depth the use and operation of this type of boat, which includes pleasure craft; equipment requirements, rules regarding carrying passengers for hire, arrangement and ventilation of fuel and engine compartments, boarding by Coast Guard, fines and penalties, and procedures for appealing USCG decisions. The addresses and commandants of all Coast Guard districts are also given.

Rules and Regulations for Small Passenger Vessels, CG-323. Exactly the same type of information as for uninspected vessels, but it also includes requirements, methods and standards of inspection for certification of this class of vessel, crew and operator requirements and licensing, navigation and radio requirements, and general operating requirements. This is very detailed and specific coverage of the law regarding passenger vessels of up to 65 feet in length.

Rules and Regulations for Cargo and Miscellaneous Vessels, CG-257. About the same as for small passenger vessels, but also includes data on cargo holds and cargo handling, and towboats.

Laws Governing Marine Inspection, CG-227. Covers methods of inspecting vessels, and the standards and requirements which must be met for the certification of different types.

Equipment Lists, CG-190. This 188-pager contains a list of every piece of equipment, mechanical and electrical, and solvents and compounds the Coast Guard has inspected and certified, together with the manufacturer's name and address. A great source directory.

sources of information

OUTBOARD BOATING CLUB
333 North Michigan Ave., Chicago, Ill. 60601
A *Handbook of Boating Laws* is available from the Outboard Boating Club in four regional editions—northeastern, southern, north central, and western states. *A Boater's Guide to State and Federal Boating Agencies* is also available.

LEGAL REQUIREMENTS

All boats must meet certain construction and equipment requirements depending on what they're used for, their size, and method of propulsion. Based on this, the Coast Guard, which enforces these requirements, has grouped all boats from skiffs to ocean-going passenger liners into the scheme shown in the chart below.

Note that steam and motor propelled vessels from 0 to 65 feet and 0 to slightly over 15 gross tons, respectively, have been further subdivided into four classes—A, 1, 2, and 3.

Pleasure vessels constitute the uninspected class; however, they must still have certain required equipment. And just to make sure they do, the Guard'll board them every so often for a general looksee. A good way to insure you're O.K. in this department is to take your boat through a U.S. Coast Guard Auxiliary courtesy inspection. If the Coast Guard catches you out of order, there can be stiff penalties and fines.

Legal requirements regarding equipment affect navigation lights, bell, whistle or horn, back-fire flame arrestor on the engine, bilge

SELLING

There are supposed to be two happy days in a boatman's life: the day he buys his first boat and the day he sells it. As in purchasing a boat, the best way to sell it is to list it with a broker. A lot of people figure they can make more money doing it themselves and saving the commission—maybe, but this would be the exception to the rule. A broker can save you a lot of headaches with the paperwork, telephone calls, inquiries, and other rigmarole that's involved. He can also get you the best price, and he knows how to talk to people to do it. Also, you don't have to worry about advertising, being on call to show the boat, or working the money problems out with the buyer; these can get somewhat ticklish. And the broker's fee for handling all this is 10% of the sale price. A very good article on "How Not to Sell A Boat" appeared in the October 1971 issue of *Motor Boating and Sailing.* Definitely worth reading. Check with your local library for a back copy or write the publisher.

PROPULSION	INSPECTED Requires formal inspect'n by USCG Marine Inspection Officer				UNINSPECTED Does not require formal inspection
	TANK VESSELS	PASSENGER VESSELS (carrying more than 6 passengers for hire)	CARGO VESSELS and TUGBOATS	OCEANOGRAPHIC VESSELS	PLEASURE and PRIVATE VESSELS (and those carrying 1 to 6 passengers for hire)
STEAM	0 to 65 ft.				
	Over 65 ft.				
MOTOR	0 to 15 gross tons				
	15 to 300 gross tons				
	Over 300 gross tons				
SAIL	0 to 700 gross tons				
	Over 700 gross tons				
NON-SELF PROPELLED	0 to 100 gross tons				
	Over 100 gross tons				

MOTORBOATS	
Class	Length
A	0 to 16 ft.
1	16 to 26 ft.
2	26 to 40 ft.
3	40 to 65 ft.

NOTES: a) A sailboat under power (inboard or outboard) is legally a motorboat. b) This chart represents a general scheme and there are exceptions to it. See *Laws Governing Marine Inspection, CG-227.*

PERIODICALS

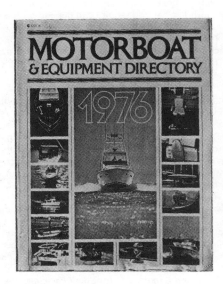

MOTORBOAT & EQUIPMENT DIRECTORY
Annual - $3/issue

Billed as the most comprehensive reference source available for selecting, buying, equipping and using a motorboat. General articles are included, and there is a special section of photos, drawings and specifications of hundreds of powerboats.
From: Motorboat Magazine, 126 Blaine Ave., Marion, Ohio 43302

SAILBOAT & EQUIPMENT DIRECTORY
Geoffrey Spranger, Ed.
Annual - $2.95/issue - 400 p. il.

This directory provides an excellent listing of production sailboats with an indication of those no longer on the market. Sizes range from 7-ft. sailing dinghies up to the 70-ft. Nicholson. Both single- and multihulls are represented as well as cruisers and racers. About 300 of these are selected for detailed descriptions with photographs and drawings. Unfortunately, the descriptions are written by the manufacturers with no independent evaluations, and price information is usually lacking. There does not seem to be any rhyme or reason as to why certain boats are given the full treatment and others just listed. Sandwiched between many advertisements are over 100 pages devoted to gear and equipment, but these chiefly are the names and addresses of companies, and other than being listed by category, no other descriptive info is given. Well worth having, but prospective yacht buyers should use this book with caution. A good number of very fine boats are not described.
From: Sail Magazine, 38 Commercial Wharf, Boston, Mass. 02110

CRUISING SAILBOATS

There're too many sailboat manufacturers to even begin listing all of them, so we've narrowed the scope to those offering vessels designed primarily for cruising and with some character to their lines. Information on this sort of boat is not as readily accessible as for the more popular fiberglass cruising-racing designs, which you'll see more typically on the water today. If you're interested in the popular types you'll have no trouble getting information through the regular media, at marinas, and from the fellows down at the yacht club. We've listed the names and addresses of some of the manufacturers of these types who've made a name for themselves and their boats, in the event you'd like to contact them for literature or at least so that you'll know who they are (they're at the end of the list). Incidentally we've listed all prices: $30,000 as $30k (k = kilo = 1,000). P & S is port and starboard.

ment in the Caribbean is available for those who wish to recover part of their costs.

BUZZARDS BAY BOATS
Harbor Rd., Mattapoisett, Mass. 02739
This is the former Allan H. Vaitses boatyard which has been building custom and limited production yachts for 18 years. Recent production boats have included the 37-ft. Herreshoff *Meadowlark,* Steve Seaton's *Menemsha 46* and *Madaket 55,* and the Cartwright *Nantucket 40.* They also offer the full range of Dick Newick-designed multihulls from 36 feet to 60 feet. All boats are available in various stages of completion or complete to the buyer's own choice of interior design.

Jongert 63 (Steve Colgate Sailing Enterprises)

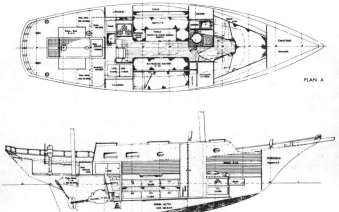

Cheoy Lee Clipper 36

Cheoy Lee Clipper 42

STEVE COLGATE SAILING ENTERPRISES, INC.
820 Second Ave., New York, N.Y. 10017
Steve, who is the North American rep for Olympic Marine of Greece, selected for his Greek charter service the *Olympic Adventure 47* designed by Ted Brewer. She is built in Greece of fiberglass-balsa core sandwich to Lloyd's specifications. Price is $94k if you wish to buy one of these well-conceived and planned yachts. A leasing arrange-

CHEOY LEE SHIPYARD
P.O. Box 5643, Kowloon, Hong Kong
Cheoy Lee Shipyard was founded over 80 years ago in Shanghai and is one of the largest and most diversified yards in the world. It is fully inspected and approved by Lloyds Register for construction in wood, steel, and fiberglass. To date over 1,000 Cheoy Lee yachts from 25' to 60' are sailing American waters, including designs by Rhodes,

Sparkman & Stephens, and Alden. Lion Yachts imports a number of Lee's stock boats to the U.S., but if you want to check with Lee directly for a particular type of design, write the above address and give them the particulars. They may have something on hand that will suit you and at a considerable saving if purchased direct.

LION YACHTS
Dauntless Shipyard, Pratt St., Essex, Conn. 06426
Lion is the eastern distributor for Cheoy Lee. Their inventory of cruising sailboats includes both wood and glass along traditional and contemporary lines. Designs by Luders, Sparkman & Stephens, Herreshoff, and Alden include a variety of rigs in lengths from 26 to 50 feet. Literature available.

DICKERSON BOATBUILDERS
Trappe Landing Rd., Trappe, Md. 21673
Dickerson offers three fiberglass boats in a choice of single and aft cabin models built along semitraditional lines. Sizes are 28 ft., 36 ft. and 41 ft. The latter two start at $30k and $46k, respectively, for bare boats. Dickerson is an old-line Maryland boatbuilding outfit with a good reputation for craftsmanship and reasonable prices.

Dickerson 36

Quoddy Pilot

PENOBSCOT BOAT WORKS, INC.
Sea St., Rockport, Maine 04856
Penobscot only builds one sailing vessel, a 32' eastport pinky called the "Quoddy Pilot." She's a charming double-ended, gaff rig sloop with a Westerberke 25 hp diesel for auxiliary power. Hull is glued strip construction of 1-1/8" cedar, covered inside and out with Vectra polypropylene cloth set in epoxy resin. Interior features include one large cabin with two berths and a drop-leaf table 'tween, forward; galley (S) and head (P), amidships; and a double berth aft of the head. Fairly roomy. Her size is 31 ft. 7 in. x 10 ft. 6 in. x 5 ft. A nice little boat for $42k, which includes sails and auxiliary ready to sailaway. Literature, photos and specs are available.

EDEY & DUFF
Harbor Rd., Mattapoisett, Mass. 02739
Twelve thousand bucks may seem like a lot for a 23-ft. cruising sloop, but *Stone Horse* is a honey. She's a fast, modern adaptation of a Crocker design built in Airex foam core fiberglass sandwich. Engine and sails are extra. Send $1.50 for the book describing the boat and her design philosophy.

SYMONS-SAILING, INC.
255 S. Ketcham Ave., Amityville, L.I., N.Y. 11701
Two of the many fiberglass British multihull imports are shown here: the 26-ft. *Telstar* trailerable cruising trimaran and the 34-ft. *Snow Goose* cruising catamaran. Both have been sailed extensively in European and North Atlantic waters. Several firms in the U.S. have begun production of cruising catamarans, and it seems that we will see more of these than heretofore. They and trimarans have much to recommend them in terms of cruising comfort. Living at a 20- to 30-degree angle of heel in a conventional single-hull boat is usually very wearying. For sailing efficiency, the *Snow Goose 34* has a diesel engine with fully-retracting drive unit. Send $1 for literature.

LARSEN YACHT SALES, INC.
Box 48, Annapolis, Md. 21404
These people represent Fairways Marine of England in the United States and have imported a neat little double-ender modeled along the lines of a Baltic fishing boat. Called the "Fisher 30," she's ketch-rigged and available with or without wheelhouse. Features include self-bailing cockpit; down below, a galley to starboard and dinette that makes into a double berth to port; and the forecabin has two berths. Other interior arrangements are available including a midship house with aft cabin. Really a tight little ship—30'0" x 9'6" x 4'3". Price ranges from $28k to $33k depending on interior arrangements and deck plan chosen. Literature and specifications available.

Fisher 30

Rosborough's 46' Brigantine

JAMES D. ROSBOROUGH
P.O. Box 188, Armdale, Nova Scotia, Canada
Rosborough designs and builds traditional wooden sailing vessels and offers stock designs ranging from a 30' ketch to an 80' barque. His most popular boat is a 46 footer available as a gaff or marconi ketch, schooner, or brigantine (which is slightly overkill for 46'). Arrangement features include great cabin aft, midship cockpit with engine room below, main saloon forward with drop-leaf table and two berths, and a private fo'c'sle with two berths. Galley can be located either forward or aft of the cockpit as the purchaser desires, and there are two heads (F&A), one with shower. All Rosborough's boats are salty and built in the traditional down east manner by Nova Scotia shipwrights. For $2 you can get brochures with photos, specifications, plans and arrangements, and descriptive commentary on the various boats offered.

Interior arrangement

Westsail 32

WESTSAIL CORP.
P.O. Box 1828, Costa Mesa, Calif. 92627
In the 19th century, Colin Archer designed a double ended sailing craft for the Norwegian government to transport harbor pilots to meet inbound vessels. One of the requirements for this pilot boat was that it be suitable for control by one man under all sailing and sea conditions. Archer later adapted the design to a life saving vessel for the Norwegian Rescue Society. Its success was such that the design was eventually used throughout Europe and America for pilot vessels. In 1924 Wm. Atkin refined the design and sail plan, and in 1967 W. I. B. Crealock adapted it to a fiberglass boat optimizing the proven

cruising lines with modern fiberglass construction. In 1971 Westsail purchased the molds and commissioned Crealock to modernize the interior arrangement and sail plan. The result is the Westsail 32, a 32' double ended fiberglass cutter (also available as a ketch) with a semi-divided main cabin—galley-navigation area and main saloon—and a private forecabin with one double and one single berth. The dinette (port) makes into a double berth and to starboard are a transom berth and an upper berth. She's got a tiny cockpit, outboard rudder with tiller, full length trunk cabin, and runs a Volvo Penta diesel for auxiliary power. Price is $40k ready-to-sail, and a kit is available. Also manufactured are the Westsail 28, 42 and 43-Aft Cockpit. Send $3 for handsome color brochure which includes specifications, drawings, optional equipment and prices.

Crotch Island Pinky

PETER VAN DINE
P.O. Box 8, Annapolis, Md. 21404
Van Dine has three small fiberglass character boats—a 21-foot Crotch Island pinky, cat ketch rigged; a dory skiff in two lengths, 12 and 16 feet; and an 1890 Chic replica, a 12-foot gaff rig sloop. An illustrated 4-page brochure is available.

CABOTCRAFT INDUSTRIES LTD.
23 Prince Andrew Place, Don Mills, Ontario, Canada M3C 2H2
The *Cabot 36* is a beautiful 35 ft.-7 in. fast cruising cutter, or sloop at the buyer's option. Her medium-displacement, Airex fiberglass foam-sandwich hull was designed by Ted Brewer, and she should sail closer to the wind and be faster than the tubby and heavy-displacement re-creations of older craft. Cabot comes with diesel engine, 100 gallons of water tankage, 12- and 110-volt wiring, gimballed three-burner stove and oven, and an unusually complete list of equipment, ordinarily available only as extras on other yachts. Price for the cutter version is $43.8k.

other sources

Morgan Out Island 41

JOHN G. ALDEN, INC.
89 Commercial Wharf, Boston, Mass. 02110

COLUMBIA YACHTS
275 McCormick Ave., Costa Mesa, Calif. 92626

IRWIN YACHT & MARINE CORP.
13055 49th St. North, St. Petersburg, Fla. 33732

ISLANDER YACHTS
777 West 17th St., Costa Mesa, Calif. 92627

JENSEN MARINE
235 Fischer, Costa Mesa, Calif. 92626

MORGAN YACHT CORP.
P.O. Box 13247, St. Petersburg, Fla. 33733

NEW BOMBAY TRADING CO.
4501 Ulmerton Rd., Clearwater, Fla. 33502

Designing your own boat can be interesting, but without the proper background, it would be, to put it mildly, a dumb thing to do. Modifying an existing design (perhaps the boat you now own) is a little more feasible, but for the novice even that's bad business. If you want to fool around with design, you've gotta get some grounding in naval architecture—or have an awful lot of money to blow on a boat that might not even float. For those who are students or aspiring yacht designers, here's some info that might help to further your avocation.

sources of information

AMATEUR YACHT RESEARCH SOCIETY (AYRS)
10822 92nd Ave. N., Seminole, Fla. 33542
(British Address: Hermitage, Newbury, Berkshire, England RG16 9RW)
The AYRS was founded in 1955 by Dr. John Morwood in England. Today it has volunteers staffing regional offices throughout the world and numbers among its membership amateur and professional boat-builders and yacht designers, experimenters, inventors, offshore sailors and those just curious about boats. The President is His Royal Highness Prince Philip, Duke of Edinburgh. The AYRS is an idea organization dedicated to research on yachts including materials, theory, design, racing, cruising, performance analyses, naval architecture, seamanship and boatbuilding. The AYRS is particularly noted for having published members' contributions in the over 6,000 pages to date in the areas of hull resistance from sailing models, home-built test tanks and full-scale yachts; sail measurements at full-scale and from home-built wind tunnels; sailing hydrofoils; multihulls; self-steering gears; rudder design; sail rigs; and sailboat performance analyses. Much effort has been devoted to the development of low-cost yachts as well as high-speed sailing craft. Although most of the AYRS members sail conventional monohulls, the group is acknowledged by the New York Public Library to be the "world authority" on multihull craft. The AYRS is a nonprofit organization with no qualifications for membership other than an interest in yachting. Membership is $15 per year which includes six of the bimonthly journals now published in the U.S. plus one or two books from England. Members in the southeast can join a subgroup called the AYRS-Florida-Caribbean Contact Group which holds sailing meetings and symposia. Some of the older publications are now out of print, but when funds become available, a new printing is made. Prices for those listed range from $1.30 to $11 to members, who receive a discount on the larger bound books such as *Design for Fast Sailing* (318 p.), *Sailing Hydrofoils* (284 p.), *Cruising Catamarans* (372 p.), *Rudder Design* (80 p.), *Sail Trimming, Testing & Theory* (124 p.), *Deepwater Seamanship* (92 p.), *Self Steering* (167 p.) and *Multihull Safety Study* (143 p.).

Issues of the *Bulletin* are shown below. Some may be out of print. (Sure is small print, ain't it—you ought to see the size of the people who wrote it).

AYRS BULLETINS

1. Catamarans	26. Sail Rigs	51. Foil & Float
2. Hydrofoils	27. Cruising Catamarans	52. Trimarans 1964
3. Sail Evolution	28. Catamarans 1959	53. Solo Cruising
4. Outriggers	29. Outriggers 1959	54. Catamarans 1965
5. Sailing Hull Design	30. Tunnel and Tank	55. Trimarans 1965
6. Outrigged Craft	31. Sailing Theory	56. Sailing Figures
7. Catamaran Construction	32. Sailboat Testing	57. Round Britain 1966
8. Dinghy Design	33. Sails 1960	58. Practical Hydrofoils
9. Sails and Aerofoils	34. Ocean Trimarans	59. Multihull Design &
10. American Catamarans	35. Catamarans 1960	Catamarans 1966
11. The Wishbone Rig	36. Floats, Foil & Fluid Flows	60. Multihull Seamanship &
12. Amateur Research	37. Aerodynamics 1	Trimarans 1966
13. Self-Steering (see overleaf)	38. Catamarans 1961	61. Sailing Analyses
14. Wingsails	39. Trimarans 1961	62. Hydrofoil Victory
15. Catamarans Design	40. Yacht Research I	63. Multihull Capsizing
16. Trimarans and Outriggers	41. Yacht Research II	64. Catamarans 1967
17. Commercial Sail	42. Catamarans 1962	65. Trimarans 1968
18. Catamaran Developments	43. Trimarans 1962	66. Foils, Ice Yachts & Sails
19. Hydrofoil Craft	44. A.Y.R.S. Yachts	67. Catamarans 1969
20. Modern Boatbuilding	45. Basic Research	68. Outriggers 1969
21. Ocean Cruising	46. Catamarans 1963	69. Multihull Safety Study
22. Catamarans 1958	47. Outriggers 1963	70. Retirement Yachts and Polars
23. Outrigger 1958	48. Yacht Electrics	71. O.S.T.A.R. 1968
24. Yacht Wind Tunnels	49. Keel Yachts	72. Catamarans 1970
25. Fiberglass	50. Catamarans 1964	

NAVAL ARCHITECTURE

UNDERSTANDING BOAT DESIGN
Edward S. Brewer, N.A., and Jim Betts
1971 - 66 p. il. - $4.95

An excellent, highly recommended first book for anyone interested in yacht design or in purchasing his first boat. In Almost outline order it covers the basic concepts, theories, and techniques of small craft design in layman's terms, though not at all simplistically. The really nice thing about Brewer's book is that you don't have to wade through theory to get to the practical information, and all the terms and formulas are nicely explained. It's all there, hull formulas, centers and heights, interpretation of drawings and offsets, power and prop data, sail and rigging plans, construction principles, materials, designing and modifying your own boat, plus a portfolio of 11 of Brewer's designs.
From: International Marine Pub. Co., Camden, Me. 04843

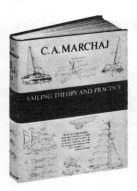

SAILING THEORY AND PRACTICE
Czeslaw A. Marchaj
1964 - 450 p. il. - $15

This is considered to be the most complete scientific analysis of the aerodynamic, hydrodynamic, and other design factors which define a yacht's behavior since Dr. Manfred Curry's classic *Yacht Racing* (rev. ed. available from Chas. Scribner's Sons, Vreeland Ave., Totowa, N.J. 07512, for $12.50). Illustrated with 335 drawings and photographs.
From: Dodd, Mead & Co., 79 Madison Ave., New York, N.Y. 10016

THE COMMONSENSE OF YACHT DESIGN
L. Francis Herreshoff
1974 - 333 p. il. - $29

This is a reprint of the two-volume work which first appeared in 1946. While study of this book will not make you a full-fledged designer, it will go a long way toward that goal. It's probably the best book in print on the subject of yacht design. In addition to treating hull design, there is good, solid information on rigs and sail plans, cabin arrangements, construction, marine hardware and esthetics. Before buying or building one of the modern center-cockpit, tubby, heavy boats, it would pay to read Herreshoff's opinions on the merits of long, narrow, shoal-draft boats.
From: Caravan-Maritime Books, 87-06 168th Place, Jamaica, N.Y. 11432

SKENE'S ELEMENTS OF YACHT DESIGN
Francis S. Kinney
1973 - 351 p. il. - $15

Once an employee-draftsman for the Herreshoff firm, Norman L. Skene wrote the original edition in 1927. It has been completely revised and updated by Kinney. Although there are some mistakes and biases, Skene's is one of the classic treatises on the naval architecture of the yacht, principally the sailing kind. Not recommended for "freshmen."
From: Dodd, Mead & Co., 79 Madison Ave., New York, N.Y. 10016

BOOKS

DESIGN FOR FAST SAILING
Edmond Bruce and Harry Morss
1976 - 318 p. il. - $22

A really fine work for those interested in the science and technology of sailing yachts—what makes the boat go and why? It's written for the amateur experimenter with a knowledge of high school math, and has sketches and instructions for building and using test tanks, wind tunnels and on-board instrumentation.
From: Amateur Yacht Research Society, 10822 92nd Ave. N., Seminole, Fla. 33542

AMERICAN SAILING CRAFT
Howard I. Chapelle
1975 - 239 p. il. - $13.50

Not to be confused with Chapelle's classic, *American Small Sailing Craft,* this is an excellent, just-republished account of some of the best old-time American sailboats complete with sketches of sail plans and lines drawings as well as descriptions of each type. Included are New Haven Sharpie, Skipjack, Friendship Sloop, Gloucester Schooner, Pinkies and American Pilot Boats.
From: International Marine Pub. Co., 21 Elm St., Camden, Maine 04843

SAILING YACHT DESIGN
Robt. G. Henry and Richards T. Miller
1965 - 160 p. il. - $6

Synthesizes a large mass of loose information into one of the best short form collections of sailing yacht design data available. Covers sailing yacht types, proportions and form, arrangements, sail plan and control, construction, measurement rules, and the role of the naval architect. An appendix includes data on a number of small and large sailing boats. Sixty-three drawings and photos.
From: Cornell Maritime Press, Inc., Box 109, Cambridge, Md. 21613

YACHT DESIGNING AND PLANNING
Howard I. Chapelle
1971 - 319 p. il. - $15

Another classic in yacht design, originally brought out in 1938 and now in an updated edition by Chapelle, who is, among other things, an advisor to the Smithsonian Institution on the history and design of sailing vessels. Chapelle's book is not only a good textbook, but makes for good reading as well. He takes you through the process of learning in the same order an architect takes when designing a boat—get your tools together (description and use of drafting tools); rough out the idea (preliminary design and considerations); draw up the design (the how and why of various types of designs, considerations, and drafting techniques); draw up the working plans (construction and joiner plans, materials, fastenings, and other considerations); the sail and rigging plan, and writing up the specifications. A 24-page appendix gives many useful tables and proportions, and includes procedures for taking off lines of half models and building cardboard half models. Great book, and recommended for advanced "freshmen" on up.
From: W. W. Norton & Co., Inc., 500 Fifth Ave., New York, N.Y. 10036

OFFSHORE SAILING

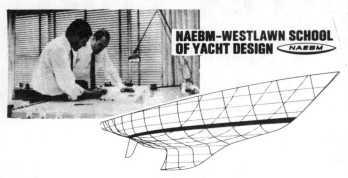

NAEBM-WESTLAWN SCHOOL OF YACHT DESIGN NAEBM

NAEBM-WESTLAWN SCHOOL OF YACHT DESIGN
537 Steamboat Rd., Greenwich, Conn. 06830

Westlawn was founded back in 1930 by Gerald T. White, a member of the Society of Naval Architects and Marine Engineers, and E. S. Nelson, to provide complete instruction in the specialized field of small craft design. Since then the school has been made a subsidiary of the National Association of Engine and Boat Manufacturers (NAEBM) and has grown to become one of the leading yacht design correspondence schools in the nation.

Yacht design involves more than just the preparation of plans for new boats. Many of the duties of the designer aren't worked out solely by draftsmanship. They involve calculations for displacement, stability, coefficients, immersion, powering, sailing rigs, propellers, and innumerable other factors of a complex science. Westlawn's three-year course covers all of this and much more. During the course you will be required to prepare complete plans, computations, specifications and all other details for fast open powerboats, cruisers, auxiliaries, and sailing boats. Many of the problems are submitted just as they would be from a client. There are more than thirty separate lesson assignments that must be completed with a grade of 75% or better to receive Westlawn's diploma.

Once you've completed the course and decide that you'd like to go into yacht designing as a profession, Westlawn will assist in getting a placement for you. The complete course with textbooks and materials runs $490 on full payment or $545 via their deferred payment plan. Complete information on the school, courses, payment plans, etc. are available from the above address.

YACHT DESIGN INSTITUTE
BROOKLIN, MAINE 04616

Ted Brewer

YACHT DESIGN INSTITUTE (YDI)
Brooklin, Maine 04616

YDI isn't quite as fancy as Westlawn, but it has a good, healthy down-to-earth attitude. Their literature is straightforward and includes background sketches of the naval architect-instructors, a descriptive lesson schedule of the course, and the school's policies regarding the student and instruction. The course consists of twnety lessons on the theory and practical application of yacht design. Price is $15 or $20 per lesson depending on whether you wish to audit (lesson and course material is provided and then you're on your own!) or take the diploma course. The latter is preferable, as all drawings and other homework are criticized thoroughly and graded by Ted and his partner, Bob Wallstrom. Price is reduced for those wishing to pay the entire amount in advance. YDI is less formal than Westlawn, gives more individual treatment, and there's the advantage of having your work supervised through correspondence by two active and prolific yacht designers. Write them for the 10-page booklet describing the Institute and its course.

Building your own boat isn't quite as risky as designing it, providing you've got a fair background in the use of tools and have a good set of plans and specifications. Specifications are not instructions on how to build a boat, but rather the requirements of good construction practice with respect to materials, fastenings, joinery work, and so forth. Other considerations are adequate working space and protection from the elements; how the boat will be moved to the water; the money supply; and the builder's capacity to maintain interest in the project to finish it. Quite often the boat is too big and requires construction skills or additional help the amateur builder cannot supply, sending the South Seas cruising dream and maybe a lot of money down the hole.

The best way to prevent this is to build the boat on paper. Consider each aspect of the project in the order it will be done and write down how it'll be handled, the skills needed, the number of men, tools and accessories like frames, jigs, and so forth; the quantity of materials and fastenings, and the time it will take to complete, taking into account bad weather (be very careful in estimating this). Add up the costs and time, then figure conservatively how many hours a week you'll be able to devote to the project. Divide the hours into the total time and you've got the number of weeks it'll take (and just to be

sources of information

AMERICAN BOAT AND YACHT COUNCIL, INC. (ABYC)
15 E. 26th St., New York, N.Y. 10010

The prime function of the ABYC is to write standards for the construction of yachts. All builders, whether amateur or professional, should purchase a copy of their *Safety Standards for Small Craft*. Price of $35 may seem steep but is well worth the money. $10 per year buys the annual supplements and updating. Sections cover most aspects of boatbuilding including ventilation of fuel and tank compartments, hatches and doors, cockpits and scuppers, metal fastenings, hull openings, water and fuel systems, engine mountings, exhaust and cooling systems, prop shafting, steering, wiring, galley stoves, refrigeration, navigation lights, and on and on.

AMERICAN BUREAU OF SHIPPING (ABS)
45 Broad St., New York, N.Y. 10004

ABS is an organization of steamship executives, shipbuilders, and marine underwriters, and though a professional group, they do have some publications of interest to the amateur builder and may be able to assist with inquiries on technical design problems (we haven't checked them out on this, but they're a pretty good group—and a lot more reasonable than the Coast Guard when it comes to approval of commercial vessel designs and specifications). Here're the publications:

Rules for Building and Classing Steel Vessels, $15. This book is the standard of the shipbuilding industry and is a must for anyone building a steel boat.

Shear Force and Bending Moment Calculations, free.

Approved Welding Electrodes, Wire-Flux and Wire Gas Combinations, $6.

These may be ordered from Book Order Dept. via the above address. A complete list of ABS publications can also be secured on request from the same place.

LLOYD'S REGISTER OF SHIPPING
17 Battery Place, New York, N.Y. 10004

Not to be confused with Lloyd's of London which insures ships and boats, this English firm is the one which surveys yachts and certifies them as being planned or built under Lloyd's supervision or to their specifications. Of interest to the builder are the fine books produced and sold by this organization. *Rules and Regulations for the Construction and Classification of Wood and Composite Yachts* with 184 pages and costing $15 is the most complete available on the subject. *Rules for the Hull Construction of Steel Yachts* is 57 pages and $10, and *Provisional Rules for the Construction of Reinforced Plastic Yachts* is 105 pages and $10. Write for a list of other books.

BOATBUILDING

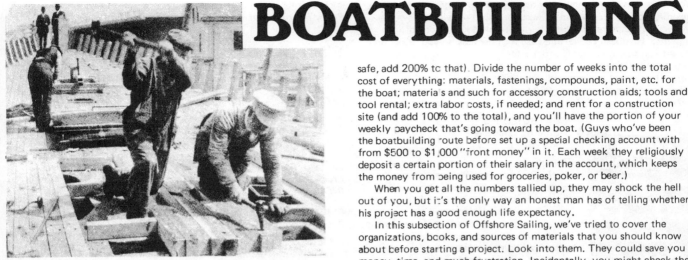

Spiking down deck planking on a Gloucester fishing schooner.

safe, add 200% to that). Divide the number of weeks into the total cost of everything: materials, fastenings, compounds, paint, etc. for the boat; materials and such for accessory construction aids; tools and tool rental; extra labor costs, if needed; and rent for a construction site (and add 100% to the total), and you'll have the portion of your weekly paycheck that's going toward the boat. (Guys who've been the boatbuilding route before set up a special checking account with from $500 to $1,000 "front money" in it. Each week they religiously deposit a certain portion of their salary in the account, which keeps the money from being used for groceries, poker, or beer.)

When you get all the numbers tallied up, they may shock the hell out of you, but it's the only way an honest man has of telling whether his project has a good enough life expectancy.

In this subsection of Offshore Sailing, we've tried to cover the organizations, books, and sources of materials that you should know about before starting a project. Look into them. They could save you money, time, and much frustration. Incidentally, you might check the the Tools subsection of Wilderness Living for additional boatbuilding aids.

PERIODICALS

BOATS & HARBORS
36 issues/yr. - $2 - 20 p. il.

This is the industrial marine "grapevine" advertiser chock full of goodies the cruising man usually figures only on finding in a marine salvage yard. Lotsa surplus, salvage-type gear including engines, fittings, hardware, deck and hull accessories, and parts. Great place to go scrounging if you're building or recommissioning; good deals and good prices on everything from soup to nuts. Good advertising rates too if you've got stuff in the boat locker to get rid of. As their dippy tri-monthly cartoon puts it, "Without Boats & Harbors you're sunk ... or sinking." Subscribe once, and you'll never be without a copy. Newspaper-size and comes out three times a month.
From: Boats & Harbors, Crossville, Tenn. 38555

BOOKS

BOAT BUILDING IN YOUR OWN BACK YARD
Sam S. Rabl
1958 - 223 p. il. - $12

This is one of the four or five best books on amateur boatbuilding in my opinion. Eminently practical and even makes the bugaboo of

steam bending easy for the amateur. Includes complete building instructions and drawings for 11 boats from 7 to 24 feet including Rabl's famous 18-ft. world cruiser, *Picaroon*.
From: Cornell Maritime Press, Box 109, Cambridge, Md. 21613

COMPLETE AMATEUR BOAT BUILDING
Michael Verney
1959 - 327 p. il. - $7.95

Provides full details on all systems of boat construction from reading plans to engine installation, plus many tables and data for building a wide variety of boats from 6 to 60 feet in wood, glass, and metal. Contains 116 drawings and 35 photos. One of the better books for amateurs.
From: The Macmillan Co., Front and Brown Sts., Riverside, N.J. 08075

SHIP SHAPE AND BRISTOL FASHION
Loren R. Borland
1969 - 208 p. il. - $5.95

Sixty-five short articles on building useful equipment and parts for cruising sailboats from truck to keel and main saloon to engine room. Includes construction data and drawings for a lot of neat and useful innovations. Very much like the old *Practical Yachting* reprints.
From: Van Nostrand Reinhold Co., 300 Pike St., Cincinnati, Ohio 45202

Wood

BOATBUILDING WITH PLYWOOD
Glenn L. Witt
1967 - 214 p. il. - $8.95

An excellent workshop book with numerous tables, drawings and photographs illustrating in a down-to-earth way, how to build a boat of sheet plywood. There is some information on double-diagonal or cold-moulded construction as well. Highly recommended.
From: Glen-L Marine Designs, 9152 Rosecrans, Bellflower, Calif. 90706

BOAT OWNER'S SHEET ANCHOR
Carl D. Lane
1969, 2nd ed. - 304 p. il. - $3.50 (pb)

Originally published in 1941 and revised in 1969, *Sheet Anchor* covers inspecting used boats, converting them, painting, rigging, and the like, including complete rebuilding if necessary. Carl's advice is down-to-earth, direct, and presupposes a fairly complete knowledge of carpentry. He doesn't have much use for fiberglass, so you won't find any info on this in his book. Strictly for the small wooden yacht owner, both sail and power. Includes many good illustrations by Carl, who himself has owned and restored more than 37 boats.

From: Hawthorn Books, Inc., 260 Madison Ave., New York, N.Y. 10016

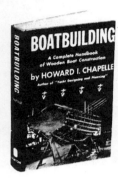

BOATBUILDING
Howard I. Chapelle
1969 - 624 p. il. - $17.50

This classic, a companion to Chapelle's *Yacht Designing and Planning,* covers the complete process of wooden boatbuilding from flat-bottom row boats to blue-water cruisers. He describes in detail the various tools, techniques, and methods used by the ship's carpenter, from laying the keel to properly fidding a mast. Beautiful technical drawings—nothing less from Howard's board—and a very salty text.
From: W. W. Norton & Co., 500 Fifth Ave., New York, N.Y. 10036

BOATBUILDING MANUAL
Robert M. Steward
1970 - 220 p. il. - $10

A practical, concise, and clearly worded guide to wooden boatbuilding, well illustrated with photographs and the author's own drawings. Steward has it well organized and covers every aspect of the subject from the preparation stage to finishing touches on brightwork. He includes lists of tools, supplies, wood strengths, and fastening sizes.
From: International Marine Publishing Co., 21 Elm St., Camden, Me. 04843

Metal

BOATBUILDING WITH STEEL
Gilbert C. Klingel
1973 - 248 p. il. - $12.50

A good appreciation for the many virtues of owning a steel yacht may be had from this book which also includes a section on *Boatbuilding with Aluminum* by Thomas Colvin. The latter is not detailed enough to be of practical use, but the major part on steel construction is well worth the price.
From: International Marine Pub. Co., 21 Elm St., Camden, Maine 04843

SHIPFITTER 3 & 2
U.S. Navy Training Manual
1970, 2nd ed. - 422 p. il. - $3.25
D 208.11:Sh 6/6/970

An excellent instruction manual on cutting, brazing, welding (oxyacetylene and arc), plumbing and pipe fitting, and general metal-working including sheetmetal. Very good section on metals and alloys, and metalworking tools. Only thing that's missing is data on corrosion and its prevention. For $3.25 it's certainly worth adding to your ship's library if you've got a metal boat.
From: Sup. of Doc., U.S. Gov. Printing Off., Washington, D.C. 20402

SMALL STEEL CRAFT - DESIGN, CONSTRUCTION AND MAINTENANCE
Ian Nicholson
1971 - 206 p. il. - $12

This is a very good British book which complements Klingel's work. There is a good discussion on the virtues and vices of steel, and the design and building information is fairly complete. Unfortunately, as with all British books, references are to addresses and practices in England, so if you are going to buy just one book on steel boats, better

stick with Klingel.
From: International Marine Pub. Co., 21 Elm St., Camden, Maine 04843

Fiberglass

FIBERGLASS KIT BOATS
Jack Wiley
1973 - 184 p. il. - $9.95

Probably the best way to go about building your own boat is to purchase a bare hull or hull plus deck and cabin top and go from there. Jack follows with pictures and words the complete construction of a cruising sailboat step-by-painful-step. This includes 62 diagrams and photographs and a list of 73 manufacturers and their addresses.
From: International Marine Pub. Co., 21 Elm St., Camden, Maine 04843

FIBERGLASS BOATS, CONSTRUCTION AND MAINTENANCE
Boughton Cobb, Jr.
1973 - 236 p. il. - $4.75 (pb)

An excellent little book on practical aspects of fiberglass boatbuilding including moulded boats, sandwich construction, hand layup, wood-fiberglass composites, covering of wooden hulls and making your own water tanks, sinks, masts and other yacht equipment.
From: Yachting Pub. Corp., 50 W. 44th St., New York, N.Y. 10036

ONE-OFF AIREX FIBREGLASS SANDWICH CONSTRUCTION
Thomas J. Johannsen
1973 - 94 p. il. - $7.50

This book is published by the firm that makes Airex foam which, though expensive, is probably the best on the market for boatbuilding. There are good sections on design and testing as well as practical construction. Some of the difficulties in bending to compound curves are glossed over. Of particular interest will be the information on conversion from single-skin fiberglass and wooden hulls to Airex laminates.
From: Chemacryl, Inc., 1051 Clinton St., Buffalo, N.Y. 14206

HOW TO REPAIR FIBERGLASS BOATS
Ferro Corp.
1969 - 36 p. il. - $3

A basic handbook on the repair of gel-coated fiberglass products with explicit and detailed step-by-step instructions on mending dents and holes. Beautiful close-up photographs on each aspect of the job. These people leave nothing to the imagination. Three bucks, however, seems a bit high for 36 pages—though it's excellent information, it isn't privileged.
From: Ferro Corp., Fiber Glass Rd., Nashville, Tenn. 37211

THE USE OF PLASTICS IN BOATBUILDING
32 p. il. - $3

Contains 18 articles from past issues of the *National Fisherman* by John Gardner and other experts on glass. Covers composite construction combining wood and plastics, covering a wooden hull with fabric and epoxy, coating an aluminum hull with plastic, and the advantages of plastics for amateur building. Includes 8 plans and 32 photos. Printed on newsprint, tabloid size (17" x 11").
From: International Marine Pub. Co., 21 Elm St., Camden, Me. 04843

Ferro-Cement

CONCRETE BOATBUILDING: ITS TECHNIQUE AND ITS FUTURE
Gainor W. Jackson and W. Morely Sutherland
1969 - 106 p. il. - $7.95

This book is primarily a starter for people who may be interested in actively investigating the construction of a concrete boat. Though there is an ample supply of how-to information, the authors deal mostly with the history of construction, going back a hundred years or so, and describe the development of concrete technology. They also compare cement with wood, steel, and fiberglass boats and tell how some of the ferro-cement boats built have performed.
From: John De Graff, Inc., 34 Oak Ave., Tuckahoe, N.Y. 10707

THE USE OF FERRO-CEMENT IN BOATBUILDING
16 p. il. - $2.50

Contains 14 articles and letters from previous issues of the *National*

Fisherman, which includes a list of 16 other articles and books on the subject, the names and addresses of three Portland cement companies, six ferro-cement building firms, and seven naval architects working in ferro-cement. Twenty-eight photographs and drawings. Tabloid size (17" x 11") on newsprint.
From: International Marine Pub., 21 Elm St., Camden, Me. 04843

FERRO-CEMENT
Bruce Bingham
1974 - 444 p. il. - $17.50

If you've finally decided to get serious about building your own ferro-cement boat, this is one of the best books you could buy. As a matter of fact, it's an excellent book on just the theory and practice of naval architecture and lofting, alone, not to mention ferro-cement construction technique. The book is fat and heavy with detailed information and profusely illustrated with some of the finest technical and perspective drawings to come along in some time, plus many, many

excellent close-up photographs. It's a true goodie!
From: Cornell Maritime Press, Cambridge, Md. 21613

PRACTICAL FERRO-CEMENT BOATBUILDING
Jay R. Benford and Herman Husen
1971 - 216 p. il. - $10

A plastic-ring bound shop manual that concentrates on detailed how-to-build information. Several different backbone and framing methods are discussed, plus tools, which includes details on making a semi-automatic wire-tying tool and other time-saving aids, setting up, applying mesh and rods, tying and compacting welded mesh, cementing the hull and deck, and curing. Has 54 drawings and plans.
From: International Marine Pub., 21 Elm St., Camden, Me. 04843

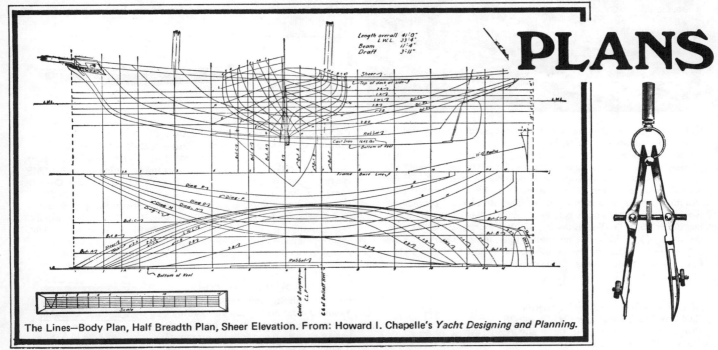

PLANS

The Lines—Body Plan, Half Breadth Plan, Sheer Elevation. From: Howard I. Chapelle's *Yacht Designing and Planning.*

A good boatbuilding project begins with a good set of plans. These can be gotten from several sources—(1) you can work them up yourself for free; (2) you can have a naval architect prepare a custom-designed set to your requirements for $500 to $2,000; (3) you can buy the rights from the designer to use someone else's custom plans (a set of review drawings—to see if you're interested—runs from $25 to $100 depending on how much of the set you need; the right to use them for construction, however, can run as high as $2,000—designers normally retain property rights to their designs and just sell the use on a one-time-only basis; the fee paid for this use is called a royalty; if you see a boat you like, you might be able to get the use of the design if you can track down the architect); or (4) you can buy a set from the designer's stock inventory at a considerably cheaper price, $50 on up to $800, which includes building rights. Some of these stock plans have been collected into catalogs which are available through several of the boating magazines. A source of info on the foregoing is *Boat Owners Buyers Guide.* It lists architects with descriptions and prices of their stock designs.

A set of plans normally consists of the Lines (sheer plan, half breadth plan, and body plan); Table of Offsets (these are the most critical because they're the actual dimensions of the boat; without these numbers the Lines are almost useless); Arrangement drawings; Deck and Interior; Sail Plan; Structural drawings (various, as necessary to illustrate certain methods of construction, dimensions and locations of structural members, and so forth); detail drawings (various, including engine placement and line-up, electrical wiring, fuel and water piping, rigging and spar features, hatches, joinery work, and interior details that may require particular attention); Specifications (written requirements concerning construction practices to be used in building the boat, and the choice of materials, fastenings, hardware, com-

pounds, paints, and so forth). There may also be details regarding engine, prop, sails, rigging, and other equipment of this class.

One particular frustration amateur builders have with plans is that they never seem to have quite enough information. This is not an oversight or evidence of a poor designer, but rather efficiency. Designers design the boat, builders build it, and the designer presumes the carpenter, welder, shipfitter, or whoever, has the experience to handle the job. If there are particular methods of construction to be employed that the designer feels the builder may not be aware of, they'll be drawn, but to slap a set of "paint by number" plans on a builder would be a cut to his ability, and likewise, take the designer three to four times longer to draw up. Amateurs should be prepared for this by learning the techniques and methods commonly used in small boat construction.

sources of plans

JIM BROWN TRIMARANS
Almar, 241 W. 35th St., National City, Calif. 92050

Jim Brown offers plans for four sizes of a cutter-rigged, plywood and fiberglass trimaran called the Searunner. Lengths are 25, 31, 37, and 40 feet. Plans have been worked up with the amateur builder in mind and include much "how to" construction details drawn in a non-technical style. As an introduction to his Searunner trimarans, Brown has put together a 128-page "catalog" which, in narrative form, covers some of the boats' features: the centerboard, central cockpit, cutter rig, hull form and construction, interiors, auxiliary engines, self-steering (for which construction data is included with each set of plans),

JIM BROWN - designed
SAILING TRIMARANS

JAY R. BENFORD
P.O. Box 399, Friday Harbor, Wash. 98250
Jay is a very articulate and experienced designer, principally of traditional sailing craft and is well-known to readers of the yachting magazines. His 66-page book, *Cruising Designs*, is a good buy at $2.50, and he is also the author of the just-published *The Benford 30*, $1. The first book includes study plans for 55 sailboats, 23 powerboats, four motor sailers and two houseboats.

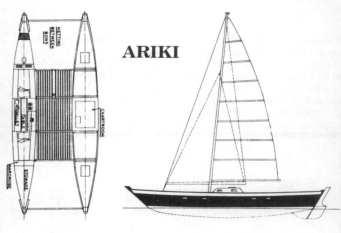

ARIKI

and safety. Each of the four sizes is also discussed in some detail. The catalog, *Searunner Trimarans*, $4, has a lot of good information in it for prospective plans buyers, but it's also got a lot more "jaw" that's of marginal use to the serious amateur builder who wants to get on with it. As an aid to the neophyte, Brown has written the 312-page *Searunner Construction*, $8, also in narrative form, which has construction procedures and advice to supplement plans. It probably would be of value if you're actually building a Searunner. Plans run: Searunner 25, $100; Searunner 31, $300; Searunner 37, $400; and Searunner 40, $450. A free newsletter (brochure), *Searunner*, is available from the above address. It tells you little about the trimarans, but a lot about what a great time people are having with them.

BRUCE BINGHAM YACHT DESIGN
P.O. Box 113, Walnut Creek, Calif. 94596
Bruce Bingham's designs for the amateur builder have appeared in many of the leading yachting magazines. *Rudder* featured his 20-ft. *Flicka* in a continuing six-month series on building in ferro-cement. His book of plans for $3 is a good buy. It includes a description of stock designs offered, contents of a typical design package and information on building and costs. Plans for 13 cruising sailboats and three powerboats are shown ranging in size from the 8-ft. *Trinka* to the 50-ft. *Sabrina*. My favorite is his 46-ft. *Andromeda* which may be built in fiberglass, ferro-cement, strip planking or cold-moulded plywood. (see the books section, a couple of pages back, for Bruce's book on ferro-cement construction: *Ferro-Cement*)

Melvin H. Jackson, Curator of Marine Transportation
SMITHSONIAN INSTITUTION
Washington, D.C. 20560
The Smithsonian Institution stocks a number of lines drawings and sail plans of traditional yachts, many of which are described in the wonderful books of Howard Chapelle: *American Small Sailing Craft* and *American Sailing Craft*. A typical set of three sheets of plans is $10.50.

SEVEN SEAS PRESS
32 Union Square, New York, N.Y. 10003
A very useful series of plans booklets is offered by this firm at prices ranging from $2.25 to $4 which includes designs by Thomas E. Colvin, Thomas C. Gillmer, John G. Hanna, Al Mason and Winthrop L. Warner. The booklets show study plans of many designs and give information on prices and addresses of where to obtain complete plans sets.

CANADIAN MULTIHULL SERVICES (CMS)
Toronto Island Airport, Toronto, Ontario, Canada M5V 1A1
"If you are about to build a multihull, but don't know where to start, talk to Pat McGrath...the 'brain' behind the operation of CMS." CMS is a design service and sells plans for Norman Cross and Lock Crowther trimarans and James Wharram catamarans. Pat is the author of *50 Multihulls You Can Build* ($4) and *Wooden Boatbuilding & Repair with Bote-Cote Epoxy* ($1). CMS also sells Bote-Cote epoxy, spars, rigging, nails and sails. "We'll help you with the selection of the right size and make of deck equipment such as winches, tracks, blocks, etc." A free list with prices of plans, books and materials is available.

YACHTING PUBLISHING CORP.
50 West 44th St., New York, N.Y. 10036
Yachting magazine features a monthly design section with four to six boats, which includes sail plan and interior arrangement drawings, specifications, and a brief description of the boat. Many of these designs have been collected into *Yachting's Book of Plans*. The most recent edition carries 84 sailboat and 66 powerboat designs and sells for $2. Incidentally, if you come across a design you like, the usual procedure is to contact the architect (address is given) and make arrangements to secure a set of plans for review.

Yachting's
BOOK OF PLANS

DESIGNS FOR
363 BOATS
YOU CAN BUILD

POWER : SAIL : INBOARD : OUTBOARD
cruisers • auxiliaries • utilities • dinghies

NAVAL ARCHITECT'S NOTEBOOK

MOTOR BOATING & SAILING BOOKS
P.O. Box 2316, New York, N.Y. 10019
Motor Boating & Sailing, like *Yachting*, features a design section each month, and many of them have been incorporated in one or more of the following books, available from the above address:
Designs For 336 Boats You Can Build, 224 p. il., $3. A detailed

collection of popular designs, 7 to 50 feet in length, from the boards of Atkin and other leading naval architects. Each includes profile sketches and arrangement plans, with principal dimensions and specifications.

Naval Architect's Notebook by David P. Martin, 96 p. il., $3.95. Includes more than three dozen new and proven designs, power and sail, for boats from 11 to 65 feet from the board of Dave Martin. Most are suitable for construction by amateur builders. Each design is accompanied by a commentary describing how the boat came to be and what it is intended to do. A special section, of interest to would-be builders, gives instructions on reading and using lines drawings and offsets, boatbuilding in marine plywood, and tricks of the amateur boatbuilder that apply to other types of construction.

Professional Designs for Amateur Boatbuilders, 204 p. il., $5. Contains plans, construction details, and instructions for 42 individual boats from the boards of William and John Atkin and other top-notch naval architects, ranging from a 12-foot sailing dinghy to a 40-foot auxiliary ketch. Included are power utilities, run-abouts, and cruisers.

In addition to the above, Motor Boating & Sailing Books offers a free list of individual designs (plans) they have for sale.

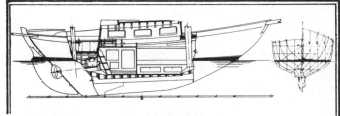

THOMAS C. GILLMER, NAVAL ARCHITECT
1 Shipwright Harbor, Annapolis, Md. 21401
Tom has put together a very nice 24-page booklet of his stock plans called *Marine Designs*. It's illustrated with many photographs of his boats and features twelve traditional types, the biggest of which is a 44-foot cruising ketch. Data on each boat include sail plan, profile and plan views of interior arrangement, commentary, and the price of working drawings which range from $48 to $275; all quite reasonable. Study plans are available for any boat at $16 a set. For a copy of *Marine Designs* send $1 to Tom at the above address.

KITS

Many would like to build their own yacht for economy, or to obtain a custom yacht or to have a much sounder vessel than is commonly available in production versions. Starting from scratch to build an entire yacht is a tremendous undertaking (it took me three years of full-time work), and anyone who completes such has my admiration. Most do not. Few realize that completion of the shell—hull, deck and cabin house—represents at the most only one-third of the man-hours required. It therefore makes a good deal of sense to start with a completed hull and go on from there. Most production yacht firms will quote on a bare hull, and the following companies specialize in such. In some cases they also furnish optional kits. For a more complete discussion of the subject, read the book earlier described: Fiberglass Kit Boats.

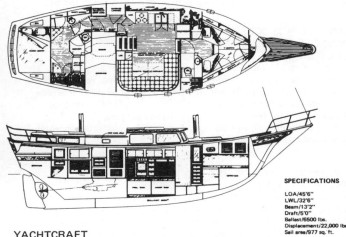

SPECIFICATIONS
LOA/45'6"
LWL/32'6"
Beam/13'2"
Draft/5'0"
Ballast/6500 lbs.
Displacement/22,000 lbs.
Sail area/977 sq. ft.

YACHTCRAFT
1922 Barranca Rd., Irvine, Calif. 92705
Yachtcraft offers eight sailing yacht kits ranging from a 34-ft. sloop through a 37-ft. motor sailer to a 55-ft. beauty. Major components kits including hull, deck and rudder range from $6,768 to about $20k. Other parts are available such as ballast, windows, liners, interior and spars. Designs are by Crealock, McGlasson and Lapworth.

GLANDER BOATS INC.
P.O. Box 1107, Tavernier, Fla. 33070
28-ft. and 33-ft. fiberglass shoal-draft hulls are offered at $4k and $7,855, respectively.

C. E. RYDER CORP.
Box 274, Bristol, R.I. 02809
This firm offers the 31-ft. *Southern Cross* heavy-displacement cutter in Airex foam sandwich. Hull price is $4,500.

GREENWICH YACHTS LTD.
535 Airport Rd. South, Richmond, B.C., Canada
Available from this company are 35-ft. and 42-ft. Colvin-designed aluminum hulls.

SIMPSON WILD INTERNATIONAL, INC.
P.O. Box 698, Kemah, Tex. 77565
The only source we know of in the U.S. for trimaran kits. Just began production of the 32-ft. *Shifter Mk. 2.*

HARSTIL INDUSTRIES, INC.
17150 Fifteen Mile Rd., Fraser, Mich. 48026
The extremely rugged *Sea Explorer 46,* heavy-displacement cruising ketch, is available for about $17k bare-hull price. Other components are available, such as stringers, bulkheads, deck, shaft log, rudder, engine beds, tanks, and so on. Of particular interest is that Harstil manufactures a 1/10 scale sailing model with hull, deck and cabin trunk molded in fiberglass. It sells for $113. This firm also builds the *Kaulua 31* fast cruising catamaran whose kit price is $9,436.

BLUE WATER BOATS, INC.
Box 625C, Woodinville, Wash. 98072
The 38-ft. ketch, *Ingrid,* is priced at $8k for a bare hull in fiberglass, and other components may also be purchased.

NORTH STAR FIBERGLASS YACHTS
800 Cacique, Santa Barbara, Calif. 93103
Two of Bruce Bingham's designs, *Flicka 20* and *Anastasia 32,* are furnished in fiberglass from bare hulls to finished craft. Hulls only are $2,450 and $5,600, respectively. Partial kits are available.

WINDWARD MARINE, INC.
3310 S. Union. Tacoma, Wash. 98409
The *Searaker 50* is a 17-ton, Monk-designed cutter or ketch supplied at any stage of construction. She has an unusually strong, hand-laminated hull of 17 layers of woven roving, mat and cloth at the sheer and 44 layers of reinforcement at the bottom of the full keel.

STARRATT & JENKS YACHT CO.
1421 Bay St. SE, St. Petersburg, Fla. 33701
The *Starratt 45* is offered in kit form at $7,000 for hull, deck and all hatches. $39 a month rents fenced space at the factory for completion of the boat.

WESTSAIL CORP.
1626 Placentia Ave., Costa Mesa, Calif. 92627
Westsail offers a 32' double-ended cutter as a kit in various stages of completion or as a complete boat. This Archer-Atkin-Creslock-designed North Sea pilot boat is more fully described under Cruising Sailboats.

DREADNOUGHT BOATWORKS
P.O. Box 221, Carpinteria, Calif. 93013

Somewhat similar to Westsail's design is Dreadnought's double-ended ketch—the Dreadnought 32. She's 32' x 10' x 5', and the manufacturers claim a 21-day passage for her from San Francisco to Honolulu. The Dreadnought 32 is a replica of the Tahiti Ketch designed by John G. Hanna in 1933, and sailed as the *Adios* twice around the globe by Tom and Janet Steel (winners of the '64 Bluewater Cruising Medal). Dreadnought Boatworks offers the Tahiti Ketch as a kit in various stages of completion; deck, rudder, tanks, or (choice of) engine can be installed in the one-piece, hand-laminated fiberglass hull prior to delivery. Cost of the kit with all these items installed (f.o.b. Carpinteria) is $8,770—this does not include the cost of the engine, only its installation. You can count on spars, rigging, a suit of sails, and an engine, all of which the purchaser must supply, to bring the cost of the boat up to $12k—still, a pretty fantastic deal. Literature, specifications, and photos are available.

DREADNOUGHT 32

BOATBUILDING GEAR

TOOLS and EQUIPMENT

Generally, the same tools used in carpentry, metalworking, painting, and so forth are used in boatbuilding. There are, of course, specialized tools for caulking, ropework, rigging, and so forth. We've got tool dealers spread throughout the Source Book—for a general roundup, check the Wilderness Living Section; for mechanics' tools, the Off-Road Touring Section; and for specialized boatbuilding tools, the Marine Equipment subsection. Boat Owners Buyers Guide is an excellent source of tool and equipment dealers, as are the three volumes of The Mariner's Catalog and Boats and Harbors. Listed below is one firm that handles woodworking tools worth calling to your attention:

Timber Scriber

#999 Straight blunt
#1000 Straight sharp
#1001 Bent sharp
#1001A Bent blunt
#1002 Single Crease

Mailing weight 2 lbs. ea.

#1001 #1001A #1002 #1000 #999   Caulking Irons

WOODCRAFT SUPPLY CORP.
313 Montvale Ave., Woburn, Mass. 01801

Woodcraft has a very good line of quality woodworking tools of the type you won't often find in a hardware store. Prices are reasonable, and amongst the boatbuilding tools there are several types of caulking iron, $3 to $5; a timber scriber, used to scribe waterlines, $6; chipping irons, scrapers, and sewing palms. They also handle a large assortment of woodworking and carpentry books. Their 46-page catalog is well-illustrated and can be had for 50¢.

GILLIOM MFG. CO.
1109 N. 2nd St., St. Charles, Mo. 63301

This company manufactures a complete line of stationary power tool kits including band saws, floor saws, drill press-lathe, table belt sander, and floor-model spindle shaper. The 18-in. band saw kit complete with 3/4-hp motor and adding in the wood necessary for the cabinet comes to $195 plus freight. This compares to about $1,200 for a new band saw of this size. A friend of mine has used this saw over many years to build many large wooden yachts and has found it to be very satisfactory. He does recommend that a 1-hp motor be used.

MATERIALS and FITTINGS

Some materials for boatbuilding can be picked up at the local lumberyard and hardware store if suitable cautions are paid to using

relatively well-seasoned and rot-resistant woods and metals not susceptible to salt air or water corrosion. Mixing of most metals is a no-no because of electrolysis. Prices at marine stores are often quite high. Commercial fishermen's supply houses are very reasonable sources for hot-dipped plough steel, galvanized hardware and rigging wire—usually at one-third the price of their marine counterparts. Try wrecking and salvage companies for seasoned oak and cedar timbers. Boatyards sometimes have a derelict lying around with fittings and timbers which could be purchased for scrap value. If you are lucky enough to find a stadium being torn down or a lot of park benches being scrapped, check the wood used in the seats. Alaskan Yellow Cedar (an excellent boat wood) is usually used because of its unique property of not producing splinters.

Listed are a few firms that might be useful to you. Other dealers will be found in the Marine Equipment subsection. Incidentally, don't forget to check the Boat Owners Buyers Guide, Mariner's Catalogs, Boats and Harbors and AYRS Journals for materials and fittings.

U.S. PLASTICS CORP.
1550 Elida Rd., Lima, Ohio 45805

U.S. Plastics carries a fantastic range of items in various types of plastic. Here's just a brief listing of the major ones: all sizes and shapes of tanks and containers, plumbing and piping, valves, sink drains, plexiglass sheeting suitable for skylights and portlights, flexible tubing and fittings, small pumps and a couple of larger ones suitable for bilge pumps ("Guzzler," hand-operated). You'll find many boatbuilding aids here, too. A very well done 110-page catalog is available free on request.

MAURICE L. CONDON, INC.
250 Ferris Ave., White Plains, N.Y. 10603

If you need mahogany (Philippine, African, Honduras), teak, sitka spruce, cedar, cypress, and so forth in plank, plywood or moulding and can't find it locally, you might try Condon. He has a good stock of marine lumber and prices are average. All prices are f.o.b. White Plains, N.Y. Price sheets are available for 25¢. Also, you might ask for shipping charges to your address; they could add quite a bit to the cost.

THE DEAN CO.
519 N.W. Tenth Drive, Gresham, Oreg. 97030

This is the only source known for veneers in quantities and prices suitable for building cold-moulded boats of any size. They supply 1/8-in. vertical grain Western Red Cedar, suitable for building boats, at the very low price of $200 per thousand square feet, plus freight. I've seen several boats built in this way with epoxy glue and coating, inside and out, (*WEST System*), and it's a good way for the amateur builder to go.

HARBOR SALES CO., INC.
1401 Russell St., Baltimore, Md. 21230

This is a good source of marine plywood, and I found them less expen-

268

sive, including freight, than purchasing A-A exterior plywood locally. Their Utile marine mahogany-type plywood is imported from Holland, and is of really excellent quality.

PAINTS and COMPOUNDS

Not everyone knows how antifouling paint works, so we'll make mention of it here. Antifouling paint is designed to dissolve slowly off the hull, and as it does, it releases toxic chemicals. Marine organisms can't get along with this, thus they stay off the hull. In salt water, bottom paint lasts about six months before a new coat is needed; in fresh water, eight to twelve months. The cooler the water, the longer the time it'll last. Quite a few bottom paints are designed to be immersed in water immediately after application; if allowed to dry, the release of toxic agents can be inhibited from 75 to 100 per cent.

Good marine paints are expensive and can run up to twice as much as house paint. Bottom paint, for example, ranges from $35 to $120 per gallon, so be prepared to pay through the nose during annual maintenance.

GOUGEON BROTHERS
706 Martin St., Bay City, Mich. 48706

Meade and his brothers, Jan and Joe, build and sail wooden boats, and in 1975 their two-tonner, *Golden Dazy*, won the two-ton Admiral's Cup races in Canada. They have developed a method where cheaper grades of wood can be used in boatbuilding—a blessing in these days of scarce traditional boat lumber. Briefly, all wooden parts are coated with three layers of a low-viscosity epoxy resin inside and out. The encapsulated wood is sealed from moisture which prevents rot and preserves the higher strength of dry wood. The technique is described in their 27-page book, *WEST System,* for $2. The Gougeons sell their epoxy resin formulation at a very low price compared to the usual—the delivered price I've had to pay is about 30% less than what it runs locally for a good grade. They also offer a metering pump and various additives including microballoons and carbon fibers. Highly recommended.

ALADDIN PRODUCTS INC.
RFD 2, Wiscasset, Maine 04578

Platt Monfort, the inventor of Git-Rot, has developed a synthetic polyester resin cement and reinforcement called Wire Plank for a very much improved synthetic ferro-cement system for boatbuilding. This overcomes most of my objections to conventional ferro-cement. Even light-displacement boats and multihulls can be made of this material. Send Platt $2 for his 64-page book, *A Revolution in Ferro Construction.*

TRAVACO LABORATORIES, INC.
345 Eastern Ave., Chelsea, Mass. 02150

Travaco is the source of Marine-Tex, a widely used epoxy, metal alloy filler, which can be drilled, tapped, and sanded, is water-proof and unaffected by chemicals or petroleum products. Other Travaco compounds include Gluvit, an epoxy waterproof sealer; Caulke-Tex, an epoxy caulking and bedding compound; TUF-Seal, an epoxy waterproof sealant for concrete and ferro-cement structures, plus Ferro 3, an additive to improve the cement's qualities; and Liquid Marine-Tex, a special epoxy compound for use with fiberglass. Detailed literature on all these is available from the above address.

INTERNATIONAL PAINT CO., INC.
21 West St., New York, N.Y. 10006

Besides good paint, International puts out an informative booklet for the practical boatman on paint; varnish; preparing wood, fiberglass, and metal surfaces for painting; hints and tips for new and old work; explanations of why and when to use various types of paints from anti-fouling to wood undercoater; painting tools and their use and maintenance; paint requirements for various size boats; and, of course, suggestions for using various types of International Paint. Great book for your boat locker. Forty pages, illustrated, and costs only 25¢.

B. F. GOODRICH, AEROSPACE AND DEFENSE PRODUCTS
500 South Main St., Akron, Ohio 44138

If you're tired of haul-outs and the high price of bottom paints, you might look into B. F. Goodrich's Nofoul, a rubber sheet material that can be applied to hulls with a special marine adhesive. It presents a mildly toxic surface that repels barnacles like anti-fouling paint, except the rubber doesn't wear away. The release rate is controlled and protection is good for five to six years instead of five to six months as with paint. Nofoul also seals leaks, protects against marine borers, cavitation, and corrosion. Specifications and sources of Nofoul can be secured from the above address.

FLO-PAINT, INC.
5-54 49th Ave., Long Island City, N.Y. 11101

Here's the line-up of Flo-Paint products. All have a good reputation:

BoatLIFE LIFE-CALK. 1 or 2 part Thiokol rubber base sealants produce lastingly watertight seams above and below water line. One-part system available in 17 oz. cartridge and new 4½ oz. squeeze tube.

BoatLIFE Rub-R-Cote. Paints on a waterproof rubber sheet over deck, hull, cabin roof. Permanent seal. Variety of colors.

BoatLIFE Plastic Finishes. Polyurethane-fortified paints. Look and wear like baked-on finish. Rich, beautiful colors, and clear. High gloss and low lustre.

BoatLIFE ANTI-FOULING. Sleek surface constantly exposing fresh toxic film to kill barnacles, worms, grass, other marine growth. Contains effective new ingredient — bio-MeT*. Brilliant colors — white, green, blue, red.

CLEAR-N-TUF. Crystal clear flexible coating for wood, metal, plastic, canvas. Revitalizes time-dulled fiberglass, varnish, paint.

BoatLIFE MetaLIFE. Guards all metal surfaces against corrosion, pitting, staining for extended time period.

BoatLIFE Plastic Canvas Seal. Restores canvas. Flexible. Seals, waterproofs.

BoatLIFE FLO-CALK. Fast-curing butyl rubber sealant. Especially good for bedding. Produces watertight hull and deck seams.

Free literature is available, which includes specifications, applications, and prices.

Type	Size	Topside	Bottom	Waterline	Deck	Varnish	Interior	Engine
DINGHY	10'	1 Qt.	1 Pt.	—	—	1½ Qts.	—	—
ROWBOAT	14'	2 Qts.	1 Qt.	—	—	—	—	—
OUTBOARD	14'	2 Qts.	1 Qt.	—	1 Pt.	1½ Qts.	—	½ Pt.
RUNABOUT	18'	2 Qts.	2 Qts.	½ Pt.	1 Qt.	1 Qt.	—	½ Pt. or 16 oz. Spray
SAILBOAT	20'	2 Qts.	3 Qts.	1 Pt.	1 Gal.	2 Qts.	—	—
RUNABOUT	24'	2 Qts.	3 Qts.	½ Pt.	1½ Qts.	3 Qts.	—	1 Pt. or 16 oz. Spray
UTILITY	24'	2 Qts.	3 Qts.	½ Pt.	1½ Qts.	1 Qt.	—	1 Pt. or 16 oz. Spray
CRUISER	25'	3 Qts.	3 Qts.	1 Pt.	2 Qts.	2 Qts.	2 Qts.	1 Pt. or 16 oz. Spray
CRUISER	32'	2 Gals.	1½ Gals.	1 Pt.	2 Qts.	3 Qts.	2 Qts.	1 Pt. or 16 oz. Spray
AUXILIARY	36'	2 Gals.	2 Gals.	1 Pt.	1 Gal.	1 Gal.	3 Qts.	1 Pt. or 2 16 oz. Spray
CRUISER	40'	2½ Gals.	2 Gals.	1 Pt.	1½ Gals.	1 Gal.	1 Gal.	1 Pt. or 2 16 oz. Spray
YACHT	60'	4 Gals.	5 Gals.	1 Qt.	3½ Gals.	2½ Gals.	3 Gals.	1½ Qt. or 2 16 oz. Spray

Paint requirements for various size boats (2 coats).

MARINE EQUIPMENT

We'd originally intended breaking this section down into the various divisions of ship's husbandry (a ship's husband is the nautical term for one who maintains and looks after the well-being of a boat)— masting and rigging, sailmaking, engineering, etc., to discuss more systematically the books, tools, supplies, equipment, and everything else you should know about, and where to get it. Turns out we're running a bit long, though, and since this book has to cover a lot of ground, we've had to leave out the discussions of equipment here and under navigation. Sorry about this.

sources of information

Commandant (G-CAS-2/81)
U.S. COAST GUARD
400 Seventh St., S.W., Washington, D.C. 20590
We've talked about the Guard already in several places, so you should have a fairly good idea of what they're about; however, here we want to call your attention to several publications regarding marine equipment that you ought to get. All are free for the asking:

Marine Communications for the Boating Public, CG-423A. Six-page brochure covering all the essentials.

Marine Emergency and Distress Information Sheet, CG-3892. A handy 5¼" x 8" card to post by your radio. Covers the transmitting drill to use if you're in trouble or you see some other vessel in trouble. This will help you avoid time-wasting mistakes.

Equipment Lists, CG-190. Contains 187 pages listing every piece of equipment, chemical, compound, or whatever that has been approved by the Guard for use at sea, with the name and address of the manufacturer. This is not necessarily an endorsement of quality, but everything listed has had to meet certain requirements.

Marine Engineering Regulations, CG-115. This 180 pager is primarily concerned with large vessel engineering, though Part 58 will be of interest to pleasure boatmen. This part covers internal combustion engines and their installation; use of LP gas for cooking and heating; refrigeration; steering apparatus; fluid power and control systems; and fuel systems and tanks. Emphasis is on design, construction, and installation.

Electrical Engineering Regulations, CG-259. Covers general requirements of the electrical system; emergency lighting and power system; and communication and alarm systems and equipment. This 150-page book is a must for recommissioning, repairing, or just plain maintenance. Emphasis is on design, construction, and installation.

NATIONAL FIRE PROTECTION ASSOCIATION (NFPA)
60 Batterymarch St., Boston, Mass. 02110
NFPA sets standards and makes recommendations on virtually every aspect of fire protection and preservation. They publish over 900 booklets of various thickness on equipment, systems, and methods of protecting everything from aardvarks to ZIP codes. Here's a list of the booklets that would be of interest to boatmen (order by number and title):

10: Extinguishers, Installation - $1.
10-A: Extinguishers, Maintenance - $1.
12: Carbon Dioxide Systems - $1.50.
17: Dry Chemical Ext. Systems - 75¢.
58: LP-Gas Storage, Use - $1.25.
302: Motor Craft (re. motor boats) - $1.25.
303: Marinas and Boatyards - $1.
306: Gas Hazards on Vessels - 75¢.
312: Vessels, Construction—Repair - 50¢.

A complete list of booklets and information on NFPA can be had by writing the above address.

HUBBEL, INC., Wiring Device Div.
Bridgeport, Conn. 06602
Publishes an excellent little 26-page manual, *More Boat Power to You,* covering marine electricity, wiring, and electrolysis. Includes tables, wiring diagrams, and many helpfull hints and tips. Free from Hubbell.

RADIO TECHNICAL COMMISSION FOR MARINE SERVICES
P.O. Box 19087, Washington, D.C. 20036
These are the people to contact about licensing your marine radio-telephone (which is considered a mobile station) and licensing yourself to operate it. For this you'll need a Restricted Radiotelephone Operator Permit which just lets you operate the set. For installing it and screwing around inside with the back off, you need a 2nd or 1st phone ticket (Radio Telephone [or Telegraph] Operator license). Get the full skinny on this and other interesting legal requirements from:

Ship Radiotelephone and Radar, SS Bul. 1007, free. A 4-page summary of some of the more important requirements affecting the installation and operation of radios on pleasure vessels.

Marine Radiotelephone Handbook, $2.50. This book contains extracts from FCC rules with explanations covering the requirements for operating marine radiotelephones. A good one to have aboard.

Both are available from the Radio Technical Commission, as are answers to your specific inquiries on this aspect of boating.

PERIODICALS

BOAT OWNERS BUYERS GUIDE
Frank T. Moss, Ed.
Annually - $2.50/issue - 364 p. il.

We covered this earlier in the section. This is just a reminder that the *Boat Owners Buyers Guide* is the best source directory there is to boating gear and everything else nautical. Sockitoimpapa!
From: Yachting Pub. Corp., 50 W. 44th St. New York, N.Y. 10036

SPYGLASS 76
1976, 3rd ed. - 384 p. il. - $5

This is a massive sailboat equipment catalog assembled from manufacturers' leaflets. The editorial section has articles on boat construction materials, sailcloth manufacture, iceboat racing, backstay adjustments, and provisioning for a cruise. The second part is an up-to-date rigging guide. The third section is an equipment directory, and all items can be ordered through the publisher of this catalog.
From: Spyglass Catalog Co., 2415 Webster St., Alameda, Calif. 94501

THE TELLTALE COMPASS
Victor Jorgensen, Ed.
Monthly - $20/yr. - 4 p.

In its six years of publication, *The Telltale Compass* has discussed many subjects of prime interest to boatmen, all naming names and pulling no punches. They cover a broad range of topics from deck shoes to designs such as a series of straightforward evaluations of the Ranger 23, the Cascade 29, the Irwin 32, the Columbia 45, the Morgan Out Island 41, and other current craft; critique of the Whistler radar, vodka as an antifreeze for water tanks, discussions on diesel fuel additives, and the pros and cons of ferro-cement; a completely frank report on the problems one sailor encountered in having his boat built in the Orient; evaluations of different kinds of electronic gear from Apelco to Zenith; reports of problems found in such boats as a Columbia 24, a Cal 20, and a Morgan 28, to name a few; plain advice on what to do and what equipment to buy in view of the new marine radio rulings; and dozens more. The 4-page reports are published monthly and edited by Vic Jorgensen who's been in the boating field some 17 years and was at one time managing editor of *The Skipper.* He's assisted by various knowledgeable boatmen in the marine field, some who remain anonymous and others who are independent enough to by-line their reports without fear of repercussion. The subscription rate of $20 a year is a little rough, but the information is prime and would be cheap at twice the price.
From: The Telltale Compass, 18418 S. Old River Dr., Lake Oswego, Oreg. 97034

sources of general gear

LANDS' END YACHT STORES, INC.
2317 N. Elston Ave., Chicago, Ill. 60614
Lands' End has the most widely acclaimed catalog in the marine field. It's well laid out, interesting, and virtually a reference work in itself on racing sailboat hardware. Usually there are a number of editorial discussions of interest to racing types included in the book.

Lands' End's inventory is mainly oriented to racing hardware for all sizes of boats and includes just about anything and everything one would need for spar fittings, rigging, roller reefing and furlings, deck hardware, and so on. Brands include Barient (winches), Yacht Specialities (steering pedestals), Mariner (blocks and general hardware), Schaefer (winches, blocks, hardware), Star (blocks and general hardware), Seaboard (winches, travelers, general hardware), Brummel (hooks), Nocro-Fico (blocks, ventilators, reefing and furling gear, general hardware), and Harken (blocks); all top names in the field. Other sailing accessories include apparel, galley gear, life rafts and preservers, navigation instruments and compasses, boating books, rope, wire, riggers tools, sail maintenance equipment, and miscellaneous odds and ends. All gear is fully illustrated and described, and in some cases technical or opinion commentary is included. Lands' End's 208-page catalog runs $2 and is well worth it if you're pretty heavy into racing.

THOMAS FOULKES
Lansdowne Rd., Leytonstone, London, England E11 3HB
This is a British discount house which exports to individuals in the U.S. and other countries. Excellent savings are possible on certain items, and I have found them to give good service. Their Ebbco micrometer drum ABS plastic sextant, which I have used in preference to my heavyweight brass job for the past few years, costs only $23, plus shipping, as compared to more than double that price from American importers. There are also good savings on Avon inflatable dinghies, Seagull outboards, stainless turnbuckles and toggles, marine fluorescent lights, Gibb winches and much more. They also are a good source for low-priced books. *Ocean Passages of the World* is only $11.50, one-third the U.S. price, and the *Nautical Almanac* is only $3.20, less than half the current price here. Send $1 for their annual 26-page catalog.

JAMES BLISS & CO., INC.
Rt. 128, Dedham, Mass. 02026
Bliss carries an extensive line of general marine gear including apparel, foul weather gear, safety and emergency, medical, maintenance, navigation, galley, and signalling accessories, charts, books, novelties,

gifts, ship models (they have a special catalog for model builders), rigging and deck hardware, binoculars, ground tackle, so forth and so on—284 pages of it in their catalog, which sells for $1. Bliss's book is an excellent marine equipment reference source if you want to know of all the things that are available. Prices are average to high.

WEST PRODUCTS CORP.
P.O. Box 707, East Boston, Mass. 02128
West manufactures most of the products it sells under the name "Sealine." Their gear is all of high quality and most items are priced at what the market will bear. Inventory includes rope; rigging and rope working tools; anchors, shackles, blocks, and other fittings and hardware; bilge pumps; chemicals and compounds; repair tapes; some nav instruments apparel, foul weather gear; flares and survival equipment; fire extinguishers; electrical panels, fittings, and tools; yacht maintenance equipment and supplies; cabin and galley gear; flags; various duffle and sea bags; boating books; and nautical gifts. West's very nicely illustrated 192-page catalog is available on request.

DEFENDER INDUSTRIES, INC.
255 Main St., New Rochelle, N.Y. 10801
The dollar you send for their annual 168-page catalog is well worth the money. This is a discount house which sells a wide variety of marine equipment and hardware. Of interest to the amateur boatbuilder and those doing their own marine maintenance are their stocks of hull sheathing and laminating materials: fiberglass, vectra polypropylene, dynel and kevlar, plus a variety of various types of epoxy and polyester resins. I've had good results from this company, although they are a bit slow through the mails.

JAY STUART HAFT
8925 North Tennyson Dr., Milwaukee, Wisc. 53217
Haft handles big boat gear for 30-footers and on up. His 78-page catalog lists several types of anchor windlasses (hand-crank and electric); a rope-chain gipsy; H & M geared sheet winches; ventilators; engine

telegraphs; cabin stoves and fireplaces; hot water heater; teak ship's wheels, 18" to 66"; teak side ladders and skylights; cabinetry hardware; gimbled oil lamps, oil and electric running lights, search lights; compasses of all types including a master's tell tale compass, binnacles; a small selection of rigging hardware; and a CQR plow anchor in weights from 5 to 105 lbs. Choice gear that you won't find in too many marine stores. Jay's catalog runs 25¢ and is worth picking up.

PAUL E. LUKE
East Boothbay, Me. 04544
This down-easter handles several models of LP gas and alcohol stoves and cabin heaters including two fireplaces; aluminum ventilators; a pedestal binnacle unit with teak wheel; and if you're looking for a good kedge anchor, Paul has them in weights from 40 to 200 lbs. at prices from $186 to $560. Materials are steel and high-strength modular iron, and the anchors are designed to be taken apart for stowage. Literature and price sheet available on request.

E & B MARINE SUPPLY
1801 Hylan Blvd., Staten I., N.Y. 10305
Good source of discount boating gear, though mainly general-type stuff (no windjammer's grab bag). E & B's line consists of Airguide and Aqua Meter compasses; Davis nav gear; Kenyon speedometers and wind instruments; marine reefers, stoves, and heaters, including Aladdin and Ratelco; bilge pumps, Jabsco pumps, and the Guzzler; electrical fittings and shore line; engine gauges, controls, and other accessories; rope; miscellaneous deck hardware and builder's hardware; maintenance equipment, and supplies; ground tackle including Danforth; winches; waterclosets, holding tanks, and survival equipment; Avon inflatable boats; fathometers by Ray Jefferson and others; Marine radiotelephones; binoculars; flags; Nicro-Fico sailboat hardware; and so forth. E & B's 170-page catalog has a lot of good deals for the $1 it costs.

GOLDBERGS' MARINE
202 Market St., Philadelphia, Pa. 19106
Goldbergs' is about the same drill as E & B, though Goldberg has more variety and more sailboat gear, including Nicro-Fico, Barient, Star, Schaefer, Seaboard and Barlow. They also handle stoves, outboard motors, weather instruments and other stuff E & B doesn't handle. Discounts are comparable to E & B's, though don't look for any slack on the sailing hardware; those manufacturers don't go that route. Goldbergs' 228-page catalog runs $2.50, and of the two (E & B's and Goldbergs') , Goldbergs' is most worth scraping the money for.

RVG: RIEBANDT VANE STEERING
Box 8433, Madeira Beach, Fla. 33738
Successful self-steering systems are vital on small craft taken on long voyages and very useful for even the weekender. Electronic types usually give trouble from salt air corrosion, and the auto-pilot type used on powerboats can get you into real trouble on a sailboat when the wind changes. The RVG gear is extremely responsive to small changes in wind velocity and direction and has been found to be accurate and dependable on a variety of boats from a Cal 25 to a 54,000-lb., 62-ft. double-ender on *all* points of sailing. A friend on mine used his on a several-thousand-mile voyage in a 42-ft. trimaran and swears by it. Most vane gears have difficulty steering when the boat is running with the wind, but the RVG seems to work well on this course on most boats. This is the only company I know who will fit the gear to the boat for you and let you know whether it's suitable or not.

KENYON MARINE
New Whitfield St., Guilford, Conn. 06437
Makes 4,000 different marine hardware items: masts, booms, spinnaker poles for boats up to 40 feet; 14 different marine stoves and ovens; 25 different instruments to measure wind speed, direction, boat speed, and other parameters; shackles, blocks and other hardware. Send $1 for catalogs.

ALEXANDER-ROBERTS
1851 Langley Ave., Santa Ana, Calif. 92705
Complete line of boat and yacht hardware from dinghies to 72-ft. Barlow winches, Ronstan fittings and Seafast turnbuckles. Line includes rigging gear, mast and spar fittings, cleats, goosenecks, jib-furling drums, reefing systems, blocks, shackles, track, etc. Free catalog.

DANFORTH
Portland, Me. 04103
Danforth is probably best known for their anchors, and they've got a lot on the market to prove it. Several models are available for vessels up to 90 feet in length at prices ranging from $22 to $280. Danforth publishes a 16-page booklet entitled *Anchors and Anchoring*, which is an in-depth discussion of the subject that includes much technical data with tables and charts. Now in its 7th edition, this little book should be in every sailor library. It's available free from the above

HI-TENSILE®

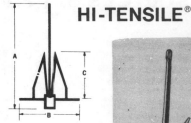

Anchor Size	Price	A Anchor Lgth.	B Stock Lgth.	C Fluke Lgth.
5-H	$ 32.50	21½	16½	11¾
12-H	$ 62.00	28¼	21½	15½
20-H	$ 95.00	35	26¾	19
35-H	$140.00	40¾	31	22

address.

Other items in the Danforth line are compasses and binnacles; fathometers, including digital read out and recording types; weather instruments and relative wind indicators; automatic pilots; electrical gauges; binoculars; plotting instruments; aluminum transom davits; electric and freon horns; searchlights and navigation lights; and an intra-ship and hailing communication system. Check it all out in their illustrated 54-page catalog, free.

PALMER-JOHNSON, INC.
61 Michigan St., Sturgeon Bay, Wisc. 54235
This is a specialty outfit that manufacturers high quality equipment for large boats. Their line is rather varied, though with some items they may have only one model or one size. At any rate, the list runs: aluminum steering sheaves and quadrants; teak cockpit gratings and companionway hatch doors (custom-built); aluminum portlights; deck deadlight prisms; various padeyes; locust (wood) and aluminum cleats; aluminum roller reefing gooseneck; various sizes and types of aluminum alloy blocks (this is Palmer's main line); foul weather suits; and wind indicating instruments. Prices are right up there, but you're paying for craftsmanship. Palmer's illustrated catalog runs $1.

SOUTHERN MARINE SUPPLY
1630 Superior Ave., Costa Mesa, Calif. 92627
Southern is one of the big general-type marine supply houses that handles just about everything nautical, most of which is name-brand stuff. It would take several pages just to give a general run-down of what they have in their big 550-page catalog (costs $5), so of course, we're not gonna do it. There are several big firms like Southern around the country with a comparable inventory and prices. It would be worthwhile to pick up a catalog from at least one of them for your reference files if you're planning on doing any major work on your boat. Incidentally Southern also publishes a free 32-page catalog, if you'd like to get a general idea of what they handle.

FAWCETT BOAT SUPPLIES, INC.
100 Compromise St., Annapolis, Md. 21404
Like Southern. Biggest outfit on the Chesapeake Bay, so we hear. Fawcett's catalog runs some 500 pages and costs $3. It's a little different from the usual one, because they make it up using original manufacturer's literature. You get everyone's blurb all nicely bound up in one easy-to-use package. A point worth mentioning: Though

Fawcett's does have a catalog and will probably work with you on an order, they're not really pushing mail-order sales—take it from there.

ATLAS BOAT SUPPLY CO., INC.
93 Chambers St., New York, N.Y. 10007
An old-line outfit similar to Southern. They don't have quite the same inventory though, nor is their book as fat. Still, a good outfit. Catalog runs $1.

PERKINS MARINE LAMP & HARDWARE CORP.
Box D, Miami, Fla. 33164
Perkins' trade name, "Perko," is a familiar mark on lamps and marine hardware found in marine stores and on boats throughout the country. This outfit has been in business for a long time, and their products are well-known throughout the marine industry. They do not sell to the general public, but will gladly assist you with any problems or questions you may have regarding marine lamps (oil and electric) and hardware. They issue a 192-page catalog of their products, which is available from the above address for $1.

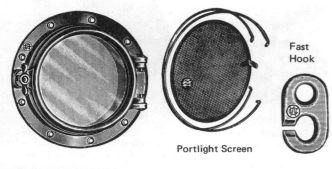

Fast Hook

Portlight Screen

WILCOX-CRITTENDEN
Box 1111, Middletown, Conn. 06457
Wilcox-Crittenden is another old-line marine hardware company like Perkins. Most marine hardware supply stores will carry a selection of their line, which bears the imprint "W-C" or "Marinium" (lightweight yacht fittings). These people do not sell to the public, but they will sell you their 112-page catalog for $1.75. This is a good reference source of what they make and the prices of same.

MASTING & RIGGING BOOKS

ENCYCLOPEDIA OF KNOTS AND FANCY ROPE WORK
Raoul Graumont and John Hensel
1952, 4th ed. - 706 p. il. - $15

This one is considered the definitive work on knots and fancy rope work. Starting with notes on the history of knots and rope making, the *Encyclopedia* then goes into the "how to" of tying and making useful and decorative articles of rope. There are more than 3600 knots described and illustrated in 348 full-page plates. The stories behind many of the knots are re-told with their associated lore.
From: Cornell Maritime Press, Box 109, Cambridge, Md. 21613

ASHLEY BOOK OF KNOTS
Clifford W. Ashley
1944 - 630 p. il. - $16.95

A comprehensive and (can you believe it?) charming book on knots, covering over 3,000 different kinds: what each looks like, where it comes from, how to tie and use it. Ashley's, however, is not as useable a book as *Encyclopedia of Knots and Fancy Rope Work*.
From: Doubleday, Inc.
501 Franklin Ave.
Garden City, L.I., N.Y. 11530

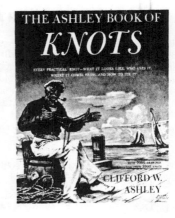

RIGGING SMALL SAILBOATS
Ken Hankinson
1973 - 96 p. il. - $4.95 (pb)

The author treats a much-neglected subject in sailing literature by telling us how to rig and adjust the rigging of small boats up to about 25 feet. Material covered includes spars, deck fittings, standing and running rigging, hull fitting installation, daggerboards and centerboards.
From: Glen-L Marine Designs, 9152 Rosecrans, Bellflower, Calif. 90706

THE MARLINSPIKE SAILOR
Harvey Garrett Smith
1971 - 143 p. il. - $7.95

This is one of my favorites. It has a very clear explanation of how to tie and make various knots and splices as well as turks heads, rope ladder, mast boots, stropped blocks, deadeyes, lanyards and much more.
From: John de Graff, Inc., 34 Oak Ave., Tuckahoe, N.Y. 10707

HANDBOOK FOR RIGGERS
W. G. Newberry
1967 - 120 p. il. - $2.95

A pocket-size gem that crams a tremendous amount of rigging data into a tiny volume. Includes wire rope breaking strengths; slings and chokers; splicing wire rope; wire rope fittings; splicing synthetic ropes; knots; safe working loads for rope and tackle; and chain strengths. Anyone doing rigging work ought to have this 4" x 6" book in his shirt pocket.
From: Internat'l Marine Pub. Co., 21 Elm St., Camden, Me. 04843

MASTING AND RIGGING
Harold A. Underhill
1946 - 314 p. il. - $13.50

If you're masting and rigging anything from a schooner to a full-rigged ship, this is *the* authoritative work on the subject. Harold Underhill is the European counterpart of Chapelle, and his many books on the technical aspects of sailing ships leave little if anything to be desired. He's a fantastic draftsman, and this book is a superb example of his work. It contains over 180 *working* drawings of bowsprits, wooden and steel masts, yards, square and stays'ls, plus smaller drawings of fittings, parts and accessories from pin rail to truck. And if you're at a loss as to where the mizzen-topgallant-stays'l-sheet makes up on a four-master, he's got that too, by way of a two-foot fold-out pin and fife rail diagram in the back of the book. Only problem is you had best be up on the jargon, 'cause this book is flat salty. Written in a how-to, documentary style with detailed instructions.
From: International Marine Pub. Co., 21 Elm St., Camden, Me. 04843

sources of gear

GIBBS YACHTING EQUIPMENT
2308 Clement St., San Francisco, Calif. 94121
Gibbs is a British-owned outfit that specializes in rigging gear for all size boats. Their inventory includes blocks, winches, roller reefing gear, mast, boom, and pole fittings and hardware, wire rope fittings, sail track, and miscellaneous fixed and sliding (track) padeyes and fairleads. All high quality equipment. Their 84-page illustrated catalog has quite a bit of "how to" information and suggestions. Cost, $1.

S & F TOOL CO.
P.O. Box 1546, Costa Mesa, Calif. 92626

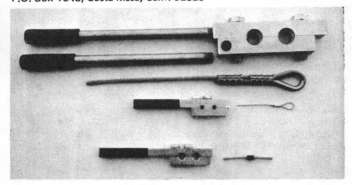

One way of putting an eye at the end of a wire rope is to swage it. This consists of compressing a sleeve of metal over the wire at the place it loops over itself. S & F has the sleeves and tools to do this for wire up to 3/8" thick. Three Swage-It kits are available from $10 to $50. S & F also handles galvanized and stainless wire rope, hardware, and fittings. Illustrated literature and price sheets are available on request.

LIPTON MARINE INDUSTRIES
Rock Ridge, Mamaroneck, N.Y. 10543
For accurate adjustment (tuning) of standing rigging, Lipton sells a cast aluminum, stainless steel meter that measures relative tension. With it you can equalize the strain on port and starboard shrouds, or reset the running backstay to exactly what it was before it was cast off. Cost for Mark I for use with wire up to 9/32" is $22.

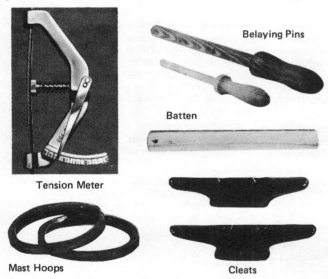

Belaying Pins

Batten

Tension Meter

Mast Hoops

Cleats

BETE MANUFACTURING CO.
P.O. Box 276, Marion, Mass. 02738
Bete is a source of steam-bent, copper-riveted, varnished, white ash mast hoops (made to special order); belaying pins of varnished white ash, 5/8" x 10", $5; 3/4" x 16", $9; black locust, standard and jamb cleats; turnbuckle boots, white ash and fiberglass battens; and white ash shroud rollers—hollow dowels split down the center; the two halves are clamped on a shroud and taped or sewed together, and when set up, they roll, thus preventing the shroud from chafing the sail (some people use bamboo or baggy wrinkle). Illustrated 4-page price sheet is available on request.

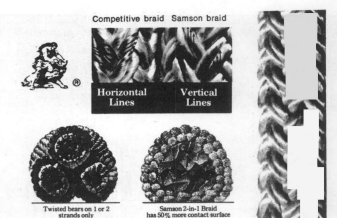

Competitive braid   Samson braid

Horizontal Lines   **Vertical Lines**

Twisted bears on 1 or 2 strands only

Samson 2-in-1 Braid has 50% more contact surface

SAMSON CORDAGE WORKS
470 Atlantic Ave., Boston, Mass. 02210
Samson manufacturers a very pliable single- and double-braid nylon yachting rope that runs smoothly through blocks, is easy to handle and coil, and very easy to "splice" (requires a special technique). The secret is in the braided construction which orients core and cover filaments parallel to the rope's axis. Samson Cordage is recommended for sheets, halyards, vangs, guys, and docking, mooring, and anchor lines. Literature with technical data, prices, and complete instructions for splicing is available from the above address.

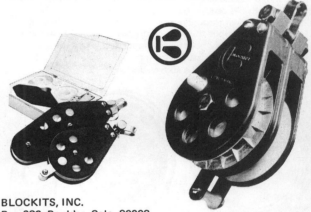

BLOCKITS, INC.
Box 386, Boulder, Colo. 80302
Gerry Cunningham is at it again. After inventing all types of gear for backpackers, he's gotten into the marine field with a very versatile block called the Blockit. The idea is to have a block that can be adapted to different needs—swivel, non-swivel; with becket, without becket, and so forth. A novel idea that could save money. At any rate, you buy a kit and put together exactly what the situation calls for. Blockit No. 1 for example, makes 2 singles and one fiddle block in 26 styles. Cost is $33. Write Gerry at the above address for his 12-page booklet *Rigging Your Boat the Blockit Way.*

SAILS
BOOKS

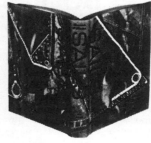

SAILS
Jeremy Howard-Williams
1970 - 400 p. il. - $12.50

Currently, this is the top seller on sails by a man who knows what its all about. Howard-Williams is with Ratsey and Lapthorn in Great Britain. In *Sails* he takes a brief look at the history of sailmaking and the consequent requirements of sail design and construction. Added to this are sections on choosing sails, sail characteristics, maintenance, faults with sails, and the chances of altering a defective sail. Also good info on tuning rigging. Many photos and illustrations.
From: John De Graff, Inc., 34 Oak Ave., Tuckahoe, N.Y. 10707

MAKE YOUR OWN SAILS

R. M. Bowker and S. A. Budd
1975, 2nd ed. - 142 p. il. - $3.95 (pb)

Subtitled "Handbook for the Amateur and Professional Sailmaker," this book is just that. Excellent for getting into the art and science of sailmaking, with chapters on tools and equipment; canvas and synthetic materials; setting up a sail loft at home; designing, laying-out, and cutting; false seaming, stitching grommets, reef points, sail slides, and so forth; use of the needle and palm, and sewing machine; sail alteration, repair and maintenance. Excellent drawings, and really a gem of a book for the price.
From: St. Martin's Press, Inc., 175 Fifth Ave., New York, N.Y. 10010

sources of sails

CHOW'S TRADING CO.

2B Captain Richard's Lane, Northport, N.Y. 11768
Chow represents Cheong Lee of Hong Kong who will custom-sew sails to your order from nylon or terylene—the British equivalent of dacron. I ordered my last sails from them and am very satisfied after almost two years of use and a savings of about 50%. Only problem is that Cheong Lee is too far away for re-cutting and adjustments, and local sailmakers often will not touch foreign sails—real chauvinism. Of the dozen or so Hong Kong mail-order sail firms, I can only endorse this one from actual experience.

VANCOUVER SAIL SUPPLY LTD.

6825 Granville St., Vancouver 14, B.C. Canada
Vancouver represents Viking Sails of Hong Kong. No evaluative info, but write them for prices and specifications.

SAILRITE KITS

12937 Venice Blvd., Mar Vista, Calif. 90066
This firm supplies sail kits for some 70 stock boats and will happily quote on any sail you dream up. I ordered a large drifter kit and the only problem I had was to find a large enough floor space to loft the whole thing and baste up the seams. You'll need a sewing machine of the zig-zag type, but otherwise the kits are very complete. Better check prices carefully though to make sure the savings are worthwhile. There's a good deal of labor involved, but it's rather fun, and you acquire the experience to repair and re-cut your old sails. Dr. Grant's sailmaking instruction manuals are excellent and may be purchased separately: *Make Your Own Mainsails* - $3, *Make Your Own Spinnakers and Staysails* - $3, *Make Your Own Stormsails* - $3, *Make Your Own Jibsails* - $3, *Sailrite Kits Sail Repair Manual* - $1.50. All five for $13. Write for Sailrite's 43-page catalog, $1.

RATSEY & LAPTHORN, INC.

Scofield St., City Island, N.Y. 10464
Ratsey sells a small kit with basic sailmaking gear, including palm, needles, twine, and beeswax in a compact box for $15. Also offers a deluxe sailmaker-rigger's kit which includes everything one would need for handling general rigging and sail maintenance jobs. Cost with carrying bag, $100. They used to offer a general sailmaker's kit with a bit more than the $15 one, but don't know whether its still available. It sold for around $25. Check at the above address for further info.

Sailmaker and Rigger's Basic Kit

Two-foot section of carpenter's folding ruler
Knife
Small marlinspike
Awl
Small fid
Pencil
Sailmaker's bench
Sewing palm
Sail needles (nos. 14, 15, 16, 17)
Roping needle
Beeswax
Dacron sewing twine
Cotton sewing twine
Pliers
Spinnaker repair tape

BACON & ASSOCIATES, INC.

P.O. Box 3150, Annapolis, Md. 21403

Bacon, as far as we know, is the only guy in the sail brokerage business. He buys and sells 'em and comes out with four legal-size descriptive lists, usually once a month:

List "AC": For centerboard-type boats. Mainsails up to 25-ft. luff, and appropriate jibs, genoas, and spinnakers.

List "AK": For fixed-keel-type boats. Mainsails from 25-ft. luff to 45-ft. luff; jibs, genoas, staysails, spinnakers, to 45-ft. luff thru 7 oz. fabric.

List "B": Big sails, heavy, working and storm sails. Sails of all sizes of 8 oz. or heavier material.

Low $$ List: Mains, jibs, genoas, spinnakers for keel boats and other sail boats. Damaged Dacrons, some excellent cottons, much-used synthetic and cotton sails. Sails of all sizes, all weights.

If you're interested in selling your used sail(s), wrap them up and send them to the above address (Bacon's been in business for a long time, he's reputable, reliable, and honest.) You can suggest your asking price or Bacon will make the decision. He lists them, and when they sell, you get 70%, he gets 30%. Incidentally, risk for loss, damage, etc. is your responsibility until the sails are actually sold. 'Member that! Any list (above) that interests you is available free on request.

COMMUNICATIONS BOOKS

ELECTRICAL AND ELECTRONIC EQUIPMENT FOR YACHTS

John French
1974 - 148 p. il. - $15

In layman's language detailed descriptions and principles of operation of direction finders, radar, sonar, navigation systems, automatic pilots, and batteries. Installation, adjustment, limitations, reliability, maintenance, and repair. Includes photographs, diagrams and charts.
From: Dodd, Mead & Co., Inc., 79 Madison Ave., New York, N.Y. 10016

MARINE ELECTRONICS HANDBOOK

Leo G. Sands
1973 - 192 p. il. - $7.95

This is a detailed technical guide on ship-to-shore radio, VHF, AM and SSB marine radiotelephones, antenna systems and radio direction finders.
From: International Marine Pub. Co., 21 Elm St., Camden, Maine 04843

VHF-FM MARINE RADIO

Leo G. Sands and Geoffrey Tellet
1968 - 343 p. il. - $6.50 (pb)

With the phasing out of conventional medium frequency radiotelephones (completely out by 1977) and the phasing in of VHF-FM, this would be the book to pick up. Covers the equipment, installation, maintenance and operation, together with locations of shore stations, FCC regulations, and channel allocations.
From: Chilton Book Co., 401 Walnut St., Philadelphia, Pa. 19106

SEA SIGNALLING SIMPLIFIED

Capt. P. J. Russell
1970, 3rd ed. - 86 p. il. - $2.50

Designed to simplify the teaching and learning of the International Code. Covers flags and pennants (in color), various usage of Morse and

Semaphore codes, and voice signalling via hailers and radio telephone. Indexed for quick referral to proper signal. Pocket-size.
From: Fernhill House Ltd., 303 Park Ave. S., New York, N.Y. 10010

OFFSHORE SAILING

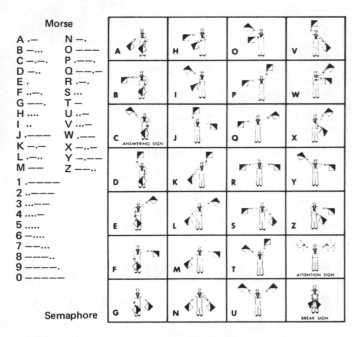

Morse

A .—	N —.
B —...	O ———
C —.—.	P .——.
D —..	Q ——.—
E .	R .—.
F ..—.	S ...
G ——.	T —
H	U ..—
I ..	V ...—
J .———	W .——
K —.—	X —..—
L .—..	Y —.——
M ——	Z ——..
1 .————	
2 ..———	
3 ...——	
4 ....—	
5	
6 —....	
7 ——...	
8 ———..	
9 ————.	
0 —————	

Semaphore

INTERNATIONAL CODE OF SIGNALS (H.O. Pub. No. 102)
U.S. Naval Oceanographic Office
$4 - S/N 0842-0008

Your boat is approaching a cove in foreign waters and you see a red and white star flare fired from two different positions on the beach. What do these flares mean? (Two beer parties. If off Martinique, the red would be the better. If off Jamaica, the white. NAVOCEANO doesn't know a thing about this. Harry Ketts told us.) Are you in distress and seeking aid, or do you require medical assistance? How would you indicate this? You see a ship at sea flying the flags AQ; what does it mean? All the answers are in this book, which would make a valuable addition to any ship's library. The International Code, adopted in 1965 by the International Governmental Maritime Consultative Organization, an agency of the United Nations, is understood by all nations and does not present a language barrier.
From: Sup. of Doc., U.S. Gov. Printing Off., Washington, D.C. 20402

ENGINEERING BOOKS

SMALL BOAT ENGINES: Inboard & Outboard
Conrad Miller
1961 - 319 p. il. - $7.95

Comprehensive and clearly illustrated handbook on the care and maintenance of gasoline and diesel engines. Miller's is a practical book geared to the layman's understanding of mechanics. Includes engine tuning, trouble shooting, and simple repairs and adjustments afloat.
From: Sheridan House, Box 254, South Station, Yonkers, N.Y. 10705

DIESEL ENGINE OPERATION AND MAINTENANCE
V. L. Maleev
1954 - 512 p. il. - $12.95

Covers principles of operation; the engine and components; fuel, cooling and exhaust systems; operation and performance; and engine installation, maintenance, and repair. In other words, just about everything you need to know to deal with any type diesel.
From: McGraw-Hill, 1221 Sixth Ave., New York, N.Y. 10020

DART UNION CO.
134 Thurbers Ave., Providence, R.I. 02905
If you're looking for a good, solid, dependable bilge pump, Dart Union's "Guzzler" is one. Available in three models from 12 gallons per minute (gpm) to 30, these babies are easy (on the old back) to operate, can be mounted in any position, are self-priming (15-foot suction lift), and are impervious to most oils, fuels, solvents, and detergents. Prices range from $30 to $97. Dart also manufactures a fire hose to fit their pumps; might be a handy thing to have. Check at the above address for literature, specifications, and prices.

BASS PRODUCTS
P.O. Box 901, Marblehead, Mass. 01945
For a good range of marine light fixtures and accessories check with Bass. This is also a good place to get 6-, 12-, and 32-volt bulbs (all types of bases). Bass has socket adapters, too; switch from screw to bayonet base. Other items include generators, panels, switches, power converters, 12-volt oscillating fans, and test instruments. Bass also handles water system accessories (galley-oriented), a couple of small stoves, marine refrigerators and a freezer. An illustrated 40-page catalog is available on request.

INLAND MARINE CO.
79 East Jackson St., Wilkes-Barre, Pa. 18701
Inland handles the Whale line of hand-operated bilge and galley pumps. These are good quality pumps manufactured in England; sizes are 8 gpm, $40; 18 gpm, $80; and 25 gpm, $89.
   If you've been having problems fitting fuel, water, or holding tanks in your hull, Inland can help you with the flexible Talamex tank, another European product. These are available in sizes from 11 to 44 gallons and constructed of plastic-lined, nylon-reinforced rubberized fabric. Prices with standard fittings range from $48 on up. Inland also handles Marlow yacht ropes, Avon inflatable boats, and the British Seagull outboard engine. Complete literature is available on request.

THE GRUNERT CO.
195 Drum Point Rd., Osborneville, N.J. 08723
Marine refrigeration is the theme here. If you've got the box, Grunert can supply you with the condensing unit and evaporator. Four models of condensers are available ranging from $571 to $775 and eight models of evaporators from $162 to $311. Grunert also offers a "Sta-Cold" unit which will provide a full day of refrigeration without drawing on the boat's electrical power. The unit is plugged into shore power at the dock to freeze up a eutectic solution. Once frozen, the solution will keep a box at even temperature for up to 18 hours. Two models are available, 6SC, $375, and 4SC, $590. Complete literature is available on request from Grunert.

MARTEC
2257 Gaylord St., Long Beach, Calif. 90813
If you've been looking for a low-drag sailboat propeller, Martec ought to be able to fix you up. They manufacture only one folding model, but in 618 different sizes at prices ranging from $174 on up. This prop looks like just the ticket. Write Martec for complete specs and prices.

STOKES MARINE INDUSTRIES
505 Race St., Coldwater, Mich. 49036
Stokes is a good supplier of converted marine engines and accessories. They have good, used diesel and gasoline inboards reconditioned in their factory and offer new engines from 19 to 120 hp at prices of $1,900 to $4,445. Send $1 for complete catalog.

J. H. WESTERBEKE CORP.
39 Avon Industrial Park, Avon, Mass. 02322
Westerbeke manufactures a very wide range of sailboat diesel engines from 7 hp to 115 hp. Send them your boat specifications for literature and a recommendation on the best engine for you. I have found them to be very responsive to mail inquiries.

GALLEY, CABIN, ETC.
BOOKS

THE SEAWIFE'S HANDBOOK
Joyce Sleightholme
1970 - 208 p. il. - $8.95

This work is for the woman sailor. It covers living afloat, crewing, cooking at sea, children aboard, first aid, clothing and much more.
From: International Marine Pub. Co., 21 Elm St., Camden, Maine 04843

CAROLYN'S SEAFOOD RECIPES
Carolyn T. Kelley
1972 - 102 p. il. - $5.95

Carolyn is the author of the monthly *National Fisherman* feature, "Getting the Best from Seafood." Her recipes are practically guaranteed to produce fine seafood menus.
From: International Marine Pub. Co., 21 Elm St., Camden, Maine 04843

sources of gear

SHIPMATE STOVE DIV., Richmond Ring Co.
Souderton, Pa. 18964
Shipmate stoves are a marine tradition and were used aboard sailing vessels before Fulton ever thought of using boiling water for anything other than coddling eggs. Go aboard the *Charles W. Morgan* at Mystic, Conn., and you'll find a wood-burning Shipmate aboard her. You can still get this model (pretty close to it, anyway) from Shipmate (no. 212) in eleven sizes; burns coal or wood. The company also manufactures small and large, gimbled and ungimbled, alcohol, bottled gas, and kerosene stoves. For the cabin, Shipmate offers an open wood or coal burning fireplace and the Skippy, a small pot-belly combination

heater and stove. Quality is unsurpassed. Illustrated literature and price sheet is available from the company.

King Cole

RATELCO, INC.
610 Pontius Ave., North, Seattle, Wash. 98109
Two models of a bulkhead-mounted cabin heater, the Cole, $95, and the King Cole, $160. The Cole is designed for small sailboats and takes up less than one square foot of space. The King Cole is a little larger, and is designed so the front screen can be removed to make it into a small fireplace. Both heaters use charcoal briquettes for fuel. Complete specs and prices available at the above address.

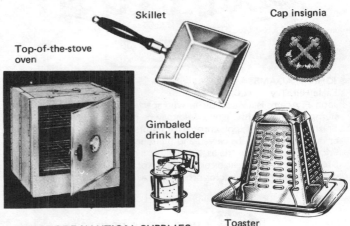

Skillet

Cap insignia

Top-of-the-stove oven

Gimbaled drink holder

Toaster

COMMODORE NAUTICAL SUPPLIES
396 Broadway, New York, N.Y. 10013
Commodore is oriented to the domestic side of boating—cabin and quarters gear, galley equipment, and apparel. Inventory includes all types of yachting clothes, caps, foul weather gear, paid crew and USPS uniforms; flags, burgees, and pennants (they'll make up flags to special order, too); figureheads and sternpieces; lamps; deck furniture; disposable bed clothing; dishes (all very "yachty"); cooking gear including a top of the stove oven ($33) and miscellaneous galley gadgets; clocks; barometers; some nav gear; boating books and logs; nautical jewelry including USPS and USCGA insignia; tools and tool kits; oddball plaques for head and wheelhouse, and some useful ones, too, on navigation procedures. Commodore's 115-page illustrated catalog is available for $1.

S. T. PRESTON & SON, INC.
102 Main St. Wharf, Greenport, N.Y. 11944

OUR 92ND YEAR

Preston has one of the largest stocks of marine prints, ship models, cannons, and other nauticana around; really some beautiful stuff. Their 126-page catalog, *Ships & Sea*, runs 25¢ and is well worth it. One section includes illustrations of all the prints they handle and the frames available, should you wish to use their framing service. Another illustrates such items as carved eagles, figureheads, old tavern signs, clocks, barometers, lamps, brassware, carved whales and figurines, and other interesting items. Truly an outstanding collection that would make any Jack Tar feel homesick. If you're in the Long Island area, make an effort to stop by Preston's shop.

FULTON SUPPLY CO., INC.
23 Fulton St., New York, N.Y. 10038

If you happen to be cruising Long Island Sound and dock at the big city, or if you happen to be lucky enough (?) to live there, Fulton's is one of *the* places to buy boating duds. Nothing fancy; in fact, it's a fisherman's store, but their gear is rugged and of good quality. Line-up includes several styles of knit European sweaters, watch caps, jackets, foul weather gear, CPO shirts, rubber boots, mittens and sailing gloves, British Breton red pants, $15, bermuda shorts, crush sailing hats, denim shirts and dungarees, khaki duds—shorts and longs, yachting caps, and various dunnage bags. Prices are average. Fulton's is more retail than mail order, but they do issue an illustrated 16-page catalog, which you can requisition from the above address, free.

JOHN T. ADAMS
Eagle Hill, Tryon, N.C. 28782

John T. Adams is a wood carver who specializes in trailboards and sternpieces for yachts. Wood used may be pine, teak, or mahogany finished in gold leaf, polychrome, or natural wood. Any animal, fish, or other design may be carved and figureheads may also be ordered. Prices range from as little as $35 for just a name banner (scroll) to $1000 plus for large eagles or intricate work; usual price for a sternpiece is about $350. A color brochure is available.

IMPORT MARINE SALES
P.O. Box 1060-B
Garden Grove, Calif. 92640

These are the people that import the QME vane self-steering gear from England. The QME comes in kit form for $75. It's no problem to put together and can be used on any sailboat up to 50 feet. A letter to the above address will get you full details, which includes a copy of a magazine article describing the performance of the QME.

The ability to operate a boat safely involves a knowledge of wind and weather; use of charts, instruments, buoys and other aids to navigation; rules of the road—inland and international; and the ability to determine position by dead reckoning, piloting and star observations, and steer a course to a dock a hundred or a thousand miles distant—and reach it on the first try. This is navigation. In this section are listed the books, charts and places to get instruments and equipment for this.

sources of information

UNITED STATES COAST GUARD
400 Seventh St., S.W., Washington, D.C. 20590

The Guard, which maintains all aids to navigation in the United States and administers the navigation laws (rules of the road), publishes several books in this department that would be worth picking up for your nav library. They're free and can be requested from the above address or picked up at your local Coast Guard district office—

Coast Guard Aids to Navigation, CG-193
Rules of the Road, International-Inland, CG-169
Rules of the Road, Great Lakes, CG-172
Rules of the Road, Western Rivers, CG-184

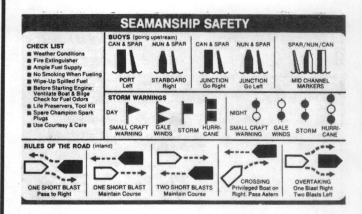

NATIONAL WEATHER SERVICE (NWS)
Gramax Bldg., Silver Spring, Md. 20910

The National Weather Service broadcasts marine weather forecasts via repeat taped messages every 4 to 6 minutes on 162.40 MHz and 162.55 MHz from stations located at key coastal cities around the nation. These tapes are updated every 2 to 3 hours and provide wind observations, visibility, sea and lake conditions and detailed local and area forecasts. Broadcasts can be received up to 40 miles from the station. The VHF-FM frequencies used for these broadcasts require narrow-band FM receivers. The National Weather Service (NWS) recommends receivers having a sensitivity of one microvolt or less and a quieting factor of 20 decibels.

Weather forecasts can also be obtained through AM radio broadcasts, TV, and marine radiotelephone broadcasts. Also the smart skipper will call the local weather bureau for a pre-cruise briefing.

Information on broadcast schedules of radio stations, National

Weather Service office telephone numbers and locations of display stations are shown on Marine Weather Service Charts for specific coastal

NOAA VHF-FM Radio Weather

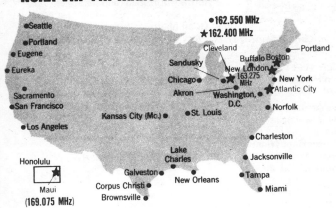

● 162.550 MHz
★ 162.400 MHz

areas. Copies of these charts are available at local marinas and marine chart dealers, or by ordering from: National Ocean Survey, Distribution Div. (C44), Riverdale, Md. 20840; price, 25¢.

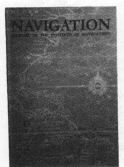

INSTITUTE OF NAVIGATION
815 Fifteenth St., N.W., Suite 832,
Washington, D.C. 20005
The Institute was founded in 1945 as a nonprofit society devoted to improving the art and science of navigation on and under the sea. Membership is open to individuals and organizations interested in this area of offshore sailing. Dues, which include a subscription to the quarterly journal, *Navigation,* are $15 per year. Unfortunately, unless you're really a nav buff, most of the articles in the journal are going to be "dry as dust" and hardly worth the $15 investment. Perhaps one day the editors will remember that all professionals were once amateurs, and it'd be nice to have something in there for them, too—*Scientific American* does it.

BOOKS

AMERICAN PRACTICAL NAVIGATOR
(H.O. Pub. No. 9)
Nathaniel Bowditch
Vol. I - 1977 - $?
Vol. II - 1975, rev. ed. - $4.80 - D 5.317:9/2/v.2

The *American Practical Navigator,* more commonly known as "Bowditch," needs little introduction to most deep-water sailors. This is where the buck stops in navigation—the final reference work on the subject. The latest edition has been divided into two volumes, as the book was becoming unwieldy. Volume II provides the tables, formulas, data and instructions for the navigator. It can either be used alone or serve as a supplement to earlier editions of Bowditch for which it has substitute material for six chapters, four appendices and three tables. The new Volume I primarily will have information on the new nautical chart systems, piloting and weather, but the majority of original material will be concerned with elaborate and sophisticated navigational systems, which few yachtsmen can afford, such as inertial and satellite navigation. Latest is that Vol. I will not be ready till the later part of '77.
From: Sup. of Doc., U.S. Gov. Printing Off., Washington, D.C. 20402

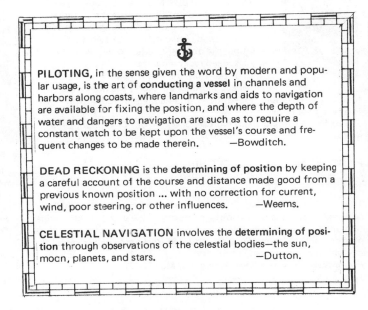

PILOTING, in the sense given the word by modern and popular usage, is the art of **conducting a vessel** in channels and harbors along coasts, where landmarks and aids to navigation are available for fixing the position, and where the depth of water and dangers to navigation are such as to require a constant watch to be kept upon the vessel's course and frequent changes to be made therein.   —Bowditch.

DEAD RECKONING is the **determining of position** by keeping a careful account of the course and distance made good from a previous known position ... with no correction for current, wind, poor steering, or other influences.   —Weems.

CELESTIAL NAVIGATION involves the **determining of position** through observations of the celestial bodies—the sun, moon, planets, and stars.   —Dutton.

RADAR NAVIGATION MANUAL
1971 - 190 p. il. - $2.75
S/N 0842-0048

Published in looseleaf form, this manual discusses the fundamentals of radar, radar operation, collision avoidance, and radar navigation.
From: Sup. of Doc., U.S. Printing Off., Washington, D.C. 20402

CELESTIAL NAVIGATION FOR YACHTSMEN
Mary Blewitt
1967 - 96 p. il. - $5.95

This would probably be the best book for a beginner to use to learn celestial navigation. Mary Blewitt is an Englishwoman who knows her stuff, and her book has been used by yachtsmen for nearly 20 years. Covers navigation by the H.O. 249 method using the *Air Almanac* for data.
From: John De Graff, Inc., 34 Oak Ave., Tuckahoe, N.Y. 10707

COASTAL NAVIGATION STEP BY STEP
Warren Norville
1975 - 203 p. il. - $15

This is a text on all aspects of piloting and dead reckoning covering: compass error, speed, time and distance problems, lines of position and radio navigation, among others.
From: International Marine Pub. Co., 21 Elm St., Camden, Maine 04843

CELESTIAL NAVIGATION STEP BY STEP
Warren Norville
1973 - 168 p. il. - $12.50

This book covers sight reduction using both the nautical and air almanacs and the tables: H.O. 214, H.O. 249 and H.O. 229 using many examples.
From: International Marine Pub. Co., 21 Elm St., Camden, Maine 04843

THE BOOK OF THE SEXTANT
Capt. H. H. Shufeldt and G. D. Dunlap
1971 - 45 p. il. - $1.75

This pamphlet from the offices of Weems and Plath covers the sextant in detail, including selecting and buying, the old instrument, adjusting, maintenance and care, altitude corrections, and how to package and ship a sextant when sending it in for repairs to Weems and Plath (where else—Baker & Lyman?).
From: International Marine Pub. Co., 21 Elm St., Camden, Me. 04843

PRIMER OF NAVIGATION

George W. Mixter, rev. by Donald McClench
1967, 5th ed. - 572 p. il. - $13.50

Mixter's book has been used by many a small boat sailor to learn the rudiments of piloting and celestial navigation. It covers just about everything one would need to know to be a competent navigator, including tools of the trade, the compass and its adjustment, aids to navigation, piloting, use of charts, radio, loran, radar, time signals, dead reckoning, the stars and planets, lines of position, use of the nautical and air almanacs and the days work. Includes a multitude of charts, graphs, illustrations, and handy samples of work forms. Really a great book.
From: Van Nostrand Reinhold Co., 300 Pike St., Cincinnati, Ohio 45202

PILOTING AND DEAD RECKONING

Capt. H. H. Shufeldt and G. D. Dunlap
1970 - 150 p. il. - $7

This is the U.S. Coast Guard Auxiliary's boating course text which is designed to give the boatman the necessary knowledge for safe navigation under piloting and dead reckoning conditions. If you're not planning on going offshore, *Piloting and Dead Reckoning* will cover all the navigation problems you'll run into.
From: Naval Institute Press, Annapolis, Md. 21402

WEATHER, WATER AND BOATING

Donald A. Whelpley
1961 - 160 p. il. - $5

Written in layman's language for the practical cruising man who wants to grasp the phenomena of weather quickly so as to readily apply it to his boating needs. Information is presented in such a manner that it is interesting and easy to retain. Covers theory and practical application including judging weather, wind, and storms from clouds and sea states. Very interesting section on old sailors' weather sayings. Good photos of clouds.
From: Cornell Maritime Press, Box 109, Cambridge, Md. 21613

SELF STEERING

Tom Herbert
1974 - 167 p. il. - $5.30

This Amateur Yacht Research Society book describes every known way in which a sailing craft can be made to steer herself. Analyzes 27 different steering systems including twin headsail and vane steering arrangements. Ninety-seven diagrams and photos.
From: Amateur Yacht Research Society, 10822 92nd Ave., N., Seminole, Fla. 33542

SCHOOLS and INSTRUCTION

Coast Navigation School

COAST NAVIGATION SCHOOL
418 E. Canon Perdido, Santa Barbara, Calif. 93102
Coast offers a piloting course for $95 and a celestial course for $150. The celestial course covers the use of H.O. 214, 229, and 249. The school supplies all text material and charts, but you supply instruments, H.O. tables, and almanacs, which can be purchased through the school. Other Coast Navigation correspondence courses include astronomy, meteorology, boating & seamanship, sailing, and preparation for various Coast Guard license examinations. Complete description of courses, prices, and time-payment plans is available on request.

INTERNATIONAL NAVIGATION SCHOOL
108 Burlingame Rd., Toronto, Ontario, Canada M8W 1Z2
Capt. John Pettit, formerly of the Royal Navy, heads up this Canadian correspondence school. He offers a 13-lesson coastal navigation course and a 15-lesson celestial course, each for $75 or both for $125. We don't have any qualitative data on his instruction though Capt. Pettit certainly seems to have the background and qualifications to teach. Descriptive brochure is available on request.

DAVIS INSTRUMENTS CORP.
643 143rd Ave., San Leandro, Calif. 94578
Davis offers a home-study course in celestial navigation for $90.

UNIVERSITY OF TENNESSEE
Center for Extended Learning, 447 Communications Bldg., Knoxville, Tenn. 37916
Their basic course is advertised at $35 plus textbooks and the intermediate course is offered at $50—both for home study.

U.S. POWER SQUADRONS (USPS)
Airport Rd. and Lumley Ave., P.O. Box 30423, Raleigh, N.C. 27612
We mentioned this fine organization in the beginning of this section. Some 442 squadrons in the U.S. offer free night school courses in: Basic Boating including piloting, Advanced Piloting, Junior Navigator, Navigator, Weather and Marine Electronics among others, which cover all areas of yacht navigation from coastal, river and lake piloting to offshore celestial navigation. Write for information.

OCEANUS SCHOOL OF THE SEA
407 Ardmore, Ho-Ho-Kus, N.J. 07423
This sounds like the ideal way to learn navigation—aboard a 47- or 50-foot yacht at sea. Owner-skippered by a Master Mariner, students sail together in the Caribbean. Courses are offered in a variety of subjects in seamanship and navigation including electronic navigation. All-inclusive price is $52 per day.

NATIONAL MARINE CORRESPONDENCE SCHOOL
28 Hamilton St., Birkenhead, Merseyside L41 1AL, England
Correspondence courses are offered in a variety of nautical subjects including the famous and challenging Royal Yachting Association coastal and yachtsmaster certificates. Basic coastal navigation course is £32.50 including air mail one way. Its principal, Capt. R. G. Morrison, says the school is using the new metric charts.

NAVIGATION GEAR
BOOKS

U.S. NAVAL OCEANOGRAPHIC OFFICE CAT. OF PUBLICATIONS
1976 - 73 p. - 75¢ - S/N 0842-0054

For a complete list of all the navigation books, manuals, systems, methods, etc. available from the government, pick up this catalog.
From: Sup. of Doc., U.S. Gov. Printing Off., Washington, D.C. 20402

TIDE TABLES

Four volumes of these are published, each covering a specific part of the world. The tables give the predicted times and heights of high and low water for every day in the year at different locations, usually prominent coastal cities, and enough info is provided so that you can figure the time of high and low tide for places in between.

East Coast, North & South America	$3.75
West Coast, North & South America	3.75
Europe & West Coast of Africa	3.75
Central & Western Pacific & Indian Oceans	3.75

From: National Ocean Survey, Distribution Division (C-44), Riverdale, Md. 20840

TIDAL CURRENT TABLES

These tables are published annually. They tabulate daily predictions of the times of slack water and the times and speeds of maximum flood and ebb currents for a number of waterways, together with differences for obtaining predictions at numerous other places. They also include current diagrams and other useful information on coastal tidal currents, plus a method for obtaining the speed of current at any time and one for determining the duration of slack water. Info on the Gulf Stream is included in the Atlantic coast table.

Atlantic Coast of North America	$3.75
Pacific Coast of North America and Asia	3.75

From: National Ocean Survey, Distribution Div. (C-44), Riverdale, Md. 20840

TIDAL CURRENT CHARTS

These tables depict the direction and speed of the tidal current for each hour of the tidal cycle, thus presenting a comprehensive view of the tidal current movement in the respective waterways as a whole, and supplying a ready means of determining for any time the direction and speed of the current at various localities throughout the areas covered. The Narragansett Bay and New York Harbor charts are to be used with the tide tables, and the rest of them require the current tables.

Boston Harbor, 3rd Edition	$1.00
Narragansett Bay to Nantucket Sound, 3rd Edition	1.00
Narragansett Bay, 1st Edition	1.00
Block Island Sound and Eastern Long Island Sound, 1st Edition	1.00
Long Island Sound and Block Island Sound, 4th Edition	1.00
New York Harbor, 7th Edition	1.00
Delaware Bay and River, 2nd Edition	1.00
Upper Chesapeake Bay, 1st Edition	1.00

Charleston Harbor, S.C., 1st Edition	1.00
San Francisco Bay, 5th Edition	1.00
Puget Sound – Northern Part, 2nd Edition	1.00
Puget Sound – Southern Part, 2nd Edition	1.00

From: National Ocean Survey, Distribution Div. (C-44), Riverdale, Md. 20840

LIGHT LISTS

Five volumes are published, each covering a particular area of the United States. The *Light List* tabulates navigational lights with their locations, candle powers, and other identifying characteristics so that at night, when you spot one, you can tell just what light you're looking at. Other aids to navigation such as fog signals and radiobeacons are also included. This is a required reference book for coastal navigation.

Vol. I - Atlantic Coast from St. Croix River, Maine to Little River, South Carolina, $4.25.
Vol. II - Atlantic and Gulf Coasts from Little River, South Carolina to Rio Grande, Texas, $5.90
Vol. III - Pacific Coast and Pacific Islands, $2.75
Vol. IV - Great Lakes, $2.00.
Vol. V - Mississippi River System, $2.75

From: Defense Mapping Agency, Hydrographic Center, Washington, D.C. 20390

AIR ALMANAC, $8.45

D 213.7:97(a)/(b). [(a) insert last digit of year; 1973:*3*; (b) insert *1* (Jan–Apr), *2* (May–Aug), *3* (Sep–Dec). Example: D 213.7:97*3*/3.]

A joint publication of the U.S. Naval Observatory and the Royal Greenwich Observatory, listing the Greenwich hour angle and declination of various celestial bodies at 10-min. intervals; time of sunrise, sunset, moonrise, moonset; and other astronomical information arranged in a form convenient for navigators. Each issue covers four months of the year. The *Air Almanac* is "faster" than the *Nautical Almanac* for working solutions to the astronomical triangle.
From: Sup. of Doc., U.S. Gov. Printing Off., Washington, D.C. 20402

NAUTICAL ALMANAC, $9

D 213.11:97(a) [(a) insert last digit of year; 1977:7]

This is of more use to the navigator of small craft, as only one volume need be purchased each year, and it is more universally available. Corrections are given for emergency use in the succeeding year. Greenwich hour angle and declination data are given for 57 stars, 4 planets and the sun and moon, plus times of sun- and moonrise and -set and twilights. Other useful data and corrections are included. This is a joint publication with the Royal Greenwich Observatory in England, and those wishing to save some money can order the British edition at £1.60 (less than one-third the U.S. price) from: Thomas Foulkes, Lansdowne Road, Leytonstone, London E11 3HB, England.
From: Sup. of Doc., U.S. Gov. Printing Off., Washington, D.C. 20402

AZIMUTHS OF THE SUN (H.O. 211), $3.50

This is a reprint of *Ageton's Dead Reckoning Altitude and Azimuth Table,* which no longer is published by the U.S. Government. It is a good deal more complicated to use than the other methods and takes more time with more chance of error. However, it is a simple, one-volume compendium which is suitable for any heavenly body with any declination from any latitude. It is an excellent backup table for a yacht, and one should be in every abandon ship kit bag or attached to your life raft along with a simple plastic sextant and the *Nautical Almanac.*
From: International Marine Pub. Co., 21 Elm St., Camden, Maine 04843

281

TABLES OF COMPUTED AZIMUTH AND ALTITUDE (H.O. 214)

These have been discontinued in favor of H.O. 229 and are no longer being printed by the U.S. Government. However, they are still offered at $8.50 per volume by the firm listed below. There are seven volumes, each covering ten degrees of latitude from 0° to 69° inclusive:

Vol. 1 - Lat. 0° to 9°
Vol. 2 - Lat. 10° to 19°
Vol. 3 - Lat. 20° to 29°
Vol. 4 - Lat. 30° to 39°
Vol. 5 - Lat. 40° to 49°
Vol. 6 - Lat. 50° to 59°
Vol. 7 - Lat. 60° to 69°

From: Nautech Maritime Corp., 445 N. Sacramento Blvd., Chicago, Ill. 60612

SIGHT REDUCTION TABLES FOR MARINE NAV. (H.O. 229)

These tables are similar to those of H.O. 214 in providing tabulated solutions to the navigational spherical triangle but are far quicker, easier and more accurate. H.O. 229 has, therefore, replaced all earlier tabular methods of navigation. The six volumes cover 16° of latitude each:

Vol. 1 - Lat. 0° to 15°, $ 6.00 (S/N 0842-0041)
Vol. 2 - Lat. 15° to 30°, $11.55 (S/N 0842-0042)
Vol. 3 - Lat. 30° to 45°, $ 9.40 (S/N 0842-0043)
Vol. 4 - Lat. 45° to 60°, $ 9.40 (S/N 0842-0044)
Vol. 5 - Lat. 60° to 75°, $ 6.00 (S/N 0842-0045)
Vol. 6 - Lat. 75° to 90°, $ 6.00 (S/N 0842-0013)

From: Sup. of Doc., U.S. Gov. Printing Off., Washington, D.C. 20402

SIGHT REDUCTION TABLES FOR AIR NAVIGATION (H.O. 249)

This method is often used by yachtsmen in conjunction with the *Air Almanac,* as it is somewhat faster. However, it is not so accurate and it is limited. Volume 1 contains tabulated altitudes and azimuths for seven selected stars, the entering arguments being latitude, local hour angle of the vernal equinox, and the name of the star. Volumes 2 and 3 contain tabulated altitudes and azimuth angles of any body within the limits of the entering arguments, which are: latitude, LHA and declination.

Vol. 1 - Selected Stars, 1975, $7.75
Vol. 2 - Lat. 0° to 39°, Dec. 0° to 29°, $5.30 (S/N 0842-0046)
Vol. 3 - Lat. 40° to 89°, Dec. 0° to 29°, $6.00 (S/N 0842-00058)

From: Sup. of Doc., U.S. Gov. Printing Off., Washington, D.C. 20402

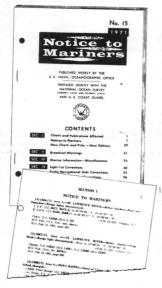

NOTICE TO MARINERS
Weekly - free

This is the world-wide *Notice to Mariners* that advises ship masters, navigators, and chart dealers of new hydrographic discoveries, changes in channels and navigation aids, and other important matters affecting navigational safety, which is used to update the latest editions of nautical charts and publications. The *Notice* also includes info on latest charts and navigational publications that have been published. Though this one is free, it's not available to the general public. If you're in the business, so to speak, you can put in a request for a subscription, but whether they'll honor it or not depends on what your needs for the *Notice* are.

From: Defense Mapping Agency, Hydrographic Center, Washington, D.C. 20390

LOCAL NOTICE TO MARINERS
Weekly - free

This is the regional *Notice* issued by each Coast Guard District Office. This publication is available to the general public on request, and contains info on changes in aids to navigation, water depths, hazards, and so forth. Just drop the commander of your local district a letter, and you'll be put on the list.

From: Commander, Coast Guard District, (check front part of this section under Coast Guard for district addresses)

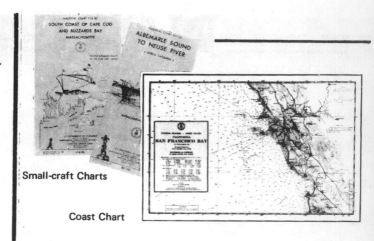

Small-craft Charts

Coast Chart

There are two basic types of charts presently in use: small-craft charts, which are identified by the letters SC following the chart number, and conventional charts.

Small-craft charts are for all purposes the same as conventional

WORLD

DEFENSE MAPPING AGENCY
Hydrographic Center, Washington, D.C. 20390

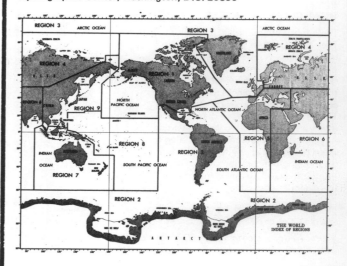

For world-wide charts of the high seas and coastal areas of all foreign countries, these are the people to contact. Their index consists of thirteen booklets in two divisions: *Numerical List of Nautical Charts and Publications,* parts I, II, and III; and catalogs of *Nautical Charts and Publications,* regions 0 thru 9. Best bet is to order all three parts of the *Numerical List* for 75¢ and take it from there.

The Defense Mapping Agency also publishes Pilot Charts. These are issued monthly for various areas of the world and are vital for anyone planning ocean crossings or long-distance water voyages. Data included in NO 16: *Pilot Chart of the North Atlantic Ocean* are: current directions and strengths, wind directions and strengths, magnetic variation, fog incidence, shipping lanes, iceberg limits, general climatology and temperatures, selected severe storm tracks, mean pressures and a host of other navigational details. An article of interest to the skipper or navigator is included on the back of each. The catch is the price. Subscription was only $6 per year, but in 1976 this was increased to $22.

EUROPE

THE HYDROGRAPHER OF THE NAVY
Ministry of Defence
Taunton, Somerset, England, U.K.
Publishes the British Admiralty charts. Good place to go for any inquiries regarding British nautical charts. However, because this

charts, except that they come in sort of a file folder and are in sections of three to four small folded sheets. The idea is to make them handy for use aboard outboards and day sailers.

Conventional charts are printed on large sheets of heavy paper, show more area, and because of this, frankly, are easier to work with in plotting courses, even if you do have to fold them when working in a cramped space. Conventional charts come in one of four types:

Harbor Charts. These are published at scales of 1:50,000 and larger, depending on the importance of the harbor and the dangers to navigation.

Coast Charts. Published at scales from 1:50,000 to 1:100,000 (approximately 1.4 nautical miles per inch). They're intended for coastwise navigation inside offshore reefs and shoals, when entering bays and harbors, and for certain inland waterways. If you're going to run inland waterways most of the time, get the small-craft charts.

General Charts. Published at scales from 1:100,000 to 1:600,000 (approximately 8.2 nautical miles per inch). Intended primarily for offshore work where you're fixing your position by landmarks, lights, buoys, and characteristic soundings. Not quite

as much topographical or hydrographical information on these as on the former two.

Sailing Charts. Published at scales smaller than 1:600,000 and used primarily for plotting courses and determining lines of position through celestial navigation.

The most important thing to keep in mind about charts is that they be up to date. Look for the date, which will be printed in the lower left corner.

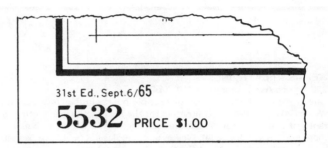

31st Ed., Sept.6/65

5532 PRICE $1.00

sources of charts

government agency isn't geared up to providing speedy service for overseas mail-order purchases, it's not the best place to go for charts. The private agencies that are listed following would be better. You can write the above address for a copy of Admiralty catalog NP131, though. It lists all Admiralty charts and publications. Include $2 with your order to cover costs and postage. An International Money Order for two bucks can be gotten at any post office.

J.D. POTTER LTD.
145 Minories, London EC3, England, U.K.
Good source of Admiralty charts and Hydrographic Office publications. Publications list available.

CAPT. O.M. WATTS LTD.
49 Albemarle St., London W1, England, U.K.
Capt. Watts, who incidentally is also the editor of *Reed's Nautical Almanac*, carries a complete line of Admiralty charts, tide tables and navigation instruments.

EDWARD STANFORD LTD.
12-14 Long Acre, London WC2, England, U.K.
Publisher of Stanford's Coloured Charts for Coastal Navigators, which covers United Kingdom coastal waters, and handles all Admiralty charts and Hydrographic Office publications plus the Blondel La Rougery charts for the north coast of France. Write for info and prices.

CANADA

HYDROGRAPHIC CHART DISTRIBUTION OFFICE (Canada)
Dept. of the Environment, P.O. Box 8080, Ottawa, Ontario, Canada K1G 3H6
This office produces and distributes Canadian nautical charts, which cost from 50¢ to $2 and are pretty much the same as NOS charts as far as symbols, markings and colors go. The following area indexes are free and can be ordered from the above address:

> *IB 1 - Great Lakes and Adjacent Waterways.*
> *IB 4 - Rainy Lake, Lake of the Woods, Lake Winnipeg, Lake Winnipegosis, and Lac La Ronge.*
> *IB 5 - St. Lawrence River—Ile d'Anticosti to Lake Ontario.*
> *IB 6 - Northwestern Canada—Mackenzie River Basin.*
> *IB 7 - Island of Newfoundland and North Shore of the Gulf of St. Lawrence.*
> *IB 8 - Nova Scotia, New Brunswick, and Prince Edward Island.*
> *IB 9 - Labrador Coast.*
> *IB 11 - Hudson Bay and Hudson Strait.*
> *IB 13 - Southern British Columbia Coast including Vancouver Island.*

> *IB 14 - Northern British Columbia Coast including Queen Charlotte Islands.*
> *IB 15 - Canadian Arctic.*
> *IB 35 - Fleuve Saint-Laurent (French)*

UNITED STATES

NATIONAL OCEAN SURVEY (NOS)
Distribution Div. (C-44), Riverdale, Md. 20840
The National Ocean Survey (NOS) is the old U.S. Coast and Geodetic Survey, and now has added the charting of the former U.S. Lake Survey publishing charts for United States coastal waters and the Great Lakes region. Most of their charts are available from local marinas or marine hardware stores for $3.25 to $3.50, or you can order directly from the above address. First, though, better order an index to the area you're interested in so you'll be able to give NOS the chart number(s) and remit the correct amount with your order. Incidentally, while ordering the index, you might also request a copy of Chart No. 1 at $1.50, which is a complete description of what the markings, symbols and colors used on charts mean. Here are the chart indexes that can be requested from the above address—they're free:

> *No. 1 - Atlantic and Gulf Coasts, Including Puerto Rico and the Virgin Islands*
> *No. 2 - Pacific Coast, Including Hawaii, Guam and Samoa Islands*
> *No. 3 - Alaska, Including the Aleutian Islands*
> *No. 4 - Great Lakes and Adjacent Waterways*

U.S. ARMY ENGINEER DISTRICT
906 Olive St., St. Louis, Mo. 63101
Mississippi River and tributaries.

LAKE SURVEY CENTER
630 Federal Bldg., Detroit, Mich. 48226
Great Lakes and New York State Canals.

BAHAMAS

TROPIC ISLE PUBLISHERS, INC.
P.O. Box 613, Coral Gables, Fla. 33134
Detailed Bahamas cruising sketch charts by Harry Kline, creator of *Yachtsman's Guide to the Bahamas.*

sources of INSTRUMENTS

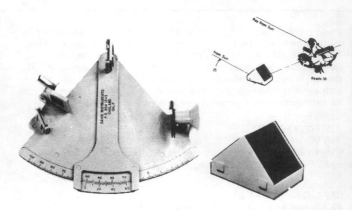

WEEMS & PLATH, INC.
222 Severn Ave., Annapolis, Md. 21403

One of the best known navigator's supply houses in the United States, Weems is one of the U.S. importers for the famous German Plath sextants, of which several models are available from $633 up, although there is a 2/3 size for $246. Weems also handles a 3-in., 8½-oz. sextant by Francis Barker & Son of England. A beautiful little vernier instrument that reads to 1', $165 complete with leather case. Other

navigational items carried by Weems include: clocks, chronometers, barometers, compasses (steering and hand-bearing), plotting instruments of all types, various nav computers, plotting board, a taffrail log, hand-held anemometer, binoculars, range finder and stadimeter, and navigational charts and books. Weems services and repairs navigational instruments, too. Write first for a quote and shipping instructions. A 25-page catalog is available.

ROBERT E. WHITE INSTRUMENTS, INC.
51 Commercial Wharf, Boston, Mass. 02110

White handles a selection of navigation instruments that includes Plath sextants, taffrail logs, binoculars, a hand bearing compass, the Mercer and Accutron chronometers, plotting instruments, and a time-speed-distance calculator. Prices are about average. Used instruments are available, and White offers maintenance and repair services for sextants, chronometers, and weather instruments (he also handles a complete line of meteorological instruments). Illustrated literature and price sheets are available.

DAVIS INSTRUMENTS CORP.
857 Thornton, San Leandro, Calif. 94577

For the budget-minded navigator, Davis has two plastic sextants, a stadimeter, hand bearing compass, pelorus, time-speed-distance calculator, and plotting instruments. Davis' fame came with its Mark 3 plastic sextant which retails for $20 and is accurate to two minutes of arc. It brought celestial navigation to those who couldn't afford it before, and with enough accuracy for around the world cruising. As a

matter of fact, a number of successful voyages have been made using only the Mark 3 for taking sights. Davis' other sextant, the Mark 12, runs $65 and is a little more accurate. Both instruments use a vernier. Considering the prices of nav instruments today, it would pay you to take a look at what Davis has to offer. Davis also furnishes a home-study course in celestial navigation at $90, and a variety of navigational aids including a small radio/compass direction finder at $70 and Blockits, among others. A 12-page illustrated brochure is available on request.

B & F ENTERPRISES
119 Foster Ave., Peabody, Mass. 01960

This surplus operation handles new and used chronometers. Prices for some of the gear are a little higher than you would expect to pay for surplus, though. An illustrated catalog of electronic and optical equipment is available on request.

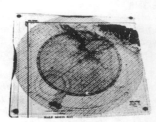

KANE MARINE
P.O. Box 1133, Burlingame, Calif. 94010

Kane has put together a little thing called the PBC Mark II Plotting Board, $25, which looks like a real winner (if you dig gadgets). The PBC consists of two movable plastic discs under which a chart is slid. One disc has degrees marked on its outer rim, the other, a series of parallel lines. By rotating the discs over the chart, courses and bearings can be plotted, drift angles calculated, variation eliminated, and a number of other handy things. Write Bud Kane, he'll tell you all about it. He's even put together a 16-page booklet, *Instant Navigation with the PBC Plotter,* which has a lot of good information.

COAST NAVIGATION SCHOOL (CNS)
418 E. Canon Perdido, Santa Barbara, Calif. 93102
CNS imports five sextants manufactured for them overseas under the name Simex. Prices range from $50 for the Simex Pilot to $435 for the Mariner. Other items include a computer for calculating time, speed, distance, course, and bearing problems, $11; star finder (almost a duplicate of H.O. 2102-D), $15; and plotting instruments. An illustrated brochure is available.

NAUTECH MARITIME CORPORATION
445 N. Sacramento Blvd., Chicago, Ill. 60612
Nautech is another general navigational tool supply outfit with several models of imported sextants from Japan ranging from $320 to $450; others at lower prices are available including the British EBBCO micrometer drum plastic sextant at $50. I have used the latter very successfully myself and highly recommend it. Other products carried include: star finder, plotting sheets, chronometers, knotmeters, compasses, distress signals, books, charts and survival gear. Of particular interest is their $200 NC-2 navigation calculator pictured below, which is programmed to solve all major navigational problems with the push of a few buttons. It can also be used as a teaching machine for celestial navigation. All you need is a sextant, nautical almanac, timepiece and the NC-2. No other tables are required. It automatically calculates computed altitudes and displays azimuths, gives most probable position in displaying latitude and longitude, calculates initial course and distance for great circle sailings, dead reckoning position, Mercator sailings, midlatitude sailings and arc-to-time conversions and vice versa. This is a powerful pocket-size machine well worth having. Another favorite of mine from their catalog is the MINI Handbearing Compass, at $63, which I use on my own boat. With the "rubber tire" around the compass, it may be thrown out on deck or dropped without damage.

*Nautech
NC-2 Navigation Calculator*

KLEID NAVIGATION, INC.
24 Lee Dr., Fairfield, Conn. 06430
Kleid is another general supplier of navigational gear, and they offer sextants including the Plath and Heath models. Davis and Ebbco plastic sextants are also available, as is a variety of other navigational gear. Write for their 28-page catalog and send 50¢ for the paperback pamphlet: *Choosing a Marine Sextant,* by Robert E. Kleid.

___ ELECTRONIC AIDS

Two items should be on every yacht sailing passages coastwise or offshore: depth sounder and radio direction finder. There has been some talk of eliminating the U.S. Government direction finding beacons, but let's hope that this will not occur. Most yachts which get into trouble do so near or on shore. They run aground or tear the bottom out on a reef. And this is no joke when the sea and wind are up. Many a boat has been battered to pieces from such. Those who have sailed the reef-laden Caribbean extensively have told me they would sail only with two depth sounders and transducers—one for backup—since they regard this electronic aid of such prime importance. As well as warning of shoal water, the depth sounder also can be used as a navigational tool by matching depths indicated or recorded with depths shown on charts. I would think radar would be an excellent aid, particularly at night or in fog. Piloting at night inshore in strange waters and sometimes even in familiar places, where beer signs conflict with buoys (which hopefully are lighted), can be very disorienting, if not downright dangerous.

Two-way radio can be used as a form of navigation, and this field, too, has proliferated in the past few years. Yachts now may only be equipped with one or more of the four types of radio communication gear listed: VHF-FM, Single Side-Band (SSB) shortwave marine transceivers, citizens band radios, and amateur radio gear. Of them all I prefer the latter, although the first two have the advantage of including international distress channels guarded 24 hours a day around the world, through which yacht-to-ship communication may be effected readily.

*Heathkit
Digital Radio/Direction
Finder
Kit.....................$200*

HEATH COMPANY
Benton Harbor, Mich. 49022
A number of Heathkits for boating are manufactured including a digital depth sounder at $150, digital radio direction finder at $200, white line depth recorder at $290 and an automatic foghorn/hailer at $100. There are also Heathkits for low power drain amateur radio transmitters and receivers and citizens band equipment suitable for yacht use. Write for 104-page catalog.

*"ECHO-LARM" is a transistorized depthfinder which reads from 0-120 ft. and will read to 240 ft. under favorable conditions. It has a unique pre-set feature which instantly alerts with a loud warning beep whenever an underwater object comes between the boat's bottom and the pre-set depth or when the depth under the boat is less than the pre-set depth.
Model 5125 $180*

RAY JEFFERSON
Main & Cotton Sts., Philadelphia, Pa. 19127
Ray Jeff manufactures a broad line of low-priced marine electronics gear from a depthfinder at $100, knotmeter at $100 and tape player at $60 to a digital depth computer at $260. Discounts from mail-order firms are often possible.

ALDEN ELECTRONIC AND IMPULSE RECORDING EQUIPMENT CO., INC.
Small Craft Div., Alden Research Center, Westborough, Mass. 01581
One of the neatest gadgets we have seen in some years for small commercial and pleasure craft is the Alden 11 Marinefax Recorder. It is a facsimile receiver which prints out weather maps from stations located over most of the world including: North Atlantic—both sides, Mediterranean, South Atlantic, North Pacific, South Pacific and Indian Oceans. The $3,000 price tag is not that high, compared to the peace of mind in receiving such a wealth of information on the weather.

RAYTHEON MARINE CO.
676 Island Pond Rd., Manchester, N.H. 03103
Raytheon makes electronic equipment for ships and yachts of high quality. Their small radar sets sell for $3,900 and $4,400, SSB radiotelephones at $800 to $3,200, VHF-FM transceivers at $340 to $700, Omega at $4,600 and Loran C at the same price.

NARCO MARINE
Commerce Drive, Ft. Washington, Pa. 19034
Narco offers at $170 an emergency SOS beacon with self-contained batteries good for up to 8 days. It is claimed that the SOS is transmitted over a 32,000-square-mile area. This is an excellent safety device for those planning to go offshore, as it broadcasts on a band monitored by overseas aircraft and is likely to be heard. The signal can be used as a homing device by rescue vessels and aircraft.

Epsco
Model 4020 A
Omega Receiver

EPSCO INC.
411 Providence Hwy., Westwood, Mass. 02090
This company makes a high-quality Loran C receiver at $4,200, and a less expensive unit at $3,000. For automatic plotting of position and track, a plotter is also available to connect to the Loran unit for $4,500. EPSCO is also into the Omega navigation business and offers a receiver for $3,000 and a radar unit at $4,500.

BENMAR
3000 W. Warner Ave., Santa Ana, Calif. 92704
Benmar offers a wide variety of high-quality marine electronics equipment including: radar at $3,500; Loran A units at $1,200 and $1,600; depth sounders from $100 to $800; autopilots; and a complete line of direction finders from $300 to $3,700.

Konel Loran A
Model KL-155
Receiver

KONEL CORP.
271 Harbor Way, S. San Francisco, Calif. 94080
Konel supplies a variety of quality electronics equipment including: SSB marine radios at $1,000 to $1,700; VHF-FM sets at $539; radars at $4,500 to $5,600; Loran units at $1,300; direction finders and depth sounders.

Decca STR 24
Synthesized VHF/FM
Radiotelephone

DECCA MARINE INC. DIV. OF ITT
40 W. 57th St., New York, N.Y. 10019
Decca manufactures a high-quality line of electronics including: radar, sonar, VHF-FM radios, SSB radios, autopilots and Loran. By the way, the world is in the process of converting from Loran A to Loran C for greater accuracy and less ambiguity. Therefore, if Loran is on your shopping list, better be certain you buy a C unit.

KENYON MARINE
Box 308, New Whitfield St., Guilford, Conn. 06437
Kenyon produces a very high quality line of instruments for both sail- and powerboats to measure: wind, speed, distance, temperature and depth. Their KS 100 dual-range speedometer is $225. Write for catalog.

SIGNET SCIENTIFIC CO.
129 E. Tujunga Ave., Burbank, Calif. 91510
Signet manufactures a complete line of on-board sailboat instrumentation. Their Mark 9 knotmeter (0-12 knots) runs $170. Log that reads to 10,000 miles is $240. Signet also makes a variety of other instruments including: knotmeters which read up to 30 knots, delta units which give speed changes in small increments for fine-tuning a yacht, boat speed recorder, close-hauled indicator, crystal clock, barometer and others. Signet produces an unusual autopilot for sailboats with tiller steering. It's electric with a ¾-amp drain and costs $650. Literature and price sheets are available on request.

INTERNATIONAL MARINE INSTRUMENTS, INC.
Faulkner St., North Billerica, Mass. 01862
This company markets the COMBI 6 instrument package for sailboats, which on one dial gives: wind speed to 99 knots, distance log from .01 to 9,999.99 miles, acceleration or deceleration with variations as small as 0.05 knots, apparent wind direction, steering director which amplifies the apparent wind direction, and boat speed to 19.9 knots, with masthead unit and thru-hull paddle wheel transducer. Price is $1,400.

| Anemometer | Close Hauled | Apparent Wind |

ANDREWS INSTRUMENTS
9033 Monroe Rd., Houston, Tex. 77017
Andrews offers a complete system of sailboat instrumentation including: knotmeters, logs, anemometers, complete wind systems, remote compass systems, course director, quartz chronometers, repeaters and the like. They also market an Omni navigational receiver.

⚓ ⚓ ⚓ CRUISING

mechanics of *entering* involve checking the vessel's papers including the log book and her cargo, if any, ascertaining the citizenship of the crew and determining whether there are any health reasons (involving humans, plants or animals) for the boat to be kept in quarantine or not allowed to remain.

Clearing. Most countries require that upon final departure you *clear* with their customs and immigration officials before proceeding to the next country. This is somewhat easier than *entering*, but be certain to *clear* from designated ports.

When entering U.S. ports from abroad, you must give notice to U.S. Customs and Immigration within 24 hours of arrival.

sources of information

BUREAU OF CUSTOMS
2100 K St., N.W., Washington, D.C. 20226
Contact these people for information regarding entering and clearing, U.S. and foreign ports of entry, dutiable merchandise, liquor and tobacco limits, and so forth. The Bureau publishes a 30-page pamphlet for travelers called *Know Before You Go* (S/N 4802-00039), 55¢ (order from Superintendent of Documents, U.S. Gov. Printing Office, Washington, D.C. 20402), which covers everything you ought to know about dutiable merchandise and customs regulations. Worth picking up.

U.S. PUBLIC HEALTH SERVICE (USPHS)
National Communicable Disease Center, Atlanta, Ga. 30333
This is the place to inquire after health requirements and animal and plant quarantine regulations for the U.S. and other countries. USPHS publishes a small booklet called *Health Information for International Travel*, which can be gotten from the above address.

THE SLOCUM SOCIETY
9206 N.E. 180th St., Bothwell, Wash. 98011
This cruising group was established in 1955 to record, encourage, and support long-distance passages in small boats. Membership is $10 a year. The society publishes the *Spray*, a quarterly magazine that supports the purposes of the organization. The Slocum Society is named after Joshua Slocum, the first man to circle the globe single-handed (1895–1898), and the magazine is named after his boat.

The Slocum Society Sailing Club exists for members who have boats. They are entitled to fly the Sailing Club burgee, the house flag of the last line Joshua Slocum worked for. The society maintains extensive files on cruising and an extensive library of books written by and about cruising people. The society was recently reorganized and the new Honorary Secretary is Richard G. McCloskey.

SEVEN SEAS CRUISING ASSOCIATION, INC. (SSCA)
P.O. Box 38, Placida, Fla. 33946
The Seven Seas Cruising Association was formed in 1952 by a group of people living aboard six sailboats. The idea was to merge for the purpose of sharing cruising experiences through the medium of a monthly printed bulletin. SSCA is now a world-wide association of cruising sailors who live aboard and cruise their own sailing craft. They are an unusual group. SSCA is very active but not yet well known, probably because the Association is particular about its membership. To become a Commodore (member), the applicant must have lived aboard his own boat for at least one year, and his yacht must be his only home. He must be recommended by two members who have been Commodores for at least one year, and candidacy lasts for three months after the applicant's letter and the two recommendations have appeared in the *SSCA Commodore's Bulletin*. A member is dropped if he knowingly breaks the laws of the country he is in or leaves unpaid

Generally, we classify cruising as to three types: inland, coastwise and offshore; and this is a logical progression to develop your skills and test your abilities and likes and dislikes. This classification does not necessarily reflect the degree of dangers which may be encountered or the amount of experience required. In many ways, offshore cruising and ocean crossings are easier than sailing inshore, where reefs and poorly-lighted and -charted harbors may abound. Some of the worst seas and winds I have ever experienced on small boats and ships have been on the Great Lakes. There are many joys in gunkholing—the leisurely exploration in a shoal-draft boat of tiny islands, creeks, rivers and the like—and for many, this is a very satisfying end-all of their cruising. However, for others the magic lies in sailing foreign—cruising about the Caribbean, where some 21 countries are located, or crossing oceans to visit European ports or the romantic islands of the South Pacific.

Legal requirements for yachtsmen change frequently, and we recommend that you join a cruising society and subscribe to some publications, such as the periodical, *Cruising World,* which we discussed earlier, to keep up with what's what. As an example, for some time, it has been particularly difficult for yachtsmen to visit Venezuela and the Galapagos Islands, among others, without prior visas. Problems have been encountered in certain Mexican ports.

For those planning to sail foreign, it is highly recommended that you have your yacht documented. All necessary forms and instructions may be secured from your nearest U.S. Coast Guard district office—addresses were given earlier. You do not have to go through any formalities to leave the U.S., but you'd best have passports for all, plus immunization cards with the necessary shots entered by type and date. Passport applications may be secured from your local U.S. Post Office, and the U.S. Public Health Service can supply the official yellow cards for your shot record. It is a good idea to leave a record with U.S. Customs of any foreign goods carried aboard abroad, such as your Pentax camera, to avoid having to pay duty when reentering the U.S. on your return. Keep a formal log book, and type up in advance many copies of your crew list with full names, birth dates and places, passport numbers and dates to ease your paper-work problems. Some have suggested carrying a small typewriter aboard to cope better with all the forms you will face when entering foreign countries. It also helps if your yacht has a short, easily-understood name, and if her hailing port is a recognized U.S. seaport (see Appendix S in Bowditch for examples of well-known U.S. ports). The U.S. Public Health Service can provide you with a *bill of health,* which will make entering foreign ports easier. Sailing with pets such as dogs and cats can make your life difficult. Many countries now either flatly forbid the entry of such or require up to six months quarantine.

Entering. This is the process of arriving in the port of a country. You are required to *enter* a foreign country at designated cities which have facilities for customs, immigration and health inspections. Consult the various cruising guides for information on these. The procedure for entering is to sail into the harbor flying the flag of the foreign country at the starboard spreader or shroud of the forward-most mast. The U.S. flag is flown at the stern, and the yellow quarantine flag is hoisted on the flag halyard. You anchor or dock at the appropriate quarantine area and wait for the officials to board and clear you for entry. At some ports, the *skipper only* may go ashore to seek out the officials. Unfortunately, some ports charge exorbitant fees, and some officials expect some extra payments. It helps to have a bottle of wine or whatever to make the affair a more social one. The

bills behind when leaving port. Commodores pay $7 per year plus at least one letter on their experiences, and others may subscribe to the *Bulletin* at $8. Back issues from 1967 through 1973 are available at $7 per year from: SSCA, P.O. Box 6354, San Diego, Calif. 92106. Write the above address for back issues from 1974.

The 30-page monthly bulletin is packed with specific information on foreign ports, islands and countries, and tips for the travelling yachtsman. The annual meeting is held in Florida each year for those in the U.S. at that time.

CRUISING INFORMATION CENTER (CIC)
Peabody Museum, East India Sq., Salem, Mass. 01970

Frederick Johnson is the director of this new fount of knowledge for the cruising sailor. The object is to help yachtsmen planning long-range cruises, and fees for their research service run from $25 to $100 or more, depending on the length of the proposed voyage and the amount of information available and supplied. CIC offers to try to handle queries ranging from detailed routing and planning for a round-the-world cruise to specific questions on where to purchase fuel and food in out-of-the-way areas.

SAIL CREW CLEARING HOUSE (SCCH)
P.O. Box 1976, Orlando, Fla. 32802

Phil Beach has begun this admirable organization which publishes the bimonthly newsletter, *World Cruise News*. SCCH was created to bring together yacht owners needing crew members for long-distance cruises, or for maintenance work, and those seeking to voyage by sail. Membership is $10 in the U.S. and $15 foreign. Crew members come from every state and 20 foreign countries. Phil has also organized the Ocean Sailing Society as a nonprofit group dedicated to acquiring, restoring, preserving and operating some of the less than 150 large and historical sailing vessels which still exist. Send $1 for information.

WIND VANE
241 K West 35th St., National City, Calif. 92050

$4 a year will pay your subscription to this quarterly 48-page bulletin written, edited and published by cruising sailors interested in the concept of self sufficiency afloat. The pages read like a *Mother Earth News* of the sea. The bulletin is filled with practical advice on living aboard your yacht at low cost.

BOOKS

CRUISING UNDER SAIL
Eric C. Hiscock
1965, 2nd ed. - 468 p. il. - $22.50

This is numero uno—the first book any serious sailor should pick up on cruising. Since publication of the first edition in 1950, *Cruising Under Sail* has held its position as one of the leading books, if not the outstanding one on the subject. Part I covers the yacht and her gear, including hull form and construction; accommodations; rig; rope and rope work; masts and standing rigging; working sails; spars and running rigging; ground tackle; and examples of cruising yachts. Part II discusses seamanship and navigation—maneuvering under sail; light-weather sails and their handling, avoiding collision; weather; aids to navigation; tides; practical navigation; management in heavy weather; and passage making. Part III covers the dinghy; the auxiliary engine; safety at sea; flags and signalling; laying up and fitting out; and ship's business. The appendix has a good list of books and a list of all the tools, supplies, hardware, and so forth you should plan to carry aboard. The book is well illustrated with photographs and line drawings—just great! The only problem (if it can be called a problem) is that it's slanted toward the British, particularly in the navigation section and the list of books.
From: Oxford Univ. Press, 16-00 Pollitt Dr., Fair Lawn, N.J. 07410

VOYAGING UNDER SAIL
Eric C. Hiscock
1970 rev. - 208 p. il. - $17.95

This is the follow-up to Hiscock's first book on general cruising. *Voyaging Under Sail* covers the special problems associated with the ocean-going cruiser; the arrangement is somewhat similar to *Cruising.* Part I covers the ocean-going yacht and her gear including the hull; construction and general arrangement; rig and rigging; sails and self-steering arrangements; mechanical and electrical equipment; some notable ocean-going yachts. Part II on voyaging discusses planning the voyage; seamanship; navigation; welfare of the crew; in port; photography (including setting up processing apparatus on the boat and a complete list of supplies and equipment you should have). The appendix contains five pages listing notable passages by various cruising boats; a book list of the specifications and particulars on more than sixty cruising boats, many of them very well known (*Spray, Islander, Svaap, Yankee*, and of course, *Wanderer II* and *III*). Add this one as no. 2 to your cruising library.
From: Oxford Univ. Press, 16-00 Pollitt Dr., Fair Lawn, N.J. 07410

THE LONG DISTANCE CRUISER
Bill Rothrock
1974 - 175 p. il. - $8.95

Subtitled: "A Somewhat Irreverent Look at the Design of...," this

book pokes many holes in the establishment design of the modern yacht where advertising men and accountants replace the naval architect. Bill has some fine thoughts on galleys, heads and crew comfort. He gives three examples of more-or-less ideal cruising yachts for the trans-ocean types. You may be outraged by some of his statements, but the book is very thought-provoking and well worth some study.
From: International Marine Pub. Co., 21 Elm St., Camden, Maine 04843

THE CRUISER'S MANUAL
Carl D. Lane
1970 - 397 p. il. - $10

This is a revised edition of one of cruising's standard reference manuals originally brought out in 1949. The book is illustrated by Lane and contains a fantastic amount of practical information on the subject. Recommended as an excellent back-up to Hiscock's *Cruising Under Sail.*
From: Funk & Wagnalls, Vreeland Ave., Totowa, N.J. 07512

SEA QUEST
Charles A. Borden
1966 - 352 p. il. - $7.95

This is a collection of facts about long voyages in small boats from ancient times to the present. Borden, who has made several voyages himself, one in a 17' sloop across the Pacific, describes with familiarity the cruises of others who have gone before him: Slocum, Gerbault, Pigeon, Robinson, Chichester, and others. The book is well illustrated with photographs, drawings, and plans of the boats used by these sailing adventurers. There's also a glossary of sea and sailing terms and an excellent bibliography and reading list of small boat voyages and sea literature. A very good reference book deserving a place in every ship's library.
From: Macrae Smith Co., 225 S. 15th St., Philadelphia, Pa. 19102

THE OCEAN SAILING YACHT
Donald M. Street, Jr.
1973 - 703 p. il. - $23.95

Don Street sails a 45-foot renovated yawl and has had many years of cruising experience. His advice on all aspects of cruising is valuable, and he treats a whole range of topics from refrigeration to navigation, seamanship, anchoring, deck hardware, ventilation for the tropics, tools and spares, and sources of supply. Don lives aboard in the Caribbean and is the author of *Cruising Guide To the Lesser Antilles.*
From: W. W. Norton & Co., Inc., 500 Fifth Ave., New York, N.Y. 10036

LOVE FOR SAIL
Mark Hassall and Jim Brown
1974 - 207 p. il. - $6.45 (pb)

This is an absorbing account of a 40,000-mile, round-the-world cruise in a 37-ft. trimaran. The book was assembled and edited by Jim Brown, designer of the yacht, from tapes recorded enroute. Emphasis is divided between the people a cruising sailor meets and the practicalities of cruising foreign: money, schools, food, costs, pests, sickness, motives and attitudes. The accounts of the four hurricanes encountered are terrifyingly realistic. This book is beautifully written and edited and should be in every sailor's library.
From: ALMAR, 241 West 35th St., Suite K, National City, Calif. 92050

OCEAN VOYAGING
David M. Parker
1975 - 216 p. il. - $12.50

If Herreshoff does not jar your thinking on offshore sailing yachts, Parker will. A veteran of 100,000 miles of ocean sailing, his words make a good deal of sense. The most important chapters are concerned with choosing the hull design, construction and interior layout, rigs and rigging, equipment and self steering.
From: John DeGraff, Inc., 34 Oak Ave., Tuckahoe, N.Y. 10707

GUIDES, SAILING DIRECTIONS & COAST PILOTS

The number of cruising guidebooks to various areas is increasing rapidly, and it is almost impossible to keep up with those which are still in print and the more local ones. We list *some* of the more permanent and useful below with the caution that you may well find others of particular use to you in libraries, from reading boating magazines and directories, and in conversations with other sailors.

THE WORLD

SAILING DIRECTIONS
Defense Mapping Agency

The Defense Mapping Agency with the assistance of pleasure boatmen, merchant seamen, and foreign oceanographic offices has put together some 70 volumes of navigation information covering the whole world. These *Sailing Directions* are published in loose leaf form at a standard price of $4.50 per volume including ring binder or $3 for contents only. All "Changes" in effect at the time are included in the selling price, and later "Changes" may be had for 35¢ each. Each volume covers a particular area of the world, for example, H.O. No. 21, *Sailing Directions for the West Indies, Vol. I* includes Bermuda, the Bahama Islands, and the Greater Antilles. The contents of any one volume start off with general info for the area, such as buoyage, signals, pilotage, regulations, cautions, oceanography, weather tendencies, and routes. From there, islands, coastal regions, and such are covered systematically for the whole area. Descriptions given include landmarks, bearings and courses, water conditions (tides and currents, depths, channels, etc.), winds, aids and hazards to navigation, anchorages, pilot requirements, harbor descriptions, facilities, and other pertinent information, plus anything else that may be of value to the mariner. In general, the *Sailing Directions* are intended for merchant ships rather than pleasure boats, so don't look for info that would just be of value to the small boatman. For a complete list of all the volumes available, request *Catalog of Nautical Charts and Publications, Introduction, Part I.*
From: Def. Map. Agency, Hydro. Cntr., Washington, D.C. 20390

OCEAN PASSAGES FOR THE WORLD
1973, 3rd ed. - $25

This is a British Admiralty publication which is excellent for planning ocean crossings and other offshore cruising. There is written material giving sailing directions and coast pilot information as well as six folded charts, which give information on routes, currents, weather and winds.
From: International Marine Pub. Co., 21 Elm St., Camden, Maine 04843

CANADA

CRUISING THE GEORGIAN BAY
CRUISING THE NORTH CHANNEL
Both from: Bellhaven House, 12 Dyas Rd., Don Mills, Ont., Canada

CARIBBEAN

A CRUISING GUIDE TO THE LESSER ANTILLES
Donald M. Street, Jr.
1974 rev. ed. - 320 p. il. - $18.50

This large-format book is the most complete sailing guide for the Windward and the Leeward Islands from Puerto Rico to Trinidad. In addition, there is good, solid information on trip preparations and proper seamanship in the Caribbean including methods of anchoring, what to bring, water safety and insurance. Of particular value are the chapters on charts, weather and tides, and an evaluation of the various sailing routes from the U.S. to the Caribbean. Sailing directions and sketch maps of many of the Caribbean Islands appear to be complete and very useful.
From: SAIL Books, Inc., 38 Commercial Wharf, Boston, Mass. 02110

A CRUISING GUIDE TO THE CARIBBEAN AND THE BAHAMAS
Jerrems C. Hart and William T. Stone
1976 - 578 p. il. - $20

This is a comprehensive guide to sailing in the entire Caribbean including the north coast of South America, Central America and Yucatan. Black-and-white charts are included.
From: Dodd, Mead & Co., 79 Madison Ave., New York, N.Y. 10016

YACHTSMAN'S GUIDE TO THE GREATER ANTILLES
Harry Kline
1976 - 256 p. il. - $4.95

Covered in this cruising guide are some of the larger islands in the Caribbean: Virgin Islands, Puerto Rico, Haiti and Dominican Republic.
From: Tropic Isle Publishers Inc., P.O. Box 866, Coral Gables, Fla. 33134

YACHTSMANS GUIDE TO THE BAHAMAS
Harry Kline
1976 - $4.95

Loaded with excellent descriptions plus hand-drawn charts describing dangers, channels, and anchorages, this is *the* sailing directions and boating guide to the Bahamas. A fantastic quantity of information—ports of entry (if you'll need a pilot), customs info, sizing-up a strange harbor, and so forth.
From: Tropic Isle Publishers, P.O. Box 866, Coral Gables, Fla. 33134

EUROPE

Best way to purchase books on cruising in European waters is directly from Thomas Foulkes, Lansdowne Road, Leytonstone, London E11 3HB, England. Their selection on cruising includes: *Inland Waterways of Great Britain, North Sea Harbors and Pilotage, Normandy Harbours and Pilotage, French Mediterranean Harbours, Holiday Cruising in the Netherlands, South Biscay Pilot, Yachtsman's 8 Language Dictionary, Channel Harbours and Anchorages, Through France to the Mediterranean, Through the Dutch Canals, Through the Belgian Canals, Through the French Canals* and a large number of local cruising guides for England including, among others, the Stanford Harbour Guides to the West Coast of Scotland, and North Foreland to The Needles. Charts and chart catalogs are also available. Send $1 for a catalog via air mail.

GREAT BRITAIN

BRITAIN'S INLAND WATERWAYS
Roger Wickson - $4.95
From: Roy Publishers, Inc., 30 E. 74th St., New York, N.Y. 10021

MEDITERRANEAN

THE ADRIATIC
H. M. Denham - $9.50
Guide to facilities and scenery on the Albanian, Yugoslavian, and

Apulian Coasts and the Gulf of Venice.
From: Transatlantic Arts, Inc., Levittown, N.Y. 11756

THE AEGEAN
H. M. Denham - $12.50
General information as well as nautical information on the Aegean Coast and Islands.
From: Transatlantic Arts, Inc. Levittown, N.Y. 11756

THE EASTERN MEDITERRANEAN
$9.50
Covers the coast of Greece from Corfu through the Ionian Islands to the shores of southern Crete and eastward to Anatoba, Cyprus.
From: Transatlantic Arts, Inc., Levittown, N.Y. 11756

MARINER IN THE MEDITERRANEAN
John Marriner
From: Aslard Coles Ltd., 1–3 Upper James St., London W–1, England

THE IONIAN ISLANDS TO RHODES
SOUTHERN TURKEY, THE LEVANT AND CYPRUS
THE TYRRHENIAN SEA
All by H. M. Denham
All from: Transatlantic Arts, Inc., Levittown, N.Y. 11756

MEXICO

BAJA CRUISING NOTES
Vern Jones
Strictly a navigation guidebook to the area.
From: SeeBreez Publications, Thousand Oaks, Calif. 91360

POWERBOATING THE WEST COAST OF MEXICO
Murray and Poole - $6.75
Cruising guide covering Guaymas-Topolobampo to Puerto Vallarta; sea, weather, and port conditions.
From: Desert-Southwest Press, Thousand Oaks, Calif. 91360

SEA GUIDE/BAJA, Vol. II
Leland Lewis - $29.50
Deluxe volume to cruising Baja waters; covers both coastlines.
From: Miller Freeman Pub., Inc., Book Dept., 500 Howard St., San Francisco, Calif. 94105

UNITED STATES

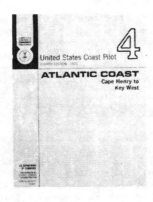

UNITED STATES COAST PILOT
National Ocean Survey

The *Coast Pilot* provides navigation information which cannot be geographically shown on nautical charts. Primarily for larger vessels, the pilots are of value to the pleasure boatman as well, since he can go anywhere a large vessel can. A *Pilot* will start off with general information covering certain government organizations and their services for mariners, emergency and distress procedures, weather broadcasts, and time signal data. Next, navigation regulations are given for the area the book covers; and then comes descriptive commentary on sections of the coast, islands, and so forth. This information includes water conditions, aids and hazards to navigation, courses and bearings, harbor data and facilities, physical descriptions of the coastline for determining position, bays, rivers and inlets. Regardless of whether you have some popular cruising guide with you or not, you should always have a *Coast Pilot* as a backup. The editions available are:
>   No. 1 - Eastport to Cape Cod - $6
>   No. 2 - Cape Cod to Sandy Hook - $6
>   No. 3 - Sandy Hook to Cape Henry - $6
>   No. 4 - Cape Henry to Key West - $6

>   No. 5 - Gulf of Mexico, Puerto Rico and Virgin Islands - $6
>   No. 7 - California, Oregon, Washington and Hawaii - $6
>   No. 8 - Dixon Entrance to Cape Spencer - $6
>   No. 9 - Cape Spencer to Beaufort Sea - $6
>   (no. 6 is not presently being used)

From: National Ocean Survey, Distribution Div. (C-44), Riverdale, Md. 20840

WATERWAY GUIDE
The Waterway Guide is published annually in three separate editions. Information contained is more for pleasure than for navigation, though facilities and services data are very good. These are shown on a chart and described in a numbered table. The *Waterway Guide* is good company for a *Coast Pilot*. The three editions available are:
>   *Northern Edition.* New York to Cape Cod, Maine, Canada, and the Barge Canals - $5.95
>   *Mid-Atlantic Edition.* New York to Georgia-Florida line, Chesapeake Bay and Intracoastal Waterway - $5.95
>   *Southern Edition.* Georgia-Florida line to the Keys, Gulf Coast to Texas, Mexico - $5.95

From: Sidney J. Wain, Inc., P.O. Box 1486, Annapolis, Md. 21404

Alaska

CRUISING GUIDE TO ALASKAN WATERS
From: J. B. Lippincott Co., E. Washington Sq., Philadelphia, Pa. 19105

East Coast

BLOCK ISLAND TO NANTUCKET
F. S. Blanchard - $7.50
Introduction to the waters off Rhode Island and southern Massachusetts.
From: Van Nostrand Reinhold Co., 300 Pike St., Cincinnati, Ohio 45202

BOATING ALMANAC
About the same drill as the *Waterway Guide,* but cluttered-looking and not as nice a presentation as the *Guide,* also smaller. Probably a little more practical info than in the *Guide,* though; but can't exactly say it's all practical for navigation. It does include complete tide and current tables and charts, and marina locations are shown on chart reproductions. The four regional editions available are:
>   1. Massachusetts, Maine, and New Hampshire - $3.25
>   2. Rhode Island, Connecticut, and Long Island - $3.25
>   3. New Jersey, Delaware Bay and River, Hudson River and Lake Champlain - $3.25
>   4. The Chesapeake Bay to North Carolina - $3.25

From: G. W. Bromley & Co., Inc., 325 Spring St., New York, N.Y. 10013

BOATING ATLAS OF TIDEWATER VIRGINIA
Color charts of Virginia seacoast, Chesapeake shores, and Tidewater rivers. Tide tables, facilities, and course protractors.
From: Paxton Co., 1111 Ingeside Rd., Norfolk, Va. 23502

CANAL GUIDE FOR THE NEW YORK STATE CANAL SYSTEM
Free
Cruising New York State canals and connecting Canadian waterways.
From: Cruising Guide Book, 146 Sheridan Ave., Albany, N.Y. 12210

CRUISING GUIDE TO THE CHESAPEAKE
F. S. Blanchard and W. T. Stone - $7.50
Covers all waterways off the Chesapeake; charts, piloting info, local lore, and anchorages. Cruising conditions from Long Island Sound to Cape Henry.
From: Dodd, Mead Co., 79 Madison Ave., New York, N.Y. 10016

CRUISING NEW JERSEY TIDEWATER
Fred Van Deventer - $4.95
Piloting and cruising, where to go ashore on Delaware River and Bay, Cape May, Atlantic Highlands, and many more locations.
From: Rutgers University Press, 30 College Ave., New Brunswick, N.J. 08903

CRUISING THE MAINE COAST
Morten Lund - $12.50
Numerous maps and photographs comprise this informative guide. Well-planned model cruise.
From: Walker and Co., 720 Fifth Ave., New York, N.Y. 10019

CRUISING GUIDE TO THE NEW ENGLAND COAST
R. F. Duncan and J. P. Ware
1972 - 619 p. il. - $15

Descriptions of harbors and facilities: tides, depth, bottom; includes charts, anchorages, history, and weather. This is one of the classics.
From: Dodd, Mead and Co., 79 Madison Ave., New York, N.Y. 10016

EASTWARD ON FIVE SOUNDS
$10.00

Guide for cruising from New York to Nantucket. Charts, anchorages, and emergency stops included.
From: Walker and Co., 720 Fifth Ave., New York, N.Y. 10019

FLORIDA CRUISE TIPS/77
1977 - $3.50

Complete description of all Florida's marinas and their facilities together with information on bridges and other obstructions and other navigational tips. Chart excerpts show location of each feature, dock and marina described.
From: Gondolier Enterprises, Inc., P.O. Box 7516, Fort Lauderdale, Fla. 33304

GUIDE TO CRUISING MARYLAND WATERS
William B. Matthews, Jr.
1976 - $5

This is a chart and tidal current atlas which covers Chesapeake Bay from the Potomac River north. Additional information is contained, such as magnetic courses between various points, index of place names, etc. Charts are also furnished for the C&O Canal, the Potomac River and the Intracoastal Waterway in Maryland.
From: State of Maryland, Dept. of Natural Resources, State Off. Bldg., Annapolis, Md. 21404

A BOOK OF CHARTS FOR CHESAPEAKE BAY
1976 - $11.95

This is an atlas of 17 shore-to-shore, fold-out charts covering the whole Bay and its navigable rivers. Also included are a planning chart of the entire Bay and brief cruising information.
From: Sidney J. Wain, Inc., P.O. Box 1486, Annapolis, Md. 21404

REED'S NAUTICAL ALMANAC 1977: American East Coast Edition
1977 - 868 p. - $11.95

This is the American edition of a classic British work which combines the most-used parts of the nautical almanac, tide tables, coast pilot and other useful tables. Not as complete as the individual publications.
From: Thomas Reed Publications, Ltd., 5-45 49th Ave., Long Island City, N.Y. 11101

MACMILLAN MARINE ATLAS
Three editions; hardbound books of carefully reproduced nautical charts in a handy size. Features include the best courses already plotted, marine facilities and shore points indicated, and enlargements of harbors and rivers. The three editions are:
    New Jersey and Delaware Waters - $7.95
    Long Island Sound and South Shore - $7.95
    New England - $7.95
From: The Macmillan Co., Front and Brown Sts., Riverside, N.J. 08075

WHERE TO GO, WHAT TO DO, HOW TO DO IT ON CAPE COD
J. M. Wilensky - $7.95
Charts of facilities and points of interest.
From: Westcott Publishing Co., Box 130, Stamford, Conn. 06940

WHERE TO GO, WHAT TO DO, HOW TO DO IT ON LONG ISLAND SOUND
Julius M. Wilensky - $8.95
Detailed information on nearly every harbor and gunkhole on both the Connecticut and the New York side. Food and provision sources plus history and sight seeing info.
From: Snug Harbor Pub. Co., Box 3312, Ridgeway Station, Stamford, Conn. 06905

YACHTSMAN'S GUIDE TO NORTHERN HARBORS
Harbors and services—Long Island and the coast of New England.
From: Seaport Publishing Co., 843 Delray Ave., Grand Rapids, Mich. 49506

Great Lakes

YACHTSMAN'S GUIDE TO THE GREAT LAKES
$2.50
Harbors and services on the Lakes, St. Lawrence, Hudson, and Richelieu Rivers, Lake Champlain, and New York State Barge Canal.
From: Seaport Publishing Co., 843 Delray Ave., Grand Rapids, Mich. 49506

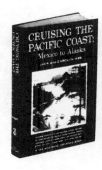

Gulf Coast

CRUISING GUIDE TO THE SOUTHERN COAST
Fessenden Blanchard - $17.50
Covers the Intracoastal Waterway from Norfolk, Virginia, to New Orleans, Louisiana, including the Florida waterways.
From: Dodd, Mead and Co., 79 Madison Ave., New York, N.Y. 10016

Mississippi River

QUIMBY'S HARBOR GUIDE TO THE MISSISSIPPI
$3.00
A "must" guide which covers everything you'll need to know about cruising the Mississippi.
From: Quimby's Harbor Guide, Box 85, Prairie du Chien, Wis. 53821

Northwest

COASTAL CRUISING
W. Dawson
Covers British Columbia, Puget Sound-San Juan waters, and southeast Alaska.
From: Mitchell Press Ltd., Vancouver, B.C. Canada

West Coast

CRUISING THE CALIFORNIA DELTA
R. E. Walters - $10.95
Charts, maps, and facilities of the Northern California Delta.
From: Miller Freeman Publications, Inc., 500 Howard St., San Francisco, Calif. 94105

CRUISING THE PACIFIC COAST (1970)
Jack and Carolyn West - $8.50
Piloting the coast; charts, harbor facilities, weather, and points of interest are covered.
From: Miller Freeman Pub., Inc., 500 Howard St., San Francisco, Calif. 94105

THE ISLANDS AND PORTS OF CALIFORNIA
Duncan Gleason - $10
Guide to coastal California.
From: Devin-Adair Co., 1 Park Ave., Old Greenwich, Conn. 06870

SEA GUIDE/SOUTHERN CALIFORNIA, Vol. I
Leland Lewis and Peter Ebling - $18.00
Point Conception to Ensenada; charts and photos.
From: Miller Freeman Pub., Inc., Book Dept., 500 Howard St., San Francisco, Calif. 94105

SEA MARINE ATLAS
W. Crawford - $10.95
Comprehensive chart book and guide covering waters from Point Arguello, Calif., to Punta Colnett, Mexico.
From: Miller Freeman Pub., Inc., Book Dept., 500 Howard St., San Francisco, Calif. 94105

Marauder - Muller Kites Ltd.

hang gliding

Picture yourself standing in a light breeze on the top of a hill. You turn your wing into the wind anticipating the takeoff,

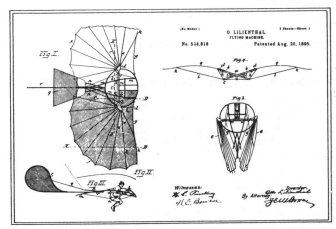

O. Lilienthal's patent office drawing.

take a few steps and then it happens. You lift off into the age-old dream of unencumbered, personal flight. Like Icarus, you escape the bonds of earth for the ultimate freedom of the sky. Hang gliding is, in fact, the oldest form of heavier-than-air flying. It was practiced by Otto Lillienthal during the last century and few people realize that all of the early flights made by the Wright Brothers at Kitty Hawk were gliding or soaring. Of course, they blew it, missed the point completely when they mounted a noisy, smelly engine on the glider and took off in another direction.

In design, hang gliders are light and simple (that's what it's all about). They may be controlled by pilot weight shift, control surfaces or a combination of both. Aside from gliding down hills or mountain slopes, hang gliders are capable of maintaining or gaining altitude utilizing up-currents of air. This is called "soaring." The most common type is "ridge soaring" where a wind is deflected upwards by a cliff or hill. Another type is "thermal soaring" where differential heating of the ground by the sun causes rising bubbles of hot air. One

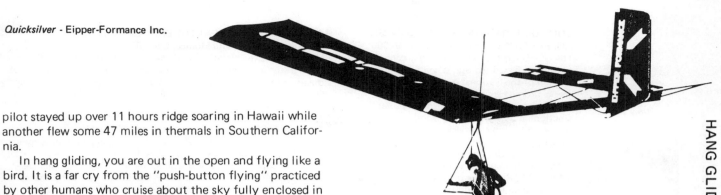

pilot stayed up over 11 hours ridge soaring in Hawaii while another flew some 47 miles in thermals in Southern California.

In hang gliding, you are out in the open and flying like a bird. It is a far cry from the "push-button flying" practiced by other humans who cruise about the sky fully enclosed in fast-moving missiles. Perhaps that's why so many airline pilots are flying hang gliders.

Most anyone can fly a hang glider (one man in Australia is otherwise confined to a wheelchair). But since just as many can crash, it is strongly recommended that you attend a school. Everyone learns faster with a coach. Instructors want you to enjoy yourself, to experience the feeling of personal flight and they'll do their best to see that you learn with a minimum of unintentional ground contact. Besides, students are tough on equipment and it's better to break their kite than yours.

Hang gliding is physically demanding initially (who do you think carries those kites *UP* the hill?). Often in the excitement of a day's flying, a student fails to realize that he is using a new set of muscles. While it may be good exercise, the legs can hurt. Later, you'll develop the muscles or use a vehicle.

There is no governmental licensing but the United States Hang Gliding Association does certify instructors and does issue licenses to members.

Typically, your instruction will include a few hours of ground school to brief you in the basics. You'll learn to set up the kite and to ground handle it. You'll begin by running with it on level ground to get the feel of it. Then you'll progress up the hill, a little farther on each flight. First you'll learn takeoffs, straight flight and landings and later you'll begin turns. Probably the three most important things you'll learn are: which way the wind is blowing, maintaining airspeed and maintaining control until you've come to a complete stop.

If you don't have any hills to foot-launch from, don't despair. You can be towed up by boat to release and fly away. They do it four times a day in the show at Cypress Gardens and no state is as flat as Florida. Launching from snow is easier because it is so simple to reach the 15-mph airspeed necessary for takeoff—even if the wind is blowing slightly downhill.

Instruction

There are hundreds of hang gliding schools so it shouldn't be necessary to travel any great distance. First, pick up the *Yellow Pages* and look under "hang gliders," then "gliders." If that doesn't do it, switch to the *White Pages* and look under "U.S. Government, Transportation Department, Federal Aviation Administration" and try a few of their numbers. Or, you can always write or call the USHGA (213) 390-3065; they'll be happy to send you to the nearest school, dealer or club.

Bailing Out

The time to think about selling your gear is before you buy it, and the best advice is to purchase the latest and best equipment, as it will be the easiest to sell whether you're

bailing out or trading up. Hang gliders are changing rapidly and sometimes last year's model is next to valueless. Ask around before you buy.

The easiest way to sell equipment is to someone in a local club. This allows inspection by the purchaser and avoids transportation and shipping problems. Try word of mouth, an announcement at a club meeting and posting notice on the local bulletin board. Next best is through the local kite shop. While they will take a cut, they'll also usually give your rig a presale checkover by disassembling and inspecting it, and making needed repairs. This provides peace of mind as well as an element of safety for both you and the buyer.

The last shot would be advertising in one of the hang gliding magazines via a classified. *Hang Glider Weekly* and *Glider Rider* offer the shortest advertising lead times.

sources of information

LAWS AND REGULATIONS

So far, there are virtually no regulations—federal, state or local—covering the sport of hang gliding. Obviously, the hang glider is an "aircraft" and, just as obviously, the person flying it a "pilot." But the sport grew so fast—no, exploded—that government agencies were taken by surprise. They knew that standard plane and pilot licensing would kill off the sport, they knew little about ultralight flight and they realized that enforcement of any rules would be impossible. After all, if an agency wishes to stop you from flying or parachuting, they can issue a notice to airports, but hang gliding doesn't require a prepared landing area. While they might bust a few flyers and close a few flying sites, they couldn't very well post a notice on every tree. Besides, such bureaucratic interference would simply serve to force the flyers ever farther from the city and farther from the occasionally required medical help.

FEDERAL AVIATION ADMINISTRATION
800 Independence Ave., S.W., Washington, D.C. 20590

In its infinite wisdom, the Federal Aviation administration issued an Advisory Circular (No. 60-10) in May of 1974. In it they profess no desire to regulate the sport at this time, but they do present a number of safety suggestions. Actually, it was a smart move. Many people are attracted to aviation through hang gliding; many who would not have looked to the sky because they thought it was too dangerous or too expensive. Hang gliding introduced them to aviation and from there they've graduated to faster, fancier modes of flight and have secured FAA licensing. Thus FAA's bailiwick is enlarged and they are justified in asking Congress for more funds. For a free copy of Advisory Circular 60-10, write: U.S. Dept. of Transportation, Publications Section TAD 443.1, Washington, D.C. 20590.

UNITED STATES HANG GLIDING ASSN.
P.O. Box 66306, Los Angeles, Calif. 90066

The USHGA is the national hang gliding association of the United States and a nonprofit division of the National Aeronautic Association. It is devoted to promoting improvement in ultralight flight, flying safety, sanctioning and establishing standards for competition, and supervising and documenting all hang gliding record attempts. It also selects and trains the United States Hang Gliding Team for international competition and is the official U.S. Representative of the Fédération Aéronautique Internationale, the governing body of international aviation sports. The USHGA has instituted a licensing program to smooth the way for flyers visiting new flying sites. There are five types of licenses called "Hang Ratings" which are issued on the basis of experience, flight demonstrations and written tests. It also conducts Instructor Certification Courses and rates those who pass. USHGA issues guidelines to clubs to promote safe flying. The annual $10 membership fee ($11, foreign) includes a subscription to the excellent *Ground Skimmer* magazine, which covers the whole spectrum of ultralight flight from humor to technical articles—excellent info source.

═══ THE HANG RATING SYSTEM. USHGA PART 104 ═══

104.07 HANG ONE
Persons who hold a Hang One rating are certified as being able to fly at Hang One rated sites up to 150 feet AGL. He has demonstrated his ability to:
a. Set up and preflight his own glider,
b. take off unassisted to make straight flights with minor corrections and good control, and
c. pass a written exam.

104.08 HANG TWO
Persons who hold a Hang Two rating are certified as being able to fly at Hang Two rated sites up to 300 feet AGL. He may fly in smooth winds to 18 mph and gusty winds up to 11 mph. He has demonstrated his ability to:
a. Make smooth alternating 90 degree "S" turns over preselected points demonstrating good airspeed control,
b. Land within 40 feet of the target,
c. Fly at least 40 feet AGL, and
d. pass a written exam.

104.09 HANG THREE
Persons who hold a Hang Three rating are certified as being able to fly at Hang Three rated sites. He may fly in smooth winds to 20 mph and gusty winds to 15 mph. He has no altitude limitations. He has:
a. Held a Hang Two rating for at least 60 days and has made 90 flights over 30 flying days,
b. Demonstrated his ability to make steep and gentle linked 180 degree "S" turns along his predetermined track.
c. made three consecutive landings within 30 feet of the target,
d. flown a standard task for the site to demonstrate that he differentiates between airspeed/groundspeed and flight path/ground track.
e. Demonstrated precise 180 degree entry turns
f. Made ten flights with a ground clearance of 75 feet, and
g. demonstrated alternating fast (max L/D) and slow (min. sink) flight in a constant direction (to demonstrate knowledge of the flying speeds and stall characteristics of his glider).
h. passed a written exam.

104.10 HANG FOUR
Persons who hold a Hang Four rating are certified as being able to fly at Hang Four rated sites. He may enter regional, national and international competition. He may participate in national and international records attempts. He has:
a. Held a Hang Three rating for four months,
b. made 60 flights of one minute or more,
c. made five flights at each of five sites, three of which are inland,
d. made five flights of five minutes,
e. made three flights soaring above takeoff for five minutes,
f. made five flights above 250 feet AGL,
g. demonstrated figure eights,
h. made three consecutive landings within 20 feet of the target on flights of at least one minute,
i. made a flight over an imaginary 15 foot barrier to land no more than 30 feet past the barrier and within 10 feet of a centerline, and
j. passed a written exam.

HANG GLIDER MANUFACTURERS' ASSOCIATION
3021 Airport Ave., Santa Monica, Calif. 90401

HMA publishes specifications and standards for the design and manufacture of ultralight aircraft. It provides a vehicle for the exchange of industry information. Copies of the Category I Specifications are available from the above address for $1.

HANG GLIDING ASSOCIATION OF CANADA
P.S.C. Box 4063, Calgary, Alberta, Canada T2T 5M9

HGAC is the Canadian national hang gliding organization functioning essentially in the same way the USHGA does, except that a great deal of financial support is received from government agencies. Membership is through provincial associations and dues vary from province to province. Addresses of the provincial associations may be secured from the above address.

_____ PERIODICALS

HANG GLIDER WEEKLY
Joe Faust, Ed.
Weekly - $12/yr. - 8 p.

A tiny-print gold mine of hang gliding information. *Hang Glider Weekly* is a free-spirited publication listing among its goals fellowship, enjoyment and "the advancement of the science of mechanical motorless flight in the realms of minimum total cost."
From: Hang Glider Weekly, P.O. Box 1860, Santa Monica, Calif. 90406

GLIDER RIDER
Tracy Knauss, Ed.
Monthly - $10/yr. - 30 p. il.

A timely, interesting and entertaining tabloid-size publication with many good photos and stories.
From: Glider Rider, P.O. Box 6009, Chattanooga, Tenn. 37401

ICARUS FLIGHT
John Dowd, Ed.
Monthly - $5/yr.

The only magazine which concentrates on rigid-wing-type hang gliders. Many timely, important tips on flying and construction.
From: Icarus Flight, 11045 Sorrento Valley Ct., San Diego, Calif. 92121

THE FLYPAPER
Catherine Buckley, Ed.
Monthly - $10/yr.

Subscription to *The Flypaper* also gets you membership in the Alberta Hang Gliding Association. It's the oldest and largest Canadian magazine covering ultralight flight.
From: Alberta Hang Gliding Assn., 131 Tenth Ave., SE, Calgary, Alberta, Canada

DRACHENFLIEGER MAGAZIN
Walter Zuerl, Ed.
Monthly - DM 36/yr.

The only hang gliding magazine printed in the German language. Slick and informative. When subscribing use an international postal money order equal to 36 Marks; check at your local post office.
From: Drachenflieger Magazin
    Luftfahrt-Verlag, Walter Zuerl
    D-8031 Steinebach/W.
    West Germany

Launching a kite.

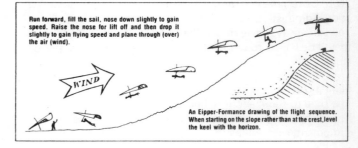

Run forward, fill the sail, nose down slightly to gain speed. Raise the nose for lift off and then drop it slightly to gain flying speed and plane through (over) the air (wind).

An Eipper-Formance drawing of the flight sequence. When starting on the slope rather than at the crest, level the keel with the horizon.

BOOKS

HANG GLIDING
Dan Poynter
1976, 7th ed. - 216 p. il. - $5.95 (pb), $9.95 (hb)

The first book to come out on the subject, now updated for the sixth time, *Hang Gliding* covers basic to advanced flying, design, materials, construction, history, the law, and lists every kite on the market with its description, photo, performance specifications and source. Over 400 manufacturers, dealers, clubs and schools are listed. A really great book that would just about be perfect—if it had an index!
The author is President of the Commission Internationale de Vol Libre (Hang Gliding) of the Fédération Aéronautique Internationale, the organization governing international aviation sports. He is a hang gliding Flight Examiner and a member of the USHGA Board of Directors as well as a pilot licensed for both powered aircraft and gliders.
From: Parachuting Publications, P.O. Box 4232-105, Santa Barbara, Calif. 93103

KITING
Dan Poynter
1975, 2nd ed. - 104 p. il. - $3.95 (pb)

Kiting is the first and only book on boat tow-launched hang gliding. It is roughly the same as *Hang Gliding* in scope as it treats this different hang gliding application.
From: Parachuting Publications, P.O. Box 4232-105, Santa Barbara, Calif. 93103

HANG GLIDING MANUAL & LOG
Dan Poynter
1976 - 24 p. il. - $1.50 (pb)

Intended primarily as a basic training manual, *Hang Gliding Manual & Log* contains all the basic essential review information necessary for making safe, enjoyable ultralight flights. It even provides space for the novice to record his first month of flying.
From: Parachuting Publications, P.O. Box 4232-105, Santa Barbara, Calif. 93103

HANG GLIDING AND FLYING CONDITIONS
Dennis Pagen
1976 - 102 p. il. - $6.15 (pb)

This book covers micrometeorology or low-level weather conditions as they pertain to the hang glider/flyer. An outstanding, scholarly work by one of the most knowledgeable writers in the field.
From: Sky Light Flight, 1184 Oneida, State College, Pa. 16801

THE FLYINGEST FLYING: HANG GLIDING
Don Dedera and Stephen McCarroll
1975 - 144 p. il. - $9.95 (pb), $14.50 (hb)

A beautiful, full-color "celebration" of this new and fast-expanding aviation sport.
From: Northland Press, P.O. Box N, Flagstaff, Ariz. 86001

HANG GLIDERS GUIDE TO ARIZONA
Wilson Baker
1975 - 50 p. il. - $4.95 (pb)

Sites, maps and conditions; a guide to flying in Arizona.
From: Sonoita Soaring Assn., P.O. Box 261, Sonoita, Ariz. 85637

HANG GLIDING AND SOARING
James E. Mrazek
1976 - 184 p. il. - $6.95 (pb)

Mrazek gives advice on evaluating, buying or building equipment, locating groups with training facilities, and choosing sites in the U.S. and Canada. Besides basic orientation, the book includes easily understood aerodynamic theory, flight techniques and a description of a typical first flight. Good info on safety tips and reading weather patterns, plus an appendix with periodicals and club addresses, and hang gliding terms—but no index! Good reading if you're interested in finding out what hanging's all about.
From: St. Martin's Press, 175 Fifth Ave., New York, N.Y. 10010

GUIDE TO ROGALLO FLIGHT—BASIC
Bob Skinner and Rich Finley
1974, 2nd ed. - 30 p. il. - $2.50 (pb)

A handbook for beginning pilots.
From: Flight Realities, 1945 Adams Ave., San Diego, Calif. 92116

other books

HANG FLIGHT
Joe Adleson and Bill Williams - $3.25 (pb)
From: Eco-Nautics, P.O. Box 1154, Redlands, Calif. 92373

THE COMPLETE BOOK OF HANG GLIDING
D. S. Halacy, Jr. - $4.95 (pb), $7.95 (hb)
From: Hawthorn Books, Inc., 260 Madison Ave., New York, N.Y. 10016

DELTA
Jean-Bernard Desfayes - $6.95 (pb)
From: Haessner Publishing, Inc., P.O. Drawer B, Newfoundland, N.J. 07435

SKYSURFING, a guide to hang gliding
Eddie Paul - $3.95 (pb)
From: Crown Publishers, 419 Park Ave. South, New York, N.Y. 10016

HANG GLIDING RAPTURE
Lorrain Doyle - $3.95 (pb)
From: Lion Press, P.O. Box 836, National City, Calif. 92050

FLY LIKE A BIRD—HANG GLIDING HANDBOOK
George Siposs - $5.95 (pb), $8.95 (hb)
From: TAB Books, Monterey & Pinola Aves., Blue Ridge Summit, Pa. 17214

FLY, THE COMPLETE BOOK OF SKY SAILING
Rick Carrier - $7.95 (hb)
From: McGraw-Hill Book Co., 1221 Ave. of the Americas, New York, N.Y. 10020

sources of books

A free listing of hang gliding publications is available from:

AVIATION BOOK COMPANY
565½ W. Glenoaks Blvd., Glendale, Calif. 91202

PARA-GEAR EQUIPMENT CO.
3839 W. Oakton, Skokie, Ill. 60076

THE TOUCHSTONE PRESS
P.O. Box 81, Beaverton, Oreg. 97005

FLIGHT RESOURCES CO-OP.
Wilton, N.H. 03086

U.S. HANG GLIDING ASSN.
P.O. Box 66306, Los Angeles, Calif. 90066

FILM

Some good films on hang gliding may be obtained from:

GIBCO FILM PRODUCTIONS
12814 Collins St., N. Hollywood, Calif. 91607
Film: *Wings on the Wind.*

SIDNEY J. BERAN
4885 Cole St., No. 6, San Diego, Calif. 92117
Film: *The Wind Dancers.*

FREE FLIGHT SYSTEMS
12424 Gladstone Ave., Sylmar, Calif. 91342
Film: *The New Freedom.*

HANG GLIDERS, ETC.

Flying wing-type hang glider

Monoplane-type hang glider

Rogallo-type hang glider

GLIDERS
$400 - $1,500

The largest, most important and most significant piece of equipment is, of course, the hang glider itself. Prices range from a low of $400 for a standard Rogallo to perhaps $1,500 for a completely assembled, fancy rigid-wing glider. Great strides in design have been made in just the past year, and these second-generation gliders offer not only greater performance, but they're also far safer. Designers are generally still employing the Rogallo principle of three main tubes, a spreader spar and a sail with an unsupported trailing edge, though they are pushing the aspect ratios further, i.e., the wings are getting longer. The popularity of the Rogallo design lies in its light weight, typically 40 lbs., which makes it very portable—ideal for car-topping and ease of on-site assembly. Comparatively, rigid-wing rigs, though they are slightly better performers, are heavy, often requiring a trailer for transport and at the site, two men to set them up. Plus they're more expensive.

Hang gliders are made of aircraft-quality materials, usually 4.5-oz./sq./yd. Dacron fabric, special alloy aluminum tubing, stainless steel cable and a number of specially designed and machined parts. A close look will reveal that the main tubes are rigidly supported by the king post (on top) and the control bar (underneath) with a number of tensioned cables.

The pilot is suspended from a point where the keel tube and cross tube meet so that by moving the control bar in front of him, he may tilt the kite in the direction he wishes to go. The body is hanging plumb.

CLOTHING

Gloves, footgear, knee pads, and so forth depend mostly upon the terrain. When learning, it is always wise to wear old but adequate protective clothing. Except on sand, you're guaranteed to wear the knees out of your pants. A high-topped boot with a fully gusseted tongue will keep out pebbles, foxtails and other debris. On the other hand, if you are training at the beach, you may tire of emptying the sand and go without footgear altogether.

SUSPENSION SYSTEMS
$25 - $90

There are three basic suspension systems and listed in order of popularity, they are: prone (so you can fly like Superman), seated (for longer flights) and supine (a comfortable reclined position which cuts down on wind resistance). They may run from $25 to $90, depending upon complexity. The suspension system is one of the most important pieces of equipment from the standpoints of both safety and comfort.

HELMETS
$10 - $30

While few flyers used them in the early days of hang gliding, nearly everyone does today. They range from hockey helmets priced under $10 to the fancy Bell Soaring Helmet at less than $30.

sources of hang gliders

So far, there aren't any large general mail-order companies servicing the hang gliding sport but all manufacturers use the mails and most of the local schools handle several lines. All manufacturers make a "standard" Rogallo and most produce some fancy, advanced, high-performance models. Standards may run from $400 to $600 while some of the second-generation gliders are in the $800 to $1,200 range. All are made of the highest quality aircraft materials. Equipment is changing rapidly and the reader is advised to send to the following for the latest brochures.

MANTA WINGS
1647 E. 14th St., Oakland, Calif. 94606

Manta has three Rogallo-type models, the 80S in six sizes from $570 to $665; the 80SK in three sizes from $620 to $675, and the 80SK2 in three sizes also from $620 to $675. Their latest, though, is the Fledgling, a high-performance, rigid-wing, tailless monoplane hang glider available in a series A for 130- to 180-lb. pilots and a larger series B. The A number has a span of 29 feet, wing area of 145 sq. ft., an aspect ratio of 6 and weighs 50 lbs. Glide angle is 8:1; sink rate,

225 fpm; and stall speed, 16 mph. The Fledgling sets up in 15 minutes without tools. For complete info on Manta's gliders and accessories, write 'em.

Super Swallow Tail

SPORT KITES, INC.
1202 E. Walnut, Santa Ana, Calif. 92701
Run by Bob and Chris Wills, Sport Kites has the SST (Super Swallow Tail) available with 90° or 100° nose and manufactured of special grade 6061-T6 aluminum tubing of uniform thickness. Features include SS cable with shrink tubing over ends; king post with quick-release turnbuckle on trailing edge keel cable; wing nuts, nose skid plate, tube plugs and so forth. Weight is 44 lbs. Available with 16- or 20-ft. keel, control bar may be 4 or 5 feet wide with grip surfaces. Tandem seating is available for flying dual. The all new Swallowtail offers large kite performance with small kite response and has consistently proven itself in hang gliding competition. Complete wings, replacement parts and custom sails are also available from Sport Kites. For more info drop a card to the above address.

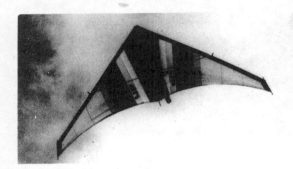

ULTRALITE PRODUCTS (UP)
Dragonfly
28011 Front St., Rancho, Calif. 92390
These people manufacture the Dragonfly, a high aspect ratio, second-generation hang glider with truncated wing tips. It has a nose angle of 102°, 20-ft. leading edges, 11-ft. keel, 2-ft. wing tips with washout and weighs in at 43 lbs. The 3.8-oz. Dacron sail has 3° of billow. A well-engineered, finely-built craft with all of Brock's fancy hardware. UP also produces the Brock 82 Standard, the Red Tail short keel and the Super Red Tail very short keel gliders. Kits, complete units, replacement parts and tools are also available.

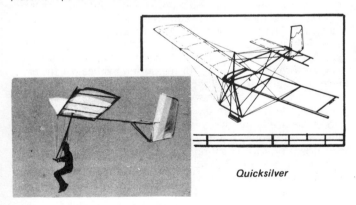

Quicksilver

EIPPER-FORMANCE, INC.
P.O. Box 246, Lomita, Calif. 90717
Dick Eipper's group, who offer the Flexi Flier, keel lengths from 15 to 20 feet, and the Quicksilver, both in kit or flyaway, and the latest off Dave Cronk's board, the Cumulus VB, available in three leading edge lengths: 16, 17 and 18 feet. Specs on the VB at wing loading of 1.25 lbs./sq. ft. are L/D max., approximately 7:1 at 25 mph; min.

sink, 250 ft./min. @ 18 mph; stall speed, 15-16 mph. Priced at $950, delivery is being limited to lads or lasses with a Hang 4 Rating. Eipper has a very nice catalog describing all their models, accessories and other gear, for $1. Request it from the above address.

DELTA WING KITES AND GLIDERS, INC.
P.O. Box 483, Van Nuys, Calif. 91408
This is Bill Bennett's outfit, and his glider line-up includes the 222B, three models of the Phoenix and two of the Skytrek; flyaway prices range from $745 to $895. In towed kites he has 8 models, three of which are gliders converted for towed flying. A complete line of spare parts and accessories is available. Delta also sells helmets, miscellaneous clothing, patches, decals and such, plus flight-training films. They offer flight instruction, too. Write for literature and prices.

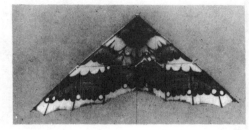

Kestrel

SKY SPORTS INC.
Rt. 83, Ellington, Conn. 06029
These people make the Kestrel, a second-generation, advanced-performance Rogallo-type glider which was created with emphasis on good air handling, price and convenience features such as disassembly without tools, removable rigging, adjustable trim and breakdown ability to a package just over half the length of the leading edge. The Kestrel is the first production Rogallo to have cross-member streamlining, and the first to use a double-surface sail which provides better performance and easier handling than common single-surfaced, high-performance designs. The Kestrel's glide ratio is 7:1; sink rate, 76m/min.; and stall speed, 25 kph. Sky Sports also has a line of standard and short-keel gliders, plus parts and accessories. Write for more info.

Marauder

MULLER KITES LTD.
P.S.C. Box 4063, Calgary, Alberta, Canada T2T 5M9
This Canadian group under the leadership of Willi Muller makes the Marauder, which placed 3rd in the World Snow Kite Championship. She's a 20-ft. x 18-ft., 222-sq. ft. Rogallo-type with a glide ratio of 6:1 @ 24 mph; min. sink is 360 fpm, and stall speed is 13 mph. Price is $745 FOB Canada. Muller also offers three other models, plans, kits and materials. For more info, write Willi.

Icarus V

FREE-FLIGHT SYSTEMS
12424 Gladstone Ave., Sylmar, Calif. 91342
Home of the Icarus V, a flying wing with pronounced sweep, washout, dihedral and a reflexed high-lift, low-moment airfoil. Performance: glide ratio, 10:1 @ 22-24 mph; min. sink, 180 fpm; stall speed, 16 mph. Free-Flight has flyaway units, kits and replacement parts. Write for data and prices. Plans to build your own are available from the designer: Taras Kiceniuk, Jr., Palomar Mountain, Calif. 92060.

ballooning

Hot air ballooning is the oldest form of aviation. It was born in France nearly 200 years ago and has been practiced with varying popularity ever since.

Like soaring or parachuting, ballooning is an end in itself rather than a means of practical transportation. A typical balloon flight consists of floating tranquilly over the countryside for a couple of hours, listening to the sounds of animals and people on the earth below, plucking leaves from treetops, and just generally enjoying the sensations of buoyancy, silence, and a new visual perspective. It's an activity that appeals to a certain kind of person and is surely as much an emotional as a physical experience.

For quite a while the sport was at an ebb, but now hot air ballooning is enjoying a renaissance of sorts. Ten years ago there were only three or four of the craft operating in the United States, but today the number is approaching 200. Still, compared to the 2500 odd sailplanes and the thousands of private aircraft that fill the sky, 200 isn't very many balloons, which accounts in part for the fact that not many people have ever seen a balloon. Another reason they're not commonly seen is that the best time to launch and fly a balloon is in the first hours after dawn, and the ideal place is the open countryside. There aren't many people out there at that time except for a few farmers.

A balloon craft, or aerostation as it's also called, is basically a large bag (envelope) of hot air with a basket (gondola) suspended from it where the pilot and passengers ride. Hot air is what makes the balloon rise, and the hotter the air with respect to the air surrounding the envelope, the faster and higher the balloon rises. This is why the cool early morning is such a good time for flights. Obviously nighttime temperatures are even better, but then the visibility is lousy, so free balloons rarely operate at night.

The bottom of the balloon is not fastened closed, but is opened wide to allow heated air to circulate and rise within the envelope. The hot air is supplied by several high-powered propane burners positioned directly under the opening or "mouth" so that their flames roar upward into the envelope. Fuel for the burners is supplied from two tanks located in the gondola (where they also serve as seats) and the burners are controlled by a flexible cable that hangs down like a light cord. The flight instruments—altimeter, compass, and rate-of-climb meter—are either mounted in a corner of the gondola or in a portable box, along with a pyrometer (high temperature thermometer) for measuring the heat of the air in the envelope. So envelope, burners, and gondola essentially make up the hot air balloon.

A balloon is very limited in its maneuverability. It can be moved vertically by increasing or decreasing the heat of the burners, but movement in a lateral direction is entirely dependent on the prevailing wind. And since a balloon moves as part of the wind it has no use for a rudder or other such steering device. The pilot is able to choose his direction to some degree, however, by climbing to an altitude where the wind is blowing in the direction he'd like to go. But for the most part, the balloonist is content to just *go* rather than to go *somewhere*.

Because of this lack of maneuverability, the pilot has to know the countryside pretty well within a radius of 15 or 20 miles (the average flight distance) so he can be prepared for whatever obstacles to flight and landing may present themselves. Ballooning is probably the safest of air sports, but, nevertheless, the pilot has to cope with the hazards of high tension power lines, towers, and trees that may come in his path.

If you think you'd like to give ballooning a try, you'd probably like to know what expenses are involved. Not dirt cheap, certainly. An average three-passenger hot air balloon costs in the neighborhood of $7,000. On the other hand, maintenance costs are zero unless you treat your balloon roughly, ripping or burning the fabric or damaging the basket or instruments. Operating costs are about $5 an hour for propane, and one tank will hold about 20 "galloons" (unit of liquid measurement used on a balloon). There are no airport storage or other type fees, because the whole unit, when deflated, fits into the gondola which can be stored in the corner of a garage or basement, and a balloon can be launched from any open field or even a parking lot.

It's probably beginning to look better and better, but there are still a few more things to take into consideration. A balloon is an aircraft and as such both it and its pilot are subject to Federal Aviation Regulations (FAR's). An aerostation must meet federal airworthiness standards for lighter-than-air craft as set forth in FAR Part 31. New balloons already possess an Airworthiness Certificate when delivered by their manufacturers, so that's no problem, but they need to be FAA inspected each year, which costs about $50 a throw.

FAR Part 61 details what you need on the way of knowledge and experience in order to qualify for a balloon pilot's license. The instruction and air time required to meet these qualifications can be acquired through a commercial school

A Japanese artist, Gengyo, painted his version of two Westerners watching a balloon ascension in 1861. The band around the balloon is lettered "CNNTCTUTION" which is probably as close as he could get to "CONSTITUTION." The original is owned by the Philadelphia Museum of Art.

for about $1,000 or through membership in a club at a much lower cost. Three licenses are available: student, private and commercial.

Certainly before making any radical decisions, you should go take a ride in a balloon. There are clubs or balloon owners near most large metropolitan areas and you can find the one nearest you by writing to the Balloon Federation of America, the FAA, or probably best, the Wind Drifters Balloon Club. Get in touch and hitch a ride. If you decide after a flight or two that you're sold on it there are three approaches to getting into ballooning: (1) join an existing club if there's one near you, and make use of club balloons and facilities; (2) start your own club by getting together enough people interested in contributing to the $7,000 or so it costs to buy a balloon (Wind Drifters also provides guidelines for groups interested in forming a balloon club); or (3) buy your own balloon and take lessons.

It's been our experience in talking to and corresponding with a number of balloonists in the course of getting this section together, that they are genuinely super-nice people. And they are so totally sold on their sport that they go out of their way to help newcomers become involved. Add this to the foregoing information on ballooning in general, and if it sounds good, maybe this is the sport for you.

BALLOONING

BALLOON FEDERATION OF AMERICA (BFA)
Suite 610, 806 Fifteenth St., N.W., Washington, D.C. 20005
BFA is a division of the National Aeronautic Association and as such serves as the official FAI representative for the sport of ballooning in the United States. Its functions are to promote, develop, and aid the art and science of free ballooning by providing information to the public, sponsoring and supervising competitions and championships, and by taking an interest in legislation and restrictions that affect the sport (since BFA is a non-profit organization, it cannot actually lobby). Dues are $10 a year and include a subscription to the Federation's quarterly journal, *Ballooning*, which covers technical and state-of-the-sport type articles, plus news on ballooning meets and competitions. BFA membership includes just about every free ballooning pilot in the United States. Since the officers and directors of the organization are spread out across the country, getting specific information is kind of difficult unless you know who's handling a particular department and write him at his home address. At this writing these are the two officers handling the BFA's paperwork:

Secretary
Steven Langjahr
3528 East Broadway
Long Beach, Calif. 90803

Membership
Carl Armstrong
P.O. Box 2592
Columbus, Ohio 43216

FEDERATION AERONAUTIQUE INTERNATIONALE
Siege Social A Paris, 6, Rue Galilee, Paris, France
The Federation Aeronautique is an organization of national aeronautical clubs throughout the world with over fifty countries represented. FAI's principal job is to coordinate the activities of member organizations for the world-wide development of aeronautics, which not only includes flying, but also soaring, ballooning, hang gliding, parachuting—actually any type of air activity. This is the organization that certifies world records in the field of aviation and promotes competitions. In the United States the National Aeronautics Association and its affiliates, like the Balloon Federation of America, is the official representative body of the FAI.

THE ALBERTA FREE-BALLOONIST SOCIETY
1712 Home Rd., N.W., Calgary 45, Alberta, Canada T3B 1G9
The Alberta Free-Balloonist Society was organized to promote lighter-than-air (LTA) aviation and to encourage interest in the sport of ballooning. Activities are primarily limited to the province of Alberta, but the group will assist anyone with an enthusiasm for LTA flight. Present membership ranges from experienced balloonists, one of whom has made flights in gas balloons over the Swiss Alps, to people who have never even seen a balloon but are interested in knowing more about the sport. The Society does not sponsor formal competitions as of now, but is working toward developing an annual balloon rally across the Canadian Rockies. The Society holds regular meetings in the winter on three areas of basic interest to the membership: gas ballooning, hot air ballooning, and airships. Membership dues are $15 a year.

WIND DRIFTERS BALLOON CLUB
2814 Empire Ave., Burbank, Calif. 91503
Wind Drifters is the largest most active balloon club in the world with a membership of 115. Its stated purpose is "promoting and professionalizing the very old and little known sport of hot air ballooning." The club is run on the lines of a flying cooperative offering two types of membership. A Flying Membership costs $300 initially and thereafter $8 a month. Of this initial fee, $100 provides the member with ground school, flight training, books, and other supplies (commercially this service runs from $650 to $1000). The remaining $200 buys a share of the club's equipment which is a Raven AX-7 (a 6-man balloon) and a Piccard AX-4 (2-man balloon). The $200 is refunded if the party has to leave the organization at any time. The other membership class is Supporting. The fee here is $15 initially and $5 a year thereafter. The supporting member does not own a share of the equipment or go through pilot training; he just enjoys ballooning and club activities. Wind Drifters offer the best (possibly the only) technical material available on ballooning, and one needn't be a club member to purchase them:

Examination Guide. This book contains 150 pages of FAR's, weather, flight planning, hot-air and gas balloon procedures and terminology. It also contains the latest question and multiple choice answer aids for passing the FAA written exams. This guide is the only one of its kind in the field.

Training Manual. Includes typical equipment detail drawings (unavailable even from the manufacturers) as well as procedures for flying, from pre-flight to deflation. Also charts, graphs, equipment certification, nomenclature, and repairs.

Flight Curriculum. Available to individuals and flight schools as a guide for learning to fly hot air balloons. Meets or exceeds requirements of Federal Regulations. Can be used as a log book certifying experience.

Introduction to Club Ballooning. A comprehensive report by the largest and most active balloon club in the United States. Includes a one year subscription to *Hot-Air* (published monthly).
The prices for the above manuals are as follows:

Any 1 book - $10	Any 4 books - $35
Any 2 books - $19	Add $8 for each
Any 3 books - $27	additional book.

Trans-Atlantic attempt by John Wise in 1873. He didn't make it.

LIGHTER-THAN-AIR SOCIETY
1800 Triplett Blvd., Akron, Ohio 44306

The Lighter-Than-Air Society has a worldwide membership of over 1000 people who are dedicated to furthering knowledge of the history, science, and techniques of buoyant flight. It has a collection of airship and balloon artifacts, as well as some 500 books, housed in the Akron Public Library. Membership is open to anyone interested in LTA flight and entitles the member to receive the club's bi-monthly publication, *Buoyant Flight*, and to a discount on all books bought through the club. Active membership, which allows one to vote and hold office, is $6; associate membership, with no office holding or voting privileges, is $2.

The Society offers Xerox copies of the following out-of-print LTA classics. Prices do not include postage or library binding, which is $2 extra.

Airship Design by Charles P. Burgess. Originally published 1927; 300 p. $11.30. OP-06527.

Pressure Airships by Thomas Blakemore and W.Watters Pagon. Originally published 1927; 311 p. $11.35. OP-04460.

Free and Captive Balloons by Ralph Upson and Charles Deforest Chandler. Originally published 1926; 331 p. $12.10. OP-04461.

Aerostatics by Edward P. Warner. Originally published 1926; 112 p. $4.25. OP-04462.

National Academy of Science (first three reports of the Durand Committee) Reports 1 and 2 bound together, and Report 3, on "Technical Aspects of the Loss of the Macon" (1936-37). $15.15. OP-15552.

The U.S. Navy Rigid Airship Manual (1927), $23.55. OP-14145. *Solomon Andrews* (2), $6. OP-24361 and OP-24362.

Order the above from University Microfilms, Inc., 300 Zeeb Rd., Ann Arbor, Michigan 48103.

A bibliography of recommended books, as well as a list of balloon clubs, schools, and organizations in the U.S. and abroad is available upon request, as is a fact sheet and membership information on the Society and a sample copy of their publication. This is a very friendly, service-oriented organization that offers help, information, and counsel to anyone interested in the science, traditions, and sport of ballooning.

It's hard to get good information on gas ballooning, probably because it isn't practiced much in the United States, though in Great Britain and on the Continent where hot air is only beginning to catch on, it's still the most popular form. At any rate, here's some very general data on gas bags:

Gas balloons can reach higher altitudes, stay aloft longer, and therefore cover greater distances than hot air balloons. The altitude record for gas is more than 100,000 feet; greatest distance covered, about 2,000 miles; and duration of flight, around 90 hours. Comparitively for hot air, it's around 35,000 feet for altitude, 200 miles for distance covered, and about 10 hours for duration of flight.

Gas bags are expensive to operate. As near as we can determine from limited data, it costs around $300 to inflate a three-passenger balloon with hydrogen, whereas a hot air balloon can be inflated on a couple of bucks worth of propane. Hydrogen is a highly flammable gas and the danger of explosion is always present, though manufacturers are careful to use wood and nonsparking metals in the balloon's construction. Even so, no one smokes in a gas balloon and everyone worries about lightning storms. Helium is an alternative and is totally safe; however, it also costs three times as much as a hydrogen fill, so it isn't used much.

Despite the high cost of hydrogen and the danger of its exploding, which would appear to be two pretty big drawbacks, some of the greatest adventures of all time have been had in gas balloons like the *Eagle*, the *America*, and the *Jambo*. Around the turn of the century, a traveling aeronaut named Thompson used his tethered gas balloon to seduce unsuspecting young ladies 2,000 feet over Portland, Oregon.

Balloon Platoon's Hail Atlantis.

BALLOON PLATOON OF AMERICA
P.O. Box 272, Bloomfield Hills, Mich. 48013

This is a young organization totally devoted to the fun of ballooning and associated socializing. Members have actually built their own club balloons from surplus parachutes, ripping and reassembling the panels to create the *Charlie Brown* and the *Hail Atlantis*, a beautiful red balloon that is decorated like the original Montgolfier with signs of the zodiac. Though the 150 members are mostly concentrated in the southeastern Michigan area, plans are being mapped to foster national and international platoons of what club spokesmen call "balloonatics." Dues are $5 a year; membership entitles you to participate in club events and to receive the quarterly publication, *Uprising*.

NATIONAL ASSOCIATION OF AMERICAN BALLOON CORPS VETERANS
116 S. Main St., Tekonsha, Mich. 49092

From the time of the French Revolution, through World War II, balloons have been used in military operations. During World War I, gas balloons tethered to truck-mounted winches were used as observation platforms during battle. Moving across the countryside with ground crews cutting away telegraph wires and other obstructions, the gas bags made fantastic targets for the enemy. At least 120 U.S. balloons were shot down in Europe. Most of the pilots were killed though some of the luckier ones parachuted to safety. The National Association of American Balloon Corps Veterans is a last-man organization made up entirely of surviving veterans of the World War I Balloon Corps. This group is a valuable source of information for anyone interested in this aspect of ballooning and military history. Their quarterly newspaper, *Haul Down and Ease Off*, though largely devoted to news of members and their activities, includes much interesting historical information on balloons of World War I.

DEPARTMENT OF TRANSPORTATION
FEDERAL AVIATION ADMINISTRATION

FEDERAL AVIATION ADMINISTRATION
800 Independence Ave. SW., Washington, D.C. 20590
Regulations affecting applicants for a balloon pilot's license are contained in FAA Regulations, Part 61, *Certification: Pilots and Flight Instructors*. A student pilot's certificate must be obtained before beginning training. Successful completion of training leads to a private pilot's certificate, lighter-than-air category with a free balloon class rating. After further training and experience a commercial rating may be obtained, qualifying an individual to fly for hire or to instruct. The following are the general requirements for student and private certificates.

Subpart C - Student Pilots

1. A student must be at least 14 years of age.
2. He must be able to read, speak, and understand the English language (some exceptions allowed).
3. No medical certificate is required, but the applicant must certify that he has no known medical defect that makes him unable to pilot a free balloon.
4. Student pilot certificates may be issued by FAA inspectors or designated pilot examiners.
5. Student pilots may solo after demonstrating to their instructor that they are familiar with Part 91 of the Federal Aviation Regulations and are proficient in the following aspects of balloon operation: preflight preparation, operation of controls, lift-off and climb, descent and landing, and emergency situations.
6. A student pilot may fly a balloon only under the supervision of a qualified instructor. He may not carry passengers or fly a balloon for hire.

Subpart D - Private Pilots
1. To be eligible for a free balloon private pilot's certificate a person must be at least 16 years of age.
2. Read, speak, and understand the English language.
3. No medical certificate required. Same as paragraph 3 above.
4. The applicant must pass a written test on such items as: (a) Federal Aviation Regulations covering pilot privileges, limitations, and flight procedures, (b) use of navigation charts, (c) recognition of weather conditions and use of weather reports, (d) operating procedures with gas and hot air balloons.
5. The applicant must have received instruction on the following pilot operations: (a) ground handling and inflation, (b) preflight checks, (c) takeoff and ascents, (d) descents and landings, (e) emergency conditions.
6. Flight experience must include at least 10 hours in free balloons, which must include 6 flights under the supervision of an instructor. These flights must include at least the following: two flights of at least 30 minutes duration, one ascent to 3,000 feet above takeoff point, and one solo flight (these requirements are for hot air balloons; requirements for gas balloons are slightly different).

An excellent aid for anyone applying for this license is the *Examination Guide* published by the Wind Drifters Balloon Club, 2814 Empire Ave., Burbank, Calif. 91503. Cost is $10, and the *Guide* covers all the information necessary to pass the FAA examination.

Since it is an aircraft, a balloon is subject to FAA Airworthiness Standards as contained in Federal Aviation Regulations, Part 31, *Airworthiness Standards: Manned Free Balloons*. Part 31 defines the term "free manned balloon" and provides detailed specifications regarding the following:

Flight requirements. Applicant must demonstrate the controllability and maneuverability of the craft in take-off, flight, and landing.

Strength requirements. Specifies load limits and safety factors.

Design construction. Sets standards for quality of materials, fastenings, method of construction, fuel cells, heaters, control systems, etc., including safety belts and running lights where applicable (night flight).

Equipment. Simply states that whatever equipment is used must work properly and not endanger the passengers or pilot.

Operating limitations and information. Sets forth criteria for flight manuals, balloon colors, and required instruments.

FAR Part 31 is available as part of Vol. IV of the Federal Aviation Regulations and Part 61 as part of Vol. IX. They can be ordered as follows:

Federal Aviation Regulations, Vol. IV. Catalog No. TD 4.6/3: v.4 Price: $3.50.

Federal Aviation Regulations, Vol. IX. Catalog No. TD 4.6/3 v.9 Price $6.00.

From: Superintendent of Documents, Government Printing Office, Washington, D.C. 20402

A Brief History of Ballooning

Though most people tend to think of balloons in terms of the hydrogen-filled craft so popular in the 19th century, the first balloon was of the hot-air type, and the first recorded instance of manned flight took place in a hot-air balloon.

The Montgolfier "Flying Machine"—1783.

In addition to the following books, there are several technical publications available through some of the organizations in the previous section—Wind Drifters, LTA Society, the FAA. There are supposedly some good books on gas ballooning published abroad, but we weren't able to track them down. If anyone knows something about them and where they can be purchased, let us know.

THE MOTOR BALLOON "AMERICA"
Edward Mabley
il. - $4.95

Walter Wellman was an American journalist and explorer who made several attempts to reach the North Pole from 1894 to 1899. In 1910 he attempted to cross the Atlantic in a balloon of his own design, the *America*. Although he didn't make it, he covered 1,010 miles and broke all existing world distance records. (He was picked up about 375 miles off Cape Hatteras.) We haven't had a chance to review this book, but it sounds like a good one, and Stephen Greene Press publishes nice things.
From: Stephen Greene Press, P.O. Box 1000, Brattleboro, Vt. 05301

This event was staged over two hundred years ago when two intrepid Frenchmen in defiance of the adage "if man were meant to fly, etc." took to the air in a cloth and paper sphere fifty feet in diameter and seventy feet tall. This first flying machine was the creation of Joseph and Etienne Montgolfier, brothers who operated a paper factory in the south of France. Their pilots, Pilatre de Rozier and the Marquis d'Arlandre, kept the craft aloft over the rooftops of Paris almost 25 minutes, heating the air in the balloon by means of a fire fed with straw. They traveled a distance of 9,000 feet. The launch took place in November of 1783 before the court of Louis XVI and Marie Antoinette over 100 years before Kitty Hawk and almost 200 years before Apollo 11 put the first man on the moon. A few months after the Montgolfiers' launching, Jacques Charliere, a member of the French Academy of Science, piloted his, the first gas balloon, on a flight that lasted one and three-quarters hours and covered a distance of 27 miles.

The balloon soon became the tool of showmen, scientists, and explorers, and almost immediately, a tool of war. The French Republicans, who put Louis and Marie Antoinette to the guillotine, used gas balloons as observation stations on the battlefield as they fought off invading neighbors. In 1849 the Austrians employed hundreds of small hot air balloons laden with bombs in their siege of Venice, and during the War Between the States, the Union Army used a corps of observation balloons to spy on Confederate encampments and movements. The Allies used a balloon corps for similar purposes during World War I and maintained the corps until the mid-thirties.

The most recent instance of the military use of balloons occurred during World War II when the Japanese launched nearly a thousand small unmanned hydrogen balloons laden with explosives to drift across the Pacific to the west coast of North America. They were supposed to start fires and generally harass an already jumpy populace. About 200 of these reached their destination and were found from Mexico to Alaska, but they landed for the most part in snow-covered wilderness areas where the explosives did little harm.

Paralleling military use, balloons were used for sporting and scientific purposes. The most spectacular instance of the use of a balloon in exploration was the 1897 attempt by the Swede Salomon August Andree to reach the North Pole in his hydrogen balloon, *Eagle*. The attempt was unsuccessful and after three days, *Eagle* was forced down on the ice. Andree and his party, prepared for that possibility, were well-clothed and provisioned, but they died of trichinosis which they contracted from eating polar bear meat.

BALLOONING
Peter L. Dixon
1972 - 208 p. il. - $1.50 (pb)

Over half this book is devoted to a history of ballooning from the first flights of the Montgolfiers through the Japanese balloon invasion during World War II. Sections that deal with the practical aspects of the modern day sport are fine as a general introduction, but there is one glaring exception on page 162, which is obviously a typographical error; hopefully corrected by now. Here the text reads: "Two to three hours of enjoyable flying [speaking of hot air flight] can be had for about $400 worth of propane." This would put the cost at over $130 an hour. The actual cost, as estimated by the manufacturers, is between $2 and $3 an hour. Nevertheless, it's the only introductory guide to ballooning generally available at this time, so it's worth getting if you are at all interested in becoming involved. Even with typos, it's fun reading.
From: Ballantine Books, Inc., 101 Fifth Ave., New York, N.Y. 10003

FLIGHT OF THE EAGLE
Per O. Sundman, translated by Mary Sandbach
$6.95

Sundman offers the most up-to-date information available on the brave, but foredoomed flight of the *Eagle*. Of all attempts at Polar conquest, this one was probably the most daring and dramatic. Swedish explorer Salomon August Andree and two companions attempted to reach the North Pole by gas balloon in the summer of 1897. Andree surely knew from the start that his chances of success were remote, but so much money, time, and prestige, both national and personal, was invested in the venture that he could not turn back. *Eagle* was forced down onto the ice after three days of flight, and the crew was obliged to set out on foot for civilization. They didn't make it, and for thirty-three years, no one knew where they'd died or why. In 1930 the bodies of the three explorers were found by seal hunters on White Island, along with ample food, clothing, and other provisions. Why did they perish? Sundman reveals that trichinosis, contracted from infected polar bear meat, was what killed them in the end. Drawing from diaries and journals, he tells a moving, personal story of a struggle for achievement and in the end for survival that is a fine contribution to literature on the great era of Polar exploration.
From: Pantheon Books, Inc., 201 E. 50 St., New York, N.Y. 10022

JAMBO: AFRICAN BALLOON SAFARI
Anthony Smith
1963 - il. - $6.50

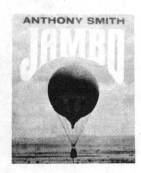

Jambo is the kind of book that every half-hearted nine-to-fiver should read just to get his perspectives straight. It is the absorbing story of an adventure that is as much spiritual as physical, and it restates the ability of ordinary human beings to do extraordinary things, like climb Mt. Everest, walk to the South Pole, and take a balloon across Africa. The book gets its name from the craft that transported zoologist Anthony Smith, along with two photographers, on their picture-taking safari. In addition to recounting adventures, encounters, and mishaps, Smith offers a lot of insights into the workings of gas balloons, their advantages and disadvantages, and the joys of ballooning in general. His enthusiasm is infectious. By the end of the first chapter you'll be ready to go anywhere with him. If you have to pick one book to read about ballooning, pick this one, because it's great.
From: E. P. Dutton and Co., Inc., 201 Park Ave. S., New York, N.Y. 10003

FLIGHT DAY

Story by
Tom Oerman

Photography by
Rick Souther

Equipment and people by
Matt Wiederkehr

1 This picture taken inside the balloon shows the pilot inspecting the deflation port (20 ft. in diam.) to make sure that the Velcro that holds it in place during flight is secure.

2 The balloon has been spread out on the ground and is being inflated with "cold" (ambient) air. The gas-operated fan at the right of the gondola is pushing about 15,000 cu. ft. of air per minute into the balloon, but since the balloon holds almost 60,000 cu. ft. it will take a few minutes to fill up. Crew members are holding the mouth of the balloon open while the pilot finishes his final walk-around inspection of the balloon before takeoff.

3 Pilot comes around the other side. All A-OK.

4 "Pouring the cobs to it"—a 10-ft. flame is blasted into the balloon to heat the cold air in a hurry. This is an older Raven balloon, so the burner here is probably only putting out about 4 million BTU's per hour. Newer burners will blast almost 20 million BTU's for fast inflation and quick response in flight.

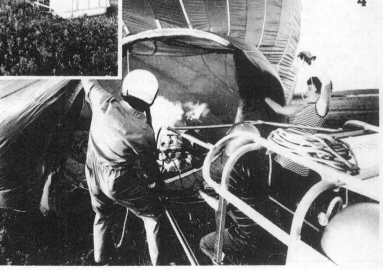

5 *When the air inside the balloon is sufficiently heated, the balloon begins to stand erect until it is upright over the gondola. The ratio here is 56,500 cu. ft. of air heated until it weighs approximately 130 lbs. less than the air it's displacing— around 100 degrees hotter than ambient. Add more heat and the balloon will lift off the ground.*

6 *Inflation complete, and preparing for lift-off.*

7 *The big moment—lift-off! The pilot is on the blast valve heating the balloon to take it to altitude while waving to the crew who will follow the balloon and retrieve it when it lands.*

8 *Up, up, and away. Altitude is increased by the addition of more heat.*

9 *The beautiful balloon is reflected in a placid rural lake as it drifts along with the wind. The pilot could skim the surface of the lake by venting some heat out of the envelope and dropping the balloon down on the water if he wanted to.*

10 *Coming back to earth.*

11 *All good things must come to an end, and this gentle voyage ends here in an open field. The pilot has ripped the deflation port on landing and the balloon drags a short distance as it deflates, then settles down on its side.*

12 *Spectators and crew group up in the field to roll up the balloon, put it in a canvas sack and stow it in the gondola. They'll load the gondola on a truck or trailer to haul it back to store until the next time. The group here is a bit young, so it's probably lemonade time, but usually the traditional wine would be passed around to celebrate another beautiful flight.*

Photos by
Raven Industries, Inc.

BALLOON SKIRT

A wide ring of fabric attached to the envelope. It encircles the burner to protect it from gusts of wind.

MANEUVERING VENT

A balloon can only be maneuvered vertically—up and down. And one of the ways to bring a balloon down quickly is via the maneuvering vent. This vent is an open seam in one of the envelope's panels, which is rigged with a Velcro fastener so that it can be opened and closed from the gondola by means of a long cable. By opening the maneuvering vent, the pilot releases some of the hot air, causing the balloon to descend. When enough air is released to achieve the desired altitude, the vent is closed.

ENVELOPE

This is the balloon itself, a roughly spherical unit which is constructed of ripstop nylon cloth or dacron polyester-coated fabric. The cloth is cut in gored panels of varying colors (Federal regulations require that balloons be of conspicuous colors) and stitched together to form the round shape. Load-bearing tape is sewn along panel seams from the crown (top) to the throat (bottom) of the envelope. The wire cable that supports the gondola or "basket" is attached to these high-tensile tapes.

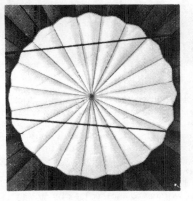

DEFLATION PORT

This is a section of panels on the crown of the envelope that is closed with Velcro or zippers, like the maneuvering vent, and controlled by a rip strap that hangs down in the gondola. This is not a maneuvering device, but is employed only in landing when a pull on the strap opens the port causing the balloon to deflate immediately.

GONDOLA

The gondola is the basket that carries the aeronaut and his passengers, as well as the fuel tanks and flight instruments. The traditional material for a gondola is wicker, because it is extremely resilient and absorbs impact well, but new materials such as fiberglass and aluminum, which are supposedly equally as shock-absorbent, are also employed. The gondola is usually 3 feet high and 3 or 4 feet square. In storage, the envelope is packed in a sack and stowed in the gondola so that the huge aerostation takes up only about 4 square feet of floor space in a garage or workshed.

Lifting Capacities of Balloon Gases
(at sea level @STP)

Gas	Relative Weight	Actual Weight kgs/m³	Actual Weight lbs/ft³	Lift kgs/m³	Lift lbs/ft³
Air	1	1.3	.081	0	0
Hot Air (200°)	0.6	0.78	.049	0.52	.032
Coal Gas (average)	0.4	0.52	.032	0.78	.049
Helium	0.14	0.18	.011	1.12	.070
Hydrogen	0.07	0.09	.0056	1.21	.075

Lift is the weight of air displaced minus the weight of the gas displacing it.

usually be purchased through balloon manufacturers, also, for approximately $75.

INSTRUMENTS

The FAA requires that all balloons be equipped with an altimeter, rate-of-climb meter, and a compass. In addition, it requires that hot-air balloons be equipped with an envelope temperature indicator—pyrometer, which is a thermometer that measures heat of high intensities. Instruments are housed in a portable box or mounted in a panel at one of the corners of the gondola.

BURNERS

A hot air balloon operates on hot or "rarified" air which is lighter than the ambient (surrounding) air of the atmosphere. To heat the thousands of cubic feet of air in the envelope, powerful propane-fueled burners are positioned over the gondola and aimed into the mouth of the balloon. These burners put out between ten and twenty million BTU's of heat per hour. On the ground the burners are used to inflate the balloon. In flight they are used to keep the balloon aloft. The pilot can cause the aerostat to ascend or descend (though not as fast as by using the maneuvering vent) by regulating burner heat. Raising the heat raises the balloon, and lowering it brings it down. This heat control is what allows the balloonist to rise up over treetops or skim over the surface of a lake.

FUEL TANKS

The propane gas which powers the burners is contained in cylindrical tanks of aluminum or stainless steel. The tanks are carried in the basket, two or three ten-gallon tanks being standard. In competition or on record flights, extra tanks may be added if weight limits permit, to increase the fuel supply and thereby extend the amount of time the balloon can remain airborne.

Tanks have fuel gauges on them, most of which begin to read out when the fuel in the tank is at 30%. Once the tank gets down to approximately 10% fuel, the pilot switches to another tank by closing off one valve and opening another.

Fuel pressure is an essential part of ballooning—without sufficient fuel pressure feeding to the burner, the efficiency of the burner is greatly reduced and, if the situation is extreme enough, the balloon will not be able to get off the ground.

Fuel pressure is dependent on two factors: quantity of fuel and temperature. Propane is a liquid which it is necessary to vaporize before burning, and vaporization of the propane is directly proportional to the ambient temperature. When flying in winter, it is usually necessary to heat the tanks to generate enough fuel pressure to take off.

Tank covers with heating systems in them have been recently developed which can be left on the tanks, and if the temperature drops, plugged in until the tank is heated and the pressure raised to approximately 80 psi, a comfortable tank pressure to take off with.

Tank covers without heating systems are also available and these are insulated covers of some thickness which serve to protect the tank—and the pilot—on rough landings. A padded cover is much nicer to whang against than a metal tank anytime.

Tanks are standard equipment on all balloons, and two or three tanks come with the balloon from the manufacturer. Extra tanks may

INFLATION FANS

Large fans are used to "cold inflate" balloons, and these are gas-operated fans specifically made for use in the field. The fan is positioned at the mouth of the balloon which is held open by crew members. When the fan is turned on, it will fill the balloon envelope at the rate of 15,000 to 20,000 cu. ft. per minute.

Fans are statically balanced for safety of operation, and are made to be both lightweight and easily portable both to and on the field. During a high wind inflation the balloon envelope may start to blow across the field, and then a crew member must run with the fan to keep it with the envelope if the inflation is to be completed (it's fun, really).

Some "purist" balloonists refuse to use a fan for inflation, preferring to "flap" the balloon up instead. However, we don't recommend this, since you need to have a crew who are willing to stand around flapping for a long time and these are hard to find.

If you decide to get a fan, look for light weight but solid construction. Be sure it's statically balanced, and look for maximum air output. There's nothing more frustrating than a small fan that takes "just hours" to fill the balloon when everyone is already "up, up and away."

Inflation fans are available through American Balloon Services, Inc., 113 Park Ave., Muscatine, Iowa 52761 or Denny Floden, 225 E. Fifth Street, Flint, Michigan 48503.

RAVEN INDUSTRIES, INC.
P.O. Box 1007, Sioux Falls, S. Dak. 57101
Raven manufactures four balloon models:

S-50 A, 56,400 cu. ft., normal rated capacity, 2, certified structurally for 4; price, $6,175.

S-55 A, 77,500 cu. ft., normal rated capacity, 3, certified for 4; price, $7,075.

S-60 A, 105,000 cu. ft., normal rated capacity, 4, certified for 4; price, $7,905.

All S models include envelope, skirt, deflation panel, single burner, lightweight aluminum frame gondola with fiberglass liner, instrument panel with altimeter, rate of climb meter, and pyrometer, and three 10-gallon aluminum fuel tanks.

RX-6, 56,400 cu. ft., normal rated capacity, 2; price, $4,850. Essentially the same system as the S-50 A, except the gondola is a molded one-piece fiberglass unit with only two 10-gallon fuel tanks.

Raven also offers the S models in a Classic Series. Difference is in the gondola: classic wicker gondola with padded black suede handrails and uprights, hand-finished laminated floor, leather-covered portable instrument case and two lightweight 20-gallon stainless steel fuel tanks. Price: add about a $1,000 plus to any one of the above S model prices.

Options and accessories are available from Raven for all of their

models. For more info write Sioux Falls, S. Dak.

RAVEN MODEL SPECIFICATIONS

	S-50A	S-55A	S-60A
Diameter (ft.)	50	55	60
Overall Height (ft.)	58	63	69
Volume (cu. ft.)	56,400	77,500	105,400
Weight (Envelope (Gondola (Fuel	465	490	520
Maximum Certified Lift*	1,400	1,450	1,500
Crew	1-4	1-4	1-4
FAI Category	AX-6	AX-7	AX-8
Standard (Nominal Burner (Rating System (Btu/hr.	11,000,000	11,000,000	11,000,000
Standard Fuel Tanks	3 ea. 10 gal.	3 ea. 10 gal.	3 ea. 10 gal.

*See chart at right

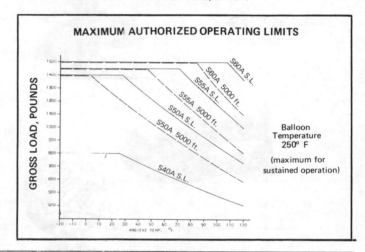

MAXIMUM AUTHORIZED OPERATING LIMITS

GROSS LOAD, POUNDS (vertical axis)

AMBIENT TEMP., °F (horizontal axis)

S60A S.L.
S60A 5000 ft.
S55A S.L.
S55A 5000 ft.
S50A S.L.
S50A 5000 ft.
S40A S.L.

Balloon Temperature 250° F
(maximum for sustained operation)

DON PICCARD—BALLOONS
P.O. Box 1902, Newport Beach, Calif. 92660
All Piccard balloons are custom-made and available in any size, though the most popular and recommended is the four-passenger AX-6 which is about 50 feet in diameter and 55 to 60 feet high. Piccard uses the traditional wicker gondola. It's suspended from the envelope by 1/8-in. vinyl coated stainless steel aircraft cable which runs through and reinforces the wicker.

Fuel: Propane preferable but will run on butane or LP gas
Fuel tanks: Two 10-gallon, aluminum alloy
Burners: Two, output 6,000,000 BTU per hour
Instruments: Altimeter, rate-of-climb meter, compass, and thermometer mounted in a portable aluminum box.

Specifications: Piccard AX-6
Diameter: 50 ft.
Height: 60 ft.
Average Weight: 284 lbs. (overall system)
Crew: 1 - 4

TheBalloonWorks

THE BALLOON WORKS
Rhyne Aerodrome, RFD 2, Statesville, N.C. 28677
Tracy Barnes' outfit which currently offers two basic systems: the Firefly and the Dragonfly, each available with a choice of three different size gondolas and four sizes of envelopes. Prices range from $4000 to $9000 depending on the system chosen and its components.

Envelopes are constructed of high temperature, deterioration resistant polyester fabric which has been urethane coated to seal it. Envelopes can be custom designed by the purchaser—choice of 2 basic panel configurations and 45 colors. Of special note is the Barnes Envelope Valve, 20' in diameter, that automatically seats itself during inflation and requires no special attention. Very effective, yet very simple.

Each system includes the Barnes designed T3-017 burner, capable of a maximum output of 20 million BTU's, and which is equipped with three redundant pilot burners to virtually eliminate difficulties with flame outs.

The triangular gondolas are handcrafted of wicker (rattan) woven into a gracefully curved shape, padded with leather and trimmed with hardwoods and plush fabrics. The 4.0T and 4.5T each hold 3 eleven gallon aluminum LPG cylinders, and the 5.0T, the largest of the baskets, holds 6 cylinders. Beautiful work!

For more info, details and prices write Tracy at the above address.

ROBERT J. RECHS
P.O. Box 483, Van Nuys, Calif. 91408

Bob Rechs offers anything your heart may desire in the way of flying machines. In addition to selling balloons by the major manufacturers, he will construct special units to a customer's requirements. Balloon services include pilot training, exhibitions, and safaris. Training costs vary from $750 to $950. Write for rates on safaris, describing your needs. Rechs also manufactures airships (blimps) for one and two passengers for use in training and sports flying. They are powered by dual engines, inflated with hot air, and cost from $10,000 on up. Training leading to airship pilot rating is offered to purchasers of blimps. Rechs also sells and instructs in the use of man-flying kites (told you he handles *anything* having to do with flying machines). Check the Soaring Section for information on these.

ROBERT J. RECHS
CONSULTANT
BALLOONS - AIRSHIPS
AND OTHER THINGS THAT FLY

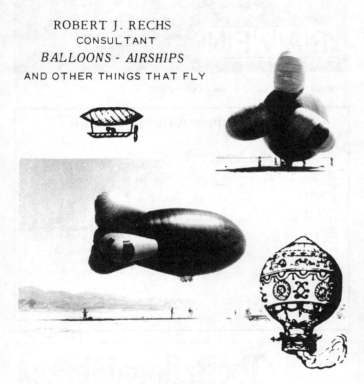

Professor C. E. Ritchell over Hartford, Conn., in 1878.

BALLOON ASCENSIONS
Rt. 11, Box 279, Statesville, N.C. 28677

Ascensions is the East Coast dealer for Piccard. In addition to sales, the company offers instruction at its Statesville location or anywhere else east of the Mississippi. The course at their base is about $850. If the instructor has to come to you in the school's mobile unit, the cost is about $980.

Ascensions also offers lectures, balloon demonstrations for promotional purposes and air shows, pleasure voyages, and gas ballooning. Write for specifics on your area of interest.

CHAUNCEY M. DUNN
4643 Wadsworth St., Denver, Colo. 80033

Chauncey Dunn set a new world record for hot air balloons on June 12, 1971, when he reached an altitude of 32,949 feet aboard his Raven S-60, *Stratsuraus*. The flight was a carefully planned and engineered undertaking involving a lot of equipment and preparation far exceeding normal operating needs.* In Peter Dixon's *Ballooning*, Mr. Dunn's reaction to the flight is quoted: "The flight was one of those seldom-reached peak experiences, a whole, a complete unit, detached from usefulness and expediency, which carries its own intrinsic value with it... in this experience there is wholeness, perfection, fulfillment, aliveness, truth and honesty, and self-sufficiency." Dunn is a dealer for Raven and offers instruction for $500 to balloon purchasers. Write for full details.

* This record has since been exceeded by Julian Nott of Hereford, England who reached 35,971 feet on July 14, 1972.

SCHOOLS, RENTALS, TOURS, ETC.

MINNESOTA HOT AIR BALLOON SCHOOL
(International Balloon Services)
1604 Euclid St., St. Paul, Minn. 55106
This school is run by Matt Wiederkehr, a balloonist totally committed to the aesthetics and excitement of the sport. Wiederkehr set two world records in his Raven S-50A on March 29, 1972. He covered 196.71 miles and remained aloft for eight hours and forty-eight minutes, breaking existing hot air records for distance and duration. He describes his finest ballooning experiences as "a benediction...a reverence that we each experience in our own way."

The Minnesota Balloon School is FAA approved, operates year round, includes in its standard ground school such aids as training films, vacuum chambers and mercury monometers to simulate altitude changes on flight instruments, tape recordings of balloon flights in strong thermal conditions, and aircraft and weather radios. The school is pioneering what may be the ultimate in hot air ballooning experiences—riding the thermals in a thermal (a hot air balloon is a self-contained "thermal" of rising warm air). Write for further information on sales and instruction. International Balloon Services is a dealer for Raven balloons.

BALLOON ENTERPRISES, INC., Division of Sky Promotions
20 Nassau St., Princeton, N.J. 08540
Balloon Enterprises operates five ballooning schools in the East:
   20 Nassau St., Princeton, N.J. 08540
   Kobelt Airport, Wallkill, N.Y. 12589
   Danbury Airport, Danbury, Conn. 06810
   RFD 1 Dingley Dell, Palmer, Mass. 01069
   c/o W. R. Walden, 1834 Main St., Sarasota, Fla. 33577
Cost for a course is $650. Check with the one nearest you for full details. In addition, Balloon Enterprises has hot air, gas, super pressure, heavy lift, and logging balloons for promotional purposes, is a Raven dealer, and operates the "World's Only Balloon Airline" (don't know exactly what that means). Included among the balloons owned by the company are *La Coquette* from *Around the World In Eighty Days*, *Great Race* from the movie of the same name, and *Great Gregory* from *The Great Bank Robbery*. If you got to see the television special, *The Great American Balloon Adventure*, the pilot of that balloon was Bob Waligunda, owner of Enterprises, and the balloon belonged to the school, too.

Matt Wiederkehr landing in 30 mph winds after his world record flight in which he broke existing records for distance and duration.

Bob Waligunda—Balloon Enterprises, Inc.

PROFESSIONAL BALLOONISTS, INC.
135 East 55th St., New York, N.Y. 10022
Balloon school located at Somerville, N.J. Course runs $850. Champagne flights which includes elementary instruction in ballooning runs $75 per person. Associated with the Chalet Club of New York City.

BALLOON EXCELSIOR
777 Beechwood Dr., Daly City, Calif. 94015
Balloon Excelsior is run by Brent Stockwell, an experienced aeronaut and member of the BFA Safety Committee. He offers a complete balloon instruction course which includes about 44 hours of classroom time and ground school, and about 12 hours of actual flight time (cost is around $900). Excelsior rents balloons, is the West Coast distributor for Piccard, and offers charter and advertising flights. It has facilities for propane refueling, launch, and chase and retrieval crews. In addition to these aeronautical services, Excelsior sells what it calls "Aerostatic Artifacts." Of special interest are plans for a do-it-youself tissue paper model flying balloon, six feet tall for $1.00, and a Robinson model flying balloon for $50. Further information on instruction, services, and balloonalia can be had from the above address.

DAEDULUS BALLOON SCHOOL
Menlo Oaks Balloon Field, Menlo Park, Calif. 94025

parachuting

The Golden Knights

Not a lot of people get into parachuting, but those who do are generally regarded by their contemporaries as madmen out to prove themselves, or satisfy some latent death-wish. Sky diving, which is probably the closest thing to the realization of man's ancient ambition to fly, has been tossed into the same image category as high wire walking and lion taming. But get below the surface, toss away the myths and misconceptions, and you have a beautiful sport. And one that for all its apparent freedom and exhilaration is probably the most controlled, regulated, and carefully supervised of any.

Sport parachuting is regulated in the U.S. by the United States Parachute Association, a non-profit organization composed of sport parachutists. These guys have joined together to promote safety in parachuting by establishing standards and procedures for safe jumping. USPA also licenses parachutists on the basis of their level of experience and ability.

The objective of sport parachuting, besides floating through the air with the greatest of ease, is to control the direction of your descent such that you can land on a predetermined target (a white disc about 3 inches in diameter) on the ground. In addition to this is the graceful execution of free-fall, various games such as tag, relay, and pass the reserve chute, or making 10, 15, and 24-1/2-man stars.

Aspiring parachutists first go through ground school training which can last from one to several sessions, depending on the instructor and the number of students in the class. Instruction consists of parachute landing falls (PLF's); chute aerodynamics; deployment; emergency procedures; aircraft exits; and body stabilization techniques in free fall. Usually you are also asked to become a member of USPA, since just about all training groups and clubs are associated with them. For all purposes, anything involving parachuting involves USPA, and if you intend doing anything in the sport, it's a lot easier being a member. Up Canada way, you'd join the Canadian Sport Parachuting Association.

The first five jumps you make (six in Canada) are static line; after this you're in free fall status and pull your own rip cord.

If you want to get into parachuting check with USPA for the club or jump center nearest you. For $1.50 they'll send a copy of *USPA Directory and General Reference Source*, which lists every club, jump center, drop zone, parachute loft, et cetera, in the U.S. and Canada. It also includes many foreign parachuting organizations. If you go to a commercial jump center, instruction averages $70 including gear and air lift for the first jump. Subsequent jumps will run $15 or less if you've picked up your own chute and stuff by then, which can set you back $150 used, and up to $300 new. If you go the club route (join up) for training it can sometimes cost less. The only thing with clubs, though, is get some background on the one you choose. As much as we hate to admit it, there are still some screw-offs around and you don't want to get involved with them when you're just getting started. Ask around, and check with USPA. If you'd like to know what good training consists of USPA will supply you with their *USPA Doctrine Part III "Novice Training."*

Parachuting can be an expensive proposition. For example air lifts run $5 to $10 and you can shoot $30 to $50 easy on a Sunday afternoon. Your reserve chute has to be repacked every 60 days whether used or not, by a licensed rigger; that's another four to five bucks. As far as equipment goes, one of the most popular chutes going—the Para-Commander—costs over $400 for the canopy alone. So before you invest, get your feet wet with an observation ride on a jump training flight. They shouldn't charge more than $7. In the armchair department, a good source of information is R. A. Gunby's book, *Sport Parachuting*, $3.95. This is the best place to get started in parachuting.

sources of information

UNITED STATES PARACHUTE ASSOCIATION
806 Fifteenth St. N.W., Washington, D.C. 20005
USPA is the national parachuting association of the United States and a non-profit division of the National Aeronautics Association. It is devoted to promoting improvement of parachute and parachutist safety, sanctioning and establishing standards for competition, and supervising and documenting all parachuting record attempts. It also selects and trains the United States Parachute Team for international competition and is the official U.S. representative of the Federation Aeronautique Internationale, the governing body of world aviation sports. USPA issues four types of licenses to parachutists on the basis of ability and experience. It also issues guidelines to clubs for training and safety procedures, though unfortunately it does not have the power to enforce them. Important publications of USPA are *Parachutist*, its monthly magazine with much good technique and equipment info (nonmember rate is $7

per year); *USPA Directory and General Reference Source*, $2, a comprehensive listing of clubs and parachuting facilities; *USPA*

MEMBERSHIP IN THE UNITED STATES PARACHUTE ASSOCIATION GIVES YOU:

- A subscription to PARACHUTIST, the world's largest parachuting publication, a national monthly news pictorial and technical magazine which is the official publication of USPA.
- Insurance protection . . . $10/$20,000 Public Liability and $5,000 Property Damage insurance.
- Eligibility for competition in USPA-sanctioned meets.
- Eligibility for participation in national and international record attempts.
- Eligibility for international parachuting licenses.
- Representation before local, state, and national government.
- A voice in the government and operation of the USPA.
- USPA insignia and credentials.
- Guidance and assistance in all sport parachuting activities.

Doctrine Part III "Novice Training," an instruction outline. In order to jump through an affiliated club you have to be a member of USPA. Dues are $20 annually and include a subscription to *Parachutist*, and $10,000 to $20,000 liability and $5,000 property damage insurance. Membership is well worth it. Frankly, just about everyone who has made a first jump and is still jumping in the U.S. is a member.

PARACHUTIST
Norman E. Heaton, Ed.
Monthly - $7/yr. - 35 p. il.

KENTUCKY

USPA AFFILIATED CLUBS

FORT CAMPBELL Sport Prcht. Club, Fort Campbell 42223, 502/647-4941.
KENTUCKY PARACHUTE ASSOCIATION, 8903 Brandywyne Dr., Louisville 40291, 502/239-0218.

DROP ZONES

ELKTON AIRPORT – (N) – U.S. Hwy 68, 1 mi. SW of Elkton, Ky. – **Mail Add**: Chris-Todd SPC, Box 453, Elkton, Ky., 265-2308 – **Open**: Sun & by arr – **Areft**: C-180 – **Tgt**: Plowed – **ASO**: Mike Kremar – **Req**: USPA, Logs – **Svcs**: MR, Partial Inv., Eqpmt Provided FJC w/Radio.
SON DZ, FORT CAMPBELL – (A/M) – Fort Campbell, Ky. – **Mail Add**: Ft. Campbell SPC, Central Accounting Off., Fort Campbell 42223 – **Open**: Sat/Sun – **Areft**: Mil. A/C – **Tgt**: Pg (100) – **ASO**: Mike Kremar – **Req**: USPA, Lic, Logs – **Svcs**: SR, MR, Cmplt. Inv., Eqpmt Provided FJC w/AO.

USPA AREA SAFETY OFFICERS

ROBERT BOSWELL, JR., c/o GCSPC, Rt. 2, Box 140, Bardstown 40004, 502/348-9521.
MIKE KREMAR, Rt. 6, Cumberland Heights, Clarksville, Tennessee 37040, 615/647-4941.

FAA GENERAL AVIATION DISTRICT OFFICES

Louisville 40205: Admin. Bldg., Bowman Field, 502/582-6116.

LOUISIANA

USPA AFFILIATED CLUBS

DELTA SKYDIVERS, INC., 2801 Berch Dr., Gretna 70053, 504/362-7281.

DROP ZONES

DELTA SKYDIVERS – (A) – Raceland, La. – **Mail Add**: Dave Bowen, 518 Burgundy St., New Orleans 70112, 504/523-6596 – **Open**: Sat/Sun & by arr – **Areft**: C-180 – **Tgt**: Pg (45) – **ASO**: Huntley Dufour, Jr. – **Req**: Logs – **Svcs**: Rentals, Eqpmt Provided FJC.
LOUISIANA TECH – (N) – 1 mi. SW of Ruston Arpt., Ruston, La. – **Mail Add**: La. Tech Parachute Team, c/o Dean of Students, La. Tech Univ., Ruston 71270 – **Open**: Sat/Sun & by arr – **Areft**: C-206, Howard – **Tgt**: Sw (35) – **ASO**: George Trousdale, Jr. – **Req**: USPA, Logs – **Svcs**: SR, Eqpmt Provided FJC.
SOUTHERN PARACHUTE CENTER, INC. – (C) – Covington-Vincent Arpt., Hwy 190W, Covington, La. – **Mail Add**: P.O. Box 1314, Covington 70433, 504/892-6311 or 892-0227 – **Open**: Daily – **Areft**: C-172, C-180 – **Tgt**: Pg (100) – **ASO**: Leon Riche, Jr. – **Req**: USPA, Logs – **Svcs**: MR, Partial Inv., Rentals, Eqpmt Provided FJC w/AO.

–23–

NATIONAL COLLEGIATE PARACHUTE LEAGUE
P.O. Box 109, Monterey, Calif. 93940

NCPL is a subsidiary of USPA. It is an association of collegiate parachuting clubs of which at least 50% of the members are associated with an accredited college or university as student, staff, or faculty member. For individual membership, a person must be a full time undergraduate student. There is no charge for individual membership apart from standard USPA dues. Clubs pay a $15 initial affiliation fee and $10 each subsequent year. NCPL hosts National Collegiate Parachuting Championships each year during Thanksgiving week and is active in promoting sport parachuting as a college varsity sport. If you're interested in starting a collegiate parachuting club or affiliating an existing club with NCPL, write the above address requesting a copy of the *Collegiate Guidebook*, which is free for the asking.

CANADIAN SPORT PARACHUTING ASSOCIATION
P.O. Box 848, Burlington, Ontario, Canada L7R 3Y7

CSPA is the Canadian national organization for parachuting, functioning essentially in the same way as USPA does in the U.S. Annual membership fee is $15. Its official publication is *Canadian Parachutist*, a bi-monthly magazine with an annual subscription rate for nonmembers or $6.

CANADIAN PARACHUTIST
John R. Smyth, Ed.
Bimonthly - $6/yr. - 40 p. il.

What Is The Canadian Sport Parachuting Assn.?

The CSPA is an Association of member clubs situated from Coast to Coast.
The CSPA:
—Through the RCFCA is Canada's representative to the Federation Aeronautique Internationale (FAI), the Governing body of world aeronautical activities.
—Is a member of the Canadian Amateur Sports Federation.
—Provides training films and public information films on sport parachuting.
—Provides the membership and Government agencies with the Technical data and safety regulations, safety manuals and bulletins necessary for safe participation in the sport.
—Provides a National magazine "The Canadian Parachutist".
—Issues and controls licences, certificates of proficiency, and a variety of ratings to sport parachutists.
—Arranges and holds Instructor and Rigger's Courses for the betterment of the sport and technical advancement of its membership.
—Organizes and trains the National Parachute Team— which has been in the top ten countries in International competition since 1960.
Provides automatic third party PL/PD insurance with its membership.
—Controls and records all official record making attempts.
—Provides a network of Safety Co-ordinators, Riggers, Instructors and advisory committee members.
—Provides liaison with all Government agencies.
—Co-ordinates the Provincial Councils of Sport Parachuting within Canada.
—Provides insignias, crests, pins, badges, diplomas and awards, trophies and other merchandise for the benefit of the membership.
—Arranges local, National and International competitions for its membership to participate in.

In closing we would like to leave you with this thought:
NASA spends billions of dollars in the struggle for the conquest of space

As part of this program—the parachute plays the ultimate role in insuring the safe return of the astronauts and their equipment. It is not a safety device . . . it is the only device.

SUBPART B — LICENSES

*140.07 Class A License — Parachutist

Persons who hold a Class A License are certified as able to jumpmaster themselves, pack their own main parachute, and compete in USPA competitions (other than the Conference and National Championships). The applicant must have:

a. Completed 25 freefall parachute jumps including:
1. 12 controlled delays of at least 10 seconds.
2. 6 controlled delays of at least 20 seconds.
3. 3 controlled delays of at least 30 seconds.
4. 10 freefall jumps landing within 50 meters of target center during which the novice selected the exit and opening points.

b. Demonstrated ability to hold heading during freefall and make 360 degree flat turns to both the right and left.

c. Demonstrated ability to safety jumpmaster himself, to include independently selecting the proper altitude and properly using correct exit and opening points.

d. Demonstrated ability to properly pack his own main parachute and conduct safety checks on his and other parachutist's equipment prior to a jump.

e. A logbook endorsement by a USPA Instructor/Examiner, a USPA Instructor, his CSO or ASO that he had received training for unintentional water landings.

f. Passed a written examination conducted by a USPA Instructor/Examiner, USPA Instructor, his CSO or ASO.

License Fee: $5.00.

*104.08 Class B License — Intermediate

Persons who hold a Class B License are certified as able to jumpmasters themselves, pack their own main parachute, are eligible for appointment as Club Safety Officer, and are recognized as having reached the level of proficiency to safely perform relative work and to participate in competition and record attempts. The applicant must have:

a. Met all requirements for the Class A license.

b. Completed 50 controlled freefall parachute jumps (refer to USPA PART 111.08, Progression) including:
1. 15 delays of at least 30 seconds;
2. 2 delays of at least 45 seconds.

c. Demonstrated his ability to complete two alternate 360 flat turns to the right and left (Figure 8) followed by a backloop in freefall in ten seconds or less.

d. Landed within 25 meters of target center on 10 jumps during which he selected the exit and opening points.

e. Demonstrated his ability to control and vary both his rate of descent and lateral movement.

f. Demonstrated his ability to move to a horizontal distance from another jumper such that they could safely pull at the same time. Demonstrate that he knows how to and has adequate control in freefall to be able to thoroughly check the sky around himself before pulling. (This demonstration of horizontal separation and looking before pulling must be done in 7 seconds or less. It will be verified by an experienced relative worker.) Demonstrate his ablity to keep track of other canopies and remain a safe distance from them.

g. Passed a written examination conducted by a USPA Instructor/Examiner, USPA Instructor, his CSO, or ASO.

License Fee: $10.00.

*104.09 Class C License — Advanced

Persons who hold a Class C License are certified as able to jumpmaster licensed parachutists, pack their own main parachute; are eligible for appointment as Club Safety Officer and Area Safety Officer; are recognized as having reached the proficiecy level to participate in competition; make relative work, night, water, and exhibition jumps; participate in record attempts; and are eligible for the Jumpmaster and Instructor Ratings. The applicant must have:

a. Met all requirements for the Class B License.

b. Completed 100 controlled freefall parachute jumps including:
1. 30 controlled delays of at least 30 seconds;
2. 5 controlled delays of at least 45 seconds.

c. Demonstrated his ability to perform a controlled international series (Figure 8, Back Loop, Figure 8, Back Loop) in freefall in less than 18 seconds.

d. Landed within 15 meters of target center on 25 freefall jumps during which the parachutist independently selected the exit point.

FAA recommends that the first jump be preceded by a review of the Federal Aviation Regulations on sport parachuting and by familiarization courses on types of parachutes, the use of jump aircraft, parachute instruments and accessories, landing falls (preferably from a jump platform) and emergency precedures.

Training is usually given at jump centers, or by clubs operating at centers, most of which are affiliated with the United States Parachute Association. The length and type of training offered will vary from one locality to another. Determination of when a jump candidate is ready to go aloft is usually made by the safety officer of the club or center. Beginners are strongly advised to make their first jumps under this type of supervision.

FEDERAL AVIATION ADMINISTRATION

FEDERAL AVIATION ADMINISTRATION
Washington, D.C. 20590

Although the FAA doesn't issue parachuting licenses, it does regulate the sport to some extent, having jurisdiction over activities and licensing of parachute riggers and parachute lofts. In order to operate within the FAA's guidelines (for safety's sake, and to avoid fines and even imprisonment), parachutists should be familiar with the applicable Federal Aviation Regulations (FAR's) listed below. These regulations are available through the Government Printing Office. Only trouble is, they're part of complete volumes of FAR's that cost $6 each, and each FAR listed is in a different volume; total of $18. But there is a way to get around this, heh, heh. Yessir you came to the right place. Step over and lemme whisper this privileged info in your ear...Parachutes, Inc. has 'em for a buck each.

FAR Part 65. CERTIFICATION: AIRMEN OTHER THAN FLIGHT CREW MEMBERS
FAA regulations governing eligibility requirements for parachute riggers certificates, both Senior and Master ratings. Those aiming for the USPA's instructor's rating must also be familiar with these requirements.

FAR Part 105. PARACHUTE JUMPING
These regulations cover jumps in particular areas, notification requirements, and who to notify, night jumps, visibility requirements, parachute and packing requirements.

FAR Part 149. PARACHUTE LOFTS
Requirements for riggers, regulations for certification of parachute lofts, loft operating standards, and a list of certified parachute lofts in the United States.

The following two books are available from: Superintendent of Documents, Government Printing Office, Washington, D.C. 20402

AIRCREW SURVIVAL EQUIPMENTMAN 3 & 2
1972 - 379 p. il. - $3.25
S/N 0847-0050

This is the Navy's manual for the parachute rigger's rating. Thorough coverage of parachutes, maintenance and packing, including chest, seat and back types. Introductory material on pressure suits, oxygen, and survival equipment. Required reading for the FAA rigger's exam or the USPA Instructor/Examiner rating.

AIRCREW SURVIVAL EQUIPMENTMAN 1 & C
1971 - 232 p. il. - $2.25
S/N 0847-0126

This is the follow-up manual for Navy personnel who want to advance to Chief in this rating. It covers packing and maintenance of cargo and deceleration parachutes, loft administration, pressure suits and survival equipment. A large section treats in depth the operation and maintenance of oxygen equipment. A vital reference work for parachutists planning high altitude jumps.

CANADIAN AIR TRANSPORTATION ADMINSTRATION
Ottawa, Ontario, Canada K1A 0N8
Here's where to write if you have any questions regarding Canadian government regulations relating to parachuting.

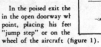
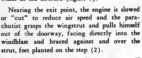
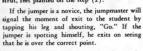
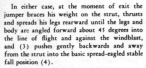

Aircraft Exits

POISED EXIT

In the poised exit the ... in the open doorway wh... point, placing his fee... "jump step" or on the ... wheel of the aircraft (figure 1).

Nearing the exit point, the engine is slowed or "cut" to reduce air speed and the parachutist grasps the wingstrut and pulls himself out of the doorway, facing directly into the windblast and braced against and over the strut, feet planted on the step (2).

If the jumper is a novice, the jumpmaster will signal the moment of exit to the student by tapping his leg and shouting, "Go." If the jumper is spotting himself, he exits on seeing that he is over the correct point.

In either case, at the moment of exit the jumper braces his weight on the strut, thrusts and spreads his legs rearward until the legs and body are angled forward about 45 degrees into the line of flight and against the windblast, and (3) pushes gently backwards and away from the strut into the basic spread-eagled stable fall position (4).

Simply, easily, and safely the jumper is in the correct falling position almost at the instant of letting go of the aircraft.

The poised ... line jumping ... line are alwa, ... immediate sta ... offers maxim ... tanglement.

All this is ... struts, steps, ... exits. Other a ... safely used t... each has its o ... the novice n ... mock-up prid ... shown here is ... approach to n...

65

SPORT PARACHUTING
R.A. Gunby
1971 - 162 p. il. - $3.50

This is a great book for anyone who's thinking about getting into sky diving, but doesn't really know much of what it's all about. From beginning to end, Gunby covers the technical aspects of sport parachuting in the simplest of terms, infusing his exposition with his own basic love for the sport. Here in one book is everything the novice needs to know along with a lot of good information that will even be of use to experienced jumpers.
From: Para-Gear, Inc., 5138 N. Broadway, Chicago, Ill. 60640

THE COMPLETE BOOK OF SKY SPORTS
Linn Emrich
Il. - $2.95 (pb), $7.95 (hb)

This book describes complete basic courses in parachuting, soaring, ballooning, gyrocraft, and power planes, providing basic costs and terminology for each. It's extensively illustrated with drawings and photographs and makes good reading even if you don't ever plan to get into any of the sports.
From: The Macmillan Co., 866 Third Ave., New York, N.Y. 10022

PERIODICALS

FREE FALL KIWI
Bimonthly - $11/yr., Air Mail

Newsy type stories and photos of jumping down under. Published every two months by the New Zealand Federation of Parachute Clubs, Inc.
From: Free Fall Kiwi, P.O. Box 51, Otaki Railway, New Zealand

SPORT PARACHUTING
Charles Ryan
1975 - 228 p. il. - $4.95 (pb)

Ryan, also author of *Jumpmaster's Handbook*, a highly readable and interesting coverage of the sport of parachuting from Tiny Broadwick's first free-fall jump in 1914 to procedures for handling night jumps, tonight. In between are chapters on getting started, student programs, emergency procedures, first aid, where to jump, jumping styles and technique for competition and relative work, and high-altitude jumping. Also a good deal of info on USPA and other parachuting clubs, plus names and addresses. Frankly, Ryan's book may have the edge over Gunby's for the newcomer to parachuting because of its readability and broader coverage of the various aspects of the sport; however, from a technical procedures standpoint, Gunby's is still the preferred basic book.
From: Henry Regnery Co., 180 N. Michigan Ave., Chicago, Ill. 60601

PARA-COMMANDER OWNER'S MANUAL
Pioneer Parachute Co.
40 p. il. - $1.50
From: Parachutes, Inc., Box 96, Orange, Mass. 01364

PARACHUTES AND PARACHUTING
Bud Sellick
223 p. il. - $8.95

This is a guidebook to the sport of parachuting that dispels a lot of myths about daredevils and skydiving nuts. It covers every aspect of the sport from its history to how to do it. Good for amateurs and professionals.
From: Prentice-Hall, Inc., Englewood Cliffs, N.J. 07632

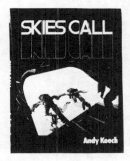

SKIES CALL
Andy Keetch
1974 - 136 p. il. - $20

One of the best books on sport parachuting to be recently published, *Skies Call* shows what parachuting is all about through some 150 fabulous photographs. It's not a "how-to" book, but rather one vividly expressing the spirit and nature of the sport through its text and illustrations by a gifted sport parachuting photographer.
From: Andy Keetch, 806 Fifteenth St. N.W., Washington, D.C. 20005

PARACHUTING FOR SPORT
Jim Greenwood
$2.95 (pb)
From: Sports Car Press, Crown Publishers, 419 Park Ave., New York, N.Y. 10016

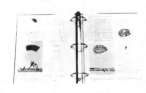

THE PARACHUTE MANUAL
Dan Poynter
1972 - 480 p. il. - $20.85 (looseleaf)

Over 2,000 illustrations covering design criteria, construction techniques, component assembly, maintenance and alteration specs and procedures. Packing instructions, mil specs, material lists and details of every parachute. This one, which took eight years to put together, tells you why as well as how, and is a must for every parachute rigger, engineer, loft or anyone who messes with jumping.
From: Parachuting Pubs., P.O. Box 4232, Santa Barbara, Calif. 93103

Basic Gear

Photos courtesy of
Parachutes Inc.

The Hustler canopy is a double "Gary Gore" with good stability and forward speed and a reasonable rate of descent. This design was used by the team which set the first official world record in accuracy for the United States.

MAIN CHUTE
$150 - $700

In jumping two chutes are used: the main and the reserve. The main chute is composed of six major parts: the pilot chute, deployment sleeve or bag, canopy, suspension lines, pack, and harness. Though generally purchased as a unit, each part can be bought separately. This way not only can worn parts be replaced, but experienced parachutists can choose the particular components that best suit their technique. The canopy (the parachute itself) comes in one of three basic types: (1) The *drag canopy* is the standard umbrella-shaped parachute that's been in use since 1920. It's mostly used by the military and has no modifications (panels removed) for forward movement or steering. It simply slows the jumper's rate of descent going straight down. The drag canopy's only use in sport parachuting is for reserve chutes. (2) The *modified drag canopy* has sections or panels of cloth removed from one side to allow air to escape. Venting the airflow out of the back of the chute moves it forward at the same time it's falling, somewhat in a steep glide, and by closing and opening some of the panels via toggle lines, the chute can be rotated to move in different directions. (3) The *lifting or wing parachute* is shaped like an aerofoil and gives a tremendous amount of forward motion relative to descent. The Hornet, by Pioneer Parachute, $500, is typical of this type. Somewhere in between the modified drag and the wing is the Para-Commander (PC) also by Pioneer. This is the big daddy of sport parachutes and is recommended only after a jumper has at least 15 jumps with a modified drag under his belt. The PC produces 11 ft. to 12 ft. of forward glide for every 10 ft. of descent, and offers the ultimate in maneuverability.

LOG BOOK
$3 - $4

A log book is required by clubs and jump centers to validate a person's jump record, and is particularly important when a jumper goes up for an advanced license. It serves as credentials in that it is a record of what the individual has done and what he or she is qualified to do.

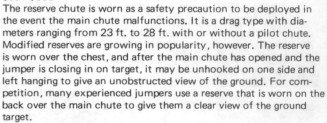

RESERVE CHUTE
$50 - $300

The reserve chute is worn as a safety precaution to be deployed in the event the main chute malfunctions. It is a drag type with diameters ranging from 23 ft. to 28 ft. with or without a pilot chute. Modified reserves are growing in popularity, however. The reserve is worn over the chest, and after the main chute has opened and the jumper is closing in on target, it may be unhooked on one side and left hanging to give an unobstructed view of the ground. For competition, many experienced jumpers use a reserve that is worn on the back over the main chute to give them a clear view of the ground target.

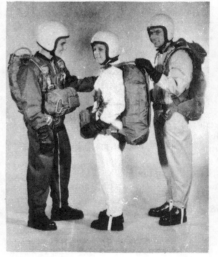

JUMPSUITS
$8 - $50

Generally just coveralls or a surplus flight suit will do, though many custom made suits with long zippers from neck to ankle are available. Snap-on stirrups (keeps suit leg down over boot) can be had through Parachutes, Inc. You'll have to put the male snap in your suit legs though. Stevens Para-Loft makes a suit with a wing in the armpit for added drag during free fall.

BOOTS
$8 - $80

You can go the military jump boot route; they're available at just about all surplus stores. But the "in" boot is a French import—the Paraboot by Richard Pontvert, $75. It has a specially-designed sole with air pockets to aid in cushioning landings.

HELMET
$30 - $40
Worn for head protection when opening chute, landing, and sometimes when doing relative work during free fall to keep the fledgings (greenhorns) from doing too much damage when they smash into you. Bell and McHal are the two brand names to look for.

GOGGLES
$1 - $6
Since cumulative wind velocity in free fall can reach 120 mph, goggles are worn for clear visibility and to protect the eyes. In addition to standard types, there are special ones made that fit over glasses.

Instruments

Since instruments can malfunction, students are trained to count seconds out loud and use sight (topography and horizon) for determining when to pop their chutes. Instruments are not generally advised till at least 15 jumps have been completed and the student is getting into delayed free falls, over 10 seconds. Remember though, instruments are strictly aids. Always be ready to count on yourself and to do your own counting.

STOPWATCH
$15 - $50
The jumper predetermines the number of seconds it will take to reach a certain altitude where he'll open up, and uses the stopwatch to count those seconds off. The crown reset type is best; only one button to work. Stopwatches are used in combination with altimeters, so that one can back the other up.

ALTIMETER
$40 - $45
Altimeters measure the changes in air pressure as you drop. They are supposed to be adjusted to the altitude of the field so that when the dial reads 0, you're on the ground. Dial calibrations range from 10,000 to 20,000 feet with a red section from 2,500 to 0 feet. Minimum safe deployment altitude for a chute is 2,500 feet.

INSTRUMENT PANELS
About $7
These are of aluminum and are used to hold stopwatch and altimeter for convenient viewing. Most often they're strapped to the top of the reserve chute. Other types strap to your wrist.

PARACHUTE ACTUATORS
$140 - $230

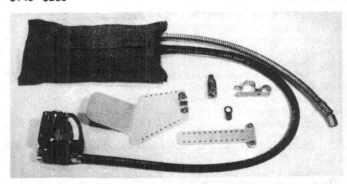

These are automatic opening devices activated mechanically, electrically or via a small explosive charge. The tripping device is air pressure controlled and will trip when the altitude changes too rapidly or when a predetermined altitude is reached. Actuators are mostly used with reserve chutes. PI uses them on mains for student instruction.

FLOTATION DEVICES
$5 - $30
There's a variety of these available for the jumper, ranging from ultra-light gadgets that attach to the wrist to conventional Mae West life vests with automatic water-activated inflators. PI and Para-Gear offer the most complete lines. Should be worn for all jumps near water.

FLASHING LIGHT
About $30
This light attaches to the helmet, flashes at four-second intervals, and is visible at night for 25 miles. The FAA requires such a light for night jumps.

SMOKE SIGNALS
$1.50 - $2
These are fuse ignited devices that call attention to the jumper. They're used either for safety purposes when jumping in a busy air traffic zone or to add drama to an exhibition jump.

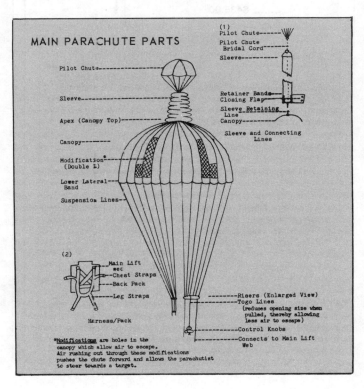

PARACHUTING

PARACHUTES, INC. (PI)
P.O. Box 69, Orange, Mass. 01364

This is the largest manufacturer/distributor of parachuting gear in the U.S. with dealers all over the world. One dollar gets you their beautiful 121-page catalog which offers everything to fill the jumper's needs. Each item is well illustrated and thoroughly described. The catalog is indexed and includes a complete glossary of parachuting terms. Offerings range from chutes and canopies to books and trophies, along with a complete line of repair fabrics, tools, and hardware. A great reference source. PI also operates a jump training center.

Para-Commander —
The Standard of the World

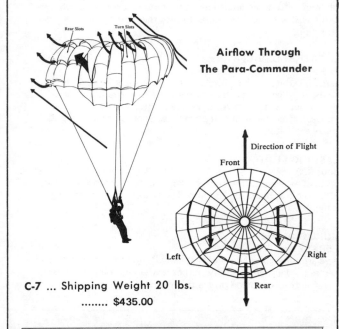

Rear Slots   Turn Slots

**Airflow Through
The Para-Commander**

Direction of Flight

Front

Left   Right

Rear

C-7 ... Shipping Weight 20 lbs.
.... **$435.00**

Technical Data
The Para-Commander is a uniquely designed and technically complex piece of equipment. It is made up of 117 parts, which include such items as panels, tapes, lines, webbing, plus 2000 yards of thread.
Design .... 24' diameter canopy
Fabric Weight (nylon taffeta) .... 2.0-2.25 oz./sq. yd.
Fabric Breaking Strength .... warp: 80 lb./in.
                                        fill: 60 lb./in.
Fabric Tear Strength .... warp: 5 lb. fill: 5 lb.
Fabric Porosity .... 3.0-10.0 cu. ft./sq. ft./min.
Suspension Lines, Tensile Strength .... 550 lb. each
Steering Lines, Tensile Strength .... 550 lb. each

Performance Data
Rate of Descent: 190 lb. suspended wt., 15.7 ft./sec.
Rate of Descent: 250 lb. suspended wt., 17.6 ft./sec.
L/D (Lift to Drag) Ratio 1.16
360° Turn .... 3-4 sec.
Deployment time: Jump and Pull .... 2.4 sec.
Deployment time: Terminal Velocity .... 1.7 sec.
Landing Force .... equal to jump from 3-3½ ft.
Maneuvers .... turn, brake, stall
Of particular interest is the lift to drag (L/D) ratio, which shows that the canopy moves 11.6 feet horizontally for every 10 feet vertically. That is, horizontal speed is 16 per cent greater ·than vertical speed in no wind. Previously, the highest L/D ratio was only 0.7 for a low porosity seven-panel TU.

COST OF PARACHUTING
PI/ELSINORE PARACHUTING CENTER

First Jump Course, complete $70.00
With Sport Parachutist Card $68.00
SECOND & SUBSEQUENT JUMPS
Second Jumps, if tickets purchased on day of first jump $14.50
Breakdown of Each Subsequent Student Jump
Instruction .... $ 2.50
With Sport Parachutist Card .... $ 2.00
Main Parachute including licensed repack .... $ 6.00
Reserve Parachute .... $ 2.00
Aircraft Ticket .... $ 4.00
Plus all day rental of:
Boots .... $ 1.50
Jump coveralls .... $ 1.50
Helmet .... $ 1.50
AIRCRAFT LIFT

Jump	Altitude	Regular Rate	Full Plane Special Rates	Before 8:30 A.M. Early Bird Rate
Static Line	2500	$4.00		$2.00
5 second delay	3000	$4.50		$2.50
10 second delay	3500	$4.50		$2.50
15 second delay	4400	$5.00		$2.50
20 second delay	5200	$5.50	$5.00	$3.00
25 Style delay	6500	$6.00		
30 second delay	7200	$6.50	$6.00	$3.50
50 second delay	10000	$8.50	$7.50	$4.50
60 second delay	12500	$9.50	$8.50	$5.00

LICENSED RIGGER SERVICES. We will repack your parachutes:
Main parachute $7.50
Reserve parachute .... $7.50 and up
Prices and schedules subject to change without notice.

THE CHUTE SHOP
Highway 202, Flemington, N.J. 08822

In addition to a complete line of new parachuting gear, Chute Shop carries unused surplus equipment at good prices. Catalog: $1.

DYNA-SOAR JUMPSUIT NO. 5084

The Dyna-Soar by North American Aerodynamics is the ultimate in R W jumpsuits. This is the first jumpsuit to provide full range variable drag. The extra heavy fabric, full cut design and balanced flares allow even the biggest man to float. Engineered braking surfaces allow you to come in hot, flare out and stop . . . Period. Once you're in, you can tuck everything away or stay open for maximum control of your position.

Standard features include extra heavy, high drag flares all around, heavy duty zippers and velcro closure on collar and cuffs.

Sizes—Small, Medium, Large and Humungus!

Colors - Red w/white trim
      Blue w/white trim
      Blue w/red trim
      Blue w/black trim
      Blue w/gold trim
      Black w/red trim
      Black w/gold trim
      Red, White and
        Blue

Ship. Wt. 6 lbs. $69.95

PARA-GEAR, INC.
5138 N. Broadway, Chicago, Ill. 60640

Complete line of parachuting equipment and a fine 128-page catalog (cost: $1). Para-Gear sells chutes, hardware, special canopies, repair fabric and tools, books, trophies, and so forth.

This complete parachute consists of the following: Harness with "D" rings, ripcord pocket, housing, ripcord with curved handle, container with easy open dot snaps and reserve tie down rings, risers, canopy with your choice of modifications, deluxe sleeve, sleeve deployment line, bridle cord and pilot chute. Shipping Weight: 34 lbs.

No. 1R. 28-ft. Canopy, 5 or 7 Double "L" Modification $240

No. 4R. 28-ft. Canopy, 5 or 7 "TU" Modification $250

If you desire an extended container for any of the above 28-ft. assemblies, add $5 to the price listed.

No. 7R. 35-ft. Canopy, 5 or 7 "TU" Modification $270

No. 10R. MARK 1 or RW PARA-COMMANDER Canopy, short sleeve, pilot chute plus complete harness and container assembly $575

STEVENS PARA-LOFT
Oakland Municipal Airport, Box 2553, Oakland, Calif. 94614

Stevens manufactures custom parachute equipment. Especially worth looking into is the Stevens Cutaway System, a device for disengaging the main chute and pulling the reserve in the event of main chute malfunction (mail order kits, complete and ready to install, $5); and the Stevens Jumpsuit which features a high-lift "wing" area between arm and waist, $33. In addition to their own equipment, they are dealers for Parachutes, Inc. No catalog of their own. They use PI's for general equipment and have brochures which describe their own.

OTHER DEALERS

MID-WEST PARACHUTE SALES & SERVICE
46901 Grand River, Mich. 48050

PHOTO-CHUTING ENTERPRISES
12619 S. Manor Dr., Hawthorne, Calif. 90250

PARA-FLIGHT, INC.
331 Cherry Hill Blvd., Cherry Hill, N.J. 08034

U.S. PARACHUTE SERVICE
6976 E. Baseline Rd., Mesa, Ariz. 85208

ELSINORE PARA-CENTER
Rt. 2, Box 501, Elsinore, Calif. 92330

MCELFISH PARACHUTE SERVICE
2615 Love Field, Dallas, Texas 75235

STRONG ENTERPRISES, INC.
542 E. Squantum St., North Quincy, Mass. 02171

Pioneer Parachute Company, Inc. (Manchester, Conn. 06040) manufactures the Para-Sail, an ascending parachute that is towed behind a motorboat, car, or snowmobile. It operates like a kite, with small slits in just about all the panels creating many little aerofoils, and these give the canopy its lift. The cost of one of these rigs is around $630. For full details write to Parachutes, Inc., the world-wide distributor for Para-Sail.

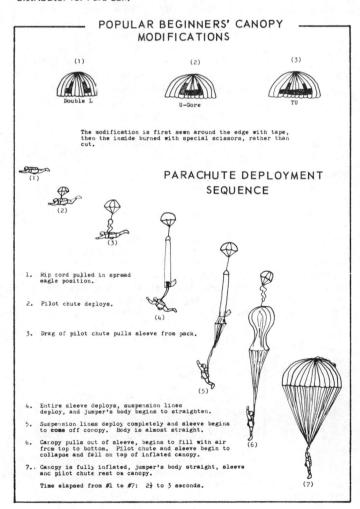

POPULAR BEGINNERS' CANOPY MODIFICATIONS

(1) Double L   (2) U-Gore   (3) TU

The modification is first sewn around the edge with tape, then the inside burned with special scissors, rather than cut.

PARACHUTE DEPLOYMENT SEQUENCE

1. Rip cord pulled in spread eagle position.

2. Pilot chute deploys.

3. Drag of pilot chute pulls sleeve from pack.

4. Entire sleeve deploys, suspension lines deploy, and jumper's body begins to straighten.

5. Suspension lines deploy completely and sleeve begins to come off canopy. Body is almost straight.

6. Canopy pulls out of sleeve, begins to fill with air from top to bottom. Pilot chute and sleeve begin to collapse and fall on top of inflated canopy.

7. Canopy is fully inflated, jumper's body straight, sleeve and pilot chute rest on canopy.

Time elapsed from #1 to #7: 2½ to 3 seconds.

FIRST AID AND MEDICAL

A knowledge of first-aid techniques is important to everyone from the armchair adventurer to the leader of a climb on Mt. Everest. The point is that injuries can and do happen whether you're in the woods, on the side of the rocks, at sea, in a gondola of a balloon or just at home—actually, accidents at home can be worse than those on adventures because you're not as prepared to expect them.

First aid, after the fact, is first and foremost an attitude. An attitude of calmness and confidence almost to the point of disassociating yourself from the traumatic occurrence that has just happened to the person you're treating. Through disassociation you remain outside the sticky wicket of emotional involvement—indecision, fear, panic—thus enabling yourself, with a light spirit, to quickly and objectively analyze the situation and determine the best of the options to apply within your total range of knowledge. Let the situation get heavy, and your total range of knowledge clouds up, thinking becomes confused to desperate, and your options dwindle to one or two—in a nutshell: mistakes. And they could be permanent! It's much better to say, "Isn't that interesting," when someone gets hurt than, "Ohhh dear God!!!" Try it.

Perhaps more important than the foregoing is first aid before the fact—an attitude of preventative awareness. This simply means being mindful of the traps and pitfalls in your environment and the usual methods that you or your comrades may have in dealing with them that can lead to "accidents." To wit: a hot air balloonist notes a line fouling his burner. He quickly reaches up to remove it and burns the hell out of his hand. An accident? Nope! A bad habit—always in a big rush, making the first move that comes to mind. Earlier, while rigging the gondola, he had removed his gloves to make an adjustment. Being eager to get moving—"Hey let's

go, gang; up, up and away!"—he had not taken the time to be *aware* that his gloves were not on.

Psychological studies indicate that only a small percentage of mishaps are truly accidental. In most cases the person sets himself up for the fall, and quite often it's subconsciously preplanned to purposely produce a result that satisfies a subconscious need (some form of attention from another person, an excuse for acting a certain way, punishment for another person or himself, and so forth).

When you get right down to it a person's attitude and lifestyle are the key factors in the development of accidents—rarely is it bad luck. Pasteur put it rightly when he said, "Luck favors the prepared mind," and being prepared to deal with an emergency by preventing it is still the best first-aid advice going.

If that doesn't work, then we hope the following info on first-aid courses, books, and medical gear will provide a second-best bet through remedial action.

The Good Samaritan

The legal problems a layman may encounter because he tried to help an injured person, and perhaps unknowingly aggravated the situation, are real. Despite the so-called Good Samaritan Doctrine, which, according to *Black's Law Dictionary,* states that if you help someone in trouble, you cannot be held negligent unless your assistance during "rescue" worsens the "position of the person in distress," it still may be difficult to prove that you did not act in a negligent manner. What constitutes negligence? That's the tricky part—in one case, a person was held negligent in administering first aid, when in fact, he had no such training to do so. The negligence here was in presuming he knew something he did not.

The best approach to the whole business is to take a first aid course which certifies you, for example from the Red Cross. Then you'll be in a better position to offer assistance as a good samaritan, and likewise, able to substantiate your methods.

sources of information

FAMILY DOCTOR

The usual advice is that if you have any specific health problems, you should consult your physician regarding preconditioning for the trip and any specialized emergency medications you should have with you. Other than that, your family doc, especially if he's an outdoors type himself, can give you guidelines for a first-aid kit, assist in getting needed prescription items, and teach you certain techniques that he feels you may need and can handle, such as suturing and giving injections.

INTERMEDIC INC.
777 3rd Ave., New York, N.Y. 10017
They offer two main services: 1. A directory of "qualified English speaking physicians in every important city in the world," and 2. "Overseas health information with respect to conditions in foreign countries, medications to carry and immunizations which are required." We've got nothing on the cost or criteria for membership so you'll have to write them for all that kind of dope.

U.S. COAST GUARD
400 7th St. S.W., Washington, D.C. 20591
The Coast Guard can often be of great help to small craft with medical emergenices by providing the afflicted person with air transportation to adequate medical facilities. If the problem isn't that critical or you're too far out, you can use their medical advisory service via radiotelephone (2181 kHz). This is tied in with AMVER, a system by which the nearest vessel to you carrying a doctor can be identified and alerted to your plight. Depending on the situation and vessel's distance, they may come to you or the doctor will advise you by radio.

TRANS CARE LTD.
The Moorhouse Nursing Home, Tilford Rd., Hindhead, Surrey, England
Gaining a reputation as "Angels of Mercy," Trans Care seems like a really good deal for sick or disabled travelers. They claim to be able to handle any medical emergency in any part of the world and provide qualified medical escorts at the low cost of one pound sterling ($1.60) per hour for overseas duties. An air-mail letter for more data on their program will cost you 31¢ to England.

aid and medical

AMERICAN NATIONAL RED CROSS
17th and D Sts., N.W., Washington, D.C. 20006
The Red Cross would probably be the easiest place to get started in first-aid training, since they have chapters all over the country and are nationally recognized for their programs. Courses offered are the 8-hr. Standard First Aid, Multimedia System, 14-hr. Standard First Aid and Personal Safety, and 40-hr. Advanced First Aid and Emergency Care. Only costs are for text and workbooks. Other courses are also offered in swimming, canoeing, boating and sailing, which you can inquire about. Upon completion of any course, a certificate wallet card is issued and badges and lapel pins are available. For more info on these courses and addresses of where to go in your area write the above address.

POISON CONTROL CENTERS
These are regional and local centers established to provide immediate first-aid information via telephone in the event a poison is ingested. Originally founded in 1957 by the American Academy of Pediatrics in Chicago for the use of physicians, the program has grown to include a control center in virtually every city of the U.S. to advise laymen as well as doctors. You'll usually find their number in the front of your phone book. If someone is suspected of having ingested a poison you should call them immediately and provide the name of the substance, if at all known. They will advise you of its toxicity and the first-aid measures that should be taken if they're necessary. For more info on the program you can contact: National Clearinghouse for Poison Control Centers, Food and Drug Administration, Washington, D.C. 20204.

U.S. PUBLIC HEALTH SERVICE (USPHS)
330 Independence Ave., S.W., Washington, D.C. 20201
USPHS's value is mainly to the traveler. They can provide information on vaccinations and shots required for travel in foreign areas, and in certain cases can administer them for free. State and local public health facilities can often provide these services, also. Check with them.

LOCAL CLUBS
Sometimes local yachting, hiking, mountaineering, or skiing clubs will offer first aid or search and rescue courses which you can sign up for. It's certainly worth looking into.

BOOKS

BEING YOUR OWN WILDERNESS DOCTOR
E. Russel Kodet, M.D., and Bradford Angier
1968 - 128 p. il. - $3.95 (pb)

Though a little dated, Kodet and Angier's book still has much good information on the specialized aspects of first aid in the wilderness. The book starts out with a "Problem-Treatment Finder" index which leads you directly to the pages giving symptoms (to be sure you'll be treating the right problem) and the best approach to handling the situation. Back part of the book gives suggested contents of a lightweight first-aid kit and additions that can be made for longer trips. As with all first-aid books, best bet is get practical experience first by taking a course and use the book as a backup.
From: Stackpole Books, Cameron and Kelker Sts., Harrisburg, Pa. 17105

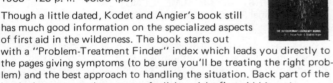

FIRST AID AFLOAT
Paul B. Sheldon, M.D.
1968 - 123 p. il. - $2.50 (pb)

A small book, but crammed with a lot more info than straight first aid—giving injections, suturing, catheterization, and so forth—techniques you may have to use when you're ten days from the nearest port. Also suggests several good medicine chests for the yacht. Information is well-presented; however, illustrations leave a bit to be desired.
From: Yachting Publishing Co., 50 W. 44th St., New York, N.Y. 10036

ADVANCED FIRST AID AFLOAT
Peter F. Eastman, M.D.
1972 - 115 p. il. - $5 (pb)

Eastman gives you an incentive to learn by presenting various hypothetical problems that could occur in horrible picture words. You can feel the urgency to do something. But he doesn't let you down, carrying through with precise instructions for administering treatment and postoperative care. An excellent manual to be kept with the ship's medicine chest—after you've memorized it! It was originally prepared for the author's son and daughter-in-law who contemplated a circum-navigation aboard their 28-ft. sloop. Users of the book should have some previous first-aid experience.
From: Cornell Maritime Press, Inc., Box 109, Cambridge, Md. 21613

FIRST AID PRINCIPLES & PROCEDURES
P. B. doCarmo and A. T. Patterson
1976 - 242 p. il. - $5.95

An excellent book to get you started in first aid. Presentation, illustrations and text are all excellent, and there's no question that the authors did their homework well. As a matter of fact, we would recommend this book over the Red Cross's *Advanced First Aid and Emergency Care* for comprehensiveness and ease of use/study. The authors state that the general aim of the book is to provide a text for students to use in university first-aid courses. Chapters include basic principles of first a d, cardiopulmonary resuscitation, hemorrhage control, soft tissue and skeletal system injuries, shock, poisoning, burns and exposure, med cal and psychological emergencies, childbirth, and first-aid skills. Start your first-aid library off with this one.
From: Prentice Hall, Inc., Englewood Cliffs, N.J. 07632

MOUNTAINEERING MEDICINE
Fred T. Darvill, M.D.
1973 rev. - 48 p. il. - $1

This one, designed for mountaineering use, contains first-aid and medical information oriented to wilderness travel at high altitudes. The booklet is light enough to be carried on your back with the rest of your stuff. Its first-aid and medical procedures are excellent, but limited, and you should supplement them with more extensive reading.
From: Darvill Outdoor Pub., P.O. Box 636, Mt. Vernon, Wash. 98273

SNAKEBITE FIRST AID
Thos. G. Glass, Jr., M.D.
1974 - 26 p. il. - $1.50 (pb) (cost includes postage)

If you want the straight skinny and the latest on snakebites, and what to do and what *not* to do, then you'd best be reading Dr. Glass's little book. Dr. Glass, who is a professor of surgery at University of Texas Medical School, lives in snake country and has treated a multitude of bites. He indicates that more problems arise because of bad first aid than through poisoning. Facts, data and procedures, accompanied by color photographs, present the information clearly and concisely. Recommended treatment methods are given for three levels of medical competence: layman, EMT and physician. Without a doubt, this book is required reading for anyone operating in snake country. The price has been kept low, so there's no excuse!
From: Thos. G. Glass, Jr., M.D., 8711 Village Dr., San Antonio, Tex. 78217

WHAT TO DO ABOUT BITES AND STINGS OF VENOMOUS ANIMALS
Robt. E. Arnold, M.D.
1973 - 122 p. il. - $1.95

Procedures for handling a bite or sting by any venomous creature in North America from a caterpillar to a water moccasin. Text and pictures identify the venomous animals and their characteristics. Included are telephone numbers of antivenin locations, both regular and emergency.
From: Collier-Macmillan, Inc., 866 Third Ave., New York, N.Y. 10022

MEDICINE FOR MOUNTAINEERING
James Wilkerson, M.D.
1976 - 350 p. il. - $7.50

"The first detailed exposition published in America of what to do *after* first aid and *before* the doctor comes—which may be a long period of time on expeditions." It was designed for two purposes: as a "text for a course in medicine for mountaineering taught by a physician" and as a reference during treatment. Excellent!
Covers just about everything that could possibly happen on a mountaineering trip and suggests the components of a complete medical kit to aid you in making up your own.
From: The Mountaineers, P.O. Box 122, Seattle, Wash. 98111

MOUNTAINEERING FIRST AID: A Guide to Accident Response and First Aid Care
Dick Mitchell
1974 - 96 p. il. - $2.50

Climber/first-aid instructor/author, Dick Mitchell, deals with remote area wounds, shock, fractures, common emergencies, high-altitude problems, preparation for rescue and evacuation.
From: Backpacker Books, Bellows Falls, Vt. 05101

EMERGENCY MEDICAL GUIDE
John Henderson, M.D.
1973, 3rd ed. - 651 p. il. - $3.95 (pb)

One of the standard reference works for upper-level first aid and emergency care. Good chapter on anatomy and physiology, which is often lightly treated in other first-aid texts, and other chapters follow through with the standard drill: principles and basic techniques, respiration, hemorrhaging, shock, skeletal injuries, soft-tissue injuries, and so forth. There are a number of specialized areas that will be of interest to the outdoorsman: plant poisoning, insect bites, snakebites (suggests several treatments that Dr. Glass—see *Snakebite First Aid*—sez are definite no-no's!), and exposure. This would be a good second book to add to your medical library, though you might want to look over *Emergency Care and Transportation of the Sick and Injured*, which a number of *Source Book* readers with first-aid background recommend over this one.
From: McGraw-Hill, Inc., 1221 Ave. of the Americas, New York, N.Y. 10020

Two-Man-4-Hand-Carry

A patient unable to stand upright can be lifted and carried by the two-man 4-hand carry. This method is best for short carries to transfer the patient to a more comfortable or convenient location.

EMERGENCY CARE AND TRANSPORTATION OF THE SICK AND INJURED (ECT)
Committee on Injuries, American Academy of Orthopaedic Surgeons
1976 rev. - 304 p. il. - $7; ECT Student workbook, $2; ECT and workbook, $8.50

"Terrific manual designed for the EMT-ambulance technician. Not only gives current treatment, but explains 'why' by going into physiology and anatomy, which the Red Cross book does not. Its major shortcoming is the presumption that a well-equipped ambulance is at one's disposal and the hospital emergency room is minutes away. Yet this 'orange book' is indispensable because of the attention it gives to diagnosis. How can you treat if you don't know what's wrong? How can you diagnose the abnormal if you are not familiar with the normal?"—Bill Schweikert (1974).
"One excellent book is *Emergency Care and Transportation of the Sick and Injured*. Under emergency conditions, especially when one's 'nerves' are on edge, and the adrenalin is pumping, this book is easy to follow."—Ted Baltes, Jr. (1974).
An ECT student workbook is available for $2; save 50¢ and get the ECT and workbook for $8.50.
From: Amer. Academy of Orthopaedic Surgeons, P.O. Box 7195, Chicago, Ill. 60680

ADVANCED FIRST AID AND EMERGENCY CARE
American National Red Cross
1973 - 318 p. il. - $2.50 (pb)

The Red Cross's textbook for their Advanced First Aid course. Not a bad book, but considering the group that's behind it, they've been sadly outclassed by some of the other first-aid books on the market which are also oriented toward the layman (i.e., not EMT-types). If you can't get ahold of doCarmo and Patterson's *First Aid Principles & Procedures*, then this one would be your next-best bet. The Red Cross also has *Standard First Aid & Personal Safety* for $1.95 (pb)—forget it!
From: Amer. Nat. Red Cross, 17th & D Sts., Washington, D.C. 20006

FROSTBITE: WHAT IT IS—HOW TO PREVENT IT—EMERGENCY TREATMENT
Bradford Washburn
1963 - 25 p. il. - 75¢
From: American Alpine Club, 113 E. 90th St., New York, N.Y. 10028

MOUNTAIN RESCUE TECHNIQUES
Wastl Mariner
1963 - 195 p. il. - $3.50
From: The Mountaineers, P.O. Box 122, Seattle, Wash. 98111

MOUNTAINEERING FIRST AID
Harvey Manning, Ed.
1968 il. - 50¢
From: The Mountaineers, P.O. Box 122, Seattle, Wash. 98111

THE TOOTH TRIP
Thomas McGuire, D.D.S.
1972 - il. - $6.95 (hb), $3.95 (pb)
From: Random House, 457 Hahn Rd., Westminster, Md. 21157

GOV. PUBLICATIONS

REFRESHER TRAINING PROGRAM FOR EMERGENCY MEDICAL TECHNICIAN—AMBULANCE COURSE GUIDE
1971 - 26 p. - 80¢
S/N 050-003-00032-9

If you want to know what an emergency medical technician (EMT) has to know, this will give you a good rundown of the subjects.

TYPICAL POISONOUS PLANTS
1973 - 23 p. il. - 70¢
S/N 017-012-00177-7

This booklet provides useful information on more than 17 varieties of poisonous plants found most commonly in the United States. It gives a complete description of each plant and points out the dangers of each. It also describes symptoms to look for in case of accidental ingestion, and tells how to administer emergency treatment until a physician arrives.

ARMY MEDICAL HANDBOOK OF BASIC NURSING
1971 - 634 p. il. - $5.25 (looseleaf)
S/N 0820-0336

Though a great part of this book lies in the EMT and RN area—intravenous administration of drugs, irrigating colostomies, and such—the chapters on Anatomy and Physiology, Disease and Injury, Emergency Medical Care and Pharmacology and Drug Administration in Addition to Basic Nursing Procedures would be of value and interest to serious first-aiders, offshore skippers and expedition medics—people who may have to attend to sick and injured party members for long periods of time before professional medical help is available. Well-written and illustrated and being GI, it shouldn't be over anyone's head.

Removing a Fish Hook

GUIDE TO MEDICAL PLANTS OF APPALACHIA
1971 - 291 p. il. - $1.75
S/N 0100-1261

MEDICAL EQUIPMENT

DRESSINGS AND BANDAGES
10¢ - $5
In general, the term *dressing* is used to describe everything which is used to cover or dress a wound. The sterile pad which is put directly on the wound is called a *compress*. A *bandage* is used to hold the compress in position over the wound. A combination compress and bandage, in which the sterile gauze pad is fastened to a gauze, muslin or adhesive bandage (like a Band-Aid) is usually referred to as a dressing. Any part of a dressing which is to come in direct contact with a wound should be absolutely sterile, and it is when packed by the manufacturer; however, if after opening the package you touch it with your fingers or clothes it won't be sterile and shouldn't (if you can get another one) be used on the wound.

Compresses come in various sizes: 2" x 2", 3" x 3", 4" x 4", and so forth, though they may also be available in rectangular shapes. A compress should be large enough to cover the entire area of the wound, and to extend at least 1 inch in every direction beyond the edges to keep them from getting contaminated. Best bet is to purchase at least 4" x 4" compresses for your first-aid kit and forget the smaller sizes—if the wound is small, you can always fold the compress over before bandaging it in place. Incidentally, materials which are likely to stick to a wound, such as cotton or adhesive tape, should never be placed directly on the wound.

The two basic types of bandages which are most commonly used are the *roller bandage* and *triangular bandage*. A roller bandage consists of a long strip of material, usually gauze or muslin, which is wound into a roll. Almost all roller bandage has been sterilized prior to packing by the manufacturer, so if you're careful to avoid contaminating it, it can be used to make a dressing. Again, it's best to get the large-width roller bandage, as you can always split it down the middle to get a smaller width as needed.

Triangular bandages are usually made of muslin and cut diagonally from a 36- to 40-in. square piece of cloth to make a triangle. They're used to make arm slings, head bandages, chest bandages, and so forth—anywhere support is needed or a dressing is to be kept in place over a large area of the body. Folding a triangular bandage makes it into a *cravat bandage* which is more functional than the triangular shape for holding dressings in place on certain parts of the body, also for tying splints in place. Usually it's best to carry at least two triangular bandages in your kit, because some wounds, like in the chest area, will require two triangulars to hold the dressing in place properly.

There are a number of specialized bandages available such as the Ace bandage (an elastic roller bandage) and the butterfly bandage (a strip with a narrow center and adhesive on each end used to hold deep cuts together in lieu of stitches, as a temporary measure or because too much time has passed to suture safely). Also, bandages are available in materials other than gauze, such as Kling and Cerlix. Some first-aiders love Kling because it sticks to itself and seems to stay in place easier. Others wouldn't touch it with a 10-ft. pole. Talk with a salesperson at your local surgical supply house. They'll be glad to tell you about new products that have come on the market and explain their good and bad points.

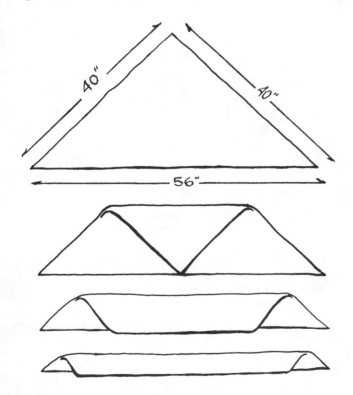

Cravat Bandage

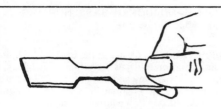

CUT 4 DIAGONAL SLASHES TOWARD CENTER OF STRIP AND FOLD UNDER EDGES TO MAKE A NONADHERENT BRIDGE. FLAME THE UNDERSIDE OF THE BRIDGE, HOLDING A MATCH OR LIGHTER JUST CLOSE ENOUGH TO SCORCH THE FABRIC. DO NOT TOUCH THE FLAMED PORTION AS THIS WILL LIE OVER THE WOUND EDGES. ALLOW HEATED PORTION TO COOL.

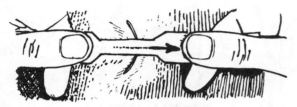

ATTACH ADHESIVE PORTION AT RIGHT ANGLE TO ONE SIDE OF LACERATION. PRESS FIRMLY TO ANCHOR IT TO THE SKIN. APPLY TRACTION TO OTHER END OF STRIP TO APPOSE SKIN EDGES. ANCHOR FREE END.

Sutureless skin closure: butterfly tape technique.

SURGICAL INSTRUMENTS
50¢ - $15

Tweezers. The sharp-nosed splinter kind are the most versatile. About 1/2 oz. - $2.

Scissors. The collapsible type are great for general use because they can't puncture anything when folded. From outdoor dealers. Only 1 oz. - $5. For your kit, though, it's still best to stick with a pair of bandage scissors. They're safer. Available in several lengths from $5 to $8.

Mosquito clamp. These neat, self-locking clamps should be about 5 in. in length. They can be used to clamp off bleeding blood vessels and to hold a needle for suturing. ¾ oz. - $5 to $8.

Suture thread and needle. Size 5-0 thread for face wounds and 3-0 for other parts of the body. Both should come in sterile packets with a curved cutting needle and about 18 in. of nylon or silk thread. Weight is negligible and the cost is about $1 per packet.

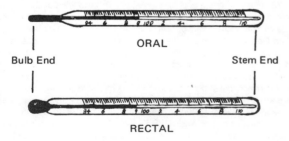

ORAL

Bulb End   Stem End

RECTAL

Thermometers

Thermometer. You can get an inexpensive glass one in a plastic case for $1 to $5, or you can make the big move up in the world and purchase an all metal, non-breakable one that reads like a stop watch for the modest price of $15 (made by Cary Thermometer Co.). Weight from 1/2 to 2 oz. Oral type probably best for field use.

Blades for Handle No. 3

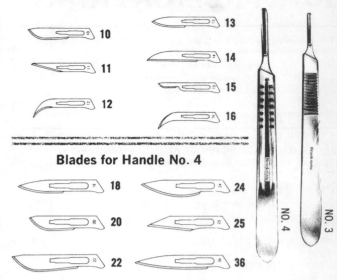

Blades for Handle No. 4

Cat gut. Size 3-0 for tying off bleeders (severed veins and arteries). Cat gut doesn't have to be removed because it will dissolve and disappear when used inside the body. It comes in sterile packets of about 18 in. and costs around $1.

Single-edge razor blades or scalpel blades. A no. 11 blade and a no. 12 curved blade are a good combination and you can get them in sterilized packets, too. It's nice to have a couple of each. No weight and approximately $1 for the works. If you want the handle it will cost you $2 to $5 more.

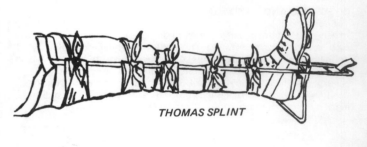

THOMAS SPLINT

AIR SPLINT

HALF LEG PLASTIC AIR SPLINT

SPLINTS AND TRACTION DEVICES
$2 - $15

In an emergency almost any firm object will serve as a splint as long as it is light, strong, and rigid. It should be long enough to reach beyond the joints, above and below the fracture. Some ready made splints fill these requirements very well. The reusable plastic blow-up kind is very light, takes up little room, and comes in different types that can be used for most any break of the arm or leg. Cost varies from $5 to $10 depending on the model. They are easy to apply and are also good for treatment of lacerations. If you have to apply traction (pulling the broken bone ends into place) to the lower extremity (leg), you should have some sort of traction device such as the Thomas Leg Splint with supporting equipment. It should be noted that use of this equipment is highly technical and in some cases, dangerous. It takes three people to apply this splint with traction, and serious damage to the patient may result if it is not used properly. So it's advisable to obtain competent instruction on its application before using.

Hypodermic syringes. Without a prescription these are illegal in a number of states. In most cases the plastic disposable syringes, which come in sterilized packets with needle, are desirable. The best size needle is 5/8 in. by 25 gauge. Not only is this type convenient, but sterility is assured. If you're afraid you'll run out of the disposable hypos, the reusable variety may be better. Two are best, of about 2-cc. size for the syringe and 3/4 in. by 26 gauge for the needle. You may also want to get a steritube in which to store the sterilized hypo. Before deciding on the syringe, consult your "how to" book and your doctor for the size, type and correct method of use. After discussing the pros and cons with your doctor, you may decide you need both systems.

RESCUE LITTER ·
About $58
Sometimes an accident victim has to be carried out. Much of the time

Stokes splint stretcher

the only feasible way to accomplish this is with the aid of a litter. The Stokes Splint Stretcher is one of the best rescue litters available and is used on ships, mountains, ski slopes, and in caves. It is essentially a wire basket supported by iron or aluminum rods. It's adaptable to a variety of uses because the casualty is strapped in and can be held securely in place regardless of the stretcher's position.

SNAKEBITE KITS

SNAKEBITE KIT
$3 - $8
There are many types of snakebite kits on the market, and they all boil down to a knife and suction device of some sort. The best medicine for snakebite though is prevention.

Most snakebites occur below the knee on the front of the leg and the foot—so don't go barefooted. As far as we know, there is no recorded instance of a snake biting through a leather boot or shoe and causing any damage—people who've been hurt got it through cloth or on the bare skin.

Snakes usually hide under rocks, logs or whatever is cool, during the heat of the day and don't come out to hunt food till the early evening and night. Sooo...don't go walking around at night in snake country. Snakes can sense infrared radiation (heat), and if they feel your warmth, they'll figure you're a small animal that'd make a tasty morsel—and, whamoo! you got it. That's the way they hunt.

As far as snakebite kits go...well, before you go chasing one down, read *Snakebite First Aid*, by Thos. G. Glass, Jr., M.D., and also the following, which you may also find enlightening:

I read with interest the very accurate analysis of snakebite and kits in the first edition of the *Source Book*. The subject is, as you say, overblown, but it is also an interest of mine. I prepared my M.S. thesis on a snakebite-related theme, "Some effects of alcoholic beverages on... rattlesnake,...scorpion,...and Gila monster venom." In the process of that mind-bending year, I did (of course) a lot of research on venenation, worked closely with the Poisonous Animals Research Lab associated with Arizona State University, and otherwise got wrapped up in the topic.

The summation of my work with regard to snakebite is as follows: People who know about such things and deal frequently with snakebite, which are precious few doctors, zoo handlers and such, generally disagree with Cutter, who is trying to sell snakebite kits. Cut-and-suction has never been demonstrated to be effective, and quite often it causes more damage than the snake did. Reasons?

The person executing the method is so rattled over the whole incident he's likely to be uncoordinated and make mistakes. Nerves, blood vessels, and tendons can be cut by someone unfamiliar with anatomy which can result in hemorrhaging (since venom acts as an anticoagulant), paralysis and other problems, and a contaminated blade can infect the cuts.

In nearly every snakebite, particularly in the case of an extremity, the venom very quickly "soaks" into the surrounding tissues mixing with lymph and blood, and unless the whole area is sucked dry (which

you just can't do) you're wasting your time. The majority of snakebites are deep and penetrating. Very infrequently are they so shallow—just beneath the skin—that the venom could be sucked out before it got to muscle tissue. Pit viper venom is primarily a proteolytic enzyme which is a long word that means it causes the destruction of protein, muscle and blood tissue in particular (that's why people can lose a finger).

Another reason why cut-and-suction may not be the best choice is there may be no venom to suck out. Not every poisonous snake releases venom with his bite. He may have just eaten and used his supply on a hapless rodent or he may have just decided to strike and released very little venom or none at all. Then again, it may not even be a poisonous snake. Snakes that aren't rattlers can rattle. This is a favorite trick of the lyre snake, bull (gopher) snake and some others. Identification of the snake is very important, and if it is poisonous it should be taken with you to the doctor or hospital.

So the question is: Why cut and suck when (a) there may be no venom at all, (b) if there is venom, it has soaked into the surrounding tissues and a sufficient quantity cannot be removed by sucking to be of any value in lessening the damage occurring, and (c) with cutting, nerves and blood vessels are very likely to be sliced thus compounding the problem rather than reducing it.

The American National Red Cross first-aid text still advocates, or at least condones, cut-and-suction. I'm a Red Cross instructor, and when my class reaches that page in the book we learn what it says. But, later, unofficially, I tell the students the other methods I've learned.

Authorities, such as there are, agree that:

(1) applying a ligature (constricting band like a rubber band—*not* a tourniquet!) above and below the bite to prevent it from spreading, is a good first step in any event;

(2) cooling the affected member (assuming it's an arm or a leg and not your fanny) in cold water (*not* ice that might cause frostbite or freeze burn) slows down both enzyme action and circulation;

(3) a disputed treatment called *cryotherapy* is advocated by some, renounced by others; read the lit and take your choice;

(4) antivenin is a possibility, but because of the chance of a dangerous reaction, it should only be administered professionally with backup facilities available.—Mrs. W. F. Dengler (1975).

So much for snakebite kits.

MEDICAL KITS

KITS
50¢ - $100
A medical or first aid kit, like a shaving kit, should be tailored to your personal needs, and you can't exactly get that with the ready made types. Commercial kits are designed for general purpose "light" first aid, where the doctor is normally only a telephone call

away. When you get away from it all, you need something that will take care of your special activities and problems, and at the same time, be light if you are carrying it. You can easily supplement a commercial kit with surgical instruments, pharmaceuticals, and certain other items, but it's usually cheaper and more efficient just to start from scratch. It also allows you to become more familiar with your kit. Check over some of the books we've listed for suggested kits, and get together with your doctor. He can be a big help, particularly if he's an outdoor type. Once you've got a list of materials, hit the local pharmacy and surgical supply store or check with some of the dealers we've listed. One thing that's great for packaging and weather-proofing individual items are tongue-and-groove, self-sealing plastic bags. They come in all sizes. For carrying everything, best we've found is a good, durable, water-tight plastic tackle box. These are available in all sizes from pocket size on up. When you're traveling light, a waterproof nylon "stuff" bag may be more feasible. Incidentally, we're always looking for good ideas in the homemade medical kit department, so if you've any ideas, let's hear 'em.

If you decide to go to the commercial types, some of the better ones are sold by Medical Supply Co. and Mine Safety Appliances Co. Both of these have Coast Guard approved kits, and both have a containerized system of packaging their supplies for fast and easy use. There are other good kits on the market, but these two companies are especially impressive.

General Purpose Personal Medical Kit

10 - 1" Band-Aids. Minor cuts and scrapes.
6 - misc. shapes Band-Aids. Minor cuts and scrapes.
6 - butterfly closures. For closing small lacerations.
5 - 2" x 2" dressings. Protecting wounds.
3 - 4" x 4" dressings. Protecting wounds.
1 - 3" x 18" petrolatum gauze. Covering and sealing sucking chest wounds; burns.
1 - 1" roller bandage. Holding dressing in place.
1 - 2" roller bandage. Holding dressing in place.
1 - Ace elastic bandage. Holding dressings in place and binding sprains, etc.
1 - ¾" roll adhesive tape. Taping bandages or dressings in place.
1 - triangular bandage. Supporting injured arm, holding dressings in place.
1 - pkg. Moleskin. Protection of blisters.
10 - cotton-tipped applicators.
4 - tongue depressors. Examining mouth; finger splints.
4 - rubber bands (wide). Ligatures for snakebite.
1 - tweezers.
1 - scissors. Cutting bandages, clothes, etc. Folding scissors are good; however, bandage scissors are preferred because of their shape and blunt lower tip which won't snag or puncture the skin.
1 - hemostat. Clamping off blood vessel till it can be tied with catgut; holding and working suturing needle.
1 - No. 0000 silk thread with curved cutting needle attached. Comes in packets or tubes. For suturing large lacerations that cannot be handled with a butterfly closure. Before trying to use this, get detailed instructions with practice from your doctor.

1 - pkg. No. 000 chromic catgut. For tying off blood vessels in severe bleeding that cannot be stopped with a compress.
1 - single-edge razor blade. Shaving hairy spots before applying adhesive tape. Misc. cutting.
4 - surgical blades: 2 - No. 11; 2 - No. 12. For lancing boils; misc. cutting (handle optional).
1 - oral thermometer.
20 - waterproof wooden matches. To waterproof, dip in melted paraffin. For emergency fire-starting, to boil water, etc.
6 - large safety pins. Misc. pinning of bandages, most often used with triangular bandage.
1 - small bottle (wide mouth) isopropyl alcohol, 70%. Sterilizing instruments.
1 - Betadine Solution, ½-oz. plas. bot. Mild antiseptic for cleaning wounds; preferred over iodine or Mercurochrome.
1 - tube Chapstick. Chapped lips.
12 - aspirins. Headaches and relief of minor pain.
12 - salt tabs. Prevent heat exhaustion and cramps due to heavy perspiring.
1 - pkg. antacid. Tums, Rolaids or your favorite. Relief of upset stomach, heartburn, etc.
10 - Lomotil, 2.5 mg. tabs. Relief of diarrhea.
10 - Dulcolax, 5 mg. tabs. Relief of constipation. (We'll straighten it out one way or t'other.)
1 - Neosporin ointment, 1-oz. tube. Antibiotic for treatment of skin infections.
1 - Butesin Picrate ointment, 1-oz. tube. Burn ointment, relief of pain.
1 - oil of cloves, ¼-oz. bot. Relief of toothache pain.
1 - Cavit, small tube. A ready-mixed temporary filling material. Emergency replacement of lost filling. Check with your dentist for sources.
4 - dimes. Put on strip of masking tape. To be sure money is available for making emergency call in event you happen to be in the vicinity of a phone booth.

The following medications require a prescription—

10 - Compazine, 5 mg. tabs. Relief of nausea and vomiting.
6 - Codeine, 30 mg. tabs. Analgesic for relief of severe pain.
6 - Acromycin, 250 mg. tabs. Antibiotic for deep wounds and severe infections.
6 - Pyrabenzamine, 5 mg. tabs. Antihistamine for relief of colds, itching from hives, insect bites, poisonous plant contact, and other situations where allergy may be a factor.
1 - Cort-Dome creme, 1%, ½-oz. tube. Relief of itching and burning skin irritations from insects and plant contact.
1 - Holocaine ophthalmic ointment, 1%, 1/8-oz. tube. Relief of pain in eyes due to snow blindness and other eye irritants.
1 - Neosporin ophthalmic ointment, 1/8-oz. tube. Treatment of eye infections.

References: *Basic Mountaineering*, ed. H. I. Mandolf, "Climbing Miseries and First Aid," T. Hornbein, M.D.; *First Aid Afloat*, Paul B. Sheldon, M.D.; *Being Your Own Wilderness Doctor*, E. R. Kodet, M.D., and Bradford Angier; *Mountaineering: Freedom of the Hills*, ed. H. Manning, "First Aid," J. Lucas, M.D., J. Stewart, M.D.; *Emergency Care, Surgical and Medical*, W. H. Cole, M.D., C. B. Puestow, M.D.; *Emergency Medical Guide*, John Henderson, M.D.

Comments on Medical Kits

I think you should include some type of reader warning before you recommend the carrying along of prescription drugs. This may be a minor issue, but it seems to me that it could be dangerous to take these drugs without a qualified person to administer them. I'm no pharmacist, but one could run into problems if one self-diagnosed himself and took one of these drugs and made a mistake. Or worse yet, giving them to someone else, in an emergency, who might be allergic, etc., to the drug. It could possibly enter into the "field of illegality." And I sure wouldn't want to take a chance on using these drugs unless I was qualified to do so. One must also consider that some nut might read this article, obtain these drugs, and in an emergency situation do a lot of harm to himself or someone else. After all, how many people are informed enough to know about these drugs?

MOUTH-TO-MOUTH RESUSCITATION

Artificial respiration may be given by inflating the patient's lungs with your breath. The inflation is accomplished via mouth-to-mouth or mouth-to-nose. Mouth-to-mouth is the preferred method; however, when the patient's jaws are tightly closed by spasm or when he has a jaw or mouth wound, the mouth-to-nose may be used.

Inflate the victim's lungs by blowing into the mouth—forcefully with adults, gently with children, only "puffs" with infants. Watch victim's chest constantly. When his chest rises, allow victim to exhale. Repeat 15 to 20 times per minute.

You just can't read the label and information sheet that is enclosed with most Rx drugs and expect to be qualified to know their proper usage. I don't know about Delaware, but one needs a prescription to obtain these drugs from a doctor. And unless you have a good friend who is a doctor, that means paying for a doctor visit, trying to get him to prescribe all of those drugs and then having them filled. That runs into a lot of bucks out here in California. And as far as Dexedrine goes, it is government controlled, and there aren't many doctors who would pass out "uppers" just like that for a survival kit.

Other prescription items are pHisoHex and Neosporin Ophthalmic. One can obtain Neosporin ointment for cuts (same as Mycitracin). This is probably the best antibiotic ointment available "over-the-counter." As far as an excellent antiseptic solution goes, the best is probably Betadine Solution (providone-iodine). It has been used in the space program and for surgical antiseptic use. Watch out for different types, though, because they make a scrub and a douche under the same name, which I believe are weaker solutions. You left out something for accidental poisoning. There aren't many things that can be used in most cases, but ipecac syrup can be carried along, and there is also a temporary universal antidote—Res-Q—that can be utilized until a doctor can be found somewhere. Another good item might be an anti-itch, anti-poison ivy, sumac, etc., liquid such as Caladryl or Zirardryl.

In conclusion, I think the medical kit is excellent. As far as the prescription drugs, suture material, etc., go, they are important if one can expertly utilize them. All I'm saying is that a lot of hikers, voyagers and wanderers, in general, have never done more than put Band-Aids on, and that some type of warning should be emphasized to warn people of the possible dangers involved in using some of these things.—Ted Baltes, Jr. (1974).

Here are some thoughts I have on the First Aid section. American Red Cross—the new Blue-and-White editions of the old Green book are pretty good.

Winter First Aid Manual, National Ski Patrol System, 2901 Sheridan Blvd., Denver, Colo. 80214, 55 pp. A specialized treatise on medical problems arising on the ski slopes. Lots on splinting and evacuation. Presumption is that a toboggan and good medical equipment are at hand and that an ambulance or emergency-aid station is located at the base. Strictly *first* aid; winter mountaineers will have to adapt this information to their own needs.

Jarvis' book on Folk Medicine is folksy and quaint, but neither useful nor sound. Angier's, Darvill's and Wilkerson's books are good, the last being excellent.

Arista Surgical Supply Co., Inc., 67 Lexington Ave., New York, N.Y. 10010. Arista sells enough to equip a first-aid kit or a hospital and will sell to all. The retail store is worth a visit, as the personnel are helpful, there is no minimum order, and one-of-a-kind bargains are displayed. Probably the best single source, except they do not sell any form of drug, serum or chemical. Mail order catalog is available.

Quite often veterinary supply houses or farm co-op stores will sell drugs and equipment that are not ordinarily available to the layman through medical sources.

Insect Sting First Aid Kit—Center Laboratories, Port Washington, N.Y. Allergy to insect bites, bee stings, drugs, pollen and certain foods may put you into anaphylactic shock, which death follows quite rapidly. If anyone in your party is sensitive to the above, this kit could be a life-saver. Available on prescription only. Contains adrenaline and hypodermic syringe for injection, an antihistamine, a bronchodilator, and hypnotic (sedative). If you're going to carry a snakebite kit, this is just as necessary.

Snake antivenin is available also from Herter's, Rt. 2, Mitchell, S. Dak. 57301.

Don't buy cheap sterile gauze or put cotton on an open wound. There is nothing worse than a doctor in the emergency room picking pieces of lint from the site—with tweezers. Likewise on putting cremes or ointments on a wound. If you're on your way to the emergency room anyway, why bother?

J&J or Duke's Elastoplast sterile dressings have been satisfactory. For covering the dressing, stay away from old-fashioned roller gauze. Kling, Cerlix and J&J's new improved gauze bandages are the only products which can be called "soft roller bandages," an item now required in ambulances. Kotex is invaluable for cases of massive bleeding and is now recommended for placement over the dressing.

Air splints are fine, but have limitations.

Advantages	Disadvantages
Comfortable, self-padding	Expensive
Convenient, fast	Easily punctured
Compact, lightweight	Sweats
Stops bleeding by compression	Impairs circulation
Permits x-rays through splint	May expand or contract due to temperature or altitude changes
Uniform pressure	Water vapor in breath may freeze walls together in cold
	Produces pressure over a fracture site
	Promotes anaerobic bacteria growth and spread of infection

I go along with the medical kit, but would add lots of strong tape (it has other uses) and an S-tube or Resuscitube. Many deaths outdoors are due to candies or chewing gum being inhaled. A tube would help in such cases.

First-aid kits—We have tried several bags and containers for the kits. Among these have been the fanny belt pack, including the Ski Patrol and Hurricane Island Outward Bound waist packs. For my personal use, I have settled on a medical equipment pack, which ties on the outside of my main pack, and a drug bag which is carried deep inside the main pack. One seldom needs drugs as fast as dressings may be needed, the interior of the pack is cooler, and the drugs are safer inside.

Flash on software. *Exploration Medicine*, by Bacharach, and available through Blackwell's, Broad St., Oxford, England, covers all facets of medical preparation of a prolonged expedition, supplies, and treatment. Even goes into psychological factors. Written apparently for Antarctic medical officers, judging by the topics covered.

I have a fairly good bibliography of medical journal articles on emergency, cold weather, and wilderness medicine. Will send it to interested parties on receipt of a stamped-self-addressed envelope.—Bill Schweikert (1974). (Box 96, Mt. Hermon, Mass. 01354)

Rather than plastic bags, I pack pills in those little plastic bottles that pharmacists use. Some are too brittle, but others work fine. And they are waterproof and easily marked. Sometimes the bottles are bigger than I need (a no-no in my book), so rather than stick in a lot of useless cotton, I put two pills in one bottle. If the pills aren't too potent (for example, Lomotil and aspirin), there's no danger. Naturally, only mix different size or colored pills, and *never* mix opposite acting or strong pills (don't mix the laxatives with the Lomotil, and don't put anything with the sleeping pills). When you have to pack light, one or two double-edge razor blades weigh a lot less than a scalpel. Tape both edges. I can't see the point of so much nonsterile gauze. For mopping up blood after minor wounds, the best things are sanitary napkins. That's what they're made for, no? Also, J&J sells nonsterile gauze pads called "gauze sponges" which are easier to use than roll gauze. Also, someone now markets nonstick roll gauze, but I've forgotten who. Also, *Consumer Reports* often tests nonprescription medicines (*The Medicine Show*, $3.50, Book Dept., Consumers Union, Orangeburg, N.Y. 10962). May I suggest, for serious climbers, that you discuss with your doctor the advisability of taking along morphine on long trips. Severe pain can prevent someone from getting the rest he may need to recuperate. Lastly, an idea from my last trip: Divide your first-aid kits between party members so a lost pack or eager bear won't leave you in a very dangerous spot. Also, I always throw a few Band-Aids and a bit of moleskin into my pockets. It's nice to have at night when your pack's out there in the cold snow and you discover a blister. Also, in designing your kit you must bear in mind the relative possibilities of large and small accidents. The longer the trip, the more small cuts and blisters will appear. But you usually can only have one major accident per trip, regardless of length, since you will end the trip as soon as it occurs. Thus, the number of Band-Aids, etc., is a function of length and party size, while the number of triangular bandages, etc., is a function of party size and danger. Lastly, you needn't bring bandages enough for a really major catastrophe, since you can always rip up T-shirts, etc.—Michael Cohen (1974).

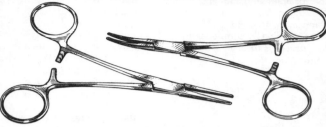

FIRST AID AND MEDICAL

Variously called "Kelly forceps" or "hemostats," these fine genuine surgical instruments belong in every workshop. They amount to a kind of extra-useful slender needle-nose plier, made to exacting surgical standards. Of top quality stainless steel perfectly polished, they are rust free, and solder won't stick to them. Excellent as heat sinks in soldering electronic connections. Narrow jaws are serrated straight across, for vise-like grip, yet won't cut insulation. Superior for reaching deep into small places to grip, manipulate or pull. Three-position ratchet locks the jaws shut with three tensions—ideal for clamping and as third hand. Acts as miniature vise, too. Release instantly. Sturdy box joint is hand-fitted, won't loosen, maintains jaw alignment. No pivot screw to work loose. 5½" and 7½" forceps jaws taper from 3/16" wide to about 1/16" at tips. 5" mosquito forceps are lighter, more delicate, for finer work.

```
M-1252.6 5½" forceps, straight............$6.50
   Three & up......................Each $5.95
M-1253.4 5½" forceps, curved............$6.50
   Three & up......................Each $5.95
M-1584.2 7½" forceps, straight............$8.25
   Three & up......................Each $7.50
M-1585.9 7½" forceps, curved............$8.25
   Three & up......................Each $7.50
M-1586.7 5" mosquito forceps, straight......$6.50
   Three & up......................Each $5.95
M-1587.5 5" mosquito forceps, curved......$6.50
   Three & up......................Each $5.95
```

BROOKSTONE COMPANY
123 Vose Farm Rd., Peterborough, N.H. 03458
"Hard-To-Find-Tools (and other things)." That just about describes 'em. They've gotten it all together in an unusual line of hand tools. Aside from an amazing array of mechanics' gear, they carry small surgical tools such as scalpels (two types), scissors (a variety), tweezers (many types), pliers, mosquito clamps, and micro-probes. Their prices seem just a tad higher than some other dealers, even with a discount of 10% on quantity orders, but their quality also seems about that much higher. A free 68-page illustrated catalog is available.

Liferaft and lifeboat kit

Contents

Adhesive bandages	2 pkg
Ammonia inhalants	1 pkg
Compress bandages, 4 in.	5 pkg
Compress bandages, 2 in.	2 pkg
Eye-dressing packet	1 pkg
Gauze bandage	1 pkg
Iodine swab	1 pkg
Petrolatum gauze dressing	3 pkg
Tourniquet, forceps, scissors, and pins	1 pkg
Triangular bandages	3 pkg
Wire splint	1 pkg
Aspirin, phenacetin, and caffeine	1 pkg

The liferaft and lifeboat first aid kit contains 24 D units and is designed to meet requirements of the U.S. Coast Guard for use in lifeboats, passenger boats, cargo ships, and other seagoing vessels.

The case has a special finish which will withstand exposure to salt water and extreme weather conditions. It has six clamps which hold the lid tightly closed; therefore the kit can withstand several hours submerged in water without damage to contents. In addition, each D unit is sealed in a polyethylene envelope.

MINE SAFETY APPLIANCES CO.
201 N. Braddock Ave., Pittsburgh, Pa. 15208
These guys have it all in mining safety equipment, including resuscitators, and a full line of first aid kits and supplies. Pocket first aid kits for $2 and Coast Guard approved chests for around $57. They also make up custom kits. All kits are packed in weather-proof cases. When writing, ask for the illustrated 24-page catalog: *First Aid Materials*, Section No. 7.

COMBINATION STETHOSCOPE

An extremely efficient model with super-sensitive diaphragm. Both a Ford and Bowles head included. Metal parts are chromium plated.

MD-740SU	Combination	$5.95
MD-741SU	Ford Single Head	2.98
MD-742SU	Bowles Single Head	2.98

PALLEY SUPPLY CO.
2263 E. Vernon Ave., Los Angeles, Calif. 90058
Palley claims to be "the world's largest surplus dealer" and they damn well might be. A load of stuff is illustrated in their 256-page catalog (it's free), which includes a number of inexpensive medical tools.—a Nova sphygmomanometer (to measure blood pressure) for $27, a combination stethoscope for $6, 5 in. bone chisels, mosquito clamps for $3, splinter tweezers for $2, as well as lots of other goodies. Fairly prompt on their mail order service as well.

OFFSHOREMAN

The OFFSHOREMAN KIT for vessels, sail or power, 26 to 42 feet in length. It meets the needs of vessels that may range as far as 1000 miles, and perhaps a day from medical help, with accommodations to eight people. The contents of this chest meets most of the average needs of medical emergencies and comfort aids. Also water and corrosion proof case. Close it, and it is sealed, ready to float.

MARINE MEDIC DIVISION, LEE MEDICAL PRODUCTS, INC.
9856 Everest St., Downey, Calif. 90242
Here's another company that deals in kits and replacement materials. Industrial kits from $2 to $60 and a specialty line in marine medical kits from $8 to $59. Cases are water and corrosion proof and will float when closed. Literature on request.

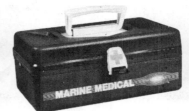

marine medical pac

$19.95

Contents: disposable plastic spoons (6), aromatic spirits of ammonia (½ ounce), motion sickness tablets (12), tincture of merthiolate (½ ounce), adhesive tape (5 yards), scissors (1), tweezers (1), antibiotic healing ointment (½ ounce), plastic bandages (20), Coca-Cola syrup (2 ounces), moist towelettes (4), pain relief tablets (50), salt tablets (100), conforming gauze bandage (2 inches x 5 yards), distilled water (8 ounces), diarrhea mixture (8 ounces), disposable cups (25), emergency first aid instructions, product use instructions.

MEDICAL SUPPLY CO.
1027 W. State St., Rockford, Ill. 61101
Their first aid kits meet both Federal Aviation specifications and Coast Guard requirements. Specialty kits range from small $2 pocket types to the large $37 Coast Guard approved life boat kit, and the $71 burn spray chest. Kits contain individual packets and are color coded for easy identification. Saunders' excellent snake bite kit goes for $5.44. Refill units and individual supplies are available. Other wares include antiseptics, ointments, ammonia capsules, plastic blow-up splints, and resuscitation equipment. Illustrated 34-page catalog available.

PAC ENTERPRISES, INC.
5045 Torresdale Ave., Philadelphia, Pa. 19124
Kits only, including three seagoing Medical Pacs (kits)—the Boat Pac at $7, the Marine Pac for $20, and the most expensive, the Yacht Pac, priced at $60—all include snake bite kits and insect repellent. They seem to be complete, but expensive, and we're not sure they sell replacements. Free literature available.

FIRST AID EMERGENCY KIT

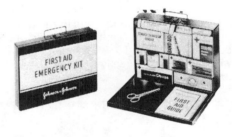

A sturdy, all-steel medicine chest type First Aid Kit. Everything packed in full view for quick and easy use. It's versatile! Can be attached to the wall as a permanent fixture or can be carried as a portable kit.

Size: 10½ x 7⅝ x 2⅛ inches. Weight 2¾ pounds.

2—Red Cross Bandages 1" x 10 yd.
1—Red Cross Bandage 2" by 10 yd.
1—Red Cross Bandage 3" x 10 yd.
1—Red Cross Cotton ½ oz.
1—Red Cross Adhesive Tape 1" x 2½ yd.
1—Red Cross Gauze 1 yd.
12—Red Cross Steri-Pad 2" x 2".

1—Esmarch Triangular Bandage
33—BAND-AID BRAND Plastic Strips.
3—Amoply Ammonia Inhalants
1—Scissors.
6—Sterile Eye Pads.
1—Johnson & Johnson First Aid Cream (Antiseptic)
1—First Aid Guide Booklet

ACME COTTON PRODUCTS CO., INC.
14 S. Franklin Ave., Valley Stream, N.Y. 11582
Naturally they carry a wide selection of cotton products including gauze pads and rolls, cotton fiber pads, cotton balls, eye pads, cotton tipped applicators, and triangular bandages. Regular and waterproof type adhesive tape is also available. Kits range from small $1 models to large $70 sizes. Fairly complete, and the cases of their four outdoor-type kits are weatherproof; cases for the other kits are wall-hanging types. Full color literature available on request.

SAFARI Cat. No. 9005
Contains:
1—1 in. x 6 yds. Gauze Bandage
1—¼ oz. USP Cotton
12—2 in. x 2 in. Gauze Pads
1—Tube Antiseptic & Burn Ointment
1—Adhesive Tape, ½ in. x 54 in.
2—3 in. x 3 in. Gauze Pads
1—Eye Pad
10—Zip-Strips Adhesive Bandages ¾ in.
1—Tin Aspirin

1—Plastic Mouth-to-Mouth Rescue Breather
1—Tweezers
1—Scissors
1—First Aid Handbook
1—Rescue Breather Instructions
1—Snakebite Kit
2—Ammonia Inhalant
12—Motion Sickness Tablets
2—Antiseptic Wipes

FORESTRY SUPPLIERS, INC.
Box 8397, 205 W. Rankin St., Jackson, Miss. 39204
That's what the name says—Forestry Suppliers—and they sell just about every kind of forestry-type do-jigger around. This includes first-aid kits, resuscitation gear, and snakebite kits by Cutter, Saunders, B-D, and MSA (Mine Safety Appliances). The first-aid stock comes mostly from MSA and it's cheaper than MSA sells it. Also some Johnson & Johnson merchandise as well. Prices are generally cheaper than elsewhere.

survival

sources of information

No one wants to be forced into a survival situation, but it can happen unexpectedly anytime, anywhere: in the wilderness, at sea, even on home grounds, such as a house afire or a screaming mob. Experts have differing opinions as to the amount of training and equipment needed for survival situations, but they all tend to agree that the most important requirement is the proper mental attitude—a together head and the will to survive. This is ninety percent of survival in any situation.

Survival conditions are, by definition, unexpected, unfamiliar, and dangerous. Your attitude is decisive in overcoming fear and clearing your mind so as to act quickly and effectively. The will to live is more entrenched in some people than others, but it can be greatly augmented by the confidence and self-assurance you get from concentrated survival training in controlled learning situations.

The equipment and training needed are really a matter of common sense and foresight, that is, researching and preparing for the particular area you'll be heading into and visualizing the potential problems to be encountered. One key to success is to read accounts of survival experiences and training manuals. In addition to this, you must become confident in executing what you have learned. Practice the techniques. Practice making a fire without matches, finding direction without a compass, and living in the woods for a week with just a knife and a canteen. If you're a boatman, blow up your raft...and spend a weekend at sea with just your survival gear. Then if it really happens, survival won't be such a stranger to you.

ARCTIC-DESERT-TROPIC INFORMATION CENTER
Aerospace Studies Institute
USAF Air University
Maxwell Air Force Base, Ala. 36112
Areas of Interest: Geographical areas of environmental extremes and effects of extremes on equipment and personnel; geography; climatology; applied psychology and sociology; anthropology; human survival.
Holdings: Books, research reports, abstracts, manuscripts, and geographical charts; ethnographic information on the USSR, Southeast Asia and the Middle East; International Geophysical Year studies; file of current research projects on nontemperate areas.
Publications: Annotated bibliographies on survival, escape and evasion, and counterinsurgency (annual); technical reports; bulletins; special studies.
Information Services: Answers inquiries, makes referrals, and provides reference and reproduction services to the Department of Defense and other Government agencies. Unclassified materials and reference services are made available to other researchers by appointment.

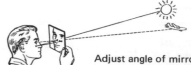

Hold mirror a few inches from face and sight at airplane through hole. Spot of light through hole will fall on face, hand, or shirt. Adjust angle of mirror until reflection of light spot in rear of mirror disappears through hole while you are sighting on airplane through hole.

Using a signal mirror.

Office of Information
USAF SURVIVAL AND SPECIAL TRAINING SCHOOL
3636th Combat Crew Training Group (Survival) (ATC)
Fairchild Air Force Base, Wash. 99011
Areas of Interest: Global Survival; physical, psychological, and technical aspects of basic survival anywhere in the world; survival equipment; POW resistance training; escape and evasion in enemy controlled territory.
Holdings: Classified and unclassified information on survival, resistance, and escape and survival topics.
Information Services: Answers inquiries; makes referrals. Write describing your area of activity and request information on survival tactics in those circumstances. Unclassified material is available to anyone; classified material is subject to standard security controls.

Outward Bound

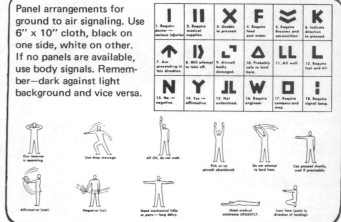

Panel arrangements for ground to air signaling. Use 6" x 10" cloth, black on one side, white on other. If no panels are available, use body signals. Remember—dark against light background and vice versa.

THE ART OF SURVIVAL
Cord C. Troebst
$5.95

This is not a "how to" book. Troebst relates and analyzes various experiences of people who have survived emergency situations to draw certain conclusions about why these people succeeded and why others failed. The material is of special interest to the pilot and sea-goer.
From: Doubleday & Co., 277 Park Ave., New York, N.Y. 10019

EQUIPMENT LISTS, CG-190
U.S. Coast Guard
184 p. - free

A 184-page book listing all products approved by the U.S. Coast Guard with their manufacturers and addresses. A fantastic source of information on all types of survival equipment and supplies, and where to get it.
From: Commandant (CMC), U.S. Coast Guard, Washington, D.C. 20591

OUTDOOR SURVIVAL SKILLS
Larry D. Olsen
1967 - 188 p. il. - $4.95

Making the valid premise that you are unlikely to have a neat survival kit handy when you most need it, Olsen stresses the caveman approach in coping with unfriendly wilderness situations. And that means making do with what nature provides using *no* artificial aids. It's a rough trip, but it's true survival in its purest form. If Olsen can do half of what he tells you how to do, he'd make the most skilled American Indian, Eskimo or Australian aborigine look like an amateur. Very well illustrated.
From: Brigham Young University Press, Provo, Utah 84601

THE SURVIVAL BOOK
P.H. Nesbitt, A.W. Pond, & W.H. Allen
1959 - 338 p. il. - $1.95 (pb)

A very comprehensive text with a wealth of practical, technical, and statistical information crammed between its covers. Designed primarily for the pilot downed on land or sea, the book describes the standard regional environments, their problems and the survival techniques to be used in coping with them. Among the 15 sections of *Survival* is one dealing with stresses and the human body, with interesting charts and statistics; another tells how to deal with the desert peoples of North Africa (especially useful to Israeli pilots). This is definitely an A-1 reference work highly recommended for the serious survival student.
From: Service Center, Funk & Wagnalls, Vreeland Ave., Totowa, N.J. 07512

HOW TO SURVIVE ON LAND AND SEA
F.C. Craighead and J.J. Craighead
1956 - 366 p. il. - $5.50

Essentially written for Navy personnel who have had to dump, but have managed to retain some of their gear. Covers survival throughout the globe. Some of the material is dated, but most of the techniques are still valid and useful: plant identification, trapping, shelter, securing water, and so forth. This is a good basic survival book.
From: Naval Institute Press, Annapolis, Md. 21402

THE BOOK OF SURVIVAL
Anthony Greenbank
1970 - 223 p. il. - 95¢

The common sense book of survival. It only assumes the determination to survive in covering an amazingly large number of crises with practical, fast-acting solutions for each. A sometimes humorous and always entertaining book, it is unusual in that it includes the everyday stuff. You don't have to be looking for bad times a thousand miles away in the wilderness, or at sea on an oak plank with an army of sharks for company. You can be in a suffocating church crowd talking tongues, in a falling elevator, or in a crowded theater when someone yells fire. Greenbank's got the answers.
From: Backpacker Books, Bellows Falls, Vt. 05101

DESERT SURVIVAL
Louis E. Roninger, Ed.
1972 - 27 p. il. - 25¢

An excellent little manual for anyone traveling in the desert Southwest. Though it's 80% text, the information is practical and right to the point. Included are driving and walking tips; clothing and equipment; much water data: life charts, preventing dehydration, finding water in the desert, and how to make a still; food lists and survival recipes; poisonous plants and animals, and data on quicksand. Well worth the two bits they ask for postage and handling.
From: Maricopa Cnty. Dept. of Civil Defense, 2035 N. 52nd St., Phoenix, Ariz. 85008

SURVIVAL, SEARCH AND RESCUE
U.S. Air Force AFM 64-5
1969 - 153 p. il. - $1.50.
D 301.7:64-5/3

A masterpiece of a handbook. Thorough and well-written with scads of excellent illustrations of shelters, plants, fish, devices (stills, snares, etc.), star charts, orienteering charts, and many tables and graphs. As a matter of fact the navigation section is exceptional. The Air Force boys have thought of everything. In the very back of the book is the "when all else fails" section—Religious Readings. Buy it...
From: SupDocs, U.S. Government Printing Office, Wash., D.C. 20402

SAFETY AND SURVIVAL AT SEA
Eric & Kenneth Lee
1971 - 296 p. il. - $8.25

First-person accounts of survival experiences backed up by the authoritative comments of two British experts on safety at sea. The subjects covered include shipwreck, living off the sea, psychological aspects of exposure afloat, search and rescue, safety and survival equipment, and treatment following rescue.
From: W. W. Norton & Co., 500 Fifth Ave., New York, N.Y. 10036

Water

The human body consists of approximately 57% water, or for a 154 lb. man, 92 pints of liquid. This level must be maintained for normal body activity. There is an obligatory water loss of about 3 to 4 pints per day through urine, feces, perspiration, and breath. The human organism can sustain this loss for a period of 6 to 8 days during which time efficiency is drastically reduced. Continued loss will eventually result in death through dehydration. In short this means you should take in at least a quart of water per day in temperate climates and a lot more in the desert to make up the obligatory loss. A good way to avoid dehydration is this: If there's plenty of water, drink more than enough to quench your thirst. If not, ration your sweat, not your water intake by keeping activity to a minimum during the day and traveling by night.

FILTERING DEVICES
$3 - $39
Cheapest thing is a funnel, filter paper, and 6 drops of iodine (careful: poison); or 5 Halazone tablets per quart of water, shake and let stand for 30 minutes. More expensive is Katadyn's $135 filter pump which clears and decontaminates water at the rate of ¾ liter per minute. It will not remove dissolved minerals or chemicals from water, however. The filter pump is 10 inches long and weighs in at 23 ozs., just on the border line of being too much for backpacking.

DESALTING DEVICE
(no data on price)
Desalting kit contains silver aluminum silicate briquettes and a plastic processing bag. Each briquette will desalt about a pint of water by precipitating dissolved salts so they can be filtered out. Kit will produce 6 to 7 times the amount of water that could be carried in the same space.

CANNED WATER
30¢ - 70¢ per can
A good source of emergency water for lifeboat, plant, or Land Rover, but if you're traveling by foot, too heavy. Common can size is 10-2/3 fl. oz., and It'll take 3 per day to maintain your normal fluid level.

BIOLOGICAL PURIFIERS
50¢ - 75¢
Halazone is the most common. Others are Globuline and 10% tincture of iodine. Don't buy surplus stuff; it may be too old and ineffective. Best to buy from a reliable source or through your druggist.

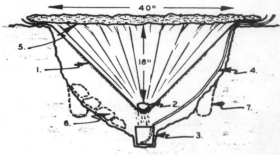
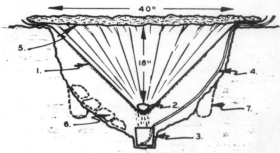
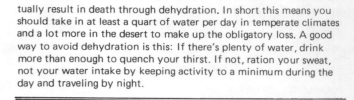

LEGEND:

1. Sheet of wettable plastic, 6-foot diameter
2. Smooth, fist-sized rock for forming cone of plastic.
3. Pail, jar, can, or cone of foil, plastic or canvas to catch water
4. Drinking tube, ¼ inch plastic, about 5 feet long. Desirable but not necessary
5. Soil to weight plastic sheet and seal space. A good closure is important
6. Line hole with broken cacti or other succulents
7. If non-potable water is available, dig a soaking trough around inside of hole. Carefully fill the trough to prevent impure water from running down and contaminating the water-catching container.

SOLAR STILLS
$5 - $36
Solar stills use the heat of the sun to distill water. The type used at sea consists of a large plastic ball inflated by lung power. Inside, sea water is dripped on a black cloth heated by the sun. Water evaporates from the cloth leaving salts and impurities behind, condenses on the plastic and drains down to a fresh water reservoir at the bottom of the globe. This type of still requires water to be handy for the process. The desert still shown above does not. It gets its water from the moist earth as it is heated and evaporated by the sun (which technically makes it a condenser). Survival Equipment Co. sells both the marine ($36) and desert ($10) types. You ought to be able to make your own desert still for $5.

Warmth

Metal Match

Matches in
Waterproof Case

MAUTZ FIRE RIBBON

SPACE Rescue Blanket

Space Blanket

FIRE LIGHTING DEVICES
50¢ - $5
Waterproof/windproof matches are good, except that they require a special surface to strike on. Make your own by soaking kitchen matches in hot paraffin. Keep them in a plastic or metal match safe. Plastic cases have a piece of flint on the bottom for when you run out of matches. Better than flint is the Metal Match and similar flint-like (pyrophoric) alloys which, when struck with a knife, produce 2800° F. sparks that will readily ignite tinder. Fire Ribbon, a flammable paste, is great for damp wood. Smear it on and light.

SPACE RESCUE BLANKET
$2 - $9
This is a light waterproof/windproof sheet made of aluminized mylar. Its shiny surface reflects back 90% of the body's radiated heat; the other side can be had in silver, or orange which makes a good signal panel. The material remains flexible down to -60°F. and can be detected by radar.

All environments considered, food ranks third in priority to water and shelter. You could probably survive for weeks without any at all. A 154 lb. man uses 2400 calories a day resting, and 4500 working heavily. For survival purposes, he can meet all of his caloric *and* nutritional requirements by eating a pemmican-based survival ration. Coman and Gurenko developed such a ration which has proven itself over extended periods of severe survival conditions (see: *The Survival Book,* p. 124). About 2 lbs. of this per day is sufficient for a 154 lb. man doing heavy work. You could get the same caloric value from 2 lbs. of peanut butter or 30 ozs. of a Wilson's meatbar, but you'd be missing certain other nutritional requirements.

SURVIVAL PROVISIONS
$2 - $25
This includes items such as pemmican, beef jerky, malted milk tablets, tropical chocolate bars, in general, high-energy foods that require no preparation. Most of the backpacking outfitters handle a full line of both survival and trail foods, some of which are suitable for survival use. Provisions are available singly or in variety packs such as the LSS-3 described on the next page.

Signaling

WHISTLE
35¢ - $1.50
A seemingly insignificant item until you find out how far one of these things can be heard. Available in chrome-plated brass or plastic.

SMOKE
$2 - $19
Good for indicating your position during the day on land or sea under low wind conditions.

SIGNAL PANELS
$1 - $3
Daytime signaling device for giving location, direction, or transmitting message. Space resuce blanket can be used as a panel.

FLARES and FLARE GUNS
$1 - $70
The hand-held kind, similar to railroad flares, are the most popular and the cheapest, but they can burn the crap out of you. Besides, they cannot be seen as far as a flare shot in the air. For this a gun is a must. Best and least expensive is the Penguin pocket flare gun, $6. It's spring-loaded, simple to operate, and shoots red, green, amber, or white flares. For greater height, visibility, and a bit more money, $18, the Very flare pistol is the ticket. In addition to regular flares, it also shoots star shells ($2 ea.), and parachute flares ($6 ea.), which present a brighter or longer lasting signal (respectively). For the average hiker or boatman, however, Penguin's flare kit will do the job without costing you a mint.

37 MM VERY PISTOL AND PARACHUTE FLARES

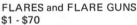

MIRROR
50¢ - $2.50
A mirror is considered second only to a radio for signaling, and an aircraft will see its flash long before the sender sees the plane. A signal mirror has a small aperture in its center for aiming the flash. If you have a metal mirror a small hole punched in the center will serve the same purpose.

STROBE FLASHER
$30 - $50
Most of the ones you see are manufactured by ACR Electronics. Its 250,000 peak lumen flash cuts through fog, rain, and snow, and is visible over 700 square miles; operates 9 hours continuously, and the battery has a 5-year shelf life.

RADIO TRANSMITTER
$185 - $560
Automatic beacons and walkie-talkie types are available, crystal controlled to transmit on distress frequencies: aircraft, 121.5 and 243.0 MHz; marine 2182 kHz and 156.8 MHz.

SURVIVAL

DYE MARKER
$2 - $4
A life jacket accessory to mark your position. Release of dye can be manually controlled. Colors are usually iridescent orange or yellow.

SHARK CHASER
$7 - $10
Chemical developed during WW II by the U.S. Naval Research Lab. Tested, but results were inconclusive as to the degree of protection offered. Shark tales of Navy and Air Force people tell it both ways—it works, and it doesn't. As it stands though, this is the only protection available on the market today, and it can't be any worse than using nothing at all. Best to buy new packets rather than surplus because the chemical may have deteriorated.

RADAR REFLECTOR
$6 - $25
Reflective device used on small boats and life rafts so they'll show up on a radar screen. Two types are available: wire mesh (less expensive) and solid (illustrated).

Diamond No. 2 found in distress by *USS Hunt*, Coast Guard vessel, on March 3, 1935, and assisted into Sandy Hook Bay. This unusual photograph is one of the few available that shows the American flag flying in a distress attitude, i.e., upside down. *Courtesy of the American Merchant Marine Library Association.*

LIFE JACKETS AND VESTS
$4 - $12
The Mae West CO_2 vest is the most common type used by aircraft crews. On boats, however, cork jackets or kapok vests are better suited to the conditions. The inflatable Mae West can be blown up by mouth if the CO_2 cartridge fails, and it has arrangements for attaching lights, dye marker, shark chaser, and radio beacon.

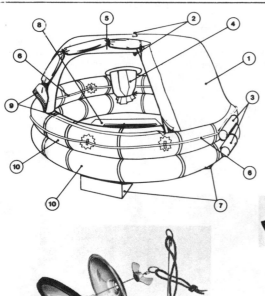

1. Fluorescent orange canopy
2. Interior and exterior lights
3. Double CO_2 inflation cylinders
4. Ventilation port and fresh water catch
5. Self-inflation canopy support tube
6. Interior and exterior life lines
7. Stabilizing pockets
8. Nylon zippered pocket for survival kit
9. Watertight nylon zippered entrance
10. Dual floatation tubes
(Not shown but included):
  Boarding ladder
  Drogue Sea anchor
  Canopy entrance ties
  Hand pump valve
  Hand pump and repair kit
  Rubber quoited life line
Fiberglass "Instant release" cannister
(tie-down and deck hardware included)

RAFTS
$20 - $1000 plus
The two basic types available are cork and air-inflated rubber. Cork rafts are better suited to larger vessels as a back-up for rubber rafts and life boats. They're stored handy on deck and in most cases are easier to deploy than the other two when things really screw up. Rubber rafts are the only efficient survival boats for aircraft and small cruising vessels because of their weight and compact storage size. A fiberglass can is used on deck and a soft valise for internal storage. Rubber rafts use CO_2 for inflation, and set-up time is about 60 to 90 seconds—zip! Rafts are usually sold with accessories (paddles, canopy, etc.), survival equipment and provisions. Revere Survival Products has the best inventory of rafts representing five manufacturers with four to six models each. Revere also has a raft repair service.

Valise Pack

Fiberglass Container

RUBBER BOAT REPAIR PLUGS are brand new G.I. surplus. Designed to be used in emergencies under combat conditions, they enable outdoorsmen to repair holes or small tears in boats quickly and easily. Made of aluminum and rubber. Oval shaped plugs are 3⅜'' long x 1⅞'' wide. Directions included.
☐ S770 Rubber Boat Repair Plug . . $1.00
                  4 for $3.50

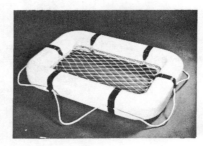

$2 - $200
Various types are available, designed for differ-ent situations and durations from three days in the wilderness to twenty at sea in a lifeboat. Hence, survival kits should be duly chosen with careful thought given to the survival situations you might find yourself in.

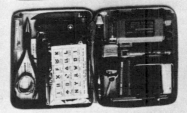

Provisions for one person for three days. Includes:
4 Cans Water   Malt Chocolate Tablets
1 Can Pemmican   4 Tropical Chocolate Bars
4 Wheat Biscuits
From: P & S Sales

LSS-1 SURVIVAL KIT
Water Purification Tablets	Antiseptic Swabs
Bouillon Cubes	Bandage Compress 4''
Fishing Kit	Sewing Kit
Waterproof Matches & Flint	Adhesive Bandages
Wrist Compass	Anti-motion Sickness Tabs.
Insect Repellent	Signal Mirror
ACR Flex Saw	Chapstick
Razor Knife	Safety Pins
Aspirin Tablets	Survival Manual
From: ACR Electronics	

LSS-2 SURVIVAL KIT
7 Red Flares & Flare Gun	Signal Mirror
Flashlight w/Batteries	Survival Blanket, 56'' x 84''
25' Parachute Cord	(also serves as panel marker)
3 Smoke Signals, Red	5' Snare Wire
Whistle & Lanyard	Strobe Signal Light
Pliers & Wire Cutter	Pocket Knife
Knife/Hacksaw	Waterproof Matches
Survival Manual	Flint
From: ACR Electronics	

LIFEBOAT SURVIVAL KIT
Fishing Kit	Hygienic Tissues	Distress Whistle	Flares
Survival Rations	Suntan Lotion	First Aid Kit	Dye Markers
Insect Repellent	Matches	Pemmican	Distress Flags
Canned Water	Flashlight with extra batteries	Signal Mirror	
From: James Bliss & Co., Inc.			

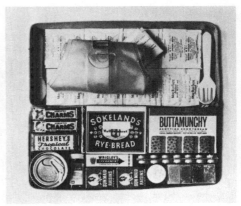

Survival Trail Kit for one person; fits in pocket.
Compass	Insect Repellent
Chocolate Bars	First Aid Items
Fishing Equipment	25' Snare Wire
Survival Instructions	
From: P & S Sales	

LSS-3 RATION PACK
Canned Meat	Chocolate Bars
Hard Candy	Water Purification Tablets
Knife, Spoon and Fork	Raisins
Chewing Gum	Rye Bread
2 qt. Water Canteen	Inst. Beef & Chicken Broth
Multiple Vitamins	Short Bread
Jelly Bars	Malted Milk Tablets
Survival Manual	
From: ACR Electronics	

Weapons

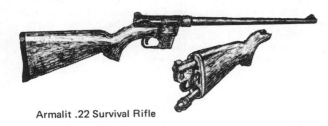

Armalit .22 Survival Rifle

Randall Attack-Survival Knife

Air Force Survival Knife

FIREARMS
$45 - $150
The only firearm specifically manufactured for survival use is the AR-7 Explorer survival rifle by Armelite, Inc. The AR-7 is the civilian version of the AR-5 Air Force survival rifle. Specs are: .22 LR rimfire, semi-automatic; 2-3/4 lbs.; overall length, 34-1/2 in.; with barrel and chamber stowed in stock, 16-1/2 in.; magazine holds 8 rounds; controlled test firing by NRA, 5/8 in. groups; stock floats with parts stowed; cost, $75. You'll have to order it through your local gun shop. There are no ''survival'' handguns manufactured (that we know of), but a .22 LR revolver can be recommended, or if you're heading into really wild country, a .357 Magnum revolver. Revolvers tend to malfunction less than automatics.

KNIVES
$8 - $67
The Air Force survival knife, 5 in. blade, with sharpening stone is found in most surplus stores. Be sure the name Camil-lus is on the blade and that it costs at least $10, or you may be getting a cheap import imitation. Randall Knives makes the Attack/Survival knife, 5½- or 7½-in. blade, with a hollow handle, about $90.

SURVIVAL

ACR ELECTRONICS CORP.
3901 N. 29th Ave., Hollywood, Fla. 33020
Here's a company that offers first rate, sophisticated electronic survival equipment for aircraft and ships at sea. Their inventory includes strobe flashers, manually and water-activated life jacket rescue lights, $10 to $150; radio transceivers and locator beacons, also manually and water activated, $185 to $560; several types of survival and ration kits from $15 to $120; and a couple of commercial rescue items for airlines. According to the grapevine, much of their gear is used by James Bond and Shaft. Product literature and prices provided on request.

JAMES BLISS & CO., INC.
Rt. 128, Dedham, Mass. 02026
Mostly marine survival gear including Winslow life rafts; cork rafts; life jackets, CO_2 and kapok; hand-held flares; electronic flashers and life vest lights; Very and Olin flare guns; compact, one-time-only flare launchers; signal mirrors, dye markers, shark chasers, whistles, first aid kits; life boat accessories, survival, and provision kits. Bliss is a full-line ship chandlery and their prices vary from good to expensive. For $1 you can get their 380-page color catalog of marine equipment. We highly recommend it if you're into boating.

REVERE SURVIVAL PRODUCTS
605 W. 29th St., New York, N.Y. 10001
Quite a selection of quality survival gear at better than reasonable prices. Revere is especially complete in the marine line—"Safety at Sea" specialists, and probably handles more makes of rubber boats than enyone else in the business. Brands include: Avon, Winslow, Dunlop, Zodiac, Pirelli, Zeebird, C-Craft, and Gladding with prices ranging from $137 to $1,125. So you'll have quite a spread to pick from. They handle life raft accessories such as paddles, sea anchors, canopies, fishing kits, canned water and rations, all Coast Guard approved. If your raft needs repair work, Revere will handle this for you too. As far as general signaling gear, they handle the ACR Electronics line at better prices than ACR; Penguin and Very flare guns; their own line of Revere flare kits; smoke cannisters, signal mirrors, and whistles. Other items include fire extinguishers, life jackets, first aid and medical kits, and a rather hard to find item: the E-Z Liner line throwing gun for shooting a line to disabled ships, rigging breeches buoys, etc., $139 for the complete kit. We can candidly recommend you hit Revere first, and use their prices as a basis for comparison; they sell at just about wholesale, and no junk. Ask for their free 32-page catalog.

PERMA-PAK
40 East 2430 South, Salt Lake City, Utah 84115
These people have an extremely wide range of low moisture (dehydrated, freeze dried) foods of good quality, and prices are some of the lowest around. Survival-wise Perma-Pak offers "Crisis Kits" for one person on a 2-day backpacking trip, to 20 people in a Civil Defense shelter or lifeboat. Foods are packed in cloth bandoliers ("chow belt"); waterproof, airtight metal tins; or cardboard carry cartons for 2 to 18 days; price: $5 to $30 depending on the size kit. If you're after long term, 12 months or more, food reserves, these can be had at prices ranging from $255 to $305, depending on quantities. If you want to build your own food kits, these are the people that can help you do it. They've got all sizes of poly-bags, plastic and metal containers, and cardboard boxes, plus the individual food packets (from soup to nuts), canned water, and so forth to pack in them. If you want to build your own food they've got the equipment, books, and accessories for this too. They've really got a Complete (w/capital C) food operation. Comprehensive literature, equipment, food, and price lists available on request.

ARMALITE, INC.
118 East 16th St., Costa Mesa, Calif. 92627
Manufactures the AR-7 Explorer survival rifle described in this section under "Survival Equipment." Literature available from manufacturer.

P & S SALES
P.O. Box 45095, Tulsa, Okla. 74145
Good source of surplus and new survival equipment at reasonable prices. Inventory includes one- and two-man life rafts; life raft repair plugs; first-aid kits; survival provision kits; pemmican; beef jerky; some K-rations; waterproof/windproof matches, Metal Match; rescue blanket; Camillus Air Force survival knife, $11; and various surplus pouches and bags useful for making up your own survival and provision kits. Ninety-page surplus and outdoor equipment catalog available. Good descriptions and well-illustrated.

RANDALL MADE KNIVES
P.O. Box 1988, Orlando, Fla. 32802
Among other quality knives, Randall makes the Attack Survival knife with a 5½- or 7½-in. blade. Price runs from $88 to $93, depending on the material you select for the blade. Knife has brass hilt, stainless steel handle, and a saw-toothed edge on the blade. Handle is hollow for storing survival items and comes with a push-on waterproof cap. For $7 extra a brass, screw-on cap is available. Fishing line, snare wire or parachute cord can be wrapped around the handle. Delivery time on this knife is about 3 weeks. Randall has a 36-page catalog of all their knives, available on request.

PENGUIN INDUSTRIES, INC.
P.O. Box 97, Parkesburg, Pa. 19365
Penguin doesn't sell to the general public, but many retail stores and mail order outlets handle their pen-size flare guns. Revere Survival Products handles one of their flare kits, and a letter to Penguin's home office ought to get you the address of a local dealer, plus some sales literature on their signaling equipment. Certainly worth looking into.

KATADYN PRODUCTS LTD.
Industriestrasse 27, CH-8309 Wallisellen, Switzerland
Amer. Rep.: Sharp Associates, P.O. Box 1618, Deming, N. Mex. 88030
Katadyn is in the water filter business and among their products they include a portable filter pump water purifier. The unit clears and decontaminates water, but will not remove dissolved chemicals or minerals. The price is $135 from Sharp Associates. Description and prices of filter and filter elements are also available from Sharp.

McELFISH PARACHUTE SERVICE
2615 Love Field Dr., Dallas, Tex. 75235
McElfish, an authorized FAA repair station for survival equipment, handles a complete line of survival gear including 2-, 5-, 8- and 12-man inflatable life rafts, all of which meet U.S. government specs for material and construction. They also sell raft repair kits. Other items in their inventory are: several styles of inflatable life vests; the EB-2BW Emergency Beacon Transmitter, signal guns, projectile and hand-held flares and smoke distress signals, strobe lights, sea water distillation kits, solar stills, dye markers, shark repellent and first-aid kits. Some items are military surplus and quite often there are good deals to be had. Have to write for current info on this, though. McElfish also handles several types of FAA-approved survival kits: three kinds of 1-man ones and six specialized ones—jungle, desert, combined jungle/desert, frigid area, sparsely settled area, and uninhabited terrain. Prices on the survival kits ain't cheap, running as high as $600 for the Sparsely Settled Area, 3-man kit. Survival equipment catalog and literature are available. Write 'em at the above address.

SURVIVAL SCHOOLS

NORTH AMERICAN WILDERNESS SURVIVAL SCHOOL (NAWSS)
46 Waterfall Village, Bloomingdale, N.J. 07403
NAWSS offers year-round coeducational courses and outings of varying lengths and serving different age groups. They are designed both
for those embarking on their first wilderness adventure and for those
wishing to advance their training. Program includes concentrated winter and summer courses, adaptive courses, custom-designed courses
and outings, and weekend and holiday outings. Subject range just
about covers the whole wilderness show: backpacking, climbing, canoeing, ski touring and mountaineering, and survival. Costs run from
$65 for a two-day course to $275 for a week's concentrated (course)
backpacking foot trip in the Dix Wilderness Area of the Adirondacks.
Complete details on request.

NATIONAL OUTDOOR LEADERSHIP SCHOOL (NOLS)
Box AA, Lander, Wyo. 82520
Another well-known wilderness school founded by Paul Petzoldt
in 1965 which includes survival training as a major part of its
curriculum, in addition to leadership training, expedition planning
and logistics, mountaineering, search and rescue, first aid, ecology,
etc. Courses are conducted in Wyoming, New England, the Pacific
Northwest, Alaska, Tennessee, and Baja California. They vary, but
generally are co-ed for ages 16 to 50 and can run up to 4 months for
semester programs. There's one thing worth noting that sets NOLS
apart from the other wilderness schools—that's Petzoldt himself.

BRIGHAM YOUNG UNIVERSITY
242 H.R. Clark Bldg., Provo, Utah 84601
BYU offers three credit-earning survival courses:

   Youth Leadership 480. This 28-day course in the Canyonlands
and mountains of southern Utah is designed for ages 15 to 50.
Students learn to live off the desert by themselves using a minimum
of equipment, "... home will often be no more than a blanket and
a juniper fire. This, along with a pocket knife, a very basic food
pack, a billy can, and maybe a canteen, is the only equipment,
which makes it very interesting indeed!" Activities include rappelling,
belaying, solo expedition, and forced marches. Tuition: $250.

   CDFR 360. (Achieving Success in Marriage in a Survival
Setting). An unusual and exciting 10-day course for married couples
set in the Wasatch Mountain wilderness. Want to really get to know
your roommate...? $220 for two bodies.

   Sociol/Psychology 357. This one is designed to develop leadership ability through productive group relationships with others via
a 10-day survival sojourn in the mountain wilderness of Utah. $110
for one body.

OUTDOOR SURVIVAL (a game)
1972 - $10
Actually five games in one and all of them fun. Its survival value is
maybe a little vague, but it sure drives home the importance of
water. Perhaps with some small changes the game could better
relate to survival situations. For example, rolling a die isn't quite
the same as making a calculated decision on how to get out of a
sticky situation, and it sorta takes the challenge out of it. A very
well-done 23-page survival manual accompanies the game, and it
has some good information that applies to the real thing.
From: Stackpole Books, Cameron & Kelker Sts., Harrisburg, Pa.
17105

Outward Bound

OUTWARD BOUND
165 West Putnam Ave., Greenwich, Conn. 06830
Outward Bound is perhaps the best known wilderness school in the
U.S. and though it is not technically in the survival category, survival
training does play an important part in its curriculum. The standard
course is for 16-1/2 to 23 year olds and averages 26 days. The
first week everyone takes part in fitness training through such
activities as running, hiking, ropes course work, swimming or other
related events. Instruction is given in safety, search and rescue, use of
equipment, food planning and preparation, route finding, travel
skills appropriate to the environment, expedition planning, and
care and protection of the environment to be used in the course.
After initial training, groups of 8 to 12 take part in short expeditions;
a solo, which is a period of wilderness solitude lasting up to three
days and nights with a minimum of equipment (you're on your
own); rock climbing and rappelling; and a final expedition of up to
4 days' duration with a minimum of instructor supervision. In addition to the standard course, there are specialized courses lasting
from 10 to 28 days, such as Managers Courses, Leadership Skill
Courses, Manpower Challenge Courses, and Seminars. At present
there are six Outward Bound schools in the U.S., which, though
they are all under one umbrella, operate somewhat autonomously
with respect to their programs. For information it's best to write
the school you're interested in rather than the home office in
Greenwich, Conn.. Their addresses follow:

School	Emphasis
Colorado Outward Bound School P.O. Box 7247 Park Hill Station Denver, Colo. 80207	Mountain wilderness environ- ment; orienteering, ecology, backpacking, mountaineering & rescue, (winter) ski moun- taineering.
Minnesota Outward Bound School 1055 E. Wayzata Blvd. Wayzata, Minn. 55391	Quetico-Superior Wilderness; orienteering, camping, search and rescue, canoeing.
Hurricane Island Outward Bound School P.O. Box 429 Rockland, Maine 04841	Island in Penobscot Bay; seamanship, navigation, ocean sailing, rescue, "castaway" bivouac experience.
Northwest Outward Bound School 3200 Judkins Rd. Eugene, Ore. 97403	Mobile courses in mountain wilderness environment; orien- teering, ecology, backpacking, mountaineering & rescue, fire fighting, (winter) ski mountain- eering.
North Carolina Outward Bound School P.O. Box 817 Morganton, N.C. 28655	Appalachian Mtn. wilderness en- vironment; orienteering, ecolo- gy, backpacking, climbing & rescue, white-water rafting.
Southwest Outward Bound School P.O. Box 2840 Santa Fe, N. Mex. 87501	Southwest wilderness environ- ment (desert & mountains); orienteering, ecology, desert skills, backpacking, moun- taineering & rescue, river rafting.
Dartmouth Outward Bound Center P.O. Box 50 Hanover, N.H. 03755	Northeast mountain and lakes re- gions; cycling, climbing, leadership training, snowshoeing & ski expeditions, winter camping.

American Youth Hostels.

Question: What can at the same time provide both exercise and transportation, is nonpolluting, is the most efficient means of using energy to move a given body weight a certain distance in a given period of time, and is economical to purchase, insure, register and license, operate, fuel, maintain and store than any other vehicle of transportation? Right—a bicycle! So what are you doing using an automobile for *every* trip you take?! That's even a better question, isn't it?

The exercise and health benefits a bicycle can provide while pedaling around town on odd errands, shopping and visiting, have long been recognized and expounded in periodicals and books. Unfortunately, though, too many bike owners use their bikes just for exercise and go to the automobile for all their transportation—even just to the corner store. The problem with this, of course, is that the bike is soon looked upon as something that involves work—exercise is work—and soon it is used less and less, even for that. The progressive attitude would be to get a bike for fun, everyday, short-distance transportation, and let the exercise benefits come as they will.

The important thing to remember in purchasing a bike is to do your "homework" well, so as to make a choice of make and model that will provide an incentive to ride as opposed to dampening your enthusiasm. A bike that takes too much "umph" to pedal will do that. *Consumer Reports* tested fifty-one 10-speed bikes and reported on their findings in the February '76 edition. Of interest was the following: "Frequently, as it happened, they would ride in succession a bike that later proved low-rated and one that was later high-rated. The tour on the better bike invariably struck our cyclists as a minor revelation. Hills that they had chugged up before, they zipped up now in a higher gear. They coasted on slight downslopes, where they had previously had to pedal. From their notes, it was evident that the bikes later rated highest in field and laboratory tests gave our cyclists the greatest return for effort and the most sport on the road."

S. S. Wilson did some analysis of the energy efficiency of using a bike for travel. He compared the energy consumed in calories by a man on bicycle to that consumed by other machines and traveling animals to move one gram of body weight one kilometer of distance (time apparently wasn't a

sources of information

BICYCLE INSTITUTE OF AMERICA (BIA)
122 E. 42nd St., New York, N.Y. 10017
The U.S. bike manufacturers' public relations association—the Bicycle Manufacturers Association is their lobbying power. Useful for information on how to start a club and get in touch with existing clubs, also for high-school-driver-education-mentality safety pamphlets and movies. Heavy on the counter-productive kinds of bikeways (see *Effective Cycling* under "Books"). Publishes *Bike Safety* which covers developments on national, state and local levels concerning laws, safety standards, and so forth, and *Boom In Bikeways* containing info on the development of bikeways and paths. Both are about 8 pages and published periodically. Of primary interest to bicyclists is BIA's 56-pg. *Bicycle Clubs Directory and Other Stuff*. Write for publications list, free.

ANTIQUE BICYCLE CLUB OF AMERICA
Dr. Roland C. Geist
260 W. 260th St., Bronx, N.Y. 10471
No dues.

FRIENDS FOR BIKECOLOGY
1035 E. De La Guerra St., Santa Barbara, Calif. 93103
Oriented toward promoting biking to preserve the environment. Student membership, $3/yr., on up to Patron, $100/yr.

THE LEAGUE OF AMERICAN WHEELMEN (LAW)
3582 Sunnyview Ave., N.E., Salem, Oreg. 97303
Founded in 1880, the League is into everything and anything concerning bicycling especially legislation, running the best Washington lobby cyclists have. Membership runs $8 per year and as a member you can receive maps of many areas, technical help for your own riding needs, tour-planning assistance and monthly copies of *The American Wheelmen Bulletin* which runs club news and activities, articles on biking by members, book reviews, bike pathway info and plenty of ads. Another LAW benefit is the annual directory of its enthusiastic members, who certainly don't seem to mind being contacted for help or advice.

touring

factor—Hmmmm?). The least efficient energy users are mice and lemmings at 60.00 calories per gram per kilometer; a light plane runs at 1.30; automobiles at about .80; a walking man, .75; a horse, about .60; and a man on bicycle, .15. For more info on this, check the March '73 edition of *Scientific American*, "Bicycle Technology."

As far as the economics of using a bike go, it requires no cost for registration, licensing, liability insurance or fuel, and maintenance is just about zero compared to a car. Supplementing automobile use with a bicycle is definitely a money-saver, particularly for short trips. Here is where wear and tear and fuel consumption are so excessive with a car— you know, stop-and-go traffic, the slow creep, parking, and so forth. Even on long trips where the auto is the only reasonable way to go, many people bring their bikes to provide hassle-free transportation at the destination. We've noted, traveling around the Connecticut Ave. Mall in downtown Washington, D.C., and the central part of Annapolis (where, on weekends, people and cars are so thick there isn't even room to change your mind), that people park on the outskirts, unrack their bikes and ride into town just as slick as grease—no fuss, no muss—and park right at the door of the shops and museums they wish to visit. The only setback (which is unfortunate) is that you'd best run a chain, interwoven between both wheels and frame and around a lamppost or parking meter, to protect your bike from theft.

What about bike touring? Well, that's the frosting on the cake. With daily and continuous use of a bike around town and to and from work, you will have built up the stamina to handle short tours to the country and longer trips, camping overnight, with no strain. On a good quality 10-speed you should be able to move along at 12 to 15 miles an hour covering 40 to 50 miles a day at a leisurely pace. Riding straight through with only a few rest stops can get you 70 to 80 miles per day with little effort, even packing camping gear.

Federal and state transportation agencies are slowly providing signs and bike pathways adjacent to city streets and country highways, and many groups, both public and private, are grinding out bike tripping info by way of books, atlases, maps and travel guides. Yep, bicycle touring is easier than it has ever been.

CANADIAN CYCLING ASSOCIATION (CCA)
333 River Rd., Vanier City, Ontario, Canada K1L 8B9
Unlike U.S. clubs, CCA, founded in 1882, is the only national bicycling organization of Canada. Its orientation is more toward racing than anything else, though there is a good bit of general biking and touring info available through them. Membership is $6 a year and gets you the *Canadian Cyclist*, a 24- to 28-page newspaper published 8 times a year. Worth joining if you do biking in Canada or want to keep up with Canadian activities.

THE WHEELMEN
Mrs. Donald Cottrell, Treasurer
6239 Anavista Dr., Flint, Mich. 48507
Robert McNair
32 Dartmouth Circle, Swarthmore, Pa. 19081
Antique high-wheeler club. Dues $5 per year.

PERIODICALS

BICYCLING!
Gail E. Heilman, Ed.
Monthly - $9.50/yr. - $1/issue - 96 p. il.

The only long-time bicycle rag, greatly improved recently due to competition, money, and contributions from the bike boom. Best feature is an authoritative, technical question-and-answer column by Dick Swann and Fred DeLong (see "Books"). Covers racing, touring, medicine, the law, politics, camping, and anything else of general interest to bikers. An occasional sloppy article still gets in, and product news and tests are the usual commercial-magazine variety, i.e., if anything mildly critical is mentioned it should be translated to mean a fatal flaw. An unwelcome trend is having novice riders test cheap bikes. Still, essential reading for any serious bicyclist. All big mail-order discounters advertise here, and they publish an annual bicycle directory.
From: Bicycling!, P.O. Box 4450, San Rafael, Calif. 94903

BIKE WORLD
John Potter, Ed.
Monthly - $8.50/yr. - 75¢/issue - 56 p. il.

Four years old and less traditional than *Bicycling!* Thinner, but compensates by often going into more depth in fewer articles, having more-critical road tests, running an excellent reader's suggestion column, and being generally California-freaky (articles on "centering" and yoga). Fewer ads, which you may or may not like, and more apt to cover safety issues and controversies well.
From: World Publications, Box 366, Mountain View, Calif. 94040

COMPETITIVE CYCLING
Jim McFadden, Ed.
Monthly - $7/yr. - 75¢/issue - 24 p. il.

The only U.S. periodical oriented toward racing, although *The LAW Bulletin* and the two magazines above have some later coverage of major events. Also has product news and tests, especially in winter. Naturally biased toward California events, but attempts nationwide coverage. Really only for the fanatic! Pretty well done considering the limited space and budget.

BOOKS

Caveat emptor! Hack writers and publishers have taken notice of bike sales, and the bike book field seems to contain a higher percentage of turkeys and "disinformation" than any other this side of true confession rags. With the exception of a couple of books, the following are among the best available and listed in rough order of their usefulness.

DeLONG'S GUIDE TO BICYCLES AND BICYCLING
Fred DeLong
1974 - 278 p. il. - $12.95 (hb)

This is it—the book that tries to cover everything, but repairs, and damn near succeeds. Explanation always has the clarity of expertise, and there's always a photo or drawing when needed. The chapter on safety is only surpassed by Forester (below); no apologies are necessary elsewhere. The medical chapter is by a bicycling M.D. There's a wealth of technical information, some unavailable elsewhere, e.g., tubing composition. Even the experienced cyclist will learn a lot, and the beginner should start here rather than with an "easier" book that'll require un-learning later.
From: Chilton Book Co., Chilton Way, Radnor, Pa. 19089

AROUND-TOWN CYCLING
Donald Pruden
1975 - $2.50 plus 40¢ postage (pb)

Anyone who commutes by bike owes it to his posterior to read Pruden, DeLong, and Forester for all the hot tips on how to stay alive till they [(sic)] run out of gas.
From: World Publications, Box 366, Mountain View, Calif. 94040

EFFECTIVE CYCLING
John Forester
1975, 2nd ed. - $7.95 (includes shipping)

A text for a college cycling course, but it only shows in its completeness. Unsurpassed for safe-riding advice including why bikeways are dangerous. Many thought-out details on equipment, maintenance, gearing and other subjects, some too original. Binding idea is how to use the bike for everyday transportation—near and far.
From: Custom Cycle Fitments, 782 Allen Court, Palo Alto, Calif. 94303

THE NEW COMPLETE BOOK OF BICYCLING
Eugene Sloan
1974 - 532 p. il. - $12.50

Sloan tries to do what DeLong did, but he's a P.R. man, not an engineer, and it shows. The book is often so shallow you can hardly get your mind damp. Another book full of useful information laced with "facts" that have to be double-checked.
From: Trident Press, 630 Fifth Ave., New York, N.Y. 10020

RICHARD'S BICYCLE BOOK
Richard Ballantine
1974, 2nd ed. - 250 p. il. - $2.95

Reviewed because it's a best seller. Contains no information or advice not better given by several books heretofore listed. Much seems to have been culled from elsewhere, and badly revised. The section on city cycling is plodding and obvious; that on bikes and equipment is misleading and incomplete; that on repairs is too simplified. So much for nepotism.
From: Ballantine Books, Inc., 201 E. 50th St., New York, N.Y. 10022

A CLOSE-UP LOOK AT BICYCLE FRAMES
Joe Kossack
1975 - 32 p. il. - $1.75 plus 40¢ postage (pb)

Some overlapping with DeLong, but one should read this and the chapter on frames by Kossack in *Traveling By Bike* for full information on this most important and irreplaceable part of the bike.
From: World Publications, Box 366, Mountain View, Calif. 94040

Recreational Reading

BEST OF BICYCLING!
Hal Aiger, et al. - $2.20

From: Bicycling!, P.O. Box 4450, San Rafael, Calif. 94930

THE CLEAR CREEK BIKE BOOK
Hal Aiger, et al.
1972 - 180 p. il. - $1.25

From: New American Library, 1301 Ave. of the Americas, New York, N.Y. 10022

BIKE TRIPPING
Tom Cuthbertson
1972 - 172 p. il. - $3.95

From: Ten Speed Press, Box 4310, Berkeley, Calif. 94704

sources of books

Two good sources for the above and other books on bicycling are:

BOOKS ABOUT BICYCLING
Box 208, Nevada City, Calif. 95959

WORLD PUBLICATIONS
Box 366, Mountain View, Calif. 94040

Hobby Horse, 1834

Racing Ordinary, 1887

Safety Racer, 1892

BICYCLES
$40 - $1,200

Yesterday it used to be rather simple to choose a bike, since coaster brakes, gearing, tires and such were relatively the same, the major difference being in the frame, either designed for a girl or boy. Today, however, with the boom in bicycling, the matter is not quite so simple. The American Bicycle Industry has evolved a voluntary standard (BMA/6) for bicycle construction, which is one thing that can be checked for. Problem, though, is that many builders do not go to the expense of submitting models for a test. In lieu of, or as an adjunct to, the BMA/6 seal of acceptance, the make of frame and the trade name of the components (brakes, derailleur, etc.) can be a guide to quality. Also, price seems to be a good indication of the craftsmanship invested by the manufacturer.

Types of Bicycles

One-speed, heavyweight, junk prices to $70. Ideal for riding on loose surfaces. Coaster brake is unsafe on long downhills. A new version laid out like a kids' "polo bike," but with motorcycle-type suspension front and rear, is great for really rough terrain but slow; about $140 at Yamaha and Kawasaki motorcycle dealers and Motocross bike dealers.

Folding or take-down bikes, 30 to 42 lbs., $70 to $220. Backup vehicle for getting from one type of transportation to another, especially for commuters, sailors and pilots. Range from heavy 1-speeds to the $220, 10-speed Gitane Get-Away.

Three-speed, 35 to 45 lbs., $60 to $110. Hub shifter, upright riding position, uncomfortable on long rides. Much harder to pedal than a good 10-speed; OK for short trips on level ground. Design is standardized, so look for quality; there are several good Japanese and English brands.

Derailleur (10-, 12-, 15-speed) lightweight, 18 to 34 lbs., $100 to $1,200 plus. For regular transportation and travel over any distance, a quality, geared, lightweight bike is the only answer. The touring bike of 40 years ago had a 3-speed hub but otherwise looked like today's 10-speeds—drop handlebars, narrow leather seat, toe clips, skinny high-pressure tires, and light brazed frame. More efficient gear shifting made it obsolete so now you have to buy a derailleur-type to get a good bike.

What To Expect For Your Money

A general description by price category follows. There are lots of bad bicycles, most of them American, but the only brands in this country unsafe enough to require a warning are Easy Rider and Lambert. Japanese bikes are usually better buys if the price is in the $100 range.

Under $100. Forget it!

$100 to $140, 34 to 29 lbs., straight gauge heavy steel frame; cheap but perhaps good derailleur; usually cottered steel cranks; steel rims; bolt-on or sometimes quick-release hubs (avoid rear wingnuts); and clincher tires. With low enough gears a good model can do anything a $500 bike can, just more slowly. If it weighs over 34 lbs. or doesn't have a lugged frame, don't buy it—unfortunately, all U.S.-made 10-speeds are in this group.

$150 to $240, 28 to 25 lbs., lugged frame of higher-quality steel; decent derailleurs; cotterless alloy cranks; alloy rims, bars and stem; good quick-release hubs; U.S. import versions usually have wide-ratio gears and clincher tires. Sidepull brakes are OK at this price. Bikes in this range are best buys for most uses—wheel weight limits speed more than total weight does, and lighter combinations of tire and rim are too fragile for city, busy-highway, or rough-road use. Almost every quality manufacturer makes a bike in this price range; don't overlook recent Japanese imports.

$250 to $400, 24 to 20 lbs., frame tubing is double-butted, high-strength steel: Reynolds 531, Columbus, or Champion; next-to-top quality on all components; sewup tires. Some touring versions have clinchers and wide-ratio gears. Definitely worth the money but not that much faster than a good $180 bike.

$400 to $1,200. Usually all Campy parts. Really only for racing, unless custom-made for touring. Some snob tourists ride such super machines, putting up with a superstiff frame, bent rims, sewup repairs, and ripoff paranoia for the slight extra speed and prestige.

BIKES and ACCESSORIES

PARTS OF A BICYCLE

1) Handlebars	10) Down tube	18) Chain
2) Brake levers	11) Tire pump	19) Rear derailleur
3) Stem	12) Gear shift levers	20) Rear sprockets
4) Head	13) Front sprockets	(freewheel)
5) Front brake	(chainwheel)	21) Rear brake
6) Fork	14) Crank	22) Saddle
7) Front hub	15) Pedal	23) Saddle post
8) Top tube	16) Toe clip	24) Seat stays
9) Seat tube	17) Front derailleur	25) Chain stays

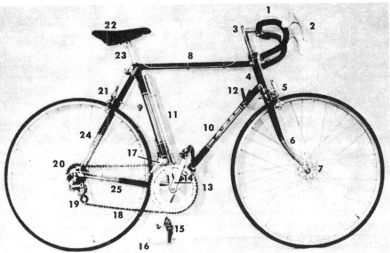

Fuji Road Racer, 23 lbs.

Bicycle Parts

Regardless of the price, most of the good bicycles come from countries that are strong in racing: Japan, France and Italy. Since the bike boom, almost every European country now exports something to the United States—some excellent, some junk. U.S. 10-speeds are always too heavy (except the 650 Schwinn), and rarely have balanced-quality components. Campagnolo (Campy, to bike freaks) components are often the best and seldom worth the price. Japanese products for serious (rather than kids') bikes are usually well-designed and made, and often innovative, which is more than can be said for most old European lines. Except for derailleurs, it's almost never a mistake to use the same that racers-on-a-budget use.

A list of all makes and models would be of doubtful utility, even if we could spare the 50 pages. Such lists are available in buyers'-type guides. Only problem is they don't give you qualitative info on each bike's components, such as the frame, brakes, derailleur, and so forth. Since almost no bike manufacturer manufactures every part of the bike himself, if you know how good various components are, by name and model, you can then be in a position to do some intelligent comparing.

If you don't have a lot of background in the components area, best bet is to check for a knowledgeable and helpful bike shop—find out where the racers shop—and let them assist you. What we're going to try and do throughout the rest of the section is provide you with enough input to ask intelligent questions at the shop.

FRAME

The frame is the heart of the bicycle. The material of which it is constructed and the way the material is joined—welded, brazed, clamped—determines the bike's capacity to be pedaled and maneuvered easily, and to endure normal riding abuse and road shock without failures. Manufacturers of low-cost bicycles use low-carbon steels to obtain maximum production at minimum cost. Though such tubing is satisfactory for kids' bikes, it makes for frames that are relatively heavy and only of moderate strength. A higher carbon content is the answer to lighter, stronger tubing, but because of the care needed in the application of heat during the construction process to avoid brittleness because of the extra carbon, production must slow down and cost go up. Unfortunately, unless the tubing used in the

frame carries the label of a known manufacturer, it's almost impossible for the layman to tell what kind of quality he's getting. Even here, careful scrutiny is called for, because labels very closely resembling those of quality tube manufacturers have been known to be stuck on a frame to influence a purchase. Familiarize yourself with the way bona-fide labels look. Labels of quality tubing are: Reynolds of England; Durifort, Vitus, and Super-Vitus, and A. H. R. of France; Columbus and Falck of Italy; Tange, Isawata, Day & Day of Japan; and Mansmann of Germany. All of these tubes are seamless.

The other aspect of a frame (actually the whole bike) is that it fits the rider. Since every human has different proportions to the parts of his body, even if two people are the exact same height, there can be some problems in getting the seat, pedals and handlebars properly related to each other—distance- and aspectwise—so the individual is operating the bike at maximum comfort and efficiency. Like a suit of clothes, the best answer is tailor-made. Such frames are available averaging $200 to $300 for the frame alone.

Since most of us would find it a bit stretchy on the wallet to go custom, the next best alternative is to know how a stock-built bike should fit for best riding efficiency and comfort. DeLong, in his *Guide to Bicycles and Bicycling*, goes into this in depth in Chap. IV—well worth reading. In general, though, a rider should be able to straddle the frame comfortably with his feet flat on the ground or the frame should be about 9" less than the inside leg length barefooted. The seat height is correct when your leg is straight, with the heel of your foot on the pedal at its lowest position.

GUARANTEED
BUILT
WITH
REYNOLDS
BUTTED
TUBES
FORKS & STAYS

GEAR CHART
(27-inch wheels) 👉

	front sprocket																
SP	26	30	32	36	38	40	42	44	45	46	47	48	49	50	51	52	54	56
13	54.0	62.3	66.5	74.8	78.9	83.1	87.2	91.4	93.5	95.5	97.6	99.7	101.8	103.8	105.9	108.0	112.1	116.3
14	50.1	57.8	61.7	69.4	73.3	77.1	81.0	84.8	86.8	88.7	90.6	92.6	94.5	96.4	98.4	100.3	104.1	108.0
15	46.8	54.0	57.6	64.8	68.4	72.0	75.6	79.2	81.0	82.8	84.6	86.4	88.2	90.0	91.8	93.6	97.2	100.8
16	43.9	50.6	54.0	60.8	64.1	67.5	70.9	74.2	75.9	77.6	79.3	81.0	82.7	84.4	86.1	87.8	91.1	94.5
17	41.3	47.6	50.8	57.2	60.4	63.5	66.7	69.9	71.5	73.1	74.6	76.2	77.8	79.4	81.0	82.6	85.8	88.9
18	39.0	45.0	48.0	54.0	57.0	60.0	63.0	66.0	67.5	69.0	70.5	72.0	73.5	75.0	76.5	78.0	81.0	84.0
19	36.9	42.6	45.5	51.2	54.0	56.8	59.7	62.5	63.9	65.4	66.8	68.2	69.6	71.1	72.5	73.9	76.7	79.6
20	35.1	40.5	43.2	48.6	51.3	54.0	56.7	59.4	60.8	62.1	63.4	64.8	66.2	67.5	68.8	70.2	72.9	75.6
21	33.4	38.6	41.1	46.3	48.9	51.4	54.0	56.6	57.9	59.1	60.4	61.7	63.0	64.3	65.6	66.9	69.4	72.0
22	31.9	36.8	39.3	44.2	46.6	49.1	51.5	54.0	55.2	56.5	57.7	58.9	60.1	61.4	62.6	63.8	66.3	68.7
23	30.5	35.2	37.6	42.3	44.6	47.0	49.3	51.7	52.8	54.0	55.2	56.3	57.5	58.7	59.9	61.0	63.4	65.7
24	29.2	33.8	36.0	40.5	42.8	45.0	47.2	49.5	50.6	51.8	52.9	54.0	55.1	56.2	57.4	58.5	60.8	63.0
25	28.1	32.4	34.6	38.9	41.0	43.2	45.4	47.5	48.6	49.7	50.8	51.8	52.9	54.0	55.1	56.2	58.3	60.5
26	27.0	31.2	33.3	37.4	39.5	41.5	43.6	45.7	46.7	47.8	48.8	49.8	50.9	51.9	53.0	54.0	56.1	58.2
27	26.0	30.0	32.0	36.0	38.0	40.0	42.0	44.0	45.0	46.0	47.0	48.0	49.0	50.0	51.0	52.0	54.0	56.0
28	25.1	28.9	30.9	34.7	36.6	38.6	40.5	42.4	43.4	44.4	45.3	46.3	47.2	48.2	49.2	50.1	52.1	54.0
30	23.4	27.0	28.8	32.4	34.2	36.0	37.8	39.6	40.5	41.4	42.3	43.2	44.1	45.0	45.9	46.8	48.6	50.4
31	22.6	26.1	27.9	31.4	33.1	34.8	36.6	38.3	39.2	40.1	40.9	41.8	42.7	43.5	44.4	45.3	47.0	48.8
32	21.9	25.3	27.0	30.4	32.1	33.8	35.4	37.1	38.0	38.8	39.7	40.5	41.3	42.2	43.0	43.9	45.6	47.2
34	20.6	23.8	25.4	28.6	30.2	31.8	33.4	34.9	35.7	36.5	37.3	38.1	38.9	39.7	40.5	41.3	42.9	45.0
36	19.5	22.5	24.0	27.0	28.5	30.0	31.5	33.0	33.8	34.5	35.2	36.0	36.8	37.5	38.2	39.0	40.5	42.0

CADENCE CHART (speed in miles per hour)

gear in inches	cadence in revolutions per minute					
	60	70	80	90	100	120
30	5.4	6.2	7.1	8.0	8.9	10.7
40	7.1	8.3	9.5	10.7	11.9	14.3
50	8.9	10.4	11.9	13.4	14.9	17.8
60	10.7	12.5	14.3	16.1	17.8	21.4
70	12.5	14.6	16.7	18.7	20.8	25.0
80	14.3	16.7	19.0	21.4	23.8	28.6
90	16.1	18.7	21.4	24.1	26.8	32.1
100	17.8	20.8	23.8	26.8	29.7	35.7

rear sprocket

DRIVE TRAIN

Gears provide the means of keeping your cadence (how many revolutions per minute you pedal) at a comfortable rate for traveling on flat surfaces with the wind and against it, up hills and down them. In the days of the heavy, one-speed bikes, pumping up a hill meant slow pedaling and required standing on the pedals to get your full weight behind each thrust to develop enough force to get up the hill—almost better to get off the thing and walk up. With gears, however, all that's necessary is to shift to a lower gear and pedal maybe a little faster.

The most efficient cadence for pedaling lies in the 60- to 70-rpm range. With gears you can stay in this range and yet still throw either power to the rear wheel for climbing and fighting headwinds, or speed, for long straight hauls.

Gearing isn't hard to understand, providing you remember the rule that power is inversely proportional to velocity. That means: more power, less speed; more speed, less power. If a large gear with 100 teeth turns a small gear with 50 teeth, every time the large gear turns once, the small gear turns twice. If we call the large gear the crank (the gear the pedals are attached to) and the small gear the rear sprocket (attached to the bike's drive wheel), we can see that with respect to the crank, we're getting twice as much speed (rpm) out of the rear sprocket. If we switch gears so that the crank would have 50 teeth and the rear sprocket 100, we'd get less speed, but more power.

Power can be understood if we think of a lever. If you stick a long handle in an axle it's easier to turn the axle against a resistance than it is with a short handle. If we slip a gear on the axle and draw a line on the gear from the axle to the outside edge where the gearteeth are, we can think of that line as a "handle." A large gear will have a longer line or "handle" than a smaller gear and thus more power can be developed through it.

For gears to provide useful information, we have to attach some numbers to them. Thus the most natural question is: How can I tell what gear my bike is in? The answer depends on three factors: the number of teeth in the crank sprocket, the number of teeth in the rear sprocket and the diameter of the rear drive wheel. Combining these numbers according to the following formula will give you a gear value:

$$\frac{\text{no. of teeth on front sprocket}}{\text{no. of teeth on rear sprocket}} \times \frac{\text{diameter of}}{\text{drive wheel}} = \text{gear number}$$

If your bike has a 50-tooth crank sprocket, a 27-tooth rear sprocket and a 27-in. rear drive wheel, it would have a gear value of 50. What does the 50 mean? The 50 means that you're getting the same results out of riding your little bike as you would from riding a high unicycle that had a 50-inch diameter wheel!

With the various combinations of gears available on 10-speed bikes, gear values can be had as low as 20 and as high as 120. For normal riding on a flat surface, though, most cyclists operate in a gear range of around 60 to 70. As it turns out, the most efficient pedaling cadence for a cyclist is also around 60 to 70 (rpm), which might make it easy to remember these two numbers. Pedaling at 60 rpm in 60 gear gives us a road speed of about 12 mph, which is the average comfortable cycling speed most people ride at—a useful figure for giving you a rough idea of how long it might take to make a trip.

Now what about all those gears and using them? Well, since the human body works most efficiently pedaling at 60 to 70 rpm, gears can be used to keep this cadence, but yet change the power delivered to the rear wheel. Terrain, wind, weather, fatigue and traffic require different amounts of power or speed. The skilled cyclist shifts gears as soon as conditions change so that increases in power or speed are supplied as needed while at the same time keeping pedaling effort low to avoid strain on muscles and ligaments, and likewise, keeping pedaling rpm in that narrow range of greatest efficiency.

Since 10 speeds are available, what would be the best combinations of crank and rear sprocket sizes to have? (As far as the rear drive wheel diameter goes, 27 inches is just about standard on all bikes.) The answer depends on whether you're into racing or touring.

A racing cyclist in top condition will use higher gears going uphill than the average person, and will want to have narrow-ratio gearing to maintain his one best pedaling cadence—for instance, 14-16-18-21-24 teeth on the freewheel (rear sprockets) and 40-52 on the chainwheel (crank sprockets).

A tourist, loaded down with pack and gear, needs the lowest gear he can get to pedal up steep grades, and wider gaps between intermediate gears to efficiently handle varying intermediate grades and headwind conditions. The average 10-speeder has top gears that are too high for efficient touring; unless you're racing, the 30mph produced by spinning an 85 gear at 120 rpm is plenty fast. Mountain

dwellers are the only ones who use higher gears regularly. An ideal gear range for touring would be 25 to 90. Unfortunately, most bikes can't have such a low range without changing cranks. For those stuck with 40-52 chainwheels or rear derailleurs that can't handle a freewheel bigger than 28 teeth, a 14-17-20-24-28 one will do.

In customizing the gearing of your bike for touring, be careful to avoid duplicating gear ratios so you don't effectively end up with only 7 speeds. Evenly spacing the intermediate ratios can help prevent this. For the common chainwheels, a 15-18-22-27-34 freewheel will give the lowest gears possible in a range of 30 to 94 without duplication. The more standard 14-17-21-26-32 is next best in the 32-to-100 range. Those with slow bikes or little interest in top speed might even consider 16-19-23-28-34 for a range of 30 to 88 with closer spacing than either of the above. With a 16-tooth difference between chainwheel sprockets, say 36-52, a stock 14-17-22-28-34 freewheel will give even spacing and a range of 28 to 100. If any gearing combination besides the above is offered on a bike, check for uneven spacing or duplication before accepting it; some supposed 10-speeds come from the factory as actual 6-speeds!

Rear Derailleur, $8 to $32. The freewheel on a 10-speed is composed of 5 progressively smaller sprockets mounted side-by-side on the rear wheel hub. In shifting gears the chain must be moved up to a larger sprocket or down to a smaller one smoothly. The most common method of doing this is by "derailing" the moving chain from one sprocket to another by pushing it sideways. When moving from a large gear to a smaller one some chain will be left over, and something must be used to take up the slack and maintain tension till the chain moves from a small sprocket to a large one again. These chain-shifting and

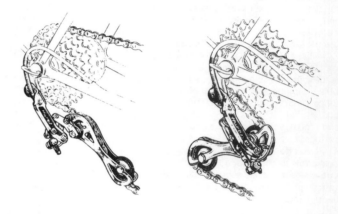

Huret Super Touring rear derailleur in two extreme positions. Note how the tensioner arm wraps excess chain for small sprockets (right).

tensioning devices are called derailleurs, which is the French word for derail. The important thing to remember about using derailleurs, which novices so often are not aware of, is that to shift gears, the chain must be moving, though there must be no pressure or force being applied to it. If you try to shift at the same time you're applying pressure to the pedals, the chain will try to stay seated in the gear it's in. Relax the pressure and the chain will jump over to the next gear easily.

Rear derailleurs can be had for as little as $8 and as much as $32 (these are the lowest mail-order prices we found, which is something to shoot for when buying over-the-counter). The $32 one is the Campy Nuovo Record, but it's for racing and can't handle freewheels over 28 teeth. Campy also makes a good touring derailleur (*not* the clumsy Gran Tourismo) but it's virtually a line-for-line copy of the Shimano Crane GS (turnabout is fair ploy!). So you might compliment Campy's taste and buy the Shimano at $18. The best buy in touring derailleurs is the Suntour at $9—almost as light and smooth-shifting as the Crane GS. No European derailleur, besides Campy, is as good, and all cost more. The Lux at $8 is equally as good for around-town bikes.

Front Derailleur, $5 to $17. This is just a cage to shove the chain back and forth between the chainwheels; the rear derailleur has the difficult job of maintaining chain tension. The best buy is the Suntour Allegro at five bucks. It has a parallelogram like a rear derailleur instead of the jam-prone pushrod found on the cheaper Simplex and Campy models, and is stronger than the similar Huret. The Campy Nuovo Record costs $17; for gramparers only.

Cotterless Crankset, $20 to $105. Campy is still the best here, but $105? In order of more-or-less descending quality, other good sets are: Shimano Dura-Ace, $65; Sakae Royal (SR) 5, $63; Sugino Mighty Compe, $46; Stronglight 99 (wide-ratio) or 93, $60; TA (available with smallest chainwheels), $50; Shimano 600, $35; and the Surgino Maxy II, $20. At the price of the latter, you'd be crazy to buy a steel crankset when your old one needs replacement. All Surgino Mighty Compe parts fit Campy, by the way. Replacement chainwheels run $7 to $11.

Chain, $5. The chain is exposed to road dirt, and one of the best ways to help attract it is to copiously squirt oil along its whole length. This, instead of providing lubrication where most needed, only holds the dirt in place to increase wear. The only place where a chain really needs lubrication is at the heavily loaded surfaces of the outer link pin and the inner link bushings. Oil 'em with an old hypodermic syringe and needle. Also remember that when replacing sprockets, replace the chain.

Pedals, $5 to $30. Rat traps provide the best nonskid surface, and Campy is tops here in the $30 range. Cheaper rat traps just as serviceable are available.

Toe Clips, $4 to $6. Toe clips can make pedaling a lot more effective and are highly recommended. Just get some practice in getting in and out of them quickly before you start riding in traffic.

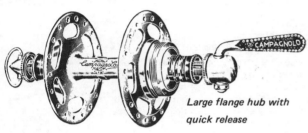

Large flange hub with

quick release

WHEELS

Hubs, $17 to $50 per pair. Quick-release hubs are just about the standard today and facilitate the easy and quick removal and replacement of wheels in the event of a needed tire repair, or for packing the bike up to travel by bus or car. Campy Nuovo Record is tops here followed by Shimano Dura-Ace, Campy Nuovo Tipo, and a bunch of Japanese hubs. Watch the Normandy and Atom axles—they bend too often.

Spokes, 10¢ ea. Dented and weavy wheels are one of the cyclist's most common problems. They can be averted by lifting your weight off the bike when hitting a bump or pothole. Broken spokes are not a common enough problem to make it worth carrying spares.

Rims, $6 to $12. Aluminum rims save weight where it counts most, but are not for riding over curbs. The best alloy clincher rim is the Super Champion, which has tubular corners for greater strength. Arraya and Mavic are also good; Fiamme rims tend to bend.

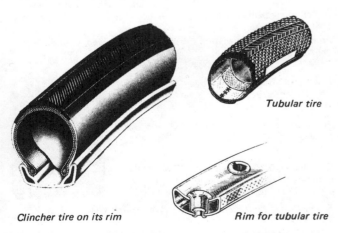

Clincher tire on its rim　　*Tubular tire*　　*Rim for tubular tire*

Tires, $7 to $25. The cyclist has a choice of either clincher or sew-up tires. Clinchers will take the beating better, but are heavier. Sewups are lighter, but don't take abuse as well and they're harder to repair. Tires intermediate in weight and puncture resistance between the heavier sewups and clinchers are available to mount on regular clincher rims: Vittoria, Clement, Michelin, Elan or Schwinn SR's, 390 gm w/90 gm tube; IRC, Nishiki or Daiwa "skinwall," 340 gm. A typical, touring-weight, cotton sewup runs about 300 gm at $10; racing, silk sewup, 220 gm at $25. There is a difference in price!

BRAKES
$15 - $96
Campy, Dura-Ace and Universal have licked the uneven action of earlier sidepull brakes, but at a price. A set of Mafac Racers at $15 works as well, better on uneven rims, and can be adjusted for all kinds of odd problems. Mafac Competition is the same brake with a shorter reach, $20. Some weight can be saved with alloy Weinman levers instead of steel Mafac, and that last increment of control can be had by using Universal 68 brake cables, which are thicker and don't stretch as much, in plastic-lined Ultra-Glide housings.

Mafac center-pull brake (front)

SADDLES
$8 - $16
Plastic or nylon saddles are not recommended. They have the same problem as plastic shoes: they're waterproof, last a lot longer, but if they don't fit immediately, they never will. Ouch! Nylon-covered, padded leather is best, though more expensive.

HANDLEBARS and STEMS
$4 - $22 each
A considerable saving in weight and quicker steering can be had for just a couple of dollars extra by getting alloy instead of steel. Get the right size, never force a too-large bar or stem into place, and always leave at least 4 cm of stem *past* the slot inside the head tube—having the bars break off in your hands is a terrible way to go.

ACCESSORIES

LIGHTS
$2 - $10
If you need to see where you're going, any bike shop can sell you a headlight powered by 2 D cells. Anything smaller is for cars to see you, not for you to see the road.

HORN
Free.
Your voice is the best. Any kind of prosthesis takes too much reaction time in the short-distance world of the urban cyclist. Time would be better spent grabbing brakes or steering, than trying to hit a horn button. Besides, lots of car drivers, through conditioning, will ignore a horn. Freon should no longer be a part of your life, anyway.

Leco child carrier

CHILD CARRIERS
$10 - $14
Several styles are available that fit over the rear wheel; however, consider a back or front child carrier, like the Gerry, worn by the rider for greater safety. At any rate, make sure the kid is strapped in with any carrier.

343

SADDLE BAGS and PANNIERS
$6 - $30

The Cannondale front pack is lightest since it doesn't need a supporting bracket. For carrying small, heavy objects consider a midframe bag that hangs from the top tube, though narrow enough not to interfere with pedaling; available through Recreational Equipment or Bikecology.

Bellwether bags on Schwinn bike

REAR CARRIERS
$4 - $8

Flat metal decks or grids that bolt to the rear of the bike frame have their place for commuter cycling to carry packages, books, or brief cases. Go for aluminum, it's lighter.

WATER BOTTLE and CARRIER
$1 - $5

Nothing like a cool hit on a long, hot run. Carry your water or soda with you in a plastic bottle. If carrying water, dampen a handkerchief and wrap it around the bottle—evaporation, as you ride, will help cool the water. Carriers are available to mount on handlebars or frame.

BIKE CARRIERS
$20 - $55

The best way to portage a bike with you when motoring is to hang it on a bike carrier at the rear or front of the car, or strap it upside down on a cartop carrier. Problem with the top carrier is that it can increase your driving windage, though if you have more than a couple of bikes to tote, the top carrier may be the only place you can fit them all. JCI has several good models.

CLOTHES
$1 - $50

If you're into racing, there are specialized shorts, jerseys, and so forth; however, for the touring cyclist, about the only thing that may make his riding more efficient and safe is specialized cycling shoes and a helmet.

Touring Kits and Tools

This is the tool kit that the Student Hosteling Program issues to its bicycle trip leaders in the United States, Canada and Europe. With it you can do most any on-the-road repairs, maintenance and cleaning. You can use this as a guide for making up your own kit, or purchase it ready-to-go from SHP (see Student Hosteling Program of New England, Inc., in Sources of Bikes and Gear).

metric box wrenches (8, 9, 10, 11mm)
metric open end wrench (9mm)
metric cone wrenches (13, 14, 15, 16mm)
metric allen keys (5, 6, 7, 8mm)
metric forward & reverse ratchet socket set (6, 7, 8, 9, 10, 11, 12mm)
chain rivet tool with spare pin
third hand brake adjusting tool
universal crank tool (cotterless cranks)
  OR
  cotter pin punch (cottered cranks)
chain nose pliers with cable cutter
fine, medium & thick blade screwdrivers

plastic repair tape & small grease rag
small box for easily lost tools
6" adjustable wrench
spoke wrench
tire irons (set of 3)
freewheel extractor
patch kit
tire pressure gauge
bike grease
bike oil
spray lubricant & protector
12" channel lock pliers
flat file, round file
magnet, tweezers, thread brush
canvas toolbag

Maintenance Books

ANYBODY'S BIKE BOOK
Tom Cuthbertson
1971 - 176 p. il. - $2.95 (pb)

The best-selling bicycle maintenance book of all time. Written in laymen's terms, simple, concise and with a sense of humor in a modern "with it" style. The author has covered almost every aspect of bicycle maintenance problems and how to cope with them. Step-by-step procedures reflect a great wealth of practical experience and knowledge drawn from many bicycle specialists. Line drawings and exploded views accompany text.

From: Ten Speed Press, 2510 Bancroft Way, Berkeley, Calif. 94704

DERAILLEUR BICYCLE REPAIR
XYZYX Information Corp.
1972, rev. ed. - 132 p. il. - $4.95

Step-by-step instructions, written in easy-to-follow style, are given for each maintenance task. This book covers all of the maintenance procedures which can be accomplished by the bicycle owner with readily available tools. Written for and tested by nonmechanical persons.

From: XYZYX Information Corp., 21116 Vanowen, Canoga Park, Calif. 91303

FIX YOUR BICYCLE
Eric Jorgensen and Joe Bergman
1972 - 100 p. il. - $3.95

From: Books about Bicycling, P.O. Box 208, Nevada City, Calif. 95959

GLENN'S COMPLETE BICYCLE MANUAL
Clarence W. Coles and Harold T. Glenn
1973 - 340 p. il. - $7.95

From: Crown Publishers, 419 Park Ave. South, New York, N.Y. 10016

sources of bikes and gear

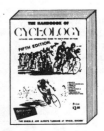

WHEEL GOODS CORP.
2737 Hennepin Ave., Minneapolis, Minn. 55408
Their 138-page catalog includes a 24-page service manual for Sturney Archer and Shimano hub shifters; Campagnolo Gran Sport, Huret Allvit, Simplex Prestige, and Shimano Lark derailleurs; and tubular tires. Catalog, called *The Handbook of Cycl-ology*, runs $2.

SINK'S BICYCLE WORLD
816 S. Washington St., Marion, Ind. 46952
Very nice selection of bicycles and accessories—in fact, there's not much that's not included in their 109-page catalog, from Mondia bikes to bike-touring gear to books. Catalog runs $2.50, though for that price it could be a bit more professional-looking. Sink's sponsors tours throughout the year. Check with 'em, if you're interested.

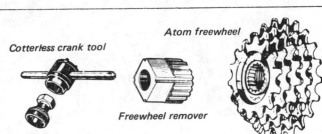

Mafac tool kit

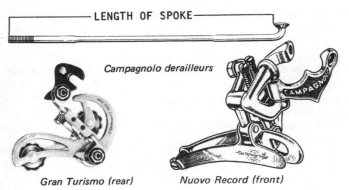

LENGTH OF SPOKE

Campagnolo derailleurs

Gran Turismo (rear)   *Nuovo Record (front)*

GENE PORTUESI
311 N. Mitchell, Cadillac, Mich. 49601
Portuesi's 72-page *Cyclo-Pedia* catalog doesn't list as many items as some of the others, but it generally describes the products more thoroughly. Includes several useful articles on bicycles and touring. Cost is $3.

Cotterless crank tool   *Atom freewheel*

Freewheel remover

VELOCIPEDE
611 E. Pine, Seattle, Wash. 98122
Sixty-page catalog of bike gear, indexed, $2.

WARES CYCLES
2656 N. 76th St.
Milwaukee, Wis. 53213
Forty-seven-page catalog plus brochures.

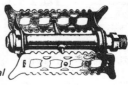

Rat-trap pedal

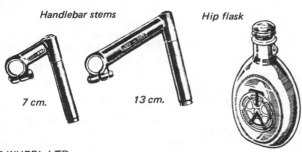

Handlebar stems   *Hip flask*

7 cm.   *13 cm.*

BIG WHEEL LTD.
340 Holly St., Denver, Colo. 80220
Has an 84-page catalog, *The Complete Handbook of Cycling* for $2.10.

Chain tool

Spoke wrench   *Pump frame mounts*

AMERICAN YOUTH HOSTELS, Metro. New York Council
535 West End Ave., New York, N.Y. 10024
Full line of bike touring and hosteling accessories and books; discounts to members. Catalog available.

JCI
717 S. Nogales St., City of Industry, Calif. 91744
Bicycle carriers for automobiles. Literature available.

BELLWETHER
1161 Mission St., San Francisco, Calif. 94103
Panniers, packs and down clothing; literature available.

STUDENT HOSTELING PROGRAM OF NEW ENGLAND, INC.
Maple Hill, Rochester, Vt. 05767
Very nice little catalog devoted strictly to specialized bike-camping equipment, from tents to panniers to clothing. They also handle 5 types of tool kits, one of which we mentioned on the previous page, ranging in price from $80 to $90. Catalog can be had from the above address. Also, you might ask for info on their student hosteling program.

345

BIKE TOURING

teaus and mountains. You can help with the cost of the research work involved by becoming a member at $10 a year (students, $5). They've already got a number of touring brochures and guidebooks available, some of which are free to members. As a member you'll also receive periodic information on their progress, and new publications as they become available, and be in a good position to assist with your input. For complete picture, write 'em.

TOURING BOOKS

FREEWHEELING: THE BICYCLE CAMPING BOOK
Raymond Bridge
1974 - 192 p. il. - $2.95

Not particularly expert, but fairly complete and well written.
From: Stackpole Books, Cameron & Kelker Sts., Harrisburg, Pa. 17105

THE SECOND TWO-WHEEL TRAVEL
Peter Tobey, Ed.
1974 - 192 p. il. - $4.70 (pb, 10½'' x 14½'')

An incomplete and hasty revision of the first edition, but still the best single introduction to bicycle touring with emphasis on camping. Especially good discussions of riding technique, gearing, and bike bags; incomplete on camping; misleading or out of date on parts, but good on most other subjects. Essential reading for the tourist, though don't believe everything they say.
From: Tobey Publishing Co., Box 428, New Canaan, Conn. 06840

BICYCLE TOURING IN EUROPE
Karen and Gary Hawkins
1973 - 184 p. il. - $2.95

The best book on many aspects of touring in general. These people have been through many kilometers and have much to say about how to make a trip enjoyable. Includes 8 appendices with conversion charts, useful addresses, equipment and map sources, and so forth.
From: Pantheon Books, Inc., 201 E. 50th St., New York, N.Y. 10022

TRAVELING BY BIKE
Editors of *Bike World* magazine
1974 - 96 p. il. - $1.95 plus 40¢ shipping (pb)

If you rip the appendix out of this one and throw it away, what's left over is definitely must reading for the serious bike tourer. Excellent articles on technique, psychology, equipment, and medical problems pertaining to bicycle travel, sharing a common emphasis on using the bicycle to go anywhere—not just for touristy rides in easy locations. The appendix? Well, it's sorta embarrassing!
From: World Publications, Box 366, Mountain View, Calif. 94040

sources of information

CLIFFORD L. FRANZ
764 Mills Ave., San Bruno, Calif. 94066
If you're interested in trading cycle-touring information, Clifford Franz is the man to get together with. He specializes in Pacific Coast info, but also has files on the rest of the country. If you'll send him route information with a hand-drawn map of local bicycle paths and tours you know about, he'll send you:
    Recommended bike routes on detailed section or state maps,
    List of campgrounds and motels along the route,
    Check list of what to take along,
    Guide to camping from a bike,
    List of names and addresses of League of American Wheelmen (LAW) officers along the route who can give you up-to-date trail information.

INTERNATIONAL BICYCLE TOURING SOCIETY
846 Prospect St., La Jolla, Calif. 92037
This group, formed in 1964, is devoted to taking bicycle tours here and abroad, usually about 12 tours a year. Volunteers within the membership suggest tours after scouting them. These are passed on to the membership at large, and those who want to go sign up. Membership in the society is open to anyone 21 and over at $7 a year, which covers the costs for newsletters and leaflets. An easy-going group that's more interested in the joys and pleasures of riding than roughing it. Write for their brochure.

BIKECENTENNIAL 76
P.O. Box 1034, Missoula, Mont. 59801
In 1976, Bikecentennial completed work on the 4,326-mile Trans-America Bicycle Trail which follows pleasant and scenic roadways from the Atlantic coast of Virginia to the Pacific coast of Oregon. And now they're at work on four new trails that will provide another 10-20,000 miles through pleasant successions of farms, forests, pla-

TOURS

HIGH HORIZONS
Box 1166, Banff, Alberta, Canada
Offers two-week cycle tours for boys and girls, 12 to 18, in the Canadian Rockies. Tours include side trips for mountaineering and backpacking; sag wagon (to carry gear and stragglers) and meals provided, $180. Adult tours are also conducted.

THE WILDERNESS INSTITUTE
P.O. Box 338, Bonners Ferry, Idaho 83805
Among other activities they conduct one-week bicycle tours through Yellowstone National Park. You provide the bicycle, they provide camping equipment, cook the meals, and transport your gear.

Somehow the mention of hosteling conjures images of rosy-cheeked Bavarian adolescents clad in knee socks and lederhosen, bicycling en masse down a travel poster Swiss mountainside, framed by a background of picturesque villages and smiling peasants. As their bicycle spokes fade into the distance, an unseen accordion strikes up a tune as a cow moos, Tyroleans yodel, and edelweiss sways enticingly in the breeze. The image is one of such complete wholesomeness that even the Mary Poppinses among us are likely to choke a little.

But before you decide to leave this to your little sister and move on to skydiving, there's something you ought to know. While hosteling is partly a bicycling-in-the-countryside type of thing (and what's wrong with that?) it is also mountain climbing, backpacking, snowshoeing, downhill and cross-country skiing, canoeing, horseback riding, sailing, and anything else you can think of. It's going it alone or with a friend or in a group of energetic outdoor people who share your interests and attitudes. It's rafting down a river, working 18th-century style with a Mennonite farmer, or spending a summer in Europe or Asia far removed from the conventional hotels and tourist traps.

A brief look at the origins of hosteling might best explain it. It originated in 1909 in Germany, where a young elementary school teacher, Richard Schirrmann, wanted to get his students out of the city and into the country where they could experience the pleasures of open space and fresh air. At first the outings were no expense because the children hiked, thereby eliminating transportation fares. But when the outings expanded into overnight trips, lodging became a problem. The action was limited until the next year, when Schirrmann got permission to use several vacant rooms in a 12th-century castle in Westphalia which housed a museum. He converted the rooms into inexpensive dormitories for schoolchildren traveling in the area. Support grew as people donated furniture and even the use of their

---

GENERAL HOSTELING GEAR

Youth Hostel membership card.
Hostel handbook for whatever country you're traveling in.
Bicycle, canoe, horse, skis, hiking boots, etc., depending on how you plan to travel.
A sheet sleeping sack to keep hostel blankets clean.
Eating utensils—knife, fork, spoon, cup, plate, and dish towel.

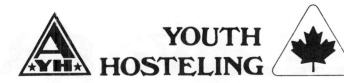

YOUTH HOSTELING

homes and barns for lodging the children. By the end of 1911 there were 17 of these "youth hostels" in Germany.

The idea spread. Other European countries established hostels, and in 1932 the first International Youth Hostel Conference was held in the Netherlands, setting up uniform standards for youth hostels and arranging for each country to honor the membership card of hostelers from every other country.

Today there are over 4,200 hostels in 47 countries, including parts of Asia, South America, Africa, and the Soviet Union.

With few exceptions youth hostels are open only to people traveling under their own steam—by bicycle, canoe, snowshoes, etc. Accommodations are quite simple, providing for only the basic needs. There are separate bunk rooms for men and women, bath and kitchen facilities, and some sort of communal recreation room. Some hostels maintain separate rooms for family groups traveling together.

Prices for an overnight stay range from 75¢ to $3, depending on the area.

From the beginning, the hosteling experience has been directed primarily at young people, but in recent years more and more people of all ages have joined in.

Membership costs vary with age: $5 if you are under 18 (Junior Membership) and $11 if you are 18 or older. Hostel rules and regulations as well as a listing of hostels by country are in a two-volume set published by AYH: *International Youth Hostel Handbook*. Volume 1, Europe: $2.45; Volume 2, Asia, Australia, Africa, and the Americas: $2.30.

Hosteling groups often take conducted tours to Europe and North Africa. These are supervised by a group leader, and you can save a good deal of money by taking advantage of them—for example, with charter air flight rates.

For more information contact:

AMERICAN YOUTH HOSTELS, INC.
National Campus, Delaplane, Va. 22025

CANADIAN YOUTH HOSTELS ASSOCIATION
National Office, 1406 West Broadway, Vancouver 9, B.C., Canada

---

Traveling With Your Bike

One of the best ways to double up on distance and cut time in half when traveling by bike is to combine it with some other form of transportation—car, bus, train or plane. Even if time isn't a problem, numerous new opportunities will flash on the imaginative cyclist who thinks in terms of packing a bike along. To wit: traffic hassles in large cities can be beat by car-carrying a bike to town, parking in a noncongested area, and pedaling in. Business or pleasure trips, where bringing a car is almost self-defeating (downtown New York), can be efficient and fun via bike, either by car-carrying it (as above) or by toting on a bus as luggage. International vacations, where budgets require a close watch (don't they all), have the stumper of how to work out a cheap, free-roaming means of transportation once you land. Bring your bike! It's easy, just think "bike" to get things rolling when you have transportation problems.

Expanding your thinking along these lines can bring innumerable, low-cost ideas. For example, Bill Marquardt, one of the contributors to *Traveling By Bike* (on previous page), gives a good insight as to how easy it really is to go all over, from state to state or country to country (U.S. to Mexico, Japan, England, etc.) by bike—plus hitchhiking, or some form of commercial transportation. The important thing to remember is that a bike will break down quickly to a small, convenient and light package which will fit the trunk of a car (even the back seat) or the baggage compartment of a bus, train or plane.

Hitching isn't too bad with a bike; useful when you run out of time, get tired or inclement weather blows up. A cyclist presents a different image than the run-of-the-mill hitcher. Motorists will stop just out of curiosity and usually provide a ride if it's not too difficult to stash the bike. Marquardt used an old sleeping bag in which to put his broken-down bike (no reference to quality). It provided protection for the bike and his benefactor's upholstery. Stopping for coffee and a

chat with a trucker at wayside stops is another means of getting a lift—sometimes. If they like your style, you've got a ride. Problem is only the independents can give rides.

Traveling by bus with a bike is much easier than several years ago. Greyhound will accept a bike at stations that operate a package express, provided it's crated to their specs. Marquardt would just stuff the two wheels and frame of his 22-lb. bike in the sleeping bag, and tell 'em it was part of his baggage—no problem. There's more than one way to skin a cat. However, if you're just planning to ship your bike (without you along), it would be better to crate it. For info on busing your bike, call the local bus station and speak to the baggage express agent. If the station doesn't have one, then ask 'em for the address of the general agent (general manager) so you can write a letter of inquiry as to the company's requirements. Rates run about $8 to $12 per 150 miles.

Railroads, in particular Amtrak, will accept a bike as extra baggage for a couple of bucks handling charge, or you can substitute it for a piece of the number of suitcases you're allowed. It will have to be packaged in a carton, though. Rail agents in some of the larger cities can provide a box at a nominal fee.

United, American, Eastern, Delta, and several of the other airlines will accept bikes as personal luggage at excess baggage fees of from $4 to $12 depending on the distance. In some cases the airline will supply a vinyl bag or carton, in others all you have to do is remove the pedals and secure the front wheel with shock cord. Best bet is to ring ahead of time and get the scoop. Incidentally, if they tell you they can't take it, but you know the plane is large enough to have the baggage space, you can demand that they handle it as air freight—costs a bit more than excess baggage.

vagabonding

Traveling is not something that all of us have the time or the means to indulge in, yet an increasing number of the young, and the not-so-young, have begun shouldering backpacks and heading out for places unknown.

Perhaps it is a form of escapism for many, but nonetheless, travelers seem to return from their ventures with a clearer understanding of what's happening in the world, and their own place in it. There is still the lure of adventure and for those who choose to look for it, adventure still exists, whether in the outbacks of New Guinea or simply in crossing the border from Persia to Afghanistan.

Travel, however, doesn't come without its problems, and for the novice they can be many. Once outside of the conducted tour and away from the tourist bureaus, a person must soon develop his own skills of survival and economy over the world's highways and travel routes.

Hopefully, the information following will smooth the way somewhat and lessen the burden of questions that the new traveler might be carrying.

PASSPORT and VISAS

The acquisition of a passport becomes one of the first requirements. This is easily done with a visit to the local post office in most communities. If the postmaster doesn't carry a supply of passport application forms, they can be obtained through one of the passport agencies located in major U.S. cities. The postmaster will have their addresses.

Once you have passport in hand it remains to have visas entered into it for the countries you will visit. Not all countries require visas. A trip through western Europe will leave the average passport unblemished. Some countries, like Mexico, will issue an individual Tourist Card rather than enter a visa into the passport. Travel agencies, airline offices, passport agencies and American Embassies abroad usually have a list of visa requirements on hand for all foreign countries. If a visa is needed, it can often be obtained through the country's embassy in Washington, D.C., or at one of its embassies in foreign capitals along your route. Do not, however, expect to get a visa at the country's frontier. Most often they will turn you around and head you back the way you came.

Next in line is a health card, called the International Certificate of Vaccination, which is usually obtainable through local state and community health clinics or hospitals. The number and type of inoculations you *might* need will be determined by the areas you plan to visit. The International Certificate of Vaccination should be stapled to the inside, last page of your passport (if you wear glasses, have the prescription entered in the health card, as you might need a new lens ground while traveling).

MONEY

The last requirement is to check money out of the bank. With today's inflation rate, it's best to check out more than you think you'll need. You should carry the greater portion of your money in the form of traveler's checks. Choose a company that's well known and has offices around the world. You might also check to see if these offices can be used as a forwarding address for your mail, en route. A supply of ten's and twenty's can be carried, with the rest in one-hundred-note checks which can be broken down later to smaller denominations at the issuing company's overseas offices. This keeps the checks less bulky to carry around in the pocket. Traveler's check numbers and the location of purchase should be recorded in two separate places, one of which might be your passport or health card. Very important, because the checks cannot be replaced when lost or stolen if you do not know the numbers.

Cashwise, about $5 worth of one-dollar bills should be carried to cover airport taxes and other miscellaneous small-change items that may come up. If you plan on dealing in a black market exchange (more on that later), bring along $50 and $100 bills in good condition for a better rate.

If you need to have money sent to you overseas, check local restrictions first on currency import. Some countries will not allow you to receive the money in U.S. dollars. What they do is change it into local currency which may be the next best thing to worthless. Bank drafts are usually the best form in which to transfer money. Have the sender work through a bank that has an agent bank in your present or projected location, and have a money draft made out to that bank for payment in U.S. dollars or traveler's checks. The American dollar may have suffered in recent years, but it is still the best recognized currency around the world.

Needless to say, your money, passport and health card should be kept with you at all times. Exceptions will be hotels in certain areas which need to keep your passport overnight to meet police regulations.

DOCUMENTS and PAPERS

Along with the foregoing, there are several other documents that are worth having along, too.

An International Student Identity card can save you piles of money in Europe and on the road to India. It is also gaining acceptance throughout the rest of the world for student discounts. There is no age limit, but one must be a registered full-time student to apply for the card and provide a 1½" x 1½" photo and two dollars with the application. The card is good for 15 months and provides discounts on railway systems through Europe to Indonesia, charter flights in Europe and admission fees to most museums and art galleries. For more info, see listing for the Council on International Education and Exchange.

For those who are not students, but would like to enjoy student discount rates, counterfeit but usable student I.D. cards are usually obtainable in major European cities and capitals along the Asian Highway at student meeting places. Try to compare the prospective card with a real one as close as possible before purchasing.

If you plan to utilize youth hostels along the way for accommodations, a card should be obtained through the American Youth Hostels, Inc., National Campus, Delaplane, Virginia 22025. There are two cards available: for those under 18, the cost is five dollars; for those 18 years and older, the cost is ten dollars. The cards are good for 15 months and come with a booklet listing all American youth hostels and information on foreign hostels.

For those who plan on doing some driving, an International Drivers License is a good thing to have. The American Automobile Association can help with obtaining this document and also provide maps and information on overseas driving conditions.

A few other items that can be brought along are a bankbook or letter from your bank that shows you have more money than immigrations police might choose to give you credit for. Also, if you plan to work along the way, and have a skill, try to bring something such as a union card or reference letter that says so on paper. It will make things much easier. Business cards and press cards can also be used to advantage at times if you can have them made up.

A large supply of passport-size photographs should be carried. Often the prints can be made cheaper once you're overseas, so it's worthwhile to ask for the negative from your first set. Some countries ask for as many as six passport photos with each visa application, so 30 to 50 pictures are considered a good supply for extensive traveling.

Maps and guidebooks would be the final items of paper needed on a journey (excepting pocket novels and a fair supply of T.P.). Good maps are produced by National Geographic (handy because they show towns having regular air service), Kummerly and Frey, Bartholomew & Sons, and Michelin. Government tourist offices sometimes provide maps of the surrounding area, though the quality is usually poor. Airlines are also a source of maps in a pinch.

BAGGAGE

Baggage is one thing that is almost always overdone by travelers. In the warmer areas of the world, one should be able to travel with nothing bigger than an ordinary airline flight bag.

Packs—backpacks—are good, but they lend themselves to too much stuffing: if something else will fit, you stuff it in, and before you know it the weight starts to get up there. Backpacks are also coming under fire from world immigration authorities who feel they brand the

bearer as economically destitute and, therefore, undesirable. On the other hand, a flight bag shows that the bearer is probably not staying long enough to worry about. The only advantage a pack will offer over a shoulder-strap flight bag is that it's a lot easier to tote if you really plan to do some remote-area hiking or hitchhiking. In the latter case, a pack seems to show a more honest need of a ride than a flight bag would, though the bag would probably be much easier to get into the car.

CLOTHES and GEAR

What do you need in the bag? Not much. Unisex fashions being what they are, a typical list might read like this:

> 2 pair good quality, but well worn-in jeans
> 2 light shirts
> 2 pair briefs
> 1 wool shirt or pullover
> 1 pair rubber sandals
> 1 light waterproof windbreaker
> 1 lightweight swimsuit
> 1 very light (1/16 in.) wool blanket (if not
> carrying a sleeping bag)

Plus, of course, you have the clothes on your back. Towels are impossible to carry if you're moving from day to day. You can use your shirt to dry with after a shower, then wash it along with your socks and underwear. If you've bought the right material, everything should be dry by the next morning. Needless to say, your clothes will get a workout in this manner, so select them for quality when purchasing.

After packing the clothes, there should still be plenty of room left over for a small toilet kit, sewing kit and medicine kit, along with other odds and ends. Incidentally, if you travel by air, the airline can often be a source of some handy articles. Many give out small sewing kits and toothbrush kits for the asking. There should be a few extra small bars of soap available in the lavatory. If your meal comes with plastic eating utensils, you might keep them for your next campout. The hostess will also provide a small supply of free writing paper and postcards, maybe even a pen. Some airlines even give out decent flight maps, which can be of some use.

Other items which can be brought along are a pair of fingernail clippers, a good quality pocketknife (corkscrew's handy, if traveling in wine country, also can opener) and, if you've packed the bag right, there should be room for an SLR camera and about 15 rolls of film (de-box your film and remember those airport x-ray units!).

Most of the foregoing items, or something similar, can be purchased en route, and often cheaper. A major exception is good quality shoes, which should be with you from the start. An inexpensive pair of suede desert boots with a black rubber sole should carry you in comfort for about a year. European hiking boots, with the waffle sole, sometimes prove to be too hot and heavy over the long haul for normal walking. The sole pattern also has a tendency to pick up mud (which can ruin a car ride for you) and small rocks (which make alot of noise at night).

Along with clothes and accessory items, you should also save a very small corner for important documents. Some can go in the bag, others should be carried on your person. Number one is your passport with the International Health Card, and right along side it, your cash. These three items should always be carried on your body. Some people make up a small sack from an old pocket and wear it around their neck. Others simply carry cash and passport in their pants pocket. If you choose the latter method, *don't* use rear pockets, and if you use the front pockets, expect a slightly bent passport out of the deal.

Once financial, political and health matters are out of the way, it remains only to buy your ticket. There is a well-known formula for traveling that balances time with money. The more time you have, the less money you will need; the less time you have, the more money you will need. If you have to travel fast, you will need to spend more money. If you can travel at your leisure, however, you can choose the cheapest forms of transportation.

AIR TRANSPORTATION

Air transportation is, in most cases, the quickest and most convenient method of getting from one place to another. It is also expensive. Many of the larger international carriers are members of the International Air Transport Association (IATA), which regulates prices between carriers so as to provide equal competition over world travel routes. This, in effect, sets the price of air tickets above what the most economical air carrier could provide. The disadvantage of high ticket costs, however, is somewhat offset by several advantages offered by IATA regulations. One of these is the mileage system.

Under the mileage system, passengers are allowed to stop off at cities between their departure and destination points as long as the total mileage between all stops does not exceed a set total. To provide equal competition between member carriers, the mileages are usually set at well over the normal straight line mileage. An example would be the maximum allotted mileage between Bangkok, Thailand, and Honolulu, Hawaii, of 8037 miles. Several carriers fly almost directly with only one or two stops between the two cities. Great if you're in a rush, but if you have the time, take another carrier and stop over, free of charge, in Saigon, Manila, Hong Kong, Taipei and Tokyo. The total mileage between all seven cities is only 7819 miles, well under the maximum allotted 8037 miles for the Bangkok-Honolulu ticket.

Another convenient item that IATA has established is the interchangeability of tickets between member airlines. Thus, if the Bangkok-Honolulu ticket were originally purchased from Pan American Airlines, it doesn't mean that you have to fly with Pan American. The ticket can be endorsed over to any other IATA carrier flying that route and, if you care to sample airlines, a different IATA carrier can be flown between each city. Needless to say, the airlines don't like seeing people do this as it cuts into their profits, but then again, they're the ones who drew up the regulations.

IATA airlines also offer savings on excursion fares, and military, clergy and youth rates (if you fit any of these categories). The excursion fares are round-trip packages usually with a time clause, such as a minimum and maximum stay period at your final destination. The savings on certain excursion fares can be substantial, so if you know exactly where you want to go and how long you want to stay, it would be worth checking into them.

One other interesting item IATA carriers have produced is the MCO or Miscellaneous Charges Order. This is a coupon which the airlines often give you as change or a refund for ticket overpayment. It's very similar in appearance to a normal airline ticket, and if payed for in cash, is usually redeemable for cash. Many travelers have found MCO's to be a good way of carrying "cash" and showing immigration personnel that they have a means of getting out of the country. Other less scrupulous travelers who are a little "short," have obtained $2 MCO's, moved the decimal point over two places, and used them to get past immigration officials. Needless to say, this act doesn't go over too well with the airlines people, or immigration, if you get pinched.

There are non-IATA carriers around and their numbers are growing. One of the main reasons is air transportation doesn't really have to be as expensive as IATA would like you to believe. One of the best known of the non-IATA airlines is Icelandic, which has offered low air fares across the North Atlantic for years. Not joining the IATA leaves the carrier free to set its own rates, and they're usually a good deal lower than competing IATA carriers. What's lost in the bargain, however, is the free interchangeability of tickets and the free list of stopovers. Non-IATA carriers are best utilized to carry you between two specific points, New York and Luxembourg are examples with Icelandic. Another non-IATA carrier across the Atlantic is International Air Bahamas, which flies between the Bahama Islands and Europe. AeroCondor, a non-IATA South American carrier, offers low fares out of Miami to Colombia and Caribbean points. Aerofloat, the world's largest airline, is steadfastly non-IATA and offers inexpensive flights between Europe and Southeast Asia. Other smaller non-IATA carriers around the world set their own prices depending on what the market will bear. South America has some of the cheapest flights available, but then you don't want to look at their airplanes too closely either...

Charter Flights

Several years ago, charter flights came on the North Atlantic scene en masse, and just about ran IATA carriers out of business. That, of course, didn't last too long. Today, though charter flights are still the cheapest way to go, costs have come up considerably and regulations have gotten more stringent. Two types of charters are presently run, the affinity charter (you have to be a member of a group or club six months in advance of departure) and the newer TGA charters. The latter is open to anyone and requires only that reservations and payment be completed 60 days in advance of departure. Several of the larger airlines have jumped on the charter bandwagon under this new system, and a fairly good selection of flights is now operated from both the east and west coasts to Europe and back. There are also several char-

ters to the Far East and South America that cater to a small market. However, almost all charters have one serious drawback—a mandatory return date—and it doesn't matter what predicament you happen to find yourself in at the time. Charter flight insurance is available to cover the cost of a regular fare ticket in the event you get caught, though. There are a limited number of one-way charters operated, but most are run for particular groups or are one-way Europe to the USA only. Many people end up on the streets trying to sell the unused portion of their return charter ticket. This is usually only possible if the prospective buyer is willing to assume the seller's identity for the duration of the flight, as most of the tickets are not legally transferable. Normally, however, there is little checking of identification on the charters.

Once in Europe, there are a large number of student organization-sponsored charters to European capitals and on to Asia, Africa and India. The Student Air Travel Association (SATA) should be contacted if you want more info on these, in care of Council on International Education Exchange (CIEE), 777 United Nations Plaza, New York, N.Y. 10017.

Private Aircraft

A final category of aircraft which might get the overinquisitive traveler out of a bind someday is: private, military, police and missionary planes. Normally they don't carry unauthorized personnel, but if you are caught out in the middle of nowhere, or have come down with something that may require hospitalization, they will sometimes take you aboard. Contact the police, military base or church ahead of time, if possible, to let them know what the problem is. Sometimes they may have only one plane servicing a wide area.

In the case of a private aircraft, it is simply a matter of catching the pilot or owner and explaining your tale of woe. In the United States and Europe, helping with the cost of gas will generally get you miles farther than the best of stories. In South America and parts of Asia, the military operates commercial flights that will accept passengers if space is available. An example is the Argentine Air Force, which operates a commercial service (L.A.D.E.) in southern Argentina that is cheaper than many of the local long-distance bus fares.

The **ABC** and **OAG Airline Guide** books. These books, each the size of a telephone directory, are published monthly with a single copy costing $7. They can be found in most of the larger libraries, and all travel agencies and airline offices. They are also carried on many airliners for use by the passengers. The guides contain listings for all commercially scheduled flights by major airlines in the world. Given is the time, day, cost, number of stopovers, and aircraft type and flight number. Listings are by city of departure or destination with maximum mileage figures usually shown. Also included in the books are currency conversion factors, lists of all airlines with addresses, airline timetables, baggage allowances, excursion fare information, flight itineraries and airport taxes. For the person who will be doing alot of flying, these books can save considerable time and money. Most airline offices or travel agencies will allow you to look through their copies.

SEA TRANSPORTATION

Liners

Over the past decade, ships have taken a terrible beating from the airplanes as far as transporting passengers is concerned. Today there are very few passenger liners left operating on regular routes. Most have either been sent to the scrap yards or rebuilt for cruising. If you can find a liner on your proposed routing, however, a sea voyage can be a beautiful way to travel.

Perhaps the best served route, and one that can still save you money over an air ticket, is the United Kingdom-Australia service. The route is served by six companies, two on a regular basis and four at irregular times of the year. The present voyage is operated via Cape Town, South Africa, on the outward leg and via Panama on the homeward journey. This may vary, however, depending on the company involved. Most American passengers board at Port Everglades, Florida,

Freighters

Ocean-going freighters for the most part are expensive. The better ships have accommodations for twelve passengers, but it's usually first class with a price to match. There is also a time problem with freighters, as their every movement is regulated by cargo. They may leave on time or they may leave several days later. They also have the nasty habit of anchoring offshore for several days when ports are crowded; passengers are expected to catch up on their reading during this period.

Freighters can and do, however, provide decent passenger-carrying service in several parts of the world. In the Pacific, they have managed to keep their fares close to those of the airlines on the West Coast-Japan route. There are also several good services operated down the coast of West Africa and from Europe and the United States to South America. In the South Pacific, a number of small cargo/passenger vessels keep the different island chains tied together. Papeete Harbor at Tahiti and Suva Harbor in the Fijian Islands are centers for this traffic. In the Caribbean area, the *S.S. Federal Maple* accepts both cabin and deck passengers on her island service between Jamaica and Trinidad. Ships of the Surinam Navigation Company provide limited passenger service between the Guianas and New Orleans.

The ABC Shipping Guide and the *Official Steamship Guide International*. Like the airline guides, these two books are standard travel agency references and are published on a monthly basis. Inside are listed most world shipping lines that deal in passenger traffic. Listings are carried by company but are cross-referenced with ports of the world and by the individual ships operated. As passenger liners have been withdrawn from service, the two volumes have shrunk some but the rapidly growing cruise market is building them back up. Fares are listed when possible but for many of the lines you will have to write directly to the company for the latest prices. Both volumes handle liners as well as passenger-carrying freighters. Ferry systems and some river-boat schedules are also covered. Of the two guides, the *ABC*, published in England, is by far the best but most American travel agencies subscribe to the *International* guide.

or in the Canal Zone, Panama. Several of the liners also stop at Acapulco, Mexico, but Mexican port taxes are extremely high and best avoided.

Several lines operate in the Northern Pacific area (Orient Overseas Lines, Pacific Far East Lines, Royal Viking Lines), but they are all first class and offer little for the budget traveler except high costs. P&O Lines, a British company, does have several sailings a year calling at Pacific ports on its Australia-U.K. service. The cost to Australia or the United Kingdom is roughly $700 to $800.

The east and west coasts of South America are connected to Europe by the services of Italia Lines, Costa Lines and Yabbara Lines. The west coast service is operated by Italia and connects Valparaiso and ports north to the Canary Islands, Spain and Italy. The east coast services call at Buenos Aires and Rio de Janeiro and return to Europe via the Canary Islands. There is no regularly operating line between South America and Africa. The closest available is a stop at the Canary Islands where a local Spanish line connects to the African mainland.

Several liners still operate across the North Atlantic connecting New York with European ports, but their costs are, for the most part, prohibitive. An exception are the Polish and Russian vessels which sail to Canadian ports from the Baltic Sea and vice versa. Fares are generally around $300 to $400, and the voyages are often uncomfortable because of rough weather.

The Indian Ocean presently offers the richest grounds for low-cost sea transportation. The Shipping Corporation of India offers a regular service between Mombasa, Kenya, and Bombay, India, with a stop usually made in the Seychelles Islands. Onward services are available from Bombay into the Persian Gulf and Red Sea areas. From the port of Madras on India's east coast there are scheduled services operated by Indian and Malaysian liners on to Penang and Singapore. At Singapore connections can be made southward to Indonesia and Australia, northward to Bangkok and Hong Kong, and eastward to Borneo. Deck passage is available on some of the ships, but this type of accommodation is rapidly being closed to Europeans because of their high complaint rate. Indonesian ships have by far the hardest decks and worst food, but they are also among the cheapest. Thai ships feature some of the best food afloat, but their routes are usually limited to the Thailand coast.

Riverboats

Coastwise and river traffic also offer opportunities for low-cost travel. There are regular coastwise mailboat services operated every day of the year along the Norwegian coast from Bergen to Kirkenes well above the Arctic Circle. A slightly less frequent service is operated along the Alaskan and Canadian coastlines by a system of car ferries. A similar car ferry service is operated in the Baltic and North Sea areas connecting Scandinavia with mainland Europe. Iceland, Greenland and the Spitsbergen Islands are also connected to Europe by seasonal shipping services.

River boats operate up the Amazon River from Belem as far as Pucallpa and Yurimaguas in Peru on the South American continent. The trip can take anywhere from a month to half a year, depending on connections. River-boat services are also operated on many of the larger rivers of Brazil plus the Orinoco River in Venezuela, the Mamore River in Bolivia and the Parana River in Argentina. On the African continent, river services are operated on sectors of the Nile, Congo, Niger and Gambia, and also on Lakes Tanganyika, Nyasa and Victoria. You are expected to put up with some discomforts on river boats—limited space, cramped cabins, bad food, stinking toilets, rats and mosquitoes, to name a few. There are river trips of shorter duration available in Burma, Thailand, India and Bangladesh. River trips of higher cost are available in the United States and Europe.

Hitching Your Way

Hitchhiking on the high seas still offers a few possibilities. American tuna clippers and shrimp boats will sometimes give American nationals a ride home in exchange for some rust scraping and paint work. This is particularly true of boats headed back to the USA for dry-docking. The South American Pacific coast ports, the Panama Canal Zone, Mexico's east coast ports and French Guiana are good bets for finding a ride home. If you're hoping to get to another country, however, most captains don't want the hassle with immigrations that it would take to land you. Private yachts are also a possibility for a "work your way" passage. Most yachts leave the United States fully crewed, but some suffer a drop-out rate by the time they reach Panama or Tahiti, thus these are good areas to try and hitch a ride. Other places in the world to stand with your thumb out would be the Canary Islands, South Africa and Australia. The Caribbean Islands see a lot of yachts, but most of these boats are not going very far. If you're game to sign on, pin a note up in the local yacht club giving your destination, experience and a phone number or address where you can be contacted. If you can contact the captain or a member of the crew directly, so much the better. Just remember that yachts take a long time to reach their destination (which might turn out to be different from yours) and that they provide a cramped space in which to get along with others you may or may not take a liking to.

Working Your Way

Finding "working" passage on larger ships is extremely hard nowadays. Unions and national hiring policies have largely put an end to what was at one time a cheap way to see the world. A freighter may occasionally take on a replacement crew member in a foreign port, but usually they are looking for experienced, skilled sailors or engineers. If you have a hankering for the sea, though, the best ships to try are those flying flags of convenience (Liberian, Panamanian, etc.) or Scandinavian vessels. Try to get on board and talk directly with the captain. If this is impossible, check with local shipping agents, consulates and seamens missions or service clubs. Every so often a ship that has been sold to new owners will take on a one-shot crew to ferry her to a new operating area. In this case, they will sign on whoever is available. Ship brokerage firms will know of recent sales and may contact the new owners for you, this is particularly true in northern European ports.

For those who would choose maritime employment as a career, the picture is pretty dark right now. A Merchant Mariner's Document must be obtained from the U.S. Coast Guard for employment on U.S. commercial vessels. As anyone who has tried knows, the Coast Guard won't give you the time of day, unless you first have a job, and no one will give you a job without first having the Document—"Catch-22" with only two parts.

A better possibility is to contact the Military Sea Transport Service (MSTS) in Brooklyn, Oakland, Seattle or New Orleans and see if they won't take your application. In this manner, the Coast Guard will issue you a Document as long as you are on MSTS roles. Even with your card, however, the unions will still put your name at the bottom of the list and charge you for doing so, usually around $40 every three months. Union dues, once you are in, are high and jobs very few and far between.

A much better bet, nowadays, is to pick up a skill in navigation, radio communications, marine engineering or cooking and try your luck on foreign flag ships. Many of these vessels do have a need for trained personnel and will take you on. Conditions aboard and wages, however, may be much lower than U.S. flag vessels.

LAND TRANSPORTATION

Land transportation is naturally much more varied than flying through the skies or cutting through the waves. The choice can run from a ride on the Orient Express to camel-backing it across the Sahara Desert.

Train

Trains are still the chief means of transportation in much of Europe, India and Japan. Most other areas of the world, however, have come to rely on the bus or private motorcars.

If you plan on traveling by train, always check beforehand on discounts offered for students, youth, and such. These are not always advertised in many Eastern countries. Student discounts are available in Indonesia, India, Pakistan, Iran, Turkey and most of Europe. The European discounts are obtainable through offices of the International Student Travel Conference (info through CIEE) and apply only to certain trains operated between major European cities. In the Middle East and Asia, the railway Station Master must be contacted and he will refer you on to the department issuing the discount. The Interna-

Rack section on the Zugspitze Railway, Bavaria.

tional Student Identity Card (available through CIEE) should be carried when applying for these discounts, which range from 20% to 50% off the normal fare.

Seasonal and time discounts are available on Canadian trains and certain U.S. Amtrak operations. In South Africa, you can ride in the caboose of a freight train with a second-class ticket. India is clamping down on "ticketless travelers" of European lineage and "out of class" passengers, so make sure you have a ticket and are in the correct class. Excuses are referred to the head office *after* you've paid the fine.

Bus

Buses now cover just about every navigable road in the world, and for the seasoned traveler, they've almost become a second home. Buses are usually the cheapest and most regularly run form of transportation, though far from the safest. World travelers can often trace their most terrified moments back to a bus trip through the Andes or along the hairpin turns of Turkey's narrow roads. There is little you can do in such a situation other than try to sit as close to an exit door as possible—and pray. In the higher mountains, it helps not to look down.

Seat reservations are available on most buses around the world now, unless you're picking it up alongside the road. If you have baggage going atop the bus or in a compartment, remove all valuable items, and be sure to have thread along to sew up knife slashes... It's not that bad on all bus lines, but it does happen. Bus stations are also a meeting place for snatch-and-run thieves. While you're occupied buying a ticket or searching for your bus, you present an easy target for the would-be thief. Make it plainly evident to bystanders that you're watching your belongings *at all times.* They'll be watching you for several minutes before they strike. Bogota, Colombia, presently claims the highest number of rip-offs in this type of business.

Bus excursion tickets exist in North America, Europe, Australia and South America. Check with the bus lines in these areas and see if their requirements—usually 30 days unlimited travel—meet your situation. The South American system is new and several companies don't seem to know they are involved in the program, so try to stick with the larger operators. In the United States, both Greyhound and Trailways feature 15-day, 30-day and longer excursion tickets. Several Australian companies, such as Greyhound and Pioneer, do the same. It's often cheaper to buy these tickets outside the country.

Truck

Trucks with very hard benches usually take over from the buses when the terrain starts getting rugged. You find this in the remote Andes and the Himalayas, also in Africa and some sections of the Middle East. Usually there are no reservations and sometimes no seat.

Trucks seldom run under any safety requirements, and ninety-nine times out of a hundred are way overloaded. Psyche yourself up to jump from the moving vehicle quickly should it appear that the brakes are going or the driver has gone asleep. It happens many times out in the "developing World" and your only protection is to keep alert...Hitchhiking trucks is possible, but the drivers usually expect a fee or tip. Several good trucking routes are the Tan-Zam Highway in East Africa, the Asian Highway from Europe to Teheran, and the central Australian routes.

Automobile

If you are going to travel overseas with your own auto, van, bus or motorcycle, you'll need a *carnet de passage* for most countries, plus insurance and proper licensing. The American Automobile Association can be contacted for full information on most requirements.

The Pan-American Highway is passable from Fairbanks, Alaska, to

Pan American Highway in Costa Rica. (From: *Central America* by Cliff Cross)

Ushuaia, Tierra del Fuego, Chile, with a sea trip necessary between Panama and either Buenaventura or Cartagena, Colombia. Most of the highway is now paved except for stretches in Canada, Panama, Ecuador and Argentina. Over these sections it is best to have headlights, windshields, gasoline tanks and brake lines protected from flying rocks. If you hitchhike these sections, stay well off the road itself when vehicles pass, as the rocks start to fly.

The route through Europe and on across the Middle East to India has now become well established, and most of the road is in passable shape. The worst section is found in eastern Turkey, which has been severely potholed due to increase of truck traffic into Teheran. Afghanistan now has some of the best highway on the route thanks to recent construction efforts. Political hassles can be more of a problem along the road to India than the highway itself. Because of the large traffic in drugs through the area, it's not out of the ordinary for a vehicle to be gone through completely and drilled or cut up just to satisfy local customs men. For those who have forgotten to bring along the proper papers, there is a large parking lot at the Pakistan border full of vehicles for which there was no *carnet de passage.* A similar lot exists in Bombay close to the wharf for vehicles being shipped into India by sea.

Africa can now be transited by motor vehicle north to south and east to west. The roads and the politics, however, are worse than in any other area. The Sahara is crossed through Algeria to Niamey in Niger on a fairly decent road, though it should only be transited during the winter months. The western road through Mauritania is for the adventurous and well-equipped only. Cars shipped into Dakar, Senegal (there is a car ferry from France) must proceed by train to Mali, as there is no road connecting the two countries. Once in Mali, however, there are several trans-Africa routes to choose from. Michelin road maps can point out the better features of each. The road on into East Africa proceeds through the Central African Republic and on through the northern Congo into Uganda. Once in Uganda, good paved roads exist into Kenya and graded roads push south through Tanzania to connect with the American-built Tan-Zam Highway to Lusaka in Zambia. Here a connection can be made with the Rhodesia-South Africa road system, providing the border is open. Again, politics manage to provide more roadblocks to travel in these areas than the roads themselves. In central Africa it is not uncommon to wait for several days at a border or be sent back 1500 miles for an official signature. The only defense for these situations is alot of patience and alot of time.

From Africa, vehicles can be shipped to India from the port of Mombasa in Kenya and from Durban in South Africa on to Fremantle

in Australia. Onwards from India cars can be shipped from the port of Madras in southern India to Penang, Malaysia, where road connections exist northward to Bangkok and Laos and southward to Singapore. There is no overland route through Burma at the present time. To complete a journey around the world in this manner calls for a very long and expensive voyage by ship across the Pacific. Several lines accept vehicles from Bangkok or Singapore to the United States or Panama.

Of the vehicles used in this type of expedition, one of the most successful has been the small French Citren *Deux Cheval* pickup model which can be made to sleep two people. It takes plenty of punishment, is simply made, light and very good on gas mileage. The VW bus model is the most popular form of vehicle for long trips, however, because of its roominess and economy. They are somewhat expensive to ship, though. American-made pickup campers and mobile homes are now being seen down the Pan-American Highway and on through South America, as parts are easily available in most South American countries. They are expensive vehicles to run, however, and the proper gasoline is not always available.

Four-wheel drive vehicles are rarely needed unless one plans to challenge particularly rough terrain. For a straight road trip, they are nothing but extra weight. A light vehicle equipped with a length of heavy nylon rope can usually travel about anywhere. If the car gets stuck a second vehicle can get it out with the rubber-band effect of the nylon rope.

Camel

Mentioned earlier were camels across the Sahara. They're still out there, but the old camel routes are becoming fewer and fewer. They still exist in central Niger and northern Mali, however. Camels are also used in the remote sections of Afghanistan and Pakistan. If you plan to ride animals for any distance, try to get to know them beforehand. They have their likes and dislikes, one of which may be you. Most often you will have to purchase the animal and then resell it after you've reached your destination. This means you should know something about appraising animals, otherwise you might be stuck with a lemon.

Donkeys and horses are used widely in Latin America to get into the mountain regions. Colombia and Argentina are made for horseback riding. Don't try to climb on a llama in Peru or Bolivia, though—they can't take it; besides, they bite. Travel by horseback may be the up-and-coming way to tour the world, as lately several crossings of the USA have been done in this manner. If you contemplate such a long trip on an animal, and will cross international borders, be sure to get a firm clearance from immigration and health authorities along the way.

Bicycle

Touring by bike is becoming popular. You should research your route and build yourself up physically before attempting a long overland trip, however. If it's going to be an overseas trip, choose a bike frame that will fit into an aircraft luggage compartment, you may want to fly back. Some countries now want to see a *carnet de passage* for a bike. Check along your route for this or you may be walking part of the distance.

Hitchhiking

Hitchhiking private cars is possible any place you can find traffic moving. The idea may not have come to the area yet, but you can always be the first with a new thing. Needless to say, not all areas of the world are equally endowed with a surplus of motor vehicles, so it stands that hitching is best where there are a lot of cars. South Africa, Australia and New Zealand stand high on the hitchhiker's honor roll, as do Canada, the USA and most of Europe. Other areas in the world where hitchhiking is gaining popularity are Malaysia, Japan, Mexico, Argentina, Brazil, and portions of North and East Africa. In other regions there are just not enough private cars, though again, if you can find just one you've got a chance.

If you plan on hitching quite a bit, try to keep your baggage at a minimum. Outside the United States, compact cars are the rule and a large backpack can be a hard item to squeeze in. If you're going through rather remote areas, or even tackling the Autobahns, keep a bit of food and water with you. Also make sure you have protection against the elements in case the weather should change suddenly.

Keep a map of your route with you and wear a good pair of shoes. Hitchhiking always seems to entail a lot of walking. Most drivers report that they like to see a person with a sign showing where they're headed—and a smile! After that, all it takes is time and a driver with a heart (usually a past hitchhiker himself).

Walking

Traveling by foot brings us down to the last category of land transportation. Several people have completed journeys around the world this way. All one needs is a good pair of boots, strong legs and lots of time. Hiking trails in the USA, Europe and Nepal become crowded during the summer seasons now, so make sure you don't mind crowds when you start off for the Mt. Everest base camp or the Sierra Nevada crest trail. Finland is being discovered as a nice area for flatland hiking in truly beautiful remote locations. Yugoslavia also offers some nice trails at higher elevations.

If you plan to tackle high altitude climbs, make sure you know what's involved and who you're going with. A large number of novice climbers have been falling off the Andes Mountains or coming down with bad cases of frostbite over the last few years. This holds true for the Himalaya range and southern Chile, also. Weather conditions can change in a few hours on the mountains and many people go unprepared for it.

GETTING AROUND

Once you've found yourself at your destination, or perhaps just a place you've taken a fancy to, there are several things that always present themselves.

One is language. Luckily, English is a more widely understood language than many people realize, largely because of the former British Empire and the present American tourist industry. In the Americas, English is found in many tourist areas south of the border. Most Caribbean Island populations speak English as do the residents of Guyana on the north coast of South America. Tucked in just below Mexico is the English-speaking nation of British Honduras, and you will find that most black people who have settled on the east coast of Central America speak English. Many Panamanians understand and speak English, as do many of the residents of southern Argentina. The second language of the Philippines is English, as it is for Malaysia, Singapore, Hong Kong, Burma, Bangladesh, India, Ceylon, Nepal, Pakistan and the West African nations of Nigeria, Ghana, Liberia, Sierra Leone, Gambia and the western Cameroons. Many people in East Africa speak English from South Africa northward to Egypt, as do many people of the Middle East. In Europe, English has become the standard language of tourism and is a second language in most Scandinavian countries.

What happens if you're not in one of these areas? A picture is worth a thousand words—draw one with your hands, and in most cases you will be understood. If a direct translation is needed, there is usually someone at a major airlines office who will speak English, as is the case for many tourist offices.

Outside of English, Spanish and French become the two great travel languages of the world. Spanish can take one through most of Latin America while French comes into play through large parts of Africa and island groups in the South Pacific and the Caribbean, not to mention the two home countries in Europe.

If you plan to spend some time in either of these geographical areas, it would be of benefit to take a course in the language before starting out. Pronunciation is the key element. Once this is mastered, it will be easy to add words to your vocabulary while traveling. Even a slight understanding of the language will open up many doors of friendship...

Money is another problem to be reckoned with while traveling. It takes a bit of thinking to keep your conversions straight when changing money or buying goods with a foreign currency. To compound problems, in the Middle East many countries use Arabic numbers on the coinage and notes. Several major airlines and some banks publish small conversion charts which can be handy as long as they're up-to-date. *Newsweek* magazine also publishes major world conversion rates in each of its weekly issues.

Money is best carried in the form of traveler's checks issued by a well-known company, and valued to American dollars. Banks will give the best exchange value when cashed. Once you have a foreign currency, try to keep track of what it represents in U.S. dollars or you may be overspending. It is sometimes difficult to change back

certain foreign currencies that may be weak on the world market, so change only small amounts at a time and be prepared to collect a souvenir bag of foreign coins. If you plan to spend down to the last dime, check beforehand on any departure or port taxes that may be levied at the last minute. Also, remember local bank holidays.

Bargaining is a way of life in most areas outside of North America and Europe. If it scares you at first, back off and watch for awhile before trying to make a purchase. It's usually not too hard to get the drift of things and see how much money changes hands for a given item. For most local food goods, there will be a set daily rate; but for tourist items, the first price may be ten times what the seller can eventually be talked down to. Plan on buying late in the day, or just before you leave, for the best prices. If the price you offer is too low (and it should be), and it's not accepted at first (which it won't be), leave. You'll more than likely be called back. If not, you can come back later and up your original price, if you really want the item.

There are many other social customs which go beyond bargaining and should be watched for and understood. Eating and passing food or any other transaction such as shaking hands is done only with the *right* hand in many areas of the world, particularly the Middle East and Africa.

Mosques and temples (Buddhist, Hindu and others) should be entered fully clothed, but with bare feet, and only upon invitation, unless it is understood that the building is open to the public. There may be other restrictions on females as to areas that can be entered. Statues should not be climbed on, especially statues of Buddha in Asia. A number of people have been thrown in jail in Thailand because they wished to have their pictures taken while nestled in the arms of Buddha.

In certain areas of the world people do not like to have their pictures taken, while in other areas they might swarm to a camera. It's best to ask people before taking their picture; but as any photographer knows, the best picture is a candid shot—just make sure you have good camera insurance, in case it doesn't work.

To clean your plate or not clean your plate may also be a problem in some regions. In South America, leaving food on the plate or a half-empty bottle is considered a sign of status and even the poorest of people will do it. Yet, in another place it might be seen as a sign of contempt for the cook. In parts of Asia, leaving a clean plate means you are still hungry and your plate will be refilled. To stop the supply of food, you are forced to leave food on the plate. It may get confusing, but you quickly pick up the local customs; if not, you end up with a swollen stomach.

Health matters can usually be taken care of by local doctors or clinics. If there is an emergency, it's a good idea to contact the nearest U.S. embassy for their advice. The embassy should also be contacted if you become involved in legal problems. As for running out of money, they can do little to help, other than wire your family in the States and request that funds be forwarded. Embassies also no longer handle traveler's mail. You are referred to **Poste Restante** (General Delivery) at the local post office. Poste Restante c/o the local post office can be used as a mailing address just about anywhere in the world. Problem is it's not always the best, but it's always there. Several of the traveler's check firms will accept user's mail, but many are now starting to charge a "search fee" for locating letters in their mail room. Transportation companies can also be used, as can banks if you are doing business with them. If people will be writing to you, inform them that *aerograms* are much cheaper to send than letters, and also less likely to be pilfered. As for banks, keep in mind that post offices and embassies (foreign and U.S.) will be closed on local holidays as well as Sundays, and in Muslim countries, on Fridays. Embassies may also close on their own national holidays.

Once the necessities are taken care of, you are free to see what the country looks like. If a local tourist office exists, it's always the best place to head for. They'll normally have piles of information and maps, and they will most likely speak your language. Many tourist departments, such as that of India, operate inexpensive tours of which you may want to take advantage. They can also provide information on local public transportation and accommodation prices. If you are planning to visit a remote area, the tourist department may be able to help you organize the expedition through other government departments.

Travel agencies are also helpful, but they exist mainly to sell tickets, tours and rooms. Giving out free information provides them with little revenue, unless there's the chance you might buy. For long-distance transportation, however, they can save you money by having volumes of recent and accurate information available on air carriers and shipping lines.

For the true explorer, there are areas of the world which hold mysteries not yet fully answered. The Andes may still hide another "Machu Picchu." There may be other "lost tribes" in the Philippines or Indian villages yet uncontacted in the jungles of Brazil. The vast expanses of the Sahara, Central Australia and Saudi Arabia's "Empty Quarter" may still hold secrets yet undiscovered. Even areas of the earth that have been previously explored remain to be gone over by the specialist with modern methods and a fine-toothed comb. Many newly independent countries need people who can help rediscover historical areas and lost cultural artifacts or help organize new museums for populations which are becoming more aware of their cultural heritage. Exploration projects cost money, but it may be that if your idea has merit and will assist the host country, you will receive government assistance. In any case, movement to a remote area of any country should be done with the prior consent of the host government.

FOOD and HEALTH

Food and good health are very important on a long trip. If you're sick, you won't enjoy a trip of any kind.

A change from normal eating habits and new types of food usually give most people a slight case of diarrhea, normally during the second week of a trip. This is the same when coming back to old eating habits after a long trip overseas.

Food is generally very cheap once outside the U.S. and Europe. Even expensive Singapore has street-side stalls where a filling Chinese dish can be had for under a dollar. India and surrounding countries have possibly the cheapest food in the world, though it doesn't always measure up to European palates. The hotter (heat, not *picante*) a food, usually the safer it is to eat. Stay away from food that has sat for any length of time. Raw fruit and vegetables are to be avoided unless you buy them yourself and do the skinning, even then make sure your own hands are clean. The culprit in most cases of diarrhea is usually water, therefore, try to stick with bottled liquids as much as possible or treat your own water and carry it with you.

Overeating can cause problems when you travel. The food may be cheap but it's best to eat in moderation. This is especially true if you're changing altitudes in mountain regions.

Vitamins are a good bet, as many areas can offer only a meal of starch in the form of potatoes or rice, but don't depend too much on them. Proper eating can keep your health problems to a minimum.

Hepatitis drags many travelers down each year. Guard against it as much as possible by watching what you eat and drink. If you come down with a case of diarrhea or dysentery, the local remedy may be better against the local germ than your imported pills; check with the local hospital or health department.

Infection must be watched for, especially in the tropics where even a pimple can give you trouble if not properly cared for. Also guard against injuries to your feet, which means wearing good walking shoes and clean socks rather than sandals or bare feet. It's hard to envision, but if something happens to your feet, you can't move.

Get inoculations at health centers and have them properly recorded on an International Health Card. Get all shots that might be related to the areas you plan to travel through. You may run into local health crews who want to give everyone on the bus an inoculation against something. This is usually done with the same needle for everyone, so impress upon them that you already have been inoculated.

A small medical kit can be carried along, though most things are readily available overseas. But aspirin, Band-Aids and prophylactics against malaria, diarrhea, stomach upset and the possible results of illicit sex should be carried. If you have forgotten anything, German travelers always seem to carry a wealth of medical supplies, so you might check with them.

ACCOMMODATIONS

If you're on the road, you have to have a place to hole up for the night, even if it's only ground space for your sleeping bag or a park bench. The particular route you're traveling and the amount of money you have to spend will largely determine where you do this.

If you choose to carry a sleeping bag you should plan on using it at least four nights out of every week otherwise it's probably not paying its way. A $15 bag will do for hostels, but for camping out

you'll need something in the neighborhood of $50 to $85 to have a bag that's both light and warm. Between the latitudes of the Tropic of Cancer and the Tropic of Capricorn only a light sleeping bag will be needed unless you plan on traveling in the mountains.

North America and Central Africa are perhaps the hardest regions in the world to find cheap accommodations. Europe has loads of cheap hotels in the south, and youth hostels or "sleep-ins" in the north. If you're going to use the hostels or sleep-ins, travel with a light sleeping bag or "sheet-bag"; otherwise, you may not be allowed to stay. Hostels are generally running around $2 to $3 in northern Europe now. Hotels have skyrocketed well over the five-dollar mark for the cheapest of rooms.

European campgrounds, which are usually located on the outskirts of town, may still charge you a price not far off that of a hostel. Many of the northern European capitals such as Amsterdam and Copenhagen now have an accommodation program for traveling youth (youth is just about everyone) during the summer months. Information on them can be obtained at the main railway stations or tourist offices. Paris and London can still be a little difficult in the field of accommodations, but something will usually turn up. Hotel and pension prices in southern Europe are low enough to warrant a night's stay inside rather than sleeping on the ground.

Youth hostels are found in many areas of the world besides Europe and are usually the cheapest means of accommodations available. Their chief drawbacks are a long list of regulations (no drinking, no smoking, no sleeping with someone else...) and their locations, which are invariably a long ways from the city center. A Youth Hostel card may or may not be needed for entrance, depending on the country and management.

The road to India has seen a large number of "hippie hotels" started up in the past few years. They begin at the Bosphorus and extend all the way across to the Orient. Most are located close to bus stops or railway stations, most have small restaurants that serve somewhat westernized food, most have small urchins that can show you their location, and most have signs on all the doors warning against drug smoking. They are also fairly cheap, and excellent sources of information for your onward trip.

Once in India, the country is loaded with cheap places to stay. In the larger cities, the YMCA's and Salvation Army Hostels have become focal points for a growing number of small inexpensive hotels. In the smaller towns, there are usually cheap hotels around the railway stations and government-run tourist bungalows and rest houses near popular tourist sights. Most railway stations also contain retirement rooms where one can hole up overnight (you must have an onward railway ticket and pay about one dollar).

Southeast Asia now has its own set of hippie hotels which are quite luxurious compared to the ones along the Asian Highway. The price, however, has gone up to the $3 and $4 range at some of them. Bangkok has several of these hotels and there are a few in Malaysia. Singapore has sadly done away with its youth hostels in an attempt to stem the flow of unkempt youth from its shores. There are, however, several underground hostels still operating. They publish no address, but their location is usually well known by travelers in the area. Prices in a crowded, shared room still average above three dollars a day. There is a local YMCA and several Chinese hotels in the $4 to $5 range. Hong Kong has a similar arrangement with the hostel addresses being advertised through small business cards and in the paper. The YMCA and Salvation Army also operate hostels in Hong Kong with prices only a few steps below those in Singapore.

Down through Indonesia accommodations again become inexpensive with the exception of Jakarta, where the cheapest beds are found on Djaksa Street several blocks behind the U.S. Embassy. Through the rest of Indonesia, small rooms in locally operated "Losmans" are available for a few dollars. In Bali, the rates drop even lower with good double rooms available for $1.25 per person.

Once in Australia, the prices for accommodations are high. A sleeping bag can come in very handy in the rural areas (which means most of the country). In the cities, the YMCA's and YWCA's plus the Salvation Army run places called "Peoples Palace," which offer the cheapest accommodations. But even these are well into the five-dollar range and up, unless there's a dormitory available.

In Japan, there is an excellent Youth Hostel program with hostels in just about every section of the country. The main tourist offices will have maps available giving their location and price range. These are not exactly cheap unless you've already priced a Japanese hotel...

Taiwan has a limited number of small hostels located throughout the country, but many are not shown on the map. Local students, however, can help you out with accommodations or tell you whom to contact. Overnight sleeping is usually allowed in the local bus stations.

Korea has a good selection of small inexpensive hotels, but they're hard to find for the foreigner. The police can usually direct you to their location and bargain the price for you. Korean universities will also take in travelers at times, especially if you can teach a few lessons of English. Korean people are very friendly and will often invite you into their home for the night if it is at all within their power.

Latin America is filled with inexpensive hotels and pensions from the Mexican border to Tierra del Fuego. They come in a wide range of price and cleanliness, however. The cheapest are right around a dollar and the sheets are changed every month. A good quality room can usually be had for around three dollars. Bed bugs are not unknown in the cheaper establishments, so make a good search before you call it a night. Most are transparent in color and can't be seen until they've sucked up half a pint of blood, so it's best to let them bite for awhile so you can find 'em.

Africa does not offer a cheap line of hotels, except for countries north of the Sahara. Southern Africa and Rhodesia both have YMCA's and the Salvation Army hostels, but through most of central Africa there is little in the offering. Several countries in East Africa have migrant hostels, which travelers can use. These are usually nothing more than buildings with floors and walls, so bring a sleeping bag. Police stations will allow you to use their facilities in many locations (this is true worldwide). Churches are also a good bet, as are overseas aid organizations such as the Peace Corps. If they can't put you up, they'll often know of the cheapest place in town. Africans are friendly people, and if you find yourself stuck, they'll try their best to help you out.

In the countryside there are always places to sleep, just remember the weather can change. Nothing will wake you up quicker or soggier than an overnight rain shower. If you intend to sleep in the open, choose a location away from roads and water. Never opt for a location if there is the *slimmest* chance that a motor vehicle may drive over it during the night. If the land is privately owned, it's a good idea to ask for permission to camp before laying out your things. It will save you some worry and the owner some buckshot.

In cities things are rougher but there are still places you can find a night's rest. Buildings under construction are possibilities, just remember that you should not be seen entering or leaving them. Also be careful of open shafts and scaffolding. School yards, church yards and graveyards are other possibilities. It is best to look a location over well during the day, then come back late at night and leave very early in the morning. Dogs can become a frustration, because once they pick you up in the wind they'll bark through the rest of the night. Parked vehicles can sometimes be used if checked out carefully. Buses are the best bet here and sometimes the driver will allow you to sleep in the bus while it's parked overnight.

If, for some reason, you find yourself without sleeping bag or hotel room, try airport, bus and railway waiting rooms. In larger cities, especially in Europe, they're open all night and you can choose your bench. If this is not possible, it's best to refer yourself to the local police station. If you don't, someone else probably will...

AOG Travel Planner & Hotel/Motel Guide. Another interesting book found in most travel agencies. It contains, among other things, a list of all motels and hotels in the United States, a list of United States colleges and universities, a list of military bases, diagrams of major U.S. airports, city maps and tourist board locations. For the international traveler, the book's main asset is a visa guide listing requirements for most foreign countries. Also contained are international airline route maps and nonstop air mileages.

EMPLOYMENT

Work is not something every overseas traveler looks for; but for some, it's one of the experiences of traveling, for others, an urgent necessity.

There is very little high-paying work available to the average traveler in overseas locations. You'll come across oil men, construction workers and executives making fabulous sums, but your chances of getting into the same pay bracket are practically nil. U.S. companies working overseas have a limit placed on them by the host country as to the number of U.S. nationals they may employ. Most companies choose their U.S. personnel for overseas operations by how much experience they've had within the company, not how much traveling they may have done. Construction and oil firms employ only highly qualified and experienced workmen on their overseas projects, and these people are usually unionized.

If you have a sellable skill such as mechanics, secretarial, medical, etc., you have a decent chance of coming across work somewhere in your travels. If you are unskilled, there will be very little available. Even for the skilled, pay scales are usually far lower than American rates for work overseas. For this reason, if it's simply money you're after, it is far better to work a couple extra weeks in the States at a decent wage than to slave away overseas for 50¢ an hour.

There are five countries in the world outside the United States where work is fairly easy to find, and pay scales are similar to U.S. levels. These are Canada, Australia, New Zealand, South Africa (including S.W. Africa) and Rhodesia. If you can work one or two of these countries into your travel route, there's a good chance you'll be able to earn enough to keep you going. There is also the chance of finding decent paying jobs in Northern Europe and Japan, but openings will be far fewer, and there will usually be a language problem.

You can work any place in the world without a work visa—as long as you're not caught. If the government does find out, they have the option of throwing you out of the country or in jail. For most countries, work visas are just too much of a hassle to obtain, unless you plan on working there for a good while. In that case, you're better off getting one.

The best way to find work overseas is to go there and search for it. There's very little you'll find by letter writing from the United States. If you do have a skill, you'll soon know where the best places are to look for work. Overseas aid missions and development organizations sometimes will take on people who show up on their doorstep with a needed skill. You've already taken care of the transportation, so all they have to do is pay you a wage, a cheaper way to go for them than to fly someone over from the States.

If you feel like working overseas more for the experience than the money, and don't fancy looking for a job, there are several organizations that will find you work for a fee. Most of the employment is in Europe and most of the work calls for little skill or experience. Pay usually averages around $200 to $400 per month with room and board sometimes included. The most trusted organization presently providing this type of employment service is the Council on International Educational Exchange, 777 United Nations Plaza, New York, N.Y. 10017. There are other agencies, good and bad, most of which have their addresses posted on U.S. college campuses. Their rates for finding you a job can be very high and a few have been known to take the money, but not supply the job, so check out the agency involved before you send them money, especially organizations located overseas.

In Europe, farm work openings are often posted in locations where youth or students hang out, such as on university campuses or at hostels. The tourist offices may also have leads on this type of work. It's popular with students, and usually available in surplus to the demand through the late summer months.

European employment offices can also be carefully examined for employment possibilities.

International voluntary agencies can provide longer stays overseas for people who have two years to commit. The Peace Corps program is well known, but there are also several other agencies that place people overseas. Even with the Peace Corps, however, skill becomes a prime requirement. Most organizations supply transportation, living allowances, readjustment allowances, housing and medical care for accepted volunteers. For people who wish to go into overseas work as a career, successful completion of a voluntary overseas assignment may open many doors. The following is a list of organizations that accept applications for overseas voluntary assignments:

Peace Corps/Vista
Action
Washington, D.C. 20525

Church World Service
475 Riverside Drive
New York, N.Y. 10001

International Voluntary Service
1555 Connecticut Ave., N.W.
Washington, D.C. 20036

V.I.D. Inc.
Box 4543
Stanford, Calif. 94305

American Friends Service Committee
160 North 15th St.
Philadelphia, Pa. 19102

Mennonite Central Committee
Box M
Akron, Pa. 17501

Service Civil International
P.O. Box A 3036
Chicago, Ill. 60690

Jesuit Volunteer Corps
P.O. Box 3928
Portland, Oreg. 97208

A very good reference book for U.S. and overseas voluntary work is *Invest Yourself,* available from the Commission on Voluntary Service and Action, 475 Riverside Drive, Rm. 665, New York, N.Y. 10027 for $1.25.

Outside of honest labor, several ways still remain to keep yourself above water while traveling.

Any country that has weak currency or overstringent customs regulations is usually a target for smuggling. It's not a trade to be taken up lightly, but if you feel a taste for illegal adventure, the opportunity is always there. A lot of people are making better than average wages working dope, gold, diamonds, precious stones, currency and antiques across international borders. If you would just like to dabble a bit, however, it's best to stick with minor transactions on the black market and the scotch and cigarette trade.

The countries of India, Ceylon, Bangladesh and Burma presently lend themselves best to minor smuggling transactions. All have a black market rate for currency, though it has rapidly diminished in India over the last few years. Your best exchange rates will be found in the streets, but your safest exchanges will be found in small shops. If there's any market at all, you, as a foreigner, will be approached by prospective dealers. Large bills in the range of $50 to $100 usually bring a better rate than $10's and $20's. Before you start to deal, you should understand what the local rate is and whom you're dealing with. If you're at all unsure, it's best to change legally at a bank or tourist office.

Scotch and cigarettes bring good profits in both India and Burma, cigarettes seeming to have a higher value in Burma and scotch more in India. Stick to well-known brands, Johnny Walker in scotch and 555's or Benson and Hedges in smokes. If you're coming in by air, you can buy the goods on the aircraft or at the departure airport's duty-free shop. You will be met on arrival by eager buyers—don't take the first price offered.

A few other countries in the world, such as Chile in South America and Guinea in Africa, also offer themselves to black marketing, but the authorities are much more unsympathetic, so it's best to keep on the up-and-up or know exactly with whom you are dealing.

If you have totally exhausted all other means of finance, there exists in several countries the possibility of selling some of your bodily fluid. Kuwait and several other Middle East nations have been known to pay good prices for blood, as has Greece. There may now, however, be a surplus over demand, so it is advisable to check with the local hospitals before planning your next meal.

A person with imagination should be able to come up with several means of making a small bundle while traveling. Americans are known to be decent salesmen and good organizers. Once you're in an area you like, look around, there's probably a way to make money that none of the natives have yet thought of.

sources of information

TRAVEL

Travel Agencies

Nearly every city in America has some sort of travel agency. Most of the better ones belong to ASTA, The American Society of Travel Agents, 360 Lexington Ave., New York, N.Y. 10017. With 10,200 members, this is the largest association of travel agents in the world. You can write them for recommendations on what travel agencies to see in your area.

INTERNATIONAL LEAGUE OF COMMERCIAL TRAVELERS & AGENTS
Stauffacherstrasse 66, CH-3000 Bernel, Switzerland
A commercial travelers' organization with a membership of over 200,000. Provides advice on contacts with foreign companies, assistance in obtaining overseas business representation, and legal aid in the event of conflicts with foreign countries.

INTOURIST
45 East 49th St., New York, N.Y. 10017
This is the official Soviet travel bureau, and their booklet, *Visiting the USSR,* is a must. Travel in the Soviet Union is considerably different from bumming around Western Europe. All stops, visits, and such are tightly programmed, and there are no provisions for the visitor to do a little independent sightseeing. If you're planning a visit to Mother Russia, start preparing well in advance of the departure date. Your itinerary has to be approved, lengths of stay in cities okayed, and the whole travel schedule given a stamp before your visa will be issued.

THOS. COOK & SON
587 Fifth Ave., New York, N.Y. 10020
Cook's is probably the best-known name in travel. A "Cook's tour" has even become part of the language. This British-based firm is the world's largest travel agency, with over 400 offices throughout the world. It has an international reputation as tour leaders although it provides a full range of travel services. Free literature.

AMERICAN EXPRESS
65 Broadway, New York, N.Y. 10006
Offices in most of the world's major cities. It provides mail pick-up service for users of its traveler's checks or credit cards. Despite advertised claims, the checks aren't as good as cash in some areas of Latin America—a lot safer, though. The American Express Credit Card is the most universally accepted of all credit card plans. Write for the booklet, *American Express Services and Offices.*

CAHILL-LAUGHLIN TOURS, INC.
655 Madison Ave., New York, N.Y. 10021
Specialists in African travel. Conducted tours or individual plans are available. Free literature from the above address.

SANBORN'S, Mexican Insurance Service
P.O. Box 1210, McAllen, Texas 78501
For the first-time traveler to Mexico, Sanborn's is a must. While not technically a travel agency, its services just about qualify the company as one. Not only will Sanborn's give you a good shake (it never oversells), but it provides you with the finest and most detailed route instructions and maps available. Dan Sanborn has personally driven every major Mexican highway and meticulously recorded every bump, turn and switchback. He is also candid in describing restaurants, gas stations and hotels. If he doesn't like them, he says so—and you can rely on his advice. One of the very best travel services to be found anywhere in the world. Very highly recommended; offices in all major border-crossing cities. Write for Dan's free *Mexico Travel Aid and Trip-Planner.*

Travel Organizations

Travel organizations are a comparatively recent phenomenon. Basically, they consist of groups of people of somewhat similar interests who are able to use their collective buying power to travel at reduced rates. In addition, these organizations offer social activities and discount prices on a wide variety of goods and services. The advantages of group purchase are the savings earned by chartering an airplane and minimal-fee use of club-owned facilities.

CLUB INTERNATIONALE
2233 Wisconsin Ave., Washington, D.C. 20007
The club is the largest in the United States, with a membership of over 25,000. Three foreign vacations are paid for in 36 monthly savings installments of $35 a person. At the end of the first and second years, members have the choice of eight- to ten-day trips to Jamaica, Puerto Rico, the Bahamas, Acapulco, Aruba, or Bermuda or a cruise through the Caribbean. Third-year choices are several 20-day grand European vacations. Year-round social activities take place at local clubs. Membership is $30 annually for three years, and there is the monthly $35 savings deposit (for the trips). Membership brochure on request.

CLUB MEDITERRANEE
516 Fifth Ave., New York, N.Y. 10036
This Paris-based club has the largest world-wide membership of any.

At last report 700,000 members were enrolled, 17,000 of them Americans. The club maintains 47 low-cost vacation villages in 13 countries. Although travel is involved in reaching these spas, the club is essentially geared for vacationing at the club-owned sites rather than actually traveling. Information available.

FOUR WINDS TRAVEL, INC.
175 Fifth Ave., New York, N.Y. 10010
Expensive, fully escorted trips to nearly every spot in the world (Timbuktu: 22 days in Central and West Africa, $1295 plus charter flight costs). They offer the usual club benefits, discounts, and so forth. Free information from them at the above address.

ADVENTURE TRAVEL CLUB
O'Hare International Airport, AMF Box 66182, Chicago, Ill. 60666
Club members receive discounts at selected hotels or motels and on car rentals, plus information sheets (passports, currency, etc.). One trip monthly. Annual membership runs $10 for an individual and $15 for individual and spouse and includes a subscription to the club bulletin issued ten times a year.

MATTERHORN SPORTS CLUB
500 Fifth Ave., New York, N.Y. 10036
This group, as the name indicates, is more sports-oriented than the other organizations. It tends to center its travel activities on skiing, mountain climbing, skin diving, sailing and the like. It attracts the younger and more athletic types, has lots of social activities, and offers discount prices on a wide variety of items.

CHALET CLUB
135 East 55th St., New York, N.Y. 10022
This outdoor adventure sports club, founded in 1954, is one of the most active in the nation. It has managed Honduras rafting trips, has a strenuous program of weekly skiing, and backpacking events (depending on the season), flies balloons, parachutes, skin-dives, and has even promoted an Antarctic expedition. Definitely not for the faint of heart or unsound of body. Membership literature available.

LINBLAD TRAVEL, INC.
133 East 55th St., New York, N.Y. 10022
Linblad tours feature the unusual—trans-Saharan Land Rover expeditions, cruises to Antarctica, trips to the Soviet Union in the winter, and the like; some itineraries change each year. Our informants (and a rather negative article in *Playboy*) tell us the tours aren't without their foul-ups, though it's probably natural considering the offbeat routes. Linblad's expeditions are relatively expensive. For example, the five-week trans-Saharan camping tour of 3100 miles costs $3000. Free illustrated literature is available.

COUNCIL ON INTERNATIONAL EDUCATIONAL EXCHANGE
777 United Nations Plaza, New York, N.Y. 10017
Over 165 North American colleges, universities, secondary schools and various educational organizations participate in this student-exchange program. Basically, it means that you go to a foreign country and a foreign student comes here. There is a wide variety of programs—summer study, hostel trips, work camps, voluntary service and just plain traveling. The council is an affiliate service of the United Nations and promotes the international exchange of ideas, possibly in the hope that understanding the other guy's problems might make wars a little less likely. Its booklet, *Taking Off,* is available from the above address. The council has also written a very fine travel manual called *Whole World Handbook.* The book is reviewed a bit further on under Books.

DRIVING

AMERICAN AUTOMOBILE ASSOCIATION (AAA)
World Wide Travel Service
8111 Gatehouse Rd., Falls Church, Va. 22042
Good source of automotive travel information including guidebooks and maps. Also a source for the International Driving Permit (IDP). Your U.S. driver's license is good in most European countries, but there are a few that require an IDP to back it up. Even in countries where it's not required, the IDP is a handy identification card. You can apply for it at the above address or at any AAA office in most major cities. For info on requirements for the IDP, check with the above address.

LANGUAGES

The long-standing bugaboo of foreign travel has been the language barrier. In recent years, this has become less of a problem because of the enormous diffusion of American, Canadian and English tourists. There are still many places where English isn't spoken, though generally they tend to be the most interesting—and the most frustrating. Learning at least a smattering of the language is not only helpful but also establishes a rapport with the natives. It really isn't as hard as it may sound. The availability of language records, tapes and simplified manuals that dispense with the intricacies of grammar and structure have made learning a foreign language relatively painless.

DOVER PUBLICATIONS, INC.
LISTEN & LEARN
RECORD SETS

These record sets have been designed specifically to meet the needs of travel and everyday life abroad as well as for class-room or home study use. Each set contains 3 12" 33⅓ records—about 90 minutes of recorded speech—prepared and spoken by eminent native speakers who are professors at Columbia, New York University, Queens College, University of Michigan, etc. Check these unusual features: (a) Dual language recording, over 800 selected foreign language sentences and phrases (over 3200 words); English is spoken first, then followed by the foreign language equivalent, which is followed by a pause sufficient for you to repeat the foreign language. (b) Practicality: no time wasted on dead wood, archaic forms, literary forms; emphasis, instead, is on living material that you can really use. (c) Modernity: the words you really need and are not likely to be in dictionaries. (d) 128- to 256-page manual containing everything on the records, both English and foreign, with phonetic transcriptions you read at sight, pronunciation guides, miscellaneous information, and in many cases extensive lists of important subsidiary vocabulary. (e) Unusual bracketing system enables you to substitute words and enlarge course. (f) Completely indexed. (g) High fidelity recording. (h) Money-back guarantee. Few other sets permit you to return sets if you are not satisfied with them.

"Excellent . . . among the very best on the market," Mario Pei, Columbia U.

Each set contains three 12" 33⅓ records, manual, album. **$9.95 each.**

Sets with **EG** contain "Essential Grammar" for language.

LISTEN AND LEARN FRENCH[EG]	98875-9
LISTEN AND LEARN SPANISH (AMERICAN)[EG]	98876-7
LISTEN AND LEARN ITALIAN[EG]	98887-2
LISTEN AND LEARN PORTUGUESE (EUROPEAN)[EG]	98881-3
LISTEN AND LEARN MODERN GREEK	98882-1
LISTEN AND LEARN MODERN HEBREW	98883-X
LISTEN AND LEARN JAPANESE[EG]	98880-5
LISTEN AND LEARN RUSSIAN	98879-1
LISTEN AND LEARN GERMAN[EG]	98878-3
LISTEN AND LEARN SWEDISH	98884-8

DOVER PUBLICATIONS
180 Varick St., New York, N.Y. 10014

Dover has a good deal for the aspiring linguist. They sell records and books for 25 different languages, including Swahili and Esperanto, all at a very modest cost. For example, French consists of three records and a follow-along book for $10. Dover also publishes excellent texts without the records, a phrase book of 100 useful sentences, and dictionaries and other learning aids. Request the catalog of language learning aids.

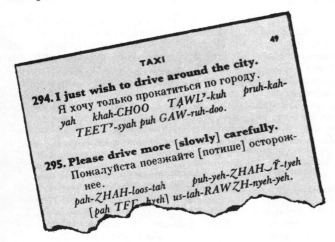

"SAY IT" PHRASE BOOKS

The original "Say It" phrase books that have helped hundreds of thousands of travelers and students. Each book contains more than 1000 useful phrases and sentences of modern language. Check features of this helpful travel aid: everything immediately useful to modern American needs; convenient pocket size (3½ x 5¼); sewnbound for years of hard use; large, clear type; phonetic transcription you can read at sight; lists of numbers, traffic signs, foods, etc.

Available for:

22026-5 ARABIC	20809-5 PORTUGUESE
20818-4 DANISH	20810-9 RUSSIAN
20817-6 DUTCH	20811-7 SPANISH
20820-6 ESPERANTO	20812-5 SWEDISH
20803-6 FRENCH	20821-4 TURKISH
20804-4 GERMAN	20815-X YIDDISH
20813-3 GREEK	20802-8 ENGLISH for Spanish-
20805-2 HEBREW	speaking people
20806-0 ITALIAN	20801-X ENGLISH for German-
20807-9 JAPANESE	speaking people
20814-1 NORWEGIAN	20816-8 ENGLISH for Italian-
20808-7 POLISH	speaking people

HARIAN PUBLICATIONS
Greenlawn, N.Y. 11740

These people primarily publish travel guides and books; however, they have produced a 12-inch long-play record and a 32-page vest-pocket reminder of 700 words that you'll get some good use of for only $2.95. This neat package is available for Spanish, French, German and Italian. If you really want to astound the natives, you can buy all four records for $10.

Superintendent of Documents
U.S. GOVERNMENT PRINTING OFFICE
Washington, D.C. 20402

Another inexpensive source of "quick" language books is the United States government. Order the following army guides from the above address and remember to use the catalog number given.

Spanish, D 101:11:30-300, 40¢
German, D 101:11:30-306, 35¢
Norwegian, D 101:11:30-310, 45¢
Swedish, D 101:11:30-312, 45¢
Japanese, D 101:11:30-341, 35¢
Korean, D 101:11:30-342, 40¢
Greek, D 101:11:30-350, 35¢

These inexpensive booklets were originally issued to servicemen stationed in those countries and are pretty easy to use. All of the phrases are spelled out phonetically.

The really inexpensive route is the local library. A lot of libraries will lend foreign language records for a week or two.

The more thorough and really professional approach is an intensive course at a language school. The two best-known names in the business are Berlitz and Cortina. Cortina has been in business since 1882. Costs are in the range of $200 to $300, but the training is really excellent. Cortina also has home-study courses.

BERLITZ SCHOOL OF LANGUAGE
Rockefeller Center, 40 West 51st St., New York, N.Y. 10020

CORTINA SCHOOL OF LANGUAGE
136 West 52nd St., New York, N.Y. 10020

There are branches of these two schools in many major cities.

____PERIODICALS

Travel periodicals published in the United States are, for the most part, geared to vacationers and tend to lean heavily on the "glamor" spots like Puerto Vallarta and the like. Filled with splashy color pictures and some breezy writing, they're fun to browse through but fall a little short of the mark when it comes to the nuts and bolts of international travel. There is one travel publication, however, that does really dig in—*The Joyer Report...*

THE JOYER REPORT
Dick Joyer, Ed.
Monthly - $12/yr.

This monthly is a newsletter crammed full of really useful travel tips, and unlike so many guidebooks that are out-of-date when issued, *The Joyer Report* is current. Included in the newsletter are items like how to go around the world for $1075, how to see 100 European cities for $88, clubs that offer charter flight membership, and a South American vacation for only $225. All subscriptions are fully guaranteed, and if you don't like the report, Dick Joyer will immediately refund your money.
From: The Joyer Report, Box 707, Corona del Mar, Calif. 92625

AMERICAS
Monthly - $10/yr.

The official publication of the Organization of American States. A good periodical for general background information on Latin America. A very slick magazine printed in three editions—English, Spanish, and Portuguese. Very good photos and stories ranging from archaeology to the contemporary culture of Latin America.
From: Americas, Pan American Union, Washington, D.C. 20006

HOLIDAY
Bimonthly - $7/yr.

Lots of color and some interesting material. Mainly geared to the vacationer with at least an upper-middle-class income.
From: Holiday, 1100 Waterway Blvd., Indianapolis, Ind. 46202

NATIONAL GEOGRAPHIC
Monthly - $10/yr.

The granddaddy of all travel magazines. Anyone who has never seen the *National Geographic* has never been to a doctor or dentist in his life. Beautiful reproductions and lots of really outstanding material. Membership in the society brings little goodies like maps of all kinds every few months: for example, the National Geographic archaeological map of Mesoamerica, which is more accurate than Mexican government maps.
From: National Geographic, 17th & M Sts., N.W., Washington, D.C. 20036

Other periodicals

TRAVEL
Monthly - $7/yr.
From: Travel, Travel Bldg., Floral Park, N.Y. 11001

BOOKS

VAGABONDING

One glance at the travel section of your local library will give you an idea of how vast as assortment of travel material is available. Row after row of guides, reminiscences, adventures, diatribes, humor, history, and lots and lots of hogwash.

One popular guidebook suggests turning right on Mexican Highway 15, marker 918, for a trip to sunny San Blas. If anyone did that, he'd find himself up to his ears in jungle—there isn't a road there. Another advises great caution while traversing a crooked, narrow, and badly-paved stretch of mountainous highway. The book was published in 1972, and there has been a four-lane freeway over those "treacherous" mountains for six years. One erstwhile guide to Mexico contained a "how-to-speak-Spanish" section. Among the useful phrases were "At what time do I pay the ticket taker of the oncoming trolley?" and "At what time does the shooting of grouse commence?"

We have tried to limit our book section to those guides and publications that have stood the test of time and reliability. We don't say that there aren't other great books; we just know that these are reliable.

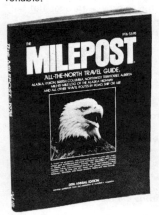

THE MILEPOST
1977 - 666 p. il. (incl. fold-out map) - $2.95

The cover says it's a "must" for all Northland travelers, and for once, we agree with the blurb. This is a handsome and fact-filled guide for northwestern Canada and Alaska. For Alaska Highway travelers, it will take you mile-by-mile in meticulous detail. Really one of the best guidebooks we've seen.
From: Alaska Northwest Pub. Co., Box 4-EEE, Anchorage, Alaska 99509

WHOLE WORLD HANDBOOK
Marjorie Cohen and Margaret E. Sherman
1977 - 367 p. - $2.95 (pb)

Published in conjunction with the Council on International Education Exchange, the **Whole World Handbook** attempts to be to travel what the **Whole Earth Catalog** is to everything else. As a travel guide, the book still has a way to go, but for the student who plans to work or study abroad, the book will have some real value. Study programs and work camps are listed by country or region. Most of the educational programs listed are U.S.-sponsored, thus university credit is assured. Also dealt with are overseas employment, transportation, eating and sleeping, visa requirements and a wealth of addresses. As the title states, the whole world is covered.

WORK   GERMANY
The Regulations
The Zentralstelle fur Arbeitsvermittlung (ZAV), 6000 Frankfurt (Main), Feuerbachstrasse 42, the official government labor agency, places U.S. and Canadian students in summer jobs throughout Germany. If you are interested in a summer job in Germany, you may apply to the ZAV through CIEE. In order to be eligible, you must be at least 18 years old, have a good command of German (how good depends on the individual job), and agree to work for at least two months. Work is available in agriculture, industry, hotels and restaurants, homes for the aged, and as chambermaids or kitchen helpers in hospitals and sanatoriums. There is no fee for this service. Write to CIEE for applications.

From: Simon and Schuster, Inc., 630 Fifth Ave., New York, N.Y. 10020

ARTHUR FROMMER TRAVEL GUIDES ($10 a Day Series)
Arthur Frommer

Frommer's $10 a Day Series cover principally lodging and meals, as opposed to transportation, though he does go into pointers on saving money on air fares in the front part of his books. Descriptions of everything from hotels to hostels to dorms are covered in detail with prices, services and the best way to take advantage of them: "The cheapest rooms in Vienna (Austria) are provided by the *Stadherberge Esterhazypark*...This...is an old air-raid bunker used for the protection of Nazi officials during wartime raids by the Allies. It has since been converted into a unique hostel (for which no hostel card is needed), and offers single rooms for 44 schillings ($2.64), which includes a continental breakfast." Complete addresses, directions, and if you get lost, phone numbers, too, are given to the lodgings listed. Descriptions are excellent.

In addition to lodgings and meals, Frommer also covers the more touristy things such as sightseeing, tours, and so forth. If you're planning a trip to any of the following countries or continents, it'd be worth your while to have the appropriate copy of the $10 a Day Series in hand: Europe, England, Greece, Hawaii, India, Ireland, Israel, Mexico and Guatemala, New Zealand, Scandinavia, South America, Spain and Morocco, Turkey. Just about all the books of the series run $3.95 each.
From: Arthur Frommer, Inc., 70 Fifth Ave., New York, N.Y. 10011

AIR TRAVEL & CHARTER FLIGHT HANDBOOK
Jens Jurgen
1973 - $4.95

The most complete book ever written on the in's and out's of air travel. Though the price of the book is abnormally high, it contains information which could easily save the reader hundreds of dollars. How to get the maximum number of stopovers per ticket, how to save money through special excursions rates, how to get the airlines to pay your hotel bill for a night, all are covered in this book, and much, much more. Sadly many of the prices and some of the information is now out-of-date, but hopefully a revised copy will be brought out in the near future.
From: Travel Information Bureau, P.O. Box 105, Kings Park, N.Y. 11754

TODAY'S OUTSTANDING BUYS IN FREIGHTER TRAVEL
Norman Ford
1976 - 176 p. il. - $3.95

Travel by freighter, like travel by passenger liner, has diminished rapidly over the last five years. For most companies, the added expense and time involved in catering to passengers is simply no longer worth the time. Ford's guide, however, lists which lines still carry a limited number of passengers on their cargo vessels. Listings are covered by regions of departure and are cross-referenced with ports and the shipping companies involved. Itineraries are given as well as price, and a brief description of the service and the ships involved. There are a few bargains but most freighters now cater only to the rich and retired.
From: Harian Pubs., Greenlawn, L.I., N.Y. 11740

LET'S GO: EUROPE
Harvard Student Agencies, Inc.
1976 - 300 p. - $4.95 (pb)

The standard student guide to Europe and North Africa. *Let's Go* is one of the few student guides that has been kept up-to-date yearly, and that's probably the reason for much of its success. Besides covering the essentials of transportation, visas, currencies and other odds and ends, the guide deals with traveling through each country of Europe, the places to see and problems that might present themselves along the way. It lists hotels, hostels and camping grounds; tourist offices and student agencies; and it usually has the latest information on transportation back to the USA and on over the Bosphorus to India. It has become a bulky book, but if you don't think you can use certain sections, tear them out.
From: Harvard Student Agencies, Inc., 4 Holyoke St., Cambridge, Mass. 02138

STUDENT GUIDE TO ASIA
Australian Union of Students
David Jenkins
1974 - 340 p. - $2.95

Australians have been traveling the road up through Asia to Europe for years, thus they're well qualified to publish one of its first guides. Unfortunately, the *Student Guide to Asia* went to print just as inflation began to sweep the world leaving many of its stated prices now far out of line. Nevertheless, it probably is the best guide for the budget traveler going through the Orient and on westward to Afghanistan. The Student Union has recently come up with several smaller guides dealing with Singapore/Malaysia and Thailand/Laos, which should update much of the information in the *Student Guide to Asia*.
From: Australian Union of Students, Travel Dept., 220 Faraday St., Carlton, Melbourne, Australia 3053

OVERLAND TO INDIA AND BEYOND - $2.40

A mimeographed publication which is constantly updated and crammed with information on the overland routes to the Middle East, India and onward to Australia. It is constantly fed new facts by travelers just off the road so it remains as one of the most up-to-date publications on travel anywhere. Securing the latest copy may be somewhat of a problem, but inquiries to the London office are usually answered with the help of a return envelope and international postal coupons. The organization also puts out a shorter work on Africa called *Overland Through Africa* and it, like the India version, is continually updated.
From: B.I.T. Information & Help Service, 146 Great Western Rd., London W II England, U.K.

OVERSEAS JOBS: THE TEN BEST COUNTRIES
Curtis W. Casewit
1972 - 222 p. - $1.50 (pb)

Though this one is a bit dated, we've included it 'cause we haven't run across any newer book of this type, and it really has some good info. The ten best countries are: Australia, Canada, Israel, Germany, Mexico, Switzerland, Italy, Sweden, England and France. In the introduction, Casewit gives you an insight as to what's involved in getting a foreign job. Discussed are finding a job, preparing a résumé, letters of application, passports and citizenship, and U.S. tax obligations. Next comes a country-by-country rundown. Coverage starts out with what the country has to offer socially, politically, laborwise, cost of living, and so forth. Then, methods of securing employment, case histories, problems to expect, miscellaneous tips, and a good number of addresses to write. Damn good book!
From: Warner Books, Inc., 315 Park Ave. So., New York, N.Y. 10010

INVEST YOURSELF - $1

A small book, but well worth the price for anyone who is interested in working as a volunteer in domestic and overseas development programs and work camps. A new issue is published each year by CVSA listing hundreds of opportunities to help with projects in the U.S. and around the world.
From: Commission on Voluntary Service and Action (CVSA), 475 Riverside Dr., Rm. 665, New York, N.Y. 10027

FODOR'S GUIDES
Eugene Fodor, Ed.

The Fodor Guide Series has, at last count, 27 books on foreign countries. In addition to his single country publications, Fodor also has a comprehensive guide to Europe and special guides to Austria, Belgium and Luxembourg, Czechoslovakia, France, Germany, Great Britain, Greece, the Netherlands, Hungary, India, Ireland, Israel, Italy, Japan and East Asia, Morocco, Portugal, Scandinavia, South America, Spain, Switzerland, Turkey, and Yugoslavia. Believe it or not, there are even more, but they cover travel in North America and Hawaii. Most of the European guides are in the $9 to $12 range, and though they may seem a bit expensive, they're big books and a tremendous amount of effort has gone into each one. Rather than trying personally to cover every inch of the area the book encompasses, Fodor has assigned recognized experts from the countries described and lets them tell you about their native lands. Good editing and good writing; factual and entertaining. Incidentally, if you don't mind using a Fodor Guide that's a year or two old, Marboro Books, 131 Varick Street, New York, N.Y. 10013, often has them for a couple of bucks. So do most used books stores.
From: McKay Publishing, 750 Third Ave., New York, N.Y. 10017

HOW TO TRAVEL WITHOUT BEING RICH
Norman D. Ford
1976 - 176 p. - $2.95 (pb)

If you want an overview of the transportation possibilities—car, bus, rail, steamer and plane—for moving around the Americas, Caribbean, Europe, Asia and Africa as cheaply as possible, then by all means pick up Ford's book. Frankly, for the price, it's one of the best deals in travel literature going. Ford's forte is to save coins by traveling the trade routes of the world. "For when you travel on vehicles and ships operated by concerns which cater principally to freight or nontourist travel, such as freighter companies and railroads, river steamers and ferries, and even ordinary buses, your fare is subject to the same influences as are the grain, wool, frozen meat and—in many cases—the *working* people you travel with." That means less cost, which to most of us vagabonding types means a lot more than conveniences and on-the-dot timetables. Emphasis is more on the Americas (Central and South) and the Caribbean than across the pond, which means more details on sideline trips off the trade routes. Ford's book is definitely recommended as a first purchase if you've been thinking about traveling—anywhere.
From: Harian Pubs., Greenlawn, L.I., N.Y. 11740

VAGABONDING IN EUROPE AND NORTH AFRICA
Ed Buryn
1973 - 243 p. il. - $6.95

Ed says tourism is nothing unless you get involved...go as a wayfarer, he says, open to all experience. Don't go just to see things, but to encounter your fellow man and to get your life into rhythm with other styles. We think Ed Buryn has captured the essential spirit of vagabonding. Maybe we call it exploring, but it's the same. "The age of discovery is never over if you are the discoverer," he says. Ed's book is the best going. His quick, easy style kindles enthusiasm. Primarily an exposition of options, suggestions, possibilities, the book stays away from "what to see, where to go" writing. Instead, Ed concentrates on meeting Europeans, hitchhiking techniques, travel hassles, equipment, modes of travel, finding a place to sleep. Take it from us, this is the book to read first.
From: Random House, 201 East 50th St., New York, N.Y. 10022

TRAVEL QUESTIONS: MEXICO
Mexican National Tourist Council
70 p. il. - free

This little booklet is undoubtedly the best thing the Mexican government has ever put out. No tourist baloney, just hard and straight material. A short introduction, a few historical and geographical items and the rest of the book is devoted to answering just about any question a first-time visitor to Mexico could ask. It's worth more to the traveler than most "guides" to Mexico.
From: Mexican Nat. Tourist Council, 405 Park Ave., New York, N.Y. 10022

MOTORING IN MEXICO
Pan American Union
1967 - 57 p. il. - 25¢

Another goodie. Extremely detailed, step-by-step guide to Mexico's major highways, complete with maps. If you get lost with this, you probably should take up knitting instead of traveling.
From: Pan American Union, Sales & Promotion Div., Washington, D.C. 20006

LATIN AMERICAN TRAVEL GUIDE/PAN AMERICAN HIGHWAY GUIDE
Ernst A. Jahn
1976 - $7.95 (pb) plus 40¢ shipping

We have it on good authority (a couple who drove a motor home clear to the tip of South America) that this book was invaluable to them. Prepared in cooperation with the Pan American Union and the American Automobile Association, this guide is a wealth of information to auto travel in Mexico, Central and South America. It's not a description of tourist attractions, but a compilation of invaluable facts and figures pertaining to visa and vaccination requirements; currency exchange rates; climatic conditions; hotels and restaurants; car rentals; banks; banking and business hours; legal holidays; travel bureaus; communications and telex data; weights and measures conversion tables; electric current and measuring systems; insurance facts; driving time between cities and daily driving averages; gasoline prices, octane ratings; average daily food expenses; U.S. sources for business info before you leave, plus airline, bus and train timetables and prices; auto and passenger shipping information with prices and frequencies; and the latest hotel prices.

Of course, the claim to fame that this book has always had has been its accurate information on the Pan American Highway, which includes a 14-page mileage table and a unique 78-page mile-by-mile profile chart showing precise altitudes and inclines of the entire length of the Highway. A record of toll roads and toll bridges, with charges listed in U.S. dollars is there, plus the latest on road conditions. All the facts and figures presented are based on firsthand experience of the author during his continuing automobile trips through all nineteen Central and South American countries.
From: Compsco Pub. Co., 663 Fifth Ave., New York, N.Y. 10022

SOUTH AMERICAN HANDBOOK - $6.95

The senior of Latin American guidebooks, having now been published for several decades. Each year it is brought up-to-date with the help of many of its users. It's a bit bulky to carry, but is well worth

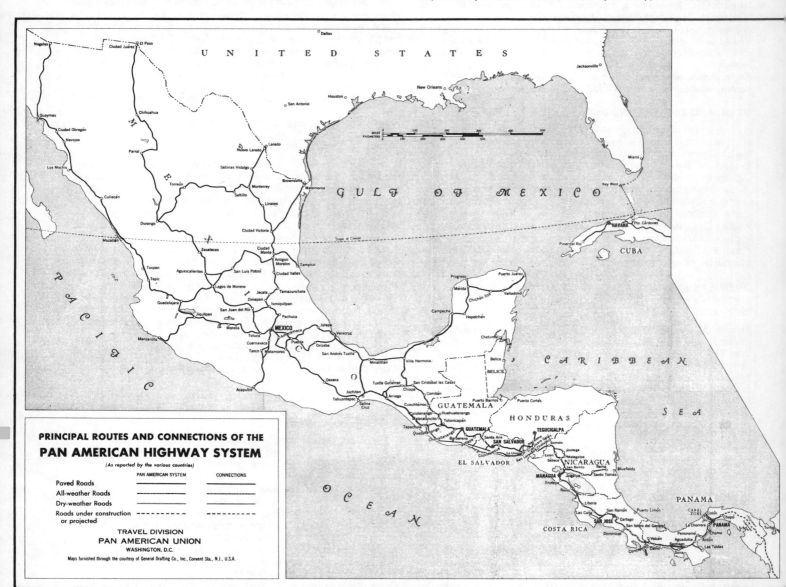

PRINCIPAL ROUTES AND CONNECTIONS OF THE
PAN AMERICAN HIGHWAY SYSTEM
(As reported by the various countries)

	PAN AMERICAN SYSTEM	CONNECTIONS
Paved Roads		
All-weather Roads		
Dry-weather Roads		
Roads under construction or projected		

TRAVEL DIVISION
PAN AMERICAN UNION
WASHINGTON, D.C.

Maps furnished through the courtesy of General Drafting Co., Inc., Convent Sta., N.J., U.S.A.

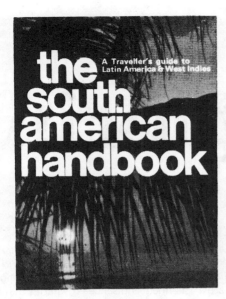

having along—a historical background is given for each country, which gives you something to read on the bus. The major travel routes through each country are covered in detail with lists of hotels, restaurants, points of interest and transportation companies. It's one of the best travel guides in the world.

From: Trade & Travel Publications, 14 Leadenhall St., London EC 3 England

MICHELIN GREEN GUIDES - $4.95 ea.
Michelin Tire Corp.

The Michelin Green Guides are published on a continuous basis and revised periodically. They offer touristic and cultural information on main places of interest and suggestions for sightseeing, and are without a doubt the best general guidebooks available to Austria, Brittany, Chateaux Loire, French Riviera, Germany, Italy, New York City, Normandy, Paris, Portugal, Spain, and Switzerland. These are the editions that are available in the English language. Each edition has an introduction to the area (or city), major driving routes, detailed info on all major and minor tourist attractions plus tips on language and culture. Really great! (See Maps section for info on Michelin maps).

From: Michelin Guides and Maps, P.O. Box 188, Roslyn Heights, N.Y. 11577

HITCH-HIKER'S GUIDE TO EUROPE
Ken Welsh
1972 - 254 p. il. - $5.95

Ken provides some good input for those who'd like to travel Europe on "less than $5 a day," which includes what to take, routes, currency hints, formalities, eating, drinking, sleeping, emergencies, local transport, useful phrases, working abroad and best buys. Covered for each country is a brief history, places to eat and sleep and what to see and do. Lotsa good tips and grapevine-type info, but contrary to the title, not a helluva lot of hitchin' data.

From: Stein and Day, Pub., 7 East 48th St., New York, N.Y. 10017

THE HITCHHIKER'S ROAD BOOK - A Guide to Traveling by Thumb in Europe
Jeff Kennedy and David E. Greenberg
1972 - 200 p. il. - $2.50 (pb)

Now here's a real hitching guide covering the whole European scene, which includes real hard-core vagabonding info, which'd do old J. London proud. For each country, Kennedy and Greenberg cover the general travel situation and environment, and then get into specifics on the cars, roads and drivers, best routes for travel in consideration of getting rides, weather, various laws you should be aware of, places to sack out from park benches to churches to hostels, and miscellaneous info, such as what you might want to try if you run out of coins. Great book! Even includes a section of city maps showing the best places to hang out for rides. Incidentally, also covered are techniques for hitching rides on boats, ferries, trains and planes. Those boys didn't miss a trick.

From: Doubleday & Co., 501 Franklin Ave., Garden City, L.I., N.Y. 11530

YUCATAN
1971 (updated to '74) - 134 p. il. - $4.95

MEXICO
1974 - 194 p. il. - $4.95

BAJA CALIFORNIA
1974 - 178 p. il. - $4.95

CENTRAL AMERICA
1974 (updated to '76) - 170 p. il. - $4.95
all by Cliff Cross

These are Cliff's travel notebooks, and they look like he pasted up the stuff for these books while he was on the road. Lotsa handwritten notes, typewritten copy, pen-drawn city maps and road routes, but all good information on travel conditions and situations particularly in reference to the highways. Cliff has included a goodly amount of black-and-white photos to give you a good idea of what you'll be seeing down Latin America way. Only criticism we have is that *Central America* falls a bit short on hard-core info compared to the other books.

From: H.P. Books, P.O. Box 5367, Tucson, Ariz. 85703

CENTRAL AMERICA
Doug Richmond
1974 - 176 p. il. - $5.95

Now if you want the straight skinny on the things that can happen and not happen to you on a run through Guatemala, Honduras, El Salvador, Nicaragua and Costa Rica, check in with Doug. It's like you were sittin' in the local pub with him over a beer..."Say Doug, what's it really like to make the run down there? You know, passports, visas, border hassles, cops, bandits, food, road conditions, and so. What's the real story?" And the way the book reads, is the way he'd probably answer. Doug, who usually sports a full beard and Levi's all the way, made the run to gather material for this book with three other people in a '68 Valiant, which apparently turned out to be a real bomb for the trip. He recommends the old-fashioned VW Beetle as best. Good photos, great writing. You should really enjoy it and come away much better informed for your run.

From: H.P. Books, P.O. Box 5367, Tucson, Ariz. 85703

exploring

This was kind of a hard section to put together, because there's so little that can be classified as pure exploring. Most "exploring" concerns a specific field of activity or scientific investigation—mountaineering, diving, caving, or archeology, paleontology, botany, and so forth. However, there are groups, sources of info, publications and other miscellaneous resource items that concern all areas of exploration, or the adventure of exploration. They didn't fit under any of the other headings, ergo: "Exploring."

There is another aspect to this section which has to do with resources that concern the very heart of exploration—the unknown, the mysterious, the anomalous, or whatever-youwantocallit. Oh sure, there've always been question marks in the realm of exploring, but mostly they've been missing links necessary to prove logical and generally reasonable events or situations. It wasn't till Charles F. Fort came along, around the turn of the century, that attention began to be focused on question marks that were illogical, unreasonable, and in some cases, downright weird.

Fort, who was born in 1874, made two false starts in zoology and journalism, finally ending up as a librarian in a newspaper morgue. At 42, he came into a modest inheritance, and from then on was able to devote his life to that which he loved best, collecting, analyzing, and correlating strange and conflicting reports on things that in themselves didn't make any sense. He spent 27 years in the New York Public Library or the British Museum checking through every available scientific journal, popular science magazine and newspaper making notes of his findings on little slips of paper, which he kept in

shoe boxes. Finally they were collected into four books, which today comprise *The Complete Books of Charles Fort* (see "Books"), *The Book of the Damned, Lo!, Wild Talents,* and *New Lands.* Here are contained the facts on thousands of cases that are a "damned" nuisance—mysteries that are ignored by orthodox science or explained away improperly. An example is the little golden airplanes discovered in South America and dated between 500 and 800 A.D. These delicately tooled images have been passed off as flying fish or possibly some form of bug. A closer study of these artifacts reveals that this answer is biologically ridiculous. Indeed, the objects are very similar to the most modern delta-wing aircraft. Is it possible that people a thousand years ago could have imagined a vertical takeoff airplane?

The popularity of Charles Fort's books led to the forming of numerous associations to carry on his work, and to the coining of the word "Fortean" to classify that phenomena, which heretofore had simply been labeled miscellaneous.

Forteans (also the name of those who hold Fort's basic outlook) insist upon keeping an open mind on everything, but at the same time, remaining skeptical—especially of professional skeptics. Forteans see it as their duty to investigate any matter that has been officially or popularly debunked so as to preserve a balance between the impossible and the improbable.

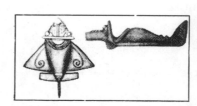

The little golden airplanes.
Top: Drawing of "original" from
Columbian National Collection.
Bottom: Similar model from
Chicago Museum. (Courtesy SITU)

Charles H. Fort (1874–1932)

The "experts" told us that stones cannot fall from the sky. Today we have a whole science devoted to the study of such non-existent stones; all major museums in the world have collections of these impossible stones. We call them meteorites.

INTERNATIONAL FORTEAN ORGANIZATION (INFO)
P.O. Box 367
Arlington, Va. 22210

This lively organization, competently headed by Paul Willis, specializes in reporting and investigating the borderlands of science—sea monsters, UFO's, abominable snowmen, frogs and blood raining from the sky, and other such unusual phenomena. "INFO is a group of skeptics; of individualists who are...ready to speculate upon an endless variety of 'cryptoscientific' subjects." Every three months the organization publishes the 54-page journal *INFO* with documentary reports and commentary on fortean-type phenomena. Interesting and well written. Membership, which includes a subscription to *INFO,* is open to anyone with an interest in the "unexplained" for $10 per year.

INSTITUTO INTERAMERICANO (II)
5133 NT, Denton, Tex. 76203

Instituto Interamericano, which has been active for about 23 years, is, essentially, a clearinghouse in the various fields of anthropology. II answers questions, arranges communication between scholars and researchers, assists in the establishment of programs of various types in areas of anthropology, assists in locating bibliographic citations, aids in preparing material for publication (editing) and, in general, attempts to assist persons working in the various fields of anthropology in contributing to the dissemination of knowledge of man, his productions and activities, past and present. The Instituto's area of interest is world-wide.

II does not have members in the usual sense of the term. What they're called are Fellows, and they are elected by the Executive Committee upon nomination by two or more other Fellows and the concurrence of the Director. Normally, though not necessarily, nominees are persons eminent in the areas of anthropology or ancillary fields.

So what's in it for the serious amateur? The Instituto Interamericano publishes a bimonthly newsletter, *The Interamerican,* a neatly done mimeograph job that's an excellent source of "grapevine" info for the active explorer. Covered are info on digs and finds, technique tips, travel data and hints, book and periodical reviews, and scads of miscellany of interest to the shoestring, penny-budget explorer. A really fabulous, entertaining, well-written and informative 8-pager. As far as we know, there's no charge for the newsletter, but we sincerely ask you to send at least a couple of bucks or more to help them cover the cost of printing and mailing. It's a great service, and one way to make sure it continues is to help support it.

ADVENTURERS CLUB OF NEW YORK
11 Seabert Lane, Kinnelon, N.J. 07405

This group, which got under way December of 1912, is composed of some 400-odd adventurers from various walks of life: travelers, hunters, fishermen, writers, newspapermen, doctors, and so forth. As would be expected, most of the membership is concentrated in the New York environs, where they get together informally once a month to trade tall tales and stories. The objective of the club is to promote fellowship among congenial men who have distinguished themselves in some form or other of adventure. And though membership in the club is open to anyone who can secure two sponsors, an aspirant must be able to establish his claim to the title of adventurer. The By-Laws state: "To qualify as an active member an applicant must relate a story of personal adventure before the Board of Governors or at a regular meeting of the Club. The Board of Governors will decide if the experience related qualifies the applicant for active membership." In lieu of this, associate membership is open to anyone who establishes that he

is an adventurer in spirit. even though circumstances have prevented him from being one in fact. Membership fees are: Active—initiation fee, $35, annual dues, $25; Associate—initiation, $45, annual dues, $35. The Club publishes a monthly bulletin, an annual called *The Adventurer* and a directory about every 5 years. For more information, write to the Secretary at the above address.

SOCIETY FOR THE INVESTIGATION OF THE UNEXPLAINED (SITU)
RD 1, Columbia, N.J. 07832

"The main objective of the society is, as the name implies, the investigation of everything of a factual nature that is as yet unexplained in all fields of the natural sciences. This means *search* as opposed to *research*; and, to this end, the greater part of our energies are devoted to fieldwork and the encouragement of on-the-spot investigations by our members."

SITU was founded in 1965 by the late Ivan T. Sanderson and maintains vast files on fortean phenomena and scientific anomalies. Much of this information is compiled into articles and published in the society's quarterly journal *Pursuit.* The journal also features new discoveries, reviews current events, and presents a cumulative bibliography. Sanderson, who was a well-known zoologist and author of many books, set a high standard for the publication, and as a result, it is one of the most interesting "exotic science" journals currently published.

You can become a corresponding member of SITU with information withdrawal privileges for $10 annual dues. Membership includes a subscription to *Pursuit.*

EXPLORERS CLUB
46 E. 70th St., New York, N.Y. 10021

"The Explorers Club, founded in 1904, is an institution of serious purpose designed for and dedicated to the search for new knowledge of the earth and outer space. To this end, the Club serves as an international focal point and catalyst in the identification and stimulation of institutional exploration, independent investigators, and students." As part of this premise, the Explorers Club has developed an Educational Program to assist young men and women who are seeking educational opportunities in exploration and field sciences. This includes a series of lectures plus a field trip to supplement academic instruction, counseling services to provide information on educational opportunities for participation in expeditionary and field science programs, and awards in the form of grants, scholarships and other types of support to help students participate in field science programs. A Research Program has also been developed to provide grants to young graduate, postgraduate and junior professional scientists who often find it difficult to obtain financial support for scientific field work because of a lack of experience or recognition.

To keep members up-to-date on what's going on, the Club publishes the *Explorers Journal* (quarterly), *Expeditions and Field Projects* (annual) and the *Explorers Club News* (5 times per year).

Membership consists of two types: Members and Fellows, and Resident and Nonresident. The category of Fellow is generally conferred on those men who have a demonstrated record of accomplishment and leadership in exploration in the physical and biological sciences. A Member is broadly interpreted to include men who can show a continuing interest in exploratory endeavor. Initiation fees for all classes of membership run $75, and annual dues from $35 up to $115 depending on whether you're a Fellow or Member and Resident or Nonresident. Full info on membership, publications and

A zoology lecture, given as part of the Explorers Club's Field Science Series Education Programs.

other services can be had by writing the above address.

CIRCUMNAVIGATORS CLUB
271 Madison Ave., New York, N.Y. 10016
This club was founded in 1902 to provide points of friendly contact among men who go to the ends of the earth in the cause of commerce, research, exploration, big game hunting, military and government service, or for the simple pleasure of travel. There are about 800 or so members, and to keep them all in touch with each other the club publishes a bimonthly magazine called *The Log.*

AMERICAN INSTITUTE FOR EXPLORATION, INC. (AIFE)
1809 Nichols Rd., Kalamazoo, Mich. 49007
This independent research and educational organization of scientists, writers, photographers and others actively engaged in exploration, was founded in '54 "to further knowledge of the world and its life through expeditions and regional studies." AIFE sponsors expeditions, provides aid to field scientists who are looking for grants, offers consulting services, and assists expeditions with gear through the AIFE equipment pool. Their areas of interest include archeology, ethnography, ethnobotany, geography, undersea exploration, bioecology, and human ecology, particularly of the Aleutian Islands, Hokkaido, the Caribbean region, North American Arctic, and Northeast Asia. The group's holdings include archeological and botanical specimens from the Aleutian Is. and Hokkaido, Japan areas; marine specimens from the Bering Sea; field notes, technical reports and photos covering expeditions; detailed medical records of Aleutian Eskimos at Atka, Nikolski, and Unalaska from 1928 to 1942, plus maps of archeological sites in the Aleutians, in addition to miscellaneous paper work from various of their expeditions. Publications to keep the 150-odd members together are somewhat irregular and include a *Field Report* and *News Letter.*

NATIONAL GEOGRAPHIC SOCIETY
17th and M Sts., N.W., Washington, D.C. 20036
This group, founded in 1888, was pretty neat in the old days (early 1900's) when individuality was still recognized. Today, though, National Geo is stiff, formal and aloof, and the only way an individual gets involved is to come with a wagon-full of laurels and be willing to be reprogrammed to the party line and the status of a common denominator. For the most part being a member means getting a copy of the monthly journal, wherein the emphasis is on good photography as opposed to good writing from the standpoint of style, individuality, excitement and novelty. Cover up the name of the author and you couldn't begin to tell who wrote what. The good news is that National Geo has excellent maps. Check the Maps section for more details.

SOCIETY FOR THE HISTORY OF DISCOVERIES
Univ. of Minnesota Library, Minneapolis, Minn. 55455
This group, founded in 1960 and numbering about 200 members, includes college and university professors in various fields and others interested in the history of geographical exploration. Scope of the Society in general deals with the expansion of Europe, including the allied fields of cartography, economic expansion, geographic thought, beginnings of colonialism, and so forth to the extent that they pertain to the age of discoveries. They publish an annual called *Terra Incogni-*

ta and a newsletter at irregular intervals. If you're into research, these people might be a good group to get together with. More info can be had from the above address.

NEW ENGLAND ANTIQUITIES RESEARCH ASSOCIATION (NEARA)
4 Smith St., Milford, N.H. 03055
NEARA is a serious amateur archeologists group that specializes in the prehistory and early history of New England and surrounding areas, especially those having unexplained stone structures, monoliths and petroglyphs—and there are a lot of them in the northeastern U.S. Most members are located in New England, where they can actively participate in the Association's field work; however, membership is open to anyone with a sincere interest in this area of exploration, particularly if you'd like to become actively involved in some way or another.

At present, NEARA investigates, correlates and maintains files on many different types of unresolved human involvement in stone- and earthwork. New members receive a site classification index to aid them in making out reports. In addition, they also receive a quarterly newsletter (actually more like a magazine), the *NEARA Journal,* which features articles and reports on discoveries, investigations, research, and so forth. The *Journal* isn't any great work of art, but they make up for it with interesting and well-written articles and news. Membership in NEARA runs $10 per year, or if you'd just like to subscribe to the *Journal,* $5. For more info, write Andy Rothovius, Secretary, at the above address.

ANCIENT COINS
FOUND ALONG NEW JERSEY COAST
Barbara Corcoran

Exciting the curiosity of believers in Pre-Columbian Trans-Atlantic contact was the discovery that ancient coins are to be found inconspicuously displayed in small museums along the Jersey coast.

A Bronze ca. 921 A.D. Byzantine coin, with markings over 1,000 years old and still beautifully clear, is to be found on an index card above an ancient Roman coin which contains no information whatsoever.

These coins are in the Cape May Courthouse Museum at the southern tip of New Jersey. Approximately 60 miles northeast in the Barnegat Historical Society Museum is another Roman coin, undated and unreasearched. This Roman coin was found on the beach at the nearby community of Beach Haven.

The avenues of thought connecting a Byzantine coin's journey from the 10th century across the Atlantic Ocean to the 20th century are waiting to be travelled...

One possible theory is that adventurous Pre-Columbian sailors from Mediterranean lands have at different times passed along the Jersey coastline. New Jersey has several bays, inlets and natural harbors which would have afforded protective "stopovers" to such sailors.

To exist today, the remainders of their visits would have to have been of a composition which under relatively good conditions could have withstood the natural weathering of a millenium, as in the case of the bronze ca. 921 A.D. Byzantine coin.

Admittedly this theory is no more than a logical guess. In presenting this brief paper, it is my purpose to point out that coins minted in the ancient Mediterranean world (and probably others) lie ignored, unreported and unresearched, in many places in America.

These interesting finds should be published and not simply dismissed as having been brought over by post-Columbian explorers or settlers. Undoubtedly more such discoveries will be made in the future.

...from the NEARA Journal, *Vol. 10 No. 3, Spring 1976*

WORLD EXPEDITIONARY ASSOCIATION
45 Brompton Rd., Knightsbridge, London SW3, England
See "Tours & Expeditions."

ARCHEOLOGICAL INSTITUTE OF AMERICA (AIA)
260 W. Broadway, New York, N.Y. 10013
The Archeological Institute's main thrust is to encourage archeological research. Their secondary objective is to provide a means for both the

professional scholar and the interested layman to follow the latest archeological discoveries and their interpretation thus forging a link between work in the field and the amateur and professional researcher at home. The primary means of doing this is through the Institute's beautifully done quarterly, *Archeology,* and the *American Journal of Archeology,* also a quarterly. *Archeology* is the group's popular magazine written principally for the layman, whereas the *Journal* is slanted more towards the scholar. When you join, you have your choice of receiving one or the other, or both, depending on the type of membership you choose.

One of the nice things about AIA is they want people who are interested in archeology to get involved and they push in that direction. For example, regional chapters are active throughout the U.S. and Canada which have been formed by members who like to get out in the field and do things. A list of addresses is available. Students, archeology buffs and other interested parties are encouraged to consult the AIA. Several helpful publications are distributed by the Institute and can be ordered from the above address. These include *Archeology in American Colleges,* $2.50; *Archeology As A Career,* 50¢; and *British Digs and American Students,* $1. The Institute is affiliated with many related organizations, and often if they can't handle an inquiry, they'll field it to an affiliate who may be able to help.

Students working an excavation under the supervision of archeologists.

We'd suggest that if you're interested in this area of exploration that you join the AIA, not only to support their programs, but also to open some doors for you to possible field-type activities here and abroad in archeology. Regular membership runs $25 a year and Student membership, $12.50. Applications are available from the above address.

Smithsonian Associates
SMITHSONIAN INSTITUTION (SI)
900 Jefferson Dr., Washington, D.C. 20560

In 1965, the Smithsonian Institution established the Smithsonian Associates program. Up until that time, SI was, as far as the American public was concerned, the Nation's attic. Except for those who worked with, or for, SI or visited the museums while in DC, the Institution wasn't totally fulfilling James Smithson's legacy. Smithson, an English scientist who was mostly into chemistry and mineralogy, was a bit miffed that, through circumstances, he had been denied what he felt was the true status of his birthright. At one point he wrote, "My name shall live in the memory of man when the titles of the Northumberlands and the Percys are extinct and forgotten." In 1826, at the age of 61, he wrote out a brief will leaving his entire fortune of about £100,000 to his nephew, and then added that if his nephew were to die without child, "I then bequeath the whole of my property to the United States of America to found at Washington, under the name of the Smithsonian Institution, an establishment for the increase and diffusion of knowledge among men." Well, Jimmy made his mark in the U.S., but at home he's still on par with the Northumberlands and Percys, for the Smithsonian is no better known in England than the British Museum is here.

At any rate, the key word to Smithson's legacy is "diffusion," and SI's principal activity till '65 was collecting. With the establishment of the Associates program and in '70 the commencing of the *Smithsonian* magazine, the final part of the legacy was on its way to being fulfilled.

The Smithsonian Associates program offers quite a number of opportunities to the exploring enthusiast, particularly if he or she qualifies for Resident Membership (lives in or in the vicinity of DC). These include lectures, films, tours, classes, workshops, and so forth, all listed in the monthly *Smithsonian Calendar,* which a Resident receives, and discounts on selected books and periodicals, and travel programs, plus opportunities to participate in volunteer programs. The National Membership is about the same, except sans those activities which would require living in the area for participation. Both memberships receive a subscription to the *Smithsonian* magazine. National Membership runs $10 annually, and Resident, slightly more.

AMERICAN MUSEUM OF NATURAL HISTORY
Central Park West at 79th St., New York, N.Y. 10024
The Museum of Natural History operates in a similar fashion to that of the Smithsonian. Associate Membership gets you a subscription to the very well done *Natural History* magazine and discounts when ordering books and articles from the Museum gift shop. For more info, drop a card to the Membership Dept. at the above address.

EXPEDITION TRAINING INSTITUTE (ETI)
P.O. Box 171, Prudential Center Station, Boston, Mass. 02199
Here's a group that is devoted entirely to finding expeditions for volunteers and volunteers for expeditions. Three programs are offered: (1) for high school students, there are ETI expeditions designed to train you in field work; (2) for college seniors and graduate students, who serve as leaders on their own expeditions which have been funded by ETI, there is a scholarship program; and (3) ETI also has a direct placement service for experienced people of all ages who will work with a scientist and share the costs. The most noteworthy aspect of ETI's effort is that they restrict their references to cost limitations of $450 to $550 for the time period of the expedition (this does not include travel expense). ETI does not create the programs that are contrived, rather, each year they select graduates who apply for grants and then list their expeditions in the organization's periodic newsletter, *Quest,* as participation opportunities for ETI's student members. Grants, in 1975, were arranged for 44 leaders, each averaging about $650. Additional grants were made to 15 students of high school age, and partial grants allowed to many others in the form of underwriting expedition costs. It's a small program, but as far as it goes, ETI is the only group working to fund graduate students and undergraduates in their own research projects.

To get involved, you have to become a member of ETI. Dues run $15 per year for students and $25 for nonstudents. You apply to be either an Assistant or a Leader. Requirements for the Assistant position are simply the ability to work under arduous conditions as a team member, an interest in field research, the time to participate in an expedition of your choice, and the cash to cover the expedition participation fee (averages about $450 or so) plus travel expenses. To be approved as a Leader, the applicant must be enrolled in a degree program of an established university or associated with a research institution.

Looks like a real good group. More info can be had by writing Richard E. Enright, Jr., at the above address.

AMERICAN POLAR SOCIETY
August Howard, Sec.
98-20 62nd Dr. - No. 7H, Rego Park, N.Y. 11374
The Polar society was organized in 1934 to band together, as a permanent group, persons interested in the history and exploration of the Arctic and Antarctic regions, in order to act as a clearinghouse of polar information, to be of aid to organizers and members of polar expeditions, and to spread knowledge of the polar regions.

Membership at $2 per year is open to all persons interested in the history and exploration of the polar regions. Benefits include the privilege of attending meetings held in large cities around the U.S. (mainly in N.Y., though) at which polar veterans and scientists give talks and lectures, and reception of *The Polar Times,* published twice a year. Other publications and information are sent to all members from time to time.

MARIAH
Lawrence J. Burke, Ed.
Quarterly - $12/yr. - $3/issue - 70 p. il.

Well, here's a new quarterly, the consumer's *Explorers Journal/National Geographic* combination—*Mariah.* Nice little book for those who want to read about what others are doing. Good writing, though light, and intriguing color photographs that'll whet your appetite for God's Country. The first edition, which came out in February of '76, carried seven articles ranging from the adventures of a rafting group running the Omo River in Ethiopia, to a ski-touring trip in California's White Mountains, with a biography of E. S. Curtis, a frontier photographer (including 3 exceptional Indian photographs of his), a sailing venture,

and a conservation feature on the fate of Admiralty Island, Alaska, with a couple of other articles in between. Though *Mariah* is certainly well done, both editorially and artwise, it just doesn't have $3 worth of information, or for that matter, entertainment. Frankly, you can get this style of writing, on essentially the same subject matter in greater depth and more of it per issue, from *Mountain Gazette* at 60¢ a copy (see Climbing, "Periodicals"). Of course, the *Gazette* isn't a slick, coffee-table number with color photos, but if your main thrust is tactile and visual stimulation, then go for the Sierra Club books. You'll get a lot better return on your investment.
From: Mariah, P.O. Box 2690, Boulder, Colo. 80302

EXPEDITION
James D. Muhly, Ed.
Quarterly - $8/yr. - 40 p. il.

This beautifully done quarterly published by the University Museum of the University of Pennsylvania covers archeological and anthropological expeditions and discoveries. The editorial slant, thought, places more emphasis on discussing what the expeditions found and their archeological or anthropological relevance as opposed to details of the expedition itself—planning, logistics, operations management, problems, and so forth. Except for that, the articles are interesting and well-written, and the photography is superb.
From: Expedition, Univ. Museum, Univ. of Pennsylvania, 33rd and Spruce Sts., Philadelphia, Pa. 19174

BOOKS

Tents. 155

weight it will be possible to carry, it must be borne in mind that the tent will become far heavier than it is found to be in the peculiarly dry atmosphere of a tent-maker's show-room. It is very convenient that a tent should admit of being pitched in more than one form : for instance, that one side should open and form an awning in hot weather ; also, that it should be easy to attach flys or awning to the tent to increase its available size during the daytime. All tents should be provided with strong covers, for pack-ropes are sure to fray whatever they press against ; and it is better that the cover should suffer than the tent itself.

Comparative Size of Tents.—The annexed diagram will show the points on which the *roominess* of a tent mainly depends.

A man wants space to sit at a table, and also to get at his luggage in order either to pack it or to unpack it ; lastly, he wants a reasonable amount of standing room. A fair-sized tent ought to include the figures drawn in the diagram ; and I have indicated, by lines and shaded spaces, the section of various descriptions of tents that would be just sufficient to embrace them.

THE ART OF TRAVEL or
SHIFTS AND CONTRIVANCES AVAILABLE IN WILD COUNTRIES
Francis Galton
1872 (rep. 1971) - 366 p. il. - $6.95

"The idea of the work occurred to me when exploring South-western Africa in 1850-51. I felt acutely at that time the impossibility of obtaining sufficient information on the subjects of which it treats. Then remembering...how every traveller discovers some useful contrivances for himself, it appeared to me that I should do welcome service to all who have to rough it—whether explorers, emigrants, missionaries or

soldiers—by collecting the scattered experiences of many such persons in various circumstances...and deducing from them what might fairly be called an *Art of Travel.*"

Galton was as good as his word, and his book, first published in 1855, ran to an eighth edition (1893) but the fifth (1872) of which this is a reprint, is the last to incorporate new material. The problems he deals with are so varied (drawing lots, finding a lost path, presents for savages) and so ingeniously solved, that few Victorian travellers set off for strange lands without a copy in their baggage. The "shifts and contrivances" for the explorer are gleaned from travellers' tales from all over the world: how the Tibetans keep warm, how the Chinese stop asses braying at night, how Hindoos catch wild duck, and so forth. A profusion of fine engravings is to be found throughout the book to add to the information, of which much is just as good today as it was yesterday. Definitely has a place in every explorer's library.
From: Stackpole Books, Cameron & Kelker Sts., Harrisburg, Pa. 17105

STRANGE STORIES, AMAZING FACTS
Editors of Readers Digest
1976 - 608 p. il. - $11.97

An excellent collection of stories, articles and photographs concerning the bizarre, the unusual, the odd, astonishing and incredible. Though not all of the contents of this book concern geographical exploration, most of it will be of interest to explorer types. Coverage is definitely broad and diversified ranging from astronomical facts and enigmas to zoological oddities. In between are polar and tropical exploration, archeology, architecture, machines and inventions, travel and journeys, and many, many mysteries. The neat thing is that the greater part of the book concerns stories most people have heard about—scuttlebutt—but really don't have the facts on. For example, what was El Dorado that the Spaniards were chasing, who was Jack the Ripper, how were the pyramids really built, who was Bridey Murphy, why can certain people of the South Pacific walk across red hot coals, can dolphins really carry on a conversation, and on, and on. Great book, great reading.
From: Readers Digest, Pleasantville, N.Y. 10570

THE SOURCEBOOK PROJECT
William R. Corliss, Researcher & Compiler

Bill Corliss is a physicist and engineer who, till 1963, worked in various supervisory capacities at Martin's Nuclear Division, G.E.'s Flight Propulsion Lab, Pratt and Whitney, and the University of California's Radiation Lab. In 1963 Bill turned to writing scientific and popular texts on various aspects of rocket propulsion, space flight and exploration. At the same time, he also commenced work on his Sourcebook Project, a monumental task of researching, collecting and organizing data relative to unusual phenomena and curious features of the natural world, the aim being to challenge science with data not easily explained (or not explainable at all) in terms of current scientific theories. Research methods included chasing down specific leads arriving daily from a multitude of sources, and "sweeps" or complete examinations of key sources. For example, the first 100 volumes of *Nature*, the *Monthly Weather Review* and the *Journal of Geophysical Research* were analyzed. Finally in 1974, the first of a series of Sourcebooks were published: *Strange Phenomena* and *Strange Artifacts*. Here's a short but typical entry from *Strange Phenomena:*

GLD-034 ELECTRICAL PHENOMENA NEAR WEYMOUTH
Anonymous; *Nature,* 126:262, August 16, 1930.
Aug. 17, 1876. *Electrical Phenomena near Weymouth.*—At Ringstead Bay, near Weymouth, Dorset, during a sultry afternoon, on ground above the cliggs, a number of globes of light were seen of the size of billiard balls, extending from a few inches above the surface to a height of 7-8 ft. They slowly rose and fell vertically, sometimes within a few inches of the observers, but always eluding the grasp. The number of these objects varied from twenty to "thousands." No sound accompanied the display, but at 10 P.M. there was a thunderstorm.

Ball lightning is intriguing and mysterious; so are the strange "resonances" that exist among the solar system planets. No one has satisfactorily explained the well-documented explosive sounds called Barisal Guns or mistpouffers. Who built the ancient canals in Florida and why? What was the purpose behind the immense megalithic alignments in Brittany? The Sourcebook Project collects and indexes original source material in these and similar areas so that researchers can focus better on the far frontiers of science. A thousand jumping-off places for further study and research are to be found in the series.

Though the Sourcebooks are privately published by Corliss,

typography and printing are of the highest caliber. Each Sourcebook comes in a 7- x 9-in., vinyl-covered, 3-ring binder and is thoroughly indexed by subject, author, source, time of event and place of event. To date, the following Sourcebooks are available:

Strange Artifacts, Vol. M1, 1974, 262 p. il., $7.95.
Strange Artifacts, Vol. M2, 1976, 287 p. il., $7.95. Both of these are Sourcebooks on ancient man and deal with unusual facts from archeology, mythology, and anthropology. Coverage includes fossil footprints, discoveries in mounds, cupmarks, ancient canals in Arizona, degeneracy of man, myths of giants in South America, fused forts of Scotland, Easter Island, Tiahuanaco, the Mexican Messiah, Stonehenge, Phoenicians in America. great building under a lake, ancient works in New York, ancient inscription on a wall at Chatata, Tenn., and much more.

Strange Life, Vol. B1, 1976, 287 p. il., $7.95. A Sourcebook on the mysteries of organic nature which covers reports that have been collected describing unknown animals, the peculiar behavior of well-known animals and data that seem to contradict the great dogma of evolution. Some of the listings are: last of the dinosaurs, Chinese accounts of the mammoth, water-monsters of the American aborigines, an attempt to prove the existence of the unicorn, footprints in the snow at South Devon, Great Britain, wolf children, the Berlin "thinking" horse, why did the foxes sing?, a compass plant, and a new underground monster.

Strange Phenomena, Vol. G1, 1974, 277 p. il., $7.95.
Strange Phenomena, Vol. G2, 1974, 264 p. il., $7.95. These two contain accounts dealing with unusual geophysical events and include: luminous portents of earthquakes, ball lightning, Texas ghost light, the Barisal guns and similar sounds, Yellowstone lake whispers, luminous footprints, the queer lights on Brown Mt., shower of fish, tornadoes—puzzling phenomena and photographs, wheels of light at sea, sound of the Aurora, the dark day in New England, snow without clouds, and so forth.

Strange Planet, Vol. E1, 1975, 283 p. il., $7.95. A compendium of articles on curious and controversial aspects of geology as originally published in *Journal of Geology, Nature, Scientific American* and similar publications. Subjects include: the great dinosaur disaster, a toad in solid rock, traditions of the deluge, legendary islands of the North Atlantic, a new magnetic reversal at 12,500 years?, Patrick County, Va. and its curious fairy stones, dry quicksand, mystery imprints stump geologists, tektites and geomagnetic reversals, erupting boulders, Carolina bays and their origin, did a comet collide with the earth in 1908?, the mystery of the Mima mounds, when the Mediterranean dried up.

Strange Universe, Vol. A1, 1975, 279 p. il., $7.95. Astronomers frequently see unusual astronomical phenomena and record them in the *Astronomical Register, Nature,* the *Monthly Notices of the Royal Astronomical Society,* and other scientific publications. *Strange Universe* is a compilation of a wide variety of these curious observations which include: Swift's forecast of Mars' satellites, the order of the

---

HANDBOOK FOR EXPEDITIONS
Brathay Exploration Group
1971 - 137 p. il. - $?

Covers planning, methods and logistics for organizing and activating expeditions of all types.
From: The Geographical, 128 Long Acre, London, England WC2E 9QH

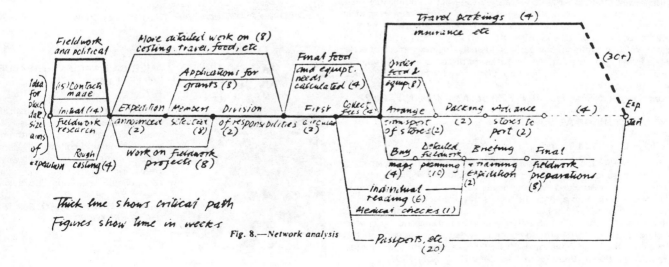

Fig. 8.—Network analysis

Thick line shows critical path
Figures show time in weeks

planets, Huth's moving star of 1801-02, the moon may be a former planet, the supposed planet Vulcan, brilliant object seen near the sun, lightning-like phenomena on the moon, evidence for weakening gravity, beam of light from Mars, dark objects crossing the sun's disk, how real are gravitational waves?, decrease in the velocity of light, possible changes in Saturn's rings, a tenth planet?, dark triangular patch under moon, and spoke-like markings on Venus.

Each Sourcebook runs $7.95; however, any 4 can be had for $29 and any 5 for $36, which is a savings of about four bucks over the individual cost. For a brochure on the above Sourcebooks, and other books in the Forteana realm that Bill handles, drop a request to the address below.

From: William R. Corliss, The Sourcebook Project, Box 107, Glen Arm, Md. 21057

THE RIDDLE OF THE PYRAMIDS
Kurt Mendelssohn
1974 - 224 p. il. - $14.95

A totally new concept as to why the pyramids of Egypt were built. Reason? To unify the peoples of Egypt toward a common goal with the ultimate objective of forming a centralized state. Why a pyramid? "It was the only means of doing something spectacular with the large labor force that they wanted to gather, and a mountain of 50° elevation was...the best they could manage." The Egyptians had tried a steeper one, but it collapsed. "The building of a distinctive mark in the landscape by making a large heap is still with us in the desire of children making a sand castle. Moreover, this primitive urge is testified to in the Bible (*Genesis*, XI, 4): 'Let us build us a city and a tower whose top may reach unto heaven; and let us make a name.' " Most of Mendelssohn's book is devoted to showing how he arrived at this theory through the history of Egypt and the construction of these mountains of stone, which, by the way, were also used as tombs. Fascinating reading, excellent photographs and line drawings.

From: Praeger Publishers, Inc., 111 Fourth Ave., New York, N.Y. 10003

THE BERMUDA TRIANGLE MYSTERY—SOLVED
Lawrence D. Kusche
1975 - 336 p. il. - $10

Kusche, a librarian at Arizona State University did his homework well, in fact, many many months of it in checking through every scrap of information he could find on the Bermuda Triangle—newspaper accounts, weather bureau reports, and other official documents. Through meticulously examining, comparing and analyzing every piece of evidence—the real and the unreal—about every disappearance, Kusche very effectively scuttles the mystery. Definitely the book to read first before any of the others.

From: Harper & Row, Inc., 10 E. 53rd St., New York, N.Y. 10022

THE MYSTERY OF ATLANTIS
Charles Berlitz
1975 - 206 p. il. - $1.75 (pb)

This is probably the fairest book on the Atlantis situation to date. Berlitz, whose forte is linguistics (Berlitz School of Languages), has examined all the lore and evidence available, and has weighed the complaints of the skeptics against the beliefs of the advocates. He's decided that Atlantis is somewhere out in the Atlantic, perhaps in the Bahamian area. But as yet, even his on-site inspections and underwater explorations have turned up no concrete evidence. So we're no further along with the puzzle, except that Charlie has added some new pieces.

From: Avon Books, 959 Eighth Ave., New York, N.Y. 10019

EDUCATIONAL EXPEDITIONS INTERNATIONAL (EEI)
68 Leonard St., Belmont, Mass. 02178

EEI is a nonprofit organization that coordinates and sponsors field research projects for scientists from all over the world. The funds and staff assistance to support the research come from amateurs and professionals who apply for places on expedition teams.

Essentially, EEI is a clearinghouse. Scientists apply for research grants from many disciplines—archeology, anthropology, astronomy, biology, ecology, geology, medicine, and marine sciences. Those ad-

THE COMPLETE BOOKS OF CHARLES FORT
Charles Fort
1974 - 1,125 p. - $15

Charles Fort worked full time for twenty-seven years at the British Museum and the New York Public Library researching scientific journals, old periodicals, newspapers, and manuscript accounts to gather material on phenomena from the borderlands between science and fantasy, *The Book of the Damned, New Lands, Lo!,* and *Wild Talents.* Here then are all these four books bound up in one volume. In what are considered to be the 4 classic works on Fortean phenomena, Fort has gathered together, organized, and commented on a host of strange and unusual happenings observed and witnessed in various parts of the world from early times to modern: flying machines before the invention of the aircraft; flying wheels; strange noises in the sky; falls of red snow, frogs, worms and jellyfish; sightings on the moon and Mars; unexplainable footprints; disruption of gravity and much more. Fort was a researcher and collector, and his objective was to slap science in the face with the facts and show the ludicrousness of many of the explanations given. Unfortunately, most readers will not find Fort a relaxing author to settle down with. He's a hair-trigger cynic who has little use for tunnel vision, and he shows it throughout his works with innuendos and sarcasm directed at anyone and everyone who is unwilling to admit to what's really "going on." For example (fr: Chap. 6 of *Lo!*):

"Flows of blood from 'holy images'—

"I take for a proposition that, though nothing can be proved—because, if all phenomenal things are continuous, there is, in a final sense, nothing phenomenal—anything can be said to be proved—because, if all phenomenal things are continuous, the most preposterous nonsense must somewhere be linked with well-established beliefs. If I had the time for an extra job, I'd ask readers to think up loony theories, and send them to me, and I'd pick out the looniest of all, and engage to find abundant data to make it reasonable to anybody who wanted to think it reasonable."

There's a lot of interesting information in *The Complete Books,* but there's also a lot of drivel you're gonna hafta go through to get to it.

From: Dover Publications, Inc., 180 Varick St., New York, N.Y. 10014

AMERICA'S ANCIENT TREASURES
Franklin Folsom
1975, rev. - 216 p. il. - $2.95 (pb)

An excellent guide to archeological sites and museums in the United States and Canada, plus museums with important archeological collections. More than 40 features on various lifeways of prehistoric Indians. Listings give data on admission fees, hours, locations and how to get there.

From: Rand McNally, P.O. Box 7600, Chicago, Ill. 60680

judged most worthy by an advisory board of scientists and educators are selected for support. The personnel requirements, logistic arrangements, and timetable are set. Then EEI works up the expedition support team, from amongst those amateurs and professionals who've applied to help out, by looking for that mixture of individuals whose collective contributions, enterprise and enthusiasm can be put to constructive use in the field.

Once selected, participants are taught what they need to know to be productive. The Chief Scientist and his colleagues provide the historical and scientific background to put the research goals in perspective. Many of EEI's staff are faculty scientists at leading institutions. Under their personal guidance, team members are instructed in field methodology, including the use of instruments, tools and equipment, surveying and mapping techniques, collecting and sampling, observations, excavations, photography and other relevant activities.

Despite the fact that you have to pay a participation fee ranging anywhere from $200 to $2,000 depending on the expedition, number of days involved and other factors, EEI trips are not tours or educational outings. They are working experiences designed to fulfill the needs and requirements of professional scientists. The environments are remote, often untamed. Extremes of climate, rugged topography, and isolation are not uncommon. As companions in the field, participants share the life-style of the professional scientist. This includes the chores connected with the research as well as those associated with bivouac living.

Expeditions are open to men and women of all ages and no professional qualifications are required. Past participants have ranged in age from 16 to 72. About one-third are teachers and students. The others come from a wide variety of professions and life experiences. Their common denominators have been curiosity, imagination and a genuine desire to learn more about themselves and the world around them.

A catalog describing forthcoming expeditions, timetables, work schedules and fees is available from the above address.

"If you are willing to work, ready to learn, tolerant of others, and have a sense of humor, please apply. We need your help in the field."

BEAMER EXPEDITIONS
P.O. Box 285, Canoga Park, Calif. 91305

Wanna chase Big Foot? Beamer'll take you. According to their write-up, "You join scientists, naturalists and trackers *searching* for Big Foot in southwestern Oregon and northwestern California. Unforgettable 22-day wilderness expeditions in an area containing rare plants, 360 bird species and 87 mammal species. You help solve a scientific mystery and keep safe an endangered species. Tracking instructions. Trailers and tents furnished."

Sounds like it could be fun. To find out, though, you've got to start paying right away. Beamer needs $3 to get the info back to you on schedules, logistics, etc., and what you'll need to pay to join his team. He plans on running trips the year round.

WORLD EXPEDITIONARY ASSOCIATION (WEXAS)
45 Brompton Rd., Knightsbridge, London SW3, England

This group, which has been in operation for about 6 years now, is oriented toward providing low-cost travel (especially air fares) for individuals and groups. As they put it, "World Expeditionary Association exists to promote low-cost air travel and to assist enterprising projects involving overseas travel, particularly expeditions. To this end, the Association offers three services: a low-cost travel programme, an information and publishing service, and grants for expeditions. Anyone is eligible to join WEXAS and use each or all of these services." Well, this is fine for residents of Great Britain, but not any great advantage to us Yanks, unless we be traveling in European and Asian areas. WEXAS does have an Onward Travel Bookings service, which can get you a booking anywhere in the world through one of their agents. Best to check with them on that. Air fare discounts range from 15 to 65% and about 80% of all their flights are on scheduled services.

For the American explorer/traveler with an international run in mind, WEXAS' most immediate benefit would be information, and they seem to have their finger in almost every pie from the Channel to the Coral Sea. They publish a quarterly magazine entitled *Expedition,* which features articles on historical and contemporary expeditions, news reports on current expeditions, quite a number of good book reviews (almost all the books are published in Great Britain) and an interesting classified section—expeditions looking for people, people looking for expeditions. Best of all, though, is WEXAS' *Off-The-Beaten-Track,* an expedition and travel handbook with a batch of really fine articles, tips, and miscellaneous info for those who want to go on their own or join up with a group. Included are many, many neat exploring and travel groups; a reader's book list of practical exploring and vagabonding books; a guide to visa and health requirements; and articles on organizing and planning the expedition, travel medicine and health, and means of getting a return on your trip through freelance photography. In addition to all this, WEXAS helps members with contacts and specialized information needs. Certainly worth joining if your exploring activities are more than just armchair. Membership runs £7.00, which could be anything, the way the pound has been running. Best to drop them a card and get the current membership fees in US dollars.

MOUNTAIN TRAVEL INC.
1398 Solano Ave., Albany, Calif. 94706

This group conducts adventure trips to all spots of the globe—hiking, climbing, river tripping, four-wheeling—to discover new territories and new experiences. Most of the trips involve walking or climbing and run from a couple of days to more than a month. Prices ain't cheap, ranging from $600 up to $3,000 plus, but they've got a good staff of trip leaders and the trips are well arranged. For more info, write for their current trip booklet—beautifully illustrated.

ARCHEOLOGICAL INSTITUTE OF AMERICA
260 W. Broadway, New York, N.Y. 10013

Each January, the Archeological Institute publishes *Fieldwork Opportunities Bulletin,* which lists job opportunities, excavations and archeological programs for volunteers and students. If you're interested in something like this, send $2 to the above address for a copy of the bulletin.

Searching along the main street of an old ghost town in Colorado for whatever turns up.

treasure

before the turn of the century. How? Well, that's the secret of the treasure hunter's success—with a metal detector.

Detectors have come a long way since the days of the WWII mine-locator types that weighed twenty pounds, were cumbersome to carry and used up expensive batteries fairly quickly. Today, detectors are lightweight, well balanced and operate for pennies per hour. They have become so sophisticated (yet easy to operate and very dependable despite the electronic complexity) that they will not only locate metallic objects, but tell you if the detected targets are valuable or not (that is, whether they are gold, silver, copper or such, or just iron) even before you dig! In fact, they'll do just about everything but dig the object for you. There are, basically, three types of detectors: the beat frequency oscillator (BFO), transmitter-receiver (TR) and very low frequency (VLF). These are discussed later. Even though detectors can be purchased for as little as $35, the median price range for a dependable instrument that, in general, measures up to today's state of detector technology is from $150 to $300. Anything on the low end, especially below $100, may not have the technology behind it; anything on the high end, when you start getting to $350 and $400 may be costing you extra for the brand name—unfortunately, status isn't useful for detecting treasure.

Treasure hunting can be pursued alone or with a group. There are approximately 100 treasure hunting clubs throughout the United States with at least one club in every state. These groups range in size from a dozen to several hundred members and are made up of men, women and children. Usually, the groups meet monthly to discuss finds and metal detectors, share ideas and plan field trips or competition meets. The beginner would do well to join one of these groups, because it is a quick way to learn the ropes. Of course, there are several good books on the subject that are reading "musts." To the treasure hunter who starts right, the cost of these books will come back quickly in the form of finds.

How do you start? First, you need to acquire a general knowledge of treasure hunting. An excellent $2 book that will give you a good overall view of the hobby is *Treasure Hunting Pays Off!* (A condensed version of this book is available, free, from Garrett Electronics.) Second, find out about the instruments. Write to several detector manufacturers and request literature on their detectors. Decide what types of treasure hunting you want to do—coin hunting, ghost-towning or maybe nugget hunting—and then select a detector that will do the job. If you want to learn more about detectors than the manufacturers' literature tells you, which in many cases is loaded with promo BS, rather than hard facts and numbers (except the price, which is always hard), read Roy Lagal's *"How To Test" Detector Field Guide* or his detector and applications manual, the *Detector Owner's Field Manual.*

Prior to the mid-50's, a treasure hunter was thought to be a professional adventurer who roamed along the Atlantic seaboard in search of Captain Kidd's chests of gold, silver and jewelry, or out West hoping to run across Jesse James's ill-gotten bank loot, perhaps hastily hidden under a rock.

Over the past twenty-five years or so, however, the term "treasure hunter" has acquired an entirely different connotation. Treasure *is* being found and by people whom you would not likely suspect...the man or woman who lives across the street or the doctor or lawyer down the block. Believe it or not, today's modern treasure hunters are finding at least a million dollars worth of valuables a month. With that kind of sum in prospect, the ghosts of Kidd and James themselves might try to make a comeback if they could learn the treasure hunter's secret to success.

What is "treasure" and what is "treasure hunting"? Treasure has been defined as anything that has value to someone. Treasure hunting is the searching for and retrieving of lost or hidden valuables. Valuables is, of course, a relative term. Examples can be a knife you lost in the backyard last week, a five-dollar gold coin you find in a ghost town, a flintlock pistol you recover from the attic of an old deserted house, or a gold nugget that has lain unnoticed for a hundred years on the floor of an old mine tunnel. Treasure hunting extends into many fields of interest: coin hunting, cache hunting (pronounced "cash" and meaning hidden or buried money), relic hunting, bottle hunting, prospecting, ghost-towning and nugget hunting. It is so all-encompassing that the treasure hunter is never without several places to search, regardless of where he or she might live.

Recently a treasure hunter, while searching for coins in an old park, found a 1776 Continental dollar valued at $12,000. A lady, searching for coins at a schoolyard, found a very old and rare 18th-century Florentine necklace. A man in Oklahoma found a cache of buried gold coins worth $38,000, and a Wisconsin man found $41,000 in rotting currency in a trash dump. A man who lives in Lewiston, Idaho, found a rare Blake and Agnell twenty-dollar gold piece valued at $300,000.

Obviously, these kinds of finds are not everyday occurrences, but it is easy, however, to walk down to the city park and, after a few hours' searching, come away with your pockets bulging with coins, some of which could easily date

Jewelry box discovered in an old deserted house in Colorado (different place). It contained five $20 gold pieces, four old and rare coins, several pieces of jewelry, two tintype photographs and a toy gun.

hunting

Photos: Courtesy of Garrett Electronics.

Find out where, near your home, the old parks and playgrounds were, as well as other places people congregated many years ago. The book, *Successful Coin Hunting* by Charles Garrett, lists over 150 places where coins and valuables can be found. After you begin to find coins and other valuables at these places, you'll probably want to branch out into other forms of treasure hunting—especially if you're a history or antiques buff. You can learn about research and tracking down potential finds, plus a lot of other good info, by reading Karl von Mueller's very well-known works (among initiates), the *Treasure Hunter's Manuals No. 6* and *No. 7.* By the time you study these books and get about 100 hours on your detector, your only problem will be deciding where, out of hundreds of good treasure-finding places, to go next.

Keep in mind, however, that treasure hunting is hard work. The stuff doesn't jump right out of the ground. You have to do a certain amount of walking to find it (worse than playing golf and heftin' your own bag). You'll need patience, but always remember that treasure is there to be found, lots of it. *You* can find your share, maybe even more than your share!

Next, the most common question...

Many treasure-hunting hobbyists rightfully ask, "May I legally keep a treasure if I find one?" A good answer might be the old adage that "possession is nine-tenths of the law" and that secrecy is the best protection both before and after the finding of a treasure. The ancient motto of "finders, keepers" is proper and fitting in covering most discoveries of treasure, especially where integrity, legality and honesty have been exercised.

If no one is aware that a treasure exists and you discover and dig it up, there should be no question, but that the treasure is yours to keep or share through mutual agreement. In this regard, a good reference is Vol. 34, Sec. 4, of *American Jurisprudence,* which states, "The rule in this country, in the absence of legislation (to the contrary) is that the title to treasure trove belongs to the finder against all the world except the true owner, and in this respect is analogous to lost property. The owner of the soil in which the treasure trove is found acquires no title thereto by virtue of his ownership of the land."

A good rule of thumb is to check conditions with law enforcement officers and secure permission from property owners before you begin your search with detectors. Rare will be the case when you are refused, especially when you show you are not planning to destroy property and that you will fill in all evidences of digging and leave the area in as good a condition as you found it.

Bailing Out

As with any other hobby, you could grow tired of treasure hunting if you don't start finding interesting things right away, and you may want to bail out. But if you do your re-

search carefully and systematically and go about the business of treasure hunting with patience, it is quite likely that you will get in even deeper. Though, if you *must* leave all that money to more persistent fellows, you'll find it easy to sell your equipment. There are countless places to advertise. Try your local drugstore or laundromat free bulletin boards. Check with a coin dealer...many coin collectors are avid detector coin hunters. Call your local insurance agent. Many of them do a lot of their own searching when clients lose rings, jewelry and such. There are many places (such as the ones just mentioned) where you can advertise your detector for sale without paying a cent. If these fail, try a simple word ad in a newspaper classified section on a multiple-day, special rate offering. If that, too, fails, sell your detector by advertising in one or more of the treasure hunting publications, such as *In The Steps Of The Treasure Hunter, Treasure,* or *Lost Treasure.*

sources of information

While there are no national clubs in the United States, there are several informal "associations" formed by subscribers to certain treasure hunting periodicals. These periodicals do a fair job of keeping subscribers up-to-date as to what is going on within each group. Reports of treasures found, club activities and individual experiences are included in each issue. Two of these periodicals are *In The Steps Of The Treasure Hunter* and *National Treasure Hunters League Quarterly* (see Periodicals).

As mentioned previously, there is at least one regional treasure hunting club in each state. Most of these groups hold monthly meetings; several have their own publication. A few sponsor once-a-year competition meets and invite treasure hunters country-wide to come and participate. Because mailing addresses and officers of most of these clubs change from year to year, it is not practical to include names and addresses here. However, if you would like the name and address of the club nearest you, write one of the major metal detector manufacturers, who normally have current information on the various clubs and their activities. A number of periodicals, such as *Treasure* and *Western & Eastern Treasures,* do a good job of reporting club activities.

PERIODICALS

WESTERN & EASTERN TREASURES
Ray Krups, Managing Ed.
Monthly - $10/yr. - $1/issue - 66 p. il.

Same general types of articles as *Treasure,* including emphasis on treasure hunting club activities and hunts. An excellent publication. *From: People's Publishing Co., P.O. Box 7030, Compton, Calif. 90224*

TREASURE
Bob Grant, Ed.
Monthly - $11.25/yr. - $1.25/issue - 74 p. il.

Each issue contains something of interest to all treasure hunters: stories of treasures found and waiting to be found; test reports on metal detectors and related equipment; personalities; reports on clubs and their activities; instructional articles; good editorial comment; book reviews. Bob Grant, no armchair editor, is active in treasure hunting and attends many treasure hunting functions. His personal activity and interest in treasure hunting are reflected in *Treasure*.
From: Jess Publishing Co., Inc., 7950 Deering Ave., Canoga Park, Calif. 91304

LOST TREASURE
John H. Latham, Ed.
Monthly - $11/24 months - $1/issue - 66 p. il.

Each issue is filled with so many "waybills" to lost treasure that an army of treasure hunters could be kept busy a lifetime searching them all out. Accounts of found treasures are also included, as well as features on books, calendar of coming events, and questions/answers. This is a publication which will keep a person's interest in treasure hunting at a high level.
From: Carter/Latham Publishing Co., Inc., P.O. Box 328, Conroe, Tex. 77301

NATIONAL TREASURE HUNTERS LEAGUE QUARTERLY
Ray Smith, Ed.
Quarterly - $5/yr. - 50 p. il.

Publication of the National Treasure Hunters League, this quarterly is devoted to reporting on activities of its subscribers, but it's also of interest to treasure hunters in general. Each issue includes several detailed "how to" articles and equipment test reports, plus many letters from people in the field.
From: National Treasure Hunters League, Box 53, Mesquite, Tex. 75149

IN THE STEPS OF THE TREASURE HUNTER
Gene Ballinger, Ed.
Bimonthly - $6/yr. - 16 p. il., tabloid-size

Dedicated to keeping the treasure hunter abreast of what is going on, each issue is put together in a very interesting and informative style. Reports on treasures found throughout the United States, "how to" articles and good editorial comment are helpful to the treasure hunter. Classified ad section.
From: "In The Steps," Calle de Sol, Elephant Butte, N. Mex. 87935

GOLD PROSPECTORS ASSOCIATION OF AMERICA NEWS
George Massie, Managing Ed.
Bimonthly - $5/yr. - 30 p. il.

Since treasure hunters love gold, treasure hunting and prospecting go hand-in-hand. This excellent publication will keep you informed about gold—where and how to find it, current information on gold pans, detectors and dredges.
From: Gold Prospectors Association of America, P.O. Box 507, Bonsall, Calif. 92003

DESERT
William and Joy Knyvett, Eds.
Monthly - $6/yr. - 75¢/issue - 48 p. il.

A top-quality publication slanted toward southwestern U.S. desert and ghost town subjects. Of particular interest to treasure hunters who like to search for relics and artifacts in ghost towns. Excellent photography and includes well-written features on desert flora and fauna, book reviews, and calendar of western events of interest to rock hounds and treasure hunters.
From: Desert, P.O. Box 1318, Palm Desert, Calif. 92260

BOOKS

TREASURE HUNTER'S MANUAL NO. 7
Karl von Mueller
1974 ed. - 330 p. il. - $6.95 (pb); $9.95 (hb)

The most complete, up-to-date guide to America's fastest-growing hobby, written by an old master of treasure hunting. Includes topics ranging from research techniques to detector operation, from legality to gold dredging.
From: Ram Publishing Co., P.O. Box 38464, Dallas, Tex. 75238

SUCCESSFUL COIN HUNTING
Charles L. Garrett
1977 ed. - 242 p. il. - $5.95 (pb)

Since 90% of today's treasure hunters spend time searching for lost coins, this book will be extremely helpful to those who hunt with a metal detector. It is the best and most complete guide to successful coin hunting and explains fully the how's, where's and when's of searching for coins and related objects. It includes a complete explanation of how to select and use the various types of coin-hunting metal detectors. Based on more than 20 years of coin hunting experience by the author, this volume contains a great amount of practical coin-hunting information that will not be found elsewhere.
From: Ram Publishing Co., P.O. Box 38464, Dallas, Tex. 75238

TREASURE HUNTING PAYS OFF!
Charles Garrett
1976 - 96 p. il. - $2 (pb)

Tells how to begin and be successful in all phases of general treasure hunting—research; coin hunting; relic, cache and bottle seeking; prospecting; use of metal/mineral detectors. Excellent guidebook for the beginner, plus tips and ideas for the experienced TH'er. An excellent book worth far more than the price would indicate.
From: Ram Publishing Co., P.O. Box 38464, Dallas, Tex. 75238

TREASURE HUNTER'S DIGEST
Jack Lewis
1975 - 287 p. il. - $7.95 (pb)

In words and pictures, from front to back, this book gives an excellent view of the world of treasure hunting. Covers land and underwater searching, prospecting, research, artifact and relic collecting and what to do with your treasures after you have found them.
From: Digest Books, Inc., 540 Frontage Rd., Northfield, Ill. 60093

THE MODERN TREASURE FINDER'S MANUAL
George Sullivan
1975 - 196 p. il. - $8.95 (hb)

Contains a great amount of research and "how to" information you need in your search for buried treasures, coins, relics and gold. Hundreds of sources of information you require as you go about the

business of treasure hunting.
From: Chilton Book Co., Chilton Way, Radnor, Pa. 19089
Thomas Nelson & Sons, Ltd., Don Mills, Ontario, Canada

GOLD PANNING IS EASY
Roy Lagal
1976 - 84 p. il. - $2 (pb)

Since gold has been found in all 50 states and since there is much still to be found, you will want to be prepared if you find a likely-looking stream or dry wash. Contains valuable "how to find" information and simple "how to recover" gold-panning techniques. Metal detector and dredge applications included.
From: Ram Publishing Co., P.O. Box 38464, Dallas, Tex. 75238

TREASURE ANTHOLOGY, Vol. 1
E. S. "Rocky" LeGaye
1973 - 206 p. il. - $6 (pb)

Of hundreds of good books about lost treasures, this one stands out because of its wide range of stories...from lost mines to buried treasures; from the Conquistadores, Frontier America and the Plantation South. A joy to read because of the author's style. Research techniques, history of treasure hunting and location maps.
From: Western Heritage Press, 1530 Bonnie Brae, Houston, Tex. 77006

Metal Detector Operation

The following two books are "musts" for those who use or plan to use metal detectors.

DETECTOR OWNER'S FIELD MANUAL
Roy Lagal
1976 - 236 p. il. - $6.95 (pb)

Ranking far above all other books about metal detectors, this book includes detector operating instructions that can be found nowhere else. Detailed descriptions of how to treasure and cache hunt, prospect, search for nuggets and black sand deposits...in short, how to use your detector exactly as it should be used. Covers BFO-TR-VLF types, PI's, PRG's, and so forth. Explains precious metals, minerals, ground conditions and more.
From: Ram Publishing Co., P.O. Box 38464, Dallas, Tex. 75238

"HOW TO TEST" (Before Buying) DETECTOR FIELD GUIDE
Roy Lagal
1973 - 76 p. il. - $2.95 (pb)

Completely explains the inner workings of the BFO, TR and discriminator types of detectors. Discusses how to test for sensitivity, stability, total response, wide scan, soil conditions, coils, Faraday shields and frequency drift so that you may avoid incompetent detector engineering and overly-enthusiastic, misleading advertising.
From: Ram Publishing Co., P.O. Box 38464, Dallas, Tex. 75238

sources of books

DESERT MAGAZINE
Book Order Dept., Box 1318, Palm Desert, Calif. 92260
Great selection of over 300 books on the West. Write for order information and listing or obtain from a copy of *Desert.* Maps, prints, gold pans, back issues of *Desert,* and so on, also available.

FRONTIER BOOKS
Box 805, Fort Davis, Tex. 79734
Many old and out-of-print treasure hunting books—ghost towns, treasure sites, history of the West—all and more are covered. List available free on request.

H. GLENN CARSON ENTERPRISES
801 Juniper Ave., Boulder, Colo. 80302
Free listing of over 200 books on all phases of treasure hunting available on request.

IN THE STEPS OF THE TREASURE HUNTER
Calle de Sol, Elephant Butte, N. Mex. 87935
Write for free listing of treasure hunting books.

WHITE'S ELECTRONICS, INC.
1011 Pleasant Valley Rd., Sweet Home, Oreg. 97386
Discover, 12 p. il. Bimonthly publication sent free on request. Presents new developments in company products, tips on how best to utilize metal detectors in various applications. Includes many photos and success "letters" from treasure hunters.

NATIONAL TREASURE HUNTERS LEAGUE
P.O. Box 53, Mesquite, Tex. 75149
A magazine published by NTHL, available free on request, contains a categorized listing and order information on the more than 400 titles of treasure hunting-related books they offer.

RAM PUBLISHING CO.
P.O. Box 38464, Dallas, Tex. 75238
This is the only group that has concentrated on publishing books about the technique of treasure hunting and metal detector operation, as opposed to the "treasure trails and tales"-type. Some good, hard-core info available here, particularly in E. S. LeGaye's book on detector circuitry operation and Roy Lagal's several books on detector usage. Prices are good, too. List is available for the asking.

WESTERN HERITAGE PRESS
1530 Bonnie Brae, Houston, Tex. 77006
Good selection of the best in the treasure hunting field. Write for list and order information.

GARRETT ELECTRONICS
2814 National Dr., Garland, Tex. 75041
Garrett has several free publications that would be worth getting, particularly the *Operating Manual.* All, of course, push Garrett instruments; but, nevertheless, there's some good info to be found in 'em—and they're free. Can't beat that.

Treasure Hunting Secrets, 32 p. il. Book on general treasure hunting. Free on request.

Operating Manual, 74 p. il. Book containing complete instructions for operating the BFO, TR and VLF-type metal detectors, including many operating and treasure hunting tips. A good source of material, if you wish to study about the various types of detectors before purchasing one. Free on request.

Start Your Own Treasure Hunting Club, 2 p. This flyer, free on request, gives ideas and tips on organizing a TH'ing club.

The Roundtable, 12 p. il. A bimonthly publication that contains information on how to be a successful treasure hunter. Discusses metal detectors and how to use them in all phases of treasure hunting. Treasure stories, finds, and so forth, are also included in each issue. Sent free on request.

FILM

GARRETT ELECTRONICS, INC.
2814 National Dr., Garland, Tex. 75041
Two 16mm outdoor adventure films with sound available for bookings to clubs or hobby groups. No charge except to pay shipping/insurance both ways.

The Silent Past. A 150-year-old "ghost" prospector leads his grandson and family in search of a lost West Texas silver mine. Shows treasure hunting with detectors in the scenic, rugged Big Bend country of Texas.

The Westward Way. A family in their motor home follows the Lewis/Clark route to the Pacific. A bit commercial, but still an interesting film which shows metal detector usage, historical sites and beautiful scenery. Send your name and address, number of families expected to view the film(s) (free treasure hunting books will be sent for each family), $2.50 to cover shipping and insurance, give name of film(s) you want and date needed.

METAL DETECTORS

In the hardware department, treasure hunting really only requires a metal detector. Of course, collaterally, you should have something to dig with. A garden trowel and a narrow spade would be good digging tools, together with a long, thin rod for probing in the earth (could save some time by precisely locating the object picked up by the detector). Two other items are also worth having along: a haversack with some old rags for wrapping and collecting your finds in, and a decent-size piece of canvas, or something similar, on which to put any dirt you dig up. That way it's easier to fill the hole in, and leave hardly a trace that you've been there—especially if you take care in removing the topsoil and grass in unit pieces.

METAL DETECTORS
$50 - $800

Metal detectors operate somewhat like magnets, in that they emit (electromagnetic) lines of force. If some substance that will conduct electricity and/or magnetic lines of force comes within range of this force field, it is affected by it, and it in turn affects the force field. The detector senses this electronically.

As simple as this may sound, it can be and is complicated by a number of factors, such as bobbing the detector up and down while walking over rough terrain, which changes the signal strength and may give the impression you've found something; mineralized soil, such as that found along the edge of the sea (salt) and out West, will conduct lines of force, and thus give a false signal or "bury" the weaker signal of a small object in its louder one; even temperature changes (moving from shade to sun or vice versa) will affect some electronic circuitry and create problems. Some detectors are designed to take some of these things into account, others are designed to take other factors into account—but there is no instrument made that can take all the problems into account in one instrument, so think about what you want the detector to do. Other factors affecting detector type and use are: the usual size and depth of the general objects searched for; the operator's desire to distinguish between ferrous (iron and Fe alloys) and nonferrous (all other conductive substances, i.e., copper, brass, gold, silver, aluminum, etc.) materials, and the operator's experience in being able to distinguish and verify the real signal from the false one before he even bends over to dig.

It's important to understand that there are different detectors made for different jobs and different degrees of experience. So take care in choosing yours.

At present, the three principal types of detectors are: the Beat Frequency Oscillator (BFO), the Transmitter-Receiver (TR) and the Very Low Frequency (VLF). A new instrument, the VLF/TR, has recently been introduced. It's a dual- or twin-circuit instrument incorporating the VLF and TR circuits. Other types of less popular detectors are the Phase Readout Gradiometer (PRG), the Pulse Inductance (PI) and the Radio Frequency (RF) two-box detectors.

BFO Types. *Advantages.* If you expect to engage in a wide range of treasure hunting experiences, including prospecting and metal/mineral identification, as well as coin and cache hunting, then the Beat Frequency Oscillator detector is the recommended type. Its broad range of accessories makes it the most versatile in the industry. The available Twin Circuit discrimination feature rounds out its coin-hunting capabilities. Its constant tone permits successful operation over rough terrain that contains negative mineralization. *Disadvantages.* In the area of coin hunting, the BFO is the more difficult instrument to learn to use. Inexperienced operators fail to recognize the weaker signals and thus cannot achieve the depth on coins as with TR detectors.

TR Types. *Advantages.* If you intend to engage primarily in *coin hunting* with occasional diversions to cache, relic and ghost-town hunting, then the Transmitter-Receiver detector is for you. The TR is easy to learn to use. Its 6-inch and 8-inch coils are lightweight. Its semi-silent tone, quickness of response, and its discriminating abilities make it by far the most desired coin-hunting detector. *Disadvantages.* No TR-type detector (regardless of make) can produce a uniform searchcoil pattern. Thus, the TR's ability as a metal/mineral identifying instrument is limited. Its quick audio response plus the large searchcoil operating characteristics make it extremely difficult to operate over rough terrain that contains iron mineralization.

VLF Types. *Advantages.* When operating in the VLF mode, these Very Low Frequency types of detectors are the deepest-seeking and easiest-to-operate over mineralized ground, and they detect as deeply in negative mineralized ground as in the air. They give fantastic all-metal depth detection in coin, cache and battlefield hunting and, with certain restrictions, excel in prospecting. *Disadvantages.* NOT for trashy areas since no VLF type will discriminate properly while maintaining mineral-free operation. Operation in the non-VLF, discrimination mode gives extra depth, but mineralized ground requires extra operating skill. Searchcoils are heavier than TR coils. The tuning "null" does not remain "fixed," thus all mineral-free types have limitations in prospecting. All types of mineral-free detectors should be backed up with a quality-built BFO.

VLF/TR Types. *Advantages.* In the VLF mode, these detectors are the easiest to operate over mineralized ground and they detect as deeply in iron-mineralized ground as in air. They give excellent all-metal depth detection in coin, cache and battlefield hunting and, with certain restrictions, excel in prospecting. In trashy areas, the operator may achieve (in VLF mode) a certain amount of discrimination. Featherweight VLF/TR searchcoils are comparable to standard TR searchcoils.

PRG Types. *Advantages.* The Pulse Readout Gradiometer is a TR type that undoubtedly has the best discriminating circuit. It is as sensitive as the VLF types. Operates perfectly on the beaches and in noniron-mineralized areas. *Disadvantages.* The instrument will not operate satisfactorily over iron-mineralized ground. It is heavier and more bulky than all other types. Its cost (approximately $800) may be difficult to justify.

PI Types. *Advantages.* The Pulse Inductance type is a radio frequency pulse type of detector. It is as sensitive as the VLF types, works perfectly over mineralized ground, and is easy to operate. *Disadvantages.* Present models will not discriminate. Its operation is much slower than other types. Its output signal is "like a bell ringing." At present, all models are imported from England and parts may be difficult to obtain.

RF Two-Box Types. *Advantages.* This type has been in use for about 30 years. It is designed to detect objects larger than baseball size. *Disadvantages.* Heavy, cumbersome, and will detect water, minerals and tree roots. Very few in use except by utility companies since the new VLF types will detect as deeply and without most of the above disadvantages.

Since the selection of the correct metal detector is a serious matter, you should read Roy Lagal's book, the ***Detector Owner's Field Manual,*** paying particular attention to the type of hunting you will be doing. Write the various manufacturers to request their literature. Study the literature carefully and thoughtfully before selecting your instrument in order to choose the "best" instrument for your particular needs. No one type of instrument will do everything perfectly. As your treasure hunting horizons expand, you may find you need two or more types of detectors in order to do everything you want to do.

SERVICE and REPAIRS

Metal detectors are known to be very reliable instruments requiring surprisingly few repairs even though they are subjected to some pretty bad operating conditions. Detectors are built so that they do not need periodic servicing...fresh batteries and reasonable care is all you need to be concerned about.

Should you think your detector does need service, please read through your instruction manual's troubleshooting section, if it has one, and try to make certain the trouble is not a fault of your operating technique or weak batteries. Manufacturers report that very often problems lie with the operator, not the detector. When you are confident the problem is the manufacturer's, not yours, wrap the detector in its original shipping carton and send it to them. You are advised NOT to let a local radio or TV repairman work on it. While metal detectors have many of the same components as radios or TV's, they are not the same to work on. Expert repair work can, in most cases, be found only at the factory or authorized repair station. Your instruction manual will tell you exactly what to do and where to send or take your detector for repair. Follow those instructions and you'll have many more years of enjoyable use from your "money-finding machine"!

_____ sources of detectors

There may be several metal detector dealers in your area; in other areas, there may be none. Because of the absence of dealers in many geographical areas, most detector manufacturers sell directly to the public through the mail. Write several manufacturers to request their product catalogs and related information. All will send you free information. Several manufacturers also distribute their products through dealers located throughout the United States, Canada and some foreign countries. Those marked with an asterisk (*) have large dealer networks, the addresses of which are listed in the major treasure hunting periodicals such as *Treasure, Western & Eastern Treasures, Treasure Search,* and *Lost Treasure.*

PACIFIC NORTHWEST INSTRUMENTS (PNI)
1309 West 21st St., Tempe, Ariz. 85282
PNI was probably the first company to enter the treasure hunting field with a complete line of all-metal construction BFO and TR detectors priced below $100. At present, their prices are at a point somewhere between the low-cost detectors and the higher-priced professional instrumentation. Ownership of the company changed hands in 1976 and, as a result, the company's product quality is being improved. PNI instruments perform well and are seen quite often throughout treasure hunting circles. PNI detectors ($60 to $230) have many unique features and should be considered, especially by those who do not wish to spend a great deal of money getting started in treasure hunting. Attractive brochure available free upon request.

METROTECH
475 Ellis St., Mountain View, Calif. 94043
This is a company about which you hear little because owner Curt Fisher wants it that way. He's satisfied to build a small quantity of first-rate, highly reliable TR detectors, and there's no problem selling what he builds. Quality, performance and dependability have been bywords in the Metrotech line for at least ten years. Prices run from $180 to $230. Free brochure upon request.

*NATIONAL TREASURE HUNTERS LEAGUE (NTHL)
P.O. Box 53, Mesquite, Tex. 75149
NTHL, headquartered in Dallas, is not a manufacturer but a distributor of approximately ten brands of detectors through branch dealers located throughout the U.S. Ray Smith, owner, stocks a complete line of related books and accessories for the treasure hunter. His quarterly publication of the same name as the organization is $5/year. One copy, however, will be sent free on request. Each issue describes all detector lines carried by NTHL and has many good articles and "found" treasure stories.

FISHER RESEARCH LABORATORY
917 East Main St., Klamath Falls, Oreg. 97601
Fisher is one of the oldest manufacturers in the business, dating back to the early 1930's. They offer a good line of TR's for the treasure-hunting hobbyist and are strong in the commercial field with the Fisher line of pipe locators. Their newest line of detectors, the VLF, ground canceling-type, are priced from $170. You may write for their free complete catalog.

A. H. ELECTRONICS
5100 Newport Dr., Unit 6, Rolling Meadows, Ill. 60008
This company builds a line of small, lightweight TR-type detectors, the A. H. Pro, with fully adjustable discrimination. Since their instruments operate with some difficulty over highly-mineralized ground, you would be wise to write, telling them where you will be operating and let them recommend the model you should have. Prices range from $230 to $350. For information concerning the A. H. Pro product line, write the factory for a free brochure.

*GARRETT ELECTRONICS, INC.
2814 National Dr., Garland, Tex. 75041
Garrett is the only company building complete lines of the most popular types of detectors: the BFO, TR and VLF/TR types. Charles Garrett, President and owner of the company, uses and continuously field-tests his products to insure customers receive perfect detector operation under all types of environmental and ground conditions. Garrett instruments are quality throughout and service to the customer is excellent. The company builds a complete line of attachments for all three detector types. A conversion kit is available for $40 which permits all types to be quickly (in about two minutes) converted to either hip, chest or sling-mount configurations. Carrying cases, suitcases, speed handles and other attachments are available. Underwater searchcoils are available for BFO detectors which permit detection of submerged metallic objects to depths of 50 feet. At this writing, the company is testing its new, self-contained detector for underwater exploration. All instruments have fully adjustable discriminating features and range in price from $150 to $300.

The company manufactures the Garrett "Gravity Trap" Gold Pan for the prospector and weekend gold-panning hobbyist.

A 32-page illustrated *Buyer's Guide* and an interesting book, *Treasure Hunting Secrets,* are available free. Treasure hunting films are available on a free loan basis.

*WHITE'S ELECTRONICS, INC.
1011 Pleasant Valley Rd., Sweet Home, Oreg. 97386
White's Electronics builds complete lines of TR and VLF-type discriminating detectors and markets them throughout its large United States and Canadian distributor network. During the past 20 years, the company has built a keen reputation with its ruggedly-built and reliable instruments. Service to the customer is excellent. Their higher-than-average prices, however, do not necessarily reflect higher-than-average performance. Several complete lines of TR's are available with prices from $80 to $300. The company's excellent GEB (Ground Exclusion Balance) instruments (VLF types) range in price from $200 to $400. Complete lines of accessories and carrying cases are available, as is a line of self-contained underwater detectors (priced from under $200) and accessories. In addition, the company offers a line of gold pans and a dry washer for the prospector and treasure hunter who wants to try his luck. A complete set of product literature and a bimonthly publication, *Discover,* are available free upon request.

GOLD MOUNTAIN
604 Walnut Circle East, Garland, Tex. 75040
While the majority of companies building inexpensive (less than $100) detectors sell their instruments through mass-market discount stores, Gold Mountain sells primarily through existing treasure hunter supply dealers. These quality-built, low-cost metal detectors utilize tough ABS plastic construction, which stands up well in the field. The company builds complete lines of BFO and TR detectors including discriminators, in the price range $80 to $140. A free product catalog is available on request.

*COMPASS ELECTRONICS CORPORATION
3700 24th Ave., Forest Grove, Oreg. 97116
Compass Electronics produces a line of TR's that range in price from $100 to $370. These instruments are known for their good balance and fast operating characteristics. The company was founded in 1972 and enjoyed a very rapid rise in popularity. Reports indicate, however, that in 1976 some problems in production and design were encountered. Compass instruments feature all-metal construction and ease of operation. Accessories and carrying cases are available for each instrument. A lower-cost ($60 to $80) all-metal line is also available. This company recently entered the mass-market, discount store field with a new line of plastic constructed detectors, the CUE line. An attractive 6-page flyer is available upon request.

Photo by Geo. F. Jackson © 1973

Caving is the lighter side of speleology. It is the absolute of sports, matching the thrills of exploring the unknown with the intellectual challenge of explaining how the underground scenery has evolved. It is an adventure into darkness, a darkness that hides some of nature's rarest beauties.

Speleology is the scientific study of caves from all points of view. It includes the discovery of caves, the techniques of exploring them, cave surveying and photography, the study of the geological and chemical problems connected with their origin and development, the physical and atmospheric conditions in caves and the study of their flora, fauna, and deposits.

Modern speleology dates back to the late-nineteenth century with the founding of the first speleological society in France in 1895. Today, most countries of the world have societies for the promotion of speleology. Here in the Western Hemisphere, the National Speleological Society, founded in 1941, is the guiding light in marshalling the efforts of scientists and explorers in a widespread program of exploration, study, and conservation.

The best way to get into caving is through a local group, the name and address of which can be gotten from the National Speleological Society (NSS). No special background is required and fellow club members will teach you the correct procedures as you cave or through special club courses. Most clubs have group equipment, so you won't need much more than a hard hat, carbide or electric head lamp, and maybe a pair of coveralls.

The number of caves to be found and their relative difficulty varies considerably with the type of region you live in. In Kansas you might be hard-pressed to find anything bigger than a rabbit hole, whereas in Missouri caves are a dime a dozen. If you live in the Northwest or Hawaii, your caving trips may be in lava tubes. If you're in northern New England, they might be to boulder caves or small, wet, crawl-type caves. Clubs will often travel to distant caving areas because there are few if any local caves, or they have a preference for certain types of caverns.

Caving can be done in a single day, a weekend, or over a period of a week or more, and a group might consist of from two to twenty people. Usually a group of four to eight is about the right size, which in the event of a mishap, allows one to stay behind with the injured party and two to go for aid. One person working a cave alone is asking for big trouble. Regardless of the size party, though, someone on the outside should be given specific information as to where you are going, how long you'll be gone, and when you'll be back. It may also be a truism to say that safety should be paramount in everyone's actions; if you've ever had to get an injured person out of a cave, you'll know that safety and caution can never be emphasized enough.

Caving can present some unusual problems. You can't see or predict what lies below. A mountaineer can fly over his peak, take aerial telephoto shots of his route, and in general plan out each step of his attack. But when a team of cave explorers enters a new cave they have no way of knowing whether they'll need a hundred or a thousand feet of rope, supplies for a day or a week, rubber rafts, diving gear, climbing hardware or whatever. So the exploration of a cave proceeds slowly, step by step, with each trip advancing a certain distance until the entire cavern has been explored, surveyed and photographed.

A Cave Map

~ N ~

CROSS - SECTIONS

ROCK FLOOR

4' STALAGMITE

DRAPERY

~ LEGEND ~

————	SURVEYED PASSAGE
- - - -	UNSURVEYED PASSAGE
- - - - -	LOW OVERHANG
⌐⌐⌐⌐	DROP OR LEDGE
⌐⌐⌐⌐⌐	STEEP SLOPE
⌂	CEILING HEIGHT (in FEET)
	MASSIVE FLOWSTONE
	COLUMNS
▲	STALAGMITE
	LARGE ROCK
	BREAKDOWN

CROSS - SECTIONS

CABLE SLIDE

LEDGE ACROSS CEILING

WATER DEPTH

UPPER LIMIT OF WALL

LAKE

SHALLOW SINK

BAKER CAVE NO. 3
WILLIAMSON, FRANKLIN CO. PA.

SURVEYED BY S. HIVNER, L. OSBORNE, &
G. GRIM, JULY 1961
YORK GROTTO, NSS
DRAWN BY S. SMELTZER

SCALE IN FEET

0 10 20 30 40 50

ENTRANCE

People who care about caves and caving aren't out to promote the activity, because they've learned from experience that it only pays off in heartbreak. A cave environment is a very closed, very delicate system that is especially vulnerable to outside influences. Careless movement and idle touching can leave marks or result in damage that will never be obliterated or repaired through natural processes. This is because there is no wind or rain to wash away foot or finger prints and few workings of nature to biodegrade trash and refuse. As an illustration of how longlasting marks can be, explorers have come upon footprints left by paleolithic cave dwellers in dry sand, footprints that have remained unchanged over thousands of years. Innocent carelessness is not the only problem. In hundreds of caves, collectors have ripped away stalagtites and stalagmites for souvenirs, and vandals have smashed and defaced walls and formations that took centuries for nature to build. So it's not difficult to see why new cave discoveries are hushed up, and cave lists only give locations in very general terms.

More and more states are finally making it a crime to damage or remove historic relics, and sometimes even formations, from a cave. Of course, such laws are often very difficult to enforce, but it's a step in the right direction. Cave owners in many cases, especially in the East, have closed their property because of the actions of a minority of cavers. A landowner's signs and his known wishes must be respected or it goes bad for everyone. If he wants you to personally sign in prior to entering his cave, do so, even if it means driving an extra five or ten miles. Caver-cave owner relations are worthy of careful attention by everyone who caves.

—Take nothing but pictures, leave nothing but footprints—
(The caver's motto)

sources of information

NATIONAL SPELEOLOGICAL SOCIETY (NSS)
Cave Ave., Huntsville, Ala. 35810
The main organization for cavers in the United States, founded in 1941, and which now has 4,000 members in 115 chapters, called Grottos, throughout the country. Members receive a monthly newsletter and a quarterly bulletin, plus the right to buy cave books at less than publisher's price. Annual convention held each summer which involves spelunking at the convention locale, lectures, slide shows, and workshops. NSS's prime objective is the education of people who are already cavers and those who wish to begin caving. In view of the problem large numbers of participants pose to cave conservation, they do not promote caving as a popular sport. NSS policy statements, conservation material, membership applications, names and addresses of local members or Grottos are available upon request to interested parties. NSS publications:

NSS News, monthly, $6 a year, free to members; covers caving activities in the U.S.
NSS Bulletin, quarterly, $6 a year, free to members; primarily devoted to scientific cave papers.

Spelunker descending into Sites Cave, Va.

AMERICAN SPELEAN HISTORY ASSOCIATES
1117 36th Ave., East, Seattle, Wash. 98102
Dedicated to the study, dissemination, and interpretation of spelean history. Publishes *Journal of Spelean History,* quarterly; for members, $5/yr. (membership dues); information on early exploration of caves and details of their history.

CAVE RESEARCH ASSOCIATES
3842 Brookdale Blvd., Castro Valley, Calif. 94546
Publishes *Caves and Karst,* a bi-monthly summarizing current research in speleology; $3.25/yr., $7.50/3 yrs.

CAVE RESEARCH FOUNDATION
206 West 18th Ave., Columbus, Ohio 43210
Responsible for all exploration in the Flint Ridge Cave System and Mammoth Cave. Membership is by invitation only.

ASSOCIATION FOR MEXICAN CAVE STUDIES
P.O. Box 7672, Austin, Tex. 78712
Goals are collection and dissemination of information on Mexican caves. Publishes the *AMCS Newsletter, Bulletin,* and *Cave Report Series,* free to interested parties. AMCS is known for the beauty and quality of its publications.

PERIODICALS

DESCENT
8 issues per year - $6/yr. - 40 p. il.

Concerned with international news of caving, but about 75% of it is British.
From: Descent, 14 Central Parade Villas, Main Rd., St. Paul's Cray, Kent BR5 3HF England

THE BRITISH CAVER
Tony Oldham, Ed.
Intermittently - $2/issue

World-wide information pertaining to caving.
From: The British Caver, 17 Freemantle Rd., Bristol, BS5 6SY, England

THE CANADIAN CAVER
Semi-annually - $1/issue

Devoted to international as well as Canadian caving.
From: The Canadian Caver, Dept. of Geology, McMaster University, Hamilton, Ontario, Canada

DEPTHS OF THE EARTH
William R. Halliday
1976 - 398 p. il. - $14.95

Well written and illustrated accounts of America's best known caves and cavers. Contains 26 chapters, a glossary, index, and an excellent four-page listing of suggested further reading arranged by chapters. Contains a lot of history.
From: Harper & Row, Inc., Keystone Industrial Park, Scranton, Pa. 18512

AMERICAN CAVES AND CAVING
William R. Halliday
1973 - 300 p. il. - $11.95

A comprehensive study of American caving technique and equipment by the Director of the Western Speleological Survey. The book describes the types of caves available to spelunkers in the U.S., limestone caves, lava tubes, glacier caves, and other, lesser known structures and includes a discussion of the geographical and geological aspects of their formation. Halliday then gets into the proper protection and clothing needed for caving and continues with a meticulous commentary on equipment. The assorted types of brake bar rigs for rappelling, mechanical ascending devices and ropes are examined. An entire chapter is devoted to the types of headlamps available and exposes their weaknesses and strengths. Techniques of belaying, vertical ascending and descending, and exploratory procedures are covered. Optional techniques and frank reasons for Halliday's preference of when and where to use what are related. Two chapters are devoted to cave medicine and first aid, and cave search and rescue, where the author's experience as a physician is apparent. Appendix includes a good list of equipment sources.
From: Harper & Row, Inc., Keystone Industrial Park, Scranton, Pa. 18512

AMERICAN CAVING ILLUSTRATED
J. Welborn Story
1965 - 302 p. il. - $4.00

Written by a caver with input from practicing spelunkers all across the country, this is one book that touches on just about every practical aspect of caving. It starts with a general discussion of caving—underground navigation, safety, conservation, and so forth—then goes on to cover equipment, food and cooking, camping, geology of caves, cave climbing (seven chapters devoted to this), first aid, rescue, cave diving, speleophotography (including underwater cave photography), surveying, and finishing up with a chapter of caving vernacular and humor, including instructions for making wine(???). To give an example of how thorough the book is, the chapter on food and cooking includes charts that give the number of calories expended for specific activities involved in a cave expedition, so that necessary food and nourishment required can be computed in advance. The chapter on camping includes instruction in survival. A glossary gives definitions of caving terms, and a supplement includes sample legal release forms (for cave owners), cave field report form, and suggested reading list. This isn't a slick trade publication; some of the printing isn't sharp and not all the photographs reproduced well. But the wealth of information more than compensates for any graphic shortcomings. Besides, it makes the book seem very fresh and honest.
From: J. Welborn Storey, P.O. Box 38051, Capitol Hill Station, Atlanta, Ga. 30334

CELEBRATED AMERICAN CAVERNS
Horace C. Hovey
1970 - 228 p. - $9.00

This classic in American speleology was first published in 1882. Detailed descriptions of Mammoth Cave, Wyandot Cave, and the Caverns of Luray are given along with some maps. This reprint is based on the 1896 printing and includes an excellent new 38-page introduction by William R. Halliday.
From: Johnson Reprint Corp., 111 Fifth Ave., New York, N.Y. 10003

CELEBRATED AMERICAN CAVES
Charles E. Mohr and Howard N. Sloane, Eds.
1955 - 340 p. - $7.50

Fifteen well known American cavers are the contributors to this book that covers the whole Western Hemisphere. The book is well illustrated and, at the time of its publication, was the first general book on American caving to appear in seventy years.
From: Rutgers University Press, 30 College Ave., New Brunswick, N.J. 08903

THE CAVES BEYOND
Joe Lawrence, Jr. and Roger W. Brucker
1955 - 1st. ed. - 283 p. - out of print.

This excellent book is by far the best ever written on the adventures of exploring a single cave. It's based on the 1954 National Speleological Society's expedition to Floyd Collins Crystal Cave and includes nineteen chapters and seven appendices. Only thing lacking is an index. The book has been out of print for many years though it is available at libraries and can often be found at used book stores. Johnson Reprint Co. has indicated they plan to reprint it later this year. This is really a terrific book, and if I had to single out the most enjoyable caving book in my library, this would be it. —Chuck Pease.
From: Johnson Reprint Corp., 111 Fifth Ave., New York, N.Y. 10003

EXPLORING AMERICAN CAVES
Franklin Folsom
1962 - 2nd ed. - 319 p. - $1.50 (pb)

First published in 1956 as a hardback, this book gives the history, geology, lore, and location of some American caves. It is a good introduction to caving although a bit dated.
From: Macmillan Co., 866 Third Ave., New York, N.Y. 10022

THE LIFE OF THE CAVE
Charles E. Mohr and Thomas L. Poulson
1966 - 232 p. il. - $3.95

This is a must for every caver's shelf. It contains probably the greatest collection of cave photography ever found in one book; over 100 color and 50 black and white photographs. Included is an appendix with a guide to scientific names, how to become a spelunker, glossary, bibliography, and index. This book is available at such a low price because it was developed jointly with the World Book Encyclopedia and produced with the cooperation of the United States Department of the Interior.
From: McGraw-Hill Book Co., 1221 Sixth Ave., New York, N.Y. 10020

THE MYSTERIOUS WORLD OF CAVES
Ernest Bauer
129 p. il. - $4.95
From: Franklin Watts, Inc., 845 Third Ave., New York, N.Y. 10022

SPELEOLOGY, THE STUDY OF CAVES
George W. Moore and Brother G. Nicholas
1964 - 120 p. il. - $2.00 (pb)

An excellent introduction to the science of speleology. Prepared in cooperation with the NSS, this book's eight chapters include introduction, origin of caves, underground atmosphere, growth of formations, cave microorganisms, cave animals, evolution of blind cave animals, and man's uses of caves.
From: National Speleological Society, Cave Ave., Huntsville, Ala. 35810

BRITISH CAVING
C. H. D. Cullingford, Ed.
1962 - 2nd ed. - 592 p. - $17.50

This is a revised and enlarged edition of an excellent speleological reference book that is of much use to both the beginner and the professional caver. Contains an extensive bibliography and is considered the textbook of speleology.
From: National Speleological Society, Cave Ave., Huntsville, Ala. 35810

BOOKS

LUMINOUS DARKNESS
Alfre Bogli and Herbert W. Franke
1966 - 84 p. il. - $14.95
From: Rand McNally Co., P.O. Box 7600, Chicago, Ill. 60680

GLACIERS OR FREEZING CAVERNS
Edwin Swift Balch
1970 - $9.00
From: Johnson Reprint Corp., 111 Fifth Ave., New York, N.Y. 10003

CAVE REGIONS OF THE OZARKS AND BLACK HILLS
Luella Agnes Owen
1970 - $7.50
From: Johnson Reprint Corp., 111 Fifth Ave., New York, N.Y. 10003

SUCKER'S VISIT TO THE MAMMOTH CAVE: Including a History of the Experience and Adventures of a Party Who Undertook to See the Cave and Have Some Fun Going There
Ralph Seymour Thompson
1970 - $5.50
From: Johnson Reprint Corp., 111 Fifth Ave., New York, N.Y. 10003

VISITING AMERICAN CAVES
Russell Gurnee and Howard Sloane
1966 - 246 p. - $4.95
From: Crown Publishers, 419 Park Ave., S., New York, N.Y. 10016

Constitution Pillar, Wyandotte Cave, Ind. Geo. Jackson © 1973.

Chuck Pease in Gouffre Berger, France. Wilton Jones.

sources of books

STATE GEOLOGICAL SURVEYS
Many of the state geological surveys have produced guide books to their caverns, which include descriptive commentary on each cave, maps, photographs, and locations. We weren't able to check out all of the states, but you can, or at least check your own state's survey for possible caving data. Addresses of state geological surveys are in the Maps Section of the *Source Book.*

ANNE OLDHAM
Rhychydwr, Crymych SA41 3RB, Dyfed, United Kingdom
Complete selection of new, old and out-of-print books on caving from all over the world. If Anne Oldham doesn't have it, or can't find it, it doesn't exist. Also handles speleo journals and periodicals. Send Anne one U.S. dollar ($1) and she'll send you back a batch of mimeo lists.

JOHNSON REPRINT CORP.
111 Fifth Ave., New York, N.Y. 10003
Specializes in bringing back old and valuable and some recently published caving books that have gone out of print.

The Problems of Publicity

Cave exploring should not be pushed publicly. The people who are caving now and those who will cave in the future should be fully educated on safe caving habits and taught strong conservation attitudes. A careless camper can burn down a forest, and in fifty or a hundred years it has regrown, but a careless caver breaks off formations that may take thousands of years to regrow—if they ever do. This is why more and more clubs are finally realizing the folly of using publicity to attract more people to their meetings.

Excluding cave surveys of Virginia (1933) and Pennsylvania (1930 & 1932) there were no books on general American cave exploration published from 1883 to 1938. From 1939 to 1954 there were only three books by Clay Perry about caves in New York and the New England states. But from 1955 through 1972 it was a different story, and at least twenty books on the generalized subject of American caving have appeared, plus numerous cave survey lists, pamphlets, magazines, etc.

In the last few years a debate over the pros and cons of publishing has emerged. The pros say that we now have information and that it should be published in order to be preserved and to be useful to both the scientist and the spelunker. Without publication much data could be lost or work duplicated unknowingly. The cons argue that caving articles and books influence more people to go caving thereby increasing the damage caused to caves. Also publication of cave lists or surveys enables novices to sometimes get themselves into predicaments from which they must be rescued, and encourages vandalism in the more accessible caves. Who is right?

Obviously you cannot expect everyone to stop compiling cave lists or writing cave adventure books. The conservationists, realizing that cave surveys will be published in any case, have attempted to convince the compilers of such lists to generalize their cave locations and not be specific. Some groups favor giving cave locations by the county. Also the lists should be controlled and not sold to the general public, but this is seldom the case. One very important message that should appear in all cave material written for the public is a note about safety and conservation. Authors should stress the fact that inexperienced cavers should contact local caving clubs and that utmost care should be taken to prevent damaging anything in a cave.

—Chuck Pease.

CAVING GEAR

A basic rule in caving is that each caver should carry three independent sources of light. These might be your main head lamp, either carbide or electric, a flashlight, and some eight-hour candles with matches. People have been known to find their way out of a cave by using matches alone. Be sure yours are in a waterproof container and in a place where they won't be lost. Many people carry two or three containers in different locations. Remember, the most important thing a spelunker needs is light.

CARBIDE LAMP
$6 - $12
Used by most cavers in the past and still preferred by many today, the carbide lamp is easy to operate and requires only water and carbide to burn. It gives off an even and spread-out light. Its biggest advantage is that the whole unit mounts on a hard hat and there's no cord to get in the way. You need to carry a container of water to feed it unless a reliable water source is available in the cave, a container for fresh carbide, and a container for spent carbide. Dumping used carbide in a cave or burying it is no longer an acceptable practice. In addition, you should carry a carbide tip cleaner and a few spare parts such as extra felt, gasket, and tip. Justrite is the standard brand for carbide lamps in the U.S., and until just a year or so ago they were building them out of solid brass. Today, they're made of plastic. Since the changeover, we haven't heard a complimentary word for Justrite from anyone. Premier solid brass carbide lamps are available for $9 to $11 from Recreational Equipment Co. and Eastern Mountain Sports.

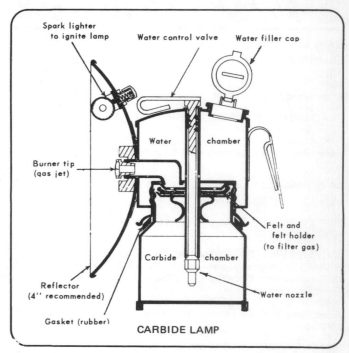

CARBIDE LAMP

Spark lighter to ignite lamp — Water control valve — Water filler cap — Water chamber — Burner tip (gas jet) — Felt and felt holder (to filter gas) — Carbide chamber — Reflector (4'' recommended) — Water nozzle — Gasket (rubber)

ELECTRIC HEAD LAMPS
$5 - $15
The electric head lamp has increased in popularity over the last few years as longer lasting batteries have been developed. Its advantages over carbide are that it gives a brighter beam of light, can be safely used when going through waterfalls without fear of it going out, and does not generate the heat that a carbide lamp does. Disadvantages are: it is heaver, on long trips spare batteries and bulbs need to be carried, and it has a cord that seems to get in your way at the most inopportune moments. Technology is rapidly approaching the point where soon cavers may have available a lightweight, long-lasting electric head lamp that can be all self-contained on the front of a hard hat. When this point is reached carbide lamps will become a thing of the past. Eastern Mountain Sports carries electric head lamps in the $9-to-$10 price range.

FLASHLIGHT
$2 - $6
A waterproof small 'C' cell flashlight makes an ideal back-up source of light and is also handy when changing carbide or batteries in your head lamp. If you can't find one locally, Eastern Mountain Sports sells a waterproof one for about $3. Spare batteries and bulb should be carried for flashlight.

You need to be warm whether you're sitting for long periods holding a survey marker or moving quickly through a long crawl way. The experienced caver will wear clothing that he can either open up or peel off when he's too hot and close up when he's too cold. Jeans are undoubtedly the most common for both male and female cavers. Sweat shirts, wool shirts, and heavy duty work shirts are quite commonly worn also. Each caver decides after some experimentation what's best. Some cave in tennis shoes, others, in hiking boots, and still others in combat boots. A wet or cold cave may require specialized clothing such as exposure or wet suits (like for skin diving), a glacier or ice cave may call for down clothing. A swimsuit may be in order for a trip through a warm stream cave, and in others you may need overboots or waders. If the cave has sharp rocks, gloves and knee pads may be required. Some of this specialized gear is discussed in other sections of the *Source Book*: wet suits in the Diving section, down clothing under Winter Bivouacking. The rest of it follows:

HARD HAT
$4 - $6
There are five types of hard hats currently available—construction hats, miners hats, rock helmets, the Bell Toptex climbing helmet and motorcycle helmets. Most cavers don't like the hats with the wide brim all the way around, since they can sometimes be troublesome in small, tight passages. Motorcycle helmets are seldom used because they're hot and you can't hear well when wearing them. Some cavers who also climb use a regular $20 rock helmet for both activities. Recreational Equipment Co. sells several good ones in this price range. The most popular caving headgear though, is the fiberglass safety hats used by miners. Sears, Roebuck and Co. and Mine Safety Appliance Co. sell these for under $10 (MSA has a much wider selection). A lamp bracket is required on any hat or helmet used, and if yours doesn't have one, MSA sells lamp brackets for $1 that can be attached with a couple of screws.

COVERALLS
$3 - $15
Some sort of coverall or flight suit is often preferred since it can be worn over regular clothes to protect them from damage. Sears, J. C. Penny, Levi-Strauss all make coveralls in the $9 to $15 price range. Palley's sells military surplus flight suits for $3 to $6.

KNEE PADS
$2 - $6
When the crawling gets rough a pair of carpenter's or Mason's rubber knee pads can make it a lot easier. Most hardware stores carry them, or check Wilderness Camping Supplies or Camp and Trail Outfitters (in the Backpacking section).

Hauling duffle through a damp passage at the 2100-ft. level.
Photo by Wilton H. Jones.

Other Gear

BIVOUACKING GEAR
For caving expeditions lasting several days some sort of bivouacking gear will be needed—cooking and mess equipment, perhaps a tent to provide a confined space for warmth and shelter against dripping water, a sleeping bag and mat, and so forth. Since caves can often be soggy places it may be wise to consider Dacron Polyester Fiberfill II in place of down for sleeping bags and jackets. There are more details on this in the Backpacking section, but clearly the major reason is that it absorbs less than 1% moisture, which makes it easier to wring out and dry. Unlike down, Fiberfill maintains its shape and won't clump up when wet or wrung out, which means it will maintain its good insulating qualities.

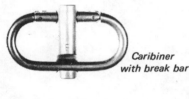

Caribiner with break bar

CAVING HARDWARE
Often the caver must borrow from the mountaineer's equipment. Pitons, piton hammers, ascenders, rope, and so forth may be needed to get him up steep walls and down into pits. Ice axes and crampons might be needed in glacier or ice caves. You might need a twenty-foot rope hand-line to help people up a steep slope or you might need two thousand feet in a deep Mexican pit cave. For a full discussion of this equipment and its use, see the Climbing Section.

Jumar ascender

Cable ladder

CABLE LADDERS
About $40
Cable ladders are not used as much as they once were. New rope climbing techniques have enabled the caver to lighten his load by replacing ladders with single ropes. Clubs sometimes still use ladders for short drops where it would take too long for each individual to rope up. The only source of ladders that we know of is Caving Supplies in England.

For a discussion on cave photography, mapping, surveying, and first aid, see (respectively) Field Photography, Land Navigation & Maps, and First Aid & Medical Sections.

BAGS
$1 - $5
For carrying supplies and lunch. The ideal thing is an Army surplus ammo pouch or gas mask bag, but there are many types available that will do just as well. You can choose one that fastens around your leg or hip or one that goes over the shoulder or on your back. And on major expeditions, Army duffel bags are very handy for lowering gear down pits and hauling it out. Palley's has an assortment of surplus bags from $1 to $5. Tupper-ware containers are great for carrying sandwiches or other foods because they seal out dust, which is to a cave what sand is to the beach.

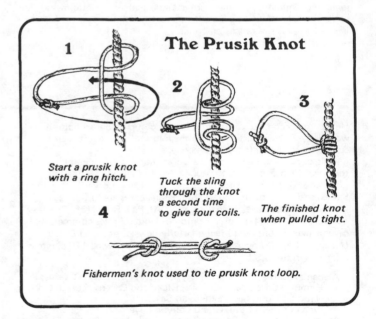

The Prusik Knot

1 Start a prusik knot with a ring hitch.

2 Tuck the sling through the knot a second time to give four coils.

3 The finished knot when pulled tight.

4 Fisherman's knot used to tie prusik knot loop.

RUBBER RAFTS
$18 - $33
Spelunkers are sometimes stopped by a large underground lake or stream. To swim across may not be feasible because of the distance or water temperature, so inflatable rubber rafts are hauled into the cave to use. Extreme caution is necessary when using them, because an overturned raft can be fatal, or at the very least, result in the loss of precious equipment. P & S Sales sells surplus one- and two-man inflatable rafts for $19 to $32.

sources of caving gear

CAVING

CAVING SUPPLIES
84 Chatsworth Rd., Cheam, Sutton, Surry, England
Good, well-rounded source of caving equipment and supplies. For a comprehensive list of over 300 items, send $1 to the above address (to cover postage & handling).

JOSEPH LEONARD CO.
1625 Blake St., Denver, Colo. 80202
U.S. distributors for the Safesport brass carbide lamp with 4" chrome reflector, $9.75. Have no specifics on the lamp except that it looks very similar to the old Justrite. Spare parts are available. Leonard does not sell directly to the public; however, a letter of inquiry may get you the address of a source.

BILL CUDDINGTON
4729 Lumary Dr., Huntsville, Ala. 35810
Technical caving gear.

BLUE WATER LTD.
P.O. Box 129, Carrollton, Ga. 30117
Technical caving gear and rope.

EASTERN MOUNTAIN SPORTS (EMS)
1041 Commonwealth Ave., Boston, Mass. 02215
Aside from carrying an exceptional line of outdoor recreational staple, including climbing, mountaineering, and orienteering equipment, they carry one type of electric head lamp and the Premier brass carbide lamp ($9), plus several caving books.

WILDERNESS CAMPING SUPPLIES
615 N. Walnut St., Bloomington, Ind. 47401
Carries a complete inventory of all cave exploring supplies and also some mountaineering equipment. One of the few sources of knee pads. Includes all carbide lamp replacement parts. No books or publications are sold. Write for further information.

RECREATIONAL EQUIPMENT, INC.
1525 11th Ave., Seattle, Wash. 98122
Premier brass carbide lamps (about $9), climbing helmets ($9 to $25). Free 73-page catalog of general recreational equipment.

GIBBS PRODUCTS
854 Padley St., Salt Lake City, Utah 84108
Sells only Gibbs ascenders, ropes, slings, and carabiners. These mechanical rope ascenders are attached to the legs for a natural method of walking up the rope. Beginners should practice outside a cave prior to using them underground. Small catalog available free.

A cave bivouac. Photo by Etienne Lemaire

CAVE TOURS

Unless you accompany some established group on an expedition or work up your own party to go cave exploring, you're left with the guided tours conducted in commercial caves.

Missouri has more commercial caves than any other state; in 1972 they had 30 in operation. Kentucky, North Carolina, Tennessee, Virginia, and West Virginia contain some of the finest caves in the United States, and many of the oldest commercial caves are in this region.

The National Caves Association (NCA), P.O. Box 3128, Chattanooga, Tenn. 37404, an organization of United States commercial cave owners, publishes a small quarterly newsletter called *Down Under*, and the October 1972 issue listed the following 170 commercial caves in the U.S.:

Alabama - Cathedral Caverns, Crystal Cave, Forbidden Caverns, Kymulga Cave, Manitou Cave, Rickwood Cavern, Russell Cave National Monument, Sequoyah Caverns.
Arizona - Colossal Cave, Grand Canyon Caverns.
Arkansas - Blanchard Springs Caverns, Bull Shoals Caverns, Diamond Caverns, Dogpatch Caverns, Hurricane River Cave, Mystery Cave, Onyx Cave, Ozark Mystery Cave, Rowland Cave, Shawnee Caverns, Wonderland Cave.
California - Bear Gulch Caves, Boyden Cave, Crystal Cave, Lava Beds Caves, LaJolla Caves, Lake Shasta Caverns, Mercer Caverns, Mitchells Caverns, Moaning Cave.
Colorado - Cave of the Winds.
Florida - Florida Caverns State Park, Ocala Caverns.
Georgia - Cave Springs Cave.
Idaho - Crystal Ice Cave, Lava Caves, Minnetonka Caves, Shoshone Ice Caves.
Illinois - Cave-in-Rock Cave.
Indiana - Blue Springs Cave, Donaldson, Hamer & Twin Caves, Endless & River Caves, Marengo Cave, Squire Boone Caverns, Wyandotte Caves.
Iowa - Crystal Lake Cave, Maquoketa Cave, Spook Cave, Wonder Cave.
Kentucky - Carter & Cascade Caves, Crystal Onyx Cave, Daniel Boone's Cave, Diamond Caverns, James & Coach Caves, Lost River Cave, Mammoth Cave National Park, Mammoth Onyx Cave, Saltpetre Cave.
Maine - Anemone Cave.
Maryland - Crystal Grottoes.
Michigan - Bear Cave.
Minnesota - Mystery Cave.
Missouri - Bridal Cave, Big Springs Onyx Caverns, Bluff Dwellers Cave, Boone Cave, Civil War Cave, Crystal Cave, Crystal Caverns, Fantastic Caverns, Fishers Cave, Honey Branch Cave, Jacobs Cave, Keener Cave, Mark Twain Cave, Marvel Cave Park, Meramec Caverns, Mystic River Cave, Old Spanish Cave, Onondaga Cave, Ozark Caverns, Ozark Wonder Cave, Rebel Cave, Round Spring Cavern, Smittle Cave, Stark Caverns, Talking Rocks, Truitt's Cave.
Montana - Lewis & Clark Cavern.
Nebraska - Robber's Cave.
Nevada - Lehman Caves.
New Hampshire - Lost River Glacial Caverns, Mystery Hill Caves, Polar Caves.
New Mexico - Carlsbad Caverns National Park, Ice Caves.
New York - Howe Caverns, Natural Stone Bridge and Caves, Secret Caverns.

Caves for the Record Book

A beginner in any sport is quite often interested in records. Where is the largest, deepest, longest, highest mountain, river, lake, cave, whatever? And a novice spelunker is no exception. Even among experienced cavers the discussion about cave depths and lengths is a never ending one. There is a certain thrill in exploring a record-breaking cave. Cave explorers by their very nature are always seeking out the unusual or unknown, and being the first to cross that unseen barrier can act as a stimulus to further exploration. At one time the magic depth barrier for caves was 1000 metres and even today only two caves are known to surpass this figure. Of course, any list of cave depths or lengths will change on a daily basis as exploration and mapping continue, sometimes even around the clock.

For many years the record for the longest cave swung back and forth between Holloch Cave in Switzerland and the Flint Ridge Cave System in Kentucky. However, the recently announced connection between Flint Ridge and Mammoth Cave has made this system more than twice as long as Holloch Cave.

It should be mentioned that while Holloch is one cave with a single entrance, the Flint-Mammoth Cave System is just that—a system of several caves that, through extensive exploration, have been shown to be connected. There are fourteen known entrances to this system, making it much more accesible. Holloch Cave presents additional problems. Explorers there must monitor the water level carefully to avoid being trapped for days or even weeks at a time.

The past four years have seen many big changes in the list of the longest known caves. In 1969 the United States had two in the top seven and five in the top sixteen. As of February 1973, the United States had four of the top five and seven of the top twelve. The roster of the deepest caves has also had several changes, but the United States is still not even listed in the fifty deepest. France and Italy continue to dominate this list with fourteen out of the top twenty. Holloch Cave retains the unique position of being the only one to appear in the top twenty for both depth and length. —Chuck Pease.

LONGEST CAVES IN THE WORLD

	Metres	Miles
1. Flint-Mammoth Cave System, Ky., USA	232,605	144.4
2. Holloch Cave, Switzerland	115,620	71.8
3. Jewel Cave, S. Dak., USA	72,300	44.9
4. Greenbriar Caverns, W. Va., USA	72,145	44.8
5. Organ-Hendricks Cave Sys., W. Va., USA	64,410	40.0*
6. Sistema Cavernario de Cuyaguateja, Cuba	52,980	32.9
7. Eisriesenwelt Cave, Austria	42,190	26.2
8. Wind Cave, S. Dak., USA	37,035	23.0*
9. Peschtschera Optimistitscheskaja, USSR	36,880	22.9
10. Complejo Palomera-Dolencias, Spain	36,390	22.6
11. Blue Spring Cave, Indiana, USA	30,400	18.9
12. Binkleys Cave, Ind., USA	28,985	18.0*
13. Ozernaja Peschtschera, USSR	26,360	16.4
14. Reseau de la Dent Crolles, France	25,715	16.0
15. Reseau Courry-Cocaliere, France	25,250	15.7
16. Ogof Ffynnon Ddu, Great Britain	25,000	15.5
17. Goule de Foussoubie, France	22,000	13.7
18. Domica Cave, Hungary & Yugoslavia	22,000	13.7
19. Dachsteinmammuthohle, Austria	20,250	12.6
20. Gran Caverna de Santo Tomas, Cuba	20,000	12.4

*These are approximate figures.

DEEPEST PITS IN THE WORLD

1. El Sotano, Mexico	410	1345
2. Abyss at Provatina, Greece	396	1298
3. Le Pot II, Isere, France	337	1105
4. Sotano de las Golongrinas, Mexico	334	1094
5. Gouffre Lepineux a la Pierre St-Martin, France/Spain	333	1091

DEEPEST PITS IN THE UNITED STATES

1. Fantastic Pit, Ellison's Cave, Georgia	155	510
2. Incredible Pit, Ellison's Cave, Georgia	134	440
3. Surprise Pit, Fern Cave, Alabama	123	404

DEEPEST CAVES IN THE WORLD

	Metres	Feet
1. Gouffre de la Pierre St-Martin, Fr./Spain	1350	4428
2. Gouffre Berger, France	1143	3749
3. Chourum des Aiguilles, France	980	3214
4. Gouffre du Cambou de Liard, France	935	3067
5. Abisso Michele Gortani, Italy	913	2995
6. Spluga della Preta, Italy	875	2870
7. Garma Ciega, Spain	853	2798
8. Reseau Felix Trombe, France	830	2722
9. Grotta del Monte Cucco, Italy	810	2657
10. Antro del Corchia, Italy	805	2640
11. Gouffre Criska, France	797	2614
12. Ghar Parau, Iran	795	2608
13. Scialet de la Combe de Fer, France	780	2558
14. Sniezna, Poland	770	2526
15. Gouffre Juhue, Spain	751	2463
16. Holloch Cave, Switzerland	750	2460
17. Gouffre Georges, France	726	2381
18. Gouffre Lonne Peyre, France	716	2348
19. Gruberhornhohle, Austria	710	2329
20. Piaggia Bella, Italy	689	2260

DEEPEST CAVES IN AMERICA

1. Sotano de San Agustin, Mexico	612	2007
2. Sotano del Rio Iglesia, Mexico	535	1755
3. Sotano de las Golondrinas, Mexico	514	1686
4. Cueva de San Agustin, Mexico	458	1504
5. El Sotano, Mexico	455	1492
6. Sotano de Tlamaya, Mexico	454	1489
7. Hoya de las Guaguas, Mexico	422	1385
8. Sotano de la Joya de Salas, Mexico	376	1234
9. Neff Canyon, Utah, USA	361	1184
10. Cueva de El Chorreadero, Mexico	345	1132

Compiled by Chuck Pease—Feb., 1973.

North Carolina - Linville Caverns.

Ohio - Crystal Cave, Olentangy Indian Caverns, Ohio Caverns, Perry Cave, Seneca Caverns, Zane Caverns.

Oklahoma - Alabaster Caverns State Park.

Oregon - Lava River Caves, Oregon Caves, Sea Lion Caves.

Pennsylvania - Crystal Cave, Indian Cave, Indian Echo Caverns, Laurel Caverns, Lincoln Caverns, Lost River Caverns, Onyx Cave, Penn's Cave, Woodward Cave, Wonderland Caverns.

South Dakota - Bethelhem Cave, Crystal Cave, Nameless Cave, Rushmore Cave, Sitting Bull Crystal Caverns, Stage Barn Cave, Wild Cat Cave, Wind Cave National Park, Wonderland Cave.

Tennessee - Bristol Caverns, Caverns of the Ridge, Crystal Cave, Cudjos Cave, Cumberland Caverns, Dunbar Cave, Indian Cave, Jewel Cave, Lost Sea, Ruby Falls, Tuckaleechee Caverns, Wonder Cave.

Texas - Cascade Caverns, Caverns of Sonora, Century Caverns, Cobb Cavern, Inner Space, Longhorn Caverns State Park, Natural Bridge Caverns, Wonder Cave.

Utah - Timpanogos Cave National Monument.

Virginia - Battlefield Crystal Caverns, Dixie Caverns, Endless Caverns, Grand Caverns, Luray Caverns, Massanutten Caverns, Melrose Caverns, Skyline Caverns.

Washington - Chelan Ice Caves, Crawford Cave.

West Virginia - Lost World, Organ Cave, Seneca Caverns, Smokehole Caverns.

Wisconsin - Cave of the Mounds, Crystal Cave, Eagle Cave, Kickapoo Caverns, Lost River Cave.

Wyoming - Spirit Mountain Caverns.

MEXICO

This country is not for the novice spelunker. Many of the caves have enormous pits and are often located far off the beaten path. You may very well have to use trails that were built by Indians hundreds of years ago to find caves that have not yet been explored, surveyed, or photographed. To go down for less than two weeks or more at one stretch is almost a waste of time. Some caves require three or four-day hikes just to reach the area.

photography

PHOTOGRAPHY

It's one thing to travel with a car-full of lenses, filters, tripods, light meters, film, and two or three cameras, seeking out and working with a selected subject, and quite another to carry the bare essentials to record the most exciting moment of a white-water kayak trip, a lightweight backpacking tour of Europe, a 15,000-ft. parachute jump, or a Caribbean wreck dive. Your outfit of camera, lenses, filters, tripods, and other accessories must be chosen carefully with due regard for versatility, weight, and bulk.

Since many trips are one-time visits to an area, enough film must be carried to get the pictures you want and in sufficient quantity to allow for the usual bad shots. An alternative is to develop the film in the field, inspect the negatives, and determine what needs to be reshot before leaving the place.

Developing black and white in the field is not at all complicated, and a number of tanks and special one-shot developers are available for this.

If you're really interested in the results of your photographic efforts and likewise want to save money, it's best to take up the whole bag and not only do your own shooting, but processing and printing, too. With the availability of discounts on quality gear through many New York mail-order shops, your initial investment in equipment can be kept down, and discount photo suppliers (for film and processing supplies) can save you much coin, compared to drugstores and commercial processors, if you're even slightly active in taking pictures. And doing your own work gives you quality control that you can't always be sure of when someone else is doing it.

Getting the hang of things, familiarizing yourself with terms, brands, and suppliers will take some effort, but in the long run it can really pay off, not only in a fun and educational hobby, but in practical results for information gathering. It's a fact that even some of the most accomplished photographers drastically overlook the value of a camera as an everyday recording device—see a cookbook recipe, shoot it; need a copy of a letter, shoot it; have to have an inventory of household items for insurance records, take pictures of all the rooms in your house; want to remember a bikini wandering down the beach, shoot it!

PERIODICALS

PHOTOGRAPHIC
Paul R. Farber, Ed.
Monthly - $9/yr. - $1/issue - 80 p. il.

This is a fine magazine, one honestly aimed at the needs of the amateur photographer. It contains articles and monthly regulars that deal with problems the non-professional is apt to encounter, avoiding heavy technical stuff without being too elementary. Recent issues have dealt with such subjects as how to process your own color transparencies, basic darkroom tricks, how to get the most out of stop bath, and a technique for flawless print mounting.

Other photography magazines seem to assume that the reader has mastered such basic things, and concern themselves with more sophisticated or specialized subjects. This makes them pretty useless to the beginner. *Photographic* is full of useful information and is the kind of magazine that ends up being read from cover to cover and then stashed away for reference.
From: Petersen Publishing Co., 8490 Sunset Blvd., Los Angeles, Calif. 90069

CAMERA 35
Willard Clark, Ed.
10 issues annually - $10/yr. - $1/issue - 84 p. il.

A pretty good, down-to-earth magazine with solid information even for the non-engineer types. All the dope is on 35mm, which is what you're likely to be working with in the field. Columns by Bob Nadler, Mike Edelson, Bill Pierce, and an on-going photo course by teacher-extraordinary, David Vestal, make each issue a good deal. Book reviews and photo essays, too. *Camera 35* is owned by American Express, so maybe you could use your card to subscribe.
From: Camera 35, P.O. Box 9500, Greenwich, Conn. 06830

MODERN PHOTOGRAPHY
Julia Scully, Ed.
Monthly - $9/yr. - $1/issue - 170 p. il.

Modern is more concerned with camera technique—the ability of the photographer to see, and interpret what he sees with his camera—than with the physics and optics of the tools of photography. While many articles are devoted to technical discussions of equipment, just as many deal with the work of contemporary photographers in an evaluative way. Good product information is given, for instance, in the annual camera buyer's guide which appears in the December issue and details pros, cons, and prices of popular cameras. A lot of good information, but it's not the kind of magazine one would sit down and read from cover to cover.
From: Modern Photography, 165 W. 46th St., New York, N.Y. 10036

POPULAR PHOTOGRAPHY
Kenneth Poli, Ed.
Monthly - $9/yr. - $1/issue - 170 p. il.

Articles devoted to the finer, more sophisticated aspects of photographic techniques, for instance, highly technical evaluations of lenses, complete with diagrams and graphs, and discussions of the photometrics of through-the-lens metering. If you're looking for this kind of information, you'll find it here. It isn't that the material is too advanced for an intelligent amateur to grasp, but it's of such a specialized nature that it's questionable whether the typical reader would find it valuable. Of general interest are new product evaluation, a question-and-answer column, beautiful photo spreads, as well as articles about noted photographers.
From: Popular Photography, P.O. Box 2775, Boulder, Colo. 80302

EASTMAN KODAK CO.
343 State St., Rochester, N.Y. 14650

Kodak's about got the market sewn up for how-to photography books. Most are well written and are valuable as quick reference information sources since they tend to avoid in-depth theory. The ones we've listed are only a few of the Kodak publications available from many photo shops. If you're interested in a full list, as well as a complete catalog of everything Kodak manufacturers, write them for the latest edition of their *Professional Products* catalog, which is free and a fine reference source in itself.

Kodak Master Photo Guide, 32 p. il., $3.95. This midget encyclopedia (3¾" x 4¾") will fit into a pocket or purse, and with its vinyl cover and coated card-weight pages, it's designed to take a lot of use. Sections and sub-sections are tab indexed and color coded for quick reference. Major divisions are Daylight Exposure, Filters, Artificial Light Exposure, Depth of Field, and Close-ups. There are nifty little computers for figuring exposures, aperture and film speed for flash, depth of field, and so forth and a wealth of charts and diagrams if you want to take time for them. The beginning photographer will consider this little book worth its weight (3 oz.) in gold. One of the handiest quick-reference books around.

Kodak Color Dataguide, $6.70. If you're working with color film, either shooting with it, or working with it in the darkroom, here's another invaluable quick-reference source. Includes basic descriptive and working data needed to correctly take, process, and print color pictures. Slanted toward advanced amateurs and professionals.

Kodak "Here's How" Series. This series offers basic, easy-to-understand information for the amateur on many phases of photography. Really a quick way to immerse yourself in the medium and learn the tools with as little sweat as possible. They're a good place for the beginner to start..Digest these and then go on to the Time-Life series or the Ansel Adams Books.

Here's How, $1.50. Bad weather pictures, remote releases in nature photography, glassware, tabletops, night photography, subject control, exposure meters.

More Here's How, $1.50. Titling, building a blind for nature photography, exhibition photographs, Kodacolor-X film, multiple flash, lenses, photographing stars.

The Third Here's How, $1. Photographing kids, wild flowers; technique articles on Kodak High Speed Ektachrome film, flash, colorslide manipulation.

The Fourth Here's How, 95¢. Movie lenses, color printing, print finishing, slide duplication, slide-tape talks, photographing antique cars.

The Fifth Here's How, $1.50. Pictorial lighting, underwater photography, aerial photography, photographing cars, dogs, flowers and glassware.

The Sixth Here's How, $1. Photographing insects, dance; candid photography, the art of seeing, movie editing, new pictures from old negatives.

The Seventh Here's How, 95¢. Color infra-red photography, top-quality slide projection, photographing motion as color, decorating your home with photographs, creating moods in pictures, time-lapse movies.

Color Photography Outdoors, $1.

Basic Scientific Photography, $1.25. Introduces the student and advanced amateur to the applications of photography for illustrating and documenting the natural sciences, archaeology and biomedicine.

Close-Up Photography, $2.75.

Filters for Black-and-White and Color Pictures, 95¢.

Adventures in Existing-Light Photography, 95¢.

Advanced Camera Techniques for 126 and 35mm Cameras, 95¢.

Color As Seen and Photographed, $1.

Flash Pictures, 95¢.

New Adventures in Outdoor Color Slides, 95¢. An inspiring book of picture-taking suggestions—close-ups of flowers, storytelling sequences, sunsets and other dramatic lighting effects.

Copying, $1.50. Covers equipment and techniques for copying photographs, paintings, drawings and documents, both in color and black-and-white. Includes 16 pages of data sheets on films for copying.

TIME-LIFE PHOTOGRAPHY SERIES
Publication date and pages vary per volume; price doesn't—$7.95 each

Life magazine was probably the major force in shaping modern concepts of photojournalism. It mastered superbly the use of photographs as a medium of visual instruction, so it would seem that a *Life* series devoted to the practical aspects of photography would have to be a winner. It is. The series is open-ended, that is, more volumes will be added later. Present volumes are:

The Camera. Outlines principles and techniques for the use of the three basic types of modern cameras: 35mm, 2¼" x 2¼", and large format (4" x 5" and 8" x 10"). There is a discussion of the fundamentals of camera optics as well as a history of the development of the camera. Includes "Camera Buyer's Guide." 235 p. il.

Light and Film. The types of film, the physics of light, and the use or artificial lighting. Includes "Guide to Camera Accessories." 227 p. il.

The Print. A step-by-step course in print-making with a discussion of film and paper. Illustrated with some of photography's greatest prints. Includes "Buyer's Guide to Darkroom Components." 227 p. il.

Color. A history of color photography, how to develop and print color at home, and how color photography works.

Photographing Nature.
Photographing Children.
Special Problems. Working around things like bad weather, unusual lighting, and so forth.

Photojournalism.
The Art of Photography.
The Great Photographers.
The Great Themes.

The Studio. The use of professional, large-format cameras and other studio equipment. Provides a guide for setting up a small commercial studio of your own.

Photography as a Tool. Scientific, industrial, and technological uses of photography, including underwater photography.

From: Time-Life Books, Time & Life Bldg., Rockefeller Ctr., New York, N.Y. 10020

PHOTOGRAPHY FOR THE SERIOUS AMATEUR
Eugen J. Skudrzyk
1971 - 367 p. il. - $12

Here's a book that covers just about every aspect of photography as it relates to the amateur. Beginning with a discussion of the value of workshops and correspondence courses, the author goes on to discuss choosing a camera and accessories, darkroom techniques, properties of lenses, nature photography, and much more. In the chapters on cameras and accessories, he names names in evaluating available cameras and lenses, and discusses special angles like buying from Hong Kong and from big New York discount dealers.
From: A. S. Barnes & Co., Cranbury, N.J. 08512

ANSEL ADAMS BOOKS
Ansel Adams
Publication date and pages vary per volume. Price $5.95 each.

The following books by master photographer Ansel Adams are considered by many to be among the best available as an introduction to photography.
The Negative
The Print
Natural Light Photography
Artificial Light Photography
From: Morgan & Morgan, Inc., 400 Warburton Ave., Hasting-on-Hudson, N.Y. 10706

AMATEUR PHOTOGRAPHERS HANDBOOK
Aaron Sussman
1973 - $8.95

The illustrations are not exactly all up to date, but the information is current and the presentation clear, concise, and easy to understand. Many consider this the "Photographer's Bible" and among the many introductory books for amateur photographers, it certainly ranks way up there. It's been around since 1941 and is in its eighth edition.
From: Thomas Crowell Co., 201 Park Ave., South, New York, N.Y. 10003

THE BLUEBOOK OF PHOTOGRAPHY PRICES
Thomas I. Perrett
$20

If you want to know how much to charge for your photos or movies, this book serves as a guide to the going prices. Perret states that the most important considerations in establishing your price are your expenses, the prices charged by your competitiors, and the future income that either you or your client will realize from the product. The price for the book is steep, but includes a three-ring binder for adding the four yearly supplements that are sent to each purchaser to keep the Bluebook up to date.
From: P.R.I., 21237 South Moneta Ave., Carson, Calif. 90745

PHOTOGRAPHY
(A Golden Handbook)
Wyatt B. Brummit, R. Will Burnett, and Herbert S. Zim
1964 - 160 p. il. - $1.25

A very basic, simplistic guide to photography directed at people with no knowledge of the subject and little technical aptitude. Explains cameras, film, working with color and black-and-white, nature photography, developing and printing, and how to deal with special problems. If you want to start at the *very* beginning, start here with this book.
From: Golden Press, 1220 Mound Ave., Racine, Wisc. 53404

PHOTOGRAPHER'S MATE 3 & 2
1966 - 644 p. il. - $9
S/N 0847-0146

Navy training manual for Photographer's Mate rating; a basic course in photography including theory and practical applications. Covers in addition to conventional still camera work, a discussion of motion picture cameras, how to take motion pictures, and processing movie film, plus such specialized things as aerial cameras and photography, and airborne photographic reconnaissance and mapping. A lot of information for six bucks.
From: Sup. of Doc., U.S. Gov. Printing Off., Washington, D.C. 20402

TOTAL PICTURE CONTROL
Andreas Feininger
1970 - $12.50

A good, basic, technical book that will teach you how to use the tools of photography: lenses, filters, camera, print paper, and so forth.
From: Chilton Book Co., 401 Walnut St., Philadelphia, Pa. 19106

THE PHOTOGRAPHY CATALOG
Norman Snyder, Ed.
1976 - 256 p. il. - $7.95

A candid coverage of the best equipment, materials, techniques and resources available to today's photographer, edited by Norman Snyder, originator of the *Life Library of Photography,* with Carole Kismaric and Don Myrus. If you're into any area of photography, either as a beginner or expert, this book is a *must* for your library. Norm, Carole and Don have done their homework on this one and tell it like it is—what's good, what's not so good, what's worth thinking about and what to skip—in cameras, darkroom gear, books, magazines, instruction, workshops, camera repair, etc., etc., et cetera. A fantastic source of "inside" info!!!!
From: Harper & Row, Inc., 10 East 53rd St., New York, N.Y. 10022

MAKING WILDLIFE MOVIES:
A Beginner's Guide
Christopher Parsons
1971 - 224 p. il. - $7.95

The devoted naturalist who wants to progress beyond observing wildlife to recording what he sees on film will find a wealth of helpful information in Parson's book. The author first covers appropriate choices of equipment and then goes into the fine points of working with various types of animals in different habitats: birds in the nest, away from the nest; large and small mammals; aquatic life in aquariums and in streams; insects and other small creatures. He even devotes a chapter to wildlife in urban areas and the problems encountered there. There are chapters on scripting, editing, and sound, and numerous drawings and illustrations to show how to set up blinds, build your own equipment, and so forth. Lots of good information.
From: Stackpole Books, Harrisburg, Pa. 17105

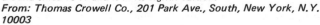 # SCHOOLS

NATIONAL CAMERA
Englewood, Colo. 80110
A complete course of instruction in camera repairs. Tuition includes all practice parts, loan of tools, subscription to bimonthly *The Camera Craftsman.* National also sells repair parts to professional camera repairmen (write for a catalog if you'd like to try repairing a camera yourself). Tuition for the course is around $1000 for a maxiumum of 39 months of study.

PHOTOGRAPHIC GEAR

CAMERAS
$25 - $1,000

On most expeditions the main considerations are weight and bulk, so most look for the smallest, lightest cameras that will still offer a wide range of features, maximum versatility and enough sharpness. 35mm single-lens reflex (SLR) cameras are generally considered the best choice. Smaller film sizes don't allow sufficient enlargement past snapshot sizes; larger cameras should be lugged around only for special purposes. 35mm is the standard size for photojournalism and increasingly for commercial photography. Larger cameras are handicapped by slower and less sharp lenses and often by vibration and film flatness problems. To compare the specific slide films used most often, a well-made 35mm Kodachrome 25 can be equal in sharpness to a 120

range. Incidentally, the Canon TX is the cheapest SLR of the group discussed here and an easy way to buy into an excellent system. Next is Minolta running a close 3rd to Canon and Nikon, and Olympus running 4th in completeness. Olympus is also the smallest, lightest, most vibration-free and just about the quietest 35mm SLR made. For backpacking, candid shots, wildlife or any other situation where a minimum of noise or weight counts, the Olympus should be a first consideration. On reliability, though, we can only give a "perhaps" because, although it gives all indications of first-class construction, it has only been on the market for a little over two years—still considered new. Also, previous Olympi were only average. Minolta, previously mentioned, does have a versatile system; however, not much to recommend it over the foregoing three; lenses, on the average

Ektachrome-X. About the only reasons for using 120 film are a picky publisher or some anticipated murals. Also, a 120 SLR outfit will weigh upwards of twice the same in 35mm.

35mm SLR's are the most versatile type of camera. Most importantly they accept interchangeable lenses, with fields of view between 220° and 1°. You compose and focus looking through the lens. This is especially important to good composition, as you see what the picture will look like and can adjust the relationships of the elements of the composition until it looks right. Viewfinder cameras merely frame what you'll get without showing various parts in and out of focus. All modern SLR's measure light through the lens; with some you match a pointer, others set exposure automatically. Either way is more accurate than any external meter for common problems like backlighting, filters, close-ups and telephoto work. For shooting within three feet, an SLR is the only way to go.

The most reliable 35mm SLR's are made by Canon, Nikon (including Nikkormat), Minolta, Pentax, Olympus and perhaps Contax. Of these, Canon and Nikon have the most complete system, widest and best lens lines, and the best reputations. Nikon has the most weird lenses; Canon, the sharpest and fastest in the normal (24- to 300mm)

seem to be less sharp. Pentax, except for Olympus, is the most compact, but still has that damn screw-thread lens mount, and versatility for the Pentax is the least for this select group of cameras. All makes come in cheaper match-pointer and more expensive autoexposure models. Canon, Nikon and Minolta have, in addition, interchangeable-everything models that, frankly, add needless complication and weight—unless you have a specific need for their features.

For those who must use 120 film (for publication, for instance), suggest you first look at a Rolleiflex, Tele-Rolleiflex or Mamiya C330 twin-lens reflex (TLR). By avoiding the large moving mirror of an SLR, they achieve much lower noise and vibration. The Mamiya takes interchangeable lenses from 55- to 250mm and focuses much closer, but weighs more. Those who need a 120 SLR for extreme close-ups (the C330 does well up to about a foot) or telephotos longer than 250mm can choose among Kowa, Mamiya (other than the C330), Hasselblad, Pentax 6x7, Bronica, and Rollei SL66 or SLX66. All share the problems of weight, bulk, noise, vibration and high price, and most have inconvenient metering. Hasselblad is the lightest, but along with Kowa, Bronica and Rollei SLX66, is limited to its own lenses with shutters. Even with 220 film, 24 exposures take the space of 72 35mm

---

CAMERAS IN COLD WEATHER

In very cold weather when the temperature drops down below zero, cameras and film cease to function as they were meant to. The lubricant on the mechanical parts of the camera can freeze up, and the film becomes so brittle that it breaks easily. Here are a few ideas for coping with a camera in the cold:

If you plan to use your camera outdoors in the cold to any extent or for an extended period of time, send it into the shop for a winter lubrication job. It's kind of like changing the oil in your car only a lot more expensive (some cameras will run as much as $100). The camera technician will disassemble the camera, remove the old lube, and relubricate with a lighter oil.

Carry your camera close to your chest or stomach inside you jacket so that body heat will keep it relatively warm. Decide on your picture before you pull it out to shoot, and when you do, work quickly and get it back inside your clothes as soon as you can. Keep a couple of rolls of film in a breast pocket so they can be warming too.

Before you go into a warm tent or cabin, put the camera in an airtight plastic bag. This will keep moisture from condensing on the lens and seeping into seams and the mechanisms. It'll freeze up later when you go back outside and jam up the works. Take the camera, in its plastic bag, to bed with you to keep it warm.

When you advance or rewind, do so slowly to keep as much stress as possible off the film. As soon as you finish with a roll, get it into an airtight container right away to keep moisture off it.

Wear two pairs of gloves—a heavy outer glove and a pair of silk liner gloves. The liners are light enough so that you can operate the camera with them on, but they can keep your fingers from freezing for four or five minutes without the outer gloves.

A belt pack worn backwards with the bag in front makes a good gadget bag. Keep it under your jacket and it'll get the benefit of some body heat. You might try a hand warmer in the bag too, for added heat.

exposures, which means changing film more often than with 35.

For places where it's difficult or impossible to change film, a half-frame 35mm camera may be in order, which takes 72 exposures on a regular 36-exposure roll. This can be publication-quality with a slow film (e.g., the '63 Everest expedition). Available, used, are several single-lens reflexes: the Olympus Pen F or FT (w/meter), the much larger autoexposure first model Konica Autoreflex (which can be switched to full-frame in mid-roll), and a lot of tiny viewfinder cameras mostly named Olympus Pen.

Unless you need a camera you can hide in your hand (the Tessina), it isn't necessary to go to half-frame for a really light, compact non-SLR camera. The Rollei 35 and Minox EL are tiny, in part because they lack range finders, etc. In order of increasing size and versatility, some good compact autoexposure range-finder cameras are the Olympus 35RC, Konica Auto S3, Canonet GIII 1.7, and Olympus 35RD, which can be recommended for backpacking, climbing and skiing. There are others. Given the limitations of one semiwide lens, pictures can be as good as any. If you know absolutely nothing about photography, the best way to learn is with one of these. They won't frustrate you with their limitations like a box camera will, and are as easy to use.

A Polaroid is excellent for making friends anywhere (except Moslem countries!), also for seeing mistakes immediately (and expensively). The folding pack film models are best for traveling and come as cheap as $20 used; as for the SX-70, do you want a camera whose shutter opens a quarter of a second after you push the button?

LENSES
$50 - $2,000

Here are a couple of basic things to bear in mind about lenses.

First of all, unlike binoculars or telescopes where the measurement given for a lens is its diameter, the measurement given for a camera lens is its focal length. Focal length is the distance from the center of the lens to the point behind it where light rays from a distant object converge in a sharp, focused image.

The *f* number of a lens is the ratio of its focal length to its diameter. The lower the f number, the faster the lens. Here *fast* refers to the lens' ability to take in light at its widest aperture. An f 1.2 lens is faster than an f 2.8 lens, and so on.

Single lens reflex cameras are built so that their lenses can be changed for special purposes. For instance, if you are taking pictures of buildings or ruins, a wide angle lens is very useful. It will enable you to get a picture of a broad subject without having to move back so far that you lose detail. In a narrow street you simply can't move back far enough anyway. For far-off subjects, a narrow-angle (telephoto) lens is needed. These are also very good for portraits. Zoom lenses have variable focal lengths, usually from moderate to longer telephoto. They're handy but very few are as sharp or as fast as the several lenses they could otherwise replace.

FILTERS
$3 - $20

It's best to take only the filters you understand and ordinarily use. For black and white three will suffice: a light green (G1) to lighten foliage or tone down skies; a medium yellow (K2) for clouds in general; a deep orange (O2) or light red (A25) for more dramatic cloud effects. For color work, a polarizing filter will intensify clouds and darken the sky. A UV filter is necessary to keep the bluish cast out of seaside and high altitude shots, and a color correcting filter will be needed to convert your color film from daylight to artificial (tungsten) light, or vice versa.

LIGHT METERS
$10 - $90

Exposure or light meters are used to determine how much light must reach the film in order to render a properly exposed negative. Some are built into the camera and others are carried as separate units. By pointing the meter at the subject, or 20 degrees below the horizon on infinity shots, you can determine what lens aperture and shutter speed is required for that particular picture. Selenium or cadmium sulfide (CDS) are the light-sensitive materials used in light meters. When exposed to light they generate an electric current which moves the dial. Because of minute variances in these elements, each light meter has a different "feel" to light. A half stop difference in black and white will never be noticed, but in color there will be a difference in color saturation. Unless your new meter checks out close to the one you've been using, don't use it for important work until you've tried a dozen pictures with it. Since two meters are a good idea for long trips, in the event one breaks or is lost, it might be worth making adjustments to one or both with respect to their readings to save mental calculations or a possible ruined picture.

FLASH UNITS
$6 - $200

There are bound to be times when a flash will be needed, either for supplemental lighting or for taking pictures in dark places or at night. You may choose either a flash gun that uses bulbs or an electronic flash unit which is a lot more efficient. Porter's Camera Store sells the Ultima Pocket Flash which uses M-2 or M-3 flashbulbs for around $6 (no weight given), and Eastern Mountain Sports carries the Mini Flash Gun which measures 2" x 1" x ¾" and weighs only 1 oz. without battery (about $6). Most camera equipment

We got this note in on first aid for a wet camera, and attached to it was the following memo:

Enclosed are suggested comments for field photography—the result of first hand experience! I was trying for a "salty" canoe shot for the book—full pack, camera slung around neck, the whole bit. As you might guess, I capsized (mickey mouse Appleby canoe) and the "camera man" didn't even get a shot as I flipped. The result was lost glasses and a dunked camera. Not knowing the proper way to dry a camera, repairs cost me $157.50—bad news! Turns out it's almost impossible to do the job yourself, but I talked with the repair man and learned a few things on how to keep the bill down. Hope it's useful.   —Mike.

Wet Camera

Oops, dunked your camera. Unfortunately it happens frequently on outdoor trips and is almost always an expensive proposition. Repair costs can easily run three quarters the cost of the camera. In fact, with the exception of better quality cameras, forget it. It's

catalogs don't give actual weights with each article (only shipping weight which isn't the same) so we can't recommend one electronic flash as especially lightweight or compact over another. The best approach is to check at a local camera store and compare different brands and sizes. Cost will range from as little as $20 for one like the Vivitar 91 (available from Solar Cine Products) on up to around $150. For an evaluation of electronic flash units see *Consumer's Guide,* February, 1970 issue, or the *Consumer Reports 1971 Buying Guide Issue.*

CAMERA HARNESS
$7 - $9

A harness is useful in skiing, climbing, or hiking where there's the danger of the camera bouncing back and forth or hitting against something if you just had it hung around your neck on a strap. A harness consists of two adjustable straps, one running around the neck and another under the arms, that fasten to the camera to hold it snugly against the chest. These work well with the lighter cameras, but the heavier SLR's and the TLR's still move around a lot. With a little imagination it seems as though it would be fairly easy to make one of these. If you want to buy one, try Recreational Equipment Co. or Eastern Mountain Sports.

TRIPODS
$7 - $70

Tripods are used to hold the camera steady when pictures are being taken at very slow shutter speeds (1/30th or slower) or for time exposures. They are essentially three-legged stands with a mounting at the top to which the camera is attached. Standard tripods vary in size and weight and can cost anywhere from $10 on up depending on how many convenience features they have. In cases where weight is a factor and a conventional tripod cannot be carried, there are camera clamps. These are C-clamps, on which the camera is mounted, that can be attached to fence posts or screwed into tree stumps or limbs to provide steady support. Most have small telescoping legs that convert them to table top tripods. They vary in weight from about 5 oz. and cost from $6 to $10. If you can't

cheaper to buy a new one.

A wet camera will soon begin to rust, and the oxidation process will freeze up gears and other moving parts unless the repair shop can get to them first. If oxidation sets in, the camera will have to be completely stripped down and soaked in a special chemical bath.

In case of an unexpected camera dunking, here's what to do:
(1) If the camera was in salt water, wash it down in fresh water as soon as possible.
(2) Don't dry the camera, put it in a plastic bag while still wet and seal tight.
(3) Rush it to a competent repair shop; every hour counts!

In the event you can't get to a repair shop within a few hours there are still several alternatives. You could force-dry the camera internally by gently warming in an oven at low heat (not over 150°F.) or you could immerse it in a bucket of water to prevent air from reaching corrodable surfaces.

As a last ditch effort, especially if the camera is not worth the cost of commercial repairs, you could partially disassemble the unit and wipe all gears and other surfaces with a cloth that has been dipped in fine machine oil.   —Mike Blevins.

get one at a local camera store, try Eastern Mountain Sports or Solar Cine Products or Forter's Camera Store. Another special steadying device is the Bushnell Optical Co. car window mount for cameras or telescopes, which clamps to a partially rolled down window.

 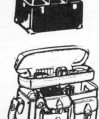

CAMERA CASES
$20 - $130

There are all sorts of camera bags and cases. If you're traveling extra light, your gear can be carefully wrapped in an ensolite or foam sleeping pad, eliminating the need for a special case. But for other situations, a special case may be in order. Since camera stores and catalogs are full of conventional camera cases, anything we say about them here would be overkill, so we'll concentrate on special types of cases.

1—Remove the foam lining pad, and place on it all the items to go in the case, arranging them with the largest pieces centered and the smaller items around the edges. Allow a minimum of ½" between various pieces. Mark the outlines of the items on the foam pad with chalk.

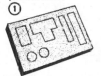

2—Then, cut out the foam, using knife provided. Cut inside the outlines to provide snug fit. For small, narrow items, simply cut a slit in foam.

Molded cases with polyfoam interiors are available from Solar Cine Products for $7 to $15. These look like small suitcases lined with thick polyfoam. You trace the outline of the camera and accessories you want to carry on the polyfoam and then cut out holes for them. This way camera equipment is snugly held in place and cushioned against shock. A deluxe version of these are the Halliburton aluminum cases ($70 to $130). Of course, this kind of case is too big to be practical traveling light, but they're perfect if you're four-wheeling over rough terrain, sailing in rough seas, or crossing the Sahara on a bumpy camel.

Recreation-Creations, Inc. sells the Sportsafe watertight (to a three-foot water depth), high-density, polyethylene camera carrying case with a 1-yr. warranty. Great for keeping gear dry in an open boat or in the event of capsize. Color is international orange and cost is around $25.

A leather pouch makes a very simple gadget bag provided each article has its own case or box since everything is going to rub shoulders. Danner Shoe Mfg. Co. sells cowhide drawstring bags for from $2.50 for a 4¾" x 7", to $5.50 for a 10" x 12".

Good buys on conventional camera cases can be had through Solar Cine Products, Spiratone, and other large mail-order houses. Try discount department stores, too.

CHANGE BAG
$5 - $9

If the film in your camera jams up or if you're in the middle of a desert or beach and need to reload, a lightproof change bag is indispensible. The camera is put inside the bag and you work with it through two hand holes. Of course, you need to know your camera pretty well to feel your way through a jam-up and straighten it out, or even just to load it, but that comes with practice. Change bags are also used for developing away from a darkroom. You just put the developing tank, reel, and cover into the bag along with the film, load it up, close the tank, and you're all set to run the chemicals through. With a little practice, this isn't much harder than loading the reel in a darkroom.

The Kodak *Index* is the starting point for ordering any of the vast number of publications produced by the company, which include such diverse subjects as amateur photographer's "hint" books, graphic arts, aerial, medical, and scientific photography, and a great many other photo related topics. It's strictly an index, however, and you won't find any descriptions of the books included. Kodak issues it annually and lists the publications alphabetically both by title and by subject matter. A handy postage-paid order blank is included in the back. Request publication L–5 (free):
From: Eastman Kodak Co., Dept. 454, 343 State St., Rochester, N.Y. 14650

Basic Photography Kit

Here are some suggestions for minimum equipment to take along on two types of trips:

TRAVELING LIGHT
One camera with regular lens   Light meter
Medium telephoto, 85- to 200mm
Camera clamp or pocket tripod   Film

There are lots of alternatives. You might carry a camera with a wide-angle lens and telephoto as an extra so that you're covered at both extremes. Or you might just stick to the regular lens to save a lot of fuss and the extra weight.

EXTENDED TRIPS
Two cameras—a 35mm compact or Nikonos plus an SLR with wide-angle (28mm, since compact lenses are so close to 35) and a telephoto. Two cameras or bodies enable you to have two different types of film going at the same time.

Lightweight tripod   Lens brush & cleaning tissue
Filters   Small penlight
Film   Sheet of plastic
Two exposure meters, or one in addition to built-in meter
Small flash gun with bulbs, or electronic flash

FILM

There are several types of film available in both color and black and white. All possess properties or characteristics that cause them to differ from one another in varying degrees. This is especially true with color film, where no one film is available that exactly duplicates the actual color in a subject or scene. Each one—Kodachrome, Ektachrome, Anscochrome has its own peculiarities. Some seem to be heavy on reds and yellows, others on blues and purples. So to recommend one film over another would be foolish. Buy one type and stick with it until you learn its properties, then try another until you find one that gives you what you want, one that you like. The manufacturer includes a data sheet with each roll or film that gives ASA rating and film characteristics (like sharpness, graininess, and so forth) and many photography books fully discuss and describe the properties of various films (*Photograpy for the Serious Amateur* by Skudrzyk for one). A big factor in choosing a film is its ASA rating. Very simply, ASA is a measure of the speed of the film. This refers to how well the film can deal with light. A *fast* film reacts more quickly to light than a slow one, hence it requires less exposure. The faster the film, the higher the ASA number; the slower, the lower the number. So if you'll be shooting indoor pictures with available light, you'll want fast film. Outdoors in bright sunlight, you can use a slow film.

How much film you carry depends on what kind of photography you'll be doing. A weekend canoe trip or backpacking trip might be covered by one roll of film (20, 24, or 36 exposures). But if taking pictures is an important or the main point of your trip, figure as many as 36 exposures a day. This is especially true if you don't

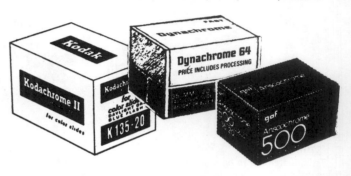

plan to visit the area again. If you're using a flashgun, two or three bulbs per roll should be enough unless you'll be doing a lot of cave shots.

Be especially careful about excessive moisture after the film has been opened. After it is exposed, put it into an airtight container (35mm color film comes in airtight aluminum cans) and keep it in the coolest spot you can find until it goes to the processor, like inside a sleeping bag or blanket roll. If your trip is extended, mail it back to the labs for processing.

FILM	RESOLUTION (LINES/MM)	MAXIMUM ENLARGEMENT NUMBER OF DIAMETERS GOOD QUALITY	TOP QUALITY
Kodacolor-X	35	3.5	2.4
Kodachrome II or X (1966)	120	12.0	8.0
Ektachrome-X	60	6.0	4.1
Kodak High Contrast Copying Film	140–160	14.0	10.0
Panatomic-X	100–120	10.0	7.0
Plus-X	90	9.0	6.2
Tri-X	60	6.0	4.1
Agfa Isopan Record	40	4.0	2.8
Adox Kb 14	100	10.0	7.0
Panatomic-X Sheet Film	48	5.0	3.5
Kodak Process Pan Sheet Film	65	6.5	4.5

Resolution and maximum enlargement that can be obtained with various roll and sheet films.

PUBLICATIONS

DIGNAN NEWSLETTER
Quarterly - $24/yr.

The Dignan Newsletter covers black-and-white and color processing and is concerned with the chemicals used in these processes. The newsletters present the most up-to-date information on formulas for photographic solutions so that the reader can compound his own. Not only does this enable him to duplicate commercial mixtures at a fraction of the cost, but by taking advantage of the latest research, he can frequently produce a better formula for his needs or for special effects. Apart from the greater control this makes possible, it also saves the photographer a lot of money, especially on color chemicals. Dignan also sells the Dignan Divided Developing System (NCF-41) for processing Kodacolor II, Vericolor II, Fujicolor II and Eastman Color 5247 negs. The beauty of it is savings and *no critical* temperature control. Three kits are available in prices ranging from $10 to $48. Write for descriptive literature.
From: Dignan Photographic, Inc., P.O. Box 4338, North Hollywood, Calif. 91607

KODAK MASTER DARKROOM DATAGUIDE (for black-and-white)
28 p. il. - $6.20

Here in one book is just about all the data needed on films, chemicals, papers, safelights, and processing to answer any darkroom question that comes up. Percentages for mixing chemicals, capacity and shelf life, properties of different developers, samples of paper types and surfaces, computers for figuring film development time and paper exposure time, and just about any other basic information you can think of. This one has the same vinyl treated cover and coated card-weight pages that make the other Kodak guides so long lasting. Probably the best quick-reference book available for the darkroom.
From: Eastman Kodak Co., 343 State St., Rochester, N.Y. 14650

Developing

For short trips, developing in the field isn't very practical. Not that it's difficult, but it does require carrying extra equipment, and maintaining the cleanliness necessary for good negatives isn't always easy. We won't even talk about color developing here. Theoretically, it can be done in the field but isn't really practical, so you may as well wait till you get back home. Black and white negatives, however, present little trouble, and if the trip or expedition is fairly long or is undertaken in a hot climate where film deterioration is a consideration, it can be worthwhile to take the time and trouble.

The equipment isn't very complicated. You'll need a change bag for loading film in complete darkness, a developing tank for your film size, plastic bottles for storing developer and fixer, a small funnel for pouring solutions from tank to bottle, paper towels or Scott tissues (Scott, as their ads trumpet endlessly, doesn't fall apart when it gets wet), to line the funnel for straining chemicals, and a few clips or clothespins for hanging film to dry.

TANKS
$6 - $10
The developing tank is a lightproof container that holds a reel onto which the film is wound. Once the film is loaded, placed in the tank, and the tank closed, the rest of the processing can be done in full light. There are metal reels and plastic reels and there are proponents of each type. After trying unsuccessfully to teach myself how to use a metal reel, I went out and bought a Paterson tank (Braun North America, 55 Cambridge Pkwy., Cambridge, Mass. 02142) with a plastic ratchet wheel; it practically loads itself. You just stick one end of the film into the spool, grab each hub of the reel, and in a back and forth twisting motion wind the film right up. It's so easy you could do it in the dark. Metal reels are just as fast if you know how to use them, just make sure you practice with some exposed film a couple of times before dousing the lights and popping a casette—to do the real thing.

CHEMICALS
$1 - $3
A gallon of developer costs about a dollar, a gallon of fixer, about 85¢. Depending on how much your tank holds, you can develop 16 to 20 rolls of films with this quantity of chemicals, which works out to about 10¢ to 13¢ a roll.

There are a couple of chemicals on the market that can make the process easier. One is Monobath, by Townley Chemical Co., which combines developer and fixer in one solution so that you only have to carry one chemical with you instead of two or three. After loading the film in the tank (this can be done in the change bag), just pour in the Monobath, leave it for up to fourteen minutes with periodic agitation, and at the end of that time the film is developed and fixed. Temperature control isn't critical, but the solution should be somewhere between 65° and 80°F.

Townley also makes Rapid Film Dryer, a solution that film is soaked in to make it dry in 3 to 5 minutes.

Another useful solution is Diafine (Bauman Photochemical Corp., 139 E. Illinois St., Chicago, Ill. 60611), a two solution developer. The fuss of carrying two solutions is offset by the fact that temperature control is not important. You can use Diafine anywhere from 65° to 90° whereas conventional developers should be kept as close to 68° as possible.

Kodak developers are available in small packets that mix up to just enough solution for a tankful of developer. These are handy to carry. Only problem here is that most developers have to be mixed at very high temperatures, like 125°F, and then cooled to 68° or 70° for use. It's easier, except for the weight and the freshness factor, to carry the developer ready mixed.

ACCESSORIES
Plastic bottles are probably the best for storing chemicals, particularly when traveling because of breakage, but at home old tinted wine bottles with corks are fine. You can use well-cleaned detergent bottles, too. If you decide to go the plastic route, check U.S. Plastic Corporation's stock first. They've got everything (listed elsewhere in this section).

For hanging film to dry, spring-loaded clothes pins work just as well as the stainless steel jobs that sell for 50¢ each.

Change bags (your portable darkroom) can be had from Spiratone for $4 to $10 depending on what size you want.

Enlarger

Lens brush

Safe light

Timer (enlarger)

Easel

Tray

Funnel and graduate

Tray thermometer

This isn't printing in the field (though you could certainly set up something for this on a boat or at a permanent base camp if you really had a need for it), but rather the finishing up process at home. Here's where you can end up spending a lot of money. If you're just interested in snapshot-size, generally good photos, you're better off having prints made commercially at a good processing house; it's cheaper. If you want to exercise some control over the quality of prints set up your own darkroom. It can be as simple as a piece of plywood set on the tub in your bathroom for workspace, to a full-blown temperature controlled, gadget-crammed lab in your basement. For aspiring photolab technicians, here's the basic gear you'll need for a store-in-the-closet-take-it-out-once-a-month darkroom.

ENLARGER
$25 - $250 and up
An enlarger projects and magnifies the negative's image by means of a lens. The image is projected onto light sensitive paper which is then processed to produce a print. The size of magnification can be adjusted by moving the enlarger head up or down on its support column and by the size of the lens used.

There are two basic types of enlarger: diffusion enlargers and condenser enlargers. A diffusion enlarger employs a lighting system that spreads or diffuses light over the negative. This is done by using a flourescent type bulb or a frosted glass between the light source and the negative. A condenser, on the other hand, uses a single point of light, like a 100-watt bulb. Diffusion types are used mostly for work with large negatives (over 4'' x 5''). Condenser enlargers are best for smaller negatives, and most of the popular enlargers—Durst, Vivitar, Bogen—are of the condenser type.

A popular rule of thumb in choosing an enlarger is to buy one of equal quality to your camera, but just about any enlarger, carefully used, can produce quality prints, expensive or not. There are several beginner's enlargers, like the Junior Fotolarger No. 1 from Porter's Camera Store for around $26. Vivitar, Spiratone, Bogen make enlargers in the $50 to $80 price range, and Durst enlargers start at around $80.

You will need an enlarger equipped with a lens and negative carrier designed for the size film you use. Try to get one that has a filter drawer above the lens for polycontrast filters. This enables you to use Kodak Polycontrast filters and paper to regulate the contrast of your print and color filters should you decide to get into color processing. Negative carriers without glass seem to be easier to use than those with it. This is because with the glass you have to worry not only about being sure your negative is dust-free, but that the glass in the carrier is clean, as well.

Consumer Reports did an evaluation of popular enlargers in their February 1970 issue, including a rating of enlarger lenses. This is a good source of information. These ratings are included in the ***Consumer Reports 1971 Buying Guide Issue***, available for $2.65 from Consumers Union, 256 Washington St., Mt. Vernon, N.Y. 10550. In this same 1971 Buying Guide there are evaluations of timers, cameras, and electronic flash units, so this is a good book to have if you're in the market for photographic equipment and want to know what you're getting.

EASEL
$7 - $50
An easel is placed under the enlarger to hold the printing paper. There are two types of easels: one is the type that adjusts to any of the common paper sizes so that it can be used for any size print; the other type is the Speed-E-Zel. Speed-E-Zels come in various sizes, each to match a popular paper size (4 x 5, 5 x 7, 8 x 10, etc.) so that you need a different one of these for each size print. The first type is the most versatile and economical, but the second type saves time if you customarily do prints all of one size. Spiratone, Solar Cine Products, and many of the mail-order discount houses sell easels for anywhere from $7 on up. Speed-E-Zels start at around $2.

TIMER
$15 - $40
A timer is used to regulate the duration of the negative's exposure onto the printing paper. A dial is set for the appropriate number of seconds of exposure, a switch pushed, and the timer automatically turns the enlarger on and off. Two of the best ones available are the Graylab 300 (about $30) and the Time-O-Lite ($35 to $40). The Time-O-Lite model P-59 has an outlet to which a foot switch can be attached. This is useful if you're burning and dodging and need your hands free. There are many less expensive timers, like the Spiratone (about $9) that perform adequately. Here again, see the *Consumer Reports,* February 1970 issue or the 1971 *Buying Guide* for ratings and evaluations of timers.

SAFELIGHTS
$5 - $14
Much of the printing work done in a darkroom requires that you be able to see to do it. So, photographic papers have been designed to be used with certain types of light without being affected by it. These are called safelights and they come with several filters so the color of the light can be changed for different types of paper. The least expensive of these is the type that screws into a standard bulb socket. Yankee safelights are an example and cost from $5 to $7 each, including filters. Kodak makes a safelight that's a separate lamp unit. The lamp runs $15 and the filters that go with it, $5 each.

TRAYS
$3 - $25 (for three)
Three solutions are used in black & white print processing and a tray is required for each. Trays come in sizes to match standard print sizes from 5 x 7 on up to 16 x 20. It's best to buy one of the large size trays so that you can process several sizes of prints. Spiratone has the best prices we've come across—three 8 x 10's for $3, three 11'' x 14'''s for $5.50.

ACCESSORIES
These include tray thermometer, graduates or measuring cup, bottles, and funnel. Chemicals have certain temperatures they work best at and a thermometer is used for this. Graduates are used for measuring and mixing solutions, and the funnel for pouring stuff back into the bottles. Spiratone has a thermometer for $2.25, and an assortment of inexpensive measures, bottles, and so forth.

sources of photographic gear

Mail Order

There are discount mail-order companies all across the country that offer big savings on name-brand cameras and equipment, darkroom gear, film, paper and many of their own brands at even greater savings. The biggest collection of them is in New York City. With a couple of exceptions, few of these people publish catalogs. Instead, they run one-, two- or multiple-page ads in the back of photography magazines where they list current bargains. Many offer good buys on used equipment, with guarantees. The following are some of the best known ones:

PORTER'S CAMERA STORE, INC.
P.O. Box 628, Cedar Falls, Iowa 50613
Porter's has a fantastically wide selection of photographic products. Not only do they sell cameras, flash units, tripods, projectors, light meters, and so forth, but in addition, things like darkroom cloth, change bags, black photographic tape, projection tables. We can't think of anything remotely connected with photography that we did not find in their catalog, even a camera clamp (about $6). Porter's carries a complete line of black and white and color film in Kodak, Fujifilm, and Agfa brands, darkroom chemicals and paper—even disposable red and white striped blazers for carnival photographers. 96-page newspaper type catalog, jumbled but indexed, is free. Film prices are about 20% below list.

SOLAR CINE PRODUCTS, INC.
4247 S. Kedzie Ave., Chicago, Ill. 60632
This is one of the best discount photography houses we've come across. They have an almost exhaustive selection of still cameras, movie cameras, and projectors. They carry six or seven different full frame miniature 35mm cameras; most of the popular 35mm SLR'S; Mamiya and Yashica TLR's, and the Kowa 2¼" square format SLR. Camera prices are from 30% to 35% below retail. For instance, in their last catalog, the Rollei 35 which lists for around $195 was offered for $146, and the Minolta SR-T 101 with f1.2 lens was going for $276, about $125 below list. Film is about 20% below regular retail prices. They also sell slide projectors, Polaroid cameras and accessories, flash units, extra lenses, tripods, exposure meters, darkroom equipment, and camera cases. These are all name brands, all at big discounts. Free catalog.

SPIRATONE, INC.
135-06 Northern Blvd., Flushing, N.Y. 11354
Spiratone handles everything the photographer needs. Only problem is it's not always easy to determine exactly what that is, because their literature consists of various sizes and shapes of brochures with mixtures of how-to information and product data. Probably the easiest way to handle it, is to ask for their "Request for Literature" form, and check off the stuff you want. Among their inventory they include two items of interest to the field photographer—change bags, $4 to $10, and a Clamp-Pod that'll attach your camera to anything up to 1¼" thick, $5. Other items are darkroom supplies and outfits from $85, lens and accessory pouches, slide accessories, infrared photography supplies, lenses, filters, and a stabilization processing system that

SPIRATONE AUTO LEVEL CONTROL STABILIZATION PROCESSOR,
automatically maintains solution level in trays
Shipping Wt., 2 cartons 24 and 6 lbs., F.O.B., N.Y.

Constructed of stainless steel, nylon and plastic, Spiratone processors are equipped with UL approved electrical components, have six high quality rubber rollers and process prints in any size from 3½x5 to 11x14", single weight or double weight, glossy or matte.

will process and deliver 4 damp-dry 8" x 10" prints a minute that have been conventionally exposed in an enlarger. Could save a lot of time messing with trays.

other discount mail-order houses

Cambridge Camera Exchange
  21 W. 4th St., New York, N.Y. 10011
Wall Street Camera Exchange
  82 Wall St., New York, N.Y. 10005
Wolk Camera
  133 N. Wabash Ave., Chicago, Ill. 60602
Olden Camera
  1265 Broadway, New York, N.Y. 10001
Bass Camera Co.
  179 W. Madison, Chicago, Ill. 60602
Executive Photo & Supply Corp.
  170 Rutledge St., Brooklyn, N.Y. 11211

Local Camera Shops

Don't neglect the local camera store as a source of good equipment at good prices. Many stores offer "professional" discounts which just about anyone can get, and a lot of places discount their merchandise anyway in order to be competitive. There are definite advantages to buying close to home. First of all you get the stuff a lot faster and you get to see what you're getting, and play with it. Second, you get to talk to a salesman who knows the equipment, so you can glean a lot of good advice along the way. Third, if anything goes wrong with something you buy, you don't have to go far to get it fixed. (By "camera store" we mean, specifically, shops that sell only photographic equipment, not the photographic sections of big department stores where the clerk isn't apt to know as much about cameras as you do. These may be good places for bargains, if you know what you want, just don't go there for advice.)

TOWNLEY CHEMICAL CORP.
115 Albany Ave., Amityville, N.Y. 11701

Townley manufactures two processing chemicals that are especially useful for developing film under less than ideal circumstances. The first is Monobath, a solution that combines developer and fixer. You just load your film, pour in the Monobath solution, and in no more than 14 minutes, film is developed and fixed. Temperature is not especially critical and can range from 70° to 80°, but the higher the temperature, the greater the contrast. Timing isn't critical either, because film can't be over-developed since contrast is predetermined. One of our staff members used this stuff on a trip through Mexico and was well satisfied with the results. Even on his 35mm negatives there was no problem with graininess. Monobath comes in two types: TC-1 for films exposed at the recommended ASA index and TC-2 for giving maximum film speed.

The second product is Rapid Film Dryer. After washing film, immerse it in this solution, agitate it for about two minutes, then remove it and hang to dry. In three to five minutes, film is dry and ready to store or print with. Solution may be reused indefinitely and does not deteriorate. Check your local photo store or write to Townley for a list of the nearest stores that carry it.

———————————————— Film

SUPERIOR BULK FILM CO.
443-450 N. Wells St., Chicago, Ill. 60610

Superior specializes in bulk movie film—Kodak, Fujifilm, and Agfa—but also carries bulk 35mm still film and bulk processing chemicals. Also sells many accessories for movie making like editors and viewers, splicers, titling equipment, movie lights and stands, and an assortment of tripods; equipment for processing your own movies. Free 73-page catalog.

MERIT DISTRIBUTING
P.O. Box 220, St. Clair Shores, Mich. 48083

Good prices on popular types of Kodak film and Polaroid film. Prices are about 20% below list. Postage and handling charges are 75¢ per order, but sometimes you can save more than that on a single roll of color film. Prices are especially good if you're ordering a lot of film at one time, since the handling charge, regardless, seems to stay the same.

PRINT FILE, INC.
Box 100, Schenectady, N.Y. 12304

Print File's negative preservers are about the handiest storage method ever devised. They are clear plastic sheets with slots for negatives and come in sizes to fit all popular film, including 4" x 5" 's and 8" x 10" 's. Each sheet has a tab at the top for recording data pertinent to the negatives and is punched to fit a three-ring binder. One of the nicest things about Print-Files is that contact prints can be made without removing the negatives. The company also sells a contact printer to work with the sheets, which consists of a metal box with a thick piece of polyfoam inside and a heavy hinged glass lid. You put the printing paper on top of the foam and the negatives in the Print-File on top of this and close the lid. This presses the negatives flat against the paper. Cost is about $16. Print-Files cost from $15 to $25 a hundred depending on film size.

THE NEGA-FILE CO., INC.
Furlong, Pa. 18925

File drawers and cases for negatives and slides in every conceivable size and shape, most of them pretty expensive. Storage envelopes for individual slides and negatives including glassine envelopes (about $8 per hundred; shipping cases for 2" x 2" slides ($10 to $14). Free 32-page catalog.

DESIGNERS
AND
MANUFACTURERS
OF

VIS®

SLIDE
FILE
FOLIOS

PLASTIC SEALING CORP.
1507 N. Gardner St., Hollywood, Calif. 90046

File folios for slides. Folios are made of a heavy gauge window, clear vinyl plastic front that has slots for mounted slides or transparencies. The back is frosty vinyl for diffused back lighting. Punched to fit a standard three-ring binder, or may be placed in standard file cabinet folders. About 40¢ each. Folio holds twenty 2" x 2" slides, twelve 2¼" x 2¼". Request current price list.

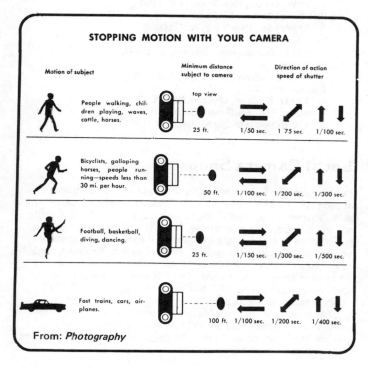

STOPPING MOTION WITH YOUR CAMERA

Motion of subject	Minimum distance subject to camera		Direction of action speed of shutter		
People walking, children playing, waves, cattle, horses.	top view	25 ft.	1/50 sec.	1/75 sec.	1/100 sec.
Bicyclists, galloping horses, people running—speeds less than 30 mi. per hour.		50 ft.	1/100 sec.	1/200 sec.	1/300 sec.
Football, basketball, diving, dancing.		25 ft.	1/150 sec.	1/300 sec.	1/500 sec.
Fast trains, cars, airplanes.		100 ft.	1/100 sec.	1/200 sec.	1/400 sec.

From: *Photography*

DANNER SHOE MANUFACTURING CO.
110 S.E. 82nd Ave., Portland, Oreg. 97216
Danner makes mostly boots, but they do sell leather pouches of garment tanned cowhide, which are good for all kinds of things, including camera gadget bags or lens bags. Prices are: 4¾" x 7", $2.50; 6½" x 9", $3.25; 7½" x 11", $4.00; and 10" x 12", $5.50. Their 24-page catalog is free.

AMERICAN GENERAL PRODUCTS, INC.
1000 First Ave., South, Seattle, Wash. 98134
If you'd like to take time-lapse photographs of a flower blooming, an egg hatching, or a seed sprouting, or maybe a sunset or moonrise, the PulsAR will do it for you. This is an electronic unit that can be attached to any movie camera or spring advance still camera. Cost of the unit is about $150. For motor driven still cameras, the Time Trigger 2 does the same thing as the PulsAR, and will trigger your camera to expose one or more frames in a range of action from two frames per second to one frame per ten minutes. Cost, about $70. Free literature.

BUSHNELL SPORTS OPTICS
2828 East Foothill Blvd., Pasadena, Calif. 91107
Most of Bushnell's catalog is devoted to binoculars and rifle scopes, but they manufacture several items that are of particular interest to the photographer: a line of fully automatic lenses for Single Lens Reflex cameras; a Spacemaster Telescope that can be adapted to work with many popular SLR cameras to provide telephoto lens capability from 750- to 3000mm (cost: $195); and several special tripods, including one to attach the camera to a car window glass for steadying. 35-page catalog, free.

BAKER MANUFACTURING CO.
P.O. Box 1003, Valdosta, Ga. 31601
Manufactures a tree stand for hunters that would also serve for the naturalist photographer. It fits trees from five to eighteen inches in diameter, can support up to 500 lbs. and is secure for sitting or standing. Its weight is 10 lbs. This tree stand climbs, that is, you get it up the tree by attaching it to your feet and the tree and going through a shinnying, foot pumping motion that's too improbable to commit to words. Price, about $35.

SWIFT INSTRUMENTS, INC.
952 Dorchester Ave., Boston, Mass. 02125
The Safari, a 60X spotting scope that can be used as a telephoto lens on 35mm cameras is one item available from Swift. The scope features hard magenta coating on all air-to-glass surfaces, built in sunshade, screw-in lens cap. Cost is around $100, and adapters for various cameras run $4 to $10. Free catalog.

PARACHUTES, INC.
24 N. Main St., Orange, Mass. 01364
Parachutists need to have their hands free, so when they want to take pictures during a jump, they use a helmet mount to hold their camera. Seems like any sport that kept the hands too busy for picture-taking—white-water kayaking, motorcycling, or whatever—could be handled with one of these mounts. PI is the only source of these that we've found. They sell a mount for still cameras and one for movie cameras, each $115. 121-page catalog of parachuting gear, $1.

Equipment Rental

F & B CECO, INC.
315 W. 43rd St., New York, N.Y. 10036
If you need a special camera for some purpose and don't want to invest in buying one, this company rents all kinds, including accessories. Fees are charged on a daily basis. They will ship rental cameras anywhere in the U.S., but you're charged the rental fee for the time in transit (except for a one day free-of-charge travel allowance for equipment shipped outside a 300-mile radius of New York City). This makes their service practical mainly to residents of NYC and nearby areas. CECO also has a sound stage facility and mobile photography studio with 4WD which can be rented. Write for a free catalog of equipment.

UNDERWATER PHOTOGRAPHY

BOOKS

PHOTOGRAPHY

There's not an awful lot of photo books for the underwater enthusiast. Here's five, but we just weren't able to get data on them for this edition. Probably Rebikoff & Cherney's *Underwater Photography* would be worth checking into, because Rebikoff has strong background in the U/W field. You might also check the Caving Section for a book entitled *American Caving Illustrated* by Jim Storey, which has a chapter on underwater cave photography.

UNDERWATER PHOTOGRAPHY
Derck Townsend
1971 - 152 p. il. - £2.10
From: George Allen & Unwin Ltd., Ruskin House, Museum St., London, England.

THE ART OF UNDERWATER PHOTOGRAPHY
Walter Starck & P. Brudza
$7.95
From: New England Divers, Inc., 42 Water St., Beverly, Mass. 01915

UNDERWATER PHOTOGRAPHY SIMPLIFIED
Jerry Greenburg
1963, - 48 p. il. - $2.00
From: New England Divers, Inc., 42 Water St., Beverly, Mass. 01915

CAMERA BELOW
Paul Tzimoulis & Hank Frey
1968 - $12
From: The Association Press, 291 Broadway, New York, N.Y. 10007

UNDERWATER PHOTOGRAPHY
Dimitri Rebikoff & P. Cherney
$5.95
From: Chilton Book Co., 40 Walnut St., Philadelphia, Pa. 19106

CAMERAS and ACCESSORIES

UNDERWATER CAMERAS AND HOUSINGS
$30 on up
If you want to take pictures underwater, you have two options: you can buy an underwater housing for your present camera and accessories or invest in a waterproof Nikonos camera, which requires no housing.

Underwater housings are waterproof cases made of metal, plexiglass, or some other synthetic, with outside controls that enable the photographer to make shutter and aperature settings, advance the film, and release the shutter. A lens port of glass or plexi-glass covers the camera lens. These ports may be simple clear glass much like a conventional glass lens cover, or they may be designed to correct optically the underwater distortion of image and color. Similar housings are also available for light meters, electronic flash units, and compasses.

Prices for housings range from as little as $30 for one that encases an Instamatic camera and flash cube, to $1500 for one for the Hasselblad EL. If you own one of the popular SLR's, you can get a plexiglass case for about $150 from Ikelite Underwater Systems. There are even cases for the TLR's and the miniatures.

With a little help from your friends or a local diving club, you can build your own housing for under $25. See the dealer's section for where to buy parts.

At this time, the only widely available camera that doesn't require a housing is the Nikonos by Nikon, Inc. It is a 35mm camera with a special body that is completely sealed so it can be used to depths of 160 feet without danger of leakage. It is available with a 35mm Nikkor f2.5 lens, a 28mm Underwater-Nikkor f3.5 lens (this one provides full compensation for underwater distortion), and a long focus 80mm Nikkor f4 lens. The Nikonos can be used on land with all but the underwater lens and its impenetrable exterior makes it ideally suited to situations where the camera will be exposed to rain, snow, mud, sand, and even radioactive dust (should be great for cavers). It isn't affected by extremes of temperature or humidity and is fully resistant to salt water corrosion, mildew, fungus, and damp rot. Clean it off by running it under a faucet.

Although it probably sounds like it ought to be outrageously expensive, especially since it's a Nikon, the Nikonos costs about the same as an average 35mm SLR. Price with the 35mm f2.5 Nikkor lens is about $220, with the 28mm f3.5 Underwater Nikkor lens, about $320. The 80mm f4 lens by itself runs about $160, viewfinders from $8 to $30, flash gun, $105. A variety of other accessories can be had, including exposure meter, close-up rings, lens hoods, filters, and so forth.

There are two moderately priced cameras on the market that can be bought with an underwater housing and flash unit. One is the Ricoh Hi-Color 35. This is a very compact full frame 35mm camera with built-in light meter and semi-automatic exposure control (set the shutter speed and the aperature automatically changes to correctly expose for the existing light conditions). It is available alone or with

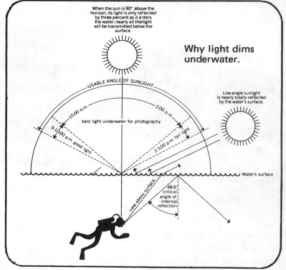

Why light dims underwater.

From: Oceans magazine

the housing. Cost with the housing is about $150. Removed from the housing, this is a very compact camera for traveling light. Check the Solar Cine catalog for a good price on this one.

Another underwater camera unit is the Konica C35 Marine. This one is fully-automatic and comes with its own underwater flash. Camera and flash have been pressure tested to depths of 120 feet. It can be taken out of the case for land use. The camera without housing weighs about 14 oz. and like the Ricoh, is a compact full frame 35mm. Cost with housing, flash, and grip is around $225.

FILM AND FILTERS
Black and white film may be used underwater, but color is almost always the photographer's choice. Unfortunately, most color film has relatively low film speeds, and color rendition is affected by the bluish cast of the water. Color correction is made by using a Kodak CC 20 R filter over the lens, which will remove some of the blue cast from the water. In very shallow water or where there is a bright sandy bottom, a CC 20 M filter may be used. In exceptionally clear waters, a slow film like Kodachrome II (ASA 25) is excellent at shallow depths. Going deeper, or in less clear water, Kodachrome X (ASA 64) gives more latitude. Both Anscochrome 100 and 200 are good for speed in low light situations, but grain might be objectionable to Kodachrome lovers. High-speed Ektachrome (ASA 160) may be pushed to an ASA of 320 with special processing, provided you make arrangements for this to done with the processor.

Equipment Rental

M & E MARINE SUPPLY CO.
P.O. Box 601, Camden, N.J. 08101
Rents underwater cameras: Calypso, Nikonos, Robot Star, and 16 mm movie cameras. Prices are low enough to make renting by mail economical but their catalog doesn't say whether or not they handle mail rentals. They also sell underwater cameras, housings, and accessories. 124-page catalog is free.

UNDERWATER LIGHTING
$30 - $400

A lot of underwater photography is done with available light, for instance, in the clear, beautiful waters of the Caribbean. Where artificial light is necessary there are several options.

Many cameras, like the Konica C35 Marine, the Nikonos, and the Ricoh Color 35 have their own amphibious flash guns. Ikelite's underwater housing for the Instamatic (about $50) includes a space for flashcubes, and Ikelite also sells a variety of underwater flash guns that work with their own and other manufacturers' housings. If you prefer electronic flash, there are waterproof housings available, again, from Ikelite, for conventional units ($60 to $80). Subsea Products, Inc. manufactures an underwater strobe for around $300, a little high for most amateurs, but a good investment for a club or someone seriously into underwater photography.

LIGHT METERS

If you're using the Nikonos or other camera which doesn't have a built-in light meter, you can buy a meter housing from Ikelite for around $13. A water-tight jar makes a good emergency housing. Use a piece of elastic or string and attach it to your wrist so that it doesn't go flying back to the surface should you let go. Preset the shutter speed before you close the jar, and then adjust lens aperture for correct exposure. Be sure not to bump it against a rock.

Home-Built Housings

Building your own underwater camera housing is relatively simple using plexiglass, providing you can also get the necessary control shafts and glands, knobs, O-rings, and lens gears.

First thing to do is send $1.95 to Hydrotech Co., Box 14444, Long Beach, Calif. 90814, for a copy of *How to Build Your Own Underwater Camera Housing* by Matt Toggweiler—74 pages of "how to" information plus good photographs on putting together housings for still and movie cameras, light meters, flash units, and so forth. Hydrotech also sells all the hardware and plastic material you'll need to build just about any size housing. Cost of the home-built job should run about $35.

Other sources of materials include:

SMALL PARTS, INC.
6901 N.E. Third Ave., Miami, Fla. 33138
Small mechanical parts of every description including fittings and "O" rings. Free catalog.

U.S. PLASTIC CORP.
1550 Elida Rd., Lima, Ohio 45805
Clear plexi-glass sheeting and cylinders of various thicknesses and dimensions, reasonable prices. Free catalog.

SEACOR, INC.
P.O. Box 22126, San Diego, Calif. 92122
Seacor is the U.S. distributor for the Konica C35 Marine camera ($225 with flash and grip), underwater housing for the Rolleiflex (called the Rolleimarin, about $600) and the Hasseacor, a super sophisticated housing for the Hasselblad E1 (about $1500). In addition, they manufacture a special underwater fisheye lens housing called the Super-Eye (about $200) and the Sea-Eye corrected underwater 21mm f3.3 lens (about $400) for the Nikonos. Seacor also carries a complete line of Nikonos cameras, lenses, and accessories and the Bolex H-16 Movie Camera with auxilliary lens and underwater housing. They handle the Halliburton aluminum camera cases. Free literature and price list available.

IKELITE UNDERWATER SYSTEMS
P.O. Box 88100, Indianapolis, Ind. 46208
Ikelite offers the most complete selection of plexiglass underwater housings for cameras and accessories available anywhere. Prices are as low as $50 for a housing for the Instamatics, on up to around $400 for motor-drive SLR's. In between are those for the 35mm compacts like the Rollei 35, for standard SLR's like the Nikon F, Nikkormat, Honeywell Pentax, etc. (about $150), for electronic flash units ($50 to $80) and for light meters (about $30). In addition, they offer waterproof flash guns that require no housing for $14 to $20. Write for their catalog, $1.

SUBSEA PRODUCTS, INC.
P.O Box 9532, San Diego, Calif. 92109
Three underwater strobe lights: Subsea Mark 150, about $539; Subsea Mark 50, about $200; and the AE 100 All Environmental Strobe Light, about $300. All feature adjustable light out put, variable light angle, even light distribution, and slave light capability. The AE 100 can be used above or below water. Subsea also manufactures extension tubes for the Nikonos to adapt it to macro-photography. Each tube costs $50. Literature giving full details, prices and specifications is available.

GIDDINGSFELGEN, INC.
578 4th St., San Francisco, Calif. 94107
Manufacturers of the Niko Mar III underwater housing for the Nikon 35mm SLR cameras. Housing includes corrective lens port, focus control, aperture control, shutter speed control, and many other features ($430). Also makes the Sea Star III Underwater Strobe ($240) and several accessories for the Nikonos including a Quick-fire bracket that enables the photographer to grip and fire the camera with one hand ($26). Also lights and housings for movie cameras. Good spec sheet available on all items.

FRENCH UNDERWATER INDUSTRIES
134 Paul Dr., Unit 8., San Rafael, Calif. 94903
Manufactures ultra-sophisticated housings for Nikon, $325, Bronica, $775, and Beaulieu movie cameras, $1995, as well as an underwater strobe, French Foto Strobe, about $200. Will also give estimates for custom housings.

Photographic Equipment. . .from Hong Kong

If you'd like to save a lot of money on top quality camera equipment and can afford to wait six to ten weeks for delivery, the Hong Kong dealers are a good source. These companies offer world-wide mail order service at savings of up to 50% over U.S. list prices. In addition to cameras, they sell light meters, electronic flash units, lenses, filters, enlargers, and, if you're interested, hi-fi equipment, radios, and watches. The cost is so low because by buying directly from the country of origin, you eliminate two or three middlemen and their markups. These are highly reputable companies, so there's no worry about being gypped.

There's only one catch to ordering cameras this way. There are certain brands that are trademarked in this country by the authorized U.S. distributors of that product. This means that only this distributor is legally able to import equipment bearing that name. For instance, only Honeywell is authorized to import Pentax cameras. If you want to buy a camera with such an import restriction, you may have to make arrangements to have the brand name obliterated or removed from the camera. Sometimes you can arrange to have this done by the Hong Kong dealer before it's shipped, but most of time, you must take care of this when you receive the merchandise (a jeweler can do a good job without damaging the camera). Customs might ask you to sign a statement certifying that you will have the trade name removed within three days of delivery.

Following is a list of camera and accessory brand names that are restricted. The list can change periodically as new brands become trademarked, so whatever brand you choose, be sure to check with Customs first.

Asahi Pentax	Gossen	Miranda	Rolleicord
Bolex	Konica	Nikkor	Rolleiflex
Canon	Leica	Nikon	Technika
Canonet	Leicaflex	Pentax	Topcon
Contaflex	Mamiya	Reflekta	Voigtlander
EXA	Mamiyaflex	Richohflex	Weston
Fujica	Minox	Rollei	

Anything valued at over $10 is subject to import duty. The present rate is 7½% on cameras, 12¼% on extra lenses, 4½% on light meters, 5½% on electronic flashes, 10% on filters, and 17½% on projectors.

Here's a rundown on a typical purchase, including duty, postage, and insurance, giving the total price and comparing it to the U.S. list price. Figures are based on those of Universal Suppliers of Hong Kong, but prices of all the Far East dealers are about the same, give or take a few dollars [We couldn't get a new list in time so these prices don't reflect the Febuary '73 dollar devaluation. Obviously that kicks the price up. We'll catch up next time around.]

Minolta SR-T 202 Single-Lens Reflex 35mm camera	
with Rokkor 50mm f 1.7 lens	$185.00
7½% import duty	13.88
postage and insurance	4.20
total cost	203.08
U.S. suggested retail price	$400.00

Add to the U.S. price state and local sales tax where applicable. Bear in mind, though that most camera stores here discount their prices below list anyway, and in addition, there are several mail-order houses that offer big savings. To get an idea of how Hong Kong prices compare to U.S. discount prices, we shopped around. The biggest discount we found on this same Minolta camera was from Wall Street Camera in New York. Their price for camera and lens was $227.95. Postage is additional. So Hong Kong prices represent a big savings no matter how you look at it. Just remember, though, shipping takes a long time. Delivery time can be cut to about two weeks if you arrange for air mail delivery. This costs an additional $12 or so.

Here's a list of the Hong Kong companies we know about with a brief description of each. When writing for their catalog or ordering, be sure to send your letter by air mail. Send payment by certified check or cashier's check. Most will accept personal checks, but you have to wait until the check clears your bank before the merchandise will be shipped, an additional delay of several weeks. U.S. Postal money orders are not honored by Hong Kong banks. Other money orders are but seem to entail the same delay as personal checks.

FAR EAST COMPANY
P.O. Box 7335, Kowloon, Hong Kong

Sells most of the popular SLR's and TLR's and extra lenses for them; compact, miniature, and 126 cartridge cameras; tripods, light meters, electronic flash units, and filters; slide projectors; movie cameras; darkroom equipment including enlargers and enlarger lenses (Durst and Hansa), trays, tanks, safelights, and so forth. All equipment is guaranteed for twelve months from date of shipment, including postage and handling. Ninety-page catalog is free if sent by surface mail, $1 if sent by airmail.

T. M. CHAN & CO.
Sheung Wan Post Office Box 3881, Hong Kong

Chan doesn't carry as many different brands as some of the other Hong Kong suppliers, no Rollei or Hasselblad if you're interested in those. They carry Bauer, Canon, Fujica, Minolta, Nikon, and Yashica movie cameras; movie and slide projectors; filters, exposure meters, and electronic flash; Durst enlargers and Schneider enlarger lenses. All equipment is guaranteed for one year from the date of purchase, and if it has to be repaired, parts and labor are furnished free. They don't mention who pays the postage and insurance in such a case, but you'd have to inquire before shipping it for repairs anyway. The catalog states that substitutions of like quality merchandise will be made if what you order is out of stock. This is only if you authorize it but it would be wise to clearly specify when you order whether or not a substitution would be acceptable to you, and if so, what brand and model you'll take instead. 144-page catalog, free.

UNIVERSAL SUPPLIERS
General Post Office Box 14803, Hong Kong

Most of the popular SLR's and TLR's and accessory lenses, filters, exposure meters, tripods, electronic flash units, slide and movie projectors, Nikkor and Schneider enlarging lenses. All merchandise fully guaranteed for one year, including postage and handling. 89-page catalog is free by surface mail or $1.65 by air mail.

MUTUAL FUNDS CO.
P.O. Box K 3265, Kowloon Central Post Office, Hong Kong

Most popular SLR's and TLR's and accessory lenses; movie and slide projectors; Bauer, Canon, Elmo Beaulieu, Fujica, Minolta, Nikon, Rollei, Sankyo, Vivitar, and Yashica movie cameras; exposure meters, electronic flash; Durst enlargers and Schneider lenses. All merchandise guaranteed for one year. Be sure to state whether or not substitutions may be made. 138-page catalog is free.

WOOD'S PHOTO SUPPLIES
60 Nathan Rd., Kowloon, Hong Kong

When you write for a catalog from Wood's be sure to specify what types of cameras you're interested in because there are different catalogs for each (actually, loose sheets with descriptions and prices). We only received information on 35mm SLR's and 8mm movie cameras— must have worded our letter wrong—but we know they carry a complete line of popular lenses, exposure meters, electronic flash units, and so forth. Based on what we received we can tell you that they carry most 35mm SLR's (no Nikon or Rollei), and the following movie cameras: Bauer, Bolex, Canon, Elmo, Eumig, Minolta, Nizo, Rollei, Sankyo, Vivitar, Yashica, and Fujica. All merchandise is guaranteed for one year, except for electronic flashes, which are guaranteed for 6 months. Wood's will take care of grinding off trade names on restricted brands unless you ask them not to. Catalogs free.

ALBERT WHITE & CO., LTD.
K.P.O. Box K-202, Kowloon, Hong Kong

Most popular SLR's and TLR's and accessory lenses; subminiature cameras; professional cameras (Rollei, Hasselblad, Linhof, etc.); electronic flash; exposure meters; 8mm and 16mm movie cameras; slide projectors; tripods; gadget bags; binoculars; telescopes; and tape gear. One year guarantee on all equipment. Other catalogs are available for office gear, men's clothing, carpets, calculators, furniture, china, and hi-fi gear. 38-page photo catalog is free by air mail.

CAVE PHOTOGRAPHY

Rolfe Schell taking movies by home-made flares in caves at Calcohtok, Mexico.

A series of 42 stereo views taken by Charles Waldack in 1866 in Mammoth Cave are thought to be the first cave photographs. These views were made with the aid of burning magnesium and were distributed nationally. *The Mammoth Cave* by W. Stump Forwood was published in 1870 and contained twelve lithographic plates that were copied from the Waldack photographs. The early cave photographers had large, fragile, cumbersome equipment to work with. It often took over an hour just to obtain one photograph.

Inexplicably, it seems that the most photogenic areas of a cave are also the most inaccessible. Today's cave explorers usually prefer the small, compact, light 35mm cameras. Many shots can be taken on one roll of film, and film changing is not difficult. A tripod is not essential but will enable one to obtain a greater variety of photographs. It will also make possible group shots, and with the use of a timer, no one needs to be left out of the photograph. Tripods must be light, collapsible, and easy to pack and carry.

Your camera and film must be protected from the mud, dust, water, and rocks of the cave. One ideal solution is an Army surplus metal ammunition case. These have rubber seals and when lined with foam rubber or some similar type of padding can even protect the camera from damage in a short fall.

Should you use color or black and white film? On most small caving trips colored slides is the film used. Slides can be sorted and stored easily and are often used for presenting lectures to your caving club or other interested groups. You can get prints or enlargements made easily if required. On the other hand if the photographs are being taken with a plan to publish them in newspapers, magazines, etc. often black and white is better.

Black and white is much cheaper so you can afford to take more photographs to start with and to discard those not needed. If you are going on a caving expedition the best plan is to have two or more people along whose primary function is to photograph the cave and cavers. One should be shooting only black and white while the other uses color. In addition, of course, some of the other expedition members will have their own cameras and sometimes may be at a point where some photographs are wanted, but the photographers may not be immediately available. Remember also that on any caving trip where people are taking pictures you will not be traveling as fast as you would if photographers were not along.

Your biggest question in regard to cave photography will probably concern lighting. The 19th century cave photographers used magnesium ribbon, calcium light, or electric arc lamps. The modern spelunker uses an electronic flash unit or flashbulbs. Electronic flash, although more expensive initially, is the best choice for several reasons. It can be recharged and used over and over, and some units have separate batteries that can be charged up and then carried as spares. An electronic unit is also quicker to use. The big disadvantage with flashbulbs is that you must carry enough of them and insure they're not broken on the trip in. Also used flashbulbs must be carried back out of the cave.

If you are planning on taking any shots of long passages or of large rooms you can handle it one of two ways. The first method is to use a tripod and leave the shutter of your camera open while you go around setting off your flashes at various locations, until the entire room or passage has been exposed to light. The camera shutter is then closed. The disadvantage here is that you must not permit any direct light, such as a carbide lamp, to be seen by the camera, because if you do you'll have a wavy line of light in your final picture. The second and better method is to have several other persons each set off separate simultaneous flashes throughout the area being photographed.

When several photographers on one cave trip are interested in conserving flashbulbs or flashes from an electronic unit this can easily be accomplished by 'riding' each others flashes. Everybody sets up his camera and uses an open shutter method; the person with the flash counts *one, two* (at this moment everyone who wants to take that picture opens his shutter), *three* and fires his flash. This method works nicely, provided there are no extraneous lights in the shot.

Another field of cave photography is motion pictures. The 1972 NSS Convention held at White Salmon, Washington, in August showed four cave films. One excellent one was "Cave of the Winding Stair" (Calif.) by Stanley R. Ulfeldt. It was filmed using natural carbide lamp lighting and very high speed black and white film!! The first cave motion pictures were taken in July 1972 in Old Salts Cave, Kentucky, by Russell Trall Neville.

One common problem with underground photography is the high humidity and the cool temperatures of many caves. Moisture can fog the camera lens or cause the formation of miniature clouds in the room. A camel's hair brush can solve the lens fogging problem and controled breathing can prevent formation of clouds. Another problem is that size is difficult to visualize in your final photograph unless you have put something into the picture for scale. Some commonly used items are a coin, knife, carbide lamp, flashlight, hardhat, or a person, depending on the size of the object being photographed.

Many of the older United States commercial caves had certain photographers do all of their initial photographic work. The history of early cave photography is a subject that still requires extensive investigation and detailed research. Many questions about the early cave photographers, their original negatives, number of views they took, dates of their work, etc. remain unanswered today, and original cave prints by these men are scarce. Some of these photographers are listed below along with the earliest known dates they worked in caves and the caves they photographed.

Carlsbad Caverns, New Mexico
Ray V. Davis - 1923
Willis T. Lee - 1923

Cave of the Winds, Colorado
William H. Jackson - 1885
(Probably taken by a Jackson Studio employee and not by Jackson himself)
W. E. Hook - 1885
and numerous others.

Howe Cavern, New York
Aaron Veeder - 1878

Luray Caverns, Virginia
C. H. James - 1881
J. D. Strickler - 1906

Mammoth Cave, Kentucky
Charles Waldack - 1866
A. F. Styles - 1867
Mandeville Thum - 1876
Mr. Sesser - 188?
Ben Hains - 1889

Wyandotte Cave, Indiana
Ben Hains - 1889

Many thanks to James F. Quinlan, Burlington, Ontario, for supplying much help in gathering the above data.
—Chuck Pease (1972).

401

index of suppliers and service organizations

... and so there ain't nothing more to write about, and I am rotten glad of it, because if I'd a knowed what a trouble it was to make a book I wouldn't a tackled it and I ain't agoing to no more.

Mark Twain